THE MAKING OF THE WEST

PEOPLES AND CULTURES

THE MAKING OF THE WEST

PEOPLES AND CULTURES

Volume II: Since 1560

LYNN HUNT
University of California at Los Angeles

THOMAS R. MARTIN
College of the Holy Cross

BARBARA H. ROSENWEIN
Loyola University Chicago

R. PO-CHIA HSIA
New York University

BONNIE G. SMITH
Rutgers University

BEDFORD/ST. MARTIN'S   Boston ◆ New York

FOR BEDFORD/ST. MARTIN'S

Executive Editor: Katherine E. Kurzman
Senior Development Editor: Elizabeth M. Welch
Project Manager: Tina Samaha
Production Supervisor: Catherine Hetmansky
Map Development Editors: Heidi Hood, Laura Arcari
Editorial Assistants: Sarah Barrash, Molly E. Kalkstein
Marketing Manager: Jenna Bookin Barry
Assistant Production Editor: Coleen O'Hanley
Copyeditor: Barbara G. Flanagan
Text Designer: Wanda Kossak
Cover Designer: Donna Lee Dennison
Photo Researchers: Carole Frohlich and Martha Shethar, The Visual Connection
Proofreaders: Mary Lou Wilshaw-Watts, Jan Cocker
Indexer: Maro Riofrancos
Composition: York Graphic Services, Inc.
Cartography: Mapping Specialists Limited
Printing and Binding: R.R. Donnelley & Sons Company

President: Charles H. Christensen
Editorial Director: Joan E. Feinberg
Director of Marketing: Karen Melton
Director of Editing, Design, and Production: Marcia Cohen
Managing Editor: Elizabeth Schaaf

Library of Congress Control Number: 00–133169
Copyright © 2001 by Bedford/St. Martin's

Manufactured in the United States of America.

5   4   3   2   1   0
f   e   d   c   b   a

For information, contact: Bedford/St. Martin's, 75 Arlington Street, Boston, MA 02116
617-399-4000
www.bedfordstmartins.com

ISBN: 0–312–18370–4 (hardcover complete edition)
ISBN: 0–312–18369–0 (paperback Volume I)
ISBN: 0–312–18368–2 (paperback Volume II)
ISBN: 0–312–18365–8 (paperback Volume A)
ISBN: 0–312–18364–X (paperback Volume B)
ISBN: 0–312–18363–1 (paperback Volume C)

Cover Art: Top left; title page spread (details): *Le 28 juillet 1830: La liberté guidant le peuple.* Eugene Delacroix (1798–1863). Louvre, Paris. © Photo RMN-Herve Lewandowski. Bottom left: *The Luncheon* (1739), Francois Boucher (1703–1770). Louvre, Paris. Courtesy of Art Resource. Right: *Lenin addressing the 2nd All-Russian Congress of Soviets* (1917). Vladimir Serov (1865–1911). Courtesy of Novosti.

A Conversation with Lynn Hunt

A RENOWNED SCHOLAR OF THE FRENCH REVOLUTION who has trained a generation of graduate students at the University of California at Berkeley, the University of Pennsylvania, and now as Eugen Weber Professor of Modern European History at the University of California at Los Angeles, Lynn Hunt has long been committed to the centrality of the Western civilization survey course to undergraduate education. In this conversation she explains why she and her coauthors Thomas R. Martin, Barbara H. Rosenwein, R. Po-chia Hsia, and Bonnie G. Smith wrote *The Making of the West: Peoples and Cultures.*

Q You taught the Western civilization survey for many years before deciding to write a textbook for the course. What inspired you to undertake such a time-consuming project at this point in your career?

A When I started teaching Western civ in the 1970s, I found the prospect daunting. How can any one person make sense of such a long time span—in my case, the West from the sixteenth century to the present? In addition, historical research was undergoing major changes: social history produced much new information about the lower classes, women, and minorities; then cultural historians began to draw attention to the importance of religious festivals, political rituals, and a variety of cultural expressions. How could these new subjects, new findings, and new methods be incorporated into the narrative of Western historical development?

Every generation needs new textbooks that synthesize the most recent findings. But after 1989 the need for a new vision became especially acute. Not only did new information need to be integrated in a course that was already jam-packed with important material about political personalities, events, and movements, but the very notion of the West was beginning to change. Just as immigration was creating a United States that was much more multiethnic and multicultural than ever before, so too historians had become much more interested in the interactions between the West and the rest of the world. Textbooks conceived and written during the era of the cold war had been oriented toward explaining the conflict between the West and their eastern-bloc opponents, eastern Europe and the Soviet Union. In the post-1989 world,

"Every generation needs new textbooks that synthesize the most recent findings."

political conflicts no longer fit into that neat mold: conflict takes place on a global stage at a time when many important social, economic, and cultural trends have became global. The new histories had to reflect these momentous changes. Since my coauthors and I have all been personally involved in the new approaches to historical research and in the effort to understand the West in a world setting, we felt we would make an effective team for integrating these perspectives and showing how they offer a more coherent and convincing view of the important issues in Western civ.

Q Textbooks for the course typically contain "Western Civilization" in the title. Why is your book named *The Making of the West: Peoples and Cultures*? What are its themes and objectives, and how are they realized?

A Our title makes two important points about our approach: (1) that the history of the West is the story of a process that is still ongoing, not a finished result with only one fixed meaning; and (2) that "the West" includes many different peoples and cultures, that is, that there is no one Western people or culture that has existed from the beginning until now. Although our book emphasizes the best of recent social and cultural history—hence our subtitle, *Peoples and Cultures*—it integrates that new material into a solid chronological framework that does full justice to political, military, and diplomatic history. We try to suggest the richness of themes available for discussion and challenge students to think critically without limiting instructors to just one or two points of view. My coauthors and I have learned from our own teaching that students need a compelling chronological narrative, one with enough familiar benchmarks to make the material readily assimilable, but also one with enough flexibility to incorporate the new varieties of historical research. We aimed for a strong central story line that could integrate the findings of social and cultural history into the more familiar accounts of wars, diplomacy, and high politics, yet we also endeavored to include the experiences of many

"Although our book emphasizes the best of recent social and cultural history—hence our subtitle, Peoples and Cultures—it integrates that new material into a solid chronological framework that does full justice to political, military, and diplomatic history."

individual women and men. Nothing makes sense in history if it cannot be related back to the actual experiences of real people. For this reason we begin each chapter with an anecdote about an individual and his or her particular experience and then incorporate that information into the discussion of

> *"Nothing makes sense in history if it cannot be related back to the actual experiences of real people."*

general themes and trends. It is, after all, the interaction between public events and private experiences that makes history of enduring interest to students. Among the ordinary people we chose for special attention, we focused in particular on those who had contacts with the world outside the West, from missionaries and soldiers to naturalists and painters.

Q Four other well-known historians join you on the author team: Thomas Martin, Barbara Rosenwein, R. Po-chia Hsia, and Bonnie Smith. How did the author team come into being? Knowing the potential dangers of a multiauthored textbook, how did you all work together to ensure a single, cohesive work?

A No one scholar can hope to offer a truly authoritative and balanced synthesis of the rich materials available on the whole course of Western history. It is hard enough for one person to teach a semester of Western civ! This kind of undertaking requires collaboration among colleagues of great expertise who can bring to their writing the experience that comes from years of teaching different kinds of students. Our team is made up of just these kinds of scholars and teachers. Each author has an international reputation for research that has helped to shape the agenda for history in the new century. Each one has taught a wide range of students with different levels of skills. We have worked intensively together over the years—meeting often, reading one another's chapters—to develop a clearly focused, integrated narrative that combines the best of new social and cultural approaches with the traditional political narrative and seeks to put Western history in a worldwide context. We have benefited as well from an exceptionally intensive review process that has provided us with helpful input from scores of scholars and teachers with expertise different from our own. They and our editors at Bedford/St. Martin's have helped ensure that the text offers a coherent, continuous narrative. Reading the book, even I can't detect a change in authorship from chapter to chapter!

> *"This kind of undertaking requires collaboration among colleagues of great expertise who can bring to their writing the experience that comes from years of teaching different kinds of students."*

Q   The authors—you in particular—are known for cutting-edge scholarship. In what ways does *The Making of the West* reflect your research and interpretations?

A   From long experience in teaching, we know that students can grasp the most recent advances in scholarship only if those advances can be put in a clear framework that builds on what the students already find familiar. And we also know, like all of our fellow Western civ instructors, that new materials have to be carefully calibrated so as not to overwhelm students who might not be familiar at all with Western history or the methods of historical criticism. For this reason, we have confined much of the explicit discussion of methods and interpretations to the features, which instructors can use or not as they see fit. The narrative itself reflects the authors' most recent research, but it never neglects to explain the relevance of social, cultural, gender, or minority history to the central political problems of an age. Our team has a distinct advantage in this regard because each of us works on topics that have clear relevance for the most "traditional" kinds of political or economic history. In my work on the cultural aspects of the French Revolution, for example, I have always tried to use those approaches to illuminate the most traditional questions: How is a new form of power created? What makes people change their minds and endorse new ideas? Tom Martin, our specialist on ancient history, has considered equally fundamental issues in his study of ancient Greek coinage. How did coins originate in Western civilization? What is the function of money in a society? How are money and power related? As a consequence of these kinds of linkages, we as a team are particularly well placed to show how social and cultural developments can illuminate the most enduring questions of history.

"As a consequence of these kinds of linkages, we as a team are particularly well placed to show how social and cultural developments can illuminate the most enduring questions of history."

Q   *The Making of the West: Peoples and Cultures* represents a major revision of *The Challenge of the West* (Heath, 1995). **From the narrative itself to features, pedagogy, maps, and artwork, the book has changed dramatically. Can you describe these revisions and explain why the authors made them? Let's start with the narrative.**

A   There is no better way to find out what works and what doesn't than by trying out an approach. Since *Challenge* was published in 1995, we have had the opportunity to teach the book and to get feedback from scores of colleagues around the country who have used it. We now have a much surer sense of how to make our case. *The Making of the West* offers much clearer signposts of the development of the argument along the way. For example, we added a third level of chapter heading to signal supporting as well as main ideas and developments, and we worked hard to provide clear and compelling chapter and section introductions

> *"Much of our excitement in this project arose from its very nature: textbook writing, unlike the scholarly books to which we were accustomed, offers historians the rare chance to revise the original work, to keep it fresh, and to make it better."*

and summaries. Although we maintained our strong chronological organization, we loosened it here and there—the scientific revolution provides one example, the World Wars of the twentieth century another—to allow the completion of a story in progress, to streamline discussion, and to underline the main themes in our narrative. While offering a clearer sense of our overall direction, we also incorporated even more material on the West's interactions with the rest of the world. And of course we brought in the new research published since 1995. Much of our excitement in this project arose from its very nature: textbook writing, unlike the scholarly books to which we were accustomed, offers historians the rare chance to revise the original work, to keep it fresh, and to make it better.

Q   **New to the book are extensive pedagogical support, recurring special features, and large map and art programs. Knowing the time pressures that teachers and students face, why did you decide to devote many pages to these elements?**

A   More and more is required of students these days (and not just in Western civ), and we know from our own teaching that students need all the help they can get in assimilating information, acquiring skills, learning about historical debate, and sampling the very newest approaches. It is a truism now, but an important one, that education must foster the ability to keep on learning how to adapt to new requirements in the future. Frankly, in *Challenge* we stuck too much to the traditional approach, expecting students to comprehend by simply reading straight through. In *The Making of the West*, we try to teach both traditional skills and new perspectives with the aim of preparing students to grasp the past and understand the history that is yet to come. For example, mastery of chronology is perhaps the most fundamental task for history students: to help them accomplish it, each chapter in our text opens with a comparative timeline that allows students to see at a glance how politics and diplomacy, economic and social trends, and intellectual, religious and cultural developments interact. A list of important dates near the close of each chapter provides a view of key events, while topic-specific timelines outline particular themes and processes. Even the running heads at the top of pages support our effort to help students keep track of chronology and stay focused on their reading by linking subject matter to time frame.

"We try to teach both traditional skills and new perspectives with the aim of preparing students to grasp the past and understand the history that is yet to come."

But like a clear narrative synthesis, strong pedagogical support is not enough on its own to encourage active learning. Setting out to revise *Challenge*, we paid special care to the boxed feature program, eager to hold to our goal of maximum flexibility for teachers while offering student readers the best introduction to historical thinking available in a survey text. We are very proud of the result: an integrated set of features that genuinely extend the narrative by revealing the process of interpretation, providing a solid introduction to the principles of historical argument, and capturing the excitement of historical investigation. The **Contrasting Views** feature, for example, provides three or four often conflicting eyewitness accounts of a central event, person, or development, such as the English civil war, Martin Luther, late-nineteenth-century migration. But it does not just present these views inertly. Introductory paragraphs provide needed context for the primary sources, and questions for debate help students focus on the big questions and alert them at the same time to the ways that history is susceptible to ongoing reinterpretation.

The **New Sources, New Perspectives** feature shows students how historians continue to develop new kinds of evidence about the past—from tree rings to Holocaust museums. This feature will fascinate students with unexpected information and also prompt them to consider how new evidence leads to new interpretations. Curious students will find suggested references for further study of these issues. Questions for Debate that appear at the end of the feature might spark a class discussion about the relationship between evidence and interpretation in our understanding of history.

Too often, textbooks seem to assume that students already know the meaning of some of the most important and contested terms in the history of the West: feudalism, the Renaissance, progress, and revolution, not to mention civilization itself. We do not make this assumption. Instead we offer a **Terms of History** feature in which we explain the meaning of these terms and show how those meanings have developed—and changed—over time. Thus, for example, the discussion of *progress* shows how the term took root in the eighteenth century and has been contested in the twentieth. For the student who is struggling to make sense of Western history, this feature explains the meaning of key terms. For a more sophisticated student, this feature can shed yet more light on the question of historical interpretation.

Since we want to emphasize the interactions between the West and the broader world, a short illustrated feature, **Did You Know?**, offers unexpected and sometimes even startling examples of cultural interchange ranging from the invention of "smoking" (derived from the New World) to the creation of polo (adapted from South Asia). History can be fun as well as provocative, after all! From our many years of teaching, we know that students learn best when they are engaged by the material.

Now, more than ever, quantitative or statistical literacy is vitally important. The **Taking Measure** feature, which appears in every chapter, highlights a chart, table, graph, or map of historical statistics that illuminates an important political, social, or cultural development. Learning how to read such information is crucial preparation for students, no matter what their eventual field of study.

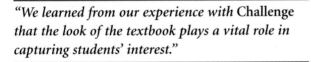

"We learned from our experience with Challenge *that the look of the textbook plays a vital role in capturing students' interest."*

Q   **Your rationale for extensive pedagogy and features is clear; what about the space devoted to art and maps?**

A   We learned from our experience with *Challenge* that the look of the textbook plays a vital role in capturing students' interest, and we were pleased to work with a publisher who similarly understood the importance of a striking, full-color design and rich art and map programs. Students have become much more attuned to visual sources of information, yet they do not always receive systematic instruction in how to "read" such visual sources. Our captions aim to help them learn how to make the most of these visually attractive and informative materials. Over 480 illustrations not only reinforce the text but show the varieties of primary sources from which historians build their narratives and interpretations. We are proud as well of our map program: fundamental to any good history book, maps take on special importance in a text intended to stress interactions between the West and the wider world, and we worked intensively with our publisher to provide the most comprehensive map program available in a survey text. Thus we offer in each chapter 4–5 full-size maps, 2–4 "spot maps"—that is, small maps on single but crucial issues that are exactly located in related discussion—and, another first for our map program, "summary maps" at the end of each chapter, which individually provide a snapshot of the West at the close of a transformative period and collectively help students visualize the West's changing contours over time.

Q   You and your coauthors have written many well-received and influential scholarly works. What response to *The Making of the West: Peoples and Cultures* would please you most?

A   We aim to communicate the vitality and excitement as well as the fundamental importance of history. The highest compliment we could receive would be to hear that reading this textbook has encouraged students to take more history courses, major in history, perhaps even want to become historians themselves. We also hope that our text helps instructors overcome the obstacles in teaching this course and perhaps even revives their own interest in the materials covered here. History is never an entirely settled matter; it is always in process. If we have succeeded in conveying some of the vibrancy of the past and the thrill of historical investigation, we will be encouraged to start rethinking and revising—as historians always must—once again.

"History is never an entirely settled matter; it is always in process."

❖ Supplements

The authors of *The Making of the West: Peoples and Cultures* oversaw development of the well-integrated ancillary program that supports their text. A comprehensive collection of print and electronic resources for students and instructors provides a host of practical learning and teaching aids.

For Students

Study Guide to Accompany **The Making of the West: Peoples and Cultures**—Volumes I (to 1740) and II (since 1560)—by Victoria Thompson, Arizona State University. This carefully developed study guide offers overview and review materials to help students master content and learn to analyze it. For each chapter in the textbook, the study guide offers a summary; an expanded outline with matching exercises; a glossary of important terms with related questions; multiple-choice and short-answer questions; and map, illustration, and documents exercises that help students synthesize the material they have learned as well as appreciate the skills historians use to understand the past. Answers for all questions and exercises, with references to relevant pages in the textbook, are provided.

The *Online Study Guide for* **The Making of the West: Peoples and Cultures** is like none other: thoroughly integrated with the text and based on the print study guide, the online study guide takes advantage of the Internet to offer structured and easily accessed help for each chapter and innovative multimedia exercises designed to reinforce themes and content. For each chapter, an initial multiple-choice test assesses student comprehension of the material and a Recommended Study Plan suggests specific exercises that cover the subject areas they still need to master. Three multiple-choice tests per chapter help students improve their command of the material. Additional exercises encourage students to think about chapter themes as well as to develop skills of analysis.

Using the highly acclaimed course-tools software developed by QuestionMark, the online study guide for *The Making of the West* allows students to keep track of their performance chapter by chapter.

Sources of **The Making of the West: Peoples and Cultures**—Volumes I (to 1740) and II (since 1560)—by Katharine Lualdi, Colby College. For each chapter in *The Making of the West*, this companion sourcebook features four important political, social, or cultural documents that either reinforce or extend text discussion. Short chapter summaries, headnotes, and discussion questions highlight chapter themes and encourage students to think critically about these primary sources.

The Bedford Series in History and Culture—Advisory Editors Natalie Z. Davis, Princeton University; Ernest R. May, Harvard University; David W. Blight, Amherst College. Any of the volumes from this highly acclaimed series of brief, inexpensive, document-based supplements can be packaged with *The Making of the West* at a reduced price. The fourteen European history titles include *Spartacus and the Slave Wars*, *Utopia*, *Candide*, *The French Revolution and Human Rights*, and *The Communist Manifesto*.

For Instructors

Instructor's Resource Manual for **The Making of the West: Peoples and Cultures**—Volumes I (to 1740) and II (since 1560)—by Michael Richards, Sweet Briar College. This comprehensive collection of tools offers both the first-time and the experienced instructor extensive teaching information for each chapter in the textbook: outlines of chapter themes, chapter summaries, lecture and discussion topics, ideas for in-class work with maps and illustrations, writing and classroom presentation assignments, and research topic suggestions. The manual also includes seven essays for instructors with titles such as "What Is Western Civilization?," "Teaching Western Civilization with Computers and Web Sites," and "Literature and the Western Civilization Classroom," as well as over a dozen reprints of frequently assigned primary sources for easy access and distribution.

Test Items to Accompany **The Making of the West: Peoples and Cultures**—Volumes I (to 1740) and II (since 1560)—by Tamara Hunt, Loyola Marymount University. In addition to twenty fill-in-the-blank, fifteen multiple-choice, ten short-answer, and four essay questions, this test bank includes for each chapter in the text a relationship-causation exercise, which asks students to place five events in chronological order and to explain a common theme that runs through them, and four map and documents exercises that test students' comprehension of chapter material and their ability to use sources. Answers for identification, multiple-choice, and short-answer questions, with references to relevant pages in the textbook, are provided. So that instructors may customize their tests to suit their classes, the answer key labels multiple-choice questions by difficulty.

The test bank is available in book format, with perforated pages for easy removal, or in Macintosh and Windows formats on disk. Easy-to-use software allows instructors to create and administer tests on paper or over a network. Instructors can generate exams and quizzes from the print test bank or write their own. A grade management function helps keep track of student progress.

Map Transparencies. A set of approximately 145 full-color acetate transparencies, free to adopters, includes all the full-size maps in the text.

CD-ROM with Presentation Manager Pro. For instructors who wish to use electronic media in the classroom, this new CD includes images, maps, and graphs from *The Making of the West: Peoples and Cultures* in an easy-to-use format that allows instructors to customize their presentations. The CD-ROM may be used with Presentation Manager Pro or with PowerPoint for instructors who wish to add their own slides to a presentation.

Using the Bedford Series in the Western Civilization Survey by Maura O'Connor. Recognizing that many instructors use a survey text in conjunction with supplements, Bedford/St. Martin's has made the fourteen Bedford Series volumes available at a discount to adopters of *The Making of the West: Peoples and Cultures.* This short guide gives practical suggestions for using volumes from the Bedford Series in History and Culture with *The Making of the West.* The guide not only supplies links between the text and the supplements but also provides ideas for starting discussions focused on a single primary-source volume.

The *Web Site for* **The Making of the West: Peoples and Cultures.** At http://www.bedfordstmartins.com/makingwest, instructors will find our useful Syllabus Manager as well as annotated pedagogical links with teaching suggestions tied to *The Making of the West.* A print guide is available for instructors looking for guidance in setting up their own Web sites.

❖ Acknowledgments

From the first draft to the last, the authors have benefited from repeated critical readings by many talented scholars and teachers. Our thanks to the following instructors, whose comments often challenged us to rethink or justify our interpretations and always provided a check on accuracy down to the smallest detail.

Dorothy Abrahamse, *California State University at Long Beach*

F. E. Beeman, *Middle Tennessee State University*

Martin Berger, *Youngstown State University*

Raymond Birn, *University of Oregon*

Charmarie J. Blaisdell, *Northeastern University*

Keith Bradley, *University of Victoria*

Paul Breines, *Boston College*

Caroline Castiglione, *University of Texas at Austin*

Carolyn A. Conley, *University of Alabama*

William Connell, *Seton Hall University*

Jo Ann H. Moran Cruz, *Georgetown University*

John P. Daly, *Louisiana Tech University*

Suzanne Desan, *University of Wisconsin at Madison*

Michael F. Doyle, *Ocean County College*

Jean C. England, *Northeastern Louisiana University*

Steven Epstein, *University of Colorado at Boulder*

Steven Fanning, *University of Illinois at Chicago*

Laura Frader, *Northeastern University*

ACKNOWLEDGMENTS

Alison Futrell, *University of Arizona*

Gretchen Galbraith, *Grand Valley State University*

Timothy E. Gregory, *Ohio State University*

Katherine Haldane Grenier, *The Citadel*

Martha Hanna, *University of Colorado at Boulder*

Julie Hardwick, *Texas Christian University*

Kenneth W. Harl, *Tulane University*

Charles Hedrick, *University of California at Santa Cruz*

Robert L. Hohlfelder, *University of Colorado at Boulder*

Maryanne Horowitz, *Occidental College*

Gary Kates, *Trinity University*

Ellis L. Knox, *Boise State University*

Lawrence Langer, *University of Connecticut*

Keith P. Luria, *North Carolina State University*

Judith P. Meyer, *University of Connecticut*

Maureen C. Miller, *Hamilton College*

Stuart S. Miller, *University of Connecticut*

Dr. Frederick Murphy, *Western Kentucky University*

James Murray, *University of Cincinnati*

Phillip C. Naylor, *Marquette University*

Carolyn Nelson, *University of Kansas*

Richard C. Nelson, *Augsburg College*

John Nichols, *University of Oregon*

Byron J. Nordstrom, *Gustavus Adolphus College*

Maura O'Connor, *University of Cincinnati*

Lawrence Okamura, *University of Missouri at Columbia*

Dolores Davison Peterson, *Foothill College*

Carl F. Petry, *Northwestern University*

Carole A. Putko, *San Diego State University*

Michael Richards, *Sweet Briar College*

Barbara Saylor Rodgers, *University of Vermont*

Sally Scully, *San Francisco State University*

Jane Slaughter, *University of New Mexico*

Donald Sullivan, *University of New Mexico*

Victoria Thompson, *Arizona State University*

Sue Sheridan Walker, *Northeastern Illinois University*

John E. Weakland, *Ball State University*

Theodore R. Weeks, *Southern Illinois University at Carbondale*

Merry Wiesner-Hanks, *University of Wisconsin at Milwaukee*

Each of us has also benefited from the close readings and valuable criticisms of our coauthors, though we all assume responsibility for our own chapters. Thomas Martin has written Chapters 1–7; Barbara Rosenwein, Chapters 8–12; Ronnie Hsia, Chapters 13–15; Lynn Hunt, Chapters 16–22; and Bonnie Smith, Chapters 23–30.

Many colleagues, friends, and family members have helped us develop this work as well. Lynn Hunt wishes to thank in particular Anne Engel, Margaret Jacob, Rick Weiche, and Melissa Verlet for their help with various aspects of this project. Tom Martin and Ronnie Hsia express warm thanks to their families for their forbearance and support. Barbara Rosenwein extends special gratitude to Steven Epstein, Naomi Honeth, Maureen Miller, and Frank, Jess, and Tom Rosenwein. Bonnie Smith thanks Julie Taddeo, Cathy Mason, Scott Glotzer,

Tamara Matheson, and Todd Shepard for research assistance.

We also wish to acknowledge and thank the publishing team who did so much to bring this book into being. Katherine E. Kurzman, executive editor for history, introduced us to Bedford/St. Martin's and guided our efforts throughout the project. Charles H. Christensen, president, and Joan E. Feinberg, editorial director, shared generous resources, mutual vision, and, best, confidence in the project and in us. Special thanks are due to many other individuals: Tina Samaha, our project manager, who with great skill and professionalism pulled all the pieces together with the help of Coleen O'Hanley, assistant production editor; photo researchers Carole Frohlich and Martha Shethar and map editors Heidi Hood and Laura Arcari, who did so much to help us realize our goals for the book's art and map programs; our original development editor, Ellen Kuhl, and the fine editors she brought to the project, Louise Townsend, Barbara Muller, and Jane Tufts; editorial assistants Sarah Barrash and Molly Kalkstein, who helped in myriad ways on many essential tasks; and our superb copyeditor, Barbara Flanagan. Last and above all, we thank Elizabeth M. Welch, senior development editor, who provided just the right doses of encouragement, prodding, and concrete suggestions for improvement. Her intelligence, skill, and determination proved to be crucial at every step of the process.

Our students' questions and concerns have shaped much of this work, and we welcome all our readers' suggestions, queries, and criticisms. Please contact us at our respective institutions or through our Web site: www.bedfordstmartins.com/makingwest.

L.H.   T.R.M.   B.H.R.   R.P.H.   B.G.S.

Brief Contents

Contents

CHAPTER 16

Wars over Beliefs, 1560–1648   563

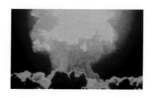

The New Globalism: Opportunities and Dilemmas, 1980 to the Present *1153*

Maps and Figures

Special Features

About the Authors

LYNN HUNT, Eugen Weber Professor of Modern European History at the University of California at Los Angeles, received her B.A. from Carleton College and her M.A. and Ph.D. from Stanford University. She is the author of *Revolution and Urban Politics in Provincial France* (1978); *Politics, Culture, and Class in the French Revolution* (1984); and *The Family Romance of the French Revolution* (1992). She is also the coauthor of *Telling the Truth about History* (1994); editor of *The New Cultural History* (1989); editor and translator of *The French Revolution and Human Rights* (1996); and coeditor of *Histories: French Constructions of the Past* (1995) and *Beyond the Cultural Turn* (1999). She has been awarded fellowships by the Guggenheim Foundation and the National Endowment for the Humanities and is a fellow of the American Academy of Arts and Sciences. She is currently preparing a CD-ROM of documents, images, and songs from the French Revolution and a book on the origins of human rights.

THOMAS R. MARTIN, Jeremiah O'Connor Professor in Classics at the College of the Holy Cross, earned his B.A. at Princeton University and his M.A. and Ph.D. at Harvard University. He is the author of *Sovereignty and Coinage in Classical Greece* (1985) and *Ancient Greece* (1996, 2000) and one of the originators of *Perseus 1.0: Interactive Sources and Studies on Ancient Greece* (1992, 1996) and www.perseus.tufts.edu, which, among other awards, was named the EDUCOM Best Software in Social Sciences (History) in 1992. He also wrote the lead article on ancient Greece for the revised edition of the Encarta electronic encyclopedia. He serves on the editorial board of STOA (www.stoa.org) and as codirector of its DEMOS project (online resources on ancient Athenian democracy). A recipient of fellowships from the National Endowment for the Humanities and the American Council of Learned Societies, he is currently conducting research on the history and significance of freedom of speech in Athenian democracy.

BARBARA H. ROSENWEIN, professor of history at Loyola University Chicago, earned her B.A., M.A., and Ph.D. at the University of Chicago. She is the author of *Rhinoceros Bound: Cluny in the Tenth Century* (1982); *To Be the Neighbor of Saint Peter: The Social Meaning of Cluny's Property, 909–1049* (1989); and *Negotiating Space: Power, Restraint,* *and Privileges of Immunity in Early Medieval Europe* (1999). She is the editor of *Anger's Past: The Social Uses of an Emotion in the Middle Ages* (1998) and coeditor of *Debating the Middle Ages: Issues and Readings* (1998) and *Monks and Nuns, Saints and Outcasts: Religion in Medieval Society* (2000). A recipient of Guggenheim and National Endowment for the Humanities fellowships, she is currently working on a history of emotions in the early Middle Ages.

R. PO-CHIA HSIA, professor of history at New York University, received his B.A. from Swarthmore College and his M.A. and Ph.D. from Yale University. He is the author of *Society and Religion in Münster, 1535–1618* (1984); *The Myth of Ritual Murder: Jews and Magic in Reformation Germany* (1988); *The German People and the Reformation* (1998); *Social Discipline in the Reformation: Central Europe, 1550–1750* (1989); *Trent 1475: Stories of a Ritual Murder Trial* (1992); and *The World of the Catholic Renewal* (1997). He has been awarded fellowships by the Woodrow Wilson International Society of Scholars, the National Endowment for the Humanities, the Guggenheim Foundation, the Davis Center of Princeton University, and the Mellon Foundation. Currently he is working on sixteenth-to-eighteenth-century cultural contacts between Europe and Asia.

BONNIE G. SMITH, professor of history at Rutgers University, earned her B.A. at Smith College and her Ph.D. at the University of Rochester. She is the author of *Ladies of the Leisure Class* (1981); *Confessions of a Concierge: Madame Lucie's History of Twentieth-Century France* (1985); *Changing Lives: Women in European History since 1700* (1989); *The Gender of History: Men, Women, and Historical Practice* (1998); and *Imperialism* (2000). She is also the coauthor and translator of *What Is Property?* (1994); editor of *Global Feminisms since 1945* (2000); and coeditor of *History and the Texture of Modern Life: Selected Writings of Lucy Maynard Salmon.* She has received fellowships from the Guggenheim Foundation, the National Endowment for the Humanities, the National Humanities Center, the Davis Center of Princeton University, and the American Council of Learned Societies. Currently she is studying the globalization of European culture and society after World War II.

16

Wars over Beliefs

1560–1648

Grand Duke of Alba

This polychrome wood sculpture from the late 1500s shows the Spanish grand duke of Alba in armor, equipped with a lance. He overshadows three potential sources of trouble: Pope Pius V, who pressed the Spanish to take aggressive action against heretics; Elizabeth I of England, who sent pirates to prey on the Spanish ships carrying gold to the armies; and Elector Augustus I of Saxony, the most influential Lutheran prince. Alba commanded the Spanish armies sent to punish the Netherlands for their rebellion against Philip II. He unleashed a reign of terror to crush the Calvinists and alarmed Protestant rulers all over Europe. Institut Amatller d'Art Hispanic.

IN MAY 1618, Protestants in the kingdom of Bohemia furiously protested the Holy Roman Emperor's attempts to curtail their hard-won religious freedoms. Protestants wanted to build new churches; the Catholic emperor wanted to stop them. Tensions boiled over when two Catholic deputy-governors tried to dissolve the meetings of Protestants. On May 23, a crowd of angry Protestants surged up the stairs of the royal castle in Prague, trapped the two Catholic deputies, dragged them screaming for mercy to the windows, and hurled them to the pavement below. One of the rebels jeered: "We will see if your [Virgin] Mary can help you!" But because they landed in a dung heap, the Catholic deputies survived. One of the two limped off on his own; the other was carried away by his servants to safety. Although no one died, this "defenestration" (from the French for "window," *la fenêtre*) of Prague touched off the Thirty Years' War (1618–1648), which eventually involved almost every major power in Europe. Before it ended, the fighting had devastated the lands of central Europe and produced permanent changes in European politics and culture.

The Thirty Years' War grew out of the religious conflicts initiated by the Reformation. When Martin Luther began the Protestant Reformation in 1517, he had no idea that he would be unleashing such dangerous forces, but religious turmoil and warfare followed almost immediately upon his break with the Catholic church. Until the early 1600s, the Peace of Augsburg of 1555 maintained relative calm in the lands of the Holy Roman Empire by granting each ruler the right to

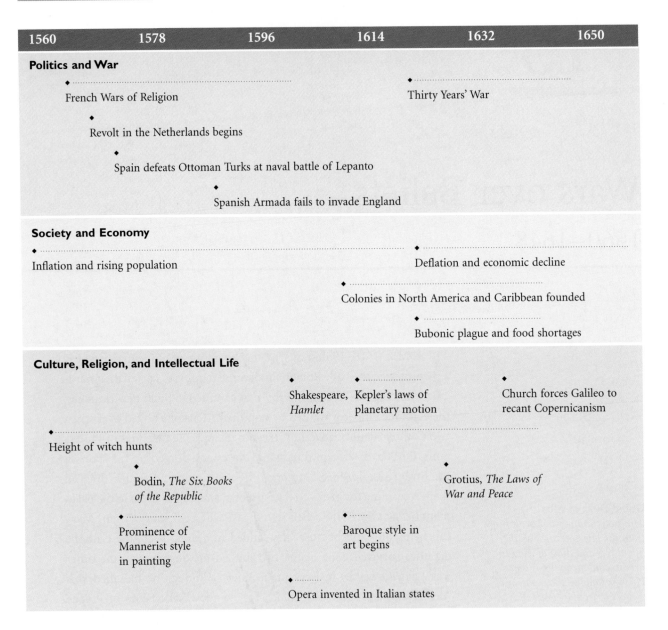

1560	1578	1596	1614	1632	1650

Politics and War

French Wars of Religion

Thirty Years' War

Revolt in the Netherlands begins

Spain defeats Ottoman Turks at naval battle of Lepanto

Spanish Armada fails to invade England

Society and Economy

Inflation and rising population

Deflation and economic decline

Colonies in North America and Caribbean founded

Bubonic plague and food shortages

Culture, Religion, and Intellectual Life

Shakespeare, *Hamlet*

Kepler's laws of planetary motion

Church forces Galileo to recant Copernicanism

Height of witch hunts

Bodin, *The Six Books of the Republic*

Grotius, *The Laws of War and Peace*

Prominence of Mannerist style in painting

Baroque style in art begins

Opera invented in Italian states

determine the religion of his territory. But in western Europe, religious strife increased dramatically after 1560 as Protestants made inroads in France, the Spanish-ruled Netherlands, and England. All in all, nearly constant warfare marked the century between 1560 and 1648. These struggles most often began as religious conflicts, but religion was never the sole motive; political power entered into every equation and raised the stakes of conflict. The Bohemian Protestants, for example, wanted both freedom to practice their religion as Protestants and national independence for the Czechs, the largest ethnic group in Bohemia. Since Bohemia had many Catholics, religious and political aims inevitably came into conflict.

The Thirty Years' War brought the preceding religious conflicts to a head and by its very violence effectively removed religion from future international disputes. Although religion still divided people *within* various states, after 1648 religion no longer provided the rationale for wars *between* European states. The orgy of mutual destruction in the Thirty Years' War left no winners in the religious struggle, and the cynical manipulation of religious issues by both Catholic and Protestant leaders showed that political interests eventually outweighed those of religion. In addition, the violence of religious conflict pushed rulers and political thinkers to seek other, nonreligious grounds for governmental authority. Few would argue for genuine toleration of religious differences, but many began to insist that the interests of states had to take priority over the desire for religious conformity.

Although particularly dramatic and deadly, the church-state crisis was only one of a series of upheavals that shaped this era. In the early seventeenth century, a major economic downturn led to food shortages, famine, and disease in much of Europe. These hit especially hard in the central European lands devastated by the fighting of the Thirty Years' War and helped shift the balance of economic power to northwestern Europe, away from the Mediterranean and central Europe. An upheaval in worldviews was also in the making, catalyzed by increasing knowledge of the new worlds discovered overseas and in the heavens. The development of new scientific methods of research would ultimately reshape Western attitudes toward religion and state power, as Europeans desperately sought alternatives to wars over religious beliefs.

❖ Religious Conflicts and State Power, 1560–1618

The Peace of Augsburg of 1555 made Lutheranism a legal religion in the predominantly Catholic Holy Roman Empire, but it did not extend recognition to Calvinists. Although the followers of Martin Luther (Lutherans) and those of John Calvin (Calvinists) similarly refused the authority of the Catholic church, they disagreed with one another about religious doctrine and church organization. Lutheranism flourished in the northern German states and Scandinavia; Calvinism spread from its headquarters in the Swiss city of Geneva. The rapid expansion of Calvinism after 1560 threatened to alter the religious balance of power in much of Europe. Calvinists challenged Catholic dominance in France, the Spanish-ruled Netherlands, Scotland, and Poland-Lithuania. In England they sought to influence the new Protestant monarch, Elizabeth I. Calvinists were not the only source of religious

contention, however. While trying to suppress the revolt of Calvinists in the Netherlands, Philip II of Spain also fought the Muslim Ottoman Turks in the Mediterranean and expelled the remnants of the Muslim population in Spain. To the east, the Russian tsar Ivan IV fought to make Muscovy the center of an empire based on Russian Orthodox Christianity. He had to compete with Lutheran Sweden and Poland-Lithuania, itself divided by conflicts among Catholics, Lutherans, and Calvinists.

French Wars of Religion, 1562–1598

Calvinist inroads in France had begun in 1555, when the Genevan Company of Pastors took charge of missionary work. Supplied with false passports and often disguised as merchants, the Calvinist pastors moved rapidly among their growing congregations, which gathered in secret in towns near Paris or in the south. Calvinist nobles provided military protection to local congregations and helped set up a national organization for the French Calvinist—or Huguenot—church. In 1562, rival Huguenot and Catholic armies began fighting a series of wars that threatened to tear the French nation into shreds (Map 16.1).

Religious Division in the Nobility. Conversion to Calvinism in French noble families often began with the noblewomen, some of whom sought intellectual independence as well as spiritual renewal in the new faith. Charlotte de Bourbon, for example, fled from a Catholic convent and eventually married William of Orange, the leader of the anti-Spanish resistance in the Netherlands. Jeanne d'Albret, mother of the future French king Henry IV, became a Calvinist and convinced many of her clan to convert, though her husband died fighting for the Catholic side. Calvinist noblewomen protected pastors, provided money and advice, and helped found schools and establish relief for the poor.

Religious divisions in France often reflected political disputes among noble families. At least one-third of the nobles—a much larger proportion than in the general population—joined the Huguenots, who usually followed the lead of the Bourbon family. The Bourbons were close relatives of the French king and stood first in line to inherit the throne if the Valois kings failed to produce a male heir. The most militantly Catholic nobles took their cues from

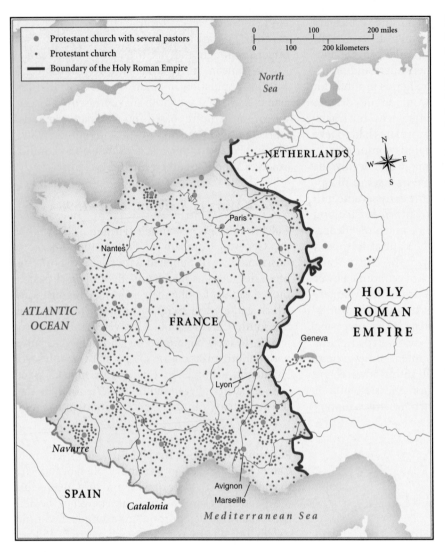

MAP 16.1 Protestant Churches in France, 1562
Calvinist missionaries took their message from their headquarters in Geneva across the border into France. The strongest concentration of Protestants was in southern France. The Bourbons, leaders of the Protestants in France, had their family lands in southwestern France in Navarre, a region that had been divided between France and Spain.

the Guise family, who aimed to block Bourbon ambitions. The Catholic Valois were caught between these two powerful factions, each with its own military organization. The situation grew even more volatile when King Henry II was accidentally killed during a jousting tournament in 1559 and his fifteen-year-old son Francis died soon after. Ten-year-old Charles IX (r. 1560–1574) became king, with his mother, Catherine de Medicis, as regent. Catherine, an Italian and a Catholic, urged limited toleration for the Huguenots in an attempt to maintain political stability, but her influence was severely limited. As one ambassador commented, "It is sufficient to say that she is a woman, a foreigner, and a Florentine to boot, born of a simple house, altogether beneath the dignity of the Kingdom of

France." In the vacuum created by the death of Henry II, the Bourbon and Guise factions consolidated their forces, and civil war erupted in 1562. Both sides committed terrible atrocities. Priests and pastors were murdered, and massacres of whole congregations became frighteningly commonplace.

St. Bartholomew's Day Massacre, 1572. Although a Catholic herself, Catherine aimed to preserve the throne for her son by playing the Guise and Bourbon factions off each other. To this end she arranged the marriage of the king's Catholic sister Marguerite de Valois to Henry of Navarre, a Huguenot and Bourbon. Just four days after the wedding in August 1572, assassins tried but failed to kill one of the Huguenot nobles allied with the Bourbons, Gaspard de Coligny. Panicked at the thought of Huguenot revenge and perhaps herself implicated in the botched plot, Catherine convinced her son to order the killing of leading Huguenots. On St. Bartholomew's Day, August 24, a bloodbath began, fueled by years of growing animosity between Catholics and Protestants. The duke of Guise himself killed Coligny. Each side viewed the other as less than human, as a source of moral pollution that had to be eradicated. In three days, Catholic mobs murdered three thousand Huguenots in Paris. Ten thousand died in the provinces over the next six weeks. The pope joyfully ordered the church bells rung throughout Catholic Europe; Spain's Philip II wrote Catherine that it was "the best and most cheerful news which at present could come to me."

The massacre settled nothing. Huguenot pamphleteers now proclaimed their right to resist a tyrant who worshiped idols (a practice that Calvinists equated with Catholicism). This right of resistance was linked to a notion of contract; upholding the true religion was part of the contract imagined as binding the ruler to his subjects. Both the right of resistance and the idea of a contract fed into the larger doctrine of constitutionalism—that a government's legitimacy rested on its upholding a constitution or contract between ruler and ruled. Constitutionalism justified resistance movements from the sixteenth century onward. Protestants and Catholics alike now saw the conflict as an international struggle for survival that required aid to coreligionists in other countries. In this way, the French Wars of Religion paved the way for wider international conflicts over religion in the decades to come.

Henry IV and the Edict of Nantes.   The religious division in France grew even more dangerous when, two years after the massacre, Charles IX died and his brother Henry III (r. 1574–1589) became king. Like his brothers before him, Henry III failed to produce an heir. Next in line to the throne was none other than the Protestant Bourbon leader Henry of Navarre. Yet because Henry III and Catherine de

Massacre Motivated by Religion
The Italian artist Giorgio Vasari painted St. Bartholomew's Night: The Massacre of the Huguenots *for a public room in Pope Gregory XIII's residence. The pope and his artist intended to celebrate a Catholic victory over Protestant heresy.*
Scala/Art Resource.

Henry IV's Paris
This painting of the Pont Neuf (new bridge) over the Seine River in Paris dates from about 1635 and shows the statue of Henry IV that was erected after his assassination in 1610. Henry IV built the bridge, the first one in Paris to have no houses on it, to link an island in the river with the two banks. This bridge is still one of the most beautiful in Paris.
Giraudon/Art Resource, NY.

Medicis saw an even greater threat to their authority in the Guises and their newly formed Catholic League, which had requested Philip II's help in rooting out Protestantism in France, they cooperated with Henry of Navarre. The Catholic League, believing that Henry III was not taking a strong enough stand against the Protestants, began to encourage disobedience. Henry III responded with a fatal trick: in 1588 he summoned the two Guise leaders to a meeting and had his men kill them. A few months later a fanatical monk stabbed Henry III to death, and Henry of Navarre became Henry IV (r. 1589–1610), despite Philip II's attempt to block his way with military intervention.

The new king soon concluded that to establish control over the war-weary country he had to place the interests of the French state ahead of his Protestant faith. In 1593, Henry IV publicly embraced Catholicism, reputedly explaining his conversion with the phrase "Paris is worth a Mass." Within a few years he defeated the ultra-Catholic opposition and drove out the Spanish. In 1598, he made peace with Spain and issued the Edict of Nantes, in which he granted the Huguenots a large measure of religious toleration. The approximately 1.25 million Huguenots became a legally protected minority

within an officially Catholic kingdom of some 20 million people. Protestants were free to worship in specified towns and were allowed their own troops, fortresses, and even courts. The Edict of Nantes pacified a religious minority too large to ignore and impossible to eradicate. Few believed in religious toleration, but Henry IV followed the advice of those neutral Catholics and Calvinists called *politiques* who urged him to give priority to the development of a durable state. Although their opponents hated them for their compromising spirit, the *politiques* believed that religious disputes could be resolved only in the peace provided by strong government. The Edict of Nantes ended the French Wars of Religion.

But the new king needed more than a good theory to strengthen state power. To ensure his own safety and the succession of his heirs, Henry had to reestablish monarchical authority. Shrewdly mixing his famous charm with bravado and cunning, Henry created a splendid image of monarchy and extended his government's control. He used paintings, songs, court festivities, and royal processions to rally subjects and officials around him. Henry also developed a new class of royal officials to counterbalance the fractious nobility. For some time the French crown had earned considerable revenue by selling offices to qualified bidders. Now, in exchange for an annual payment, officeholders could not only own their offices but also pass them to heirs or sell them to someone else. Because these offices carried prestige and often ennobled their holders, rich middle-class merchants and lawyers with aspirations to higher social status found them attractive. By buying offices they could become part of a new social elite known as the "nobility of the robe" (named after the robes that magistrates wore, much like those judges wear today). The monarchy acquired a growing bureaucracy, though at the cost of granting broad autonomy to new officials who could not be dismissed. Nonetheless, new income raised by the increased sale of offices reduced the state debt and helped Henry build the base for a strong monarchy. His efforts did not, however, prevent his own assassination in 1610 after nineteen unsuccessful attempts.

Challenges to Spanish Power

Although he failed to prevent Henry IV from taking the French throne, Philip II of Spain (r. 1556–1598) was the most powerful ruler in Europe (Map 16.2). In addition to the western Habsburg lands in

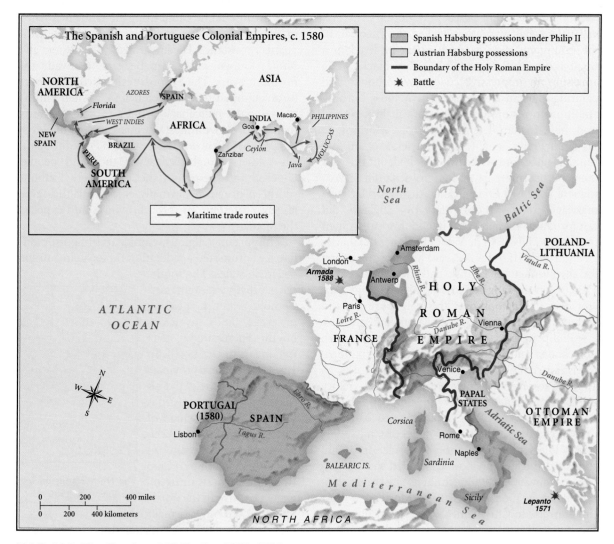

MAP 16.2 The Empire of Philip II, r. 1556–1598
Spanish king Philip II drew revenues from a truly worldwide empire. In 1580 he was the richest European ruler, but the demands of governing such far-flung territories eventually drained many of his resources.

Spain and the Netherlands, he had inherited from his father, Charles V, all the Spanish colonies recently settled in the New World of the Americas. Gold and silver funneled from the colonies supported his campaigns against the Ottoman Turks and French and English Protestants. But all of the money of the New World could not prevent his eventual defeat in the Netherlands, where Calvinist rebels established an independent Dutch Republic that soon vied with Spain, France, and England for commercial supremacy.

Philip II, the Catholic King. A deeply devout Catholic, Philip II came to the Spanish throne at age twenty-eight. He built a great gray granite structure, half-palace, half-monastery, called the Escorial, in the mountains near Madrid. There he lived in a small room and dressed in somber black, while amassing an impressive collection of books and paintings. His austere personal style hid a burning ambition to restore Catholic unity in Europe and lead the Christian defense against the Muslims. In his quest Philip benefited from a series of misfortunes. He had four wives, who all died, but through them he became part of four royal families: Portuguese, English, French, and Austrian. His brief marriage to Mary Tudor (Mary I of England) did not produce an heir, but it and his subsequent marriage to Elisabeth de Valois, the sister of Charles IX and Henry III of France, gave him reason enough for involvement in English and French affairs. In 1580, when the king of Portugal died without a direct heir, Philip took over this neighboring realm with its rich empire in Africa, India, and the Americas.

Philip insisted on Catholic unity in his own possessions and worked to forge an international Christian coalition against the Ottoman Turks. In 1571, he achieved the single greatest military victory of his reign when he joined with Venice and the papacy to defeat the Turks in a great sea battle off the Greek coast at Lepanto. Fifty thousand sailors and soldiers fought on the allied side, and eight thousand died. Spain now controlled the western Mediterranean. But Philip could not rest on his laurels. Between 1568 and 1570, the Moriscos—Muslim converts to Christianity who remained secretly faithful to Islam—had revolted in the south of Spain, killing 90 priests and 1,500 Christians. The victory at Lepanto destroyed any prospect that the Turks might come to their aid, yet Philip took stern measures against the Moriscos. He forced 50,000 to leave their villages and resettle in other regions. In 1609, his successor, Philip III, ordered their expulsion, and by 1614 some 300,000 Moriscos had been forced to relocate to North Africa.

The Revolt of the Netherlands. The Calvinists of the Netherlands were less easily intimidated than the Moriscos: they were far from Spain and accustomed to being left alone. In 1566, Calvinists in the Netherlands attacked Catholic churches, smashing stained-glass windows and statues of the Virgin Mary. Philip sent an army, which executed more than 1,100 people during the next six years. Prince William of Orange (whose name came from the lands he owned in southern France) took the lead of the anti-Spanish resistance. He encouraged adventurers and pirates known as the Sea Beggars to invade the northern ports. The Spanish responded with more force, culminating in November 1576 when Philip's long-unpaid mercenary armies sacked Antwerp, then Europe's wealthiest commercial city. In eleven days of horror known as the Spanish Fury, the Spanish soldiers slaughtered seven thousand people. Shocked into response, the ten largely Catholic southern provinces formally allied with the seven largely Protestant northern provinces and expelled the Spaniards.

Important religious, ethnic, and linguistic differences promoted a federation rather than a union of Dutch states. The southern provinces remained Catholic, French-speaking in parts, and suspicious of the increasingly strict Calvinism in the north. In 1579, the southern provinces returned to the Spanish fold. Despite the assassination in 1584 of William of Orange, after he had been outlawed as "an enemy of the human race" by Philip II, Spanish troops never regained control in the north. Spain would not formally recognize Dutch independence until 1648, but by the end of the sixteenth century the Dutch Republic was a self-governing state sheltering a variety of religious groups.

The Netherlands during the Revolt, c. 1580

Rembrandt's Depiction of Dutch Life
Rembrandt's painting known as The Night Watch *(1642) shows members of a voluntary militia company in action. In fact, it is a group portrait, probably commissioned by the guardsmen themselves. Once responsible for defending the city, the militia companies had become eating and drinking clubs for prosperous businessmen. The painting demonstrates Rembrandt's interest in every aspect of daily life in the Dutch Republic.*
Rijksmuseum, Amsterdam.

The Dutch Republic.   The princes of Orange resembled a ruling family in the Dutch Republic (sometimes incorrectly called "Holland" after the most populous of the seven provinces), but their powers paled next to those of local interests. Urban merchant and professional families known as "regents" controlled the towns and provinces. This was no democracy: governing explicitly included "the handling and keeping quiet of the multitude." In the absence of a national bureaucracy, a single legal system, or a central court, each province governed itself and sent delegates to the one common institution, the States General, which carried out the wishes of the strongest individual provinces and their ruling families.

Well situated for maritime commerce, the Dutch Republic developed a thriving economy based on shipping and shipbuilding. Whereas elites in other countries focused on their landholdings, the Dutch looked for investments in trade. After the

Dutch gained independence, Amsterdam became the main European money market for two centuries. The city was also a primary commodities market and a chief supplier of arms—to allies, neutrals, and even enemies. Dutch entrepreneurs produced goods at lower prices than anyone else and marketed them more efficiently. Dutch merchants favored free trade in Europe because they could compete at an advantage. They controlled many overseas markets thanks to their preeminence in seaborne commerce: by 1670, the Dutch commercial fleet was larger than the English, French, Spanish, Portuguese, and Austrian fleets combined.

Since the Dutch traded with anyone anywhere, it is perhaps not surprising that Dutch society tolerated more religious diversity than the other European states. One-third of the Dutch population remained Catholic, and the secular authorities allowed them to worship as they chose in private. Because Protestant sects could generally count on toleration from local regents, they remained peaceful. The Dutch Republic also had a relatively large Jewish population because many Jews had settled there after being driven out of Spain and Portugal; from 1597, Jews could worship openly in their synagogues. This openness to various religions helped make the Dutch Republic one of Europe's chief intellectual and scientific centers in the seventeenth and eighteenth centuries.

Elizabeth I's Defense of English Protestantism

As the Dutch revolt unfolded, Philip II became increasingly infuriated with Elizabeth I (r. 1558–1603), who had succeeded her half-sister Mary Tudor as queen of England. Philip had been married to Mary and had enthusiastically seconded Mary's efforts to return England to Catholicism. When Mary died in 1558, Elizabeth rejected Philip's proposal of marriage and promptly brought Protestantism back to England. Eventually she provided funds and troops to the Dutch Protestant cause. As Elizabeth moved to solidify her personal power and the authority of the Anglican church (Church of England), she had to squash uprisings by Catholics in the north and at least two serious plots against her life. In the long run, however, her greater challenges came from the Calvinist Puritans and Philip II.

Puritanism and the Church of England. The Puritans were strict Calvinists who opposed all vestiges of Catholic ritual in the Church of England. After Elizabeth became queen, many Puritans returned from exile abroad, but Elizabeth resisted their demands for drastic changes in church ritual and governance. She had assumed control as "supreme governor" of the Church of England, replacing the pope as the ultimate religious authority, and appointed all bishops. The Church of England's Thirty-Nine Articles of Religion, issued in 1563, incorporated elements of Catholic ritual along with Calvinist doctrines. Puritan ministers angrily denounced the Church of England's "popish attire and foolish disguising, . . . tithings, holy days, and a

Glorifying the Ruler
This exquisite miniature (c. 1560) attributed to Levina Teerlinc, a Flemish woman who painted for the English court, shows Queen Elizabeth I dressed in purplish blue, participating in an Easter Week ceremony at which the monarch washed the feet of poor people before presenting them with money, food, and clothing. The ceremony was held to imitate Christ's washing of the feet of his disciples; it showed that the queen could exercise every one of the ruler's customary roles.
Private collection.

thousand more abominations." To accomplish their reforms, Puritans tried to undercut the bishops' authority by placing control of church administration in the hands of a local presbytery made up of the minister and the elders of the congregation. Elizabeth rejected this Calvinist "presbyterianism."

Even though Puritans lost on almost every national issue about church organization, their influence steadily increased in local parishes. Known for their emphasis on strict moral lives, the Puritans opposed traditional forms of merrymaking such as maypole festivals and dances and regarded Sunday fairs as an insult to the Sabbath (observed by Puritans as the day of rest and worship). They abhorred the "hideous obscenities" that took place in theaters and tried to close them down. Every Puritan father—with the help of his wife—was to "make his house a little church" by teaching the children to read the Bible. At Puritan urging, a new translation of the Bible, known as the King James Bible after Elizabeth's successor, James I, was authorized in 1604. Believing themselves God's elect and England an "elect nation," the Puritans also pushed Elizabeth to help Protestants on the continent.

Triumph over Spain. Although enraged by Elizabeth's aid to the Dutch rebels, Philip II bided his time as long as she remained unmarried and her Catholic cousin Mary, Queen of Scots (Mary Stuart), stood next in line to inherit the English throne. In 1568, Scottish Calvinists forced Mary to abdicate the throne of Scotland in favor of her year-old son James (eventually James I of England), who was then raised as a Protestant. Mary spent nearly twenty years under house arrest in England, fomenting plots against Elizabeth. In 1587, when Mary's letter offering her succession rights to Philip was discovered, Elizabeth overcame her reluctance to execute a fellow monarch and ordered Mary's beheading. In response, Pope Sixtus V decided to subsidize a Catholic crusade under Philip's leadership against the heretical queen, "the English Jezebel."

At the end of May 1588, Philip II sent his *armada* (Spanish for "fleet") of 130 ships from Lisbon toward the English Channel. The Spanish king's motives were at least as much political and economic as they were religious; he now had an excuse to strike at the country whose pirates raided his shipping and encouraged Dutch resistance, and he hoped to use his fleet to ferry thousands of troops from the Netherlands across the channel to invade England itself. After several inconclusive engagements, the English scattered the Spanish Armada by sending blazing fire ships into its midst. A gale then forced the Spanish to flee around Scotland. When the Armada limped home in September, half the ships had been lost and thousands of sailors were dead or starving. Protestants throughout Europe rejoiced; Elizabeth struck a medal with the words "God blew, and they were scattered." In his play *King John* a few years later (1596), William Shakespeare wrote, "This England never did, nor never shall, Lie at the proud foot of a conqueror." Philip and Catholic Spain suffered a crushing psychological blow. A Spanish monk lamented, "Almost the whole of Spain went into mourning."

By the time Philip II died in 1598, his great empire had begun to lose its luster. The Dutch revolt ground on, and Henry IV seemed firmly established in France. The costs of fighting the Dutch, the English, and the French mounted, and in the 1590s pervasive crop failures and an outbreak of the plague made hard times even worse. An overburdened peasantry could no longer pay the taxes required to meet rising expenses. In his novel *Don Quixote* (1605), the Spanish writer Miguel de Cervantes captured the sadness of Spain's loss of grandeur. Cervantes himself had been wounded at Lepanto, been held captive in Algiers, and then served as a royal tax collector. His hero, a minor nobleman, wants to understand "this

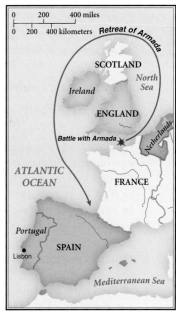

Retreat of the Spanish Armada, 1588

thing they call reason of state," but he reads so many romances and books of chivalry that he loses his wits and wanders the countryside hoping to re-create the heroic deeds of times past. He refuses to believe that these books are only fantasies: "Books which are printed under license from the king . . . can such be lies?" Don Quixote's futile adventures incarnated the thwarted ambitions of a declining military aristocracy.

England could never have defeated Spain in a head-to-head battle on land, but Elizabeth made the most of her limited means and consolidated the country's position as a Protestant power. In her early years, she held out the prospect of marriage to many political suitors but never married. She cajoled Parliament with references to her female weaknesses, but she knew Latin, French, and Italian and showed steely-eyed determination in protecting the monarchy's interests. Her chosen successor, James I (r. 1603–1625), came to the throne as king of both Scotland and England. Shakespeare's tragedies *Hamlet* (1601), *King Lear* (1605), and *Macbeth* (1606), written about the time of James's succession, might all be read as commentaries on the uncertainties faced by Elizabeth and James. In each play, family relationships are linked to questions about the legitimacy of government, just as they were for Elizabeth and James. But Elizabeth's story, unlike those of Shakespeare's tragedies, had a happy ending; she left James secure in a kingdom of growing weight in world politics.

The Clash of Faiths and Empires in Eastern Europe

State power in eastern Europe was also tied up with religion, but in less predictable ways than in western Europe. In the east, the most contentious border divided Christian Europe from the Islamic realm of the Ottoman Turks. After their defeat at Lepanto in 1571, the Ottomans were down but far from out. Even in the Mediterranean, they continued their attacks, seizing Venetian-held Cyprus in 1573. Ottoman rule went unchallenged in the Balkans, where the Turks allowed their Christian subjects to cling to the Orthodox faith rather than forcibly converting them to Islam. Orthodox Christians thus enjoyed relative toleration and were unlikely to look to western Europe for aid. Even less inclined to turn westward were the numerous and prosperous Jewish communities of the Ottoman Empire, augmented by Jews expelled from Spain.

Orthodox Christians in Russian lands received official protection from the Muscovite tsars, but on occasion some suffered the effects of official displeasure. Building on the base laid by his grandfather Ivan III, Tsar Ivan IV (r. 1533–1584) stopped at nothing in his endeavor to make Muscovy the center of a mighty Russian empire. Given to unpredictable fits of rage, Ivan tortured priests, killed numerous *boyars* (nobles), and murdered his own son with an iron rod during a quarrel. His epithet "the Terrible" reflects not only the terror he unleashed but also the awesome impression he evoked. Cunning, intelligent, morbidly suspicious, and cruel, Ivan came to embody barbarism in the eyes of westerners. An English visitor wrote that Ivan's actions had bred "a general hatred, distreccion [distraction], fear and discontentment throw [throughout] his kingdom. . . . God has a great plague in store for this people." Such warnings did not keep away the many westerners drawn to Moscow by opportunities to buy furs and sell western cloth and military hardware.

Ivan brought the entire Volga valley under Muscovite control and initiated Russian expansion eastward into Siberia. In 1558, he struck out to the west, vainly attempting to seize the decaying state of the German crusader (Teutonic) knights in present-day Estonia and Latvia to provide Russia direct access to the Baltic Sea. Two formidable foes blocked Ivan's plans for expansion: Sweden (which then included much of present-day Finland) and Poland-Lithuania. Their rulers hoped to annex the eastern Baltic provinces themselves. Poland and the grand duchy of Lithuania

Russia, Poland-Lithuania, and Sweden in the Late 1500s

united into a single commonwealth in 1569 and controlled territory stretching from the Baltic Sea to deep within present-day Ukraine and Belarus. It was the largest state lying wholly within the boundaries of Europe.

Poland-Lithuania, like the Dutch Republic, constituted one of the great exceptions to the general trend in early modern Europe toward greater monarchical authority; the Polish and Lithuanian nobles elected their king and severely circumscribed his authority. Noble converts to Lutheranism or Calvinism feared religious persecution by the Catholic majority, so the Polish-Lithuanian nobility insisted that their kings accept the principle of religious toleration as a prerequisite for election. The numerous Jewish communities prospered under the protection of the king and nobles.

Poland-Lithuania threatened the rule of Ivan's successors in Russia. After Ivan IV died in 1584, a terrible period of chaos known as the Time of Troubles ensued, during which the king of Poland-Lithuania tried to put his son on the Russian throne. In 1613, an army of nobles, townspeople, and peasants finally drove out the intruders and put on the throne a nobleman, Michael Romanov (r. 1613–1645), who established an enduring new dynasty. With the return of peace, Muscovite Russia resumed the process of state building. Reorganizing tax gathering and military recruitment and continuing to create a service nobility to whom the peasantry was increasingly subject, the first Romanovs laid the foundations of the powerful Russian empire that would emerge in the late seventeenth century under Peter the Great.

❖ The Thirty Years' War and the Balance of Power, 1618–1648

Although the eastern states managed to avoid civil wars over religion, the rest of Europe was drawn into the final and most deadly of the wars of religion, the Thirty Years' War. It began in 1618 with conflicts between Catholics and Protestants within the Holy Roman Empire and eventually involved most European states. By its end in 1648, many central European lands lay in ruins and the balance of power had shifted away from the Habsburg powers—Spain and Austria—toward France, England, and the Dutch Republic. Constant warfare created immediate turmoil, but it also fostered the growth of armies and the power of the bureaucracies that fed them with men and money. Out of the carnage would emerge centralized and powerful states that made increasing demands on ordinary people.

The Course of the War

The fighting that devastated central Europe had its origins in a combination of political weakness, ethnic competition, and religious conflict. The Austrian Habsburgs officially ruled over the huge Holy Roman Empire, which comprised eight major ethnic groups, but they could govern only with local cooperation. The emperor and four of the seven electors who chose him were Catholic; the other three electors were Protestants. The Peace of Augsburg of 1555 was supposed to maintain the balance between Catholics and Lutherans, but it had no mechanism for resolving conflicts; tensions rose as the new Catholic religious order, the Jesuits, won many Lutheran cities back to Catholicism and as Calvinism, unrecognized under the Peace, made inroads into Lutheran areas. By 1613, two of the three Protestant electors had become Calvinists. The long and complex war that grew out of these tensions took place in four phases: Bohemian (1618–1625), Danish (1625–1630), Swedish (1630–1635), and French (1635–1648).

Bohemian Phase. War first broke out in Bohemia after the defenestration of Prague in May 1618. The Austrian Habsburgs held not only the imperial crown of the Holy Roman Empire but also a collection of separately administered royal crowns, of which Bohemia was one. When the Catholic Habsburg heir Archduke Ferdinand was crowned king of Bohemia in 1617, he began to curtail the religious freedom previously granted to Protestants and thereby set in motion a fatal chain of events. After the defenestration, the Czechs, the largest ethnic group in Bohemia, established a Protestant assembly to spearhead resistance. A year later, when Ferdinand was elected emperor (as Ferdinand II, r. 1619–1637), the rebellious Bohemians deposed him and chose in his place the young Calvinist Frederick V of the Palatinate (r. 1616–1623). A quick series of clashes ended in 1620 when the imperial armies defeated the outmanned Czechs at the Battle of White Mountain, near Prague. Like the martyrdom of the religious reformer Jan Hus in 1415, White Mountain became an enduring symbol of the Czechs' desire for self-determination. They would not gain their independence until 1918.

White Mountain did not end the war. Private mercenary armies (armies for hire) began to form during the fighting, and the emperor had virtually no control over them. The meteoric rise of one commander, Albrecht von Wallenstein (1583–1634), showed how political ambition could trump religious conviction. A Czech Protestant by birth, Wallenstein offered in 1625 to raise an army for the Catholic emperor and soon had in his employ

125,000 soldiers, who occupied and plundered much of Protestant Germany with the emperor's approval.

Danish and Swedish Phases. The Lutheran king of Denmark Christian IV (r. 1596–1648) responded to Wallenstein's depredations by invading northern Germany to protect the Protestants and to extend his own influence. Despite Dutch and English encouragement, Christian lacked adequate military support, and Wallenstein's forces defeated him. Emboldened by his general's victories, Ferdinand issued the Edict of Restitution in 1629, which outlawed Calvinism in the empire and reclaimed Catholic church properties confiscated by the Lutherans.

With Protestant interests in serious jeopardy, Gustavus Adolphus (r. 1611–1632) of Sweden marched into Germany in 1630. Declaring his support for the Protestant cause, he clearly intended to gain control over trade in northern Europe, where he had already ejected the Poles from present-day Latvia and Estonia. His highly trained army of some 100,000 soldiers made Sweden, with a population of only one million, the supreme power of northern Europe. Now the primacy of political motives became obvious: the Catholic French government under the leadership of Cardinal Richelieu offered to subsidize the Lutheran Gustavus. Richelieu hoped to block Spanish intervention in the war and win influence and perhaps territory in the Holy Roman Empire. The agreement between the Lutheran and Catholic powers to fight the Catholic Habsburgs showed that state interests now outweighed all other considerations.

Gustavus defeated the imperial army and occupied the Catholic parts of southern Germany before he was killed at the battle of Lützen in 1632. Once again the tide turned, but this time it swept Wallenstein with it. Because Wallenstein was rumored to be negotiating with Protestant powers, Ferdinand dismissed his general and had his henchmen assassinate him.

French Phase. France openly joined the fray in 1635 by declaring war on Spain and soon after forged an alliance with the Calvinist Dutch to aid them in their struggle for independence from Spain. The French king Louis XIII (r. 1610–1643) and his chief minister Richelieu (1585–1642) had hoped to profit from the troubles of Spain in the Netherlands and from the conflicts between the Austrian

A Ruler Rides in Majesty
This caparison (ornamental covering) of wool and silk was decorated with the arms of Gustavus Adolphus of Sweden. It was manufactured in 1621 for the king's official entry into Stockholm.
© LSH Fotoavdelnigen. Foto Goran Schmidt/Livrustkammaren, Stockholm.

The Horrors of the Thirty Years' War
The French artist Jacques Collot produced this engraving of the Thirty Years' War as part of a series called The Miseries and Misfortunes of War *(1633). The actions depicted resemble those in Hans Grimmelshausen's novel* The Adventures of a Simpleton, *based on Grimmelshausen's personal experience of the Thirty Years' War.*
The Granger Collection.

emperor and his Protestant subjects. Religion took a backseat as the two Catholic powers France and Spain pummeled each other. The Swedes kept up their pressure in Germany, the Dutch attacked the Spanish fleet, and a series of internal revolts shook the cash-strapped Spanish crown. In 1640, peasants in the rich northeastern province of Catalonia rebelled, overrunning Barcelona and killing the viceroy; the Catalans resented government confiscation of their crops and demands that they house and feed soldiers on their way to the French frontier. The Portuguese revolted in 1640 and proclaimed independence like the Dutch. In 1643, the Spanish suffered their first major defeat at French hands. Although the Spanish were forced to concede independence to Portugal (part of Spain only since 1580), they eventually suppressed the Catalan revolt.

France too faced exhaustion after years of rising taxes and recurrent revolts. In 1642 Richelieu died. Louis XIII followed him a few months later and was succeeded by his five-year-old son Louis XIV. With an Austrian queen mother serving as regent and an Italian cardinal, Mazarin, providing advice, French politics once again moved into a period of instability, rumor, and crisis. All sides were ready for peace.

The Effects of Constant Fighting

When peace negotiations began in the 1640s, they did not come a moment too soon for the ordinary people of Europe. Warfare left much of central Europe in shambles and taxed to the limit the resources of people in all the countries involved. The desperate efforts of rulers to build up bigger and bigger armies left their mark on the new soldiers and eventually on state structures as well.

The Experience of Ordinary People. People caught in the paths of rival armies suffered most. Some towns had faced up to ten or eleven prolonged sieges during the fighting. In 1648, as negotiations dragged on, a Swedish army sacked the rich cultural capital Prague, plundered its churches and castles, and effectively eliminated it as a center of culture and learning. Even worse suffering took place in the countryside. Peasants fled their villages, which were often burned down. At times, desperate peasants revolted and attacked nearby castles and monasteries. War and intermittent outbreaks of plague cost some German towns one-third or more of their population. One-third of the inhabitants of Bohemia also perished.

One of the earliest German novels, *The Adventures of a Simpleton* (1669) by Hans Grimmelshausen, recounts the horror of the Thirty Years' War. In one scene, the boy Simplicius looks up from his bagpipe to find himself surrounded by unidentified enemy cavalrymen, who drag him back to his father's farm; ransack the house; rape the maid, his mother, and his sister; force water mixed with dung (called "the Swedish drink" after the Swedish armies) down the hired farmhand's throat; and hold the feet of Simplicius's father to the fire until he tells where he hid his gold and jewels. The invaders then torture neighbors with thumbscrews, throw one alive into the oven, and strangle another with a crude noose. Simplicius hides in the woods but can still hear the cries of the suffering peasants and see his family's house burn down.

The Growth of Armies.   Soldiers did not fare all that much better than peasants as rulers sought to expand their armies by any means possible. Governments increasingly short of funds often failed to pay the troops, and frequent mutinies, looting, and pillaging resulted. Armies attracted all sorts of displaced people desperately in need of provisions. In the last year of the Thirty Years' War, the Imperial-Bavarian Army had 40,000 men entitled to draw rations—and more than 100,000 wives, prostitutes, servants, children, maids, and other camp followers forced to scrounge for their own food. The bureaucracies of early-seventeenth-century Europe simply could not cope with such demands: armies and their hangers-on had to live off the countryside. The result was scenes like those witnessed by Simplicius.

The Thirty Years' War accelerated developments in military armament and tactics. To get more firepower, commanders followed the lead of Gustavus Adolphus in spreading out the soldiers firing guns; rather than bunching those firing muskets together, they set up long, thin lines of three to five ranks firing in turn. Tightly packed formations of pike-carrying foot soldiers pushed the battle forward. Everywhere, the size of armies increased dramatically. Most armies in the 1550s had fewer than 50,000 men, but Gustavus Adolphus had 100,000 men under arms in 1631; by the end of the seventeenth century, Louis XIV of France could count on 400,000 soldiers. The cost of larger armies and weapons such as cannon and warships strained the resources of every state. Maintaining discipline in these huge armies required harsher methods. Drill, combat training, and a clear chain of command became essential. Newly introduced "uniforms" created—as their name suggests—standardization, but uniforms soon lost their distinctiveness in the conditions of early modern warfare. An Englishman who fought for the Dutch army in 1633 described how he slept on the wet ground, got his boots full of water, and "at peep of day looked like a drowned ratt."

Although foreign mercenaries still predominated in many armies, rulers began to recruit more of their own subjects. Volunteers proved easiest to find in hard times, when the threat of starvation induced men to accept the bonus offered for signing up. A Venetian general explained the motives for enlisting: "To escape from being craftsmen [or] working in a shop; to avoid a criminal sentence; to see new things; to pursue honour (though these are very few) . . . all in the hope of having enough to live on and a bit over for shoes, or some other trifle."

The Peace of Westphalia, 1648

The comprehensive settlement provided by the Peace of Westphalia—named after the German province where negotiations took place—would serve as a model for resolving conflict among warring European states. For the first time, a diplomatic congress addressed international disputes, and the signatories to the treaties guaranteed the resulting settlement. A method still in use, the congress was the first to bring *all* parties together, rather than two or three at a time.

The Winners and Losers.   France and Sweden gained most from the Peace of Westphalia. Although France and Spain continued fighting until 1659, France acquired parts of Alsace and replaced Spain as the prevailing power on the continent. Baltic conflicts would not be resolved until 1661, but Sweden took several northern territories from the Holy Roman Empire (Map 16.3).

The Habsburgs lost the most. The Spanish Habsburgs recognized Dutch independence after eighty years of war. The Swiss Confederation and the German princes demanded autonomy from the Austrian Habsburg rulers of the Holy Roman Empire. Each German prince gained the right to establish Lutheranism, Catholicism, or Calvinism in his state,

MAP 16.3 The Thirty Years' War and the Peace of Westphalia, 1648
The Thirty Years' War involved many of the major continental European powers. The arrows marking invasion routes show that most of the fighting took place in central Europe in the lands of the Holy Roman Empire. The German states and Bohemia sustained the greatest damage during the fighting. None of the combatants emerged unscathed because even ultimate winners such as Sweden and France depleted their resources of men and money.

a right denied to Calvinist rulers by the Peace of Augsburg in 1555. The independence ceded to German princes sustained political divisions that would remain until the nineteenth century and prepared the way for the emergence of a new power, the Hohenzollern Elector of Brandenburg, who increased his territories and developed a small but effective standing army. After losing considerable territory in the west, the Austrian Habsburgs turned eastward to concentrate on restoring Catholicism to Bohemia and wresting Hungary from the Turks.

The Peace of Westphalia permanently settled the distributions of the main religions in the Holy Roman Empire: Lutheranism would dominate in the north, Calvinism in the area of the Rhine River,

and Catholicism in the south. Most of the territorial changes in Europe remained intact until the nineteenth century. In the future, international warfare would be undertaken for reasons of national security, commercial ambition, or dynastic pride rather than to enforce religious uniformity. As the *politiques* of the late sixteenth century had hoped, state interests now outweighed motivations of faith in political affairs.

The Growth of State Authority. Warfare increased the reach of states: to field larger armies, governments needed more revenue and more officials to supervise the supply of troops, the collection of taxes, and the repression of resistance to higher taxes. In France the rate of land tax paid by peasants doubled in the eight years after France joined the war. In addition to raising taxes, governments frequently resorted to currency depreciation, which often resulted in inflation and soaring prices; the sale of new offices; forced loans to raise money in emergencies; and manipulation of the embryonic stock and bond markets. When all else failed, they declared bankruptcy; the Spanish government, for example, did so three times in the first half of the seventeenth century.

Poor peasants and city workers could hardly bear new demands for money, and the governments' creditors and high-ranking nobles resented monarchical intrusions. Opposition to royal taxation often set off uprisings. From Portugal to Muscovy, ordinary people resisted new impositions by forming makeshift armies and battling royal forces. With their colorful banners, unlikely leaders, strange names (the Nu-Pieds, or "Barefooted," in France, for instance), and crude weapons, the rebels usually proved no match for state armies, but they did keep officials worried and troops occupied.

As the demand for soldiers and for the money to supply them rose, the number of state employees multiplied, paperwork proliferated, and appointment to office began to depend on university education in the law. Monarchs relied on advisers who now took on the role of modern prime ministers. Axel Oxenstierna, for example, played a central part in Swedish governments between 1611 and 1654; continuity in Swedish affairs, especially after the death of Gustavus Adolphus, largely depended on him. As Louis XIII's chief minister, Richelieu arranged support for the Lutheran Gustavus even though Richelieu was a cardinal of the Catholic church. His priority was *raison d'état* ("reason of state"), that is, the state's interest above all else. He silenced Protestants within France because they had become too independent and crushed noble and popular resistance to Louis's policies. He set up *intendants*—delegates from the king's council dispatched to the provinces—to oversee police, army, and financial affairs.

To justify the growth of state authority and the expansion of government bureaucracies, rulers carefully cultivated their royal images. James I of England explicitly argued that he ruled by divine right and was accountable only to God: "The state of monarchy is the supremest thing on earth; for kings are not only God's lieutenant on earth, but even by God himself they are called gods." He

The Arts and State Power
Diego Velázquez painted King Philip IV of Spain and many members of his court. This painting of 1634–1635 shows Philip on horseback. In the seventeenth century, many rulers hired court painters to embellish the image of royal majesty. Philip IV commissioned this painting for his new palace called Buen Retiro.
All rights reserved. © Museo Nacional Del Prado – Madrid.

advised his son to maintain a manly appearance (his own well-known homosexual liaisons did not make him seem less manly to his subjects): "Eschew to be effeminate in your clothes, in perfuming, preening, or such like, and fail never in time of wars to be galliardest and bravest, both in clothes and countenance." Clothes counted for so much that most rulers regulated who could wear which kinds of cloth and decoration, reserving the richest and rarest such as ermine and gold for themselves.

Just as soldiers had to learn new drills for combat, courtiers had to learn to follow precise rituals at court. In Spain, court regulations set the wages, duties, and ceremonial functions of every official. Hundreds, even thousands, of people made up such a court. The court of Philip IV (r. 1621–1665), for example, numbered seventeen hundred. In the 1630s he built a new palace near Madrid. There the courtiers lived amid extensive parks and formal gardens, artificial ponds and grottoes, an iron aviary (which led some critics to call the whole thing a "chicken coop"), a wild animal cage, a courtyard for bullfights, and rooms filled with sculptures and paintings. State funerals, public festivities, and court display, like the acquisition of art and the building of sumptuous palaces, served to underline the power and glory of the ruler.

❖ Economic Crisis and Realignment

The devastation caused by the Thirty Years' War deepened an economic crisis that was already under way. After a century of rising prices, caused partly by massive transfers of gold and silver from the New World and partly by population growth, in the early 1600s prices began to level off and even to drop, and in most places population growth slowed. With fewer goods being produced, international trade fell into recession. Agricultural yields also declined. Just when states attempted to field ever-expanding standing armies, peasants and townspeople alike were less able to pay the escalating taxes needed to finance the wars. Famine and disease trailed grimly behind economic crisis and war, in some areas causing large-scale uprisings and revolts. Behind the scenes, the economic balance of power gradually shifted as northwestern Europe began to

dominate international trade and broke the stranglehold of Spain and Portugal in the New World.

From Growth to Recession

Population grew and prices rose in the second half of the sixteenth century. Even though religious and political turbulence led to population decline in some cities, such as war-torn Antwerp, overall rates of growth remained impressive: in the sixteenth century, parts of Spain doubled in population and England's population grew by 70 percent. The supply of precious metals swelled too. Improvements in mining techniques in central Europe raised the output of silver and copper mines, and in the 1540s new silver mines had been discovered in Mexico and Peru. Spanish gold imports peaked in the 1550s, silver in the 1590s. (See "Taking Measure," below). This flood of precious metals combined with population

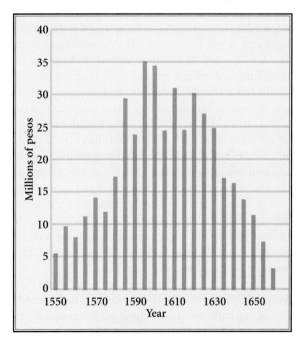

TAKING MEASURE **The Rise and Fall of Silver Imports to Spain, 1550–1660**
Gold and silver from the New World enabled the king of Spain to pursue aggressive policies in Europe and around the world. At what point did silver imports reach their highest level? Was the fall in silver imports precipitous or gradual? What can we conclude about the resources available to the Spanish king?
From Earl J. Hamilton, *American Revolution and the Price Revolution in Spain, 1501–1650* (Cambridge, Harvard University Press, 1934).

growth to fuel an astounding inflation in food prices in western Europe—400 percent in the sixteenth century—and a more moderate rise in the cost of manufactured goods. Wages rose much more slowly, at about half the rate of the increase in food prices. Governments always overspent revenues and by the end of the century most of Europe's rulers faced deep deficits.

Recession did not strike everywhere at the same time, but the warning signs were unmistakable. From the Baltic to the East Indies, foreign trade slumped as war and an uncertain money supply made business riskier. After 1625, silver imports to Spain declined, in part because so many of the native Americans who worked in Spanish colonial mines died from disease and in part because the ready supply of precious metals was progressively exhausted. Textile production fell in many countries and in some places nearly collapsed, largely because of decreased demand and a shrinking labor force. Even the relatively limited trade in African slaves stagnated, though its growth would resume after 1650 and skyrocket after 1700. African slaves were first transported to the new colony of Virginia in 1619, foreshadowing a major transformation of economic life in the New World colonies.

Demographic slowdown also signaled economic trouble. Overall, Europe's population may actually have declined, from 85 million in 1550 to 80 million in 1650. In the Mediterranean, growth apparently stopped in the 1570s. The most sudden reversal occurred in central Europe as a result of the Thirty Years' War: one-fourth of the inhabitants of the Holy Roman Empire perished in the 1630s and 1640s. The population continued to increase only in England and Wales, the Dutch Republic and the Spanish Netherlands, and Scandinavia.

Crop production eventually reflected these differences. Where the population stagnated or declined, agricultural prices dropped because of less demand, and farmers who produced for the market suffered. Many reacted by converting grain-growing land to pasture or vineyards (the prices of other foods fell less than the price of grain). Interest in improvement of the land diminished. In some places peasants abandoned their villages and left land to waste, as had happened during the plague epidemic of the late fourteenth century. The only country that emerged unscathed from this downturn was the Dutch Republic, principally because it had long excelled in agricultural innovation. Inhabiting Europe's most densely populated area, the Dutch developed systems of field drainage, crop rotation, and animal husbandry that provided high yields of grain for both people and animals. Their foreign trade, textile industry, crop production, and population all grew. After the Dutch, the English fared best; unlike the Spanish, the English never depended on New World gold and silver, and unlike most continental European countries, England escaped the direct impact of the Thirty Years' War.

Historians have long disagreed about the causes of the early-seventeenth-century recession. Some cite the inability of agriculture to support a growing population by the end of the sixteenth century; others blame the Thirty Years' War, the states' demands for more taxes, the irregularities in money supply resulting from rudimentary banking practices, or the waste caused by middle-class expenditures in the desire to emulate the nobility. To this list of causes, recent researchers have added climatic changes. (See "New Sources, New Perspectives," page 584.) Cold winters and wet summers meant bad harvests, and these natural disasters ushered in a host of social catastrophes. When the harvest was bad, prices shot back up and many could not afford to feed themselves.

Consequences for Daily Life

The recession of the early 1600s had both short-term and long-term effects. In the short term it aggravated the threat of food shortages and increased the outbreaks of famine and disease. In the long term it deepened the division between prosperous and poor peasants and fostered the development of a new pattern of late marriages and smaller families.

Famine and Disease.   Outside of England and the Dutch Republic, grain had replaced meat as the essential staple of most Europeans' diets because meat had become too expensive. Most people consumed less butter, eggs, poultry, and wine and more grain products, ranging from bread to beer. The average adult European now ate more than four hundred pounds of grain per year. Peasants lived on bread, soup with a little fat or oil, peas or lentils, garden vegetables in season, and only occasionally a piece of meat or fish. In most places the poor existed on the verge of starvation; one contemporary observed that "the fourth part of the inhabitants of the parishes of England are miserable people and (harvest time excepted) without any subsistence."

The threat of food shortages haunted Europe whenever harsh weather destroyed crops. Local markets were vulnerable to problems of food distribution: customs barriers inhibited local trade, overland transport moved at a snail's pace, bandits disrupted traffic, and the state or private contractors commandeered available food for the perpetually warring armies. Usually the adverse years differed from place to place, but from 1594 to 1597 most of Europe suffered from shortages; the resulting famine triggered revolts from Ireland to Muscovy. To head off social disorder, the English government drew up a new Poor Law in 1597 that required each community to support its poor. Many other governments also increased relief efforts.

Most people, however, did not respond to their dismal circumstances by rebelling or mounting insurrections. They simply left their huts and hovels and took to the road in search of food and charity. Overwhelmed officials recorded pitiful tales of suffering. Women and children died while waiting in line for food at convents or churches. Husbands left their wives and families to search for better conditions in other parishes or even other countries. Those left behind might be reduced to eating chestnuts, roots, bark, and grass. In eastern France in 1637, a witness reported, "The roads were paved with people. . . . Finally it came to cannibalism." Eventually compassion gave way to fear as these hungry vagabonds, who sometimes banded together to beg for bread, became more aggressive, occasionally threatening to burn a barn if they were not given food.

Successive bad harvests led to malnutrition, which weakened people and made them more susceptible to such epidemic diseases as the plague, typhoid fever, typhus, dysentery, smallpox, and influenza. Disease did not spare the rich, although many epidemics hit the poor hardest. The plague was feared most: in one year it could cause the death of up to half of a town's or village's population, and it struck with no discernible pattern. Nearly 5 percent of France's entire population died just in the plague of 1628–1632.

The Changing Status of the Peasantry.
Other effects of economic crisis were less visible than famine and disease, but no less momentous. The most im-

The Life of the Poor
This mid-seventeenth-century painting by the Dutch artist Adriaen Pietersz van de Venne depicts the poor peasant weighed down by his wife and child. An empty food bowl signifies their hunger. In retrospect, this painting seems unfair to the wife of the family; she is shown in clothes that are not nearly as tattered as her husband's and is portrayed entirely as a burden, rather than as a help in getting by in hard times. In reality, many poor men abandoned their homes in search of work, leaving their wives behind to cope with hungry children and what remained of the family farm.
Allen Memorial Art Museum, Oberlin College, Oberlin, Ohio, Mrs. F. F. Prentiss Fund, 1960.

portant was the peasantry's changing status. Peasants faced many obligations, including rent and various fees for inheriting or selling land and tolls for using mills, wine presses, or ovens. States collected direct taxes on land and sales taxes on such consumer goods as salt, an essential preservative.

NEW SOURCES, NEW PERSPECTIVES

Tree Rings and the Little Ice Age

The economic crisis of the seventeenth century had many causes, and historians disagree about what they were and which were more important. One cause that has inspired intense debate is global cooling. Glaciers advanced, average temperatures fell, and winters were often exceptionally severe. Canals and rivers essential to markets froze over. Great storms disrupted ocean traffic (one storm changed the escape route of the Spanish Armada). Entire villages were demolished by glacier advance. Even in the valleys far from the mountains, cooler weather meant lower crop yields, which quickly translated into hunger and greater susceptibility to disease, leading in turn to population decline. Some historians of climate refer to the entire period 1600–1850 as the little ice age because glaciers advanced during this time and retreated only after 1850; others argue for the period 1550–1700 as the coldest, but either time frame includes the seventeenth century. Since systematic records of European temperatures were kept only from the 1700s onward, how do historians know that the weather was cooler? Given the current debates about global warming, how can we sift through the evidence to come up with a reliable interpretation?

Information about climate comes from various sources. The advance of glaciers can be seen in letters complaining to the authorities. In 1601, for example, panic-stricken villagers in Savoy (in the French Alps) wrote, "We are terrified of the glaciers . . . which are moving forward all the time and have just buried two of our villages." Yearly temperature fluctuations can be determined from the dates of wine harvests; growers harvested their grapes earliest when the weather was warmest and latest when it was coolest. Scientists study ice cores taken from Greenland to determine temperature variations; such studies seem to indicate that the coolest times were the periods 1160–1300; the 1600s; and 1820–1850. The period 1730–1800 appears to have been warmer. Recently, scientists have developed techniques for sampling corals in the tropics and sediments on oceanic shelves.

But most striking are data gathered from tree rings (the science is called *dendrochronology* or *dendroclimatology*). Timber samples have been taken from very old oak trees and also from ancient beams in buildings and archaeological digs and from logs left long undisturbed in northern bogs and riverbeds. In cold summers, trees lay down thinner growth rings; in warm ones, thicker rings.

Protestant and Catholic churches alike exacted a tithe (a tax equivalent to one-tenth of the parishioner's annual income); often the clergy took their tithe in the form of crops and collected it directly during the harvest. Any reversal of fortune could force peasants into the homeless world of vagrants and beggars, who numbered as much as 1 to 2 percent of the total population.

In the seventeenth century the mass of peasants in western Europe became more sharply divided into prosperous and poor. In England, the Dutch Republic, northern France, and northwestern Germany, the peasantry was disappearing: improvements gave some peasants the means to become farmers who rented substantial holdings, produced for the market, and in good times enjoyed relative comfort and higher status. Those who could not afford to plant new crops such as maize (American corn) or buckwheat or to use techniques that ensured higher yields became simple laborers with little or no land of their own. The minimum plot of land needed to feed a family varied depending on the richness of the soil, available improvements in agriculture, and distance from markets. For example,

The Frozen Thames

This painting by Abraham Hondius of the frozen Thames River in London dates to 1677. In the 1670s and 1680s the Thames froze several times. Hondius himself depicted another such view in 1684. Diarists recorded that shopkeepers even set up their stalls on the ice. In other words, the expected routines of daily life changed during the cooling down of the seventeenth century. Contemporaries were shocked enough by the changes to record them for posterity. Museum of London.

Information about tree rings confirms the conclusions drawn from wine harvest and ice core samples: the seventeenth century was relatively cold. Recent tree ring studies have shown that some of the coldest summers were caused by volcanic eruptions; according to a study of more than one hundred sites in North America and Europe, the five coldest summers in the past four hundred years were in 1601, 1641, 1669, 1699, and 1912 (four out of five in the seventeenth century), and all but the summer of 1699 came in years following recorded eruptions.

QUESTIONS FOR DEBATE

1. What were the historical consequences of global cooling in the seventeenth century?

2. Why would trees be especially valuable sources of information about climate?

FURTHER READING

H. H. Lamb, *Climate, History and the Modern World*, 2nd ed., 1995.

Patrick R. Galloway, "Long-Term Fluctuations in Climate and Population in the Preindustrial Era," *Population and Development Review* 12 (1986): 1–24.

only two acres could support a family in Flanders, as opposed to ten acres in Muscovy. One-half to four-fifths of the peasants did not have enough acreage to support a family. They descended deeper into debt during difficult times and often lost their land to wealthier farmers or to city officials intent on developing rural estates.

As the recession deepened, women lost some of their economic opportunities. Widows who had been able to take over their late husbands' trade now found themselves excluded by the urban guilds or limited to short tenures. Many women went into domestic service until they married, some for their entire lives. When town governments began to fear the effects of increased mobility from country to town and town to town, they carefully regulated women's work as servants, requiring them to stay in their positions unless they could prove mistreatment by a master.

Effects on Marriage and Childbearing. Demographic historians have shown that European families reacted almost immediately to economic crisis. During bad harvests they postponed marriages and

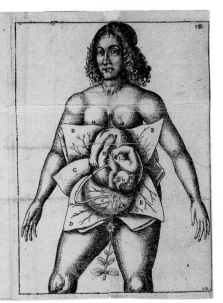

The Figure Explained:

Being a Diſſection of the WOMB, with the uſual manner how the CHILD lies therein near the time of its Birth.

B B. The inner parts of the *Chorion* extended and branched out.

C. The *Amnios* extended.

D D. The Membrane of the Womb extended and branched.

E. The Fleſhy ſubſtance call'd the *Cake* or *Placenta*, which nouriſhes the Infant, it is full of Veſſels.

F. The Veſſels appointed for the Navel ſtring.

G. The Navel ſtring carrying nouriſhment from the *Placenta* to the Navel.

H H H. The manner how the Infant lieth in the Womb near the time of its Birth.

I. The Navel ſtring how it enters into the Navel.

The *Midwives Book* (1671)
The English woman Jane Sharp wrote the first book on midwifery by a woman. She endeavored to provide as much scientific information about the female body as was available at the time.
British Library.

had fewer children. When hard times passed, more people married and had more children. But even in the best of times, one-fifth to one-quarter of all children died in their first year, and half died before age twenty. In 1636, an Englishman described his grief when his twenty-one-month-old son died: "We both found the sorrow for the loss of this child, on whom we had bestowed so much care and affection . . . far to surpass our grief for the decease of his three elder brothers, who dying almost as soon as they were born, were not so endeared to us as this [one] was."

Childbirth still carried great risks for women, about 10 percent of whom died in the process. Even in the richest and most enlightened homes, childbirth often occasioned an atmosphere of panic. To allay their fears, women sometimes depended on magic stones and special pilgrimages and prayers. Midwives delivered most babies; physicians were scarce, and even if they did attend a birth they were generally less helpful. The Englishwoman Alice Thornton described in her diary how a doctor bled her to prevent a miscarriage after a fall; her son died anyway in a breech birth that almost killed her too.

It might be assumed that families would have more children to compensate for high death rates, but beginning in the early seventeenth century and continuing until the end of the eighteenth, families in all ranks of society started to limit the number of children. Because methods of contraception were not widely known, they did this for the most part by marrying later; the average age at marriage dur-

ing the seventeenth century rose from the early twenties to the late twenties. The average family had about four children. Poorer families seem to have had fewer children, wealthier ones more. Peasant couples, especially in eastern and southeastern Europe, had more children than urban couples because cultivation still required intensive manual labor.

The consequences of late marriage were profound. Young men and women were expected to put off marriage (*and* sexual intercourse) until their mid- to late twenties—if they were among the lucky 50 percent who lived that long and not among the 10 percent who never married. Because both the Reformation and Counter-Reformation had stressed sexual fidelity and abstinence before marriage, the number of births out of wedlock was relatively small (2–5 percent of births); premarital intercourse was generally tolerated only after a couple had announced their engagement.

The Economic Balance of Power

Just as the recession produced winners and losers among ordinary people, so too it created winners and losers among the competing states of Europe. The economies of southern Europe declined, whereas those of the northwest emerged stronger. Competition in the New World reflected and reinforced this shift as the English, Dutch, and French rushed to establish trading outposts and permanent settlements to compete with the Spanish and Portuguese.

Regional Differences. The crisis of the seventeenth century ended the dominance of Mediterranean economies, which had endured since the time of the Greeks and Romans, and ushered in the new powers of northwestern Europe with their growing Atlantic economies. With expanding populations and geographical positions that promoted Atlantic trade, England and the Dutch Republic vied with France to become the leading mercantile powers. Northern Italian industries were eclipsed; Spanish commerce with the New World dropped. Amsterdam replaced Seville, Venice, Genoa, and Antwerp as the center of European trade and commerce. The plague also had differing effects. Whereas central Europe and the Mediterranean countries took generations to recover from its ravages, northwestern Europe quickly replaced its lost population, no doubt because this area's people had suffered less from the effects of the Thirty Years' War and from the malnutrition related to the economic crisis.

East-west differences would soon overshadow those between northern and southern regions. Because labor shortages coincided with economic recovery, peasants in western Europe gained more independence and all but the remnants of serfdom disappeared. By contrast, from the Elbe River east to Muscovy, nobles reinforced their dominance over peasants, thanks to cooperation from rulers and lack of resistance from villagers, whose community traditions had always acknowledged nobles' rights of lordship.

The price rise of the sixteenth century prompted Polish and eastern German nobles to increase their holdings and step up their production of grain for western markets. To raise production, they demanded more rent and dues from their peasants, whom the government decreed must stay in their villages. Although noble landlords lost income in the economic downturn of the first half of the seventeenth century, their peasants gained nothing. Those who were already dependent became serfs—completely tied to the land. A local official might complain of "this barbaric and as it were Egyptian servitude," but he had no power to fight the nobles. In Muscovy the complete enserfment of the peasantry would eventually be recognized in the Code of Laws in 1649. Although enserfment produced short-term profits for landlords, in the long run it retarded economic development in eastern Europe and kept most of the population in a stranglehold of illiteracy and hardship.

Competition in the New World. Many European states, including Sweden and Denmark, rushed to join the colonial competition because they considered it a branch of mercantilist policy. According to the doctrine of mercantilism, governments should sponsor policies to increase national wealth. To this end, they chartered private joint-stock companies to enrich investors by importing fish, furs, tobacco, and precious metals, if they could be found, and to develop new markets for European

"Savages" of the New World
Europeans found the "savages" of the New World fascinating and terrifying. Both sides are captured in Paolo Farinati's 1595 painting America. *The half-dressed savage appears much like a noble Italian; he holds a crucifix in his right hand, signifying his conversion to Christianity. But to his right his comrades are roasting human flesh. Europeans were convinced that many native peoples were cannibals.*
Villa della Torre, Mezzane de Sotto, Verona.

products. Because Spain and Portugal had divided among themselves the rich spoils of South America, other prospective colonizers had to carve niches in seemingly less hospitable places, especially North America and the Caribbean (Map 16.4). Eventually the English, French, and Dutch would dominate commerce with these colonies.

English settlement policies had an unfortunate precedent in Ireland, where in the 1580s English armies drove the Irish clans from their strongholds and claimed the land for English and Scottish Protes-

tant colonists. When the Irish resisted with guerrilla warfare, English generals waged total war, destroying harvests and burning villages; one general lined the path to his headquarters with Irish heads. A few decades later, the English would use the same tactics against another group of "savages," this time in the New World.

Some colonists in North America justified their mission by promising to convert the native population to Christianity. As the English colonizer John Smith told his followers in Virginia, "The growing

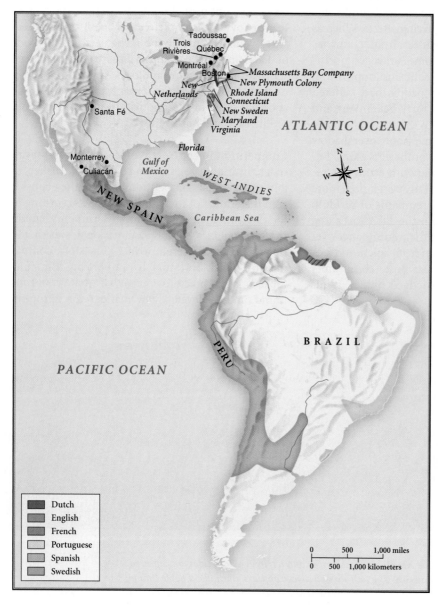

MAP 16.4 European Colonization of the Americas, c. 1640
Europeans established themselves first in coastal areas. The English, French, and Dutch set up most of their colonies in the Caribbean and North America because the Spanish and Portuguese had already colonized the easily accessible regions in South America. Vast inland areas still remained unexplored and uncolonized in 1640.

provinces addeth to the King's Crown; but the reducing heathen people to civility and true religion bringeth honour to the King of Heaven." Catholic France and Spain were more successful, however, than Protestant England in their efforts to convert American natives. Protestantism did not mesh well with native American cultures because it demanded an individual conversion experience based on a Christian notion of sin. Catholicism, in contrast, stressed shared rituals, which were more accessible to the native populations.

In establishing permanent colonies, the Europeans created whole new communities across the Atlantic. Careful plans often fell afoul of the hazards of transatlantic shipping, however. Originally, the warm climate of Virginia made it an attractive destination for the Pilgrims, a small English sect that, unlike the Puritans, attempted to separate from the Church of England. But the *Mayflower*, which had sailed for Virginia with Pilgrim emigrants, landed far to the north in Massachusetts, where in 1620 the settlers founded New Plymouth Colony. As the religious situation for English Puritans worsened, wealthier people became willing to emigrate, and in 1629 a prominent group of Puritans incorporated themselves as the Massachusetts Bay Company. They founded a virtually self-governing colony headquartered in Boston.

Colonization gradually spread. Migrating settlers, including dissident Puritans, soon founded new settlements in Connecticut and Rhode Island. Catholic refugees from England established a much smaller colony in Maryland. By the 1640s, the British North American colonies had more than fifty thousand people—not including the Indians, whose numbers had been decimated in epidemics and wars—and the foundations of representative government in locally chosen colonial assemblies. By contrast, French Canada had only about three thousand European inhabitants by 1640. Because the French government refused to let Protestants emigrate from France and establish a foothold in the New World, it denied itself a ready population for the settling of permanent colonies abroad. Both England and France turned their attention to the Caribbean in the 1620s and 1630s when they occupied the islands of the West Indies after driving off the native Caribs. These islands would prove ideal for a plantation economy of tobacco and sugar cane.

❖ A Clash of Worldviews

The countries that moved ahead economically in this period—England, the Dutch Republic, and to some extent France—turned out to be the most receptive to new secular worldviews. Although *secularization* did not entail a loss of religious faith, it did prompt a search for nonreligious explanations for political authority and natural phenomena. During the late sixteenth and early seventeenth centuries, art, political theory, and science all began to break some of their bonds with religion. The visual arts, for example, more frequently depicted secular subjects. Scientists and scholars sought laws in nature to explain politics as well as movements in the heavens and on earth. A "scientific revolution" was in the making. Yet traditional attitudes did not disappear. Belief in magic and witchcraft pervaded every level of society. People of all classes accepted supernatural explanations for natural phenomena, a view only gradually and partially undermined by new ideas.

The Arts in an Age of Religious Conflict

Two new forms of artistic expression—professional theater and opera—developed to express secular values in an age of conflict over religious beliefs. The greatest playwright of the English language, William Shakespeare, never referred to religious disputes in his plays, and he always set his most personal reflections on political turmoil and uncertainty in faraway times or places. Religion played an important role in the new Mannerist and baroque styles of painting, however, even though many rulers commissioned paintings on secular subjects for their own uses.

Theater in the Age of Shakespeare. Permanent professional theater companies appeared for the first time in Europe in the last quarter of the sixteenth century. In previous centuries, traveling companies made their living by playing at major religious festivals and by repeating their performances in small towns and villages along the way. In London, Seville, and Madrid, the first professional acting companies performed before paying audiences in the 1570s. A huge outpouring of playwriting followed. The Spanish playwright Lope de Vega (1562–1635) alone wrote more than fifteen hundred plays. Between 1580 and 1640, three hundred English playwrights produced works for a hundred different acting companies. Theaters did a banner business despite Puritan opposition in England and Catholic objections in Spain. Shopkeepers, apprentices, lawyers, and court nobles crowded into open-air theaters to see everything from bawdy farces to profound tragedies.

The most enduring and influential playwright of the time was the Englishman William Shakespeare (1564–1616), son of a glovemaker, who wrote three dozen plays and acted in one of the chief troupes. Although Shakespeare's plays were not set in contemporary England, they reflected the concerns of his age: the nature of power and the crisis of authority. His greatest tragedies—*Hamlet* (1601), *King Lear* (1605), and *Macbeth* (1606)—show the uncertainty and even chaos that result when power is misappropriated or misused. In each play, family relationships are linked to questions about the legitimacy of government, just as they were for Elizabeth I herself. Hamlet's mother marries the man who murdered his royal father and usurped the crown; two of Lear's daughters betray him when he tries to divide his kingdom; Macbeth's wife persuades him to murder the king and seize the throne. Some of Shakespeare's female characters, like Lady Macbeth, are as driven, ambitious, powerful, and tortured as the male protagonists; others, like Queen Gertrude in *Hamlet*, reflect the ambiguity of women's role in public life—they were not expected to act with authority, and their lives were subject to men's control.

Shakespeare's stories of revenge, exile, political instability, broken families, betrayal, witchcraft, madness, suicide, and murder clearly mirror the anxieties of the period. One character in the final act describes the tragic story of Prince Hamlet as one "Of carnal, bloody, and unnatural acts; Of accidental judgments, casual slaughters; Of deaths put on by cunning and forced cause." Like many real-life people, Shakespeare's tragic characters found little peace in the turmoil of their times.

Mannerism and the Baroque in Art.   New styles of painting reflected similar concerns less directly, but they too showed the desire for changed standards. In the late sixteenth century the artistic style

Mannerist Painting
With its distortion of perspective, crowding of figures, and mysterious allusions, El Greco's painting The Dream of Philip II *(1577) is a typical mannerist painting. Philip II can be seen in his usual black clothing with a lace ruffle as his only decoration.*
© National Gallery, London.

known as Mannerism emerged in the Italian states and soon spread across Europe. Mannerism was an almost theatrical style that allowed painters to distort perspective to convey a message or emphasize a theme. The most famous Mannerist painter, called El Greco because he was of Greek origin, trained in Venice and Rome before he moved to Spain in the

Baroque Painting
*The Flemish baroque painter Peter
Paul Rubens used monumental
canvases to glorify the French queen
Marie de Medici, wife of Henry IV
and mother of Louis XIII. Between
1622 and 1625, Rubens painted
twenty-four panels like this one to
decorate Marie's residence in Paris.
Their gigantic size (some were more
than twenty feet wide), imposing
figures captured in rich colors, and
epic settings characterized the use
of the baroque to exalt secular
rulers. In this scene, Henry is shown
handing over government to his
wife on behalf of his young son
(Henry was assassinated in 1610).*
Giraudon/Art Resource, NY.

1570s. His paintings encapsulated the Mannerist style: he crowded figures or objects into every available space, used larger-than-life or elongated figures, and created new and often bizarre visual effects. This style departed abruptly from precise Renaissance perspective. The religious intensity of El Greco's pictures shows that faith still motivated many artists, as it did much political conflict.

The most important new style in seventeenth-century high art was the baroque, which, like Mannerism, originated in the Italian states. As is the case with many historical categories, *baroque* was not used as a label by people living at the time; in the eighteenth century, art critics coined the word to mean shockingly bizarre, confused, and extravagant, and until the late nineteenth century, art historians and collectors largely disdained the baroque. Stylistically, the baroque rejected Renaissance classicism: in place of the classical emphasis on line, harmonious design, unity, and clarity, the baroque featured curves, exaggerated lighting, intense emotions, release from restraint, and even a kind of artistic sensationalism.

In church architecture and painting the baroque melodramatically reaffirmed the emotional depths of the Catholic faith and glorified both church and monarchy. The Catholic church encouraged the expression of religious feeling through art because its emotional impact helped strengthen the ties between the faithful and the Counter-Reform church (the label given the Catholic church in the aftermath of the Protestant Reformation, when it offered its own internal reforms). As an urban and spectacular style, the baroque was well suited to public festivities and display. Along with religious festivals, civic processions, and state funerals that served the interests of the church and state, baroque portraits, such as the many portraits of Philip IV by Diego Velázquez, celebrated authority.

Closely tied to the Counter-Reformation, the baroque style spread from Rome to other Italian states and then into central Europe. The Catholic Habsburg territories, including Spain and the Spanish Netherlands, embraced the style. The Spanish built baroque churches in their American colonies as part of their massive conversion campaign. Within Europe, Protestant countries largely resisted the baroque, as we can see by comparing Flemish painters from the Spanish Netherlands with Dutch artists. The first great baroque painter was an Italian-trained Fleming, Peter Paul Rubens (1577–1640). A devout Catholic, Rubens painted vivid, exuberant pictures on religious themes, packed with figures. His was an extension of the theatrical baroque style, conveying ideas through broad gestures and dramatic poses. The great Dutch Protestant painters of the next generation, such as Rembrandt van Rijn (1606–1669), sometimes used biblical subjects, but their pictures were more realistic and focused on everyday scenes. Many of them suggested the Protestant concern for an inner life and personal faith rather than the public expression of religiosity.

Church Music and Opera.   As in the visual arts, differences in musical style during the late sixteenth and early seventeenth centuries reflected religious divisions. The new Protestant churches developed their own distinct music, which differentiated their worship from the Catholic Mass and also marked them as Lutheran or Calvinist. Lutheran composers developed a new form, the strophic hymn, or chorale, a religious text set to a tune that is then enriched through harmony. Calvinist congregations, in keeping with their emphasis on simplicity and austerity, avoided harmony and more often sang in unison, thereby encouraging participation.

A new secular musical form, the opera, grew up parallel to the baroque style in the visual arts. First influential in the Italian states, opera combined music, drama, dance, and scenery in a grand sensual display, often with themes chosen to please the ruler and the aristocracy. Operas could be based on typically baroque sacred subjects or on traditional stories. Like Shakespeare, opera composers often turned to familiar stories their audiences would recognize and readily follow. One of the most innovative composers of opera was Claudio Monteverdi (1567–1643), whose work contributed to the development of both opera and the orchestra. His earliest operatic production, *Orfeo* (1607), was the first to require an orchestra of about forty instruments and to include instrumental as well as vocal sections.

The Natural Laws of Politics

In reaction to the wars over religious beliefs, jurists and scholars not only began to defend the primacy of state interests over those of religious conformity but also insisted on secular explanations for politics. Machiavelli had pointed in this direction with his prescriptions for Renaissance princes in the early sixteenth century, but the intellectual movement gathered steam in the aftermath of the religious violence unleashed by the Reformation. Religious toleration could not take hold until government could be organized on some principle other than one king, one faith. The French *politiques* Michel de Montaigne and Jean Bodin started the search for those principles. During the Dutch revolt against Spain, the jurist Hugo Grotius gave new meaning to the notion of "natural law"—laws of nature that give legitimacy to government and stand above the actions of any particular ruler or religious group. His ideas would influence John Locke and the American revolutionaries of the eighteenth century.

Montaigne and Bodin.   Michel de Montaigne (1533–1592) was a French magistrate who resigned his office in the midst of the wars of religion to write about the need for tolerance and open-mindedness. Although himself a Catholic, Montaigne painted on the beams of his study the words "All that is certain is that nothing is certain." To capture this need for personal reflection in a tumultuous age of religious discord, he invented the essay as a short and pithy form of expression. He revived the ancient doctrine of skepticism, which held that total certainty is never attainable—a doctrine, like toleration of religious differences, that was repugnant to Protestants and Catholics alike, both of whom were certain that their religion was the right one. He also questioned the common European habit of calling newly discovered peoples in the New World barbarous and savage: "Everyone gives the title of barbarism to everything that is not in use in his own country."

The French Catholic lawyer Jean Bodin (1530–1596) sought systematic secular answers to the problem of disorder in *The Six Books of the Republic* (1576). Comparing the different forms of government throughout history, he concluded that there were three basic types of sovereignty: monarchy, aristocracy, and democracy. Only strong monarchical power offered hope for maintaining order, he insisted. Bodin rejected any doctrine of the right to resist tyrannical authority: "I denied that it was the function of a good man or of a good citizen to offer violence to his prince for any reason, however great a tyrant he might be" (and, it might be added, whatever his ideas on religion). Bodin's ideas helped lay the foundation for absolutism, the idea that the monarch should be the sole and uncontested source of power. Nonetheless, the very discussion of types of governments in the abstract implied that they might be subject to choice rather than simply being God-given, as most rulers maintained.

Grotius and Natural Law. Hugo Grotius (1583–1645) argued that natural law stood beyond the reach of either secular or divine authority; it would be valid even if God did not exist. Natural law should govern politics, by this account, not Scripture, religious authority, or tradition. Not surprisingly, these ideas got Grotius into trouble. His work *The Laws of War and Peace* (1625) was condemned by the Catholic church. The Dutch Protestant government arrested him for his part in religious controversies; his wife helped him escape prison by hiding him in a chest of books. He fled to Paris, where he got a small pension from Louis XIII and served as his ambassador to Sweden. The Swedish king Gustavus Adolphus claimed that he kept Grotius's book under his pillow even while at battle. Grotius was one of the first to argue that international conventions should govern the treatment of prisoners of war and the making of peace treaties.

At the same time that Grotius expanded the principles of natural law, most jurists worked on codifying the huge amount of legislation and

jurisprudence devoted to legal forms of torture. Most states and the courts of the Catholic church used torture when the crime was very serious and the evidence seemed to point to a particular defendant but no definitive proof had been established. The judges ordered torture—hanging the accused by the hands with a rope thrown over a beam, pressing the legs in a leg screw, or just tying the hands very tightly—to extract a confession, which had to be given with a medical expert and notary present and had to be repeated without torture. Children, pregnant women, the elderly, aristocrats, kings, and even professors were exempt.

Grotius's conception of natural law directly challenged the use of torture. To be in accord with natural law, Grotius argued, governments had to defend natural rights, which he defined as life, body, freedom, and honor. Grotius did not encourage rebellion in the name of natural law or rights, but he did hope that someday all governments would adhere to these principles and stop killing their own and one another's subjects in the name of religion. Natural law and natural rights would play an important role in the founding of constitutional governments from the 1640s forward and in the establishment of various charters of human rights in our own time.

The Origins of the Scientific Revolution

Although the Catholic and Protestant churches encouraged the study of science and many prominent scientists were themselves clerics, the search for a secular, scientific method of determining the laws of nature eventually challenged the traditional accounts of natural phenomena. (See "Did You Know?" page 594.) Christian doctrine had incorporated the scientific teachings of ancient philosophers, especially Ptolemy and Aristotle; now these came into question. A revolution in astronomy challenged the Ptolemaic view, endorsed by the Catholic church, which held that the sun revolved around the earth. Startling breakthroughs took place in medicine, too, which laid the foundations for modern anatomy and pharmacology. By the early seventeenth century, a new scientific method had been established based on a combination of experimental observation and mathematical deduction. Conflicts between the new science and religion followed almost immediately.

DID YOU KNOW?

The Gregorian Calendar: 1582

The Catholic church relied on the work of astronomers when it undertook a major reform of the calendar in 1582. Every culture has some kind of calendar by which it groups days to mark time, but the length of the day, the week, and the month have varied throughout much of human history. At different moments in the past, West Africans, for example, used four-day weeks, central Asians five-day weeks, and Egyptians ten-day weeks. These different systems became uniform when most of the world's countries adopted the Gregorian calendar. The spread of the use of the Gregorian calendar, which happened only very gradually after its introduction in 1582, marked the extension of Western influence in the world.

The Gregorian calendar got its name from Pope Gregory XIII, who ordered calendar reform to compute more accurately the exact date on which Easter—the Christian holiday commemorating the resurrection of Jesus—should fall. Easter was supposed to fall on the first Sunday after the first full moon after the vernal equinox. But over the years the dates had become confused because

no one had been able to calculate the exact length of a solar year (365.242199 days). As a result, the calendar had become increasingly out of phase with the seasons; by 1545, the vernal (spring) equinox had moved ten days from its proper date. In 1582, when the reform took effect, October 5 became October 15, thus omitting ten days and setting the vernal equinox straight—but causing any number of legal complications.

Although the Gregorian calendar was based on a truer calculation of the length of a year and thus required less adjustment than previous calendars, it was not immediately adopted, even in Christian Europe, in part because any change would have been difficult to enforce given the state of communications at the time. Because the pope had sponsored the reform, the Catholic countries embraced it first; Protestant countries used it only after 1700. England accepted it in 1752. Adoption followed in Japan in 1873, Egypt in 1875, Russia in 1918, and Greece in 1923. The Greek Orthodox church never accepted it, so Easter in that church is about one week later than elsewhere in Christianity.

Even though the Gregorian calendar is astronomically correct, it still has bothersome defects: the months are different in length, and holidays do not fall on the same day in each year. Two other calendars have been proposed. The International Fixed Calendar would divide the year into thirteen

The Revolution in Astronomy. The traditional account of the movement of the heavens derived from the second-century Greek astronomer Ptolemy, who put the earth at the center of the cosmos. Above the earth were fixed the moon, the stars, and the planets in concentric crystalline spheres; beyond these fixed spheres dwelt God and the angels. The planets revolved around the earth at the command of God. In this view, the sun revolved around the earth; the heavens were perfect and unchanging, and the earth was "corrupted." Ptolemy insisted that the

planets revolved in perfectly circular orbits (because circles were more "perfect" than other figures). To account for the actual elliptical paths that could be observed and calculated, he posited orbits within orbits, or epicycles.

In 1543, the Polish clergyman Nicolaus Copernicus (1473–1543) began the revolution in astronomy by publishing his treatise *On the Revolution of the Celestial Spheres*. Copernicus attacked the Ptolemaic account, arguing that the earth and planets revolved around the sun, a view known as *heliocentrism* (a

Calendar
This painting by Aldo Durazzi shows Gregory XIII presiding over the council of 1582 that reformed the calendar. The Catholic church sponsored the work of many astronomers and other scientists.
Archivio di Stato, Siena. Photo Lensini Fabrio.

months of twenty-eight days with an additional day at the end. The World Calendar would divide the year into four quarters of ninety-one days each with an additional day at the end of the year; the first month in each quarter would have thirty-one days and the second and third thirty days each. Neither has been adopted. Logic does not always win this kind of argument, for changing the length of the months seems almost equivalent to changing which side of the road you drive on; once a system is learned, no one really wants to give it up and start all over again. The same is true for the numbering of the years, which was set by the Council of Nicea in 325. The year 1 was designated as the year it was believed Jesus was born. Today scholars have determined that the date was wrong by several years, and many object in any case to the use of a calendar based on the birth of Jesus. But if that dating system were eliminated, what would replace it? Where should a common calendar begin?

sun-centered universe). He discovered that by placing the sun instead of the earth at the center of the system of spheres, he could eliminate many epicycles from the calculations. In other words, he claimed that the heliocentric view simplified the mathematics. Copernicus died soon after publishing his theories, but when the Italian monk Giordano Bruno (1548–1600) taught heliocentrism, perhaps with the aim of establishing a new religion, the Catholic Inquisition (set up to seek out heretics) arrested him and burned him at the stake.

For the most part, however, Copernicus's ideas attracted little sustained attention until the early seventeenth century, when astronomers systematically collected evidence that undermined the Ptolemaic view. A leader among them was the Danish astronomer Tycho Brahe (1546–1601), who was educated in Copenhagen and Leipzig. While at university he lost part of his nose in a duel and for the rest of his life he wore a metal insert to replace the missing part. Brahe designed and built new instruments for observing the heavens and trained a whole

The Trial of Galileo
In this anonymous painting of the trial held in 1633, Galileo appears seated on a chair in the center facing the church officials who accused him of heresy for insisting that the sun, not the earth, was the center of the universe (heliocentrism). Catholic officials forced him to recant or suffer the death penalty, but the trial did more damage in the long term to the Catholic church's reputation than it did to Galileo's.
Private collection, New York.
© Photograph by Erich Lessing/ Art Resource.

generation of astronomers. His observation of a new star in 1572 and a comet in 1577 called into question the Aristotelian view that the universe was unchanging. Brahe still rejected heliocentrism, but the assistant he employed when he moved to Prague in 1599, Johannes Kepler (1571–1630), was converted to the Copernican view. Kepler continued Brahe's collection of planetary observations and used the evidence to develop his three laws of planetary motion, published between 1609 and 1619. Kepler's laws provided mathematical backing for heliocentrism and directly challenged the claim long held, even by Copernicus, that planetary motion was circular. Kepler's first law stated that the orbits of the planets are ellipses, with the sun always at one focus of the ellipse.

The Italian Galileo Galilei (1564–1642) provided more evidence to support the heliocentric view and also challenged the doctrine that the heavens were perfect and unchanging. In 1609, he learned that two Dutch astronomers had built a telescope. He quickly invented a better one and observed the earth's moon, four satellites of Jupiter, the phases of Venus (a cycle of changing physical appearances), and sunspots. The moon, the planets, and the sun were no more perfect than the earth,

he insisted, and the shadows he could see on the moon could only be the product of hills and valleys like those on earth. Galileo portrayed the earth as a moving part of a larger system, only one of many planets revolving around the sun, not as the fixed center of a single, closed universe.

Because he recognized the utility of the new science for everyday projects, Galileo published his work in Italian, rather than Latin, to appeal to a lay audience of merchants and aristocrats. But he meant only to instruct an educated elite. The new science, he claimed, suited "the minds of the wise," not "the shallow minds of the common people." After all, his discoveries challenged the commonsensical view that it is the sun that rises and sets while the earth stands still. If the Bible were wrong about motion in the universe, as Galileo's position implied, the error came from the Bible's use of common language to appeal to the lower orders. The Catholic church was not mollified by this explanation. In 1616 the church forbade Galileo to teach that the earth moves and in 1633 accused him of not obeying the earlier order. Forced to appear before the Inquisition, he agreed to publicly recant his assertion that the earth moves to save himself from torture and death. Afterward he lived under house arrest and could publish his work only in the Dutch Republic, which had become a haven for iconoclastic scientists and thinkers.

Breakthroughs in Medicine. Until the mid-sixteenth century, medical knowledge in Europe had been based on the writings of the second-century Greek physician Galen, who was a contemporary of Ptolemy. Galen derived his knowledge of the anatomy of the human body from partial dissections. In the same year that Copernicus challenged the traditional account in astronomy (1543), the Flemish scientist Andreas Vesalius (1514–1564) did the same for anatomy. He published a new illustrated anatomical text, *On the Construction of the Human Body*, that revised Galen's work. Drawing on public dissections in the medical faculties of European universities, Vesalius at first hesitated to entirely reject Galen, but in his second edition of 1555 he explicitly refuted his predecessor. Theophrastus Bombastus von Hohenheim, better known as Paracelsus (1493–1541), went even further than Vesalius. He burned Galen's text at the University of Basel, where he was a professor of medicine. Paracelsus experimented with new drugs, performed operations (at the time most academic physicians taught medical theory, not practice), and pursued his interests in magic, alchemy, and astrology. He helped establish the modern science of pharmacology.

The Englishman William Harvey (1578–1657) also used dissection to examine the circulation of blood within the body, demonstrating how the heart worked as a pump. The heart and its valves were "a piece of machinery," Harvey insisted. They obeyed mechanical laws just as the planets and earth revolved around the sun in a mechanical universe. Nature could be understood by experiment and rational deduction, not by following traditional authorities.

Scientific Method: Bacon and Descartes. In the 1630s, the European intellectual elite began to accept the new scientific views. Ancient learning, the churches and their theologians, and even cherished popular beliefs seemed to be undermined by a new standard of truth—scientific method, which was based on systematic experiments and rational deduction. Two men were chiefly responsible for spreading the prestige of scientific method: the English politician Sir Francis Bacon (1561–1626) and the French mathematician and philosopher René

Descartes (1596–1650). They represented the two essential halves of scientific method: respectively, inductive reasoning through observation and experimental research and deductive reasoning from self-evident principles.

In *The Advancement of Learning* (1605), Bacon attacked reliance on ancient writers and optimistically predicted that scientific method would lead to social progress. The minds of the medieval scholars, he said, had been "shut up in the cells of a few authors (chiefly Aristotle, their dictator) as their persons were shut up in the cells of monasteries and colleges," and they could therefore produce only "cobwebs of learning" that were "of no substance or profit." Advancement would take place only through the collection, comparison, and analysis of information. Knowledge, in Bacon's view, must be empirically based (that is, gained by observation and experiment). Bacon ardently supported the scientific method over popular beliefs, which he rejected as "fables and popular errors." Claiming that God had called the Catholic church "to account for their degenerate manners and ceremonies," Bacon looked to the Protestant English state, which he served as lord chancellor, for leadership on the road to scientific advancement.

Although he agreed with Bacon's denunciation of traditional learning, Descartes saw that the attack on tradition might only replace the dogmatism of the churches with the skepticism of Montaigne—that nothing at all was certain. A Catholic who served in the Thirty Years' War, Descartes aimed to establish the new science on more secure philosophical foundations, those of mathematics and logic (Descartes invented analytic geometry). In his *Discourse on Method* (1637), he argued that mathematical and mechanical principles provided the key to understanding all of nature, including the actions of people and states. All prior assumptions must be repudiated in favor of one elementary principle: "I think, therefore I am." Everything else could—and should—be doubted, but even doubt showed the certain existence of someone thinking. Begin with the simple and go on to the complex, he asserted, and believe only those ideas that present themselves "clearly and distinctly." Descartes believed that rational individuals would see the necessity of strong state power and that only "meddling and restless spirits" would plot against it. He insisted that human reason could not only unravel the secrets of nature but also prove the existence of God. Although he hoped to secure the authority of both church and state, his reliance on human reason alone irritated authorities, and his books were banned in many places. He moved to the Dutch Republic to work in peace. Scientific research, like economic growth, became centered in the northern, Protestant countries, where it was less constrained by church control.

Magic and Witchcraft

Despite the new emphasis on clear reasoning, observation, and independence from past authorities, science had not yet become separate from magic. Many scholars, like Paracelsus, studied alchemy alongside other scientific pursuits. Elizabeth I maintained a court astrologer who was also a serious mathematician, and many writers distinguished between "natural magic," which was close to experi-

Persecution of Witches
This engraving from a pamphlet account of witch trials in England in 1589 shows three women hanged as accused witches. At their feet are frogs and toads, which were supposed to be the witches' "familiars," sent by the devil to help them ruin the lives of their neighbors by causing disease or untimely deaths among people and livestock. The ferret on the woman's lap was reported to be the devil himself in disguise.
Lambeth Palace Library.

mental science, and demonic "black magic." The astronomer Tycho Brahe defended his studies of alchemy and astrology as part of natural magic. For many of the greatest minds, magic and science were still closely linked.

In a world in which most people believed in astrology, magical healing, prophecy, and ghosts, it is hardly surprising that many of Europe's learned people also firmly believed in witchcraft, the exercise of magical powers gained by a pact with the devil. The same Jean Bodin who argued against religious fanaticism insisted on death for witches—and for those magistrates who would not prosecute them. In France alone, 345 books and pamphlets on witchcraft appeared between 1550 and 1650. Trials of witches peaked in Europe between 1560 and 1640, the very time of the celebrated breakthroughs of the new science. Montaigne was one of the few to speak out against executing accused witches: "It is taking one's conjectures rather seriously to roast someone alive for them," he wrote in 1580.

Belief in witches was not new in the sixteenth century. Witches had long been thought capable of almost anything: passing through walls, flying through the air, destroying crops, and causing personal catastrophes from miscarriage to demonic possession. What was new was the official persecution, justified by the notion that witches were agents of Satan whom the righteous must oppose. In a time of economic crisis, plague, warfare, and the clash of religious differences, witchcraft trials provided an outlet for social stress and anxiety, legitimated by state power. At the same time, the trials seem to have been part of the religious reform movement itself. Denunciation and persecution of witches coincided with the spread of reform, both Protestant and Catholic. The trials concentrated especially in the German lands of the Holy Roman Empire, the boiling cauldron of the Thirty Years' War.

The victims of the persecution were overwhelmingly female: women accounted for 80 percent of the accused witches in about 100,000 trials in Europe and North America during the sixteenth and seventeenth centuries. About one-third were sentenced to death. Before 1400, when witchcraft trials were rare, nearly half of those accused had been men. Explanations for this gender difference have raised many controversies. Some historians argue that the trials expressed a fundamental hatred of women that came to a head during conflicts over the Reformation. Official descriptions of witchcraft oozed lurid details of sexual orgies, incest, homosexuality, and cannibalism, in which women acted as the devil's sexual slaves. In this view, Catholic and Protestant reforming clergy attacked the presumably wild and undisciplined sexuality of women as the most obvious manifestation of popular unruliness and heretical tendencies. Lawyers and judges followed their lead.

Other historians see in the trials a social dimension that helps explain the prominence of women. Accusers were almost always better off than those they accused. The poorest and most socially marginal people in most communities were elderly spinsters and widows. Because they were thought likely to hanker after revenge on those more fortunate, they were singled out as witches. Another commonly accused woman was the midwife, who was a prime target for suspicion when a baby or mother died in childbirth. Although sometimes venerated for their special skill, midwives also numbered among the thousands of largely powerless women persecuted for their supposed consorting with the devil.

Witchcraft trials declined when scientific thinking about causes and effects raised questions about the evidence used in court: how could judges or jurors be certain that someone was a witch? The tide turned everywhere at about the same time, as physicians, lawyers, judges, and even clergy came to suspect that accusations were based on popular superstition and peasant untrustworthiness. As early as the 1640s, French courts ordered the arrest of witch-hunters and released suspected witches. In 1682, a French royal decree treated witchcraft as fraud and imposture, meaning that the law did not recognize anyone as a witch. In 1693, the jurors who had convicted twenty witches in Salem, Massachusetts, recanted, claiming: "We confess that we ourselves were not capable to understand. . . . We justly fear that we were sadly deluded and mistaken." The Salem jurors had not stopped believing in witches; they had simply lost confidence in their ability to identify them. This was a general pattern. Popular attitudes had not changed; what had changed was elites' attitudes. When physicians and judges had believed in witches and persecuted them officially, with torture, witches had gone to their deaths in record numbers. But when the same groups distanced themselves from popular beliefs, the trials and the executions stopped.

IMPORTANT DATES

1562	French Wars of Religion begin
1566	Revolt of Calvinists in the Netherlands against Spain begins
1569	Formation of commonwealth of Poland-Lithuania
1571	Battle of Lepanto marks victory of West over Ottomans at sea
1572	St. Bartholomew's Day Massacre of French Protestants
1588	Defeat of the Spanish Armada by England
1598	French Wars of Religion end with Edict of Nantes
1601	William Shakespeare, *Hamlet*
1618	Thirty Years' War begins
1625	Hugo Grotius publishes *The Laws of War and Peace*
1629	English Puritans set up the Massachusetts Bay Company and begin to colonize New England
1633	Galileo Galilei is forced to recant his support of heliocentrism
1635	French join the Thirty Years' War by declaring war on Spain
1648	Peace of Westphalia ends the Thirty Years' War

Conclusion

The witchcraft persecutions reflected the traumas of these times of religious war and economic decline. Marauding armies combined with economic depression, disease, and the threat of starvation to shatter the lives of many ordinary Europeans. Some people blamed the poor widow or upstart midwife for their problems; others joined desperate revolts; still others emigrated to the New World to seek a better life. Even rulers confronted frightening choices: forced abdication, death in battle, or assassination often accompanied their religious decisions, and economic shocks could threaten the stability of their governments.

Religious conflicts shaped the destinies of every European power in this period. These conflicts came to a head in 1618–1648 in the Thirty Years' War, which cut a path of destruction through central Europe and involved most of the European powers.

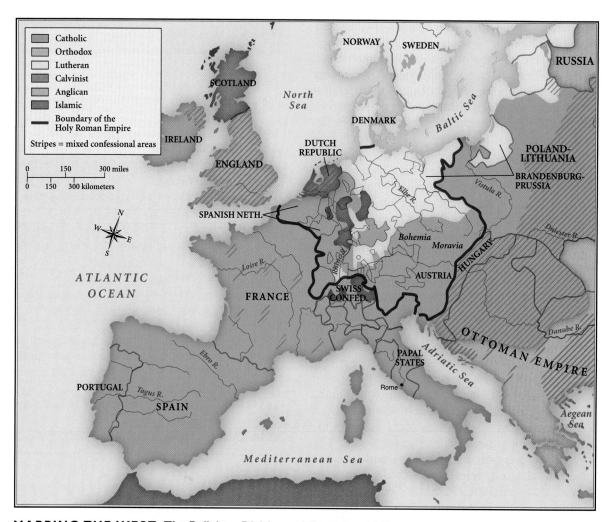

MAPPING THE WEST The Religious Divisions of Europe, c. 1648

The Peace of Westphalia recognized major religious divisions within Europe that have endured for the most part to the present day. Catholicism dominated in southern Europe, Lutheranism had its stronghold in northern Europe, and Calvinism flourished along the Rhine River. In southeastern Europe, the Islamic Ottoman Turks accommodated the Greek Orthodox Christians under their rule but bitterly fought the Catholic Austrian Habsburgs for control of Hungary.

Repulsed by the effects of religious violence on international relations, European rulers agreed to a peace that effectively removed disputes between Catholics and Protestants from the international arena. The growing separation of political motives from religious ones did not mean that violence or conflict had ended, however. Struggles for religious uniformity within states would continue, though on a smaller scale. Bigger armies required more state involvement, and almost everywhere rulers emerged from these decades of conflict with expanded powers. The growth of state power directly changed the lives

of ordinary people: more men went into the armies and most families paid higher taxes. The constant extension of state power is one of the defining themes of modern history; religious warfare gave it a jump start.

For all their power, rulers could not control economic, social, or intellectual trends, much as they often tried. The economic downturn of the seventeenth century produced unexpected consequences for European states even while it made life miserable for many ordinary people; economic power and vibrancy shifted from the Mediterranean world to the northwest because the countries of northwestern Europe—England, France, and the Dutch Republic especially—suffered less from the fighting of the Thirty Years' War and recovered more quickly from the loss of population and production during bad times.

In the face of violence and uncertainty, some began to look for secular alternatives in art, politics, and science. Although it would be foolish to claim that everyone's mental universe changed because of the clash between religious and secular worldviews, a truly monumental shift in attitudes had begun. Secularization combined a growing interest in nonreligious forms of art, such as theater and opera, the search for nonreligious foundations of political authority, and the establishment of scientific method as the standard of truth. Proponents of these changes did not renounce their religious beliefs or even hold them less fervently, but they did insist that attention to state interests and scientific knowledge could serve as a brake on religious violence and popular superstitions.

Suggested References

Religious Conflicts and State Power, 1560–1618

The personalities of rulers such as Elizabeth I of England and Philip II of Spain remain central to the religious and political conflicts of this period. Recent scholarship also highlights more structural factors, especially in the French Wars of Religion and the rise of the Dutch Republic.

Cameron, Euan, ed. *Early Modern Europe: An Oxford History.* 1999.

Holt, Mack P. *The French Wars of Religion, 1562–1629.* 1995.

Israel, Jonathan. *The Dutch Republic: Its Rise, Greatness, and Fall, 1477–1806.* 1995.

Kamen, Henry. *Philip of Spain.* 1997.

Mattingly, Garrett. *The Defeat of the Spanish Armada.* 2nd ed. 1988.

Roberts, Penny. *A City in Conflict: Troyes during the French Wars of Religion.* 1996.

Strong, Roy. *The Cult of Elizabeth: Elizabethan Portraiture and Pageantry.* 1977.

The Thirty Years' War and the Balance of Power, 1618–1648

As ethnic conflicts erupt again in eastern Europe, historians have traced their roots back to the intertwined religious, ethnic, and dynastic struggles of the Thirty Years' War.

Asch, Ronald G. *The Thirty Years War: The Holy Roman Empire and Europe, 1618–48.* 1997.

Lee, Stephen J. *The Thirty Years War.* 1991.

Parker, Geoffrey. *The Military Revolution: Military Innovation and the Rise of the West, 1500–1800.* 1988.

———, ed. *The Thirty Years' War.* 2nd ed. 1997.

*Rabb, Theodore K. *The Thirty Years' War.* 2nd ed. 1972.

Economic Crisis and Realignment

Painstaking archival research has enabled historians to reconstruct the demographic, economic, and social history of this period. Recently, attention has focused more specifically on women, the family, and the early history of slavery.

Ashton, Trevor H., ed. *Crisis in Europe.* 1965.

Braudel, Fernand. *The Mediterranean and the Mediterranean World in the Age of Philip the Second.* 2 vols. Trans. Siân Reynolds. 1972–1973.

De Vries, Jan. *The Economy of Europe in an Age of Crisis, 1600–1750.* 1982.

Parry, J. H. *The Age of Reconnaissance.* 1981.

Pouncy, Carolyn Johnston, ed. and trans. *The "Domostroi": Rules for Russian Households in the Time of Ivan the Terrible.* 1994.

Spierenburg, Pieter. *The Broken Spell: A Cultural and Anthropological History of Preindustrial Europe.* 1991.

Wiesner, Merry E. *Women and Gender in Early Modern Europe.* 1993.

A Clash of Worldviews

The transformation of intellectual and cultural life has long fascinated scholars. Recent works have developed a new kind of study called "microhistory," focused on one person (like Ginzburg's Italian miller) or a series of individual stories (as in Roper's analysis of witchcraft in the German states).

Baroque architecture: http://www.lib.virginia.edu:80/dic/colls/arh102/index.html.

*Drake, Stillman, ed. *Discoveries and Opinions of Galileo.* 1957.

The Galileo Project: http://riceinfo.rice.edu/Galileo.

Ginzburg, Carlo. *The Cheese and the Worms: The Cosmos of a Sixteenth-Century Miller.* Trans. John and Anne Tedeschi. 1992.

Jacob, James. *The Scientific Revolution.* 1998.

Roper, Lyndal. *Oedipus and the Devil: Witchcraft, Sexuality, and Religion in Early Modern Europe.* 1994.

Skinner, Quentin. *The Foundations of Modern Political Thought.* Vol. 2, *The Age of Reformation.* 1978.

Thomas, Keith. *Religion and the Decline of Magic.* 1971.

Zagorin, Perez. *Francis Bacon.* 1998.

*Primary sources.

State Building and the Search for Order

1648–1690

IN ONE OF HER HUNDREDS OF LETTERS to her daughter, the French noblewoman Marie de Sévigné told a disturbing story about a well-known cook. The cook got upset when he did not have enough roast for several unexpected guests at a dinner for King Louis XIV. Early the next morning, when the fish he had ordered did not arrive on time, the cook felt personally dishonored. He rushed up to his room, put his sword against the door, and ran it through his heart on the third try. The fish arrived soon after. The king regretted the trouble his visit had caused, but others soon filled in for the chief cook. That evening, Sévigné wrote, there was "a very good dinner, light refreshments later, and then supper, a walk, cards, hunting, everything scented with daffodils, everything magical."

Reading this account now produces puzzlement and shock. It is difficult to comprehend how anyone could care that much about a shipment of fish. The story nonetheless reveals an important aspect of state building in the seventeenth century: to extend state authority, which had been challenged during the wars over religion and threatened by economic recession, many rulers created an aura of overwhelming power and brilliance around themselves. Louis XIV, like many rulers, believed that he reigned by divine right. He served as God's lieutenant on earth and even claimed certain godlike qualities. The great gap between the ruler and ordinary subjects accounts for the extreme reaction of Louis's cook, and even leading nobles such as Sévigné came to see the king and his court as somehow "magical."

Louis XIV in Roman Splendor
Images of Louis appear everywhere in his chateau at Versailles. This plaster relief by Antoine Coysevox in the Salon de la Guerre *(War Hall) represents Louis as Mars, the Roman god of war, riding roughshod over his enemies.*
Giraudon/Art Resource, NY.

1640	1652	1664	1676	1688	1700

Politics and War

Peace of Westphalia; Fronde in France

Austria breaks Turkish siege of Vienna

Poland-Lithuania confronts The Deluge

"Glorious Revolution" in England

Society and Economy

Russian legal code of serfdom

Uprising in Russia of Stenka Razin

La Salle claims Louisiana for France

Height of mercantilism

Great Fire of London

"Black Code" to regulate slavery in French colonies

Culture, Religion, and Intellectual Life

Hobbes, *Leviathan*

Molière, *The Middle-Class Gentleman*

Locke, *Two Treatises of Government*

Bernini, St. Peter's Square

Newton, *Principia Mathematica*

Louis XIV suppresses Jansenists

Madame de Lafayette, *The Princess of Clèves*

Revocation of the Edict of Nantes

Louis XIV moves into castle at Versailles

Louis XIV's model of state building was known as *absolutism,* a system of government in which the ruler claimed sole and uncontestable power. Although absolutism exerted great influence, especially in central and eastern Europe, it faced competition from *constitutionalism,* a system in which the ruler had to share power with parliaments made up of elected representatives. Constitutionalism led to weakness in Poland-Lithuania, but it provided a strong foundation for state power in England, the British North American colonies, and the Dutch Republic. Constitutionalism triumphed in England, however, only after one king had been executed as a traitor and another had been deposed.

Although the differences between absolutism and constitutionalism turned out to be very significant in the long run, these two methods of state building faced similar challenges in the mid-seventeenth century. Competition in the international arena required resources, and all states raised taxes in this period, provoking popular protests and rebellions. The wars over religion that culminated in the Thirty Years' War left many economies in dire straits, and, even more significant, they created a need for new explanations of political authority. Monarchs still relied on religion to justify their divine right to rule, but they increasingly sought secular defenses of their powers too. Absolutism and constitutionalism were the two main responses to the threat of disorder and breakdown left as a legacy of the wars over religion.

The search for order took place not only at the level of states and rulers but also in intellectual, cultural, and social life. In science, the Englishman Isaac Newton explained the regular movement of the universe with the law of gravitation and thereby consolidated the scientific revolution. Artists sought means of glorifying power and expressing order and symmetry in new fashion. As states consolidated their power, elites endeavored to distinguish themselves more clearly from the lower orders. The upper classes emulated the manners developed at court and tried in every way to distance themselves from anything viewed as vulgar or lower class. Officials, clergy, and laypeople all worked to reform the poor, now seen as a major source of disorder. Whether absolutist or constitutionalist, seventeenth-century states all aimed to extend control over their subjects' lives.

❖ Louis XIV: Model of Absolutism

French king Louis XIV (r. 1643–1715) personified the absolutist ruler who shared his power with no one. Louis personally made all important state decisions and left no room for dissent. In 1651, he reputedly told the Paris high court of justice, "*L'état, c'est moi*" ("I am the state"), emphasizing that state authority rested in him personally. Louis cleverly manipulated the affections and ambitions of his courtiers, chose as his ministers middle-class men who owed everything to him, built up Europe's largest army, and snuffed out every hint of religious or political opposition. Yet the absoluteness of his power should not be exaggerated. Like all rulers of his time, Louis depended on the cooperation of many others: local officials who enforced his decrees, peasants and artisans who joined his armies and paid his taxes, creditors who loaned crucial funds, and nobles who might stay home and cause trouble rather than join court festivities organized to glorify the king.

The Fronde, 1648–1653

Absolutism was not made in a day. Louis XIV built on a long French tradition of increasing centralization of state authority, but before he could extend it he had to weather a series of revolts known as the *Fronde*. Derived from the French word for a child's slingshot, the term was used by critics to signify that the revolts were mere child's play. In fact, however, they posed an unprecedented threat to the French crown. Louis was only five when he came to the

throne in 1643 upon the death of his father, Louis XIII, who with his chief minister Cardinal Richelieu had steered France through increasing involvement in the Thirty Years' War, rapidly climbing taxes, and innumerable tax revolts. Louis XIV's mother, Anne of Austria, and her Italian-born adviser and rumored lover Cardinal Mazarin (1602–1661) ruled in the young monarch's name. French nobles and magistrates suspected the motives of the foreign-born Anne and Mazarin. Some of them hoped to use the crisis created by Louis XIII's death to move France toward a constitutional government.

To meet the financial pressure of fighting the Thirty Years' War, Mazarin sold new offices, raised taxes, and forced creditors to extend loans to the government. In 1648, a coalition of his opponents presented him with a charter of demands that, if granted, would have given the parlements (high courts) a form of constitutional power with the right to approve new taxes. Mazarin responded by arresting the leaders of parlements. He soon faced a series of revolts that at one time or another involved nearly every social group in France.

The Fronde posed an immediate menace to the young king. Fearing for his safety, his mother and

Anne of Austria
Wife of Louis XIII and mother of Louis XIV, Anne served as regent during her son's youth but delegated most authority to Cardinal Mazarin, her Italian-born adviser. She is shown here praying with Louis and his younger brother Philippe. The painting emphasizes her religious devotion.
Laurie Platt Winfrey, Inc.

members of his court took Louis and fled Paris. With civil war threatening, Mazarin and Anne agreed to compromise with the parlements. The nobles saw an opportunity to reassert their claims to power against the weakened monarchy and renewed their demands for greater local control, which they had lost when the religious wars ended in 1598. Leading noblewomen often played key roles in the opposition to Mazarin, carrying messages and forging alliances, especially when male family members were in prison. While the nobles sought to regain power and local influence, the middle and lower classes chafed at the constant tax increases. Conflicts erupted throughout the kingdom as nobles, parlements, and city councils all raised their own armies to fight either the crown or each other, and rampaging soldiers devastated rural areas and disrupted commerce. In places, such as the southwestern city of Bordeaux, the urban poor revolted as well.

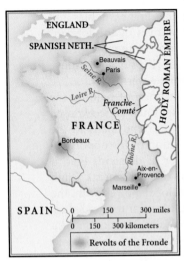

The Fronde, 1648–1653

Despite the glaring weakness of central power, the monarchy survived. Neither the nobles nor the judges of the parlements really wanted to overthrow the king; they simply wanted a greater share in power. But Louis XIV never forgot the humiliation and uncertainty that marred his childhood. Years later he recalled an incident in which a band of Parisians invaded his bedchamber to determine whether he had fled the city, and he declared the event an affront not only to himself but also to the state. His own policies as ruler would be designed to prevent the repetition of any such revolts.

Court Culture as a Form of State Power

When Cardinal Mazarin died in 1661, Louis XIV decided to rule without a first minister. He described the dangers of his situation in memoirs he wrote later for his son's instruction: "Everywhere was disorder. My Court as a whole was still very far removed from the sentiments in which I trust you will find it." Louis listed many other problems in the kingdom, but none occupied him more than his attempts to control France's leading nobles, some of whom came from families that had opposed him militarily during the Fronde.

Typically quarrelsome, the French nobles had long exercised local authority by maintaining their own fighting forces, meting out justice on their estates, arranging jobs for underlings, and resolving their own conflicts through dueling. Louis set out to domesticate the warrior nobles by replacing violence with court ritual. Using a systematic policy of bestowing pensions, offices, honors, gifts, and the threat of disfavor or punishment, he induced the nobles to cooperate with him and made himself the center of French power and culture. At Louis's court the great nobles vied for his favor, attended the ballets and theatricals he put on, and learned the rules of etiquette he supervised—in short, became his clients, dependent on him for advancement. Access to the king was the most valued commodity at court. Nobles competed for the honor of holding his shirt when he dressed; foreign ambassadors squabbled for places near him; and royal mistresses basked in the glow of his personal favor.

Participation at court required constant study. The preferred styles changed without notice, and the tiniest lapse in attention to etiquette could lead to ruin. Madame de Lafayette described the court in her novel *The Princess of Clèves* (1678): "The Court gravitated around ambition. Nobody was tranquil or indifferent—everybody was busily trying to better his or her position by pleasing, by helping, or by hindering somebody else." Occasionally the results were tragic, as in the suicide of the cook recounted by Marie de Sévigné. Elisabeth Charlotte, duchess of Orléans, the German-born sister-in-law of Louis, complained that "everything here is pure self-interest and deviousness," but she gloried in the special privileges of her closeness to the king, which included the right to a military honor guard and a special cloth to stand on during daily Mass.

Politics and the Arts. Louis XIV appreciated the political uses of every form of art. Mock battles, extravaganzas, theatrical performances, even the king's dinner—Louis's daily life was a public performance designed to enhance his prestige. Calling himself the Sun King, Louis adorned his court with statues of Apollo, Greek god of the sun. He also emulated the style and methods of ancient Roman emperors. At a celebration for the birth of his first son in 1662, Louis dressed in Roman attire, and many engravings and paintings showed him as a Roman emperor. Sculpture and paintings adorned his palace; commissioned histories vaunted his achievements; and coins and medals spread his likeness throughout the realm.

The king's officials treated the arts as a branch of government. The king gave pensions to artists who worked for him and sometimes protected writers from clerical critics. The most famous of these was the playwright Molière, whose comedy *Tartuffe* (1664) made fun of religious hypocrites and was loudly condemned by church leaders. Louis forced Molière to delay public performances of the play but resisted calls for his dismissal. Louis's ministers set up royal academies of dance, painting, architecture, and music and took control of the Académie française (French Academy), which to this day decides on correct usage of the French language. A royal furniture workshop at the Gobelins tapestry works in Paris turned out the delicate and ornate pieces whose style bore the king's name. Louis's government also regulated the number and locations of theaters and closely censored all forms of publication.

Music and theater enjoyed special prominence. Louis commissioned operas to celebrate royal marriages, baptisms, and military victories. His favorite composer, Jean-Baptiste Lully, an Italian who began as a cook's assistant and rose to be virtual dictator of French musical taste, wrote sixteen operas for court performances as well as many ballets. Louis himself danced in the ballets if a role seemed especially important. Playwrights presented their new plays directly to the court. Pierre Corneille and Jean-Baptiste Racine wrote tragedies set in Greece or Rome that celebrated the new aristocratic virtues which Louis aimed to inculcate: a reverence for order and self-control. All the characters were regal or noble, all the language lofty, all the behavior aristocratic. The king's sister-in-law called the plays of Corneille "the best entertainment I have."

The Palace of Versailles. Louis glorified his image as well through massive public works projects. Military facilities, such as veterans' hospitals and new fortified towns on the frontiers, represented his military might. Urban improvements, such as the reconstruction of the Louvre palace in Paris, proved his wealth. But his most remarkable project was the construction of a new palace at Versailles, twelve miles from the turbulent capital.

Building began in the 1660s. By 1685, the frenzied effort engaged 36,000 workers, not including

Palace of Versailles

In this defining statement of his ambitions, Louis XIV emphasized his ability to impose his own personal will, even on nature itself. The sheer size and precise geometrical design of the palace underlined the presence of an all-powerful personality, that of the Sun King. The palace became a national historical monument in 1837 and was used for many momentous historical occasions, including the signing of the peace treaty after World War I.

Giraudon/Art Resource, NY.

Louis XIV Visits the Royal Tapestry Workshop
This tapestry was woven at the Gobelins tapestry workshop between 1673 and 1680. It shows Louis XIV (wearing a red hat) and his minister Colbert (dressed in black, holding his hat) visiting the workshop on the outskirts of Paris. The artisans of the workshop scurry around to show Louis all the luxury objects they manufacture. Louis bought the workshop in 1662 and made it a national enterprise for making tapestries and furniture.
Giraudon/Art Resource, NY.

the thousands of troops who diverted a local river to supply water for pools and fountains. Royal workshops produced tapestries, carpets, mirrors, and porcelains. Even the gardens designed by landscape architect André Le Nôtre reflected the spirit of Louis XIV's rule: their geometrical arrangements and clear lines showed that art and design could tame nature and that order and control defined the exercise of power. Le Nôtre's geometrical landscapes were imitated in Spain, the Italian states, Austria, the German states, and later as far away as St. Petersburg in Russia and Washington, D.C. Versailles symbolized Louis's success in reining in the nobility and dominating Europe, and other monarchs eagerly mimicked French fashion and often conducted their business in French.

Yet for all its apparent luxury and frivolity, life at Versailles was often cramped and cold. Fifteen thousand people crowded into the palace's apartments, including all the highest military officers, the ministers of state, and the separate households of each member of the royal family. Refuse collected in the corridors during the incessant building, and thieves and prostitutes overran the grounds.

By the time Louis actually moved from the Louvre to Versailles in 1682, he had reigned as monarch for thirty-nine years. After his wife's death in 1683, he secretly married his mistress, Françoise d'Aubigné, marquise de Maintenon, and conducted most state affairs from her apartments at the palace.

Her opponents at court complained that she controlled all the appointments, but her efforts focused on her own projects, including her favorite: the founding in 1686 of a royal school for girls from impoverished noble families. She also inspired Louis XIV to pursue his devotion to Catholicism.

Enforcing Religious Orthodoxy

Louis believed that as king he must defend the Catholic faith against Protestants and dissident Catholics; orthodox Catholicism was an essential pillar of his rule. One of his advisers, Bishop Jacques-Benigne Bossuet (1627–1704), explained the principle of divine right that justified the king's actions: "We have seen that kings take the place of God, who is the true father of the human species. We have also seen that the first idea of power which exists among men is that of the paternal power; and that kings are modeled on fathers." The king, like a father, should instruct his subjects in the true religion, or at least make sure that others did so. Some questioned Louis's understanding of the finer points of doctrine: according to his sister-in-law, Louis himself "has never read anything about religion, nor the Bible either, and just goes along believing whatever he is told."

Louis's campaign for religious conformity first focused on the Jansenists, Catholics whose doctrines and practices resembled some aspects of

Protestantism. Following the posthumous publication of the book *Augustinus* (1640) by the Flemish theologian Cornelius Jansen (1585–1638), the Jansenists stressed the need for God's grace in achieving salvation. They emphasized the importance of original sin; and, in their austere religious practice, resembled the English Puritans. Prominent among the Jansenists was Blaise Pascal (1623–1662), a mathematician of genius, who wrote his *Provincial Letters* (1656–1657) to defend Jansenism against charges of heresy. Many judges in the parlements likewise endorsed Jansenist doctrine.

Louis feared any doctrine that gave priority to considerations of individual conscience over the demands of the official church hierarchy. He preferred teachings that stressed obedience to authority. Therefore, in 1660 he began enforcing various papal bulls (decrees) against Jansenism and closed down Jansenist theological centers. Jansenists were forced underground for the rest of his reign.

After many years of escalating pressure on the Calvinist Huguenots, Louis revoked the Edict of Nantes in 1685 and eliminated all of the Calvinists' rights. Louis considered the Edict (1598), by which his grandfather Henry IV granted the Protestants religious freedom and civil rights, a temporary measure, and he fervently hoped to reconvert the Huguenots to Catholicism. He closed their churches and schools, banned all their public activities, and exiled those who refused to embrace the state religion. Thousands of Huguenots emigrated to England, Brandenburg-Prussia, or the Dutch Republic. Many now wrote for publications attacking Louis XIV's absolutism. Protestant European countries were shocked by this crackdown on religious dissent and would cite it when they went to war against Louis.

Extending State Authority at Home and Abroad

Louis XIV could not have enforced his religious policies without the services of a nationwide bureaucracy. *Bureaucracy*—a system of state officials carrying out orders according to a regular and routine line of authority—comes from the French word *bureau*, for "desk," which came to mean "office," both in the sense of a physical space and a position of authority. Louis personally supervised the activities of his bureaucrats and worked to ensure his

supremacy in all matters. The ultimate goal of developing absolute power at home was the pursuit of French glory abroad.

Bureaucracy and Mercantilism. Louis extended the bureaucratic forms his predecessors had developed, especially the use of intendants, officials who held their positions directly from the king rather than owning their offices, as crown officials had traditionally done. Louis handpicked them to represent his will against entrenched local interests such as the parlements, provincial estates, and noble governors. The intendants reduced local powers over finances and insisted on more efficient tax collection. Despite the doubling of taxes in Louis's reign, the local rebellions that had so beset the crown from the 1620s to the 1640s subsided in the face of these better-organized state forces.

Louis's success in consolidating his authority depended on hard work, an eye for detail, and an ear to the ground. In his memoirs he described how he operated:

> to learn each hour the news concerning every province and every nation, the secrets of every court, the mood and weaknesses of each Prince and of every foreign minister; to be well-informed on an infinite number of matters about which we are supposed to know nothing; to elicit from our subjects what they hide from us with the greatest care; to discover the most remote opinions of our courtiers and the most hidden interests of those who come to us with quite contrary professions [claims].

To gather all this information, Louis relied on a series of talented ministers, usually of modest origins, who gained fame, fortune, and even noble status from serving the king. Most important among them was Jean-Baptiste Colbert (1619–1683), the son of a wool merchant turned royal official. Colbert had managed Mazarin's personal finances and worked his way up under Louis XIV to become head of royal finances, public works, and the navy. Like many of Louis's other ministers, he founded a family dynasty that eventually produced five ministers of state, an archbishop, two bishops, and three generals.

Colbert used the bureaucracy to establish a mercantilist policy. According to the economic doctrine of *mercantilism*, governments must intervene to increase national wealth by whatever means

Wars of Louis XIV

1667–1668   War of Devolution
Enemies: Spain, Dutch Republic, England, Sweden
Ended by Treaty of Aix-la-Chapelle in 1668, with
France gaining towns in Spanish Netherlands
(Flanders)

1672–1678   Dutch War
Enemies: Dutch Republic, Spain, Holy Roman Empire
Ended by treaty of Nijmegen, 1678–1679, which gave
several towns in Spanish Netherlands and Franche-
Comté to France

1688–1697   War of the League of Augsburg
Enemies: Holy Roman Empire, Sweden, Spain, England
Ended by treaty of Rijswijk, 1697, with Louis returning
all his conquests made since 1678 except Strasbourg

possible. Such government intervention inevitably increased the role and eventually the number of bureaucrats needed. Under Colbert, the French government established overseas trading companies, granted manufacturing monopolies, and standardized production methods for textiles, paper, and soap. A government inspection system regulated the quality of finished goods and compelled all craftsmen to organize into guilds, in which masters could supervise the work of the journeymen and apprentices. To protect French production, Colbert rescinded many internal customs fees but enacted high foreign tariffs, which cut imports of competing goods. To compete more effectively with England and the Dutch Republic, Colbert also subsidized shipbuilding, a policy that dramatically expanded the number of seaworthy vessels. Such mercantilist measures aimed to ensure France's prominence in world markets and to provide the resources needed to fight wars against the increasingly long list of enemies. Although later economists questioned the value of this state intervention in the economy, virtually every government in Europe embraced mercantilism.

Colbert's mercantilist projects extended to Canada, where in 1663 he took control of the trading company that had founded New France. He transplanted several thousand peasants from western France to the present-day province of Quebec, which France had claimed since 1608. To guard his investment, Colbert sent fifteen hundred soldiers to join the settlers. Of particular concern to the French government were the Iroquois, who regularly interrupted French fur-trading convoys. Shows of French military force, including the burning of Indian villages and winter food supplies, forced the Iroquois to make peace with New France, and from 1666 to 1680, French traders moved westward with minimal interference. In 1672, fur trader Louis Jolliet and Jesuit missionary Jacques Marquette reached the upper Mississippi River and traveled downstream as far as Arkansas. In 1684, French explorer Sieur de La Salle went all the way down to the Gulf of Mexico, claiming a vast territory for Louis XIV and calling it Louisiana after him. Louis and Colbert encouraged colonial settlement as part of their rivalry with the English and the Dutch in the New World.

The Army and War.   Colonial settlement occupied only a small portion of Louis XIV's attention, however, for his main foreign policy goal was to extend French power in Europe. In pursuing this purpose, he inevitably came up against the Spanish and Austrian Habsburgs, whose lands encircled his. To expand French power Louis needed the biggest possible army. His powerful ministry of war centralized the organization of French troops. Barracks built in major towns received supplies from a central distribution system. The state began to provide uniforms for the soldiers and to offer veterans some hospital care. A militia draft instituted in 1688 supplemented the army in times of war and enrolled 100,000 men. Louis's wartime army could field a force as large as that of all his enemies combined.

Absolutist governments always tried to increase their territorial holdings, and as Louis extended his reach, he gained new enemies. In 1667–1668, in the first of his major wars after assuming personal control of French affairs, Louis defeated the Spanish armies but had to make peace when England, Sweden, and the Dutch Republic joined the war. In the Treaty of Aix-la-Chapelle in 1668, he gained control of towns on the border of the Spanish Netherlands. Pamphlets sponsored by the Habsburgs accused Louis of aiming for "universal monarchy," or domination of Europe. The chorus of denunciation would only grow over the years.

In 1672, Louis XIV opened hostilities against the Dutch because they stood in the way of his acquisition of more territory in the Spanish Netherlands. He declared war again on Spain in 1673. By now the Dutch had allied themselves with their former Spanish masters to hold off the French. Louis also marched his troops into territories of the Holy Roman Empire, provoking many of the German princes to join with the emperor, the Spanish, and the Dutch in an alliance against Louis, now denounced as a "Christian Turk" for his imperialist ambitions. But the French armies more than held their own. Faced with bloody but inconclusive results on the battlefield, the parties agreed to the Treaty of Nijmegen of 1678–1679, which ceded several Flemish towns and Franche-Comté to Louis, linking Alsace to the rest of France. These territorial additions were costly: French government deficits soared, and increases in taxes touched off the most serious antitax revolt of Louis's reign, in 1675.

Louis had no intention of standing still. Heartened by the Habsburgs' seeming weakness, he pushed eastward, seizing the city of Strasbourg in 1681 and invading the province of Lorraine in 1684. In 1688,

he attacked some of the small German cities of the Holy Roman Empire and was soon involved again in a long war against a Europe-wide coalition. As Louis's own mental powers diminished with age, he seems to have lost all sense of measure. His armies laid waste to German cities such as Mannheim; his government ordered the local military commander to "kill all those who would still wish to build houses there." Between 1689 and 1697, a coalition made up of England, Spain, Sweden, the Dutch Republic, the Austrian emperor, and various German princes fought Louis XIV to a stalemate. When hostilities ended in the Peace of Rijswijk in 1697, Louis returned many of his conquests made since 1678 with the exception of Strasbourg (Map 17.1). Louis never lost his taste for war, but his allies learned how to set limits on his ambitions.

Louis was the last French ruler before Napoleon to accompany his troops to the battlefield. In later generations, as the military became more professional, French rulers left the fighting to their generals. Although Louis had eliminated the private armies

MAP 17.1 Louis XIV's Acquisitions, 1668–1697
Every ruler in Europe hoped to extend his or her territorial control, and war was often the result. Louis XIV steadily encroached on the Spanish Netherlands to the north and the lands of the Holy Roman Empire to the east. Although coalitions of European powers reined in Louis's grander ambitions, he nonetheless incorporated many neighboring territories into the French crown.

of his noble courtiers, he constantly promoted his own military prowess in order to keep his noble officers under his sway. He had miniature battle scenes painted on his high heels and commissioned tapestries showing his military processions into cities, even those he did not take by force. He seized every occasion to assert his supremacy, insisting that other fleets salute his ships first.

War required money and men, which Louis obtained by expanding state control over finances, conscription, and military supply. Thus absolutism and warfare fed each other, as the bureaucracy created new ways to raise and maintain an army and the army's success in war justified further expansion of state power. But constant warfare also eroded the state's resources. Further administrative and legal reform, the elimination of the buying and selling of offices, and the lowering of taxes—all were made impossible by the need for more money.

The playwright Corneille wrote, no doubt optimistically, "The people are very happy when they die for their kings." What is certain is that the wars touched many peasant and urban families. The people who lived on the routes leading to the battlefields had to house and feed soldiers; only nobles were exempt from this requirement. Everyone, moreover, paid the higher taxes that were necessary to support the army. By the end of Louis's reign, one in six Frenchmen had served in the military.

❖ Absolutism in Central and Eastern Europe

Central and eastern European rulers saw in Louis XIV a powerful model of absolutist state building, yet they did not blindly emulate the Sun King, in part because they confronted conditions peculiar to their regions. The ruler of Brandenburg-Prussia had to rebuild lands ravaged by the Thirty Years' War and unite far-flung territories. The Austrian Habsburgs needed to govern a mosaic of ethnic and religious groups while fighting off the Ottoman Turks. The Russian tsars wanted to extend their power over an extensive but relatively impoverished empire. The great exception to absolutism in eastern Europe was Poland-Lithuania, where a long crisis virtually destroyed central authority and sucked much of eastern Europe into its turbulent wake.

Brandenburg-Prussia and Sweden: Militaristic Absolutism

Brandenburg-Prussia began as a puny, landlocked state on the Elbe River, but it had a remarkable future. In the nineteenth century, it would unify the disparate German states into modern-day Germany. The ruler of Brandenburg was an elector, one of the seven German princes entitled to select the Holy Roman Emperor. Since the sixteenth century the ruler of Brandenburg had also controlled the duchy of East Prussia; after 1618 the state was called Brandenburg-Prussia. Through marriages and alliances, including French support in the Thirty Years' War, Brandenburg-Prussia slowly added lands on the Rhine and the Baltic coast. Each territory had its own laws and representative institutions, called *estates*. Despite meager resources, Frederick William of Hohenzollern, the Great Elector of Brandenburg-Prussia (r. 1640–1688), succeeded in welding these scattered lands into an absolutist state.

Pressured first by the necessities of fighting the Thirty Years' War and then by the demands of reconstruction, Frederick William set four main tasks for himself: establishing his personal authority at the expense of the estates, founding a strong standing army, creating an efficient bureaucracy, and extending his territory. To force his territories' estates to grant him a dependable income, the Great Elector struck a deal with the Junkers (nobles) of each land: in exchange for allowing him to collect taxes, he gave them complete control over their enserfed peasants and exempted them from taxation. The tactic worked. By the end of his reign the estates met only on ceremonial occasions.

Supplied with a steady income, Frederick William could devote his attention to military and bureaucratic consolidation. Over forty years he expanded his army from eight thousand to thirty thousand men. (See "Taking Measure," page 613.) The army mirrored the rigid domination of nobles over peasants that characterized Brandenburg-Prussian society: peasants filled the ranks, and Junkers became officers. Each group learned discipline and obedience, with peasants serving the nobles and nobles serving the elector. Nobles also served the elector by taking positions as bureaucratic officials, but military needs always had priority. The elector named special war commissars to take charge not only of military affairs but also of tax collection. To

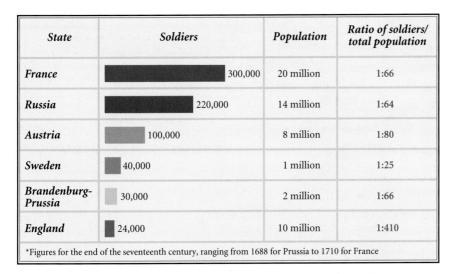

State	Soldiers	Population	Ratio of soldiers/ total population
France	300,000	20 million	1:66
Russia	220,000	14 million	1:64
Austria	100,000	8 million	1:80
Sweden	40,000	1 million	1:25
Brandenburg-Prussia	30,000	2 million	1:66
England	24,000	10 million	1:410

*Figures for the end of the seventeenth century, ranging from 1688 for Prussia to 1710 for France

TAKING MEASURE
The Seventeenth-Century Army
The figures in this chart are only approximate, but an important story. What conclusions can be drawn about the relative weight of the military in the different European states? Why would England have such a smaller army than the others? Is the absolute or the relative size of the military the most important indicator?
From André Corvisier. *Armées et sociétés en Europe de 1494 à 1789.* (Paris: Presses Universitaires de France, 1976), 126.

hasten military dispatches, he also established one of Europe's first state postal systems.

As a Calvinist ruler, Frederick William avoided the ostentation of the French court, even while following the absolutist model of centralizing state power. He boldly rebuffed Louis XIV by welcoming twenty thousand French Huguenot refugees after Louis's revocation of the Edict of Nantes. In pursuing foreign and domestic policies that promoted state power and prestige, Frederick William adroitly switched sides in Louis's wars and would stop at almost nothing to crush resistance at home. In 1701, his son Frederick I (r. 1688–1713) persuaded Holy Roman Emperor Leopold I to grant him the title "king in Prussia." Prussia had arrived as an important power.

Across the Baltic, Sweden also stood out as an example of absolutist consolidation. In the Thirty Years' War, King Gustavus Adolphus's superb generalship and highly trained army had made Sweden the supreme power of northern Europe. The huge but sparsely populated state included not only most of present-day Sweden but also Finland, Estonia, half of Latvia, and much of the Baltic coastline of modern Poland and Germany. The Baltic, in short, was a Swedish lake. After Gustavus Adolphus died, his daughter Queen Christina (r. 1632–1654) conceded much authority to the estates. Absorbed by religion and philosophy, Christina eventually abdicated and converted to Catholicism. Her successors temporarily made Sweden an absolute monarchy.

In Sweden (as in neighboring Denmark-Norway), absolutism meant simply the estates standing aside while the king led the army in lucrative foreign campaigns. The aristocracy went along because it staffed the bureaucracy and reaped war profits. Intrigued by French culture, Sweden also gleamed with national pride. In 1668, the nobility demanded the introduction of a distinctive national costume: should Swedes, they asked, "who are so glorious and renowned a nation . . . let ourselves be led by the nose by a parcel of French dancing-masters"? Sweden spent the forty years after 1654 continuously warring with its neighbors. By the 1690s, war expenses began to outrun the small Swedish population's ability to pay, threatening the continuation of absolutism.

An Uneasy Balance: Austrian Habsburgs and Ottoman Turks

Holy Roman Emperor Leopold I (r. 1658–1705) ruled over a variety of territories of different ethnicities, languages, and religions, yet in ways similar to his French and Prussian counterparts, he gradually consolidated his power. Like all the Holy Roman emperors since 1438, Leopold was an Austrian Habsburg. He was simultaneously duke of Upper and Lower Silesia, count of Tyrol, archduke of Upper and Lower Austria, king of Bohemia, king of Hungary and Croatia, and ruler of Styria and Moravia (Map 17.2). Some of these territories were provinces in the

MAP 17.2 State Building in Central and Eastern Europe, 1648–1699
The Austrian Habsburgs had long contested the Ottoman Turks for dominance of eastern Europe, and by 1699, they had pushed the Turks out of Hungary. In central Europe, the Austrian Habsburgs confronted the growing power of Brandenburg-Prussia, which had emerged from relative obscurity after the Thirty Years' War to begin an aggressive program of expanding its military and its territorial base. As emperor of the Holy Roman Empire, the Austrian Habsburg ruler governed a huge expanse of territory, but the emperor's control was in fact only partial because of guarantees of local autonomy.

Holy Roman Empire; others were simply ruled from Vienna as Habsburg family holdings. Leopold needed to build up his armies and state authority in order to defend the Holy Roman Empire's international position, which had been weakened by the Thirty Years' War, and to push back the Ottoman Turks who steadily encroached from the southeast.

The Austrian Version of Absolutism. To forge a powerful central state, Leopold had to modernize his army and gain control over far-flung provinces that cherished their independent ways. The emperor and his closest officials took control over recruiting, provisioning, and strategic planning and worked to replace the mercenaries hired during the Thirty Years' War with a permanent standing army that promoted

professional discipline. When Leopold joined the coalition against Louis XIV in 1672, his new imperial troops fought well; and thanks to the emperor's astute diplomacy, the Austrians played a critical role in keeping Louis XIV's ambitions in check.

To pay for the army and staff his growing bureaucracy, Leopold had to gain the support of local aristocrats and chip away at provincial institutions' powers. As punishment for rebelling against Austrian rule, the Bohemians lost their right to elect a monarch; the Austrians named themselves hereditary rulers of Bohemia. To replace Bohemian nobles who had supported the 1618 revolt against Austrian authority, the Habsburgs promoted a new nobility made up of Czechs, Germans, Italians, Spaniards, and even Irish who used German as their common tongue, professed Catholicism, and loyally served the Austrian dynasty. Bohemia became a virtual Austrian colony. "You have utterly destroyed our home, our ancient kingdom, and have built us no new one in its place," lamented a Czech Jesuit in 1670, addressing Leopold. "Woe to you! . . . The nobles you have oppressed, great cities made small. Of smiling towns you have made straggling villages." Austrian censors prohibited publication of this protest for over a century.

Battle for Hungary. In addition to holding Louis XIV in check on his western frontiers, Leopold had to confront the ever-present challenge of the Ottoman Turks to his east. Hungary was the chief battle zone between Austria and the Turks for more than 150 years. In 1682, when war broke out again, Austria controlled the northwest section of Hungary; the Turks occupied the center; and in the east, the Turks demanded tribute from the Hungarian princes who ruled Transylvania. In 1683, the Turks pushed all the way to the gates of Vienna and laid siege to the Austrian capital; after reaching this high-water mark, however, Turkish power ebbed. With the help of Polish cavalry, the Austrians finally broke the siege and turned the tide in a major counteroffensive. By the Treaty of Karlowitz of 1699, the Ottoman Turks had to surrender almost all of Hungary to the Austrians.

Hungary's "liberation" from the Turks came at a high price. The fighting laid waste vast stretches of Hungary's central plain, and the population may have declined as much as 65 percent since 1600. To repopulate the land, the Austrians settled large communities of foreigners: Romanians, Croats, Serbs, and Germans. Magyar (Hungarian) speakers became a minority, and the seeds were sown for the poisonous nationality conflicts in nineteenth- and twentieth-century Hungary, Romania, and Yugoslavia.

Once the Turks had been beaten back, Austrian rule over Hungary tightened. In 1687, the Habsburg dynasty's hereditary right to the Hungarian crown was acknowledged by the Hungarian diet, a parliament revived by Leopold in 1681 to gain the support of Hungarian nobles. The diet was dominated by nobles who had amassed huge holdings in the liberated territories. They formed the core of a pro-Habsburg Hungarian aristocracy that would buttress the dynasty until it fell in 1918. As the

Turks retreated from Hungary, Leopold systematically rebuilt churches, monasteries, roadside shrines, and monuments in the flamboyant Austrian baroque style.

Ottoman State Authority. The Ottoman Turks also pursued state consolidation, but in a very different fashion from the Europeans. The Ottoman state centralized its authority through negotiation with and incorporation of bandit armies, which European rulers typically suppressed by armed force. In the seventeenth century, mutinous army officers often deposed the Ottoman ruler, or sultan, in a palace coup, but because the Ottoman state had learned to manage constant crises, the state itself survived and rarely faced peasant revolts. Rather than remaining in their villages and resisting state authorities, Ottoman peasants often left to become bandits who periodically worked for the state as

The Siege of Vienna, 1683
In this stylized rendition by Frans Geffels, the Ottoman Turks bombard the city, which had been surrounded for two months. The forces commanded by Polish king Jan Sobieski are arriving in the foreground to help lift the siege.
Museen der Stadt, Wien (detail).

mercenaries. Leaders of bandit gangs entered into negotiation with the Ottoman sultan, sometimes providing thousands of bandit mercenaries to the sultan's armies and even taking major official positions. Similarly, the Ottomans avoided revolt by the elites by playing them off against each other, absorbing some into the state bureaucracy and pitting one level of authority against another. This constantly shifting social and political system explains how the coup-ridden Ottoman state could appear "weak" in Western eyes and still pose a massive military threat on Europe's southeastern borders. In the end, the Ottoman state lasted longer than Louis XIV's absolute monarchy.

Russia: Foundations of Bureaucratic Absolutism

Superficially, seventeenth-century Russia seemed a world apart from the Europe of Louis XIV. Straddling Europe and Asia, it stretched across Siberia to the Pacific Ocean. Western visitors either sneered or shuddered at the "barbarism" of Russian life, and Russians reciprocated by nursing deep suspicions of everything foreign. But under the surface, Russia was evolving along paths much like the rest of absolutist Europe; the tsars wanted to claim unlimited autocratic power, but they had to surmount internal disorder and come to an accommodation with noble landlords.

Serfdom and the Code of 1649. When Tsar Alexei (r. 1645–1676) tried to extend state authority by imposing new administrative structures and taxes in 1648, Moscow and other cities erupted in bloody rioting. The government immediately doused the fire. In 1649, Alexei convoked the Assembly of the Land (consisting of noble delegates from the provinces) to consult on a sweeping law code to organize Russian society in a strict social hierarchy that would last for nearly two centuries. The code of 1649 assigned all subjects to a hereditary class according to their current occupation or state needs. Slaves and free peasants were merged into a serf class. As serfs they could not change occupations or move; they were tightly tied to the soil and to their noble masters. To prevent tax evasion, the code also forbade townspeople to move from the community where they resided. Nobles owed absolute obedience to the tsar and were required to serve in the army, but in return no other group could own estates worked by serfs. Serfs became the chattel of their lord, who could sell them like horses or land. Their conditions of life differed little from those of the slaves on the plantations in the Americas.

Some peasants resisted enserfment. In 1667, Stenka Razin, a Cossack from the Don region in southern Russia, led a rebellion that promised liberation from "the traitors and bloodsuckers of the peasant communes"—the great noble landowners, local governors, and Moscow courtiers. Captured

Stenka Razin in Captivity
After leading a revolt of thousands of serfs, peasants, and members of non-Russian tribes of the middle and lower Volga region, Razin was captured by Russian forces and led off to Moscow, as shown here, where he was executed in 1671. He has been the subject of songs, legends, and poems ever since. Novosti Photo Library (London).

four years later by the tsar's army, Razin was dismembered, his head and limbs publicly displayed, and his body thrown to the dogs. Thousands of his followers also suffered grisly deaths, but his memory lived on in folk songs and legends. Landlords successfully petitioned for the abolition of the statute of limitations on runaway serfs, the use of state agents in searching for runaways, and harsh penalties against those who harbored runaways. The increase in Russian state authority went hand in hand with the enforcement of serfdom.

The Tsar's Absolute Powers. To extend his power and emulate his western rivals, Tsar Alexei wanted a bigger army, exclusive control over state policy, and a greater say in religious matters. The size of the army increased dramatically from 35,000 in the 1630s to 220,000 by the end of the century. The Assembly of the Land, once an important source of noble consultation, never met again after 1653. Alexei also imposed firm control over the Russian Orthodox church. In 1666, a church council reaffirmed the tsar's role as God's direct representative on earth. The state-dominated church took action against a religious group called the Old Believers, who rejected church efforts to bring Russian worship in line with Byzantine tradition. Old Believer leaders, including the noblewoman Fedosia Morozova, endured exile, prison, and torture; whole communities of Old Believers starved or burned themselves to death rather than submit. Religious schism opened a gulf between the Russian people and the crown.

Nevertheless, modernizing trends prevailed. As the state bureaucracy expanded, adding more officials and establishing regulations and routines, the government intervened more and more in daily life. Decrees regulated tobacco smoking, card playing, and alcohol consumption and even dictated how people should leash and fence their pet dogs. Western ideas began to seep into educated circles in Moscow. Nobles and ordinary citizens commissioned portraits of themselves instead of only buying religious icons. Tsar Alexei set up the first Western-style theater in the Kremlin, and his daughter Sophia translated French plays. The most adventurous nobles began to wear German-style clothing. Some even argued that service and not just birth should determine rank. A long struggle over Western influences had begun.

Poland-Lithuania Overwhelmed

Unlike the other eastern European powers, Poland-Lithuania did not follow the absolutist model. Decades of war weakened the monarchy and made the great nobles into virtually autonomous warlords. They used the parliament and demands for constitutionalism to stymie monarchical power. The result was a precipitous slide into political disarray and weakness.

In 1648, Ukrainian Cossack warriors revolted against the king of Poland-Lithuania, inaugurating two decades of tumult known as the Deluge. Cossack bands had formed from runaway peasants and poor nobles in the no man's land of southern Russia and Ukraine. The Polish nobles who claimed this potentially rich land scorned the Cossacks as troublemakers; but to the Ukrainian peasant population they were liberators. In 1654, the Cossacks offered Ukraine to Russian rule, provoking a

Poland-Lithuania in the Seventeenth Century

Russo-Polish war that ended in 1667 when the tsar annexed eastern Ukraine and Kiev. Neighboring powers tried to profit from the chaos in Poland-Lithuania; Sweden, Brandenburg-Prussia, and Transylvania sent armies to seize territory.

Many towns were destroyed in the fighting, and as much as a third of the Polish population perished. The once prosperous Jewish and Protestant minorities suffered greatly: some 56,000 Jews were killed either by the Cossacks, Polish peasants, or Russian troops, and thousands more had to flee or convert to Christianity. One rabbi wrote, "We were slaughtered each day, in a more agonizing way than cattle: they are butchered quickly, while we were being executed slowly." Surviving Jews moved from towns to *shtetls* (Jewish villages), where they took up petty trading, moneylending, tax gathering, and tavern leasing—activities that fanned peasant anti-Semitism. Desperate for protection amid the war, most Protestants backed the violently anti-Catholic Swedes, and the victorious Catholic majority branded them as traitors. Some Protestant refugees fled to the Dutch Republic and England. In Poland-Lithuania it came to be assumed that a good Pole was a Catholic. The commonwealth had ceased to be an outpost of toleration.

The commonwealth revived briefly when a man of ability and ambition, Jan Sobieski (r. 1674–1696), was elected king. He gained a reputation throughout Europe when he led 25,000 Polish cavalrymen into battle in the siege of Vienna in 1683. His cavalry helped rout the Turks and turned the tide against the Ottomans. Married to a politically shrewd French princess, Sobieski openly admired Louis XIV's France. Despite his efforts to rebuild the monarchy, he could not halt Poland-Lithuania's decline into powerlessness.

Elsewhere the ravages of war had created opportunities for kings to increase their power, but in Poland-Lithuania the great nobles gained all the advantage. They dominated the Sejm (parliament), and to maintain an equilibrium among themselves, they each wielded an absolute veto power. This "free veto" constitutional system soon deadlocked parliamentary government. The monarchy lost its room to maneuver, and with it much of its remaining power. An appalled Croat visitor in 1658 commented on the situation:

> Among the Poles there is no order in the state, and the subjects are not afraid either of the king or the judge. Everybody who is stronger thinks to have the right to oppress the weaker, just as the wolves and bears are free to capture and kill cattle. . . . Such abominable depravity is called by the Poles "aristocratic freedom."

The Polish version of constitutionalism fatally weakened the state and made it prey to neighboring powers.

❖ Constitutionalism in England

In the second half of the seventeenth century, western and eastern Europe began to move in different directions. The farther east one traveled, the more absolutist the style of government and the greater the gulf between landlord and peasant. In eastern Europe, nobles lorded over their serfs but owed almost slavish obedience in turn to their rulers. In western Europe, even in absolutist France, serfdom had almost entirely disappeared and nobles and rulers alike faced greater challenges to their control. The greatest challenges of all would come in England.

This outcome might seem surprising, for the English monarchs enjoyed many advantages compared with their continental rivals: they needed less money for their armies because they had stayed out of the Thirty Years' War, and their island kingdom was in theory easier to rule because the population they governed was only one-fourth the size of France's and relatively homogeneous ethnically. Yet the English rulers failed in their efforts to install absolutist policies. The English revolutions of 1642–1660 and 1688–1689 overturned two kings, confirmed the constitutional powers of an elected parliament, and laid the foundation for the idea that government must guarantee certain rights under the law.

England Turned Upside Down, 1642–1660

Disputes about the right to levy taxes and the nature of authority in the Church of England had long troubled the relationship between the English crown and Parliament. For over a hundred years, wealthy English landowners had been accustomed to participating in government through Parliament and expected to be consulted on royal policy. Although England had no one constitutional document, a variety of laws, judicial decisions, charters and petitions granted by the king, and customary procedures all regulated relations between king and parliament. When Charles I tried to assert his authority over Parliament, a civil war broke out in 1642. It set in motion an unpredictable chain of events, which included an extraordinary ferment of religious and political ideas. Some historians view the English civil war of 1642–1646 as the last great war of religion because it pitted Puritans against those trying to push the Anglican church toward Catholicism; others see in it the first modern revolution because it gave birth to democratic political and religious movements.

Charles I versus Parliament.   When Charles I (r. 1625–1649) succeeded his father, James I, he faced an increasingly aggressive Parliament that resisted new taxes and resented the king's efforts to extend his personal control. In 1628, Parliament forced Charles to agree to a Petition of Right by which he promised not to levy taxes without its consent. Charles hoped to avoid further interference with his plans by simply refusing to call Parliament into session between 1629 and 1640. Without it, the king's ministers had to find every loophole possible to raise revenues. They tried to turn "ship money," a levy on seaports in times of emergency, into an annual tax collected everywhere in the country. The crown won the ensuing court case, but many subjects still refused to pay what they considered to be an illegal tax.

Religious tensions brought conflicts over the king's authority to a head. The Puritans had long agitated for the removal of any vestiges of Catholicism, but Charles, married to a French Catholic, moved in the opposite direction. With Charles's encouragement, the archbishop of Canterbury, William Laud (1573–1645), imposed increasingly elaborate ceremonies on the Anglican church. Angered by these moves toward "popery," the Puritans poured forth vituperative pamphlets and sermons. In response Laud hauled them before the feared Court of Star Chamber, which the king personally controlled. The court ordered harsh sentences for Laud's Puritan critics; they were whipped, pilloried, branded, and even had their ears cut off and their noses split. When Laud tried to apply his policies to Scotland, however, they backfired completely: the stubborn Presbyterian Scots rioted against the imposition of the Anglican prayer book—the Book of Common Prayer—and in 1640 they invaded the north of England. To raise money to fight the war, Charles called Parliament into session and unwittingly opened the door to a constitutional and religious crisis.

The Parliament of 1640 did not intend revolution, but reformers in the House of Commons (the lower house of Parliament) wanted to undo what they saw as the royal tyranny of the 1630s. Parliament removed Laud from office, ordered the execution of an unpopular royal commander, abolished the Court of Star Chamber, repealed recently levied taxes, and provided for a parliamentary assembly at least once every three years, thus establishing a constitutional check on royal authority. Moderate reformers expected to stop there and resisted Puritan pressure to abolish bishops and eliminate the Anglican prayer book. But their hand was forced in January 1642, when Charles and his soldiers invaded

**Artemisia Gentileschi, *Painting*
(an allegorical self-portrait)**
Like all monarchs of his time, King Charles I of England spent lavishly on clothing, furniture, and art. Among the many paintings commissioned by him was this painting by the Italian woman artist Gentileschi (1630s), which shows the artist herself at work. Gentileschi lived at the English court and worked for Charles between 1638 and 1641. She painted as well for King Philip IV of Spain and for many Italian patrons. Coming from the hand of a woman, the painting must be seen as a kind of wry commentary on women's exclusion from most cultural endeavors. The figure supposedly represents an allegory of painting. Most allegories—symbolic figures standing for abstract concepts—relied on female figures, not because women did these things but because women could be imagined as symbols. The Italian word for painting, *moreover, like many Romance-language words for abstractions, is gendered female (la pittura). But Gentileschi portrays herself, not an abstract female figure, as if to say that real women can paint too.*
The Royal Collection. © 1998 Her Majesty Queen Elizabeth II.

Parliament and tried unsuccessfully to arrest those leaders who had moved to curb his power. Faced with mounting opposition within London, Charles quickly withdrew from the city and organized an army. The stage was set for a civil war between king and parliament.

Civil War and the Challenge to All Authorities.

The war lasted four years (1642–1646) and divided the country. The king's army of royalists, known as Cavaliers, enjoyed most support in northern and western England. The parliamentary forces, called Roundheads because they cut their hair short, had their stronghold in the southeast, including London. Although Puritans dominated on the parliamentary side, they were divided among themselves about the proper form of church government: the Presbyterians wanted a Calvinist church with some central authority, whereas the Independents favored entirely autonomous congregations free from other church government (hence the term *congregationalism*, often associated with the Independents). Putting aside their differences for the sake of military unity, the Puritans united under an obscure member of the House of Commons, the country gentleman Oliver Cromwell (1599–1658), who sympathized with the Independents. After Cromwell skillfully reorganized the parliamentary troops, his New Model Army defeated the Cavaliers at the battle of Naseby in 1645. Charles surrendered in 1646.

Although the civil war between king and Parliament had ended in victory for Parliament, divisions within the Puritan ranks now came to the fore: the Presbyterians dominated Parliament, but the Independents controlled the army. Both factions' leaders belonged to the social and political elite, but the Independents favored more far-reaching political and religious changes than the Presbyterians. Their disputes drew lower-class groups into the debate. (See "Contrasting Views," page 622.) The most

England during the Civil War

important were the Levellers, who emerged among disgruntled soldiers when Parliament tried to disband the New Model Army. In 1647, the Levellers honed their ideas about the nature of political authority in a series of debates between soldiers and officers at an army camp near London. They insisted that Parliament meet annually, that members be paid so as to allow common people to participate, and that all male heads of households be allowed to vote. Their proposed democracy excluded servants, the propertyless, and women but nonetheless "leveled" social differences (hence their name) by offering political access to artisans, shopkeepers, and modest farmers. Cromwell and other army leaders rejected the Levellers' demands as threatening to property owners. Cromwell insisted, "You have no other way to deal with these men but to break them in pieces. . . . If you do not break them they will break you."

Just as political differences between Presbyterians and Independents helped spark new democratic political movements, so too their conflicts over church organization fostered the emergence of new religious doctrines. The new sects had in common only their emphasis on the "inner light" of individual religious inspiration and a disdain for hierarchical authority. Their emphasis on equality before God and democracy within the church appealed to the middle and lower classes. The Baptists, for example, insisted on adult baptism because they believed that Christians should choose their own church and that every child should not automatically become a member of the Church of England. The Quakers demonstrated their beliefs in equality and the inner light by refusing to doff their hats to men in authority. Manifesting their religious experience by trembling, or "quaking," the Quakers believed that anyone—man or woman—inspired by a direct experience of God could preach.

Parliamentary leaders feared that the new sects would overturn the whole social hierarchy. Rumors abounded, for example, of naked Quakers running through the streets waiting "for a sign." Some sects did advocate sweeping change. The Diggers promoted rural communism—collective ownership of all property. Seekers and Ranters questioned just about everything. One notorious Ranter, John Robins, even claimed to be God. A few men advocated free love. These developments convinced the political elite that tolerating the new sects would lead to skepticism, anarchism, and debauchery.

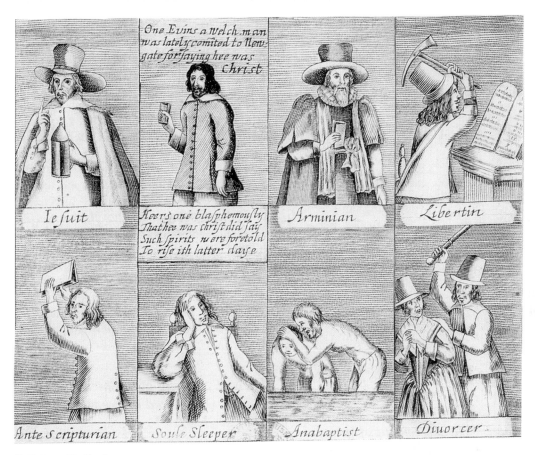

Religious Radicals

The Puritans in Parliament had opposed the Catholic leanings of the Church of England (shown as the Arminian here) and worried that Catholic missionary groups, such as the Jesuits (top left), might gain access to England. But they also detested the nonconformist Protestant sects that sprang up during the civil war: some individuals, called Ranters or Seekers, supposedly claimed they were Jesus come again; Arians rejected the doctrine of the Trinity; libertines attacked all sacramental objects of religion, anti-scripturians rejected the authority of the Bible; soul sleepers denied the afterlife; Anabaptists refused infant baptism; the family of love did not keep the sabbath; and some advocated easier divorce. It should be remembered that pamphlets such as this one represented the views of those who opposed these tendencies. It is questionable, for example, whether Arians believed in free love, libertines attacked religious objects, or those in favor of easier divorce beat their wives.
British Library.

In keeping with their notions of equality and individual inspiration, many of the new sects provided opportunities for women to become preachers and prophets. The Quakers thought women especially capable of prophecy. One prophet, Anna Trapnel, explained her vocation: "For in all that was said by me, I was nothing, the Lord put all in my mouth, and told me what I should say." Women presented petitions, participated prominently in street demonstrations, distributed tracts, and occasionally even dressed as men, wearing swords and joining armies. The duchess of Newcastle complained in 1650 that women were "affecting a Masculinacy . . . practicing the behaviour . . . of men." The outspoken women in new sects like the Quakers underscored the threat of a social order turning upside down.

Oliver Cromwell. At the heart of the continuing political struggle was the question of what to do with the king, who tried to negotiate with the Presbyterians in Parliament. In late 1648, Independents

The English Civil War

The civil war between Charles I and Parliament (1642–1646) excited furious debates about the proper forms of political authority, debates that influenced political thought for two centuries or more. The Levellers, who served in the parliamentary army, wanted Parliament to be more accountable to ordinary men like themselves (Document 1). When the king came to trial in January 1649, he laid out the royalist case for the supremacy of the king (Document 2). After the restoration of the monarchy in 1660, Lucy Hutchinson wrote a memoir in which she complained that *Puritan* had become a term of political slander. Her memoir shows how religious terms had been politicized by the upheaval (Document 3). Thomas Hobbes in his famous political treatise *Leviathan* (1651) develops the consequences of the civil war for political theory (Document 4).

1. The Levellers, "The Agreement of the People, as Presented to the Council of the Army" (October 28, 1647)

Note especially two things about this document: (1) it focuses on Parliament as the chief instrument of reform and demands proportional or democratic representation; and (2) it claims that government depends on the consent of the people.

. . . Since, therefore, our former oppressions and scarce-yet-ended troubles have been occasioned, either by want of frequent national meetings in Council [Parliament], or by rendering those meetings ineffectual, we are fully agreed and resolved to provide that hereafter our representatives be neither left to an uncertainty for the time nor made useless to the ends for which they are intended. In order whereunto we declare:—

That the people of England, being at this day very unequally distributed by Counties, Cities, and Borough for the election of their deputies in Parliament, ought to be more indifferently [equally] proportioned according to the number of the inhabitants. . . .

That the power of this, and all future Representatives of this Nation, is inferior only to theirs who choose them, and doth extend, without the consent or concurrence of any other person or persons [the king], to the enacting, altering, and repealing of laws, to the erecting and abolishing of offices and courts, to the appointing, removing, and calling to account magistrates and officers of all degrees, to the making war and peace, to the treating with foreign States [in other words, Parliament is the supreme power, not the king]. . . .

These things we declare to be our native rights, and therefore are agreed and resolved to maintain them with our utmost possibilities against all opposition whatsoever. . . .

Source: Samuel Rawson Gardiner, *The Constitutional Documents of the Puritan Revolution, 1625–1660* (1906), 333–35.

2. Charles I's Refusal of the Jurisdiction of the Court Appointed to Try Him (January 21, 1649)

Charles argued that his trial was illegal. He cast himself as the true defender of English liberties and accused Parliament of going against both the Bible and English law.

The duty I owe to God in the preservation of the true liberty of my people will not suffer me at this time to be silent: for, how can any free-born subject of England call life or anything he possesseth his own, if power without right daily make new, and abrogate the old fundamental laws of the land which I now take to be the present case? . . . Now I am most confident this day's proceeding cannot be warranted by God's laws; for, on the contrary, the authority of obedience unto Kings is clearly warranted, and strictly commanded in both the Old and New Testament. . . .

Then for the law of this land, I am no less confident, that no learned lawyer will affirm that an impeachment can lie against the King, they all going in his name: and one of the maxims is, that the King can do no wrong.

Thus you see that I speak not for my own right alone, as I am your King, but also for the true liberty of all my subjects, which consists not in the power of government, but in living under such laws, such a government, as may give themselves the best assurance of their lives, and property of their goods.

Source: Stuart E. Prall, ed., *The Puritan Revolution: A Documentary History* (Gloucester, Mass.: Peter Smith, 1973), 186–88.

3. *Lucy Hutchinson,* Memoirs of the Life of Colonel Hutchinson *(1664–1671)*

Lucy Hutchinson wrote her memoir to defend her Puritan husband, who had been imprisoned upon the restoration of the monarchy.

If any were grieved at the dishonour of the kingdom, or the griping of the poor, or the unjust oppressions of the subject by a thousand ways invented to maintain the riots of the courtiers and the swarms of needy Scots the king had brought in to devour like locusts the plenty of this land, he was a puritan; if any showed favour to any godly, honest person, kept them company, relieved them in want, or protected them against violent and unjust oppression, he was a puritan. . . . In short, all that crossed the views of the needy courtiers, the proud encroaching priests, the thievish projectors, the lewd nobility and gentry . . . all these were puritans; and if puritans, then enemies to the king and his government, seditious, factious hypocrites, ambitious disturbers of the public peace, and finally the pest of the kingdom.

Source: Christopher Hill and Edmund Dell, eds., *The Good Old Cause: The English Revolution of 1640–1660, Its Causes, Course and Consequences* (London: Lawrence and Wishart, 1949), 179–80.

4. *Thomas Hobbes,* Leviathan *(1651)*

In this excerpt, Hobbes depicts the anarchy of a society without a strong central authority, but he leaves open the question of whether that authority should be vested in "one Man" or "one Assembly of men," that is, a king or a parliament.

During the time men live without a common Power to keep them all in awe, they are in that condition which is called Warre; and such a warre, as is of every man, against every man. . . . In such condition, there is no place for Industry; because the fruit thereof is uncertain: and consequently no Culture of the Earth; no Navigation, nor use of the commodities that may be imported by Sea; no commodious Building; no Instrument of moving, and removing such things as require much force; no Knowledge of the face of the Earth; no account of Time; no Arts; no Letters; no Society; and which is worst of all, continuall feare, and danger of violent death; And the life of man, solitary, poore, nasty, brutish, and short.

The only way to erect such a Common Power, as may be able to defend them from the invasion of Forraigners, and the injuries of one another, and thereby to secure them in such sort, as that by their owne industrie, and by the Fruites of the Earth, they may nourish themselves and live contentedly; is, to conferre all their power and strength upon one Man, or upon one Assembly of men, that may reduce all their wills, by plurality of voices, unto one Will. . . . This is more than Consent, or Concord; it is a reall Unitie of them all, in one and the same Person, made by Covenant of every man with every man. . . . This done, the Multitude so united in one Person, is called a COMMON-WEALTH, in latine CIVITAS. This is the Generation of that great LEVIATHAN, or rather (to speake more reverently) of that *Mortall God,* to which wee owe under the *Imortall God,* our peace and defence.

Source: Thomas Hobbes, *Leviathan,* ed. Richard E. Flathman and David Johnston (New York: Norton, 1997), 70, 95.

QUESTIONS FOR DEBATE
1. Which of these views do you find most persuasive?
2. Why did Hobbes's arguments about political authority upset supporters of both monarchy and Parliament?

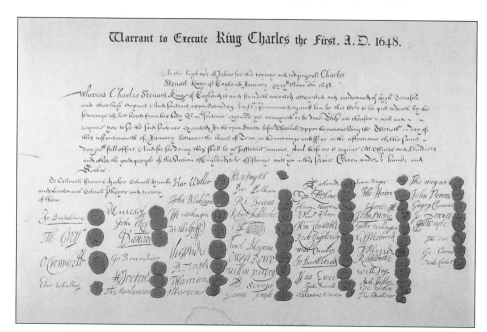

Death Warrant of Charles I
Parliament voted to try Charles I for treason, and the trial began in January 1649. A week later the court found Charles to be a "tyrant, traitor, murderer, and public enemy" and ordered his execution. When the monarchy was restored in 1660, everyone who signed Charles I's death warrant was hunted down and executed. Mary Evans Picture Library.

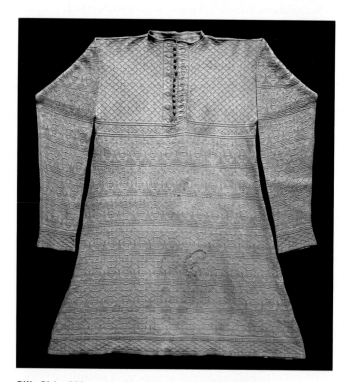

Silk Shirt Worn by Charles I at His Execution
The blood is still visible on the shirt worn by Charles I for his beheading. After his head was severed, many people rushed forward to dip their handkerchiefs in the blood, which some believed to have miraculous qualities. His wife and son fled to France. Museum of London Photographic Library.

in the army purged the Presbyterians from Parliament, leaving a "rump" of about seventy members. This Rump Parliament then created a high court to try Charles I. The court found him guilty of attempting to establish "an unlimited and tyrannical power" and pronounced a death sentence. On January 30, 1649, Charles was beheaded before an enormous crowd, which reportedly groaned as one when the axe fell. Although many had objected to Charles's autocratic rule, few had wanted him killed. For royalists, Charles immediately became a martyr, and reports of miracles, such as the curing of blindness by the touch of a handkerchief soaked in his blood, soon circulated.

The Rump Parliament abolished the monarchy and the House of Lords (the upper house of Parliament) and set up a Puritan republic with Oliver Cromwell as chairman of the Council of State. Cromwell did not tolerate dissent from his policies. He saw the hand of God in events and himself as God's agent. Pamphleteers and songwriters ridiculed his red nose and accused him of wanting to be king, but few challenged his leadership. When his agents discovered plans for mutiny within the army, they executed the perpetrators; new decrees silenced the Levellers. Although Cromwell allowed the various Puritan sects to worship rather freely and permitted Jews with needed skills to return to England for the first time since the thirteenth century, Catholics could not worship publicly, nor could Anglicans use the Book of Common Prayer. The elites—many of them were still Anglican—were troubled by Cromwell's religious policies but pleased to see some social order reestablished.

The new regime aimed to extend state power just as Charles I had before. Cromwell laid the foundation for a Great Britain made up of England, Ireland, and Scotland by reconquering Scotland and subduing Ireland. Anti-English rebels in Ireland had seized the occasion of troubles between king and Parliament to revolt in 1641. When his position was secured in 1649, Cromwell went to Ireland with a large force and easily defeated the rebels, massacring whole garrisons and their priests. He encouraged expropriating the lands of the Irish "barbarous wretches," and Scottish immigrants resettled the northern county of Ulster. This seventeenth-century English conquest left a legacy of bitterness that

Oliver Cromwell
Shown here preparing for battle, Cromwell lived an austere life but believed fiercely in his own personal righteousness. As leader he tolerated no opposition. When he died, he was buried in Westminster Abbey, but in 1661 his body was exhumed and hanged in its shroud. His head was cut off and displayed outside Westminster Hall for nearly twenty years.
Courtesy of the National Portrait Gallery, London.

the Irish even today call "the curse of Cromwell." In 1651, Parliament turned its attention overseas, putting mercantilist ideas into practice in the first Navigation Act, which allowed imports only if they were carried on English ships or came directly from the producers of goods. The Navigation Act was aimed at the Dutch, who dominated world trade; Cromwell tried to carry the policy further by waging naval war on the Dutch from 1652 to 1654.

At home, however, Cromwell faced growing resistance. His wars required a budget twice the size of Charles I's, and his increases in property taxes and customs duties alienated landowners and merchants. The conflict reached a crisis in 1653: Parliament considered disbanding the army, whereupon Cromwell abolished the Rump Parliament in a military coup and made himself Lord Protector. He now silenced his critics by banning newspapers and using networks of spies and mail readers to keep tabs on his enemies. Although he assumed some trappings of royalty, he refused the crown. When he died in 1658, one opponent claimed, "There were none that cried but dogs." Cromwell intended that his son should succeed him, but his death only revived the prospect of civil war and political chaos. In 1660, a newly elected, staunchly Anglican Parliament invited Charles II, the son of the executed king, to return from exile.

The "Glorious Revolution" of 1688

Most English welcomed back the king in 1660. According to one royalist, throughout the realm "the ways were strewed with flowers, the bells ringing, the streets hung with tapestry, fountains running with wine." The restoration of royal authority in 1660 whisked away the more austere elements of Puritan culture and revived old traditions of celebration—drinking, merrymaking, and processions of young maidens in royalist colors. But the religious policies of Charles II and his successor, James II, ensured that conflicts between king and Parliament would erupt once again.

The Restored Monarchy. In 1660, the traditional monarchical form of government was reinstated, restoring the king to full partnership with Parliament. Charles II (r. 1660–1685) promised "a liberty to tender consciences" in an attempt to extend religious toleration, especially to Catholics, with whom

Great Fire of London, 1666
This view of London shows the three-day fire at its height. The writer John Evelyn described the scene in his diary: "All the sky was of a fiery aspect, like the top of a burning oven, and the light seen above 40 miles round about for many nights. God grant mine eyes may never behold the like, who now saw above 10,000 houses all in one flame; the noise and cracking and thunder of people, the fall of towers, houses, and churches, was like an hideous storm." Everyone in London at the time felt overwhelmed by the catastrophe, and many attributed it to God's punishment for the upheavals of the 1640s and 1650s.
Museum of London Photographic Library.

he sympathized. Yet more than a thousand Puritan ministers lost their positions, and after 1664, attending a service other than one conforming with the Anglican prayer book was illegal.

Natural disasters marred the early years of Charles II's reign. The plague stalked London's rat-infested streets in May 1665 and claimed more than thirty thousand victims by September. Then in 1666, the Great Fire swept the city. Diarist Samuel Pepys described its terrifying progress: "It made me weep to see it. The churches, houses, and all on fire and flaming at once, and a horrid noise the flames made, and the cracking of houses at their ruine." The crown now had a city as well as a monarchy to rebuild.

The restoration of monarchy made some in Parliament fear that the English government would come to resemble French absolutism. This fear was not unfounded. In 1670, Charles II made a secret agreement, soon leaked, with Louis XIV in which he promised to announce his conversion to Catholicism in exchange for money for a war against the Dutch. Charles never proclaimed himself a Catholic, but in his Declaration of Indulgence (1673) he did suspend all laws against Catholics and Protestant dissenters. Parliament refused to continue funding the Dutch war unless Charles rescinded his Declaration of Indulgence. Asserting its authority further, Parliament passed the Test Act in 1673, requiring all government officials to profess allegiance to the Church of England and in effect disavow Catholic doctrine. Then in 1678, Parliament precipitated the so-called Exclusion Crisis by explicitly denying the throne to a Roman Catholic. This action was aimed at the king's brother and heir, James, an open convert to Catholicism. Charles refused to allow it to become law.

The dynastic crisis over the succession of a Catholic gave rise to two distinct factions in Parliament: the Tories, who supported a strong, hereditary monarchy and the restored ceremony of the Anglican church, and the Whigs, who advocated parliamentary supremacy and toleration for Protestant dissenters such as Presbyterians. Both labels were originally derogatory: *Tory* meant an Irish Catholic bandit; *Whig* was the Irish Catholic designation for a Presbyterian Scot. The Tories favored James's succession despite his Catholicism, whereas the Whigs opposed a Catholic monarch. The loose moral atmosphere of Charles's court also offended some Whigs, who complained tongue in cheek that Charles was father of his country in much too literal a fashion (he had fathered more than one child by his mistresses but produced no legitimate heir).

Parliament's Revolt against James II. Upon Charles's death, his brother, James, succeeded to the throne as James II (r. 1685–1688). James pursued pro-Catholic and absolutist policies even more aggressively than his brother. When a male heir—who would take precedence over James's two adult Protestant daughters and be reared a Catholic—was born, Tories and Whigs banded together. They invited the Dutch ruler William, prince of Orange and the husband of James's older daughter, Mary, to invade England. James fled to France and hardly any blood was shed. Parliament offered the throne jointly to William (r. 1689–1702) and Mary (r. 1689–1694) on the condition that they accept a bill of rights guaranteeing Parliament's full partnership in a constitutional government.

In the Bill of Rights, William and Mary agreed not to raise a standing army or to levy taxes without Parliament's consent. They also agreed to call meetings of Parliament at least every three years, to guarantee free elections to parliamentary seats, and to abide by Parliament's decisions and not suspend duly passed laws. The agreement gave England's constitutional government a written, legal basis by formally recognizing Parliament as a self-contained, independent body that shared power with the rulers. Victorious supporters of the coup declared it the "Glorious Revolution." Constitutionalism had triumphed over absolutism in England.

The propertied classes who controlled Parliament eagerly consolidated their power and prevented any resurgence of the popular turmoil of the 1640s. The Toleration Act of 1689 granted all Protestants freedom of worship, though non-Anglicans were still excluded from the universities; Catholics got no rights but were more often left alone to worship privately. In Ireland the Catholics rose to defend James II, but William and Mary's troops brutally suppressed them. With the Whigs in power and the Tories in opposition, wealthy landowners now controlled political life throughout the realm. The factions' differences, however, were minor; essentially, the Tories had less access to the king's patronage. A contemporary reported that King William had said "that if he had good places [honors and land] enough to bestow, he should soon unite the two parties."

❖ Constitutionalism in the Dutch Republic and the Overseas Colonies

When William and Mary came to the throne in England in 1689, the Dutch and the English put aside the rivalries that had brought them to war against each other in 1652–1654, 1665–1667, and 1672–1674. Under William, the Dutch and the English together led the coalition that blocked Louis XIV's efforts to dominate continental Europe. The English and Dutch had much in common: oriented toward commerce, especially overseas, they were the successful exceptions to absolutism in Europe. Also among the few outposts of constitutionalism in the seventeenth century were the British North American colonies, which developed representative government while the English were preoccupied with their revolutions at home. Constitutionalism was not the only factor shaping this Atlantic world; as constitutionalism developed in the colonies, so too did the enslavement of black Africans as a new labor force.

The Dutch Republic

When the Dutch Republic gained formal independence from Spain in 1648, it had already established a decentralized, constitutional state. The individual provinces granted power over foreign policy to the Estates General, an assembly made up of deputies from each province, but local authorities jealously guarded most of the power. Rich merchants called *regents* effectively controlled the internal affairs of each province and through the Estates General named the *stadholder*, the executive officer responsible for defense and for representing the state at all ceremonial occasions. They almost always chose one of the princes of the house of Orange, but the prince of Orange resembled a president more than a king. One foreign visitor observed that the Dutch "behave as if all men were created equal," but in fact real power remained in the hands of the regents, not the common people.

The decentralized state encouraged and protected trade, and the Dutch Republic soon became Europe's financial capital. The Bank of Amsterdam offered interest rates less than half those available in England and France. Praised for their industriousness, thrift, and cleanliness—and maligned as greedy, dull "butter-boxes"—the Dutch dominated overseas commerce with their shipping (Map 17.3). They imported products from all over the world: spices, tea,

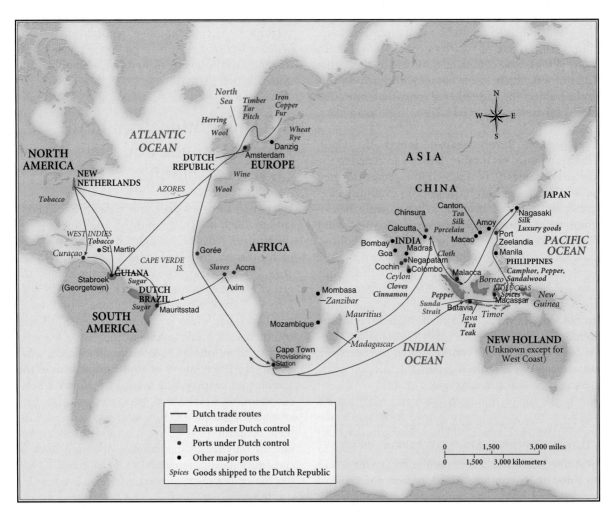

MAP 17.3 Dutch Commerce in the Seventeenth Century
Even before gaining formal independence from the Spanish in 1648, the Dutch had begun to compete with the Spanish and Portuguese all over the world. In 1602, a group of merchants established the Dutch East India Company, which soon offered investors an annual rate of return of 35 percent on the trade in spices with countries located on the Indian Ocean. Global commerce gave the Dutch the highest standard of living in Europe and soon attracted the envy of the French and the English.

and silk from Asia; sugar and tobacco from the Americas; wool from England and Spain; timber and furs from Scandinavia; grain from eastern Europe. (See "Did You Know?", page 630.) One English traveler in 1660 described the riches of Amsterdam as superior to those of Venice and called the Hague "the most pleasant place in the world." A widely reprinted history of Amsterdam that appeared in 1662 described the city as "risen through the hand of God to the peak of prosperity and greatness. . . . The whole world stands amazed at its riches and from east and west, north and south they come to behold it."

The Dutch rapidly became the most prosperous and best-educated people in Europe. Middle-class people supported the visual arts, especially painting, to an unprecedented degree. Artists and engravers produced thousands of works, and Dutch artists were among the first to sell to a mass market. Whereas in other countries kings, nobles, and churches bought art, Dutch buyers were merchants, artisans, and shopkeepers. Engravings, illustrated histories, and oil paintings, even those of the widely acclaimed Rembrandt van Rijn (1606–1669), were all relatively inexpensive. One foreigner commented that "pictures are very common here, there being scarce an ordinary tradesman whose house is not decorated with them." The pictures reflected the Dutch interest in familiar daily details: children at play, winter landscapes, and ships in port.

The family household, not the royal court, determined the moral character of this intensely commercial society. Dutch society fostered public enterprise in men and work in the home for women, who were expected to filter out the greed and materialism of commercial society by maintaining domestic harmony and virtue. Relative prosperity decreased the need for married women to work, so Dutch society developed the clear contrast between middle-class male and female roles that would become prevalent elsewhere in Europe and in America more than a century later. As one contemporary Dutch writer explained, "The husband must be on the street to practice his trade; the wife must stay at home to be in the kitchen."

Extraordinarily high levels of urbanization and literacy created a large reading public. Dutch presses printed books censored elsewhere (printers or authors censored in one province simply shifted operations to another), and the University of Leiden attracted students and professors from all over Europe. Dutch tolerance extended to the works of Benedict Spinoza (1633–1677), a Jewish philosopher and biblical scholar who was expelled by his synagogue for alleged atheism but left alone by the Dutch authorities. Spinoza strove to reconcile religion with science and mathematics, but his work scandalized many Christians and Jews because he seemed to equate God and nature. Like nature, Spinoza's God followed unchangeable laws and could not be influenced by human actions, prayers, or faith.

Dutch learning, painting, and commerce all enjoyed wide renown in the seventeenth century, but this luster proved hard to maintain. The Dutch lived in a world of international rivalries in which strong central authority gave their enemies an advantage. Though inconclusive, the naval wars with England drained the state's revenues. Even more dangerous

A Typical Dutch Scene from Daily Life
Jan Steen painted The Baker Arent Oostward and His Wife *in 1658. Steen ran a brewery and tavern in addition to painting, and he was known for his interest in the details of daily life. Dutch artists popularized this kind of "genre" painting, which showed ordinary people at work and play.* Rijksmuseum, Amsterdam.

Tobacco and the Invention of "Smoking"

In the early seventeenth century, a "new astonishing fashion," wrote a German ambassador, had come to the Dutch Republic from the New World. For a long time there was no word for what you did with tobacco; *smoking* came to be commonly used as a term only in the seventeenth century. Until then one spoke of "a fog-drinking bout," "drinking smoke," or "drinking tobacco." One Jesuit preacher called it "dry drunkenness." The analogy to inebriation is not entirely far-fetched, for nicotine (named after the French ambassador to Portugal, Jean Nicot, who brought tobacco to France in the mid-sixteenth century) does have an effect more comparable to alcohol than to caffeine; nicotine is a nerve toxin that dulls the nervous system. It is not known exactly where in the Americas tobacco had its birthplace, but its use was widespread by the time the Europeans arrived. Mayans and Aztecs smoked ceremonial pipes, Incas used tobacco as a medicine, and Indians in Brazil took snuff.

Spain began exporting tobacco to other European countries in the sixteenth century. The Spanish did not exploit the possibilities of producing tobacco on plantations; tobacco growing began in earnest in the seventeenth century only with the spread of black slavery. Virginia and Maryland expanded their exports of tobacco sixfold between 1663 and 1699. Until 1700, Amsterdam dominated the curing process; half the tobacco factories in Amsterdam were owned by Jewish merchants of Spanish or Portuguese descent.

Smoking spread geographically from western to eastern Europe, socially from the upper classes downward, and from men to women. At first the Spanish preferred cigars, the British pipes, and the French snuff. In the eighteenth century, both upper- and middle-class women took snuff, which was considered an aristocratic taste. Before the end of the nineteenth century, women did not regularly take tobacco in any form other than snuff. A woman smoking a pipe or cigar was a favorite target of cartoonists in the eighteenth and nineteenth centuries. This changed with the Russian invention of the cigarette in the mid-nineteenth century. Women began to smoke cigarettes in the late 1800s as a sign of emancipation.

Source: Wolfgang Schivelbusch, *Tastes of Paradise: A Social History of Spices, Stimulants, and Intoxicants,* trans. David Jacobson, 1993.

The Vice of Tobacco
In this engraving of 1628,
The Vice of Tobacco, *the Dutch artist Gillis van Scheyndel portrays smoking as similar to excessive drinking, a habit that makes people sick and leads them astray. Pipes often symbolized the folly and futility of a life given over to materialistic pleasures. The company of revelers is led on by a pipe-smoking ape who has features like a devil.*
Koninklijke Bibliotheek.

were the land wars with France, which continued into the eighteenth century. The Dutch survived these challenges but increasingly depended on alliances with other powers, such as England. At the end of the seventeenth century, the regent elite became more exclusive, more preoccupied with ostentation, less tolerant of deviations from strict Calvinism, and more concerned with imitating French styles. Dutch architecture, painting, and intellectual life eventually came under French influence.

Freedom and Slavery in the New World

The French and English also increasingly overshadowed the Dutch in the New World colonies. While the Dutch concentrated on shipping, including the slave trade, the seventeenth-century French and English established settler colonies that would eventually provide fabulous revenues to the home countries. Many European governments encouraged private companies to vie for their share of the slave trade, and slavery began to take clear institutional form in the New World in this period. Even while slavery offered only a degrading form of despotism to black Africans, whites found in the colonies greater political and religious freedom than in Europe.

The Rise of the Slave Trade. After the Spanish and Portuguese had shown that African slaves could be transported and forced to labor in South and Central America, the English and French endeavored to set up similar labor systems in their new Caribbean island colonies. White planters with large tracts of land bought African slaves to work fields of sugarcane, and as they gradually built up their holdings, the planters displaced most of the original white settlers, who moved to mainland colonies. After 1661, when Barbados instituted a slave code that stripped all Africans of rights under English law, slavery became codified as an inherited status that applied only to blacks. The result was a society of extremes: the very wealthy whites, about 7 percent of the population in Barbados; and the enslaved, powerless black majority. The English brought little of their religious or constitutional practices to the Caribbean. Other Caribbean colonies followed a similar pattern of development. Louis XIV promulgated a "black code" in 1685 to regulate the legal status of slaves in the French colonies. Although one

of his aims was to prevent non-Catholics from owning slaves in the French colonies, the code had much the same effect as the English codes on the slaves themselves: they had no legal rights.

The highest church and government authorities in Catholic and Protestant countries alike condoned the gradually expanding slave trade; the governments of England, France, Spain, Portugal, the Dutch Republic, and Denmark all encouraged private companies to traffic in black Africans. The Dutch West India Company was the most successful of them. In 1600, about 9,500 Africans were exported from Africa to the New World every year; by 1700, this had increased nearly fourfold to 36,000 annually. Historians advance several different factors for the increase in the slave trade: some claim that improvements in muskets made European slavers more formidable; others cite the rising price for slaves which made their sale more attractive for Africans; still others focus on factors internal to Africa such as the increasing size of African armies and their use of muskets in fighting and capturing other Africans for sale as slaves. Whatever the reason, the way had been prepared for the development of an Atlantic economy based on slavery.

Constitutional Freedoms in the English Colonies. Virtually left to themselves during the upheavals in England, the fledgling English colonies in North America developed representative government on their own. Almost every colony had a governor and a two-house legislature. The colonial legislatures constantly sought to increase their power and resisted the efforts of Charles II and James II to reaffirm royal control. William and Mary reluctantly allowed emerging colonial elites more control over local affairs. The social and political elite among the settlers hoped to impose an English social hierarchy dominated by rich landowners. Ordinary immigrants to the colonies, however, took advantage of plentiful land to carve out their own farms using white servants and, later, in some colonies, African slaves.

For native Americans, the expanding European presence meant something else altogether. They faced death through disease and warfare and the accelerating loss of their homelands. Unlike white settlers, native Americans believed that land was a divine gift provided for their collective use and not subject to individual ownership. As a result,

Europeans' claims that they owned exclusive land rights caused frequent skirmishes. In 1675–1676, for instance, three tribes allied under Metacomet (called King Philip by the English) threatened the survival of New England settlers, who savagely repulsed the attacks and sold their captives as slaves. Whites portrayed native Americans as conspiring villains and sneaky heathens, who were akin to Africans in their savagery.

❖ The Search for Order in Elite and Popular Culture

The early success of constitutionalism in England, the Dutch Republic, and the English North American colonies would help to shape a distinctive Atlantic world in the eighteenth century. Just how constitutionalism was linked to the growing commerce with the colonies remains open to dispute, however, since the constitutional governments, like the absolutist ones, avidly pursued profits in the burgeoning slave trade. Freedom did not mean liberty for everyone. One of the great debates of the time—and of much of the modern world that followed—concerned the meaning of freedom: for whom, under what conditions, with what justifiable limitations could freedom be claimed?

There was no freedom without order to sustain it, and most Europeans feared disorder above all else. In 1669, the English writer Margaret Cavendish, duchess of Newcastle, cataloged some of the sources of disorder in her time: "I wish Men were as Harmless as most Beasts are, then surely the World would be more Quiet and Happy than it is, for then there would not be such Pride, Vanity, Ambition, Covetousness, Faction, Treachery, and Treason, as is now." Cavendish wrote not long after the restoration of the monarchy in England, and her thoughts echoed the titanic struggles that had taken place over the nature of authority, not only in England but throughout Europe. Political theories, science, poetry, painting, and architecture all reflected in some measure the attempts to ground authority—to define the relation between freedom and order—in new ways. Authority concerned not just rulers and subjects but also the hierarchy of groups in society. As European states consolidated their powers,

elites worked to distinguish themselves from the lower classes. They developed new codes of correct behavior for themselves and tried to teach order and discipline to their social inferiors.

Social Contract Theory: Hobbes and Locke

The turmoil of the times prompted a major rethinking of the foundations of all authority. Two figures stood out prominently amid the cacophony of voices: Thomas Hobbes and John Locke. Their writings fundamentally shaped the modern subject of political science. Hobbes justified absolute authority; Locke provided the rationale for constitutionalism. Yet both argued that all authority came not from divine right but from a "social contract" between citizens.

Hobbes.   Thomas Hobbes (1588–1679) was a royalist who sat out the English civil war of the 1640s in France, where he tutored the future king Charles II. Returning to England in 1651, he published his masterpiece, *Leviathan* (1651), in which he argued for unlimited authority in a ruler. Absolute authority could be vested in either a king or a parliament; it had to be absolute, he insisted, in order to overcome the defects of human nature. Believing that people are essentially self-centered and driven by the "right to self-preservation," Hobbes made his case by referring to science, not religion. To Hobbes, human life in a state of nature—that is, any situation without firm authority—was "solitary, poor, nasty, brutish, and short." He believed that the desire for power and natural greed would inevitably lead to unfettered competition. Only the assurance of social order could make people secure enough to act according to law; consequently, giving up personal liberty, he maintained, was the price of collective security. Rulers derived their power, he concluded, from a contract in which absolute authority protects people's rights.

Hobbes's notion of rule by an absolute authority left no room for political dissent or nonconformity, and it infuriated both royalists and supporters of Parliament. He enraged royalists by arguing that authority came not from divine right but from the social contract between citizens. Parliamentary supporters resisted Hobbes's claim that rulers must possess absolute authority to prevent the greater evil of anarchy; they believed that a constitution should guarantee shared power between king and parliament and protect individual rights under the law. Like Machiavelli before him, Hobbes became associated with a cynical, pessimistic view of human nature, and future political theorists often began their arguments by refuting Hobbes.

Locke. Rejecting both Hobbes and the more traditional royalist defenses of absolute authority, John Locke (1632–1704) used the notion of a social contract to provide a foundation for constitutionalism. Locke experienced political life firsthand as physician, secretary, and intellectual companion to the earl of Shaftesbury, a leading English Whig. In 1683, during the Exclusion Crisis, Locke fled with Shaftesbury to the Dutch Republic. There he continued work on his *Two Treatises of Government*, which, when published in 1690, served to justify the Glorious Revolution of 1688. Locke's position was thoroughly anti-absolutist. He denied the divine right of kings and ridiculed the common royalist idea that political power in the state mirrored the father's authority in the family. Like Hobbes, he posited a state of nature that applied to all people. Unlike Hobbes, however, he thought people were reasonable and the state of nature peaceful.

Locke insisted that government's only purpose was to protect life, liberty, and property, a notion that linked economic and political freedom. Ultimate authority rested in the will of a majority of men who owned property, and government should be limited to its basic purpose of protection. A ruler who failed to uphold his part of the social contract between the ruler and the populace could be justifiably resisted, an idea that would become crucial for the leaders of the American Revolution a century later. For England's landowners, however, Locke helped validate a revolution that consolidated their interests and ensured their privileges in the social hierarchy. Although he himself owned shares in the Royal African Company and justified slavery, Locke's writings were later used by abolitionists in their campaign against slavery.

Locke defended his optimistic view of human nature in the immensely influential *Essay Concerning Human Understanding* (1690). He denied the existence of any innate ideas and asserted instead that each human is born with a mind that is a tabula rasa (blank slate). Everything humans know, he claimed, comes from sensory experience, not from anything inherent in human nature. Locke's views promoted the belief that "all men are created equal," a belief that challenged absolutist forms of rule and ultimately raised questions about women's roles as well. Not surprisingly, Locke devoted considerable energy to rethinking educational practices; he believed that education crucially shaped the human personality by channeling all sensory experience.

The Scientific Revolution Consolidated

New breakthroughs in science lent support to Locke's optimistic view of human potential. Building on the work of Copernicus, Kepler, and Galileo (see Chapter 16), the English scientist Isaac Newton finally synthesized astronomy and physics with his law of gravitation. His work further enhanced the prestige of science, but he sought no conflict with religious authorities. Indeed, many clergy applauded his refutation of atheism and his success in explaining the orderliness of God's creation. Some rulers supported scientific activity as another form of mercantilist intervention to enhance state power. Science also gained a broader audience among upper-class men and women.

Newton. A Cambridge University student at the time of Charles II's restoration, Isaac Newton (1642–1727) was a pious Anglican who aimed to reconcile faith and science. By proving that the physical universe followed rational principles, Newton argued, scientists could prove the existence of God and so liberate humans from doubt and the fear of chaos. Newton applied mathematical principles to formulate three physical laws: (1) in the absence of force, motion continues in a straight line; (2) the rate of change in the motion of an object is a result of the forces acting on it; and (3) the action and reaction between two objects are equal and opposite. The basis of Newtonian physics thus required understanding mass, inertia, force, velocity, and acceleration—all key concepts in modern science.

Extending these principles to the entire universe in his masterwork, *Principia Mathematica* (1687), Newton united celestial and terrestrial mechanics—astronomy and physics—with his law of gravitation. This law held that every body in the universe exerts over every other body an attractive force directly proportional to the product of their masses and inversely proportional to the square of the distance between them. The law of gravitation explained Kepler's elliptical planetary orbits just as it accounted for the motion of ordinary objects on earth. Once set in motion, the universe operated like clockwork, with no need for God's continuing intervention. Gravity, although a mysterious force, could be expressed mathematically. In Newton's words, "From the same principles [of motion] I now demonstrate the frame of the System of the World." The English poet Alexander Pope later captured the intellectual world's appreciation of Newton's accomplishment:

Nature and Nature's laws lay hid in night
God said, Let Newton be! and all was light.

Newton's science was not just mathematical and deductive; he experimented with light and helped establish the science of optics. Even while making these fundamental contributions to scientific method, Newton carried out alchemical experiments in his rooms at Cambridge University and spent long hours trying to calculate the date of the beginning of the world and of the second coming of Jesus. Not all scientists accepted Newton's theories immediately, especially on the continent, but within a couple of generations his work was preeminent, partly because of experimental verification. His "frame of the System of the World" remained the basis of all physics until the advent of relativity theory and quantum mechanics in the early twentieth century.

Public Interest in Science. Absolutist rulers saw science as a means for enhancing their prestige and glory. Frederick William, the Great Elector of Brandenburg-Prussia, for example, set up agricultural experiments in front of his Berlin palace, and various German princes supported the work of Gottfried Wilhelm Leibniz (1646–1716), one of the inventors of calculus. A lawyer, diplomat, and scholar who wrote about metaphysics, cosmology, and history, Leibniz helped establish scientific societies in the German states. Government involvement in science was greatest in France, where it became an arm of mercantilist policy; in 1666, Colbert founded the Royal Academy of Sciences, which supplied fifteen scientists with government stipends.

Constitutional states supported science less directly but nonetheless provided an intellectual environment that encouraged its spread. The English Royal Society, the counterpart to the Royal Academy of Sciences in France, grew out of informal meetings of scientists at London and Oxford rather than direct government involvement. It received a royal charter in 1662 but maintained complete independence. The society's secretary described its business to be "in the first place, to scrutinize the whole of Nature and to investigate its activity and powers by means of observations and experiments; and then in course of time to hammer out a more solid philosophy and more ample amenities of civilization." Whether the state was directly involved or not, thinkers of the day now tied science explicitly to social progress.

Because of their exclusion from most universities, women only rarely participated in the new scientific discoveries. In 1667, nonetheless, the English Royal Society invited Margaret Cavendish, a writer of poems, essays, letters, and philosophical treatises, to attend a meeting to watch the exhibition of experiments. She attacked the use of telescopes and microscopes because she detected in the new experimentalism a mechanistic view of the world that exalted masculine prowess and challenged the Christian belief in freedom of the will. She also urged the formal education of women, complaining that "we are kept like birds in cages to hop up and down in our houses." "Many of our Sex may have as much wit, and be capable of Learning as well as men," she insisted, "but since they want Instructions, it is not possible they should attain to it."

Freedom and Order in the Arts

Even though Newtonian science depicted an orderly universe, most artists and intellectuals had experienced enough of the upheavals of the seventeenth century to fear the prospect of chaos and disintegration. The French mathematician Blaise Pascal vividly captured their worries in his *Pensées* ("Thoughts") of 1660: "I look on all sides, and I see only darkness everywhere. Nature presents to me nothing which is not a matter of doubt and concern. . . . It is incomprehensible that God should exist, and incomprehensible that He should not exist." Poets, painters, and architects all tried to make sense of the individual's place within what Pascal called "the eternal silence of these infinite spaces."

Milton. The English Puritan poet John Milton (1608–1674) gave priority to individual liberty. In 1643, in the midst of the civil war between king and Parliament, he published writings in favor of divorce. When Parliament enacted a censorship law aimed at such literature, Milton responded in 1644 with one of the first defenses of freedom of the press, *Areopagitica* ("Tribunal of Opinion"). Milton served as secretary to the Council of State during Cromwell's rule and earned the enmity of Charles II by writing a justification for the execution of his father, Charles I, based on biblical precedents.

In forced retirement and now totally blind, in 1667 Milton published his epic poem *Paradise Lost,* which some have read as a veiled commentary on English affairs. The poet used Adam and Eve's Fall to meditate on human freedom and the tragedies of rebellion. Although Milton wanted to "justify the ways of God to man," his Satan, the proud angel who challenges God, is so compelling as to be heroic. In the end, Adam and Eve learn to accept moral responsibility and face the world "all before them." Individuals learn the limits to their freedom, yet personal liberty remains essential to their definition as human.

The Varieties of Artistic Style. The dominant artistic styles of the time—the baroque and the classical—both submerged the individual in a grander design. The baroque style proved to be especially suitable for public displays of faith and power that overawed individual beholders. The combination of religious and political purposes in baroque art is best exemplified in the architecture and sculpture of Gian Lorenzo Bernini (1598–1680), the papacy's official artist. His architectural masterpiece was the gigantic square facing St. Peter's Basilica in Rome (1656–1671). His use of freestanding open colonnades and a huge open space is meant to impress the individual observer with the power of the popes and the Catholic religion. Bernini also sculpted tombs for the popes and a large statue of Constantine, the first Christian emperor of Rome—perfect examples of the marriage of power and religion.

Gian Lorenzo Bernini,
Ecstasy of St. Teresa of Ávila (c. 1650)
This ultimate statement of baroque sculpture captures all the drama and even sensationalism of a mystical religious faith. Bernini based his figures on a vision reported by St. Teresa in which she saw an angel: "In his hands I saw a great golden spear, and at the iron tip there appeared to be a point of fire. This he plunged into my heart several times so that it penetrated my entrails. When he pulled it out I felt that he took them with it, and left me utterly consumed by the great love of God." Scala/Art Resource, NY.

In 1665, Louis XIV hired Bernini to plan the rebuilding of the Louvre palace in Paris but then rejected his ideas as incompatible with French tastes. The one tangible result of his visit to Paris, a marble bust of Louis XIV, captured the king's strength and dynamism.

Although France was a Catholic country, French painters, sculptors, and architects, like their

French Classicism
In his 1638 painting Moses Saved from the Floods of the Nile, *the French painter Nicolas Poussin sets a biblical story in an antique Roman landscape, with a pyramid serving as the sole reference to Egypt. The austerity and statuesque poses of the figures convey the ideals of classicism rather than the exuberance of the baroque style.*
Giraudon/Art Resource, NY.

patron Louis XIV, preferred the standards of classicism to those of the baroque. French artists developed classicism to be a French national style, distinct from the baroque style that was closely associated with France's enemies, the Austrian and Spanish Habsburgs. As its name suggests, classicism reflected the ideals of the art of antiquity; geometric shapes, order, and harmony of lines took precedence over the sensuous, exuberant, and emotional forms of the baroque. Rather than being overshadowed by the sheer power of emotional display, in classicism the individual could be found at the intersection of converging, symmetrical, straight lines. These influences were apparent in the work of the leading French painters of the period,

Nicolas Poussin (1594–1665) and Claude Lorrain (1600–1682), both of whom worked in Rome and tried to re-create classical Roman values in their mythological scenes and Roman landscapes.

Dutch painters found the baroque and classical styles less suited to their private market, where buyers sought smaller-scale works with ordinary subjects. Dutch artists came from common stock themselves—Rembrandt's father was a miller, and the father of Jan Vermeer (1632–1675) was a silk worker. Their clients were people like themselves who purchased paintings much as they bought tables and chairs. Rembrandt occasionally worked on commission for the prince of Orange but even he painted ordinary people, suffusing his canvases with a radiant, otherworldly light that made the plainest people and objects appear deeply spiritual. Vermeer's best-known paintings show women working at home, and, like Rembrandt, he made ordinary activities seem precious and beautiful. In Dutch art, ordinary individuals had religious and political significance.

Art might also serve the interests of science. One of the most skilled illustrators of insects and flowers was Maria Sibylla Merian (1646–1717), a German-born painter-scholar whose engravings were widely celebrated for their brilliant realism and microscopic clarity. Merian eventually separated from her husband and joined a sect called the Labadists (after their French founder, Jean de Labadie), who did not believe in formal marriage ties and established a colony in the northern Dutch province of Friesland. After moving there with her daughters, Merian went with missionaries from the sect to the Dutch colony of Surinam in South America and painted watercolors of the exotic flowers, birds, and insects she found in the jungle around the cocoa and sugarcane plantations. In the seventeenth century, many women became known for their still-lifes and especially their paintings of flowers. Paintings by the Dutch artist Rachel Ruysch, for example, fetched higher prices than those received by Rembrandt.

Women and Manners

Poetry and painting imaginatively explored the place of the individual within a larger whole, but real-life individuals had to learn to navigate their own social worlds. Manners—the learning of individual self-discipline—were essential skills of social navigation, and women usually took the lead in teaching them. Women's importance in refining social relationships quickly became a subject of controversy.

The Cultivation of Manners. The court had long been a central arena for the development of individual self-discipline. Under the tutelage of their mothers and wives, nobles learned to hide all that was crass and to maintain a fine sense of social distinction. In some ways, aristocratic men were expected to act more like women; just as women had long been expected to please men, now aristocratic men had to please their monarch or patron by displaying proper manners and conversing with ele-

European Fascination with Products of the New World
In this painting of a banana plant, Maria Sibylla Merian offers a scientific study of one of the many exotic plants and animals found by Europeans who traveled to the colonies overseas. Merian was fifty-one when she traveled to the Dutch South American colony of Surinam with her daughter. Courtesy of Hunt Institute for Botanical Documentation, Carnegie Mellon University, Pittsburgh, PA.

gance and wit. Men as well as women had to master the art of pleasing—foreign languages (especially French), dance, a taste for fine music, and attention to dress.

As part of the evolution of new aristocratic ideals, nobles learned to disdain all that was lowly. The upper classes began to reject popular festivals and fairs in favor of private theaters, where seats were relatively expensive and behavior was formal. Clowns and buffoons now seemed vulgar; the last king of England to keep a court fool was Charles I.

Music and the Refinement of Manners
In Emanuel de Witte's Woman at the Clavecin, *the artist celebrates the importance of music in the Dutch home. The woman herself remains a mystery, but the sumptuous setting of heavy curtains, mirrors, and chandeliers signals that clavichord music was associated with refinement.*
The Netherlands Institut of Cultural Heritage, Rijswijk, the Netherlands; Museum Boijmans-Van Beuningen, Rotterdam.

Chivalric romances that had entranced the nobility down to the time of Cervantes's *Don Quixote* (1605) now passed into popular literature.

The greatest French playwright of the seventeenth century, Molière (the pen name of Jean-Baptiste Poquelin, 1622–1673), wrote sparkling comedies of manners that revealed much about the new aristocratic behavior. Son of a tradesman, Molière left law school to form a theater company, which eventually gained the support of Louis XIV. His play *The Middle-Class Gentleman* first performed at the royal court in 1670, revolves around the yearning of a rich, middle-class Frenchman, Monsieur Jourdain, to learn to act like a *gentil-homme* (meaning both "gentleman" and "noble-man" in French). Monsieur Jourdain buys fancy clothes, hires private instructors in dancing, music, fencing, and philosophy, and lends money to a debt-ridden noble in hopes of marrying his daughter to him. Only his sensible wife and his daughter's love for a worthier commoner stand in his way. The

women in the family, including the servant girl Nicole, are reasonable, sincere, and keenly aware of what behavior is appropriate to their social station, whereas Jourdain stands for social ambition gone wild. The message for the court seemed to be a reassuring one: Only true nobles by blood can hope to act like nobles. But the play also showed how the middle classes were learning to emulate the nobility; if one could learn to *act* nobly through self-discipline, could not anyone with some education and money pass himself off as noble?

As Molière's play demonstrated, new attention to manners trickled down from the court to the middle class. A French treatise on manners from 1672 explained:

If everyone is eating from the same dish, you should take care not to put your hand into it before those of higher rank have done so. . . . Formerly one was permitted . . . to dip one's bread into the sauce, provided only that one had not already bitten it.

Nowadays that would be a kind of rusticity. Formerly one was allowed to take from one's mouth what one could not eat and drop it on the floor, provided it was done skillfully. Now that would be very disgusting.

The key words *rusticity* and *disgusting* reveal the association of unacceptable social behavior with the peasantry, dirt, and repulsion. Similar rules now governed spitting and blowing one's nose in public. Ironically, however, once the elite had successfully distinguished itself from the lower classes through manners, scholars became more interested in studying popular expressions. They avidly collected proverbs, folktales, and songs—all of these now curiosities. In fact, many nobles at Louis XIV's court read fairy tales.

Debates about Women's Roles. Courtly manners often permeated the upper reaches of society by means of the *salon,* an informal gathering held regularly in private homes and presided over by a socially eminent woman. In 1661, one French author claimed to have identified 251 Parisian women as hostesses of salons. Although the French government occasionally worried that these gatherings might be seditious, the three main topics of conversation were love, literature, and philosophy. Hostesses often worked hard to encourage the careers of budding authors. Before publishing a manuscript, many authors would read their compositions to a salon gathering. Corneille, Racine, and even Bishop Bossuet sought female approval for their writings.

Some women went beyond encouraging male authors and began to write on their own, but they faced many obstacles. Marie-Madeleine de La Vergne, known as Madame de Lafayette, wrote several short novels that were published anonymously because it was considered inappropriate for aristocratic women to appear in print. Following the publication of *The Princess of Clèves* in 1678, she denied having written it. Hannah Wooley, the English author of many books on domestic conduct, published under the name of her first husband. Women were known for writing wonderful letters (Marie de Sévigné was a prime example), many of which circulated in handwritten form; hardly any appeared in print during their authors' lifetimes. In the 1650s, despite these limitations, French women began to turn out best-sellers in a new type of literature, the novel. Their success prompted the philosopher Pierre Bayle to remark in 1697 that "our best French novels for a long time have been written by women."

The new importance of women in the world of manners and letters did not sit well with everyone. Although the French writer François Poulain de la Barre (1647–1723), in a series of works published in the 1670s, used the new science to assert the equality of women's minds, most men resisted the idea. Clergy, lawyers, scholars, and playwrights attacked women's growing public influence. Women, they complained, were corrupting forces and needed restraint. Only marriage, "this salutary yoke," could control their passions and weaknesses. Salons drew fire as promoting unrestrained social ambition; women were accused of raising "the banner of prostitution in the salons, in the promenades, and in the streets." Some feared the new manners would make men effeminate: "Thus, the entire nation, formerly full of courage, grows soft and becomes effeminate, and the love of pleasure and money succeeds that of virtue." Molière wrote plays denouncing women's pretension to judge literary merit. English playwrights derided learned women by creating characters with names such as Lady Knowall, Lady Meanwell, and Mrs. Lovewit. A real-life target of the English playwrights was Aphra Behn (1640–1689), one of the first professional woman authors, who supported herself by journalism and wrote plays and poetry. Her short novel *Oroonoko* (1688) told the story of an African prince wrongly sold into slavery. The story was so successful that it was adapted by playwrights and performed repeatedly in England and France for the next hundred years. Behn responded to her critics by demanding that "the privilege for my masculine part, the poet in me" be heard and by arguing that there was "no reason why women should not write as well as men."

Reforming Popular Culture

The illiterate peasants who made up most of Europe's population had little or no knowledge of the law of gravity, upper-class manners, or novels, no matter who authored them. Their culture had three main elements: the knowledge needed to work at farming or in a trade; popular forms of entertainment such as village fairs and dances; and their religion, which shaped every aspect of life and death. What changed most noticeably in the seventeenth century was the social elites' attitude toward lower-class culture. The division between elite and popular culture widened as elites insisted on their difference from the lower orders and tried to instill new forms of discipline in their social inferiors. Historians have learned much of what they know about popular culture from the attempts of elites to change it.

Popular Religion. In the seventeenth century, Protestant and Catholic churches alike pushed hard to change popular religious practices. Their campaigns against popular "paganism" began during the sixteenth-century Protestant Reformation and Catholic Counter-Reformation but reached much of rural Europe only in the seventeenth century. Puritans in England tried to root out maypole dances, Sunday village fairs, gambling, taverns, and bawdy ballads because they interfered with sober observance of the Sabbath. In Lutheran Norway, pastors denounced a widespread belief in the miracle-working powers of St. Olaf. *Superstition* previously meant "false religion" (Protestantism was a superstition for Catholics, Catholicism for Protestants). In the seventeenth century it took on its modern meaning of irrational fears, beliefs, and practices, which anyone educated or refined would avoid. *Superstition* became synonymous with popular or ignorant beliefs.

The Catholic campaign against superstitious practices found a ready ally in Louis XIV. While he reformed the nobles at court through etiquette and manners, Catholic bishops in the French provinces trained parish priests to reform their flocks by using catechisms in local dialects and insisting that parishioners attend Mass. The church faced a formidable challenge. One bishop in France complained in 1671, "Can you believe that there are in this diocese entire villages where no one has even heard of Jesus Christ?" In some places, believers sacrificed animals to the Virgin, prayed to the new moon, and worshiped at the sources of streams as in pre-Christian times.

Like its Protestant counterpart, the Catholic campaign against ignorance and superstition helped extend state power. Clergy, officials, and local police worked together to limit carnival celebrations, to regulate pilgrimages to shrines, and to replace "indecent" images of saints with more restrained and decorous ones. In Catholicism, the cult of the Virgin Mary and devotions closely connected with Jesus, such as the Holy Sacrament and the Sacred Heart, took precedence over the celebration of more popular saints who seemed to have pagan origins or were credited with unverified miracles. Reformers everywhere tried to limit the number of feast days on the grounds that they encouraged lewd behavior.

New Attitudes toward Poverty. The campaign for more disciplined religious practices helped generate a new attitude toward the poor. Poverty previously had been closely linked with charity and virtue in Christianity; it was a Christian duty to give alms to the poor, and Jesus and many of the saints had purposely chosen lives of poverty. In the sixteenth and seventeenth centuries, the upper classes, the church, and the state increasingly regarded the poor as dangerous, deceitful, and lacking in character. "Criminal laziness is the source of all their vices," wrote a Jesuit expert on the poor. The courts had previously expelled beggars from cities; now local leaders, both Catholic and Protestant, tried to reform their character. Municipal magistrates collected taxes for poor relief, and local notables organized charities; together they transformed hospitals into houses of confinement for beggars. In Catholic France, upper-class women's religious associations, known as *confraternities,* set up asylums that confined prostitutes (by arrest if necessary) and rehabilitated them. Confraternities also founded hospices where orphans learned order and respect. Such groups advocated harsh discipline as the cure for poverty.

Although hard times had increased the numbers of poor and the rates of violent crime as well, the most important changes were attitudinal. The elites wanted to separate the very poor from society either to change them or to keep them from contaminating others. Hospitals became holding pens for society's unwanted members, where the poor joined the disabled, the incurably diseased, and the insane. The founding of hospitals demonstrates the connection between these attitudes and state building. In 1676, Louis XIV ordered every French city to establish a hospital, and his government took charge of their finances. Other rulers soon followed the same path.

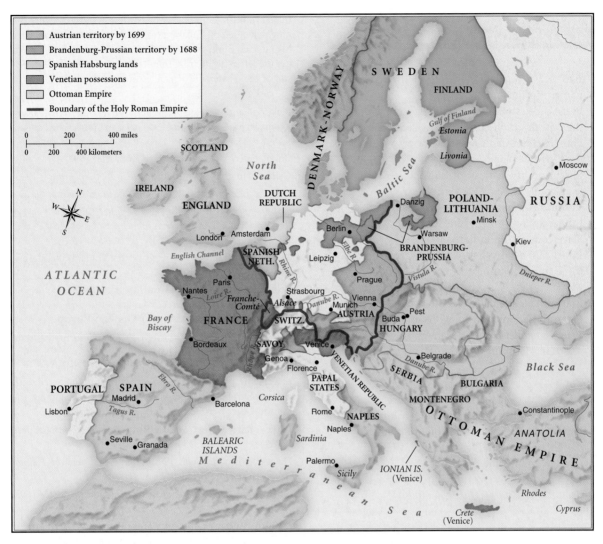

MAPPING THE WEST Europe at the End of the Seventeenth Century

A map can be deceiving. Although Poland-Lithuania looks like a large country on this map, it had been fatally weakened by internal conflicts. In the next century it would disappear entirely. The Ottoman Empire still controlled an extensive territory, but outside of Anatolia its rule depended on intermediaries. The Austrian Habsburgs had pushed the Turks out of Hungary and back into the Balkans. At the other end of the scale, the very small Dutch Republic had become very rich through international commerce. Size did not always prove to be an advantage.

Conclusion

The search for order took place on various levels, from the reform of the disorderly poor to the establishment of more regular bureaucratic routines in government. The biggest factor shaping the search for order was the growth of state power.

Whether absolutist or constitutionalist in form, seventeenth-century states all aimed to penetrate more deeply into the lives of their subjects. They wanted more men for their armed forces, higher taxes to support their projects, and more control over foreign trade, religious dissent, and society's unwanted.

IMPORTANT DATES

1642–1646 Civil war between King Charles I and Parliament in England

1648 Peace of Westphalia ends Thirty Years' War; the Fronde revolt challenges royal authority in France; Ukrainian Cossack warriors rebel against the king of Poland-Lithuania

1649 Execution of Charles I of England; new Russian legal code

1651 Thomas Hobbes publishes *Leviathan*

1660 Monarchy restored in England

1661 Slave code set up in Barbados

1667 Louis XIV begins first of many wars that continue throughout his reign

1670 Molière's play, *The Middle-Class Gentleman*

1678 Marie-Madeline de La Vergne (Madame de Lafayette) anonymously publishes her novel *The Princess of Clèves*

1683 Austrian Habsburgs break the Turkish siege of Vienna

1685 Louis XIV revokes toleration for French Protestants granted by the Edict of Nantes

1687 Isaac Newton publishes *Principia Mathematica*

1688 Parliament deposes James II and invites his daughter, Mary, and her husband, William of Orange, to take the throne

1690 John Locke's *Two Treatises of Government*, *Essay Concerning Human Understanding*

Some tearing had begun to appear, however, in the seamless fabric of state power. In England, the Dutch Republic, and the English North American colonies, property owners successfully demanded constitutional guarantees of their right to participate in government. In the eighteenth century, moreover, new levels of economic growth and the appearance of new social groups would exert pressures on the European state system. The success of seventeenth-century rulers created the political and economic conditions in which their critics would flourish.

Suggested References

Louis XIV: Model of Absolutism

Recent studies have examined Louis XIV's uses of art and imagery for political purposes and have also rightly insisted that absolutism could never be entirely absolute because the king depended on collaboration and cooperation to enforce his policies. Some of the best sources for Louis XIV's reign are the letters written by important noblewomen. The Web site of the Château of Versailles includes views of rooms in the castle.

Beik, William. *Absolutism and Society in Seventeenth-Century France: State Power and Provincial Aristocracy in Languedoc.* 1985.

Burke, Peter. *The Fabrication of Louis XIV.* 1992.

Collins, James B. *The State in Early Modern France.* 1995.

*Forster, Elborg, trans. *A Woman's Life in the Court of the Sun King: Elisabeth Charlotte, Duchesse d'Orléans.* 1984.

Ranum, Oreste. *The Fronde: A French Revolution, 1648–1652.* 1993.

*Sévigné, Madame de. *Selected Letters.* Trans. Leonard Tancock. 1982.

Versailles: http://www.chateauversailles.com.

Absolutism in Central and Eastern Europe

Too often central and eastern European forms of state development have been characterized as backward in comparison with those of western Europe. Now historians emphasize the patterns of ruler-elite cooperation shared with western Europe, but they also underscore the weight of serfdom in eastern economies and political systems.

Barkey, Karen. *The Ottoman Route to State Centralization.* 1994.

Davies, Norman. *God's Playground: A History of Poland.* Vol. 1, *The Origins to 1795.* 1981.

Dukes, Paul. *The Making of Russian Absolutism, 1613–1801.* 1990.

Kivelson, Valerie A. *Autocracy in the Provinces: The Muscovite Gentry and Political Culture in the Seventeenth Century.* 1996.

Vierhaus, Rudolf. *Germany in the Age of Absolutism.* Trans. Jonathan B. Knudsen. 1988.

Wilson, Peter H. *German Armies: War and German Politics, 1648–1806.* 1998.

Constitutionalism in England

Though recent interpretations of the English revolutions emphasize the limits on radical change, Hill's portrayal of the radical ferment of ideas remains fundamental.

Carlin, Norah. *The Causes of the English Civil War.* 1999.

Cust, Richard, and Ann Hughes, eds. *The English Civil War.* 1997.

*Primary sources.

*Graham, Elspeth, et al., eds. *Her Own Life: Autobiographical Writings by Seventeenth-Century English Women.* 1989.

*Haller, William, and Godfrey Davies, eds. *The Leveller Tracts, 1647–1653.* 1944.

Hill, Christopher. *The World Turned Upside Down: Radical Ideas during the English Revolution.* 1972.

Israel, Jonathan, ed. *The Anglo-Dutch Moment: Essays on the Glorious Revolution and Its World Impact.* 1991.

Mack, Phyllis. *Visionary Women: Ecstatic Prophecy in Seventeenth-Century England.* 1992.

Manning, Brian. *Aristocrats, Plebeians, and Revolution in England, 1640–1660.* 1996.

*Pincus, Steven Carl Anthony. *England's Glorious Revolution and the Origins of Liberalism: A Documentary History of Later Stuart England.* 1998.

Constitutionalism in the Dutch Republic and the Overseas Colonies

Studies of the Dutch Republic emphasize the importance of trade and consumerism. Recent work on the colonies has begun to explore the intersecting experiences of settlers, native Americans, and African slaves.

*Campbell, P. F. *Some Early Barbadian History.* 1993.

Delâge, Denys. *Bitter Feast: Amerindians and Europeans in Northeastern North America, 1600–64.* Trans. Jane Brierley. 1993.

*Foster, William C., ed. *The La Salle Expedition to Texas: The Journal of Henri Joutel, 1684–1687.* Trans. Johanna S. Warren. 1998.

Israel, Jonathan. *Dutch Primacy in World Trade, 1585–1740.* 1989.

Merrell, James Hart. *Into the American Woods: Negotiators on the Pennsylvania Frontier.* 1999.

Price, J. L. *The Dutch Republic in the Seventeenth Century.* 1998.

Schama, Simon. *The Embarrassment of Riches: An Interpretation of Dutch Culture in the Golden Age.* 1988.

Thornton, John. *Africa and Africans in the Making of the Atlantic World, 1400–1800.* 1992.

The Search for Order in Elite and Popular Culture

Historians do not always agree about the meaning of popular culture: was it something widely shared by all social classes or a set of activities increasingly identified with the lower classes, as Burke argues? The central Web site for Dutch museums allows the visitor to tour rooms and see paintings in scores of Dutch museums, many of which have important holdings of paintings by Rembrandt and Vermeer. The website on Isaac Newton links to many other sites on his scientific and mathematical discoveries.

Burke, Peter. *Popular Culture in Early Modern Europe.* 1978.

Davis, Natalie Zemon. *Women on the Margins: Three Seventeenth-Century Lives.* 1995.

DeJean, Joan E. *Tender Geographies: Women and the Origins of the Novel in France.* 1991.

Dobbs, Betty Jo Teeter and Margaret C. Jacob. *Newton and the Culture of Newtonianism.* 1994.

Dutch Museums: http://www.hollandmuseums.nl.

Elias, Norbert. *The Civilizing Process: The Development of Manners.* Trans. by Edmund Jephcott. 1978.

*Fitzmaurice, James, ed. *Margaret Cavendish: Sociable Letters.* 1997.

Isaac Newton: http://www.newtonia.freeserve.co.uk.

Todd, Janet M. *The Secret Life of Aphra Behn.* 1997.

18

The Atlantic System and Its Consequences

1690–1740

JOHANN SEBASTIAN BACH (1685–1750), composer of mighty organ fugues and church cantatas, was not above amusing his Leipzig audiences, many of them university students. In 1732 he produced a cantata about a young woman in love—with coffee. Her old-fashioned father rages that he won't find her a husband unless she gives up the fad. She agrees, secretly vowing to admit no suitor who will not promise in the marriage contract to let her brew coffee whenever she wants. Bach offers this conclusion:

> *The cat won't give up its mouse,*
> *Girls stay faithful coffee-sisters*
> *Mother loves her coffee habit,*
> *Grandma sips it gladly too—*
> *Why then shout at the daughters?*

London Coffeehouse
This gouache (a variant on water-color painting) from about 1725 depicts a scene from a London coffeehouse located in the courtyard of the Royal Exchange (merchants' bank). Middle-class men (wearing wigs) read newspapers, drink coffee, smoke pipes, and discuss the news of the day. The coffeehouse draws them out of their homes into a new public space.
British Museum, Bridgeman Art Library, NY.

Bach's era might well be called the age of coffee. European travelers at the end of the sixteenth century had noticed Middle Eastern people drinking a "black drink," *kavah*. Few Europeans sampled it at first, and the Arab monopoly on its production kept prices high. This changed around 1700 when the Dutch East India Company introduced coffee plants to Java and other Indonesian islands. Coffee production then spread to the French Caribbean, where African slaves provided the plantation labor. In Europe, imported coffee spurred the development of a new kind of meeting place: the first coffeehouse opened in London in 1652, and the idea spread quickly to other European cities. The coffeehouses became

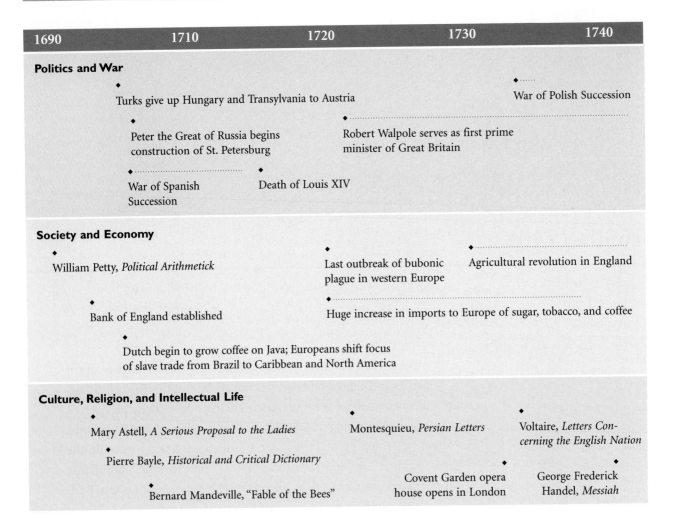

1690	1710	1720	1730	1740

Politics and War

Turks give up Hungary and Transylvania to Austria

War of Polish Succession

Peter the Great of Russia begins construction of St. Petersburg

Robert Walpole serves as first prime minister of Great Britain

War of Spanish Succession

Death of Louis XIV

Society and Economy

William Petty, *Political Arithmetick*

Last outbreak of bubonic plague in western Europe

Agricultural revolution in England

Bank of England established

Huge increase in imports to Europe of sugar, tobacco, and coffee

Dutch begin to grow coffee on Java; Europeans shift focus of slave trade from Brazil to Caribbean and North America

Culture, Religion, and Intellectual Life

Mary Astell, *A Serious Proposal to the Ladies*

Montesquieu, *Persian Letters*

Voltaire, *Letters Concerning the English Nation*

Pierre Bayle, *Historical and Critical Dictionary*

Covent Garden opera house opens in London

George Frederick Handel, *Messiah*

Bernard Mandeville, "Fable of the Bees"

gathering places for men to drink, read newspapers, and talk politics. As a London newspaper commented in 1737, "There's scarce an Alley in City and Suburbs but has a Coffeehouse in it, which may be called the School of Public Spirit, where every Man over Daily and Weekly Journals, a Mug, or a Dram . . . devotes himself to that glorious one, his Country."

European consumption of coffee, tea, chocolate, and other novelties increased dramatically as European nations forged worldwide economic links. At the center of this new world economy was an "Atlantic system" that bound together western Europe, Africa, and the Americas. Europeans bought slaves in western Africa, transported and sold them in their colonies in North and South America and the Caribbean, bought the commodities such as

coffee and sugar that were produced by the new colonial plantations, and then sold the goods in European ports for refining and reshipment. This Atlantic system first took clear shape in the early eighteenth century; it was the hub of European expansion all over the world.

Coffee was one example among many of the new social and cultural patterns that took root between 1690 and 1740. Improvements in agricultural production at home reinforced the effects of trade overseas; Europeans now had more disposable income for "extras," and they spent their money not only in the new coffeehouses and cafés that sprang up all over Europe but also on newspapers, musical concerts, paintings, and novels. A new middle-class public began to make its presence felt in every domain of culture and social life.

Although the rise of the Atlantic system gave Europe new prominence in the global context, European rulers still focused most of their political, diplomatic, and military energies on their rivalries within Europe. A coalition of countries succeeded in containing French aggression, and a more balanced diplomatic system emerged. In eastern Europe, Prussia and Austria had to contend with the rising power of Russia under Peter the Great. In western Europe, both Spain and the Dutch Republic declined in influence but continued to vie with Britain and France for colonial spoils in the Atlantic. The more evenly matched competition among the great powers encouraged the development of diplomatic skills and drew attention to public health as a way of encouraging population growth.

In the aftermath of Louis XIV's revocation of the Edict of Nantes in 1685, a new intellectual movement known as the Enlightenment began to germinate. French Protestant refugees began to publish works critical of absolutism in politics and religion. Increased prosperity, the growth of a middle-class public, and the decline in warfare after Louis XIV's death in 1715 all fostered the development of this new critical spirit. Fed by the popularization of science and the growing interest in travel literature, the Enlightenment encouraged greater skepticism about religious and state authority. Eventually the movement would question almost every aspect of social and political life in Europe. The Enlightenment began in western Europe in those countries—Britain, France, and the Dutch Republic—most affected by the new Atlantic system. It too was a product of the age of coffee.

❖ The Atlantic System and the World Economy

Although their ships had been circling the globe since the early 1500s, Europeans did not draw most of the world into their economic orbit until the 1700s. Western European trading nations sent ships loaded with goods to buy slaves from local rulers on the western coast of Africa; then transported the slaves to the colonies in North and South America and the Caribbean and sold them to the owners of plantations producing coffee, sugar, cotton, and tobacco; and bought the raw commodities produced

in the colonies and shipped them back to Europe, where they were refined or processed and then sold to other parts of Europe and the world. The Atlantic system and the growth of international trade helped create a new consumer society.

Slavery and the Atlantic System

Spain and Portugal had dominated Atlantic trade in the sixteenth and seventeenth centuries, but in the eighteenth century European trade in the Atlantic rapidly expanded and became more systematically interconnected (Map 18.1, inset). By 1630, Portugal had already sent 60,000 African slaves to Brazil to work on the new plantations (large tracts of lands farmed by slave labor), which were producing some 15,000 tons of sugar a year. Realizing that plantations producing staples for Europeans could bring fabulous wealth, the European powers grew less interested in the dwindling trade in precious metals and more eager to colonize. Large-scale planters of sugar, tobacco, and coffee displaced small farmers who relied on one or two servants. Planters and their plantations won out because slave labor was cheap and therefore able to produce mass quantities of commodities at low prices.

State-chartered private companies from Portugal, France, Britain, the Dutch Republic, Prussia, and even Denmark exploited the 3,500-mile coastline of West Africa for slaves. Before 1675, most blacks taken from Africa had been sent to Brazil, but by 1700 half of the African slaves landed in the Caribbean (Figure 18.1). Thereafter, the plantation economy began to expand on the North American mainland. The numbers stagger the imagination. Before 1650, slave traders transported about 7,000 Africans each year across the Atlantic; this rate doubled between 1650 and 1675, nearly doubled again in the next twenty-five years, and kept going until the 1780s (Figure 18.2). In all, more than 11 million Africans, not counting those who died at sea or in Africa, were transported to the Americas before the slave trade began to wind down after 1850. Many traders gained spectacular wealth, but companies did not always make profits. The English Royal African Company, for example, delivered 100,000 slaves to the Caribbean, imported 30,000 tons of sugar to Britain, yet lost money after the few profitable years following its founding in 1672.

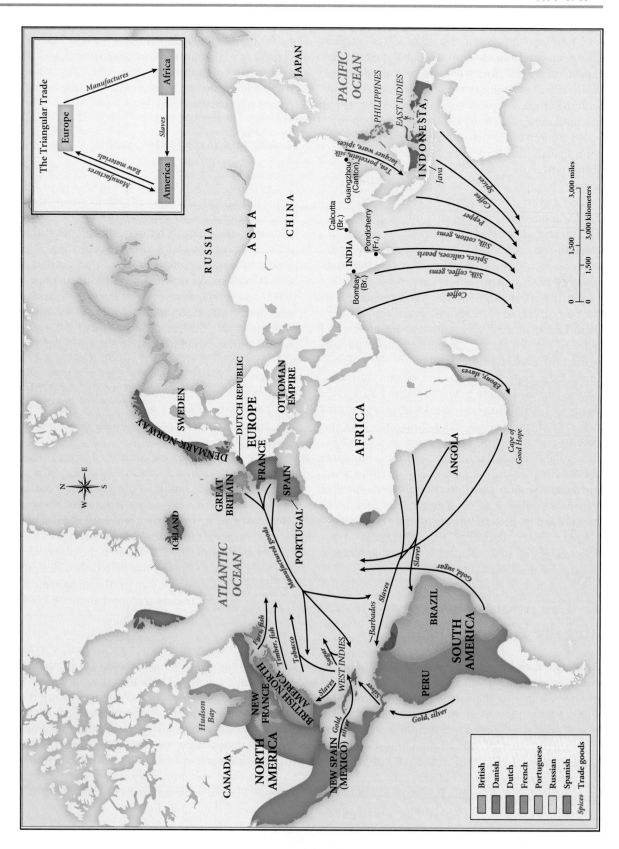

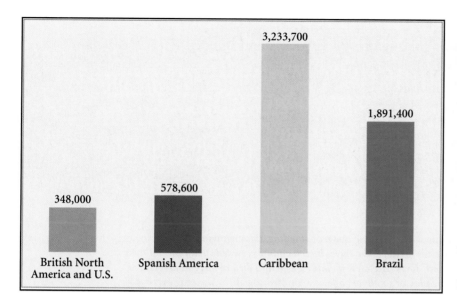

FIGURE 18.1 African Slaves Imported into American Territories, 1701–1810
During the eighteenth century, planters in the newly established Caribbean colonies imported millions of African slaves to work the new plantations that produced sugar, coffee, indigo, and cotton for the European market. The vast majority of African slaves transported to the Americas ended up in either the Caribbean or Brazil. Adapted from Philip D. Curtin, *The Atlantic Slave Trade: A Census* (Madison: University of Wisconsin Press, 1969).

The Life of the Slaves. The balance of white and black populations in the New World colonies was determined by the staples produced. New England merchants and farmers bought few slaves because they did not own plantations. Blacks—both slave and free—made up only 3 percent of the population in eighteenth-century New England, compared with 60 percent in South Carolina. On the whole, the British North American colonies contained a higher proportion of African Americans from 1730 to 1765 than at any other time in American history. The imbalance of whites and blacks was even more extreme in the Caribbean; in the early 1700s, the British sugar islands had a population of about 150,000 people, only 30,000 of them Europeans. The rest were African slaves, as most indigenous people died fighting Europeans or the diseases brought by them.

The slaves suffered terrible experiences. Most had been sold to European traders by Africans from the west coast who acquired them through warfare or kidnapping. The vast majority were between fourteen and thirty-five years old. Before being crammed onto the ships for the three-month trip, their heads were shaved, they were stripped naked, and some were branded with red-hot irons. The men and women were separated and the men shack-led with leg irons. Sailors and officers raped the women whenever they wished and beat those who refused their advances. In the cramped and appalling conditions of the voyage, as many as one-fourth of the slaves died in transit.

Once they landed, slaves were forced into degrading and oppressive conditions. As soon as masters bought slaves, they gave them new names, often only first names, and in some colonies branded them as personal property. Slaves had no social identities of their own; they were expected to learn their master's language and to do any job assigned. Slaves worked fifteen- to seventeen-hour days and were fed only enough to keep them on their feet. Brazilian slaves consumed more calories than the poorest Brazilians do today, but that hardly made them well fed. The manager of a plantation in Barbados insisted in 1711, "It is the greatest misfortune in this island that few planters give [the slaves] . . . a bellyful" of corn. The death rate among slaves was high, especially in Brazil, where quick shifts in the weather, lack of clothing, and squalid living conditions made them susceptible to a variety of deadly illnesses.

Not surprisingly, despite the threat of torture or death on recapture, slaves sometimes ran away. (See

◀ **MAP 18.1 European Trade Patterns, c. 1740**
By 1740, the European powers had colonized much of North and South America and incorporated their colonies there into a worldwide system of commerce centered on the slave trade and plantation production of staple crops. Europeans still sought spices and luxury goods in China and the East Indies, but outside of Java, few Europeans had settled permanently in these areas.

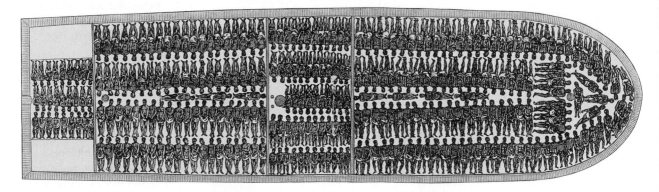

Conditions on Slave Ships
Although the viewer cannot tell if the slaves are lying down or standing, this engraving, inspired by the campaign to abolish slavery, has a clear message: the slaves had to endure crowded conditions on their long passage across the Atlantic. Most slaves (like crew members, who also died in large numbers) fell victim to dysentery, yellow fever, measles, or smallpox; a few committed suicide by jumping overboard.
North Wind Picture Archive.

"New Sources, New Perspectives," page 652). In Brazil, runaways hid in *quilombos* (hideouts) in the forests or backcountry. When it was discovered and destroyed in 1695, the *quilombo* of Palmares had thirty thousand fugitives who had formed their own social organization complete with elected kings and councils of elders. Outright revolt was uncommon, especially before the nineteenth century, but other forms of resistance included stealing food, breaking tools, and feigning illness or stupidity. Slaveholders' fears about conspiracy and revolt lurked beneath the surface of every slave-based society. In 1710, the royal governor of Virginia reminded the colonial legislature of the need for unceasing vigilance: "We are not to Depend on Either Their Stupidity, or that Babel of Languages among 'em; freedom Wears a Cap which Can Without a Tongue, Call Togather all Those who Long to Shake off the fetters of Slavery." Masters defended whipping and other forms of physical punishment as essential to maintaining discipline. Laws called for the castration of a slave who struck a white person.

Effects on Europe. Plantation owners often left their colonial possessions in the care of agents and collected the revenue to live as wealthy landowners back home, where they built opulent mansions and gained influence in local and national politics. William Beckford, for example, had been sent from Jamaica to school in England as a young boy. When he inherited sugar plantations and shipping companies from his father and older brother, he moved

the headquarters of the family business to London in the 1730s to be close to the government and financial markets. His holdings formed the single most powerful economic interest in Jamaica, but he preferred to live in England where he could collect art for his many luxurious homes, hold political office (he served as lord mayor of London and in Parliament), and even lend money to the government.

The slave trade permanently altered consumption patterns for ordinary people. Sugar had been prescribed as medicine before the end of the sixteenth century, but the development of plantations in Brazil and the Caribbean made it a standard food item. By 1700, the British sent home 50 million pounds of sugar a year, a figure that doubled by 1730. During the French Revolution of the 1790s, sugar shortages would become a cause for rioting in Paris. Equally pervasive was the spread of tobacco; by the 1720s, Britain imported two hundred shiploads of tobacco from Virginia and Maryland every year, and men of every country and class smoked pipes or took snuff.

The Origins of Racism. The traffic in slaves disturbed many Europeans. As a government memorandum to the Spanish king explained in 1610: "Modern theologians in published books commonly report on, and condemn as unjust, the acts of enslavement which take place in provinces of this Royal Empire." Between 1667 and 1671, the French Dominican monk Father Du Tertre published three volumes in which he denounced the mistreatment of slaves in the French colonies.

In the 1700s, however, slaveholders began to justify their actions by demeaning the mental and spiritual qualities of the enslaved Africans. White Europeans and colonists sometimes described black slaves as animal-like, akin to apes. A leading New England Puritan asserted about the slaves: "Indeed their *Stupidity* is a *Discouragement*. It may seem, unto as little purpose, to *Teach*, as to *wash an Aethiopian* [Ethiopian]." One of the great paradoxes of this time was that talk of liberty and self-evident rights, especially prevalent in Britain and its North American colonies, coexisted with the belief that some people were meant to be slaves. Although Christians believed in principle in a kind of spiritual equality between blacks and whites, the churches often defended or at least did not oppose the inequities of slavery.

World Trade and Settlement

The Atlantic system helped extend European trade relations across the globe. The textiles that Atlantic shippers exchanged for slaves on the west coast of Africa, for example, were manufactured in India and exported by the British and French East India Companies. As much as one-quarter of the British exports to Africa in the eighteenth century were actually re-exports from India. To expand its trade in the rest of the world, Europeans seized territories and tried to establish permanent settlements. The eighteenth-century extension of European power prepared the way for western global domination in the nineteenth and twentieth centuries.

The Americas. In contrast to the sparsely inhabited trading outposts in Asia and Africa, the colonies in the Americas bulged with settlers. The British North American colonies, for example, contained about 1.5 million nonnative (that is, white settler and black slave) residents by 1750. While the Spanish competed with the Portuguese for control of South America, the French competed with the British for control of North America. Spanish and

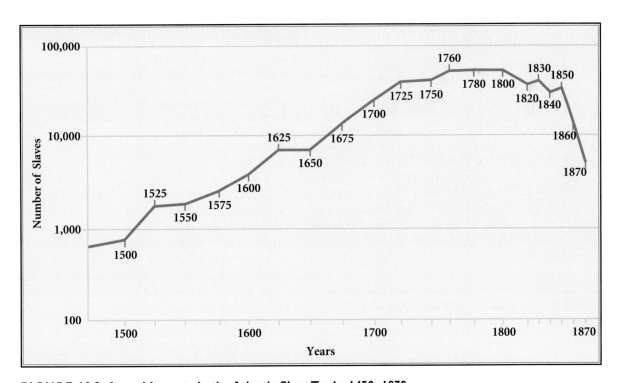

FIGURE 18.2 Annual Imports in the Atlantic Slave Trade, 1450–1870
The importation of slaves to the American territories reached its height in the second half of the eighteenth century and began to decline around 1800. Yet despite the abolition of the slave trade by the British in 1807, commerce in slaves did not seriously diminish until after the revolutions of 1848.
Adapted from Philip D. Curtin, *The Atlantic Slave Trade: A Census* (Madison: University of Wisconsin Press, 1969). Reprinted by permission of the University of Wisconsin Press.

Oral History and the Life of Slaves

Because slaves imported from Africa to the New World did not speak the language of their captors, historians have found it difficult to reconstruct slave life from the point of view of the slaves themselves. Ship records provide information about the number of slaves captured and transported, the deaths on the voyages across the Atlantic, and the prices paid for slaves when they finally arrived. This information comes from the point of view of slave traders, and it says very little about the realities of life on board ship or at the plantations. Scholars have attempted to fill in this blank by using a variety of overlapping sources. The most interesting and controversial of them are oral histories taken from descendants of slaves. In some former slave societies, descendants of slaves still tell stories about their ancestors' first days under slavery. The controversy comes from using twentieth-century memories to get at eighteenth-century lives.

One of the regions most intensively studied in this fashion is Dutch Surinam, on the northeast coast of South America between present-day Guyana and French Guiana. It is a good source of oral histories because 10 percent of the African slaves transported there between the 1680s and the 1750s escaped from the plantations and fled into the nearby rain forests. There they set up their own societies and developed their own language in which they carried on the oral traditions of the first runaway slaves. The twentieth-century descendants of the runaway slaves recount:

In slavery, there was hardly anything to eat. It was at the place called Providence Plantation. They

Slaves of Surinam in the 1770s
John Gabriel Stedman published an account of his participation in a five-year expedition against the runaway slaves of Surinam that took place in the 1770s. He provided drawings such as the one reproduced here, which shows Africans who have just come off a slave ship. Schomburg Center for Research in Black Culture/New York Public Library.

whipped you there till your ass was burning. Then they would give you a bit of plain rice in a calabash [a bowl made from the tropical American tree known as calabash]. . . . And the gods told them that this is no way for human beings to live. They would help them. Let each person go where he could. So they ran.

British settlers came to blows over the boundary between the British colonies and Florida, which was Spanish.

Local economies shaped colonial social relations; men in French trapper communities in Canada, for example, had little in common with the men and women of the plantation societies in Barbados or Brazil. Racial attitudes also differed from place to place. The Spanish and Portuguese tolerated intermarriage with the native populations in both America and Asia. Sexual contact, both inside and outside marriage, fostered greater racial variety in the Span-

From other sources, historians have learned that there was a major slave rebellion at Providence Plantation in 1693.

By comparing such oral histories to written accounts of plantation owners, missionaries, and Dutch colonial officials, historians have been able to paint a more richly detailed picture not only of slavery but also of runaway slave societies, which were especially numerous in South America. At the end of the eighteenth century, a Portuguese-speaking Jew wrote his own history of plantation life based on records from the local Jewish community that are now lost. Because the Dutch, unlike most other Europeans, allowed Jews to own slaves, Portuguese-speaking Jews from Brazil owned about one-third of the plantations and slaves in Surinam. This eighteenth-century chronicler, David de Ishak Cohen Nassy, wrote his version of Surinam's first slave revolt:

> There was in the year 1690 a revolt on a plantation situated on the Cassewinica Creek, behind Jews Savannah, belonging to a Jew named Imanuël Machado, where, having killed their master, they fled, carrying away with them everything that was there. . . . The Jews . . . in an expedition which they undertook against the rebels, killed many of them and brought back several who were punished by death on the very spot.

The oral histories told about the revolt from the runaway slaves' perspective:

> There had been a great council meeting [of runaway slaves] in the forest. . . . They decided to burn a different one of his plantations from the place where he had whipped Lanu [one of the runaway slaves] because they would find more tools there. This was the Cassewinica Plantation, which had many slaves. They knew all about this plantation from slavery times. So, they attacked.

> It was at night. They killed the head of the plantation, a white man. They took all the things, everything they needed.

The runaway slaves saw the attack as part of their ongoing effort to build a life in the rain forest, away from the whites.

Over the next decades, the runaway slaves fought a constant series of battles with plantation owners and Dutch officials. Finally in 1762, the Dutch granted the runaway slaves their freedom in a peace agreement; offered them tools, gunpowder, and other necessities; and allowed them to trade in the main town of the colony in exchange for agreeing to return all future runaways. The runaways had not destroyed the slave system, but they had gained their own independence alongside it. From their oral histories it is possible to retrace their efforts to build new lives in a strange place, in which they combined African practices with New World experiences.

Source: Richard Price, *Alabi's World* (Baltimore: Johns Hopkins University Press, 1990), 17, 9.

QUESTIONS FOR DEBATE

1. What did runaway slaves aim to accomplish when they attacked plantations?
2. Why would runaway slaves make an agreement with the Dutch colonial officials to return future runaways?
3. Can oral histories recorded in the twentieth century be considered accurate versions of events that took place in the eighteenth century? How can they be tested?

FURTHER READING

Richard Price, *Alabi's World*. 1990.

John Gabriel Stedman, *Narrative of a Five Years' Expedition Against the Revolted Negroes of Surinam*, edited, and with an introduction and notes, by Richard Price and Sally Price. 1988.

ish and Portuguese colonies than in the French or the English territories (though mixed-race people could be found everywhere). By 1800, *mestizos*, children of Spanish men and Indian women, accounted for more than a quarter of the population in the Spanish colonies, and many of them aspired to join the local elite. Greater racial diversity seems not to have improved the treatment of slaves, however, which was probably harshest in Portuguese Brazil.

Where intermarriage between colonizers and natives was common, conversion to Christianity proved most successful. Although the Indians

India Cottons and Trade with the East
This brightly colored cotton cloth was painted and embroidered in Madras in southern India sometime in the late 1600s. The male figure with a mustache may be a European, but the female figures are clearly Asian. Europeans—especially the British—discovered that they could make big profits on the export of Indian cotton cloth to Europe. They also traded Indian cottons in Africa for slaves and sold large quantities in the colonies.
Victoria and Albert Museum, London.

maintained many of their native religious beliefs, many Indians in the Spanish colonies had come to consider themselves devout Catholics by 1700. Indian carpenters and artisans in the villages produced innumerable altars, retables (painted panels), and sculpted images to adorn their local churches, and individual families put up domestic shrines. Yet the clergy remained overwhelmingly Spanish: the church hierarchy concluded that the Indians' humility and innocence made them unsuitable for the priesthood.

In the early years of American colonization, many more men than women emigrated from Europe. Although the sex imbalance began to decline at the end of the seventeenth century, it remained substantial; two and one-half times as many men as women were among the immigrants leaving Liverpool, England, between 1697 and 1707, for example. Women who emigrated as indentured servants ran great risks: if they did not die of disease during the voyage, they might end up giving birth to illegitimate children (the fate of at least one in five servant women) or being virtually sold into marriage. Many upper-class women were kept in seclusion, especially in the Spanish and Portuguese colonies.

The uncertainties of life in the American colonies provided new opportunities for European women and men willing to live outside the law,

however. In the 1500s and 1600s, the English and Dutch governments had routinely authorized pirates to prey on the shipping of their rivals, the Spanish and Portuguese. Then, in the late 1600s, English, French, and Dutch bands made up of deserters and crews from wrecked vessels began to form their own associations of pirates, especially in the Caribbean. Called *buccaneers* from their custom of curing strips of beef, called *boucan* by the native Caribs of the islands, the pirates governed themselves and preyed on everyone's shipping without regard to national origin. In 1720, the trial of buccaneers associated with Calico Jack Rackham in Jamaica revealed that two women had dressed as men and joined the pirates in looting and plundering English ships. Mary Read and Anne Bonny escaped death by hanging only because they were pregnant. After 1700, the colonial governments tried to stamp out piracy. As one British judge argued in 1705, "A pirate is in perpetual war with every individual and every state. . . . They are worse than ravenous beasts."

Africa and Asia.   White settlements in Africa and Asia remained small and almost insignificant, except for their long-term potential. Europeans had little contact with East Africa and almost none with the continent's vast interior. A few Portuguese trading posts in Angola and Dutch farms on the Cape of Good Hope provided the only toeholds for future expansion. In China the emperors had welcomed Catholic missionaries at court in the seventeenth century, but the priests' credibility diminished as they squabbled among themselves and associated with European merchants, whom the Chinese considered pirates. "The barbarians [Europeans] are like wild beasts," one Chinese official concluded, "and are not to be ruled on the same principles as citizens." In 1720, only one thousand Europeans resided in Guangzhou (Canton), the sole place where foreigners could legally trade for spices, tea, and silk.

Europeans exercised more influence in Java in the East Indies and in India. Dutch coffee production in Java and nearby islands increased phenomenally in the early 1700s, and many Dutch settled there to oversee production and trade. In India, Dutch, English, French, Portuguese, and Danish companies competed for spices, cotton, and silk; by the 1740s the English and French had become the leading rivals in India, just as they were in North America. Both countries extended their power as India's Muslim rulers lost control to local Hindu princes, rebellious Sikhs, invading Persians, and their own provincial governors. A few thousand Europeans lived in India, though many thousand more soldiers were stationed there to protect them. The staple of trade with India in the early 1700s was calico—lightweight, brightly colored cotton cloth that caught on as a fashion in Europe.

Europeans who visited India were especially struck by what they viewed as exotic religious practices. In a book published in 1696 of his travels to western India, an Anglican minister described the fakirs (religious mendicants or beggars of alms), "some of whom show their devotion by a shameless appearance, walking naked, without the least rag of clothes to cover them." Such writings increased European interest in the outside world but also fed a European sense of superiority that helped excuse the more violent forms of colonial domination.

The Birth of Consumer Society

Worldwide colonization produced new supplies of goods, from coffee to calico, and population growth in Europe fueled demand for them. Beginning first in Britain, then in France and the Italian states,

and finally in eastern Europe, population surged, growing by about 20 percent between 1700 and 1750. The gap between a fast-growing northwest and a more stagnant south and central Europe now diminished, as regions that had lost population during the seventeenth-century downturn recovered. Cities, in particular, grew. Between 1600 and 1750, London's population more than tripled, and Paris's more than doubled.

Although contemporaries could not have realized it then, this was the start of the modern "population explosion." It appears that a decline in the death rate, rather than a rise in the birthrate, explains the turnaround. Three main factors contributed to this decline in the death rate: better

The Exotic as Consumer Item
In this painting by the Venetian woman Rosalba Carriera (1675–1757), Africa (the title of the work) is represented by a young black girl wearing a turban. Carriera was known for her use of pastels. In 1720, she journeyed to Paris where she became an associate of Antoine Watteau and helped inaugurate the rococo style in painting.
Staatliche Kunstsammlungen Dresden, Gemaldegalerie Alte Meister.

weather and hence more bountiful harvests, improved agricultural techniques, and the plague's disappearance after 1720.

By the early eighteenth century, the effects of economic expansion and population growth brought about a consumer revolution. The British East India Company began to import into Britain huge quantities of calicoes. British imports of tobacco doubled between 1672 and 1700; at Nantes, the center of the French sugar trade, imports quadrupled between 1698 and 1733. Tea, chocolate, and coffee became virtual necessities. In the 1670s, only a trickle of tea reached London, but by 1720 the East India Company sent 9 million pounds to England—a figure that rose to 37 million pounds by 1750. By 1700, England had two thousand coffeehouses; by 1740, every English country town had at least two. Paris got its first cafés at the end of the seventeenth century; Berlin opened its first coffeehouse in 1714; Bach's Leipzig boasted eight by 1725.

The birth of consumer society did not go unnoticed by eye witnesses. In the English economic literature of the 1690s, writers began to express a new view of humans as consuming animals with boundless appetites. Such opinions gained a wide audience with the appearance of Bernard Mandeville's poem "Fable of the Bees" (1705), which argued that private vices might have public benefits. In the poem a hive of bees abolishes evil in its society, only to discover that the society has also disappeared. Mandeville insisted that pride, self-interest, and the desire for material goods (all Christian vices) in fact promoted economic prosperity: "every part was full of Vice, Yet the whole mass a Paradise." Many authors attacked the new doctrine of consumerism, and the French government banned the poem's publication. But Mandeville had captured the essence of the emerging market for consumption.

❖ New Social and Cultural Patterns

The impact of the Atlantic system and world trade was most apparent in the cities, where people had more money for consumer goods. But rural changes also had significant long-term influence, as a revolution in agricultural techniques made it possible to feed more and more people with a smaller agricultural workforce. As population increased, more people moved to the cities, where they found themselves caught up in innovative urban customs such as attending musical concerts and reading novels. Along

Agricultural Revolution
This English painting of a manor in Gloucestershire from about 1730 demonstrates the concrete effects of the agricultural revolution. Fields are enclosed as far as the eye can see, and large groups of men and women work together to farm the consolidated plots of land owned by the wealthy local landlord. The individual peasant family working its own small plot of land has disappeared in favor of a new and more hierarchical labor structure.
Cheltenham Art Gallery & Museums, Gloucestershire. Bridgeman Art Library, NY.

with a general increase in literacy, these activities helped create a public that responded to new writers and artists. Social and cultural changes were not uniform across Europe, however; as usual, people's experiences varied depending on whether they lived in wealth or poverty, in urban or rural areas, or in eastern or western Europe.

Agricultural Revolution

Although Britain, France, and the Dutch Republic shared the enthusiasm for consumer goods, Britain's domestic market grew most quickly. In Britain, as agricultural output increased 43 percent over the course of the 1700s, the population increased by 70 percent. The British imported grain to feed the growing population, but they also benefited from the development of techniques that together constituted an agricultural revolution. No new machinery propelled this revolution—just more aggressive attitudes toward investment and management. The Dutch and the Flemish had pioneered many of these techniques in the 1600s, but the British took them further.

Four major changes occurred in British agriculture that eventually spread to other countries. First, farmers increased the amount of land under cultivation by draining wetlands and by growing crops on previously uncultivated common lands (acreage maintained by the community for grazing). Second, those farmers who could afford it consolidated smaller, scattered plots into larger, more efficient units. Third, livestock raising became more closely linked to crop growing, and the yields of each increased. (See "Taking Measure," opposite.) For centuries, most farmers had rotated their fields in and out of production to replenish the soil. Now farmers planted carefully chosen fodder crops such as clover and turnips that added nutrients to the soil, thereby eliminating the need to leave a field fallow (unplanted) every two or three years. With more fodder available, farmers could raise more livestock, which in turn produced more manure to fertilize grain fields. Fourth, selective breeding of animals combined with the increase in fodder to improve the quality and size of herds. New crops had only a slight impact; potatoes, for example, were introduced to Europe from South America in the 1500s, but because people feared they might cause leprosy, tuberculosis, or fevers, they were not grown in quantity until the late 1700s. By the 1730s and 1740s,

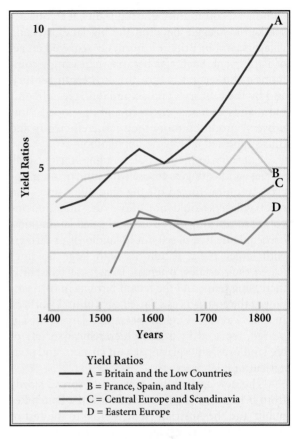

TAKING MEASURE Relationship of Crop Harvested to Seed Used, 1400–1800
The impact and even the timing of the agricultural revolution can be determined by this figure, based on yield ratios (the number of grains produced for each seed planted). Britain, the Dutch Republic, and the Austrian Netherlands all experienced huge increases in crop yields after 1700. Other European regions lagged behind right into the 1800s.
From Peter J. Hugill, *World Trade since 1431: Geography, Technology, and Capitalism* (Johns Hopkins University Press, 1995), p. 56. Reprinted by permission of Johns Hopkins University Press.

agricultural output had increased dramatically, and prices for food had fallen because of these interconnected innovations.

Changes in agricultural practices did not benefit all landowners equally. The biggest British landowners consolidated their holdings in the "enclosure movement." They put pressure on small farmers and villagers to sell their land or give up their common lands. The big landlords then fenced off ("enclosed") their property. Because enclosure eliminated community grazing rights, it frequently sparked a struggle between the big landlords and villagers, and in Britain it normally required an act of Parliament. Such acts became increasingly common in the second half of the eighteenth century, and by the century's end six million acres of common lands had been enclosed and developed. "Improvers" produced more food more efficiently and thus supported a growing population.

Contrary to the fears of contemporaries, small farmers and cottagers (those with little or no property) were not forced off the land all at once. But most villagers could not afford the litigation involved in resisting enclosure, and small landholders consequently had to sell out to landlords or farmers with larger plots. Landlords with large holdings leased their estates to tenant farmers at constantly increasing rents, and the tenant farmers in turn employed the cottagers as salaried agricultural workers. In this way the English peasantry largely disappeared, replaced by a more hierarchical society of big landlords, enterprising tenant farmers, and poor agricultural laborers.

The new agricultural techniques spread slowly from Britain and the Low Countries (the Dutch Republic and the Austrian Netherlands) to the rest of western Europe. Outside a few pockets in northern France and the western German states, however, subsistence agriculture (producing just enough to get by rather than surpluses for the market) continued to dominate farming in western Europe and Scandinavia. In southwestern Germany, for example, 80 percent of the peasants produced no surplus because their plots were too small. Unlike the populations of the highly urbanized Low Countries (where half the people lived in towns and cities), most Europeans, western and eastern, eked out their existence in the countryside.

In eastern Europe, the condition of peasants worsened in the areas where landlords tried hardest to improve their yields. To produce more for the Baltic grain market, aristocratic landholders in Prussia, Poland, and parts of Russia drained wetlands, cultivated moors, and built dikes. They also forced peasants off lands the peasants worked for themselves, increased compulsory labor services (the critical element in serfdom), and began to manage their estates directly. Some eastern landowners grew fabulously wealthy. The Potocki family in the Polish Ukraine, for example, owned three million

Treatment of Serfs in Russia
Visitors from western Europe often remarked on the cruel treatment of serfs in Russia. This drawing by one such visitor shows the punishment that could be inflicted by landowners. Serfs could be whipped for almost any reason, even for making a soup too salty or neglecting to bow when the lord's family passed by. Their condition actually deteriorated in the 1700s, as landowners began to sell serfs much like slaves. New decrees made it illegal for serfs to contract loans, enter into leases, or work for anyone other than their lord. Some landlords kept harems of serf girls. Although the Russian landlords' treatment of serfs was even more brutal than that in the German states and Poland, upper classes in every country regarded the serfs as dirty, deceitful, brutish, and superstitious. New York Public Library Slavonic Division.

acres of land and had 130,000 serfs. The Eszterházy family of Hungary owned seven million acres; and the Lithuanian magnate Karol Radziwill controlled six hundred villages. In parts of Poland and Russia the serfs hardly differed from slaves in status, and their "masters" ran their huge estates much like American plantations.

Social Life in the Cities

Because of emigration from the countryside, cities grew in population and consequently exercised more influence on culture and social life. Between 1650 and 1750, cities with at least ten thousand inhabitants increased in population by 44 percent. From the eighteenth century onward, urban growth would be continuous. Along with the general growth of cities, an important south-to-north shift occurred in the pattern of urbanization. Around 1500, half of the people in cities of at least ten thousand residents could be found in the Italian states, Spain, or Portugal; by 1700, the urbanization of northwestern and southern Europe was roughly equal. Eastern Europe, despite the huge cities of Istanbul and Moscow, was still less urban than western Europe. London was by far the most populous European city, with 675,000 inhabitants in 1750; Berlin had 90,000 people, Warsaw only 23,000.

Urban Social Classes. Many landowners kept a residence in town, so the separation between rural and city life was not as extreme as might be imagined, at least not for the very rich. At the top of the ladder in the big cities were the landed nobles. Some of them filled their lives only with conspicuous consumption of fine food, extravagant clothing, coaches, books, and opera; others held key political, administrative, or judicial offices. However they spent their time, these rich families employed thousands of artisans, shopkeepers, and domestic servants. Many English peers (highest-ranking nobles) had thirty or forty servants at each of their homes.

The middle classes of officials, merchants, professionals, and landowners occupied the next rung down on the social ladder. London's population, for example, included about 20,000 middle-class families (constituting, at most, one-sixth of the city's population). In this period the middle classes began to develop distinctive ways of life that set them apart from both the rich noble landowners and the lower classes. Unlike the rich nobles, the middle classes lived primarily in the cities and towns, even if they owned small country estates. They ate more moderately than nobles but much better than peasants or laborers. For breakfast the British middle classes ate toast and rolls and, after 1700, drank tea. Dinner, served midday, consisted of roasted or boiled beef or mutton, poultry or pork, and vegetables. Supper was a light meal of bread and cheese with cake or pie. Beer was the main drink in London, and many families brewed their own. Even children drank beer because of the lack of fresh water.

In contrast to the gigantic and sprawling country seats of the richest English peers, middle-class houses in town had about seven rooms, including four or five bedrooms and one or two living rooms, still many more than the poor agricultural worker. New household items reflected society's increasing wealth and its exposure to colonial imports: by 1700, the middle classes of London typically had mirrors in every room, a coffeepot and coffee mill, numerous pictures and ornaments, a china collection, and several clocks. Life for the middle classes on the continent was quite similar, though wine replaced beer in France.

Below the middle classes came the artisans and shopkeepers (most of whom were organized in professional guilds), then the journeymen, apprentices, servants, and laborers. At the bottom of the social scale were the unemployed poor, who survived by intermittent work and charity. Women married to artisans and shopkeepers often kept the accounts, supervised employees, and ran the household as well. Every household from the middle classes to the upper classes employed servants; artisans and shopkeepers frequently hired them too. Women from poorer families usually worked as domestic servants until they married. Four out of five domestic servants in the city were female. In large cities such as London, the servant population grew faster than the population of the city as a whole.

Signs of Social Distinction. Social status in the cities was readily visible. Wide, spacious streets graced rich districts; the houses had gardens and the air was relatively fresh. In poor districts the streets were narrow, dirty, dark, humid, and smelly, and the houses were damp and crowded. The poorest people were homeless, sleeping under bridges or in abandoned homes. A Neapolitan prince described his homeless neighbors as "lying like filthy animals, with no distinction of age or sex." In some districts, rich and poor lived in the same buildings, with the poor having to clamber to the shabby, cramped apartments on the top floors.

Like shelter, clothing was a reliable social indicator. The poorest workingwomen in Paris wore woolen skirts and blouses of dark colors over petticoats, bodice, and corset. They also donned caps of various sorts, cotton stockings, and shoes (probably their only pair). Workingmen dressed even more drably. Many occupations could be recognized by their dress: no one could confuse lawyers in their dark robes with masons or butchers in their special

The Seedy Side of City Life

The English painter and engraver William Hogarth chronicled every aspect of social life in London. In Night *(1738), he completes a cycle of engravings about greed and carelessness in city life. The Salisbury Flying Coach has overturned in Charing Cross Road, narrowly missing a bonfire. Despite the statue of King Charles I in the background, this is a sordid street filled with taverns, a quack pulling teeth, and urchins up to no good. About to be showered with the contents of a chamber pot is a drunken magistrate known for his anti-alcohol legislation. He is oblivious to the ills of the city that surround him, but Hogarth knew them well.*
Carole Frohlich Archive.

aprons, for example. People higher on the social ladder were more likely to sport a variety of fabrics, colors, and unusual designs in their clothing and to own many different outfits. Social status was not an abstract idea; it permeated every detail of daily life.

The Growth of a Literate Public

The ability to read and write also reflected social differences. People in the upper classes were more literate than those in the lower classes; city people were more literate than peasants. Protestant countries appear to have been more successful at promoting education and literacy than Catholic

countries, perhaps because of the Protestant emphasis on Bible reading. Widespread popular literacy was first achieved in the Protestant areas of Switzerland and in Presbyterian Scotland, and rates were also very high in the New England colonies and the Scandinavian countries. In France, literacy doubled in the eighteenth century thanks to the spread of parish schools, but still only one in two men and one in four women could read and write. Despite the efforts of some Protestant German states to encourage primary education, primary schooling remained woefully inadequate almost everywhere in Europe: few schools existed, teachers received low wages, and no country had yet established a national system of control or supervision.

Despite the deficiencies of primary education, a new literate public arose especially among the middle classes of the cities. More books and periodicals were published than ever before. Britain and the Dutch Republic led the way in this powerful outpouring of printed words. The trend began in the 1690s and gradually accelerated. In 1695, the British government allowed the licensing system, through which it controlled publications, to lapse, and new newspapers and magazines appeared almost immediately. The first London daily newspaper came out in 1702, and in 1709 Joseph Addison and Richard Steele published the first literary magazine, *The Spectator*. They devoted their magazine to the cultural improvement of the increasingly influential middle class. By the 1720s, twenty-four provincial newspapers were published in England, and by the 1730s the new *Gentleman's Magazine*, a kind of *Reader's Digest* of news, literature, and humor, enjoyed a large national circulation. In the London coffeehouses, an edition of a single newspaper might reach ten thousand male readers. Women did their reading at home. Newspapers on the continent lagged behind and often consisted mainly of advertising with little critical commentary. France, for example, had no daily paper until 1777.

New Tastes in the Arts

The new literate public did not just read newspapers; its members now pursued an interest in painting, attended concerts, and besieged booksellers in search of popular novels. Because increased trade and prosperity put money into the hands of the growing middle classes, a new urban audience began to compete with the churches, rulers, and courtiers as chief patrons for new work. As the public for the arts expanded, printed commentary on them emerged, setting the stage for the appearance of political and social criticism. New artistic tastes thus had effects far beyond the realm of the arts.

Rococo Painting. Developments in painting reflected the tastes of the new public, as the rococo style challenged the hold of the baroque and classical schools, especially in France. Like the baroque, the rococo emphasized irregularity and asymmetry, movement and curvature, but it did so on a much smaller, subtler scale. Many rococo paintings depicted scenes of intimate sensuality rather than the monumental, emotional grandeur favored by classical and baroque painters. Personal portraits and pastoral paintings took the place of heroic landscapes and grand, ceremonial canvases. Rococo

paintings adorned homes as well as palaces and served as a form of interior decoration rather than as a statement of piety. Its decorative quality made rococo art an ideal complement to newly discovered materials such as stucco and porcelain, especially the porcelain vases now imported from China.

Rococo, like *baroque,* was an invented word (from the French word *rocaille,* meaning "shell-work") and originally a derogatory label, meaning "frivolous decoration." But the great French rococo painters, such as Antoine Watteau (1684–1721) and François Boucher (1703–1770), were much more than mere decorators. Although both emphasized the erotic in their depictions, Watteau captured the melancholy side of a passing aristocratic style of life, and Boucher painted middle-class people at home during their daily activities. Both painters thereby contributed to the emergence of new sensibilities in art that increasingly attracted a middle-class public.

Rococo Painting
Painted originally as a shop sign for an art merchant, Gersaint's Shopsign *(1721) by Antoine Watteau demonstrates the new rococo style. The colors are muted and the atmosphere is light and airy. The subject matter—the sale of art, gilded mirrors, and toiletries to the new urban aristocrats and middle classes—is entirely secular and even commercial. The canvas reflects the new urban market for art and slyly notes the passing of a era: a portrait of the recently deceased Louis XIV is being packed away on the left-hand side of the painting. Watteau painted the sign in eight days while suffering from the tuberculosis that would kill him just a few months later.*
Erich Lessing/Art Resource, NY.

Music for the Public. The first public music concerts were performed in England in the 1670s, becoming much more regular and frequent in the 1690s. City concert halls typically seated about two hundred, but the relatively high price of tickets limited attendance to the better-off. Music clubs provided entertainment in smaller towns and villages. On the continent, Frankfurt organized the first regular public concerts in 1712; Hamburg and Paris began holding them within a few years. Opera continued to spread in the eighteenth century; Venice had sixteen public opera houses by 1700, and in 1732 Covent Garden opera house opened in London.

The growth of a public that appreciated and supported music had much the same effect as the extension of the reading public: like authors, composers could now begin to liberate themselves from court patronage and work for a paying audience. This development took time to solidify, however, and court or church patrons still commissioned much eighteenth-century music. Bach, a German Lutheran, wrote his *St. Matthew Passion* for Good Friday services in 1729 while he was organist and choirmaster for the leading church in Leipzig. He composed secular works (like the "Coffee Cantata") for the public and a variety of private patrons.

The composer George Frederick Handel (1685–1759) was among the first to grasp the new directions in music. He began his career playing second violin in the Hamburg opera orchestra and then moved to Britain in 1710. After distinguishing himself with operas and music composed for the British court, he turned to composing oratorios, a form he introduced in Britain. The oratorio combined the drama of opera with the majesty of religious and ceremonial music and featured the chorus over the soloists. Handel's most famous oratorio, *Messiah* (1741), reflected his personal, deeply felt piety but also his willingness to combine musical materials into a dramatic form that captured the enthusiasm of the new public. In 1740, a poem published in the *Gentleman's Magazine* exulted: "His art so modulates the sounds in all, / Our passions, as he pleases, rise and fall." Music had become an integral part of the new middle-class public's culture.

Novels. Nothing captured the imagination of the new public more than the novel, the literary genre whose very name underscored the eighteenth-century taste for novelty. Over three hundred French novels appeared between 1700 and 1730. During this unprecedented explosion, the novel took on its modern form and became more concerned with individual psychology and social description than with the picaresque adventures popular earlier (such as Cervantes's *Don Quixote*). The novel's popularity was closely tied to the expansion of the reading public, and novels were available in serial form in periodicals or from the many booksellers who popped up to serve the new market.

Women figured prominently in novels as characters, and women writers abounded. The English novel *Love in Excess* (1719) quickly reached a sixth printing, and its author, Eliza Haywood (1693?–1756), earned her living turning out a stream of novels with titles such as *Persecuted Virtue, Constancy Rewarded,* and *The History of Betsy Thoughtless*—all showing a concern for the proper place of women as models of virtue in a changing world. Heywood had first worked as an actress when her husband deserted her and her two children, but she soon turned to writing plays and novels. In the 1740s, she began publishing a magazine, *The Female Spectator*, which argued in favor of higher education for women.

Haywood's male counterpart was Daniel Defoe (1660?–1731), a merchant's son who had a diverse and colorful career as a manufacturer, political spy, novelist, and social commentator. Defoe wrote about schemes for national improvement, the state of English trade, the economic condition of the countryside, the effects of the plague, and the history of pirates, as well as such novels as *Robinson Crusoe* (1719) and *Moll Flanders* (1722). The story of the adventures of a shipwrecked sailor, *Robinson Crusoe* portrayed the new values of the time: to survive, Crusoe had to meet every challenge with fearless entrepreneurial ingenuity. He had to be ready for the unexpected and be able to improvise in every situation. He was, in short, the model for the new man in an expanding economy. Crusoe's patronizing attitude toward the black man Friday now draws much critical attention, but his discovery of Friday shows how the fate of blacks and whites had become intertwined in the new colonial environment.

Religious Revivals

Despite the novel's growing popularity, religious books and pamphlets still sold in huge numbers, and most Europeans remained devout, even as their religions were changing. In this period a Protestant revival known as Pietism rocked the complacency of the established churches in the German Lutheran states, the Dutch Republic, and Scandinavia. Pietists believed in a mystical religion of the heart; they wanted a more deeply emotional, even ecstatic religion. They urged intense Bible study, which in turn promoted popular education and contributed to the increase in literacy. Many Pietists attended catechism instruction every day and also went to morning and evening prayer meetings in addition to regular Sunday services.

As a grassroots movement, Pietism appealed to both Lutherans and Calvinists, some of whom left their churches to form new sects. One of the most remarkable disciples of Pietism was the English woman Jane Leade (1623–1704), who founded the sect of Philadelphians (from the Greek for "brotherly love"), which soon spread to the Dutch Republic and the German states. Leade's visions and studies of mysticism led her to advocate a universal, nondogmatic church that would include all reborn Christians. Philadelphic societies maintained only loose ties to one another, however, and despite Leade's organizational aims they soon went off in different directions.

Catholicism also had its versions of religious revival, especially in France. A French woman, Jeanne Marie Guyon (1648–1717), attracted many noblewomen and a few leading clergymen to her own Catholic brand of Pietism, known as Quietism. Claiming miraculous visions and astounding prophecies, she urged a mystical union with God through prayer and simple devotion. Despite papal condemnation and intense controversy within Catholic circles in France, Guyon had followers all over Europe.

Even more influential were the Jansenists, who gained many new adherents to their austere form of Catholicism despite Louis XIV's harassment and repeated condemnation by the papacy. Under the pressure of religious and political persecution, Jansenism took a revivalist turn in the 1720s. At the funeral of a Jansenist priest in Paris in 1727, the crowd who flocked to the grave claimed to witness a series of miraculous healings. Within a few years a cult formed around the priest's tomb, and clandestine Jansenist presses reported new miracles to the reading public. When the French government tried to suppress the cult, one enraged wit placed a

sign at the tomb that read, "By order of the king, God is forbidden to work miracles here." Some believers fell into frenzied convulsions, claiming to be inspired by the Holy Spirit through the intercession of the dead priest. Although the Catholic church, the French state, and even some Jansenists ultimately repudiated the new cult, its remarkable emotional power showed that popular expressions of religion could not be easily contained. After midcentury, Jansenism became even more politically active as its adherents joined in opposition to crown policies on religion.

❖ Consolidation of the European State System

The spread of Pietism and Jansenism reflected the emergence of a middle-class public that now participated in every new development, including religion. The middle classes could pursue these interests because the European state system gradually stabilized. Warfare settled three main issues between 1690 and 1740: a coalition of powers held Louis XIV's France in check on the continent; Great Britain emerged from the wars against Louis as the preeminent maritime power; and Russia defeated Sweden in the contest for supremacy in the Baltic. After Louis XIV's death in 1715, Europe enjoyed the fruits of a more balanced diplomatic system, in which warfare became less frequent and less widespread. States could then spend their resources establishing and expanding control over their own populations, both at home and in their colonies.

The Limits of French Absolutism

When the seventy-six-year-old Louis XIV lay on his deathbed suffering from constipation and gangrene in 1715, he must have felt depressed by the unraveling of his accomplishments. Not only had his plans for territorial expansion been thwarted, but his incessant wars had exhausted the treasury, despite new taxes. In 1689, Louis's rival, William III, prince of Orange and king of England and Scotland (r. 1689–1702), had set out to forge a European alliance that eventually included Britain, the Dutch Republic, Sweden, Austria, and Spain. The allies fought Louis to a stalemate in the War of the League of Augsburg, sometimes called the Nine Years' War (1689–1697), but hostilities resumed four years later in the War of the Spanish Succession, which brought France's expansionist ambitions to a grinding halt.

The War of the Spanish Succession, 1701–1713. When the mentally and physically feeble Charles II (r. 1665–1700) of Spain died in 1700 without a direct heir, all of Europe poised for a fight over the spoils. The Spanish succession could not help but be a burning issue, given Spain's extensive territories in Italy and the Netherlands and colonies overseas. It seemed a plum ripe for picking. Spanish power had declined steadily since its golden age in the sixteenth century: the gold and silver of the New World had been exhausted, and the Spanish kings neglected manufactures, debased their coinage, and failed to adopt the new scientific ideas and commercial practices developed by the Dutch and the British. As a consequence, they lacked the resources for international competition.

Before Charles died, he named Louis XIV's second grandson, Philip, duke of Anjou, as his heir, but his bequest resolved nothing. Louis XIV and the Austrian emperor Leopold I had competing dynastic claims to the Spanish crown, and Leopold refused to accept Charles's deathbed will. The ensuing War of the Spanish Succession proved disastrous for the French because most of Europe once again allied against them, fearing the consequences of French control over Spanish territories. The French lost several major battles and had to accept disadvantageous terms in the Peace of Utrecht of 1713–1714 (Map 18.2). Although Philip was recognized as king of Spain, he had to renounce any future claim to the French crown, thus barring unification of the two kingdoms. Spain surrendered its territories in Italy and the Netherlands to the Austrians and Gibraltar to the British; France ceded possessions in North America (Newfoundland, the Hudson Bay area, and most of Nova Scotia) to Britain. France no longer threatened to dominate European power politics.

The Death of Louis XIV and the Regency. At home, Louis's policy of absolutism had fomented bitter hostility. Nobles fiercely resented his promotions of commoners to high office. The duke of Saint-Simon complained that "falseness, servility, admiring glances, combined with a dependent and cringing attitude, above all, an appearance of being nothing without him, were the only ways of pleasing him." Even some of the king's leading servants, such as Archbishop Fénelon, who tutored the king's grandson, began to call for monarchical reform. An admirer of Guyon's Quietism, Fénelon severely criticized the court's excesses: the "steady stream of extravagant adulation, which reaches the point of idolatry"; the constant, bloody wars; and the misery of the people.

On his deathbed, Louis XIV gave his blessing and some sound advice to his five-year-old great-grandson and successor, Louis XV (r. 1715–1774): "My child, you are about to become a great King. Do not imitate my love of building nor my liking for war." Squabbling over control of the crown began immediately. The duke of Orléans (1674–1723), nephew of the dead king, was named regent. He revived some of the parlements' powers and tried to give leading nobles a greater say in political affairs as a way to restore confidence and appease aristocratic critics. The regent also moved the court back to Paris, away from the atmosphere of moral rigidity and prudery that Louis had enforced in his last years at Versailles.

Financial problems plagued the Regency as they would beset all succeeding French regimes in the eighteenth century. In 1719, the regent appointed the Scottish adventurer and financier John Law to the top financial position of controller-general. Law founded a trading company for North America and a state bank that issued paper money and stock (without them trade depended on the available supply of gold and silver). The bank was supposed to offer lower interest rates to the state, thus cutting the cost of financing the government's debts. The value of the stock rose rapidly in a frenzy of speculation, only to crash a few months later. With it vanished any hope of establishing a state bank or issuing paper money for nearly a century.

France finally achieved a measure of financial stability under the leadership of Cardinal Hercule de Fleury (1653–1743), the most powerful member of the government after the death of the regent. Fleury aimed to avoid adventure abroad and keep social peace at home; he balanced the budget and carried out a large project for road and canal construction. Colonial trade boomed. Peace and the acceptance of limits on territorial expansion inaugurated a century of French prosperity.

English and French Claims after the Peace of Utrecht, 1714

Hudson Bay

Newfoundland

English claim

French claim

English claim

Nova Scotia

SWEDEN

St. Petersburg

Moscow

DENMARK-NORWAY

Baltic Sea

SCOTLAND

Edinburgh

North Sea

IRELAND

Dublin

GREAT BRITAIN

ENGLAND

London

Utrecht

DUTCH REPUBLIC

Hanover

BRANDENBURG-PRUSSIA

Berlin

Elbe R.

POLAND-LITHUANIA

Warsaw

RUSSIA

Kiev

English Channel

Austrian Neth.

Cologne

Rhine R.

HOLY ROMAN EMPIRE

Vistula R.

ATLANTIC OCEAN

Paris

Loire R.

FRANCE

SWISS CONFED.

AUSTRIA

Vienna

Buda

Pest

HUNGARY

Danube R.

SAVOY

MILAN VENICE

GENOA

Marseille

TUSCANY PAPAL STATES

Corsica

Rome

Black Sea

OTTOMAN EMPIRE

Constantinople

PORTUGAL

Madrid

SPAIN

Lisbon

Minorca (Gr. Br.)

BALEARIC IS.

Sardinia

KINGDOM OF NAPLES

Gibraltar (Gr. Br.)

Sicily

Mediterranean Sea

0   200   400 miles

0   200   400 kilometers

0   500   1000 miles

0   500   1000 kilometers

Territories gained after the Peace of Utrecht, 1714

- French Bourbon lands
- Spanish Bourbon lands
- Austrian Habsburg lands
- Prussian lands
- Great Britain
- To Great Britain
- To the Austrian Empire
- The Jacobite rising of 1715
- Main areas of fighting during the War of the Spanish Succession, 1701–1713
- Boundary of the Holy Roman Empire

MAP 18.2 Europe, c. 1715

Although Louis XIV succeeded in putting his grandson Philip on the Spanish throne, France emerged considerably weakened from the War of Spanish Succession. France ceded large territories in Canada to Britain, which also gained key Mediterranean outposts from Spain, as well as a monopoly on providing slaves to the Spanish colonies. Spanish losses were catastrophic. Philip had to renounce any future claim to the French crown and give up considerable territories in the Netherlands and Italy to the Austrians.

British Rise and Dutch Decline

The British and the Dutch had joined in a coalition against Louis XIV under their joint ruler William III, who was simultaneously stadholder of the Dutch Republic and, with his English wife, Mary (d. 1694), ruler of England, Wales, and Scotland. After William's death in 1702, the British and Dutch went their separate ways. Over the next decades, the English monarchy incorporated Scotland and subjugated Ireland, becoming "Great Britain." At the same time Dutch imperial power declined; even though Dutch merchants still controlled a substantial portion of world trade, by 1700 Great Britain dominated the seas and the Dutch, with their small population of less than two million, came to depend on alliances with bigger powers.

From England to Great Britain. English relations with Scotland and Ireland were complicated by the problem of succession: William and Mary had no children. To ensure a Protestant succession, Parliament ruled that Mary's sister, Anne, would succeed William and Mary and that the Protestant House of Hanover in Germany would succeed Anne if she had no surviving heirs. Catholics were excluded. When Queen Anne (r. 1702–1714) died leaving no children, the elector of Hanover, a Protestant great-grandson of James I, consequently became King George I (r. 1714–1727). The House of Hanover—it was renamed the House of Windsor during World War I—still occupies the British throne.

Support from the Scots and Irish for this solution did not come easily because many in Scotland and Ireland supported the claims to the throne of the deposed Catholic king, James II, and, after his death in 1701, his son James Edward. Out of fear of this "Jacobitism" (from the Latin *Jacobus* for "James"), Scottish Protestant leaders agreed to the Act of Union of 1707, which abolished the Scottish Parliament and affirmed the Scots' recognition of the Protestant Hanoverian succession. The Scots agreed to obey the Parliament of Great Britain, which would include Scottish members in the House of Commons and the House of Lords. A Jacobite rebellion in Scotland in 1715, aiming to restore the Stuart line, was suppressed. The threat of Jacobitism nonetheless continued into the 1740s.

The Irish—90 percent of whom were Catholic—proved even more difficult to subdue. When James

II had gone to Ireland in 1689 to raise a Catholic rebellion against the new monarchs of England, William III responded by taking command of the joint English and Dutch forces and defeating James's Irish supporters. James fled to France, and the Catholics in Ireland faced yet more confiscation and legal restrictions. By 1700, Irish Catholics, who in 1640 had owned 60 percent of the land in Ireland, owned just 14 percent. The Protestant-controlled Irish Parliament passed a series of laws limiting the rights of the Catholic majority: Catholics could not bear arms, send their children abroad for education, establish Catholic schools at home, or marry Protestants. Catholics could not sit in Parliament, nor could they vote for its members unless they took an oath renouncing Catholic doctrine. These and a host of other laws reduced Catholic Ireland to the status of a colony; one English official commented in 1745, "The poor people of Ireland are used worse than negroes." Most of the Irish were peasants who lived in primitive housing and subsisted on a meager diet that included no meat.

The Parliament of Great Britain was soon dominated by the Whigs. In Britain's constitutional system, the monarch ruled with Parliament. The crown chose the ministers, directed policy, and supervised administration, while Parliament raised revenue, passed laws, and represented the interests of the people to the crown. The powers of Parliament were reaffirmed by the Triennial Act in 1694, which provided that Parliaments meet at least once every three years (this was extended to seven years in 1716, after the Whigs had established their ascendancy). Only 200,000 propertied men could vote, out of a population of more than 5 million people, and, not surprisingly, most members of Parliament came from the landed gentry. In fact, a few hundred families controlled all the important political offices.

George I and George II (r. 1727–1760) relied on one man, Sir Robert Walpole (1676–1745), to help them manage their relations with Parliament. From his position as First Lord of the Treasury, Walpole made himself into first or "prime" minister, leading the House of Commons from 1721 to 1742. Although appointed initially by the king, Walpole established an enduring pattern of parliamentary government in which a prime minister from the leading party guided legislation through the House of Commons. Walpole also built a vast patronage machine that dispensed government jobs to win

Sir Robert Walpole at a Cabinet Meeting
Sir Robert Walpole and George II developed government by a cabinet, which consisted of Walpole as first lord of the treasury, the two secretaries of state, the lord chancellor, the chancellor of the exchequer, the lord privy seal, and the lord president of the council. Walpole's cabinet was the ancestor of modern cabinets in both Great Britain and the United States. Its similarities to modern forms should not be overstated, however. The entire staff of the two secretaries of state, who had charge of all foreign and domestic affairs other than taxation, numbered twenty-four in 1726.
The Fotomas Index, U.K.

support for the crown's policies. Some complained that his patronage system corrupted politics, but Walpole successfully used his political skills to convince the ruling class not to rock its own boat. Walpole's successors relied more and more on the patronage system and eventually alienated not only the Tories but also the middle classes in London and even the North American colonies.

The partisan division between the Whigs, who supported the Hanoverian succession and the rights of dissenting Protestants, and the Tories, who had backed the Stuart line and the Anglican church, did not hamper Great Britain's pursuit of economic, military, and colonial power. In this period, Great Britain became a great power on the world stage by virtue of its navy and its ability to finance major military involvement in the wars against Louis XIV. The founding in 1694 of the Bank of England—which, unlike the French bank, endured—enabled the government to raise money at low interest for foreign wars. The bank's success can be measured by the amount of money it lent in wartime: by the 1740s, the government could borrow more than four times what it could in the 1690s.

The Dutch Eclipse. When William of Orange (William III of England) died in 1702, he left no heirs, and for forty-five years the Dutch lived without a stadholder. The merchant ruling class of some two thousand families dominated the Dutch Republic more than ever, but they presided over a country that counted for less in international power politics. In some areas, Dutch decline was only relative: the Dutch population was not growing as fast as others, for example, and the Dutch share of the Baltic trade decreased from 50 percent in 1720 to less than 30 percent by the 1770s. After 1720, the Baltic countries—Prussia, Russia, Denmark, and Sweden—began to ban imports of manufactured goods to protect their own industries, and Dutch trade in particular suffered. The output of Leiden textiles dropped to one-third of its 1700 level by 1740. Shipbuilding, paper manufacturing, tobacco processing, salt refining, and pottery production all dwindled as well. The Dutch East India Company saw its political and military grip loosened in India, Ceylon, and Java.

The biggest exception to the downward trend was trade with the New World, which increased with escalating demands for sugar and tobacco. The Dutch shifted their interest away from great power rivalries toward those areas of international trade and finance where they could establish an enduring presence.

Russia's Emergence as a European Power

Dutch and British commerce and shipbuilding so impressed Russian tsar Peter I (r. 1689–1725) that he traveled incognito to their shipyards in 1697 to learn their methods firsthand. But the tsar intended to build a strong absolutist state in Russia, avoiding the weaknesses of decentralization that plagued the Dutch. As Britain gained dominance on the seas in the West, Peter aimed for dominance on land in the East. Known to history as Peter the Great, he dragged Russia kicking and screaming all the way to great power status. Although he came to the throne while still a minor (on the eve of his tenth birthday), grew up under the threat of a palace coup, and enjoyed little formal education, his accomplishments soon matched his seven-foot-tall stature. Peter transformed public life in Russia and established an absolutist state on the western model. His westernization efforts ignited an enduring controversy: did Peter set Russia on a course of inevitable westernization required to compete with the West, or did he forever and fatally disrupt Russia's natural evolution into a distinctive Slavic society?

Peter the Great's Brand of Absolutism.   Peter reorganized government and finance on western models; he streamlined the ministries and assigned each a foreign adviser. Like other absolute rulers, he strengthened his army. With ruthless recruiting methods, which included branding a cross on every recruit's left hand to prevent desertion, he forged an army of 200,000 men and equipped it with modern weapons. He created schools for artillery, engineering, and military medicine and built the first navy in Russian history. Not surprisingly, taxes tripled.

The tsar allowed nothing to stand in his way. He did not hesitate to use torture and executed thousands. He allowed a special guards regiment unprecedented power to expedite cases against those suspected of rebellion, espionage, pretensions to the throne, or just "unseemly utterances" against him. Opposition to his policies reached into his own family: because his only son, Alexei, had allied himself with Peter's critics, he threw him into prison, where the young man mysteriously died.

To control the often restive nobility, Peter insisted that all noblemen engage in state service. A Table of Ranks (1722) classified them into military, administrative, and court categories, a codification of social and legal relationships in Russia that would last for nearly two centuries. All social and material advantages now depended on serving the crown. Because the nobles lacked a secure independent status, Peter could command them to a degree that was unimaginable in western Europe. State service was

Peter the Great Modernizes Russia
In this popular print, a barber forces a protesting noble to conform to Western fashions. (The barber is sometimes erroneously identified as Peter himself.) Peter ordered all nobles, merchants, and middle-class professionals to cut off their beards or pay a huge tax to keep them. An early biographer of Peter, the French writer Jean Rousset de Missy (1730), claimed that those who lost their beards saved them to put in their coffins, in fear that they would not enter heaven without them. Most western Europeans applauded these attempts to change Russian customs, but many Russians deeply resented the attack on traditional ways.
Carole Frohlich Archive.

not only compulsory but also permanent. Moreover, the male children of those in service had to be registered by the age of ten and begin serving at fifteen. To increase his authority over the Russian Orthodox church, Peter allowed the office of patriarch (supreme head) to remain vacant, and in 1721 he replaced it with the Holy Synod, a bureaucracy of laymen under his supervision. To many Russians, Peter was the Antichrist incarnate.

Westernization.   With the goal of Westernizing Russian culture, Peter set up the first greenhouses, laboratories, and technical schools and founded the

Russian Academy of Sciences. He ordered translations of western classics and hired a German theater company to perform the French plays of Molière. He replaced the traditional Russian calendar with the western one,* introduced Arabic numerals, and brought out the first public newspaper. He ordered his officials and the nobles to shave their beards and dress in western fashion, and he even issued precise regulations about the suitable style of jacket, boots, and cap (generally French or German). He published a book on manners for young noblemen and experimented with dentistry on his courtiers.

Peter did not undertake these reforms alone. Elite men who were eager for social mobility and willing to adopt Western values cooperated with him. Peter encouraged foreigners to move to Russia to offer their advice and skills, especially for building the new capital city, St. Petersburg. The new capital, named after Peter, was meant to symbolize Russia's opening to the West. Construction began in 1703 in a Baltic province that had been recently conquered from Sweden. By the end of 1709, forty thousand recruits a year found themselves assigned to the work. Peter ordered skilled workers to move to the new city and commanded all landowners possessing more than forty serf households to build houses there. In the 1720s, a German minister described the city "as a wonder of the world, considering its magnificent palaces, . . . and the short time that was employed in the building of it." By 1710, the permanent population of St. Petersburg reached eight thousand. At Peter's death in 1725, it had forty thousand residents.

As a new city far from the Russian heartland around Moscow, St. Petersburg represented a decisive break with Russia's past. Peter widened that gap by every means possible. At his new capital he tried to improve the traditionally denigrated, secluded status of women by ordering them to dress in European styles and appear publicly at his dinners for diplomatic representatives. Imitating French manners, he decreed that women attend his new social salons of officials, officers, and merchants for con-

Russian Rococo
Peter the Great's insistence on incorporating western European influences extended even to tableware. This silver tureen might have been fashioned in Paris or any other western European center of decorative art. Its motifs and trim reveal rococo influences.
State Historical Museum, St. Petersburg.

versation and dancing. A foreigner headed every one of Peter's new technical and vocational schools, and for its first eight years the new Academy of Sciences included no Russians. Upper-class Russians learned French or German, which they often spoke even at home. Such changes affected only the very top of Russian society, however; the mass of the population had no contact with the new ideas and ended up paying for the innovations either in ruinous new taxation or by building St. Petersburg, a project that cost the lives of thousands of workers. Serfs remained tied to the land, completely dominated by their noble lords.

Despite all his achievements, Peter could not ensure his succession. In the thirty-seven years after his death in 1725, Russia endured six different rulers: three women, a boy of twelve, an infant, and an imbecile. Recurrent palace coups weakened the monarchy and enabled the nobility to loosen Peter's rigid code of state service. In the process the serfs' status only worsened. They ceased to be counted as legal subjects; the criminal code of 1754 listed them as property. They not only were bought and sold like cattle but also had become legally indistinguishable from them. Westernization had not yet touched the lives of the serfs.

The Balance of Power in the East

Peter the Great's success in building up state power changed the balance of power in eastern Europe. Overcoming initial military setbacks, Russia eventually defeated Sweden and took its place as the

---

*Peter introduced the Julian calendar, then still used in Protestant but not Catholic countries. Later in the eighteenth century, Protestant Europe abandoned the Julian for the Gregorian calendar. Not until 1918 was the Julian calendar abolished in Russia, at which point it had fallen thirteen days behind Europe's Gregorian calendar.

leading power in the Baltic region. Russia could then turn its attention to eastern Europe, where it competed with Austria and Prussia. Once mighty Poland-Lithuania became the playground for great power rivalries.

The Decline of Sweden. Sweden had dominated the Baltic region since the Thirty Years' War and did not easily give up its preeminence. When Peter the Great joined an anti-Swedish coalition in 1700 with Denmark, Saxony, and Poland, Sweden's Charles XII (r. 1697–1718) stood up to the test. Still in his teens at the beginning of the Great Northern War, Charles first defeated Denmark, then destroyed the new Russian army, and quickly marched into Poland and Saxony. After defeating the Poles and occupying Saxony, Charles invaded Russia. Here Peter's rebuilt army finally defeated him at the battle of Poltava (1709).

The Russian victory resounded everywhere. The Russian ambassador to Vienna reported, "It is commonly said that the tsar will be formidable to all Europe, that he will be a kind of northern Turk." Prussia and other German states joined the anti-Swedish alliance, and war resumed. Charles XII died in battle in 1718, and complex negotiations finally ended the Great Northern War. By the terms of the

Treaty of Nystad (1721), Sweden ceded its eastern Baltic provinces—Livonia, Estonia, Ingria, and southern Karelia—to Russia. Sweden also lost territories on the north German coast to Prussia and the other allied German states (Map 18.3). An aristocratic reaction against Charles XII's incessant demands for war supplies swept away Sweden's absolutist regime, essentially removing Sweden from great power competition.

Prussian Militarization. Prussia had to make the most of every military opportunity, as it did in the Great Northern War, because it was much smaller in size and population than Russia, Austria, or France. King Frederick William I (r. 1713–1740) doubled the size of the Prussian army; though much smaller than those of his rivals, it was the best-trained and most up-to-date force in Europe. By 1740, Prussia had Europe's highest proportion of men at arms (1 of every 28 people, versus 1 in 157 in France and 1 in 64 in Russia) and the highest proportion of nobles in the military (1 in 7 noblemen, as compared with 1 in 33 in France and 1 in 50 in Russia).

The army so dominated life in Prussia that the country earned the label "a large army with a small state attached." So obsessed was he with his soldiers

MAP 18.3 Russia and Sweden after the Great Northern War, 1721
After the Great Northern War, Russia supplanted Sweden as the major power in the north. Although Russia had a much larger population from which to draw its armies, Sweden made the most of its advantages and gave way only after a great military struggle.

that the five-foot-five-inch-tall Frederick William formed a regiment of "giants," the Grenadiers, composed exclusively of men over six feet tall. Royal agents scoured Europe trying to find such men and sometimes kidnapped them right off the street. Frederick William, the "Sergeant King," was one of the first rulers to wear a military uniform as his everyday dress. He subordinated the entire domestic administration to the army's needs. He also installed a system for recruiting soldiers by local district quotas. He financed the army's growth by subjecting all the provinces to an excise tax on food, drink, and manufactured goods and by increasing rents on crown lands. Prussia was now poised to become one of the major players on the continent.

The War of Polish Succession, 1733–1735. Prussia did not enter into military conflict foolishly. During the War of Polish Succession it stood on the sidelines, content to watch others fight. The war showed how the balance of power had changed since the heyday of Louis XIV: France had to maneuver within a complex great power system that now included Russia, and Poland-Lithuania no longer controlled its own destiny. When the king of Poland-Lithuania died in 1733, France, Spain, and Sardinia went to war against Austria and Russia, each side supporting rival claimants to the Polish throne.

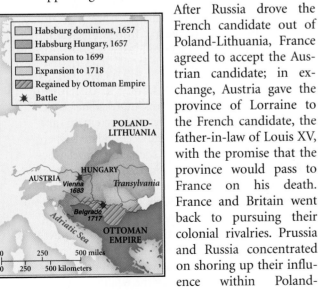

After Russia drove the French candidate out of Poland-Lithuania, France agreed to accept the Austrian candidate; in exchange, Austria gave the province of Lorraine to the French candidate, the father-in-law of Louis XV, with the promise that the province would pass to France on his death. France and Britain went back to pursuing their colonial rivalries. Prussia and Russia concentrated on shoring up their influence within Poland-Lithuania.

Austrian Conquest of Hungary, 1657–1730

Austria did not want to become mired in a long struggle in Poland-Lithuania because its armies still faced the Turks on its southeastern border. Even though the Austrians had forced the Turks to recognize their rule over all of Hungary and Transylvania in 1699 and occupied Belgrade in 1717, the Turks did not stop fighting. In the 1730s, the Turks retook Belgrade, and Russia now claimed a role in the struggle against the Turks. Moreover, Hungary, though "liberated" from Turkish rule, proved less than enthusiastic about submitting to Austria. In 1703, the wealthiest Hungarian noble landlord, Ferenc Rákóczi (1676–1735), led a combined noble and peasant revolt against the Austrians. Rákóczi raised an army of seventy thousand men who pledged to fight for "God, Fatherland, and Liberty." Although the rebels did not win the ensuing war, which lasted until 1711, they forced the Austrians to recognize local Hungarian institutions, grant amnesty, and restore confiscated estates in exchange for confirming hereditary Austrian rule. Austria had more than sufficient reason to avoid committing itself to a long war against France.

The Power of Diplomacy

No single power emerged from the wars of the first half of the eighteenth century clearly superior to the others, and the idea of maintaining a balance of power guided both military and diplomatic maneuvering. The Peace of Utrecht had explicitly declared that such a balance was crucial to maintaining peace in Europe, and in 1720 a British pamphleteer wrote, "There is not, I believe, any doctrine in the law of nations, of more certain truth . . . than this of the balance of power." It was the law of gravity of European politics. This system of equilibrium often rested on military force, such as the leagues formed against Louis XIV or the coalition against Sweden. All states counted on diplomacy, however, to resolve issues even after fighting had begun.

To meet the new demands placed on it, the diplomatic service, like the military and financial bureaucracies before it, had to develop regular procedures. The French set a pattern of diplomatic service that the other European states soon imitated. By 1685, France had embassies in all the important capitals. Nobles of ancient families served as ambassadors to Rome, Madrid, Vienna, and London, whereas royal officials were chosen for Switzerland, the Dutch Republic, and Venice. Most held their appointments for at least three or four years, and all went off with elaborate written instructions that included explicit statements of policy as well as full accounts of the political conditions of the country to which they were posted. The ambassador selected and paid for his own staff. This practice could make the journey to a new post very cumbersome, because the staff might be as large as eighty people, and they brought along all their own furniture, pictures, silverware, and tapestries. It took one French ambassador ten weeks to get from Paris to Stockholm.

By the early 1700s, French writings on diplomatic methods were read everywhere. François de Callières's manual *On the Manner of Negotiating with Sovereigns* (1716) insisted that sound diplomacy was based on the creation of confidence, rather than deception: "The secret of negotiation is to harmonize the real interests of the parties concerned." Callières believed that the diplomatic service had to be professional—that young attachés should be chosen for their skills, not their family connections. These sensible views did not prevent the development of a dual system of diplomacy, in which rulers issued secret instructions that often negated the official ones sent by their own foreign offices. Secret diplomacy had some advantages because it allowed rulers to break with past alliances, but it also led to confusion and, sometimes, scandal, for the rulers often employed unreliable adventurers as their confidential agents. Still, the diplomatic system in the early eighteenth century proved successful enough to ensure a continuation of the principles of the Peace of Westphalia (1648); in the midst of every crisis and war, the great powers would convene and hammer out a written agreement detailing the requirements for peace.

The Power of Numbers

Successful diplomacy could smooth the road toward peace, but success in war still depended on sheer numbers—of men and muskets. Because each state's strength depended largely on the size of its army, the growth and health of the population increasingly entered into government calculations. The publication in 1690 of the Englishman William Petty's *Political Arithmetick* quickened the interest of government officials everywhere; Petty offered statistical estimates of human capital—that is, of pop-

ulation and wages—to determine Britain's national wealth. This "political arithmetic" inevitably drew attention to public health issues. Although hospitals were transformed in this period from public charities into medical institutions focused more narrowly on disease, health care remained precarious at best.

Political Arithmetic.   A large, growing population could be as vital to a state's future as access to silver mines or overseas trade, so government officials devoted increased effort to the statistical estimation of total population and rates of births, deaths, marriages, and fertility. In 1727, Frederick William I of Prussia founded two university chairs to encourage population studies, and textbooks and handbooks advocated state intervention to improve the population's health and welfare.

Physicians used the new population statistics to explain the environmental causes of disease, another new preoccupation in this period. Petty devised a quantitative scale that distinguished healthy from unhealthy places largely on the basis of air quality, an early precursor of modern environmental studies. After investigating specific cities, German medical geographers urged government campaigns to improve public sanitation. Everywhere, environmentalists gathered and analyzed data on climate, disease, and population, searching for correlations to help direct policy. As a result of these efforts, local governments undertook such measures as draining low-lying areas, burying refuse, and cleaning wells, all of which eventually helped lower the death rates from epidemic diseases.

Public Hygiene and Health Care.   Urban growth made public hygiene problems more acute. Cities were the unhealthiest places because excrement (animal and human) and garbage accumulated where people lived densely packed together. A traveler described the streets of Madrid in 1697 as "always very dirty because it is the custom to throw all the rubbish out of the window." Paris seemed to a visitor "so detestable that it is impossible to remain there" because of the smell; even the facade of the Louvre palace in Paris was soiled by the contents of night commodes that servants routinely dumped out of windows every morning. Only the wealthy could escape walking in mucky streets, by hiring men to carry them in sedan chairs or to drive them in coaches.

Founded originally as charities concerned foremost with the moral worthiness of the poor, hospitals gradually evolved into medical institutions that defined patients by their diseases. The process of diagnosis changed as physicians began to use specialized Latin terms for illnesses. The gap between medical experts and their patients increased, as physicians now also relied on postmortem dissections in the hospital to gain better knowledge, a practice most patients' families resented. Press reports of body snatching and grave robbing by surgeons and their apprentices outraged the public well into the 1800s.

Despite the change in hospitals, individual health care remained something of a free-for-all in which physicians competed with bloodletters, itinerant venereal-disease doctors, bonesetters, druggists, midwives, and "cunning women," who specialized in home remedies. Physicians often followed popular prescriptions for illnesses because they had nothing better to offer. Recipes for cures were part of most people's everyday conversation. The various "medical" opinions about childbirth highlight the confusion people faced. Midwives delivered most babies, though they sometimes encountered criticism, even from within their own ranks. One consulting midwife complained that ordinary midwives in Bristol, England, made women in labor drink a mixture of their husband's urine and leek juice. By the 1730s, female midwives faced competition from male midwives, who were known for using instruments such as forceps to pull the baby out of the birth canal. Women rarely sought a physician's help in giving birth, however; they preferred the advice and assistance of trusted local midwives. In any case, trained physicians were few in number and almost nonexistent outside cities.

Public and private hygiene improved only gradually. Patients were as likely to die of diseases caught in the hospital as to be cured there. Antiseptics were virtually unknown. The wealthy preferred treatment at home, sometimes by private physicians. The medical profession, with nationwide organizations and licensing, had not yet emerged, and no clear line separated trained physicians from quacks. For example, if a woman of the prosperous classes had breast cancer, she could have a doctor remove the breast tumors in a short, painful operation without anesthesia; but many opted instead to use folk remedies such as a plaster of mutton suet, beeswax, and flaxseed. Unfortunately, usually neither the surgery nor the concoctions proved effective.

Insanity was treated as a physical rather than an emotional ailment. Doctors believed most madness was caused by "melancolia," a condition they attributed to disorders in the system of bodily "humors." Their prescribed treatments included blood transfusions; ingestion of bitter substances such as coffee, quinine, and even soap; immersion in water; various forms of exercise; and burning or cauterizing the body to allow black vapors to escape.

Hardly any infectious diseases could be cured, though inoculation against smallpox spread from the Middle East to Europe in the early eighteenth century, thanks largely to the efforts of Lady Mary Wortley Montagu, who learned about the technique while living in Constantinople. (See "Did You Know?," page 674.) After 1750, physicians developed successful procedures for wide-scale vaccination, although even then many people resisted the idea of inoculating themselves with a disease. Other diseases spread quickly in the unsanitary conditions of urban life. Ordinary people washed or changed clothes rarely, lived in overcrowded housing with poor ventilation, and got their water from contaminated sources, such as refuse-filled rivers.

Until the mid-1700s, most people considered bathing dangerous. Public bathhouses had disappeared from cities in the sixteenth and seventeenth centuries because they seemed a source of disorderly behavior and epidemic illness. In the eighteenth century, even private bathing came into disfavor because people feared the effects of contact with water. Fewer than one in ten newly built private mansions in Paris had baths. Bathing was hazardous, physicians insisted, because it opened the body to disease. One manners manual of 1736 admonished, "It is correct to clean the face every morning by using a white cloth to cleanse it. It is less good to wash with water, because it renders the face susceptible to cold in winter and sun in summer." The upper classes associated cleanliness not with baths but with frequently changed linens, powdered hair, and perfume, which was thought to strengthen the body and refresh the brain by counteracting corrupt and foul air.

Lady Mary Wortley Montagu and Inoculation for Smallpox

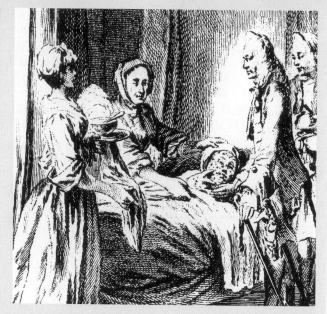

The Scourge of Smallpox

This engraving from a hospital report of 1750 shows a patient being tended in a smallpox hospital for the poor in London. The patient's face has been disfigured by the disease.
British Museum.

Daughter of a duke, wife of an ambassador, and mother-in-law of a prime minister, Lady Mary Wortley Montagu (1689–1762) might have confined herself to socializing in the highest circles and managing a large household. But her life changed as a result of two unexpected circumstances: in 1715 she caught smallpox, which left her disfigured by pitted skin and the loss of her eyelashes (her brother died of the dread disease); and in 1716 her husband was named the British ambassador to the Ottoman Empire. She undertook the long voyage with him and wrote letters filled with vivid descriptions of life in eastern Europe and the Ottoman Empire. She returned from Constantinople in 1718, determined to introduce a Turkish invention, inoculation against smallpox. Lady Mary studied inoculation in several Turkish towns and tried it on her son while still in the Ottoman Empire. In 1717, she wrote a friend describing how inoculation was carried out by old women who used needles to prick the skin with smallpox "venom." The children fell ill after eight days but recovered completely.

In 1721, when a new smallpox epidemic threatened England, Lady Mary called on her physician to inoculate her daughter with two additional physicians attending as witnesses. One of the observers immediately inoculated his own son: the newspapers picked up the story, and within a few weeks six convicted criminals had volunteered to serve as guinea pigs in front of a crowd of witnesses including scientists from the English Royal Society. All six survived, but when two new patients died after inoculation in the following months, clergymen and physicians attacked

the practice. One physician denounced "an Experiment practiced only by a few *Ignorant Women,* amongst an illiterate and unthinking People." Montagu printed a stinging rejoinder under the anonymous signature "Turkey Merchant." Although she won this battle as inoculation spread in use, she never published anything under her own name in her lifetime.

Ridiculed by some male contemporaries for her meddling in public affairs, Montagu had the last word after her death when her letters about the Ottoman Empire were published, revealing her as a correspondent with a talent for description of foreign customs and a wide-ranging interest in philosophical and literary matters. Lady Mary incarnated the new perspective gained by travel, in which close study of another culture challenged preconceptions and might even suggest important innovations to bring back home.

❖ The Birth of the Enlightenment

Economic expansion, the emergence of a new consumer society, and the stabilization of the European state system all generated optimism about the future. The intellectual corollary was the *Enlightenment*, a term used later in the eighteenth century to describe the loosely knit group of writers and scholars who believed that human beings could apply a critical, reasoning spirit to every problem they encountered in this world. The new secular, scientific, and critical attitude first emerged in the 1690s, scrutinizing everything from the absolutism of Louis XIV to the traditional role of women in society. After 1740, criticism took a more systematic turn as writers provided new theories for the organization of society and politics, but even by the 1720s and 1730s, established authorities realized they faced a new set of challenges.

Popularization of Science and Challenges to Religion

The writers of the Enlightenment glorified the geniuses of the new science and championed scientific method as the solution for all social problems. (See "Terms of History," page 676.) One of the most influential popularizations was the French writer Bernard de Fontenelle's *Conversations on the Plurality of Worlds* (1686). Presented as a dialogue between an aristocratic woman and a man of the world, the book made the Copernican, sun-centered view of the universe available to the literate public. By 1700, mathematics and science had become fashionable pastimes in high society, and the public flocked to lectures explaining scientific discoveries. Journals complained that scientific learning had become the passport to female affection: "There were two young ladies in Paris whose heads had been so turned by this branch of learning that one of them declined to listen to a proposal of marriage unless the candidate for her hand undertook to learn how to make telescopes." Such writings poked fun at women with intellectual interests, but they also demonstrated that women now participated in discussions of science.

The New Skepticism. Interest in science spread in literate circles because it offered a model for all forms of knowledge. As the prestige of science increased, some developed a skeptical attitude toward attempts to enforce religious conformity. A French Huguenot refugee from Louis XIV's persecutions, Pierre Bayle (1647–1706), launched an internationally influential campaign against religious intolerance from his safe haven in the Dutch Republic. His *News from the Republic of Letters* (first published in

A Budding Scientist
In this engraving, Astrologia, *by the Dutch artist Jacob Gole (c. 1660–1723), an upper-class woman looks through a telescope to do her own astronomical investigations. Women with intellectual interests were often disparaged by men, yet some middle- and upper-class women managed to pursue serious interests in science. One of the best known of these was the Italian Laura Bassi (1711–1778), who was a professor of physics at the University of Bologna. Such a position was all but impossible to attain since women were not allowed to attend university classes in any European country. Yet because many astronomical observatories were set up in private homes rather than public buildings or universities, wives and daughters of scientists could make observations and even publish their own findings.*
Bibliotèque Nationale de France.

Progress

Believing as they did in the possibilities of improvement, many Enlightenment writers preached a new doctrine about the meaning of human history. They challenged the traditional Christian belief that the original sin of Adam and Eve condemned human beings to unhappiness in this world and offered instead an optimistic vision: human nature, they claimed, was inherently good, and progress would be continuous if education developed human capacities to the utmost. Science and reason could bring happiness in this world. The idea of novelty or newness itself now seemed positive rather than threatening. Europeans began to imagine that they could surpass all those who preceded them in history, and they began to think of themselves as more "advanced" than the "backward" cultures they encountered in other parts of the world.

More than an intellectual concept, the idea of progress included a new conception of historical time and of Europeans' place within world history. Europeans stopped looking back, whether to a lost Garden of Eden or to the writings of Greek and Roman antiquity. Growing prosperity, European dominance overseas, and the scientific revolution oriented them toward the future. Europeans began to call their epoch "modern" to distinguish it from the Middle Ages (a new term), and they considered their modern period superior in achievement. Consequently, Europeans took it as their mission to bring their modern, enlightened ways of progress to the areas they colonized.

The economic and ecological catastrophes, destructive wars, and genocides of the twentieth century cast much doubt on this rosy vision of continuing progress. As the philosopher George Santayana (1863–1952) complained, "The cry was for vacant freedom and indeterminate progress: *Vorwarts! Avanti! Onward! Full Speed Ahead!*, without asking whether directly before you was a bottomless pit." In the movement toward *postmodernism*, which began in the 1970s, critics argued that we should no longer be satisfied with the modern; the modern brought us calamity and disaster, not reason and freedom. They wanted to go beyond the modern, hence "postmodernism." The most influential postmodern historian, the Frenchman Michel Foucault, argued in the 1970s and 1980s that history did not reveal a steady progress toward enlightenment, freedom, and humanitarianism but rather a descent into greater and greater social control, what he called a "carceral [prisonlike] society." He analyzed the replacement of torture with the prison, the birth of the medical clinic, and the movements for sexual liberation and declared that all simply ended up teaching people to watch themselves more closely and to cooperate in the state's efforts to control their lives.

Historians are now chastened in their claims about progress. They would no longer side with the German philosopher Georg W. F. Hegel who proclaimed in 1832, "The history of the world is none other than the progress of the consciousness of freedom." They worry about the nationalistic claims inherent, for example, in the English historian Thomas Babington Macaulay's insistence that "the history of England is emphatically the history of progress" (1843). But most would not go so far as Foucault in denouncing modern developments. As with many other historical questions, the final word is not yet in: is there a direction in human history? Or is history, as many in ancient times thought, a set of repeating cycles?

FURTHER READING

Bury, J. B. *The Idea of Progress: An Inquiry into Its Origin and Growth.* 1932.

Foucault, Michel. *Discipline and Punish: The Birth of the Prison.* Trans. Alan Sheridan. 1977.

1684) bitterly criticized the policies of Louis XIV and was quickly banned in Paris and condemned in Rome. After attacking Louis XIV's anti-Protestant policies, Bayle took a more general stand in favor of religious toleration. No state in Europe officially offered complete tolerance, though the Dutch Republic came closest with its tacit acceptance of Catholics, dissident Protestant groups, and open Jewish communities. In 1697, Bayle published the *Historical and Critical Dictionary*, which cited all the errors and delusions that he could find in past and present writers of all religions. Even religion must meet the test of reasonableness: "Any particular dogma, whatever it may be, whether it is advanced on the authority of the Scriptures, or whatever else may be its origins, is to be regarded as false if it clashes with the clear and definite conclusions of the natural understanding [reason]."

Although Bayle claimed to be a believer himself, his insistence on rational investigation seemed to challenge the authority of faith. As one critic complained, "It is notorious that the works of M. Bayle have unsettled a large number of readers, and cast doubt on some of the most widely accepted principles of morality and religion." Bayle asserted, for example, that atheists might possess moral codes as effective as those of the devout. Bayle's *Dictionary* became a model of critical thought in the West.

Other scholars challenged the authority of the Bible by subjecting it to historical criticism. Discoveries in geology in the early eighteenth century showed that marine fossils dated immensely farther back than the biblical flood. Investigations of miracles, comets, and oracles, like the growing literature against belief in witchcraft, urged the use of reason to combat superstition and prejudice. Comets, for example, should not be considered evil omens just because such a belief had been passed on from earlier generations. Defenders of church and state published books warning of the dangers of the new skepticism. The spokesman for Louis XIV's absolutism, Bishop Bossuet, warned that "reason is the guide of their choice, but reason only brings them face to face with vague conjectures and baffling perplexities." Human beings, the traditionalists held, were simply incapable of subjecting everything to reason, especially in the realm of religion.

State authorities found religious skepticism particularly unsettling because it threatened to undermine state power too. The extensive literature of criticism was not limited to France, but much of it was published in French, and the French government took the lead in suppressing the more outspoken works. Forbidden books were then often published in the Dutch Republic, Britain, or Switzerland and smuggled back across the border to a public whose appetite was only whetted by censorship.

The Young Voltaire Challenges Church and State. The most influential writer of the early Enlighten-

ment was a French man born into the upper middle classes, François Marie Arouet, known by his pen name, Voltaire (1694–1778). Voltaire took inspiration from Bayle: "He gives facts with such odious fidelity, he exposes the arguments for and against with such dastardly impartiality, he is so intolerably intelligible, that he leads people of only ordinary common sense to judge and even to doubt." In his early years Voltaire suffered arrest, imprisonment, and exile, but he eventually achieved wealth and acclaim. His tangles with church and state began in the early 1730s, when he published his *Letters Concerning the English Nation* (the English version appeared in 1733), in which he devoted several chapters to Newton and Locke and used the virtues of the British as a way to attack Catholic bigotry and government rigidity in France. Impressed by British toleration of religious dissent (at least among Protestants), Voltaire spent two years in exile in Britain when the French state responded to his book with yet another order for his arrest.

Voltaire also popularized Newton's scientific discoveries in his *Elements of the Philosophy of Newton* (1738). The French state and many European theologians considered Newtonianism threatening because it glorified the human mind and seemed to reduce God to an abstract, external, rationalistic force. So sensational was the success of Voltaire's book on Newton that a hostile Jesuit reported, "The great Newton, was, it is said, buried in the abyss, in the shop of the first publisher who dared to print him. . . . M. de Voltaire finally appeared, and at once Newton is understood or is in the process of being understood; all Paris resounds with Newton, all Paris stammers Newton, all Paris studies and learns Newton." The success was international too. Before long, Voltaire was elected a fellow of the Royal Society in London and in Edinburgh, as well as to twenty other scientific academies. Voltaire's fame continued to grow, reaching truly astounding proportions in the 1750s and 1760s (see Chapter 19).

Travel Literature and the Challenge to Custom and Tradition

Just as scientific method could be used to question religious and even state authority, a more general skepticism also emerged from the expanding knowledge about the world outside of Europe. During the seventeenth and eighteenth centuries, accounts of travel to exotic places dramatically increased as travel writers used the contrast between their home societies and other cultures to criticize the customs of European society.

Travel and Relativism in Morals. In their travels to the new colonies, visitors sought something resembling "the state of nature," that is, ways of life that preceded sophisticated social and political organization—although they often misinterpreted different forms of society and politics as having no organization at all. Travelers to the Americas found "noble savages" (native peoples) who appeared to live in conditions of great freedom and equality; they were "naturally good" and "happy" without taxes, lawsuits, or much organized government. In China, in contrast, travelers found a people who enjoyed prosperity and an ancient civilization. Christian missionaries made little headway in China, and visitors had to admit that China's religious systems had flourished for four or five thousand years with no input from Europe or from Christianity. The basic lesson of travel literature in the 1700s, then, was that customs varied: justice, freedom, property, good government, religion, and morality all were relative to the place. Europe—and Christianity—might be seen as just one of many options, as relatively and not absolutely true.

Europeans from all countries began to travel more, though most limited their itineraries to Europe. Philosophers and scientists traveled to exchange thoughts; even monarchs such as Peter the Great journeyed in search of new ideas. One critic complained that travel encouraged free thinking and the destruction of religion: "Some complete their demoralization by extensive travel, and lose whatever shreds of religion remained to them. Every day they see a new religion, new customs, new rites."

From Travel Account to Political Commentary. Travel literature turned explicitly political in Montesquieu's *Persian Letters* (1721). Charles-Louis de Secondat, baron of Montesquieu (1689–1755), the son of an eminent judicial family, was a high-ranking judge in a French court. He published *Persian Letters* anonymously in the Dutch Republic, and the book went into ten printings in just one year—a best-seller for the times. Montesquieu tells the story of two Persians, Rica and Usbek, who leave

their country "for love of knowledge" and travel to Europe. They visit France in the last years of Louis XIV's reign, writing of the king: "He has a minister who is only eighteen years old, and a mistress of eighty. . . . Although he avoids the bustle of towns, and is rarely seen in company, his one concern, from morning till night, is to get himself talked about." Other passages ridicule the pope. Beneath the satire, however, was a serious investigation into the foundation of good government and morality. Montesquieu chose Persians for his travelers because they came from what was widely considered the most despotic of all governments, in which rulers had life and death powers over their subjects. In the book, the Persians constantly compare France to Persia, suggesting that the French monarchy might verge on despotism itself.

The paradox of a judge publishing an anonymous work attacking the regime that employed him demonstrates the complications of the intellectual scene in this period. Montesquieu's anonymity did not last long, and soon Parisian society lionized him. In the late 1720s, he sold his judgeship and traveled extensively in Europe, including an eighteen-month stay in Britain. In 1748, he published a widely influential work on comparative government, *The Spirit of Laws*. The Vatican soon listed both *Persian Letters* and *The Spirit of Laws* in its index of forbidden books.

Raising the Woman Question

Many of the letters exchanged in *Persian Letters* focused on women, marriage, and the family because Montesquieu considered the position of women a sure indicator of the nature of government and morality. Although Montesquieu was not a feminist, his depiction of Roxana, the favorite wife in Usbek's harem, struck a chord with many women. Roxana revolts against the authority of Usbek's eunuchs and writes a final letter to her husband announcing her impending suicide: "I may have lived in servitude, but I have always been free, I have amended your laws according to the laws of nature, and my mind has always remained independent." Women writers used the same language of tyranny and freedom to argue for concrete changes in their status. Feminist ideas were not entirely new, but they were presented systematically for the first time and represented a fundamental challenge to the ways of traditional societies.

The most systematic of these women writers was the English author Mary Astell (1666–1731), the daughter of a businessman and herself a supporter of the Tory party and the Anglican religious establishment. In 1694, she published *A Serious Proposal to the Ladies,* in which she advocated founding a private women's college to remedy women's lack of education. Addressing women, she asked, "How can you be content to be in the World like Tulips in a Garden, to make a fine *shew* [show] and be good for nothing?" Astell argued for intellectual training based on Descartes' principles, in which reason, debate, and careful consideration of the issues took priority over custom or tradition. Her book was an immediate success: five printings appeared by 1701. In later works, Astell criticized the relationship between the sexes within marriage: "If absolute sovereignty be not necessary in a state, how comes it to be so in a family? . . . If all men are born free, how is it that all women are born slaves?" Her critics accused her of promoting subversive ideas and of contradicting the Scriptures.

Astell's work inspired other women to write in a similar vein. The anonymous *Essay in Defence of the Female Sex* (1696) attacked "the Usurpation of Men; and the Tyranny of Custom," which prevented women from getting an education. In 1709, Elizabeth Elstob published a detailed account of the prominent role women played in promoting Christianity in English history. She criticized men who "would declare openly they hated any Woman who knew more than themselves." Other women wrote poetry about the same themes. In the introduction to the work of one of the best-known poets, Elizabeth Singer Rowe, a friend of the author, complained of the "notorious Violations on the Liberties of Freeborn English Women" that came from "a plain and an open design to render us meer [mere] Slaves, perfect Turkish Wives."

Most male writers unequivocally stuck to the traditional view of women. Throughout the 1700s, male commentators complained about women's interest in reading novels, which they thought encouraged idleness and corruption. The French theologian Drouet de Maupertuis published an essay, *Dangerous Commerce between the Two Sexes* (1715), in which he harped once again on the traditional theme of women's self-centeredness: "Women love neither their husbands nor their children nor their lovers," he concluded. "They love themselves." Although the French writer François Poullain de la

IMPORTANT DATES

1690s   Beginning of rapid development of plantations in Caribbean
1694   Bank of England established; Mary Astell's *A Serious Proposal to the Ladies* argues for the founding of a private women's college
1697   Pierre Bayle publishes *Historical and Critical Dictionary,* detailing errors of religious writers
1699   Turks forced to recognize Habsburg rule over Hungary and Transylvania
1703   Peter the Great of Russia begins construction of St. Petersburg, founds first Russian newspaper
1713–1714   Peace of Utrecht
1714   Elector of Hanover becomes King George I of England
1715   Death of Louis XIV
1719   Daniel Defoe publishes *Robinson Crusoe*
1720   Last outbreak of bubonic plague in western Europe
1721   Treaty of Nystad; Montesquieu publishes *Persian Letters* anonymously in the Dutch Republic
1733   War of the Polish Succession; Voltaire's *Letters Concerning the English Nation* attacks French intolerance and narrow-mindedness
1741   George Frederick Handel composes the *Messiah*

Barre (1647–1723) had asserted the equality of women's minds in a series of works published in the 1670s, most men resisted this idea. Bayle argued, for example, that women were more profoundly tied to their biological nature than were men; by nature less capable of discernment but for this very reason, more inclined to conform to God's wishes.

Such opinions about women often rested on biological suppositions. In the absence of precise scientific knowledge about reproduction, scientists of the time argued heatedly with one another about women's biological role. In the long-dominant Aristotelian view, only the male seed carried spirit and individuality. At the beginning of the eighteenth century, more physicians and surgeons began to champion the doctrine of *ovism*—that the female egg was essential in making new humans. During the decades that followed, male Enlightenment writers would continue to debate women's nature and appropriate social roles.

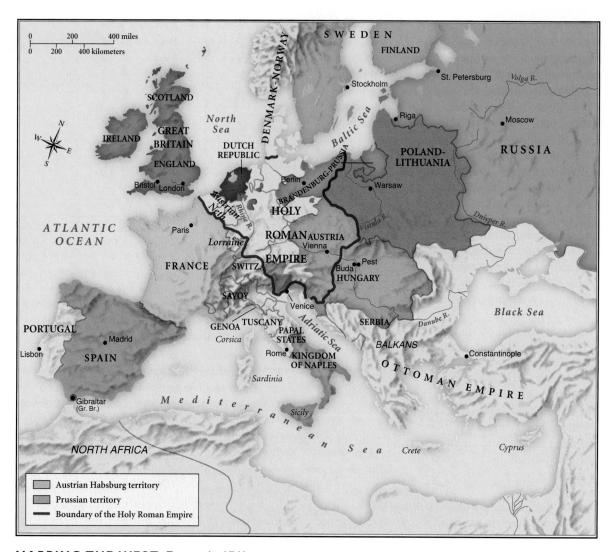

MAPPING THE WEST Europe in 1740

By 1740, Europe had achieved a kind of diplomatic equilibrium in which no one power predominated. But the relative balance should not deflect attention from important underlying changes: Spain, the Dutch Republic, Poland-Lithuania, and Sweden had all declined in power and influence while Great Britain, Russia, Prussia, and Austria had solidified their positions, each in a different way. France's ambitions had been thwarted, but its combination of a big army and rich overseas possessions made it a major player for a long time to come.

Conclusion

Europeans crossed a major threshold in the first half of the eighteenth century. They moved silently but nonetheless momentously from an economy governed by scarcity and the threat of famine to one of ever increasing growth and the prospect of continuing improvement. Expansion of colonies overseas and economic development at home created greater wealth, longer life spans, and higher expectations for

the future. In these better times for many, a spirit of optimism prevailed. People could now spend money on newspapers, novels, and travel literature as well as on coffee, tea, and cotton cloth. The growing literate public avidly followed the latest trends in religious debates, art, and music. Everyone did not share equally in the benefits: slaves toiled in abjection in the Americas; serfs in eastern Europe found themselves ever more closely bound to their noble lords; and rural folk almost everywhere tasted fewer fruits of consumer society.

Politics changed too as population and production increased and cities grew. Experts urged government intervention to improve public health, and states found it in their interest to settle many international disputes by diplomacy, which itself became more regular and routine. The consolidation of the European state system allowed a tide of criticism and new thinking about society to swell in Great Britain and France and begin to spill throughout Europe. Ultimately, the combination of the Atlantic system and the Enlightenment would give rise to a series of Atlantic revolutions.

Suggested References

The Atlantic System and the World Economy

It is easier to find sources on individual parts of the system than on the workings of the interlocking trade as a whole, but work has been rapidly increasing in this area. The Dunn book nonetheless remains one of the classic studies of how the plantation system took root. Eze's reader should be used with caution, as it sometimes distorts the overall record with its selections.

Blackburn, Robin. *The Making of New World Slavery: From the Baroque to the Modern, 1492–1800.* 1997.

Dunn, Richard S. *Sugar and Slaves: The Rise of the Planter Class in the English West Indies, 1624–1713.* 1972.

*Eze, Emmanuel Chukwudi. *Race and the Enlightenment: A Reader.* 1997.

Jordan, Winthrop D. *The White Man's Burden: Historical Origins of Racism in the United States.* 1974.

Mintz, Sidney W. *Sweetness and Power: The Place of Sugar in Modern History.* 1985.

Morgan, Philip D. *Slave Counterpoint: Black Culture in the Eighteenth-Century Chesapeake and Low Country.* 1998.

Slave movement during the eighteenth and nineteenth centuries: http://dpls.dacc.wisc.edu/slavedata/.

Smith, Alan K. *Creating a World Economy: Merchant Capital, Colonialism, and World Trade, 1400–1825.* 1991.

New Social and Cultural Patterns

Many of the novels of the period provide fascinating insights into the development of new social attitudes and customs. In particular, see Daniel Defoe's *Robinson Crusoe* (1719) and *Moll Flanders* (1722); the many novels of Eliza Heywood; and Antoine François Prévost's *Manon Lescaut* (1731), a French psychological novel about a nobleman's fatal love for an unfaithful woman, which became the basis for an opera in the nineteenth century.

*Primary sources.

Artwork of Boucher, Chardin, and Watteau: http://mistral.culture.fr/lumiere/documents/peintres.html.

De Vries, Jan. *European Urbanization, 1500–1800.* 1984.

Earle, Peter. *The Making of the English Middle Class: Business, Society, and Family Life in London, 1660–1730.* 1989.

Handel's Messiah: The New Interactive Edition (CD-ROM). 1997.

Raynor, Henry. *A Social History of Music, from the Middle Ages to Beethoven.* 1972.

Roche, Daniel. *The People of Paris: An Essay in Popular Culture in the Eighteenth Century.* Trans. Marie Evans. 1987.

Consolidation of the European State System

Studies of rulers and states can be supplemented by work on "political arithmetic" and public health.

Aspromourgos, Tony. *On the Origins of Classical Economics: Distribution and Value from William Petty to Adam Smith.* 1996.

Black, Jeremy, ed. *Britain in the Age of Walpole.* 1984.

Brewer, John. *The Sinews of Power: War, Money, and the English State, 1688–1783.* 1990.

Brockliss, Laurence, and Colin Jones. *The Medical World of Early Modern France.* 1997.

Campbell, Peter R. *Power and Politics in Old Regime France, 1720–1745.* 1996.

Hughes, Lindsey. *Russia in the Age of Peter the Great.* 1998.

Frey, Linda, and Marsha Frey. *Societies in Upheaval: Insurrections in France, Hungary, and Spain in the Early Eighteenth Century.* 1987.

Lawrence, Susan C. *Charitable Knowledge: Hospital Pupils and Practitioners in Eighteenth-Century London.* 1996.

Raeff, Marc. *Understanding Imperial Russia: State and Society in the Old Regime.* Trans. Arthur Goldhammer. 1984.

The Birth of the Enlightenment

The definitive study of the early Enlightenment is the book by Hazard, but many others have contributed biographies of individual figures or, more recently, studies of women writers.

Besterman, Theodore. *Voltaire.* 1969.

Grendy, Isobel. *Lady Mary Wortley Montagu.* 1999.

Hazard, Paul. *The European Mind: The Critical Years, 1680–1715.* 1990.

*Hill, Bridget, ed. *The First English Feminist: Reflections upon Marriage and Other Writings by Mary Astell.* 1986.

*Jacob, Margaret C. *The Enlightenment: A Brief History with Selected Readings.* 2000.

Rothkrug, Lionel. *The Opposition to Louis XIV: The Political and Social Origins of the French Enlightenment.* 1966.

Smith, Hilda L. *Reason's Disciples: Seventeenth-Century English Feminists.* 1982.

The Promise of Enlightenment

1740–1789

Catherine the Great
At the time of this portrait by Johann Baptist Edler von Lampi of 1793, the Russian empress Catherine the Great had ruled for thirty-one years and was only three years from her death. Born Sophia Augusta Frederika of Anhalt-Zerbst in 1729, she was the daughter of a minor German prince. When she married the future tsar Peter III in 1745, she promptly learned Russian and adopted Russian Orthodoxy. Peter, physically and mentally frail, proved no match for her, and she took his place on his death in 1762. The painter of this portrait was a native of northern Italy who had worked at the Austrian court in Vienna before being summoned to St. Petersburg. He painted many portraits of the Russian court and royal family between 1792 and 1797.
Art Resource, NY.

IN THE SUMMER OF 1766, Empress Catherine II ("the Great") of Russia wrote to Voltaire, one of the leaders of the Enlightenment:

It is a way of immortalizing oneself to be the advocate of humanity, the defender of oppressed innocence. . . . You have entered into combat against the enemies of mankind: superstition, fanaticism, ignorance, quibbling, evil judges, and the powers that rest in their hands. Great virtues and qualities are needed to surmount these obstacles. You have shown that you have them: you have triumphed.

Over a fifteen-year period Catherine corresponded regularly with Voltaire, a writer who, at home in France, found himself in constant conflict with authorities of church and state. Her admiring letter shows how influential Enlightenment ideals had become by the middle of the eighteenth century. Even an absolutist ruler such as Catherine endorsed many aspects of the Enlightenment call for reform; at this same time, Catherine set up a commission to write a new law code, and she introduced reforms in favor of education and religious toleration. She too wanted to be an "advocate of humanity."

Catherine's letter aptly summed up Enlightenment ideals: progress for humanity could be achieved only by rooting out the wrongs left by superstition, religious fanaticism, ignorance, and outmoded forms of justice. Enlightenment writers used every means at their disposal—from encyclopedias to novels to personal interaction with rulers—to argue for reform. Everything had to be examined in the cold light of reason,

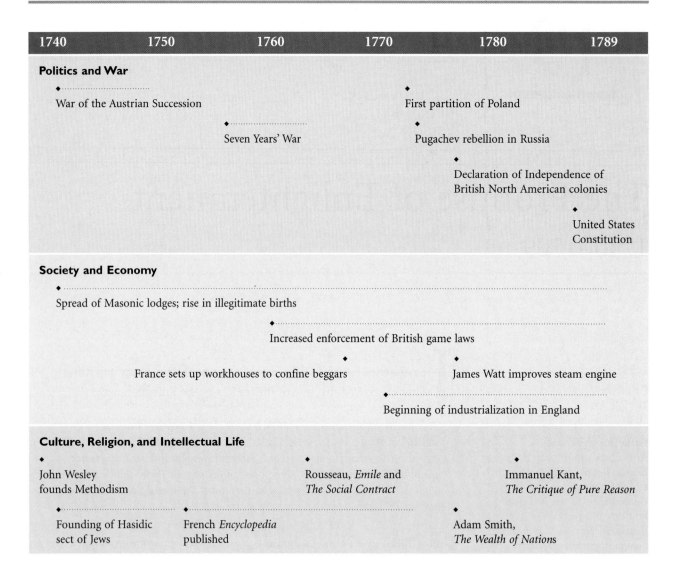

| 1740 | 1750 | 1760 | 1770 | 1780 | 1789 |

Politics and War

War of the Austrian Succession

Seven Years' War

First partition of Poland

Pugachev rebellion in Russia

Declaration of Independence of British North American colonies

United States Constitution

Society and Economy

Spread of Masonic lodges; rise in illegitimate births

Increased enforcement of British game laws

France sets up workhouses to confine beggars

James Watt improves steam engine

Beginning of industrialization in England

Culture, Religion, and Intellectual Life

John Wesley founds Methodism

Rousseau, *Emile* and *The Social Contract*

Immanuel Kant, *The Critique of Pure Reason*

Founding of Hasidic sect of Jews

French *Encyclopedia* published

Adam Smith, *The Wealth of Nations*

and if it did not promote the improvement of humanity, it should be jettisoned. As a result, Enlightenment writers attacked the legal use of torture to extract confessions and supported religious toleration. They favored the spread of education to eliminate ignorance and criticized censorship by state or church. These ideas spread far and wide through the book trade, some of it clandestine; coffeehouses; lending libraries; local academies; Masonic lodges (social clubs organized with the rituals of masons' guilds); and salons, sophisticated evening discussions organized by upper-class women.

Catherine's correspondence with Voltaire should not blind us to the limitations of Enlightenment. While a new elite of middle- and upper-class men and women embraced the Enlightenment, the lower classes had little contact with the new ideas. The continuing rise in population, the start of industrialization, and wars between the great powers shaped their lives more profoundly. States had to balance conflicting social pressures: on the one hand, rulers pursued those Enlightenment reforms that might enhance state power; and on the other hand, they feared changes that might unleash popular discontent. Catherine herself felt pulled in different directions. She had staged a coup against her husband Tsar Peter III; when he was killed, she succeeded him. German-born and educated, she aimed to bring Western ideas, culture, and reforms to Russia, but above all she intended to maintain and even extend her authority. When faced with a massive uprising of the serfs, she not only suppressed the revolt but also increased the powers of the nobles over their serfs. All reform-minded rulers faced similar potential challenges to their authority.

Even if the movement for reform had its limits, Catherine's letter should not be read as a cynical ploy. It reflected a very real shift in the basis of authority. Governments, almost all of them still ruled by hereditary monarchs, now had to respond to a new force known as "public opinion." The Russian educated public was minuscule, but Catherine nevertheless felt the need to justify her policies to her broader public, the intellectuals of western Europe. Other rulers confronted a much more aggressive, home-grown public that now read newspapers and closely followed political developments. Rulers had to portray themselves as modern, open to reform, and responsive to this public. By 1789, when revolution erupted in France, public opinion had begun to demand democracy—that is, government by, for, and of the people. Most Enlightenment writers did not embrace democracy, however; between the 1740s and the 1780s, they still looked to rulers to effect reform and addressed the educated classes as their audience. Writers such as Voltaire expressed little interest in the future of peasants or lower classes; they favored neither revolution nor political upheaval. Yet their ideas paved the way for something much more radical and unexpected. The American Declaration of Independence in 1776 showed how Enlightenment ideals could be translated into democratic political practice. After 1789, democracy would come to Europe as well.

❖ The Enlightenment at Its Height

The Enlightenment emerged as an intellectual movement before 1740 but reached its peak only in the second half of the eighteenth century. The writers of the Enlightenment called themselves *philosophes* (French for "philosophers"), but that term is somewhat misleading. Whereas philosophers concern themselves with abstract theories, the philosophes were public intellectuals dedicated to solving the real problems of the world. They wrote on subjects ranging from current affairs to art criticism, and they wrote in every conceivable format. The Swiss philosophe Jean-Jacques Rousseau,

for example, wrote a political tract, a treatise on education, a constitution for Poland, an analysis of the effects of the theater on public morals, a best-selling novel, an opera, and a notorious autobiography. The philosophes wrote for a broad educated public of readers who snatched up every Enlightenment book they could find at their local booksellers', even when rulers or churches tried to forbid their publication. Between 1740 and 1789, the Enlightenment acquired its name and, despite heated conflicts between the philosophes and state and religious authorities, gained support in the highest reaches of government. (See "Terms of History," page 687.)

The Men and Women of the Republic of Letters

Although *philosophe* is a French word, the Enlightenment was distinctly cosmopolitan; philosophes could be found from Philadelphia to Moscow and from Edinburgh to Naples. The philosophes considered themselves part of a grand "republic of letters" that transcended national political boundaries. They were not republicans in the usual sense, that is, people who supported representative government and opposed monarchy. Many, like Voltaire, warmly endorsed reform programs proposed by monarchs. What united them were the ideals of reason, reform, and freedom. The French editors of the *Encyclopedia* (published from 1751 to 1772) declared that they would "overturn the barriers that reason never erected" and "give back to the arts and sciences the liberty that is so precious to them." In 1784, the German philosopher Immanuel Kant summed up the program of the Enlightenment in two Latin words: *sapere aude,* "dare to know"—have the courage to think for yourself.

The philosophes used reason to attack superstition, bigotry, and religious fanaticism, which they considered the chief obstacles to free thought and social reform. Voltaire took religious fanaticism as his chief target: "Once fanaticism has corrupted a mind, the malady is almost incurable. . . . The only remedy for this epidemic malady is the philosophical spirit." Enlightenment writers did not necessarily oppose organized religion, but they strenuously objected to religious intolerance. They believed that the systematic application of reason could do what religious belief could not: improve the human

Bookbinding

In this plate from the Encyclopedia, *the various stages in bookbinding are laid out from left to right. Binding was not included in the sale of books; owners had to order leather bindings from a special shop. The man at (a) is pounding the pages to be bound on a marble block. The woman at (b) is stitching the pages with a special frame. The worker at (c) cuts the pages, and at (d) the volumes are pressed to prevent warping. This illustration is typical of the hundreds of plates in the* Encyclopedia *in its effort to represent precisely and thoroughly every stage in artisanal production.*

condition by pointing to needed reforms. Reason meant critical, informed, scientific thinking about social issues and problems. In the multivolume *Encyclopedia*, scores of collaborators gathered knowledge about every aspect of economic, social, and cultural life, from the secrets of manufacturing to theories of music. The chief editor of the *Encyclopedia*, Denis Diderot (1713–1784), explained their purpose: "All things must be examined, debated, investigated without exception and without regard for anyone's feelings."

The philosophes believed that the spread of knowledge would encourage reform in every aspect of life, from the grain trade to the penal system. Chief among their desired reforms was intellectual freedom, the freedom to use one's own reason and to publish the results. The philosophes wanted freedom of the press and freedom of religion, which they considered "natural rights" guaranteed by "natural law." In their view, progress depended on these

freedoms. As Voltaire asserted, "I quite understand that the fanatics of one sect slaughter the enthusiasts of another sect . . . [but] that Descartes should have been forced to flee to Holland to escape the fury of the ignorant . . . these things are a nation's eternal shame."

Most philosophes, like Voltaire, came from the upper classes, yet Rousseau's father was a modest watchmaker in Geneva, and Diderot was the son of a cutlery maker. Although it was a rare phenomenon, some women were philosophes, such as the French noblewoman Émilie du Châtelet (1706–1749), who wrote extensively about the mathematics and physics of Leibniz and Newton. (Her lover Voltaire learned much of his science from her.) Few of the leading writers held university positions, except those who were German or Scottish. Universities in France were so dominated by the clergy and unreceptive to Enlightenment ideals that they took the lead in banning Enlightenment books.

Enlightenment

In 1784, in an essay titled "What Is Enlightenment?," the German philosopher Immanuel Kant gave widespread currency to a term that had been in the making for several decades. The existence of an online database of French literature enables us to trace the actual appearance of the equivalent terms in French: *siècle de lumière(s)* or *siècle éclairé*—"century of light(s)" or "enlightened century." The term *enlightened century* became common beginning only in the 1760s. The even more common term *century of light(s)* first appeared in the inaugural volume of the *Encyclopedia* in 1751 and was soon taken up by all the major French Enlightenment writers. Closely related to Enlightenment was the French term *philosophe*, which was first used to mean "proponent of Enlightenment" in the 1740s. A clandestine tract of 1743 titled *Le Philosophe* explained that the philosophe was the man who saw through popular errors.

The Enlightenment gave itself its own name, and the name clearly had propaganda value. The philosophes associated Enlightenment with philosophy, reason, and humanity; religious tolerance; natural rights; and criticism of outmoded customs and prejudices. They tied Enlightenment to "progress" and to the "modern," and it came into question, just as these other terms did, when events cast doubt on the benefits of progress and the virtues of modernity. Although some opposed the Enlightenment from the very beginning as antireligious, undermining of authority, and even atheistic and immoral, the French Revolution of 1789 galvanized the critics of Enlightenment who blamed every excess of revolution on Enlightenment principles. Some critics believed that a conspiracy of Masonic lodges lay behind both the Enlightenment and the French Revolution.

For most of the nineteenth century, condemnation of the Enlightenment came from right-wing sources: those who opposed modernity, secularization, revolution, and sometimes any form of liberalization viewed the Enlightenment with distrust and even disdain. Some of the more extreme of these critics denounced a supposed "Jewish-Masonic conspiracy," believing that Jews and Freemasons benefited most from the spread of Enlightenment principles and worked secretly to jointly undermine Christianity and established monarchical authorities. Adolf Hitler and his followers shared these suspicions, and during World War II the Germans confiscated the records of Masonic lodges in every country they occupied. They sent the documents back to Berlin so that a special office could trace the links of this supposed conspiracy. They found nothing.

After the catastrophes of World War II, the Enlightenment came under attack for the first time from left-wing critics, those who had previously supported modernity, secularization, and even revolution. In a book published right after World War II, *Dialectic of Enlightenment*, Max Horkheimer and Theodor W. Adorno, two German Jewish refugees from Hitler's regime who had fled to the United States, denounced the Enlightenment as "self-destructive" and even "totalitarian" because its belief in reason led not to freedom but to greater bureaucratic control. They asked "why mankind, instead of entering into a truly human condition, is sinking into a new kind of barbarism," and they answered, because we have trusted too much in the Enlightenment and its belief in reason and science. Reason and science might have been tools of criticism of church and state in the eighteenth century, but in the twentieth century, Horkheimer and Adorno insisted, they resulted in concentration camps, ecological disasters, and a deadening mass culture incarnated by Hollywood films. Reason provided the technology to transport millions of Jews to their deaths in scientifically sound gas chambers. Reason invented the atomic bomb and gave us the factories that pollute the atmosphere. The masses did not rise up against these uses of reason because they were distracted by a mass culture that emphasized entertainment rather than reflection. These criticisms of the Enlightenment, however extreme and sometimes outlandish, show how central the Enlightenment remains to the very definition of modern history.

Sources: ARTFL (American Resource, Treasury of the French Language): http://humanities.uchicago.edu/ARTFL/ARTFL .html, Max Horkheimer and Theodor W. Adorno, *Dialectic of Enlightenment*, trans. John Cumming (New York: Continuum, 1993; first published 1947), xi, 6.

Enlightenment ideas developed instead through personal contacts; letters that were hand-copied, circulated, and sometimes published; salon readings of manuscripts; and letters to the editor and book reviews in periodicals. Commenting on the exchanges found in French and Italian newspapers, one writer exclaimed, "Never have new ideas had such rapid circulation at long distance." The salons gave intellectual life an anchor outside the royal court and the church-controlled universities. The best known was the Parisian salon of Madame Marie-Thérèse Geoffrin (1699–1777), a wealthy middle-class widow who had been raised by her grandmother and married off at fourteen to a much older man. Creating a salon was her way of educating herself and participating directly in the movement for reform. She brought together the most exciting thinkers and artists of the time; her social gatherings provided a forum for new ideas and an opportunity to establish new intellectual contacts. In the salon the philosophes could discuss ideas they might hesitate to put into print and thus test public opinion and even push it in new directions. Madame Geoffrin corresponded extensively with influential people across Europe, including Catherine the Great and King Stanislaw August Poniatowski of Poland-Lithuania. One Italian visitor commented, "There is no way to make Naples resemble Paris unless we find a woman to guide us, organize us, *Geoffrinize* us."

Women's role in creating salons provoked criticism from men who resented their power. (See "Contrasting Views," page 690.) Nevertheless, women's salons helped galvanize intellectual life and reform movements all over Europe. Wealthy Jewish women created nine of the fourteen salons in Berlin at the end of the eighteenth century, and in Warsaw, Princess Zofia Czartoryska gathered around her the reform leaders of Poland-Lithuania. Middle-class women in London used their salons to raise money to publish women's writings. Salons could be tied closely to the circles of power: in France, for example, Louis XV's mistress, Jeanne-Antoinette Poisson, first made her reputation as hostess of a salon frequented by Voltaire and Montesquieu. When she became Louis XV's mistress in 1745, she gained the title Marquise de Pompadour and turned her attention to influencing artistic styles by patronizing architects and painters.

Conflicts with Church and State

Madame Geoffrin did not approve of discussions that attacked the Catholic church, but elsewhere voices against organized religion could be heard.

Madame Geoffrin's Salon in 1755
This 1812 painting by Anicet Charles Lemonnier claims to depict the best-known Parisian salon of the 1750s. Lemonnier was only twelve years old in 1755 and so could not have based his rendition on firsthand knowledge. Madame Geoffrin is the figure in blue on the right facing the viewer. The bust is of Voltaire. Rousseau is the fifth person to the left of the bust (facing right) and behind him (facing left) is Raynal.
Giraudon/Art Resource, NY.

Criticisms of religion required daring because the church, whatever its denomination, wielded enormous power in society, and most influential people considered religion an essential foundation of good society and government. Defying such opinion, the Scottish philosopher David Hume (1711–1776) boldly argued in *The Natural History of Religion* (1755) that belief in God rested on superstition and fear rather than on reason. Hume soon met kindred spirits while visiting Paris; he attended a dinner party consisting of "fifteen atheists, and three who had not quite made up their minds."

Before the scientific revolution, virtually every European believed in God. After Newton, however, and despite Newton's own deep religiosity, people could conceive of the universe as an eternally existing, self-perpetuating machine, in which God's intervention was unnecessary. In short, such people could become either *atheists*, who did not believe in any kind of God, or *deists*, who believed in God but gave him no active role in earthly affairs. For the first time, writers claimed the label *atheist* and disputed the common view that atheism led inevitably to immorality.

Deists continued to believe in a benevolent, all-knowing God who had designed the universe and set it in motion. But deists usually rejected the idea that God directly intercedes in the functioning of the universe, and they often criticized the churches for their dogmatic intolerance of dissenters. Voltaire was a deist, and in his popular *Philosophical Dictionary* (1764) he attacked most of the claims of organized Christianity, both Catholic and Protestant. Christianity, he argued, had been the prime source of fanaticism and brutality among humans. Throughout his life, Voltaire's motto was *Ecrasez l'infâme*—"Crush the infamous thing" (the "thing" being bigotry and intolerance). The French authorities publicly burned his *Philosophical Dictionary*.

Criticism of religious intolerance involved more than simply attacking the churches. Critics also had to confront the states to which churches were closely tied. In 1761, a judicial case in Toulouse provoked an outcry throughout France that Voltaire soon joined. When the son of a local Calvinist was found hanged (he had probably committed suicide), authorities accused the father, Jean Calas, of murdering him to prevent his conversion to Catholicism. (Since Louis XIV's revocation of the Edict of Nantes in 1685, it had been illegal to practice Calvinism

Voltaire

In this marble bust by Jean-Antoine Houdon (1741–1828), Voltaire seems the same age as he does in the Lemonnier painting on page 688. However, Houdon began turning out a series of busts of eminent people only in 1771, so it seems likely that Lemonnier imported a later sculpture into his painting of Madame Geoffrin's salon in 1755. This bust shows Voltaire in his old age (he died in 1778).
Art Resource, NY.

publicly in France.) The all-Catholic parlement of Toulouse tried to extract a confession using torture—breaking all Calas's bones—and then executed him when he still refused to confess. Voltaire launched a successful crusade to rehabilitate Jean Calas's good name and to restore the family's properties, which had been confiscated after his death. Voltaire's efforts eventually helped bring about the extension of civil rights to French Protestants and encouraged campaigns to abolish the legal use of torture.

Critics also assailed state and church support for European colonization and slavery. One of the most popular books of the time was the *Philosophical and Political History of European Colonies and Commerce in the Two Indies*, published in 1770 by Abbé Guillaume Raynal (1713–1796), a French Catholic clergyman. Raynal and his collaborators described in excruciating detail the destruction of native populations by Europeans and denounced the inhumanity and irrationality of European ways.

Women and the Enlightenment

During the Enlightenment, women's roles in society became the subject of heated debates. Some men resented what they saw as the growing power of women, especially in the salons. Rousseau railed against their corrupting influence: "Every woman at Paris gathers in her apartment a harem of men more womanish than she." Male writers were divided in their attitudes. Many argued for greater education for women and for women's equality with men in marriage, but others still insisted on the natural weakness of women and their unsuitability for public affairs. Rousseau's *Emile* (Document 1) offered his own influential answer to the question of how women should be educated. The *Encyclopedia* ignored the contributions of salon women and praised women who stayed at home; in the words of one typical contributor, women "constitute the principal ornament of the world. . . . May they, through submissive discretion and through simple, adroit, artless cleverness, spur us [men] on to virtue." Many women objected to these characterizations. The editor of a prominent newspaper for women, Madame de Beaumer, wrote editorials blasting the masculine sense of superiority (Document 2). Many prominent women writers specifically targeted Rousseau's book because it proved to be the most influential educational treatise of the time (Document 3). Their ideas formed the core of nineteenth-century feminism.

1. Jean-Jacques Rousseau, Emile (1762)

Rousseau used the character of Emile's wife-to-be, Sophie, to discuss his ideas about women's education. "Woman is made to please and to be subjugated to man," he claimed. Sophie is educated for a domestic role as wife and mother, and she is taught to be obedient, always helpful to her husband and family, and removed from any participation in the public world. Despite his insistence on the differences between men's and women's roles, many women enthusiastically embraced Rousseau's ideas, for he placed great emphasis on maternalism, breastfeeding, and childrearing. Many women not only took to heart Rousseau's ideas about childrearing, some began to publish manuals for mothers. Rousseau's own children, however, suffered the contradictions that characterized his life. By his own admission, he abandoned to a foundling hospital all the children he had by his lower-class common-law wife because he did not think he could support them properly; if their fate was like that of most abandoned children of the day, they met an early death.

There is no parity between man and woman as to the importance of sex. The male is only a male at certain moments; the female all her life, or at least throughout her youth, is incessantly reminded of her sex and in order to carry out its functions she needs a corresponding constitution. She needs to be careful during pregnancy; she needs rest after childbirth; she needs a quiet and sedentary life while she nurses her children; she needs patience and gentleness in order to raise them; a zeal and affection that nothing can discourage. . . .

The relative duties of the two sexes are not and cannot be equally rigid. When woman complains about the unjust inequalities placed on her by man she is wrong; this inequality is by no means a human institution or at least it is not the work of prejudice but of reason. She to whom nature has entrusted the care of the children must hold herself accountable for them. . . .

On the good constitution of mothers depends primarily that of the children; on the care of women depends the early education of men; and on women, again, depend their morals, their passions, their tastes, their pleasures, and even their happiness. Thus the whole education of women ought to be relative to men. To please them, to be useful to them, to make themselves loved and honored by them, to educate them when young, to care for them when grown, to counsel them, to console them, and to make life agreeable and sweet to them—these are the duties of women at all times, and should be taught them from their infancy.

Source: Susan Groag Bell and Karen M. Offen, *Women, the Family, and Freedom: The Debate in Documents*, vol. 1, *1750–1880* (Stanford: Stanford University Press, 1983), 46–49.

2. Madame de Beaumer, editorial in Le Journal des Dames ("The Ladies' Journal"), 1762

Madame de Beaumer (d. 1766) was the first of three women editors of Le Journal des Dames. *She ran it for two years and published many editorials defending women against their male critics.*

The success of the *Journal des Dames* allows us to triumph over those frivolous persons who have regarded this periodical as a petty work containing only a few bagatelles suited to help them kill time. In truth, Gentlemen, you do us much honor to think that we could not provide things that unite the useful to the agreeable. To rid you of your error, we have made our Journal historical, with a view to putting before the eyes of youth striking images that will guide them toward virtue. . . . An historical *Journal des Dames*! these Gentlemen reasoners reply. How ridiculous! How out of character with the nature of this work, which calls only for little pieces to amuse [ladies] during their toilette. . . . Please, Gentlemen *beaux esprits* [wits], mind your own business and let us write in a manner worthy of our sex; I love this sex, I am jealous to uphold its honor and its rights. If we have not been raised up in the sciences as you have, it is you who are the guilty ones.

Source: Bell and Offen, 27–28.

3. Catharine Macaulay, Letters on Education *(1787)*

Catharine Sawbridge Macaulay-Graham (1731–1791) was one of the best-known English writers of the 1700s. She wrote immensely popular histories of England and also joined in the debate provoked by Rousseau's Emile.

There is another prejudice . . . which affects yet more deeply female happiness, and female importance; a prejudice, which ought ever to have been confined to the regions of the east, because [of the] state of slavery to which female nature in that part of the world has been ever subjected, and can only suit with the notion of a positive inferiority in the intellectual powers of the female mind. You will soon perceive, that the prejudice which I mean, is that degrading difference in the culture of the understanding, which has prevailed for several centuries in all European societies. . . . Be no longer niggards [misers], then O ye parents, in bestowing on your offspring, every blessing which nature and fortune renders them capable of enjoying! Confine not the education of your daughters to what is regarded as the ornamental parts of it, nor deny the graces to your sons. . . . Let your children be brought up together; let their sports and studies be the same. . . .

Among the most strenuous asserters of a sexual difference in character, Rousseau is the most conspicuous, both on account of that warmth of sentiment which distinguishes all his writing, and the eloquence of his compositions: but never did enthusiasm and the love of paradox, those enemies of philosophical disquisition, appear in more strong opposition to plain sense than in Rousseau's definition of this difference. He sets out with a supposition, that Nature intended the subjection of the one sex to the other; that consequently there must be an inferiority of intellect in the subjected party; but as man is a very imperfect being, and apt to play the capricious tyrant, Nature, to bring things nearer to an equality, bestowed on the woman such attractive graces, and such an insinuating address, as to turn the balance on the other scale. . . .

The situation and education of women . . . is precisely that which must necessarily tend to corrupt and debilitate both the powers of mind and body. From a false notion of beauty and delicacy, their system of nerves is depraved before they come out of the nursery; and this kind of depravity has more influence over the mind, and consequently over morals, than is commonly apprehended.

Source: Bell and Offen, 54–55.

QUESTIONS FOR DEBATE

1. Why would women in the eighteenth century read Rousseau with such interest and even enthusiasm?
2. Why does Madame de Beaumer address herself to male readers if the *Journal des Dames* is intended for women?
3. Why would Macaulay focus so much of her analysis on Rousseau? Why does she not just ignore him?
4. Was the Enlightenment intended only for men?

The book strongly opposed slavery and predicted the appearance of a black hero who would lead a rebellion of slaves "against the blind avarice of European and American colonists." Raynal was forced into exile as soon as the book appeared; like many other Enlightenment books, his work was banned by both the Catholic church and the French government.

The Enlightenment belief in natural rights led many to denounce slavery. An article in the *Encyclopedia* proclaimed, "There is not a single one of these hapless souls . . . who does not have the right to be declared free . . . since neither his ruler nor his father nor anyone else had the right to dispose of his freedom." Some Enlightenment thinkers, however, took a more ambiguous or even negative view. Montesquieu, for example, ridiculed arguments in favor of slavery yet argued that it was less irrational in hot climates because no one would work there without being compelled. Writing on national character, Hume judged blacks to be "naturally inferior to the whites," concluding, "There never was a civilized nation of any other complexion than white." Efforts to study the types of animals in nature led some scientists to rank humans according to their race, with European whites on top and African blacks at the bottom of the scale.

Enlightenment critics of church and state advocated reform, not revolution. Although he lived near the French-Swiss border in case he had to flee arrest, Voltaire, for example, made a fortune in financial speculations, wrote a glowing history called *The Age of Louis XIV* (1751), and lived to be celebrated in his last years as a national hero even by many former foes. Other philosophes also lived respectably, believing that published criticism, rather than violent action, would bring about necessary reforms. As Diderot said, "We will speak against senseless laws until they are reformed; and, while we wait, we will abide by them." Those few who lived long enough to see the French Revolution in 1789 resisted its radical turn, for the philosophes generally regarded the lower classes—"the people"—as ignorant, violent, and prone to superstition, hence in need of leadership from above. They pinned their hopes on educated elites and enlightened rulers.

Despite the philosophes' preference for reform, in the long run their books often had a revolutionary impact. For example, Montesquieu's widely reprinted *Spirit of the Laws* (1748) warned against the dangers of despotism, opposed the divine right of kings, and favored constitutional government. In his somewhat rosy view, Great Britain was "the one nation in the world which has political liberty as the direct object of its constitution." His analysis of British constitutionalism inspired French critics of absolutism and would greatly influence the American revolutionaries.

The Individual and Society

The controversy created by the most notorious conflicts between the philosophes and the various churches and states of Europe drew attention away from a subtle but profound transformation in worldviews. In previous centuries, questions of theological doctrine and church organization had been the main focus of intellectual and even political interest. The Enlightenment writers shifted attention away from religious questions toward the secular study of society and the individual's role in it. Religion did not drop out of sight, but the philosophes tended to make religion a private affair of individual conscience, even while rulers and churches still considered religion very much a public concern.

The Enlightenment interest in secular society produced two major results: it advanced the secularization of European political life that had begun after the Wars of Religion of the sixteenth and seventeenth centuries, and it laid the foundations for the social sciences of the modern era. Not surprisingly, then, many historians and philosophers consider the Enlightenment to be the origin of "modernity," which they define as the belief that human reason, rather than theological doctrine, should set the patterns of social and political life. This belief in reason as the sole foundation for secular authority has often been contested, but it has also proved to be a powerful force for change.

Although most of the philosophes believed that human reason could understand and even remake society and politics, they disagreed about what that reason revealed. Among the many different approaches were two that proved enduringly influential, those of the Scottish philosopher Adam Smith and the Swiss writer Jean-Jacques Rousseau. Smith provided a theory of modern capitalist society and devoted much of his energy to defending free markets as the best way to maximize individual efforts. The modern discipline of economics took shape around the questions raised by Smith. Rousseau set out the principles of a more communitarian philosophy, one that emphasized the needs of the community over those of the individual. His work led both toward democracy and toward communism and continues to inspire heated debate in political science and sociology.

Adam Smith.　Adam Smith (1723–1790) optimistically believed that individual interests naturally harmonized with those of the whole society. He claimed, "The study of his own [the individual's] advantage necessarily leads him to prefer what is most advantageous to the society." To explain how this natural harmonization worked, he published *An Inquiry into the Nature and Causes of the Wealth of Nations* in 1776. Like Bernard Mandeville before him but much more systematically, Smith insisted that individual self-interest, even greed, was quite compatible with society's best interest: the laws of supply and demand served as an "invisible hand" ensuring that individual interests would be synchronized with those of the whole society. Market forces—"the propensity to truck, barter, and exchange one thing for another"—naturally brought individual and social interests in line.

Smith rejected the prevailing mercantilist views that the general welfare would be served by accumulating national wealth through agriculture or the hoarding of gold and silver. Instead, he argued that the division of labor in manufacturing increased productivity and generated more wealth for society and well-being for the individual. By performing a manufacturing task over and over again, a person functioned as a part in a well-running machine. In his much-cited example of the manufacture of pins, Smith showed that when the manufacturing process was broken down into separate operations—one man to draw out the wire, another to straighten it, a third to cut it, a fourth to point it, and so on—workers who could make only one pin a day on their own could make thousands working together.

To maximize the effects of market forces and the division of labor, Smith endorsed a concept called *laissez-faire* (that is, "to leave alone") to free the economy from government intervention and control. He insisted that governments eliminate all restrictions on the sale of land, remove restraints on the grain trade, and abandon duties on imports. He believed that free international trade would stimulate production everywhere and thus ensure

Major Works of the Enlightenment

1748　Charles-Louis de Secondat, baron of Montesquieu, *Spirit of Laws*

1751　Beginning of publication of the French *Encyclopedia*

1755　David Hume, *The Natural History of Religion*

1762　Jean-Jacques Rousseau, *The Social Contract* and *Emile*

1764　Voltaire, *Philosophical Dictionary*

1770　Abbé Guillaume Raynal, *Philosophical and Political History of European Colonies and Commerce in the Two Indies*

1776　Adam Smith, *An Inquiry into the Nature and Causes of the Wealth of Nations*

1781　Immanuel Kant, *The Critique of Pure Reason*

the growth of national wealth. He insisted: "The natural effort of every individual to better his own condition, when suffered to exert itself with freedom and security, is so powerful a principle, that it is alone, and without any assistance, not only capable of carrying the society to wealth and prosperity, but of surmounting a hundred impertinent obstructions with which the folly of human laws too often encumbers its operations." Governments should restrict themselves to providing "security," that is, national defense, internal order, and public works. Smith recognized that government had an important role in providing a secure framework for market activity, but he placed most emphasis on freeing individual endeavor from what he saw as excessive government interference.

Jean-Jacques Rousseau.　Much more pessimistic about the relation between individual self-interest and the good of society was Jean-Jacques Rousseau (1712–1778). In Rousseau's view, society itself threatened natural rights or freedoms: "Man is born free, and everywhere he is in chains." Rousseau first gained fame by writing a prize-winning essay in 1749 in which he argued that the revival of science and the arts had corrupted social morals, not improved them. This startling conclusion seemed to oppose some of the Enlightenment's most cherished beliefs. Rather than improving society, he claimed, science and art raised artificial barriers between

Rousseau's Worries
Jean-Jacques Rousseau's novel The New Heloise *(1761) sold better than any other work in French in the second half of the eighteenth century. But Rousseau himself was deeply concerned about the effects of novel reading, especially on young women. The first of these illustrations for the novel (on the left) by Moreau the Younger, was rejected by Rousseau because the couple (Julie and Saint Preux) are shown in direct physical contact. He accepted the engraving on the right, by Gravelot, because it only hinted at passion.* Bibliothèque Nationale.

people and their natural state. Rousseau's works extolled the simplicity of rural life over urban society. Although he participated in the salons and contributed to the *Encyclopedia*, Rousseau always felt ill at ease in high society, and he periodically withdrew to live in solitude far from Paris. Paradoxically, his "solitude" was often paid for by wealthy upper-class patrons, who lodged him on their estates, even as his writings decried the upper-class privilege that made his efforts possible.

Rousseau explored the tension between the individual and society in various ways. In his best-selling novel *The New Heloise* (1761), he told the story of Julie, who gives up her penniless lover Saint Preux to marry someone else to please her father. Rousseau completely transformed the medieval story of Heloise and Abelard to focus on the conflict between social demands for virtue in marriage and Julie's intensely personal feelings. Julie learns to live a virtuous, domestic life with her husband and sacrifices her feelings for Saint Preux; her death at the end of the novel makes her into a saintly heroine, but it also raises questions about the cost to the individual of social virtue. In his work on education, *Emile* (1762), Rousseau tried to find a less tragic solution to the conflict between the individ-

ual and society. Without relying solely on books and free from the supervision of the clergy, who controlled most schools, the boy Emile works alone with his tutor to develop practical skills and independent ways of thinking. After developing his individuality, Emile joins society through marriage to Sophie, who received the education Rousseau thought appropriate for women. (See "Contrasting Views," page 690.)

In *The Social Contract* (1762), Rousseau proposed a political solution to the tension between the individual and society. Whereas earlier he had argued that society corrupted the individual by taking him out of nature, in this work Rousseau insisted that the right kind of political order could make people truly moral and free. In other words, he hoped to generalize the solution advanced in *Emile* to all of society. Individual moral freedom could be achieved only by learning to subject one's individual interests to "the general will," that is, the good of the community. Individuals did this by entering into a social contract not with their rulers, but with one another. If everyone followed the general will, then all would be equally free and equally moral because they lived under a law to which they had all consented.

These arguments threatened the legitimacy of eighteenth-century governments. Rousseau derived his social contract from human nature, not from history, tradition, or the Bible. He implied that people would be most free and moral under a republican form of government with direct democracy, and his abstract model included no reference to differences in social status. He roundly condemned slavery: "To decide that the son of a slave is born a slave is to decide that he is not born a man." Not surprisingly, authorities in both Geneva and Paris banned *The Social Contract* for undermining political authority. Rousseau's works became a kind of political bible for the French revolutionaries of 1789, and his attacks on private property inspired the communists of the nineteenth century such as Karl Marx. Rousseau's rather mystical concept of the general will remains controversial. The "greatest

good of all," according to Rousseau, was liberty and equality, but he also insisted that the individual could be "forced to be free" by the terms of the social contract. He provided no legal protections for individual rights. Rousseau's particular version of democracy might not preserve the individual freedoms so important to Adam Smith.

Spreading the Enlightenment

The spread of the Enlightenment followed a distinct geographic and social pattern: it flourished in places where an educated middle class provided an eager audience for ideas of constitutionalism and reform. It therefore found its epicenter in the triangle formed by London, Amsterdam, and Paris and diffused outward to eastern and southern Europe and North America (Map 19.1). Where constitutionalism and

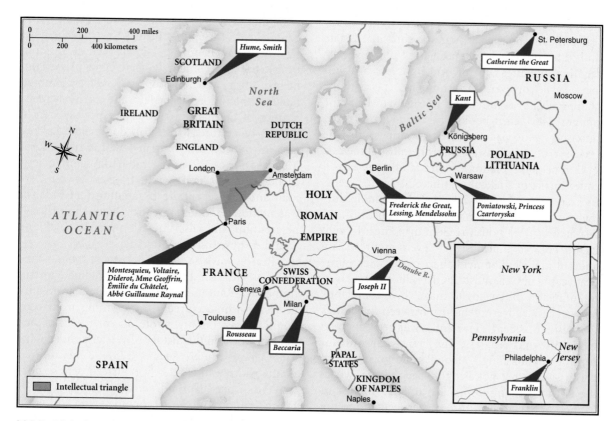

MAP 19.1 Centers of the Enlightenment
Paris was the heart of the Enlightenment because most philosophes, whatever their nationality, spoke and wrote French. Both Catherine the Great and Frederick the Great corresponded in French with their favorite French philosophes. Many French philosophes traveled to London where they met with their English and Scottish counterparts. Montesquieu and Voltaire wrote extensively about English customs. Dutch printers published books censored in France and made them available throughout Europe and the American colonies.

the guarantee of individual freedoms were most advanced, as in Great Britain and the Dutch Republic, the movement had less of an edge because there was, in a sense, less need for it. Scottish and English writers concentrated on economics, philosophy, and history rather than politics or social relations. Dutch printers made money publishing the books that were forbidden in France. In British North America, Enlightenment ideas helped stiffen growing colonial resistance to British rule after 1763. In places with small middle classes, such as Spain, the Italian states, and Russia, governments successfully suppressed writings they did not like. Italian philosophes, such as the Milanese penal reformer Cesare Beccaria (1738–1794), got moral support from their French counterparts in the face of stern censorship at home.

The French Enlightenment.   The hot spot of the Enlightenment was France. French writers published the most daring critiques of church and state and suffered the most intense harassment and persecution. Voltaire, Diderot, and Rousseau all faced arrest, exile, or even imprisonment. The Catholic church and royal authorities routinely forbade the publication of their books, and the police arrested publishers who ignored their warnings. Yet the French monarchy was far from the most autocratic in Europe, and Voltaire, Diderot, and Rousseau all ended their lives as cultural heroes. France seems to have been curiously caught in the middle during the Enlightenment: with fewer constitutional guarantees of individual freedom than Great Britain, it still enjoyed much higher levels of prosperity and cultural development than most other European countries. In short, French elites had reason to complain, the means to make their complaints known, and a government torn between the desires to censor dissident ideas and to appear open to modernity and progress. The French government controlled publishing—all books had to get official permissions—but not as tightly as in Spain, where the Catholic Inquisition made up its own list of banned books, or in Russia, where Catherine the Great allowed no opposition.

By the 1760s, the French government regularly ignored the publication of many works once thought offensive or subversive. In addition, a growing flood of works printed abroad poured into France and circulated underground. In the Dutch Republic and Swiss cities, private companies made fortunes smuggling illegal books into France over mountain passes and back roads. Foreign printers provided secret catalogs of their offerings and sold their products through booksellers who were willing to market forbidden books for a high price. Among such books were not only the philosophical treatises of the Enlightenment but also pornographic books and pamphlets (some by Diderot) lampooning the Catholic clergy and leading members of the royal court. In the 1770s and 1780s, lurid descriptions of sexual promiscuity at the French court helped undermine the popularity of the throne.

The German Enlightenment.   In the German states the Enlightenment followed a very different course. Whereas the French philosophes often took a violently anticlerical and combative tone, their German counterparts avoided direct political confrontations with authorities. Gotthold Lessing (1729–1781) complained in 1769 that Prussia was still "the most slavish society in Europe" in its lack of freedom to criticize government policies. As a playwright, literary critic, and philosopher, Lessing promoted religious toleration for the Jews and spiritual emancipation of Germans from foreign, especially French, models of culture, which still dominated. Lessing also introduced the German Jewish writer Moses Mendelssohn (1729–1786) into Berlin salon society. Mendelssohn labored to build bridges between German and Jewish culture by arguing that Judaism was a rational and undogmatic religion. He believed persecution and discrimination against the Jews would end as reason triumphed.

Reason was also the chief focus of the most influential German thinker of the Enlightenment, Immanuel Kant (1724–1804). Kant, a university professor who lectured on everything from economics to astronomy, wrote one of the most important works in the history of Western philosophy, *The Critique of Pure Reason* (1781). Kant admired Adam Smith and especially Rousseau, whose portrait he displayed proudly in his lodgings. Just as Smith founded modern economics and Rousseau modern political theory, Kant in *Critique of Pure Reason* set the foundations for modern philosophy. In this complex book, Kant established the doctrine of *idealism*, the belief that true understanding can come only from examining the ways in which ideas are formed in the mind. Ideas are shaped, Kant argued, not just by sensory information (a position central to *empiricism,* a philosophy based on John Locke's writings) but also by the operation on that information of mental categories such as space and time. In Kant's philosophy these "categories of understanding" were neither sensory nor supernatural; they were entirely ideal and abstract and located in the human mind. For Kant the supreme philosophical questions—Does God exist? Is personal immortality possible? Do humans have free will?—were unanswerable by reason alone. But like Rousseau, Kant insisted that true moral freedom could be achieved only by living in society and obeying its laws.

The Limits of Reason: Roots of Romanticism and Religious Revival

As Kant showed, reason had its limits: it could not answer all of life's pressing questions. In reaction to what some saw as the Enlightenment's excessive reliance on the authority of human reason, a new artistic movement called *romanticism* took root. Although it would not fully flower until the early nineteenth century, romanticism traced its emphasis on individual genius, deep emotion, and the joys of nature to thinkers like Rousseau who had scolded the philosophes for ignoring those aspects of life that escaped and even conflicted with the power of reason. Rousseau's autobiographical *Confessions,* published posthumously in 1782, caused an immediate sensation because it revealed so much about his inner emotional life, including his sexual longings and his almost paranoid distrust of other Enlightenment figures.

The appeal to feelings and emotions also increased interest in the occult. In the 1780s, a charismatic Austrian physician turned "experimenter," Franz Mesmer, awed crowds of aristocrats and middle-class admirers with his Paris demonstrations of "animal magnetism." He passed a weak electrical current through tubs filled with water or iron filings, around which groups of his disciples sat, holding hands; with this process of "mesmerism" he claimed to cure their ailments. (The word *mesmerize,* meaning "hypnotize" or "hold spellbound," is derived from Mesmer's name.)

A novel by the young German writer Johann Wolfgang von Goethe (1749–1832) captured the early romantic spirit with its glorification of emo-

tion. *The Sorrows of Young Werther* (1774) told of a young man who resembles Rousseau's Julie in many respects: he loves nature and rural life and is unhappy in love. When the woman he loves marries another, he falls into deep melancholy and eventually kills himself. Reason cannot save him. The book spurred a veritable Werther craze: there were Werther costumes, Werther engravings and embroidery, medallions, a perfume called Eau de Werther, and, unfortunately, a few imitations of Werther's suicide. The young Napoleon Bonaparte, who was to build an empire for France, claimed to have read Goethe's novel seven times.

Religious revivals underlined the limits of reason in a different way. Much of the Protestant world experienced an "awakening" in the 1740s. In the German states, Pietist groups founded new communities; and in the British North American colonies, revivalist Protestant preachers drew thousands of fervent believers in a movement called the Great Awakening. In North America bitter conflicts between revivalists and their opponents in the established churches prompted the leaders on

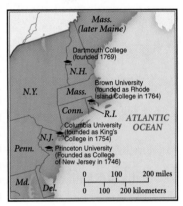

New Colleges in North America

both sides to set up new colleges to support their beliefs. These included Princeton, Columbia, Brown, and Dartmouth, all founded between 1746 and 1769.

Revivalism also stirred eastern European Jews at about the same time. Israel ben Eliezer (c. 1700–1760), later known as Ba'al Shem Tov (or the Besht, from the initials), laid the foundation for the Hasidic sect in the 1740s and 1750s. Teaching outside the synagogue system, Ba'al Shem Tov traveled the Polish countryside offering to cure men of their evil spirits. He invented a new form of popular prayer, in which the believer aimed to annihilate his own personality in order to let the supernatural speak through him. His followers, the *Hasidim* (Hebrew for "most pious" Jews), often prayed at the top of their lungs, joyfully swaying and clapping their hands. They scorned the formality of the regular synagogues in favor of their own prayer houses, where they gathered in rustic clothing and broad fur

A Hasid and His Wife
The followers of Ba'al Shem Tov were known as Hasidim ("most pious Jews"). They insisted on wearing Polish peasant-style clothing even if they themselves were not peasants.
The Hasidim stressed devotion to the rebbe ("teacher and spiritual guide").
Encyclopedia of Jewish History.

hats to emphasize their piety and simplicity. Their practices soon spread all over Poland-Lithuania.

Most of the waves of Protestant revivalism ebbed after the 1750s, but in Great Britain the movement known as *Methodism* continued to grow through the end of the century. John Wesley (1703–1791), the Oxford-educated son of an Anglican cleric, founded Methodism, a term evoked by Wesley's insistence on strict self-discipline and a methodical approach to religious study and observance. In 1738, Wesley had a mystical experience in which he felt the need to submit his life totally to Christ. Immediately afterward, he began to travel all over the British Isles, preaching a new brand of Protestantism that emphasized an intense personal experience of salvation and a life of thrift, abstinence, and hard work. In meadows and brickyards, in mine pits and copperworks, wherever ordinary people played or worked, Wesley would mount a table or a box to speak or begin a hymn. He slept in his followers' homes, ate their food, and treated their illnesses with various remedies, including small electric shocks for nervous diseases (Wesley eagerly followed Benjamin Franklin's experiments with electricity). In fifty years, Wesley preached forty thousand sermons, an average of fifteen a week. Not surprisingly, his preaching disturbed the Anglican authorities, who refused to let him preach in the churches. In response, Wesley began to ordain his

own clergy. Nevertheless, during Wesley's lifetime the Methodist leadership remained politically conservative; Wesley himself wrote many pamphlets urging order, loyalty, and submission to higher authorities. He denounced political agitation in the 1770s because he said it threatened to make Great Britain "a field of blood" ruled by "King Mob."

❖ Society and Culture in an Age of Enlightenment

Religious revivals and the first stirrings of romanticism show that all intellectual currents did not flow in the same channel. Similarly, some social and cultural developments manifested the influence of Enlightenment ideas but others did not. The traditional leaders of European societies—the nobles—responded to Enlightenment ideals in contradictory fashion: many simply reasserted their privileges and resisted the influence of the Enlightenment, but an important minority embraced change and actively participated in reform efforts. The expanding middle classes saw in the Enlightenment a chance to make their claim for joining society's governing elite. They bought Enlightenment books, joined Masonic lodges, and patronized new styles in art, music, and literature. The lower classes had much less contact with the Enlightenment. Economic growth affected them much more. Continuing population increase contributed to a rise in prices for basic goods, but the industrialization of textile manufacturing, which began in this period, made cotton clothing more accessible to those at the bottom of the social scale. Social change, however, was neither uniform nor painless. Most peasants remained tied to the land and their lords; those who moved to the cities in search of work did not always find their situations better.

The Nobility's Reassertion of Privilege

Nobles made up about 3 percent of the European population, but the proportion and their way of life varied greatly from country to country. At least 10 percent of the population in Poland was noble and 7 to 8 percent in Spain, in contrast to only 2 percent in Russia and between 1 and 2 percent in the rest of western Europe. Polish and Spanish nobles in particular often lived in poverty; titles did not guarantee wealth. The wealthiest European nobles luxuriated in almost unimaginable opulence. Many of the English peers, for example, owned more than ten thousand acres of land (the average western European peasant owned about five acres), invested widely in government bonds and trading companies, kept several country residences with scores of servants as well as houses in London, and occasionally even had their own private orchestras as well as libraries of expensive books, greenhouses for exotic plants, kennels of pedigree dogs, and collections of antiques, firearms, and scientific instruments.

In the face of the commercialization of agriculture and inflation of prices, European aristocrats converted their remaining legal rights (called *seigneurial dues*, from the French *seigneur*, for "lord") into money payments and used them to support an increasingly expensive lifestyle. Peasants felt the squeeze as a result. French peasants, for instance, paid a wide range of dues to their landlords, including payments to grind grain at the lord's mill, bake bread in his oven, press grapes at his winepress, and various inheritance taxes on the land. In addition, peasants had to work without compensation for a specified number of days every year on the public roads. They also paid taxes to the government on salt, an essential preservative, and on the value of their land; customs duties if they sold produce or wine in town; and the tithe on their grain (one-tenth of the crop) to the church.

In Britain, the landed gentry could not claim these same onerous dues from their tenants, but they tenaciously defended their exclusive right to hunt game. The game laws kept the poor from eating meat and helped protect the social status of the rich. The gentry enforced the game laws themselves by hiring gamekeepers who hunted down poachers and even set traps for them in the forests. According to the law, anyone who poached deer or rabbits while armed or disguised could be sentenced to death. After 1760, the number of arrests for breaking the game laws increased dramatically. In most other countries, too, hunting was the special right of the nobility and a cause of deep popular resentment.

Even though Enlightenment writers sharply criticized nobles' insistence on special privileges, most aristocrats maintained their marks of distinction. The male court nobility continued to sport swords, plumed hats, makeup, and powdered hair, while middle-class men wore simpler and more somber clothing. Aristocrats had their own seats in church and their own quarters in the universities. Frederick II ("the Great") of Prussia (r. 1740–1786) made sure that nobles dominated both the army officer corps and the civil bureaucracy. Catherine II of Russia (r. 1762–1796) granted the nobility vast tracts of land, the exclusive right to own serfs, and exemption from personal taxes and corporal punishment. Her Charter of the Nobility of 1785 codified these privileges in exchange for the nobles' political subservience to the state. In many countries, including Spain and France, the law prohibited aristocrats from engaging directly in retail trade. In Austria, Spain, the Italian states, Poland-Lithuania, and Russia, most nobles consequently cared little about Enlightenment ideas; they did not read the books of the philosophes and feared reforms that might challenge their dominance of rural society.

In France, Britain, and the western German states, however, the nobility proved more open to the new ideas. Among those who personally corresponded with Rousseau, for example, half were nobles, as were 20 percent of the 160 contributors to the *Encyclopedia*. It had not escaped their notice that Rousseau had denounced inequality. In his view, it was "manifestly contrary to the law of nature . . . that a handful of people should gorge themselves with superfluities while the hungry multitude goes in want of necessities."

The Middle Class and the Making of a New Elite

Enlightenment ideals helped break down the traditional barriers between the aristocracy and the middle class in western Europe and were in turn further energized by this development. The Enlightenment offered middle-class people an intellectual and cultural route to social improvement; it gave them the chance to join with nobles in a new mixed elite, united by common interests in reform and new cultural tastes. Intermarriage, the spread of businesslike attitudes among the nobility, and the middle-class emulation of noble ways encouraged this intermixing of the elite. Although middle-class people had many reasons to resent the nobles, they also aspired to be like them. The richest hoped to buy themselves a title and share all the special privileges accorded nobles.

The term *middle class* referred to the middle position on the social ladder; it comprised the families who did not have legal titles like the nobility above them but who did not work with their hands like the peasants, artisans, or workers below them. Most middle-class families lived in towns or cities and earned their living in some professional capacity—as doctors, lawyers, or lower-level officials or through investment in land, trade, or manufacturing. In the eighteenth century, the ranks of the middle class—also known as the *bourgeoisie* after *bourg*, the French word for "town," or *bourgeois*, the French word for "city dweller"—grew steadily in western Europe as a result of economic expansion. In France, for example, the overall population grew by about one-third in the 1700s, but the bourgeoisie nearly tripled in size.

Lodges and Learned Societies. Nobles and middle-class professionals mingled in Enlightenment salons and joined the new Masonic lodges and local learned societies. The Masonic lodges began as social clubs with elaborate secret rituals based on those of the masons' guilds. Their members were known as *freemasons* because that was the term given to apprentice masons when they were deemed "free" to practice as masters of their guild. Although not explicitly political in aim, the lodges encouraged equality among members, and both aristocrats and middle-class men could join. In France, women set up their own Masonic lodges. Members wrote constitutions for their lodges and elected their own officers, thus promoting a direct experience of constitutional government.

Freemasonry arose in Great Britain and spread eastward: the first French and Italian lodges opened in 1726; Frederick II of Prussia founded a lodge in 1740; and after 1750, freemasonry spread in Poland, Russia, and British North America. Despite the papacy's condemnation of freemasonry in 1738 as subversive of religious and civil authority, lodges continued to multiply throughout the eighteenth century because they offered a place for socializing outside of the traditional channels and a way of declaring one's interest in the Enlightenment and reform. In short, freemasonry offered a kind of secular religion. After 1789 and the outbreak of the French Revolution, conservatives would blame the lodges for every kind of political upheaval, but in the 1700s many high-ranking nobles became active members and saw no conflict with their privileged status.

Nobles and middle-class professionals also met in local learned societies, which greatly increased in number in this period. They gathered to discuss such practical issues as new scientific innovations

Neoclassical Style
In this Georgian interior of Syon House on the outskirts of London, various neoclassical motifs are readily apparent: Greek columns, Greek-style statuary on top of the columns, and Roman-style mosaics in the floor. The Scottish architect Robert Adams created this room for the duke of Northumberland in the 1760s. Adams had spent four years in Italy and returned in 1758 to London to decorate homes in the "Adams style," meaning the neoclassical manner. Fotomas Index, UK.

or methods to eliminate poverty. The societies, or academies, brought the Enlightenment down from the realm of books and ideas to the level of concrete reforms. They sponsored essay contests, such as the one won by Rousseau in 1749, or the one set by the society in Metz in 1785 on the question "Are there means for making the Jews happier and more useful in France?" The Metz society approved essays that argued for granting the Jews civil rights.

New Cultural Styles.   Shared tastes in travel, architecture, and the arts helped solidify the intermingled elite of nobility and middle class. "Grand tours" of Europe often led upper-class youths to recently discovered Greek and Roman ruins at Pompeii, Herculaneum, and Paestum in Italy. These excavations aroused enthusiasm for the neoclassical style in architecture and painting, which began pushing aside the rococo and the long dominant baroque. Urban residences and new government buildings soon reflected the neoclassical emphasis on purity and clarity of forms. As one German writer noted, with considerable exaggeration, "Everything in Paris is in the Greek style." In the 1760s and 1770s in Britain, the upper classes began building magnificent houses in the neoclassical style called Georgian (after the reigning king, George III), and pottery, furniture, fabrics, cutlery, and even wall-

paper incorporated classical themes and allowed middle-class people to emulate the richest aristocrats.

This period also supported artistic styles other than neoclassicism. Frederick II of Prussia built himself a palace in the earlier rococo style and gave it a French name, *Sans-souci* ("worry-free"), and filled it with the works of French masters of the rococo. The new emphasis on emotion and family life, represented in Rousseau's *The New Heloise*, was reflected in a growing taste for moralistic family scenes in painting. The paintings of Jean-Baptiste Greuze (1725–1805), much praised by Diderot, depicted ordinary families at moments of domestic crisis. Such subjects appealed in particular to the middle-class public, which now attended the official painting exhibitions in France that were held regularly every other year after 1737. Court painting nonetheless remained much in demand. Marie-Louise-Elizabeth Vigée-Lebrun (1755–1842), who painted portraits at the French court, reported that in the 1780s "it was difficult to get a place on my waiting list. . . . I was the fashion."

The English engraver and painter William Hogarth (1697–1764) ranged from noble portraits to popular moralistic print series. He sold his engravings to the middle class but he still hoped to have his work taken seriously as high art. The English potter Josiah Wedgwood (1730–1795) almost

Jean-Baptiste Greuze, *The Beloved Mother* (1765)
Greuze made his reputation as a painter of moralistic family scenes. In this one, a mother has just finished breast-feeding her infant, a practice urgently advocated at just this time by Rousseau. The contented mother is surrounded by adoring children and an admiring husband. Diderot praised Greuze's work as "morality in paint," but in later years Greuze began to depict much more ambiguous scenes, often with an erotic subtext. Art Resource, NY.

single-handedly created a mass market for domestic crockery by appealing to middle-class desires to emulate the rich and royal. His designs of special tea sets for the British queen, for Catherine the Great of Russia, and for leading aristocrats allowed him to advertise his wares as fashionable. As he said, "Few ladies dare venture at anything out of the common stile 'till authorized by their betters." By 1767, he claimed that his Queensware pottery had "spread over the whole Globe," and indeed by then his pottery was being marketed in France, Russia, Venice, the Ottoman Empire, and British North America.

Although wealthy nobles still patronized Europe's leading musicians, music too began to reflect the broadening of the elite and the spread of Enlightenment ideals as classical forms replaced the baroque style. Complex polyphony gave way to melody, which made the music more accessible to ordinary listeners. The violin's tone became stronger and more resonant, and it overcame a reputation as fit only for village dances. Mass sections of string instruments became the backbone of professional orchestras, which now played to large audiences of well-to-do listeners in sizable concert halls. The public concert gradually displaced the private recital, and a new attitude toward "the classics" developed: for the first time in the 1770s and 1780s, concert groups began to play older music rather than simply playing the latest commissioned works.

This laid the foundation for what we still call *classical* music today, that is, a repertory of the greatest music of the eighteenth and early nineteenth centuries. Because composers now created works that would be performed over and over again as part of a classical repertory, rather than occasional pieces for the court or noble patrons, they deliberately attempted to write lasting works. As a result, the major composers began to produce fewer symphonies: the Austrian composer Franz Joseph Haydn (1732–1809) wrote more than one hundred symphonies, but his successor Ludwig van Beethoven (1770–1827) would create only nine.

The two supreme masters of the new musical style of the eighteenth century show that the transition from noble patronage to classical concerts was far from complete. The Austrians Haydn and Wolfgang Amadeus Mozart (1756–1791) both wrote for noble patrons, but by the early 1800s their compositions had been incorporated into the canon of concert classics all over Europe. Incredibly prolific, both excelled in combining lightness, clarity, and profound emotion. Both also wrote numerous Italian operas, a genre whose popularity continued to grow: in the 1780s, the Papal States alone boasted forty opera houses. Haydn spent most of his career working for a Hungarian noble family, the Eszterházys. Asked why he had written no string quintets (at which Mozart excelled), he responded simply: "No one has ordered any."

Reading Matters. The Enlightenment created a new public for reading that extended far beyond the narrow confines of standard secondary and higher education. In secondary school, whether lay- or church-run, boys studied Latin, Greek, philosophy, and logic but spent little time on mathematics, science, history, or modern languages. Girls learned domestic skills, some music, and one or two foreign languages, but they did not receive the classical education considered essential for government service or intellectual life. Boys and girls read Enlightenment books at home, not in school. The universities of many countries appeared rigid and behind the times. As an Austrian reformer complained about the universities in his country, "Critical history, natural sciences—which are supposed to make enlightenment general and combat prejudice—were neglected or wholly unknown."

Shaped by coffeehouses, Masonic lodges, and public concerts more than by formal schooling, the new reading public fed a frenzied increase in publication. By the end of the eighteenth century, six times as many books were being published in the German states, for instance, as at the beginning. One Parisian author commented that "people are certainly reading ten times as much in Paris as they did a hundred years ago." Although religious books still predominated, books on history, the arts, and the sciences proliferated. Provincial towns in Britain, France, the Dutch Republic, and the German states published their own newspapers; by 1780, thirty-seven English towns had local newspapers. Newspapers advertised arithmetic, dancing, and drawing lessons, and they did not always stick to high-minded subjects; they also advertised cures for venereal disease and abortifacients. Lending libraries multiplied, and, in England especially, even small villages housed secular book clubs. Women benefited as much as men from the spread of print. As one Englishman observed, "By far the greatest part of ladies now have a taste for books." Catherine Macaulay (1731–1791) published best-selling histories of Britain, and in France Stéphanie de Genlis (1746–1830) wrote children's books—a genre that was growing in importance as middle-class parents became more interested in education.

The novel had become a respectable and influential genre. Among the most widely read novels were those of the English printer and writer Samuel Richardson (1689–1761). In *Clarissa Harlowe* (1747–1748), a long novel in eight volumes, Richardson told the story of a young woman from a heartless upper-class family who is torn between her family's choice of a repulsive suitor and her attraction to Lovelace, an aristocratic rake. Although she runs off with Lovelace to escape her family, she resists his advances; after being drugged and raped by Lovelace—despite the frantic pleas of readers of the first volumes to spare her—Clarissa dies of what can only be called a broken heart. One woman complained to Richardson, "I verily believe I have shed a pint of tears, and my heart is still bursting." The French writer Diderot compared Richardson to Moses, Homer, Euripides, and Sophocles.

Novels aroused criticism, however, because they sympathetically portrayed characters from the lower classes. Even Richardson attacked his fellow English novelist Henry Fielding: "I found the characters and situations so wretchedly low and dirty, that I imagined I could not be interested for any one of them. . . . It is beyond my conception, that a man of family, and who had some learning, and who really is a writer, should descend so excessively low, in all his pieces. Who can care for any of his people?" Although Richardson wrote *Clarissa* as a kind of manual of virtuous female conduct, critics worried that novels undermined morals with their portrayals of low-life characters, the seductions of virtuous women, and other examples of immoral behavior.

Spotlight on Children. As the rates of child mortality gradually declined in the 1700s, children became the focus of much new attention. Rousseau's *Emile* attracted so many readers because it offered an educational approach for gently drawing the best out of children rather than repressing their natural curiosity and love of learning. The book helped

change attitudes in the new elite toward children, who were no longer viewed only as little sinners in need of harsh discipline. Paintings now showed individual children playing at their favorite activities rather than formally posed with their families. Books about and for children became popular. *The Newtonian System of the Universe Digested for Young Minds*, by "Tom Telescope," was published in Britain in 1761 and reprinted many times. In 1730, no shops specialized in children's toys in Britain; by 1780, such shops could be found throughout the country. In 1762, John Spilsbury, a London engraver and mapmaker, invented the jigsaw puzzle when he mounted a map on a sheet of wood and cut around the borders of the countries using a fine-bladed saw. Babies' and children's clothing now differed in style from adult clothing: childhood was seen as a separate stage of life, and children were no longer considered miniature adults.

The Enlightenment's emphasis on reason, self-control, and childhood innocence made parents increasingly anxious about their children's sexuality. Moralists and physicians wrote books about the evils of masturbation, "proving" that it led to physical and mental degeneration and even madness. One English writer linked masturbation to debility of body and of mind; infertility; epilepsy; loss of memory, sight, and hearing; distortions of the eyes, mouth, and face; a pale, sallow, and bluish complexion; wasting of the limbs; idiotism; and death itself. The Enlightenment taught the middle and upper classes to value their children and to expect their improvement through education, but at the same time it encouraged excessive concern about children being left too much to their own devices.

Life on the Margins

The upper and middle classes worried most about the increasing numbers of poor people. Although booming foreign trade—French colonial trade increased tenfold in the 1700s—fueled a dramatic economic expansion, the results did not necessarily trickle all the way down the social scale. The population of Europe grew by nearly 30 percent, with especially striking gains in England, Ireland, Prussia, and Hungary. (See "Taking Measure," page 704.) Even though food production increased, shortages and crises still occurred periodically. Prices went up in many countries after the 1730s and continued to

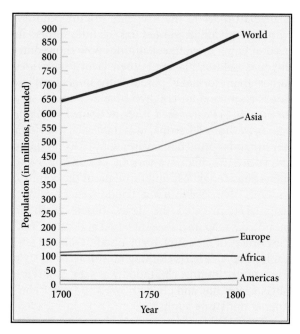

TAKING MEASURE World Population Growth, 1700–1800

Asia had many more people than Europe, and both Asia and Europe were growing much more rapidly in the 1700s than Africa or the Americas. The population stagnation in Africa has been the subject of much scholarly controversy. What are the advantages of a growing population? What are the disadvantages?
Adapted from Andre Gundar Frank, *Reorient: Global Economy in the Asian Age* (Berkeley: University of California Press), 1998.

rise gradually until the early nineteenth century; wages in many trades rose as well, but less quickly than prices. Peasants who produced surpluses to sell in local markets and shopkeepers and artisans who could increase their sales to meet growing demand prospered. But those at the bottom of the social ladder—day laborers in the cities and peasants with small holdings—lived on the edge of dire poverty, and when they lost their land or work, they either migrated to the cities or wandered the roads in search of food and work. In France alone, 200,000 workers left their homes every year in search of seasonal employment elsewhere. At least 10 percent of Europe's urban population depended on some form of charity.

The growing numbers of poor overwhelmed local governments. In some countries, beggars and vagabonds had been locked up in workhouses since the mid-1600s. The expenses for running these overcrowded institutions increased 60 percent in England between 1760 and 1785. After 1740, most German towns created workhouses that were part workshop, part hospital, and part prison. Such institutions also appeared for the first time in Boston, New York, and Philadelphia. To supplement the inadequate system of religious charity, offices for the poor, public workshops, and workhouse-hospitals, the French government created *dépôts de mendicité*, or beggar houses, in 1767. The government sent people to these new workhouses to labor in manufacturing, but most were too weak or sick to work, and 20 percent of them died within a few months of incarceration. The ballooning number of poor people created fears about rising crime. To officials, beggars seemed more aggressive than ever. The handful of police assigned to keep order in each town or district found themselves confronted with increasing incidents of rural banditry and crimes against property.

Persistence of Popular Culture. An increase in literacy, especially in the cities, allowed some lower-class people to participate in new tastes and ideas. One French observer insisted, "These days, you see a waiting-maid in her backroom, a lackey in an anteroom reading pamphlets. People can read in almost all classes of society." In France, however, only 50 percent of men and 27 percent of women could read and write in the 1780s (although that was twice the rate of a century earlier). Literacy rates were higher in England and the Dutch Republic, but much lower in eastern Europe. About one in four Parisians owned books, but the lower classes overwhelmingly read religious books, as they had in the past.

Whereas the new elite might attend salons, concerts, or art exhibitions, peasants enjoyed their traditional forms of popular entertainment, such as fairs and festivals, and the urban lower classes relaxed in cabarets and taverns. Sometimes pleasures were cruel. In Britain, bullbaiting, bearbaiting, dogfighting, and cockfighting were all common forms of entertainment that provided opportunities for organized gambling. Even "gentle" sports frequented by the upper classes had their violent side, showing that the upper classes had not become so different as they sometimes thought. Cricket matches, whose rules were first laid down in 1744, were often accompanied by brawls among fans (not unlike soccer matches today, though on a much smaller scale). Many Englishmen enjoyed what one observer called a "battle royal with sticks, pebbles and hog's dung."

Changes in Sexual Behavior. As population increased and villagers began to move to cities to better their prospects, sexual behavior changed too. The rates of births out of wedlock soared, from less than 5 percent of all births in the seventeenth century to nearly 20 percent at the end of the eighteenth. Historians have disagreed about the causes and meaning of this change. Some detect in this pattern a sign of sexual liberation and the beginnings of a modern sexual revolution: as women moved out of the control of their families, they began to seek their own sexual fulfillment. Others view this change more bleakly, as a story of seduction and betrayal: family and community pressure had once forced a man to marry a woman pregnant with his child, but now a man could abandon a pregnant lover, just by moving away.

Increased mobility brought freedom for some women, but it also aggravated the vulnerability of those newly arrived in cities from the countryside. For them, desperation, not reason, often ruled their choices. Women who came to the city as domestic servants had little recourse against masters or fellow servants who seduced or raped them. The result was a startling rise in abandoned babies. Most European cities established foundling hospitals in the 1700s, but infant and child mortality was 50 percent higher in such institutions than for children brought up at home. Some women tried herbs, laxatives, or crude surgical means of abortion; a few, usually servants who would lose their jobs if their employers discovered they had borne a child, resorted to infanticide.

European states had long tried to regulate sexual behavior but without much consistent success. Every country had laws against prostitution, adultery, fornication, sodomy, and infanticide. Despite official denunciations, sexual entertainment for men grew increasingly commercialized in this period of economic growth, and houses of prostitution became more specialized, developing into flagellation clubs and bagnios, which combined brothel and bathhouse. Reformers advocated lessening of punishments for fornication, which often included some form of public humiliation, and they criticized the harshness of laws against infanticide, but they showed no mercy for "sodomites" (as male homosexuals were called), who in some places, in particular the Dutch Republic, were systematically persecuted and imprisoned or even executed. Male homosexuals attracted the attention of authorities because they had begun to develop networks and special meeting places. The stereotype of the effeminate, exclusively homosexual male seems to have appeared for the first time in the eighteenth century, perhaps as part of a growing emphasis on separate roles for men and women.

Roots of Industrialization

Although it was only starting to take hold, industrialization would eventually transform European society. The process began in England in the 1770s and 1780s and included four interlocking trends: (1) population increased dramatically, by more than 50 percent in England in the second half of the eighteenth century; (2) manufacturers introduced steam-driven machinery to increase output; (3) they established factories to concentrate the labor of their workers; and (4) the production of cotton goods, which were lighter and more versatile than woolens, increased tenfold. Together these factors sparked the Industrial Revolution, which would change the face of Europe—indeed, of the entire world—in the nineteenth century.

Innovations in the technology of cotton production permitted manufacturers to make use of the growing supply of raw cotton shipped from the plantations of North America and the Caribbean. In 1733, the Englishman John Kay patented the flying shuttle, which weavers operated by pulling a cord that drove the shuttle to either side, enabling them to "throw" yarn across the loom rather than draw it back and forth by hand. When the flying shuttle came into widespread use in the 1760s, weavers began producing cloth more quickly than spinners could produce the thread. The shortage of spun thread propelled the invention of machines to speed the process of spinning: the spinning jenny and the water frame, a power-driven spinning machine, were introduced in the 1760s. In the following decades, water frames replaced thousands of women spinners working at home by hand. In 1776, the Scottish engineer James Watt developed an improved steam engine, and, in the 1780s, Edmund

Handloom Weaving
This plate from the Encyclopedia *demonstrates handloom weaving of gold-threaded fabrics (tassels, trims, fringes, borders). Fancy threads could not be used on the early mechanical looms, which were suitable only for basic cotton thread. This kind of handloom weaving continued well into the 1800s.* Stock Montage, Inc.

Cartwright, an English clergyman and inventor, designed a mechanized loom, which when perfected could be run by a small boy and yield fifteen times the output of a skilled adult weaver working a handloom. By the end of the century, all the new power machinery was assembled in large factories that hired semiskilled men, women, and children to replace skilled weavers.

Historians have no single explanation for why England led the Industrial Revolution. Some have emphasized England's large internal market, increasing population, supply of private investment capital from overseas trade and commercial profits, or natural resources such as coal and iron. Others have cited England's greater opportunities for social mobility, its relative political stability in the eighteenth century, or the pragmatism of the English and Scottish inventors who designed the necessary machinery. These early industrialists hardly had a monopoly on ingenuity, but they did come out of a tradition of independent capitalist enterprise. They

also shared a culture of informal scientific education through learned societies and popular lectures (one of the prominent forms of the Enlightenment in Britain). For whatever reasons, the combination of improvements in agricultural production, growth in population and foreign trade, and willingness to invest in new machines and factories appeared first in this relatively small island.

Although the rest of Europe did not industrialize until the nineteenth century, textile manufacturing—long a linchpin in the European economy—expanded dramatically in the eighteenth century even without the introduction of new machines and factories. Textile production increased because of the spread of the "putting-out" or "domestic" system. Hundreds of thousands of families manufactured cloth in every country from Britain to Russia. Under the putting-out system, manufacturers supplied the families with raw materials, such as woolen or cotton fibers. Working at home in a dimly lit room, a whole family labored together. The mother and her children washed the fibers and carded and combed them. Then the mother and oldest daughters spun them into thread. The father, assisted by the children, wove the cloth. The cloth was then finished (bleached, dyed, smoothed, and so on) under the supervision of the manufacturer in a large workshop, located either in town or in the countryside. This system had existed in the textile industry for hundreds of years, but in the eighteenth century it expanded immensely, drawing in thousands of peasants in the countryside, and it included not only textiles but also the manufacture of such products as glassware, baskets, nails, and guns. The spread of the domestic system of manufacturing is sometimes called *proto-industrialization* to signify that the process helped pave the way for the full-scale Industrial Revolution.

All across Europe, thousands of people who worked in agriculture became part-time or full-time textile workers. Peasants turned to putting-out work because they did not have enough land to support their families. Men labored off-season and women often worked year-round to augment their meager incomes. At the same time, population growth and general economic improvement meant that demand for cloth increased because more people could afford it. Studies of wills left by working-class men and women in Paris at the end of the eighteenth century show that people owned more clothes of greater variety. Working-class men in Paris began to wear underclothes, something rare at the beginning of the century. Men and women now bought night-clothes; before, Europeans had slept naked except in cold weather. And white, red, blue, yellow, green, and even pastel shades of cotton now replaced the black, gray, or brown of traditional woolen dress.

❖ State Power in an Era of Reform

All rulers recognized that manufacturing created new sources of wealth, but the start of industrialization had not yet altered the standard forms of competition between states: commerce and war. The diffusion of Enlightenment ideas of reform had a more immediate impact on the ways European monarchs exercised power than did industrialization. Historians label many of the sovereigns of this time "enlightened despots" or "enlightened absolutists," for they aimed to combine Enlightenment reforms with absolutist powers. Catherine the Great's admiring relationship with Voltaire showed how even the most absolutist rulers championed reform when it suited their own goals. Voltaire considered the nobles and the established churches the real obstacles to reform, and, like many other Enlightenment writers, he looked to monarchs such as Catherine and Frederick the Great of Prussia to overcome their resistance.

Every European ruler tried to introduce reforms in this period, including improvements in the condition of the peasantry in Austria, freer markets in grain in France, extension of education in Prussia, and new law codes almost everywhere. Success or failure in the competition for trade and territory directly affected these reform efforts. French losses in the Seven Years' War, for example, prompted the French crown to introduce far-reaching reforms that provoked violent resistance and helped pave the way for the French Revolution of 1789. Reform proved to be a two-edged sword.

War and Diplomacy

Europeans no longer fought devastating wars over religion that killed hundreds of thousands of civilians; instead, professional armies and navies battled for control of overseas empires and for dominance on the European continent. Rulers continued to expand their armies: the Prussian army, for example, nearly tripled in size between 1740 and 1789. Widespread use of flintlock muskets required deployment in long lines, usually three men deep, with each line in turn loading and firing on command. Military strategy became cautious and calculating, but this did not prevent the outbreak of hostilities. The instability of the European balance of power resulted in two major wars, a diplomatic reversal of alliances, and the partition of Poland-Lithuania among Russia, Austria, and Prussia. By 1789, Prussia had confirmed its rise to great-power status, the British had eclipsed the French overseas, and once-great Poland-Lithuania had been reduced in size and importance.

War of the Austrian Succession, 1740–1748. The difficulties over the succession to the Austrian throne typified the dynastic complications that

Maria Theresa and Her Family
In this portrait by Martin van Meytens (1695–1770), Austrian empress Maria Theresa is shown with her husband, Francis I, and eleven of their sixteen children. Their eldest son eventually succeeded to the Austrian throne as Joseph II, and their youngest daughter, Maria Antonia, or Marie-Antoinette, became the queen of France.
Giraudon/Art Resource, NY.

repeatedly threatened the European balance of power. In 1740, Holy Roman Emperor Charles VI died without a male heir. Most European rulers recognized the emperor's chosen heiress, his daughter Maria Theresa, because Charles's Pragmatic Sanction of 1713 had given a woman the right to inherit the Habsburg crown lands. The new king of Prussia, Frederick II, who had just succeeded his father a few months earlier in 1740, saw his chance to grab territory and immediately invaded the rich Austrian province of Silesia. France joined Prussia in an attempt to further humiliate its traditional enemy Austria, and Great Britain allied with Austria to prevent the French from taking the Austrian Netherlands (Map 19.2). The War of the Austrian Succession (1740–1748) soon expanded to the overseas colonies of Great Britain and France as well. Maria Theresa (r. 1740–1780) survived only by conceding Silesia to Prussia in order to split the Prussians off from France. The Peace of Aix-la-Chapelle of 1748 recognized Maria Theresa as the heiress to the Austrian lands, and her husband, Francis I, became Holy

Roman Emperor, thus reasserting the integrity of the Austrian Empire.

The fighting between France and Great Britain quickly extended to India, where a series of naval battles left the British in control of the seas. The peace of 1748 failed to resolve the colonial conflicts, and British and French trading companies continued to fight unofficially for domination in India. French and British colonials in North America also fought each other all along their boundaries, enlisting native American auxiliaries. Britain tried but failed to isolate the French Caribbean colonies during the war, and hostilities and suspicions continued unabated.

Seven Years' War, 1756–1763. In 1756, a major reversal of alliances—what historians call the "Diplomatic Revolution"—reshaped relations among the great powers. Prussia and Great Britain signed a defensive alliance, prompting Austria to overlook two centuries of hostility and ally with France. Russia and Sweden soon joined the Franco-Austrian

MAP 19.2 War of the Austrian Succession, 1740–1748

The accession of a twenty-three-year-old woman, Maria Theresa, to the Austrian throne gave the new king of Prussia, Frederick II, an opportunity to invade the province of Silesia. France joined on Prussia's side, Great Britain on Austria's. In 1745, the French defeated the British in the Austrian Netherlands and helped instigate a Jacobite uprising in Scotland. The rebellion failed and British attacks on French overseas shipping forced the French to negotiate. The peace treaties guaranteed Frederick's conquest of Silesia, which soon became the wealthiest province of Prussia. France came to terms with Great Britain to protect its overseas possessions; Austria had to accept the peace settlement after a formal public protest.

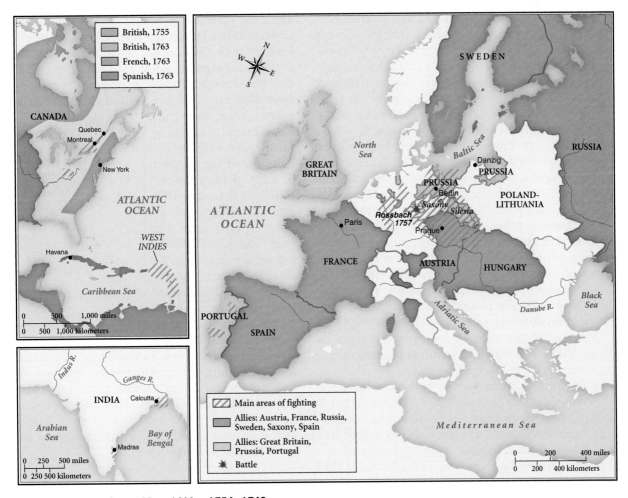

MAP 19.3 The Seven Years' War, 1756–1763

In what might justly be called the first worldwide war, the French and British fought each other on the European continent, in the West Indies, and in India. Their international struggle coincided with a realignment of forces within Europe caused by the desire of Austria, France, and Russia to check Prussian growth. Fearing, with reason, a joint Austrian-Russian attack, Frederick II of Prussia invaded Saxony in August 1756. Despite overwhelming odds, Frederick managed time and again to emerge victorious, until the Russians withdrew and the coalition against Prussia fell apart. The treaty between Austria and Prussia simply restored the status quo. The changes overseas were much more dramatic. Britain gained control over Canada and India but gave back to France the West Indian islands of Guadeloupe and Martinique. Britain was now the dominant power on the seas.

alliance. When Frederick II invaded Saxony, an ally of Austria, with his bigger and better-disciplined army, the long-simmering hostilities between Great Britain and France over colonial boundaries flared into a general war that became known as the Seven Years' War (1756–1763).

Fighting soon raged around the world (Map 19.3). The French and British battled on land and sea in North America (where the conflict was called the French and Indian War), the West Indies, and India. The two coalitions also fought each other in central Europe. At first, in 1757, Frederick the Great surprised Europe with a spectacular victory at Rossbach in Saxony over a much larger Franco-Austrian army. But in time, Russian and Austrian armies encircled his troops. Frederick despaired: "I believe all is lost. I will not survive the ruin of my country." A fluke of history saved him. Empress Elizabeth of

Russia (r. 1741–1762) died and was succeeded by the mentally unstable Peter III, a fanatical admirer of Frederick and things Prussian. Peter withdrew Russia from the war. (This was practically his only accomplishment as tsar. He was soon mysteriously murdered, probably at the instigation of his wife, Catherine the Great.) In a separate peace treaty Frederick kept all his territory, including Silesia.

Although Prussia suffered great losses in the fighting—some 160,000 Prussian soldiers died either in action or of disease—the army helped vault Prussia to the rank of leading powers. In 1733, Frederick II's father, Frederick William I, had instituted the "canton system," which enrolled peasant youths in each canton (or district) in the army, gave them two or three months of training annually, and allowed them to return to their family farms the rest of the year. They remained "cantonists" (reservists) as long as they were able-bodied. In this fashion, the Prussian military steadily grew in size; by 1740, Prussia had the third or fourth largest army in Europe even though it was tenth in population and thirteenth in land area. Under Frederick II, Prussia's military expenditures rose to two-thirds of the state's revenue. Virtually every nobleman served in the army, paying for his own support as officer and buying a position as company commander. Once retired, the officers returned to their estates, coordinated the canton system, and served as local officials. In this way, the military permeated every aspect of rural society, fusing army and agrarian organization. The army gave the state great power, but the militarization of Prussian society also had a profoundly conservative effect: it kept the peasants enserfed to their lords and blocked the middle classes from access to estates or high government positions.

The Anglo-French overseas conflicts ended more decisively than the continental land wars. British naval superiority, fully achieved only in the 1750s, enabled Great Britain to decisively defeat the French in their competition for colonial supremacy; the British routed the French in North America, India, and the West Indies. In the Treaty of Paris of 1763, France ceded Canada to Great Britain and agreed to remove its armies from India, in exchange for keeping its rich West Indian islands. Eagerness to avenge this defeat would motivate France to support the British North American colonists in their War of Independence just fifteen years later.

The First Partition of Poland, 1772. Eighteenth-century Poland-Lithuania was large but weak, and it became prey to the absolutist powers that surrounded it. Under Catherine the Great, Russia successfully battled the Ottoman Empire in intermittent fighting from 1768 to 1774 and promoted Greek efforts at independence from the Turks. Fearful of increasing Russian influence in the Balkans and the prospect of complete Russian domination of Poland, in 1772 Frederick the Great of Prussia proposed that large chunks of Polish-Lithuanian territory be divided among Austria, Prussia, and Russia. Despite the protests of the Austrian empress Maria Theresa that the partition

The First Partition of Poland, 1772

would spread "a stain over my whole reign," she agreed to split one-third of Poland-Lithuania's territory and half of its people among the three powers. Conflicts between Catholics, Protestants, and Orthodox Christians were used to justify this cynical move. Russia took over most of Lithuania, effectively ending the Polish-Lithuanian commonwealth.

State-Sponsored Reform

In the aftermath of the Seven Years' War, all the belligerents faced pressing needs for more money to fund their growing armies, to organize navies to wage overseas conflicts, and to counter the impact of inflation. Rather than simply raise taxes as they had in the past, the enlightened absolutists—Frederick II in Prussia, Catherine II in Russia, Maria Theresa and Joseph II (r. 1780–1790) in Austria, Louis XV (r. 1715–1774) and Louis XVI (r. 1774–1792) in France—all proposed similar programs to increase economic and military power by modernizing society. In short, they tried to make tax increases more palatable by promising general social reforms. To harness Enlightenment ideals to their own ends, they appointed reform-minded ministers and gave them a mandate to inventory the country's resources in order to make taxes more equitable and standardize their collection, establish state independence from the church, make the legal system more predictable and accessible, and, in some instances, extend education and religious toleration. As one adviser to Joseph II put it, "A properly constituted state must be exactly analogous to a machine . . . and the ruler must be the foreman, the mainspring . . . which sets everything else in motion." Such reforms always threatened the interests of traditional groups, however, and the spread of Enlightenment ideas aroused sometimes unpredictable desires for more change.

Administrative and Legal Reforms. The reforming monarchs did not invent government bureaucracy, but in Austria and Prussia especially they insisted on greater attention to merit, hard work, and professionalism, which made bureaucrats more like modern civil servants. As Joseph II of Austria explained, government must be organized according to "uniform principles," and it must unite "a single mass of people all subject to impartial guidance." In this view, the ruler should be a benevolent, enlightened administrator who worked for the general well-being of his or her people. Frederick II of Prussia, who drove himself as hard as he drove his officials, boasted, "I am the first servant of the state."

Legal reform, both of the judicial system and of the often disorganized and irregular law codes, was central to the work of many reform-minded monarchs. Although Frederick II favored all things French in culture—he insisted on speaking French in his court and prided himself on his personal friendship with Voltaire—he made Prussian justice the envy of Europe. His institution of a uniform civil justice system created the most consistently administered laws and efficient judiciary of the time. Joseph II also ordered the compilation of a unified law code, a project that required many years for completion. Catherine II of Russia began such an undertaking even more ambitiously. In 1767, she called together a legislative commission of 564 deputies and asked them to consider a long document called the *Instruction*, which represented her hopes for legal reform based on the ideas of Montesquieu and the Italian writer Cesare Beccaria. Montesquieu had insisted that punishment should fit the crime; he criticized the use of torture and brutal corporal punishment. In his influential book *On Crimes and Punishments* (1764), Beccaria argued

Dividing Poland, 1772
In this contemporary depiction, Catherine the Great, Joseph II, and Frederick II point on the map to the portion of Poland-Lithuania each plans to take. The artist makes it clear that Poland's fate rested in the hands of neighboring rulers, not its own people.
Mansell/Time, Inc.

that laws should be printed for everyone to read and administered in rational procedures, that torture should be abolished as inhumane, and that the accused should be presumed innocent until proven guilty. Despite much discussion and hundreds of petitions and documents about local problems, little came of Catherine's commission because the monarch herself—despite her regard for Voltaire and his fellow philosophes—was not very committed to reform.

The Church and Education. Rulers everywhere wanted more control over church affairs, and they used Enlightenment criticisms of the organized churches to get their way. In Catholic countries, many government officials resented the influence of the Jesuits, the major Catholic teaching order. The

Jesuits trained the Catholic intellectual elite, ran a worldwide missionary network, enjoyed close ties to the papacy, and amassed great wealth. Critics mounted campaigns against the Jesuits in many countries, and by the early 1770s the Society of Jesus had been dissolved in Portugal, France, and Spain. In 1773, Pope Clement XIV (r. 1769–1774) agreed under pressure to disband the order, an edict that held until a reinvigorated papacy restored the society in 1814. Joseph II of Austria not only applauded the suppression of the Jesuits but also required Austrian bishops to swear fidelity and submission to him. Under Joseph, the Austrian state supervised seminaries, reorganized diocesan boundaries, abolished comtemplative monastic orders, and confiscated their property to pay for education and poor relief.

Enlightened absolutists tried to gain greater state authority over education, even while extending education to the lower classes. Joseph II launched the most ambitious educational reforms of the period. In 1774, once the Jesuits had been disbanded, a General School Ordinance in Austria ordered state subsidies for local schools, which the state would regulate. By 1789, one-quarter of the school-age children attended school. In Prussia the school code of 1763 required all children between the ages of five and thirteen to attend school. Although not enforced uniformly, the Prussian law demonstrated Frederick II's belief that modernization depended on education. Catherine II of Russia also tried to expand elementary education—and the education of women in particular—and founded engineering schools.

Religious Toleration. Many rulers favored religious toleration, but no one achieved more than Joseph II of Austria, who had become Holy Roman Emperor and co-regent with his mother, Maria Theresa, in 1765. Joseph was able to carry out his most radical policies only when he ruled alone after 1780, but then he acted swiftly and sometimes brutally. His own brother described him as "imbued with arbitrary, brutal principles and the most severe, brutal and violent despotism." These qualities nevertheless enabled Joseph to push through reforms that might otherwise have been resisted. In 1781, he granted freedom of religious worship to Protestants, Orthodox Christians, and Jews. For the first time

these groups were allowed to own property, build schools, enter the professions, and hold political and military offices.

The efforts of other rulers to extend religious toleration proved more limited. The French state regarded Protestants as heretics until 1787, when Louis XVI signed an edict of toleration restoring their civil rights—but still they could not hold political office. Great Britain continued to deny Catholics freedom of open worship and the right to sit in Parliament. Most European states limited the rights and opportunities available to Jews. In Russia, only wealthy Jews could hold municipal office, and the Polish and Lithuanian Jews in the territory incorporated into Russia were restricted to certain places of residence. In Prussia, Frederick the Great called the Jews "useless to the state" and imposed special taxes on them. Even in Austria, where Joseph encouraged toleration, the laws forced Jews to take German-sounding names, and in the Papal States, the pope encouraged forced baptism. The leading philosophes opposed persecution of the Jews in theory but often treated them with undisguised contempt. Diderot's comment was all too typical: the Jews, he said, bore "all the defects peculiar to an ignorant and superstitious nation."

Limits of Reform

When government leaders introduce reforms, they often run into resistance from groups who feel threatened by innovation. Such was the experience of the absolutist rulers, who on many occasions faced upsurges of reaction that forced a quick backpedal. The most contentious area of reform was agricultural policy. Whereas Frederick II and Catherine II reinforced the authority of nobles over their serfs, Joseph II tried to remove the burdens of serfdom in the Habsburg lands. In 1781, he abolished the personal aspects of serfdom: serfs could now move freely, enter trades, or marry without their lords' permission. Joseph abolished the tithe to the church, shifted more of the tax burden to the nobility, and converted peasants' labor services into cash payments.

The Austrian nobility furiously resisted these far-reaching reforms. When Joseph died in 1790, his brother Leopold II had to revoke most reforms to appease the nobles. On his deathbed, Joseph recognized the futility of many of his efforts; as his epitaph he suggested, "Here lies Joseph II, who was unfortunate in all his enterprises." Prussia's Frederick II, like Joseph, encouraged such agricultural innovations as planting potatoes and turnips (new crops that could help feed a growing population), experimenting with cattle breeding, draining swamplands, and clearing forests. But Prussia's noble landlords, the Junkers, continued to expand their estates at the expense of poorer peasants, and Frederick did nothing to ameliorate serfdom except on his own domains.

Reforming ministers also tried to stimulate agricultural improvement in France. Unlike most other western European countries, France still had about 100,000 serfs; though their burdens weighed less heavily than those in eastern Europe, serfdom did not entirely disappear until 1789. A group of economists called the *physiocrats* urged the French government to deregulate the grain trade and make the tax system more equitable to encourage agricultural productivity. In the interest of establishing a free market, they also insisted that urban guilds be abolished because they prevented free entry into the trades. Their proposed reforms applied the Enlightenment emphasis on individual liberties to the

economy; Adam Smith took up many of the physiocrats' ideas in his writing in favor of free markets. The French government heeded some of this advice and gave up its system of price controls on grain in 1763, but it had to reverse this decision in 1770 when grain shortages caused a famine.

French reform efforts did not end there. To break the power of the parlements, the thirteen high courts of law that had led the way in opposing royal efforts to increase and equalize taxation, Louis XV appointed a reform-minded chancellor who replaced the parlements with courts in which the judges no longer owned their offices and thus could not sell them or pass them on as an inheritance. Justice would then be more impartial. Nevertheless, the judges of the displaced parlements aroused widespread opposition to what they portrayed as tyrannical royal policy. The furor calmed down only when Louis XV died in 1774 and his successor, Louis XVI, yielded to aristocratic demands and restored the old parlements. Louis XV died one of the most despised kings in French history, resented both for his high-handed reforms and his private vices. Underground pamphlets lampooned Louis, describing his final mistress, Madame Du Barry, as a prostitute who pandered to the elderly king's well-known taste

Russian Peasants

This engraving from the 1700s shows Russian peasants in their one-room hut. Two or more married brothers, their wives, children, and parents would share the space with poultry and livestock. Cooking took place in one corner, which was always diagonally across from the icon corner (left), where socializing took place. The fathers and younger men slept on benches, the rest of the family in the loft (right). In the winter, everyone slept near the oven.

Fotomas Index, UK.

for young girls. This often pornographic literature linked despotism to the supposedly excessive influence of women at court. Rousseau was not alone in attacking the feminizing influence of powerful women.

Louis XVI tried to carry out part of the program suggested by the physiocrats, and he chose one of their disciples, Jacques Turgot (1727–1781), as his chief minister. A contributor to the *Encyclopedia*, Turgot pushed through several edicts that again freed the grain trade, suppressed many guilds, converted the peasants' forced labor on roads into a money tax payable by all landowners, and reduced court expenses. He also began making plans to introduce a system of elected local assemblies, which would have made government much more representative. Faced with broad-based resistance led by the parlements and his own courtiers, as well as with riots against rising grain prices, Louis XVI dismissed Turgot, and one of the last possibilities to overhaul France's government collapsed.

The failure of reform in France paradoxically reflected the power of Enlightenment ideas; everyone now endorsed Enlightenment ideals but used them for different ends. The nobles in the parlements blocked the French monarchy's reform efforts using the very same Enlightenment language spoken by the crown's ministers. But unlike Austria, the other great power that faced persistent aristocratic resistance to reform, France had a large middle-class public that was increasingly frustrated by the failure to institute social change, a failure that ultimately helped undermine the monarchy itself. Where Frederick II, Catherine II, and even Joseph II used reform to bolster the efficiency of absolutist government, attempts at change in France backfired. French kings found that their ambitious programs for reform succeeded only in arousing unrealistic hopes.

❖ Rebellions against State Power

Although traditional forms of popular discontent had not disappeared, Enlightenment ideals and reforms changed the rules of the game in politics. Governments, especially in western Europe, now had to respond to public opinion; they had become accountable for their actions to a much wider range of people than ever before. In Britain and France, ordinary people rioted when they perceived government as failing to protect them against shortages created by free trade in grains. Monarchs justified their policies by appealing to the public, but they could not always control the consequences of the intensification of political interest. The growth of informed public opinion had its most dramatic consequences in the North American colonies, where a struggle over the British Parliament's right to tax turned into a full-scale war for independence. The American War of Independence showed that once put into practice, Enlightenment ideals could have revolutionary implications.

Food Riots and Peasant Uprisings

Population growth, inflation, and the extension of the market system put added pressure on the already beleaguered poorest classes of people. Seventeenth-century peasants and townspeople had rioted to protest new taxes. In the eighteenth century, they reacted violently when they feared that officials might fail to protect them from food shortages, either by freeing the grain market, which would benefit big farmers, or by requisitioning grain for the armies or the big cities. Other eighteenth-century forms of collective violence included riots against religious minorities, against militia recruiting, against turnpikes and tollgates, against attempts to arrest smugglers, and against enclosures of common fields. People sometimes rioted to express fear and anger in reaction to unexplained epidemics or to protest the execution of criminals who had captured the popular imagination.

In the last half of the eighteenth century, the food supply became the focus of political and social conflict. The poorer people in the villages and the towns believed it was the government's responsibility to ensure enough food for them, and in fact many governments did stockpile grain to make up for the occasional bad harvest. At the same time, in keeping with Adam Smith's and the French physiocrats' free market proposals, governments wanted to allow grain prices to rise with market demand, because higher profits would motivate producers to increase the overall supply of food.

But free trade in grain also meant selling to the highest bidder, even if that bidder was a foreign merchant. In the short run, in times of scarcity, big landowners and farmers could make huge profits by selling grain outside their hometowns or villages. This practice enraged poor farmers, agricultural workers, and city wageworkers, who could not afford the higher prices. Lacking the political means to affect policy, they could enforce their desire for old-fashioned price regulation only by rioting. Most did not pillage or steal grain but rather forced the sale of grain or flour at a "just" price and blocked the shipment of grain out of their villages to other markets. Women often led these "popular price fixings," as they were called in France, in desperate attempts to protect the food supply for their children.

Such food riots occurred regularly in Britain and France in the last half of the eighteenth century. One of the most turbulent was the so-called Flour War in France in 1775. Turgot's deregulation of the grain trade in 1774 caused prices to rise in several provincial cities. Rioting spread from there to the Paris region, where villagers attacked grain convoys heading to the capital city. Local officials often ordered merchants and bakers to sell at the price the rioters demanded, only to find themselves arrested by the central government for overriding free trade. The government brought in troops to restore order and introduced the death penalty for rioting.

Frustrations with serfdom and hopes for a miraculous transformation provoked the Pugachev rebellion in Russia beginning in 1773. An army deserter from the southeast frontier region, Emelian Pugachev (1742–1775) claimed to be Tsar Peter III, the dead husband of Catherine II. Pugachev's appearance seemed to confirm peasant hopes for a "redeemer tsar" who would save the people from oppression. He rallied around him Cossacks like himself who resented the loss of their old tribal independence. Now increasingly enserfed or forced to pay taxes and endure army service, these nomadic bands joined with other serfs, rebellious mineworkers, and Muslim minorities. Catherine dispatched a large army to squelch the uprising, but

The Pugachev Rebellion, 1773

Pugachev eluded them and the fighting spread. Nearly three million people eventually participated, making this the largest single rebellion in the history of tsarist Russia. When Pugachev urged the peasants to attack the nobility and seize their estates, hundreds of noble families perished. Foreign newspapers called it "the revolution in southern Russia" and offered fantastic stories about Pugachev's life history. Finally, the army captured the rebel leader and brought him in an iron cage to Moscow, where he was tortured and executed. In the aftermath, Catherine tightened the nobles' control over their serfs and harshly punished those who dared to criticize serfdom.

Public Opinion and Political Opposition

Peasant uprisings might briefly shake even a powerful monarchy, but the rise of public opinion as a force independent of court society caused more enduring changes in European politics. Across much of Europe and in the North American colonies, demands for broader political participation reflected Enlightenment notions about individual rights. Aristocratic bodies such as the French parlements, which had no legislative role like that of the British Parliament, insisted that the monarch consult them on the nation's affairs, and the new educated elite wanted more influence too. Newspapers began to cover daily political affairs, and the public learned the basics of political life, despite the strict limits on political participation in most countries.

Monarchs turned to public opinion to seek support against aristocratic groups that opposed reform. Gustavus III of Sweden (r. 1771–1792) called himself "the first citizen of a free people" and promised to deliver the country from "insufferable aristocratic despotism." Shortly after coming to the throne, Gustavus proclaimed a new constitution that divided power between the king and the legislature, abolished the use of torture in the judicial process, and assured some freedom of the press.

In France both the parlements and the monarch appealed to the public through the printed word. The crown hired writers to make its case; the magistrates of the parlements wrote their own rejoinders. French-language newspapers published in the Dutch Republic provided many people in France with detailed accounts of political news and also gave voice to pro-parlement positions. One of the

IMPORTANT DATES

1740–1748 War of the Austrian Succession: France, Spain, and Prussia versus Austria and Great Britain

1751–1772 *Encyclopedia* published in France

1756–1763 Seven Years' War fought in Europe, India, and the American colonies

1762 Jean-Jacques Rousseau, *The Social Contract* and *Emile*

1764 Voltaire, *Philosophical Dictionary*

1770 Louis XV of France fails to break the power of the French law courts

1772 First partition of Poland

1773 Pugachev rebellion of Russian peasants

1776 American Declaration of Independence from Great Britain; James Watt improves the steam engine, making it suitable for new industrial projects; Adam Smith, *The Wealth of Nations*

1780 Joseph II of Austria undertakes a wide-reaching reform program

1781 Immanuel Kant, *The Critique of Pure Reason*

1785 Catherine the Great's Charter of the Nobility grants nobles exclusive control over their serfs in exchange for subservience to the state

1787 Delegates from the states draft a new United States Constitution

new French-language newspapers printed inside France, *Le Journal des Dames* ("The Ladies' Journal"), was published by women and mixed short stories and reviews of books and plays with demands for more women's rights.

The Wilkes affair in Great Britain showed that public opinion could be mobilized to challenge a government. In 1763, during the reign of George III (r. 1760–1820), John Wilkes, a member of Parliament, attacked the government in his newspaper, *North Briton*, and sued the crown when he was arrested. He won his release as well as damages. When he was reelected, Parliament denied him his seat, not once but three times.

The Wilkes episode soon escalated into a major campaign against the corruption and social exclusiveness of Parliament, complaints the Levellers had first raised during the English Revolution of the late 1640s. Newspapers, magazines, pamphlets, handbills, and cheap editions of Wilkes's collected works

all helped promote his cause. Those who could not vote demonstrated for Wilkes. In one incident eleven people died when soldiers broke up a huge gathering of his supporters. The slogan "Wilkes and Liberty" appeared on walls all over London. Middle-class voters formed a Society of Supporters of the Bill of Rights, which circulated petitions for Wilkes; they gained the support of about one-fourth of all the voters. The more determined Wilkesites proposed sweeping reforms of Parliament, including more frequent elections, more representation for the counties, elimination of "rotten boroughs" (election districts so small that they could be controlled by one big patron), and restrictions of pensions used by the crown to gain support. These demands would be at the heart of agitation for parliamentary reform in Britain for decades to come.

Popular demonstrations did not always support reforms. In 1780, the Gordon riots devastated London. They were named after the fanatical anti-Catholic crusader Lord George Gordon, who helped organize huge marches and petition campaigns against a bill the House of Commons passed to grant limited toleration to Catholics. The demonstrations culminated in a seven-day riot that left fifty buildings destroyed and three hundred people dead. Despite the continuing limitation on voting rights in Great Britain, British politicians were learning that public opinion could be ignored only at their peril.

Political opposition also took artistic forms, particularly in countries where governments restricted organized political activity. A striking example of a play with a political message was *The Marriage of Figaro* (1784) by Pierre-Augustin Caron de Beaumarchais (1732–1799), a watchmaker, a judge, a gunrunner in the American War of Independence, and a French spy in Britain. *The Marriage of Figaro* was first a hit at court, when Queen Marie-Antoinette had it read for her friends. But when her husband, Louis XVI, read it, he forbade its production on the grounds that "this man mocks at everything that should be respected in government." When finally performed publicly, the play caused a sensation. The chief character, Figaro, is a clever servant who gets the better of his noble employer. When speaking of the count, he cries, "What have you done to deserve so many rewards? You went to the trouble of being born, and nothing more." Two years later, Mozart based an equally famous but somewhat tamer opera on Beaumarchais's story.

Revolution in North America

Oppositional forms of public opinion came to a head in Great Britain's North American colonies, where the result was American independence and the establishment of a republican constitution that stood in stark contrast to most European regimes. The successful revolution was the only blow to Britain's increasing dominance in world affairs in the eighteenth century, and as such it was another aspect of the power rivalries existing at that time. Yet many Europeans saw the American War of Independence, or the American Revolution, as a triumph for Enlightenment ideas. As one German writer exclaimed in 1777, American victory would give "greater scope to the Enlightenment, new keenness to the thinking of peoples and new life to the spirit of liberty."

The American revolutionary leaders had been influenced by a common Atlantic civilization; they participated in the Enlightenment and shared political ideas with the opposition Whigs in Britain.

Supporters demonstrated for Wilkes in South Carolina and Boston, and the South Carolina legislature donated a substantial sum to the Society of Supporters of the Bill of Rights. In the 1760s and 1770s, both British and American opposition leaders became convinced that the British government was growing increasingly corrupt and despotic, and both were concerned with the lack of representation in Parliament. British radicals wanted to reform Parliament so the voices of a broader, more representative segment of the population would be heard. The colonies had no representatives in Parliament, and colonists claimed that "no taxation without representation" should be allowed. Indeed, they denied that Parliament had any jurisdiction over the colonies, insisting that the king govern them through colonial legislatures and recognize their traditional British liberties. The failure of the "Wilkes and Liberty" campaign to produce concrete results convinced many Americans that Parliament was hopelessly tainted and that they would have to stand up for their rights as British subjects.

Overthrowing British Authority
The uncompromising attitude of the British government went a long way toward dissolving long-standing loyalties to the home country. During the American War of Independence, residents of New York City pulled down the statue of the hated George III.
Lafayette College Art Collection, Easton, Pennsylvania.

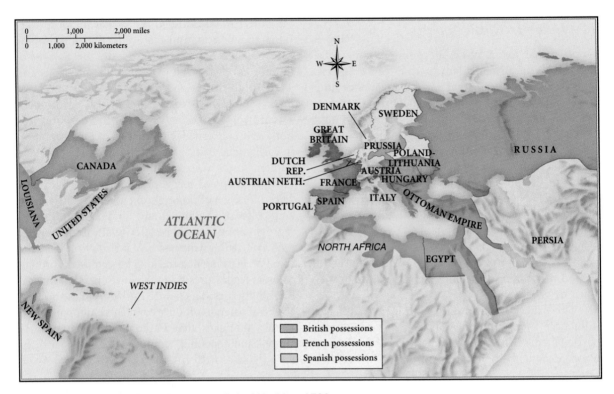

MAPPING THE WEST Europe and the World, c. 1780

Although Great Britain lost control over the British North American colonies, which became the new United States, European influence on the rest of the world grew dramatically in the eighteenth century. The slave trade linked European ports to African slave-trading outposts and to plantations in the Caribbean, South America, and North America. The European countries on the Atlantic Ocean benefited most from this trade. Yet almost all of Africa, China, Japan, and large parts of India still resisted European incursion, and the Ottoman Empire, with its massive territories, still towered over most European countries.

The British colonies remained loyal to the crown until Parliament's encroachment on their autonomy and the elimination of the French threat at the end of the Seven Years' War transformed colonial attitudes. Unconsciously, perhaps, the colonies had begun to form a separate nation; their economies generally flourished in the eighteenth century, and between 1750 and 1776 their population almost doubled. With the British clamoring for lower taxes and the colonists paying only a fraction of the tax rate paid by the Britons at home, Parliament passed new taxes, including the Stamp Act in 1765, which required a special tax stamp on all legal documents and publications. After violent rioting in the colonies, the new tax was repealed, but in 1773 a new Tea Act revived colonial resistance, which culminated in the so-called Boston Tea Party of 1773. Colonists dressed as Indians boarded

British ships and dumped the imported tea (by this time an enormously popular beverage) into Boston's harbor. The British government tried to clamp down on the unrest, but British troops in the colonies soon found themselves fighting locally organized militias.

Political opposition in the American colonies turned belligerent when Britain threatened to use force to maintain control. In 1774, the First Continental Congress convened, composed of delegates from all the colonies, and unsuccessfully petitioned the crown for redress. The next year the Second Continental Congress organized an army with George Washington in command. After actual fighting had begun, in 1776, the congress proclaimed the Declaration of Independence. An eloquent statement of the American cause written by Thomas Jefferson, the Declaration of Independence was couched in the language of universal human rights, which enlightened Europeans could be expected to understand. George III denounced the American "traitors and rebels," calling them "misled by dangerous and ill-designing men." But European newspapers enthusiastically reported on every American response to "the cruel acts of oppression they have been made to suffer." In the War of Independence (1775–1783), France boosted the American cause by entering on the colonists' side in 1778. Spain too saw an opportunity to check the growing power of Britain, though without actually endorsing American independence out of fear of the response of its Latin American colonies. Spain declared war on Britain in 1779; in 1780, Great Britain declared war on the Dutch Republic in retaliation for Dutch support of the rebels. The worldwide conflict that resulted was more than Britain could handle. The American colonies achieved their independence in the peace treaty of 1783.

The newly independent states still faced the challenge of republican self-government. The Articles of Confederation, drawn up in 1777 as a provisional constitution, proved weak because they gave the central government few powers. In 1787, a constitutional convention met in Philadelphia to draft a new constitution. It established a two-house legislature, an indirectly elected president, and an independent judiciary. The Constitution's preamble insisted explicitly, for the first time in history, that government derived its power solely from the people and did not depend on divine right or on the tradition of royalty or aristocracy. The new educated elite of the eighteenth century had now created government based on a "social contract" among male, property-owning, white citizens. It was by no means a complete democracy, and women and slaves were excluded from political participation. But the new government represented a radical departure from European models. In 1791, a Bill of Rights was appended to the Constitution outlining the essential rights (such as freedom of speech) that the government could never overturn. Although slavery continued in the American republic, the new emphasis on rights helped fuel a movement for its abolition in both Britain and the United States.

Interest in the new republic was greatest in France. The United States Constitution and various state constitutions were published in French with commentary by leading thinkers. Even more important in the long run were the effects of the American war. Dutch losses to Great Britain aroused a widespread movement for political reform in the Dutch Republic, and debts incurred by France in supporting the American colonies would soon force the French monarchy to the edge of bankruptcy and then to revolution. Ultimately, the entire European system of royal rule would be challenged.

Conclusion

The American Revolution was the most profound practical result of the general European movement known as the Enlightenment. When he looked back many years later on the Declaration of Independence, Thomas Jefferson said he hoped it would be "the signal of arousing men to burst the chains under which monkish ignorance and superstition had persuaded them to bind themselves." What began as a cosmopolitan movement of a few intellectuals in the first half of the eighteenth century reached a relatively wide audience among the educated elite of men and women. The spirit of reform swept from the salons and coffeehouses into the halls of government. Reasoned, scientific inquiry into the causes of social misery and laws defending individual rights and freedoms gained adherents everywhere.

For most Europeans, however, Enlightenment remained a promise rather than a reality. Rulers such as Catherine the Great had every intention of retaining their full, often unchecked, powers, even as they corresponded with leading philosophes, announced support for their causes, and entertained them at their courts. Moreover, would-be reformers often found themselves thwarted by the resistance of nobles, by the priorities rulers gave to waging wars, or by popular resistance to deregulation of trade that stripped away protection against the uncertainties of the market. Yet even the failure of reform contributed to the ferment in Europe after 1770. Peasant rebellions in eastern Europe, the "Wilkes and Liberty" campaign in Great Britain, the struggle over reform in France, and the revolution in America all occurred at about the same time, and their conjunction convinced many Europeans that the world was in fact changing. Just how much it had changed, and whether the change was for better or for worse, would become more evident in the next ten years.

Suggested References

The Enlightenment at Its Height

The interpretive study by Gay remains useful even though it is over thirty years old. Starobinski's intellectual biography of Rousseau shows the unities in the life and work of this enduringly controversial figure. Much more emphasis has been placed in recent studies on the role of women; on this point see Goodman and Landes. Equiano, an ex-slave, offers one of the earliest firsthand views of the experience of slavery. Voltaire's *Candide* is an accessible introduction to the thought of the philosophes.

*Equiano, Olaudah. *The Interesting Narrative and Other Writings*. Ed. Vincent Carretta. 1995.

Gay, Peter. *The Enlightenment: An Interpretation*. 2 vols. 1966, 1969.

Goodman, Dena. *The Republic of Letters: A Cultural History of the French Enlightenment*. 1994.

Griswold, Charles. *Adam Smith and the Virtues of Enlightenment*. 1999.

Jacob, Margaret C. *Living the Enlightenment: Freemasonry and Politics in Eighteenth-Century Europe*. 1991.

Landes, Joan B. *Women and the Public Sphere in the Age of the French Revolution*. 1988.

Starobinski, Jean. *Jean-Jacques Rousseau: Transparency and Obstruction*. Trans. Arthur Goldhammer. 1988.

*Voltaire. *Candide*. Ed. and trans. Daniel Gordon. 1999.

Voltaire Foundation: http://www.voltaire.ox.ac.uk.

Society and Culture in an Age of Enlightenment

Recent work has drawn attention to the lives of ordinary people. The personal journal of the French glassworker Ménétra is a rarity: it offers extensive documentation of the inner life of an ordinary person during the Enlightenment. Ménétra claimed to have met Rousseau. Even if not true, the claim shows that Rousseau's fame was not limited to the upper classes.

Darnton, Robert. *The Great Cat Massacre and Other Episodes in French Cultural History*. 1984.

Gullickson, Gay L. *Spinners and Weavers of Auffay: Rural Industry and the Sexual Division of Labor in a French Village, 1750–1850*. 1986.

Hull, Isabel V. *Sexuality, State, and Civil Society in Germany, 1700–1815*. 1996.

Jarrett, Derek. *England in the Age of Hogarth*. 1986.

McManners, John. *Death and the Enlightenment*. 1981.

*Ménétra, Jacques Louis. *Journal of My Life*. Trans. Arthur Goldhammer. Introd. Daniel Roche. 1986.

Mozart Project: http://www.frontiernet.net/~sboerner/mozart/biography/.

Stone, Lawrence. *The Family, Sex, and Marriage in England, 1500–1800*. Abridged ed. 1979.

Trumbach, Randolph. *Sex and the Gender Revolution*. 1998.

State Power in an Era of Reform

Biographies and general histories of this period tend to overemphasize the individual decisions of rulers. Although these are incontestably important, side-by-side reading of Büsch, Frederick II's writings on war, and Showalter's book on the wars themselves offers a broader view that puts Frederick II's policies into the context of military growth and its impact on society.

Blanning, T. C. W. *Joseph II and Enlightened Despotism*. 1970.

Büsch, Otto. *Military System and Social Life in Old Regime Prussia, 1713–1807: The Beginnings of the Social Militarization of Prusso-German Society*. Trans. John G. Gagliardo. 1997.

Crankshaw, Edward. *Maria Theresa*. 1996.

Cronin, Vincent. *Catherine, Empress of All the Russias*. 1996.

*Frederick II, King of Prussia. *Frederick the Great on the Art of War*. Ed. and trans. Jay Luvaas. 1999.

Showalter, Dennis E. *The Wars of Frederick the Great*. 1996.

Venturi, Franco. *The End of the Old Regime in Europe, 1768–1776: The First Crisis*. Trans. R. Burr Litchfield. 1989.

Rebellions against State Power

Exciting work has focused on specific instances of riot and rebellion. One of the most interesting studies is Thompson's work on the British repression of poaching and its significance for British social and political history. Palmer's overview remains valuable, especially for its comparative aspects.

Alexander, John T. *Autocratic Politics in a National Crisis: The Imperial Russian Government and Pugachev's Revolt, 1773–1775*. 1969.

Palmer, R. R. *The Age of Democratic Revolution: A Political History of Europe and America, 1760–1800*. Vol. 1, *The Challenge*. 1959.

*Rakove, Jack N. *Declaring Rights: A Brief History with Documents*. 1998.

Thomas, P. D. G. *John Wilkes: A Friend to Liberty*. 1996.

Thompson, E. P. *Whigs and Hunters: The Origin of the Black Act*. 1975.

Wood, Gordon S. *The Radicalism of the American Revolution*. 1992.

*Primary sources.

The Cataclysm of Revolution

1789–1800

Fall of the Bastille
The Bastille prison is shown here in all its imposing grandeur. The moment depicted is that of the surrender of the fortress's governor, Bernard René de Launay. Because so many of the besieging citizens had been killed (only one of the defenders died), popular anger ran high and de Launay was to be the sacrificial victim. As the hastily formed citizens' guard marched him off to city hall, huge crowds taunted and spat at him. When he lashed out at one of the men nearest him, he was immediately stabbed and shot. A pastry cook cut off the governor's head, which was promptly displayed as a trophy on a pike held high above the crowd. Royal authority had been successfully challenged and even humiliated.
Chateau de Versailles, France/
Bridgeman Art Library, NY.

O N OCTOBER 5, 1789, AN INCIDENT OCCURRED in France that reflected the trauma and unpredictability of revolutionary times. As tensions mounted over the rising price of bread and uncertainties about the future direction of the country, rumors spread that officers guarding the king at his palace at Versailles had stomped in drunken fury on the red, white, and blue cockades that adorned the hats of supporters of the emerging revolutionary movement. Outraged at this insult and determined to get the king's help in securing more grain for the hungry, a crowd of several thousand women marched in a drenching rain twelve miles from the center of Paris to Versailles. They sent delegates to talk with the king and demanded an audience with the deputies of the newly formed National Assembly, which met nearby. Before the evening was over, thousands of men had marched from Paris to reinforce the women. The atmosphere turned ominous as the crowd camped out all night near the palace.

Early the next morning, an angry mob forced its way into the palace grounds and broke into the royal family's private apartments. To prevent further bloodshed—two of the royal bodyguards had already been killed and their heads paraded on pikes—the king agreed to move his family and his government back to Paris. A dramatic procession guarded by thousands of ordinary men and women made its way back to Paris. The people's proud display of cannons and pikes underlined the fundamental transformation that was occurring. Ordinary people had forced the king of France to respond to their grievances. The French

1789	1791	1793	1795	1797	1800

Politics and War

- Dutch Patriot revolt
- War between France and Austria
- Poland disappears in the Third Partition
- Revolt in Austrian Netherlands
- Second Partition of Poland
- Napoleon Bonaparte comes to power
- French Revolution begins
- Beginning of slave revolt in St. Domingue (Haiti)
- Fall of Robespierre

Society and Economy

- Bread shortages and abolition of serfdom and seigneurial rights in France; Declaration of Rights of Man and Citizen
- Abolition of slavery in French colonies
- Divorce legalized in France
- Women's clubs forbidden in France

Culture, Religion, and Intellectual Life

- Civil Constitution of the Clergy
- De-Christianization movement and establishment of revolutionary calendar in France; nationalist revival in German states begins
- Thermidorian reaction and revival of Catholicism in France

monarchy was now in danger, and if such a powerful and long-lasting institution could come under fire, then could any monarch of Europe rest easy?

Although entirely unpredicted when it erupted in 1789, the French Revolution followed a series of upheavals that began in the 1770s with the American fight for independence from Great Britain. In 1787 in the Dutch Republic and in 1788 in the Austrian Netherlands and Poland, protesters mounted campaigns for political reform that threatened the very existence of the governments in place. Unlike these protest movements, all of which failed in achieving their aims, the French Revolution exceeded everyone's expectations. It had its immediate origins in a constitutional crisis provoked by a growing government deficit, traceable to French involvement in the American War of Independence. The constitutional crisis came to a head on July 14, 1789, when armed Parisians captured the Bastille, a royal fortress and symbol of monarchical authority in the center of the capital. In the march to Versailles

of October 1789—soon known as "the October days"—the common people of Paris showed once again their determination to shape unfolding events.

In its early days, the French Revolution grabbed the attention of the entire world because it seemed to promise universal human rights, constitutional government, and broad-based political participation. In the words of its most famous slogan, it pledged "liberty, equality, and fraternity." Many Europeans greeted 1789 as the dawn of a new era. Wrote an enthusiastic German, "One of the greatest nations in the world, the greatest in general culture, has at last thrown off the yoke of tyranny." Others expressed horror at the violence that accompanied the dramatic events. In 1790, the British politician Edmund Burke denounced the "vilest of women" and the "cruel ruffians and assassins" who participated in the march to Versailles. He saw anarchy and terror where others saw liberation.

As events unfolded with astonishing rapidity after 1789, the French Revolution became *the* model

Women's March to Versailles, October 5, 1789

This anonymous engraving shows a crowd of armed women marching to Versailles to confront the king. The sight of armed women frightened many observers and demonstrated that the Revolution was not only men's affair. Note the middle-class woman in a hat at the far left. She is obviously reluctant to join in but is being pulled along by the market women in their simple caps.

Musée de la Ville de Paris/Musée Carnavalet, Paris/Giraudon/Art Resource, NY.

of modern revolution and in the process set the enduring patterns of all modern politics. Republicanism, democracy, terrorism, nationalism, and military dictatorship all took their modern forms during the French Revolution. The revolutionaries used a blueprint based on the Enlightenment idea of reason to remake all of society and politics: they executed the king and queen, established a republic for the first time in French history, abolished nobility, and inaugurated bold programs for political reeducation that included reforming the calendar, introducing the metric system, and celebrating festivals of reason to replace Christianity. When they encountered resistance to their programs, they set up a government of terror to compel obedience. As a result, the Revolution became linked in some minds with violence and intimidation, and some see in it the origins of modern *totalitarianism*—that is, governments that try to control every aspect of life, including daily activities, while limiting all forms of political dissent.

The Revolution might have remained a strictly French affair if war had not involved the rest of Europe. After 1792, huge French republican armies, fueled by patriotic nationalism, marched across Europe, promising liberation from traditional monarchies but often delivering old-fashioned conquest and annexation. French victories spread revolutionary ideas far and wide, from the colonies in the Caribbean, where the first successful slave revolt established the republic of Haiti, to Poland and Egypt. The army's success ultimately undermined the republic and made possible the rise of Napoleon Bonaparte, a remarkable young general who brought France more wars, more conquests, and a form of military dictatorship.

The breathtaking succession of regimes in France between 1789 and 1799 and the failure of the republican experiment after ten years of upheaval raised disturbing questions about the relationship between rapid political change and violence. Do all revolutions inevitably degenerate into terror or wars of conquest? Is a regime democratic if it does not allow poor men, women, or blacks to vote? The French Revolution raised these questions and many more. The questions resonated in many countries because the French Revolution seemed to be only the most extreme example of a much broader political and social movement at the end of the eighteenth century.

❖ The Revolutionary Wave, 1787–1789

From Philadelphia to Warsaw, the new public steeped in Enlightenment ideas now demanded to be heard. In 1787, at the same time the recently independent United States of America was preparing a new constitution, a broad-based Dutch Patriot movement challenged the powers of the ruling Dutch stadholder. In the Austrian Netherlands (present-day Belgium and Luxembourg), the upper classes resisted, in the name of constitutional liberties, the reforms of Emperor Joseph II of Austria. In Warsaw, patriotic reformers hoped to lead Poland out of the quagmire of humiliating political impotence, dependence on Russia, and large territorial losses in the partition of 1772. All these movements included calls for more representative government, but only the French revolt developed into a full-fledged revolution.

Europe on the Eve of Revolution

In the early spring of 1787, few felt the tremors forewarning a cataclysm. Many Europeans enthusiastically greeted the American experiment in republican government, but most did not consider the changes taking place far away in a former colony a likely model for their much older, more populous, and traditional states. The Enlightenment had spread into most of the circles of high society in western Europe without affecting the social prominence of aristocrats or the political control of kings and queens. In fact, the European monarchies seemed more securely established than ever, and the French monarchy appeared as sturdy as any. Montesquieu and Rousseau, the leading political theorists of the Enlightenment, taught that republics suited only small countries, not big ones like France or Austria.

After suffering humiliation at the hands of the British in the Seven Years' War (1756–1763), the French had regained international prestige by supporting the victorious Americans, and the monarchy had shown its eagerness to promote reforms. In 1787, for example, the French crown granted civil rights to Protestants.

Europeans in general were wealthier, healthier, more numerous, and better educated than they had ever been before. They had more newspapers and books to read, more concerts to attend, and more coffeehouses to enjoy, all subtle signs of economic growth and development. Ironically, political agitation would be most dramatic in some of the wealthiest and best-educated societies within Europe, such as the Low Countries. The eighteenth-century revolutions were a product of long-term prosperity and high expectations; the short-term downturn and depression after 1786 seemed all the more disappointing after the preceding decades of robust growth.

Historians have sometimes referred to the revolts of the 1780s as the *Atlantic revolutions* because so many protest movements arose in countries on both shores of the North Atlantic in the late 1700s. Most scholars agree now, however, that the French Revolution differed greatly from the others: not only was France the richest, most powerful, and most populous state in western Europe, but its revolution was also more violent, more long-lasting, and more influential in its effects. (See "Terms of History," page 728.)

Interpretation of the Revolutionary Outbreak

Many different explanations for the French Revolution have been offered. The Marxist interpretation, presented by the nineteenth-century revolutionary philosopher Karl Marx and his modern followers, was one of the most influential. Marx saw the French Revolution as the classic example of a *bourgeois*, that is, middle-class, revolution. According to the Marxist interpretation, the *bourgeoisie* (middle class) overthrew the monarchy because of its association with the remnants of feudalism. French revolutionaries used the term *feudalism* to refer to everything that seemed outdated in their nation's economic and social systems, particularly the legal privileges long held by the aristocracy and the seigneurial rights of landowners, such as the many dues landlords levied on their tenants—payments for the use of the lord's baking oven or winepress, for example. Marxists believed the remains of the feudal order needed to be swept away to facilitate the development of capitalism.

Recent historians have successfully challenged many aspects of the Marxist interpretation, especially the link between revolution and capitalism. They argue that the French Revolution did not foster the development of capitalism and that a capitalist middle class composed of merchants and manufacturers did not lead the revolt. A kind of middle class did play an important role in the protest movements of the 1780s across Europe, but this middle class comprised lawyers, journalists, intellectuals, and lower-ranking officials rather than capitalist manufacturers. Moreover, the middle classes did not start most protest movements, which began only when aristocratic elites themselves challenged their rulers' powers. Once the uprisings began, the participation of men and women from the urban lower classes propelled the movements, just as it had during the English Revolution of the mid-seventeenth century. The volatility of this combination of upper, middle, and lower classes ultimately defeated each revolution. The appeal to "the people" as the source of legitimacy pitted one group against another and opened the way to new and sometimes dangerous forms of political mobilization. According to this interpretation, concerns about politics and power completely overshadowed interests in economic change.

Protesters in the Low Countries and Poland

If the eighteenth-century revolutions began in the British North American colonies with the War of American Independence, they took their next step on the other side of the Atlantic. Political protests in the Dutch Republic attracted European attention because Dutch banks still controlled a hefty portion of the world's capital at the end of the eighteenth century, even though the Dutch Republic's role in international politics had diminished. Revolts also broke out in the neighboring Austrian Netherlands and Poland. Although none of these movements ultimately succeeded, they showed how quickly political discontent could boil over in this era of rising economic and political expectations.

The Dutch Patriot Revolt, 1787. The Dutch Patriots, as they chose to call themselves, wanted to follow the American example and reduce the powers of the kinglike stadholder, the prince of Orange, who favored close ties with Great Britain. Government-sponsored Dutch banks owned 40 percent of the British national debt, and by 1796 they held the entire foreign debt of the United States. Relations with the British deteriorated during the American War of Independence, however, and by the middle of the 1780s, agitation in favor of the Americans had boiled over into an attack on the stadholder.

The Patriots began their protest in the relatively restricted circles of middle-class bankers, merchants, and writers who supported the American cause. They soon gained a more popular audience by demanding political reforms in a petition campaign and forming armed citizen militias of men, called Free Corps. Parading under banners that read "Liberty or Death," they forced local officials to set up new elections to replace councils that had been packed with Orangist supporters through patronage or family connections. The future American president John Adams happened to be visiting Utrecht when such a revolt occurred. He wrote admiringly to Thomas Jefferson that "in no instance, of ancient or modern History, have the People ever asserted more unequivocally their own inherent and unalienable Sovereignty."

In 1787, the protest movement coalesced when a national assembly of the Free Corps joined with a group of Patriot Regents (the upper-class officials who ran the cities) to demand "the true republican form of government in our commonwealth," that is, the reduction of stadholder powers. The Free Corps fought the prince's troops and soon got the upper hand. In response, Frederick William II of Prussia, whose sister had married the stadholder, intervened

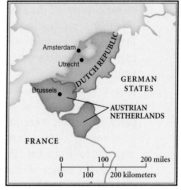

The Low Countries in 1787

with tacit British support. Thousands of Prussian troops soon occupied Utrecht and Amsterdam, and the House of Orange regained its former position.

Revolution

Many of our most important political labels and concepts—*left* and *right*, *terrorist*, and even *revolution* itself—come from the French Revolution. *Left* and *right* correlated spatial locations in the hall of the National Assembly with political positions. Those deputies who favored extensive change sat in the seats on the speaker's left hand; the Jacobins became the most prominent group on the left. On the right were the deputies who preferred a more cautious and conservative stance; royalists were most consistently on the right. A *terrorist* was someone who supported the revolutionary regime of the Terror (1793–1794), but it came to mean anyone who used terror to achieve his or her political ends.

Revolution provided the context for all these changes in meaning. It had previously meant cyclical change that brought life back to a starting point, as a planet makes a revolution around the sun. Revolutions could come and go, by this definition, and change nothing fundamental in the structure of society. After 1789, *revolution* came to mean a self-conscious attempt to leap into the future by reshaping society and politics and even the human personality. A revolutionary official analyzed the meaning of the word in 1793: "A revolution is never made by halves; it must either be total or it will abort. . . . *Revolutionary* means outside of all forms and all rules; *revolutionary* means that which affirms, consolidates the revolution, that which removes all the obstacles which impede its progress." In short, *revolution* soon had an all-or-nothing meaning; you were either for the revolution or against it. There could be no in between.

Revolution still has the same meaning given it by the French revolutionaries, but it is now an even more contested term because of its association with communist theory. In the nineteenth century, Karl Marx incorporated the French Revolution into his new doctrine of communism. In his view, the middle-class French revolutionaries had overthrown the monarchy and the "feudal" aristocracy to pave the way for capitalist development. In the future, the proletariat (industrial workers) would overthrow the capitalist middle class to install a communist government that would abolish private property. Since Marxists claimed the French Revolution as the forerunner of the communist revolution in the nineteenth and twentieth centuries, it was perhaps inevitable that those who opposed communism would also criticize the French Revolution.

The Patriots fell to the fatal combination of outside intervention and their own internal social divisions. Many of the Patriot Regents from the richest merchant families resisted the growing power of the Free Corps. The Free Corps wanted a more democratic form of government and encouraged the publication of pamphlets and cartoons attacking the prince and his wife, the rapid spread of clubs and societies made up of common people, and crowd-pleasing public ceremonies, such as parades and bonfires, that sometimes turned into riots. As divisiveness within the Patriot ranks increased, the prince of Orange was able to muster his own popular support. In the aftermath of the Prussian invasion in September 1787, the Orangists got their revenge: lower-class mobs pillaged the houses of prosperous Patriot leaders, forcing many to flee to the United States, France, or the Austrian Netherlands. Those Patriots who remained nursed their grievances until the French republican armies invaded in 1795.

The Belgian Independence Movement. If Austrian emperor Joseph II had not tried to introduce reforms, the Belgians of the ten provinces of the Austrian Netherlands might have remained tranquil. Yet Joseph, inspired by Enlightenment ideals, made changes that both extended civil rights and enhanced his own power. He abolished torture, decreed toleration for Jews and Protestants (in this resolutely Catholic area), and suppressed monasteries. His 1787 reorganization of the administrative and judicial systems eliminated many offices that belonged to nobles and lawyers. The upper classes felt their power was being usurped.

Belgian resistance to Austrian reforms consequently began as a reactionary movement, which was intended to defend historic local liberties against an

The most influential example of this view is that of the French scholar François Furet. An ex-communist, Furet argues that the French Revolution can be seen as the origin of totalitarianism: "Today the Gulag [the Soviet system of prison camps for dissidents] is leading to a rethinking of the Terror precisely because the two undertakings are seen as identical." The Soviet Gulag and the Terror were identical systems for repressing all avenues of dissent. The French Revolution ended up in totalitarianism during the Terror because it incarnated what Furet calls "the illusion of politics," that is, the belief that people can transform social and economic relationships through political revolution. The French revolutionaries became totalitarian, in Furet's view, however, because they wanted to establish a kind of political and social utopia (a perfect society), in which reason alone determined the shape of political and social life. Because this dream was impossible given human resistance to rapid change, the revolutionaries had to use force to achieve their goals. In other words, revolution itself was a problematic idea, according to Furet.

Controversy about the relationship between the French Revolution and totalitarianism continues. Critics of Furet argue that he focuses too narrowly on the Terror, which, after all, lasted only about one year, from mid-1793 to mid-1794. The French Revolution included many different political experiments: constitutional monarchy (1789–1792), a democratic republic (which preceded and succeeded the period of the Terror), and, later, a more authoritarian republic and then an empire under Napoleon Bonaparte. Is the central meaning of the French Revolution to be found in any single one of these periods or in the very fact of the succession of different phases? France went on in the nineteenth and twentieth centuries to have another constitutional monarchy, one more empire, and four more republics—and never another period of terror. Which kind of experiment was more significant in its lasting effects? Since the French government today is a democratic republic, might it not be argued that this tradition—democratic republicanism—was the most lasting outcome of the French Revolution? In short, *revolution* as a term remains as contested as the events that gave rise to it.

FURTHER READING

Furet, François. *Interpreting the French Revolution.* Trans. Elborg Forster. 1981.

Hunt, Lynn. *Politics, Culture, and Class in the French Revolution.* 1984.

---

overbearing reform-minded government. The upper classes initiated the resistance. The countess of Yves, for example, wrote pamphlets against Joseph's reforms and provided meeting places for the rebels. The movement nonetheless soon attracted democrats, who wanted a more representative government and organized clubs to give voice to their demands. At the end of 1788, a secret society formed armed companies to prepare an uprising. By late 1789, each province had separately declared its independence, and the Austrian administration had collapsed. Delegates from the various provinces declared themselves the United States of Belgium, a clear reference to the American precedent.

Once again, however, internal squabbling doomed the rebels. The democrats denounced aristocratic authority. "The nobles have no acquired right over the people," one writer proclaimed. In the face of increasing democratic ferment, aristocratic leaders drew to their side the Catholic clergy and peasants, who had little sympathy for the democrats of the cities. Every Sunday in May and June 1790, thousands of peasant men and women, led by their priests, streamed into Brussels carrying crucifixes, nooses, and pitchforks to intimidate the democrats and defend the church. Faced with the choice between the Austrian emperor and "our current tyrants," the democrats chose to support the return of the Austrians under Emperor Leopold II (r. 1790–1792), who had succeeded his brother.

Polish Patriots. A reform party calling itself the Patriots also emerged in Poland, which had been shocked by the loss of a third of its territory in the First Partition of 1772. The Patriots sought to overhaul the weak commonwealth along modern western European lines. Reformers included a few leading aristocrats; middle-class professionals and clergy who espoused Enlightenment ideas; and King Stanislaw August Poniatowski (r. 1764–1795). A nobleman who owed his crown solely to the dubious honor of being Catherine the Great's discarded lover but who was also a favorite correspondent of the Parisian salon hostess Madame Geoffrin, Poniatowski saw in moderate reform the only chance for his country to escape the consequences of a century's misgovernment and cultural decline. Ranged against the Patriots stood most of the aristocrats and the formidable Catherine the Great, determined to uphold imperial Russian influence.

Watchful but not displeased to see Russian influence waning in Poland, Austria and Prussia allowed the reform movement to proceed. In 1788, the Patriots got their golden chance. Bogged down in war with the Ottoman Turks, Catherine could not block the summoning of a reform-minded parliament, which with King Stanislaw's aid outmaneuvered the antireform aristocrats. Amid much oratory denouncing Russian overlordship, the parliament enacted the constitution of May 3, 1791, which established a hereditary monarchy with somewhat strengthened authority, at last freed the two-house legislature from the individual veto power of every aristocrat, granted townspeople limited political rights, and vaguely promised future Jewish emancipation. Abolishing serfdom was hardly mentioned. Modest though they were, the Polish reforms did not endure. Catherine II could not countenance the spread of revolution into eastern Europe and within a year engineered the downfall of the Patriots and further weakened the Polish state.

The Beginning of the French Revolution, 1787–1789

The French Revolution began with a fiscal crisis caused by a mounting deficit. After trying every available avenue to raise needed funds, Louis XVI (r. 1774–1792) was forced to call a meeting of the Estates General, a body which had not met since 1614. After the Estates General opened in May 1789, a constitutional stalemate soon pitted deputies of the commons against deputies of the nobility. Fear of a noble-led conspiracy inspired the people of Paris to revolt and attack the Bastille prison on July 14, 1789. Unlike the revolts elsewhere in Europe, the fall of the Bastille would open the way to a rev-

olutionary movement that lasted ten years and reshaped modern European, even world, politics.

Fiscal Crisis. France's fiscal problems stemmed from its support of the Americans against the British in the American War of Independence. About half of the French national budget went to paying interest on the debt that had accumulated. In contrast to Great Britain, which had a national bank to help raise loans for the government, the French government lived off relatively short-term, high-interest loans from private sources including Swiss banks,

Marie-Antoinette
In this gouache of 1775 by T. Gautier d'Agoti, Marie-Antoinette Playing the Harp, *the queen is shown playing music and surrounded by figures of the court. At the time she was only twenty years old, having married the future Louis XVI at age fifteen in 1770. Her mother, Maria Theresa, frequently wrote to advise her on her behavior at court and expressed disapproval because Marie-Antoinette had a reputation for being frivolous and flirtatious.*
Photo Bulloz.

government annuities, and advances from tax collectors.

For years the French government had been trying unsuccessfully to modernize the tax system to raise more revenue and respond to widespread criticism that the system was unfair. The peasants bore the greatest burden of taxes, whereas the nobles and clergy were largely exempt. Tax collection was also far from systematic: private contractors collected many taxes and pocketed a large share of the proceeds. The failure of the crown's various reform efforts left it at the mercy of its creditors at the end of the American War of Independence. With the growing support of public opinion, the bond and annuity holders from the middle and upper classes now demanded a clearer system of fiscal accountability. Declaring bankruptcy, as many rulers had in the past, was no longer an option.

In a monarchy the ruler's character is always crucial. Louis XVI was the model of a virtuous husband and father, but he took a limited view of his responsibilities in this time of crisis. Many complained that he showed more interest in hunting or in his hobby of making locks than in the problems of government. His wife, Marie-Antoinette, was blond, beautiful, and much criticized for her extravagant taste in clothes, elaborate hairdos, and supposed indifference to popular misery. "The Austrian bitch," as underground writers called her, had been the target of an increasingly nasty pamphlet campaign in the 1780s. By 1789, the queen had become an object of popular hatred; when confronted by the inability of the poor to buy bread, she was mistakenly reported to have replied, "Let them eat cake." The king's ineffectiveness and the queen's growing unpopularity helped undermine the monarchy as an institution.

Faced with a mounting deficit, in 1787 Louis called an Assembly of Notables, a group of hand-picked nobles, clergymen, and officials that had last met in 1626. After considering royal proposals for a more uniform land tax, the abolition of internal tariffs, and the establishment of a state bank, the assembly refused to cooperate. Next the king tried his old rival the parlement of Paris. When it too refused to agree to his proposals, he ordered the parlement judges into exile in the provinces. Overnight, the judges (members of the nobility because of the offices they held) became popular heroes for resisting the king's "tyranny"; in reality, however, the judges, like the notables, wanted reform only on their own terms. Nobles in the parlement and in the Assembly

REVEIL DU TIERS ETAT.

Ma fainte, il était tems que je me réveillasse, car l'oppression de mes fers me donnais le cochemar un peu trop fort.

The Third Estate Awakens
This print, produced after the fall of the Bastille (note the heads on pikes outside the prison), shows a clergyman (First Estate) and a noble (Second Estate) alarmed by the awakening of the commoners (Third Estate). The Third Estate breaks the chains of oppression and arms itself to battle for its rights. The message is that social conflicts lay behind the political struggles in the Estates General.
Musée Carnavale/Photo Bulloz.

of Notables saw an opportunity to make themselves partners in running France. Louis finally gave in to their demands that he call a meeting of the Estates General, which had last met 175 years before.

The Estates General. The calling of the Estates General galvanized public opinion. Who would determine the fate of the nation? There were three estates, or orders, in the Estates General. The deputies in the First Estate represented some 100,000 clergy of the Catholic church, which owned about 10 percent of the land and collected its own taxes (the tithe) on peasants. The deputies of the Second Estate represented the nobility, about 400,000 men and women who owned about 25 percent of the land, enjoyed many tax exemptions, and collected seigneurial dues and rents from their peasant tenants. The deputies of the Third Estate represented everyone else, at least 95 percent of the nation. In 1614, at the last meeting of the Estates General, each order had voted separately, and either the clergy or the nobility could therefore veto any decision of the Third Estate. Before the elections to the Estates General in 1789, the king agreed to double the number of deputies for the Third Estate (making them equal in number to the other two combined), but he left it to the Estates General to decide whether the estates would continue to vote separately by order rather than by individual head. Voting by order would conserve the traditional powers of the clergy and nobility; voting by head would give the Third Estate an advantage since many clergymen and even some nobles sympathized with the Third Estate.

As the state's censorship apparatus broke down, pamphleteers by the hundreds denounced the traditional privileges of the nobility and clergy and called for voting by head rather than order. Critics charged that the interests of the Third Estate clashed with those of the nobility; the clergy were caught in between because most ordinary clergy were not nobles but many bishops and archbishops were. The middle class, made more self-confident by the boom in trade and its participation in the Enlightenment, would no longer settle for crumbs from the political table. In the most vitriolic of all the pamphlets, *What Is the Third Estate?*, the middle-class clergyman Abbé Emmanuel-Joseph Sieyès charged that the nobility contributed nothing at all to the nation's well-being; they were "a malignant disease which preys upon and tortures the body of a sick man."

In the winter and spring of 1789, thousands of men (and a few women by proxy) held meetings to elect deputies and write down their grievances. The effect was electric. Although educated men dominated the meetings at the regional level, the humblest peasants also voted in their villages and burst forth with complaints, especially about taxes. As one villager lamented, "The last crust of bread has been taken from us." The long series of meetings raised expectations that the Estates General would help the king to solve all the nation's ills.

These new hopes soared just at the moment France experienced an increasingly rare but always dangerous food shortage. (See "Taking Measure," below.) Bad weather damaged the harvest of 1788, causing bread prices to rise in many places in the spring and summer of 1789 and threatening starvation for the poorest people. A serious slump in textile production had been causing massive unemployment since 1786, when France signed a free-trade treaty with Great Britain, opening the door to the more rapidly industrializing—and therefore cheaper—British suppliers. In the biggest French

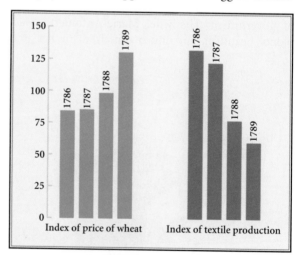

TAKING MEASURE Wheat Prices and Textile Production in France, 1786–1789

This chart, comparing yearly averages against an index set at 100 (based on the average of all four years), shows the dramatic change over time in wheat prices and textile production. The price of wheat steadily increased in the years just prior to the French Revolution, while the production of textiles dramatically declined. What would be the consequences of this movement in opposite directions? Which groups in the French population would be especially at risk? From Ernest Labrousse et al., *Historie économique et sociale de la France* (Paris: Presses Universitaries de France, 1970), 553.

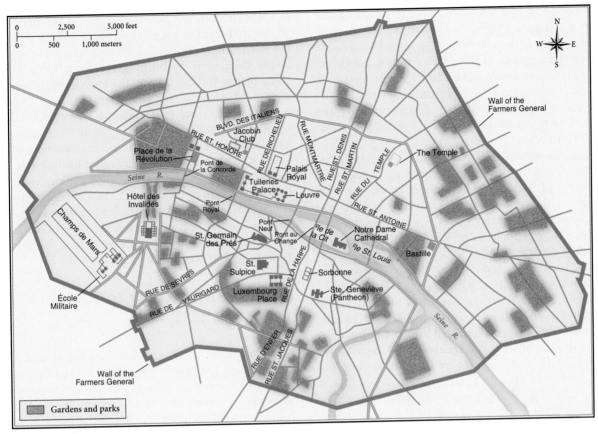

MAP 20.1 Revolutionary Paris, 1789
The French Revolution began with the fall of the Bastille prison on July 14, 1789. The huge fortified prison was located on the eastern side of the city in a neighborhood of working people. Before attacking the Bastille, crowds had torn down many of the customs booths located in the wall of the Farmers General (the private company in charge of tax collection), and taken the arms stored in the Hôtel des Invalides, a veterans hospital on the western side of the city where the upper classes lived. In other words, the crowds had roamed throughout the city.

cities, thousands of textile workers were out of work and hungry, adding another volatile element to an already tense situation.

In May 1789, some 1,200 deputies journeyed to the king's palace of Versailles for the opening of the Estates General. Many readers avidly followed the developments in newspapers that sprouted overnight. Although most nobles insisted on voting by order, the deputies of the Third Estate refused to proceed on that basis. After six weeks of stalemate, on June 17, 1789, the deputies of the Third Estate took unilateral action and declared themselves and whoever would join them the "National Assembly," in which each deputy would vote as an individual. Two days later the clergy voted by a narrow margin to join them. A constitutional revolution was under

way, for now the elected deputies of "the nation" displaced the old estates in which nobles and clergy dominated. As one new newspaper asserted, "The day of the seventeenth will be forever memorable." Barred from their meeting hall on June 20, the deputies met on a nearby tennis court and swore an oath not to disband until they had given France a constitution that reflected their newly declared authority. This "tennis court oath" expressed the determination of the Third Estate to carry through a constitutional revolution.

July 14, 1789: The Fall of the Bastille. At first Louis appeared to agree to the new representative assembly, but he also ordered thousands of soldiers to march to Paris (Map 20.1). The deputies who supported the new National Assembly feared a plot by the king and high-ranking nobles to arrest them and disperse the assembly. "Everyone is convinced that the approach of the troops covers some violent design," one deputy wrote home. Their fears were confirmed when on July 11 the king fired Jacques Necker, the Swiss Protestant finance minister and the one high official regarded as sympathetic to the deputies' cause.

The popular reaction in Paris to Necker's dismissal and the threat of military force changed the course of the French Revolution. When the news spread, the common people in Paris began to arm themselves and attack places where either grain or arms were thought to be stored. A deputy in Versailles reported home: "Today all of the evils overwhelm France, and we are between despotism, carnage, and famine." On July 14, 1789, an armed crowd marched on the Bastille, a fortified prison that symbolized royal authority. After a chaotic battle in which one hundred armed citizens died, the prison officials surrendered. The angry crowd hacked to death the governor of the prison and flaunted his head on a pike.

The fall of the Bastille (an event now commemorated as the French national holiday) set an important precedent. The common people showed themselves willing to intervene violently at a crucial political moment. All over France, food riots turned into local revolts. The officials in one city wrote of their plight: "Yesterday afternoon [July 19] more than seven or eight thousand people, men and women, assembled in front of the two gates to the city hall. . . . We were forced to negotiate with them and to promise to give them wheat . . . and to reduce the price of bread." Local governments were forced out of power and replaced by committees of "patriots" loyal to the revolutionary cause. The patriots relied on newly formed National Guard units composed of civilians. One of their first du-

The Great Fear, 1789

ties was to calm the peasants in the countryside, who feared that the beggars and vagrants crowding the roads might be part of an aristocratic plot to starve the people by burning crops or barns. In some places, the Great Fear (the term used by historians to describe this rural panic) turned into peasant attacks on aristocrats or on seigneurial records of peasants' dues kept in the lord's château. The king's government began to crumble. One of Louis XVI's brothers and many other leading aristocrats fled into exile. In Paris, the marquis de Lafayette, a hero of the American War of Independence and a noble deputy in the National Assembly, became commander of the new National Guard. The Revolution thus had its first heroes, its first victims, and its first enemies.

❖ From Monarchy to Republic, 1789–1793

Until July 1789, the French Revolution followed a course much like that of the protest movements in the Low Countries. Unlike the Dutch and Belgian uprisings, however, the French Revolution did not come to a quick end. The French revolutionaries first tried to establish a constitutional monarchy based on the Enlightenment principles of human rights and rational government. The constitutional monarchy failed, however, when the king tried to raise a counter-revolutionary army. When war broke out in 1792, new tensions culminated in a second revolution that deposed the king and established a republic in which all power rested in an elected legislature.

The Revolution of Rights and Reason

For two years after July 1789, the deputies of the National Assembly strove to establish an enlightened, constitutional monarchy. The National Assembly included the lawyers and officials who had represented the Third Estate in 1789 as well as most of the deputies from the clergy and a substantial number of nobles. Their first goal was to write a constitution, but they faced more immediate problems. In the countryside, peasants refused to pay seigneurial dues to their landlords, and the persistence of peasant violence raised alarms about the potential for a general peasant insurrection.

Major Events of the French Revolution

1789

May 5   The Estates General opens at Versailles

June 17   The Third Estate decides to call itself the National Assembly

June 20   "Tennis court oath" shows determination of deputies to carry out a constitutional revolution

July 14   Fall of the Bastille

August 4   Night session of the National Assembly abolishes "feudalism"

August 26   National Assembly passes Declaration of the Rights of Man and Citizen

October 5–6   Women march to Versailles and join with men in bringing the royal family back to Paris

1790

July 12   Civil Constitution of the Clergy

1791

June 20   Louis and Marie-Antoinette attempt to flee in disguise and are captured at Varennes

1792

April 20   Declaration of war on Austria

August 10   Insurrection in Paris and attack on Tuileries palace lead to suspension of the king

September 2–6   Murder of prisoners in "September massacres" in Paris

September 22   Establishment of the republic

1793

January 21   Execution of Louis XVI

March 11   Beginning of uprising in the Vendée

May 31–June 2   Insurrection leading to arrest of the Girondins

July 27   Robespierre named to the Committee of Public Safety

September 29   Convention establishes General Maximum on prices and wages

October 16   Execution of Marie-Antoinette

1794

February 4   Slavery abolished in the French colonies

March 13–24   Arrest, trial, and executions of so-called ultrarevolutionaries

March 30–April 5   Arrest, trial, and executions of Danton and his followers

July 27   "The Ninth of Thermidor" arrest of Robespierre and his supporters (executed July 28–29)

1795

October 26   Directory government takes office

April 1796–October 1797   Succession of Italian victories by Bonaparte

May 1798–October 1799   Bonaparte in Egypt and Middle East

1799

November 9   Bonaparte's coup of 18 Brumaire

The Night of August 4, 1789.   In response to peasant unrest, the National Assembly decided to make sweeping changes. On the night of August 4, 1789, noble deputies announced their willingness to give up their tax exemptions and seigneurial dues, thereby freeing the peasants from some of their most pressing burdens. By the end of the night, amid wild enthusiasm, dozens of deputies had come to the podium to relinquish the tax exemptions of their own professional groups, towns, or provinces. The National Assembly decreed the abolition of what it called "the feudal regime"—that is, it freed the few remaining serfs and eliminated all special privileges in matters of taxation, including all seigneurial dues on the land (a few days later the deputies insisted on financial compensation for some of these dues, but most peasants refused to pay). Peasants had achieved their goals, and most now turned conservative. The Assembly also mandated equality of opportunity in access to official posts. Talent, rather than birth, was to be the key to success. Enlightenment principles were beginning to become law.

The Declaration of the Rights of Man and Citizen. Passed three weeks later, the Declaration of the Rights of Man and Citizen, was the National Assembly's most stirring statement of Enlightenment principles. In words reminiscent of the American Declaration of Independence, whose author Thomas Jefferson was in Paris at the time, it proclaimed, "Men are born and remain free and equal in rights." The Declaration granted freedom of religion, freedom of the press, equality of taxation, and equality before the law. It established the principle of national sovereignty: since "all sovereignty rests essentially in the nation," the king derived his authority henceforth from the nation rather than from tradition or divine right. By pronouncing all "men" free and equal, the Declaration immediately created new dilemmas. Did women have equal rights with men? What about free blacks in the colonies? How could slavery be justified if all men were born free? Did religious toleration of Protestants and Jews include equal political rights? Women never received the right to vote during the French Revolution, though Protestant and Jewish men did. Women were theoretically citizens under civil law but without the right to full political participation.

Some women did not accept their exclusion, viewing it as a betrayal of the promised new order.

In addition to joining demonstrations, such as the march to Versailles in October 1789, women wrote petitions, published tracts, and organized political clubs to demand more participation. In her Declaration of the Rights of Women of 1791, Olympe de Gouges (1748–1793) played on the language of the official Declaration to make the point that women should also be included. In Article I, she announced, "Woman is born free and lives equal to man in her rights." She also insisted that since "woman has the right to mount the scaffold," she must "equally have the right to mount the rostrum." De Gouges linked her complaints to a program of social reform in which women would have equal rights to property and public office and equal responsibilities in taxes and criminal punishment.

MAP 20.2 Redrawing the Map of France, 1789–1791

Before 1789, France had been divided into provinces, each with its own administration. Some provinces had their own law codes. As it began its deliberations, the new National Assembly determined to install uniform administrations and laws for the entire country. Discussion of the administrative reforms began in October 1789 and was completed on February 15, 1790, when the Assembly voted to divide the provinces into eighty-three departments, with names based on their geographical characteristics: Basses-Pyrenees for the Pyrenees mountains, Haute-Marne for the Marne River, and so on. By eliminating the old names of provinces, with their historical associations, and supplanting them with geographical ones, the Assembly aimed to show that reason would now govern all French affairs.

Que ce jour est heureux mes Soeurs, oui les doux nom
de mere et d'épouse est bien préférable à celui de nonne
il vous rend tous les droits de la Nature ainsi qu'à nous

Decret de l'Assemblée National qui Supprime les Ordres Religieux et Religieuses.
Le Mardi 16 Fevr 1790.

Anticlerical Sentiments
This satirical anti-Catholic engraving celebrates the National Assembly's decree of February 16, 1790, which
abolished all religious orders. Nuns and monks are depicted as overjoyed at being released from their reli-
gious vows and encouraged to marry. In fact, many resisted the destruction of their way of life. Actions
taken against the Catholic church alienated a considerable number of French people from the Revolution.
Snark/Art Resource, NY.

The Constitution and the Church.   Unresponsive
to calls for women's equality, the National Assembly turned to preparing France's first written constitution. The deputies gave voting rights only to
white men who passed a test of wealth. The Constitution defined them as the "active citizens"; all
others were "passive." Despite this limitation, the
Constitution produced fundamental changes in
French government. France became a constitutional
monarchy in which the king was simply the leading
state functionary. A one-house legislature was responsible for making laws. The king could hold up
enactment of laws but could not veto them absolutely. The deputies abolished all the old administrative divisions of the provinces and replaced
them with a national system of eighty-three departments (*départements*) with identical administrative and legal structures (Map 20.2). All officials
were elected; no offices could be bought and sold.
The deputies also abolished the old taxes and re-

placed them with new ones that were supposed
to be uniformly levied. The new government had
difficulty collecting taxes, however, because many
people had expected a substantial cut in the tax rate.
The new administrative system survived, nonetheless, and the departments are still the basic units of
the French state today.

When the deputies turned to reforming the
Catholic church, they created conflicts that would
erupt again and again over the next ten years. Following a long tradition of state involvement in
church affairs but with the new aim of countering
aristocratic domination of high church offices, the
National Assembly passed a Civil Constitution of the
Clergy in July 1790. The constitution set pay scales
for the clergy and provided that the voters elect their
own parish priests and bishops just as they elected
other officials. Motivated partly by the ongoing financial crisis, the National Assembly confiscated all
the church's property and promised to pay clerical

salaries in return. The impounded property served as a guarantee for the new paper money, called *assignats*, issued by the government. The *assignats* soon became subject to inflation because the government began to sell the church lands to the highest bidders in state auctions. The sales increased the landholdings of wealthy city dwellers and prosperous peasants but cut the ground out from under the *assignats*.

The government's offensive on the church did not stop at confiscation of church lands. Convinced that monastic life encouraged idleness and a decline in the nation's population, the deputies outlawed any future monastic vows and encouraged monks and nuns to return to private life on state pensions. Many monks took the opportunity, but few nuns did; for nuns, the convent was all they knew. As the Carmelite nuns of Paris responded, "If there is true happiness on earth, we enjoy it in the shelter of the sanctuary."

In November 1790, the National Assembly required all clergy to swear an oath of loyalty to the Civil Constitution of the Clergy. Pope Pius VI in Rome condemned the constitution, and half of the French clergy refused to take the oath. The oath of allegiance permanently divided the Catholic population, which had to choose between loyalty to the old church and commitment to the Revolution with its "constitutional" church. The revolutionary government lost many supporters by passing laws against the clergy who refused the oath and by forcing them into exile, deporting them forcibly, or executing them as traitors. Riots and demonstrations led by women greeted many of the oath-taking priests who showed up to replace those who refused.

The End of Monarchy

Louis XVI was reluctant to recognize the new limits on his powers, and the reorganization of the Catholic church particularly offended him. On June 20, 1791, the royal family escaped in disguise from the Tuileries palace in Paris and fled to the eastern border of France, where they hoped to gather support to overturn the Revolution from Austria, whose emperor, Leopold II, was the brother of Marie-Antoinette. The plans went awry when a postmaster recognized the king from his portrait on the new French money, and the royal family was arrested at Varennes, forty miles from the Austrian border. The National Assembly tried to depict this incident as a

kidnapping, but the "flight to Varennes" touched off demonstrations in Paris against the royal family, whom some now regarded as traitors. Cartoons circulated depicting the royal family as animals being returned "to the stable."

War with Austria and Prussia.   The Constitution that Louis finally endorsed in 1791 provided for the immediate election of a new Legislative Assembly. In a rare act of self-denial, the deputies of the National Assembly declared themselves ineligible for the new Assembly. Those who had experienced the Revolution firsthand now departed from the scene, opening the door to men with little previous experience in national politics. The status of the king might have remained uncertain if war had not intervened, but by early 1792 everyone seemed intent on war with Austria. Louis and Marie-Antoinette hoped that war would lead to the definitive defeat of the Revolution, whereas the deputies who favored a republic hoped that war would reveal the king's treachery and lead to his downfall. On April 21, 1792, Louis declared war on Leopold. Prussia immediately entered on the Austrian side. Thousands of French aristocrats, including two-thirds of the army officer corps, had already emigrated, including both the king's brothers, and they were gathering along France's eastern border in expectation of joining Leopold's counterrevolutionary army.

When fighting broke out in 1792, all the powers expected a brief and relatively contained war. Instead, it would continue despite brief interruptions for the next twenty-three years. In 1792, the French were woefully unprepared, and in the first battles the Austrians promptly routed the French armies, joking that the new French motto was "Conquer or Run."

The Second Revolution of August 10, 1792.   As the French frantically reorganized their armies to replace the thousands of aristocratic officers who had emigrated, the authority of the Legislative Assembly came under fire. In June 1792, an angry crowd invaded the hall of the Assembly in Paris and threatened the royal family. In response, Lafayette left his command on the eastern front and came to Paris to insist on punishing the demonstrators. His appearance only fueled distrust of the army commanders, which increased to a fever pitch when the Prussians crossed the border and advanced on Paris. The Prussian commander, the duke of Brunswick, issued

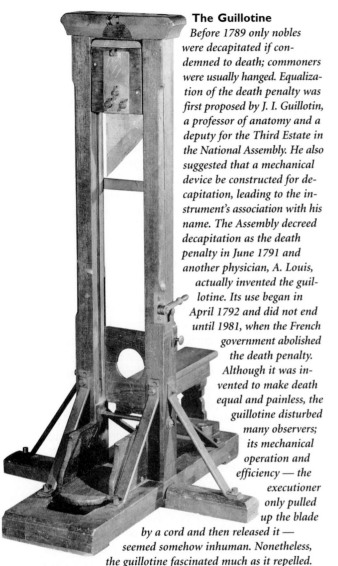

The Guillotine

Before 1789 only nobles were decapitated if condemned to death; commoners were usually hanged. Equalization of the death penalty was first proposed by J. I. Guillotin, a professor of anatomy and a deputy for the Third Estate in the National Assembly. He also suggested that a mechanical device be constructed for decapitation, leading to the instrument's association with his name. The Assembly decreed decapitation as the death penalty in June 1791 and another physician, A. Louis, actually invented the guillotine. Its use began in April 1792 and did not end until 1981, when the French government abolished the death penalty. Although it was invented to make death equal and painless, the guillotine disturbed many observers; its mechanical operation and efficiency — the executioner only pulled up the blade by a cord and then released it — seemed somehow inhuman. Nonetheless, the guillotine fascinated much as it repelled. Reproduced in miniature, painted onto snuffboxes and china, worn as jewelry, and even serving as a toy, the guillotine became a part of popular culture, celebrated as the people's avenger by supporters of the Revolution and vilified as the preeminent symbol of the Terror by opponents.
Musée Carnavalet/Photo Bulloz.

wives and daughters, had followed every twist and turn in revolutionary fortunes. Political clubs had multiplied since the founding in 1789 of the first and most influential of them, the Jacobin Club (named after the former monastery in Paris where the first club met). Newspapers, pamphlets, posters, and cartoons proliferated. Every local district in Paris had its club, where men and women listened to the news of the day and discussed their options.

Faced with the threat of military retaliation and frustrated with the inaction of the Legislative Assembly, on August 10, 1792, leaders of the local district governments of Paris (called *sections*) organized an insurrection and attacked the Tuileries palace, where the king resided. The king and his family had to escape into the meeting room of the Legislative Assembly, where the frightened deputies ordered new elections—this time by universal male suffrage (no wealth qualifications as in the Constitution of 1791)—for a National Convention that would write yet another constitution. When it met, the Convention abolished the monarchy and on September 22, 1792, established the first republic in French history. The republic would answer only to the people, not to any royal authority. Lafayette and other liberal aristocrats who had supported the constitutional monarchy fled into exile.

Violence soon exploded again. Early in September 1792, as the Prussians approached Paris, hastily gathered mobs stormed the overflowing prisons to seek out traitors who might help the enemy. In an atmosphere of near hysteria, eleven hundred inmates were killed, including many ordinary and completely innocent people. The princess of Lamballe, one of the queen's favorites, was hacked to pieces and her mutilated body displayed beneath the windows where the royal family was kept under guard. These "September massacres" showed the dark side of popular revolution, in which the common people demanded instant revenge on supposed enemies and conspirators.

Republican Rivals and the Execution of the King.
The National Convention faced a dire situation. It needed to write a new constitution for the republic while fighting a war with external enemies and confronting increasing resistance at home. The Revolution had divided the population: for some it had not gone far enough toward providing food, land, and retribution against enemies; for others it had

a manifesto—the Brunswick Manifesto—announcing that Paris would be totally destroyed if the royal family suffered any violence.

The ordinary people of Paris did not passively await their fate. Known as *sans-culottes* ("without breeches")—because men who worked with their hands wore long trousers rather than the knee breeches of the upper classes—tailors, shoemakers, cabinetmakers, and shopkeepers, along with their gone too far by dismantling the church and the monarchy. The French people had never known any government other than monarchy. Only half the population could read and write at even a basic level. In this situation, symbolic actions became very important. Any public sign of monarchy was at risk, and revolutionaries soon pulled down statues of kings and burned reminders of the former regime.

The fate of Louis XVI and the future direction of the republic divided the deputies elected to the National Convention. The deputies came from very similar social backgrounds and shared many political beliefs; most of them were middle-class lawyers and professionals who had developed their ardent republican beliefs in the national network of Jacobin Clubs. After the fall of the monarchy in August 1792, however, the Jacobins divided into two factions. The Girondins (named after a department in southwestern France, the Gironde, which provided some of its leading orators) met regularly at the salon of Jeanne Roland, the wife of a minister. They resented the growing power of Parisian militants and tried to appeal to the departments outside of Paris. The Mountain (so called because its deputies sat in the highest seats of the Convention), in contrast, was closely allied with the Paris militants.

The first showdown between the Girondins and the Mountain occurred during the trial of the king in December 1792. Although the Girondins agreed that the king was guilty of treason, many of them argued for clemency, exile, or a popular referendum on his fate. After a long and difficult debate, the Convention supported the Mountain and voted by a very narrow majority to execute the king. Louis XVI went to the guillotine on January 21, 1793, sharing the fate of Charles I of England in 1649. "We have just convinced ourselves that a king is only a man," wrote one newspaper, "and that no man is above the law."

❖ The Terror and the Republic of Virtue

The execution of the king did not end the new regime's problems. The continuing war required even more men and money, and the introduction of a national draft provoked massive resistance in some parts of France. In response to growing pressures,

the National Convention set up a highly centralized government designed to provide food, direct the war effort, and punish counterrevolutionaries. Thus began "the Terror," in which the guillotine became the most frightening instrument of a government that suppressed almost every form of dissent. The leader of this government, Maximilien Robespierre, aimed to create a "Republic of Virtue," in which the government would teach, or force, citizens to become virtuous republicans through a massive program of political reeducation. These policies only increased divisions, which ultimately led to Robespierre's fall from power and to a dismantling of government by terror.

Robespierre and the Committee of Public Safety

The conflict between the Girondins and the Mountain did not end with the execution of Louis XVI. Militants in Paris agitated for the removal of the deputies who had proposed a referendum on the king, and in retaliation the Girondins tried to single out Parisian leaders for punishment. First the Girondins engineered the arrest of Jean-Paul Marat, a deputy who styled himself in his newspaper "the friend of the people" and urged violent measures against enemies of the republic. Marat was acquitted. Then the Girondins devised a special commission to investigate the situation in Paris, ordering the arrest of various local leaders. In response, Parisian militants organized an armed demonstration and invaded the National Convention on June 2, 1793, forcing the deputies to decree the arrest of their twenty-nine Girondin colleagues. The Convention agreed to the establishment of paramilitary bands called "revolutionary armies" to enforce the distribution of grain and hunt down hoarders and political suspects and to the increased use of revolutionary courts to try political suspects and execute the guilty. In a series of decrees over the next few months, the Convention also tried to stabilize prices; on September 29, 1793, it established a General Maximum on the prices of thirty-nine essential commodities and on wages.

Setting the course for government and the war increasingly fell to the Committee of Public Safety, set up by the Convention on April 6, 1793. Composed of twelve deputies elected by the Convention, the committee gradually established its paramount

An Anti-Jacobin Satire
In The Purifying Pot of the
Jacobins *(1793), the anonymous
artist makes fun of the Jacobin
Club's penchant for constantly
examining the political correctness of its members. Those who
failed the test suffered harsh,
sometimes fatal consequences.*
Art Resource, NY.

authority. When Maximilien Robespierre (1758–1794) was named to the committee on July 27, 1793, he became in effect its guiding spirit and the chief spokesman of the Revolution. A lawyer from northern France known as "the incorruptible" for his stern honesty and fierce dedication to democratic ideals, Robespierre remains one of the most controversial figures in world history because of his association with the Terror. In September 1793, again in response to popular pressure, the deputies of the Convention voted to "put Terror on the agenda." Robespierre took the lead in implementing this decision. Although he originally opposed the death penalty and the war, he was convinced that the emergency situation of 1793 required severe measures, including death for those, such as the Girondins, who opposed the committee's policies.

Robespierre was the theorist of the Terror and the chief architect of the Republic of Virtue. Like many other educated eighteenth-century men, he had read all the classics of republicanism from Tacitus and Plutarch to Montesquieu and Rousseau. But he took them a step further. He spoke eloquently about "the theory of revolutionary government" as "the war of liberty against its enemies." He defended the people's right to democratic government, while in practice he supported many emergency measures

that restricted their liberties. He personally favored a free market economy, as did almost all middle-class deputies, but in this time of crisis he was willing to enact price controls and requisitioning. Like Rousseau, he believed the republic would have to reform its citizens by establishing a new civic religion. In a famous speech to the Convention, he insisted: "The first maxim of your policies must be to lead the people by reason and the people's enemies by terror . . . without virtue, terror is deadly; without terror, virtue is impotent." *Terror* was not an idle term; it seemed to imply that the goal of democracy justified what we now call totalitarian means, that is, the suppression of all dissent.

Through a series of desperate measures, the Committee of Public Safety set the machinery of the Terror in motion. It sent deputies out "on mission" to purge unreliable officials, work with local leaders of the Jacobin Clubs and other popular societies to uncover dissidents, and organize the war effort. In the first universal draft of men in history, every unmarried man and childless widower between the ages of eighteen and twenty-five was declared eligible for conscription into the army. Revolutionary tribunals set up in Paris and provincial centers tried political suspects. In October 1793, the Revolutionary Tribunal in Paris convicted Marie-Antoinette of treason and sent her to the guillotine. The Girondin leaders and Madame Roland were also guillotined, as was Olympe de Gouges. The government confiscated all the property of convicted traitors.

The Terror won its greatest success on the battlefield. As of April 1793, France faced war with Austria, Prussia, Great Britain, Spain, Sardinia, and the Dutch Republic—all fearful of the impact of revolutionary ideals on their own populations. The execution of Louis XVI, in particular, galvanized European governments; according to William Pitt, the British prime minister, it was "the foulest and most atrocious act the world has ever seen." To face this daunting coalition of forces, the French republic tapped a new and potent source of power, nationalist pride, in decrees mobilizing young and old alike:

> *The young men will go to battle; married men will forge arms and transport provisions; women will make tents and clothing and serve in hospitals; children will make bandages; old men will get themselves carried to public places to arouse the courage of warriors and preach hatred of kings and unity of the republic.*

Scientists contributed improvements in iron production, forges were set up in the parks and gardens of Paris to produce thousands of guns, and citizens everywhere helped collect saltpeter for gunpowder. By the end of 1793, the French nation in arms had stopped the advance of the allied powers, and in the summer of 1794 it invaded the Austrian Netherlands and crossed the Rhine River. The army was ready to carry the gospel of revolution and republicanism to the rest of Europe.

The Republic of Virtue, 1793–1794

The program of the Terror went beyond pragmatic measures to fight the war and internal enemies to include efforts to "republicanize everything"—in other words, to effect a cultural revolution. The government utilized every possible means to transform the old subjects of the monarchy into virtuous republican citizens. While censoring writings deemed counterrevolutionary, the government encouraged republican art, set up civic festivals, and in some places directly attacked the churches in a campaign known as *de-Christianization*. In addition to drawing up plans for a new program of elementary ed-

ucation, the republic set about politicizing every aspect of daily life, from the naming of babies to the measurement of space and time.

Republican Culture.   Refusing to tolerate opposition, the republic left no stone unturned in its endeavor to get its message across. Songs—especially the new national anthem, "La Marseillaise"—placards, posters, pamphlets, books, engravings, paintings,

Representing Liberty
Liberty was represented by a female figure because in French the noun is feminine (la liberté). *This painting by a woman, Jeanne-Louise Vallain, from 1793–1794 captures the usual attributes of liberty: she is soberly seated, wearing a Roman-style toga, and holding a pike with a Roman liberty cap on top. Her Roman appearance signals that she is the representation of an abstract quality. The fact that she holds an instrument of battle suggests that women might be active participants. Liberty is holding the Declaration of the Rights of Man and Citizen as it was revised in 1793. This painting was most likely hung in a central location in the Paris Jacobin Club.* Musée de la Revolution Française, Vizille.

sculpture, even everyday crockery, chamberpots, and playing cards conveyed revolutionary slogans and symbols. Foremost among them was the figure of Liberty (an early version of the Statue of Liberty now in New York harbor), which appeared on coins and bills, letterheads and seals, and as statues in festivals. Hundreds of new plays were produced and old classics revised. To encourage the production of patriotic and republican works, the government sponsored state competitions for artists. Works of art were supposed to "awaken the public spirit and make clear how atrocious and ridiculous were the enemies of liberty and of the Republic."

At the center of this elaborate cultural campaign were the revolutionary festivals modeled on Rousseau's plans for a civic religion. The festivals first emerged in 1789 with the spontaneous planting of liberty trees in villages and towns. The Festival of Federation on July 14, 1790, marked the first anniversary of the fall of the Bastille. Under the Convention, the well-known painter Jacques-Louis David (1748–1825), who was a deputy and associate of Robespierre, took over festival planning. David aimed to destroy the mystique of monarchy and to make the republic sacred. His Festival of Unity on August 10, 1793, for example, celebrated the first anniversary of the overthrow of the monarchy. In front of the statue of Liberty built for the occasion, a bonfire consumed the crowns and scepters of royalty while a cloud of three thousand white doves rose into the sky. This was all part of preaching the "moral order of the Republic . . . that will make us a people of brothers, a people of philosophers."

De-Christianization. Some revolutionaries hoped the festival system would replace the Catholic church altogether. They initiated a campaign of de-Christianization that included closing churches (Protestant as well as Catholic), selling many church buildings to the highest bidder, and trying to force even those clergy who had taken the oath of loyalty to abandon their clerical vocations and marry. Some of the greatest churches in Christendom became storehouses for arms or grain, or their stones were sold off to contractors. The medieval statues of kings on the facade of Notre Dame cathedral were beheaded. Church bells were dismantled and church treasures melted down for government use.

In the ultimate step in de-Christianization, extremists tried to establish a Cult of Reason to supplant Christianity. In Paris in the fall of 1793, a goddess of Liberty, played by an actress, presided over a Festival of Reason in Notre Dame cathedral. Local militants in other cities staged similar festivals, which alarmed deputies in the Convention, who were wary of turning rural, devout populations against the republic. The Committee of Public Safety halted the de-Christianization campaign, and Robespierre with David's help tried to institute an alternative, the Cult of the Supreme Being, in June 1794. Robespierre objected to the de-Christianization campaign's atheism; he favored a Rousseau-inspired deistic religion without the supposedly superstitious trappings of Catholicism. Neither cult attracted many followers, but both show the depth of the commitment to overturning the old order and all its traditional institutions.

Politicizing Daily Life. In principle the best way to ensure the future of the republic was through the education of the young. The deputy Georges-Jacques Danton (1759–1794), Robespierre's main competitor as theorist of the Revolution, maintained that "after bread, the first need of the people is education." The Convention voted to make primary schooling free and compulsory for both boys and girls. It took control of education away from the Catholic church and tried to set up a system of state schools at both the primary and secondary levels, but it lacked trained teachers to replace those the Catholic religious orders provided. As a result, opportunities for learning how to read and write may have diminished. In 1799, only one-fifth as many boys enrolled in the state secondary schools as had studied in church schools ten years earlier.

Although many of the ambitious republican programs failed, almost all aspects of daily life became politicized. Already in 1789, the colors one wore had political significance. The tricolor—the combination of red, white, and blue that was to become the flag of France—was devised in July 1789, and by 1793 everyone had to wear a cockade with the colors. Using the formal forms of speech (in French, *vous* for "you") or the title Monsieur or Madame might identify someone as an aristocrat; true patriots used the informal *tu* and Citizen instead. Some people changed their names or gave their children new kinds of names; biblical and saints' names such as Jean, Pierre, Joseph, or Marie gave way to names recalling heroes of the ancient

The Revolutionary Tricolor
This painting by an anonymous artist probably shows a deputy in the uniform prescribed for those sent to supervise military operations. His dress prominently displays the revolutionary tricolor — red, white, and blue — both on his official sash and on the trim of his hat. Plumes had once been reserved to nobles; now nonnobles could wear them on their hats, but they still signaled dignity and importance. Dress became a contested issue during the Revolution, and successive governments considered prescribing some kind of uniform, at least for the deputies in the legislature.
Louvre/Reunion des Musées Nationaux.

one. Its basis was reason and republican principles. Year I dated from the beginning of the republic on September 22, 1792. Twelve months of exactly thirty days each received new names derived from nature: Pluviôse (roughly equivalent to February), for example, recalled the rain of late winter (*la pluie* is French for "rain"). Instead of seven-day weeks, ten-day *décades* provided only one day of rest every ten days and pointedly eliminated the Sunday of the Christian calendar. The five days left at the end of the calendar year were devoted to special festivals called *sans-culottides*. The calendar remained in force for twelve years despite continuing resistance to it. More enduring was the new metric system based on units of ten that was invented to replace the hundreds of local variations in weights and measures. Other countries in Europe and throughout the world eventually adopted the metric system.

Successive revolutionary legislatures had also changed the rules of family life. The state took responsibility for all family matters away from the Catholic church: birth, death, and marriage registration now happened at city hall, not the parish church. Marriage became a civil contract and as such could be broken. The new divorce law of September 1792 was the most far-reaching in the West: a couple could divorce by mutual consent or for reasons such as insanity, abandonment, battering, or criminal conviction. Thousands of men and women took advantage of the law to dissolve unhappy marriages, even though the pope had condemned the measure. (In 1816, the government revoked the right to divorce, and not until the 1970s did French divorce laws return to the principles of the 1792 legislation.) The revolutionary government also limited fathers' rights over their children; they could not imprison them without cause or control their lives after the age of twenty-one. In one of its most influential actions, the National Convention passed a series of laws that created equal inheritance among all children in the family, including girls. The father's right to favor one child, especially the oldest male, was considered aristocratic and hence antirepublican.

Resisting the Revolution

By intruding into religion, culture, and daily life, the republic inevitably provoked resistance. Shouting curses against the republic, uprooting liberty trees, carrying statues of the Virgin Mary in procession,

Roman republic (Brutus, Gracchus, Cornelia), revolutionary heroes, or flowers and plants. Such changes symbolized adherence to the republic and to Enlightenment ideals rather than to Catholicism.

Even the measures of time and space were revolutionized. In October 1793, the Convention introduced a new calendar to replace the Christian

Charlotte Corday

In this anonymous painting, Charlotte Corday has just stabbed Marat to death in his bath. Her gaily decorated hat seems incongruous in the gruesome setting. Corday stabbed Marat when she gained admission to his bathroom, where he spent hours every day writing and even receiving visitors. The twenty-five-year-old Corday was tried the next day and amazed even her opponents by remaining absolutely calm and convinced of the rightness of her act.
Musée Carnavalet/Laurie Platt Winfrey, Inc.

hiding a priest who would not take the oath, singing a royalist song—all these expressed dissent with the new symbols, rituals, and policies. Resistance also took more violent forms, from riots over food shortages or religious policies to assassination and full-scale civil war.

Women's Resistance. Many women, in particular, suffered from the hard conditions of life that persisted in this time of war, and they had their own ways of voicing discontent. The long bread lines in the cities exhausted the patience of women already overwhelmed by the demands of housekeeping, childrearing, and working as shop assistants, fishwives, laundresses, and textile workers. Police spies reported their constant grumbling, which occasionally turned into spontaneous demonstrations or riots over high prices or food shortages.

Other forms of resistance were more individual. One young woman, Charlotte Corday, assassinated Jean-Paul Marat in July 1793. Corday fervently supported the Girondins, and she considered it her patriotic duty to kill the deputy who, in the columns of his paper *The Friend of the People*, had constantly demanded more heads and more blood. Marat was immediately eulogized as a great martyr: Corday went to the guillotine vilified as a monster but confident that she had "avenged many innocent victims."

Rebellion and Civil War. Violent resistance broke out for various reasons in many parts of France. In the early years of the Revolution, Catholics rioted in places with large Protestant or Jewish populations, which tended to support the Revolution and the religious toleration and civil rights it promised. The arrest of the Girondin deputies in June 1793 sparked insurrections in several departments. After the government retook the city of Lyon, one of the centers of the revolt, the deputy on mission ordered sixteen hundred houses demolished. Special courts sentenced almost two thousand people to death. The name of the city was changed to Ville Affranchie (Liberated Town).

Nowhere was resistance to the republic more persistent and violent than in the Vendée region of western France. Between March and December 1793, peasants, artisans, and weavers joined under noble leadership to form a "Catholic and Royal Army." One rebel group explained its motives: "They [the republicans] have killed our king, chased away our priests, sold the goods of our church, eaten everything we have and now they want to take our bodies [in the draft]." The uprising took two different forms: in the Vendée itself, a counterrevolutionary army organized to fight the republic; in nearby Brittany, resistance took the form of guerrilla bands, which united to attack a target and then quickly melted into the countryside. Great Britain provided money and underground contacts for these attacks, which were almost always aimed at towns. Town officials sold church lands, enforced measures against the clergy, and supervised conscription. In many ways this was a civil war between town and country, for the townspeople were the ones who supported the Revolution and bought church lands for themselves. The peasants had gained most of what they wanted in 1789 with the abolition of seigneurial dues, and they resented the government's demands for money and manpower and actions taken against their local clergy.

For several months in 1793, the Vendée rebels stormed the largest towns in the region. Both sides committed horrible atrocities. At the small town of Machecoul, for example, the rebels massacred five hundred republicans, including administrators and National Guard members; many were tied together, shoved into freshly dug graves, and shot. By the fall, however, republican soldiers had turned back the rebels. A republican general wrote to the Committee of Public Safety claiming, "There is no more Vendée, citizens, it has perished under our free sword along with its women and children. . . . Following the orders that you gave me I have crushed children under the feet of horses, massacred women who at least . . . will engender no more brigands." "Infernal columns" of republican troops marched through the region to restore control, military courts ordered thousands executed, and republican soldiers massacred thousands of others. In one especially gruesome incident, the deputy Jean-Baptiste Carrier supervised the drowning of some two thousand Vendée rebels, including a number of priests. Barges loaded with prisoners were floated into the Loire River near Nantes and then sunk. Controversy still rages about the rebellion's death toll. Estimates of rebel deaths alone range from about 20,000 to 250,000 and higher. Many thousands of republican soldiers and civilians also lost their lives. Even the low estimates reveal the carnage of this catastrophic confrontation between the republic and its opponents.

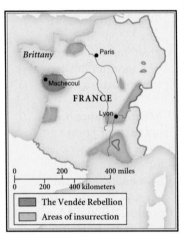

The Vendée Rebellion, 1793

The Fall of Robespierre and the End of the Terror, 1794–1799

In an atmosphere of fear of conspiracy that was fueled by overt resistance in places like the Vendée, Robespierre tried simultaneously to exert the Convention's control over popular political activities and to weed out opposition among the deputies. As a result, the Terror intensified until July 1794, when a group of deputies joined within the Convention to order the arrest and execution of Robespierre and his followers. The Convention then ordered elections and drew up a new republican constitution that gave executive power to five directors. This Directory government maintained power during four years of seesaw battles between royalists and former Jacobins. Ultimately it gave way to Napoleon Bonaparte.

The Revolution Devours Its Own.   In the fall of 1793, the Convention cracked down on popular clubs and societies. First to be suppressed were women's political clubs. Founded in early 1793, the Society of Revolutionary Republican Women played a very active part in *sans-culottes* politics. The society agitated for harsher measures against the republic's enemies and insisted that women have a voice in politics even if they did not have the vote. Women set up their own clubs in many provincial towns and also attended the meetings of local men's organizations. The closing of women's clubs marked an important turning point in the Revolution. From then on the *sans-culottes* and their political organizations came increasingly under the thumb of the Jacobin deputies in the National Convention.

The Convention severely limited women's participation in the public sphere because the deputies associated women's groups with political disorder and social upheaval. As one deputy stated, women's clubs consisted of "adventuresses, knights-errant, emancipated women, amazons." Another deputy continued, "Women are ill suited for elevated thoughts and serious meditations." In subsequent years physicians, priests, and philosophers amplified such opinions by formulating explanations for women's "natural" differences from men to justify their inferior status.

In the spring of 1794, the Committee of Public Safety moved against its critics among leaders in Paris and deputies in the Convention itself. First a handful of men labeled "ultrarevolutionaries"—in fact a

A Women's Club
In this gouache by the Lesueur brothers, The Patriotic Women's Club, *the club president urges the members to contribute funds for poor patriot families. Women's clubs focused on philanthropic work but also discussed revolutionary legislation and the debates in the National Assemblies. The colorful but sober dress indicates that the women are middle class.*
Musée de la Ville de Paris/Musée Carnavalet, Paris/Giraudon/Art Resource, NY.

motley collection of local Parisian politicians—were arrested and executed. Next came the other side, the "indulgents," so called because they favored a moderation of the Terror. Included among them was the deputy Danton, himself once a member of the Committee of Public Safety and a friend of Robespierre, despite the striking contrast in their personalities. Danton was the Revolution's most flamboyant orator and, unlike Robespierre, a high-living, high-spending, excitable politician. At every critical turning point in national politics, his booming voice had swayed opinion in the National Convention. Now, under government pressure, the Revolutionary Tribunal convicted him and his friends of treason and sentenced them to death.

With the arrest and execution of these leaders in Paris, the prophecies of doom for the Revolution seemed about to be realized. "The Revolution," as one of the Girondin victims of 1793 had remarked, "was devouring its own children." The middle-class leaders were killing each other. Even after the major threats to the committee's power had been eliminated, the Terror continued and even worsened. A law passed in June 1794 denied the accused the right of legal counsel, reduced the number of jurors necessary for conviction, and allowed only two judgments: acquittal or death. The category of political crimes expanded to include "slandering patriotism" and "seeking to inspire discouragement." Ordinary people risked the guillotine if they expressed any discontent. (Ironically, the guillotine had been introduced just a few months before the king's execution as a way of making capital punishment more humane and uniform.) The rate of executions in Paris rose from five a day in the spring of 1794 to twenty-six a day in the summer. The political atmosphere darkened even though the military situation improved. At the end of June, the French armies decisively defeated the main Austrian army and advanced through the Austrian Netherlands to Brussels and Antwerp. The emergency measures for fighting the war were working, yet Robespierre and his inner circle had made so many enemies that they could not afford to loosen the grip of the Terror.

The Terror hardly touched many parts of France. But overall the experience was undeniably traumatic. Across the country the official Terror cost the lives of at least 40,000 French people, most of them living in the regions of major insurrections or near the borders with foreign enemies, where suspicion of collaboration ran high. As many as 300,000 people went to prison as suspects between March 1793 and August 1794 (that is, one out of every fifty French). The toll for the aristocracy and the clergy was especially high. Many leading nobles perished under the guillotine, and thousands emigrated. Thirty thousand to forty thousand clergy who refused the oath emigrated, at least two thousand (including many nuns) were executed, and thousands were imprisoned. The clergy were singled out in particular in the civil war zones: 135 priests were massacred at Lyon in November 1793 and 83 shot in one day during the Vendée revolt. Yet many victims of the Terror were peasants or ordinary working people.

The final crisis of the Terror came in July 1794. Conflicts within the Committee of Public Safety and the National Convention left Robespierre isolated. On July 27, 1794 (the ninth of Thermidor, Year II, according to the revolutionary calendar), Robespierre appeared before the Convention with yet another list of deputies to be arrested. Many feared they would be named, and they shouted him down and ordered him arrested along with his followers on the committee, the president of the Revolutionary Tribunal in Paris, and the commander of the Parisian National Guard. An armed uprising led by the Paris city government failed to save Robespierre when most of the Parisian *sections* and two-thirds of the National Guard took the side of the Convention. Robespierre tried to kill himself with a pistol but only broke his jaw. The next day he and scores of followers went to the guillotine.

The Thermidorian Reaction and the Directory, 1794–1799.   The men who led the attack on Robespierre in Thermidor (July 1794) did not intend to reverse all his policies, but that happened nonetheless. Newspapers attacked the Robespierrists as "tigers thirsting for human blood." The new government released hundreds of suspects and arranged a temporary truce in the Vendée. It purged Jacobins from local bodies and replaced them with their opponents. It arrested some of the most notorious "terrorists" in the National Convention, such as Carrier, and put them to death. Within the year the new leaders abolished the Revolutionary Tribunal and closed the Jacobin Club in Paris. Popular demonstrations met severe repression. In southeastern France, in particular, a "White Terror" replaced the Jacobins' "Red Terror." Former officials and local Jacobin leaders were harassed, beaten, and often murdered by paramilitary bands who had tacit support from the new authorities. Those who remained in the National Convention prepared yet another constitution in 1795, setting up a two-house legislature and an executive body—the Directory, headed by five directors.

The Directory regime tenuously held on to power for four years, all the while trying to fend off challenges from the remaining Jacobins and the resurgent royalists. The puritanical atmosphere of the Terror gave way to the pursuit of pleasure—low-cut dresses of transparent materials, the reappearance of prostitutes in the streets, fancy dinner parties, and "victims balls" where guests wore red ribbons around their necks as reminders of the guillotine. Bands of young men dressed in knee breeches and rich fabrics picked fights with known Jacobins and disrupted theater performances with loud antirevolutionary songs. All over France people banded together and petitioned to reopen churches closed during the Terror. If necessary they broke into a church to hold services with a priest who had been in hiding or a lay schoolteacher who was willing to say Mass.

Although the Terror had ended, the revolution had not. In 1794, the most democratic and most repressive phases of the Revolution ended both at once. Between 1795 and 1799, the republic endured in France, but it directed a war effort abroad that would ultimately bring to power the man who would dismantle the republic itself.

❖ Revolution on the March

Beginning in 1792, war raged almost constantly until 1815. At one time or another, and sometimes all at once, France faced every principal power in Europe. The French republic—and later the French Empire under its supreme commander, Emperor Napoleon Bonaparte—proved an even more formidable opponent than the France of Louis XIV. New means of mobilizing and organizing soldiers enabled the French to dominate Europe for a generation. The influence of the Revolution as a political model and the threat of French military conquest combined to challenge the traditional order in Europe.

Arms and Conquests

The allied powers had a chance to defeat France in 1793, when the French armies verged on chaos because of the emigration of noble army officers and the problems of integrating new draftees. At that moment, however, Prussia, Russia, and Austria were preoccupied with clamping down on Poland. For France, this diversion meant a reprieve.

Because of the new national draft, the French had a huge and powerful fighting force of 700,000 men by the end of 1793. But the army faced many problems in the field. As many as a third of the recent draftees deserted before or during battle. Uniforms fashioned out of rough cloth constricted movements, tore easily, and retained the damp of muddy battlefields, exposing the soldiers to the elements and the spread of disease. At times the soldiers were fed only moldy bread, and if their pay was late, they sometimes resorted to pillaging and looting. Generals might pay with their lives if they lost a key battle and their loyalty to the Revolution came under suspicion. France nevertheless had one overwhelming advantage: its soldiers, drawn largely from the peasantry and the lower classes of the cities, fought for a revolution that they and their brothers and sisters had helped make. The republic was their government, and the army was in large measure theirs too; many officers had risen through the ranks by skill and talent rather than by inheriting or purchasing their positions. One young peasant boy wrote to his parents, "Either you will see me return bathed in glory, or you will have a son who is a worthy citizen of France who knows how to die for the defense of his country."

When the French armies invaded the Austrian Netherlands and crossed the Rhine in the summer of 1794, they proclaimed a war of liberation. But as they annexed more and more territory, "liberated" people in many places began to view them as an army of occupation (Map 20.3). Those just across the northern and eastern borders of France reacted most positively to the French invasion. In the

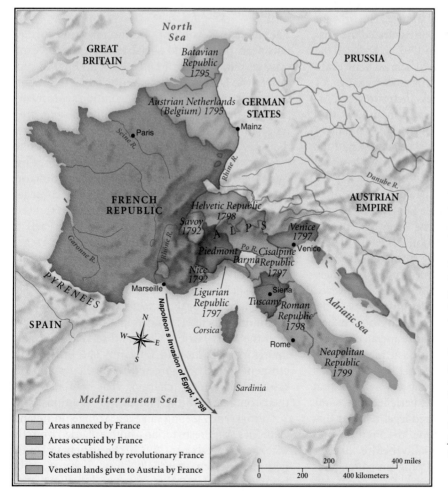

MAP 20.3 French Expansion, 1791–1799
The influence of the French Revolution on neighboring territories is dramatically evident in this map. The French directly annexed the papal territories in southern France in 1791, Nice and Savoy in 1792, and the Austrian Netherlands in 1795. They set up a series of sister republics in the former Dutch Republic and in various Italian states. Local people did not always welcome these changes. For example, the French made the Dutch pay a huge war indemnity, support a French occupying army of 25,000 soldiers, and give up some southern territories. One of the generals who invaded the Dutch Republic wrote, "Holland has done nothing to avoid being classed among the general order of our conquests. . . . It follows from this that there can be no reason to treat her any differently from a conquered country." The sister republics faced a future of subordination to French national interests.

Austrian Netherlands, Mainz, Savoy, and Nice, French officers organized Jacobin Clubs that attracted middle-class locals. The clubs petitioned for annexation to France, and French legislation was then introduced, including the abolition of seigneurial dues. Despite resistance, especially in the Austrian Netherlands, these areas remained part of France until 1815, and the legal changes were permanent. Like Louis XIV a century before, most deputies in the National Convention considered the annexed territories within France's "natural frontiers"—the Rhine, the Alps, and the Pyrenees.

The Directory government that came to power in 1795 was torn between defending the new frontiers and launching a more aggressive policy of creating semi-independent "sister" republics wherever the armies succeeded. When Prussia declared neutrality in 1795, the French armies swarmed into the Dutch Republic, abolished the stadholderate, and, with the revolutionary penchant for renaming, created the new Batavian Republic, a satellite of France. The brilliant young general Napoleon Bonaparte defeated the Austrian armies in northern Italy in 1797 and created the Cisalpine Republic. Next he overwhelmed Venice and then handed it over to the Austrians in exchange for a peace agreement that lasted less than two years. After the French attacked the Swiss cantons in 1798, they set up the Helvetic Republic and curtailed many of the Catholic church's privileges. They conquered the Papal States in 1798 and installed a Roman Republic; the pope fled to Siena.

The same year, 1798, Bonaparte took a great army, originally raised to invade England, across the Mediterranean Sea to Egypt. The Directory government hoped that an occupation of Egypt would strike a blow at British trade by cutting the route to India and thus compensate France for its losses there years before. Once the army disembarked, however, the British admiral Horatio Nelson destroyed the French fleet while it was anchored in Aboukir Bay. In the face of determined resistance and an outbreak of the bubonic plague, Bonaparte's armies retreated from a further expedition in Syria. But the French occupation of Egypt lasted long enough for that largely Muslim country to experience the same kinds of Enlightenment-inspired legal reforms that had been introduced in Europe: the French abolished torture, introduced equality before the law, eliminated religious taxes, and proclaimed religious toleration.

The revolutionary wars had an immediate impact on European life at all levels of society. Thousands of men died in every country involved, with perhaps as many as 200,000 casualties in the French armies alone in 1794 and 1795. No accurate statistics documenting casualties in these wars exist, but we do know that more soldiers died in hospitals as a result of their wounds than on the battlefields. Constant warfare hampered world commerce and especially disrupted French overseas shipping. (The abolition of slavery in the French colonies in 1794 also cut off one lucrative market for the French port cities.) In contrast to the prosperous times that preceded the French Revolution, times were now hard almost everywhere, because the dislocations of internal and external commerce provoked constant shortages.

European Reactions to Revolutionary Change

The French Revolution profoundly transformed European politics and social relations. (See "Contrasting Views," page 752.) In 1789, an English supporter, the Unitarian minister Richard Price, wrote enthusiastically about the Revolution's prospects: "Behold, the light . . . after setting AMERICA free, reflected to FRANCE, and there kindled into a blaze that lays despotism in ashes, and warms and illuminates EUROPE." The governing elites of Europe became alarmed, however, when the revolutionaries abolished monarchy and nobility and encouraged popular participation in politics. Democrats and reformers from many countries flooded to Paris to witness events firsthand. Supporters of the French Revolution in Great Britain, like the earlier reformers of the 1760s and 1770s, joined constitutional and reform societies that sprang up in many cities. The most important of these societies, the London Corresponding Society, founded in 1792, corresponded with the Paris Jacobin Club and served as a center for reform agitation in England. The British government quickly suppressed the societies and harassed their leaders, charging that their ideas and their contacts with the French were seditious.

Pro-French feeling ran even stronger in Ireland. Catholics and Presbyterians, both excluded from the vote, came together in 1791 in the Society of United Irishmen, which eventually pressed for secession from England. In 1798, the society timed a rebellion

FRENCH LIBERTY. BRITISH SLAVERY.

The English Rebuttal
In this caricature, James Gillray satirizes the French version of liberty. Gillray, a supporter of the Tories in Britain, produced thousands of political caricatures.
British Museum.

to coincide with a French invasion, but the French sent too few soldiers and the British mercilessly repressed the revolt. Thirty thousand people were killed. Twice as many regular British troops (seventy thousand) as fought in any of the major continental battles were required to put down the rebellion.

Those countries near France with a substantial middle class and access to newspapers and other publications generally sympathized the most with French ideas. Yet even countries close to France sometimes fiercely resisted French occupation, often in the form of banditry. In the German Rhineland, for example, gangs of bandits preyed on the French and on Jews. One German traveler reported, "It is characteristic of the region in which the bandits are based that these two nations [the French and the Jews] are hated. So crimes against them are motivated not just by a wish to rob them but also by a variety of fanaticism which is partly political and partly religious." Because the French offered the Jews religious toleration and civil and political rights wherever they conquered, anti-French groups sometimes attacked Jews.

Many leading intellectuals in the German states, including the philosopher Immanuel Kant, initially supported the revolutionary cause, but after 1793 most of them turned against the popular violence and military aggressiveness of the Revolution. One of the greatest writers of the age, Friedrich Schiller

(1759–1805), typified the turn in sentiment against revolutionary politics:

Freedom is only in the realm of dreams
And the beautiful blooms only in song.

The German states, still run by many separate rulers, experienced a profound artistic and intellectual revival, which eventually connected with anti-French nationalism. This renaissance included a resurgence of intellectual life in the universities, a thriving press (1,225 journals were launched in the 1780s alone), and the multiplication of Masonic lodges and literary clubs.

Not surprisingly, the areas farthest from France—Russia, the Ottoman Empire, the Balkans, Austria, Hungary, and the Scandinavian states—were generally least affected by the French Revolution. One exception was the United States, where opinion fiercely divided on the virtues of the French Revolution. Sweden was a second exception. Gustavus III (r. 1771–1792) was assassinated in Stockholm by a nobleman who claimed that "the king has violated his oath . . . and declared himself an enemy of the realm." The king's murder changed little in Sweden's power structure, however; his son Gustavus IV (r. 1792–1809) was convinced that the French Jacobins had sanctioned his father's assassination, and he insisted on avoiding "licentious liberty." Although just across the border from France, Spain's royal

Consequences of the French Revolution

Contemporaries instantly grasped the cataclysmic significance of the French Revolution and began to argue about its lessons for their own countries. A member of the British Parliament, Edmund Burke, ignited a firestorm of controversy with his *Reflections on the Revolution in France* (Document 1). He condemned the French revolutionaries for attempting to build a government on abstract reasoning rather than taking historical traditions and customs into account; his book provided a foundation for the doctrine known as *conservatism*, which argued for "conserving" the traditional foundations of society and avoiding the pitfalls of radical or revolutionary change. Burke's views provoked a strong response from the English political agitator Thomas Paine. Paine's pamphlet *Common Sense* (1776) helped inspire the British North American colonies to demand independence from Great Britain. In *The Rights of Man* (Document 2), written fifteen years later, Paine attacked the traditional order as fundamentally unjust and defended the idea of a revolution to uphold rights. Joseph de Maistre, an aristocratic opponent of both the Enlightenment and the French Revolution, put the conservative attack on the French Revolution into a deeply religious and absolutist framework (Document 3). In contrast, Anne-Louise-Germaine de Staël, an opponent of Napoleon and one of the most influential intellectuals of the early nineteenth century, took the view that the violence of the Revolution had been the product of generations of superstition and arbitrary rule, that is, rule by an absolutist Catholic church and monarchical government (Document 4).

1. Edmund Burke, Reflections on the Revolution in France *(1790)*

Born in Ireland and a supporter of the American colonists in their opposition to the British Parliament, Edmund Burke (1729–1797) opposed the French Revolution, warning his countrymen against the dangerous abstractions of the French. He argued the case for tradition, continuity, and gradual reform based on practical experience— what he called "a sure principle of conservation."

Can I now congratulate the same nation [France] upon its freedom? Is it because liberty in the abstract may be classed amongst the blessings of mankind, that I am seriously to felicitate a madman, who has escaped from the protecting restraint and wholesome darkness of his cell, on his restoration to the enjoyment of light and liberty? Am I to congratulate an highwayman and murderer, who has broke prison, upon the recovery of his natural rights? . . .

Government is not made in virtue of natural rights, which may and do exist in total independence of it; and exist in much greater clearness, and in a much greater degree of abstract perfection: but their abstract perfection is their practical defect. By having a right to every thing they want every thing. Government is a contrivance of human wisdom to provide for human *wants*. . . .

The science of constructing a commonwealth, or renovating it, or reforming it, is, like every other experimental science, not to be taught *a priori* [based on theory rather than on experience]. Nor is it a short experience that can instruct us in that practical science; because the real effects of moral causes are not always immediate; but that which in the first instance is prejudicial may be excellent in its remoter operation; and its excellence may arise even from the ill effects it produces in the beginning. . . .

All the pleasing illusions, which made power gentle, and obedience liberal, which harmonized the different shades of life, and which, by a bland assimilation, incorporated into politics the sentiments which beautify and soften private society, are to be dissolved by this new conquering empire of light and reason. All the decent drapery of life is to be rudely torn off. All the super-added ideas, furnished from the wardrobe of a moral imagination, which the heart owns, and the understanding ratifies, as necessary to cover the defects of our naked shivering nature, and to raise it to dignity in our own estimation, are to be exploded as a ridiculous, absurd, and antiquated fashion.

On this scheme of things, a king is but a man; a queen is but a woman; a woman is but an animal; and an animal not of the highest order. All homage paid to the sex in general as such, and without distinct views, is to be regarded as romance and folly. Regicide, and parricide, and sacrilege, are but fictions of superstition. . . .

In the groves of *their* academy, at the end of every visto [vista], you see nothing but the gallows. Nothing is left which engages the affections on the part of the commonwealth. . . . To make us love our country, our country ought to be lovely.

Source: *Two Classics of the French Revolution: Reflections on the Revolution in France (Edmund Burke) and The Rights of Man (Thomas Paine)* (New York: Doubleday Anchor Books, 1973), 19, 71–74, 90–91.

2. *Thomas Paine,* The Rights of Man *(1791)*

In his reply to Burke, The Rights of Man, *which sold 200,000 copies in two years, Thomas Paine (1737–1809) defended the idea of reform based on reason, advocated a concept of universal human rights, and attacked the excesses of privilege and tradition in Great Britain. Elected as a deputy to the French National Convention in 1793 in recognition of his writings in favor of the French Revolution, Paine narrowly escaped condemnation as an associate of the Girondins.*

Before anything can be reasoned upon to a conclusion, certain facts, principles, or data, to reason from, must be established, admitted, or denied. Mr. Burke, with his usual outrage, abuses the *Declaration of the Rights of Man,* published by the National Assembly of France, as the basis on which the Constitution of France is built. This he calls "paltry and blurred sheets of paper about the rights of man."

Does Mr. Burke mean to deny that *man* has any rights? If he does, then he must mean that there are no such things as rights any where, and that he has none himself; for who is there in the world but man? . . .

Hitherto we have spoken only (and that but in part) of the natural rights of man. We have now to consider the civil rights of man, and to show

how the one originates from the other. Man did not enter into society to become *worse* than he was before, nor to have fewer rights than he had before, but to have those rights better secured. His natural rights are the foundation of all his civil rights. . . .

Every civil right has for its foundation some natural right pre-existing in the individual, but to the enjoyment of which his individual power is not, in all cases, sufficiently competent. Of this kind are all those which relate to security and protection. . . .

A constitution is not a thing in name only, but in fact. It has not an ideal, but a real existence; and wherever it cannot be produced in a visible form, there is none. A constitution is a thing *antecedent* to a government, and a government is only the creature of a constitution. The constitution of a country is not the act of its government, but of the people constituting a government. . . .

Can then Mr. Burke produce the English Constitution? If he cannot, we may fairly conclude, that though it has been so much talked about, no such thing as a constitution exists, or ever did exist, and consequently that the people have yet a constitution to form.

Source: *Two Classics of the French Revolution: Reflections on the Revolution in France (Edmund Burke) and The Rights of Man (Thomas Paine)* (New York: Doubleday Anchor Books, 1973), 302, 305–306, 309.

3. *Joseph de Maistre,* Considerations on France *(1797)*

An aristocrat born in Savoy, Joseph de Maistre (1753–1821) believed in reform but he passionately opposed both the Enlightenment and the French Revolution as destructive to good order. He believed that Protestants, Jews, lawyers, journalists, and scientists all threatened the social order because they questioned the need for absolute obedience to authority in matters both religious and political. De Maistre set the foundations for reactionary conservatism, a conservatism that defended throne and altar.

In a word, if there is no moral revolution in Europe, if the religious spirit is not reinforced in this part of the world, the social bond will dissolve. Nothing can be predicted, and anything must be expected, but if there is to be improvement in this matter, either France is called upon to produce it, or there is no more analogy, no more induction, no more art of prediction.

This consideration especially makes me think that the French Revolution is a great epoch and that its consequences, in all kinds of ways, will be felt far beyond the time of its explosion and the limits of its birthplace. . . .

There is a satanic quality to the French Revolution that distinguishes it from everything we have ever seen or anything we are ever likely to see in the future. Recall the great assemblies, Robespierre's speech against the priesthood, the solemn apostasy [renunciation of vows] of the clergy, the desecration of objects of worship, the installation of the goddess of reason, and that multitude of extraordinary actions by which the provinces sought to outdo Paris. All this goes beyond the ordinary circle of crime and seems to belong to another world.

Source: Joseph de Maistre, *Considerations on France*, trans. Richard A. Lebrun (Cambridge: Cambridge University Press, 1994), 21, 41.

4. Anne-Louise-Germaine de Staël, Considerations on the Main Events of the French Revolution *(1818)*

De Staël published her views long after the Revolution was over, but she had lived through the events herself. She was the daughter of Jacques Necker, Louis XVI's Swiss Protestant finance minister. Necker's dismissal in July 1789 had sparked the attack on the Bastille. De Staël published novels, literary tracts, and memoirs and became one of the best-known writers of the nineteenth century. In her writings she defended the Enlightenment; though she opposed the violence unleashed by the Revolution, she traced it back to the excesses of monarchical government.

Once the people were freed from their harness there is no doubt that they were in a position to commit any kind of crime. But how can we explain their depravity? The government we are now supposed to miss so sorely [the former monarchy] had had plenty of time to form this guilty nation. The priests whose teaching, example, and wealth were supposed to be so good for us had supervised the childhood of the generation that broke out against them. The class that revolted in 1789 must have been accustomed to the privileges of feudal nobility which, as we are also assured, are so peculiarly agreeable to those on whom they weigh [the peasants]. How does it happen, then, that the seed of so many vices was sown under the ancient institutions? . . . What can we conclude from this, then?—That no people had been as unhappy for the preceding century as the French. If the Negroes of Saint-Domingue have committed even greater atrocities, it is because they had been even more greatly oppressed.

Source: Vivian Folkenflik, ed. *An Extraordinary Woman: Selected Writings of Germaine de Staël* (New York: Columbia University Press, 1987), 365–66.

QUESTIONS FOR DEBATE
1. Which aspect of the French Revolution most disturbed these commentators?
2. How would you align each of these writers on a spectrum running from extreme right to extreme left in politics?
3. How would each of these writers judge the Enlightenment that preceded the French Revolution?

government suppressed all news from France, fearing that it might ignite the spirit of revolt. This fear was not misplaced because even in Russia, for instance, 278 outbreaks of peasant unrest occurred between 1796 and 1798. One Russian landlord complained, "This is the self-same . . . spirit of insubordination and independence, which has spread through all Europe."

Poland Extinguished, 1793–1795

The spirit of independence made the Poles and Lithuanians especially discontent, for they had already suffered a significant loss of territory and population. "I shall fight Jacobinism, and defeat it in Poland," vowed Catherine the Great in 1792. Frightened by reports of a few friends of the

REVOLUTION ON THE MARCH

French Revolution cropping up throughout eastern Europe—even in St. Petersburg—Catherine determined to smite the moderate reformers in Warsaw. Prussia joined her, fearing a regenerated, pro-French Poland. While Prussian and Austrian troops battled the French in the west, a Russian army easily crushed Polish resistance. In effect for barely a year, Poland's constitution of May 3, 1791, was abolished, and Prussia and Russia helped themselves to generous new slices of Polish territory in the Second Partition of 1793 (Map 20.4).

Poland's reform movement became even more pro-French. Some leaders fled abroad, including Tadeusz Kościuszko (1746–1817), an officer who had been a foreign volunteer in the War of American Independence and who now escaped to Paris. In the spring of 1794, Kościuszko returned from

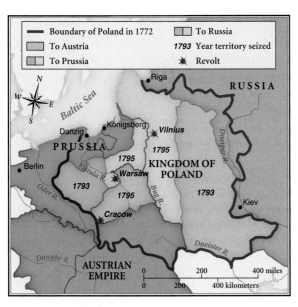

MAP 20.4 The Second and Third Partitions of Poland, 1793 and 1795

In 1793, after Russian armies invaded Poland, Russia and Prussia agreed to another partition of Polish territories. Prussia took over territory that included 1.1 million Poles while Russia gained 3 million new inhabitants. Austria gave up any claims to Poland in exchange for help from Russia and Prussia in acquiring Bavaria. When Kościuszko's nationalist uprising failed in 1794, Russia, Prussia, and Austria agreed to a final division. Prussia absorbed an additional 900,000 Polish subjects, including those in Warsaw; Austria incorporated 1 million Poles and the city of Cracow; Russia gained another 2 million Poles. The three powers determined never to use the term "Kingdom of Poland" again.

France as "dictator," empowered by his fellow conspirators to lead a national revolt. He incited an uprising at Cracow, which then spread to Warsaw and the old Lithuanian capital, Vilnius. Kościuszko faced an immediate, insoluble dilemma. He could win only if the peasants joined the struggle—highly unlikely unless villagers could be convinced that serfdom would end. But such a drastic step risked alienating the nobles who had started the revolt. So Kościuszko compromised. In his proclamation of May 7, 1794, he summoned the peasantry to the national cause and promised a reduction of their obligations as serfs, but not freedom itself. He received an equally equivocal response. Armed with scythes, a few peasant bands joined the insurrection, but most let their lords fight it out alone. Urban workers displayed more enthusiasm; at Warsaw, for example, a mob hanged several Russian collaborators, including an archbishop in his full regalia.

The uprising failed. Kościuszko led his troops to a few victories over the surprised Russians, but when Catherine's forces regrouped, they routed the Poles and Lithuanians. Kościuszko and other Patriot leaders languished for years in Russian and Austrian prisons. Taking no further chances, Russia, Prussia, and Austria wiped Poland completely from the map in the Third Partition of 1795. "The Polish question" would plague international relations for more than a century as Polish rebels flocked to any international upheaval that might undo the partitions. Beyond all this maneuvering lay the unsolved problem of Polish serfdom, which isolated the nation's gentry and townspeople from the rural masses.

Revolution in the Colonies

The Caribbean colonies lay far from France, but inevitably they felt the effects of revolution. From the beginning, political leaders in Paris feared the potential for conflict in the colonies, as aspirations for broader political rights might threaten French authority. The Caribbean colonies were crucial to the French economy. Twice the size in land area of the neighboring British colonies, they also produced nearly twice as much revenue in exports. The slave population had doubled in the French colonies in the twenty years before 1789. St. Domingue (present-day Haiti) was the most important French colony, with its approximately 465,000 slaves, 30,000 whites, and 28,000 free people of color, who were employed primarily to apprehend runaway slaves and assure plantation security.

Despite the efforts of a Paris club called the Friends of Blacks, most French revolutionaries did not consider slavery a pressing problem. As one deputy explained, "This regime [in the colonies] is oppressive, but it gives a livelihood to several million Frenchmen. This regime is barbarous but a still greater barbarity will result if you interfere with it without the necessary knowledge."

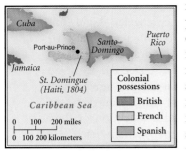

St. Domingue on the Eve of the Revolt, 1791

In August 1791, however, the slaves in northern St. Domingue organized a large-scale revolt with the slogan "Listen to the voice of Liberty which speaks in the hearts of all." To restore authority over the slaves, the Legislative Assembly in Paris granted civil and political rights to the free blacks—an action that alienated the white planters and merchants, who in 1793 signed an agreement with Great Britain, now France's enemy in war, declaring British sovereignty over the island. To complicate matters further, Spain, which controlled the rest of the island and had entered on Great Britain's side in the war, offered freedom to individual slave rebels who joined the Spanish armies as long as they agreed to maintain the slave regime for the other blacks.

The few thousand French republican troops on the island were outnumbered, and to prevent complete military disaster the French commissioner freed all the slaves in his jurisdiction in August 1793 without permission from the government at home. In February 1794, the National Convention formally abolished slavery and granted full rights to all black men in the colonies. These actions had the desired effect. One of the ablest black generals allied with the Spanish, the ex-slave François Dominique Toussaint L'Ouverture (1743–1803), changed sides and committed his troops to the French. The French eventually appointed Toussaint governor of St. Domingue as a reward for his efforts. The vicious fighting and flight of whites left the island's economy in ruins; in 1800, the plantations produced one-fifth of what they had in 1789. In the zones Toussaint controlled, army officers or officials took over the great estates and kept all those working in

Toussaint L'Ouverture

The leader of the St. Domingue slave uprising appears in his general's uniform, sword in hand. This portrait appeared in one of the earliest histories of the revolt, Marcus Rainsford's **Historical Account of the Black Empire of Hayti** *(London, 1805). Toussaint, a former slave who educated himself, fascinated many of his contemporaries in Europe as well as the New World by turning a chaotic slave rebellion into an organized and ultimately successful independence movement.* North Wind Picture Archives.

agriculture under military discipline. The former slaves were bound to their estates like serfs and forced to work the plantations in exchange for an autonomous family life and the right to maintain personal garden plots.

Toussaint remained in charge until 1802, when Napoleon sent French armies to regain control of the island. They arrested Toussaint and transported him to France, where he died in prison. The arrest prompted the English poet William Wordsworth to write of him:

There's not a breathing of the common wind
That will forget thee; thou hast great allies;
Thy friends are exultations, agonies,
And love, and man's unconquerable mind.

Toussaint became a hero to abolitionists every-where, a potent symbol of black struggles to win freedom. Napoleon attempted to restore slavery, sending Polish volunteers to do much of the gruel-ing work, but the remaining black generals defeated his armies and in 1804 proclaimed the Republic of Haiti.

The Rise of Napoleon Bonaparte

Toussaint had followed with interest Napoleon's rise to power in France; he once wrote to Bonaparte, "From the First of the Blacks to the First of the Whites." He was not alone in his fascination, for the story of the rise of Napoleon Bonaparte (1769–1821) is one of the most remarkable in Western history. It would have seemed astonishing in 1795 that the twenty-six-year-old son of a noble family from the island of Corsica off the Italian coast would within four years become the supreme ruler of France and one of the greatest military leaders in world history. In 1795, he was a penniless artillery officer, only re-cently released from prison as a presumed Robes-pierrist. Thanks to some early military successes and links to Parisian politicians, he was named comman-der of the French army in Italy in 1796.

Bonaparte's astounding success in the Italian campaigns of 1796–1797 launched his meteoric ca-reer. With an army of fewer than fifty thousand men, he defeated the Piedmontese and the Austrians. In quick order he established client republics depen-dent on his own authority; he negotiated with the Austrians himself; and he molded the army into his

Bonaparte in Egypt
This engraving, based on Antoine Jean Gros's painting Napoleon Visiting the Victims of the Plague at Jaffa *(1804), is meant to glorify Bonaparte's courage: he is not afraid to touch the victims of the plague. Yet it also signals a terrible problem in Bonaparte's campaign for domination in the western Mediterranean. He has won many battles at this moment in 1799, but he is losing the war through attrition, disease, and mounting resistance.*
National Library of Medicine, Bethesda/Visual Image Presentations.

personal force by paying the soldiers in cash taken as tribute from the newly conquered territories. He mollified the Directory government by sending home wagonloads of great Italian masterpieces of art, which were added to Parisian museum collections after being paraded in victory festivals. (Most are still there.) Even the failures of the Egyptian campaign did not dull his luster. Bonaparte had taken France's leading scientists with him on the expedition, and his soldiers had discovered a slab of black basalt dating from 196 B.C. written in both hieroglyphic and Greek. Called the *Rosetta stone* after a nearby town, it enabled scholars to finally decipher the hieroglyphs used by the ancient Egyptians. When his army was pinned down after its initial successes, Napoleon slipped out of Egypt and made his way secretly across the Mediterranean to southern France.

In October 1799, Bonaparte arrived home at just the right moment. The war in Europe was going badly; the departments of the former Austrian Netherlands had revolted against new conscription laws; deserters swelled the ranks of the rebels in western France; a royalist army had tried to take the city of Toulouse in the southwest; and many government leaders wanted to revise the Constitution of 1795. Amidst increasing political instability, generals in the field had become virtually independent, and the troops felt more loyal to their units and generals than to the republic. As one army captain wrote, "In a conquering people the military spirit must prevail over other social conditions." Its victories had made the army a parallel and rival force to the state.

Disillusioned members of the government saw in Bonaparte's return an occasion to overturn the Constitution of 1795. On November 9, 1799 (18 Brumaire, Year VIII by the revolutionary calendar), the conspirators persuaded the legislature to move out of Paris to avoid an imaginary Jacobin plot. But when Bonaparte marched into the meeting hall the next day and demanded changes in the Constitution, he was greeted by cries of "Down with the dictator." His quick-thinking brother Lucien, president of the Council of Five Hundred (the lower house), saved Bonaparte's coup by summoning troops guarding the hall and claiming that the deputies had tried to assassinate the popular general. The soldiers ejected the deputies, and a hastily assembled rump legislature voted to abolish the Directory and establish a new three-man executive called the consulate. Bonaparte became First Consul, a title revived from the ancient Roman republic.

Shortly after the coup, a new constitution was submitted to the voters. Millions abstained from voting, and the government falsified the results to give an appearance of even greater support to the new regime. Altogether it was an unpromising beginning; yet within five years Bonaparte would crown himself Napoleon I, emperor of the French. A new order would rise from the ashes of the republic, and the French armies would recover from their reverses of 1799 to push the frontiers of French influence even farther eastward.

Conclusion

In 1799, no one knew what course Napoleon Bonaparte would follow. Inside France, political apathy had overtaken the original enthusiasm for revolutionary ideals. Yet the political landscape had been permanently altered by the revolutionary cataclysm.

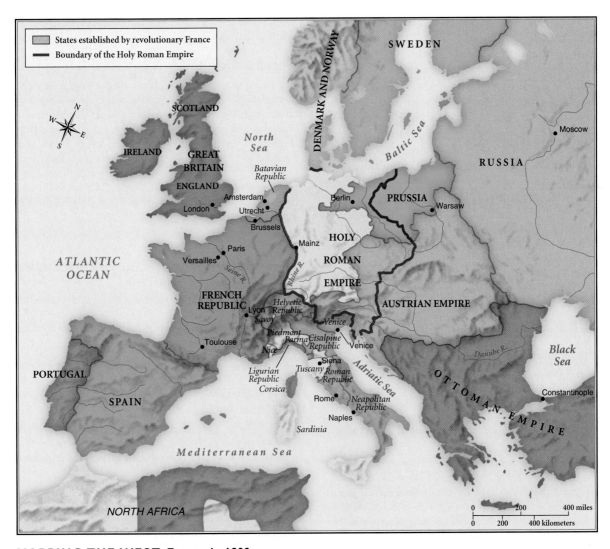

MAPPING THE WEST Europe in 1800

France's expansion during the revolutionary wars threatened to upset the balance of power in Europe. A century earlier the English and Dutch had allied and formed a Europe-wide coalition to check the territorial ambitions of Louis XIV. Thwarting French ambitions after 1800 would prove to be even more of a challenge to the other European powers. The Dutch had been reduced to satellite status, as had most of the Italian states. After 1800, even Austria and Prussia would suffer devastating losses to the French on the battlefield. Only a new coalition of European powers could stop France in the future.

Between 1789 and 1799, monarchy as a form of government had given way to a republic whose leaders were elected. Aristocracy based on rank and birth had been undermined in favor of civil equality and the promotion of merit. The people who marched in demonstrations, met in clubs, and, in the case of men, voted in national elections for the first time had insisted that government respond to them. Thousands of men had held elective office.

A revolutionary government had tried to teach new values with a refashioned calendar, state festivals, and a civic religion. Its example would inspire future revolutionaries.

But the French Revolution also had its darker side. The divisions created by the Revolution within France endured in many cases until after World War II. Even now, French public-opinion surveys ask if it was right to execute the king in 1793 (most believe Louis XVI was guilty of treason but should not have been executed). The revolutionaries proclaimed human rights and democratic government as a universal goal, but they also explicitly excluded women, even though they admitted Protestant, Jewish, and eventually black men. They used the new spirit of national pride to inspire armies that conquered other peoples. Their ideals of universal education, religious toleration, and democratic participation could not prevent the institution of new forms of government terror to persecute, imprison, and kill dissidents. These paradoxes created an opening for Napoleon Bonaparte, who rushed in with his remarkable military and political skills to push France—and with it all of Europe—in new directions.

Suggested References

The Revolutionary Wave, 1787–1789

In the 1950s and 1960s, historians debated vehemently about whether the French Revolution should be considered part of a more general phenomenon of Atlantic revolutions, as R. R. Palmer argues. Recent work on the Dutch Republic and the Austrian Netherlands has developed nuanced comparisons that show both similarities with and differences from the French Revolution. Historians of France have focused more single-mindedly on the French origins of revolution. The most influential book on the meaning of the French Revolution is still the classic study of Tocqueville, who insisted that the Revolution continued the process of state centralization undertaken by the monarchy.

*Baker, Keith Michael, ed. *The Old Regime and the French Revolution.* University of Chicago Readings in Western Civilization, vol. 7. 1987.

Chartier, Roger. *The Cultural Origins of the French Revolution.* Trans. Lydia G. Cochrane. 1991.

Lefebvre, Georges. *The Coming of the French Revolution.* Trans. with a new preface, R. R. Palmer. 1989.

Palmer, R. R. *The Age of the Democratic Revolution: A Political History of Europe and America, 1760–1800.* Vol. 2, *The Struggle.* 1964.

Polasky, Janet L. *Revolution in Brussels, 1787–1793.* 1987.

Te Brake, Wayne. *Regents and Rebels: The Revolutionary World of an Eighteenth-Century Dutch City.* 1989.

*Primary sources.

Tocqueville, Alexis de. *The Old Regime and the French Revolution.* Trans. Stuart Gilbert. 1955. Originally published 1856.

From Monarchy to Republic, 1789–1793

From 1789 onward, commentators on the French Revolution have differed over its meaning: was it a revolution for human rights and democracy (the positions of Paine and Wollstonecraft) or a dangerous experiment in implementing reason and destroying religion and tradition (Burke and Tocqueville)? The collections edited by Blanning and Kates sample some of the newer versions of these enduring controversies. Among the most important additions to the debate have been new works on women, Jews, Protestants, and slaves.

Blanning, T. C. W., ed. *The French Revolution: Class War or Culture Clash?* 2nd ed. 1998.

*Hunt, Lynn, ed. *The French Revolution and Human Rights: A Brief Documentary History.* 1996.

Images of the French Revolution: http://chnm.gmu.edu/revolution.

Kates, Gary, ed. *The French Revolution: Recent Debates and New Controversies.* 1998.

*Levy, Darline Gay, Harriet Branson Applewhite, and Mary Durham Johnson, eds. *Women in Revolutionary Paris, 1789–1795.* 1979.

Schama, Simon. *Citizens: A Chronicle of the French Revolution.* 1989.

* *Two Classics of the French Revolution:* Reflections on the Revolution in France (*Edmund Burke*) *and* The Rights of Man (*Thomas Paine*). 1973.

*Wollstonecraft, Mary. *A Vindication of the Rights of Woman.* Ed. Miriam Brody. 1992.

The Terror and the Republic of Virtue

The most controversial episode in the French Revolution has not surprisingly provoked conflicting interpretations. Soboul offers the Marxist interpretation, which Furet specifically opposes. Very recently interest has shifted from these broader interpretive issues back to the principal actors themselves: Robespierre, the Jacobins, and women's clubs have all attracted scholarly attention.

Desan, Suzanne. *Reclaiming the Sacred: Lay Religion and Popular Politics in Revolutionary France.* 1990.

Furet, François. *Interpreting the French Revolution.* Trans. Elborg Forster. 1981.

Godineau, Dominique. *The Women of Paris and Their French Revolution.* Trans. Katherine Streip. 1998.

Haydon, Colin, and William Doyle, eds. *Robespierre.* 1999.

Higonnet, Patrice L. R. *Goodness beyond Virtue: Jacobins during the French Revolution.* 1998.

Hunt, Lynn. *Politics, Culture, and Class in the French Revolution.* 1984.

Palmer, R. R. *Twelve Who Ruled: The Year of the Terror in the French Revolution.* 1989.

Soboul, Albert. *The Sans-Culottes: The Popular Movement and Revolutionary Government, 1793–1794.* Trans. Remy Inglis Hall. 1980.

Sutherland, D. M. G. *France, 1789–1815: Revolution and Counterrevolution.* 1986.

Revolution on the March

In the past, controversy about the Revolution in France raged while its influence on other places was relatively neglected. This imbalance is now being redressed in studies of the colonies and the impact of the revolutionary wars on areas from Egypt to Ireland. Recent work pays close attention to the social background of soldiers as well as their experiences in warfare.

Beaucour, Fernand Emile, Yves Laissus, and Chantal Orgogozo. *The Discovery of Egypt.* Trans. Bambi Ballard. 1990.

Blackburn, Robin. *The Overthrow of Colonial Slavery, 1776–1848.* 1988.

Blanning, T. C. W. *The French Revolutionary Wars, 1787–1802.* 1996.

Elliot, Marianne. *Partners in Revolution: The United Irishmen and France.* 1982.

Forrest, Alan I. *The Soldiers of the French Revolution.* 1990.

James, C. L. R. *Black Jacobins: Toussaint L'Ouverture and the San Domingo Revolution,* 2nd ed. 1989.

BONAPARTE

Napoleon and the Revolutionary Legacy

1800–1830

Napoleon as Military Hero
In this painting from 1800–1801,
Napoleon Crossing the Alps at
St. Bernard, *Jacques-Louis David
reminds the French of Napoleon's
heroic military exploits. Napoleon
is a picture of calm and compo-
sure while his horse shows the
fright and energy of the moment.
David painted this propagandistic
image shortly after one of his
former students went to the
guillotine on a trumped-up charge
of plotting to assassinate the
new French leader. The former
organizer of republican festivals
during the Terror had became
a kind of court painter for the
new regime.*
© Photo RMN/Herve Lewandowski.

I N HER NOVEL *FRANKENSTEIN* (1818), the prototype for modern
thrillers, Mary Shelley tells the story of a Swiss technological genius who creates a humanlike monster in his pursuit of scientific
knowledge. The monster, "so scaring and unearthly in his ugliness," ter-
rifies all who encounter him and ends by destroying Dr. Frankenstein's
own loved ones. Despite desperate chases across deserts and frozen landscapes, Frankenstein never manages to trap the monster, who is last seen
hunched over his creator's deathbed.

Frankenstein's monster can be taken as a particularly horrifying
incarnation of the fears of the postrevolutionary era, but just what did
Shelley intend? Did the monster represent the French Revolution, which
had devoured its own children in the Terror? Shelley was the daughter
of Mary Wollstonecraft, an English feminist who had defended the
French Revolution and died in childbirth when Mary was born. Did the
monster stand for the dangerous possibilities that might be unleashed
by science and industry in the new age of industrial growth? She was
also the wife of the romantic poet Percy Bysshe Shelley, who often wrote
against the ugliness of contemporary life and celebrated nature and the
"beautiful idealisms of moral excellence." Whatever the meaning—and
Mary Shelley may well have intended more than one—the novel makes
the forceful point that humans cannot always control their own crea-
tions. The Enlightenment and the French Revolution had celebrated the
virtues of human creativity, but Shelley shows that innovation often has
a dark and uncontrollable side.

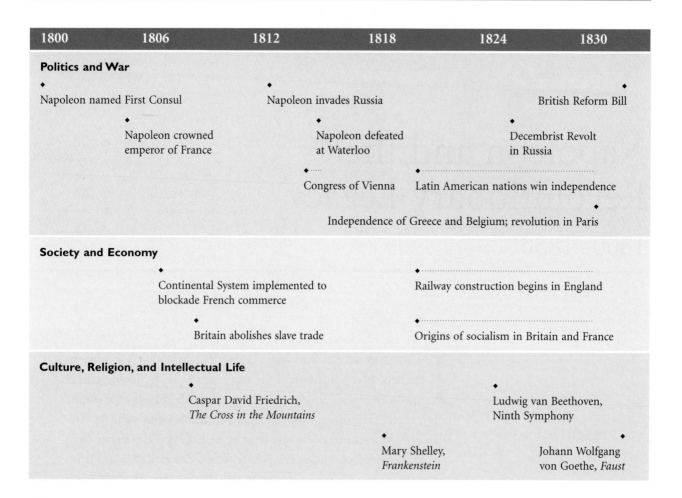

1800	1806	1812	1818	1824	1830

Politics and War

Napoleon named First Consul

Napoleon crowned emperor of France

Napoleon invades Russia

Napoleon defeated at Waterloo

Congress of Vienna

British Reform Bill

Decembrist Revolt in Russia

Latin American nations win independence

Independence of Greece and Belgium; revolution in Paris

Society and Economy

Continental System implemented to blockade French commerce

Britain abolishes slave trade

Railway construction begins in England

Origins of socialism in Britain and France

Culture, Religion, and Intellectual Life

Caspar David Friedrich, *The Cross in the Mountains*

Mary Shelley, *Frankenstein*

Ludwig van Beethoven, Ninth Symphony

Johann Wolfgang von Goethe, *Faust*

Those who witnessed Napoleon Bonaparte's stunning rise to European dominance after 1800 might have cast him as either Frankenstein or his monster. Though short and physically unimpressive, like the scientist Frankenstein, Bonaparte created something dramatically new: the French Empire with himself as emperor. Like the former kings of France, he ruled under his first name. This Corsican artillery officer who spoke French with an Italian accent ended the French Revolution even while maintaining some of its most important innovations. Bonaparte transformed France from a democratically elected republic to an empire with a new aristocracy based on military service. But he kept the revolutionary administration and most of its laws that ensured equal treatment to all citizens. Although he tolerated no opposition at home, he prided himself on bringing French-style changes to peoples elsewhere.

Bonaparte continued the revolutionary policy of conquest and annexation until it reached grotesque dimensions. His foreign policies made many see him as a monster hungry for dominion; he turned the sister republics of the revolutionary era into kingdoms personally ruled by his relatives, and he exacted tribute from subject peoples wherever he triumphed. Eventually resistance to the French armies and the ever-mounting costs of military glory toppled Napoleon. The powers allied against him met and agreed to restore the monarchical governments that had been overthrown by the French, shrink France back to its prerevolutionary boundaries, and maintain this settlement against future demands for change.

Although the people of Europe longed for peace and stability in the aftermath of the Napoleonic whirlwind, they lived in a world that was deeply unsettled by two parallel revolutions: the Industrial

Revolution and the French Revolution. The Industrial Revolution spread from Great Britain to the continent in the early 1800s in the form of factories and railroads. Even those who resisted the impact of the French Revolution with its Napoleonic sequel had to confront the underlying changes in social and economic structures that resulted from industrialization. These changes inevitably reinforced the legacy of the French Revolution, which included equality before the law, religious toleration, and, eventually, nationalism. Profoundly affected by French military occupation, many peoples organized to demand ethnic and cultural autonomy, first from Napoleon and then from the restored governments after 1815. Alongside nationalism, other new ideologies such as liberalism and socialism emerged under the impact of the Industrial and French Revolutions. These offered their adherents a doctrine that explained social change and advocated political transformation. In 1830, the development of liberalism, socialism, and nationalism shocked Europe with a new round of revolutions in France, Belgium, Poland, and some of the Italian states. By then the spread of industry, the growing awareness of social problems, and aspirations for national self-determination had reinvigorated the force of the revolutionary legacy.

❖ From Consulate to Empire: The Napoleonic State

When Napoleon Bonaparte came to power in 1799, his coup d'état appeared to be just the latest in a long line of upheavals in revolutionary France. Within the year, however, he had effectively ended the French Revolution and set France on a new course toward an authoritarian state. As emperor after 1804, he dreamed of European integration in the tradition of Augustus and Charlemagne, but he also mastered the details of practical administration. To achieve his goals, he compromised with the Catholic church and with exiled aristocrats willing to return to France. His most enduring accomplishment, the new Civil Code, tempered the principles of the Enlightenment and the Revolution with an insistence on the powers of fathers over children, husbands over wives, and employers over workers.

His influence spread into many spheres as he personally patronized scientific inquiry and encouraged artistic styles in line with his vision of imperial greatness.

The End of the French Republic

Napoleon had no long-range plans to establish himself as emperor and conquer most of Europe. Yet by seizing every opportunity, he first gained control over the new French government and then eliminated the republic and put an empire in its place. The deputies of the legislature who engineered the coup d'état of November 1799 picked him as one of three provisional consuls (the title drew on the ancient Roman precedent) only because he was a

Francisco de Goya, _The Colossus_ (1808–1812)
The Spanish painter Goya might be imagined as capturing Frankenstein's monster or Napoleon himself as the new giant overwhelming much of Europe. Goya painted for the Spanish court before Napoleon invaded and occupied the country; after an illness left him deaf, he turned toward darkly imaginative works such as this one.
Museo del Prado, Madrid.

Napoleon's Coronation as Emperor
In The Coronation of Napoleon and Josephine *(1805–1807), Jacques-Louis David shows Napoleon crowning his wife at the ceremony of 1804. Napoleon orchestrated the entire event and took the only active role in it: Pope Pius VII gave his blessing to the ceremony, but Napoleon crowned himself.*
Scala/Art Resource, NY.

famous general. Napoleon immediately asserted his leadership over the other two consuls in the process of drafting another constitution—the fourth since 1789 and the third for the republic established in 1792.

Toward Empire. The constitution of 1799 made Napoleon the First Consul with the right to pick the Council of State, which drew up all laws. He quickly exerted control by choosing men loyal to him. Government was no longer representative in any real sense: the new constitution eliminated direct elections for deputies and granted no independent powers to the three houses of the legislature. Napoleon and his advisers chose the legislature's members out of a small pool of "notables." Almost all men over twenty-one could vote in the plebiscite (referendum) to approve the constitution, but their only option was to choose Yes or No.

Napoleon's most urgent task was to reconcile to his regime Catholics who had been alienated by revolutionary policies. Although nominally Catholic, Napoleon held no deep religious convictions. "How can there be order in the state without religion?" he asked cynically. "When a man is dying of hunger beside another who is stuffing himself, he cannot accept this difference if there is not an authority who tells him: 'God wishes it so.'" In 1801, a concordat with Pope Pius VII (r. 1800–1823) ended a decade of church-state conflict. The pope validated all sales of church lands, and the government agreed to pay the salaries of bishops and priests who would swear loyalty to the state. Catholicism was officially recognized as the religion of "the great majority of French citizens." (The state also paid Protestant pastors' salaries.) The pope thus brought the huge French Catholic population back into the fold and Napoleon gained the pope's support for his regime.

Napoleon continued the centralization of state power that had begun under the absolutist monarchy of Louis XIV and resumed under the Terror. As First Consul he appointed prefects who directly supervised local affairs in every *département*, or region. He created the Bank of France to facilitate government borrowing and relied on gold and silver coinage rather than paper money. He made good use of budgets and improved tax collection, but he also frequently made ends meet by exacting tribute from the territories he conquered. The government directly managed every aspect of education: at the new *lycées*, the state-run secondary schools for boys from better-off families, students wore military uniforms, and drumrolls signaled the beginning and end of classes. (Without the military trappings, the lycées are now coeducational and still the heart of the French educational system.) Napoleon took little interest in girls' education, believing that they should spend most of their time at home learning religion, manners, and such "female occupations" as sewing and music.

Napoleon promised order and an end to the upheavals of ten years of revolutionary turmoil, but his regime severely limited political expression. He never relied on mass executions to achieve control, but he refused to allow those who opposed him to meet in clubs, influence elections, or publish newspapers. A decree reduced the number of newspapers in Paris from seventy-three to thirteen (and then finally to four), and the newspapers that remained became government organs. Government censors had to approve all operas and plays, and they banned "offensive" artistic works even more frequently than their royal predecessors. The minister of police, Joseph Fouché, once a leading figure in the Terror of 1793–1794, could impose house arrest, arbitrary imprisonment, and surveillance of political dissidents. Political contest and debate shriveled to almost nothing. When a bomb attack on Napoleon's carriage failed in 1800, Fouché suppressed the evidence of a royalist plot and instead arrested hundreds of former Jacobins. More than one hundred of them were deported and seven hundred imprisoned.

Napoleon feared the influence of fervent supporters of the republic more than that of supporters of the monarchy. In 1802, his intentions became clear: he planned to eliminate the republic. He named himself First Consul for life, and in 1804,

Empire Style
Philibert-Louis Debucourt made a reputation with paintings and engravings of everyday life such as this one, Frascati Café. *Napoleon admired neoclassicism, and its influence can be seen in the Greek columns and archways of the room as well as in the high empire waists of the women's dresses. Note that some men now wear pantaloons—the forebears of modern trousers—rather than the knee breeches of the Old Regime aristocracy.*
The Metropolitan Museum of Art, Harris Brisbane Dick Fund, 1935. (35.100.31)

with the pope's blessing, he crowned himself emperor. Once again, plebiscites approved his decisions, but no alternatives were offered.

The Civil Code. This was government from the top down, yet it was government based on law. The revolutionary governments had tried to unify and standardize France's multiple legal codes, but only Napoleon successfully established a new one, partly because he personally presided over the commission that drafted the new Civil Code, completed in 1804. Called the Napoleonic Code as a way of further exalting his image, it defined and assured property rights, guaranteed religious liberty, and established a uniform system of law that provided equal treatment for all adult males and affirmed the right of men to choose their professions.

The code sharply curtailed women's rights in almost every aspect of public and private life. Napoleon wanted to restrict women to the private sphere of the home. One of his leading jurists remarked, "There have been many discussions on the equality and superiority of the sexes. Nothing is more useless than such disputes. . . . Women need protection because they are weaker; men are free because they are stronger." The law obligated a husband to support his wife, but he alone controlled any property held in common; a wife could not sue in court, sell or mortgage her own property, or contract a debt without her husband's consent.

The Civil Code modified even those few revolutionary laws that had been favorable to women and in some instances denied women rights they had had under the monarchy. Divorce was still possible but severely restricted, especially for women. Adultery was an acceptable grounds for divorce, but the law considered a wife's infidelity more reprehensible than a husband's. A wife could petition for divorce only if her husband brought his mistress to live in the family home. In contrast, a wife convicted of adultery could be imprisoned for up to two years. The code's framers saw these discrepancies as a way to reinforce the family and make women responsible for private virtue, while leaving public decisions to men. The French code was imitated in many European and Latin American countries and the French colony of Louisiana, where it had a similar negative effect on women's rights. Not until 1965 did French wives gain legal status equal to that of their husbands.

Imperial Rule

Napoleon's charismatic personality dominated the new regime. He worked hard at establishing his reputation as an efficient administrator with broad intellectual interests: he met frequently with scientists, jurists, and artists, and stories abounded of his unflagging energy. He set an example by rising at 2:00 A.M., after only four or five hours' sleep, and working for three hours before going back to bed from 5:00 to 7:00 A.M. When not on military campaigns, he worked on state affairs, usually until 10:00 P.M., taking only a few minutes for each meal. "Authority," declared his adviser Sieyès, "must come from above and confidence from below."

As emperor, Napoleon cultivated personal symbolism to enhance his image as a hero. His face and name adorned coins, engravings, histories, paintings, and public monuments. His favorite painters embellished his legend by depicting him as a warrior-hero of mythic proportions. In his imperial court, Napoleon staged his entrances carefully to maximize his personal presence: his wife and courtiers were dressed in regal finery, and he was announced with great pomp—but he usually arrived dressed in a simple military uniform with no medals.

Believing that "what is big is always beautiful," Napoleon embarked on ostentatious building projects that would outshine even those of Louis XIV. Government-commissioned architects built the Arc de Triomphe, the Stock Exchange, fountains, and even slaughterhouses. Most of his new construction reflected his neoclassical taste for monumental buildings set in vast empty spaces. Old, winding streets with their cramped houses were demolished to make way for Napoleon's grand designs.

Despite appearances, Napoleon did not rule alone. Among his most trusted officials were men who had served with him in Italy and Egypt. His chief of staff Alexandre Berthier, for example, became minister of war, and the chemist Claude Berthollet, who had organized the scientific part of the expedition to Egypt, became vice president of the Senate in 1804. Napoleon's bureaucracy was based on a patron-client relationship, with Napoleon as the ultimate patron. Some of Napoleon's closest associates married into his family.

Napoleon reinstituted a social hierarchy in France by rewarding merit and talent, regardless of social origins. He used the Senate to dispense his patronage and personally chose as senators the nation's most illustrious generals, ministers, prefects, scientists, rich men, and former nobles. Intending to replace both the old nobility of birth and the republic's strict emphasis on equality, in 1802 he took the first step toward creating a new nobility by founding a Legion of Honor. (Members of the legion received lifetime pensions along with their titles.) Napoleon usually equated honor with military success. By 1814, the legion had 32,000 members, only 5 percent of them civilians.

In 1808, Napoleon introduced a complete hierarchy of noble titles, ranging from princes down to barons and chevaliers. All Napoleonic nobles had served the state. Titles could be inherited but had to be supported by wealth—a man could not be a duke without a fortune of 200,000 francs, or a chevalier without 3,000 francs. To go along with their new titles, Napoleon gave his favorite generals huge fortunes, often in the form of estates in the conquered territories.

Napoleon's own family reaped the greatest benefits. He made his older brother, Joseph, ruler of the newly established kingdom of Naples in 1806, the same year he installed his younger brother Louis as king of Holland. He proclaimed his twenty-three-year-old stepson Eugène de Beauharnais viceroy of Italy in 1805 and established his sister Caroline and brother-in-law General Murat as king and queen of Naples in 1808 when he moved Joseph to the throne of Spain. Napoleon wanted to establish an imperial

succession, but he lacked an heir. In thirteen years of marriage, his wife Josephine had borne no children, so in 1809 he divorced her and in 1810 married the eighteen-year-old Princess Marie-Louise of Austria. The next year she gave birth to a son to whom Napoleon immediately gave the title king of Rome.

The New Paternalism

Since Napoleon shared the rewards of rule with his own family, it is perhaps not surprising that he brought a familial model of power to his empire, instilling his personal version of paternalism. The Civil Code not only reasserted the Old Regime's patriarchal system of male domination over women but also insisted on a father's control over his children, which revolutionary legislation had limited. For example, if children under age sixteen refused to follow their fathers' commands, they could be sent to prison for up to a month with no hearing of any sort. At the same time, the code required fathers to provide for their children's welfare. Napoleon himself encouraged the foundation of private charities to help indigent mothers, and one of his decrees made it easier for women to abandon their children anonymously to a government foundling hospital. Napoleon hoped such measures would discourage abortion and infanticide, especially among the poorest classes in the fast-growing urban areas.

In periods of economic crisis the government opened soup kitchens, but in time-honored fashion it also arrested beggars and sent them to newly established workhouses. The state also intervened in prostitutes' lives. Migration from the countryside and wartime upheavals had caused a surge of prostitution in French cities. The authorities arrested prostitutes who worked on their own, but they tolerated brothels, which could be supervised by the police, and required the women in them to have monthly medical examinations for venereal disease.

The new paternalism extended to relations between employers and employees. The state required all workers to carry a work card attesting to their good conduct, and it prohibited all workers' organizations. The police considered workers without cards as vagrants or criminals and could send them to workhouses or prison. After 1806, arbitration boards settled labor disputes, but they took

Medal of the Legion of Honor

"Men are led through baubles," Napoleon once remarked, but "a little cash does not hurt." He gave this medal to members of the Legion of Honor and added a small pension. Never missing an occasion to glorify his own image, Napoleon had his portrait installed in the center of the star and garland.
© Photo Musée de L'Armee, Paris.

employers at their word while treating workers as minors, demanding that foremen and shop superintendents represent them. Occasionally strikes broke out, led by secret, illegal journeymen's associations, yet many employers laid off employees when times were hard, deducted fines from their wages, and dismissed them without appeal for being absent or making errors. These limitations on workers' rights won Napoleon the support of French business.

Patronage of Science and Intellectual Life

Napoleon did everything possible to promote French scientific inquiry, especially that which could serve practical ends. (See "Did You Know?," page 771.) He closely monitored the research institutes established during the Revolution, sometimes intervening personally to achieve political conformity. An impressive outpouring of new theoretical and practical scientific work rewarded the state's efforts. Experiments with balloons led to the discovery of laws about the expansion of gases, and research on fossil shells prepared the way for new theories of evolutionary change later in the nineteenth century. The surgeon Dominique-Jean Larrey developed new techniques of battlefield amputation and medical care during Napoleon's wars, winning an appointment as an officer in the Legion of Honor and becoming a baron with a pension.

Napoleon had his own forward-looking vision for modernizing French society through science and central administration, but to maintain his control he stifled dissent. Napoleon considered most writers useless or dangerous, "good for nothing under any government." Some of the most talented French writers of the time had to live in exile. The best-known expatriate was Germaine de Staël (1766–1817), known as Madame de Staël, the daughter of Louis XVI's chief minister Jacques Necker. When explaining his desire to banish her, Napoleon exclaimed, "She is a machine in motion who stirs up the salons." While exiled in the German states, Madame de Staël wrote a novel, *Corinne* (1807), whose heroine is a brilliant woman thwarted by a patriarchal system, and *On Germany* (1810), an account of the important new literary currents east of the Rhine. Her books were banned in France.

Although Napoleon restored the strong authority of state and religion in France, many royalists and

Germaine de Staël
One of the most fascinating intellectuals of her time, Anne-Louise Germaine de Staël seemed to irritate Napoleon more than any other person did. Daughter of Louis XVI's Swiss Protestant finance minister, Jacques Necker, and wife of a Swedish diplomat, Madame de Staël frequently criticized Napoleon's regime. She published best-selling novels and influential literary criticism and whenever allowed to reside in Paris she encouraged the intellectual and political dissidents from Napoleon's regime.
Photographie Bulloz.

Catholics still criticized him as an impious usurper. (See "Contrasting Views," page 778.) François-René de Chateaubriand (1768–1848) admired Napoleon as "the strong man who has saved us from the abyss," but he preferred monarchy. In his view, Napoleon had not properly understood the need to defend Christian values against the Enlightenment's excessive reliance on reason. Chateaubriand wrote his *Genius of Christianity* (1802) to draw attention to the power and mystery of faith. He warned, "It is to the vanity of knowledge that we owe almost all our misfortunes. . . . The learned ages have always been followed by ages of destruction."

How the Orient Became Oriental

As a result of Napoleon's expedition to conquer Egypt in 1798, Europeans began to study systematically what they named "the Orient" (from *oriēns*, Latin for "rising sun"), meaning the lands east of Europe. Napoleon took with him 151 French scientific experts in everything from architecture to mineralogy. Their mission was to discover and record the natural and human history of Egypt. While some set up the Institute of Egypt in Cairo to conduct scientific experiments, others traveled with army units, collecting information and data on Egypt.

Of course, Europeans had visited the Middle East before, but they had never so rigorously studied its cultures. Although Napoleon's occupation of Egypt eventually failed, enthusiasm for "Orientalism" spread far and wide; scholarly societies set up professorships and periodicals dedicated to Oriental studies, and before long romantic poets, novelists, and painters flocked to North Africa and the Middle East in search of new themes for their work.

Europeans viewed the Orient as exotic but also backward. In the introduction to the twenty-three-volume *Description of Egypt* published by French scholars of the Institute of Egypt between 1809 and 1828, Jean-Baptiste Fourier wrote, "Napoleon wanted to offer a useful European example to the Orient, and finally also to make the inhabitants' lives more pleasant, as well as to procure for them all the advantages of a perfect civilization." According to Fourier, "This country [Egypt], which has transmitted its knowledge to so many nations, today is plunged into barbarism." Civilization vs. barbarism; advancement vs. backwardness, science vs. superstition: before long Europeans had set up a series of mutually reinforcing categories to distinguish their culture from that of the Orient. It is probably fair to say that Orientalism led to much new knowledge but also to many unpleasant stereotypes of non-Western peoples and cultures.

It is important to remember, moreover, that *West* and *East* are relative terms; they can be defined only in relation to each other. Americans sometimes call Japan, for instance, the "Far East," following European usage, but it is closest to the western, not the eastern, half of the United States. For Japan, in fact, the United States is the "Far East."

Source: Edward W. Said, *Orientalism* (New York: Pantheon Books, 1978), quote from page 85.

Eugène Delacroix, *The Death of Sardanapalus* (1826–1827)
All of the exoticism, violence, and erotic imagery of the East are on view in this romantic painting that aims to recapture a moment in ancient history when the Assyrian king Sardanapalus first killed his harem before killing himself. Delacroix was presumably influenced by a play by Byron on the subject, though Delacroix's rendition is much less favorable to the king than Byron's.
© Photo RMN/Herve Lewandowski.

❖ "Europe Was at My Feet": Napoleon's Conquests

Napoleon left an indelible stamp on French institutions and political life, yet his fame and much of his power rested on his military conquests. Building on innovations introduced by the republican governments before him, Napoleon revolutionized the art of war with tactics and strategy based on a highly mobile army. By 1812, he ruled an empire more extensive than any since the time of ancient Rome (Map. 21.1). Yet that empire had already begun to crumble, and with it went Napoleon's power at home. Napoleon's empire failed because it was based on a contradiction: Napoleon tried to reduce virtually all of Europe to the status of colonial dependents when Europe had long consisted of independent states. The result, inevitably, was a great upsurge in nationalist feeling that has dominated European politics to the present.

MAP 21.1 Napoleon's Empire at Its Height, 1812
In 1812, Napoleon had at least nominal control of almost all of western Europe. Even before he made his fatal mistake of invading Russia, however, his authority had been undermined in Spain and seriously weakened in the Italian and German states. His efforts to extend French power sparked resistance almost everywhere: as Napoleon insisted on French domination, local people began to think of themselves as Italian, German, or Dutch. Thus Napoleon inadvertently laid the foundations for the nineteenth-century spread of nationalism.

Following the Wars
Louis-Léopold Boilly's Reading of the XIth and XIIth Bulletins of the Grand Army *shows ordinary people on the home front eagerly reading Napoleon's own bulletins of the army's progress.*
Collection Privée/Photo Bulloz.

The Grand Army and Its Victories, 1800–1807

Napoleon attributed his military success "three-quarters to morale" and the rest to leadership and superiority of numbers at the point of attack. Conscription provided the large numbers: 1.3 million men age twenty to twenty-four were drafted between 1800 and 1812, another million in 1813–1814. So many willingly served because the republic had taught them to identify the army with the nation. Military service was both a patriotic duty and a means of social mobility. The men who rose through the ranks to become officers were young, ambitious, and accustomed to the new ways of war. Consequently, the French army had higher morale than the armies of other powers, most of which rejected conscription as too democratic and continued to restrict their officer corps to the nobility. Only in 1813–1814 did French morale plummet, as the military tide turned against Napoleon.

When Napoleon came to power in 1799, France had been at war for almost seven years, and its military position was precarious. Desertion was rampant, and the generals competed with one another for predominance. Napoleon ended this squabbling

by uniting all the armies into one Grand Army under his personal command. By 1812, he commanded 700,000 troops; while 250,000 soldiers fought in Spain, others remained garrisoned in France. In any given battle, between 70,000 and 180,000 men, not all of them French, fought for France. Life on campaign was no picnic—ordinary soldiers slept in the rain, mud, and snow and often had to forage for food—but Napoleon nonetheless inspired almost fanatical loyalty. A brilliant strategist who carefully studied the demands of war, he outmaneuvered virtually all his opponents. He fought alongside his soldiers in some sixty battles and had nineteen horses shot from under him. One opponent said that Napoleon's presence alone was worth 50,000 men.

Napoleon had a pragmatic and direct approach to strategy: he went for the main body of the opposing army and tried to crush it in a lightning campaign. He gathered the largest possible army for one great and decisive battle and then followed with a relentless pursuit to break enemy morale altogether. His military command, like his domestic role, was personal and highly centralized. He essentially served as his own operations officer: "I alone know what I have to do," he insisted. This style worked as long as Napoleon could be on the battlefield, but he failed to train independent subordinates to take over in his absence. He also faced constant difficulties in supplying a rapidly moving army, which could not always live off the land.

One of Napoleon's greatest advantages was the lack of coordination among his enemies. Britain dominated the seas but did not want to field huge land armies. On the continent, the French republic had already set up satellites in the Netherlands and Italy, which served as a buffer against the big powers to the east, Austria, Prussia, and Russia. By maneuvering diplomatically and militarily, Napoleon could usually take these on one by one. After reorganizing the French armies in 1799, for example, Napoleon won striking victories against the Austrians at Marengo and Hohenlinden in 1800, forcing them to agree to peace terms. Once the Austrians had withdrawn, Britain agreed to the Treaty of Amiens in 1802, effectively ending hostilities on the continent. Napoleon considered the peace with Great Britain merely a truce, however, and it lasted only until 1803.

Napoleon used the breathing space not only to consolidate his position before taking up arms again but also to send an expeditionary force to St. Domingue to regain control of the island. Continuing resistance among the black population and an epidemic of yellow fever forced Napoleon to withdraw his troops from St. Domingue and abandon his plans to extend his empire to the Western Hemisphere. As part of his retreat, he sold the Louisiana Territory to the United States in 1803.

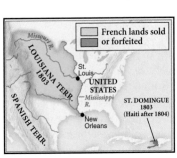

France's Retreat from America

When war resumed in Europe, the British navy once more proved its superiority by blocking an attempted French invasion and by defeating the French and their Spanish allies in a huge naval battle at Trafalgar in 1805. France lost many ships; the British lost no vessels, but their renowned admiral Lord Horatio Nelson died in the battle. On land, Napoleon remained invincible. In 1805, Austria took up arms again when Napoleon demanded that it declare neutrality in the conflict with Britain. Napoleon promptly captured 25,000 Austrian soldiers at Ulm in Bavaria in 1805. After marching on to Vienna, he again trounced the Austrians, who had been joined by their new ally, Russia. The battle of Austerlitz, often considered Napoleon's greatest victory, was fought on December 2, 1805, the first anniversary of his coronation.

After maintaining neutrality for a decade, Prussia now declared war on France. In 1806, the French promptly destroyed the Prussian army at Jena and Auerstadt. In 1807, Napoleon defeated the Russians at Friedland. Personal negotiations between Napoleon and the young tsar Alexander I (r. 1801–1825) resulted in a humiliating settlement imposed on Prussia, which paid the price for temporary reconciliation between France and Russia; the Treaties of Tilsit turned Prussian lands west of the Elbe River into the kingdom of Westphalia under Napoleon's brother Jerome, and Prussia's Polish provinces became the duchy of Warsaw. Alexander recognized Napoleon's conquests in central and western Europe and promised to help him against the British in exchange for Napoleon's support against the Turks. Neither party kept the bargain. Napoleon once again had turned the divisions among his enemies in his favor.

The Impact of French Victories

Wherever the Grand Army conquered, Napoleon's influence soon followed. By annexing some territories and setting up others as satellite kingdoms with much reduced autonomy, Napoleon attempted to colonize large parts of Europe (see Map 21.1). But even where he did not rule directly or through his relatives, his startling string of victories forced the other powers to reconsider their own methods of rule.

Rule in the Colonized Territories. Napoleon brought the disparate German and Italian states together to rule them more effectively and to exploit their resources for his own ends. In 1803, he consolidated the tiny German states by abolishing some of them and attaching them to larger units. In July 1806, he established the Confederation of the Rhine, which soon included almost all the German states except Austria and Prussia. The Holy Roman Emperor gave up his title, held since the thirteenth century, and became simply the emperor of Austria. Napoleon established three units in Italy: the territories directly annexed to France and the satellite kingdoms of Italy and Naples. Italy had not been so unified since the Roman Empire.

Napoleon forced French-style reforms on both the annexed territories, which were ruled directly from France, and the satellite kingdoms, which were usually ruled by one or another of Napoleon's relatives but with a certain autonomy. French reforms included abolishing serfdom, eliminating seigneurial dues, introducing the Napoleonic Code, suppressing monasteries, and subordinating church to state, as well as extending civil rights to Jews and other religious minorities. The experience in the kingdom of Westphalia was typical of a French satellite. When Jerome Bonaparte and his wife Catherine arrived as king and queen in 1807, they relied on French experts who worked with a hand-picked committee of Germans to write a constitution and install legal reforms. The Westphalian army had the first Jewish officers in the German states, and the army, administration, and judiciary were all opened to the middle classes. As time passed, however, the German subjects began to chafe under French rule. German officials enforced French decrees only halfheartedly, and the French army had to forbid its soldiers to frequent local taverns and shops because their presence often started fights.

As the example of Westphalia shows, reactions to Napoleonic innovations were mixed. Napoleon's chosen rulers often made real improvements in roads, public works, law codes, and education. The removal of internal tariffs fostered economic growth by opening up the domestic market for goods, especially textiles. By 1814, Bologna had five hundred factories and Modena four hundred. Yet almost everyone had some cause for complaint. Republicans regretted Napoleon's conversion of the sister republics into kingdoms after his coronation. Tax increases and ever-rising conscription quotas

Consolidation of German and Italian States, 1812

also fomented discontent. The annexed territories and satellite kingdoms paid half the French war expenses.

Almost everywhere, conflicts arose between Napoleon's desire for standardized, central government and local insistence on maintaining customs and traditions. Sometimes his own relatives sided with the countries they ruled. Napoleon's brother Louis, for instance, would not allow conscription in the Netherlands because the Dutch had never had compulsory military service. When Napoleon tried to introduce an economic policy banning trade with Great Britain, Louis's lax enforcement prompted the frustrated emperor to complain that "Holland [the leading province in the Netherlands] is an English province." In 1810, Napoleon annexed the satellite kingdom because his brother had become too sympathetic to Dutch interests.

Pressure for Reform in Prussia and Russia. Napoleon's victories forced defeated rulers to rethink their political and cultural assumptions. After the crushing defeat of Prussia in 1806 left his country much reduced in territory, Frederick William III (r. 1797–1840) appointed a reform commission, and on its recommendation he abolished serfdom and allowed nonnobles to buy and enclose land. Peasants gained their personal independence from their noble landlords, who could no longer sell them to pay gambling debts, for example, or refuse them permission to marry. Yet the lives of the former serfs remained bleak; they were left without land and their landlords no longer had to care for them in hard times. The king's advisers also overhauled the army to make the high command more efficient and to open the way to the appointment of middle-class officers. Prussia instituted these reforms to try to compete with the French, not to promote democracy. As one reformer wrote to Frederick William, "We must do from above what the French have done from below."

Reform received lip service in Russia. Tsar Alexander I had gained his throne after an aristocratic coup deposed and killed his autocratic and capricious father, Paul (r. 1796–1801), and in the early years of his reign the remorseful young ruler created Western-style ministries, lifted restrictions on importing foreign books, and founded six new universities; reform commissions studied abuses; nobles were encouraged voluntarily to free their serfs (a few actually did so); and there was even talk of drafting a constitution. But none of these efforts reached beneath the surface of Russian life, and by the second decade of his reign Alexander began to reject the Enlightenment spirit that his grandmother Catherine the Great had instilled in him.

The Continental System. The one power always standing between Napoleon and total dominance of Europe was Great Britain. The British ruled the seas and financed anyone who would oppose Napoleon. In an effort to bankrupt this "nation of shopkeepers" by choking its trade, Napoleon inaugurated the Continental System in 1806. It prohibited all commerce between Great Britain and France, as well as between Great Britain and France's dependent states and allies. At first the system worked: British exports dropped 20 percent in 1807–1808, and industrial production declined 10 percent; unemployment and a strike of 60,000 workers in northern England resulted. The British retaliated by confiscating merchandise on ships, even those of powers neutral in the wars, that sailed to or from ports from which the British were excluded by the Continental System.

In the midst of continuing wars, moreover, the system proved impossible to enforce, and widespread smuggling brought British goods into the European market. British industrial growth continued, despite some setbacks; calico-printing works, for example, quadrupled their production, and imports of raw cotton increased 40 percent. At the same time, French and other continental industries benefited from the temporary protection from British competition.

Resistance to French Rule, 1807–1812. Smuggling British goods was only one way of opposing the French. Almost everywhere in Europe, resistance began as local opposition to French demands for money or draftees, but it eventually prompted that patriotic defense of the nation known as nationalism (see page 791). In southern Italy, gangs of bandits harassed the French army and local officials; 33,000 Italian bandits were arrested in 1809 alone. But resistance continued via a network of secret societies, called the *carbonari* ("charcoal-burners"), which got its name from the practice of marking each new member's forehead with a charcoal mark. Throughout the nineteenth century the *carbonari* played a leading role in Italian nationalism. In the

German states, intellectuals wrote passionate defenses of the virtues of the German nation and of the superiority of German literature.

No nations bucked Napoleon's reins more than Spain and Portugal. In 1807, Napoleon sent 100,000 troops through Spain to invade Portugal, Great Britain's ally. The royal family fled to the Portuguese colony of Brazil, but fighting continued, aided by a British army. When Napoleon got his brother Joseph named king of Spain in place of the senile Charles IV (r. 1788–1808), the Spanish clergy and nobles raised bands of peasants to fight the French occupiers. Even Napoleon's taking personal command of the French forces failed to quell the Spanish, who for six years fought a war of national independence that pinned down thousands of French soldiers. Germaine de Staël commented that Napoleon "never understood that a war might be a crusade. . . . He never reckoned with the one power that no arms could overcome— the enthusiasm of a whole people."

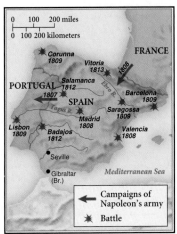

The Spanish War for Independence, 1807–1813

More than a new feeling of nationalism was aroused in Spain. Peasants hated French requisitioning of their food supplies and sought to defend their priests against French anticlericalism. Spanish nobles feared revolutionary reforms and were willing to defend the old monarchy in the person of the young Ferdinand VII, heir to Charles IV, even while Ferdinand himself was congratulating Napoleon on his victories. The Spanish Catholic church spread anti-French propaganda that equated Napoleon with heresy. As the former archbishop of Seville wrote to the archbishop of Granada in 1808, "You realize that we must not recognize as king a free-mason, heretic, Lutheran, as are all the Bonapartes and the French nation." In this tense atmosphere, the Spanish peasant rebels, assisted by the British, countered every French massacre with atrocities of their own. They tortured their French prisoners (boiling one general alive) and lynched collaborators.

Napoleon's Mamelukes Massacre the Spanish
In one of the paintings he produced to criticize Napoleon's occupation of Spain, Second of May 1808
at the Puerta del Sol *(1814), Goya depicts the brutal suppression of the Spanish revolt in Madrid
against Napoleon. Napoleon used Mamelukes, Egyptian soldiers descended from freed Turkish slaves.
For the Spanish Christians—and for European viewers of the painting—use of these mercenaries
made the event even more horrifying. Europeans considered Muslims, and Turks in particular, as
menacing because the Europeans had been fighting them for centuries.*
Museo del Prado, Madrid.

From Russian Winter to Final Defeat, 1812–1815

Despite opposition, Napoleon ruled over an extensive empire by 1812. He controlled more territory than any European ruler had since Roman times. Only two major European states remained fully independent—Great Britain and Russia—but once allied they would successfully challenge his dominion and draw many other states to their side. Britain sent aid to the Portuguese and Spanish rebels, while Russia once again prepared for war. Tsar Alexander I made peace with Turkey and allied himself with Great Britain and Sweden. In 1812, Napoleon invaded Russia with 250,000 horses and 600,000 men, including contingents of Italians, Poles, Swiss, Dutch, and Germans. This daring move proved to be his undoing.

Invasion of Russia, 1812. Napoleon followed his usual strategy of trying to strike quickly, but the Russian generals avoided confrontation and retreated eastward, destroying anything that might be useful to the invaders. In September, on the road to Moscow, Napoleon finally engaged the main Russian force in the gigantic battle of Borodino (see Map 21.1). French casualties were 30,000 men, including 47 generals; the Russians lost 45,000. The French soldiers had nothing to celebrate around their campfires: as one soldier wrote, "Everyone . . . wept for some dead friend." Once again the Russians retreated, leaving Moscow undefended. Napoleon entered the deserted city, but the victory turned hollow because the departing Russians had set the wooden city on fire. Within a week, three-fourths of it had burned to the ground. Still Alexander refused to negotiate, and French morale plunged with

Napoleon: For and Against

Napoleon and Hitler are the two most controversial figures in all of modern Western history, and they are often compared with each other. What they shared was a desire to dominate Europe by military force, and they both came very close to achieving that goal. But they differed entirely in ideas: to take just the most important example, Napoleon offered emancipation to the Jews wherever he ruled, whereas Hitler tried to eliminate them as a group, ultimately by murdering as many as he could.

Napoleon enthralled Europe. The Prussian philosopher Georg W. F. Hegel dubbed him "world history on horseback." After his final exile, Napoleon presented himself as a martyr to the cause of liberty whose goal was to create a European "federation of free people." Few were convinced by this "gospel according to St. Helena" (Document 1). Followers such as Emmanuel de Las Cases burnished the Napoleonic legend (Document 2), but detractors such as Benjamin Constant viewed him as a tyrant (Document 3). For all his defects, Napoleon fascinated even those who were too young to understand his rise and fall. The French romantic poet Victor Hugo celebrated both the glory and the tragedy of Napoleonic ambitions (Document 4).

1. Napoleon's Own View from Exile

As might be expected, Napoleon put the most positive possible construction on his plans for France. In exile he wrote letters and talked at length to Emmanuel de Las Cases (1766–1842), an aristocratic officer in the royal navy who rallied to Napoleon in 1802, served in the Council of State, and later accompanied him to St. Helena. Much of what we know about Napoleon's views comes from a book published by Las Cases in 1821.

March 3, 1817:

In spite of all the libels, I have no fear whatever about my fame. Posterity will do me justice. The truth will be known; and the good I have done will be compared with the faults I have committed. I am not uneasy as to the result. Had I succeeded, I would have died with the reputation of the greatest man that ever existed. As it is, although I have failed, I shall be considered as an extraordinary man: my elevation was unparalleled, because unaccompanied by crime. I have fought fifty pitched battles, almost all of which I have won. I have framed and carried into effect a code of laws that will bear my name to the most distant posterity. I raised myself from nothing to be the most powerful monarch in the world. Europe was at my feet. I have always been of the opinion that the sovereignty lay in the people. In fact, the imperial government was a kind of republic. Called to the head of it by the voice of the nation, my maxim was, *la carrière est ouverte aux talents* ["careers open to talent"] without distinction of birth or fortune, and this system of equality is the reason that your oligarchy hates me so much.

Source: R. M. Johnston, *The Corsican: A Diary of Napoleon's Life in His Own Words* (Boston: Houghton Mifflin, 1921), 492.

2. Napoleon's Own History of France

Las Cases included in his book parts of a history of France that Napoleon himself had undertaken to write. Napoleon here argues that his ascent to the throne was legitimate, though he did not come from the Bourbon family of kings, and that he reconciled the old nobles to the new regime by creating a new standard of nobility in the Legion of Honor. In short, he offered something for everyone.

No prince mounted the throne with more legitimate rights than Napoleon. The throne was tendered to Hugh Capet by some bishops and some nobles; the imperial throne was given to Napoleon by the will of all the citizens, verified three times in a solemn manner. Pope Pius VII, chief of the Roman, Catholic, and Apostolic religion, the religion of the majority of Frenchmen, crossed the Alps to anoint the Emperor with his own hands, surrounded by all the bishops of France, by all the cardinals of the Roman Church, and by the deputies of all the cantons of the Empire. . . .

The Emperor bound up the wounds of the Revolution; all the émigrés returned and that list of proscribed persons was destroyed. The prince performed the most kindly glorious act, that of recalling to their country, and thus reestablishing, more than twenty thousand families. Their unsold property was returned to them; and wiping clean the slate of the past, he welcomed equally to all employments individuals of all the classes, whatever their conduct had been. . . . All titles were forgotten; there were no longer aristocrats or Jacobins, and the establishment of the Legion of Honor, which was the reward for military, civil, and judicial service, united side by side the soldier, the scholar, the artist, the prelate, and the magistrate; it was a symbol of reunion of all the estates, of all the parties.

Source: Emmanuel de Las Cases, *Le Mémorial de Sainte-Hélène* (Paris: Garnier Frères, n.d.) 3:430–34, translated and excerpted by David H. Pinkney, *Napoleon, Historical Enigma* (Lexington: D. C. Heath, 1969), 1–2.

3. Benjamin Constant, Spokesman for the Liberal Opposition to Napoleon

Benjamin Constant (1767–1830) came from an old French Calvinist family that had fled to Switzerland to escape persecution. Constant spent the early years of the French Revolution in a minor post at a minor German court. He moved to Paris in 1795 and became active in French politics during the Directory. Under Napoleon he went into exile, where he published a romantic novel (Adolphe, 1806) and pamphlets like this one attacking Napoleon. He reconciled to Napoleon during the Hundred Days and then opposed the restored Bourbon monarchy. In this selection, written during his exile, he expresses his hostility to Napoleon as a usurper dependent on war to maintain himself in power.

Surely, Bonaparte is a thousand times more guilty than those barbarous conquerors who, ruling over barbarians, were by no means at odds with their age. Unlike them, he has chosen barbarism; he has preferred it. In the midst of enlightenment, he has sought to bring back the night. He has chosen to transform into greedy and bloodthirsty nomads a mild and polite people: his crime lies in this premeditated intention, in his obstinate effort to rob us of the heritage of all the enlightened generations who have preceded us on this earth. But why have we given him the right to conceive such a project?

When he first arrived here, alone, out of poverty and obscurity, and until he was twenty-four, his greedy gaze wandering over the country around him, why did we show him a country in which any religious idea was the object of irony? [Constant refers here to de-Christianization during the French Revolution.] When he listened to what was professed in our circles, why did serious thinkers tell him that man had no other motivation than his own interest? . . .

[Napoleon] judged France by her own words, and the world by France as he imagined her to be. Because immediate usurpation was easy, he believed it could be durable, and once he became a usurper, he did all that usurpation condemns a usurper to do in our century.

It was necessary to stifle inside the country all intellectual life: he banished discussion and proscribed the freedom of the press.

The nation might have been stunned by that silence: he provided, extorted or paid for acclamation which sounded like the national voice. . . . War flung onto distant shores that part of the French nation that still had some real energy. It prompted the police harassment of the timid, whom it could not force abroad. It struck terror into men's hearts, and left there a certain hope that chance would take responsibility for their deliverance: a hope agreeable to fear and convenient to inertia. How many times have I heard men who were pressed to resist tyranny postponing this, during wartime till the coming of peace, and in peacetime until war commences!

I am right therefore in claiming that a usurper's sole resource is uninterrupted war. Some object:

what if Bonaparte had been pacific? Had he been pacific, he would never have lasted for twelve years. Peace would have re-established communication among the different countries of Europe. These communications would have restored to thought its means of expression. Works published abroad would have been smuggled into the country. The French would have seen that they did not enjoy the approval of the majority of Europe.

Source: Benjamin Constant, "Further Reflections on Usurpation," in *Political Writings*, trans. Biancamaria Fontana (Cambridge: Cambridge University Press, 1988), 161–63.

4. Victor Hugo, "The Two Islands," 1825

Victor Hugo (1802–1885) was France's greatest romantic poet and novelist, author of The Hunchback of Notre Dame *and* Les Misérables. *His father was a Napoleonic general, but his mother was an equally ardent royalist. In this early poem, Hugo compares Napoleon to one of Napoleon's favorite icons, the eagle, symbol of empire. The two islands of the title are Corsica, Napoleon's birthplace, and St. Helena, his place of final exile and death.*

These Isles, where Ocean's shattered spray
    Upon the ruthless rocks is cast,
Seem like two treacherous ships of prey,
    Made by eternal anchors fast.
The hand that settled bleak and black
Those shores on their unpeopled rack,
And clad in fear and mystery,
    Perchance thus made them tempest-torn,

That Bonaparte might there be born,
And that Napoleon there might die.
. . . .
He his imperial nest hath built so far and high,
He seems to us to dwell within that tranquil sky,
Where you shall never see the angry tempest break.
    'Tis but beneath his feet the growling storms
      are sped,
    And thunders to assault his head
Must to their highest source go back.
The bolt flew upwards: from his eyrie [nest] riven,
Blazing he falls beneath the stroke of heaven;
    Then kings their tyrant foe reward—
They chain him, living, on that lonely shore;
And earth captive giant handed o'er
    To ocean's more resistless guard.

. . . .
Shame, hate, misfortune, vengeance, curses sore,
On him let heaven and earth together pour:
    Now, see we dashed the vast Colossus low.
    May he forever rue, alive and dead,
    All tears he caused mankind to shed,
    And all the blood he caused to flow.

Source: Henry Carrington, *Translations from the Poems of Victor Hugo* (London: Walter Scott, 1885), 34–41.

QUESTIONS FOR DEBATE
1. Which of these views of Napoleon has the most lasting value as opposed to immediate dramatic effect?
2. Based on these selections, what was Napoleon's greatest accomplishment? His greatest failure?
3. Victor Hugo called Napoleon "the vast Colossus." Why did he pick this larger-than-life metaphor even when writing lines critical of Napoleon's legacy of tears and bloodshed?

worsening problems of supply. Weeks of constant marching in the dirt and heat had worn down the foot soldiers, who were dying of disease or deserting in large numbers.

In October Napoleon began his retreat; in November came the cold. Napoleon himself reported that on November 14 the temperature fell to −4 degrees Fahrenheit. A German soldier in the Grand Army described trying to cook fistfuls of raw bran with snow to make something like bread. For him the retreat was "the indescribable horror of all possible plagues." Within a week the Grand Army lost 30,000 horses and had to abandon most of its artillery and food supplies. Russian forces harassed the retreating army, now more pathetic than grand. By December only 100,000 troops remained, one-sixth the original number, and the retreat had turned into a rout: the Russians had captured 200,000 soldiers, including 48 generals and 3,000 other officers.

Napoleon had made a classic military mistake that would be repeated by Adolf Hitler in World War II: fighting a war on two distant fronts simultaneously. The Spanish war tied down 250,000 French troops and forced Napoleon to bully Prussia and Austria into supplying soldiers of dubious loyalty for the Moscow campaign. They deserted at the first opportunity. The fighting in Spain and Portugal also exacerbated the already substantial logistical and communications problems involved in marching to Moscow.

The End of Napoleon's Empire.   Napoleon's humiliation might have been temporary if the British and Russians had not successfully organized a coalition to complete the job. Napoleon still had resources at his command; by the spring of 1813 he had replenished his army with another 250,000 men. With British financial support, Russian, Austrian, Prussian, and Swedish armies met the French outside Leipzig in October 1813 and defeated Napoleon in the Battle of the Nations. One by one, Napoleon's German allies deserted him to join the German nationalist "war of liberation." The Confederation of the Rhine dissolved, and the Dutch revolted and restored the prince of Orange. Joseph Bonaparte fled Spain, and a combined Spanish-Portuguese army under British command invaded France. In only a few months the allied powers crossed the Rhine and marched toward Paris. In March 1814, the French Senate deposed Napoleon, who abdicated when his remaining generals refused to fight. Napoleon went into exile on the island of Elba off the Italian coast. His wife Marie-Louise refused to accompany him. The allies restored to the throne Louis XVIII (r. 1814–1824), the brother of Louis XVI (whose son was known as Louis XVII even though he died in prison in 1795 without ever ruling).

Napoleon had one last chance to regain power because Louis XVIII lacked a solid base of support. The new king tried to steer a middle course through a charter that established a British-style monarchy with a two-house legislature and guaranteed civil rights. But he was caught between returning emigré nobles who demanded a complete restoration of their lands and powers and those who had supported either the republic or Napoleon during the previous twenty-five years. Sensing an opportunity, Napoleon escaped from Elba in early 1815 and, landing in southern France, made swift and unimpeded progress to Paris. Although he had left in ignominy, now crowds cheered him and former

soldiers volunteered to serve him. The period known as the "Hundred Days" (the length of time between his escape and his final defeat) had begun. Louis XVIII fled across the border, waiting for help from France's enemies.

Napoleon quickly moved his reconstituted army into present-day Belgium. At first it seemed that he might succeed in separately fighting the two armies arrayed against him—a Prussian army and a joint force of Belgian, Dutch, German, and British troops led by Sir Arthur Wellesley (1769–1852), duke of Wellington. But the Prussians evaded him and joined with Wellington at Waterloo. Completely routed, Napoleon had no choice but to abdicate again. This time the victorious allies banished him permanently to the remote island of St. Helena, far off the coast of West Africa, where he died in 1821 at the age of fifty-two.

The cost of Napoleon's rule was high: 750,000 French soldiers and 400,000 others from annexed and satellite states died between 1800 and 1815. Yet no other military figure since Alexander the Great had made such an impact on world history. (See "Contrasting Views," page 778.) His plans for a united Europe, his insistence on spreading the legal reforms of the French Revolution, his social welfare programs, and even his inadvertent awakening of national sentiment set the agenda for European history in the modern era.

❖ The "Restoration" of Europe

Even while Napoleon was making his last desperate bid for power, his enemies were meeting in the Congress of Vienna (1814–1815) to decide the fate of postrevolutionary Europe. Although interrupted by the Hundred Days, the Congress of Vienna settled the boundaries of European states, determined who would rule each nation, and established a new framework for international relations based on periodic meetings, or congresses, between the major powers. This congress system, or "concert of Europe," helped prevent another major war until the 1850s, and no conflict comparable to the Napoleonic wars would occur again until 1914.

Many of Europe's rulers hoped to nullify revolutionary and Napoleonic reforms and thus

The Congress of Vienna
*An unknown French engraver caricatured the efforts of the diplomats at the Congress of Vienna,
complaining that they used the occasion to divide the spoils of European territory. At the far left
is Metternich preparing to take Venice and Lombardy (northern Italy).*
Historisches Museum der Stadt Wien.

"restore" their old regimes. Some of the returning rulers so detested French innovations that they tore French plants out of their gardens and threw French furniture out of their palaces. The most successful rulers compromised between old traditions and new ideas. Total negation of the revolutionary legacy might work for a time, but in the long run, accommodation was unavoidable.

The Congress of Vienna, 1814–1815

The Vienna settlement established a new equilibrium that relied on cooperation among the major powers while guaranteeing the status of smaller states. The revolutionary and Napoleonic wars had produced a host of potentially divisive issues. In addition to determining the boundaries of France, the congress had to decide the fate of Napoleon's duchy of Warsaw, the German province of Saxony, the Netherlands, the states once part of the confederation of the Rhine, and various Italian territories. All had either changed hands or been created during the wars. These issues were resolved by face-to-face negotiations among representatives of the five major powers: Austria, Russia, Prussia, Britain, and France. With its aim to establish a long-lasting,

negotiated peace endorsed by all parties, both winners and losers, the Congress of Vienna provided a model for the twentieth-century League of Nations and United Nations.

Austria's chief negotiator, Prince Klemens von Metternich (1773–1859), took the lead in devising the settlement. A well-educated nobleman who spoke five languages, Metternich served as a minister in the Austrian cabinet from 1809 to 1848. More than anyone else, he shaped the post-Napoleonic order. Although his penchant for womanizing made him a security risk in the eyes of the British Foreign Office (he even had an affair with Napoleon's younger sister), he worked with the British prime minister Robert Castlereagh (1769–1822) to ensure a moderate agreement that would check French aggression and yet maintain its great-power status. Metternich and Castlereagh believed that French aggression must be contained because it had threatened the European peace since the days of Louis XIV, but that France must remain a major player precisely so that no one European power might dominate the others. In this way France could help Austria and Britain counter the ambitions of Prussia and Russia. Castlereagh hoped to make Britain the arbiter of European affairs, but he knew this could be accomplished only through adroit diplomacy because the British constitutional monarchy had little in common with most of its more absolutist continental counterparts.

The task of ensuring France's status at the congress fell to Prince Charles Maurice de Talleyrand (1754–1838), an aristocrat and former bishop who had embraced the French Revolution, served as Napoleon's foreign minister, and ended as foreign minister to Louis XVIII after helping to arrange the emperor's overthrow. Informed of Talleyrand's betrayal, Napoleon called him "excrement in silk stockings." When the French army failed to oppose Napoleon's return to power in the Hundred Days, the allies took away all territory conquered since 1790 and required France to pay an indemnity and support an army of occupation until it had paid. Talleyrand nonetheless successfully argued that the restored French monarchy could succeed only if it retained its great-power status and fully participated in the negotiations.

The goal of the congress was to achieve postwar stability by establishing secure states with guaranteed borders (Map 21.2). Where possible, the

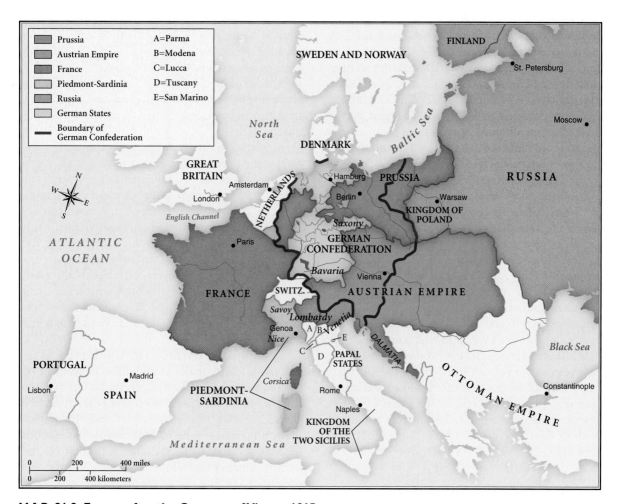

MAP 21.2 Europe after the Congress of Vienna, 1815
The diplomats meeting at the Congress of Vienna could not simply "restore" Europe to its prerevolutionary borders. Too much had changed since 1789. France was forced to return to its 1789 borders and Spain and Portugal regained their former rulers. The Austrian Netherlands and the Dutch Republic were united in a new kingdom of the Netherlands, the German states were joined in a Germanic Confederation that built upon Napoleon's Confederation of the Rhine, and Napoleon's Grand Duchy of Warsaw became the kingdom of Poland with the tsar of Russia as king.

congress simply restored traditional rulers, as in Spain and the Italian states. Where restoration was impossible, it rearranged territory to balance the competing interests of the great powers. Thus the congress turned the duchy of Warsaw into a new Polish kingdom but made the tsar of Russia its king. (Poland would not regain its independence until 1918.) The former Dutch Republic and the Austrian Netherlands, both annexed to France, now united as the new kingdom of the Netherlands under the restored stadholder. Prussia gained territory in Saxony and on the left bank of the Rhine to compensate for its losses in Poland. To make up for its losses in Poland and Saxony, Austria reclaimed the Italian provinces of Lombardy and Venetia and the Dalmatian coast. Austria now presided over the German Confederation, which replaced the defunct Holy Roman Empire and also included Prussia. The lesser powers were not forgotten. The kingdom of Piedmont-Sardinia took Genoa, Nice, and part of Savoy. Sweden obtained Norway from Denmark but had to accept Russia's conquest of Finland. Finally, various international trade issues were also resolved. At the urging of Great Britain, the congress agreed to condemn in principle the slave trade, abolished by Great Britain in 1807. In reality, however, the slave trade continued in many places until the 1840s.

To impart spiritual substance to this very calculated settlement of political affairs, Tsar Alexander proposed a Holy Alliance that would ensure divine assistance in upholding religion, peace, and justice. Prussia and Austria signed the agreement, but Great Britain refused to accede to what Castlereagh called "a piece of sublime mysticism and nonsense." Pope Pius VII also refused on the grounds that the papacy needed no help in interpreting the Christian truth. Despite the reassertion of traditional religious principle, the congress had in fact given birth to a new diplomatic order: in the future, the legitimacy of states depended on the treaty system, not on divine right.

The Emergence of Conservatism

The French Revolution and Napoleonic domination of Europe had shown contemporaries that government could be changed overnight, that the old hierarchies could be overthrown in the name of reason, and that even Christianity could be written off or at least profoundly altered with the stroke of

a pen. The potential for rapid change raised many questions about the proper sources of authority. Kings and churches could be restored and former revolutionaries locked up or silenced, but the old order no longer commanded automatic obedience. The old order was now merely *old*, no longer "natural" and "timeless." It had been ousted once and therefore might fall again. People insisted on having reasons to believe in their "restored" governments. The political doctrine that justified the restoration was *conservatism.*

Conservatives benefited from the disillusionment that permeated Europe after 1815. In the eyes of most Europeans, Napoleon had become a tyrant who ruled in his own interests. Conservatives believed it was crucial to analyze the roots of such tyranny so established authorities could use their knowledge of history to prevent its recurrence. They saw a logical progression in recent history: the Enlightenment based on reason led to the French Revolution, with its bloody guillotine and horrifying Terror, which in turn spawned the authoritarian and militaristic Napoleon. Conservative intellectuals therefore either rejected Enlightenment principles or at least subjected them to scrutiny and skepticism.

The most influential spokesman of conservatism was Edmund Burke (1729–1799), the British critic of the French Revolution. He argued that the revolutionaries erred in thinking they could construct an entirely new government based on reason. Government, Burke said, had to be rooted in long experience, which evolved over generations. All change must be gradual and must respect national and historical traditions.

Like Burke, later conservatives believed that religious and other major traditions were an essential foundation for any society. Conservatives blamed the French Revolution's attack on religion on the skepticism and anticlericalism of such Enlightenment thinkers as Voltaire, and they defended both hereditary monarchy and the authority of the church, whether Catholic or Protestant. The "rights of man," according to conservatives, could not stand alone as doctrine based simply on nature and reason. The community too had its rights, more important than those of any individual, and established institutions best represented those rights. The church, the state, and the patriarchal family would provide an enduring social order for everyone. Faith, sentiment, history, and tradition must fill the vacuum left by the failures of reason and excessive belief in individual rights. Across Europe these views were taken up and elaborated by government advisers, professors, and writers. Not surprisingly, they had their strongest appeal in ruling circles and guided the politics of men such as Metternich in Austria and Alexander I in Russia.

The restored monarchy in France provided a major test for conservatism because the returning Bourbons had to confront the legacy of twenty-five years of upheaval. Louis XVIII tried to ensure a measure of continuity by maintaining Napoleon's Civil Code. He also guaranteed the rights of ownership to church lands sold during the revolutionary period and created a parliament composed of a Chamber of Peers nominated by the king and a Chamber of Deputies elected by very restricted suffrage (fewer than 100,000 voters in a population of 30 million, or about 3 percent). In making these concessions, the king tried to follow a moderate course of compromise, but the Ultras (ultraroyalists) pushed for complete repudiation of the revolutionary past. When Louis returned to power after Napoleon's final defeat, armed royalist bands attacked and murdered hundreds of Bonapartists and former revolutionaries. In 1816, the Ultras insisted on abolishing divorce and set up special courts to punish opponents of the regime. More extreme measures were to come.

The Revival of Religion

The experience of revolutionary upheaval and nearly constant warfare prompted many to renew their religious faith once peace returned. In France, the Catholic church sent missionaries to hold open-air "ceremonies of reparation" to express repentance for the outrages of revolution. In Rome, the papacy reestablished the Jesuit order, which had been disbanded during the Enlightenment. In the Italian states and Spain, governments used religious societies of laypeople to combat the influence of reformers and nationalists such as the Italian *carbonari*.

Revivalist movements, especially in Protestant countries, could on occasion challenge the status quo, not support it. In parts of Protestant Germany and Britain, religious revival had begun in the eighteenth century with the rise of Pietism and Methodism, movements that stressed individual religious experience rather than reason as the true path to moral and social reform. The English Methodists followed John Wesley (1703–1791), who preached an emotional, morally austere, and very personal "method" of gaining salvation. The Methodists, or Wesleyans, gradually separated from the Church of England and in the early decades of the nineteenth century attracted thousands of members in huge revival meetings that lasted for days.

Shopkeepers, artisans, agricultural laborers, miners, and workers in cottage industry, both male and female, flocked to the new denomination, even though at first Methodism seemed to emphasize conservative political views: Methodist statutes of 1792 had insisted that "none of us shall either in writing or in conversation speak lightly or irreverently of the government." In their hostility to rigid doctrine and elaborate ritual and their encouragement of popular preaching, however, the Methodists fostered a sense of democratic community and even a rudimentary sexual equality. From the beginning, women preachers traveled on horseback to preach in barns, town halls, and textile dye houses. The Methodist Sunday schools that taught thousands of poor children to read and write eventually helped create greater demands for working-class political participation.

The religious revival was not limited to Europe. In the United States, the second "Great Awakening" began around 1790 with huge camp meetings that brought together thousands of worshippers and scores of evangelical preachers, many of them Methodist. (The original Great Awakening took place in the 1730s and 1740s, sparked by the preaching of George Whitefield, a young English evangelist and follower of John Wesley.) Men and women danced to exhaustion, fell into trances, and spoke in "tongues." During this period, Protestant sects began systematic missionary activity in other parts of the world, with British and American missionary societies taking the lead in the 1790s and early 1800s. In the British colony of India, for example, Protestant missionaries argued for the reform of Hindu customs. *Sati*—the burning of widows on the funeral pyres of their husbands—was abolished by the British administration of India in 1829. Missionary activity by Protestants and Catholics would become one of the arms of European imperialism and cultural influence in the nineteenth century.

❖ Forces for Social and Cultural Change

Conservatives hoped to clamp a lid on European affairs, but the lid kept threatening to fly off. In France in 1820, an assassin killed Louis XVIII's nephew, inspiring a like-minded group to try, unsuccessfully, to blow up Britain's Tory cabinet. Rapid urban growth and the spread of industry created new social tensions and inspired new political doctrines to explain the meaning of economic and social changes. These doctrines soon galvanized opponents of the conservative Vienna settlement. Cutting across and drawing on the turmoil in society and politics was romanticism, a new international movement in the arts and literature that originated in reaction to the Enlightenment in the eighteenth century and dominated artistic expression in the first half of the nineteenth.

Industrial and Urban Growth in Britain

Historians today use the term *Industrial Revolution* to describe the set of changes that brought steam-driven machinery, large factories, and a new working class first to Britain, then to the rest of Europe, and eventually to the rest of the world. French and English writers of the 1820s introduced the term to capture the drama of contemporary change and to draw a parallel with the French Revolution. But we should not take the comparison too literally. Unlike the French upheaval, the Industrial Revolution was not over in a decade. From Great Britain in the second half of the eighteenth century it spread slowly; even by the 1830s it had little effect on the continent outside of northern France, Belgium, and the Rhineland. Most Europeans were still peasants working in the old ways.

Factories and Workers. Steam-driven machines first brought workers together in factories in the textile industry. By 1830, more than one million people in Britain depended on the cotton industry for employment, and cotton cloth constituted 50 percent of the country's exports. Factories quickly sprang up in urban areas, where the growing population provided a ready source of labor. The rapid expansion of the British textile industry had as its colonial corollary the destruction of the hand manufacture of textiles in India. The British put high import duties on Indian cloth entering Britain and kept such duties very low for British cloth entering India. The figures are dramatic: in 1813, the Indian city of Calcutta exported to England £2,000,000 of cotton cloth; by 1830, Calcutta was importing from England £2,000,000 of cotton cloth. When Britain abolished slavery in its Caribbean colonies in 1833, British manufacturers began to buy raw cotton in the southern United States, where slavery still flourished. (See "Taking Measure," page 787.)

Factories drew workers from the urban population surge, which had begun in the eighteenth century and now accelerated. The reasons for urban growth are not entirely clear. The population of such new industrial cities as Manchester and Leeds increased 40 percent in the 1820s alone. Historians long thought that factory workers came from the countryside, pushed off the land by the field enclosures of the 1700s. But recent studies have shown that the number of agricultural laborers actually increased during industrialization in Britain, suggesting that a growing birthrate created a larger population and fed workers into the new factory system.

The new workers came from several sources: families of farmers who could not provide land for all their children, soldiers demobilized after the Napoleonic wars, artisans displaced by the new machinery, and children of the earliest workers who had moved to the factory towns. A system of employment that resembled family labor on farms or in cottage industry also developed in the new factories. Entire families came to toil for a single wage, although family members performed different tasks. Workdays of twelve to seventeen hours were typical, even for children, and the work was grueling. Community ties remained important as workers migrated from rural to urban areas to join friends and family from their original villages.

As urban factories grew, their workers gradually came to constitute a new socioeconomic class with a distinctive culture and traditions. Like *middle class*, the term *working class* came into use for the first time in the early nineteenth century. It referred to the laborers in the new factories. In the past, workers had labored in isolated trades: water and wood carrying, gardening, laundry, and building. In contrast, factories brought working people together with machines, under close supervision by their employers. They soon developed a sense of

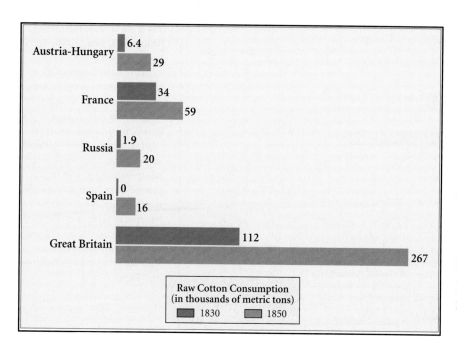

Austria-Hungary 6.4 / 29
France 34 / 59
Russia 1.9 / 20
Spain 0 / 16
Great Britain 112 / 267

Raw Cotton Consumption
(in thousands of metric tons)
■ 1830   ■ 1850

TAKING MEASURE
**Raw Cotton Consumption,
1830–1850**
*The consumption of raw cotton
correlates with the level of industrialization in the textile
industry. Great Britain already
imported more raw cotton in
1830 than any other country in
Europe, and it widened the gap
in the next generation. But the
rate of increase was even greater
in Austria-Hungary, Russia, and
Spain (but not France). Can you
calculate the rate of increase
between 1830 and 1850?*
From B. R. Mitchell, *European
Historical Statistics 1750–1970*
(New York: Columbia University
Press, 1975), FD13.

common interests and organized societies for mutual help and political reform. From these would
come the first labor unions.

The new factories and new technology threatened some people's very existence, especially in hard
times. To protect livelihoods at risk from the introduction of new technology, bands of handloom
weavers, fearing their displacement by machines,
wrecked factory machinery and burned mills in the
Midlands, Yorkshire, and Lancashire. To restore order and protect industry, the government sent in an
army of twelve thousand regular soldiers and made
machine wrecking punishable by death. The rioters
were called *Luddites* after the fictitious figure Ned
Ludd, whose signature appeared on their mani-
festos. (The term is still used to describe those who
resist new technology.)

Other workers focused their organizing efforts
on reforming Parliament, whose members were
chosen in elections dominated by the landowning
elite. One reformer complained that the members
of the House of Commons were nothing but "toad-
eaters, gamblers, public plunderers, and hirelings."
Reform clubs held large open-air meetings, and ordinary people eagerly bought cheap newspapers that
clamored for change. In August 1819, sixty thousand people attended an illegal meeting held in
St. Peter's Fields in Manchester. When the local
authorities sent the cavalry to arrest the speaker,

panic resulted; eleven people were killed and many
hundreds injured. Punsters called it the Battle of
Peterloo or the Peterloo Massacre. An alarmed government passed the Six Acts, which forbade large
political meetings and restricted press criticism,
suppressing the reform movement for a decade.

The Rise of the Railroad.   Steam-driven engines
were not limited to factory production. They appeared in the 1820s in a dramatic new form when
the English engineer George Stephenson perfected
an engine to pull wagons along rail tracks. Suddenly,
railroad building became a new industry. (See "Taking Measure," page 788.) The idea of a railroad was
not new: iron tracks had been used since the seventeenth century to haul coal from mines in wagons pulled by horses. A railroad system as a mode
of transport, however, developed only after Stephenson's invention of a steam-powered locomotive.

New companies soon manufactured rails and
laid track, with Parliament's permission. In 1830, the
Liverpool and Manchester Railway line opened
to the cheers of crowds and the congratulations
of government officials, including the duke of
Wellington, the hero of Waterloo and now prime
minister. In the excitement, some of the dignitaries
gathered on a parallel track. Another engine, George
Stephenson's famous Rocket, approached at high
speed. Most of the gentlemen scattered to safety, but

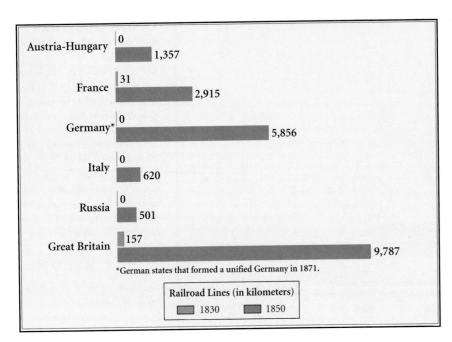

Austria-Hungary — 0 / 1,357
France — 31 / 2,915
Germany* — 0 / 5,856
Italy — 0 / 620
Russia — 0 / 501
Great Britain — 157 / 9,787

*German states that formed a unified Germany in 1871.

Railroad Lines (in kilometers)
1830   1850

TAKING MEASURE
Railroad Lines, 1830–1850
Great Britain quickly extended its lead in the building of railroads. The extension of commerce and, before long, the ability to wage war would depend on the development of effective railroad networks. These statistics might be taken as predicting a realignment of power within Europe after 1850. What do the numbers say about the relative position of Germany (the German states, including Prussia but excluding Austria) and Austria-Hungary and Germany and France?
From B. R. Mitchell, *European Historical Statistics 1750–1970* (New York: Columbia University Press, 1975), F1.

former cabinet minister William Huskisson fell and was hit. In a few hours he died, the first official casualty of the newfangled railroad. Despite the tragedy, the line was an immediate success, carrying up to 110 passengers and freight in each direction. One of the many commentators described it as "a kind of miracle exhibited before my astonished eyes."

Railroads were dramatic and expensive—the most striking symbol of the new industrial age. Placed on the new tracks, steam-driven carriages could transport people and goods to the cities and link coal and iron deposits to the new factories. They gave industrialization a big push forward as every European country soon tried to set up its own railroad system.

The New Ideologies

Although traditional ways of life still prevailed in much of Europe, new modes of thinking about the changes in the social and political order arose in direct response to what some have called the "dual revolution" of the French Revolution and the Industrial Revolution. The 1820s and 1830s were an era of "isms"—conservatism, liberalism, nationalism, romanticism, and, newest on the scene, socialism. The French Revolution had caused people to

ask questions about the best possible form of government, and its effects had made clear that people acting together could change their political system. The events of the 1790s and the following decades, however, also produced enormous differences of opinion over what constituted the ideal government. Similarly, the Industrial Revolution, first in Britain and then in western Europe, posed fundamental questions about changes in society and social relations: How did the new social order differ from the earlier one, which was less urban and less driven by commercial concerns? Who should control this new order? Should governments try to moderate or accelerate the pace of change? Answers to these questions about the social and political order were called *ideologies*, a word coined during the French Revolution. An *ideology* is a coherent set of beliefs about the way a society's social and political order should be organized. In the 1830s and 1840s, new political and social movements organized around these ideologies.

Liberalism. As an ideology, liberalism traced its origins to the writings of John Locke in the seventeenth century and the Enlightenment philosophy of the eighteenth. The adherents of *liberalism* defined themselves in opposition to conservatives on one end of the political spectrum and revolutionaries on the other. Unlike conservatives, liberals supported the Enlightenment ideals of constitutional guarantees of personal liberty and free trade in economics, believing that greater liberty in politics and economic matters would promote social improvement and economic growth. For that reason, they also generally applauded the social and economic changes produced by the Industrial Revolution, while opposing the violence and excessive state power promoted by the French Revolution. The leaders of the rapidly expanding middle class composed of manufacturers, merchants, and professionals favored liberalism.

Liberals' demands varied from country to country. In divided countries like Italy, liberals allied with movements for national unification. In France and Britain, liberals agitated largely for parliamentary reforms, including more middle-class representation, but also wanted economic changes, notably free trade, because they believed lifting tariffs would lower prices, increase consumption, and consequently stimulate economic activity. Economic liberalism was much less important in countries such as Spain, where commercial and industrial change had not yet affected much of society. Nowhere did liberals favor democracy, however, because they feared that extending the vote to all men (let alone women) would lead to anarchy and disorder.

The foremost exponent of early-nineteenth-century liberalism was the English philosopher and jurist Jeremy Bentham (1748–1832). He called his brand of liberalism *utilitarianism* because he held that the best policy is the one that produces "the greatest good for the greatest number" and is thus the most useful, or utilitarian. Liberalism and utilitarianism were closely identified in England. Such views clearly challenged aristocratic dominance, which relied on policies that defended the privileges of a small minority. Bentham's criticisms spared no institution; he railed against the injustices of the British parliamentary process, the abuses of the prisons and the penal code, and the educational system. In his zeal for social engineering, he proposed elaborate schemes for managing the poor and model prisons that would emphasize rehabilitation through close supervision rather than corporal punishment. British liberals like Bentham wanted government involvement, including deregulation of trade, but they shied away from any association with revolutionary violence.

Bentham and many other liberals joined the abolitionist, antislavery movement that intensified between the 1790s and 1820s. One English abolitionist put the matter in these terms: "[God] has given to us an unexampled portion of civil liberty; and we in return drag his rational creatures into a most severe and perpetual bondage." The contradiction between calling for more liberty at home and maintaining slavery in the West Indies seemed intolerable to British liberals and to many religious groups, especially the Quakers, who since the 1780s had taken the lead in forming antislavery societies in both the United States and Great Britain. Agitation by such groups as the London Society for Effecting the Abolition of the Slave Trade succeeded in gaining a first victory in 1807 when the British House of Lords voted to abolish the slave trade. Throughout the 1820s, antislavery activism expanded in the United States, Great Britain, and France because the slave trade still continued in

Railroads in Britain
A commemorative mug shows an early railway carriage. The mug was manufactured to celebrate the opening of the Sheffield and Rotherham line on October 31, 1838. Items such as this spread awareness of railroads to people who lived far from the places first linked together.
Fitzwilliam Museum, University of Cambridge.

some countries and because slavery itself had not been abolished. As one disappointed British abolitionist explained in 1830:

> We supposed that when by the abolition of the slave trade the planters could get no more slaves, they would not only treat better those whom they then had in their power, but that they would gradually find it to their advantage to emancipate them. . . . We did not sufficiently take into account the effect of unlimited power.

The abolitionists' efforts would bear fruit in 1833 when Britain abolished slavery in all its colonies.

Socialism.   The newest ideology of the 1820s, *socialism*, took up where liberalism left off: socialists believed that the liberties advocated by liberals benefited only the middle class, the owners of factories and businesses, not the workers. They sought to reorganize society totally rather than to reform it piecemeal through political measures. Many were *utopians* who believed that ideal communities are based on cooperation rather than competition. Like Thomas More, whose book *Utopia* (1516) gave the movement its name, the utopian socialists believed that society would benefit all its members only if private property did not exist.

Socialists criticized the new industrial order for dividing society into two classes: the new middle class, or *capitalists*, who owned the wealth; and the working class, their downtrodden and impoverished employees. Such divisions tore the social fabric, and, as their name suggests, the socialists aimed to restore harmony and cooperation through social reorganization. Robert Owen (1771–1858), a successful Welsh-born manufacturer, founded British socialism. In 1800, he bought a cotton mill in New Lanark, Scotland, and began to set up a model factory town, where workers labored only ten hours a day (instead of seventeen, as was common) and children between the ages of five and ten attended school rather than working in the factory. Owen moved to the United States in the 1820s to put his principles once more into action in the community in Indiana he named New Harmony. The experiment collapsed after three years, a victim of internal squabbling. But out of Owen's experiments and writings, such as *The Book of the New Moral World*

(1820), would come the movement for producer cooperatives (businesses owned and controlled by their workers), consumers' cooperatives (stores in which consumers owned shares), and a national trade union.

Owen's utopian counterparts in France were Claude Henri de Saint-Simon (1760–1825) and Charles Fourier (1772–1837). Saint-Simon was a noble who had served as an officer in the War of American Independence and lost a fortune speculating in national property during the French Revolution. Fourier traveled as a salesman for a Lyon cloth merchant. Both shared Owen's alarm about the effects of industrialization on social relations. Saint-Simon—who coined the terms *industrialism* and *industrialist* to define the new economic order and its chief animators—believed that work was the central element in the new society and that it should be controlled not by politicians but by scientists, engineers, artists, and industrialists themselves. To correct the abuses of the new industrial order, Fourier urged the establishment of utopian communities that were part garden city and part agricultural commune; all jobs would be rotated to maximize happiness. Fourier hoped that a network of small, decentralized communities would replace the state. The emancipation of women was essential to Fourier's vision of a harmonious community: "The extension of the privileges of women is the fundamental cause of all social progress." Fourier's projects sometimes included outlandish predictions; he envisioned a world in which the oceans would turn into lemonade and the population would include 37 million poets equal to Homer, 37 million mathematicians equal to Newton, and 37 million dramatists equal to Molière.

After Saint-Simon's death in 1825, some of his followers established a quasi-religious cult with elaborate rituals and a "he-pope" and "she-pope," or ruling father and mother. Saint-Simonians lived and worked together in cooperative arrangements and scandalized some by advocating free love. They set up branches in the United States and Egypt. In 1832, Saint-Simonian women founded a feminist newspaper, *The Free Woman*, asserting that "with the emancipation of woman will come the emancipation of the worker." These early utopian socialists were lonely voices. Their emphasis on community and cooperation gained more adherents after 1830.

Nationalism. Nationalists could be liberals, socialists, or even conservatives. Their ability to cross political lines helped nationalism to influence the course of modern world history more than any other ideology. *Nationalism* holds that all peoples derive their identities from their nations, which are defined by common language, shared cultural traditions, and sometimes religion. When such "nations" do not coincide with state boundaries, as they often did not in the nineteenth and twentieth centuries, nationalism can produce violence and warfare as different national groups compete for control over territory.

The French showed the power of national feeling in their revolutionary and Napoleonic wars, but they also provoked nationalism in the people they conquered. Once Napoleon and his satellite rulers departed, nationalist sentiment turned against other outside rulers—the Ottoman Turks in the Balkans, the Russians in Poland, and the Austrians in Italy. Intellectuals took the lead in demanding unity and freedom for their peoples. They collected folktales, poems, and histories and prepared grammars and dictionaries of their native languages. Students, middle-class professionals, and army officers formed secret societies to promote national independence and constitutional reform.

Nationalist aspirations were especially explosive for the Austrian Empire, which included a variety of peoples united only by their enforced allegiance to the Habsburg emperor. The empire included three main national groups: the Germans, who made up one-fourth of the population; the Magyars of Hungary (which included Transylvania and Croatia); and the Slavs, who together formed the largest group in the population but were divided into different nationalities such as Poles, Czechs, Croats, and Serbs. The empire also included Italians in Lombardy and Venetia and Romanians in Transylvania. Efforts to govern such diverse peoples preoccupied Metternich, chief minister to the weak Habsburg emperor Francis I (r. 1792–1835). Metternich's domestic policy aimed to restrain nationalist impulses, and it largely succeeded until the 1840s.

As a conservative, Metternich believed that the experience of the French Revolution proved the superiority of monarchy and aristocracy as forms of government and society. But he did not hesitate to use new methods of governing when necessary.

Consequently, he set up a secret police on the Napoleonic model. The secret police opened letters of even the highest officials, reported any "suspicious" conversations, and followed travelers. Censorship in the Italian provinces was so strict that even the works of Dante were expurgated, and Metternich announced that "the Lombards must forget that they are Italians."

In reaction, novelists, playwrights, and poets used their pens to arouse nationalist sentiment. Membership grew in secret societies such as the *carbonari*; before the fall of Napoleon, many had been anti-French, but now the societies turned anti-Austrian and supported political rights and national self-determination. The societies had no common program across Italy and no central organization, but they attracted tens of thousands of members, including physicians, lawyers, officers, and students.

The new Germanic Confederation had a federal assembly, but it largely functioned as a tool of Metternich's policies. The only sign of resistance came from university students, who formed nationalist student societies, or *Burschenschaften*. In 1817, they held a mass rally at which they burned books they did not like, including Napoleon's Civil Code. One of their leaders, Friedrich Ludwig Jahn, spouted such xenophobic (antiforeign) slogans as "If you let your daughter learn French, you might just as well train her to become a whore." Metternich was convinced that the *Burschenschaften* in the German states and the *carbonari* in Italy were linked in an international conspiracy; in 1820, when a student assassinated the playwright August Kotzebue because he ridiculed the student movement, Metternich convinced the leaders of the biggest German states to pass the Karlsbad Decrees dissolving the student societies and more strictly censoring the press. No evidence for a conspiracy was found.

Tsar Alexander faced similar problems in Poland, his "congress kingdom" (so called because the Congress of Vienna had created it), which in 1815 was one of Europe's most liberal states. The tsar reigned in Poland as a limited monarch, having bestowed a constitution that provided for an elected parliament, a national army, and guarantees of free speech and a free press. But by 1818, Alexander had begun retracting his concessions. Polish students and military officers responded by forming secret nationalist societies to plot for change by illegal means. The government then cracked down, arresting student leaders and dismissing professors who promoted reforms. By the 1820s, Polish nationalists and the Russian imperial government were on a collision course.

Romanticism

More of an artistic movement than a true ideology, *romanticism* glorified nature, emotion, genius, and imagination. It proclaimed these as antidotes to the Enlightenment and to classicism in the arts, challenging the reliance on reason, symmetry, and cool geometric spaces. Classicism idealized models from Roman history; romanticism turned to folklore and medieval legends. Classicism celebrated orderly, crisp lines; romantics sought out all that was wild, fevered, and disorderly. Chief among the arts of romanticism were poetry, music, and painting, which captured the deep-seated emotion characteristic of romantic expression. Romantics might take any political position, but they exerted the most political influence when they expressed nationalist feelings.

Romantic Poetry. Romantic poetry celebrated overwhelming emotion and creative imagination. George Gordon, Lord Byron (1788–1824) explained his aims in writing poetry:

> *For what is Poesy but to create*
> *From overfeeling, Good and Ill, and aim*
> *At an external life beyond our fate,*
> *And be the new Prometheus of new man.*

Prometheus was the mythological figure who brought fire from the Greek gods to human beings. Byron did not seek the new Prometheus among the men of industry; he sought him within his own "overfeeling," his own intense emotions. Byron became a romantic hero himself when he rushed off to act on his emotions by fighting and dying in the Greek war for independence from the Turks. An English aristocrat, Byron nonetheless claimed, "I have simplified my politics into a detestation of all existing governments."

Romantic poetry elevated the wonders of nature almost to the supernatural. In a poem that became one of the most beloved exemplars of romanticism, "Tintern Abbey" (1798), the English poet William Wordsworth (1770–1850) compared

Lord Byron

George Gordon, Lord Byron (1788–1824), lived a short, tumultuous life, wrote enduring romantic poetry, loved both women and young men, and died a heroic death fighting for Greek independence. In the midst of the Napoleonic wars, he left Britain in 1809 for a two-year trip through Spain and Portugal, Greece, Turkey, and Turkish-controlled Albania. He visited the Turkish rulers in Greece and Albania and collected souvenir costumes, such as that worn in this portrait by Thomas Philips (1813). As a result of this trip, he became passionately involved in things Greek; when the Greek rebellion broke out, he promptly joined the British Committee that gathered aid for the Greeks. He died of a fever in Greece where he had gone to distribute funds.
National Portrait Gallery, London.

himself to a deer even while making nature seem filled with human emotions:

> *I came among these hills; when like a roe*
> *I bounded o'er the mountains, by the sides*
> *Of the deep rivers, and the lonely streams,*
> *Wherever nature led.*

Nature, wrote Wordsworth, "to me was all in all." It allowed him to sing "the still, sad music of humanity" and was "a presence that disturbs me with the joy of elevated thoughts; a sense sublime." Like many poets of his time, Wordsworth greeted the French Revolution with joy; in his poem "French Revolution" (1809), he remembered his early enthusiasm: "Bliss was it in that dawn to be alive." But gradually he became disenchanted with the revolutionary experiment and celebrated British nationalism instead; in 1816, he published a poem to commemorate the "intrepid sons of Albion [England]" who died at the battle of Waterloo.

Their emphasis on authentic self-expression at times drew romantics to exotic, mystical, or even reckless experiences. Such transports drove one leading German poet to the madhouse and another to suicide. Some romantics depicted the artist as possessed by demons and obsessed with hallucinations. This more nightmarish side was captured, and perhaps criticized, by Mary Shelley in *Frankenstein.* The aged German poet Johann Wolfgang von Goethe (1749–1832) likewise denounced the extremes of romanticism, calling it "everything that is sick." In his epic poem *Faust* (1832), he seemed to warn of the same dangers Shelley portrayed in her novel. In Goethe's retelling of a sixteenth-century legend, Faust offers his soul to the devil in return for a chance to taste all human experience—from passionate love to the heights of power—in his effort to reshape nature for humanity's benefit. Faust's striving, like Frankenstein's, leaves a wake of suffering and destruction. Goethe did not make the target of his warning explicit, but the French revolutionary legacy and industrialization both seemed to be releasing "faustian" energies that could turn destructive.

Romantic Painting and Music. Romanticism in painting also idealized nature and often expressed anxiety about the coming industrial order. These concerns came together in an emphasis on natural landscape. The German romantic painter Caspar David Friedrich (1774–1840) depicted scenes—often in the mountains, far from any factory—that captured the romantic fascination with the sublime power of nature. His melancholy individual figures looked lost in the vastness of an overpowering nature. Friedrich hated the new modern world and considered industrialization a disaster. His landscapes often had religious meaning as well, as in his controversial painting *The Cross in the Mountains* (1808), which showed a Christian cross standing alone in a mountain scene. It symbolized the steadfastness of faith but seemed to separate religion from the churches and attach it to mystical experience.

Many other artists developed similar themes. The English painter Joseph M. W. Turner (1775–1851) depicted his vision of nature in mysterious, misty seascapes, anticipating later artists by blurring

William Blake, *The Circle of the Lustful* (1824)
An English romantic poet, painter, engraver, and printmaker, Blake always sought his own way. Self-taught, he began writing poetry at age twelve and apprenticed to an engraver at fourteen. His works incorporate many otherworldly attributes; they are quite literally visionary— imagining other worlds. In this engraving of hell, the figures twist and turn and are caught up in a kind of spiritual ether. Blake, "Circle of the Lustful"/ Birmingham Museums and Art Gallery.

Caspar David Friedrich, *Wanderer above the Sea of Fog* (1818)

Friedrich, a German romantic painter, captured many of the themes most dear to romanticism: melancholy, isolation, and individual communion with nature. He painted trees reaching for the sky and mountains stretching into the distance. Nature to him seemed awesome, powerful, and overshadowing of human perspectives. The French sculptor David d'Angers said of Friedrich, "Here is a man who has discovered the tragedy of landscape."

Co Elke Walford, Hamburg/Hamburger Kunsthalle.

the outlines of objects. The French painter Eugène Delacroix (1798–1863) chose contemporary as well as medieval scenes of great turbulence to emphasize light and color and break away from what he saw as "the servile copies repeated *ad nauseum* in academies of art." Critics denounced the new techniques as "painting with a drunken broom." To broaden his experience of light and color, Delacroix traveled in the 1830s to North Africa and painted many exotic scenes in Morocco and Algeria.

The towering presence of the German composer Ludwig van Beethoven (1770–1827) in early nineteenth-century music helped establish the direction for musical romanticism. His music, ac-

cording to one leading German romantic, "sets in motion the lever of fear, of awe, of horror, of suffering, and awakens just that infinite longing which is the essence of Romanticism." Beethoven transformed the symphony into a connected work with recurring and evolving musical themes. Romantic symphonies conveyed the impression of growth, a metaphor for the organic process with an emphasis on the natural that was dear to the romantics. For example, Beethoven's Sixth Symphony, the *Pastoral* (1808), used a variety of instruments to represent sounds heard in the country. Beethoven's work showed remarkable diversity ranging from religious works to symphonies, sonatas, and concertos. Some of his work was explicitly political; his Ninth Symphony (1824) employed a chorus to sing the German poet Friedrich Schiller's verses in praise of universal human solidarity.

Romantic Nationalism. If romantics had any common political thread, it was the support of nationalist aspirations, especially through the search for the historical origins of national identity. In the German states, the Austrian Empire, Russia and other Slavic lands, and Scandinavia, romantic poets and writers collected old legends and folktales that expressed a shared cultural and linguistic heritage stretching back to the Middle Ages. These collections showed that Germany, for example, had always existed even if it did not currently take the form of a single unified state. Romantic nationalism permeated the enormously popular historical novels of Sir Walter Scott (1771–1832) and *The Betrothed* (1825–1827), a novel by Alessandro Manzoni (1785–1873) that constituted a kind of bible for Italian nationalists.

Scott's career incorporates many of the strands of romanticism. He translated Goethe and published Scottish ballads that he heard as a child. After achieving immediate success with his poetry, he switched to historical novels, but he also wrote a nine-volume life of Napoleon and edited historical memoirs. His novels are almost all renditions of historical events, from *Rob Roy* (1817), with its account of Scottish resistance to the English in the early eighteenth century, to *Ivanhoe* (1819), with its tales of medieval England. The influence of Scott's historical novels was immense. One historian claimed that *Ivanhoe* was more historically true than any scholarly work: "There is more history in the novels of Walter Scott than in half of the historians."

❖ Political Challenges to the Conservative Order

As the spread of romanticism shows, the challenges to the conservative order ran deep but not always in the same political direction. Yet in many places, discontent with the conservative Vienna settlement threatened to rise over its banks as liberals, nationalists, and socialists expressed their exasperation. The revolutionary legacy kept coming to the surface to challenge Europe's rulers. Isolated revolts threatened the hold of some conservative governments in the 1820s, but most of them were quickly bottled up. Then in 1830, successive uprisings briefly overwhelmed the established order. Across Europe, angry protesters sought constitutional guarantees of individual liberties and national unity and autonomy.

Political Revolts in the 1820s

Combinations of liberalism and nationalism fueled political upheavals in the 1820s in Spain and Italy, Russia, Greece (Map 21.3), and across the Atlantic in the Spanish and Portuguese colonies of Latin Amer-

ica. Most revolts failed, but those in Greece and Latin America succeeded, largely because they did not threaten the conservative order in Europe.

Uprisings in Spain and Italy. The restoration of regimes after Napoleon's fall disappointed those who dreamed of constitutional freedoms. When Ferdinand VII regained the Spanish crown in 1814, he quickly restored the prerevolutionary nobility, church, and monarchy. He had foreign books and newspapers confiscated at the frontier and allowed the publication of only two newspapers. Not surprisingly, such repressive policies disturbed the middle class, especially the army officers who had encountered French ideas. Many responded by joining secret societies. In 1820, disgruntled soldiers demanded that Ferdinand proclaim his adherence to the Constitution of 1812, which he had abolished in 1814. When the revolt spread, Ferdinand convened the *cortes* (parliament), which could agree on virtually nothing. Ferdinand bided his time, and in 1823 a French army invaded and restored him to absolute power. The French acted with the consent of the other great powers, who had met to discuss the Spanish situation and agree on a course of

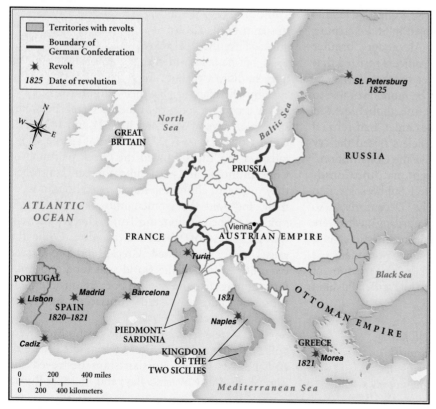

MAP 21.3 Revolutionary Movements of the 1820s
The revolts of the 1820s took place on the periphery of Europe, in Spain, Italy, Greece, Russia, and in the Spanish and Portuguese colonies of Latin America. Rebels in Spain and Russia wanted national independence. Although the Italian revolts failed, as did the uprisings in Spain and Russia, the Greek and Latin American independence movements succeeded.

action. The restored Spanish government tortured and executed hundreds of rebels; thousands were imprisoned or forced into exile.

The uprising in Spain proved contagious. Hearing of the Spanish struggles, rebellious soldiers in the kingdom of Naples joined forces with the *carbonari* and demanded a constitution. When a new parliament met, it too broke down over internal disagreements. The promise of reform sparked rebellion in the northern Italian kingdom of Piedmont-Sardinia, where rebels urged Charles Albert, the young heir to the Piedmont throne, to fight the Austrians for Italian unification. He vacillated; but in 1821, after the rulers of Austria, Prussia, and Russia met and agreed on intervention, the Austrians defeated the rebels in Naples and Piedmont. Liberals were arrested in many Italian states, and the pope condemned the secret societies as "at heart only devouring wolves." Despite the opposition of Great Britain, which condemned the "indiscriminate" suppression of revolutionary movements, Metternich convinced the other powers to agree to his muffling of the Italian opposition to Austrian rule.

The Decembrist Revolt in Russia.

Aspirations for constitutional government surfaced in Russia when Alexander I died suddenly in 1825. On the December day that the troops assembled in St. Petersburg to take an oath of loyalty to Alexander's brother Nicholas as the new tsar, rebel officers insisted that the crown belonged to another brother, Constantine, whom they hoped would be more favorable to constitutional reform. Constantine, though next in the line of succession after Alexander, had refused the crown. The soldiers nonetheless raised the cry "Long live Constantine, long live the Constitution." (Some troops apparently thought that "the Constitution" was Constantine's wife.) Soldiers loyal to Nicholas easily suppressed the Decembrists (so called after the month of their uprising), who were so outnumbered that they had no realistic chance to succeed. The subsequent trial, however, made the rebels into legendary heroes. Of their imprisonment at hard labor, the Russian poet Alexander Pushkin (1799–1837) wrote:

The heavy-hanging chains will fall,
The walls will crumble at a word,
And Freedom greet you in the light,
And brothers give you back the sword.

Pushkin would not live to see this freedom. For the next thirty years, Nicholas I (r. 1825–1855) used a new political police, the Third Section, to spy on potential opponents and stamp out rebelliousness.

Greek Independence from the Turks.

The Greek movement for independence eventually succeeded, largely because it was a nationalist movement against the Ottoman Turks, who enjoyed little support in Christian Europe and whose authority had been declining steadily. As the French ambassador explained to Chateaubriand when the writer visited Istanbul in 1807, "To make an alliance with Turkey is the same as putting your arms around a corpse to make it stand up!" Serbs revolted against Turkish rule in the Balkans and won virtual independence by 1817. A Greek general in the Russian army, Prince Alexander Ypsilanti, tried to lead a revolt against the Turks in 1820, but he failed when the tsar, urged on by Metternich, disavowed him. Metternich feared rebellion even by Christians against their Turkish rulers.

Nationalistic Movements in the Balkans, 1815–1830

A second revolt, this time by Greek peasants, sparked a wave of atrocities in 1821 and 1822. The Greeks killed every Turk who did not escape; in retaliation the Turks hanged the Greek patriarch of Constantinople, and in the areas they still controlled they pillaged churches, massacred thousands of men, and sold the women into slavery. Western opinion turned against the Turks; Greece, after all, was the home of Western civilization. While the great powers negotiated, Greeks and pro-Greece committees around the world sent food and military supplies; like the English poet Byron, a few enthusiastic European and American volunteers joined the Greeks.

The Greeks held on until the great powers were willing to intervene. In 1827, a combined force of British, French, and Russian ships destroyed the Turkish fleet at Navarino Bay; and in 1828, Russia

Greek Independence
From 1836 to 1839 the Greek painter Panagiotis Zographos worked with his two sons on a series of scenes from the Greek struggle for independence from the Turks. Response was so favorable that one Greek general ordered lithographic reproductions for popular distribution. Nationalistic feeling could be thus encouraged even among those who were not directly touched by the struggle. Here Turkish sultan Mehmet the Conqueror, exulting over the fall of Constantinople in 1453, views a row of Greeks under the yoke, a sign of submission. Collection, Visual Connection.

declared war on Turkey and advanced close to Istanbul. The Treaty of Adrianople of 1829 gave Russia a protectorate over the Danubian principalities in the Balkans and provided for a conference among representatives of Britain, Russia, and France, all of whom had broken with Austria in support of the Greeks. In 1830, Greece was declared an independent kingdom under the guarantee of the three powers; in 1833, the son of King Ludwig of Bavaria became Otto I of Greece. Nationalism, with the support of European public opinion, had made its first breach in Metternich's system.

Wars of Independence in Latin America. Across the Atlantic, national revolts also succeeded after a series of bloody wars of independence. Taking advantage of the upheavals in Spain and Portugal that began under Napoleon, restive colonists from Mexico to Argentina rebelled. Their leader was Simon Bolívar, son of a slave owner, who was educated in Europe on the works of Voltaire and Rousseau. Although Bolívar fancied himself a Latin American Napoleon, he had to acquiesce to the formation of a series of independent republics between 1821 and 1823, even in Bolivia, which is named after him. At the same time, Brazil (then still a monarchy) separated from Portugal (Map 21.4). The United States recognized the new states, and in 1823 President James Monroe announced his Monroe Doctrine, closing the Americas to European intervention—a

prohibition that depended on British naval power and British willingness to declare neutrality. Great Britain dominated the Latin American economies, which had suffered great losses during the wars for independence. The new Latin American states would be politically unstable for years to come.

Revolution and Reform, 1830–1832

In 1830 a new wave of liberal and nationalist revolts broke against the bulwark of conservatism. The revolts of the 1820s served as warning shots, but the earlier uprisings had been largely confined to the peripheries of Europe. Now revolution once again threatened the established order in western Europe.

The French Revolution of 1830. Louis XVIII's younger brother and successor, Charles X (r. 1824–1830), brought about his own downfall by steering the monarchy in an increasingly repressive direction. In 1825, a Law of Indemnity compensated nobles who had emigrated during the Revolution for the loss of their estates, and a Law of Sacrilege in the same year imposed the death penalty for such offenses as stealing religious objects from churches. Charles enraged liberals when he dissolved the legislature, removed many wealthy and powerful voters from the rolls, and imposed strict censorship. Spontaneous demonstrations in Paris led to fighting on July 26, 1830. After three days of street battles in

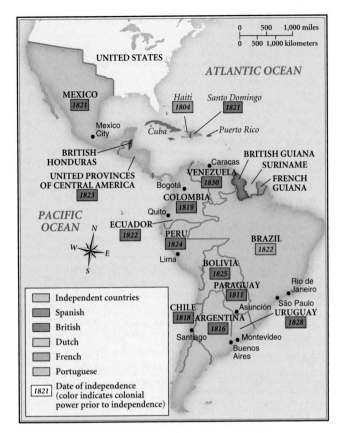

MAP 21.4 Latin American Independence, 1804–1830

The French lost their most important remaining American colony in 1804 when St. Domingue declared its independence as Haiti. But the impact of the French Revolution did not end there. Napoleon's occupation of Spain and Portugal seriously weakened those countries' hold on their Latin American colonies. Despite the restoration of the Spanish and Portuguese rulers in 1814, most of their colonies successfully broke away in a wave of rebellions between 1811 and 1830. Meanwhile a revolt in Spain in 1820–1823 led to a constitutional regime. For example, the Spanish general sent to suppress the revolt in Mexico ended up joining the rebels' cause and helping them establish independence in 1821.

which 500 citizens and 150 soldiers died, a group of moderate liberal leaders, fearing the reestablishment of a republic, agreed to give the crown to Charles X's cousin Louis-Philippe, duke of Orléans.

Charles X went into exile in England, and the new king extended political liberties and voting rights. Although the number of voting men nearly doubled, it remained minuscule—approximately 170,000 in a country of 30 million, between 5 and 6 percent. Such reforms did little for the poor and

working classes, who had manned the barricades in July. Dissatisfaction with the 1830 settlement boiled over in Lyon in 1831, when a silk-workers' strike over wages turned into a rebellion that died down only when the army arrived. Revolution had broken the hold of those who wanted to restore the pre-1789 monarchy and nobility, but it had gone no further this time than installing a more liberal, constitutional monarchy.

Belgian Independence from the Dutch.   The success of the July Revolution in Paris ignited the Belgians, whose country had been annexed to the kingdom of the Netherlands in 1815. Differences in traditions, language, and religion separated the largely Catholic Belgians from the Dutch. An opera about a seventeenth-century insurrection in Naples provided the spark, and students in Brussels rioted, shouting "Down with the Dutch."

The riot turned into revolt. King William of the Netherlands appealed to the great powers to intervene; after all, the Congress of Vienna had established his kingdom. But Great Britain and France opposed intervention and invited Russia, Austria, and Prussia to a conference that guaranteed Belgium independence in exchange for its neutrality in international affairs. Belgian neutrality would remain a cornerstone of European diplomacy for a century. After much maneuvering, the crown of the new kingdom of Belgium was offered to a German prince, Leopold of Saxe-Coburg, in 1831. Belgium, like France and Britain, now had a constitutional monarchy.

Revolts in Italy and Poland.   The Russian tsar and the Austrian emperor would have supported intervention in Belgium had they not been preoccupied with their own revolts. Anti-Austrian uprisings erupted in a handful of Italian states, but they fizzled without the hoped-for French aid. The Polish revolt was more serious. Once again, in response to news of revolution in France, students raised the banner of rebellion, this time in Warsaw in November 1830. Polish aristocrats soon formed a provisional government. Despite some victories on the battlefield, the provisional government got no support from Britain or France and was defeated. In reprisal, Nicholas abolished the Polish constitution that Alexander had granted and ordered thousands of Poles executed or banished.

The British Reform Bill of 1832. The British had long been preoccupied with two subjects: the royal family and elections for control of Parliament. In 1820, the domestic quarrels between the new king George IV (r. 1820–1830) and his German wife Caroline seemed to threaten the future of the monarchy. When George IV came to the throne, he tried to divorce Caroline, and he refused to have her crowned queen. He hoped to use rumors of her love affairs on the continent to win his case, but the divorce trial provoked massive demonstrations in support of Caroline. Women's groups gathered thousands of signatures on petitions supporting her, and popular songs and satires portrayed George as a fat, drunken libertine. Caroline's death a few months after George's coronation ended the Queen Caroline Affair. The monarchy survived but with a tarnished reputation.

The 1820s had brought into British government new men who were open to change. Sir Robert Peel (1788–1850), the secretary for home affairs, revised the criminal code to reduce the number of crimes punishable by death and introduced a municipal police force in London, called the *Bobbies* after him. In 1824, the laws prohibiting labor unions were repealed, and though restrictions on strikes remained, workers could now organize themselves legally to confront their employers collectively. In 1828, the appointment of the duke of Wellington, the hero of Waterloo, as prime minister kept the Tories in power, and his government pushed through a bill in 1829 allowing Catholics to sit in Parliament and hold most public offices.

When in 1830, and again in 1831, the Whigs in Parliament proposed an extension of the right to vote, Tory diehards, principally in the House of Lords, dug in their heels and predicted that even the most modest proposals would doom civilization itself. Even though the proposed law would not grant universal male suffrage, mass demonstrations in favor of it took place in many cities. One supporter of reform described the scene: "Meetings of almost every description of persons were held in cities, towns, and parishes; by journeymen tradesmen in their clubs, and by common workmen who had no trade clubs or associations of any kind." In this "state of diseased and feverish excitement" (according to its opponents), the Reform Bill of 1832 passed, after the king threatened to create enough new peers to obtain its passage in the House of Lords.

Although the Reform Bill altered Britain's political structure in significant ways, the gains were not revolutionary. One of the bill's foremost backers, historian and member of Parliament Thomas Macaulay, explained, "I am opposed to Universal Suffrage, because I think that it would produce a destructive revolution. I support this plan, because I am sure that it is our best security against a revolution." Although the number of male voters increased by about 50 percent, only one in five Britons could now vote, and voting still depended on holding property. Nevertheless, the bill gave representation to new cities in the industrial north for the first time and set a precedent for further widening suffrage. Exclusive aristocratic politics now gave way to a mixed middle-class and aristocratic structure that would prove more responsive to the problems of a

MAPPING THE WEST Europe in 1830

By 1830, the fragilities of the Congress of Vienna settlement had become apparent. Rebellion in Poland failed, but Belgium won its independence from the kingdom of the Netherlands, and a French revolution chased out the Bourbon ruler and installed Louis-Philippe, who promised constitutional reform. Most European rulers held on to their positions in this period of ferment, but they had to accommodate to some extent the new demands created by industrialization, desires for constitutional guarantees of rights, and growing nationalist sentiment.

fast-growing industrial society. Those disappointed with the outcome would organize with renewed vigor in the 1830s and 1840s.

Conclusion

The agitations and uprisings of the 1820s and early 1830s showed that the revolutionary legacy still smoldered and might erupt into flames again at any moment. The efforts of the great powers to maintain the European peace by shoring up established governments and damping down aspirations for constitutional freedoms and national

autonomy sometimes failed. Belgium separated from the Netherlands, Greece achieved independence from the Turks, Latin American countries shook off the rule of Spain and Portugal, and the French installed a more liberal monarchy than the one envisioned by the Congress of Vienna. Yet Metternich's vision of a conservative Europe still held: Russia clamped down on Poland, Austria stifled any sign of Italian nationalism, and the elites of Britain and France managed to maintain their hold by compromising at the right moment.

In her novel *Frankenstein,* Mary Shelley had captured some of the deepest worries of the age; human creativity might have an unpredictably destructive side in spite of every good intention. Although she did not intend her novel as a brief in support of political conservatism—she hated what Metternich stood for—she did tap into European fears about the changes taking place. The French and Industrial Revolutions promised to transform European life, for better or worse. Napoleon Bonaparte had used the French revolutionary legacy to propel his attempted colonization of much of Europe. Others used the revolutionary legacy to argue for new ideologies that would become even more important in the future. The machines of industrialization seemed to some Europeans just as horrible as Frankenstein's monster; others welcomed them as promising a brighter future. In the years to come industrialization would proceed even faster, and revolution would return to shatter the order so carefully nurtured by Metternich and his colleagues.

Suggested References

From Consulate to Empire: The Napoleonic State

Much has been written about Napoleon as a military leader, but only recently has his regime within France attracted interest. Historians now emphasize the mixed quality of Napoleon's rule. He carried forward some revolutionary innovations and halted others.

*Arnold, Eric A., Jr., ed. *A Documentary Survey of Napoleonic France.* 1994.

Crook, Malcolm. *Napoleon Comes to Power: Democracy and Dictatorship in Revolutionary France, 1795–1804.* 1998.

Ellis, Geoffrey James. *Napoleon.* 1996.

Kafker, Frank A., and James M. Laux. *Napoleon and His Times: Selected Interpretations.* 1989.

Lyons, Martyn. *Napoleon Bonaparte and the Legacy of the French Revolution.* 1994.

Napoleon Foundation: http://www.napoleon.org.

Wilson-Smith, Timothy. *Napoleon and His Artists.* 1996.

"Europe Was at My Feet": Napoleon's Conquest

Recent work shows how powerfully Napoleon's armies affected every European state. Whether annexed, allied, or simply defeated, every nation had to come to terms with this dynamo of activity.

*Brunn, Geoffrey. *Napoleon and His Empire.* 1972.

Connelly, Owen. *Napoleon's Satellite Kingdoms.* 1965.

Dallas, Gregor. *The Final Act: The Roads to Waterloo.* 1997.

Gates, David. *The Napoleonic Wars, 1803–1815.* 1997.

Simms, Brendan. *The Impact of Napoleon: Prussian High Politics, Foreign Policy, and the Crisis of the Executive, 1797–1806.* 1997.

The "Restoration" of Europe

New visions of diplomacy are emerging in recent scholarship, but internal affairs are relatively understudied. As a consequence, Artz's book is still a good introduction.

Artz, Frederick B. *Reaction and Revolution, 1814–1832.* 1934.

Johnson, Paul. *The Birth of the Modern: World Society, 1815–1830.* 1991.

Schroeder, Paul W. *The Transformation of European Politics, 1763–1848.* 1994.

Seward, Desmond. *Metternich: The First European.* 1991.

Forces for Social and Cultural Change

The new ideologies have been the subject of a steady stream of excellent work, ranging from individual figures such as Fourier to the antislavery movement and the origins of working-class activism. The Web site Romantic Chronology provides access to a wealth of information about every aspect of romanticism.

Beecher, Jonathan. *Charles Fourier: The Visionary and His World.* 1986.

Berlin, Sir Isaiah. *The Roots of Romanticism.* 1999.

Davis, David Brion. *The Problem of Slavery in the Age of Revolution, 1770–1823.* 1975.

*Hugo, Howard E., ed. *The Romantic Reader.* 1957.

Romantic Chronology: http://english.ucsb.edu:591/rchrono/.

Thompson, E. P. *The Making of the English Working Class.* 1964.

Wright, Beth S. *Painting and History during the French Restoration: Abandoned by the Past.* 1997.

Political Challenges to the Conservative Order

Recent work in British history has been particularly impressive, but in general this is an understudied period of European history. Unsuccessful revolts attract less attention than successful ones, but even the Greek, Latin American, and Belgian independence movements need to be better integrated into European history.

Clark, Anna. "Queen Caroline and the Sexual Politics of Popular Culture in London, 1820," *Representations* 31 (1990): 47–68.

Colley, Linda. *Britons: Forging the Nation, 1707–1837.* 1992.

Di Scala, Spencer. *Italy: From Revolution to Republic, 1700 to the Present.* 2nd ed. 1998.

Spitzer, Alan B. *The French Generation of 1820.* 1987.

*Primary sources.

22

Industrialization, Urbanization, and Revolution

1830–1850

Drink and the Working Classes
The title of this lithograph (c. 1830) by the German artist Franz Bur-chard Dörbeck seems to be simply descriptive. He called it Two Drunken Day Laborers. *Like many lithographs about social types, however, this one cuts more than one way. On the one hand, it seems to criticize workingmen's propensity to drink. The Prussian government supported anti-alcohol campaigns because it feared that the rapidly growing lower classes would turn to drink, prostitution, and crime as they moved to the cities. On the other hand, the lith-ograph was intended to be humor-ous, and the artist seems to treat his working-class subjects with affection and understanding. The lower classes themselves used humor to soften the edges of their often harsh lives.*
Stadtmuseum Berlin; photo: Hans-Joachim Bartsch, Berlin.

A POPULAR GERMAN LITHOGRAPH published around 1830 shows two drunken workingmen standing in front of a water pump in Berlin. In the lithograph's caption, one says, "What'd you think, Schulze, what if that were Kümmel [the Berlin liqueur made with caraway]?" His comrade responds, "Yeah, that would be my first wish if I could wish three times." "So, and the second?" "That all [water] pumps were full of Kümmel."* The lithograph quickly cuts to the core of social life in the turbulent 1830s and 1840s, in particular fears of lower-class behavior. Rapid industrial and urban growth created unprece-dented social problems as peasants and workers streamed into the cities. For example, the population of Berlin more than doubled between 1819 and 1849, reaching 412,000. By 1840, more than half the residents of Berlin had been born outside the city. Many feared that these newcom-ers would precipitate the disintegration of traditional lifestyles. Over-crowding, disease, prostitution, crime, and drinking all seemed to be on the increase. The lithograph focused on drink because it was an issue the censors agreed could be aired for public discussion. In 1832, the king of Prussia ordered all local authorities to promote temperance societies, and within fifteen years, 600,000 German men had taken the pledge to abstain from alcohol.

---

*Translation from Mary Lee Townsend, *Forbidden Laughter: Popular Humor and the Lim-its of Repression in Nineteenth-Century Prussia* (Ann Arbor: University of Michigan Press, 1992), 10.

1830	1834	1838	1842	1846	1850

Politics and War

◆
Algeria invades and begins
conquest of Algeria

◆
First Opium War

◆
Chartist demonstrations in Britain;
revolutions throughout Europe

◆
Corn Laws repealed in Britain

◆
Austria suppresses Italian revolts; Russia invades Hungary

Society and Economy

◆
Spread of industry to continent; rapid growth of cities

◆
Famine strikes Ireland; peasant insurrection in Austrian Galicia

◆
Cholera epidemic

◆
German customs union (*Zollverein*); new British Poor Law

◆
British Factory Act; abolition of slavery in the British Empire

◆
Cholera epidemic

◆
Abolition of slavery in French colonies

Culture, Religion, and Intellectual Life

◆
Romanticism in painting, literature, and music

◆
Marx and Engels, *The Communist Manifesto*

◆
George Sand,
Indiana

◆
Dickens,
Oliver Twist

◆
Invention of photography

In this case, the medium was part of the message, for lithography was a new artistic technology and consequently a sign of the increasing influence of technology on social life. Lithography (from the Greek *lithos,* "stone") was invented by a German engraver in 1798, but, like the steam engine perfected in 1776, its use spread across Europe only in the nineteenth century. In lithography, an artist used a greasy crayon to trace an image on a flat stone; the grease attracted the ink while the blank areas repelled it. The inked stone was embedded in a printing press that could produce thousands of identical images. By creating pictures of every class in society and their problems and by publishing their images in daily and weekly newspapers, artists enlightened a mass audience about social and political problems created by industrial and urban growth. Even criticisms of modern ways relied on modern forms to make their point.

Lithographs helped ordinary people make sense, even while making fun, of the changes taking place around them. Industrial and urban growth unleashed profound and sometimes frightening transformations in everyday life. Seeing the advantages of Great Britain's burgeoning railway network, other European countries soon hurried to lay down their own iron tracks. Factory machinery groaned and growled, dark clouds of grit billowed out of smokestacks, and men, women, and children trudged out to labor for twelve, fourteen, sometimes seventeen hours a day. Even without factories, cities ballooned in size as peasants left their villages to seek a better life. Builders could not keep up, and overcrowding soon provided a receptive environment for epidemic diseases such as cholera, tuberculosis, and typhus. To many commentators, the cities seemed a cesspool of crime, corruption, and degradation, dangerous places that required close police supervision.

The shock of industrial and urban growth generated an outpouring of commentary on the need for social reforms. Lithographs played a vital role in creating sympathy for the downtrodden. The French artist Honoré Daumier, for example, published no fewer than four thousand prints and caricatures criticizing the social inequalities exacerbated by economic development. Painters, poets, and especially novelists joined in the chorus warning about rising tensions. Many who wrote on social issues expected middle-class women to organize their homes as a domestic haven from this heartless process of upheaval. Yet despite the emphasis on

Life as a Married Couple

In this 1846 lithograph by Honoré Daumier titled All That One Would Want, *the wife follows meekly behind her husband. Daumier is criticizing the provision of Napoleon's Civil Code which required the wife to go to live wherever her husband chose. In his lithographs, Daumier satirized landlords, judges, lawyers, politicians, and even King Louis-Philippe himself. In the early 1830s, his political satires landed him in prison with a six-month sentence. His work always took the side of the lowly and downcast and made most fun of the high and mighty in society. His massive output of caricatures typifies an era of preoccupation with the consequences of rapid social change.*
Jean-Loup Charmet.

domesticity, middle-class women participated in public issues too: they set up reform societies that fought prostitution and helped poor mothers, and they agitated for temperance (abstention from alcohol) and joined the campaigns to abolish slavery. Middle-class men and women frequently denounced the lower classes' appetites for drink, tobacco, and cockfighting, but they remained largely silent when British traders received government support in forcing the Chinese to accept imports of opium.

Social and economic changes kept the ideological pots boiling. One German entrepreneur confidently predicted, "The locomotive is the hearse which will carry absolutism and feudalism to the graveyard." In fact, however, the consequences of industrialization and urbanization proved less than straightforward. Nationalists, liberals, socialists, and communists offered competing visions of a new social order: they all agreed that change was necessary, but they disagreed about both the means and the ends of change.

In 1848, the rapid transformation of European society provided the combustible material for a new set of revolutionary outbreaks, more consuming than any since 1789. As in 1789, food shortages and constitutional crises acted as the tinderbox, but now class tensions and nationalist impulses ignited outbreaks in capitals across Europe, not only in Paris. Some revolutionaries, such as Karl Marx, the theorist of communism, saw this as the beginning of a new age of class warfare. Because of internal quarrels and conflicts, the revolutionaries of 1848 eventually went down to defeat.

❖ The Advance of Industrialization and Urbanization

Industrialization and urbanization transformed Europe and eventually most of the world in the nineteenth and twentieth centuries. Because they are not single events but rather long-term processes that continue to the present, it is impossible to give them precise beginning and ending dates. Nevertheless, historians have shown that both processes accelerated quite suddenly in the first half of the nineteenth century and touched off loud complaints about their effects. Great Britain led the way in both industrialization and urbanization, but contemporaries did not fully understand their linkage; even today, scholars debate the connection between industrial and urban growth. Rulers quickly saw the advantages in industrialization, and in the 1830s and 1840s many of them encouraged railroad construction and the mechanization of manufacturing. States exercised little control over the consequences of industrial and urban growth, and many officials, preachers, and intellectuals worried that unchecked growth would destroy traditional social relationships and create disorder. Some held out the constancy of rural life as an antidote to the ravages of industrialization and urbanization, but population growth produced new tensions in the countryside too.

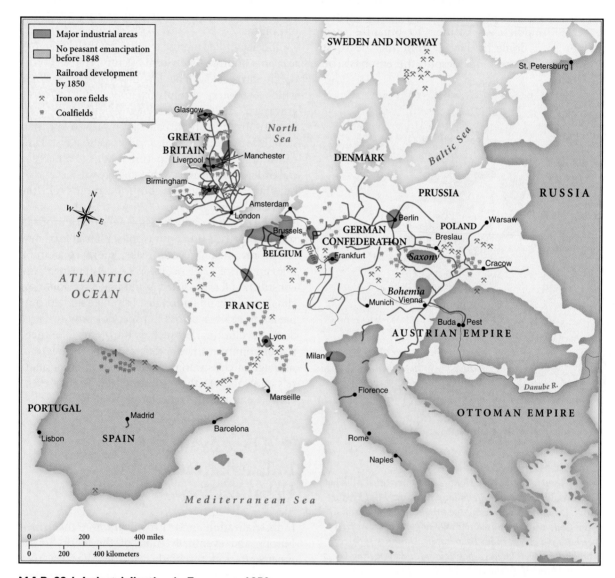

MAP 22.1 Industrialization in Europe, c. 1850

Industrialization first spread in a band across northern Europe that included Great Britain, northern France, Belgium, the northern German states, the region around Milan in northern Italy, and Bohemia. Much of Scandinavia and southern and eastern Europe were left out of this first phase of industrial development. Although railroads were not the only factor in promoting industrialization, the map makes clear the interrelationship between railroad building and the development of new industrial sites of coal mining and textile production.

	Austria	Belgium	France	German states (including Prussia)	Great Britain
1830	214	*	1,863	1,800	22,800
1835	251	2,639	2,506	2,100	28,100
1840	473	3,930	3,003	3,200	34,200
1845	689	4,919	4,202	4,400	46,600
1850	877	5,821	4,434	5,100	50,200

Output of coal (in thousands of metric tons)
*Data not available

TABLE 22.1 Coal Output, 1830–1850
Like the quantities for railroad mileage and raw cotton consumption provided pages 787–788, these figures for coal production show the economic dominance of Great Britain throughout the period 1830–1850. As long as coal remained the essential fuel of industrialization, Britain enjoyed a clear advantage. Although it produced more coal than any other European country, rates of increase in the production of coal were comparable or even higher in other countries, showing that some countries were starting to catch up with Britain.
From B. R. Mitchell, *European Historical Statistics, 1750–1970* (New York: Columbia University Press, 1975), D2.

Engines of Change

Great Britain had led the way in the development of factories and railroads since the late eighteenth century. In the 1830s and 1840s, industrialization spread to continental Europe, first to Belgium, northern France, and northern Italy and then eastward to Prussia, Austria, and eventually Russia. Despite striking industrial growth, factory workers remained a minority everywhere. In the 1840s, factories in England employed only 5 percent of the workers; in France, 3 percent; in Prussia, 2 percent. But these small figures hide a broader transformation as the nature of work changed in many sectors even without the introduction of factories.

Railroads and Steam. In the 1840s alone, railroad track mileage more than doubled in Great Britain, and British investment in railways jumped tenfold. The British also began to build railroads in India. Canal building waned in the 1840s: the railroad had won out.

Britain's success with rail transportation led other countries to develop their own projects. Railroads grew spectacularly in the United States in the 1830s and 1840s. Belgium, newly independent in 1830, opened the first continental European railroad with state bonds backed by British capital in 1835. By 1850, France had 2,000 miles of railroad and the German states nearly twice as many; Great

Britain had 6,000 miles and the United States 9,000 miles. In all, the world had 23,500 miles of track by midcentury.

Railroad building spurred both industrial development and state power (Map 22.1). Governments everywhere participated in the construction of railroads, which depended on private and state funds to pay for the massive amounts of iron, coal, heavy machinery, and human labor required to build and run them. Demand for iron products accelerated industrial development. Until the 1840s, cotton had led industrial production; between 1816 and 1840, cotton output more than quadrupled in Great Britain. But from 1830 to 1850, Britain's output of iron and coal doubled (Table 22.1). Similarly, Austrian output of iron doubled between the 1820s and the 1840s. One-third of all investment in the German states in the 1840s went into railroads.

As railroads created new transportation networks for raw materials and finished goods, the steam engine provided power for textile factories, mining, locomotives, and steamboats. The number of steamboats in Great Britain increased from two in 1812 to six hundred in 1840. Between 1840 and 1850, steam-engine power doubled in Great Britain and increased even more rapidly elsewhere in Europe, as those adopting British inventions strove to catch up. The power applied in German manufacturing, for example, rose from 60,000 to 360,000 hp (units horsepower) during the 1840s but still amounted to only a little more than a quarter of the British figure. German coal and iron output were only 6 or 7 percent of the British output. Steam-powered engines made Britain the world leader in manufacturing. By midcentury, more than half of Britain's national income came from manufacturing and trade.

Industrialization Moves Eastward.

Industrialization spread slowly east from key areas in Prussia (near Berlin), in Saxony, and in Bohemia. The Austrian Empire, with industrialization centered in Bohemia, produced more cotton cloth than either Prussia or Saxony. Cotton production in the Austrian Empire tripled between 1831 and 1845, with Bohemia accounting for half of the empire's mechanized cotton spinning and three-fourths of its cotton weaving. By 1847, coal production, also concentrated in Bohemia, had increased fourfold in just over twenty years.

The advance of industrialization in eastern Europe was slow, in large part because serfdom still survived there, hindering labor mobility and tying up investment capital: as long as peasants were legally tied to the land as serfs, they could not migrate to the new factory towns, and landlords felt little incentive to invest their income in manufacturing. The problem was worst in Russia, where industrialization had hardly begun and would not take off until the end of the nineteenth century. Nevertheless, even in Russia signs of industrialization could be detected: raw cotton imports (a sign of a growing textile industry) increased sevenfold between 1831 and 1848, and the number of factories doubled along with the size of the industrial workforce.

Although Great Britain consciously strove to protect its industrial supremacy, thousands of British engineers defied laws against the export of machinery or the emigration of artisans. The best known of them, John Cockerill, set up a machine works in Belgium that was soon selling its products as far east as Poland and Russia. Cockerill claimed to know of every innovation within ten days of its appearance in England. Only slowly, thanks to such pirating of British methods and to new technical schools, did most continental countries begin closing the gap. Belgium became the fastest-growing industrial power on the continent: between 1830 and 1844, the number of steam engines in Belgium quadrupled, and Belgians exported seven times as many steam engines as they imported. Even so, by 1850, continental Europe still lagged almost twenty years behind Great Britain in industrial development.

The Formation of the Working Class.

As industrialization proceeded, factories increasingly became the workplace of laboring people, replacing the dispersed households of preindustrial artisans. But this process stretched over years, indeed decades. Many peasants kept their options open by combining factory work with agricultural labor. From Switzerland to Russia, people worked in agriculture during the spring and summer and in manufacturing in the fall and winter. In this way, workers and their families ensured their food supply and maintained the rhythms of life on the land. Unstable industrial wages made such arrangements essential. Some new industries idled periodically: for example, iron forges stopped for several months when the water level in streams dropped, and blast furnaces shut down for repairs several weeks every year. In hard times, factory owners simply closed their doors until demand for their goods improved.

In addition, workers continued to toil at home in putting-out, or cottage, industries. In the 1840s, for example, two-thirds of the manufacturing workers in Prussia and Saxony labored at home for contractors or merchants who supplied raw materials and then sold the finished goods. Women worked in the putting-out system as much as or even more than men—they plaited straw and embroidered in Hungary, made pots in Denmark, fashioned lace in Great Britain and France, and spun cotton almost everywhere.

Some of the old forms of putting-out work changed during this period, even when factories did not supplant cottage industries. Little or no technological innovation prompted the change; instead, labor was organized in a different way. Tailoring, for example, which had been the province of male artisans preparing entire garments in small shops, was now broken up into piecework that was farmed out to women working at home for much lower "piece rates."

Even though factories employed only a small percentage of the population, they attracted much attention. Factories produced wealth without regard to the pollution they caused or the exhausted state of their workers; industry created unheard-of riches and new forms of poverty all at once. "From this foul drain the greatest stream of human industry flows out to fertilize the whole world," wrote the French aristocrat Alexis de Tocqueville after visiting the new English industrial city of Manchester in the 1830s. "From this filthy sewer pure gold flows. Here humanity attains its most complete development and its most brutish, here civilization works its miracles and civilized man is turned almost into a savage." Studies by physicians set the life expectancy of workers in Manchester at just seventeen years (partly because of high rates of infant mortality), whereas the average life expectancy in England was forty years in 1840. (See "New Sources, New Perspectives," page 810.) In some parts of Europe, city leaders banned factories, hoping to insulate their towns from the effects of industrial growth. Visitors invariably complained about the smoke and soot. One American visitor in Britain in the late 1840s described how "in the manufacturing town, the fine soot or *blacks* darken the day, give white sheep the color of black sheep, discolor the human saliva, contaminate the air, poison many plants, and corrode monuments and buildings."

As factory production expanded, local and national governments collected information about the workers. Investigators detailed the pitiful condition of factory workers. A French physician in the eastern town of Mulhouse described the "pale, emaciated women who walk barefooted through the dirt" to reach the factory. The young children who worked in the factory appeared "clothed in rags which are greasy with the oil from the looms and frames." A report to the city government in Lille, France, in 1832 described "dark cellars" inhabited by the cotton workers, where "the air is never renewed, it is infected; the walls are plastered with garbage. . . . If a bed exists, it is a few dirty, greasy planks; it is damp and putrescent straw."

Authorities worried in particular about the effects on families. A doctor in the Prussian town of Breslau (population 111,000 in 1850), for example, reported that in working-class districts "several persons live in one room in a single bed, or perhaps a whole family, and use the room for all domestic duties, so that the air gets vitiated [polluted]. . . . Their diet consists largely of bread and potatoes. These are

clearly the two main reasons for the scrofula [a disease related to tuberculosis] which is so widespread here; the diet is also the cause of the common malformation of limbs."

Government inquiries often focused on women and children. In Great Britain, the Factory Act of 1833 outlawed the employment of children under the age of nine in textile mills (except in the lace and silk industries) and limited the workdays of children age nine to thirteen to nine hours a day and those age thirteen to eighteen to twelve hours. These figures give some sense of the drudgery of factory work: adults worked even longer hours. Reports on conditions in other industries prompted further legislation. When investigating commissions showed that women and young children, sometimes under age six, were hauling coal trucks through low, cramped passageways in coal mines, the British Parliament passed a Mines Act in 1842 prohibiting the employment of women and girls underground. One nine-year-old girl, Margaret Gomley, described her typical day in the mines as beginning at 7:00 A.M. and ending at 6:00 P.M.: "I get my dinner at 12 o'clock, which is a dry muffin, and sometimes butter on, but have no time allowed to stop to eat it, I eat it while I am thrusting the load. . . . They flog us down in the pit, sometimes with their hand upon my bottom, which hurts me very much." In 1847, the Central Short Time Committee, one of Britain's many social reform organizations, successfully pressured Parliament to limit the workday of women and children to ten hours. The continental countries followed the British lead, but since most did not insist on government inspection, enforcement was lax.

Urbanization and Its Consequences

Industrial development spurred urban growth wherever factories were located in or near cities, yet cities grew even with little industry. Here, too, Great Britain led the way: half the population of England and Wales lived in towns by 1850, while in France and the German states the urban population was only about a quarter of the total. Both old and new cities teemed with growing population in the 1830s and 1840s. In the 1830s alone, London grew by 130,000 people, Manchester by 70,000, and Birmingham by 40,000. Paris grew by 120,000 just

Statistics and the Standard of Living of the Working Class

From the very beginning of industrialization, experts argued about whether industrialization improved or worsened the standard of living of the working class. For every claim, there was a counterclaim, and most often these claims came in the form of statistics. Some experts argued that factories offered higher-paying jobs to workers; others countered that factories took work away from artisans such as handloom weavers and left them on the verge of starvation. Supporters of industrialization maintained that factories gave women paying work; opponents insisted that factories destroyed the family by taking women away from the home. Through mass production, industrialization made goods cheaper and therefore more available; by polluting the air, it destroyed health, lowered life expectancy, and ruined the environment. Karl Marx and Friedrich Engels would give the debate even more of an edge by tying it to the ideology of communism. In 1844, Engels described to Marx his aim in writing *The Condition of the Working Class in England*: "I shall present the English with a fine bill of indictment. At the bar of world opinion I charge the English middle classes with mass murder, wholesale robbery and all the other crimes in the calendar."[*] The stakes of the argument were not small.

The controversy about the benefits and costs of industrialization has continued in different forms right down to the present, in part because it is an argument directly inspired by the ideologies—liberalism, socialism, communism—that emerged as explanations of and blueprints for economic and social change. In the 1830s and 1840s, liberals insisted that industrialization would promote greater prosperity for everyone, whereas conservatives complained that it destroyed traditional ways of life and socialists warned that it exaggerated inequality and class division. In the 1950s and 1960s, defenders of capitalist free enterprise still advanced the argument about prosperity, but now they were opposed by communists who argued that state control of production could sidestep the horrors of early capitalist exploitation. Newly developing countries looked to the history of the 1830s and 1840s for lessons about the likely impact of industrialization on their countries in the 1950s and beyond. The scholarly debates therefore attracted worldwide attention, and all sides called on statistics to make their competing cases.

Unfortunately, the statistics can be interpreted in many different ways. Did it matter more that wages for factory workers went up or that life expectancy went down? If an increase in sugar consumption in Great Britain from 207,000 tons in 1844 to 290,000 tons in 1847 meant an overall increase in the standard of living, how does that square with the hundreds of thousands of deaths in Ireland at the same time or the increasing disparity throughout Great Britain between rich and poor? Some convergence of opinion has taken place, however. Most now agree that by sometime between 1820 and 1845 (the exact date depending on the scholar), conditions in Great Britain had become better than before the Industrial Revolution. And there is no doubt that the debate itself

---

[*]Quoted in R. M. Hartwell et al., *The Long Debate on Poverty* (Surrey, England: Institute of Economic Affairs, 1972), 185.

between 1841 and 1846, Vienna by 125,000 between 1827 and 1847, and Berlin by 180,000 between 1815 and 1848. (See "Taking Measure," page 812.)

Massive rural emigration, not natural increase (births to women already living in cities), accounted for this remarkable increase. Agricultural improvements had increased the food supply and hence the rural population, but the land could no

longer support the people living on it. City life and new factories beckoned those faced with hunger and poverty. They also attracted emigrants from other lands: thousands of Irish emigrated to English cities, Italians went to French cities, and Poles flocked to German cities. Settlements sprang up outside the old city limits but gradually became part of the urban area. As cities grew, their medieval walls came down.

has had one major positive effect: since making one's point depends on having statistics to prove it, the debate itself has encouraged a staggering amount of research into quantitative measures of just about everything imaginable, from measures of wages and prices to rates of mortality and even average heights (height being correlated, it is thought, to economic well-being). British soldiers in the nineteenth century were taller on average than those in any other country except the United States, and people who believe that industrialization improved the standard of living are happy to seize on this as evidence for their case.

One example of a recently developed statistic shows both how powerful and how debatable such sources can be. This table adapted from a recent study by Jeffrey G. Williamson, provides a simple measure—based on complex calculations—of the gap in wages between British farm and nonfarm laborers for the period 1797 to 1851. The index measures the attractiveness of nonfarm (basically city, mining, and factory) work. It shows that nonfarm wages rose faster than farm wages, but only after 1820 or so. By 1851, nonfarm wages had far outstripped those on the farm. What can we conclude? Although these data seem to support the view that the standard of living of workers improved sometime in the 1820s and continued to do so afterward, Williamson does not conclude that factory workers were better off than farmers; instead, he argues that the gap indicates that farm people did not migrate quickly enough to the city to satisfy urban labor demands. In short, he seems to consider the gap between farm and nonfarm wages to be a problem of "labor-market disequilibrium." The lesson to be learned is that all historians' conclusions depend on the questions they ask and the sources they use—and few sources are as open to different interpretations as statistics.

Trends in the British Nominal-Wage Gap, 1797–1851 (1797=100)

Year	Index
1797	100
1805	86.6
1810	96.7
1815	105.1
1827	132.4
1835	134.7
1851	148.3

The gap is calculated as the difference between the weighted average of nonfarm unskilled earnings (common laborers, porters, police, guards, watchmen, coal miners, and so on) and the farm-earnings rate, divided by the farm-earnings rate. Thus, it is the percentage differential by which nonfarm unskilled wages exceeded farm wages.

Source: Jeffrey G. Williamson, "Leaving the Farm to Go to the City: Did They Leave Quickly Enough?" in John A. James and Mark Thomas, *Capitalism in Context: Essays on Economic Development and Cultural Change in Honor of R. M. Hartwell* (Chicago: University of Chicago Press, 1994), 159–183, table p. 182.

QUESTIONS FOR DEBATE

1. What is a good measure of the standard of living in the first half of the nineteenth century? How would you measure it today?
2. How do you explain the initial decline in nonfarm wages relative to farm wages and the subsequent rise?
3. What are the virtues of using statistical measures to determine the standard of living? What are the defects?

FURTHER READING

Morgan, Kenneth. *The Birth of Industrial Britain: Economic Change 1750–1850.* 1999.

Thompson, Noel W. *The Real Rights of Man: Political Economies for the Working Class, 1775–1850.* 1998.

At the same time, cities incorporated parks, cemeteries, zoos, and greenways, all imitations of the countryside, which itself was being industrialized by railroads and factories. "One can't even go to one's land for the slightest bit of gardening," grumbled a French citizen, annoyed by new industrial potteries in town, "without being covered with a black powder that spoils every plant that it touches."

Overcrowding and Disease. The rapid influx of people caused serious overcrowding in the cities because the housing stock expanded much more slowly than population growth. In Paris, 30,000 workers lived in lodging houses, eight or nine to a room, with no separation of the sexes. One contemporary observed: "The difficulty of finding lodgings is for the worker a constant ordeal and a

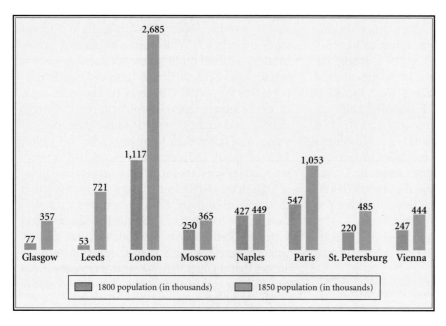

TAKING MEASURE
Population of Major European Cities, 1800–1850
Although London was by far the biggest city in mid-nineteenth-century Europe, it was not the fastest growing. According to these figures for population in 1800 and 1850, which city was the fastest growing? How much was population growth in these cities due to industrialization? What problems might have been created by especially rapid growth?
From B. R. Mitchell, *European Historical Statistics, 1750–1970* (New York: Columbia University Press, 1975), B4.

perpetual cause of misery." In 1847 in St. Giles, the Irish quarter of London, 461 people lived in just twelve houses. Men, women, and children huddled together on piles of filthy rotting straw or potato peels because they had no money for fuel to keep warm.

Severe crowding worsened already dire sanitation conditions. Garbage and refuse littered the unpaved streets of poor districts, and smog, smoke, and putrid smells fouled the air. Water was scarce and had to be fetched daily from nearby fountains. Despite the diversion of water from provincial rivers to Paris and a tripling of the number of public fountains, Parisians had enough water for only two baths annually per person (the upper classes enjoyed more baths, of course; the lower classes, fewer). In London, private companies that supplied water turned on pumps in the poorer sections for only a few hours three days a week. Sewage removal was practically nonexistent. Residents dumped refuse into streets or courtyards, and human excrement collected in cesspools under apartment houses. At mid-century, London's approximately 250,000 cesspools were emptied only once or twice a year. In rapidly growing British industrial cities such as Manchester, one-third of the houses contained no latrines. Human waste ended up in the rivers that supplied drinking water. The horses that provided transportation inside the cities left droppings everywhere, and city dwellers often kept chickens, ducks, goats, pigs, geese, and even cattle, as well as dogs and cats, in their houses. The result was a "universal atmosphere of filth and stink."

Such conditions made cities prime breeding grounds for disease; those with 50,000 people or more had twice the death rates of rural areas. In 1830–1832 and again in 1847–1851, devastating outbreaks of cholera swept across Asia and Europe (touching the United States as well in 1849–1850). Today we know that a waterborne bacterium causes the disease, but at the time no one understood the disease and everyone feared it. The usually fatal disease induced violent vomiting and diarrhea and left the skin blue, eyes sunken and dull, and hands and feet ice cold. While cholera particularly ravaged the crowded, filthy neighborhoods of rapidly growing cities, it also claimed many rural as well as some well-to-do victims. In Paris, 18,000 people died in the 1832 epidemic and 20,000 in that of 1849; in London, 7,000 died in each epidemic; in Russia, the epidemic was catastrophic, claiming 250,000 victims in 1831–1832 and a million in 1847–1851 (Map 22.2).

Rumors and panic followed in the epidemics' wakes. Everywhere the downtrodden imagined conspiracies: in Paris in April 1832, a crowd of workers attacked a central hospital, believing the doctors were poisoning the poor but using cholera as a hoax to cover up the conspiracy. Eastern European peasants burned estates and killed physicians and officials.

DIPHTHERIA.   SCROFULA.   CHOLERA.

FATHER THAMES INTRODUCING HIS OFFSPRING TO THE FAIR CITY OF LONDON.

Lithograph of London
This English lithograph draws attention to the connection between contaminated water supplies—in this case the Thames River in London—and epidemic disease—diphtheria, scrofula, and cholera are cited at the bottom of the print. The title, Father Thames Introducing His Offspring to the Fair City of London, *is particularly jarring; a monsterlike figure drags a dead body out of the slime and presents it to the fair maiden who represents London. The subtitle, "A Design for a Fresco in the New Houses of Parliament" challenges the political leadership to recognize the social problems festering nearby.*
Hulton Getty/Liaison Agency.

Daguerreotype of Paris
Daguerre experimented extensively with producing an image on a metal plate before he came up with a viable photographic process in 1837. In 1839, the French government bought the rights and made the process freely available. This picture of a Parisian boulevard seems to depict empty streets because with the long exposure required to capture the image, moving objects did not register. The image is also reversed (as if seen in a mirror). Because of these technical problems, the early photographic process proved most suitable for portraits.
Bayrisches National Museum.

Although devastating, cholera did not kill as many people as tuberculosis, Europe's number-one deadly disease. But tuberculosis took its victims one by one and therefore had less impact on social relations.

Raging epidemics spurred a growing concern for public health. When news of the cholera out-break in eastern Europe reached Paris in 1831, the city set up commissions in each municipal district to collect information about lower-class housing and sanitation. In Great Britain, reports on sanitation conditions among the working class led to the passage of new public health laws.

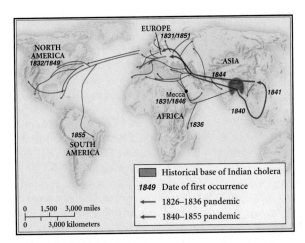

MAP 22.2 The Spread of Cholera, 1826–1855
Contemporaries did not understand the causes of the cholera epidemics in the 1830s and the 1840s in Europe. Western Europeans knew only that the disease marched progressively from east to west across Europe. Nothing seemed able to stop it. It appeared and died out for reasons that could not be grasped at the time. Nevertheless, the cholera epidemics prompted authorities in most European countries to set up public health agencies to coordinate the response and study sanitation conditions in the cities.

Middle-Class Fears.   The middle and upper classes feared the urban threats to their settled, comfortable ways of life. The more prosperous classes lived in large, well-appointed apartments or houses with more light, more air, and more water than in lower-class dwellings. But the lower classes lived nearby, sometimes in the cramped upper floors of the same apartment houses. Middle-class reformers often considered the poor to be morally degenerate because of the circumstances of urban life. In their view, overcrowding led to sexual promiscuity and illegitimacy. They depicted the lower classes as dangerously lacking in sexual self-control. A physician visiting Lille, France, in 1835 wrote of "individuals of both sexes and of very different ages lying together, most of them without nightshirts and repulsively dirty. . . . The reader will complete the picture. . . . His imagination must not recoil before any of the disgusting mysteries performed on these impure beds, in the midst of obscurity and drunkenness."

Officials collected statistics on illegitimacy that seemed to bear out these fears: one-quarter to one-half of the babies born in the big European cities in the 1830s and 1840s were illegitimate, and alarmed medical men wrote about thousands of infanticides. Between 1815 and the mid-1830s in France, 33,000 babies were abandoned at foundling hospitals every year; 27 percent of births in Paris in 1850 were illegitimate, compared with only 4 percent of rural births. By collecting such statistics, physicians and administrators in the new public health movement hoped to promote legislation to better the living conditions for workers, but at the same time they helped stereotype workers as helpless and out of control.

Sexual disorder seemed to go hand in hand with drinking and crime. Beer halls and pubs dotted the urban landscape. By the 1830s, Hungary's twin cities of Buda and Pest had eight hundred beer and wine houses for the working classes. One London street boasted twenty-three pubs in three hundred yards. Police officials estimated that London had 70,000 thieves and 80,000 prostitutes. In many cities, nearly half the urban population lived at the level of bare subsistence, and increasing numbers depended on public welfare, charity, or criminality to make ends meet.

Everywhere reformers warned of a widening separation between rich and poor and a growing sense of hostility between the classes. The French poet Amédée Pommier wrote of "These leagues of laborers who have no work, / These far too many arms, these starving mobs." Clergy joined the chorus of physicians and humanitarians in making dire predictions. A Swiss pastor noted: "A new spirit has arisen among the workers. Their hearts seethe with hatred of the well-to-do; their eyes lust for a share of the wealth about them; their mouths speak unblushingly of a coming day of retribution." In 1848 it would seem that that day of retribution had arrived.

Agricultural Perils and Prosperity

Rising population created increased demand for food and spurred changes in life in the countryside too. Peasants and farmers planted fallow land and chopped down forests and drained marshes to open up more land for farming. Still, Europe's ability to feed its expanding population remained questionable: although agricultural yields increased by 30 to 50 percent in the first half of the nineteenth century, population grew by nearly 100 percent.

Railroads and canals improved food distribution, but much of Europe—particularly in the east—remained isolated from markets and vulnerable to famines.

Most people still lived on the land, and the upper classes still dominated rural society. Successful businessmen bought land avidly, seeing it not only as the ticket to respectability but also as a hedge against hard times. Hardworking, crafty, or lucky commoners sometimes saved enough to purchase holdings that they had formerly rented or slowly acquired slivers of land from less fortunate neighbors. In France at midcentury, almost two million economically independent peasants tended their own small properties. But in England, southern Italy, Prussia, and eastern Europe, large landowners, usually noblemen, consolidated and expanded their estates by buying up the land of less successful nobles or peasants. As agricultural prices rose, the big landowners pushed for legislation to allow them to continue converting common land to private property.

Wringing a living from the soil under such conditions put pressure on traditional family life. For example, men often migrated seasonally to earn cash in factories or as village artisans, while their wives, sisters, and daughters did the traditional "men's work" of tending crops. The threat of subdivision of the land encouraged rudimentary forms of birth control. In France, for instance, the Napoleonic Code provided for an equal distribution of inheritance among all heirs; as a result, land was divided over generations into such small parcels that less than 25 percent of all French landowners could support themselves. In the past, population growth had been contained by postponing marriage (leaving fewer years for childbearing) and by high rates of death in childbirth and infant mortality. Now, as child mortality declined outside the industrial cities and people without property began marrying earlier, Europeans became more aware of birth control methods. Contraceptive techniques improved; for example, the vulcanization of rubber in the 1840s made condoms more reliable. When such methods failed and population increase left no options open at home, people emigrated, often to the United States. Some 800,000 Germans had moved out of central Europe by 1850, while in the 1840s famine drove tens of thousands of Irish abroad. Between 1816 and 1850, five million Europeans left their home countries for new lives overseas. When France colonized Algeria in the 1830s and 1840s, officials

Bearbaiting
This colored engraving from 1821 of Charley's Theater in London shows that bearbaiting did not attract only the lower classes, as reformers often implied. Top hats were most often worn by middle-class men, who seem to be enjoying the spectacle of dogs taunting the bear as much as the working-class men present. At this time, bearbaiting, like bullbaiting, began to come under fire as cruel to animals.
Mary Evans Picture Library.

tried to attract settlers by emphasizing the fertility of the land; they offered the prospect of agricultural prosperity in the colony as an alternative to the rigors of industrialization and urbanization at home.

Despite all the challenges to established ways of life, rural political power remained in the hands of traditional elites. The biggest property owners dominated their tenants and sharecroppers, often demanding a greater yield without contributing to improvements that would enhance productivity. They also controlled the political assemblies and often personally selected the parish clergy and local officials. Such power not surprisingly provoked resentment. As one Italian critic wrote, "Great landowner is often the synonym for great ignoramus." Nowhere did the old rural social order seem more impregnable than in Russia. Most Russian serfs remained tied to the land, and troops easily suppressed serfs' uprisings in 1831 and 1842. By midcentury, peasant emancipation remained Russia's great unresolved problem.

❖ Reforming the Social Order

In the 1830s and 1840s, Europeans organized to reform the social evils created by industrialization and urbanization. They acted in response to the outpouring of government reports, medical accounts, and literary and artistic depiction of new social problems. Middle-class women often took the lead in establishing new charitable organizations that tried to bring religious faith, educational uplift, and the reform of manners to the lower classes. Middle-class men and women too expected women to soften the rigors of a rapidly changing society, but this expectation led to some confusion about women's proper role: should they devote themselves to social reform in the world or to their own domestic spaces? Many hoped to apply the same zeal for reform to the colonial peoples living in places administered by Europeans.

Cultural Responses to the "Social Question"

The "social question," an expression reflecting the deeply shared concern about social changes, pervaded all forms of art and literature. The dominant artistic movement of the time, romanticism, gener-

ally took a dim view of industrialization. The English-born painter Thomas Cole (1801–1848) complained in 1836: "In this age . . . a meager utilitarianism seems ready to absorb every feeling and sentiment, and what is sometimes called improvement in its march makes us fear that the bright and tender flowers of the imagination shall all be crushed beneath its iron tramp." When Cole went to the United States to paint, he depicted "primeval forests, virgin lakes and waterfalls"—that is, a landscape untouched by machinery. Yet culture itself underwent important changes as the growing capitals of Europe attracted flocks of aspiring painters and playwrights; the 1830s and 1840s witnessed an explosion in culture as the number of would-be artists increased dramatically and new technologies such as photography and lithography brought art to the masses. Many of these new intellectuals would support the revolutions of 1848.

Romantic Concerns about Industrial Life. Because romanticism tended to glorify nature and reject industrial and urban growth, romantics often gave vivid expression to fears of economic and social transformation. The English poet Elizabeth Barrett Browning, best known for her love poems, decried child labor in "The Cry of the Children" (1843):

> For, all day, we drag our burden tiring
> Through the coal-dark underground,
> Or, all day, we drive the wheels of iron
> In the factories, round and round

Architects of the period sought to recapture a preindustrial world. When the British Houses of Parliament were rebuilt after they burned down in 1834, the architect Sir Charles Barry constructed them in a Gothic style reminiscent of the Middle Ages. This medievalism was taken even further by A. W. N. Pugin, who prepared the Gothic details for the Houses of Parliament. In his polemical book *Contrasts* (1836), Pugin denounced modern conditions and compared them unfavorably with those in the 1400s. To underline his view, Pugin wore medieval clothes at home.

Romantic painters specialized in landscape as a way of calling attention to the sublime wonders of nature, but sometimes even landscapes showed the power of new technologies. In *Rain, Steam, and*

Joseph M. W. Turner, *The Fighting Téméraire Tugged to Her Last Berth to Be Broken Up* **(1838)**
Turner's painting captures the clash of old and new as a steamer belching smoke tows a wooden sailing ship to its last berth, where it will be destroyed. Turner muses about the passing of old ways but also displays his mastery of color in the final blaze of sunset, itself another sign of the passing of time. Turner considered painting to be closely related to poetry; he was an avid reader of the romantic poets, especially Byron.
National Gallery, London.

Speed: The Great Western Railway (1844), the leading English romantic painter, Joseph M. W. Turner (1775–1851), portrayed the struggle between the forces of nature and the means of economic growth. Turner was fascinated by steamboats: in *The Fighting "Téméraire" Tugged to Her Last Berth to Be Broken Up* (1838), he featured the victory of steam power over more conventional sailing ships. An admirer described it as an "almost prophetic idea of smoke, soot, iron, and steam, coming to the front in all naval matters."

The Depiction of Social Conditions in Novels. The novel was the art form best suited to presenting social problems. Thanks to increased literacy, the spread of reading rooms and lending libraries, and serialization in newspapers and journals, novels reached a large reading public. Unlike the fiction of the eighteenth century, which had focused on indi-

vidual personalities, the great novels of the 1830s and 1840s specialized in the portrayal of social life in all its varieties. Manufacturers, financiers, starving students, workers, bureaucrats, prostitutes, underworld figures, thieves, and aristocratic men and women filled the pages of works by popular writers such as Honoré de Balzac and Charles Dickens. Pushing himself to exhaustion and a premature death to get out of debt, the French writer Balzac (1799–1850) cranked out ninety-five novels and many short stories. He aimed to catalog the social types that could be found in French society. Many of his characters, like himself, were driven by the desire to climb higher in the social order.

Charles Dickens (1812–1870) worked with a similar frenetic energy and for much the same reasons. When his father was imprisoned for debt in 1824, the young Dickens took a job in a shoe-polish factory. In 1836, he published a series of literary sketches of daily life in London to accompany a volume of caricatures by the artist George Cruikshank, whose work resembled the lithograph that opens this chapter. Dickens then produced a series of novels that appeared in monthly installments and attracted thousands of readers. In them he paid close attention to the distressing effects of industrialization and urbanization. In *The Old Curiosity Shop* (1841), for example, he depicts the Black Country, the manufacturing region west and northwest of Birmingham, as a "cheerless region," a "mournful place," in which tall chimneys "made foul the melancholy air." In addition to publishing such enduring favorites as *Oliver Twist* (1838) and *A Christmas Carol* (1843), he ran charitable organizations and pressed for social reforms. For Dickens, the ability to portray the problems of the poor went hand in hand with a personal commitment to reform.

Novels by women often revealed the bleaker side of women's situations. *Jane Eyre* (1847), a novel by Charlotte Brontë, describes the difficult life of an orphaned girl who becomes a governess, the only occupation open to most single middle-class women. Although in an economically weak position, Jane Eyre refuses to achieve respectability and security through marriage, the usual option for women. The French novelist George Sand (Amandine-Aurore Dupin, 1804–1876) took her social criticism a step further. She announced her independence in the 1830s by dressing like a man and smoking cigars. Like many other women writers of the time, she published her work under a male pseudonym while creating female characters who prevail in difficult circumstances through romantic love and moral idealism. Sand's novel *Indiana* (1832), about an unhappily married woman, was read all over Europe. Her notoriety—she became the lover of the Polish pianist Frédéric Chopin, among others, and threw herself into socialist politics—made the term *George-Sandism* a common expression of disdain for independent women.

The Explosion of Culture. As artists became more interested in society and social relations, ordinary citizens crowded cultural events. Museums opened to the public across Europe, and the middle classes began collecting art. Popular theaters in big cities drew thousands from the lower and middle classes every night; in London, for example, some

George Sand

In this lithograph by Alcide Lorentz of 1842, George Sand is shown in one of her notorious male costumes. Sand published numerous works, including novels, plays, essays, travel writing, and an autobiography. She actively participated in the revolution of 1848 in France, writing pamphlets in support of the new republic. Disillusioned by the rise to power of Louis-Napoleon Bonaparte, she withdrew to her country estate and devoted herself exclusively to her writing.
The Granger Collection.

24,000 people attended eighty "penny theaters" nightly. The audience for print culture also multiplied. In the German states, for example, the production of new literary works doubled between 1830 and 1843, as did the number of periodicals and newspapers and the number of booksellers. Thirty or forty private lending libraries offered books in Berlin in the 1830s, and reading rooms in pastry shops stocked political newspapers and satirical journals. Young children and ragpickers sold cheap prints and books door to door or in taverns.

The advent of photography in 1839 provided an amazing new medium for artists. Daguerreotypes, named after their inventor, French painter Jacques Daguerre (1787–1851), prompted one artist to claim that "from today, painting is dead." Although this prediction was highly exaggerated, photography did open up new ways of portraying reality. Visual images, whether in painting, on the stage, or in photography, heightened the public's awareness of the effects of industrialization and urbanization.

The number of artists and writers swelled. Estimates suggest that the number of painters and sculptors in France, the undisputed center of European art at the time, grew sixfold between 1789 and 1838. Not everyone could succeed in this hothouse atmosphere as writers and artists furiously competed for public attention. Their own troubles made some of them more keenly aware of the hardships faced by the poor. In one of many bitingly critical journals and booklets published in Berlin appeared the following "Lies Chronicle": "In Ipswich in England a mechanical genius has invented a stomach, whose extraordinary efficient construction is remarkable. This artificial stomach is intended for factory workers there and is adjusted so that it is fully satisfied with three lentils or peas; one potato is enough for an entire week."

The Varieties of Social Reform

Lithographs, novels, even joke booklets helped drive home the need for social reform, but religious conviction also inspired efforts to help the poor. Moral reform societies, Bible groups, Sunday schools, and temperance groups all aimed to turn the poor into respectable people. In 1844, for example, 450 different relief organizations operated in London alone. States supported these efforts by encouraging education and enforcing laws against the vagrant poor.

The Religious Impulse for Social Reform. Religiously motivated reformers first had to overcome the perceived indifference of the working classes. Protestant and Catholic clergy complained that workers had no interest in religion; less than 10 percent of the workers in the cities attended religious services. In a report on the state of religion in England and Wales in 1851, the head of the census Horace Mann commented that "the masses of our working population . . . are *unconscious secularists*. . . . These are never, or but seldom seen in our religious congregations." To combat such indifference, British religious groups launched the Sunday school movement, which reached its zenith in the 1840s. By 1851, more than half of all working-class chil-

dren between five and fifteen were attending Sunday school, even though very few of their parents regularly went to religious services. The Sunday schools taught children how to read at a time when few working-class children could go to school during the week.

Women took a more prominent role than ever before in charitable work. Catholic religious orders, which by 1850 enrolled many more women than men, ran schools, hospitals, leper colonies, insane asylums, and old-age homes. New Catholic orders, especially for women, were established, and Catholic missionary activity overseas increased. Protestant women in Great Britain and the United States established Bible, missionary, and female reform societies by the hundreds. Chief among their concerns was prostitution, and many societies dedicated themselves to reforming "fallen women" and castigating men who visited prostitutes. As a pamphlet of the Boston Female Moral Reform Society explained, "Our mothers, our sisters, our daughters are sacrificed by the thousands every year on the altar of sin, and who are the agents in this work of destruction: Why, our fathers, our brothers, and our sons." Elizabeth Fry, an English Quaker minister, toured Europe in the 1830s helping set up institutions for female prisoners modeled on the school and manufacturing shop she had organized at Newgate Prison in London.

Catholics and Protestants alike promoted the temperance movement. In Ireland, England, the German states, and the United States, temperance societies organized to fight the "pestilence of hard liquor." The first societies had appeared in the United States as early as 1813, and by 1835 the American Temperance Society claimed 1.5 million members. The London-based British and Foreign Temperance Society, established in 1831, matched its American counterpart in its opposition to all alcohol. In the northern German states, temperance societies drew in the middle and working classes, Catholic as well as Protestant. Temperance advocates saw drunkenness as a sign of moral weakness and a threat to social order. Industrialists pointed to the loss of worker productivity, and efforts to promote temperance often reflected middle- and upper-class fears of the lower classes' lack of discipline. One German temperance advocate insisted, "One need not be a prophet to know that all efforts to combat the widespread and rapidly spreading

Temperance Broadsheet
This broadsheet from the 1830s linked the temperance movements in Ireland, where it was established in 1829, England, and Scotland. Queen Victoria became patron of the British and Foreign Temperance Society upon her accession to the throne in 1837. The account is melodramatic: drink leads to crime, disease, and even hanging.
Mansell Collection/Time Inc.

pauperism will be unsuccessful as long as the common man fails to realize that the principal source of his degradation and misery is his fondness of drink." Yet temperance societies also attracted working-class people who shared the desire for respectability.

Education and Reform of the Poor. Social reformers saw education as one of the main prospects for uplifting the poor and the working class. In addition to setting up Sunday schools, British churches founded organizations such as the National Society for the Education of the Poor in the Principles of the Established Church and the British and Foreign School Society. Most of these emphasized Bible reading. More secular in intent were the Mechanics Institutes, which provided education for workers in the big cities.

In 1833, the French government passed an education law that required every town to maintain a primary school, pay a teacher, and provide free education to poor boys. As the law's author, François Guizot, argued, "Ignorance renders the masses turbulent and ferocious." Girls' schools were optional, although hundreds of women taught at the primary level, most of them in private, often religious schools. Despite these efforts, only one out of every thirty children went to school in France, many fewer than in Protestant states such as Prussia, where 75 percent of children were in primary school by 1835. Popular education remained woefully undeveloped in most of eastern Europe. Peasants were specifically

excluded from the few primary schools in Russia, where Tsar Nicholas I blamed the Decembrist Revolt of 1825 on education.

Above all else, the elite sought to impose discipline and order on working people. Popular sports, especially blood sports such as cockfighting and bearbaiting, suggested a lack of control, and long-standing efforts in Great Britain to eliminate these recreations now gained momentum through organizations such as the Society for the Prevention of Cruelty to Animals. By the end of the 1830s, bullbaiting had been abandoned in Great Britain. "This useful animal," rejoiced one reformer in 1839, "is no longer tortured amidst the exulting yells of those who are a disgrace to our common form and nature." The other blood sports died out more slowly, and efforts in other countries generally lagged behind those of the British.

When private charities failed to meet the needs of the poor, governments often intervened. Great Britain sought to control the costs of public welfare by passing a new poor law in 1834, called by its critics the "Starvation Act." The law required that all able-bodied persons receiving relief be housed together in workhouses, with husbands separated from wives and parents from children. Workhouse life was designed to be as unpleasant as possible so that poor people would move on to regions of higher employment. British women from all social classes organized anti–poor law societies to protest the separation of mothers from their children in the workhouses.

Domesticity and the Subordination of Women.

Many women viewed charitable work as the extension of their domestic roles: they promoted virtuous behavior and morality and thus improved society. In one widely read advice book, Englishwoman Sarah Lewis suggested in 1839 that "women may be the prime agents in the regeneration of mankind." But women's social reform activities concealed a paradox. According to the set of beliefs that historians call the doctrine or ideology of domesticity, women should live their lives entirely within the domestic sphere; they should devote themselves to the home. The English poet Alfred, Lord Tennyson, captured this view in a popular poem published in 1847: "Man for the field and woman for the hearth; / Man for the sword and for the needle she. . . . All else confusion." Many believed that maintaining proper and distinct roles for men and women was critically important to maintaining social order in general.

Most women had little hope of economic independence. The notion of a separate, domestic sphere for women prevented them from pursuing higher education, work in professional careers, or participation in politics through voting or holding office, all activities deemed appropriate only to men. Laws everywhere codified the subordination of women. Many countries followed the model of Napoleon's Civil Code, which classified married women as legal incompetents along with children, the insane, and criminals. In Great Britain, which had no national law code, the courts upheld the legality of a husband's complete control. For example, in 1840 a court ruled that "there can be no doubt of the general dominion which the law of England attributes to the husband over the wife." In some countries, such as France and Austria, unmarried women enjoyed some rights over property, but elsewhere laws explicitly defined them as perpetual minors under paternal control.

Distinctions between men and women were most noticeable in the privileged classes. Whereas boys attended secondary schools, most middle- and upper-class girls still received their education at home or in church schools, where they were taught to be religious, obedient, and accomplished in music and languages. As men began to wear practical clothing—long trousers and short jackets of solid, often dark colors, no makeup (previously common for aristocratic men), and simply cut hair—women continued to dress for decorative effect, now with tightly corseted waists that emphasized the differences between female and male bodies. Middle- and upper-class women had long hair that required hours of brushing and pinning up, and they wore long, cumbersome skirts. Advice books written by women detailed the tasks that such women undertook in the home: maintaining household accounts, supervising servants, and organizing social events.

Scientists reinforced stereotypes. Once considered sexually insatiable, women were now described

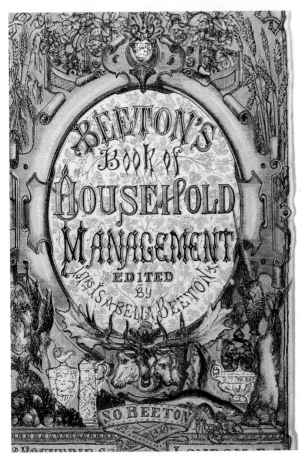

A Manual of Domesticity

Beeton's Book of Household Management *appeared in book form in 1861 after it had been published in* The Englishwoman's Domestic Magazine *by Mrs. Beeton's husband in the 1850s. In more than a thousand pages, it codified the domestic expectations of middle-class women. Mrs. Beeton, who died in childbirth at age twenty nine, advised women on almost every aspect of domestic life, from the management of servants to how to spend evenings at home (the lady does needlework; the man reads aloud from an edifying work).* Pix Producers, Inc.

as incapacitated by menstruation and largely uninterested in sex, an attitude that many equated with moral superiority. Thus was born the "Victorian woman," a figment of the largely male medical imagination. Physicians and scholars considered women mentally inferior. In 1839, Auguste Comte, an influential early French sociologist, wrote, "As for any functions of government, the radical inaptitude of the female sex is there yet more marked . . . and limited to the guidance of the mere family."

Some women denounced the ideology of domesticity; according to the English writer Ann Lamb, for example, "the duty of a wife *means* the obedience of a Turkish slave." Middle-class women who did not marry, however, had few options for earning a living; they often worked as governesses or ladies' companions for the well-to-do. Most lower-class women worked because of financial necessity; as the wives of peasants, workers, or shopkeepers, they had to supplement the family's meager income by working on the farm, in a factory, or in a shop. For them, domesticity might have been an ideal; rarely a reality. Families crammed into small spaces had no time or energy for "separate spheres."

Abuses and Reforms Overseas

Like the ideals of domesticity, the ideals of colonialism often conflicted with the reality of economic interests. In the first half of the nineteenth century, those economic interests changed as European colonialism underwent a subtle but momentous transformation. Colonialism became *imperialism*—a word coined only in the mid-nineteenth century—as Europeans turned their interest away from the plantation colonies of the Caribbean toward the new colonies in Asia and Africa. Whereas colonialism most often led to the establishment of settler colonies, direct rule by Europeans, the introduction of slave labor from Africa, and the wholesale destruction of indigenous peoples, imperialism usually meant more indirect forms of economic exploitation and political rule. Europeans still profited from their colonies, but now they also aimed to reform colonial peoples in their own image—when it did not conflict too much with their economic interests to do so.

Abolition of Slavery. Colonialism—as opposed to imperialism—rose and fell with the enslavement

Abolitionism

In 1807, Charles James Fox introduced a bill prohibiting British participation in the slave trade. This statue of a black slave kneeling in gratitude was included in Fox's memorial in Westminster Abbey. Although Parliament passed Fox's bill, other countries proved less eager to give up the slave trade, which actually expanded in the 1830s and 1840s. Britain abolished slavery in its colonies in 1833, France in 1848. Human bondage continued in the United States and Brazil until 1863 and 1888, respectively.
National Monuments Record © Crown Copyright NMR.

of black Africans. The antislavery movement spread slowly but decisively following the British withdrawal from the slave trade in 1807. The new Latin American republics abolished slavery in the 1820s and 1830s after they defeated the Spanish with armies that included many slaves. British missionary and evangelical groups condemned the conquest, enslavement, and exploitation of native

African populations and successfully blocked British annexations in central and southern Africa in the 1830s. British reformers finally obtained the abolition of slavery in the British Empire in 1833. Antislavery petitions to Parliament bore 1.5 million signatures, including those of 350,000 women on one petition alone. In France, the new government of Louis-Philippe took strong measures against clandestine slave traffic, virtually ending French participation during the 1830s. Slavery was abolished in the remaining French Caribbean colonies in 1848.

Slavery did not disappear immediately just because the major European powers had given it up. The transatlantic trade in slaves actually reached its peak numbers in the early 1840s. Human bondage continued unabated in Brazil, Cuba (still a Spanish colony), and the United States. Some American reformers supported abolition, but it remained a minority movement. Like serfdom in Russia, slavery in the Americas involved a quagmire of economic, political, and moral problems that worsened over time.

Historians debate the causes of the end of the African slave trade and of African slavery as a form of labor in the New World. Some argue that industrialization made slavery superfluous because with steam-driven machinery free labor proved itself more productive in the long run. Yet the British textile manufacturers relied heavily on imports of cotton from the southern slave states of the United States. Others place more emphasis on the antislavery campaign itself, arguing that slavery was incompatible with the humanitarian values of a reforming era. This explanation has trouble, however, in accounting for the fact that the French and Dutch governments also abolished slavery even though neither faced major public reform campaigns. Whatever the reason for abolition, slavery, and with it the old-style colonialism, was on the wane.

Economic and Political Imperialism. Despite the abolition of slavery, Britain and France had not lost interest in overseas colonies. Using the pretext of an insult to its envoy, France invaded Algeria in 1830 and after a long military campaign established political control over most of the country in the next two decades. By 1850, more than seventy thousand French, Italian, and Maltese colonists had settled there, often confiscating the lands of native peoples. The new French administration of the colony made

efforts to balance native and settler interests, however, and eventually France would not only incorporate Algeria into France but also try to assimilate its native population to French culture. France also imposed a protectorate government over the South Pacific island of Tahiti.

The British likewise increased their holdings overseas. Although they granted Canada greater self-determination in 1839, they annexed Singapore (1819) and New Zealand (1840). They also extended their control in India through the administration of the East India Company, a private group of merchants chartered by the British crown. The British educated a native elite to take over much of the day-to-day business of administering the country and used native soldiers to augment their military control. By 1850, only one in six soldiers serving Britain in India was European.

The East India Company also tried to establish a regular trade with China in opium, a drug long known for its medicinal uses but increasingly bought in China as a recreational drug. (See "Did You Know?," page 824.) The Chinese government did its best to keep the highly addictive drug away from its people, both by forbidding western merchants to venture outside the southern city of Guangzhou (Canton) and by banning the export of precious metals and the import of opium. These measures failed. By smuggling opium into China and bribing local officials, British traders

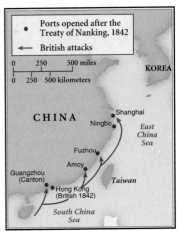

The First Opium War, 1839–1842

built up a flourishing market, and by the mid-1830s they were pressuring the British government to force an expanded opium trade on the Chinese. When in 1839 the Chinese authorities expelled British merchants from southern China, Britain retaliated by bombarding Chinese coastal cities. In 1842, it dictated to a defeated China the Treaty of Nanking, by which the British forced the opening of four more Chinese ports to Europeans, took sovereignty over the island of Hong Kong, received a substantial war indemnity, and were assured of a continuation of

Opium Addiction in Nineteenth-Century Britain

Great Britain fought two opium wars with China (1839–1842 and 1856–1858) that drew world attention to the problem of Chinese drug addiction. In Great Britain itself, the government did not regulate or restrict opium use until 1868. Pharmacists and grocers sold pills, lozenges, enemas, vinegars, and wines prepared with opium, which came from the heads of poppy plants imported first from the Ottoman Empire and, after 1750, from India. Tincture of opium (opium dissolved in alcohol), known as *laudanum*, was widely used as a sedative, and even children's opiates could be bought almost anywhere. Laudanum mixed with egg yolk was sold as a cure for hemorrhoids, and opiates were a popular remedy for toothache and diarrhea. Most doctors considered opium a good cure for delirium tremens, caused by alcohol abuse.

Death by overdose was a well-known phenomenon, but public opinion turned against the drug only when it became associated with abuse by the lower classes. Parliamentary inquiries in the 1830s denounced the use of opiates by working-class mothers, who gave their children Godfrey's Cordial or Street's Infant Quietness to make them sleep while they worked. Officials also worried that workers took opium and laudanum as a cheap substitute for alcohol, whose use was widely and loudly denounced by temperance societies. The concern about opiates followed from the general trend toward "reforming" lower-class behavior.

Well-known cases of addiction among writers and poets also attracted attention. The writer Thomas De Quincey stirred up controversy when he published his *Confessions of an English Opium-Eater* in 1821, but it was reissued many times during the nineteenth century. In the book, De Quincey discusses his and the romantic poet Samuel Taylor Coleridge's addiction. De Quincey calls himself the "pope" of the "true church" of opium and describes weaning himself from the drug in 1819 to escape the hallucinatory dreams

Opium Den in London ▶
This woodcut by Gustave Doré (c. 1870) shows that opium smoking persisted in Britain at least to the 1870s. Doré was a French book illustrator who came to London in 1869–1871 and produced illustrations of the poorer neighborhoods in the city. His taste for the grotesque is apparent in the figures watching the smokers. Doré also illustrated a book of Coleridge's poetry.
Print Collection, Miriam and Ira D. Wallach Division of Arts, Prints and Photographs. New York Public Library. Astor, Lenox and Tilden Foundation.

the opium trade. In this case, reform took a backseat to economic interest, despite the complaints of religious groups in Britain.

❖ The Ferment of Ideologies

Although reform organizations grew rapidly in the 1830s and 1840s, many Europeans found them insufficient to solve the problems created by industrialization and urbanization. They turned to movements inspired by the new political ideologies that had taken shape in the aftermath of the French Revolution. Liberals sought constitutional guarantees of rights and economic growth through free trade. Socialists developed new organizations to speak for the working classes and demand changes in the nature of work itself. But the most potent ideology—nationalism—looked past social problems to concentrate on achieving political autonomy and self-determination for groups identified by common languages and cultures rather than by class.

The Spell of Nationalism

Nationalists sought political autonomy for their ethnic group—a people linked by language and shared traditions. Although nationalism was still nascent in the first half of the nineteenth century among the peasants and workers of most countries, ethnic heritage was increasingly a major determinant of personal and political identity. Poles,

that haunted him. He had terrifying nightmares of living in China in houses in which tables and sofas turned into crocodiles multiplied ten thousand times. But he relapsed and soon took bigger and bigger doses right into the 1840s. De Quincey and Coleridge were only the best-known cases of opium addiction: Byron, Shelley, Elizabeth Barrett Browning, Walter Scott, and Charles Dickens all took opiates at one time or another, as did many leading doctors and preachers.

The history of opium use in the nineteenth century raises significant questions: why did British authorities condemn its use at home even while forcing opium on the Chinese? Why was lower-class use of opiates especially disturbing to officials? Why did so many writers experiment with the drug? The history of opium is a fascinating example of the West's interaction with the rest of the world: it was first cultivated by ancient Sumerians and passed on to the Assyrians, Babylonians, Egyptians, and then Greeks; the Portuguese brought it to Europe in the sixteenth century as part of their trade with China; and its modern derivative heroin is now the subject of worldwide smuggling and official regulation.

Sources: Virginia Berridge and Griffith Edwards, *Opium and the People: Opiate Use in Nineteenth-Century England* (New York: St. Martin's Press, 1981); Thomas De Quincey, *The Confessions of an English Opium-Eater and Other Essays* (London: Macmillan, 1924).

Italians, Germans, Irish, and Russians all pursued nationalist goals (Map 22.3).

Polish nationalism became more self-conscious after the collapse of the revolt in 1830 against Russian domination. Ten thousand Poles, mostly noble army officers and intellectuals, fled Poland in 1830 and 1831. Most of them took up residence in western European capitals, especially Paris, where they mounted a successful public relations campaign for worldwide support. Their intellectual hero was the poet Adam Mickiewicz (1798–1855), whose mystical writings portrayed the Polish exiles as martyrs of a crucified nation with an international Christian mission: "Your endeavors are for all men, not only for yourselves. You will achieve a new Christian civilization."

Mickiewicz formed a Polish Legion to fight for national restoration, but rivalries and divisions among the Polish nationalists prevented united action until 1846, when Polish exiles in Paris tried to launch a coordinated insurrection for Polish independence. Poles in Cracow responded, and in a manifesto the rebels proclaimed, "All free nations of the world are calling on us not to let the great principle of nationality fail." Plans for an uprising in the Polish province of Galicia in the Austrian Empire collapsed, however, when peasants instead revolted against their noble Polish masters. Slaughtering some two thousand aristocrats, a desperate rural population served the Austrian government's end by defusing the nationalist challenge. Class interests and national identity were not always the same.

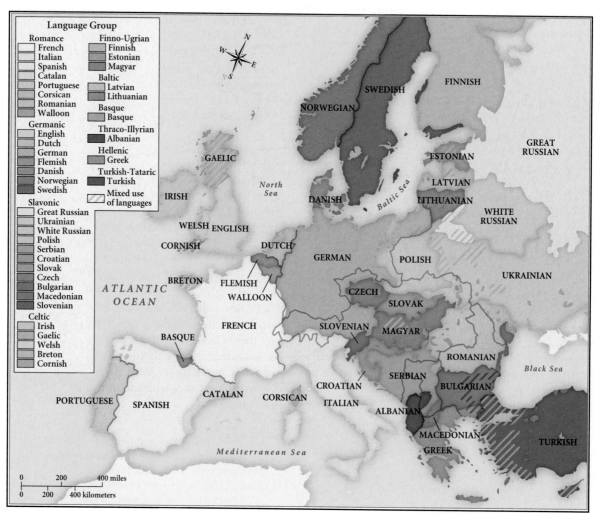

MAP 22.3 Languages of Nineteenth-Century Europe

Even this detailed map of linguistic diversity understates the number of different languages and dialects spoken in Europe. In Italy, for example, few Italians spoke Italian as their first language. Instead, they spoke local dialects such as Piedmontese or Ligurian, and some might speak better French than Italian if they came from the regions bordering France. The map does underline the inherent contradictions of nationalism in eastern Europe, where many linguistic regions incorporated other languages, and the result was constant conflict. But even in Spain, France, and Great Britain, linguistic diversity continued right up to the beginning of the 1900s.

One of those most touched by Mickiewicz's vision was Giuseppe Mazzini (1805–1872), a fiery Italian nationalist and republican journalist. Exiled in 1831 for his opposition to Austrian rule in northern Italy, Mazzini founded Young Italy, a secret society that attracted thousands with its message that Italy would touch off a European-wide revolutionary movement. The conservative order throughout Europe felt threatened by Mazzini's charismatic leadership and conspiratorial scheming, but he lacked both European allies against Austria and widespread support among the Italian masses.

Nationalism was an especially volatile issue in the Austrian Empire because Austria ruled over so many different nationalities (Map 22.3). The 1830s and 1840s saw the spread of nationalism among Magyars, Czechs, Slovaks, Serbs, Slovenes, Croats, and Romanians, in addition to Poles and Italians, all ethnic groups within the empire. Each of these peoples produced leaders who called for a cultural revival in language, literature, and education, as well as political rights. Scholars compiled dictionaries and created standard literary languages to replace peasant dialects; writers used the rediscovered vernacular instead of Latin or German; and historians glorified the national past. During the revolutions of 1848, however, it would become evident that these different ethnic groups disliked each other as much as they disliked their Austrian masters.

In the German states, teachers of German language, literature, law, and history embraced nationalism. German economic unification took a step forward with the foundation in 1834, under Prussian leadership, of the *Zollverein*, or "customs union," of most of the German states. Economist Friedrich List argued for external tariffs that would promote industrialization and cooperation across the boundaries of the German states so that an economically united Germany might compete with the rest of Europe. German nationalists sought a government uniting German-speaking peoples, but they could not agree on its boundaries. Austria was not part of the Customs Union: would the unified German state include both Prussia and the Austrian Empire? If it included Austria, what about the non-German territories of the Austrian Empire? And could the powerful and conservative kingdom of Prussia coexist in a unified German state with other, more liberal but smaller states? These questions would vex German history for decades to come.

In Russia, nationalism took the form of opposition to western ideas. Russian nationalists, or "Slavophiles" (lovers of the Slavs), opposed the "Westernizers," who wanted Russia to follow western models of industrial development and constitutional government. The Slavophiles favored maintaining rural traditions infused by the values of the Russian Orthodox church. Only a return to Russia's basic historical principles, they argued, could protect the country against the corrosion of rationalism and materialism. Slavophiles sometimes criticized the regime, however, because they believed the state exerted too much power over the church. The conflict between Slavophiles and Westernizers continues to shape Russian cultural and intellectual life to the present day.

Although nationalism was a more potent force in eastern Europe, nationalist movements arose in western Europe as well. The most significant of these was in Ireland. The Irish had struggled for centuries against English occupation, but Irish nationalists developed strong organizations only in the 1840s. In 1842, a group of writers founded the Young Ireland movement that aimed to recover Irish history and preserve the Gaelic language (spoken by at least one-third of the peasantry). Daniel O'Connell (1775–1847), a Catholic lawyer and landowner who sat in the British House of Commons, hoped to force the British Parliament to repeal the Act of Union of 1801, which had made Ireland part of Great Britain. In 1843, London newspapers reported "monster meetings" that drew crowds of as many as 300,000 people in support of repeal of the union. In response the British government arrested O'Connell and convicted him of conspiracy. Although his sentence was overturned, O'Connell withdrew from politics, partly because of a terminal brain disease. More radical leaders, who preached insurrection against the English, replaced him.

Liberalism in Economics and Politics

Nationalism overshadowed liberalism in eastern Europe, but liberalism had a strong base in the industrializing countries of western Europe. British liberals emphasized free markets, in part because they already enjoyed constitutional guarantees and in part because British industry no longer needed direct government protection. On the continent, liberals gave priority to constitutional reform. Free trade was in fact unthinkable in most other European countries because the British, dominant in technology and industrial production, could swamp rivals unprotected by tariffs.

British liberals wanted government to limit its economic role to maintaining the currency, enforcing contracts, and financing major enterprises like the military and the railroads. As historian and member of Parliament Thomas Macaulay (1800–1859) explained in 1830:

Our rulers will best promote the improvement of the nation by strictly confining themselves to their own legitimate duties, by leaving capital to find its most lucrative course, commodities their fair price, industry and intelligence their natural reward, idleness and folly their natural punishment, by maintaining peace, by defending property, by diminishing the price of law, and by observing strict economy in every department of the State.

Liberals of the 1830s sought to lower or eliminate British tariffs, especially through repeal of the Corn Laws, which benefited landowners by preventing the import of cheap foreign grain. They also advocated noninterference in employer-employee relations. This hands-off policy caused workers to feel ambivalent about liberalism: although food would cost less if tariffs on grain imports were cut, they would face unemployment and low wages should the government not protect them from their employers.

Liberals had widely supported the Reform Bill of 1832, hoping to gain more votes in Parliament for their economic program. When landholders in the House of Commons thwarted efforts to lower grain tariffs, two Manchester cotton manufacturers set up an Anti–Corn Law League. They appealed to the middle classes against the landlords, whom they labeled "a bread-taxing oligarchy" and "blood-sucking vampires," and attracted working-class backing by promising lower food prices. The league established local branches, published newspapers and the journal *The Economist* (founded in 1843 and now one of the world's most influential periodicals), and campaigned in elections. They eventually won the support of the Tory prime minister Sir Robert Peel, whose government repealed the Corn Laws in 1846.

Unlike their British counterparts, continental liberals focused on political, not economic, reform. Landowners, iron and steel manufacturers, and sugar interests fiercely resisted a French free-trade association founded in 1845. Liberals on the continent did not oppose a strong state or state intervention in the economy; they usually supported freeing internal trade while maintaining tariffs against imports.

Before 1848, continental liberals failed to win political reforms, a failure that opened the way to more radical groups. In France, Louis-Philippe's government brutally repressed working-class and republican insurrections in Lyon and Paris in the early 1830s and forced the republican opposition underground. But the French king's increasingly restrictive governments also thwarted liberals' hopes for reforms by suppressing many political organizations and reestablishing censorship. The

regime antagonized all manner of opponents: supporters of the old monarchy, nostalgic Bonapartists, die-hard republicans, and newly organizing workers and artisans.

Repression muted criticism in most other European states as well. Nevertheless, the rulers of Prussia, the smaller German states, and the Austrian Empire all encountered reform movements. In the pockets of industrialization in those countries, industrialists wanted more political clout. Metternich's government allowed liberal societies to form; indeed, in the Austrian Empire even some state bureaucrats favored economic liberalism, especially university-trained middle-class officials. Members of the societies scrutinized British institutions and economic writings, hoping to apply their ideas at home. The British example occasionally attracted noble landowners, as the remarkable career of the Hungarian count Stephen Széchenyi (1791–1860) illustrates. As an army officer, Széchenyi had spent years abroad, where he had come into contact with British liberalism. Back in Hungary, he introduced British agricultural techniques on his own lands and wrote books criticizing the social system. He advocated eliminating seigneurial burdens and equalizing taxation. In the 1830s, he helped establish projects to start up steamboat traffic on the Danube, to import machinery and technicians for steam-driven textile factories, and to construct Hungary's first railway line, from Budapest to Vienna.

In the 1840s, however, Széchenyi's efforts paled before those of the flamboyant Magyar nationalist Lajos Kossuth (1802–1894). After spending four years in prison for sedition, Kossuth grabbed every opportunity to publicize American democracy and British political liberalism, all in a fervent nationalist spirit. In 1844, he founded the Protective Association, whose members bought only Hungarian products; to Kossuth, boycotting Austrian goods was crucial to ending "colonial dependence" on Austria. Born of a lesser landowning family without a noble title, Kossuth did not hesitate to attack "the cowardly selfishness of the landowner class."

Even in Russia, stereotyped in the West as corrupt, lifeless, and dominated by "regimented Tatars," signs of liberal, even socialist, opposition appeared in the 1830s and 1840s. Small "circles" of young noblemen serving in the army or bureaucracy met in cities, especially Moscow, to discuss the latest western ideas and to criticize the Russian state: "The world is undergoing a transformation, while we vegetate in our hovels of wood and clay," wrote one. Out of these groups came such future revolutionaries as Alexander Herzen (1812–1870), described by the police as "a daring free-thinker, extremely dangerous to society." Tsar Nicholas I (r. 1825–1855) banned Western liberal writings as well as all books about the United States. He sent nearly ten thousand people a year into exile in Siberia as punishment for their political activities.

Socialism and the Early Labor Movement

Socialism had many variants in the 1830s and 1840s, but all railed against the inequalities caused by industrialization and considered liberalism an inadequate response. Socialists envisioned a future society in which workers would share a harmonious, cooperative, and prosperous life. They built on the theoretical and practical ideas laid out in the early nineteenth century by Count Henri de Saint-Simon, Charles Fourier, and Robert Owen, whose moralistic reform fervor they shared. They saw the positive potential of industrialization and hoped that economic planning and working-class organization would solve the problems caused by industrial growth, including the threat of increasingly mechanical, unfeeling social relations.

Socialism and Women. Given the focus on reconstructing social relationships, women not surprisingly participated actively in the socialist movements of the day, even though socialist men often shared the widespread prejudice against women's political activism. In Great Britain many women joined the Owenites and helped form cooperative societies and unions. They defended women's working-class organizations against the complaints of men in the new societies and trade unions. As one woman wrote, "Do not say the unions are only for men . . . 'tis a wrong impression, forced on our minds to keep us slaves!" Women's influence in the Owenite movement helped turn it toward community experimentation. Socialism no longer concentrated exclusively on work and consumer organization; Owenites now became interested in free religious thought, women's rights, marriage reform, and popular education. Rousing speakers such as Emma Martin (1812–1851) forcefully put the case: "One great evil is the depraved

and ignorant condition of woman; this evil can only be removed by Socialism." Martin's speeches often stirred turbulent opposition as clergymen urged their congregations to shout her down. Occasionally, she was jeered, chased, and even stoned by mobs, so much did her ideas and very presence challenge conventional expectations.

The French activist Flora Tristan (1801–1844) devoted herself to reconciling the interests of male and female workers. She had seen the "frightful reality" of London's poverty and made a reputation reporting on British working conditions. Tristan published a stream of books and pamphlets urging male workers to address women's unequal status, arguing that "the emancipation of male workers is *impossible* so long as women remain in a degraded state." Influenced by Fourier and Owen, Tristan advocated a Universal Union of Men and Women Workers and proposed workers' palaces to educate children and care for aged and injured laborers. Despite political harassment, she traveled around France speaking out for her beliefs and attempting to organize workers.

Collectivists and Communists. Tristan's advocacy of working-class associations reflected a general trend within socialism, even though most male socialists ignored her plea for women's participation. The French socialist Louis Blanc (1811–1882) explained the importance of working-class associations in *Organization of Labor* (1840), which deeply influenced the French labor movement. Similarly, Pierre-Joseph Proudhon (1809–1865) urged workers to form producers' associations so that the workers could control the work process and eliminate profits made by capitalists. His 1840 book *What Is Property?* argues that property is theft: labor alone is productive, and rent, interest, and profit unjust.

After 1840, some socialists began to call themselves "communists," emphasizing their desire to replace private property by communal, collective ownership. The Frenchman Étienne Cabet (1788–1856) first used the word *communist*. In 1840, he published *Travels in Icaria*, a novel describing a communist utopia in which a popularly elected dictatorship efficiently organized work, reduced the workday to seven hours, and made work tasks "short, easy, and attractive."

French socialist ideas circulated throughout Europe, from Belgium and the German states to

Russia. They evoked most response in areas of incipient industrialization where artisans and workers felt intensely threatened by the prospect of change. The German tailor Wilhelm Weitling (1808–1871) developed an influential variant of socialism that had deeply religious overtones. His book *Guarantees of Harmony and Freedom* (1842) argues for a communal society but also emphasizes faith as necessary to life. In his view, "Jesus, too, was a communist." Weitling made a profound impression on workers' societies in the western German states.

Out of the churning of socialist ideas of the 1840s emerged two men whose collaboration would change the definition of socialism and remake it into an ideology that would shake the world for the next 150 years. Karl Marx (1818–1883) and Friedrich Engels (1820–1895) seemed unlikely revolutionaries. Both were the sons of prosperous German-Jewish families that had converted to Christianity. Marx studied philosophy at the University of Berlin and then edited a liberal newspaper until the Prussian government suppressed it. He left for Paris, where he met Engels. While working in the offices of his wealthy family's cotton manufacturing interests in Manchester, England, Engels had been shocked into writing *The Condition of the Working Class in England in 1844* (1845), a sympathetic depiction of industrial workers' dismal lives. In Paris, where German and eastern European intellectuals could pursue their political interests more freely than at home, Marx and Engels threw themselves into organizing German workers living outside the German states. Marx read voraciously, especially histories of the French Revolution, and promptly earned a reputation as a fearsome critic of other socialists and would-be reformers. He attacked Weitling, destroyed much of his influence, and set up the Communist League, in whose name he and Engels published the *Communist Manifesto* (1848). It eventually became the touchstone of Marxist and communist revolution all over the world. In declaring himself a communist, Marx wanted to differentiate his ideology from that of what he called "utopian socialists," whom he considered mere fanciful dreamers.

Negligible as was Marx's and Engels's influence in the 1840s, they had already begun their lifework of scientifically understanding the "laws" of capitalism and fostering revolutionary organizations. Their principles and analysis of history were in place: communists, the *Manifesto* declared, must aim for "the downfall of the bourgeoisie [capitalist class] and the ascendancy of the proletariat [working class], the abolition of the old society based on class conflicts and the foundation of a new society without classes and without private property." Unlike many utopian socialists, Marx and Engels embraced industrialization because they believed it would eventually bring on the proletarian revolution and lead inevitably to the abolition of exploitation, private property, and class society.

Working-Class Organization. Socialism accompanied, and in some places incited, an upsurge in working-class organization in western Europe. British workers founded cooperative societies, local trade unions, and so-called friendly societies for mutual aid, associations that frightened the middle classes. A newspaper exclaimed in 1834, "The trade unions are, we have no doubt, the most dangerous institutions that were ever permitted to take root."

Even when not unionized, British workers joined in the political campaigns of the huge Chartist movement. Called *Chartism* because its members endorsed a document known as the People's Charter, the new movement brought together thousands of workers, poor people, and middle-class radicals who wanted a democratic government. They demanded universal manhood suffrage, vote by secret ballot, equal electoral districts, annual elections, and the elimination of property qualifications for and the payment of stipends to members of Parliament. They denounced their opponents as seeking "to keep the people in social slavery and political degradation." Many women took part by founding female political unions, setting up Chartist Sunday schools, organizing boycotts of unsympathetic shopkeepers, and joining Chartist temperance associations. Nevertheless, the People's Charter refrained from calling for woman suffrage because the movement's leaders feared that doing so would alienate potential supporters.

The Chartists organized a massive campaign during 1838 and 1839, with large public meetings, fiery speeches, and torchlight parades. Presented with petitions for the People's Charter signed by more than a million people, the House of Commons refused to act. In response to this rebuff from middle-class liberals, the Chartists allied themselves in the 1840s with working-class strike movements in the manufacturing districts and associated with various European revolutionary movements. But at the same time they—like their British and continental allies—distanced themselves from women workers. Chartists complained that workingwomen undermined men's manhood, taking men's jobs and turning the men into "women-men" or "eunuchs." Continuing agitation and organization prepared the way for a last wave of Chartist demonstrations in 1848.

Continental workers were less well organized because trade unions and strikes were illegal everywhere except Great Britain. Nevertheless, artisans and skilled workers in France formed mutual aid societies that provided insurance, death benefits, and education. Workers in new factories rarely organized, but artisans in the old trades, such as the silk workers of Lyon, France, created societies to resist mechanization and wage cuts.

The new workers' press, such as the Saint-Simonian *People's Beehive* (1839), spread the ideas of socialist harmony and economic reform among the working classes. In eastern and central Europe, however, socialism and labor organization—like liberalism—had less impact than in western Europe. Guild-based organizations survived in the German states, for example, but cooperative societies and workers' newspapers did not appear until 1848. Farther east, the working classes were even smaller, and labor organizing reached few people.

The New Historical Imagination

In an age of competing ideologies, every ideology offered its own reading of history as a way to buttress its analysis of the direction change should take. Nationalism, in particular, fostered an enthusiasm for history, because history substantiated claims for a common national identity. German nationalists, for example, avidly read such massive books as Friedrich C. Schlosser's eighteen-volume *General History for the German People* (1844–1856). In Great Britain the equally famous histories by Thomas Macaulay described the British people as "the greatest and most highly civilized people that the world ever saw." Macaulay aimed to broaden history to include everyday life as well as politics, war, and diplomacy.

History entered the lifeblood of literature and painting as well. Romanticism had given history a special glamour, opening the way for a commercially successful genre, the historical novel. Readers devoured novels like Alexandre Dumas's *The Three Musketeers* (1844), set in the reign of Louis XIII in the 1620s. Dumas, the grandson of a Haitian slave, recounts the adventures of four soldiers who valiantly serve the queen of France and foil the plots of Cardinal Richelieu. Governments appreciated the value of paintings with a historical theme in reinforcing their own legitimacy. To link himself to the growing cult of Napoleon, for example, Louis-Philippe commissioned four paintings of the emperor's victories for the new Gallery of Battles at Versailles, now transformed into a museum. This effort culminated in 1840 when the government, led by the new prime minister Adolphe Thiers (himself a noted historian of the French Revolution), arranged to return Napoleon's ashes to the Invalides church in Paris. Although the spectacular public funeral showed Louis-Philippe's eagerness to establish his connections to Napoleonic history, it would not succeed in its goal of stifling demands for reform.

Nationalism and the new historical imagination also influenced musical romanticism. The Polish composer and pianist Frédéric Chopin (1810–1849) became a powerful champion in the West for the cause of his native land, with music that incorporated Polish folk rhythms and melodies. Opera, long a favorite with the public, experienced an abrupt transformation about 1830. Before this time, operatic plots had generally derived from classical mythology or had been contemporary social satires; now the public demanded passionate tragedy, usually with a picturesque medieval or Renaissance setting. The operatic portrayal of heroines as sexually pure, noble-minded, emotionally vulnerable, and tragic victims mirrored the redefinition of women's character in contemporary middle-class opinion.

Alongside the burst of interest in the political and artistic uses of history came a new trend in historical writing that valued professional training above literary skill. The foremost practitioner of this new scholarship was Leopold von Ranke (1795–1886), a professor at the University of Berlin who taught many of the leading German historians of the nineteenth century. Ranke tried to understand the past objectively, on its own terms, rather than as lessons for present-day purposes. He organized small seminars of young men for the close study of documents. His reliance on source materials instead of legend or tradition helped reshape the study of history into a discipline based on critical methods. The most immediate response to this approach came in the history of religion. In 1835, the German scholar David Friedrich Strauss published the two-volume *Life of Jesus*, in which he argues that the Gospels were not history but only imaginative stories that reflected Jewish myths in Roman times. Widely reprinted, Strauss's book caused a storm of controversy. In the 1840s, a series of new books followed Strauss's lead; some of them ended with proclamations that Jesus never existed.

The study of geology prompted the examination of other religious doctrines. A three-volume work published in 1830–1833 by the British geologist Charles Lyell (1797–1875) with the bland title *Principles of Geology* ignited debate. Lyell argues that the earth is much older than the dating of the biblical story of creation (assumed by many to be 4004 B.C.). Questioning religious assumptions enraged those whose beliefs rested on biblical certainty. Un-

der Lyell's influence, Charles Darwin (1809–1882) would begin to sketch out the essentials of his theory of evolution by natural selection. Geology, opera, nationalist histories, and historical novels all helped foster new forms of historical sensibility. But a sense of history did nothing to quiet the storm of ideological discontent. Liberals, socialists, and nationalists all vied for public support for their answers to the political and social questions raised by industrialization, urbanization, and the demand for national self-determination.

❖ The Revolutions of 1848

Food shortage, overpopulation, and unemployment helped turn ideological turmoil into revolution. In 1848, demonstrations and uprisings toppled governments, forced rulers and ministers to flee, and offered revolutionaries an opportunity to put liberal, socialist, and nationalist ideals into practice (Map 22.4). Of the major powers only Great Britain

MAP 22.4 The Revolutions of 1848
The attempts of rulers to hold back the forces of change collapsed suddenly in 1848 when once again the French staged a revolution that inspired many others in Europe. This time, cities all over central and eastern Europe joined in as the spirit of revolt inflamed one capital after another. Although all of these revolutions eventually failed because of social and political divisions, the sheer scale of rebellion forced rulers to reconsider their policies.

and Russia remained untouched, the former because it already had constitutional government and the latter because its autocratic government had stamped out all signs of dissent. In the end, all the revolutions failed because liberal, socialist, and nationalist movements quarreled with one another, leaving an opening for rulers and their armies to return to power.

The Hungry Forties

In 1845, an airborne blight destroyed Europe's potato crop. The next year, other crops failed when drought gripped southern Europe and excessive rain fell on northern Europe. Farmers who could produce something got higher prices, but marginal cultivators and farm laborers starved. Urban workers lost their jobs because rural people could no longer afford industrial goods. At the same time, workers faced escalating food prices. (In the best of times urban workers paid 50 to 80 percent of their income for a diet consisting largely of bread; now even bread was beyond their means.) An aristocrat from Silesia, a province in Prussia, described the political consequences: "As long as there was a sure, and honest livelihood, none of the Silesian weavers paid any attention to communistic agitation . . . despair was aroused among them by hunger."

Overpopulation hastened famine in some places, especially Ireland, where even in years of good harvest the food supply had barely kept pace with explosive population growth. Potatoes were the principal food for Irish peasants, and the poor ate little else. Potatoes yielded more food value per acre than grains: a family of four might live off one acre of potatoes but would require at least two acres of grain. As potato cultivation increased, greater food production spurred population growth as peasants, assured of a food supply, had more children. Irish peasants often sought security in large families, trusting that their children might help work the land and care for them in old age. Thus Irish population growth surpassed that of the rest of Europe. By the 1840s, Ireland was especially

The Potato Blight and Irish Famine
In this painting by Daniel McDonald, The Discovery of the Potato Blight *(1852), a family is shown digging up its potato crop only to find that the potatoes had rotted from blight. This discovery spelled disaster for this family and thousands like it. The blight spores were airborne. After they landed on potato plants they killed the leaves, which fell to the ground. The spores were washed into the earth, where they infected the underground tubers. The crop could even look normal and still be infected.*

vulnerable to the potato blight, which returned in 1846, 1848, and 1851. Out of a population of 8 million, as many as 1 million people died of starvation and disease. Corpses lay unburied on the sides of roads, and whole families were found dead in their cottages, half-eaten by dogs. Hundreds of thousands emigrated to England, the United States, and Canada.

Throughout Europe, famine jeopardized social peace. In age-old fashion, rumors circulated about large farmers selling to other localities or hoarding grain to drive up prices. Believing that governments should ensure fair prices that would make food accessible, crowds took over village and town streets to protest, often attacking markets or bakeries. In villages across Europe they threatened officials with retribution. "If the grain merchants do not cease to take away grains . . . we will go to your homes and cut your throats and those of the three bakers . . . and burn the whole place down." So went one threat from French villagers in the hungry winter of 1847. Although harvests improved in 1848, by then many people had lost their land or become hopelessly indebted, and they strongly resented those who had prospered from high prices.

Had the crisis affected only the food supply, rural and urban people might have found outwork such as spinning, weaving, or other artisan-type production to make up for what the land failed to yield. But high food prices also drove down the demand for manufactured goods resulting in increased unemployment. Industrial workers' wages had been rising—in the German states, for example, wages rose an average of 5.5 percent in the 1830s and 10.5 percent in the 1840s—but the cost of living rose about 16 percent each decade, canceling out wage increases. Seasonal work and regular unemployment were already the norm when the crisis of the late 1840s exacerbated the uncertainties of urban life. "The most miserable class that ever sneaked its way into history" is how Friedrich Engels described underemployed and starving workers in 1847.

Another French Revolution

The specter of hunger tarnished the image of established rulers and amplified voices critical of them. Louis-Philippe's government had blocked all moves for electoral reform, and, beginning in 1847,

opposition leaders in France sponsored political meetings under the cover of banquets at which they demanded liberalization of Louis-Philippe's regime. In February 1848, the banquet campaign turned into a revolution as the people of Paris took to the streets. They demanded and got the establishment of a republic, which soon came under pressure from those who favored greater democracy and even socialism. In June 1848, the republican army crushed an uprising by workers in Paris. In the midst of this class conflict and political turmoil, an overwhelmingly rural electorate chose as president Louis-Napoleon Bonaparte, nephew of Emperor Napoleon. His election marked the end of the revolution of 1848 in France and the opening of a new period in French history.

The February Revolution. Demonstrations began on the rainy, chilly morning of February 22, 1848. At first the police and the army dispersed the students, workers, and the unemployed who gathered to build barricades. The next day, however, the crowd came back in a fighting mood. Forty or fifty people died when panicky soldiers opened fire on the crowd. On February 24, faced with fifteen hundred barricades and a furious populace, Louis-Philippe abdicated and fled to England. A hastily formed provisional government declared France a republic once again. Its most noteworthy leader was Alphonse de Lamartine (1790–1869), a romantic poet, eloquent orator, and historian of the French Revolution. Lamartine's conviction that he was destined to lead the people enabled him to face down the crowds who demanded immediate responses to hunger and unemployment.

The new republican government issued liberal reforms—an end to the death penalty for political crimes, the abolition of slavery in the colonies, and freedom of the press—and agreed to introduce universal adult male suffrage despite misgivings about political participation by peasants and unemployed workers. For middle-class liberals, these measures more than sufficed. Many in the lower classes, however, wanted more. To address the gnawing problem of unemployment and appease the one socialist in the provisional government, Louis Blanc, the government allowed Paris officials to organize a system of "national workshops" to provide the unemployed with construction work and wages of two francs a day. This was not a living wage, but the workshops did attract many desperately poor men to Paris. When women protested their exclusion, the city set up a few workshops for women workers, with even lower wages. To meet a mounting deficit, the provisional government then levied a 45 percent surtax on property taxes, alienating peasants and landowners.

The establishment of the republic politicized many segments of the population. Outside Paris, city after city announced support for the reforms and established similar workshops for the unemployed. Priests showed solidarity with the republic by blessing hundreds of liberty trees, reminders of the French Revolution of 1789. Scores of newspapers and political clubs inspired grassroots democratic fervor. Meeting in concert halls, theaters, and government auditoriums, clubs became a regular evening attraction for the citizenry. Women also formed clubs, published women's newspapers, and demanded representation in national politics. In a twist on domestic ideology, some argued that political activity followed naturally from motherhood. "This holy function of motherhood," one activist claimed, "gives women the right to intervene not only in all acts of civic life, but also in all acts of political life."

The June Days. Street-corner activism alarmed middle-class liberals and conservatives. To ensure its control, the republican government paid some unemployed youths to join a mobile guard with its own uniforms and barracks. Tension between the government and the workers in the national workshops rose. Soon competing groups paraded for their causes in massive demonstrations. The communist Étienne Cabet led one demonstration of 150,000 workers. Faced with rising radicalism in Paris and other big cities, the voters elected a largely conservative National Assembly in April 1848; most of the deputies chosen were middle-class professionals or landowners, who favored either a restoration of the monarchy or a moderate republic.

The Assembly immediately appointed a five-man executive committee to run the government and pointedly excluded known supporters of workers' rights. Suspicious of all demands for rapid change, the deputies dismissed a petition to restore divorce and voted down women's suffrage, 899 to 1.

The Vésuviennes, 1848

This lithograph satirizes women's political ambitions, referring to a women's club named the Vésuviennes (after the recent eruption of Mount Vesuvius in Italy). The artist implies that women have left their children at home in the care of their hapless husbands so that they can actively participate in politics. Some scholars claim that this particular club was invented by the police to ridicule women. Meetings of feminist clubs were often disrupted by men hostile to their aims. Bibliothèque National de France.

When the numbers enrolled in the national workshops in Paris rocketed from a predicted 10,000 to 110,000, the government ordered the workshops closed to new workers, and on June 21 it directed that those already enrolled move to the provinces or join the army.

The workers of Paris responded to these measures on June 23 by taking to the streets in the tens of thousands. In the June Days, as the following week came to be called, the government summoned the army, the National Guard, and the newly recruited mobile guard to fight the workers. Provincial volunteers came to help put down the workers, who had been depicted to them as lazy ruffians intent on destroying order and property. One observer breathed a sigh of relief: "The Red Republic [red being associated with demands for socialism] is lost forever; all France has joined against it. The National Guard, citizens, and peasants from the remotest parts of the country have come pouring in." The republic's army crushed the workers; more than 10,000, most of them workers, were killed or injured, 12,000 were arrested, and 4,000 eventually were convicted and deported.

Louis-Napoleon Bonaparte. When the National Assembly adopted a new constitution calling for a presidential election in which all adult men could vote, the electorate chose Louis-Napoleon Bonaparte, nephew of the dead emperor. Lamartine's moment of glory had passed: he came in fifth with less than 18,000 votes. (Bonaparte got more than 5.5 million votes out of some 7.4 million cast.) Bonaparte had lived most of his life outside of France, and the leaders of the republic expected him to follow their tune. In uncertain times, the name promised something to everyone. Even many workers supported him because he had no connection with the blood-drenched June Days.

In reality, Bonaparte's election had spelled the end of the Second Republic, just as his uncle had dismantled the first one established in 1792. In 1852, on the forty-eighth anniversary of Napoleon I's coronation as emperor, Louis-Napoleon declared himself Emperor Napoleon III. (Napoleon I's son died and never became Napoleon II, but Napoleon III wanted to create a sense of legitimacy and so used the Roman numeral III.) Political division and class conflict had proved fatal to the Second Republic. Although the revolution of 1848 never had a period of terror like that in 1793–1794, it nonetheless ended in similar fashion, with an authoritarian government that tried to play monarchists and republicans off against each other.

Nationalist Revolution in Italy

Italian nationalists hoped to unite a diverse collection of territories: the kingdom of Piedmont-Sardinia, ruled by King Charles Albert; Lombardy and Venetia under Austrian control; the principalities

Uprising in Milan, 1848
In this painting by an unknown artist, Fighting at the Tosa Gate, *the Milanese are setting up barricades to oppose their Austrian rulers. Whole families are involved. The flag of green, white, and red is the flag of the Cisalpine Republic of the Napoleonic period whose capital was Milan. The three colors would be incorporated into the national flag of Italy after unification.*
Scala/Art Resource, NY.

of central Italy, including the Papal states; and the kingdom of the Two Sicilies, comprising Naples and Sicily and governed by a branch of the Bourbons.

The Divisions of Italy, 1848

When Giuseppe Verdi's opera *Macbeth* was performed in Venice in 1847, audiences leaped to their feet at the words "The fatherland has been betrayed . . . brothers we must hasten to save it." In January 1848, a revolt broke out in Palermo, Sicily, against the Bourbon ruler. Then came the electrifying news of the February Revolution in Paris. In Milan a huge nationalist demonstration quickly degenerated into battles between Austrian forces and armed demonstrators. In Venice an uprising drove out the Austrians. Peasants in the south occupied large landowners' estates. Across central Italy revolts mobilized the poor and unemployed against local rulers. Peasants demanded more land, and artisans and workers called for higher wages, restrictions on the use of machinery, and unemployment relief.

But class divisions and regional differences stood in the way of national unity. Property owners, businessmen, and professionals wanted liberal reforms and national unification under a conservative regime; intellectuals, workers, and artisans dreamed of democracy and social reforms. Some nationalists favored a loose federation; others wanted a monarchy under Charles Albert of Piedmont-Sardinia; still others urged rule by the pope; a few shared Mazzini's vision of a republic with a strong central government. Many leaders of national unification spoke Italian only as a second language; most Italians spoke regional dialects.

As king of the most powerful Italian state, Charles Albert inevitably played a central role. After some hesitation caused by fears of French intervention, he led a military campaign against Austria. It soon failed, partly because of dissension over goals and tactics among the nationalists. Determined republicans in Milan, for example, wanted an independent Lombard republic, not union with conservative, monarchical Piedmont. The pope refused to join the war on Austria, and Charles Albert proved unwilling to press beyond his initial successes.

Although Austrian troops defeated the rebels in the north in the summer of 1848, democratic and nationalist forces prevailed at first in the south. In the fall the Romans drove the pope from the city and declared Rome a republic. For the next few months republican leaders, such as Mazzini and Giuseppe Garibaldi (1807–1882), congregated in Rome to organize the new republic. These efforts eventually faltered when foreign powers intervened. The new president of republican France, Louis-Napoleon Bonaparte, sent an expeditionary force to secure the papal throne for Pius IX. Mazzini and Garibaldi fled. Although revolution had been defeated in Italy, the memory of the Roman republic and the commitment to unification remained, and they would soon emerge again with new force.

Revolt and Reaction in Central Europe

News of the February Revolution in Paris sparked popular demonstrations in the "three Germanies"—Prussia, Austria, and the "third Germany," comprising the other thirty-six kingdoms, duchies, and city-states included in the German Confederation of 1815. "My heart beat with joy. The monarchy had fallen. Only a little blood had been shed for such a high stake, and the great watchwords Liberty, Equality, Fraternity were again inscribed on the banner of the movement." So responded one Frankfurt woman to Louis-Philippe's overthrow. Most German rulers lost their nerve in the face of popular revolts in March 1848. But revolutionaries did not succeed in filling the vacuum. Middle-class leaders feared lower-class demands for democracy and social reform and were quickly distracted by nationalist aspirations and ethnic conflicts. In the end, all the rulers returned to power.

The "Three Germanies," 1848

Revolutions of 1848

1848

January Uprising in Palermo, Sicily

February Revolution in Paris; proclamation of republic

March Insurrections in Vienna, German cities, Milan, and Venice; autonomy movement in Hungary; Charles Albert of Piedmont-Sardinia declares war on Austrian Empire

May Frankfurt parliament opens

June Austrian army crushes revolutionary movement in Prague; June Days end in defeat of workers in Paris

July Austrians defeat Charles Albert and Italian forces

November Insurrection in Rome

December Francis Joseph becomes Austrian emperor; Louis-Napoleon elected president in France

1849

February Rome declared a republic

April Frederick William of Prussia rejects crown of united Germany offered by Frankfurt parliament

July Roman republic overthrown by French intervention

August Russian and Austrian armies combine to defeat Hungarian forces

Prussia and the Frankfurt Parliament. At first, the German revolutions looked much like the French, with different social groups combining in giant marches to demand political liberalization. The Prussian army's efforts to clear the square in front of Berlin's royal palace on March 18, 1848, provoked panic and street fighting around hastily assembled barricades. The next day the crowd paraded wagons loaded with dead bodies under King Frederick William IV's window, forcing him to salute the victims killed by his own army. In a state of near collapse, the king promised to call an assembly to draft a constitution and adopted the German nationalist flag of black, red, and gold.

The goal of German unification soon took precedence over social reform or constitutional changes within the separate states. One noble official wrote, "The lightning has struck, and Germany will not allow itself to be lulled back to sleep." In

March and April, most of the German states agreed to elect delegates to a federal parliament at Frankfurt that would attempt to unite Germany. Local princes and even the more powerful kings of Prussia and Bavaria seemed to totter. In Bavaria, students marched to the "Marseillaise" and called for a republic. Yet the revolutionaries' weaknesses soon became apparent. The eight hundred delegates to the Frankfurt parliament had little practical political experience: "a group of old women," one socialist called them; a "Professors Parliament" was the common sneer. These delegates had no access to an army, and they dreaded the demands of the lower classes for social reforms. Unemployed artisans and workers smashed machines; peasants burned landlords' records and occasionally attacked Jewish moneylenders; women set up clubs and newspapers to demand their emancipation from "perfumed slavery."

The advantage lay with the princes, who retained legal authority and control over the armed forces. The most powerful German states, Prussia and Austria, expected to determine whether and how Germany should unite. While the Frankfurt parliament laboriously prepared a liberal constitution for a united Germany—one that denied self-determination to Czechs, Poles, and Danes within its proposed German borders—the Prussian king Frederick William IV (r. 1840–1860) recovered his confidence. First his army crushed the revolution in Berlin in the fall of 1848. Prussian troops then intervened to help other local rulers put down the last wave of democratic and nationalist insurrections in the spring of 1849. When the Frankfurt parliament finally concluded its work, offering the emperorship of a constitutional, federal Germany to the king of Prussia, Frederick William contemptuously refused this "crown from the gutter."

Ethnic Divisions in the Austrian Empire. By the summer of 1848, the Austrian Empire had reached the verge of complete collapse. Just as Italians were driving the Austrians out of their lands in northern Italy and Magyar nationalists were demanding political autonomy for Hungary, on March 13, 1848, in Vienna, a student-led demonstration for political reform turned into rioting, looting, and machine-breaking. Metternich resigned, escaping to England in disguise. Emperor Ferdinand promised a constitution, an elected parliament, and the end of censorship. The beleaguered authorities in Vienna could not refuse Magyar demands for home rule, and Széchenyi and Kossuth both became ministers in the new Hungarian government. The Magyars were the largest ethnic group in Hungary but still did not make up 50 percent of the population, which included Romanians, Slovaks, Croats, and Slovenes who preferred Austrian rule to domination by local Magyars.

The ethnic divisions in Hungary foreshadowed the many political and social divisions that would doom the revolutionaries. Fears of peasant insurrection prompted the Magyar nationalists around Kossuth to abolish serfdom. This measure alienated the largest noble landowners. In Prague, Czech nationalists convened a Slav congress as a counter to the Germans' Frankfurt parliament and called for a reorganization of the Austrian Empire that would recognize the rights of ethnic minorities. Such assertiveness by non-German peoples provoked German nationalists to protest on behalf of German-speaking people in areas with a Czech or Magyar majority.

Revolution of 1848 in Eastern Europe
This painting by an unknown artist shows Ana Ipatescu leading a group of Romanian revolutionaries in Transylvania in opposition to Russian rule. The Transylvanian provinces of Moldavia and Walachia had been under Russian domination since the 1770s and occupied directly since 1829. In April 1848, local landowners began to organize meetings. Paris-educated nationalists spearheaded the movement, which demanded the end of Russian control and various legal and political reforms. By August the movement had split between those who wanted independence only and those who pushed for the end of serfdom and for universal manhood suffrage. In response, the Russians invaded Moldavia and the Turks moved into Walachia. By October the uprising was over. Russia and Turkey agreed to control the provinces jointly.
The Art Archive.

The Austrian government slowly took advantage of these divisions. To quell peasant discontent and appease liberal reformers, it abolished all remaining peasant obligations to the nobility in March 1848. Rejoicing country folk soon lost interest in the revolution. Class conflicts flared in Vienna, where the middle classes had little sympathy for the starving artisans and workers. The new Hungarian government alienated the other nationalities when it imposed the Magyar language on them. Similar divisions sapped national unity in the Polish and Czech lands of the empire.

Military force finally broke up the revolutionary movements. The first blow fell in Prague in June 1848; General Prince Alfred von Windischgrätz, the military governor, bombarded the city into submission when a demonstration led to violence (including the shooting death of his wife, watching from a window). After another uprising in Vienna a few months later, Windischgrätz marched 70,000 soldiers into the capital and set up direct military rule. In December the Austrian monarchy came back to life when the eighteen-year-old Francis Joseph (r. 1848–1916), unencumbered by promises extracted by the revolutionaries from his now feeble uncle Ferdinand, assumed the imperial crown after intervention by leading court officials. In the spring of 1849, General Count Joseph Radetsky defeated the last Italian challenges to Austrian power in northern Italy, and his army moved east, joining with Croats and Serbs to take on the Hungarian rebels. The Austrian army teamed up with Tsar Nicholas I, who marched into Hungary with more than 300,000 Russian troops. Hungary was put under brutal martial law. Széchenyi went mad, and Kossuth found refuge in the United States. Social conflicts and ethnic divisions weakened the revolutionary movements from the inside and gave the Austrian government the opening it needed to restore its position.

Aftermath to 1848

Although the revolutionaries of 1848 failed to achieve most of their goals, their efforts left a profound mark on the political and social landscape. Between 1848 and 1851, the French served a kind of republican apprenticeship that prepared the population for another, more lasting republic after 1870.

No French government could henceforth rule without extensive popular consultation. In Italy, the failure of unification did not stop the spread of nationalist ideas and the rooting of demands for democratic participation. In the three Germanies, the revolutionaries of 1848 turned nationalism from an idea of professors and writers into a popular enthusiasm. The very idea of a Frankfurt parliament and the insistence on brandishing a German national flag at demonstrations showed that German nationalism had become a practical reality. The initiation of artisans, workers, and journeymen into democratic clubs increased political awareness in the lower classes and helped prepare them for broader political participation. Almost all the German states had a constitution and a parliament after 1850. The spectacular failures of 1848 thus hid some important underlying successes.

The absence of revolution in 1848 was just as significant as its presence. No revolution occurred in Great Britain, the Netherlands, or Belgium, three places where industrialization and urbanization had developed most rapidly. In Great Britain the prospects for revolution actually seemed quite good: the Chartist movement took inspiration from the European revolutions in 1848 and mounted several gigantic demonstrations to force Parliament into granting all adult males the vote. But Parliament refused and no uprising occurred, in part because the government had already proved its responsiveness. The middle classes in Britain had been co-opted into the established order by the Reform Bill of 1832, and the working classes had won parliamentary regulation of children's and women's work.

The other notable exception to revolution among the great powers was Russia, where Tsar Nicholas I maintained a tight grip through police surveillance and censorship. The Russian schools, limited to the upper classes, taught Nicholas's three most cherished principles: autocracy (the unlimited power of the tsar), orthodoxy (obedience to the church in religion and morality), and nationality (devotion to Russian traditions). These provided no space for political dissent. Social conditions also fostered political passivity: serfdom continued in force and the slow rate of industrial and urban growth created little discontent.

For all the differences between countries, some developments touched all of them in similar manner.

The Crystal Palace, 1851

This color lithograph by George Baxter provides a good view of the exterior of the main building for the Exhibition of the Works of Industry of All Nations in London. The building was designed by Sir Joseph Paxton (1801–1865) to gigantic dimensions: 1,848 feet long by 456 feet wide; 135 feet high; 772,784 square feet of ground floor area covering no less than 18 acres.
© The Bridgeman Art Library International Ltd.

The Crystal Palace and the Colonies

This colored lithograph by Peter Mabuse offers a view of one of the colonial displays at the Crystal Palace exhibition of 1851. The tented room and ivory carved throne are meant to recall India, Britain's premier colony. In a sermon given on the occasion of the opening of the exhibition, Reverend George Clayton attributed Britain's national greatness to its colonial presence: "Great she [Britain] truly is—great in her trade and commerce—great in her laws and constitution—great in her freedom, both civil and religious—great in the power, the character, and the virtues of her queen . . . great in the resources of her wealth, in the number and extent of her colonial possessions—great in the multitude of her subjects—great in the moral and Christian bearing of a large proportion of her people—great in the cultivation of the mind and morals of the rising population of her inhabitants—great in the distribution of her Bibles, in her mission to the heathen, in the emancipation of the slave, and in the circulation of her countless tracts for the instruction of universal man."
© The Bridgeman Art Library International Ltd.

IMPORTANT DATES

1830–1832 Cholera epidemic sweeps across Europe

1830 France invades and begins conquest of Algeria

1831 British and Foreign Temperance Society established

1832 George Sand, *Indiana*

1833 Factory Act regulates work of children in Great Britain; abolition of slavery in the British Empire

1834 German customs union (*Zollverein*) established under Prussian leadership

1835 Belgium opens first continental railway built with state funds

1839 Beginning of Opium War between Britain and China; invention of photography

1841 Charles Dickens, *The Old Curiosity Shop* (1841)

1846 Famine strikes Ireland; Corn Laws repealed in England; peasant insurrection in Austrian province of Galicia

1847 Charlotte Brontë, *Jane Eyre* (1847)

1848 Last great wave of Chartist demonstration in Britain; Karl Marx and Friedrich Engels, *The Communist Manifesto*; revolutions of 1848 throughout Europe; abolition of slavery in French colonies; end of serfdom in Austrian Empire

1851 Crystal Palace exhibition in London

European states continued to expand their bureaucracies. For example, in 1750 the Russian government employed approximately 10,500 functionaries; a century later it needed almost 114,000. In Great Britain a swelling army of civil servants produced parliamentary studies on industrialization, foreign trade, and colonial profits, while new agencies such as the British urban police forces (10,000 strong in the 1840s) intruded increasingly in ordinary people's lives. States wanted to take children out of the fields and factories where they worked with their families and educate them. In some German cities the police reported people who cleared snow off their roofs after the permitted hour or smoked in the street. A few governments even prescribed the length of sermons.

Although much had changed, the aristocracy remained the dominant power almost everywhere. As army officers, aristocrats put down revolutionary forces. As landlords, they continued to dominate the rural scene and control parliamentary bodies. They also held many official positions in the state bureaucracies. One Italian princess explained, "There are doubtless men capable of leading the nation . . . but their names are unknown to the people, whereas those of noble families . . . are in every memory." Aristocrats kept their authority by adapting to change: they entered the bureaucracy and professions, turned their estates into moneymaking enterprises, and learned how to invest shrewdly.

The reassertion of conservative rule hardened gender definitions. Women everywhere had participated in the revolutions, especially in the Italian states, where they joined armies in the tens of thousands and applied household skills toward making bandages, clothing, and food. Schoolgirls in Prague had thrown desks and chairs out of windows and helped build students' barricades. Many women in Paris had supported the new republic and seized the occasion of greater political openness to demand women's rights, only to experience isolation as their claims were denied by most republican men. Men in the revolutions of 1848 almost always defined universal suffrage as a male right. When workingmen gained the vote and women did not, the notion of separate spheres penetrated even into working-class life: political participation became one more way to distinguish masculinity from femininity. As conservatives returned to power, all signs of women's political activism disappeared. The French feminist movement, the most advanced in Europe, fell apart after the June Days when the increasingly conservative republican government forbade women to form political clubs and arrested and imprisoned two of the most outspoken women leaders for their socialist activities.

In May 1851, Europe's most important female monarch presided over a midcentury celebration of peace and industrial growth that helped dampen the still-smoldering fires of revolutionary passion. Queen Victoria (r. 1837–1901), who herself promoted the notion of domesticity as women's sphere, opened the international Exhibition of the Works of Industry of All Nations in London on May 1. A monument of modern iron and glass architecture had been built to house the display; the building was more than a third of a mile long and so tall that it was built over the trees of its Hyde Park site. Soon

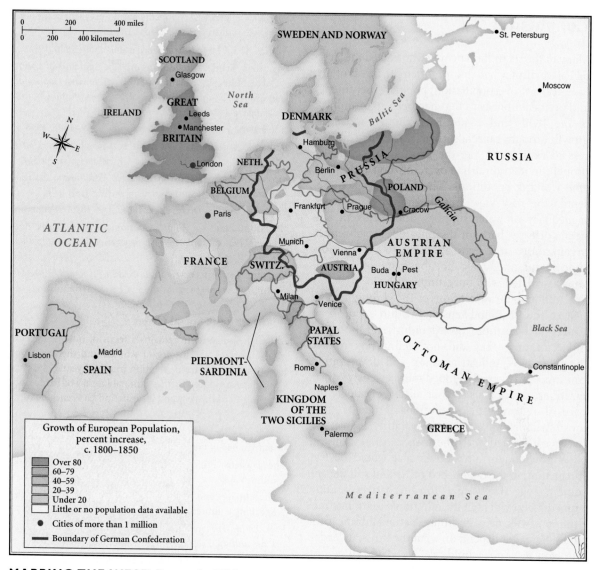

MAPPING THE WEST Europe in 1850

This map of population growth between 1800 and 1850 reveals important trends that would not otherwise be evident. Population growth correlated for the most part with industrialization; industrializing areas such as England, Belgium, and northern Italy also experienced great increases in population compared with places with little or no industrialization, such as Spain, Portugal, and southern Italy. Population also grew, however, in more agricultural regions such as East Prussia, Poland, and Ireland. Ireland's rapid population growth does not appear on this map because by 1850 more than a million people had died or emigrated because of the famine of 1846–1851.

people referred to it as the "Crystal Palace"; its nine hundred tons of glass created an aura of fantasy, and the abundant goods from all nations inspired satisfaction and pride. One German visitor described it as "this miracle which has so suddenly appeared to dazzle the inhabitants of our globe." In the place of revolutionary fervor, the Crystal Palace offered a government-sponsored spectacle of what industry, hard work, and technological imagination could produce.

Conclusion

Many of the six million people who visited the Crystal Palace display had not forgotten the threat of disease, fears of overpopulation, popular resentments, and political upheavals that had been so prominent in the 1830s and 1840s. Even though industrial growth brought railroads, cheaper clothing, and access to exhibitions like the Crystal Palace, it also brought in its train urban overcrowding and miserable working conditions. The Crystal Palace presented the rosy view, but the housing shortages, inadequacy of water supplies, and recurrent epidemic diseases had not disappeared. Social reform organizations still drew attention to prostitution, child abandonment, alcohol abuse, and other problems associated with burgeoning cities.

Although the revolutions of 1848 brought to the surface the profound tensions within a European society in transition toward industrialization and modernization, they did not definitively resolve those tensions. Industrialization and urbanization continued, workers developed more extensive organizations, and liberals and socialists fought over the pace of reform. The revolutions produced their most striking impact negatively rather than positively: confronted with the menace of revolution, elites now sought alternatives that would be less threatening to the established order and still permit some change. This search for alternatives became immediately evident in the question of national unification in Germany and Italy. National unification would hereafter depend on what the Prussian leader Otto von Bismarck would call "blood and iron," not speeches and parliamentary resolutions.

Suggested References

The Advance of Industrialization and Urbanization

The spread of industrialization has elicited much more historical interest than the process of urbanization because the analysis of industrialization occupied a central role in Marxism. Some of the best recent work on urbanization, such as Kudlick's book on cholera, combines an interest in urban history with an interest in the history of public health. The

Spartacus Internet Encyclopedia has an excellent section on the textile industry and its transformation.

Ashton, T. S. *The Industrial Revolution, 1760–1830.* 1997.

Engerman, Stanley. "Reflections on 'The Standard of Living Debate.'" In John A. James and Mark Thomas, *Capitalism in Context: Essays on Economic Development and Cultural Change in Honor of R. M. Hartwell.* 1994.

Hobsbawm, E. J. *The Age of Revolution, 1789–1848.* 1996.

Kudlick, Catherine J. *Cholera in Post-Revolutionary Paris: A Cultural History.* 1996.

Mokyr, Joel, ed. *The British Industrial Revolution: An Economic Perspective.* 2nd ed. 1999.

Pinkney, David H. *Decisive Years in France, 1840–1847.* 1986.

*Pollard, S., and C. Holmes. *Documents of European Economic History.* Vol. 1, *The Process of Industrialization, 1750–1870.* 1968.

Spartacus Internet Encyclopedia, British History 1700–1950: http://www.spartacus.schoolnet.co.uk/Britain.html.

Reforming the Social Order

Although romanticism remains a focus of interest for cultural historians, the history of women and the origins of feminism have attracted attention in recent years. The Web site Gallica, produced by the National Library of France, offers a wealth of imagery and information on French cultural history.

Davidoff, Leonore, and Catherine Hall. *Family Fortunes: Men and Women of the English Middle Class, 1780–1850.* 1987.

The Dickens Project: http://humwww.ucsc.edu/dickens/index.html.

Gallica: Images and Texts from Nineteenth-Century French-Speaking Culture: http://gallica.bnf.fr/.

Lees, Lynn. *The Solidarities of Strangers: The English Poor Laws and the People, 1700–1948.* 1998.

Moses, Claire Goldberg. *French Feminism in the Nineteenth Century.* 1984.

*Murray, Janet Horowitz. *Strong-Minded Women and Other Lost Voices from Nineteenth-Century England.* 1982.

Roberts, James S. *Drink, Temperance, and the Working Class in Nineteenth-Century Germany.* 1984.

Rodner, William S. *J. M. W. Turner: Romantic Painter of the Industrial Revolution.* 1997.

Townsend, Mary Lee. *Forbidden Laughter: Popular Humor and the Limits of Repression in Nineteenth-Century Prussia.* 1992.

*Primary sources.

The Ferment of Ideologies

Ideologies are too often studied in an exclusively national context, so broader generalizations are difficult. The important exception to this national focus in the wide-ranging study by Anderson. The works by Clark and Taylor show how gender entered in to working-class organization and socialist ideology.

Anderson, Benedict. *Imagined Communities: Reflections on the Origin and Spread of Nationalism.* 1983.

Clark, Anna. *The Struggle for the Breeches: Gender and the Making of the British Working Class.* 1995.

*Mather, F. C., ed. *Chartism and Society: An Anthology of Documents.* 1980.

Sewell, William H., Jr. *Work and Revolution in France: The Language of Labor from the Old Regime to 1848.* 1980.

Taylor, Barbara. *Eve and the New Jerusalem: Socialism and Feminism in the Nineteenth Century.* 1983.

The Revolutions of 1848

Interest in the revolutions of 1848 has revived of late, perhaps because the recent upsurge of ethnic violence in the Balkans has prompted scholars to look again at this critical period. Not to be overlooked is the excellent treatment of the Irish famine by O'Grada.

Blackbourn, David. *The Long Nineteenth Century: A History of Germany, 1780–1918.* 1998.

Lincoln, W. Bruce. *Nicholas I: Emperor and Autocrat of All the Russias.* 1978.

O'Grada, Cormac. *The Great Irish Famine.* 1989.

Randers-Pehrson, Justine Davis. *Germans and the Revolution of 1848–1849.* 1999.

Sperber, Jonathan. *The European Revolutions, 1848–1851.* 1994.

Spira, Gyorgy. *The Nationality Issue in the Hungary of 1848–49.* 1992.

*Walker, Mack. *Metternich's Europe.* 1968.

Politics and Culture of the Nation-State

c. 1850–1870

Aïda Poster
Aïda (1871), Giuseppe Verdi's opera of human passion and state power, became a staple of Western culture, bringing people across Europe into a common cultural orbit. Written to celebrate the opening of the Suez Canal, Aïda also celebrated Europe's better access to Asian resources provided by the new waterway. As the poster shows, the opera ushered in another wave of Egyptomania.
Madeline Grimoldi.

I N 1859, THE NAME VERDI SUDDENLY APPEARED scrawled on walls across the disunited cities of the Italian peninsula. The graffiti seemed to celebrate the composer Giuseppe Verdi, whose operas thrilled crowds of Europeans. Verdi was a particular hero among Italians, however, for his stories of downtrodden groups struggling against tyrannical government seemed to refer specifically to their plight. As his operatic choruses thundered out calls to rebellion in the name of the nation, Italian audiences were sure that Verdi meant for them to throw off Austrian and papal rule and unite in a new version of the ancient Roman Empire. Yet the graffiti was doubly political, a call to arms in the days before mass media. For VERDI also formed an acronym for *Vittorio Emmanuele Re* ("king") *d'I*talia, and in 1859 it summoned Italians to unite immediately under Victor Emmanuel II, king of Sardinia and Piedmont—the one leader with a nationalist, modernizing profile. The graffiti did its work, for the very next year Italy united as a result of warfare, popular uprisings, and hard bargaining by political realists.

In the wake of the failed revolutions of 1848, European statesmen and the politically conscious public increasingly rejected the politics of idealism in favor of *Realpolitik*—a politics of tough-minded realism aimed at strengthening the state and tightening social order. Claiming to distrust the romanticism and high-minded ideologies of the revolutionaries and hoping to control nationalism and other movements for reform, Realpolitikers believed in playing power politics, establishing a strong government, and using violence to attain their goals. Two

1850	1854	1858	1862	1866	1870

Politics and War

Continuing Russian expansion into Asia

Taiping rebellion ends

Franco-Prussian War

Second Empire in France

Crimean War

Italy unified

Meiji Restoration begins in Japan

Sepoy Mutiny in India

U.S. Civil War

German Empire established; Paris Commune

Austro-Hungarian monarchy established; Second Reform Bill in Britain

Society and Economy

Urban improvements and expansion of government bureaucracy and services; Britain continues to pursue free-trade policies

International Workingmen's Association formed in London

Abolition of serfdom in Russia

Suez Canal opened

Culture, Religion, and Intellectual Life

Positivism and Darwinism become popular theories among middle classes; Wagner's musical compositions

Pope Pius IX issues *The Syllabus of Errors*

Verdi's *Aïda* debuts in Cairo

Realism in literature and painting

Crystal Palace exhibition in Britain

Universal Exposition in Paris

particularly skilled practitioners of Realpolitik, the Italian Camillo di Cavour and the Prussian Otto von Bismarck, succeeded in unifying Italy and Germany, respectively, not by consensus but by war and diplomacy. Most leading figures of these decades, enmeshed like Verdi's operatic heroes in violent political maneuverings, advanced state power by harnessing the forces of nationalism and liberalism that had led to earlier romantic revolts.

Many ingredients went into making modern nation-states and empires during these momentous decades. Continued economic development was crucial, as was a growing sense of national identity and common purpose forged by both culture and government policy. As productivity and wealth increased, governments took vigorous steps to im-

prove the urban environment, monitor public health, and promote national sentiment. State support for cultural developments ranging from public schools to opera productions helped establish a common fund of knowledge and even shared political beliefs. Authoritarian leaders such as Bismarck and the new French emperor Napoleon III believed that a better quality of life would not only calm revolutionary impulses, ensure social order, and build state power but also keep political liberals at bay.

Culture also built a sense of belonging. Reading novels, attending art exhibitions, keeping up-to-date at the newly fashionable world's fairs, and attending theater and opera created a greater sense of being French or German or British but also of being European. Cultural works increasingly rejected romanticism, featuring instead realistic aspects of ordinary people's lives. Artists painted nudes in shockingly blunt ways, eliminating romantic hues and poses. Verdi's celebrated opera *La Traviata* showed a frolicking courtesan menacing a middle-class family. The Russian author Leo Tolstoy depicted the bleak life of soldiers in the Crimean War while his countryman Fyodor Dostoevsky wrote of criminals and murders in urban neighborhoods.

Realpolitik cared less for the costs than for the outcomes of state building. Advancing state power entailed stamping out resistance to colonial expansion. At home it uprooted neighborhoods in favor of public buildings, roads, and parks. The process of national expansion was often brutal, bringing war, arrests, protests, and outright civil war—all of these the centerpieces of Verdi's operas as well. As the wars of German unification drew to a close in 1871, an uprising of Parisians threw the new terms of nation building into question as citizens challenged the central government's intrusion into everyday life and its failure to count the costs. For the most part, the powerful Western state did not take shape automatically during these years. Instead, its growth occasioned warfare and dislocation, shrewd policy and heated debate. Realpolitik produced all of these, as well as a general climate of modern opinion that valued realism and hard facts.

❖ The End of the Concert of Europe

The revolutions of 1848 had weakened the concert of Europe, driving out its architect Metternich and allowing the forces of nationalism to flourish. It became more difficult for countries to control their competing ambitions and act together. In addition, the dreaded resurgence of Bonapartism in the person of Napoleon III (Louis-Napoleon, the nephew of Napoleon I) added to the volatility in international politics as France sought to reassert itself. One of Napoleon's targets was Russia, formerly a mainstay of the concert of Europe. While Russia pursued its own goals of expanded borders, France helped engineer the Crimean War of 1854–1856. Taking a huge toll in human life, the war weakened Russia and Austria and made way for a massive shift in the distribution of European power.

Napoleon III and the Quest for French Glory

Louis-Napoleon Bonaparte encouraged the resurgence of French grandeur and the cult of his famous uncle as part of nation building. "There are certain men who are born to serve as a means for the march of the human race," he wrote. "I consider myself to be one of these." On December 2, 1851, the anniversary of Napoleon I's coronation in 1804, he staged a political coup that allowed him to revise the constitution and declare himself eligible for a second presidential term, provided male voters approved. Napoleon won easily, partly because he promised not to restrict voter eligibility, as monarchists in the Assembly had proposed. Exactly one year later he declared himself Emperor Napoleon III (r. 1852–1870) and proclaimed the Second Empire. The French traded in dreams of political liberty for a strong man's promises of order and national glory.

Napoleon III acted as Europe's schoolmaster, showing its leaders how to combine economic liberalism and nationalism with authoritarian rule. Under the banner of "Order and Progress," he ruthlessly repressed opposition in small towns and cities alike, deporting, sometimes with no provocation, thousands of Parisians who appeared suspicious to harsh prison colonies outside of France. For example, Pauline Roland, a former Saint-Simonian who had become a newspaper editor, was convicted of opposing the coup in Paris and sent to a penal colony even though she had been far from the capital when the coup took place. Pro-republican professors were thrown out of work, cafés where men might discuss politics were closed, and a rubber-stamp legislature (the *Corps législatif*) reduced representative government to a facade. Imperial style replaced republican rituals. Napoleon's opulent court dazzled the public, and the emperor cultivated a masculine image of strength and majesty by wearing military uniforms (like his namesake) and by conspicuously maintaining mistresses. Napoleon's wife, Empress Eugénie, however, followed middle-class conventions such as separate spheres for men and women by serving as a devoted mother to her only son and supporting many volunteer charities. The authoritarian, apparently old-fashioned order imposed by Napoleon satisfied the many peasants who opposed urban radicals.

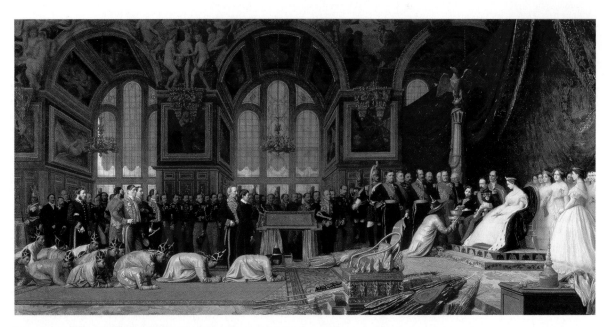

Napoleon III and Eugénie Receive the Siamese Ambassadors
At a splendid gathering of their court, the emperor Napoleon III, his consort Eugénie, and their son and heir greet ambassadors from Siam, whose exoticism and servility before the imperial family are the centerpiece of this depiction. Amidst the grandeur of the Napoleonic dynasty, the West towers above the East.
Giraudon/Art Resource, NY.

Yet Napoleon III was simultaneously a modernizer, and he promoted a strong economy, public works programs, and jobs, which lured the middle and working classes away from radical politics. International trade fairs, artistic expositions, and the magnificent rebuilding of Paris helped sustain French prosperity as Europe recovered from the hard times of the late 1840s. Empress Eugénie wore lavish gowns, encouraging French silk production and keeping Paris at the center of the lucrative fashion trade. The emperor's policies advanced commerce, most notably in a free-trade agreement with England, the Cobden-Chevalier Treaty (1860). The regime also launched a major financial innovation by backing an investment bank, the Crédit Mobilier. Such new institutions led the way in financing railroad expansion, and railway mileage increased fivefold during Napoleon III's reign.

When an economic recession struck in the late 1850s, the regime was once again subject to criticism and Napoleon III was forced to seek new alliances. Conservatives opposed Napoleon's free-trade and foreign policies, so he tried to woo political liberals by introducing democratic features into his governing methods. He encouraged the formation of working-class organizations and in the following years allowed the Corps législatif more power of deliberation. Although some historians have judged Napoleon III to be enigmatic and shifty because of these abrupt changes, his maneuvers were pragmatic responses to the fluid economic and political conditions.

On the international scene, Napoleon III's main goals were to overcome the containment of France imposed by the Congress of Vienna, realign continental politics to benefit France, and acquire international glory like a true Bonaparte. To realign European politics, Napoleon pitted France first against Russia in the Crimean War, then against Austria in the War of Italian Unification, and finally against Prussia in the Franco-Prussian War of 1870. Beyond Europe, Napoleon's army continued to enforce French rule in Algeria and Southeast Asia and tried to install Habsburg emperor Francis Joseph's brother Maximilian as ruler of Mexico and ultimately of all Central America—an assault that ended in 1867 with Maximilian's execution. Napoleon's foreign policy transformed relations among the great powers by causing a breakdown in the international system of peaceful diplomacy established at the Congress of Vienna. While his encouragement of projects like the Suez Canal to connect the Mediterranean and the Red Seas proved visionary, this push for worldwide influence eventually destroyed him: the French overthrew him after Prussia easily defeated his army in 1870.

The Crimean War, 1853–1856: Turning Point in European Affairs

Napoleon first flexed his diplomatic muscle in the Crimean War (1853–1856), which began as a conflict between the Russian and Ottoman Empires but ended as a war with long-lasting consequences for much of Europe. While professing to uphold the concert of Europe, Russia continued to build state power by making further inroads into Asia and the Middle East. In particular Tsar Nicholas I wanted to absorb much of the Ottoman Empire, fast becoming known as "the sick man of Europe" because of its disintegrating authority. To this end, Russia claimed an official right to protect Orthodox Christians within the declining empire. Nevertheless Napoleon III maneuvered Tsar Nicholas to be more aggressive in Russia's claims when he suddenly declared the rights of France as protector of Christians in the Ottoman Empire. As Russia became increasingly belligerent, war erupted in October 1853 between the two eastern empires (Map 23.1).

Behind the widening war lay the question of Europe's balance of power. The other great powers feared that increased Russian authority in Ottoman-controlled southeastern Europe would adversely affect their interests. To protect its Mediterranean routes to East Asia, Britain prodded the Ottomans to stand up to Russia. The Austrian government still resented its dependence on Russia in putting down Hungarian revolutionaries in 1849 and felt threatened by continuing Russian expansion into the Balkans. This anxiety helped Napoleon III gain a promise of Austrian neutrality during the war, thus fracturing the conservative Russian-Austrian coalition that had quashed French ambitions since 1815. In the fall of 1853, the Russians blasted the wooden Turkish ships to bits at the Ottoman port of Sinope on the Black Sea; in 1854, France and Great Britain, enemies in war for more than a century, declared war on Russia to defend the Ottoman Empire's sovereignty and territory.

Faced with attacking the massive Russian Empire, the opposition settled for limited military goals focused on capturing the Russian naval base at Sevastopol on the Black Sea in the Crimea. Even so, the Crimean War was spectacularly bloody. British and French troops landed in the Crimea in September 1854 and waged a long siege of the fortified city, but it fell only after a year of savage and costly combat. Generals on both sides demonstrated their incompetence; and governments failed to provide combatants with even minimal supplies, sanitation, or medical care. Russian military leadership proved most inept, but the British was not much better: the British commander in chief, a veteran of Waterloo, still harangued his troops to beat "the French." Like many of his fellow officers and soldiers, he would die of cholera during the war. The war claimed a massive toll. Three-quarters of a million men died, more than two-thirds from disease and starvation.

In the midst of this unfolding catastrophe, Alexander II (r. 1855–1881) ascended the Russian

MAP 23.1 The Crimean War, 1853–1856
The most destructive war in Europe between the Napoleonic Wars and World War I, the Crimean War drew attention to the conflicting ambitions around territories of the declining Ottoman Empire. Importantly for state building in these decades, the war fractured the alliance of conservative forces from the Congress of Vienna, allowing Italy and Germany to come into being as unified states and permitting Napoleon III to pursue his ambitions for France.

throne following the death of his father, Nicholas I, in 1855. The new tsar hoped for some minimal Russian triumph so he could negotiate peace from a position of strength, but as the casualties mounted and the possibility of victory dwindled, he yielded. As a result of the Peace of Paris, signed on March 30, 1856, Russia lost the right to base its navy in the Straits of Dardanelles and the Black Sea, which were declared neutral waters. Moldavia and Walachia (which soon merged to form Romania) became autonomous Turkish provinces under the victors' protection.

Some historians have called the Crimean War one of the most senseless conflicts in modern history because competing claims in southeastern Europe could have been settled by diplomacy had it not been for Napoleon III's driving ambition. Yet the war was full of consequence. New technologies were introduced into warfare, though their use was not yet perfected: the railroad, shell-firing cannon,

breech-loading rifles, the telegraph, and steam-powered ships. The relationship of the home front to the battlefront was beginning to change with the use of the telegraph and increased press coverage. Home audiences received news from the Crimean front lines more rapidly and in more detail than ever before. The news stunned even those who longed for the excitement of battle: reports of incompetence, poor sanitation, and the huge death toll outraged the public, and some people went to the front to help out or take photographs. One admirable figure rose above the carnage—Florence Nightingale (1820–1910). She seized the moment to escape the confines of middle-class domesticity by organizing a battlefield nursing service to care for the British sick and wounded. Through her tough-minded organization of nursing units, she secured additional personnel and medical supplies for her hospital and improved the sanitary conditions of the troops. (See "Did You Know?,"

The Mission of Mercy
Florence Nightingale organized British health care services during the Crimean War, inspiring a committed cadre of women volunteers to leave domestic life for the battlefront. As disease took its heavy toll, Nightingale introduced sanitary measures into the care of the wounded and sick. This romantic portrayal of her greeting the wounded at Scutari hardly captures the strenuous and tough-minded efforts involved in her work.
National Portrait Gallery, London.

Mrs. Seacole: The Other Florence Nightingale

Another highly skilled medical worker besides Florence Nightingale made an impact on the battlefields in Crimea. Mary Seacole (1805–1881), daughter of a free-black Jamaican woman and a Scottish army officer, had learned about medicine from her mother and from doctors who passed through Kingston, staying at the family boardinghouse. In addition to having a gift for healing, especially curing tropical diseases and cholera, Mrs. Seacole (as she was always called) had a passion for travel. She supported her visits to the southern United States, Panama, Europe, and elsewhere by healing and by provisioning hospitals, travelers, and the sick. Before any trip, she spent weeks preserving fruits and meats, preparing homeopathic treatments, and stitching garments—all to sell to her fellow travelers. In England when the Crimean War broke out, she chafed—like Nightingale herself—to be at the battlefront. "Now, no sooner had I heard of a war somewhere, than I longed to witness it," she wrote, and in 1855 arrived in Crimea.

Nineteenth-century armies relied on informal groups of camp followers and local provisioners to supply the ill with food, clothing, and medicine. With contagious diseases rampant among the troops, Mrs. Seacole used her healing arts to save lives. Her efforts, however, ruined her financially, and, unlike Nightingale, she was not wealthy. Returning to England, she became highly decorated, and grateful veterans tried to help her out. Resourceful as ever, Mrs. Seacole wrote her autobiography, a wonderful saga of travel, hardship, and devotion to medicine and curing the ill.

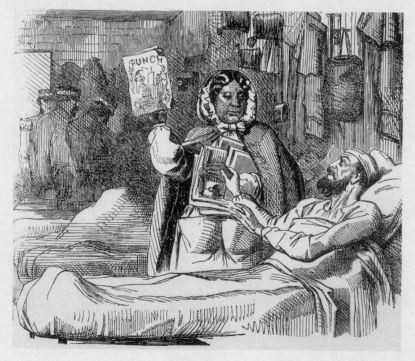

Mrs. Seacole in the Crimean War
Until well into the nineteenth century, armies lacked well-organized supply and medical units. Women, often called "camp followers" and long considered to be prostitutes, actually did much of the service work that in the twentieth-century army would be regularized as part of military service. Mary Seacole was part of a group who made a business from provisioning the forces. Mary Evans Picture Library.

above.) Back in England following the war, she spearheaded the campaign for military reform and pioneered nursing as a profession.

More immediately, the war accomplished Napoleon III's goal of severing the alliance between the Habsburgs and Russia, the two conservative powers on which the Congress of Vienna peace settlement had rested since 1815. It thus ended Austria's and Russia's grip on European affairs and undermined their ability to contain the forces of liberalism and nationalism. The defeat was cataclysmic for Russia, as its autocracy was forced to abolish serfdom, embark on long-overdue internal reforms, and strive to renovate the empire.

Spirit of Reform in Russia

Defeat in the Crimean War not only thwarted Russia's territorial ambition but also forced it on the path of reform. Hundreds of peasant insurrections had erupted during the decade before the Crimean War. Serf defiance ranged from malingering while at forced labor to boycotting vodka to protest its heavy taxation. "Our own and neighboring households were gripped with fear," one aristocrat reported, because everyone expected "a serf rising at any minute."

Although industrial development and liberal ideology spread in eastern Europe, the Russian economy stagnated compared with western Europe's. Old-fashioned farming techniques led to depleted soil and food shortages, and the nobility was often contemptuous of ordinary people's suffering. Nonetheless, through sympathetic portrayals of serfs and frank depiction of brutal masters, such as in novelist Ivan Turgenev's *A Hunter's Sketches* (1852), a spirit of reform grew. A Russian translation of Harriet Beecher Stowe's antislavery novel *Uncle Tom's Cabin* (1852) also appeared in the 1850s and struck a responsive chord. When Russia lost the Crimean War, the educated public, including some government officials, found the poor performance of serf-conscripted armies a disgrace and the system of serf labor an intolerable liability.

Emancipation of the Serfs. Confronted with the need for change, Alexander proved more flexible than his father Nicholas I. Well educated and more widely traveled, he ushered in what came to be known as the age of Great Reforms, granting Russians new rights from above as a way of ensuring that change would not be forced from below through violent action. The most dramatic reforms were the emancipation of 22 million privately owned serfs in 1861 and 25 million state-owned peasants a few years later. Other important innovations included the creation of a judicial system that limited landowners' rights to mete out justice arbitrarily and the establishment of regional self-governing councils, or *zemstvos*, in 1864 to promote local government. Realistic officials knew, however, that these reforms were not designed to introduce democracy but rather to preserve the social hierarchy. One aristocratic landowner described the serfs' emancipation as "even more necessary for the welfare of our class than for the serfs."

By the terms of emancipation, communities of former serfs, headed by male village elders, received grants of land. The community itself, called a *mir*, had full power to allocate this land among

Emancipation of the Russian Serfs
The Crimean War came as a harsh warning that the Russian Empire sorely needed social reform in an age of growing state power. The plight of tens of millions of serfs was often dire compared with the condition of western Europeans, and the emancipation of 1861 was seen as key to stabilizing both state and society.
Hulton Getty/Liaison.

individuals and to direct their economic activity. Thus, although emancipation partially laid the groundwork for a modern labor force in Russia, communal landowning and decision making prevented unlimited mobility and the development of a pool of free labor. The condition attached to these so-called land grants was that peasants were not *given* land along with their personal freedom: they were forced to "redeem" the land they farmed by paying the government through long-term loans, which in turn compensated the original landowners. With much land going to the nobility, most peasants ended up owning less land than they had tilled as serfs. These conditions, especially the huge burden of debt and communal regulations, blunted Russian agricultural development for decades. But idealistic reformers believed the emancipation of the serfs, once treated by the nobility virtually as livestock, produced miraculous results. As one of them put it, "The people are without any exaggeration transfigured from head to foot. . . . The look, the walk, the speech, everything is changed."

As with serf emancipation in Prussia in 1810 and in Austria in 1848, landowners benefited most from the change because they received the best land. Fearful of alienating the nobility, the tsar's government compensated them not only for the loss of land but also for the loss of peasant services. Through the *zemstvos*, the aristocrats could provide considerable leadership in neglected local matters such as education, public health, and welfare. Generally dominated by the nobility, some of whom were expanding their political involvement, *zemstvos* were essentially a conservative structure, but they became a countervailing political force to the distant central government. Some nobles profited from the relaxation of censorship, of restrictions on travel, and of controls on university teaching to continue the trend of Westernization begun under Peter the Great, even coming to agree with liberals in western Europe that the Russian system of political autocracy and religious orthodoxy had grave disadvantages.

Another reform swept away much of Russia's abuse-ridden judicial system. One conservative writer exclaimed, "At the mere recollection of it [the old court system] one's hair stands on end and one's flesh begins to creep." Judicial reform gave all Russians, even former serfs, access to modern civil courts, rather than leaving them at the mercy of a landowner's version of justice or secret, blatantly preferential practices. The Western principle of equality of all persons before the law, regardless of social rank, was introduced in Russia for the first time.

Military reform followed in 1874 when the government ended the twenty-five-year period of conscription that had kept the army both inefficient and too small for modern needs. A six-year term and attention to education, efficiency, and humane treatment of recruits made the Russian army more competitive with those in western Europe. Service in the army had formerly been so like a lifetime sentence that villages had held funerals for its conscripts. Soldiers returned home from the reduced term somewhat more educated and patriotic.

From Reform to Rebellion. Alexander's reforms assisted modernizing and market-oriented landowners just as enclosures and emancipation had done much earlier in western Europe. Other landowners, unprepared for modern competition, mortgaged or sold their estates and remained confined within the traditional mindset of provincial life. The changes diminished the personal prerogatives of the nobility, leaving their authority weakened and sparking intergenerational rebellion. "An epidemic seemed to seize upon [noble] children . . . an epidemic of fleeing from the parental roof," one observer noted.

A new sense of an expanding public life took shape. Rejecting aristocratic leisure, youthful rebels from the upper class valued practical activity and sometimes identified with peasants and workers. Some formed communes where they hoped to do humble manual labor or start small businesses, whereas others turned to higher education, especially the sciences. Rebellious daughters of the nobility flouted parental expectations by cropping their hair short, wearing black, and escaping from home through phony marriages so they could study in European universities. This repudiation of traditional society led Turgenev to label radical youth as *nihilists* (from the Latin for "nothing"), a term that meant a lack of belief in any values whatsoever.

The atmosphere of reform also produced resistance among Russian-dominated nationalities, including an uprising by the Poles in 1863. Although Alexander II had begun extending his reforms to the Congress Kingdom of Poland (the part of Poland that came under Russian control after the Congress of Vienna), aristocratic and middle-class nationalists revolted for full independence. By 1864, Alexander II's army regained control of the Russian section of the former Poland, having used reforms to buy peasant loyalty and support in defeating the rebels. In the Caucasus and elsewhere Alexander responded to nationalist unrest with repression and programs of intensive Russification—a tactic meant to reduce the threat of future rebellion by national minorities within the empire by forcing them to adopt Russian language and culture.

In this era of the Great Reforms, the tsarist regime only partially succeeded in transforming itself into a modern authoritarian state., Political pragmatism in Russia produced a hybrid: economic growth and the spread of liberal ideas accompanied the evolution of a bureaucratic autocracy ruling over a multinational state. Elsewhere the sense of citizenship took shape in the nineteenth century, but in imperial Russia the persistence of autocracy and the abuse of large numbers of the population hurt this development.

❖ War and Nation Building

With the concert of Europe a thing of the past and with Russia absorbed by its own crises, nationalist ambitions flourished in other parts of the West. Politicians in the German and Italian states used the opportunity to unify their countries quickly and violently through warfare. When disunity threatened, the United States also waged a bloody civil war to ensure continued expansion and the consolidation of its national borders. Historians sometimes treat the rise of Italy, Germany, and a powerful United States as seemingly inevitable, but underneath the ferment lay incredible uncertainty. And for all the winners, there were as many losers and even more unpersuaded: the Austrian Empire, Ireland, and millions of individuals whose allegiances were local rather than national or imperial.

Cavour, Garibaldi, and the Process of Italian Unification

The disunited states of the Italian peninsula were tiny compared with Russia and France, but after the Crimean War the disintegrating diplomatic equilibrium in Europe allowed a unified Italy to emerge as a potential power. Despite the failure of the revolutions of 1848, the issue of *Risorgimento* (literally meaning "rebirth" but associated with the movement for Italian unification) continued to percolate. This time the clear leader of Risorgimento would be the kingdom of Piedmont-Sardinia, in the economically modernizing north of Italy. The kingdom rallied to the operas of Verdi, but it was fortified with railroads, a modern army, and the support of France against the Austrian Empire, which still dominated the peninsula.

Cavour. The architect of the new Italy was the pragmatic Camillo di Cavour (1810–1861), prime minister of the kingdom of Piedmont-Sardinia from 1852 until his death. A rebel, economic liberal, and gambler in his youth, the young Cavour also conducted agricultural experiments on his aristocratic father's land. He organized steamship companies, played the stock market, and inhaled the heady air of modernization during his travels to Paris and London. Verdi called Cavour "the man whom every Italian will call the father of his country"—although like 90 percent of the peninsula's residents Cavour did not speak Italian, but Piedmontese, a dialect.

Cavour had begun his quest for a united Italy by making economic development rather than democratic uprising the means to his end. As prime minister to the capricious and scheming king, Victor Emmanuel II (r. 1861–1878), he capitalized on favorable conditions to develop a healthy Piedmontese economy, a modern army, and a liberal political climate through reforms such as freedom of the press. Gradually, he focused most of his immense energy on plotting the expansion of Piedmont so it would dominate the unification process (Map 23.2).

To unify Italy, however, Piedmont would have to confront Austria, which governed the provinces of Lombardy and Venetia and exerted strong influence over most of the peninsula. Cavour turned for help to Napoleon III. He admired French success in advancing the liberal economic goals that he saw as essential for Italian independence. Napoleon, in turn, championed national self-determination when it might weaken powers like Austria. In the summer of 1858 at a meeting in the French mountain spa of Plombières, Cavour promised Napoleon the city of Nice and the region of Savoy in exchange for French help in driving the Austrians out of Italy. Napoleon III expected that once the

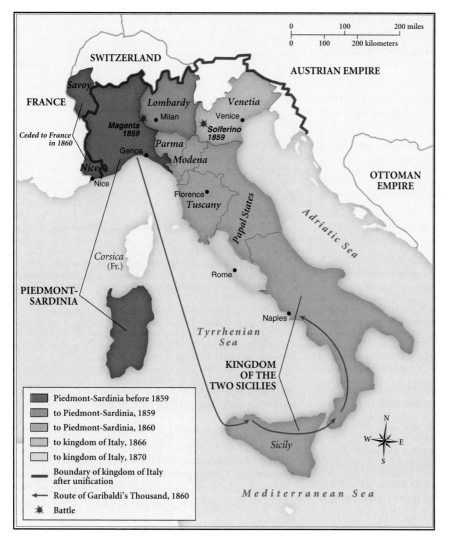

MAP 23.2 Unification of Italy, 1859–1870
The many states of the Italian peninsula had different languages, ways of life, and economic interests. In the north, the kingdom of Sardinia, which included the commercially advanced state of Piedmont, had much to gain from a unified market and a more extensive pool of labor. Although King Victor Emmanuel's and Garibaldi's armies brought these states together as a single country, it would take decades to construct a culturally, socially, and economically unified nation.

Austrians were gone, he, not they, would influence the peninsula. Sure of French help, Cavour provoked the Austrians to invade northern Italy in April 1859, and using the newly built Piedmontese railroad to move troops, the French joined the Piedmontese army. Once war broke out, the cause of Piedmont became the cause of nationalist Italians everywhere, even those who had supported romantic republicanism in 1848. Putting aside their former aspirations, political liberals in Tuscany and other central Italian states rose up on the side of Piedmont. "During the war of independence, I do not want liberty," said one, "but dictatorship: the dictatorship of a soldier."

Napoleon III was not a reliable ally, however. In June 1859, French and Piedmontese troops soundly defeated the Habsburg forces at Solferino and Magenta. Hoping to prevent a sweeping Piedmontese victory that might lessen his own control, Napoleon signed a peace treaty with Habsburg emperor Francis Joseph one month later. Its terms gave Lombardy but not Venetia to Piedmont, and the rest of Italy remained disunited. The treaty allowed both France and Austria to avoid the financial and political losses a prolonged war would entail. It enraged Cavour, but events proved that Napoleon's anxiety over growing Piedmontese strength was well founded.

Garibaldi. Napoleon's plans for controlled liberation of Lombardy and Venetia and a partitioned Italy were derailed as support for Piedmont continued to swell inside Italy and as a financially strapped Austria stood by helplessly. Ousting their rulers, citizens of Parma, Modena, Tuscany, and the Papal States (except Rome, which French troops had occupied) elected to join Piedmont. In May 1860, Giuseppe Garibaldi (1807–1882), a committed republican, inspired guerrilla fighter, and veteran of the revolutions of 1848, set sail from Genoa with a thousand red-shirted volunteers (many of them teenage boys) to liberate Sicily, where peasant revolts against landlords and the corrupt government were under way. Garibaldi's rallying cry was "Italy and Victor Emmanuel," but he was also known as a democratic populist. Garibaldi's expedition to Sicily forced Cavour to expand his vision of Piedmont's leadership to include poor and agrarian southern Italy. Rapid victories on the island followed by the Red Shirts' invasion of the southern mainland alarmed Cavour, who dispatched the Piedmontese army south to keep Garibaldi from reaching Rome, where he would surely confront the French with his ragtag army.

In the autumn of 1860, the forces of King Victor Emmanuel and Garibaldi finally met in Naples. Although some of his supporters still clamored for social reform and a republic, Garibaldi threw his support to the king, and the two unlikely allies rode together through the streets to the wild cheering of the crowd. Public celebrations and holidays were becoming increasingly important to nation building, and, after warfare had done its work, this parade bound rulers and ruled in support of the nation-state. In 1861, the kingdom of Italy was proclaimed with Victor Emmanuel as king.

Exhausted by a decade of overwork, Cavour died within months of leading the unification, leaving lesser men to organize the new Italy. Consensus among Italy's elected political leaders was often elusive once the war was over, and admirers of Cavour, such as Verdi (who had been made senator), fled the heated political scene. The wealthy commercial north and impoverished agricultural south remained at odds, as they do even today. Many southern peasants continued to rebel against the old, inequitable patterns of landholding, whereas the northern politicians who dominated the government concentrated economic benefits in their own area. Italian borders did not yet seem final because Venetia and Rome remained outside them, under Austrian and French control, respectively. But

Seamstresses of the Red Shirts
Sewing uniforms and making battle flags, European women like these Italian volunteers saw themselves as contributors to the nation. Donating their domestic skills and raising the next generation of citizens to be patriotic, many nineteenth-century women participated in nation building as "republican mothers."

the legend of an Italian struggle for freedom symbolized by the figure of Garibaldi and his Red Shirts papered over these defects and sentimentalized the Realpolitik that had made unification possible.

Bismarck and the Realpolitik of German Unification

The most momentous act of nation building for the future of Europe and of the world was the creation of a united Germany in 1871. This too was the work of Realpolitik, undertaken once the concert of Europe was smashed and the champions of the status quo defeated. Employing the old military order to wage war, yet with the support of economic modernizers who saw profits in one huge national market, the Prussian state brought a vast array of cities and kingdoms under its control within a single decade. From then on, Germany prospered, continuing to consolidate its economic and political might. By the end of the nineteenth century it would be the foremost continental power.

Bismarck's Rise to Power.   The architect of a unified Germany was Otto von Bismarck (1815–1898), the Prussian minister-president. Bismarck came from a traditional Junker (Prussian landed nobility) family on his father's side; his mother's family included high-ranking bureaucrats and literati of the middle class. Obeying his mother's wishes, the young Bismarck had gone to the university, but he spent his time there gambling and womanizing. Only a course on the economic foundations of politics interested him academically. After failing in the civil service he worked to modernize operations on his landholdings and read widely. Otherwise, by his own admission he led a loutish life.

In 1846, Bismarck experienced a religious conversion, married a pious Lutheran woman, and acquired a seriousness of purpose. In 1851, he became the Prussian representative to the restored assembly of the various German states. There Prussia's impotence and the Habsburg domination of German affairs repelled him. He learned a formative lesson in Realpolitik: despite ideological similarities between the Prussian and Austrian monarchies and past alliances to contain revolutionary France, the multinational Habsburg Empire, with its overbearing diplomacy, blocked the full flowering of the Prussian state.

In 1862, William I (king of Prussia, r. 1861–1888; German emperor, r. 1871–1888) appointed Bismarck prime minister in hopes that he would quash the growing power of the liberals in the Prussian parliament. The liberals, representing the prosperous professional and business classes, had gained parliamentary strength at the expense of conservative landowners during the decades of industrial expansion. Indeed, the liberals' wealth was crucial to the Prussian state's ability to augment its power. Desiring Prussia to be like western Europe, Prussian liberals advocated the extension of political rights, increased civilian control of the military, and other reforms. William I, along with members of the traditional Prussian elite, rejected the western European model. In fact, William wanted to consolidate state control by ending the citizen militia system, integrating the militia into the regular army, and lengthening the term of military service.

The issue of the military, on which Prussian bureaucratic and political strength had depended, gave Bismarck his first critical victory. When the liberals rejected the tax increase needed to expand the army, Bismarck announced that the king's agents would collect taxes despite parliament, and he proceeded with the military buildup. He also gave his own appraisal of contemporary politics, specifically his view of liberal ideals: "Germany looks not to Prussia's liberalism, but to its power," he preached. "The great questions of the day will not be settled by speeches and majority decisions— that was the great mistake of 1848 and 1849—but by blood and iron."

Wars of Unification.   After his triumph over the parliament, Bismarck led Prussia into a series of wars, against Denmark in 1864, against Austria in 1866, and, finally, against France in 1870. Using war as a political tactic, he kept the disunited German states from choosing Austrian leadership and instead united them around Prussia, forcing what was known as a *kleindeutsch*, or "small German," alternative that did not include Austria. The war with Denmark was a prelude to imposing the *kleindeutsch* solution and finally resolving the Austro-Prussian rivalry that had existed since the eighteenth century. When the Danish king suggested incorporating into Denmark the provinces of Schleswig and Holstein, with their mixed Danish and German populations, Bismarck drew Austria into a joint war with Prussia against Denmark in 1864. The allied victory resulted in an agreement that Prussia would administer Schleswig, and Austria, Holstein. Such an arrangement stretched Austria's geographic interests far from its central European base.

Austria proved weaker than Prussia. By the time France and Piedmont defeated the Habsburgs in 1859, Austria's state debt had swollen to five times its annual revenues, and because economic development did not grow at the same pace, Austria could not afford Prussian-style military modernization. Internally the empire had to contend with disaffected nationalities, particularly the Magyars, whose oppression after 1849 fueled their nationalism. Despite these problems, the Austrian government still behaved as if it had the same power and prestige as in the days of Metternich. Bismarck encouraged these pretensions. Then, fomenting disputes over the administration of Schleswig and Holstein, he goaded Austria into declaring war on Prussia itself. In the summer of 1866, Austria went to war with the support of most small states in the German Confederation. Within seven weeks the modernized Prussian army, using railroads and breech-loading rifles against the out-dated Austrian military, had won decisively. Victory allowed Bismarck to drive Austria from the German Confederation and to create a North German Confederation led by Prussia. This confederation subsequently adopted a common political and economic program, permitting it to compete more effectively in the growing industrial marketplace and to spearhead reform. Bavaria and the other independent southern German states found themselves clients of Prussia, and some clamored for annexation (Map 23.3).

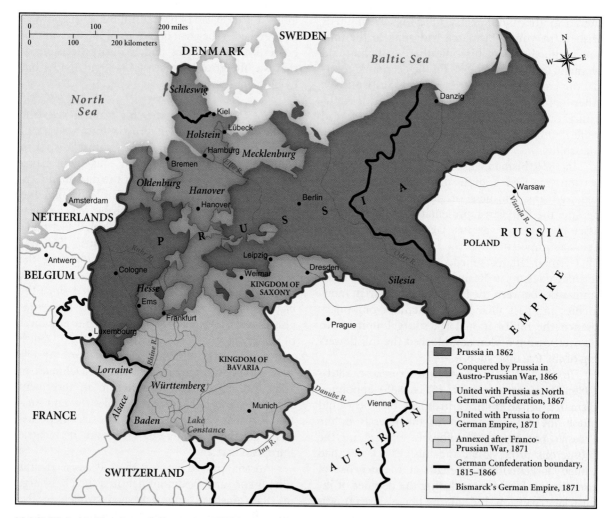

MAP 23.3 Unification of Germany, 1862–1871

In a complex series of diplomatic maneuvers, Bismarck welded disunited kingdoms and small states into a major continental power independent of the other dominant German dynasty, the Habsburg monarchy. Prussia's use of force unified Germany politically, and almost immediately that unity unleashed the new nation's economic potential. An aristocratic and agrarian elite remained firmly in power, but a rapidly growing working class would soon become a political force to be reckoned with.

Emperor William I of Germany, 1871
The defeat of France in the Franco-Prussian War of 1870–1871 ended with the proclamation of the king of Prussia as emperor of a unified Germany. Otto von Bismarck, who had orchestrated the wars of unification, appropriately appears in this artistic rendering as the central figure attired in heroic white. But the event in the French palace of Versailles symbolized the militaristic and antagonistic side of state building, especially the Franco-German rivalry that would disastrously motivate European politics in the future.
AKG London.

To bring the remaining German states into the rapidly developing nation, Bismarck next moved to entrap France in a war with Prussia. During the Austro-Prussian War, Bismarck had suggested to Napoleon III that his neutrality would bring France territory, but the emperor's actual announcement of such expansion whipped up German nationalism. The atmosphere was charged, and in 1868 an issue arose that would precipitate war between France and Prussia. A military coup in Spain sent that country's leaders shopping for a new king from among Europe's royal families. They chose a German prince of the minor branch of the Prussian ruling family. His candidacy threatened the French with Prussian rulers on two of their borders. As pressure mounted, the candidacy was withdrawn, but the French remained furious. In the summer of 1870, the French ambassador accosted William I at the German spa of Ems and demanded both an apology and promises that Prussia would never again make such a claim on the Spanish throne. "If he refuses, it's war," the French foreign minister remarked. When William sent a telegram to Bismarck about the incident, Bismarck saw his opportunity to stir up nationalist

journalism in both countries. Although William's message contained only complaints about the French ambassador's public harangue, Bismarck edited the so-called Ems telegram to make it look as if William had insulted France and then released the revised version to journalists. The inflamed French public demanded war. The parliament gladly declared it.

The French declaration of war on July 19, 1870, set in motion the alliances Prussia had created with the other German states. Bonapartism and Bismarck's diplomacy had isolated France from such potential allies as Austria, Russia, and Great Britain, and all three states sat by as the Prussians captured Napoleon III with his army on September 2, 1870. "Thank God," remarked Alexander II of Russia on hearing of Napoleon's defeat. "Sevastopol is now avenged."

The Second Empire fell on September 4, 1870. With Prussian forces still besieging Paris and the French political future uncertain, in January 1871 in the Hall of Mirrors at Versailles, King William of Prussia was proclaimed the kaiser of a new, imperial Germany. The terms of the peace signed in May 1871 required France to cede the rich industrial provinces of Alsace and Lorraine to Germany and to pay a multibillion-franc indemnity. Without French protection for the papacy, Rome became part of Italy. Germany was now poised to dominate continental politics.

The German Nation Takes Shape. Prussian military might served as the foundation for German state building, and a complex constitution ensured the continued political dominance of the aristocracy and monarchy. The kaiser, who remained Prussia's king, controlled the military and appointed Bismarck to the powerful position of Reich's chancellor. The German states balanced monarchical authority somewhat through the Bundesrat, a body composed of representatives from each state. The Reichstag, an assembly elected by universal male suffrage, ratified all budgets. In framing this constitutional settlement, Bismarck accorded rights such as suffrage in the belief that the masses would uphold autocracy out of their fear of "the domination of finance capital"—shorthand for "liberal power." He balanced this move, however, with an electoral system in which the votes from the upper classes counted more than those from the lower.

Bismarck had little to fear from the liberals, who became dizzy with German military success. The new National Liberal Party came to blend its belief in economic progress and constitutionalism with militaristic nationalism and support for the Prussian social hierarchy that Bismarck represented. Once associated with demands for political rights and constitutional reform to protect ordinary people from abuses by monarchs and aristocrats, German nationalism came more to connote military superiority. Bismarck, who later instituted many social welfare programs that benefited the German people, did nothing to discredit a vision of Prussia as a military nation led by powerful heroes like himself: "The old women, when they hear my name, fall upon their knees and beg me for their lives," he wrote to his wife during one of his wars. "Attila was a lamb compared with me." During the next decades, German ascendancy was fostered by Bismarck's flexible leadership in foreign and domestic affairs, the continuing expansion of industry, and the flowering of German culture and national pride.

Francis Joseph and the Creation of the Austro-Hungarian Monarchy

There was no blueprint for nation building. Just as the Crimean War left Russia searching for solutions to its social and political problems, so the confrontation with Cavour and Bismarck left the Habsburg Empire at bay. At first, the Habsburg Empire emerged from the revolutions of 1848 and 1849 renewed by the ascension of Francis Joseph (r. 1848–1916), who favored absolutist rule. Francis Joseph took charge of the government, working tirelessly on policies and documents and enhancing his authority through stiff, formal court ceremonies. Because the emperor insisted on grandeur and decorum, the Viennese became expert in recognizing degrees of nobility according to symbols such as insignia on carriages or one's position in funeral processions. Francis Joseph ruled by playing to the popular fascination with the trappings of power; he also stubbornly resisted change, compromising only under duress.

Despite the emperor's adherence to tradition, some changes occurred. Official standards of honesty and efficiency improved, and the government promoted local education. Although the German language was used by the administration and taught by the schools, the government respected the rights of national minorities—the Czechs and Poles, for instance—to receive education and to communicate with officials in their native tongue. Above all, the government abolished most internal customs barriers, freed trade with Germany, and sold off much of the state railway system, giving impetus to a boom in private railway construction. Foreign investment flowed into Austria; the capital city of Vienna underwent extensive rebuilding; and people found jobs as industrialization progressed.

In a fast-paced age, the emperor could not match Bismarck in advancing the power of the state. Francis Joseph's rigid adherence to absolutism often frustrated the modernizing bureaucrats. Prosperous liberals resented the swarm of police informers, the virtually free hand of the Catholic church in education and in civil institutions such as marriage, and their own lack of representation in such important policy matters as taxation and finance. Money for military modernization and warfare dried up, and Francis Joseph was forced to modify his absolutist system. He created a more modern parliament, the Reichsrat, in which German liberals predominated and which almost immediately imposed rigid economies on the military similar to those demanded by Prussian liberals in Berlin. However, the emperor lacked Bismarck's craftiness to override the liberals.

After Prussia's victory over Francis Joseph's scaled-back armies in 1866, the most disaffected but wealthy part of the empire, Hungary, became the key to stability, even to the empire's existence.

The Austro-Hungarian Monarchy, 1867

The leaders of the Hungarian agrarian elites made a simple demand: Magyar home rule over the Hungarian kingdom. Negotiating from a position of strength, the Magyar leadership forced the emperor to accept a "dual monarchy." This agreement restored the Hungarian parliament, gave it control of internal policy (including the right to decide how to treat Hungary's national minorities), and made the Hungarian contribution to the joint army a matter of negotiation every

decade. Although the Habsburg emperor Francis Joseph was crowned king of Hungary and Austro-Hungarian foreign policy was coordinated from Vienna, the Hungarians mostly ruled themselves after 1867 and hammered out any policies of joint interest, such as taxation and tariffs, in cumbersome and acrimonious negotiations with Vienna.

The dual monarchy of Austria-Hungary was designed specifically to address the Hungarian demands, but in so doing it strengthened the voices of Czechs, Slovaks, and at least half a dozen additional national groups in the Habsburg Empire wanting the same kind of consideration and self-rule. Czechs who helped the empire advance industrially failed to gain Hungarian-style liberties, and no one achieved the full range of reforms desired by the middle class of every nationality. For some of the dissatisfied ethnic groups, Pan-Slavism—that is, the transnational loyalty of all ethnic Slavs—became a rallying cry as the various Slav peoples saw themselves as having a common heritage. Instead of looking toward Vienna, they turned to the largest Slavic country—Russia—as a focal point for potential national unity. As the nation-state grew in strength, transnational movements like Pan-Slavism in Austria-Hungary would emerge to provide alternative allegiances for those not

Muslim Quarter and Bazaar
Nineteenth-century Europeans were a diverse people, composed of many religions, ethnicities, and ways of life. In the Balkans, many were Muslims, as this marketplace in Sarajevo, Bosnia, illustrates. The goal of finding a common cultural ground eluded the peoples of the Balkans. The Habsburg monarchy, which annexed Bosnia-Herzegovina in 1908, exerted its influence in the area to keep peoples divided and to play one against the other. Graphische Sammlung Albertina, Wien.

recognized as equal citizens in their home countries. Although a growing sense of national identity contributed to nation building during this period, it was increasingly a divisive and destabilizing concept.

Political Stability through Gradual Reform in Great Britain

In contrast to the turmoil on the continent, Britain appeared the epitome of liberal progress. By the 1850s, the monarchy symbolized domestic tranquillity and propriety. Unlike their predecessors, Queen Victoria (r. 1837–1901) and her husband, Prince Albert, were considered models of morality, emblematic of British stability and middle-class virtues. Britain's parliamentary system incorporated new ideas and steadily brought more men into the political process. Economic prosperity further fortified ongoing political reform, resulting in relative social peace, at least in England itself.

Whereas some countries were powder kegs of antagonistic political interests and others (such as Italy and Germany) were just being born, Great Britain was united under a single government, despite Ireland's continued suffering and its growing demands for reform. Smooth governmental decision making was fostered by an ever-changing party system. Some historians believe that the presence of a woman on the British throne allowed the monarchical system slowly to lose its prerogatives to a male electorate. Strained by the repeal of the Corn Laws in 1846, the Tory Party evolved into the Conservatives, who favored a more status-oriented politics but still went along with the developing liberal consensus around economic development and representative government. The Whigs changed names, too, and became the Liberals; the inclusion of radical members of Parliament in the government built new levels of support for liberalism. In 1867, the Conservatives, led by Benjamin Disraeli (1804–1881), passed the Second Reform Bill, which made a million more men eligible to vote. After 1867, the Conservatives and Liberals developed into more efficient political organizations with recognized platforms that targeted a wider variety of male voters.

Political parties supported reforms because pressure groups now influenced the party system.

The Law Amendment Society and the Social Science Association, for example, lobbied for laws to improve social conditions, and groups like the Reform Union and the Reform League worked for a broader male franchise. Under pressure from women's groups, the government addressed family and marital issues with the Matrimonial Causes Act of 1857, which facilitated divorce, and the Married Women's Property Act of 1870, which allowed married women to own property and keep the wages they earned. Reformist activism, much of it by the middle class, added to the political process a continuous and extensive network of groups that

Queen Victoria and Prince Albert
Mid-nineteenth-century rulers started using the new photographic technology to make themselves respectable and celebrated figures. Queen Victoria and her consort Prince Albert were expert publicists, often posing as an ordinary middle-class couple and the epitome of domestic order. Their photos were sold or given away on small cards called cartes de visites, *a means used by many leaders to spread their fame.*
The Royal Archives © Her Majesty Queen Elizabeth II.

rejected the revolutionary politics common on the continent and instead pressed for change from within the British political structure.

Not everyone favored reform, especially reforms aimed at expanding the electorate. Lower-class voters, charged an angry critic, were full of "blockheadism, gullibility, bribability, amenability to beer and balderdash." But the government overlaid liberalism with plush ceremonies that united critics and activists and, more important, different social classes. Whereas previous monarchs' sexual infidelities had inspired bawdy songs and incited crowds to riot, the monarchy of Queen Victoria and Prince Albert, with its newly devised celebrations of royal marriages, anniversaries, and births, drew respectful, though still exuberant crowds. The scheme promoting the monarchy in this way was so successful that the term *Victorian* came to symbolize almost the entire century and could refer to anything from manners to political institutions. Recalling the royal past, the aristocracy began building gigantic country houses in such traditional English architectural styles as Queen Anne and Georgian. Other building projects used a refurbished design of the thatched-roof cottage associated with the rural countryside. Like the ubiquitous monuments to Garibaldi that suggested unity, not political tensions, in the new Italy, these symbols of Merrie Olde England evoked a common past to harmonize the dislocations of rapid urbanization and industrialization. As one poet expressed it:

> Forget the spreading of the hideous town;
> Think rather of the pack-horse on the down,
> And dream of London, small, and white,
>   and clean.

Britain's politicians were as devoted to Realpolitik as were those in Germany, Italy, or France, but robust industry, a liberal consensus, and an expanding overseas empire underwrote Britain's special success in creating the sense of a shared political destiny. Acquiring its expanding empire inflicted the same toll of violence as did German, Italian, and U.S. nation building. The violence was far beyond the view of most British people, however, allowing them to imagine their nation as peaceful, advanced, and united.

Civil War and Nation Building in the United States and Canada

In North America, increasing nationalism and powerful economic growth characterized the nation-building experience. The United States entered a midcentury period of upheaval with a more democratic political culture than Europe had. Virtually universal white male suffrage, a rambunctiously independent press, and mass political parties endorsed the accepted view that sovereignty derived from the people.

The United States continued to expand its territory to the west (Map 23.4). In 1848, victory in its war with Mexico almost doubled the size of the country: Texas was officially annexed, and large portions of California and the Southwest extended U.S. borders into former Mexican land. Politicians and citizens alike favored banning the native Indian peoples from these western lands. Complicating matters, however, was the question of whether the West would be settled by free white farmers or whether southern slaveholders could bring in their slaves.

The issue polarized the country. In the North, the new Republican Party emerged to demand "free soil, free labor, free men," although few Republicans endorsed the abolitionists' demand to end slavery. With the 1860 election of Republican Abraham Lincoln to the presidency, most of the slaveholding states seceded to form the Confederate States of America. Between 1861 and 1865, the United States was torn apart by a devastating civil war.

Under Lincoln's leadership, the North fought to uphold the Union. Lincoln did not initially aim to abolish slavery, but in January 1863 his Emancipation Proclamation came into force as a wartime measure, officially freeing all slaves in the Confederate states and turning the war into a fight not only for union but also for liberation from slavery. After the summer of 1863, the North's superior industrial strength and military might overpowered and physically destroyed much of the South. By April 1865, the North had prevailed, even though a Confederate sympathizer had assassinated Lincoln. Distancing the United States still further from the colonial, plantation model, constitutional amendments ended slavery and promised free African American men full political rights.

Battle of Fredericksburg, 1863

President Abraham Lincoln cemented North and South by military means in the U.S. Civil War, which destroyed large sections of the Southeast. A war with huge casualties inflicted by the industrial development of modern weaponry, the Civil War took place on farmlands and in cities and towns. This depiction by a local artist captures the disorderly setting of the battle of Fredericksburg in the summer of 1863.
Corbis/Bettmann.

MAP 23.4 United States Expansion, 1850–1870

Like Russia, the United States expanded into adjacent regions to create a continental nation-state. Conquering indigenous peoples and taking over their territories, the United States differed from Russia, however, by herding native peoples into small confined spaces called reservations so that settlers could acquire thousands of square miles for farming and other enterprises. Gradually some Native Americans acquired the right to vote, and the United States government granted full citizenship for all in 1925.

Northerners hailed their victory as the triumph of American values, but racism remained entrenched throughout the Union. By 1871, northern interest in promoting African American political rights was waning, and southern whites began regaining control of state politics, often by organized violence and intimidation. The end of northern occupation of the South in 1877 put on hold for nearly a century the promise of rights for blacks.

The North's triumph had profound effects elsewhere in North America. It allowed the reunited United States to contribute to Napoleon III's defeat in Mexico in 1867. The United States also demanded the annexation of Canada in retribution for Britain's partiality to the Confederacy because of its dependence on cotton. To head off this threat, the British government allowed Canadians to form a united, self-governing dominion. According dominion status answered Canadian appeals for home rule and lessened domestic opposition to Britain's owning Canada in the first place.

❖ Instituting Social Order

In this age of nation building, government officials developed mechanisms to forge internal social unity and order that served to clean up or offset the violence by which the state was expanding. Confronted with growing populations and crowded cities, governments throughout Europe intervened in more areas of everyday life. (See "Taking Measure," page 868.) Many liberal theorists advocated a laissez-faire government that left social and economic life largely to private enterprise. But waves of revolution and epidemics convinced officials that the state needed to guard social peace by attending to the health and safety of its citizens. Along with continuing industrial development, expanding public institutions in Europe during the 1850s and 1860s affected the psychological, physical, and social life of ordinary citizens. Nevertheless, having confidence in the benefits of European institutions in general, bureaucrats, missionaries, and explorers pressed European influence beyond the nation-state's boundaries into the farthest reaches of the globe.

Bringing Order to the Cities

Dramatic changes in the urban environment made many European cities the backdrop for displays of state power and national solidarity. Efforts to improve sanitation and control disease also redounded to the state's credit. Governments focused their refurbishing efforts on their capital cities, although many noncapital cities acquired handsome parks, widened streets, and erected stately museums and massive city halls. In 1857, Francis Joseph ordered the destruction of the old Viennese city walls and their replacement with concentric boulevards lined with major public buildings such as the opera house and government offices. Napoleon III initiated similar embellishment of Paris, making it the symbol of his regime's grandeur. Opera houses and ministries tangibly represented national wealth and power, and the broad boulevards allowed crowds to observe royal pageantry. These wider roads were also easier for troops to navigate than the twisted, narrow medieval streets that in 1848 had concealed insurrectionists in cities like Paris and Vienna—an advantage that convinced some otherwise reluctant officials to approve the expense. Impressive parks and public gardens showed the state's control of nature, while they helped order people's leisure time. The revamped city inspired awe for the nation-state or empire.

One effect of refurbished cities was to highlight class differences. Construction first required destruction; buildings and entire neighborhoods of housing for the poor disappeared, and thousands of city dwellers were dislocated. The boulevards often served as boundaries marking rich and poor sections of the city. In Vienna, wealthy inhabitants even suggested walling off major streets so they might obtain a more secure separation from the poor. In Paris, the process of urban change was called *Haussmannization*, named for the prefect Georges-Eugène Haussmann, who implemented a grand design that included eighty-five miles of new city streets, many lined with showy dwellings for the wealthy. Tens of thousands of poor people lost their homes, as old buildings were torn down. London experienced more piecemeal urban development. British city planners nonetheless saw advantages in rebuilding for an industrial nation, and large commercial streets replaced slums and lower-class neighborhoods.

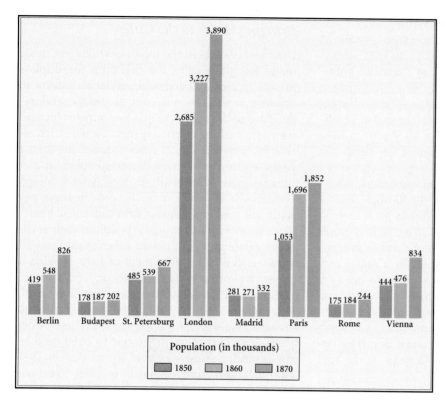

TAKING MEASURE
**Urban Population Growth,
1850–1870**
*As state building and industrial-
ization advanced, population
grew in capital, commercial,
and manufacturing cities and
towns. As this graph shows,
major cities gained hundreds of
thousands of new inhabitants,
and the outdated urban environment was usually strained
beyond its capacity. Industrial
and commercial cities like Leeds,
Essen, Düsseldorf, and Lodz doubled and even quintupled in
size, however.*
B.R. Mitchell, *International Historical Statistics, 1750–1993* (New
York: Macmillan, 1998), 74–76.

Other improvements in London seemed only decorative: old building facades, for example, were given a new look with graceful plasterwork and pillars. Those who undertook these embellishments, which often strike twentieth-century observers as manifestations of Victorian excess and bad taste, believed that ornamentation would blot out the ugliness of commerce and industry. Public beauty would enhance pedestrians' lives and lift their spirits. Moreover, the size and spaciousness of the many new banks and insurance companies built in London "help[ed] the impression of stability," as an architect put it, and this would foster social order.

Amid signs of economic prosperity, the devastation caused by repeated epidemics of diseases such as cholera debilitated city dwellers and gave the strong impression of social decay. Poor sanitation allowed typhoid bacteria to spread through sewage and into water supplies, infecting rich and poor alike. In 1861, Britain's Prince Albert reputedly died of typhus, commonly known as a "filth disease." Unregulated urban slaughterhouses and

tanneries; heaps of animal excrement in chicken coops, pigsties, and stables; human waste alongside buildings; open cesspools; and garbage everywhere facilitated the spread of disease. The many corpses that had to be buried during epidemics also posed health problems. As society grew more prosperous, the stench, diseases, and "morbid air" of cities indicated such a degree of failure, disorder, and danger that sanitation became a government priority.

Scientific research, increasingly undertaken in public universities and hospitals, provided the means to promote public health and control disease. Initial efforts to improve public sanitation relied on the *miasmatic theory* of disease, which traced sickness to breathing in putrid odors. The germ theory advanced by France's Louis Pasteur (1822–1895), whose three young daughters had died of typhus, was not only more accurate but also had widespread sanitary application. Seeking a method to prevent wine from spoiling, Pasteur began his work in the mid-1850s by studying fermentation. He found that the growth of living organisms caused fermentation, and he suggested that certain organisms—bacteria and parasites—might be responsible for human and animal diseases. Pasteur further demonstrated that heating foods such as wine and milk to a certain temperature, a process that soon became known as *pasteurization*, killed these organisms and made food safe. In the mid-1860s, the English surgeon Joseph Lister (1827–1912) applied the germ theory in medicine. He connected Pasteur's theory of bacteria to infection and developed antiseptics for treating wounds. Using carbolic acid for sterilization, as Lister suggested, hastened the decline of puerperal fever, a condition that was caused by the dirty hands of physicians and midwives and that killed innumerable women after childbirth.

Even though the germ theory proved that "morbid air" did not cause disease, air pollution still bothered city dwellers, prompting the most fastidious to move to elegant suburbs, where they could breathe fresher air and also escape the sight of their poorer neighbors. Land development and new roads also gave workers displaced by urban renewal a chance to live outside the city. By the mid-1860s, the Viennese, like residents of other capitals, could travel the city and reach rings of inner and outer suburbs by streetcar or horse-drawn omnibuses.

Meanwhile, governments undertook projects to improve sewer systems and drainage. In Paris, huge underground collectors provided a watertight terminus for accumulated sewage. In addition, Haussmann was determined to provide fresh water for every Parisian dwelling. To do so, he piped in water from less-contaminated sources in the countryside. Such ventures were imitated throughout Europe: the Russian Empire's port city Riga (now in Latvia), for example, organized its first water company in 1863. Improved sanitation testified to progress and a more active role for the state. Modernization of the city also encouraged new values. Citizens came to prize these material improvements

Vienna Opera House
The era of nation building saw the construction of architectural monuments in the center of capital cities to display cultural power and to bring music, art, and science to the people. Vienna's center was rebuilt around imposing facades like that of the Imperial Opera House, which opened in 1869.
Hulton Getty/Liaison Agency.

Paris Sewer

The Paris sewers were rebuilt in Napoleon III's Second Empire as models of modern hygiene sponsored by the state. Their construction was part of the effort to eliminate smells and signs of germs from both public and private life. As society opted for hygiene, sewers became emblematic of dangerous and diseased peoples who were threats to social well-being and order.
Corbis/Bettmann.

and came to develop a deeper feeling of national and local pride.

Ordinary people often supported better public works despite the governmental expansion and higher taxes such improvements entailed. Shopkeepers agitated for paved streets to end the difficulties of transporting goods along muddy or flooded roadways. When public toilets for men became a feature of modern Paris, women petitioned the government unsuccessfully for decades for similar facilities. On the lookout for disease and sanitary dangers, the average person became more aware of smells and the foul air that had been an accepted part of daily life for thousands of years. A citizen of Voronezh in central Russia reported to the Moscow papers that "an enormous cloud of white dust [hung] constantly over the city," injuring the lungs and eyes. To show that they were becoming more "civilized," the middle and lower-middle classes bathed more regularly and even perfumed themselves, something aristocrats had been doing for centuries. Middle-class concerns for refinement and health coincided with the quest of governments for order.

Expanding the Reach of Bureaucracy

Central to enacting new programs to build social order and enhance the nation was an expansion of state bureaucracies. The nation-state required citizens to follow a growing catalog of regulations, as government authority reached further into the realm of everyday life. The regular censuses that Britain, France, and the United States had begun early in the nineteenth century became routine in most other countries as well. Censuses provided the state with such personal details of its citizens' lives as age, occupation, marital status, residential patterns, and fertility. Governments then used these data for a variety of endeavors, ranging from setting quotas for military conscription to predicting needs for new prisons. Reformers like Florence Nightingale, who gathered medical and other statistics to support sanitary and military reform, believed that such quantitative information made government less susceptible to corruption, special deals, and inefficiency. In 1860, Sweden introduced taxation based on income, which opened an area of private life—one's earnings from work or investment—to government scrutiny. The extension of bureaucracy pleased those who thought centralized policies would help society operate more fairly and efficiently than the capricious rule of local notables, but those who believed in laissez-faire often opposed such "intrusions."

To bring about their vision of social order, most governments, including those of Britain, Italy, Austria, and France, also expanded their regulation and investigation of prostitution. Venereal disease, especially syphilis, was a scourge of the era that, like typhus, infected individuals and whole families. Officials blamed prostitutes for its spread. The police picked up any suspect woman on the street and passed her to public health doctors who examined her for syphilis. If the woman was infected with the disease she was sent to a medical institution for mandatory treatment, which usually meant a period of incarceration. To control prostitution in cities, French public planners stipulated that brothels could be built only in designated neighborhoods. As states began monitoring prostitution and other social matters like public health and housing, they had to add new departments and agencies. In 1867, Hungary's bureaucracy handled fewer than 250,000 individual cases, ranging from health to poverty issues; twenty years later it dealt with more than a million.

As government bureaucracies grew, new jobs opened. The looming question was who would get these influential, relatively secure, and higher-status positions. Would the old aristocracy and their clients fill them? Or would the government hire people based on merit and skill? In the Austro-Hungarian monarchy, an effort to open bureaucratic posts to native speakers prompted various nationalities to demand that their language replace German as the official language of local administration. The middle classes in the empire lobbied to eliminate aristocrats' stranglehold on the top positions and to keep civil service jobs from becoming a reward for political loyalty. In Britain, a civil service law passed in 1870 required competitive examinations for government posts—an idea in the air since the West had come in contact with the Chinese examination system. The push for reform in Sweden transformed the bureaucracy from an aristocratic bastion to a civil service in which more than two-thirds of all jobs went to members of the middle class. Not only did government impose new standards of order, but citizens also insisted that the state itself conform to middle-class ideas of competence and opportunity.

Schooling Society

Bureaucrats and reformers called for radical changes in the scope, curriculum, and personnel of schools—from kindergarten to university—to make the general population more fit for citizenship and useful in furthering economic progress. Ongoing expansion of the electorate along with lower-class activism prompted one British aristocrat to exclaim, "We must now educate our masters!" The growth of commerce and the state was partly behind a craze for learning, which made traveling lecturers, public forums, reading groups, and debating societies popular among the middle and working classes. Governments also introduced compulsory schooling to reduce illiteracy (more than 70 percent in Italy and Spain in the 1870s and even higher in eastern than in western Europe).

Even a few hours of lessons each day were said to teach important social habits and the responsi-

bilities of citizenship, along with practical knowledge. The impulse to strengthen the educational system came from a variety of quarters: liberals, nationalists, conservatives, and radicals all believed in bettering educational opportunities. However, the ends differed: to train people for the civil service or industry, to encourage civic loyalty, to instill patterns of obedience, to develop "modern" attitudes.

Primary education had traditionally emphasized religious instruction, with church doctrine, biblical maxims, and obedience at the core of the curriculum. Initially, various denominations had supervised schools and charged tuition, making primary education an option chosen only by prosperous or religious parents. Curricular changes in the 1850s and 1860s aimed at introducing secular and scientific instruction, because many leaders felt that liberal rationalism should supplant religiosity as a guiding principle. In 1861, an English commission on education concluded that instead of the Bible, "the knowledge most important to a labouring man is that of the causes which regulate the amount of his wages, the hours of his work, the regularity of his employment, and the prices of what he consumes."

Accomplishing this instruction was another matter. For example, the Netherlands and Switzerland had fully functioning systems of public primary schools in the 1830s, and Sweden ordered towns and parishes to provide primary schooling after 1842. Yet school attendance was virtually impossible to enforce, because it often conflicted with family interests. Rural parents depended on their children to perform farm chores and believed that they would gain useful knowledge in the fields or the household. Urban homemakers needed their children to help with domestic tasks such as fetching water, disposing of waste, tending the younger children, and scavenging for household necessities such as stale bread from bakers or soup from local missions. Secondary and university education was even more of a luxury, reserved for the top echelons of society, and officials argued endlessly about the curriculum of higher education. In many countries people debated whether future leaders should have traditional education in religion, a classical education based on Latin and Greek, or a liberal arts education grounded in science, mathematics, and modern languages. In Russia, for example, the government considered technical subjects and science potentially subversive and closely monitored university professors.

Amid the controversy over the best kind of education, the secondary school became more systematized, reflecting the demands of both an industrial society and a bureaucratic state. In Prussia, a system of secondary schools (*Gymnasia*) offered a liberal arts curriculum that trained students for a variety of careers. Those who left after a few years entered the lower ranks of the bureaucracy; higher-level positions in government and the professions were reserved for graduates and those who went to the university. In the 1860s, however, new *Realschulen*, less prestigious at the time, emphasized math, science, and modern languages for those who would not attain a Gymnasium degree or go on to attend the university. Typically, those trying for a business or technical career pursued the Realschulen education. Like many other countries, Prussia ultimately developed an intricate educational system to track the various career paths and social strata of its students.

Girls and young women were educated separately from boys, just as they were prepared for separate spheres in their adult lives. Reformers pushed for more advanced and more complex courses for young women than the fare they were initially offered. In France and Russia, for example, government leaders themselves saw that "public education has had in view only half the population—the male sex," as the Russian minister of education wrote to Tsar Alexander II in 1856. Both Napoleon III and Alexander II sponsored secondary- and university-level courses for women as part of their program to control the modernization of society. Nonetheless, higher education for women remained a hotly contested issue because religion, sewing, deportment, and writing appeared more than adequate. Yet reformers from across the political spectrum concurred that well-educated mothers—those who knew some science, history, and literature—would rear their children better and prove more satisfactory companions to their husbands.

Young women who attended universities in Zurich and Paris in the 1860s, where medical training was open to them, often aspired to an education that would qualify them to move into social roles other than those of wife and mother. The expansion of the medical profession and the opportunities in

public health appealed to women's reforming zeal. By joining a profession only men had previously entered, these women appeared to weaken the system of separate spheres. Yet many women wanted to practice medicine to protect female patients' modesty and to bring feminine values to health care. Women doctors claimed to perform examinations and treatments with more discretion and concern for female patients than shown by male doctors. In Britain the founders of two women's colleges, Girton (1869) and Newnham (1871) at Cambridge University, believed that exacting standards in women's higher education would provide an example of a modern curriculum in this stronghold of traditional learning. Reformers maintained that low standards of scholarship prevalent in the men's colleges of Cambridge and Oxford reinforced the gentlemanly ideal that education served primarily as a mark of social status. Rewarding merit and competition in women's education, they hoped, would lead to improved education for men too. As in primary-school reform, better education for women served a variety of ends.

The expansion of preschool education offered an opportunity for large numbers of women to enter teaching, a field once dominated by men. Influenced by the German reformer Friedrich Froebel, hundreds of women founded nurseries, kindergartens, primary schools, and day-care centers. Education in many of these institutions was based on Enlightenment ideas, which held that instruction and supervision by mothers from an early age started developmental processes on the right footing. In Italy, women founded schools as a way to expand knowledge and teach civics lessons, thus providing a service to the fledgling state. Yet the idea of women theorizing about educational development and teaching citizenship also aroused intense opposition: "I shudder at philosophic women," wrote one critic of female kindergarten teachers. Seen as radical because it enticed middle-class women out of the home, the cause of early childhood education, or the "kindergarten movement," was as controversial as most other educational reforms.

Spreading Western Order beyond the West

In an age of nation building, colonies took on new importance, adding a political dimension, including direct rule from the homeland, to the economic role that global trade already played in national prosperity. Great-power jockeying and securing colonial trade provided motives for continued global expansion as the 1850s opened. Gaining strategic commercial and military advantages remained an important motivation for some European overseas ventures in this age of Realpolitik. The Crimean War had shown the great powers that the Mediterranean basin was pivotal in European trade. Napoleon III, remembering his uncle's campaign in Egypt, took an interest in building the Suez Canal, which would connect the Mediterranean with the Red Sea and the Indian Ocean and thus dramatically shorten the route to Asia. The canal was completed in 1869 and formally opened by Empress Eugénie with a gala celebration. Canal fever spread: Verdi composed the opera *Aïda* (set in ancient Egypt), but the Franco-Prussian War of 1870 delayed its premiere.

After midcentury, however, Great Britain, France, and Russia revised their colonial policies by instituting direct rule, expanding colonial bureaucracies, and in many cases providing a wider array of social and cultural services such as schools. In the 1850s and 1860s, provincial governors and local officials promoted the extension of Russian borders to gain control over many nomadic tribes in central and eastern Asia. As in areas like Poland and the Ukraine, they instituted educational and religious policies that they felt were central to social order. The state redefined its self-interest as it expanded the quest for order far beyond its borders.

Imperial expansion was a matter of push, pull, and paradox. The French government pushed to establish its dominion over Cochin China (modern southern Vietnam) in the 1860s. But missionaries in the area, ambitious French naval officers stationed in Asia, and even some local peoples pulled the French government to commit resources to successive attacks in the region. Likewise, driving into the North African hinterland, the French army occupied all of Algeria by 1870; Napoleon established a governmental agency for "Algeria and the colonies," and the number of immigrants reached one-quarter million by 1870. There was also a pull: French rule in Algeria, like European rule in many other parts of the non-European world, was aided by the attraction of European goods, technology, and institutions to the local peoples. Merchants and local leaders cooperated in building railroads,

sought bank loans and trade from the French, and sent their children to schools that provided a European education. Like the rural and working classes at home, many local peoples resisted the invasions, died from European-spread diseases, or did not benefit from this expansion. By 1872, the native population in Algeria had declined by more than 20 percent from five years earlier.

Great Britain, the era's mightiest colonial power, made a dramatic change of course toward direct political rule during these decades. Before the 1850s, British liberals desired the commercial opportunities offered by colonies, but, believing in laissez-faire, they also wanted to spend as few public resources as possible in governing them. Thus, political involvement in colonial affairs remained minimal, whereas trading treaties multiplied. In India, for example, the British government exercised control indirectly through the East India Company, and many regional rulers maintained their thrones by awarding the company commercial advantages. Since the eighteenth century, the East India Company had expanded its dominion over various kingdoms on the Indian subcontinent whenever a regional throne fell vacant and built railroads throughout the countryside. Contrary to strict laissez-faire beliefs, British institutions gradually arose in India, inspired in part by historian Thomas Macaulay, who two decades earlier in the House of Commons had called for an activist colonial policy to form "a class of persons, Indians in blood and colour, but English in taste, in opinion, in morals, and in intellect." An expanding British bureaucratic and economic presence allowed some Indian merchants to grow wealthy

Indian Resistance, 1857

and send their children to British schools. Other local men enlisted in the British-run Indian army.

Resistance and resentment grew as British institutions became more widespread. In 1857, Indian troops, both Muslim and Hindu, violently

Photographs and Their Messages

After almost a century of experimentation, photography was invented in France and Britain in 1839, by a handful of different men, working independently. Photography immediately expanded people's access to visual information. Ordinary people were quick to have their photographs taken to send to distant relatives or to make visual records for themselves. Governments also understood photography to be an important resource. In the Crimean War, photographers began to substitute for official illustrators and mapmakers who customarily sketched out the vistas of towns and roads, including the placement of public buildings, natural lines of defense, and fortifications necessary for army maneuvers. Army illustrators flocked to this unrecorded region, but so did photographers. One was Carol Popp de Szathmari of Budapest, who took photos of both Russian and Turkish camps; he later sold a photo album of the war containing more than two hundred pictures. It was in this war that newspapers also began printing lithographs of wartime destruction to buildings. As in many wars, photographs of human carnage were not generally shown. An eager public bought both newspapers and albums and strengthened their allegiance to the nation-state and its wars.

Since the Crimean War, historians have recognized the importance of photography for the data it provides. Photographers recorded the vast interest in Asia and the Middle East as evidenced in the thousands of extant photographs of monuments of Egypt, Turkey, and Japan taken in the second half of the nineteenth century. *Social Life of the Chinese: A Daguerreotype of Daily Life in China* was a popular album of photos published in 1868. Historians have also believed that images of the great personages made the study of the past more vivid and more knowable. Using photos of furniture and fashions that salesmen carried from city to city in the 1850s and 1860s, historians have been able to visualize everyday life better. Individual portraits of ordinary people taken in intricately designed photography studios have similarly given a sense of what constituted people's physical reality or their fantasies of what it should be.

Recently, however, photography in this period has come to yield new interpretations, especially about people's values. The earliest photos started inching the West toward its modern celebrity cult. Photos of renowned professors were sold right outside their classroom doors, while great poets, kings and queens, businessmen, and public figures had their likenesses taken. The widespread distribution of these photos in magazines, in books, and on individual cards, called *cartes de visites*, made all of these personalities more popular. Political knowledge was spread on these little cards. The execution of Maximilian in 1867, for example, was memorialized in photos of

rebelled against regulations that violated their religious practices. Ignoring the Hindu ban on beef and the Muslim prohibition on pork, the British forced Indian soldiers to use cartridges greased with cow and pig fat. The infuriated soldiers stormed and conquered Delhi and declared the independence of the Indian nation—an uprising that became known as the Sepoy Mutiny. Simultaneously the Rani Lakshmibai, widow of the ruler of the state of Jhansi in central India, led a separate military revolt when the East India Company tried to take over her lands after her husband died. Brutally put down by the British as the record of pho-

tography would show, the Sepoy Mutiny and the Jhansi revolt gave birth to Indian nationalism. (See "New Sources, New Perspectives," above.) They also persuaded the British government to take direct control of India rather than work through the East India Company. "Despotism is a legitimate mode of government . . . with barbarians, provided the end be improvement," the liberal thinker John Stuart Mill proclaimed after the rebellions. The Government of India Act of 1858 redefined India as the concern of the British cabinet in London; the resulting colonial civil service reinforced the trend to direct governmental control of all colonies.

Sepoy Mutiny, 1857
Photographers were on the scene at Lucknow in India to capture the destruction of the Sepoy Mutiny. The West viewed the mutiny as resulting from the savagery of the Asians, while the damage inflicted by the British served to remind Westerners and colonized peoples alike of the superior power of European civilization. Photography was an integral part of the advance of imperialism, recording its progress and transmitting news from the rest of the world. Gernsheim Collection, Harry Ransom Humanities Center/University of Texas (Austin).

his dead body that were affixed to cards and sold to the public. The British royal family had *cartes de visites* made of the Prince of Wales and Princess Alexandra on their marriage to build allegiance to the monarchy.

Photography allowed people to manipulate reality. Historians have recently seen the genius of Queen Isabella II of Spain, whose chaotic administration was made to look orderly by her official photographer's expert shots of tidy parts of cities and public buildings. The queen had set this pub-

licist to work as early as 1852 to change the image of her reign. Even battlefield shots, historians have recently admitted, were often staged after the fact. Whereas once historians might have looked at images of mid-nineteenth-century Balkan peasants for the information about costumes, now they see further: that these photos were taken to build allegiance to Balkan liberation from Ottomans and Habsburgs. The photograph—on the surface a portrayal of a single reality—may have still more to yield the imaginative viewer.

In China, Christian missionaries from European countries, carrying their message of Christian salvation, provided an opening for Western powers to enhance their position there. Directing the Christian message to a population that had almost doubled during the preceding century and now numbered about 430 million, missionaries spread Christianity among people already disturbed by demographic growth, defeat in the Opium War, and economic pressures from European trade. These contacts with the West had helped generate the mass movement known as the Taiping (Heavenly Kingdom). The leader, Hung Hsui-ch'uan

(Hong Xinquan), who believed he was the younger brother of Jesus Christ, attracted millions of followers by preaching an end to the ruling Qing dynasty, the reform of morals, the elimination of foreigners, more equal treatment of women, and land reform. By the mid-1850s, the Taiping controlled half of China. The Qing regime, its dynasty threatened, promised the British and French greater economic and political influence in exchange for aid. The result was a bloody civil war that lasted until 1864 with some 30–60 million Chinese killed (compared with 600,000 dead in the U.S. Civil War, 1861–1865). When peace finally came, Western governments controlled much of the Chinese customs service and had virtually unlimited access to the country.

Japan alone was able to escape European domination. Through Dutch traders at Nagasaki, the Japanese had become keenly aware of the rising Western challenge to China but also of the important industrial, military, and commercial innovations of European society. Thus in 1854, when American commodore Matthew Perry declared that he had "opened" Japan to trade, contacts with Europe had already given the Japanese a healthy appetite for Western goods and knowledge. Curiosity, ambition, and fear that the United States would attack its cities with superior weapons motivated the trade agreements that followed Perry's arrival, but relations with the West became increasingly tense. In 1867, the ruling Tokugawa shogun (the dominant military leader) abdicated under pressure from reformers, who restored the emperor to full power. The goal of the Meiji Restoration was to establish Japan as a modern, technologically powerful state free from Western control. Even the word *Meiji*, chosen by the new emperor to name his reign, meant "enlightened rule," as the regime professed to combine "Western science and Eastern values" as a way of "making new"—hence, *restoration*. The Meiji Restoration ultimately inspired other countries to resist the intensifying pressure of Europeans.

❖ Artistic and Intellectual Visions of Social Order

Artists and writers helped build the age of realism and social order with their complex reactions to the rising nation-state and its expanding reach. After 1848, many artists and writers expressed profound grievances, notably about the brutal repression of revolutionary activists, and real concerns about the effect of enfranchising working-class men. Infused with commercial values and organized by officials, daily life seemed tawdry and hardly bearable to many artists. Unlike the romantics of the first half of the century, however, artists of the 1850s and 1860s often had difficulty depicting heroic alternatives or recapturing an ideal past. "How tired I am of the ignoble workman, the inept

bourgeois, the stupid peasant, and the odious priest," wrote the French novelist Gustave Flaubert, frustrated by his inability to romanticize these figures as previous generations had done. Such disenchantment promoted the literary and artistic style called *realism*. In contrast, intellectuals proposed theories called *positivism* and *Darwinism*, which appraised social change and even political upheaval as part of human progress. Realism, positivism, and Darwinism shared a claim to look at society with a detached eye and to depict social order starkly.

The Arts Confront Social Reality

The quest for national power enlisted culture in its cause. A hungry reading public devoured biographies of political leaders, past and present, and credited heroes with creating the triumphant nation-state. Energetic and commanding figures such as the Italian Garibaldi ultimately served as substitutes for both the divine-right king and the active democratic citizen. As literacy spread through schooling, all classes of readers responded to the mid-nineteenth-century novel and to an increasing number of artistic, scientific, and natural history exhibitions. Whether reading the same novels or attending musical events together, citizens came to be schooled in a common artistic style called *realism*.

The Realist Novel. A well-financed press and commercially minded publishers produced an age of best-sellers out of the craving for realism. The novels of Charles Dickens (1812–1870) appeared in serial form in magazines and periodicals, and each installment attracted eager buyers for the latest plot twist. His characters came from contemporary English society and included starving orphans, grasping lawyers, heartless bankers, and ruthless opportunists. *Hard Times* (1854) depicted the difficult life of sensitive members of the middle class as well as the grinding poverty and ill health of workers. *Bleak House* (1852) used dark humor to portray the judicial bureaucracy's intrusion into private life, while Dickens's other novels linked social ills to poorhouses and other bureaucratic institutions. Professing to depict ordinary reality, popular novels like Dickens's helped form a shared culture among people in distant parts of a nation much as state institutions did.

The novelist George Eliot (the pseudonym of Mary Ann Evans, 1819–1880) was also celebrated and widely read. Her novels examined contemporary moral values and deeply probed private dilemmas: works like *The Mill on the Floss* (1860) and *Middlemarch* (1871–1872) showed heroines vacillating between a world of imagination and the "real" world of family. Depicting rural society—high and low—Eliot allowed Britons to see one another's predicaments, wherever they lived. Eliot knew the pain of ordinary life from her own experience: she was a social outcast because she lived with a married man. Despite her fame, she was not received in polite society. Her depictions of social order emphasized the fragility and torment of institutions such as the family and marriage—conventionally upheld as the bulwark of stability.

French writers scorned dreams of political utopias and ideals of transcendent beauty, preferring instead to show the world as it was. In *Madame Bovary* (1857), Gustave Flaubert (1821–1880) told the story of a bored doctor's wife who, full of romantic longings and eager for distraction, has one love affair after another and becomes so hopelessly indebted that she commits suicide. Serialized in a Paris journal, *Madame Bovary* scandalized French society for its brutal depiction of marriage and frank picture of women's sexuality. The poet Charles-Pierre Baudelaire (1821–1867), called "Satanic" by his critics, wrote explicitly about sex, gaining shocked attention from the buying public on whom writers now depended. In *Les Fleurs du mal* ("Flowers of Evil," 1857), he expressed sexual passion, described drug- and wine-induced fantasies, and spun out visions condemned as perverse. Both Flaubert and Baudelaire attacked a range of social conventions, but the French authorities fought back, successfully prosecuting the two writers on obscenity charges. The issue was social and artistic order: "Art without rules is no longer art," the prosecutor maintained.

During the era of the Great Reforms, Russian writers debated whether western European values were insidiously transforming their culture. Rather than dividing the nation, this discussion about the nature of Russian culture united people around a national issue. From one viewpoint, Ivan Turgenev (1818–1883) created a powerful novel of Russian life, *Fathers and Sons* (1862), a story of nihilistic

An Age of Great Books

1851	Auguste Comte, *System of Positive Politics*
1852	Harriet Beecher Stowe, *Uncle Tom's Cabin*
1854	Charles Dickens, *Hard Times*
1857	Gustave Flaubert, *Madame Bovary*
	Charles Baudelaire, *Les Fleurs du mal*
1859	Charles Darwin, *On the Origin of Species*
	John Stuart Mill, *On Liberty*
1866	Fyodor Dostoevsky, *Crime and Punishment*
1867	Karl Marx, *Das Kapital*
1869	John Stuart Mill, *The Subjection of Women*
1871–1872	George Eliot, *Middlemarch*

children rejecting the older, romantic generation's spiritual values and espousing science instead. Popular in the West, Turgenev aroused anger in Russian readers for the way he criticized both romantics and the new generation of hardheaded "materialists." From another point of view, Fyodor Dostoevsky (1821–1881) satirized Turgenev's writing in *The Possessed* (1871–1872) and other works by showing the dark, ridiculous, and neurotic side of nihilists and thus holding up Turgenev as a softheaded romantic. Dostoevsky was exiled to Siberia late in the 1840s for participating in a political study group; there his contact with many common criminals provided him with models for his brand of literary antihero featured in *Notes from the Underground* (1864) and *Crime and Punishment* (1866). His highly intelligent characters are often personally tormented and condemned to lead absurd lives. Dostoevsky used these antiheroes to emphasize spirituality and traditional Russian values, but with a "realistic" spin by planting such values in ordinary people, not elevated, noble, unrealistic types.

Painting and Sculpture. Unlike writers, visual artists across Europe depended on government commissions, and government-sponsored exhibitions drew a more limited set of buyers. Prince Albert of England was an active patron of the arts, purchasing works for official collections and for himself until his death in 1861. Having artwork

Gustave Courbet, *Wrestlers* (1850)
Courbet painted his dirty, grunting wrestlers in the realist style, which rejected the hazy romanticism of revolutionary Europe. These muscular men summed up the resort to physical struggle during the state-building decades as well as conveyed the art world's recognition that Realpolitik had taken over the governance of society.
Museum of Fine Arts, Budapest/The Bridgeman Art Library, NY.

displayed at government-sponsored exhibitions (called *salons* in Paris, the center of the art world) was the best way for an artist to gain prominence and earn a living. Officially appointed juries selected works of art to appear in the salon and then chose prize winners from among them. By the Second Empire, thousands of paintings were shown annually, with hundreds of thousands of people from all classes in attendance. Nearly a million people visited the art portion of the international exposition held in Paris in 1855.

After 1848, the repression of political opposition lessened the romantic glorification of workers, country folk, and nature. Instead of idealizing their

subjects, artists took the lead of novelists in realistically depicting society. French painter Gustave Courbet (1819–1877) portrayed groaning laborers at backbreaking work because he believed an artist should "never permit sentiment to overthrow logic." Art could foster "democracy" by showing the world as it was and hiding neither the shabbiness nor the depravity of life.

These realist painters also rejected grand historic scenes and instead traced the course of social change, particularly the reconstruction of cities. Paris, artists found, had become a visual spectacle, a place of grand boulevards where urban residents performed as part of the cityscape. The artists' canvases showed the renovated city as a stage for individual ambition and display. *Universal Exhibition* (1867) by Édouard Manet (1823–1883) used the world's fair of 1867 as the background; figures from all social classes in the foreground were separated from one another by the planned urban spaces as they promenaded, gazing at the Paris scene and watching one another to learn the new social rules of modern life.

Manet's work removed the rose-colored glasses through which polite society seemed to view women and sexuality. His famous *Déjeuner sur l'herbe* ("Luncheon on the Grass," 1863) was deemed scandalous because it portrayed two women, one naked and the other half-dressed, on a picnic in a woods with fully clothed contemporary men. Manet's *Olympia* (1865) depicted a white courtesan lying on her bed, attended by a black woman. Both nudes shocked audiences because they showed women's bodies in realistic settings instead of mythologizing and romanticizing them. This disregard for the classical traditions of the fine arts was too much for the critics: "A sort of female gorilla," one wrote of *Olympia*. "Her greenish, bloodshot eyes appear to be provoking to the public," wrote another. Shocking at first, graphic portrayals that shattered comforting illusions became a feature of modern art.

Opera. Unlike most of the visual arts, opera was commercially profitable, accessible to most classes of society, and thus effective artistically for reaching the nineteenth-century public. Verdi used musical theater to contrast noble ideals with the corrosive effects of power, love of country with the

Édouard Manet, *Déjeuner sur l'herbe* ("Luncheon on the Grass," 1863)
The leading painters of the Parisian art world rejected the highly idealized paintings of nudes and romanticized historical scenes. In Manet's portrayal of a picnic, the clothed men made the nude and seminude women, with their garments tossed about, seem out of place and even lewd. Such critical art annoyed many genteel citizens in the art-viewing public.
Giraudon/Art Resource, NY.

inevitable call for sacrifice and death, and the lure of passion with the need for social order. His *La Traviata* (1853) stunned audiences with the tragedy of a tubercular Parisian courtesan who falls in love with a respectable middle-class man. In a series of lyrical arias, the characters express the lure of a heartfelt passion at odds with the need for stable families.

The German Richard Wagner (1813–1883) was the most flamboyant and musically innovative composer of this era. Wagner hoped to revolutionize opera by fusing music and drama to arouse the audience's fear, awe, and engagement with his vision. His music was lush and harmonically daring, and it strove for overpowering emotional climaxes. Exiled from most German states because of his revolu-

tionary activities in 1848, Wagner spent much of the 1850s working on a gigantic cycle of four operas, *Der Ring des Nibelungen,* which reshaped ancient German myths into a modern, nightmarish allegory of a world doomed by its obsessive pursuit of money and power and redeemable only through unselfish love. Despairing of seeing *The Ring* actually staged, Wagner produced other operas, most notably the comedy *Die Meistersinger* (1862–1867), a nationalistic tribute to German art. Wagner's flair for publicity, musical innovation and dramatization, and nationalistic themes ultimately made him a major force in philosophy, politics, and the arts. He thus excelled in fulfilling the nationalizing and unifying potential of literature, art, music, and other cultural works.

No matter how controversial, opera, like the other arts, helped unite isolated individuals into a community or public with a shared, if debated, cultural experience. The arts provided visions of social structure, political values, and real life—visions that themselves were ordered by the realist style.

Religion and Secular Order

Organized religion formed one bulwark of traditional social and political order after the revolutions of 1848, but the expansion of state power set the stage for clashes over influence. Should religion have the same hold on government and public life as in the past, thus competing with the national loyalty? The views were mixed and would remain so. In the 1850s, many politicians supported religious institutions and attended public church rituals because they were another source of order. Simultaneously, some nation builders, intellectuals, and economic liberals came to reject the competing jurisdiction and religious worldview of established churches, particularly Roman Catholicism. Bismarck would later be one of these. "Do not interfere with what we teach and write," one intellectual proposed to the clergy in still another view of the relationship between religion and society, "and we will not question your control over the people." Protestant churches claimed limited authority over secular life, though they inspired social reform. The Roman Catholic church, however, insisted on its political influence and explicitly attacked nineteenth-century visions of progress and reform embodied in such institutions as secular public schools. Competition between church and state for power and influence heated up in this age of Realpolitik.

Catholic Reaction. The Catholic church felt assaulted by a growing rationalism that replaced religious faith for many people and by the state building of Italy and Germany that competed for people's traditional loyalty. Conversely, rulers of these new countries found that the loyalty demanded by the church drained patriotism. In addition, nation building had resulted in the extension of liberal rights to Jews, whom Christians often considered enemies. Provocatively attacking reform and changing values, Pope Pius IX (r. 1846–1878) issued *The Syllabus of Errors* (1864), which put the church and the pope at odds "with progress, with liberalism, and with modern civilization." In 1870, the First Vatican Council approved the dogma of papal infallibility. This teaching proclaimed that the pope, under certain circumstances, must be regarded by Catholics as speaking divinely revealed truth on issues of morality and faith. Liberal-minded Catholic intellectuals and clergy found themselves obliged either to submit to the new dogma or to be excommunicated.

Religious doctrine continued to have powerful popular appeal, but the place of organized religion in society at large was changing. On the one hand, church attendance declined among workers and artisans; on the other, many in the upper and middle classes and most of the peasantry remained faithful. The Orthodox church of Russia and eastern Europe with its Pan-Slavic appeal fostered nationalism among oppressed Serbs and became a rallying point. Other churches did the same for ethnic minorities in other, scattered rural areas. Women's spiritual beliefs became more intense, with both Roman Catholic and Russian Orthodox women's religious orders increasing in size and number; men, by contrast, were falling away from religious devotion. In 1854, the pope's announcement of the doctrine of the Immaculate Conception (stating that Mary, alone among all humans, had been born without original sin) was followed by an outburst of popular religious fervor, especially among women. In 1858, a peasant girl from Lourdes in southern France, Bernadette Soubirous, began having visions of the Virgin Mary. According to Bernadette, Mary, calling herself "the Immaculate Conception," told the young girl to drink from the ground, at which point a spring appeared. Crowds, mostly of women, besieged the area to be cured of ailments by the waters of Lourdes. In 1867, less than ten years later, a railroad track was laid to Lourdes to enable millions of pilgrims to visit the shrine on church-organized trips. The Catholic church thus showed that it was not passé but that it could use such modern means as railroads, medical verifications of miraculous cures, journalism, and political lobbying to make Lourdes itself the center of a brisk commercial as well as religious culture.

The Challenge of Natural Science. Almost contemporaneously with Bernadette's vision, the English naturalist Charles Darwin (1809–1882) published

On the Origin of Species (1859), a challenge to the Judeo-Christian worldview that humanity was a unique creation of God. Darwin argued that life had taken shape over countless millions of years before humans existed and that human life was but the result of this slow development, or evolution.

Darwin Ridiculed, c. 1860

Charles Darwin's theories claimed that humans evolved from animal species and rejected the long-standing explanation of a divine human origin. His scientific ideas so diverged from people's beliefs that cartoonists lampooned both the respectable Darwin and his theory. Despite the controversy, evolution withstood the test of further scientific study.
Hulton Getty/Liaison.

Science thus called into question the divine character of both natural and human order, much as Enlightenment thinkers and French revolutionaries had done more than half a century earlier.

Evolutionary theory was in the air before Darwin's book appeared: Charles Lyell's *Principles of Geology* (1832–1834) had suggested that the earth's geological structure had developed over an immense span of time. As a young scientist on an expedition to South America, Darwin had read Lyell's work and had begun to consider various scientific puzzles in the environments he visited. Why, he pondered, did species of animals vary from one tropical island to another even though climate and other natural conditions were roughly the same? As early as the 1840s, Darwin was applying theories of evolution to biological life and suggesting that new biological forms arise from older ones as the most fit forms survive and reproduce.

Darwin's thought also reflected the gloomy predictions of the economist Thomas Malthus (1766–1834) that population growth would outstrip the food supply unless checked by famine or disease. Instead of the Enlightenment vision of nature and society as harmonious, Darwin saw the constant turmoil of all species, including humans, struggling to survive. In this fight, only the hardiest prevail and in the selection of sexual partners pass their natural strength to the next generation. That generation in turn might face harsh conditions. In this perpetual challenge to meet the forces of nature, Darwin suggested, some species die out whereas those with better-adapted characteristics survive in a new environment.

Darwin's theories angered adherents of traditional Christianity because the idea of evolution undercut the story of creation described in Genesis. Instead of God miraculously bringing the universe and all life into being in six days, Darwin held that life developed from lower forms through a primal battle for survival and through the sexual selection of mates—processes called *natural selection*. An eminently respectable Victorian gentleman, Darwin announced that the Bible gave a "manifestly false history of the world." Darwin's theories also undermined certain liberal, secular beliefs. Enlightenment principles, for example, had glorified nature as tranquil and noble and had viewed human nature as essentially rational. The theory of natural selection, in which the fittest survive, suggested a different kind of human society, one based in a hostile environment where combative individuals and groups constantly fight one another.

The mechanisms by which characteristics are passed from generation to generation eluded Darwin, but the Austrian monk and botanist Gregor Mendel (1822–1884) was laying the foundation for this understanding in Darwin's lifetime. Working in obscurity on pea plants in his monastery garden, Mendel discovered the principles of heredity in the 1860s from which the science of genetics developed. His discoveries received little attention at the time, but would prove momentous in the twentieth century.

Darwin's findings and other innovative biological research provoked further studies and influenced contemporary beliefs. Investigation into the female reproductive cycle led German scientists to discover the principle of spontaneous ovulation—the automatic release of the egg by the ovary whether sexual intercourse took place or not. This discovery caused theorists to conclude that men had aggressive and strong sexual drives because reproduction depended on their sexual arousal. In contrast, the spontaneous and cyclical release of the egg independent of arousal indicated that women were passive and lacked sexual feeling. Scientists now vied with the clergy in making weighty pronouncements on social roles.

Darwin, who shared the stereotypical social assumptions of his age, was among those who used his findings to explain the social order. The legal, political, and economic privilege of white European men in the nineteenth century, he maintained, naturally derived from their being more highly evolved than white women or people of color. Although Darwin pointed to a common ancestor for all races, he held that people of color, or "lower races," were far behind whites in intelligence and civilization. As for women, "the chief distinction in the intellectual powers of the two sexes," Darwin declared, "is shewn by man's attaining to a higher eminence in whatever he takes up." The body of his thought came to be known as *Darwinism*. As others applied Darwin's theories to explain social life, they emphasized white, middle-class, and male superiority. A school of Social Darwinism arose to lobby for public policy based on this vulgarized version of evolution and natural selection.

From Natural Science to Social Science

Darwin's thought accelerated the search for alternatives to the religious understanding of social order as being divinely ordained. Even before *Origin of Species* appeared, select members of the English middle class had formed the National Association for the Advancement of Social Science in 1857, and the French Society for Sociology was founded in 1872. The impulse for such new organizations came partly from the theories of the French social philosopher Auguste Comte (1798–1857), whose ideas formed the basis of a "positive science" of society and politics. *Positivism* claimed that careful study of facts would generate accurate, or "positive," laws of society. Comte's *System of Positive Politics, or Treatise on Sociology* (1851) proposed that social scientists construct knowledge of the political order as they would an understanding of the natural world, that is, according to informed investigation. This idea inspired people to believe they could solve the problems spawned by economic and social change. Comte also promoted women's participation in reform because he deemed "womanly" compassion and love as equally fundamental to social harmony as was scientific public policy. Positivism led not only to women's increased social and political activism but to the fields of anthropology, psychology, economics, and sociology, which developed during this period, largely under the banner of positivism.

For a time, the influential English philosopher John Stuart Mill (1806–1873) became an enthusiast of Comte, whose theories led Mill to espouse widespread reform and mass education and to support the complete enfranchisement of women. His political treatise *On Liberty* (1859) couched his aspiration for a general social improvement in a concern that superior people not be brought down or confined by the will of the masses. *On Liberty* also argued for individual liberties protected from state intrusion and for freedom of expression for those whose views ran counter to state interests. Mill's writings reflected anxiety for the status of the individual in a nation with a growing electorate of differing interests and a multiracial empire.

Stretching liberal principles to embrace an array of issues, Mill became notorious for advocating the extension of rights and freedom to women. On this subject Mill felt the profound influence of his wife, Harriet Taylor Mill (1808–1858), with whom he studied marriage, women's rights, and divorce. After his wife's death, Mill intensified his activities on behalf of women's rights, notably by introducing a woman suffrage bill into the House of Commons. The bill's defeat prompted Mill to publish *The Subjection of Women* (1869), a work recapitulating his studies with his wife. Translated into many languages and influential in eastern Europe, Scandinavia, and the western hemisphere, *The Subjection of Women* presented the family as maintaining an older kind of politics devoid of modern concepts of rights and freedom. Mill also proposed that the aura of women's voluntary obedience and love in marriage was necessary to mask gross marital inequality. According to Mill, to create "not a forced slave, but a willing one," society trained women "from the very earliest years in the belief that their ideal of a character is the very opposite to that of men; not self-will and government by self-control, but submission and yielding to the control of others." Critiquing the century's most basic beliefs about men's and women's roles, *The Subjection of Women* became a respected guide for a growing women's movement committed to expanding liberal rights.

The more progressive side of Mill's social thought was soon lost in the flood of Social Darwinist theories. Even before *Origin of Species*, Herbert Spencer's *Social Statics* (1851) advocated the study of society from many intellectual perspectives to arrive at a true picture of its workings. Spencer promoted laissez-faire and unadulterated competition, and his claim that the "unfit" should be allowed to perish in the name of progress was greatly reinforced by Darwin's work. Spencer's opposition to public education, social reform, and any other attempt to soften the harshness of the struggle for existence struck a receptive chord among the middle and upper classes and contributed to the surge of Social Darwinism in the next decades.

These various visions of social order would become dominant in future national debates over policy in the West. The influence of Darwinism and Mill's liberalism, like that of the arts, religion, and science, would be to shape the public, giving it common subjects for discussion and setting the terms of social and political thought. In an age of nation building, culture often enhanced the political call for realistic, hardheaded thinking about social order.

❖ Contesting the Political Order of the Nation-State

By the end of the 1860s, the unchecked growth of the state and the ongoing process of economic change had led to palpable tensions in European society. Protests abounded, but in France anger at defeat in the Franco-Prussian War and at economic hardship made these tensions erupt into a bitter if brief civil war. In the spring of 1871, the people of Paris—blaming the centralized state for the French surrender to the Germans—declared Paris a *commune*, a community of equals without bureaucrats and pompous politicians. The economist and philosopher Karl Marx heard of the bloody struggle between the people of Paris and the new republican government while living in England and produced his *Civil War in France* (1871). Translated along with his other writings, it provided workers with a popular and politically galvanizing account of events. From the 1870s on, these two phenomena—the writings of Karl Marx and the fury of working people—renewed fear among the middle classes that both nation-state and society might be violently destroyed.

Marxist Ideas and the Working-Class Movement

After a period of repression in the 1850s, workers' organizations slowly reemerged as a political force in the West. Like other interest groups, workers' organizations were part of a pattern of *horizontal allegiances*, in which people with similar backgrounds or with similar goals came together to shape the political process. Such allegiances replaced or coexisted with the *vertical allegiances* that reflected not similarity and equality but hierarchy and subordination. The family was one example of a vertical structure increasingly displaced as a source of social identity by peer groups in schools, factories, and clubs.

IMPORTANT DATES

1850s–1860s Positivism and Darwinism become popular in social and political thought

1850s–1870s Realism in the arts

1852 The Second Empire begins in France

1854–1856 Britain and France clash with Russia in the Crimean War

1857 Sepoy Mutiny in India

1861 Victor Emmanuel declared king of a unified Italy; abolition of serfdom in Russia

1861–1865 Civil War in the United States

1867 Second Reform Bill, increasing the ranks of male voters, passed by English Parliament; Austro-Hungarian monarchy established

1868 The Meiji Restoration begins in Japan

1869–1871 Women's colleges founded at Cambridge University

1870 Bismarck manipulates the Ems telegram and sparks the Franco-Prussian War

1871 Franco-Prussian War ends; German Empire proclaimed at Versailles; Parisians form Commune in March to oppose the central government; the French army crushes the Commune in May

In the 1850s, governments often outlawed unions, fearing they would challenge the established political order. Unions that existed were thus secret, poorly coordinated, and shaped by a wide range of programs for change, including the ideas of former printer Pierre-Joseph Proudhon (1809–1865). In the 1840s, Proudhon had coined the explosive phrase "Property is theft," suggesting that ownership robbed propertyless people of their rightful share of the earth's benefits. He opposed the centralized state and proposed that society be organized instead around natural groupings of men (but not women) in artisans' workshops. These workshops and a central bank crediting each worker for his labor would replace government and would lead to a *mutualist* social organization. Proudhon heartily opposed any mingling of men and women in political life; he believed the mutualist organization of men in public should be matched by the seclusion of their wives laboring at home for their husbands' comfort.

In 1864, a London meeting of German, Italian, British, and French workers formed the International Workingmen's Association. One leader, Russian nobleman Mikhail Bakhunin (1814–1876), argued that the existence of the state was the root of social injustice. According to Bakhunin, the slightest infringement on freedom, especially by the central state and its laws, was unacceptable. These ideas were the fundamental tenets of the political theory of *anarchism*, which advocated the destruction of all state power. Besides Bakhunin, another of the new organization's sponsors was Karl Marx (1818–1883), who constantly battled mutualism and anarchism. These doctrines, Marx insisted, were emotional and wrongheaded, lacking the sound, scientific basis of his own theory, subsequently called *Marxism*.

Marx's analysis, expounded most notably in *Das Kapital* ("Capital"), adopted the liberal idea, dating back to John Locke in the seventeenth century, that human existence was defined by the requirement to work as a way of fulfilling basic needs such as food, clothing, and shelter. Marx and Engels's *Communist Manifesto* of 1847 had many romantic ingredients, but *Capital*, published between 1867 and 1894, was based on mathematical calculations of production and profit that would justify a Realpolitik for the working classes. Marx held that the fundamental organization of any society, including its politics and culture, derived from the relationships arising from work or production. This idea, known as *materialism*, meant that the foundation of a society rested on class relationships—such as those between serf and medieval lord, slave and master, or worker and capitalist. Marx called the class relationships that developed around work the *mode of production*: for instance, feudalism, slavery, or capitalism. Rejecting the liberal focus on individual rights, he emphasized the unequal class relations caused by feudal lords, slaveholders, and the capitalists or bourgeoisie—that is, those who took control of the "means of production" in the form of the capital, land, tools, or factories necessary to fulfill basic human needs. When capitalist control disappeared, a classless society of workers—that is, a *socialist* one—would arise.

Economic liberals saw the free market ultimately producing balance and a harmony of interests, but Marx saw social organization and productive life not as harmonious but in conflict because of economic oppression. He believed that workers' awareness of their oppression would produce class consciousness among those in the same predicament and ultimately lead them to revolt against their exploiters. Such revolt, not reform or legislation, would be the mechanism for historical change. Capitalism would be overthrown by these workers—the *proletariat*—and the reign of socialism would ensue. Tough-minded theories that social conflict was necessary for progress were common to Marx and Darwin.

Marx was never precise about what socialism would entail, except that it would involve workers' control of production in large factories. A socialist utopia meant an end to private ownership of the means of production, which would in turn end class conflict and the need for a state to prop up the propertied classes. Like many male intellectuals at midcentury, Marx accorded little analytical importance to inequalities based on race and sex, concluding, for example, that the condition of women would automatically improve in a socialist utopia. The possibility of this socialist utopia continued to inspire many working-class men to organize, and some governments came to recognize an advantage in unions: they could render worker protests more predictable and more controllable.

The conditions of working-class life remained harsh, and a wave of strikes erupted in the late 1860s. In France alone, 40,000 workers participated in strikes in 1869, followed by more than 85,000 in 1870. The strikers included artisans and industrial workers who felt overworked and underpaid because of the continuing pace and expense of technological innovation. More often than not, the strikes focused on economic issues. But at times, such as in the Paris Commune, protest questioned the entire political system.

The Paris Commune versus the French State

The bloody and bitter struggle over the Paris Commune developed from mutualist and socialist political ideas that churned to the surface in Paris as the Franco-Prussian War ended. The weaknesses of the French state first became apparent in the late 1860s when Napoleon III was forced to grant liberal re-

forms such as freedom of the press and a more independent legislature. But the Haussmannization of Paris, which had displaced workers from their homes in the heart of the city, embittered many Parisians against the state. As the Prussians pressed on to Paris in 1870, the besieged Parisians demanded new republican liberties and a more balanced distribution of power between the central government and localities.

By the winter of 1870–1871, the Parisian population was suffering from the harsh weather and a Prussian siege that deprived them of sufficient food to feed more than 2 million people. As rumors of coups filled the air, Parisians demanded to elect their own local government to handle the emergency (Map 23.5). Given the threat to the nation, the temporary head of state, Adolphe Thiers, called the Parisians a "vile multitude" and sent the army into Paris in mid-March. For Parisians, this

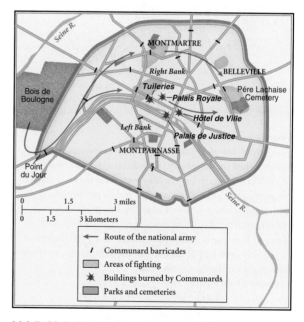

MAP 23.5 The Paris Commune, 1871
The war between the French government and the Paris Commune took place on the streets of Paris and resulted in widespread destruction of major buildings, most notably the Tuileries Palace adjacent to the Louvre. Many government records were destroyed in what some saw as a civil war; bitterness, like destruction of property, was great on both sides. The government defeat of the Communards brought the execution of thousands of people.

Woman Incendiary
The Paris Commune galvanized women activists, many of whom hoped to reform social conditions. For the short time of the Commune's existence they implemented cooperative programs for work and engaged in public political debate — something women were forbidden by law to do. However, in the aftermath of the Commune, their public image was changed from seriousness of purpose to one of half-clothed degeneracy as a way of illustrating the disorderliness of the Commune's resistance to the state.
Jean Loup Charmet.

decision revealed the utter despotism of the centralized government, and they declared themselves a self-governing commune on March 28, 1871. Other French municipalities would do the same, in an attempt to form a decentralized state of independent, confederated units.

In the Paris Commune's two months of existence, its forty-member council, its National Guard, and its many other improvised offices found themselves at cross-purposes. Trying to maintain "communal" instead of "national" values, Parisians quickly developed a wide array of political clubs, local ceremonies, and self-managed, cooperative workshops. Women workers, for example, banded together to make National Guard uniforms on a cooperative rather than a profitmaking basis. Beyond liberal political equality, the Commune proposed to liberate the worker and ensure "the absolute equality of women laborers." Thus a *commune* in contrast to a *republic* was meant to entail a social revolution. But Communards often disagreed on what specific route to take to change society: mutualism, anticlericalism, feminism, international socialism, and anarchism were but a few of the proposed avenues to social justice.

In the meantime, the provisional government at Versailles struck back to reinstitute national order. It quickly stamped out similar uprisings in other French cities. On May 21, the army entered Paris. In a week of fighting, both Communards and the army set the city ablaze (the Communards did so to slow the progress of government troops). Both sides executed hostages, and in the wake of victory the army shot tens of thousands of citizens found on the streets. Just to be in the city meant treason: Parisian insurgents, one citizen commented, "deserved no better judge than a soldier's bullet." The Communards had fatally promoted a kind of antistate in an age of growing national power, and the French establishment saw all Parisians as traitors.

This reaction soon succumbed to a different interpretation of the Commune as the work of the *pétroleuse*, or "woman incendiary." Adolphe Thiers roused the French to battle by describing the Commune as basically a case of women run mad, crowding the streets in frenzy and fury. Other writers portrayed women of the Commune as sexually depraved: "They tossed much more than their caps over windmills. . . . Soon all the rest of their clothing followed." Within a year, writers were blaming the burning of Paris on women — "shameless slatterns, half-naked women, who kindled courage and breathed life into arson." Revolutionary men often became heroes in the history books, but women in political situations were characterized as "sinister females, sweating, their clothing undone, their bosoms almost bare, [who] passed from man to man."

Defeat in the Franco-Prussian War, the Commune, and the civil war were all horrendous blows

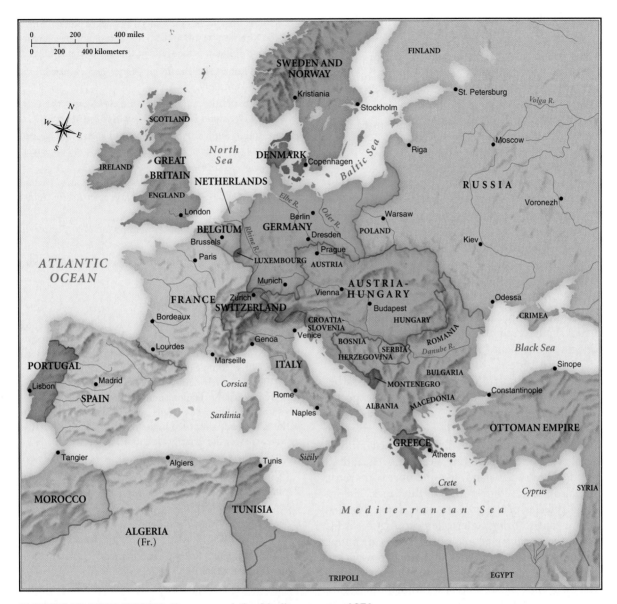

MAPPING THE WEST Europe and the Mediterranean, 1871

European nation-states consolidated their power by building unified state structures and by developing the means for the diverse peoples within their borders to became socially and culturally integrated. They were also rapidly expanding outside their boundaries, extending the economic and political reach of the nation-state. North Africa and the Middle East—parts of the declining Ottoman Empire—had particular appeal because of their resources and their potential for further European settlement. They offered a gateway to the rest of the world.

from which the French state struggled to recover. Key to restoring order in France after 1870 were instilling family virtues, fortifying religion, and claiming that the Commune had resulted from the collapsed boundaries between the male political sphere and the female domestic sphere. Karl Marx disagreed: he analyzed the Commune as a class struggle of workers attacking bourgeois interests, which were embodied in the centralized state. Executions and deportations by the thousands virtually shut down the French labor movement and kept resentment smoldering. The French would spend the next decades struggling to rebuild political and social unity.

Conclusion

Throughout modern history the development of nation-states has been neither inevitable nor uniform nor peaceful. This was especially true in the nineteenth century, when ambitious politicians, resilient monarchs, and determined bureaucrats transformed very different countries into various kinds of states by a variety of methods and policies. Nation building was most dramatic in Germany and Italy, where states unified through military force and where people of many political tendencies ultimately agreed that national unity surpassed most other causes. Compelled by military defeat to shake off centuries of tradition, the Austrian and Russian monarchs instituted reforms as a way of keeping their systems viable. In eastern Europe, the middle class was far less powerful than in western Europe, and reform came from above to preserve autocratic power rather than from popular agitation to democratize it.

After decades of romantic fervor idealizing society, politics, and culture, hardheaded realism became a much-touted norm, often with unexpected consequences. Darwin and Marx breathed the air of realism and their theories were disturbing to those who maintained an Enlightenment faith in social and political harmony. Realist novels and art jarred polite society, and, like the operas of Verdi, they also portrayed dilemmas of the times. The internal policies of the growing state apparatus that were meant to bring order often brought disorder. When the ordinary people of the Paris Commune rose up to protest the loss of French power and prestige but also to defy the trend toward state building, their actions raised difficult questions. How far should the power of the state extend in both domestic and international affairs? Would nationalism be a force for war or for peace? As these issues ripened, the next decades saw extraordinary economic advance and an unprecedented surge in European global power.

Suggested References

The End of the Concert of Europe

The inglorious Crimean War has often been left behind in historiography despite its impact on European politics. Much of the best new literature focuses not only on politi-

cal changes but on the war's social impact in Russia. Engel and the Kingston-Mann and Mixter anthology give searching looks at Russian peasant life in this age of transition.

Edgerton, Robert B. *Death or Glory: The Legacy of the Crimean War.* 1999.

Engel, Barbara Alpern. *Between the Fields and the City: Women, Work, and Family in Russia, 1861–1914.* 1994.

Hazareesingh, Sudhir. *From Subject to Citizen: The Second Empire and the Emergence of Modern French Democracy.* 1998.

Kingston-Mann, Esther, and Timothy Mixter, eds. *Peasant Economy, Culture, and Politics of European Russia, 1800–1921.* 1991.

*Seacole, Mary. *Wonderful Adventures of Mrs. Seacole in Many Lands.* 1857.

Wortman, Richard S. *Scenarios of Power: Myth and Ceremony in Russian Monarchy.* 1995.

War and Nation Building

Nation building has produced a varied literature ranging from biographies to studies of ceremonials and the presentation of royalty as celebrities and unifying figures. Two Web sites show the complexities of this process. Brown University's Victorian Web demonstrates the connections among royalty, politicians, religion, and culture. Bucknell University's Russian Studies site opens to the strains of the Russian national anthem, composed in the reign of Nicholas I to foster reverence for the dynasty and homeland.

Blackbourn, David. *Fontana History of Germany, 1780–1918: The Long Nineteenth Century.* 1997.

Breuilly, John. *The Formation of the First German Nation-State, 1800–1871.* 1996.

DiScala, Spencer. *Italy: From Revolution to Republic, 1700 to the Present.* 1995.

Homans, Margaret. *Royal Representations: Queen Victoria and British Culture, 1837–1876.* 1998.

Russian Studies: **http://www.departments.bucknell.edu/Russian/**.

Smith, Paul. *Disraeli: A Brief Life.* 1996.

The Victorian Web: **http://landow.stg.brown.edu/victorian/victov.html**.

Instituting Social Order

Nation building entailed state-sponsored activities stretching from promoting education to rebuilding cities. New histories show the process of creating a sense of nationality through government management of people's environment, so that citizenship became part of seemingly nonpolitical life.

---

*Primary sources.

Eley, Geoff, and Ronald Grigor Suny. *Becoming National: A Reader.* 1996.

Hamm, Michael F. *Kiev: A Portrait, 1800–1917.* 1993.

Johanson, Christine. *Women's Struggle for Higher Education in Russia, 1855–1900.* 1987.

Jordan, David. *Transforming Paris: The Life and Labor of Baron Haussmann.* 1995.

Lebra-Chapman, Joyce. *The Rani of Jhansi: A Study in Female Heroism in India.* 1986.

Rotenberg, Robert. *Landscape and Power in Vienna.* 1995.

Slezkine, Yuri. *Arctic Mirrors: Russia and the Small Peoples of the North.* 1994.

Wohl, Anthony. *Endangered Lives: Public Health in Victorian Britain.* 1983.

Artistic and Intellectual Visions of Social Order

Like the biographies of politicians, the lives of artists and intellectuals have proven crucial to understanding this period of realism and Realpolitik. They show artists, intellectuals, and scientists addressing the central issues of their day amidst dramatic social change.

Bordenheimer, Rosemarie. *The Real Life of Mary Ann Evans: George Eliot, Her Letters and Fiction.* 1994.

*Darwin, Charles. *Autobiography.* 1969.

Gieson, Gerald L. *The Private Science of Louis Pasteur.* 1996.

Kaufman, Suzanne. "Lourdes, Popular Religion, and Tourism." In Shelley Baranowski and Ellen Furlough, eds. *Being Elsewhere: Tourism, Consumer Culture, and Identity in Modern Europe and North America.* 2000.

Mayr, Ernst. *One Long Argument: Charles Darwin and the Genesis of Modern Evolutionary Thought.* 1991.

*Turgenev, Ivan. *A Hunter's Sketches.* 1852.

Contesting the Political Order of the Nation-State

The teachings of Karl Marx and the story of the Paris Commune haunted Europeans at the time, and have since fascinated historians. The following works capture the fear of the working classes that shaped middle-class thought in the nineteenth century, and they show the energy that working- and middle-class people alike put into politics and into developing political theories, especially in this period of political transformation.

Gullickson, Gay. *Unruly Women of Paris: Images of the Commune.* 1996.

McClellan, David. *Karl Marx: His Life and Thought.* 1978.

Nord, Philip. *The Republican Moment: Struggles for Democracy in Nineteenth-Century France.* 1995.

CHAPTER

24

Industry, Empire, and Everyday Life

1870–1890

Charles J. Staniland,
***The Emigrant Ship,* c. 1880**
*Migration, a constant human
activity since prehistoric times,
swelled dramatically with the
dislocations caused by economic
change, political revolutions, and
religious persecution of the mid-
to late nineteenth century. Despite the difficult conditions of
travel, the lure of opportunity in
developing lands, especially the
United States, enticed millions of
Europeans, traveling singly or
with their families. The influx
provided a supply of cheap labor
that helped the Western Hemisphere prosper.*
Bradford Art Galleries and Museums,
West Yorkshire, UK/The Bridgeman
Art Library International Ltd.

BETWEEN 1870 AND 1890, MARIANNE NORTH, an unmarried English woman, traveled the globe several times. The end of the
nineteenth century was a time of vast migration, some of it in
search of a better life, some of it for imperial conquest, and some of it,
as in the case of Marianne North, in pursuit of knowledge. North was a
botanical illustrator and "plant hunter," one of those avid Europeans
who on their own or under government sponsorship searched the
world over for plants to classify, grow, and put to commercial use.
North ventured to North and South America, India, Java, Borneo,
South Africa, and many other distant points setting up her easel and
making scientific drawings of plants. She discovered at least five new
species (officially named after her) and a new type of tree as well as
collecting thousands of plants to send back to botanical gardens in
England. When she became too frail to travel, she organized a permanent museum in London to display her botanical drawings to the public. Her goal was promoting ordinary people's knowledge of the British
Empire: "I want them to know," she announced, "that cocoa doesn't
come from the coconut."

Historians have aptly labeled the decades from 1870 to 1890 an era
of industry and empire in the West. Empires were spreading rapidly,
and this expansion was knit into the fabric of industrial growth and the
everyday life of all social classes. Industrial output soared in the West,
as industrialization spread from Britain to central and eastern Europe
and new products kept appearing on the market. A growing appetite

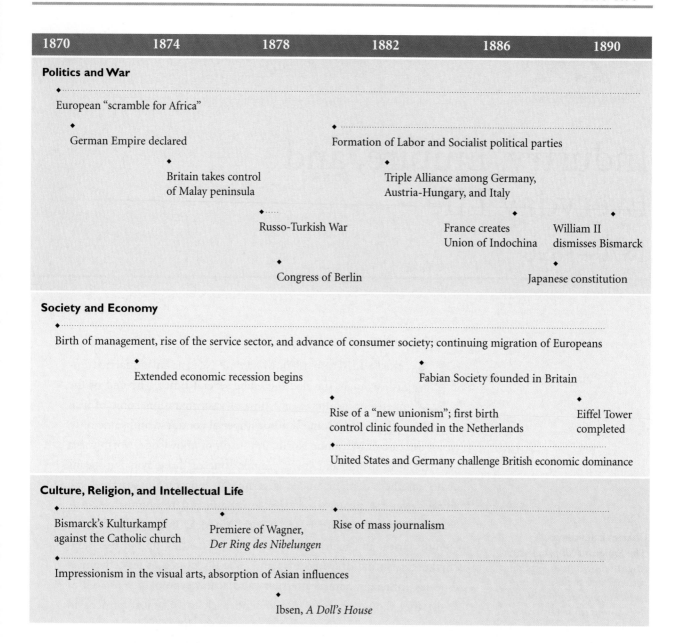

| 1870 | 1874 | 1878 | 1882 | 1886 | 1890 |

Politics and War

European "scramble for Africa"

German Empire declared

Formation of Labor and Socialist political parties

Britain takes control
of Malay peninsula

Triple Alliance among Germany,
Austria-Hungary, and Italy

Russo-Turkish War

France creates
Union of Indochina

William II
dismisses Bismarck

Congress of Berlin

Japanese constitution

Society and Economy

Birth of management, rise of the service sector, and advance of consumer society; continuing migration of Europeans

Extended economic recession begins

Fabian Society founded in Britain

Rise of a "new unionism"; first birth
control clinic founded in the Netherlands

Eiffel Tower
completed

United States and Germany challenge British economic dominance

Culture, Religion, and Intellectual Life

Bismarck's Kulturkampf
against the Catholic church

Premiere of Wagner,
Der Ring des Nibelungen

Rise of mass journalism

Impressionism in the visual arts, absorption of Asian influences

Ibsen, *A Doll's House*

for these goods, many of them for household consumption, was partly responsible for an intensified search for raw materials around the globe. Informal educators like Marianne North made people more knowledgeable about the connections among industry, empire, and their own lives.

Those connections were tight, as many Europeans benefited from the enforced labor of millions of Asians and Africans under the "new imperialism"—one name for the accelerated race for empire. Beginning in these decades, the "new im-perialism" was merely the final gulp of global territory that Europeans had been acquiring since the late fifteenth century. They explored and took political control of the interior of Africa and worked to dominate even more of Asia until by the beginning of the twentieth century they controlled more than 80 percent of the world's surface. Control was not narrowly political: Europeans tried to stamp other continents with European-style borders, place-names, architecture, clothing, languages, domestic customs, and other cultural features.

As Europeans forced open the globe, millions seized the opportunity to move vast distances, still another change in everyday life. Some movement was temporary migration to the colonies to serve in the colonial civil service, for instance, and some was permanent—to North and South America or Australia in search of work or personal safety. Some was simply to other cities or regions in Europe. The costs of this unprecedented imperial migration were also part of everyday life: among them social dislocation for tens of millions of people and violence against indigenous peoples in European colonies.

Marianne North, Pitcher Plant
Migration by wealthy Europeans increasingly occurred in the quest for knowledge and adventure, and as the West prospered travel and world tourism did too. As a woman amateur, Marianne North initially gained an official audience for her scientific drawings, reports, and specimens only because she traveled in the "best circles." Once seen, however, her canvases, like this one of a pitcher plant, were prized by scientists and curators alike.
Trustees of the Royal Botanic Gardens, Kew.

The intertwined progress of industry and empire affected politics in paradoxical ways. As urban people became more educated and more united by common experiences of neighborhood and work life, they came to share political interests and make greater demands for participation. Politics became part of their everyday lives because governments, growing bigger as their territories, economies, and population expanded, intervened more in daily affairs. At the same time, political participation of ordinary citizens increased, with suffrage opening up to more men from all social classes. Bureaucrats organized both ordinary citizens and the colonized with programs intended to unify: social reform, education, and public ceremonials. Citizens were also unified by pride in their nations' conquests and their common access to a mushrooming array of colonial goods. Europe officially brimmed with confidence and hope, while the paradoxes of industrial and imperial progress played themselves out in distant colonies, urban slums, and declining standards of living in rural areas.

❖ The Advance of Industry

The end of the Franco-Prussian War and the Paris Commune in 1871 saw an initial burst of prosperity. Paris, Berlin, Vienna, and Rome experienced a frenzy of building, and many workers' wages increased. Industry turned out a cornucopia of products that improved people's material well-being. Beginning in 1873, however, a series of downturns in business threatened both entrepreneurs and the working class. Business people sought remedies in further innovation, in new managerial techniques, and in revolutionizing marketing, most visibly in the development of the department store. Governments played their part by changing business law and supporting the drive for global profits. The steady advance of industry and the rise of a consumer economy further transformed the work lives of millions of people.

Industrial Innovation

Industrial, technological, and commercial innovation together characterized nineteenth-century Europe. New products ranging from the bicycle, typewriter, and telephone to the internal combustion engine provided dizzying proof of industrial progress. Many independent tinkerers or inventor-manufacturers created new products, but sophisticated engineers also invented revolutionary technologies. For example, in 1885 the German engineer Karl Benz devised a workable gasoline engine; six years later France's Armand Peugeot constructed a car and tested it by chasing a bicycle race. Electricity became more widely used after 1880, providing power to light everything from private drawing rooms to government office buildings. The Eiffel Tower in Paris, constructed for the International Exhibit of 1889, stood as a monument to the age's engineering wizardry; visitors rode to its summit in electric elevators.

To fuel this explosive industrial growth, the leading industrial nations mined and produced massive quantities of coal, iron, and steel during the 1870s and 1880s; production of iron increased from 11 million to 23 million tons. (Even in relatively underdeveloped Spain, iron-ore mining unearthed a total of 6 million tons in 1890, up from 130,000 tons in 1861—an almost 5,000 percent increase.) Steel output grew just as impressively in the industrial nations, increasing from 500,000 to 11 million tons in the 1870s and 1880s. Manufacturers used the metal to build the more than 100,000 locomotives that pulled trains during these years—trains that transported 2 billion people annually.

Historians used to contrast a "second" Industrial Revolution, with its concentration on heavy industrial products, to the "first" revolution of the eighteenth and early nineteenth centuries, in which innovations in textile making and the use of steam energy predominated. But many historians now believe this distinction applies mainly to Britain: in countries where industrialization came later, the two stages occurred simultaneously. Numerous textile mills were installed on the continent later than in Britain, for instance, at the same time as blast furnaces were constructed. Although industrialization led to the decline of cottage production in traditional crafts like weaving, home industry—or *outwork*—persisted in garment making, metalwork, and such "finishing trades" as porcelain painting and button polishing. The coexistence of home and factory enterprise continued through all the changes in manufacturing, to the present day.

Industrial innovations also transformed agriculture. Chemical fertilizers boosted crop yields,

Universal Exposition of 1889
French politicians launched the Universal Exposition, or World's Fair, of 1889 in Paris to celebrate what they called the "progress resulting from one hundred years of freedom." The exposition featured the latest industrial inventions as well as musical and artistic displays from the cultures France had conquered. The greatest attraction, however, was the Eiffel Tower, constructed in two years to much criticism. Tens of thousands flocked to ascend this masterpiece of engineering technology—the same technology Gustave Eiffel had used to provide the iron skeleton supporting the Statue of Liberty. Jean-Loup Charmet.

and reapers and threshers mechanized harvesting. In the 1870s, Sweden produced a cream separator, a first step toward mechanizing dairy farming. Wire fencing and barbed wire replaced wooden fencing and stone walls, both of which were labor-intensive to create. Refrigeration, developed during this period, allowed fruits, vegetables, and meat to be transported without spoiling, thus diversifying and increasing the urban food supply. Tin from colonial trade facilitated large-scale commercial canning, which made many foods available year-round to people in the cities.

Challenge to British Dominance. During these decades, Britain's rate of industrial growth slowed, as its entrepreneurs remained wedded to older, successful technologies. Although Great Britain maintained its high output of industrial goods and profited from a multitude of worldwide investments, two countries began surpassing it in research, technical education, innovation, and rate of growth: Germany and the United States.

In the aftermath of the Franco-Prussian War, Germany received the territories of Alsace and Lorraine, which had textile industries as well as rich iron deposits. Investing heavily in research, German businesses rapidly devised new industrial processes and began to mass-produce goods that other countries had originally manufactured. Germany also spent as much money on education as on its military in the 1870s and 1880s. This investment resulted in highly skilled engineers and technical workers whose productivity enabled Germany's electrical and chemical engineering capabilities to soar.

The United States began an intensive exploitation of its vast natural resources, including coal, ores, gold, and oil. The value of U.S. industrial goods spurted from $5 billion in 1880 to $13 billion two decades later. Whereas German accomplishments rested more on state promotion of industrial efforts, U.S. growth often involved innovative entrepreneurs, such as Andrew Carnegie in iron and steel and John D. Rockefeller in oil. The three-way industrial rivalry created by Germany and the United States challenging Britain's dominance would soon have political and diplomatic repercussions.

Areas of Slower Industrialization. With the exception of Belgium, the first continental country to industrialize, other countries trailed the three leaders in the pervasiveness of industry. French industry grew steadily, but French businesses remained smaller than those in Germany and the United States: although France had some huge mining, textile, and metallurgical establishments, many businessmen retired early to imitate the still-enviable aristocratic way of life. Industrial development in Spain, Austria-Hungary, and Italy was primarily a local phenomenon. Austria-Hungary had densely industrialized areas around Vienna and in Styria and Bohemia, but the rest of the country remained tied to traditional, unmechanized agriculture. Italy's economy continued to industrialize in the north while remaining rural and agricultural in the south. The Italian government spent more on building Rome into a grand capital than it invested in economic growth. A mere 1.4 percent of Italy's 1872 budget went to education and science, compared with 10.8 percent in Germany. The commercial use of electricity helped Scandinavians, who were poor in coal and ore, to industrialize in the last third of the nineteenth century. Sweden and Norway became leaders in the use of hydroelectric power and the development of electrical products; Denmark developed a major commercial sector in animal and dairy products. Despite these innovations, however, Scandinavia retained its mostly rural character, at a time when traditional farm life was becoming increasingly difficult.

Russia's road to industrialization was torturous, slowed partly by its relatively small urban labor force. Many Russian peasants who may have

Trans-Siberian Railroad
Begun in 1892, the Trans-Siberian railroad, the major east–west transportation line across the Russian Empire, took several decades to complete. From farms in western Siberia the line brought goods to markets in major cities, and in the more sparsely populated east the railroad mostly served to transport troops to secure imperial conquests and guard frontiers. The railroad also became a feature of around-the-world tourism; voyagers traveled in luxurious, if very slow, trans-Siberian railway coaches.
Sovfoto.

wished to take advantage of the opportunities of industrialization were tied to the *mir*, or landed community, by the terms of the serf emancipation. Some villages sent men and women to cities, but on the condition that they return for plowing and harvesting. Nevertheless, by the 1890s, Moscow, St. Petersburg, and a few other cities had substantial working-class populations. Minister of Finance Sergei Witte attracted foreign capital, entrepreneurs, and engineers and used them to construct railroads, including the Trans-Siberian Railroad (1891–1916), which upon completion stretched 5,787 miles from Moscow to Vladivostok. The burgeoning of the railroads combined with growth in metallurgical and mining operations lifted Russia as an industrial and military power. As in most of eastern Europe, the peasants bore the main burden of financing Russia's industrial growth, especially in the form of higher taxes on vodka. Thus neither they nor the underpaid Russian workers could afford to buy the goods their country produced. Russia was a prime example of the complexities of industrialization and its uneven benefits.

Facing Economic Crisis

Although innovations and business expansion often conveyed a sense of optimism, economic conditions were far from rosy throughout the 1870s and 1880s. Within two years of the end of the Franco-Prussian War, prosperity abruptly gave way to a severe economic depression in many industrial countries. The crisis of 1873 was followed by almost three decades of economic fluctuations, most alarmingly a series of sharp downturns whose severity varied from country to country. People of all classes lost their jobs or businesses and faced consequences ranging from long stretches of unemployment to bankruptcy. Economists of the day were stunned by the relentlessness and pervasiveness of the slump. Because economic ties bound industrialized western Europe to international markets, recession affected the economies of such diverse regions as Australia, South Africa, California, Newfoundland, and the West Indies.

These dramatic fluctuations differed from the economic cycles that were the rule before 1850, in which failure on the land led to higher food prices and then to failure in manufacturing. Although suffering problems of its own, agriculture was no

longer so dominant that its fate determined the welfare of other sectors of the economy. By the 1870s, industrial and financial setbacks were sending businesses into long-term tailspins. In France, for example, the textile industry slumped early in the 1870s and revived only in the late 1880s; facing growing competition from Asian imports, the vital Italian silk industry did not recover until the 1890s. Innovation created new or modernized industries on an unprecedented scale, but economic disaster constantly loomed. Politicians, economists, and bureaucrats struggled in vain to understand this paradox and control its impact.

As industrialization advanced, entrepreneurs encountered fundamental problems. First, the start-up costs of new enterprises skyrocketed. Textile mills had required relatively modest amounts of capital in comparison to factories producing steel and iron. Industrialization had become what modern economists call *capital-intensive* rather than *labor-intensive*: its growth required the purchase of expensive machinery, not merely the hiring of more workers. Second, the distribution and consumption of goods were inadequate to sustain industrial growth. Increased productivity in both agriculture and industry led to rapidly declining prices. Wheat, for example, dropped to one-third its 1870 price by the 1890s. Consumers, however, did not always benefit from this deflation as wages were slashed and unemployment rose during the economic downturns; nor could they always afford the new goods. Industrialists had made their fortunes by emphasizing production, not consumption. The series of slumps refocused entrepreneurial policy on finding ways to enhance sales and distribution and to control markets and prices.

In response to nervous business owners and to those fearful of potential social unrest, governments took steps to foster economic prosperity. New laws spurred the development of the limited-liability corporation, which protected investors from personal responsibility for the firm's debt. Before limited liability, businesses drew the necessary capital primarily from their own family assets, and financial backers were individually responsible for the firm's financial difficulties. In one case in England, a former partner who had failed to have his name removed from a legal document after leaving the business remained responsible to creditors when the company went bankrupt. He lost everything he owned except a watch and the equivalent of $100. The end of personal liability greatly increased investor confidence about financing business ventures.

Public financing in stocks and bonds promised wider opportunity to gain high profits. Stock markets had existed prior to the changes in liability laws, but they had dealt mainly in government bonds and in government-sponsored enterprises such as railroads. By the end of the century, stock markets traded heavily in industrial corporate stock owned by many individuals, and investors thus raised money from a larger pool of private capital than before. At the center of an international economy linked by telegraph, telephone, railways, and steamships, the London Stock Exchange in 1882 traded industrial shares worth £54 million, a value that surged to £443 million by 1900. Banks competed with the stock exchange in financing industry.

Less personal financial liability and new sources of capital did not eliminate business difficulties, however. In another adaptive move, firms in the same industry banded together in cartels and trusts to control prices and competition. Cartels flourished particularly in German chemical, iron, coal, and electric industries. For example, the Rhenish-Westphalian Coal Syndicate, founded in 1893, eventually dominated more than 95 percent of coal production in Germany. Although business owners might continue to advocate free trade, cartels broke with free-trade practices by restricting output and setting prices. Smaller businesses trying to compete and consumers had no effective means of resisting these new business techniques.

Trusts appeared first in the United States. In 1882, John D. Rockefeller created the Standard Oil Trust by acquiring stock from many different oil companies and placing it under the direction of trustees. The trustees then controlled so much of the companies' stock that they could set prices for the entire industry. They could even dictate to the railroads the rates for transporting the oil. Trusts and cartels also oversaw the *vertical integration* of industries, in which, for example, a steel company acquired mining operations in ore and coal as well as railroads to distribute its output. Such acquisitions ensured access to raw materials, lower production costs, and greater control of product distribution.

Like the practices of cartels and trusts, government imposition of tariffs expressed declining faith in classical liberal economics. Much of Europe had adopted free trade after midcentury, but during the recessions of the 1870s huge trade deficits—caused when imports exceed exports—had soured many Europeans on the concept. A country with a trade deficit had less capital available to invest internally; fewer jobs were created, and the chances of social unrest increased. Farmers in many European countries were hurt when improvements in transportation made it possible to import perishable food, such as grain from the United States and Ukraine. France and Germany were particularly vulnerable to trade deficits in the last three decades of the century. In response, governments in both countries approved tariffs throughout these decades. Farmers, capitalists, and even many workers supported these taxes on imports to prevent competition from foreign goods. Governments in the West responded to calls for economic nationalism, and by the early 1890s all but Belgium, Britain, and the Netherlands had ended free trade.

Revolution in Business Practices

Industrialists tried to minimize the damage of economic downturns by revolutionizing the everyday conduct of their businesses. A generation earlier, a factory owner was directly involved in every aspect of his business and often learned to run the firm through trial and error. In the late 1800s, industrialists began to hire managers to run their increasingly complex day-to-day operations. Managers who specialized in sales and distribution, finance, and purchase of raw materials made decisions and oversaw the implementation of their policies. Lower-level managers supervised workers to ensure productivity. One German steel magnate told his managers to hire "supervisors and supervisors of supervisors to watch what our men are doing." The managerial class formed a useful buffer between owners and workers.

The White-Collar Sector. The rise of the manager was accompanied by the emergence of a "white-collar" service sector of office workers. Businesses employed secretaries, file clerks, and typists to guide the flow of business information. Banks that accepted savings from the general

Remington Typewriter Company Office
The typewriter symbolized the beginnings of the service revolution, which would take almost a century to unfold, as a sector of work developed that was performed neither by owners nor by factory workers. Like these typists, service workers processed information, dealt with managerial knowledge, or performed various service tasks such as health care. Typing was seen as the perfect work for genteel ladies, both because it was comparatively clean and because women's nimble fingers were seen as best suited for the skill.
The Granger Collection.

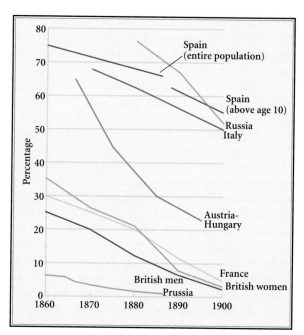

TAKING MEASURE **The Decline of Illiteracy**
The development of mass politics and the consolidation of the nation-state depended on building a cohesive group of citizens, informed about the progress of the nation. Increasing literacy was thus a national undertaking but one with national variations ranging from low levels of illiteracy in Prussia to high levels in Austria-Hungary and Russia. Even in regions of high illiteracy, however, governments successfully encouraged people to read.
Theodore Hamerow, *The Birth of New Europe: State and Society in the Nineteenth Century* (Chapel Hill: University of North Carolina Press, 1983), 85.

public and that invested those funds heavily in business needed tellers and clerks; railroads, insurance companies, and government-run telegraph and telephone companies all needed armies of white-collar employees.

Workers with mathematical skills and literacy acquired in the new public primary schools staffed this service sector, which provided in particular clean work for educated, middle-class women. (See "Taking Measure," above right.) Female employees eventually predominated in service jobs. In Paris the number of women in white-collar work tripled between 1866 and 1886. Early in the century, middle-class women had tended businesses with their husbands, but then the ideology of domesticity had dictated that middle-class women should not work

outside the home. By the late nineteenth century, however, the costs of middle-class family life, especially children's education, were becoming a burden. Many middle-class people could not even afford to marry. So whether to help pay family expenses or to support themselves, unmarried and a greater number of married women of the respectable middle class took jobs. Employers, as one put it, found in the new women workers a "quickness of eye and ear, and the delicacy of touch" essential to office work. By hiring women for newly created clerical jobs, business and government contributed to a dual labor market in which certain categories of jobs were predominantly male and others were overwhelmingly female. In the absence of competition, businesses in the service sector saved significantly by paying women chronically low wages—much less than they would have had to pay men for the same work.

The Department Store.   Finally, the rise of consumer capitalism transformed the scale of consumption the way industrial capitalism had transformed the scale of production. The principal institution of this change was the department store. Founded after midcentury in the largest cities, department stores gathered such an impressive variety of goods in one place that consumers popularly called them "marble palaces" or "the eighth wonder of the world." Created by daring entrepreneurs such as Aristide and Marguerite Boucicaut of the Bon Marché in Paris and John Wanamaker of Wanamaker's in Philadelphia, department stores eventually replaced the single-item stores that people entered knowing clearly what they wanted to purchase.

These modern palaces sought to stimulate consumer whims and desires with luxurious fabrics, delicate laces, and richly embellished tapestries. The items spilled over railings and counters, not in the calculated order inherent in rational ideals of the nineteenth century, but in intentional and glorious disarray. Shoppers no longer bargained over prices; instead they reacted to sales, a new marketing technique that could incite a buy-

ing frenzy. As most men lacked the time for shopping expeditions, department stores appealed mostly to women, who came out of their domestic sphere into a new public role. Women explained their forays outside the home as necessary to enhance their home and family lives. Attractive sales-girls, another variety of service workers, were hired to inspire customers to buy. Shopping was not only an urban phenomenon: glossy mail-order catalogs from the Bon Marché or Sears, Roebuck arrived regularly in rural areas, replete with all the luxuries and household items contained in the exotic, faraway dream world of the city.

Consumerism joined hands with empire. Wealthy travelers like Marianne North traveled on well-appointed oceanliners, carrying quinine, antiseptics, and other medicines as well as cameras, revolvers, and the latest in rubber goods and apparel. Coffee, tea, sugar, tobacco, cocoa, and cola were stimulants from the colonies whose consumption became more widespread. Tons of palm oil from Africa were turned into both margarine, adding fat to the European diet, and fine soap, allowing Westerners to see themselves as cleaner and more civilized. Industry and empire jointly shaped everyday life as a voracious desire to consume and own— whether industrial goods or colonies—took root in Western culture.

Crespin and Dufayel Department Store
The department store marked the definitive transition of European society from one of subsistence and scarcity to one of relative abundance. Centralizing the sale of all varieties of goods, department stores displayed more consumer items than any single person could possibly use. This particular Parisian department store was relatively subdued in its displays, but others ran sales and so seductively arranged goods that Europe's uninitiated consumers were often tempted into irrational purchasing.
Jean-Loup Charmet.

❖ The New Imperialism

In the last third of the nineteenth century, industrial demand and rampant business rivalry added fuel to the contest for territory in Africa and Asia. A "new imperialism"—unlike the trader-based domination of preceding centuries—brought direct rule of these two continents by European nations. The race to imperial conquest constituted an integral component of European nation building, whose champions came to connect industrial prosperity and imperial expansion with national identity. "Nations are not great except for the activities they undertake," declared a French advocate of huge imperial acquisitions in 1885. Conquering foreign territory appeared to heap glory on the nation-state. While the "new imperialism" aimed to advance Western religions and culture, simultaneously the expansion of the West increased the subjection of local peoples, inflicting violence and altering everyday life. Said to benefit all, it paradoxically intensified discord among the European powers and even among ordinary citizens.

Taming the Mediterranean

European countries eyed the African and Asian shores of the Mediterranean for reasons based on the old imperialism: the chance to profit through trade. Great Britain and France were especially eager to do business with Egypt, where the combined value of imports and exports had jumped from 3.5 million Egyptian pounds in 1838 to 21 million in 1880 (and would grow to 60 million in 1913). European capital investment in the region also rose, first in ventures such as the Suez Canal in the 1860s and then in the laying of thousands of miles of railroad track and the creation of telegraph systems. Improvement-minded rulers in Asia and Africa paid dearly for modernization: whereas European bankers charged 5 percent interest on loans at home, they charged non-Europeans 12 percent or more, a difference they justified by determining foreign investments to be a greater risk. High rates of return on loans made foreign investments very attractive, and the completion of harbors, dams, canals, and railroads increased the Middle East's desirability as a market for European exports and as an intermediate stop on the way to trade with Asia.

After India fell to direct British rule in 1858, Egypt felt the next blow of Britain. Britain and France had pursued a stake in Egypt since the Napoleonic Wars, and in 1875 British prime minister Benjamin Disraeli bought a massive share in the Suez Canal for Britain. This purchase gave the khedive Ismail (r. 1863–1879), Egypt's profligate ruler, money to make payments on high-interest loans to European creditors. In 1879, the British and the French took over the Egyptian treasury to secure their own financial investments. Nationalist groups protested this heavy-handed encroachment on Egyptian sovereignty. By this time some 88 percent of the India trade was using the Suez Canal, and to protect European interests Britain used the nationalist threat as an excuse to bombard Alexandria and invade Egypt in 1882.

The Suez Canal and British Invasion of Egypt, 1882

After defeating the nationalist forces, however, the British did not restore the khedive's independent rule but instead ran the government from behind the scenes. Despite heated parliamentary opposition at home, the British reshaped the Egyptian economy to their own needs. In keeping with the demands of modernization, they brought in new agricultural machinery, created irrigation systems, and abolished forced labor. They also reorganized agriculture, changing the system from one based on multiple crops that maintained the country's self-sufficiency to one that emphasized the production of a few crops—mainly cotton, raw silk, wheat, and rice, which were especially useful to European manufacturing. Colonial powers, local landowners, and moneylenders profited from these agricultural changes, while the bulk of the rural population barely eked out an existence.

The rest of the Mediterranean and the Ottoman Empire felt the heightened presence of the European powers. With Algeria increasingly dominated by the French military, French settlers now moved onto land taken from indigenous people. As a further guarantee of their Mediterranean claims, the French occupied neighboring Tunisia in 1881. Elsewhere, businessmen from Britain, France, and Germany flooded Asia Minor with cheap goods, driving artisans from their trades and into low-paid work building railroads or processing tobacco. Instead of basing wage rates on gender (as they did at home), Europeans used ethnicity and religion, paying Muslims less than Christians, and Arabs less than other ethnic groups. Such practices, as well as contact with European technology and national-ism, planted the seeds for anticolonial movements.

Scramble for Africa

Sub-Saharan Africans also felt the heavier hand of European ambition after the British takeover of the Egyptian government. Economic relations between Africans and Europeans were not new, but contact between the two continents had principally in-volved the trade of African slaves for European manufactured goods. The slave trade had drastically diminished by this time, and Europeans' principal objective was expanding trade in Africa's raw mate-rials, such as palm oil, cotton, diamonds, cocoa, and rubber. Additionally, with its industrial and naval supremacy and its empire in India, Britain hoped to keep the southern and eastern coasts of Africa se-cure for stopover ports on the route to Asia.

Except for the French conquest of Algeria, commerce had rarely involved direct political con-trol in Africa. Yet in the 1880s, European influence turned into direct control as one African territory after another fell to European military force (Map 24.1). The French, Belgians, Portuguese, Italians, and Germans jockeyed to dominate peoples, land, and resources—"the magnificent cake of Africa," as King Leopold II of Belgium (r. 1865–1909) put it. Driven by insatiable greed, Leopold claimed the Congo region of central Africa, thereby initiating competition with France for that territory and in-flicting on its peoples unparalleled acts of cruelty. German chancellor Otto von Bismarck, who saw colonies mostly as political bargaining chips, sent out explorers in 1884 and established German con-trol over Cameroon and a section of East Africa. Faced with competition, the British poured millions of pounds into preserving their position by domi-nating the continent "from Cairo to Cape Town," as the slogan went, and the French cemented their hold on large portions of western Africa.

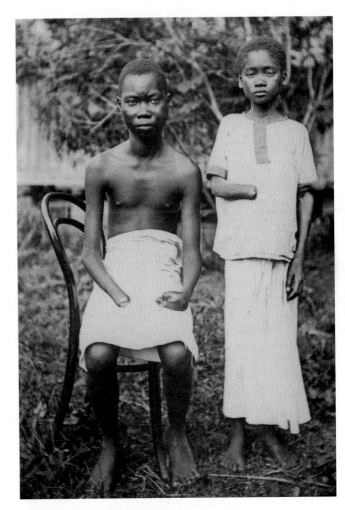

The Violence of Colonization
King Leopold, ruler of the Belgian Congo, was so greedy that his agents squeezed the last drop of rubber and other resources from local peoples. Missionaries reported such atrocities as the killing of workers whose quotas were even slightly short or the amputation of hands for the same offense. Belgian agents collected amputated hands and sent them to govern-ment officials to show Leopold that they were enforcing his kind of discipline.
Anti-Slavery International.

The scramble for Africa escalated tensions in Europe and prompted Bismarck to call a confer-ence of European nations at Berlin. The fourteen nations at the conference, held in a series of meet-ings in 1884 and 1885, decided that settlements along the African coast guaranteed rights to inter-nal territory. This agreement led to the strictly lin-ear dissection of the continent; geographers and diplomats cut across indigenous boundaries of

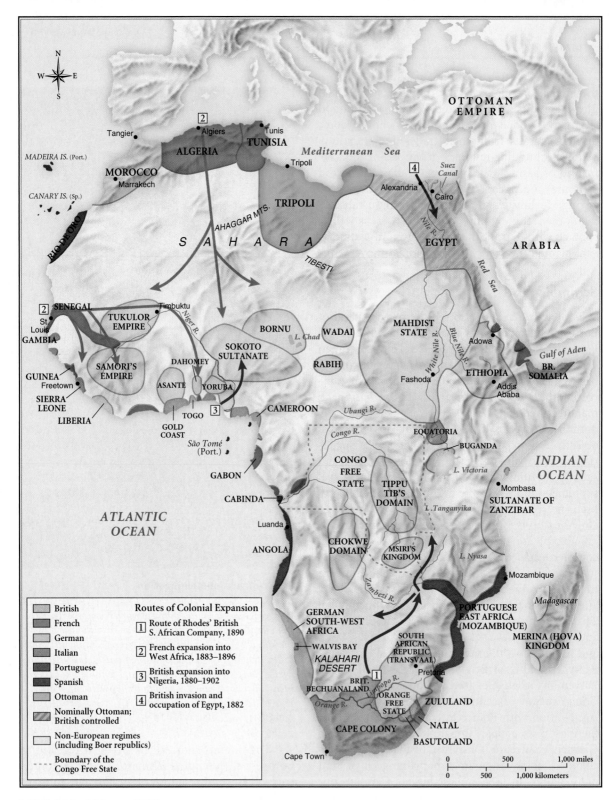

MAP 24.1 Africa, c. 1890

The "scramble for Africa" entailed a real reversal of European trading practices, which were generally limited to the coastline. Trying to conquer, economically penetrate, and rule the interior resulted in a map of the continent that made sense only to the imperial powers, for it divided ethnic groups and made territorial unities that had nothing to do with Africans' sense of geography or patterns of settlement. Nor did it conform in any way to Africans' own political organization.

African culture and ethnic life. The Berlin conference also banned the sale of alcohol and controlled the sale of arms to native peoples. In theory the meeting was supposed to reduce bloodshed and temper ambitions in Africa, but in reality European leaders were intent on maintaining and expanding their power, and utterly rapacious individuals like King Leopold continued to plunder the continent and terrorize its people. The news from Berlin only whetted the popular appetite for more imperialist ventures.

Technological development of powerful guns, railroads, steamships, and medicines dramatically expanded and facilitated Western domination, accelerating the penetration of all the continents after more than three centuries of exploration and trade. The gunboats that forced the Chinese to open their borders to opium played a part in forcing African ethnic groups to give up their independence. Quinine and guns were also an important factor in African conquest. Before the development of medicinal quinine in the 1840s and 1850s, the deadly tropical disease malaria had threatened to decimate any European party embarking on exploration or military conquest, giving Africa the nickname "White Man's Grave." The use of quinine, extracted from cinchona bark from the Andes, to treat malaria sent death rates among missionaries, adventurers, traders, and bureaucrats plummeting. A Dutch cartel, successfully experimenting with cinchona cultivation in Indonesia, broke the South American hold on quinine production and cornered the market until World War II.

While quinine saved white lives, technology to take lives was also advancing. Improvements to the breech-loading rifle and the development of the machine gun, or "repeater," between 1862 and the 1880s dramatically increased firepower. Europeans carried on a brisk trade selling inferior guns to Africans on the coast, but peoples of the interior used bows and arrows. Muslim slave traders and European Christians alike crushed African resistance with blazing gunfire: "The whites did not seize their enemy as we do by the body, but thundered from afar," claimed one local African resister. "Death raged everywhere—like the death vomited forth from the tempest."

Nowhere did this destructive capacity have greater effect than in southern Africa, where farmers of European descent and prospectors, rather than military personnel, battled the Xhosa, Zulu, and other African peoples for control of the frontier regions of Transvaal, Natal, the Orange Free State, Rhodesia, and the Cape Colony. Although the Dutch originally settled the area in the seventeenth century, the British had gained control by 1815. Thereafter descendants of the Dutch, called *Boers* (Dutch for "farmers"), were joined by British immigrants in their fight to wrest farmland and mineral resources from natives. British businessman and politician Cecil Rhodes (1853–1902), sent to South Africa for his health just as diamonds were being discovered in 1870, cornered the diamond market and claimed a huge amount of African territory with the help of official charters from the British government, all before he turned forty. Pushing hundreds of miles into the interior of southern Africa (a region soon to be named Rhodesia after him), Rhodes moved into gold mining too. His ambition for Britain and for himself was boundless: "I contend that we are the finest race in the world," he explained, "and that the more of the world we inhabit the better it is." Although notions of

Malian Young Men's House
Europeans claimed that sub-Saharan Africans had no culture and especially no technical knowledge. Skilled road builders, textile designers, and manufacturers of weapons, these Africans had also constructed intricate mosques, private dwellings, and communal buildings such as this one for young men in Mali. European painters, architects, and sculptors soon adapted features from African styles and even wholly modeled their designs on those of artists beyond the West.
Carollee Pelos/Jean-Louis Bourgeois.

European racial superiority had been advanced before, racist attitudes now justified converting trade with Africans into conquest and political control of their lands. Within just a few decades Darwinism had evolved from a contribution to science to a racist justification for imperialism.

Wherever necessary to ensure profit and domination, Europeans destroyed African economic and political systems or transformed them into instruments of their rule. A British governor of the Gold Coast put the matter succinctly in 1886: the British would "rule the country as if there were no inhabitants," as if local traditions of political and economic life did not exist. Indeed, most Europeans considered Africans barely civilized despite the wealth local rulers and merchants accumulated in their international trade in raw materials and slaves and despite individual African people's accomplishments in dyeing, road building, and architecture. Unlike the Chinese and Indians, whom Europeans credited with a scientific and artistic heritage, Africans were seen as valuable only for manual labor. By confiscating Africans' land, Europeans forced native peoples to work for them to earn a living and to pay the taxes they imposed. Subsistence agriculture, often performed by women and slaves, thus declined in favor of mining and farming cash crops. Standards of living dropped for Africans who lost their lands without realizing the Europeans were claiming permanent ownership. Systems of family and community unity provided support networks for Africans during this upheaval in everyday life.

Acquiring Territory in Asia

Britain justified the invasion of African countries as strategically necessary to preserve control of India's quarter of a billion people, but in reality from the 1870s on, the expansion of European power was occurring around the world. Much of Asia, with India as the centerpiece, was integrated into Western empires.

After two centuries of British authority, a system of rule emerged in which close to half a million Indians governed a region the British called *India* under the supervision of a few thousand British men. Indians also collected taxes and distributed patronage. As in Africa, colonial rule meant attaching subordinated peoples to the government not only through such mechanisms as native armies and civil service but also through intervention in everyday life. Thus, ordinary Indians benefited in some places from improved sanitation and medicine, which allowed the population to surge. Upper-class Indians attended British-style schools and served in a British-style bureaucracy, often coming to reject Indian customs such as infanticide, child marriage, and *sati*—a widow's self-immolation on her husband's funeral pyre. British notions of a scientific society attracted some in these upper classes, while the unity that British rule gave to what were once small localities and princedoms with separate allegiances promoted nationalism among the new, Western-educated elite.

Domination was also blatant: in 1876, the British Parliament declared Queen Victoria the empress of India. British policy forced the end to indigenous production of finished goods such as cotton textiles that would compete with Britain's own manufactures. Instead the British wanted cheaper raw materials such as wheat, cotton, and jute to supply their industries. Enclaves of British civil servants, who sought prosperity and social advancement for governing the vast subcontinent, enforced segregation and an inferior status on all classes of Indians. Discriminated against but educated, the Indian elite in 1885 founded the Indian National Congress, which challenged Britain's right to rule. In the next century, the Congress would develop into a mass movement.

British Colonialism in the Malay Peninsula and Burma, 1826–1890

To the east, British military forces took control of the Malay peninsula in 1874 and of the interior of Burma in 1885. In both areas, political instability often threatened secure trade. The British depended on the region's tin, oil, rice, teak, and rubber as well as its access to the interior trade routes of China. The presence of British troops guaranteed the order necessary to expand railroads for more efficient export of raw materials and the development of Western systems of communication. Once secured, the relative tranquillity also allowed the British to build factories and from there to create an industrial base in China.

The British rapidly added to their holdings in Asia partly to counter Russian and French annexations. Since 1865, Russia had been absorbing the small Muslim states of central Asia, including Turkestan and provinces of Afghanistan (Map 24.2). Besides extending into the Ottoman Empire, Russian tentacles reached Persia, India, and China, often encountering British ambition. The Trans-Siberian Railroad allowed Russia to begin integrating Siberia—considered a colony in the eighteenth and early nineteenth centuries. Using favorable treaties backed by the threat of military action, in 1887 France created the Union of Indochina from the ancient states of Cambodia, Tonkin, Annam, and Cochin China (the latter three now constitute Vietnam). Laos was added to Indochina in 1893.

The Union of Indochina, 1893

Like the British, the French brought some Western programs to the societies they brutally conquered. Modern projects in the Mekong Delta, for example, increased the amount of cultivated land and spurred rapid growth in the food supply; the French also improved sanitation and public health in Indochina. Such changes proved a mixed blessing, however, because they led to population growth that strained the societies' other resources. Furthermore, landowners and French imperialists siphoned off most of the profits from economic improvement. The French also undertook a cultural mission to transform Saigon and other cities into centers of French civilization. Tree-lined boulevards that emulated Paris were constructed in an urban building program. French literature, theater, and art diverted not only colonial officials but also upper-class Indochinese. Nonetheless, contact with Western culture would eventually spawn Indochinese nationalism, influenced by Western models but rejecting Western rule.

Japan's Imperial Agenda

Japan escaped the "new" European imperialism by its rapid transformation into a modern industrial nation with its own imperial agenda. A Japanese print of the 1880s illustrates both traditional ways

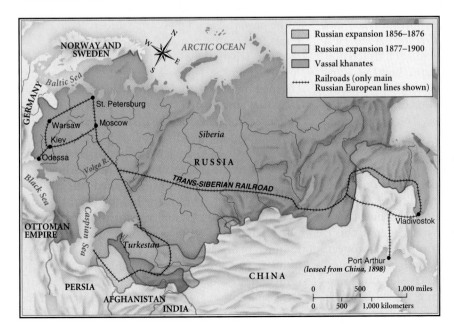

MAP 24.2 Expansion of Russia in Asia, 1865–1895
Russian administrators and military men continued enlarging Russia, bringing in Asians of many different ethnicities, ways of life, and religions. Simultaneously, land-hungry peasants in western Russia followed the path of expansion into Siberia and Muslim territories in the south. In some cases they drove native peoples from their lands, but in others they settled unpopulated frontier areas. As in all cases of imperial expansion, local peoples resisted any expropriation of their livelihood.

Modernization in Japan
Japan modernized with breathtaking speed, as this view of a railroad station demonstrates. Japan both borrowed from the West and loyally supported its own traditions. Thus, while many Japanese donned Western clothes, others remained wedded to local costumes and to native scenery such as cherry trees. In this woodcut by Ando Hiroshige II—son of the artist imitated by many in the West—the train schedule appears across the top of the depiction.
Laurie Platt Winfrey Inc.

and the Western influence behind Japan's burgeoning power. The picture's costumed women, strolling with their parasols amidst flowering cherry trees, might have been rendered centuries earlier; but a steaming locomotive in the background symbolizes change. The Japanese embraced foreign trade and industry under the leadership of the Satcho Hito clan, whose accession to power in 1868 ushered in the Meiji Restoration. "All classes high and low shall unite in vigorously promoting the economy and welfare of the nation," ran one of the first pronouncements of the new regime. The Japanese had long acquired knowledge from other countries. Unlike China, which had rejected it, Japan had endorsed the challenge from the West.

In the 1870s, Japanese government officials traveled to Europe and the United States to study technological and industrial developments. Western dress became the rule at the imperial court, and when fire destroyed Tokyo in 1872 a European directed the rebuilding in Western architectural style. Opposition to such changes was not tolerated, as the new central government, led by some of the old *samurai*, or warrior elite, crushed massive rebellions by any who resisted modernization. The Japanese adapted samurai traditions such as spiritual discipline and the drive to excel to a large, technologically modern military, which was filled by universal conscription. By 1894, Japan had become powerful enough to force traders to accept its terms for commerce and diplomatic relations.

The Japanese government instigated the turn toward industry. Japanese legal scholars, following German models, helped draft a constitution in 1889 that emphasized state power rather than individual rights. The state also stimulated economic development by building railroads and shipyards and establishing financial institutions. Then in the 1880s, when the cost of modernization had drained resources, the government auctioned off its businesses to private entrepreneurs, thereby collecting essential revenue to stabilize its finances. State support led daring innovators like Iwasaki Yataro, founder of the Mitsubishi firm, to develop heavy industries such as mining and shipping. In Japan, unlike the rest of Asia, the adaptation of Western-style enterprises became a patriotic goal. Like its Western models, Japan started intervening in nationalist and imperialist struggles elsewhere in Asia. This interference ultimately provoked war with its traditionally more powerful neighbors China and Russia.

The Paradoxes of Imperialism

Imperialism ignited constant, sometimes heated debate because of the many paradoxes in its meaning and scope. Although it was meant to stabilize great-power status, imperialism intensified distrust in international politics. New countries vied with old ones for a share of world influence. In securing India's borders, for example, the British faced Russian expansion in Afghanistan and along the borders of China. Moreover, imperial competition made areas of Europe, such as the Balkans, more volatile than ever as states sought status and national security in the control of disputed territory.

Politicians debated the economic value of empire. The search for new markets often proved more costly than profitable to societies. Britain, for example, spent enormous amounts of tax revenues to maintain its empire even as its industrial base began to decline. Yet for certain businesses, colonies provided crucial markets: late in the century, French colonies bought 65 percent of France's exports of soap and 41 percent of its metallurgical exports. Imperialism provided huge numbers of jobs

to people in European port cities, but—whether they benefited or not—taxpayers in all parts of a nation paid for colonial armies, increasingly costly weaponry, and administrators.

Motives for imperialism were equally paradoxical. Goals such as fostering national might, boosting national loyalty, and the centuries-old effort to Christianize peoples often proved unattainable or difficult to measure. Many believed that through imperialist ventures, "a country exhibits before the world its strength or weakness as a nation," as one French politician announced. Governments worried that imperialism—because of its expense and the constant possibility of war—might weaken rather than strengthen them. Another French statesman argued that France "must keep its role as the soldier of civilization." But, as French rule in Indochina showed, it was unclear if imperialists should emphasize soldiering—that is, conquest and conflict—or the more encompassing goal of exporting culture and religion.

Hoping to Christianize colonized peoples, European missionaries ventured to newly secured areas of Africa and Asia. A woman missionary working among the Tibetans reflected a common view when she remarked that the native peoples were "going down, down into hell, and there is no one but me . . . to witness for Jesus amongst them." Europeans were confident in their religious and

An ABC for Baby Patriots (1899)
Pride in empire began at an early age, when learning the alphabet from this kind of book helped develop an imperial sensibility. The subject of geography became important in schools during the decades between 1870 and 1890 and helped young people know what possessions they could claim as citizens. In British schools, the young celebrated the holiday Empire Day with ceremonies and festivities emphasizing imperial power.
Bodleian Library, Oxford.

cultural superiority. In the judgment of many, Asians and Africans were a class beneath Europeans, variously characterized as lying, lazy, self-indulgent, or irrational. One English official pontificated that "accuracy is abhorrent to the Oriental mind." At the height of imperialism, such beliefs offered still another justification for conquest and dominion: the civilizing process of colonization would eventually make conquered peoples grateful for what Europe had brought them. Viewing other races as "degenerate" helped promote Western notions of progress, but this cultural pride prompted "civilizers" such as missionaries paradoxically to collaborate with the most brutal military measures to accomplish their goals.

Western scholars and travelers had long gathered ideas and knowledge about Asian and African languages and cultures, and they claimed during these years to have garnered a totally objective and scientific view of history and society. Yet even the best scholars generally considered foreign cultures in terms of their own biases, characterizing Islam's Muhammad as a mere imitation of Jesus, for example. Alternatively, some Europeans—from novelists to military men—considered conquered peoples better than Europeans because they were unspoiled by civilization. "At last some local color," enthused one colonial officer, fresh from industrial cities of Europe, on seeing Constantinople. This romantic, misinformed, "orientalizing" vision of an ancient center of culture, similar to eighteenth-century condescension toward the "noble savage," had little to do with the reality of conquered peoples' lives. A look back at these paradoxical efforts suggests that Europe itself became conflicted as it underwent profound changes in the course of further industrialization and imperial expansion.

❖ The Transformation of Culture and Society

Advancing industrialization and empire not only made the world an interconnected marketplace but transformed everyday culture and society. Success in manufacturing and foreign ventures created millionaires, and the expansion of a professional middle class and development of a service sector resulted in more people affluent enough to own property, see some of the world, and provide their children a more cosmopolitan education. Price deflation caused by industrial success and imperial conquest changed everyday life: consumers in the West could purchase goods that poured in from around the world. Many Europeans grew healthier, partly because of improved diet and partly because of the efforts of reformers who sponsored government programs aimed at promoting the fitness necessary for citizens of imperial powers.

Industrial and imperial advance simultaneously challenged many working-class people in the West, buffeting them with the threat of replacement with machinery while offering new opportunities for mobility as European societies opened up the globe. Their experience of the internationalizing force of imperialism was different from that of the middle class: from the mid-nineteenth century on, millions migrated to the United States, Canada, Australia, Argentina, Brazil, and Siberia and, as frequently, from country to city and back. In the process they transported and imported culture. Artists captured the imperial and industrial spectacle in increasingly iconoclastic works influenced by styles from beyond the West. Their art, like the everyday lives of those they depicted, was transformed in the industrial, imperial crucible.

The "Best" Circles

The profits from industry and empire added new members to the upper class, or "best" circles, so called at the time because of their members' wealth, education, and social status. People in the best circles often came from the aristocracy, which retained much of its power and was still widely emulated. Increasingly, however, aristocrats had to share their social position with new millionaires from the ranks of the bourgeoisie. In fact, the very distinction between aristocrat and bourgeois became blurred, as monarchs gratefully endowed millionaire industrialists and businesspeople with aristocratic titles, in thanks for their contributions to the national wealth. Moreover, down-at-the-heels aristocrats were only too willing to offer their children in marriage to families from the newly rich. Such arrangements brought a much-needed infusion of funds to old, established families and the cachet of an aristocratic title to upstart families. Thus the American heiress Winaretta Singer (of Singer sewing machine fame) married Prince Edmond de Polignac of France, and Jeanette

Lord and Lady Curzon on a Tiger Shoot
Big-game hunting became the imperial sport of choice, and real adventurers came to see fox hunting and other traditional pastimes of the elites as effeminate if not decadent. European hunters took the sport over from local Africans and Asians who had previously depended on the hunt for their livelihood. Now these Africans and Asians served the European amateurs, many of whom were in wretched physical shape. Some women enjoyed hunting too. As a gesture of chivalry, men would let the woman issue the coup de grace, or death shot, if a tiger materialized during a hunt.
India Office Library/British Library.

Jerome, daughter of a wealthy New York financier, married England's Lord Randolph Churchill (their son Winston later became England's prime minister). Even millionaires without official connections to the aristocracy discarded the modest ways of a century earlier to build palatial country homes and villas, engage in conspicuous displays of wealth, and wall themselves off from the poor in suburbs or new sections of town inhabited only by the rich. To justify their success, the wealthy often appealed to Social Darwinist principles, which indicated that their accumulation of money demonstrated the natural superiority of the rich over the poor.

Sport and leisure brought upper-class men together in their favorite activity—hunting—as this activity was reshaped by imperial contact. Fox and bird hunting had been aristocratic pastimes in parts of Europe for centuries, but big-game hunting in Asia and Africa now became the rage. European hunters forced native Africans, who had depended on hunting for income or food and for group unity, to work as guides, porters, and domestics on hunts instead. Mastering foreign games like polo or activities like big-game hunting demonstrated that Europeans could conquer both territory and the more intangible things like culture. (See "Did You Know?," page 910.) Collectors on the hunts brought exotic specimens back to Eu-

rope for zoological exhibits, natural history museums, and traveling displays, all of which flourished during this period. Stags' heads, elephant tusks, and animal skins also decorated European homes.

Members of the upper class did their best to exclude others by controlling their children's social lives. Marriageable women in the upper and middle classes were closely watched to preserve their chastity and to keep them from socializing with lower-class men. Upper-class men had liaisons with lower-class women—part of the double standard that saw promiscuity as normal for men and as immoral for women—but few thought of marrying them. Parents still arranged many marriages directly, but other marriages were initiated during visiting days, on which occasions prominent hostesses held an open house under rather formal conditions. Such regular social contact sometimes provided the foundation for matrimonial decisions.

Ritualistic visits filled the everyday lives of upper-class women. Instead of working for pay, they devoted themselves to having children, directing staffs of servants, and maintaining standards of etiquette and social conduct. Women took their role seriously by keeping detailed accounts of their expenditures and monitoring their children's religious and intellectual development. The pursuit of fashion in home furnishing took on imperial

Polo and Social Class

Today's historians often see the implantation of sports by the imperial powers in colonized regions as a form of domination. By organizing teams of cricket or rugby players in West Africa, India, or the Caribbean, for instance, the British were said to be inventing identities and traditions that were based on Western ideas of what sports and sportsmen were. In this interpretation, imperialists replaced local cultures with their own.

But imperialism has always been a two-way street despite great differences in power. While planting cricket in the colonies, the British upper classes became hooked on polo, an Asian sport that imperial forces picked up in India. Played on horseback, *puhluh* was a team sport that allowed a cavalry-based fighting force (both men and horses) to stay in shape during long, idle intervals. Chutneys, curries, verandahs, jodphurs, and the game of pachisi were some of the many borrowings from India by the West in the nineteenth century. It was polo, however, that has lost most of its associations with imperial borrowing, seeming to many the essence of Britain's celebrated, aristocratic way of life.

Anglo-Indian Polo Team
Team sports underwent rapid development during the imperial years, as spectators rooted for the success of their football team in the same spirit they rooted for their armies abroad. Some educators believed that team sports formed the male character so that men could be more effective soldiers against peoples of other races. Thus this mixed team of polo players was uncharacteristic. In cricket, soccer, and other sports, city challenged city, nation challenged nation, and race often challenged race.
Hulton Getty Collection/Liaison Agency.

motifs in these decades, featuring Persian-inspired designs in textiles, Oriental carpets, wicker furniture, and Chinese porcelains. With the importation of plants such as azaleas and rhododendrons from around the world, gardens replaced parks and lawns—another domestic element for upper-class women to oversee. Being an active consumer of fashion in clothing was time-consuming. In contrast to men's plain garments, upper-class women's costumes were elaborate, ornate, and dramatic, featuring constricting corsets, long voluminous skirts, bustles, and low-cut necklines for evening wear. Upper-class women, symbols of elite leisure, fervently tried to offset the drabness of industrial life

with the rigorous practice of art and music. One Hungarian observer wrote, "The piano mania has become almost an epidemic in Budapest as well as Vienna." Some women were also quite active outside the home, engaging in religious and philanthropic activities and taking a particular interest in the welfare of lower-class women.

The Rise of Middle-Class Professionals

Below the richest best circles or "upper crust," the "solid" middle class was expanding, most notably in western and central Europe: the Russian government often sought out foreigners from Germany and other parts of central Europe to build its professional and entrepreneurial classes. Growing numbers of doctors, lawyers, managers, professors, and successful journalists found their positions enhanced by the prestige of science and information, and they established their position as masters of a complex body of knowledge. Government legislation began to allow professional people to determine who would and would not be admitted to "the professions." Such legislation had both positive and negative effects: groups could set their own standards, but otherwise qualified people were sometimes prohibited from working because they lacked the established credentials. The German medical profession, for example, was granted authority to control licensing, which led to more rigorous university training for future doctors but also pushed midwives out of medicine and caused the arrest of healers not trained in medical school. Science, too, became the province of the trained specialist rather than the amateur genius; scientists were likely to be employed by universities and institutes, funded by the government, and provided with equipment and assistants. Like other members of the middle class, professors of science were intensely patriotic, often interpreting their work as part of an international struggle for prestige and excellence. Without more staff and equipment, one French scientist threatened in 1880, "we will be far behind the German and Dutch laboratories."

Although professionals could sometimes mingle with those at the apex of society, their lives remained more modest. They employed at least one servant, to give the appearance of leisure to the middle-class woman in the home. Professional men working at home did so from the best-appointed, if not lavish, room. Middle-class domesticity substituted cleanliness and polish for upper-class conspicuous consumption. The soap and tea used in the middle-class home were becoming signs—along with hard work—of a racial superiority and higher status not accessible to the colonized peoples who actually produced those goods.

Professional Sports and Organized Leisure

As nations competed for territory and economic markets, male athletes banded together to organize team sports that eventually replaced village games. Large audiences now backed a particular team, as soccer, rugby, and cricket drew mass followings and integrated migrants as well as the lower and higher classes into a common culture. The heightened emphasis on group competition also found favor with the reading public; newspapers reported the results of all sorts of contests, including the Tour de France bicycle race, sponsored by tire makers who wanted to prove the superiority of their product.

Victorian Women's Bicycle Race

The bicycle represented freedom for millions of young people, and many credit it with changes in social customs that gradually appeared in these decades. In clubs or groups of friends, the young went off riding for miles; for young women the bicycle was particularly liberating, giving them exercise and a chance to see a bit more of the world. Their clothing changed subtly too as full skirts and abundant petticoats were soon found cumbersome and even unsafe. The bicycle also provided easier transportation for working people. Collection of Sally Fox.

Tests of speed measured by clocks and involving the use of machines like bicycles and cars replaced older forms of competition such as cockfighting and sack racing. Competitive sports began to be seen as valuable to national strength and spirit. "The Battle of Waterloo was won on the playing fields of Eton," ran the wisdom of the day, suggesting that the games played in school could mold the strength and character of an army.

Team sports—like civilian military service—helped differentiate male and female spheres and thus promoted social order based on distinction between the sexes. Some team sports for women emerged, such as soccer, field hockey, and rowing, but in general women were encouraged to engage in individual sports. "Riding improves the temper, the spirits and the appetite," wrote one sportswoman. "Black shadows and morbid fancies disappear from the mental horizon." Rejecting the idea of women's natural frailty, reformers introduced exercise and gymnastics into schools for girls, often with the idea that these would strengthen them for motherhood and thus help build the nation-state. So-called Swedish exercises for young women spread through respectable homes across Europe, while more sophisticated women practiced yoga.

The middle classes believed their leisure pursuits should be edifying as well as fun. Thus mountain climbing became a popular middle-class hobby. As the editor of a Swedish publication of 1889 explained, "The passion for mountain-climbing can only be understood by those who realize that it is the step-by-step achievement of a goal which is the real pleasure of the world." Working-class people adopted middle-class habits by joining clubs for such pursuits as bicycling, touring, and hiking. Laborers and their families also sought the benefits of fresh air and exercise by visiting the beach, taking the train into the countryside, and enjoying day trips on river steamships. Clubs that sponsored trips often had such names as the Patriots or the Nationals, again associating physical fitness with national strength. The new emphasis on healthy recreation gave individuals a greater sense of individual freedom and power and thereby contributed to a developing sense of citizenship based less on constitutions and rights than on an individual nation's exercise of raw power. A farmer's son in the 1890s boasted that with a bicycle, "I was king of the road, since I was faster than a horse."

Working People's Strategies

Working people had for centuries migrated from countryside to city and from country to country to make a living. After the middle of the nineteenth century, empire and industry were powerful factors in migration. Older cities of Europe like Riga, Marseille, and Hamburg offered secure ports of entry and jobs—now in industry—and global trade, while new colonies provided land, posts for soldiers and administrators, and the possibility of unheard-of wealth in diamonds, gold, and other natural resources. City workers adapted to new conditions as industry made further inroads into the social and economic fabric.

Migration. Some Europeans followed an imperialist pattern of migration, moving well beyond their national borders. (See "Contrasting Views," page 914.) In parts of Europe, the land simply could not produce enough to support a rapidly expanding population. For example, the vast forests of Sicily that had once supplied the Greek navies with wood to build ships had been replaced by nearly worthless, eroded soil. By the end of the nineteenth century, hundreds of thousands of Sicilians were leaving, often temporarily, to find work in the industrial cities of northern Europe or the United States. The British Isles, especially Ireland, yielded one-third of all European emigrants between 1840 and 1920, first because of the potato famine and then because of uncertain farm tenancy and periodic economic crisis. Between 1886 and 1900, half a million Swedes out of a population of 4.75 million quit their country (Figure 24.1). Millions of rural Jews, especially those of eastern Europe, left their villages for economic reasons, but Russian Jews also fled in the face of vicious anti-Semitism. Russian mobs brutally attacked Jewish communities, destroying homes and businesses and even murdering some Jews. "People who saw such things never smiled anymore, no matter how long they lived," recalled one Russian Jewish woman who migrated to the United States in the early 1890s.

Commercial and imperial prosperity determined destinations. Most migrants went to North and South America, Australia, and New Zealand, as news of opportunity reached Europe. Moreover, the railroad and steamship made journeys across and out of Europe more affordable, more comfortable,

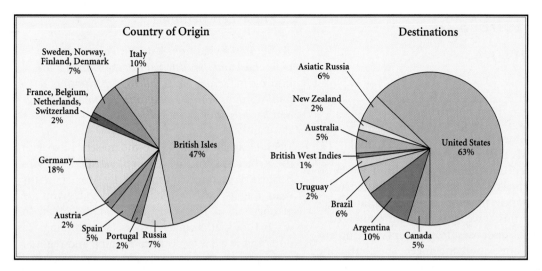

FIGURE 24.1 European Emigration, 1870–1890

The suffering caused by economic change and by political persecution motivated people from almost every European country to leave their homes for greater security elsewhere. North America attracted more than two-thirds of these migrants, many of whom followed reports of vast quantities of available land in both Canada and the United States. Both countries were known for following the rule of law and for economic opportunity in urban as well as rural areas.

Theodore Hamerow, *The Birth of New Europe: State and Society in the Nineteenth Century* (Chapel Hill: University of North Carolina Press, 1983), 169.

and faster, even though most travel was in steerage, with baggage and supplies and few amenities. Once established elsewhere, migrants frequently sent money back home and thus remained part of the family economy; European farm families often received a good deal of their income from sons and daughters who had left. Nationalist commentators in Slovakia, Poland, Hungary, and other parts of eastern and central Europe bemoaned the loss of ethnic vigor, but peasants themselves welcomed the arrival of "magic dollars" from their kin. Migrants appreciated the chance to begin anew without the deprivation and social constrictions of the old world. One settler in the United States was relieved to escape the meager peasant meal of rye bread and herring: "God save us from . . . all that is Swedish," he wrote home sourly.

Migration out of Europe often meant the end to the old way of life. Workingmen and -women immediately had to learn new languages and civic practices and to compete for jobs in growing cities where they formed the cheapest pool of labor, often in factories or sweatshops. Women who stayed at home, however, tended to associate with others like themselves, preserving traditional ways. More insulated at home, they might never learn the new

language or never put their peasant dresses away. Their children and husbands more often devalued their pasts as they were forced to build a life in schools and factories of the new world.

Simultaneously, rapid industrial development accelerated the urbanization of Europe. More common than international migration was internal migration from rural areas to European cities. Cities of more than 100,000 grew the most, but every urban area attracted migrants seeking employment. However, more people still lived in rural areas of under 2,000 people than lived in towns and cities. Migration back to those rural areas occurred at harvest time. The most urbanized countries were Great Britain and Belgium, followed by Germany, France, and the Netherlands. In Russia, only 7 percent of the population lived in cities of 10,000 or more; in Portugal the figure was 12 percent. But migration of all types continued unabated, whatever the population density. Ongoing modernization meant that peasants and city workers had to adapt to survive and to preserve their life. Temporary migrants to the cities worked as masons, cabdrivers, or factory hands to supplement declining income from agriculture; in the winter, those remaining on the land turned to cottage industry

Experiences of Migration

Migration helped to shape Europe long before the nineteenth century, but in this particular century millions of migrants moved thousands of miles from the lands of their birth. The accelerated pace of movement, the vast distances traveled, and the permanent relocation of this wave of migration generated a wide range of responses, from acceptance and enthusiasm to opposition and anger. The conflicting reactions to migration appeared in official reports, local newspapers, poems, and very personal letters. While many government officials could point with relief at the economic benefits of emigration (Document 1), people left behind were often heart-broken and suffered destitution (Document 2). Migrants themselves had vastly differing experiences, provoking a great debate over migration that continues today (Documents 3 and 4).

1. The Government View

The preamble to the Hungarian census for 1890 was blunt and unambiguous on the subject. It saw emigration exclusively in financial terms:

Emigration has proved to be a veritable boom. The impoverished populace has been drawn off to where it has found lucrative employment; the position of those left behind, their work opportunities and standard of living, have undoubtedly improved thanks to the rise in wages, and thanks to the substantial financial aid coming into the country: sums of from 300,000 to 1,500,000 florints.

Source: Quoted in Julianna Puskas, "Consequences of Overseas Migration for the Country of Origin: The Case of Hungary," in *Roots of the Transplanted: Late 19th Century East Central and Southeastern Europe*, Dirk Hoerder and Inge Blank, eds. (Boulder: East European Monographs, 1994), I: 397.

2. Those Left Behind

Teofila Borkowska from Warsaw, Poland, reacted to her husband's resettlement in the United States in two letters from 1893 and 1894. Stripped of a family group, Teofila had a difficult time surviving, and her husband never did return.

1893. Dear Husband: Up to the present I live with the Rybickis. I am not very well satisfied, perhaps because I was accustomed to live for so many years quietly, with you alone. And today you are at one end of the world and I at the other, so when I look at strange corners [surroundings], I don't know what to do from longing and regret. I comfort myself only that you won't forget me, that you will remain noble as you have been. . . . I have only the sort of friends who think that I own thousands and from time to time someone comes to me, asking me to lend her a dozen roubles.

1894. Up to the present I thought and rejoiced that you would still come back to Warsaw, but since you write that you won't come I comply with the will of God and with your will. I shall now count the days and weeks [until you take me to America]. May our Lord grant it to happen as soon as possible, for I am terribly worried. Such a sad life! I go almost to nobody, for as long as you were in Warsaw everything was different. Formerly we had friends, and everybody was glad to see us, while now, if I go to anybody, they are afraid I need something from them and they show me beforehand a different face. . . . They all do it, even those who were so good formerly. Now they show themselves as they are. You write me to try to earn something with Wladzia [a cousin owning a dressmaking shop]. But I have not earned yet a grosz from her.

Source: Letter from Teofila Borkowska to Wladyslaw Borkowski, in William Thomas and Florian Znaniecki, *The Polish Peasant in Europe and America* (New York: Dover, 1958), July 21, 1893, April 12, 1894, II: 874–75.

3. Migration Defended

In some cases emigrants were said to be unpatriotic and cowardly for leaving their homeland just to avoid hard economic times. Sweden, which more than a million left because of bad economic conditions in the countryside, saw accusation and counteraccusation fly. To charges against Swedish emigrants, one journalist, Isador Kjelberg, wrote:

Patriotism? Let us not misuse so fine a word! Does patriotism consist of withholding the truth from the workingman by claiming that "things are bad in America"? I want nothing to do with such patriotism! If patriotism consists of seeking, through lies, to persuade the poorest classes to remain under the yoke, like mindless beasts, so that we others should be so much better off, then I am lacking in patriotism. I love my country, as such, but even more I love and sympathize with the human being, the worker. . . . Among those who most sternly condemn emigration are those who least value the human and civic value of the workingman. . . . They demand that he remain here. What are they prepared to give him to compensate the deprivations this requires? . . . It is only cowardly, unmanly, heartless, to let oneself become a slave under deplorable circumstances which one *can* overcome.

Source: Quoted in H. Arnold Barton, *A Folk Divided: Homeland Swedes and Swedish Americans, 1840–1940* (Carbondale: Southern Illinois University Press, 1994), 72–73.

An anonymous Swedish poem joined the political defense of migration along with an economic motivation:

I'm bound for young America,
Farewell old Scandinavia.
I've had my fill of cold and toil,
All for the love of mother soil.
You poets with your rocks and rills
Can stay and starve—on words, no frills.

Me, I've got a stomach 'neath my hide,
No bonds can keep me on this side.
There, out west, a man breathes free,
While here one slaves, a tired bee,
Gathering honey to fill the hive
Of wise old rulers, on us they thrive.

In toil we hover before their thrones,
While they take to slumber, like lazy drones.
Drunk with our nectar they've set us afright,
But opportunity has knocked, and we'll take our flight.

Source: Quoted in ibid., 137.

4. The Perils of Migration

A contrasting view of emigration to the United States appeared in a Slovak song:

My fellow countryman, Rendek from Senica,
    the son of poor parents
Went out into the wide world. In Pittsburgh
    he began to toil.
From early morning till late at night he filled
    the furnaces with coal.
Faster, faster, roared the foreman, every day.
A letter came from home:
I want to board the ship,
Wrote his young wife.

Rendek toiled harder
So as to see his wife.
But alas! He was careless
And on Saturday evening late
He received his injuries.

At home his widow waited
For the card which would never come.
I, his friend, write this song
To let you know
What a hard life we have here.

Source: Quoted in Frantisek Bielik, Horst Hogh and Anna Stvrtecka, "Slovak Images of the New World: 'We Could Pay Off Our Debts'" in Hoerder and Blank, eds., *Roots of the Transplanted*, I:388.

QUESTIONS FOR DEBATE
1. Did the vast nineteenth-century migration ultimately enrich or diminish European culture and society?
2. How would you characterize the experience of migration for families and individuals?
3. How did migration affect the national identity of both receiving countries and European countries of origin?

making bricks, pottery, sieves, shawls, lace, locks, and samovars. To maintain their status as independent artisans, handweavers sent their wives and daughters to towns to work in factories.

Adaptation to Industrial Change. Changes in technology and management practices eliminated outmoded jobs and often made the work of those who survived job cuts more difficult. Workers complained that new machinery sped up the pace of work to an unrealistic level. For example, new furnaces at a foundry in suburban Paris required workers to turn out 50 percent more metal per day than they had produced using the old furnaces. Stepped-up productivity demanded much more physical exertion to tend and repair machines, often at a faster pace, but workers did not receive additional pay for their extra efforts. Workers also grumbled about the proliferation of managers; many believed that foremen, engineers, and other supervisors interfered with their work. For women, supervision sometimes brought on-the-job harassment, as in the case of female workers in a German food-canning plant who kept their jobs only in return for granting sexual favors to the male manager.

As new machines replaced old, managers established formal skill levels, from the most knowledgeable machinist to the untrained carrier of supplies. On the one hand, the introduction of machinery "deskilled" some jobs—traditional craft ability was not a prerequisite for operating many new machines. Employers could increasingly use untrained workers, often women, and pay them less than skilled workers. On the other hand, inventions always demanded new skills, especially for those who had to understand work processes or repair machinery. Employers began to use the concept of skill (based in the old craft traditions) to segment the labor force, but sometimes the designations were arbitrary.

Already prevalent in such trades as garment making, the trend toward breaking down and separating work processes into discrete tasks continued. For example, builders employed excavators, scaffolders, and haulers to do the "dirty work," hiring fewer highly paid carpenters. Those filling unskilled jobs could not count on regular employment and spent much of their time searching out temporary jobs. On the other end of the scale, foremen were no longer the most skilled workers,

but supervisors chosen, as one worker complained, for the "pushing powers . . . of driving fellow men."

Many in the urban labor force continued to do outwork at home. Every branch of industry, from metallurgy to toy manufacturing to food processing, employed women at home—and their work was essential to the family economy. They painted tin soldiers, wrapped chocolate, made cheese boxes, decorated porcelain, and polished metal. Factory owners liked to employ outworkers because their low piece rates made them desperate for work under any conditions, and they were willing to work extremely long days. A German seamstress at her new sewing machine reported that she "pedaled at a stretch from six o'clock in the morning until midnight. . . . At four o'clock I got up and did the housework and prepared meals." Owners could lay off women at home during slack times and rehire them whenever needed with less fear of organized protest.

Economic change and the periodic recurrence of hard times had uneven consequences for people's everyday lives. In the late nineteenth century, joblessness and destitution always threatened. Some city workers prospered by comparison to those left behind in rural areas, though a growing number lost the steadiness of traditional artisanal work. By and large, however, the urban working class was better informed, more visible, and more connected to the progress of industry and empire.

Reform Efforts for Working-Class People

The cycle of boom and bust, the uneven prosperity of industrialism, and the upheaval of migration caused social problems that many in the middle and upper classes sought to address through reform organizations and charities. Settlement houses, clinics, and maternal and child wellness societies seemed to rise overnight in cities, quickly becoming a common sight. Young men and women, often from universities, flocked to staff these new organizations, especially the settlement houses, where the reformers took up residence in poor neighborhoods to study and help the people. Believing in the scientific approach to social problems, they thought that study would uncover the causes of social ills and point the way to solutions. One group devoted to this enterprise was the Fabian Society in London, a small organization established in 1884. Committed to a socialism based on reform and state planning rather than revolution, the Fabians helped found the Labour Party in 1893 as a way of incorporating social improvement into politics. Still other reformers were motivated by a strong religious impulse. "There is Christ's own work to be done," wrote one woman who volunteered to inspect workhouse conditions. Religious fervor added a moral component to reform efforts.

Impelled as well by a Social Darwinist fear that Europeans would lack the fitness to survive in a competitive world, philanthropists, industrialists, and government agencies intervened more and more in the lives of working-class families. They sponsored health clinics and milk centers to provide good medical care and food for children and instructed mothers in child-care techniques, including breast-feeding—an important way, reformers maintained, to promote infant health. Some schools distributed free lunches, medicine, and clothing and inspected the health and appearance of their students. These attempts to improve urban life had their downside, however, as when government officials or private reformers deemed themselves the overseers of the working-class family and entered apartments with impunity. Such intrusions pressured poor, overworked mothers to conform to standards for their children—such as finding them respectable shoes and other clothing—that they often could not afford.

To counteract the burdens facing the working-class family, some professionals began to make available birth-control information in the belief that small families were more likely to survive the rigors of urban life. In the 1880s, Aletta Jacobs (1851–1929), a Dutch physician, opened the first birth-control clinic, which specialized in promoting the new, German-invented diaphragm. Jacobs was moved to act by the plight of women in Amsterdam slums who were worn out by numerous pregnancies and whose lives, she believed, would be greatly improved by limiting their fertility. But reformers were sharply divided over whether birth control was moral. Some also believed that contraception would increase the sexual exploitation of women if the threat of pregnancy and its responsibilities were overcome so easily.

Reproductive issues framed another significant government reform in these decades: legislation that would "protect" women from certain kinds of work. In such cases the fear was not that families were too large but that women were not producing healthy enough children and were stealing jobs from men. Moreover, protective legislation was considered crucial to national development; as one French official put it, such laws provided the foundation on which a nation could "achieve the plenitude of its economic and political power." Protection further divided work into jobs for men and jobs for women, which paid less. Women across Europe were barred from night work and from such "dangerous" trades as pottery allegedly for health reasons, even though medical statistics demonstrated that women became sick on the job less often than men. But lawmakers and working-men claimed that women's work in potteries endangered reproduction, and women who had worked in the trade were forced to find other, lower-paying jobs or remain at home. The new laws did not prevent women from earning their livelihood, but they made the task harder by limiting their access to well-paying jobs.

Artistic Responses to Industrial and Imperial Change

In the 1870s and 1880s, the arts explored the consequences of global expansion and economic innovation, often in the same Darwinistic and gloomy terms that fed reformers' anxieties. Despite expansion and innovation, Darwin's theory held out the possibility that strong civilizations could fail to keep up with changing conditions and could thus decay and collapse. French writer Émile Zola (1840–1902), influenced by fears of social degeneration, produced a series of novels set in industrializing France about a family plagued by alcoholism and madness. Zola's protagonists, who led violent strikes and once even castrated an oppressive grocer, raised real anxieties about the future of civilization. Zola had less concern for exploring character than for describing the effects of industrial society on individuals: his *Au bonheur des dames* (*Women's Paradise*, 1883) depicts the supposedly refined upper-class shopper as a "queen drunk with love," all too quickly abandoning decorum to the "seductions" of the new department stores of Paris.

Other writers envisioned a widespread deterioration that threatened all of society—men and women, aristocrats and peasants, rural folk and urbanites, peasants and imperialists. Emilia Pardo Bazán (1859–1921) penned dramas of incest and murder among wealthy landowning families in rural Spain. In *The Mayor of Casterbridge* (1886), English novelist Thomas Hardy traced the path of a common man who sells his wife at a country fair and later rises to a position of power, only to find that he cannot escape his murky past. Hardy's vision was fatalistic; his characters battle forces beyond their control. Earlier urban writers such as Dickens had already brought attention to working-class lives, and now authors like Hardy examined rural conditions under the microscope of realism.

Some heroines were becoming more tough-minded. Norwegian playwright Henrik Ibsen (1828–1906) created the character of Nora, a woman who shocked audiences of *A Doll's House* (1879) by leaving a loveless and oppressive marriage. Olive Schreiner (1855–1920) went even further: in *The Story of an African Farm* (1889), the heroine rejects the role of submissive wife and describes the British Empire as a "dirty little world, full of confusion." By questioning British institutions, Schreiner, like Ibsen, helped launch a critical mindset about a range of social issues.

Creating new traditions or reviving old ones was another cultural response to the rapid, often disorienting pace of industrial and imperial change. Often these traditions served a unifying or nationalizing end. Country people used mass-produced textiles to design traditional-looking costumes and developed ceremonies based on a mythical past. Such customs amused city dwellers and brought tourist business to villages. So-called folk motifs also interested urban architects and industrial designers, who turned to rural artistic styles for models of household goods, decorative objects, and clothing. In the last decades of the century, architects copied Swiss chalets or Russian country homes to achieve a rustic look. Borrowing from Indian motifs, English designers William Morris (1834–1896) and his daughter May Morris (1862–1938) designed fabrics, wallpaper, and household items from such natural styles as the silhouettes of plants. Replacing what seemed "dead" and "ornate" styles of the early industrial years, "living flowers should inspire a living ornament," as May Morris explained. Some designers were inspired by socialist ideas and hoped the enthusiasm for handcrafted products would improve conditions for struggling artisans and help preserve unique styles in an age of increasing mass production.

Painters and sculptors, although patronized by wealthy collectors, continued to depend on the fancies of official taste. Government purchases of art for museums and government-sponsored exhibits of new works still determined an artist's success. But even artists in the government's good graces felt intense competition from a popular industrial invention—the camera. Photographers could produce cheap copies of paintings and create more realistic portraits than painters could, at affordable prices. In response, painters altered their style, at times trying to make their work look as different from photographs as possible.

As art departed from photographic realism, it nonetheless commented on the changing economic scene, especially the fact that a growing segment of service workers did less physical work and had more energy for leisure. The works of French painter Georges Seurat (1859–1891), for example, depicted the newly created parks with their walking paths and Sunday bicyclists; white-collar workers in their store-bought clothing, carrying books or newspapers, paraded like the well-to-do. Another French artist, Edgar Degas (1834–1917), focused on portraying women—from ballet dancers to laundry women—in various states of exertion and fatigue. Fatigue marked almost a romantic nostalgia for a past that was seen to require relentless physical labor from sunrise to sunset. When depicting the bleak outskirts of cities where industries were often located and where the desperately poor lived, Dutch-born Vincent Van Gogh (1853–1890) avoided the intense colors he typically used for the countryside.

Degas, Van Gogh, and Seurat, although their styles varied, have been characterized as avant-garde and impressionist. French artist Édouard Manet (1832–1883) used the term *impressionist* to emphasize the artist's attempt to capture a single moment by focusing on the ever-changing light and color found in everyday vision. Using splotches and dots, impressionists moved away from the precise realism of earlier painters; their challenge to the norm made impressionists simultaneously avant-garde. Claude Monet (1840–1926), for example, was fascinated by the way light transformed an object, and he often portrayed the same place—a bridge or a railroad station—at different times of day. Van Gogh used vibrant colors in great swirls to

Mary Cassatt, In the Loge (1879)
Cassatt patterned her work on artistic styles from East Asia. Sprigs of cherry blossoms and hairstyles that looked Chinese or Japanese often appeared in her paintings of mothers, children, and society women. Cassatt incorporated the color schemes from Japan, which poster artists were also using to advertise everything from world's fairs to cabarets and steamship travel. The arts of Asia and Africa were brightening the European public sphere.
The Hayden Collection, courtesy, Museum of Fine Arts, Boston.

capture sunflowers, corn stacks, and the starry evening sky. Such distortions of reality made the impressionists' visual style seem outrageous to those accustomed to realism, but others enthusiastically greeted impressionism's luminous quality. Industry contributed to the new style, as factories produced a range of pigments that allowed artists to use a wider, more intense spectrum of colors.

In both composition and style, impressionists borrowed heavily from Asian art and architecture. The concept of the fleetingness of situations came from a centuries-old and well-developed Japanese concept—*mono no aware* (serenity before and sensitivity to the fleetingness of life). The color, line, and delicacy of Japanese art (which many impressionists collected) is evident, for example, in Monet's later paintings of water lilies, his studies of wisteria, and even his re-creation of a Japanese gar-

den at his home in France as the subject for artistic study. Similarly, the American expatriate Mary Cassatt (1845–1926) used the two-dimensionality of Japanese art in her *In the Loge* (1879) and other paintings. Other artists, like Degas, imitated Asian art's use of wandering and conflicting lines to orchestrate space on a canvas, and Van Gogh filled the background of portraits with copies of intensely colored Japanese prints.

Music would soon be saturated with Asian influence too, but for the moment, like material culture, it was more likely to explore folk themes from hard-pressed rural life and to tout cultural nationalism. Czech composer Antonín Dvořák (1841–1904) employed popular national melodies in his *Moravian Duets* (1876) and *Slavonic Dances* (1878), and Norwegian composer Edvard Grieg's (1843–1907) music for Ibsen's play *Peer Gynt* (1875) integrated rural legends into music for urban audiences. In 1876, the most important operatic composer of the day, the anti-Semitic and increasingly reactionary Richard Wagner premiered his monumental cycle of four music dramas, *Der Ring des Nibelungen*. Although Wagner was steeped in Asian philosophy, the *Ring* was hailed as a triumphal celebration of German nationalism. While claiming to present universal beauty, music and the other arts were increasingly promoted as a national accomplishment, like empire. The work of Beethoven was now said to have made German unification possible by serving as a magnificent "call to battle." Thus the arts participated in nationalizing peoples thrown together by migration, technological change, and the forces of empire.

❖ The Birth of Mass Politics

Struggles for political voice, especially through the vote, accompanied imperial and economic expansion. The growth of industry and urban development heightened networks of political communication and consciousness, continuing the work of nationalizing institutions such as schools, urban agencies, and government bureaucracy. As national consciousness grew among workers, western European governments continued to allow more men to vote; even high-ranking politicians such as William Gladstone, the prime minister of Great Britain, had to campaign by railroad to win votes from a far-flung electorate. Although only men profited from electoral reform, the era's expanding franchise marked the beginning of mass politics—a hallmark of the twentieth-century West. Germany had manhood suffrage, but in more autocratic monarchies to the east—notably Russia and the Ottoman Empire—violence and ethnic conflict resulted from attempts to dominate minorities in ways that often resembled rule of colonized peoples.

Workers, Politics, and Protest

Despite widespread migration and social dislocation, workers coalesced politically to exert pressure on governments and businesses. Strikes and activism came in reaction to industrial innovation and an uneven economy, but community bonds forged by homemakers and neighborhood groups were a necessary precondition for collective worker action. School officials or police looking for truant children and delinquents met a phalanx of housewives ready to hide the children or to lie for their neighbors. When landlords evicted tenants, women would gather in the streets and replace household goods as fast as they were removed from the rooms of ousted families. Meeting on doorsteps or at fountains, laundries, pawnshops, and markets, women initiated rural newcomers into urban ways and developed a unity similar to that created by workers in the factory. Like strikes, other political activism grew not just from the shop floor but also in neighborhoods and on city streets.

Unions and Strikes. As the nineteenth century entered its final decades, the uncertainties of economic life led workers to organize formal unions, which attracted the allegiance of millions. Instead of simply gathering workers' contributions and paying out assistance in hard times, as the mutual aid societies had done early in the century, unions demanded a say in working conditions and aimed, as one union's rule book put it, "to ensure that wages never suffer illegitimate reductions and that they always follow the rises in the price of basic commodities." Strikes had occurred before the late nineteenth century, but in the wake of the revolutions of 1848 and the Paris Commune, businesses and governments viewed massive numbers of striking workers as the first step to political unrest and destructive violence. Even so, strong unions appealed to some industrialists because a union could make strikes more predictable (or even prevent them), present demands more coherently, and provide a liaison for labor-management relations.

From the 1880s on, the pace of collective action for more pay, lower prices, and better working conditions accelerated. In 1888, for example, hundreds of young women who made matches, the so-called London matchgirls, struck to end the fining system, under which they could be penalized an entire day's wage for being a minute or two late to work. This system, the matchgirls maintained, helped companies reap profits of more than 20 percent. Newspapers and philanthropists picked up the strikers' story, helping them win their case. Soon after, London dockworkers and gasworkers protested their precarious working conditions. Across Europe the number of strikes and demonstrations rose from 188 in 1888 to 289 in 1890. On May 1, 1890, sixty thousand workers took to the streets of Budapest to agitate for suffrage and safer working conditions. Day laborers on Hungarian farms struck in 1891.

Housewives, who often demonstrated in support of strikers, carried out their own protests against high food prices. In keeping with centuries of women's protest, they confiscated merchants' goods and sold them at what they considered a just price. "There should no longer be either rich or poor," argued organized Italian peasant women. "All should have bread for themselves and for their children. We should all be equal." Fearing threats to industrial and agricultural productivity, governments increasingly responded with force, even though most strikes were about the conditions of everyday life for workers and not about political revolution.

Craft-based unions of skilled artisans, such as carpenters and printers, were the most active and cohesive, but from the mid-1880s on, a *new unionism* attracted transport workers, miners, matchgirls, and dockworkers. These new unions were nationwide groups with salaried managers who could plan massive general strikes across the trades, focusing on such common goals as the eight-hour workday, and thus paralyze an entire nation. Although they never totally eliminated vibrant local or single-craft unions or religiously affiliated organizations, the large unions of the industrialized countries of western Europe, like cartels and trusts, increasingly influenced business practices and society's views of workers.

Political Parties. New political parties also engaged the masses in political life by addressing working-class issues. Workingmen helped create the Labour Party in England, the Socialist Party in France, and the Social Democratic Parties of Sweden, Hungary, Austria, and Germany—most of them inspired by Marxist theories. Germany was home to the largest socialist party in Europe after 1890. Historians attribute the extraordinary strength of the German Social Democratic Party, with its millions of voters, to the lack of middle-of-the-road alternatives to the conservative parties.

Workingwomen joined these parties, but in much smaller numbers than men. Not able to vote in national elections and usually responsible for housework in addition to their paying jobs, women had little time for party meetings. Furthermore, their low wages hardly allowed them to survive, much less to pay party or union dues. Many workingmen opposed their presence, fearing women would dilute the union's masculine camaraderie. Contact with women would mean "suffocation," one Russian workingman believed, and end male union members' sense of being "comrades in the revolutionary cause." The shortage of women's voices in unions and political parties paralleled women's exclusion from government; it helped make the middle-class belief in separate spheres part of a working-class ideology that glorified the heroic struggles of a male proletariat against capitalism. Marxist leaders continued to maintain that injustice to women was caused by capitalism and would disappear in the socialist society following the coming revolution. As a result, although the new political organizations encouraged women's support, they downplayed women's concerns about lower wages and sexual coercion.

Socialist parties attracted workingmen because they promised the triumph of new male voters who could become a powerful collective force in national elections. Those who accepted Marx's assertion that "workingmen have no country," however, wanted an international movement that could address workers' common interests. In 1889, some four hundred socialists from across Europe (joined by many onlookers and unofficial participants) met in Paris to form the Second International, a federation of working-class organizations and political parties replacing the First International founded by Marx before the Paris Commune. In

disarray after the bloody end to the Paris Commune and the outlawing of socialist parties in Germany between 1878 and 1890, socialists had nonetheless gained enormous strength from the growth of working-class organizations. Unlike the First International, this meeting adopted a Marxist revolutionary program from the start, but it also advocated suffrage where it still did not exist and better working conditions in the immediate future.

Members of the Second International determined to rid the organization of anarchists, who flourished in the less industrial parts of Europe—Russia, Italy, and Spain. In these countries anarchism attracted some industrial workers, but it got heavy support from peasants, small property owners, and agricultural day laborers, for whom the industrially based theories of Marx had less appeal. In an age of crop failures and stiff international competition in agriculture, many rural people looked to the possibility of life without the domination of large landowners and government. Many advocated extreme tactics, including physical violence and even murder. "We want to overthrow the government . . . with violence since it is by the use of violence that they force us to obey," wrote one Italian anarchist. In the 1880s, anarchists bombed stock exchanges, parliaments, and businesses and were punished for violence even without proof—as in the Haymarket Riot in Chicago in 1886, where political hysteria over anarchism caused the trial and execution of innocent anarchists and labor activists. "There are no innocents in bourgeois society," said one anarchist, echoing in reverse the general feeling toward his kind. Members of the Second International felt such random violence was counterproductive.

Outside the informal ties of neighborhoods and of the factory, a range of organizations forged worker solidarity through popular community activities that intertwined politics with everyday life. The gymnastics and choral societies that had once united Europeans in nationalistic fervor now served working-class goals. Songs emphasized worker freedom, progress, and eventual victory. "Out of the dark past, the light of the future shines forth brightly," went one Russian workers' song. Socialist gymnastics, bicycling, and marching societies rejected competition and prizes as middle-class preoccupations, but they valued physical fitness for what it could do to the "outer and inner organism" and for helping workers in the "struggle for existence"—a reflection of Darwinian thinking about "survival of the fittest." Workers also held festivals and gigantic parades, most notably on May 1, proclaimed by the Second International as a labor holiday. Like religious processions of an earlier time, parades were rituals that fostered unity. European governments at the time frequently prohibited such public gatherings, fearing they were tools for agitators.

Expanding Political Participation in Western Europe

Western European countries moved toward mass politics more rapidly than did countries to the east. Ordinary people everywhere in the West were becoming aware of politics through newspapers, which, combined with industrial and imperial progress, were an important nationalizing force. In western Europe in particular, people's access to newspapers and their political participation meant that politicians depended for election more on the will of the people and less on the power of small cliques.

Mass Journalism. The rise of mass journalism after 1880 gave Europeans ready access to information (and misinformation) about politics and world events. The invention of automatic typesetting and the production of newsprint from wood pulp lowered the costs of printing; the telephone allowed reporters to communicate news to their papers almost instantly. Once philosophical and literary in content, daily newspapers now emphasized the sensational, using banner headlines, dramatic pictures, and gruesome or lurid details—particularly about murders and sexual scandals—to sell papers as well as their political point of view, whether it was liberal, conservative, or socialist. In the hustle and bustle of industrial society, one editor wrote, "you must strike your reader right between the eyes." A series of articles in 1885 in London's *Pall Mall Gazette* on the "white slave trade" warned the innocent not to read further. The author then proceeded to describe how young women were "snared, trapped," and otherwise forced into prostitution through sexual violation and drugs. Stories of imperial adventurers and exaggerated accounts of wasted women pottery or mine workers and their unborn babies similarly drew ordinary people to a mass, daily, and highly commercial press.

Journalism created a national community of up-to-date citizens, whether they could vote or not. Stories of crime and corruption appealed to the growing body of publicly educated, critical readers. Newspapers were not meant for quiet reflection at home or in the upper-class club but for quick reading on mass transportation and on the streets. Elites grumbled that the sensational press was itself a sign of social decay. But for up-and-coming people from the working and middle classes it provided an avenue to success. As London, Paris, Vienna, Berlin, and St. Petersburg became centers not only of politics but of news, a number of European politicians got their start working for daily newspapers. In this context of growing political literacy, politicians in western Europe sought to incorporate more people into the political process.

British Political Reforms. In the fall of 1879, William Gladstone (1809–1898), leader of the British Liberals, whose party was then out of power, waged an experimental campaign in northern England and in Scotland for a seat in the House of Commons. During this campaign, Gladstone spoke before thousands of workingmen and -women, calling for greater self-determination in India and Africa and summoning his audiences to "honest, manful, humble effort" in the middle-class tradition of "hard work." Newspapers around the country highlighted his trip, and their reports along with mass meetings fueled public interest in politics. Queen Victoria bristled at Gladstone's speaking tour and at his attacks on her empire and vowed that he would never again serve as prime minister. Gladstone's Liberals won, however, and he did become prime minister.

Gladstone's campaign exemplified the trend toward expanded participation in Britain's political life. The process had begun with the Reform Bill of 1832, which extended the franchise to middle-class men. The Ballot Act of 1872 made voting secret, a reform supported by those who wished to limit the influence of landlords and employers, who without secrecy would know how everyone voted. Most significant, the Reform Act of 1884 doubled the electorate, to around 4.5 million men, enfranchising many urban workers and artisans and thus diminishing traditional aristocratic influence in the countryside.

As many British men entered political life as voters for the first time, Liberals and Conservatives alike found it necessary to establish national political clubs as a means to gain party loyalty. These clubs competed with the insular groups of parliamentary elites, who ruled through "wire-pulling," as one member of the House of Lords put it. These small cliques had heretofore determined the course of party politics. In contrast, broadly based interest groups such as unions, businessmen's associations, and national political clubs began to open up politics by appealing to many more voters.

British political reforms immediately affected Irish politics by arming disaffected tenant farmers with the secret ballot, making them less like colonized peoples than before. The political climate in Ireland was explosive mainly because of the repressive tactics of absentee landlords, many of them English and Protestant. These landlords evicted unsuccessful and prosperous tenants alike so they could raise rents for newcomers. In 1879, opponents formed the Irish National Land League and launched protests that charged the tense political atmosphere. Irish tenants elected a solid bloc of nationalist representatives to the British Parliament.

The Irish members of Parliament, voting as a group, had sufficient strength to defeat legislation proposed by either the Conservatives or the Liberals. Irish leader Charles Parnell (1846–1891) demanded support for home rule—a system giving Ireland its own parliament—in return for Irish votes. Gladstone, who served four nonconsecutive terms as prime minister between 1868 and 1894, accommodated Parnell with bills on home rule and tenant security. But Conservatives called home rule "a conspiracy against the honor of Britain." When they were in power (1885–1886 and 1886–1892), they cracked down on Irish activism. Scandals reported in the press ultimately ended Parnell's political career. The first came late in the 1880s, when journalists at the London *Times* fabricated letters implicating Parnell in the assassination of English officials. Parnell was cleared of this charge, but in 1890 the news broke of his affair with a married woman, and he died in disgrace soon after. Following his death, Irish home rule remained as divisive an issue as ever among the British.

France's Third Republic. In France, the Third Republic was a hotly contested political institution from its beginning in 1870 to its collapse seventy years later. Inflamed by the press, intrigue and scandal threatened popular politics in France,

Charles Parnell, Irish Hero
Charles Parnell gained the support of both the moderates and the radicals working for Irish home rule. Many saw Ireland as the first of England's colonial conquests—a land that was both ruled and exploited economically like a colony. Son of a landowning Protestant and a skilled parliamentary politician, Parnell threw himself into the Irish cause by paralyzing the British Parliament's conduct of business and was even able to bring down the government. In retaliation the government used forgeries and other unsavory means to destroy Parnell, but in the end scandal in his personal life lost him the vital support of the public.
Mary Evans Picture Library.

where universal manhood suffrage already existed as a result of classical liberalism's expansion to politics but where effective participation was still not secured. Following the Second Empire's defeat in the Franco-Prussian War, the Third Republic began shakily with monarchist political factions—Bonapartist, Orléanist, and Bourbon—struggling to control the National Assembly and to restore their respective families to power. But the republican form of government, which French supporters had been trying to solidify for almost a century, was saved when the compromise candidate of the monarchists, the comte de Chambord, stubbornly refused to accept the tricolored flag. Associating the tricolor with revolution, he would accept only the flag of the Bourbons and thus lost the chance to revive the monarchy. In 1875, a new constitution created a ceremonial presidency and a premiership dependent on support from an elected Chamber of Deputies. An alliance of businessmen, shopkeepers, professionals, and rural property owners hoped the new system would prevent the kind of strong-arm politics that had ended previous republics.

Fragile constitutional compromises, menaced by a highly partisan press, kept the Third Republic on shaky ground in the midst of destabilizing economic downturns, widespread corruption, and growing anti-Semitism. Support for the government was rocked by newspaper stories about members of the Chamber of Deputies selling their votes to business interests, and the press contributed to unrest by linking economic swings to the alleged machinations of Jewish businessmen. As a result, public sentiment turned against Jews for the failures of republican government and the economy. Confidence in republican politics plummeted in 1887 when the president's son-in-law was discovered to have sold memberships in the Legion of Honor. An aborted coup by the dashing and highly popular general Georges Boulanger soon thereafter showed the fragility of the republic, and thus of political liberalism. Had Boulanger not lost his will at the last moment, his followers might have thrust him into power, replacing a republic with a strongman yet again.

Republican leaders attempted to coalesce citizens by fortifying civic institutions, most notably by instituting compulsory and free public education through legislation in the 1880s. In public schools, secular, republican-minded teachers supplanted Catholic clergy, who often favored a restored monarchy, and a centralized curriculum featured patriotic primers and courses in French geography, literature, and history. To perpetuate a republican ethos, the government established secular public high schools for young women, seen as the educators of future citizens. Mandatory military service for men inculcated the values of national identity and pride in place of regional and rural identities. In short, it turned peasants into Frenchmen.

Political Liberalism Refused. Although many western European leaders believed in economic liberalism, constitutionalism, and efficient central government, these ideals did not always translate into universal manhood suffrage and other forms of political liberalism in the less powerful western European countries. Spain and Belgium abruptly awarded suffrage to all men in 1890 and 1893, respectively, but both governments remained monarchies. Denmark and Sweden continued to limit political participation, and reform in the Netherlands in 1887 and 1896 increased manhood suffrage to only 14 percent. An 1887 law in Italy gave the vote to all men who had a primary school education, but this affected only 14 percent of the men.

In Italy the accession of liberals to power under the constitutional monarchy ironically led to decades of political and economic insecurity. The process of unification left a towering debt and massive pockets of discontent, including Catholic supporters of the pope and impoverished citizens in the south. Without receiving the benefits of nation building—the common experiences of compulsory education, urban improvements, industrial progress, and the vote—the average Italian feared the devastating effects of national taxes and the draft on the family economy.

Power Politics in Central and Eastern Europe

Germany, Austria-Hungary, and Russia diverged from the political paths taken by western European countries. These countries industrialized at varying rates—Germany rapidly and Russia far more slowly. Literacy and the development of a civic, urban culture were more advanced in Germany and Austria-Hungary than in Russia. Even Russia, however, saw the development of a modern press, although with a far smaller readership than elsewhere. Nonetheless in all three countries, agrarian political forces remained powerful, often working to block political, social, and economic change.

Bismarck's Germany. Bismarck had upset the European balance of power, first by humiliating France in the Franco-Prussian War and then by creating a powerful, unified Germany, exemplified in explosive economic growth and in rapid development of every aspect of the nation-state, from transport to its thriving capital city, Berlin (Map 24.3). His goals achieved, he now desired stability and a respite from war and so turned to diplomacy. Fearing that France would soon seek revenge against the new Reich and needing peace to consolidate the nation, he pronounced Germany "satisfied," meaning that it sought no new territory. To ensure Germany's long-term security in Europe, in 1873 Bismarck forged an alliance with Austria-Hungary and Russia, called the Three Emperors' League. The three conservative powers shared a strong interest in maintaining the political status quo.

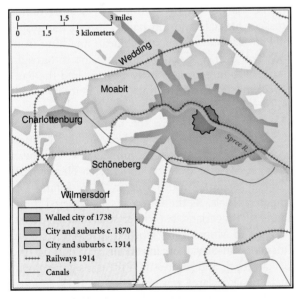

MAP 24.3 Expansion of Berlin to 1914
"A capital city is essential for the state to act as a pivot for its culture," the German historian Heinrich von Treitschke asserted. No capital city grew as dramatically as Berlin after German unification in 1871. Industrialists and bankers set themselves up in the new capital, while workers migrated there for jobs, swelling the population. The city was newly dotted with military monuments and with museums to show off its culture.

At home, Bismarck, who owned land and invested heavily in industry, joined with the liberals to create a variety of financial institutions such as a central bank to further German commerce and industry. Bismarck aggressively opposed the Catholic church because its influence, especially in southern Germany and among ethnic minorities, impeded the growth of nationalist sentiment. Watching with alarm as the new Catholic Center Party made overtures to workers, he mounted a full-blown *Kulturkampf* (culture war). The government expelled the Jesuits in 1872, increased state power over the clergy in Prussia in 1873, and introduced obligatory civil marriage in 1875. Urged on by German liberals, Bismarck had miscalculated his own ability to manipulate politics. Both conservatives and Catholics rebelled against policies of religious repression.

The Kulturkampf ended during the pontificate of Leo XIII (r. 1878–1903), a cultured scholar and humanist who confronted the skeptical intellectual climate inhospitable to Catholicism and to religion in general. Encouraging up-to-date scholarship in Catholic institutes and universities, he also tried to develop an effective niche for Catholic politics by accepting aspects of democracy while opposing socialism. Because Catholicism had identified itself so strongly with monarchism, Leo's ideas marked a dramatic turn. His encyclical *Rerum Novarum* (1891), which articulated his political principles, urged Catholics to develop a social conscience that would allow for a rebirth of religious and political unity among the classes. During these dark days of war on Catholic culture, Leo's pontificate fortified beleaguered Catholics across Europe.

In a climate of economic crisis after the mid-1870s, Bismarck reevaluated Germany's situation and decided that the most pressing problems came not from Catholics but from social unrest and liberal economic policies. He stopped persecuting Catholics and turned his attention to socialists and liberals. He used unsuccessful assassination attempts on Emperor William I as a pretext to outlaw the Social Democratic Party in 1878. Simultaneously, hoping to wean the working class from socialism, Bismarck sponsored an accident and disability insurance program—the first of its kind in Europe and an important step in broadening the mandate of government to encompass social welfare. In 1879, he assembled a conservative

IMPORTANT DATES

1860s–1890s Impressionism flourishes in the arts; absorption of Asian influences

1870s–1890s Vast emigration from Europe continues; the new imperialism

1872 Bismarck begins the Kulturkampf against Catholic influence

1873 Extended economic recession begins; the impact is global

1876 Invention of the telephone

1882 The Triple Alliance formed between Germany, Austria-Hungary, and Italy

1882–1884 Bismarck sponsors social welfare legislation

1884 British Parliament passes the Second Reform Act, doubling the size of the male electorate

1884–1885 European nations carve up Africa at the Berlin conference

1888 Japan adopts constitution based on European models

1889 Socialists meet in Paris and establish the Second International

Reichstag coalition that put through tariffs protecting German agriculture and industry from foreign competition but also raising the prices of consumer goods. Ending his support for laissez-faire economics, Bismarck also severed his working relationship with political liberals.

Authoritarian Austria-Hungary. Like Germany, Austria-Hungary frequently relied on liberal economic policies and for a time in the 1870s even had political liberals in power. From the 1860s, liberal businessmen succeeded in industrializing parts of the empire, and the prosperous middle classes erected conspicuously large homes, giving themselves a prominence in urban life that rivaled the aristocracy's. They persuaded the government to enact free-trade provisions in the 1870s and to search out foreign investment to build up the infrastructure, such as railroads.

Yet despite such influences, Austria-Hungary remained resolutely monarchist and authoritarian. Liberals in Austria—most of them ethnic Germans—saw their influence eroded under the leadership of Count Edouard von Taaffe, Austrian

prime minister from 1879 to 1893. Taaffe built a coalition of clergy, conservatives, and Slavic parties and used its power to weaken the liberals. In Bohemia, for example, he designated Czech as an official language of the bureaucracy and school system, thus breaking the German speakers' monopoly on officeholding. Reforms outraged people at whose expense other ethnic groups received benefits, and those who won concessions, such as the Czechs, continued to clamor for even greater autonomy. In this way the government played nationalities off against one another and ensured the monarchy's predominance as the central mechanism for holding competing interest groups together in an era of rapid change.

Despite the success of these divide-and-rule tactics, Emperor Francis Joseph and his ministers feared the influence of the most powerful Slavic nation—Russia—on the ethnic minorities living within Austria-Hungary. Following its defeat in the Crimean War, Russia wanted to refurbish its tattered reputation as a great power, and to accomplish this goal it stirred up the emotions of discontented Slavs living in Austria-Hungary and in the Balkans under Ottoman rule. Slavophile Russian officials and journalists spread the gospel of Pan-Slavism, which could mean anything from loose cultural cooperation among Slavs to outright political union. Francis Joseph considered the Pan-Slavic movement dangerous to the stability of his empire.

The Balkans, where the competing forces of modernization and Ottoman decay aroused political ambition, became the scene of the next European struggle. Slavs of Bulgaria and Bosnia-Herzegovina revolted against Turkish rule in 1876, killing Ottoman officials. As the Ottomans slaughtered thousands of Bulgarians, two other small Balkan states, Serbia and Montenegro, rebelled against the sultan. Russian Pan-Slavic organizations sent aid to the Balkan rebels and so pressured the tsar's government that Russia declared war on Turkey in 1877, supposedly to protect Orthodox Christians. With help from Romania and Greece, Russia defeated the Ottomans and by the Treaty of San Stefano (1878) created a large, pro-Russian Bulgaria.

The Russo-Turkish War and the ensuing treaty sparked an international uproar that almost resulted in general war. Austria-Hungary and Britain feared that an enlarged Bulgaria would become a

Russian satellite that would enable the tsar to dominate the Balkans. British prime minister Disraeli moved warships into position against Russia. The public was drawn into foreign policy: the music halls and newspapers of England echoed a new *jingoism*, or political sloganeering that throbbed with sentiments of war. "We don't want to fight, but by Jingo if we do, We've got the ships, we've got the men, we've got the money too!"

The other great powers, however, did not want a European-wide war, and in 1878 they attempted to revive the concert of Europe by meeting at Berlin under the auspices of Bismarck, who saw this potential war as inopportune. The Congress of Berlin rolled back the Russian victory by partitioning the large Bulgarian state that Russia had carved out of Ottoman territory and denying any part of Bulgaria full independence from the Ottomans (Map 24.4). Austria occupied (but did not annex) Bosnia and Herzegovina as a way of gaining clout in the Balkans, and Britain received the island of Cyprus. Serbia and Montenegro became fully independent.

Nonetheless, the Congress failed to resolve the question of Slavic movements and Russian influence over them, and the Balkans remained a site of political unrest and great-power rivalries.

Following the Congress of Berlin, the European powers attempted to guarantee stability through a complex series of alliances and treaties. Anxious about Balkan instability and Russian aggression, Austria-Hungary forged a defensive alliance with Germany in 1879. The Dual Alliance, as it was called, offered protection against Russia, whose threat to Hungarian control of its Slavic peasantry, a German diplomat wrote, "was on [the Hungarian government's] mind day and night." In 1882, Italy joined this partnership (henceforth called the Triple Alliance), largely because of Italy's imperial rivalries with France. Trying to rebuild monarchical solidarity, Bismarck convinced both Austria-Hungary and Russia to join Germany in a revived Three Emperors' League, which lasted from 1881 to 1887. Because tensions between Russia and Austria-Hungary remained high, Bismarck signed

MAP 24.4 The Balkans, c. 1878

After mid-century, the map of the Balkans would almost constantly be redrawn. This resulted in part from the weakness of the dominant Ottoman Empire, but also from the ambitions of inhabitants themselves and from great power rivalry. In tune with the growing sense of national identities based on shared culture, history, and ethnicity, various Balkan peoples sought to emphasize small-group identities rather than merging around a single dominant group such as the Serbs.

the Reinsurance Treaty (1887) with Russia to stifle Habsburg illusions about having a free hand against rivals for Slavic loyalty.

Unrest in Russia. Although Russia enjoyed some international success during these decades, its internal affairs were in disarray. By 1871, the era of Great Reforms had run its course, and Russia remained almost the only European country without a constitutional government. Reform-minded youth increasingly turned to revolutionary groups for solutions to political and social problems. One such group, the Populists, wanted to rouse the debt-ridden peasantry to revolt. Other people formed tightly coordinated terrorist bands with the goal of assassinating public officials and thus forcing change. The secret police, relying on informers among the peasantry and the revolutionaries, rounded up hundreds of members of one of the largest groups, Land and Liberty, and subjected them to torture, show trials, and imprisonment. When in 1877 a young radical, Vera Zasulich, tried unsuccessfully to assassinate the chief of the St. Petersburg police, the people of the capital city applauded her act and acquittal, so great was their horror at the brutal treatment of young radicals from respectable families.

Writers added to the intense debate over Russia's future. Novelists Leo Tolstoy, author of the

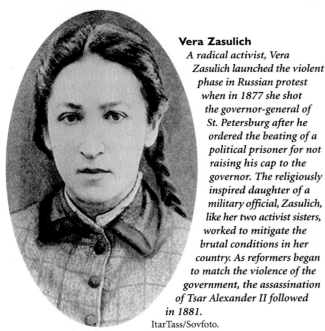

Vera Zasulich
A radical activist, Vera Zasulich launched the violent phase in Russian protest when in 1877 she shot the governor-general of St. Petersburg after he ordered the beating of a political prisoner for not raising his cap to the governor. The religiously inspired daughter of a military official, Zasulich, like her two activist sisters, worked to mitigate the brutal conditions in her country. As reformers began to match the violence of the government, the assassination of Tsar Alexander II followed in 1881.
ItarTass/Sovfoto.

MAPPING THE WEST The West and the World, c. 1890 ▶
European influence was reaching its height in the late nineteenth century as European trade and political reach spanned the globe. Needing markets for the vast quantities of goods that poured from European factories and equally needing the raw materials to produce the goods, governments asserted that the Western way of life should be spread to the rest of the world and that resources would be best used by Europeans. Explorations and scientific discoveries continued both to build the knowledge base of European peoples and to enhance their ability for greater conquest. Simultaneously, millions of Europeans left their homes to find a better life elsewhere.

epic *War and Peace* (1869), and Fyodor Dostoevsky both opposed the revolutionaries' desire to overturn the social order; they believed that Russia above all required spiritual regeneration. Tolstoy's novel *Anna Karenina* (1877) tells the story of an impassioned, adulterous love affair, but it also weaves in the spiritual quest of Levin, a former "progressive" landowner who, like Tolstoy, eventually rejects modernization and idealizes the peasantry's tradition of stoic endurance. Dostoevsky had a different outlook and satirized Russia's radicals in *The Possessed* (1871), a novel in which a group of revolutionaries carries out one central act: the murder of one of its own members. In Dostoevsky's view the radicals could only act destructively and were incapable of offering any positive solution to Russia's ills.

The more radical revolutionary groups sought to change Russia by violent action rather than by spiritual uplift. In 1881, the People's Will, a splinter group of Land and Liberty impatient with its failure to mobilize the peasantry, killed Tsar Alexander II in a bomb attack. His death, however, failed to provoke the general uprising the terrorists expected. Instead the peasants thought the assassination of the "tsar liberator" was directed against them. Alexander III (r. 1881–1894), rejecting further liberal reforms that his father had proposed on the eve of his death, unleashed a new wave of oppression against religious and ethnic minorities and gave the police virtually unchecked power. Intensified Russification aggravated old grievances among oppressed nationalities such as the Poles, but it also turned the once-loyal German middle and upper classes of the Baltic provinces against Russian rule, with serious long-term consequences.

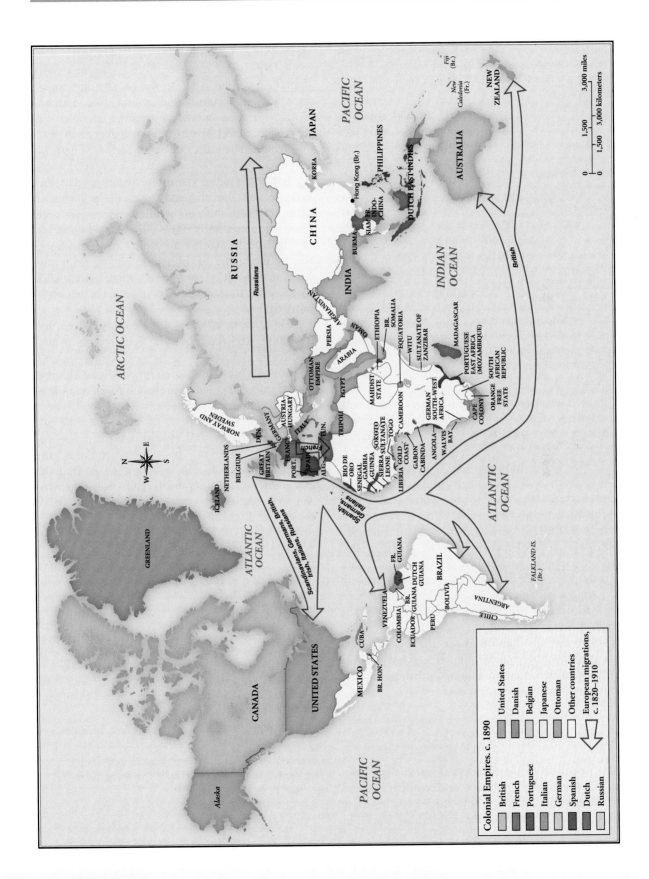

Colonial Empires. c. 1890

- British
- French
- Portuguese
- Italian
- German
- Spanish
- Dutch
- Russian

- United States
- Danish
- Belgian
- Japanese
- Ottoman
- Other countries

European migrations, c. 1820–1910

The five million Russian Jews, confined to the eighteenth-century Pale of Settlement (the name for the restricted territory in which they were permitted to live), endured particularly severe oppression. Local officials instigated pogroms against Jews, whose distinctive language, dress, and isolation in ghettos made them easy targets in an age when the Russian government was enforcing cultural uniformity and national identity. Government officials encouraged people to blame Jews for escalating taxes and living costs—though the true cause was the policy of making the peasantry pay for industrialization by raising taxes.

Russia: The Pale of Settlement in the Nineteenth Century

As the tsar responded to internal turmoil with even greater repression, Bismarck's delicate alliance of the three conservative powers was unraveling. A brash but deeply insecure young kaiser, William II (r. 1888–1918), mounted the German throne in 1888. William chafed under Bismarck's tutelage, and his advisers flattered the young man into thinking that his own personal talent made Bismarck a hindrance, even a rival. William dismissed Bismarck in 1890 and, because he ardently supported German nationalism, let the alliance with Russia lapse in favor of a strong relationship with the supposedly kindred Austria-Hungary. Fatefully, he had opened the door to a realignment of the great powers. Unsettled internal politics in eastern Europe and the Balkans made the international scene more dangerous and unpredictable while imperial rivalries intensified antagonisms among the European nation-states and empires.

Conclusion

The period from the 1870s to the 1890s has been called the age of industry and empire because Western society pursued both these ends in a way that rapidly transformed Europe and the world. In these decades the West appeared at the top of its form. Industrial innovation and national growth caused much of Europe to thrive and become more populous and urban. Europeans proudly spread their "superior" culture globally and, like Marianne North, searched out whatever other peoples and places could offer by way of knowledge, experience, and wealth. The great powers undertook a new imperialism, and as they tightened connections with the rest of the globe, European culture, society, and everyday life also changed under the influence of other civilizations. In politics, reformers drew lower-class men into active citizenship by extending suffrage; humanitarian commitment prompted the development of philanthropic agencies and promoted the development of a more activist state that worked to make citizens of imperial countries more fit.

Yet as workers struck for improved wages and conditions and the impoverished migrated to find a better life, Western society showed its fissures and divisions. While newspapers, novels, and the arts helped inform people of profound social and international changes, they also raised questions about poverty and hopelessness. By the 1890s, the advance of industry and empire was bringing unprecedented tensions to national politics, the international scene, and everyday life around the globe. Racism, anti-Semitism, and ethnic chauvinism were spreading, sanctioned in most strata of society, and the costs of empire to conquered peoples were beyond measure.

Suggested References

The Advance of Industry

Industry advanced on every front, from the development of new products and procedures to the reorganization of work life and consumption. Trebilcock's classic work on the creation of an economic infrastructure contrasts with more recent studies (such as Rappaport's) on the impact of consumers and taste in driving economic change.

Coffin, Judith. *The Politics of Women's Work: The Paris Garment Trades, 1750–1915*. 1996.

Crossick, Geoffrey, and Serge Jaumin, eds. *Cathedrals of Consumption: The European Department Store, 1850–1939*. 1999.

Franzoi, Barbara. *At the Very Least She Pays the Rent: Women and German Industrialization*. 1985.

Good, David. *The Economic Rise of the Habsburg Empire.* 1984.

Marks, Steven G. *Road to Power: The Trans-Siberian Railroad and the Colonization of Asian Russia, 1850–1917.* 1991.

Rappaport, Erika. *Shopping for Pleasure: Women in the Making of London's West End.* 2000.

Trebilcock, Clive. *The Industrialization of the Continental Powers.* 1981.

The New Imperialism

New studies of imperialism show not only increasing conquest and the creation of an international economy but also the social and cultural impulses behind it. The University of Pennsylvania's African studies Web site offers an exciting look at African history, politics, and culture—some of it from this era. Depictions of African art and architecture, such as that confiscated for Western museums, are especially vivid.

African Studies Center: http://www.sas.upenn.edu/African _Studies/AS.html.

Baumgart, Winfried. *Imperialism: The Idea and Reality of British and French Colonial Expansion.* 1989.

Comaroff, Jean, and John Comaroff. *Of Revelation and Revolution: Christianity, Colonialism, and Consciousness in South Africa.* 1991.

Crosby, Alfred W. *Ecological Imperialism: The Biological Expansions of Europe, 900–1900.* 1993.

Ferro, Marc. *Colonization: A Global History.* 1997.

Hane, Mikiso. *Modern Japan: A Historical Survey.* 1992.

Harrison, Robert T. *Gladstone's Imperialism in Egypt: Techniques of Domination.* 1995.

Headrick, Daniel R. *The Tools of Empire: Technology and European Imperialism in the Nineteenth Century.* 1981.

Rotberg, R. I. *The Founder: Cecil Rhodes and the Pursuit of Power.* 1988.

Wesseling, H. L. *Divide and Rule: The Partition of Africa, 1880–1914.* 1996.

The Transformation of Culture and Society

Historians have come to see that industrial development and the spread of imperialism affected the smallest details of everyday life as well as the larger phenomena of class formation and massive regional and global migration. Beckles, Stodart, and Blakely give particularly rich portrayals of cultural mixture, exploitation, and resistance under the colonial regime.

Beckles, Hilary McD., and Brian Stodart, eds. *Liberation Cricket: West Indies Cricket Culture.* 1995.

Blakely, Allison. *Blacks in the Dutch World: The Evolution of Racial Imagery in Modern Society.* 1993.

*Bonnell, Victoria, ed. *The Russian Worker.* 1983.

MacKenzie, John. *The Empire of Nature: Hunting, Conservation, and British Imperialism.* 1988.

Maynes, Mary Jo. *Taking the Hard Road: Life Course in French and German Workers' Autobiographies in the Era of Industrialization.* 1995.

McKlintock, Anne. *Imperial Leather: Race, Gender, and Sexuality in the Colonial Contest.* 1995.

Moch, Leslie Page. *Moving Europeans: Migration in Western Europe since 1650.* 1993.

Worobec, Christine D. *Peasant Russia: Family and Community in the Post-Emancipation Period.* 1991.

The Birth of Mass Politics

Historical study of politics in this period entails looking at both government policies and the activism based on neighborhood solidarity, the growth of unions, and the rise of the mass media. The Avalon Project at the Yale Law School provides access to major treaties and conventions, making it an excellent resource for this period.

Applegate, Celia. *A Nation of Provincials: The German Idea of Heimat.* 1990.

Avalon Project at Yale Law School: http://www.yale.edu/lawweb/avalon/avalon.htm.

Hoppen, K. Theodore. *Ireland since 1800: Conflict and Conformity.* 1999.

McReynolds, Louise. *The News under Russia's Old Regime.* 1991.

Rogger, Hans. *Jewish Policies and Right-Wing Politics in Imperial Russia.* 1986.

Ross, Ellen. *Love and Toil: Motherhood in Outcast London, 1870–1918.* 1993.

Todorova, Maria. *Imagining the Balkans.* 1997.

*Verga, Giovanni. *The House by the Medlar Tree.* 1981.

Weiner, Joel H., ed. *Papers for the Millions: The New Journalism in Britain, 1850s to 1914.* 1988.

*Primary sources.

Modernity and the Road to War

c. 1890–1914

I N THE FIRST DECADE OF THE TWENTIETH CENTURY, a wealthy young Russian man traveled from one country to another to find relief from neurasthenia, a common malady in those days. Its symptoms included fatigue, lack of interest in life, depression, and sometimes physical sickness. In 1910, the young man encountered Sigmund Freud, a Viennese physician whose unconventional treatment—eventually called *psychoanalysis*—took the form of a conversation about the patient's dreams, sexual experiences, and everyday life. Over the course of four years, Freud uncovered his patient's deeply rooted fear of castration disguised as a phobia for wolves—thus the name Wolf-Man by which he comes down to us. Freud worked his cure, as the Wolf-Man himself put it, "by bringing repressed ideas into consciousness." Freud's theories laid the groundwork for an understanding of the human psyche that has endured, with modifications and some controversy, to our own time.

The Wolf-Man was symptomatic of the age. Born into a family that owned vast estates, he reflected the growing prosperity of Europeans, albeit on a grander scale than most. Simultaneously, countless individuals seemed anguished and mentally disturbed, and suicides abounded—the Wolf-Man's own sister and father died from intentional drug overdoses. European society as a whole subjected itself to agonized questioning about the family, gender relationships, empire, religion, and the consequences of technology and progress. "Ours is a society ceaselessly racked," the novelist Émile Zola wrote in 1896: "We are sickened by our industrial progress, by science; we live in a fever, and we like to dig

Heading into War
In this colorful poster from 1907, itself a product of improved technology, a Belgian munitions factory displays all its peacetime wares, including a motorcycle. Dogs and rifles in tow, a group of men takes off to hunt in the latest automobile. The road to modernity was speedy and laden with new weaponry, as was the road to World War I.
Musée Communal de Herstal, Belgique.

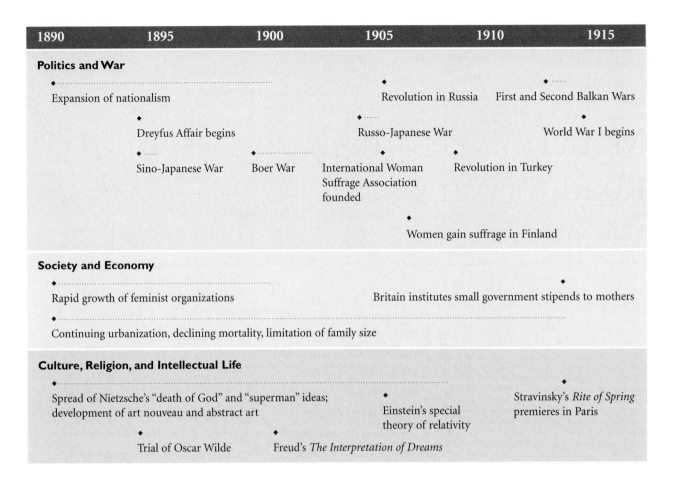

1890	1895	1900	1905	1910	1915

Politics and War

Expansion of nationalism

Revolution in Russia   First and Second Balkan Wars

Dreyfus Affair begins

Russo-Japanese War   World War I begins

Sino-Japanese War   Boer War   International Woman Suffrage Association founded   Revolution in Turkey

Women gain suffrage in Finland

Society and Economy

Rapid growth of feminist organizations   Britain institutes small government stipends to mothers

Continuing urbanization, declining mortality, limitation of family size

Culture, Religion, and Intellectual Life

Spread of Nietzsche's "death of God" and "superman" ideas; development of art nouveau and abstract art   Einstein's special theory of relativity   Stravinsky's *Rite of Spring* premieres in Paris

Trial of Oscar Wilde   Freud's *The Interpretation of Dreams*

deeper into our sores." Every sign of imperial wealth brought on an apparently irrational sense of Europe's decline. British writer H. G. Wells saw in this era "humanity upon the wane . . . the sunset of mankind."

Conflict reigned throughout Europe. Governments expanded the male electorate during this period in the hope of making politics more harmonious and manageable. Ethnic chauvinism, anti-Semitism, and militant nationalism only increased the violence of political rhetoric, however. Women suffragists along with politically disadvantaged groups such as the Slavs and Irish demanded full rights, but the liberal ethos of tolerance receded before a wave of political assassinations and public brutality. Colonized peoples developed a variety of liberation movements, many of them matching the progressive values but also the violence of the colonizing powers. At the same time, imperial competition among the great powers grew more heated, fueling an arms race that threatened to turn Europe, the "most civilized" continent in

the world according to its leaders, into a savage battleground.

These were just some of the conflicts associated with *modernity*—a term often used to describe the accelerated pace of life, the rise of mass politics, and the decline of a rural social order that were so visible in the West from the late nineteenth century on. (See "Terms of History," page 936.) *Modernity* also refers to the response of artists and intellectuals to this rapid change. The celebrated "modern" art, music, science, and philosophy of this period still resonate for their brilliant, innovative qualities. Yet these same innovations were often considered offensive at the time: cries of outrage at the new music echoed in concert halls, while educated people were utterly shocked at Freud's ideas that sexual drives motivate even the smallest children. Every advance in science and the arts simultaneously had consequences that undermined the middle-class faith in artistic and scientific progress.

When the heir to the Austro-Hungarian throne was assassinated in June 1914, few gave any thought to the global significance of the event, least of all Wolf-Man, whose treatment with Freud was just ending and who viewed that fateful day of June 28 simply as the day he "could now leave Vienna a healthy man." Yet the assassination was the catalyst for an eruption of political and societal discord that had simmered for several decades, as the nations of Europe lurched from one diplomatic crisis to another. The consequences of the resulting war, World War I, like the insights of Freud, would shape modern life.

❖ Private Life in an Age of Modernity

Transformations in private life accompanied industrialization, an improved standard of living, and the spread of democratic politics. A falling birthrate, a rising divorce rate, and growing activism for marriage reform provoked intense debate by the turn of the century. With relations between men and women changing, some imagined that distinct gender roles were disappearing. Women's visibility in public life prompted one British songwriter in the late 1890s to write:

Rock-a-bye baby, for father is near
Mother is "biking" she never is here!
Out in the park she's scorching all day
Or at some meeting is talking away!

Some saw women's emergence into the public sphere as progress, others as decay. Homosexuality became a distinct way of life and a major political topic. This trend was seen as a sign of either modern enlightenment or sin, depending on one's point of view. Freud and other scientists tried to study such phenomena dispassionately and eventually formulated new theories of the human personality. Public discussions of private life—which often found their way into political rhetoric and social programs—demonstrated the interconnections of private and public concerns.

The Population Dilemma

Urgent population concerns clogged the agendas of politicians and reformers in the 1890s. (See "Taking Measure," below.) The staggering population

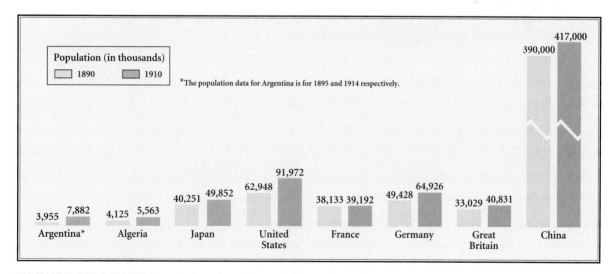

Population (in thousands)
☐ 1890   ☐ 1910

*The population data for Argentina is for 1895 and 1914 respectively.

	Argentina*	Algeria	Japan	United States	France	Germany	Great Britain	China
1890	3,955	4,125	40,251	62,948	38,133	49,428	33,029	390,000
1910	7,882	5,563	49,852	91,972	39,192	64,926	40,831	417,000

TAKING MEASURE Population Growth Worldwide, 1890–1910
Countries in the West were undergoing a demographic revolution in these decades as birthrates declined sharply. Yet population in many countries soared because of improved health, while other nations such as Argentina and the United States also received vast numbers of immigrants. Exceptions were China and other regions suffering the effects of imperialism; France's growth stagnated because the French had drastically curtailed reproduction beginning early in the century.

B. R. Mitchell, *International Historical Statistics: Africa, Asia, and Oceania, 1750–1993*, Third Edition (London: Macmillan Reference, 1998), 3, 56, 57; Mitchell, *International Historical Statistics: the Americas, 1750–1993*, Fourth Edition (London: Macmillan Reference, 1998), 6, 24; Mitchell, *International Historical Statistics: Europe, 1750–1993*, Fourth Edition (London: Macmillan Reference, 1998), 4, 8.

Modern

In one of his earliest writings from the first century, the Roman author Tacitus claimed that he could "hardly keep from laughing at some of the ancients, and from falling asleep at others."* He was advocating the distinct writing style of "our own day" and thus championing what we might call a "modern" approach to literature. But although he had the concept, there was not yet a word. *Modernus* was introduced into Latin only in the sixth century. After that, the idea of the "modern" can be found everywhere in the culture of the West. Shakespeare referred to "modern" ideas in his plays, and a huge quarrel erupted in the seventeenth century between the "ancients and the moderns" over whether people of earlier millennia should be imitated in their learning and style. By the second half of the nineteenth century, historians were heatedly debating where "modern" history began: with Abraham? with Charlemagne? with the Renaissance or the scientific revolution?

Despite the many claims to being "modern," the term has fastened itself most firmly around the period from the end of the nineteenth century through the first half of the twentieth. Its most specific historical use has been to describe the art, music, and dance that flourished at that time. When used in this sense, *modern* indicates a sharp break with lyrical romantic and classical music and dance and also with the conventions for representing objects in the arts. The blurred images of the impressionists and the jarring music of Schoenberg are part of modern art. The sexual rawness of *Madame Bovary* and *Les Fleurs du mal* (see Chapter 23) initiated a further ingredient into the multifaceted meanings of the word *modern* in the arts. Sometimes this intellectual break with the cultural past is referred to as *modernism*.

Simultaneously the term *modern* referred at the end of the nineteenth century to social phenomena. At this same historical moment, women who went to work or entered universities or began careers in the new field of social work were called "modern" women. They believed that by showing themselves capable and rational they could attain social progress and the end of

*"A Dialogue on Oratory," in *The Complete Works of Tacitus* (New York: Modern Library, 1942), 751.

---

increases of the eighteenth century had continued through the nineteenth. At the turn of the century, cities looked chaotic, filled with unwanted peoples of many ethnicities and races, as empire and industry changed the urban landscape. Influenced by Social Darwinist warnings of racial decay and armed with new types of statistical data, Western leaders faced a dramatic population dilemma.

Rising Population. Across Europe, population in cities and countries soared. Germany increased in size from 41 million people in 1871 to 64 million in 1910; tiny Denmark, from 1.7 million in 1870 to 2.7 million in 1911. Such growth resulted from improvements in sanitation and public health that extended longevity and reduced infant mortality.

As people lived longer, cities struggled to cope with their burgeoning populations. Urban building, which disrupted the day-to-day life of millions, had consumed Paris and Vienna in the 1860s–1880s,

and now Berlin, Budapest, and Moscow were torn apart and rebuilt. William II pulled down eighteenth-century Berlin and reconstructed the city with modern business and government buildings; the completion of new roadways and mass-transport systems helped push Berlin's population to over 4 million. In Moscow, an estimated 100,000 immigrants arrived each year from the countryside, and the Russian government undertook massive renovations. "Moscow has been transformed," reported a guidebook in 1903, becoming "overstimulating, full of bright colors that strike the eye and involuntarily attract attention." Rebuilding for population growth was not confined to capitals of the most powerful states: Balkan cities like Sofia, Belgrade, and Bucharest gained tree-lined boulevards, public buildings, and improved sanitation.

Falling Birthrate. There was, however, a countertrend: while the absolute size of the population restrictions placed on them. Feminists were also called "modern" when they worked optimistically for improvement in the condition of women. Some of them lived different lives from those women who had large families and confined themselves to the domestic sphere. This departure from tradition also made them appear "modern."

In seeking an education and hoping for progress toward rationality and uniformity in the law, these women were invoking a meaning of the "modern" dating back to the Enlightenment. Progress, rational thought, and science have also been taken as the bedrock of the modern. Modern social theory, such as that of Freud, Weber, or Nietzsche, was so rationally oriented it even calculated the limitations in the attainment of social progress or the achievement of rational thought.

Modernization—another derivative of the term *modern*—refers to the kind of scientific and technological progress that came with industrialization and the rise of commercial agriculture as they began to shape the nineteenth and twentieth centuries. Indoor plumbing, electricity, telephones, and automobiles were signs of "modernity." As a result, "modern" artists painted teeming cities, industrial workers, world's fairs, and other scenes associated with "modernization" of the late nineteenth century. In the second decade of the twentieth century, other artists started converting parts of industrial products like the toilet and the automobile into works of art.

Modern may be so popular a term because it contains paradoxical meanings that make it multipurpose. While associated with the triumph of industry and rational thought at the turn of the century, cultural modernism brought a glorification of the so-called primitive and non-Western, whether in representational art, music, literature, or philosophy. The great innovative composer Richard Wagner gained his inspiration from Indian philosophy, while the philosopher Nietzsche read deeply in Asian religious writings. Picasso derived much of his "modern" style from African art, while the clean lines of "modern" architecture—the turn away from Victorian curlicues and gaudy colors—were modeled on the pure forms of native American, African, and Middle Eastern dwellings. Freud, it is suggested, gained his ideas for psychoanalysis from the various therapies of African and Asian peoples.

Complex, paradoxical, and dense with meaning, *modern* may not always be precise enough to be useful. But its very breadth explains why *modern* remains a crucial—and contested—term of history.

---

was rising in much of the West, the birthrate (measured in births per thousand people) was falling. The birthrate had been decreasing in France since the eighteenth century; other European countries began experiencing the decline late in the nineteenth century. The Swedish rate dropped from thirty-five births per thousand people in 1859 to twenty-four per thousand in 1911 and would fall even more in the next two decades. England and Wales experienced a similar slump, and even populous Germany went from forty births per thousand in 1875 to twenty-seven per thousand in 1913.

Community norms more than individual decision making had traditionally limited the size of families. For example, hard-pressed agrarian communities of early modern Europe often called for couples to postpone marriage until they were too old to produce large numbers of children. This group control had balanced population with resources, but rapid economic and social change broke the grip of community decision making. In an age of agricultural industrialization, farm families needed fewer hands and individual couples increasingly practiced birth control to limit their family's size. Abstinence was a common method, but the spread of new birth-control practices that would encompass most of the globe by the end of the twentieth century mainly accounted for modern Europe's ebbing birthrate. In cities, pamphlets and advice books for those with enough money and education spread information about coitus interruptus—the withdrawal method of preventing pregnancy. Technology also played a role in curtailing reproduction: diaphragms and condoms, improved after the vulcanization of rubber in the 1840s, proved fairly reliable in preventing conception. Abortions were legion in cities, with the most conservative figures showing that in Paris some 100,000 were performed annually during these decades.

Large German Family
Improved medicine, hygiene, and diet at the turn of the century helped more people survive infancy and childhood. Thus in many cases family size grew larger, as this photo from a working-class apartment suggests. Even those opposed to birth control were appalled that lower-class families were becoming larger than those of the "best circles," where family limitation was increasingly practiced.
AKG London.

The wider use of birth control stirred controversy. Critics accused middle-class women, whose fertility was falling most rapidly, of holding a "birth strike." Others thought women were creating an identity "independent of love"—that is, independent of men and motherhood. Anglican bishops, meeting early in the twentieth century, deplored family limitation, especially by artificial means, as "demoralizing to character and hostile to national welfare." In France, where fertility decline was startling, politicians worried about a crisis in masculinity. They suggested that men of the "best" classes were failing to produce new generations of leaders, and many feared that a declining population would keep France from competing militarily with Germany. As schools and industry took over the father's role of teaching sons a trade, moreover, critics charged that men had abandoned the family hearth for taverns or radical political activism. In response to these perceived problems, physicians, statisticians, and reformers founded the National Alliance for Increasing the French Population in 1896. At the same time German activists started the German League for the Preservation of the People.

The Social Darwinist focus on national peril in a menacing world converted the debate on family issues into anxieties over class and race. A falling birthrate among the middle and upper classes was seen as leading to social decay and national catastrophe. United States president Theodore Roosevelt (1858–1919), for example, warned that women's refusal to have large families "form[ed] one of the most unpleasant and unwholesome features of modern life." The "quality" of those being born worried activists and politicians: if the "best" classes had fewer children, they asked, what would society look like when peopled mostly by the "worst" classes? The decline in fertility, one German nationalist warned, would make the country a "conglomerate of alien peoples, above all Slavs and probably East European Jews as well."

The fear that one's nation or "race" was being polluted by the presence of "aliens," the mentally ill, the severely disabled, and "nonproductive" elderly was a feature of *eugenics,* a pseudoscience popular among wealthy, educated Europeans at the turn of the century. As a famed Italian criminologist put it, such classes were not people but "orangutans"; thus "the more reason for us to destroy them as soon as one is sure that they are and will remain orangutans." Applying Darwin's idea of the survival of the fittest to humans, eugenicists favored increased fertility for "the fittest" and limitations on the fertility of "degenerates," leading even to their sterilization or elimination. Politicians worked eugenicist rhetoric into electoral campaigns, inflaming fears of ethnic minorities and the poor where once they had sought consensus among all groups.

Reforming Marriage

An array of politicians, feminists, and population experts saw marriage reform as one way to address the problems of declining birthrates and a potentially "degenerate" population. Women, they felt, would be more inclined to reproduce if the shackles in the traditional system of marriage were removed and wives were no longer treated as second-class citizens. To win support for the passage of new laws, activists pointed out that for more than a century outmoded relationships such as those of master and slave or lord and serf had been eliminated but that married women still lacked basic rights. "Give birth, give birth, without stopping," one French woman complained, "but if married, your child will be the *property* of its father."

Feminists and reform-minded men successfully lobbied for changes in the legal relationships of married men and women. Across most of Europe, married women gained the legal right to their wages and to their own property. Sweden, which made men's and women's control over property equal in marriage, allowed women to work without a husband's permission. The German law code of 1900 eliminated phrases about women owing obedience to their husbands and about men's paternal power, although it limited divorce more than the earlier laws of some individual German states. Other countries, among them France (1884), legalized divorce and made it less complicated, and thus less costly, to obtain.

Reformers had good reason to believe that these legal changes would result in an upswing of the birthrate. Given the existing constraints of motherhood—no financial resources to leave the home, no legal rights to their own children, little recourse in the event of an abusive or miserable marriage—women were reluctant to have more than two or three, if any, children. Divorce would allow unhappy couples to separate and undertake a new, more loving, and thus more fertile marriage. Greater financial parity in marriage was seen as a way to promote better health and a higher standard of living for women and their children. Swedish reformer Ellen Key (1849–1926) thought financially secure motherhood was a basic right of all women, married and single. Key, one of the most widely read reformers of the time, appealed both to "populationists" and to feminists in her advocacy of better living conditions for mothers and their children. By the early twentieth century, several countries had passed legislation that provided government subsidies to needy mothers. Great Britain, for example, mandated small maternal allowances in 1913. Like the earlier development of social security legislation in Germany and other countries, the system of subsidizing indigent mothers helped lay the foundations of the modern welfare state—a state concerned not only with war and diplomacy but with the everyday life of its citizens.

The conditions of marriage, motherhood, and other aspects of women's lives varied throughout Europe: women could get university degrees in Austrian universities long before they could at Oxford or Cambridge. A greater number of legal reforms occurred in western Europe, however. In much of rural eastern Europe the father's power over the extended family remained almost dictatorial. According to a survey of family life in eastern Europe in the early 1900s, fathers married off their children so young that 25 percent of women in their early forties had been pregnant more than ten times. A woman in Russia could obtain a divorce only if witnesses would testify that they had seen her husband having sex with another woman. Yet reform of everyday customs occurred, as community control gave way to individual practice in places, even though the pace of such change was slower than it was in western Europe. For instance, in some Balkan villages, a kind of extended-family system called the *zadruga* survived from earlier times, in which all the nuclear families shared a common great house, but now individual couples developed a degree of privacy by building one-room sleeping dwellings surrounding the great house. Among the middle and upper classes of eastern Europe, many grown children were coming to believe they had a right to select a marriage partner, not just to accept the spouse their parents chose for them based on economic or social reasons.

New Women, New Men, and the Politics of Sexual Identity

Rapid economic and institutional change set the stage for even bolder behaviors among some middle-class women, and the increasing availability of white-collar jobs for the educated meant that more European women could afford to adopt an independent way of life. So-called new women dressed more practically, with fewer petticoats and looser corsets, biked and hiked through city streets and down country lanes, lived apart from the family in women's clubs or apartments, and supported themselves. The growing number of women living on their own and freely moving in public spaces was a shocking phenomenon to the middle classes.

Many women acted in ways that further challenged accepted views of women's economic dependence and relative seclusion in the traditional middle-class family. Italian educator Maria Montessori (1870–1952), for example, went to medical school and secretly gave birth to an illegitimate child. Artists like the German painter Gabriele Münter lived openly with their lovers. Some writers portrayed these unconventional women sympathetically. Norwegian novelist and Nobel laureate Sigrid Undset in *Jenny* (1911) described an unmarried woman's reflections on her pregnancy: "She could provide for the child. . . . She had had enough of this sickly desire of clinging to somebody, to be cuddled and petted and called little girl." But in this time of social transformation, others protested the threat to gender roles: the new woman, German philosopher Friedrich Nietzsche wrote, had led to the "uglification of Europe."

Not just gendered behavior but sexual identity fueled discussion. Among books in the new field of "sexology," which studied sex scientifically from a clinical and medical point of view, *Sexual Inversion* (1894) by Havelock Ellis was popular. Ellis, a British medical doctor, postulated a new personality type—the homosexual—identifiable by such traits as effeminate behavior and a penchant for the arts in males and physical passion for members of their own sex in both males and females. Homosexuals joined the discussion, calling for recognition that they composed a legitimate and natural "third sex" and were not just people behaving sinfully. Much of this debate remained confined to physicians, psychologists, and intellectuals, but it

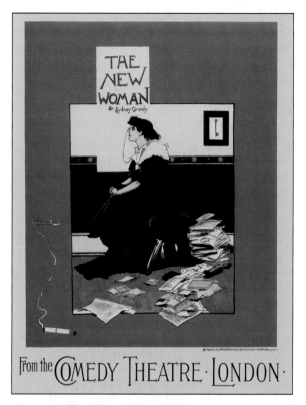

Sydney Grundy, *The New Woman* (1900)
By the opening of the twentieth century the "new woman" had become a much-discussed phenomenon. Artists painted portraits of this independent creature, while novelists and playwrights like Henrik Ibsen and Nobel Prize winner Sigrid Undset depicted her ambition to throw off the wifely role—or at least to shape that role more to her own personality. The new woman was also well educated: she had been to university, or wrote as a journalist, or entered professions such as law and medicine.
Jean-Loup Charmet.

began the trend toward considering sexuality in general as a fundamental part of human identity.

Sexual identity, including male homosexuality, became a wider public issue via the press. In the spring of 1895, reporters covered the trial of Irish playwright Oscar Wilde (1854–1900), who was sentenced to two years in prison for indecency—a charge that referred to his sexual affairs with young men. After Wilde's conviction one newspaper rejoiced, "Open the windows! Let in the fresh air!" The reading public lapped up such sensational stories. Beyond the infamous Wilde case, journalists revealed that married men of the ruling classes sometimes had sexual relations with other men. Between 1907 and 1909, for example, German newspapers publicized the courts-martial of men in Kaiser William II's closest circle who were condemned for homosexuality and transvestitism.

Attention to sexual behavior intensified concerns about falling birthrates and the solidity of the

Oscar Wilde
The Irish-born writer Oscar Wilde symbolized the sufferings experienced by homosexuals in the late nineteenth century. Tried for and convicted of having sexual relations with another man, Wilde served time in prison—a humiliation for a husband, father, acclaimed author, and witty playwright. Wilde's writings aimed to suggest that the complexities of human society made narrow moral codes harmful.
Library of Congress.

family. During the scandals over the kaiser's entourage, the public received assurances from the government itself that William's own family life "provides the entire country with a fine model." In a time of growing nationalism, sexuality took on patriotic overtones: the accused homosexual elite in Germany were said by journalists to be out to "emasculate our courageous master race." Although these cases paved the way for growing sexual openness in the next generations, sexual issues would simultaneously become regular weapons in politics.

Sciences of the Modern Mind

Scientists also found cause for alarm when they looked at population and the conditions of everyday life in industrial society and discovered a host of complaints such as fatigue and irritability. Most of these illnesses originated in the "nerves," they reasoned, which were troubled by the hectic pace and demands of urban living. Sciences of the mind such as psychology and psychoanalysis arose to treat everyone, not just the insane.

New Approaches to Mental Ailments.   Nervous illness was yet another cause of national decline, according to Social Darwinists. A rash of books in the 1890s expounded on this subject. The most widely translated of them, *Degeneration*, written by Hungarian-born physician Max Nordau (1849–1923), blamed overstimulation for both individual and national deterioration. According to Nordau, increasingly bizarre modern art, male lethargy, and female hysteria were all symptoms of overstimulation and reflected a general downturn in the human species. The standard Social Darwinist cure for such mental decline was imperial adventure, renewed virility, and increased childbearing.

Medical scientists promised new and better approaches to nervous ailments. Some researchers attempted to classify and quantify mental characteristics. Italian psychiatrist Cesare Lombroso (1836–1909) devised typologies for criminal minds by evaluating the physical features of deviants and created the field of criminology. The French psychologist Alfred Binet (1857–1911) designed intelligence tests that he maintained could measure the capacity of the human mind more accurately than schoolteachers could. In Russia, physiologist Ivan Pavlov (1849–1936) proposed that conditioning mental reflexes—that is, causing a subject to associate a desired response with a previously unrelated stimulus—could modify behavior. His most famous case involved a dog. Knowing that the dog would begin to salivate after seeing its food, Pavlov rang a bell to announce dinner. Once he established the connection between the sound of the bell and the sight of the food, Pavlov withdrew the food and found that the dog would still salivate (the desired response) when the bell rang (the previously unrelated stimulus). Such experiments formed the basis of modern psychology.

Freud and Psychoanalysis. Sigmund Freud (1856–1939) devised an approach to modern anxieties that, he claimed, avoided traditional moral evaluations of human behavior. He became convinced that the human psyche was far from rational. Dreams, he explained in *The Interpretation of Dreams* (1900), reveal a repressed part of personality—the "unconscious"—where all sorts of desires are more or less hidden. These desires appear only involuntarily, in the form of dreams, symptoms of physical illness, and abnormal behavior. Freud also believed that the human psyche is made up of three competing parts: the ego, the part that is most in touch with external reality; the id (or libido), the part that contains instinctive drives and sexual energies; and the superego, the part that serves as the force of conscience. Like Darwin's ideas, Freud's notions challenged accepted liberal belief in a unified, rational self that acted in its own interest. They also undermined the social implications of this belief, namely, that society would move in a consistently progressive direction.

Freud shocked many contemporaries by insisting that all children have sexual drives from the moment of birth, but he also believed that many of these sexual impulses have to be repressed for children to attain maturity and for society to remain

Freud's Office

Sigmund Freud's therapy room, where his patients experienced the "talking cure," was filled with imperial trophies such as Oriental rugs and African art objects. Freud himself was fascinated by cures brought about through shamanism, trances, and other practices of non-Western medicine as well as through drug-induced mental states. In 1938, Freud fled to England to escape the Nazis. This photo shows his office in London.
Mary Evans Picture Library/Sigmund Freud copyrights.

civilized. Attaining one's adult sexual identity is always a painful process because it depends on repressing infantile urges, which include bisexuality and incest. Thus, the Wolf-Man's nightmare of white wolves outside his window symbolized his unresolved sexual feelings for members of his family. Freud claimed that certain aspects of gender roles—such as motherhood—are normal and that throughout their lives women in general achieve far less than men do. At the same time, he believed that adult gender identity results not from anatomy alone (motherhood is not the only way to be female) but from inescapable mental processing of life experiences as well. He thus made gender more complicated than simple biology would suggest. Finally, Freud's psychoanalytic theory maintained that girls and women have powerful sexual feelings, an assertion that broke with ideas of women's passionlessness.

The influence of psychoanalysis became pervasive in the twentieth century. For example, free association of ideas and interpretation of dreams are mainstays in psychoanalysis: the "talking cure," as it was quickly labeled, gave rise to a general acceptance of talking out one's problems. (Ironically, Freud always had his patients lie on a couch facing away from him because he did not like to be looked at by his patients when they spoke.) As psychoanalysis became a respected means of recovering mental health, terms such as *neurosis, unconscious,* and *libido* came into widespread use, and patients faced little social stigma.

Yet despite its revolutionary content and impact, psychoanalysis reflected the many contradictions at work in turn-of-the-century Europe. For example, Freud attributed girls' complaints about unwanted sexual advances or abuse to fantasy caused by "penis envy," an idea that led members of the new profession of social work to believe that most instances of such abuse had not actually occurred. On the one hand, Freud was a meticulous scientist, examining symptoms, urging attention to the most minute evidence from everyday life, and demanding that sexual life be regarded with a rational rather than a religious eye. On the other hand, he was a pessimistic visionary who had abandoned the optimism of the Enlightenment and pre-Darwinian science by claiming that humans were motivated by irrational drives toward death and destruction and

that these shaped society's collective mentality. Freud would later interpret World War I's vast devastation of humanity as bearing out his bleak conclusions. (See "New Sources, New Perspectives," page 944.)

❖ Modernity and the Revolt in Ideas

Although the intellectuals and artists who participated in the turmoil of turn-of-the-century society did not know it at the time, their rejection of accepted values, beliefs, and artistic forms announced a new era. Philosophers who emphasized the role of the irrational and the accidental in day-to-day life challenged the belief that fundamental social laws could be discovered. In science, theories that time is relative and that energy and mass are interchangeable rocked established truths about time, space, matter, and energy. Art and music became unrecognizable. Artists and musicians who deliberately produced shocking, lurid works were, like Freud, heavily influenced by advances in science and critical thinking. Amidst contradictions such as the blending of the scientific and the irrational, intellectuals and artists helped launch the disorienting revolution in ideas and creative expression that we now identify collectively as *modernism.*

The Challenge to Positivism

Late in the nineteenth century, many philosophers and social thinkers rejected the century-old faith that in science one could discover enduring social laws based on rationally determined principles. This belief, called *positivism,* had emphasized the permanent nature of fundamental laws and had motivated reformers' attempts to perfect legislation based on studies of society. Challenging positivism, the philosophers Wilhelm Dilthey (1833–1911) in Germany and John Dewey (1859–1952) in the United States declared that human understanding was founded on the conditions of day-to-day existence. Because experience is ever changing, theories and standards cannot be constant or enduring. And just as scientific theory was modified over time, so must social theories and practice react pragmatically to the immediate conditions at hand.

Psychohistory and Its Lessons

In the nineteenth century, history books mostly told about the workings of public officials, religious institutions, and dynasties. They recounted the deeds of kings and emperors, discussed royal genealogy, and described wars and peace treaties. Determined to be factual, historians laid out the fine points of laws, charters, and treaties along with battles, strategies, and territorial gains whose records lay in official state archives.

Much has changed since then, partly because of the rise of psychology and psychoanalysis as the twentieth century opened. Confronted with strikes, mass demonstrations, anarchist deeds, anti-Semitism, and other forms of political violence, some observers tried to explain a phenomenon they called *crowd psychology*. According to this view, neither political ideas alone nor the actions of a politician as described in parliamentary records gives the full account of the past. Instead, new social observers suggested that psychic states are important factors in shaping some public events.

Not surprisingly, Sigmund Freud studied great historic figures like Leonardo da Vinci from a psychoanalytic perspective, exploring the person's work in relation to repressed childhood fantasies. Freud also explained the outbreak of World War I as more of a psychic than a diplomatic event. He showed the ways in which the war's pursuit could be connected to a form of collective death wish. In his studies, both individual and national histories were susceptible to psychoanalytic accounts.

It was not until the 1950s, however, that prominent historians turned to psychoanalysis, devising from it a genre called *psychohistory*. In 1957, William Langer, president of the American Historical Association, charged his fellow scholars with using a foolish conservatism in their methods. Unlike scientists, he claimed, historians did not experiment in their historical work, for instance by adopting new ideas like psychoanalysis that might advance their understanding of the past. Others joined the debate, finding the traditional history that ascribed actions to ambition, greed, hate, and great intelligence as superficial in its argument and lacking in explanatory force. Or they criticized it for attributing historical events to social forces and thereby discounting any kind of personal agency. A third criticism of history by those interested in psychology and psychoanalysis was that, if it did take human agency into account, it usually saw historical figures as acting rationally in their self-interest. Trauma, the irrational, uncontrollable drives, and unconscious motivations had no role to play in understanding historical figures.

Soon thereafter a major study by the German-born psychoanalyst Erik Erikson, *Young Man Luther* (1958), announced that the Protestant Reformation originated in the childhood traumas of Martin Luther. Identity crises stemming from his relationship with his father caused Luther to search for and reject father figures, not only his own father but the pope. Erikson's book caused a stir among historians, changing the way people approached Luther but also causing resistance. Not only did one need to know a great deal of psychology to duplicate Erikson's effort, one almost had to exclude other influences that historians considered important.

Not surprisingly, some of the most compelling examples of psychohistory have focused on the lives of individuals and the development of political movements that occurred during the period when Freud was setting the terms for psychoanalysis, roughly from the end of the nineteenth century to the beginning of World War II. Historians interested in psychoanalysis have tried to find in Kaiser William II's childhood answers to his rejection of Bismarck, his turn to an aggressive foreign policy, and his participation in World War I. Nietzsche's and Freud's intimate friend Lou Andreas-Salomé, a powerful intellectual during these years, was seen as having a "bisexual" personality because she published her writing, an occupation that suggested a masculine nature.

Kaiser William and Edward VII's Family

Psychotherapy aimed to cure the individual in good part by discussing family relationships and the fantasies built around them. Psychohistory often draws its analyses from these same relationships, as in the case of Martin Luther, for example, and his father. The royal families of Europe are ripe for such analysis because, as the photo shows, German and British monarchs (Edward VII, right; and William, second from right) were closely related; so too were the Russians, Germans, and British. These relationships raise potential questions about the outbreak of World War I.
Hulton Getty Picture Library/Liaison Agency.

On a collective level, analyses of Hitler's and Mussolini's followers have seen mass psychic needs and traumas as motivating their blind worship of these vicious dictators. But the intense nationalism that most people in the modern world have increasingly felt for their countries has also become a phenomenon that psychohistorians examine.

Psychohistory remains controversial to this day. While its practitioners expand the field of historical explanation, its critics find that it can be formulaic by fitting the behavior of historical characters into Freud's schema. Other critics find that psychohistory is too imprecise and speculative because it is not based on the same kinds of hard, documentary evidence that historians have been trained to use. Nonetheless, psychohistorians have made a good case that if we are going to look at personalities, character, and relationships, we should do so in the most informed way possible. Their rationale makes psychohistory a necessity.

QUESTIONS FOR DEBATE

1. What are the advantages and disadvantages of psychohistory?

2. How would you set out to investigate the psychological reasons for the actions of William II, Emmeline Pankhurst, Marie Curie, or Gavrilo Princip? Would you look at their character, their childhood, their social background, or other parts of their lives?

3. Can we write history without investigating psychology? Should we avoid "psychologizing" when thinking about the past?

FURTHER READING

Rudolph Binion, *Frau Lou: Nietzsche's Wayward Disciple.* 1968.

Erik Erikson, *Young Man Luther: A Study in Psychoanalysis and History.* 1958.

Journal of Psychohistory.

Thomas A. Kohut, *Wilhelm II and the Germans: A Study in Leadership.* 1991.

The turn-of-the-century thinkers, called *relativists* and *pragmatists*, influenced thinking about society throughout the twentieth century.

In the same vein, German sociologist and political theorist Max Weber (1864–1920) was pessimistic about the ability of government bureaucracy—once seen as a rational alternative to monarchy—to deal effectively with all the variables of modern society. Watching government and the electorate expand, Weber maintained that the sheer numbers involved in policymaking would often make decisive action impossible—especially in times of crisis, when a charismatic leader might usurp power because of his ability to make flexible and instinctive decisions. Thus the development of impartial forms of government such as bureaucracy carried the potential for undermining the rule of law and for eroding the modern commitment to constitutional government.

The most radical and influential of these scholars was the German philosopher Friedrich Nietzsche (1844–1900). Early in his career he developed one of his most challenging ideas, based on the distinction between the "Apollonian," or rational, side of human existence and the "Dionysian" side, with its expression of more primal urges. Nietzsche believed that people generally cling to the rational, Apollonian explanations of life because Dionysian ideas about nature, death, and love such as those found in Greek tragedy are too disturbing. Nietzsche maintained that all assertions of scientific fact and theory were mere illusions. Knowledge of nature had to be expressed in mathematical, linguistic, or artistic representation; truth thus existed only in the representation itself, for humans could never experience unfiltered knowledge of nature or reality. This aspect of Nietzsche's philosophy would lead to the late-twentieth-century school of thought called *postmodernism*.

Much of Nietzsche's writing took the form of aphorisms—short, disconnected statements of truth or opinion—a form that broke with the logical rigor of traditional Western philosophy. Nietzsche used aphorisms to convey the impression that his ideas were a single individual's unique perspective, not universal truths that thinkers since the Enlightenment had claimed were attainable. Influenced by a range of Asian philosophy, Nietzsche was convinced that late-nineteenth-century Europe was witnessing the decline of dogmatic truth, most notably in religion—hence his announcement that

"God is dead, we have killed him." Far from arousing dread, the death of God, according to Nietzsche, would give birth to a joyful quest for new "poetries of life" to replace worn-out religious rules. Not the rule-bound bourgeois but the untethered "superman" was Nietzsche's highly influential model.

Nietzsche's thought was inspiring from the outset, but over time it would be used for destructive ends. As a teacher he was so compelling that his first students thought they were hearing another Socrates. But after he contracted syphilis and became insane for the last eleven years of his life, his sister endeavored to spread his fame. Most important for twentieth-century politics, she edited Nietzsche's diatribes against middle-class values into attacks on Jews. She revised his concepts about each individual's "will to power" and of "superman" so as to advocate displays of military might. The popular teachings of French philosopher Henri Bergson (1859–1941) were similarly distorted. Bergson proposed the existence of an *élan vital*, or intuitive creative force, that could spark individuals and nations to superior accomplishments. Racists, nationalists, and militarists reduced these very complicated philosophies to simple-minded creeds that justified violent anti-Semitism and competition for empire.

Revolutionizing Science

While philosophers questioned the ability of science to provide timeless truths, scientific inquiry itself flourished. The scientific method gained authority beyond the traditional sciences, especially in fields such as history and psychology, and many people still held to positivist assumptions that natural laws could be understood and the universe consequently mastered. Technological breakthroughs, improvements in hygiene, and other fruits of scientific inquiry earned science great prestige with the public. Around the turn of the century, however, discoveries by pioneering researchers shook the foundations of traditional scientific certainty and challenged accepted knowledge about the nature of the universe.

Some scientists' findings undermined the principles of time, space, matter, energy, and the immutability of physical entities on which science had rested since Isaac Newton two centuries earlier. In 1896, Antoine Becquerel (1852–1908) discovered

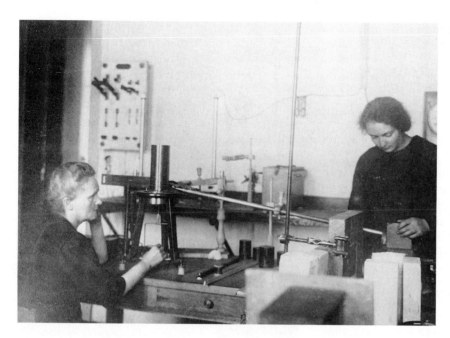

Marie Curie and Her Daughter
Recipient of two Nobel Prizes, Marie Curie came from Poland to western Europe to study science. Curie's extraordinary career made her the epitome of new womanhood; her daughter Irene Joliot-Curie followed her mother into the field and also won a Nobel Prize. Both women died of leukemia caused by their exposure to radioactive materials. Today a reconstruction of the Curie laboratory as a museum contains a display of the intense radioactivity still in scientific instruments they used a century ago. ACJC–Archives Curie et Joliot-Curie.

radioactivity and suggested the mutability of elements by the rearrangement of their atoms. French chemist Marie Curie (1867–1934) and her husband, Pierre Curie (1859–1906), isolated the elements polonium and radium, which are more radioactive than the uranium Becquerel used. From these and other discoveries, scientists concluded that atoms are composed of subatomic particles moving about a core. Instead of being solid, as scientists had believed since ancient times, atoms are largely empty space and act not as a concrete substance but as an intangible electromagnetic field. German physicist Max Planck (1858–1947) announced his influential quantum theorem in 1900; it demonstrated that energy is emitted in irregular packets, not in a steady stream.

New research transformed astronomy as well as physics. Scientists had already demonstrated that light has a uniform velocity regardless of the direction it travels from the earth and that the velocity is not relative to the motion of the earth. Thus older theories of light on which scientists had relied were no longer tenable. It was in this unsettled situation that physicist Albert Einstein (1879–1955) published his special theory of relativity in 1905. Einstein, who had been expelled from high school as a disruptive influence on other students, had later studied physics with teachers ignorant of the intellectual transformation taking place in sci-

entific thought. But on his own, working in a Swiss patent office, he proclaimed in his 1905 paper that space and time are not absolute categories but instead vary according to the vantage point of the observer. Only the speed of light is constant. That same year he also suggested that the solution to problems in Planck's quantum theorem lay in considering light both as little packets *and* as waves. These theories continued to undercut Newtonian physics as well as commonsense understanding.

Einstein later proposed yet another blurring of two distinct physical properties, mass and energy. He expressed this equivalence in the formulation of $E = mc^2$, or energy equals mass times the square of the speed of light. In 1916, his general theory of relativity connected the force, or gravity, of an object with its mass and postulated a fourth mathematical dimension to the universe. Much more lay ahead, once Einstein's theories of energy were developed: television, nuclear power, and, within forty years, nuclear bombs.

The findings of Planck, Einstein, and others revolutionized the physical sciences, but these theories were often not accepted immediately largely because power and time-honored beliefs were at stake. Einstein struggled against mainstream science and its professional institutions. Even Planck, who had excellent university positions because of family connections, tried desperately for years to get senior researchers to accept his findings. Marie Curie faced such resistance that even after she became the first person ever to receive a second Nobel Prize (1911), the prestigious French Academy of Science turned down her candidacy for membership that year.

These prejudices ultimately broke down. Max Planck institutes were established in German cities, streets across Europe were named after Marie Curie and other scientific pioneers, and Einstein's name became synonymous with genius. These scientists achieved what historians call a *paradigm shift*—that is, in the face of understandable resistance they transformed the foundations of science and came themselves to supersede other names.

Religion Confronts Modernity

A growing acceptance of scientific and social scientific accounts of human society led to a decline in religious fervor among urban elites and the working class alike. Migration and urbanization also loosened the churches' social power. "The educated middle class, especially the young people, are losing touch altogether with the House of God," one Protestant clergyman wrote in 1911. Wealthy Catholic men often tended their businesses or played sports rather than attending Mass. Religion, for some men, was best left to women.

Churches fought secularization. Some theologians wanted to modernize religion by applying scholarly methods to the Bible, although many, especially papal policymakers, opposed liberalization to regain lost prestige and active church members. Pius X (r. 1903–1914) condemned Catholic modernists who wanted Catholicism to reconcile with scientific claims. Some Protestants and Catholics took a different approach by countering intellectual and political challenges to their authority through increased missionary efforts abroad and among the urban poor. Pope Leo XIII (r. 1878–1903) called for a more active ministry among the working classes; in response, the church in Hungary channeled some of its efforts away from its traditional constituency in villages and toward ministering to workers in cities. In Austria-Hungary, Francis Joseph and his officials, faced with mounting discontent, strictly observed the rituals of their Catholic faith hoping they would draw the masses away from spectacles such as the annual

workers' May Day parade. In Orthodox Russia, the reactionary policies of Alexander III (r. 1881–1894) and his son Nicholas II (r. 1894–1917) opposed freethinking in both intellectual and religious matters. They equated the Orthodox religion with political loyalty.

Modern Art

The same conflicts between traditional values and new ideas raged in the arts, as artists distanced themselves from classical Western norms and from the conventions of polite society. Their rebellion, however, was far more disorganized than the

Pablo Picasso, *Les Demoiselles d'Avignon* (1907)
Impressionists had borrowed heavily from Asian art, but many artists in Pablo Picasso's generation leaned on Africa for inspiration. In Les Demoiselles d'Avignon, *Picasso used the elongated, angular limbs found in African carvings, while the faces resemble African masks. The artists Amadeo Modigliani, Barbara Hepworth, and Constantin Brancusi excelled in sculpture featuring the smooth forms and lively compositions of African wooden statuary.*
PICASSO, Pablo. *Les Demoiselles d'Avignon.* Paris (June – July 1907). Oil on canvas, 8' × 7'8". The Museum of Modern Art, New York. Acquired through the Lillie P. Bliss Bequest. Photograph © The Museum of Modern Art, New York © 2001 Estate of Pablo Picasso/ Artists Rights Society, NY.

impressionist revolt a generation earlier. Many new, almost incomprehensible types of visual art emerged to challenge the historic and realistic scenes still favored, for example, by the powerful German monarchy and by some buyers for museums and important collections. Modernism in the arts ushered in a proliferation of competing artistic styles and disagreement about art's relationship to society.

Art for Industrial Society. Some modern artists tried both to challenge and to comfort urbanites caught up in the rush of modern life. Abandoning the soft colors of impressionism as too subtle for a dynamic industrial society, a group of Parisian artists exhibiting in 1905 combined blues, greens, reds, and oranges so intensely that they were called *fauves,* or "wild beasts." A leader of the short-lived fauvism, Henri Matisse (1869–1954), soon struck out in a new direction, targeting the expanding class of white-collar workers. Matisse dreamed of "an art . . . for every mental worker, be he businessman or writer, like an appeasing influence, like a mental soother, something like a good armchair in which to rest from physical fatigue."

The mathematical, scientific tenor of the day appeared in the French artist Paul Cézanne's (1839–1906) focus on structure in painting. Cézanne used rectangular daubs of paint in his scenes of nature and portraits of people to capture a geometric vision of his subjects. Accentuating the lines and planes found in nature, Cézanne's art, like science, was removed from the realm of ordinary perception. The dishes, fruit, and drapery of his still lifes of the 1890s took geometric form, as did the human body. With Cézanne one of the most powerful new trends in the visual arts took shape.

Following in Cézanne's footsteps, Spanish artist Pablo Picasso (1881–1973) initiated *cubism,* a style with a radical emphasis on planes and surfaces that converted people into bizarre, inhuman, almost unrecognizable forms. Picasso's painting *Les Demoiselles d'Avignon* (1907) depicted the bodies of the *demoiselles,* or young ladies (prostitutes in this case), as fragmented and angular, with their heads modeled on African masks. Continuing along the path of impressionism and fauvism, Picasso's work showed the profound influences of African, Asian, and South American arts, but his depiction of these features was less decorative and

more brutal than those by Matisse, for example. Like explorers, botanists, and foreign journalists, he was bringing knowledge of the empire into the imperial homeland, this time in a distinctly disturbing form.

Art as Political Criticism. Political critique also shaped painting. "Show the people how hideous is their actual life, and place your hands on the causes of its ugliness" was the anarchist challenge at the time. Picasso, who had spent his youth in the heart of working-class Barcelona, a hotbed of anarchist thought, aimed to replace middle-class sentimentality in art with truth about industrial society. In 1912, Picasso and French painter Georges Braque (1882–1963) devised a new kind of collage that incorporated bits of newspaper, string, and other artifacts. The effect was a canvas that appeared to be cluttered with refuse. The newspaper clippings Picasso included described battles and murders, suggesting the shallowness of Western pretensions to high civilization.

Although Paris was still the center of the art world, artists in the thriving cities of central and eastern Europe and Scandinavia also combined radical stylistic change with political critique. They formed associations (*secessions*) to express their own rebellion against officially approved styles. "The whole empire is littered with monuments to soldiers and monuments to Kaiser William of the same conventional type," one artist complained. Such groups as the Berlin Secession and the Vienna Workshop were at the forefront in experimenting with form and in portraying the psychological complexity of the self. Their joint exhibits of work by ethnically diverse artists criticized the growing nationalism that determined official purchases of sculpture and painting.

Scandinavian and eastern European artists produced anguished works. Like the vision of Freud, their style of portraying inner reality—called *expressionism*—broke with middle-class optimism. Norwegian painter Edvard Munch (1863–1944), who participated in German exhibitions, aimed "to make the emotional mood ring out again as happens on a gramophone." His painting *The Scream* (1895) used twisting lines and a depiction of tortured skeletal human form to convey the horror of modern life that many artists perceived. German avant-garde artist Gabriele Münter

(1877–1962) and Russian painter Wassily Kandinsky (1866–1944) opened their "Blue Rider" exhibit in Munich featuring "expressive" work that made use of geometric forms and striking colors. The artists of the Blue Rider group imitated the paintings of children and the mentally ill to achieve their depiction of psychological reality. Kandinsky, who employed these forms and colors to express an inner, spiritual truth, is often credited with producing the first fully abstract paintings.

The expressionism of Oskar Kokoschka (1886–1980) was even more intense, displaying ecstasy, horror, and hallucinations. As a result, his work—like that of other expressionists and cubists before World War I—was a commercial failure in an increasingly complex marketplace. Alongside government purchases arose a system of dealers who sponsored exhibits of "their" artists' work and who relied on favorable reviews by professional art critics. With styles changing rapidly, the "old masters" of Renaissance and baroque art gained status as classics, selling for ever higher prices. Experts in authenticating and judging these older works of art, among them the American art critic and historian Bernard Berenson (1865–1959), who set himself up outside Florence, Italy, as the ultimate arbiter, made it possible for international buyers to purchase with confidence. Trade in art became professionalized, as had medicine and government work before it, even as modern artists sought to shatter traditional norms.

Art Nouveau.   Only one innovative style emerged an immediate commercial success: *art nouveau* ("new style") won approval from government, critics, and the masses. Creating everything from dishes and advertising posters to streetlamps and even entire buildings in this new style, designers manufactured beautiful things for the general public. As one French official said about the first version of art nouveau coins issued in 1895, "Soon even the most humble among us will be able to have a masterpiece in his pocket."

Like the earlier arts and crafts movement in Britain, art nouveau featured intertwined vines and flowers; women with long, wavy hair; and other similar motifs. Adapted from Asian design, the organic and natural elements of art nouveau were meant to offset the fragmentation of factory and office work with images depicting the unified forms of nature. The impersonality of machines was replaced by softly curving bodies of female nudes that would psychologically soothe the individual viewer—an idea that directly contrasted with Picasso's artistic vision. Gustav Klimt (1862–1918), son of a Czech goldsmith, flourished in Viennese high society because his paintings captured the psychological essence of dreamy, sensuous women, their bodies Eastern-inspired mosaics liberally dotted with gold. Art nouveau was the notable exception to the public outcries over innovations in the visual arts.

Musical Iconoclasm

"Astonish me!" was the motto of modern dance and music, both of which shocked audiences in the concert halls of Europe. American dancer Isadora Duncan (1877–1927) took Europe by storm at the turn of the century when, draped in a flowing garment, she danced barefoot in the first performance of modern dance. Drawing on sophisticated Japanese practices, hers was nonetheless called a primitive style that "lifted from their seats people who had never left theater seats before except to get up and go home." Similarly, experimentation with forms of bodily expression animated the Russian Ballet's performance in 1913 of *Rite of Spring* by Igor Stravinsky (1882–1971), the tale of an orgiastic dance to the death performed to ensure fertile soil and a bountiful harvest. The star, Vaslav Nijinsky (1890–1950), was noted for his grace and meticulous execution of classical ballet steps, but his choreography of *Rite of Spring* created a scandal. Nijinsky and the troupe struck awkward poses and danced to rhythms intended to sound primitive. At the work's premiere in Paris, one journalist reported that "the audience began shouting its indignation. . . . Fighting actually broke out among some of the spectators." Such controversy made *Rite of Spring* a box-office hit, although its choreographer was called a "lunatic" and the music itself "the most discordant composition ever written."

Music had been making this turn for several decades. Having heard Asian musicians at international expositions, French composers like Claude Debussy (1862–1918) transformed their style to reflect non-European musical patterns and themes. The twentieth century opened with *Scheherazade* by Frenchman Maurice Ravel (1875–1937) and

**Léon Bakst, *Nijinsky in L'Après-Midi d'un Faune*
("Nijinsky in The Afternoon of a Faun," 1912)**
*Theater sets, costume designs, and performance itself reso-
nated with the experimental climate of early-twentieth-
century Europe. Léon Bakst, a Russian painter and set
designer, used the art nouveau style to capture the faunlike
character of ballet star Vaslav Nijinsky. Yet on the eve of
World War I Nijinsky was part of a revolution in ballet that
introduced jerky, awkward, pounding movements to indicate
the primal nature of dance.*
Wadsworth Atheneum, Hartford. The Ella Gallup Sumner and Mary
Catlin Sumner Collection Fund.

Madame Butterfly by the Italian composer Giacomo
Puccini (1858–1924), both with non-Western subject matter.

Sound became jarring to many listeners. Austrian composer Richard Strauss (1864–1949) upset
convention by using several keys simultaneously in
his compositions. Like the fragmented representation of reality in cubism, atonality or several tonalities at once distorted familiar harmonic patterns
for the audience. Strauss's operas *Salome* (1905)
and *Elektra* (1909) took biblical and classical heroines and expressed through them the modern fascination with violence and obsessive passion. A
newspaper critic claimed that Strauss's dissonant
works "spit and scratch and claw each other like
enraged panthers." The Hungarian pianist Béla
Bartók (1881–1945) incorporated folk melodies
into his compositions as Edvard Grieg and other
nationalist composers had before him, but he composed so that two folk melodies could be played simultaneously in different keys. Bartók's aim was to
elevate the virtues of Hungarian ethnicity above
the Habsburg Empire's unifying multinationalism.
His music disturbed some audiences because of its
nationalism and others because of its dissonance.

The early orchestral work of Austrian composer Arnold Schoenberg (1874–1951), who also
wrote cabaret music to earn a living, shocked even
Strauss. In *Theory of Harmony* (1911) he proposed
eliminating tonality altogether; a decade later he
devised a new twelve-tone scale. "I am aware of
having broken through all the barriers of a dated
aesthetic ideal," Schoenberg wrote of his music.

Modernists in music, like modernists in other
arts, felt they were shattering old norms and values
with their concern for abstract forms. But new aesthetic models distanced these artists from their audiences, separating high from low culture even
more and ending the support of many in the upper
classes, who found this music not only incomprehensible but unpleasant. The artistic elite and the
social elite parted ranks. "Anarchist! Nihilist!"
shouted Schoenberg's audiences, showing their
contempt for modernism and bringing the language of politics into the arts.

❖ Politics in a New Key

New political challenges accompanied the revolution in intellectual life. To some observers, Queen
Victoria's death in 1901 after a reign of more than
sixty years symbolized the uncertainties that lay
ahead in European politics. "It isn't only the Queen
who has disappeared," commented a diplomat's
wife. "It is the century." The Crystal Palace exhibit

Queen Victoria had opened in 1851 had exemplified people's unshakable faith in progress. Now, fifty years later, that optimism had been tempered by an apprehensive, even pessimistic feeling about the future, especially among the upper classes. Cracks in the political consensus and changing political tactics had undermined upper-class control of politics. Liberalism had opened the door to expanded political representation and tolerance for diverse opinions. Political activists, however, were no longer satisfied with the liberal rights sought by reformers a century earlier. Militant nationalists, anti-Semites, socialists, suffragists, and many others demanded changes that alarmed traditional liberals. Mass politics soon threatened social unity, especially in central and eastern Europe, where governments often answered reformers' demands with refusal and repression.

The Growing Power of Labor

European leaders watched with dismay the rise of working-class political power late in the century. Unions gained members among factory workers, while Labor and Socialist Parties won seats in parliaments as men in the lower classes received the vote. In Germany, Kaiser William II had allowed antisocialist laws to lapse after dismissing Bismarck as chancellor in 1890. Through continuous grassroots organizing, the Social Democratic Party (SPD), founded by socialists in 1875, became the largest parliamentary group in the Reichstag by 1912. In France, competing political parties merged in 1905 to form the French Section of the Workers' International (SFIO). These massive workers' parties in central and western Europe voted representatives favorable to labor into parliaments, where they focused on passing legislation that benefited laborers and their families.

Electoral victories raised issues for socialists. Some felt uncomfortable sitting with the upper classes in parliaments. Others worried that their participation in cabinets would produce reform but compromise their ultimate goal of revolution. Often these deputies refused seats in the government. Between 1900 and 1904, the Second International wrestled with the issue of reformism. The International hotly debated the "revisionist" theories of Eduard Bernstein, who criticized many Marxist tenets and proposed that socialism be achieved by evolutionary rather than revolutionary means. German Marxists responded that reformism only buttressed capitalism. The topic touched off stormy discussions, sometimes pitting delegates from France, England, and Belgium who had attained some political authority and favored reform against more intransigent German socialists who were denied ministerial posts by military and aristocratic statesmen or refused them.

Russian socialists had even less political power than their German counterparts and could gain no ground against a rigidly authoritarian government. Most of these socialists operated in exile because the Russian government outlawed political parties until 1905 and persecuted activists. The foremost activist, V. I. Lenin (1870–1924), became a radical after his brother was executed for plotting to assassinate the tsar. Jailed and sent to Siberia during the 1890s for his left-wing politics, Lenin migrated to western Europe after his release and earned his reputation among Russian Marxists there with his hard-hitting journalism and political intrigue. Lenin advanced the theory that a highly disciplined party elite would lead a lightly industrialized Russia immediately into socialism. At a 1903 party meeting of Russian Marxists, he briefly gained the upper hand when a group of his opponents walked out of the proceedings. In ensuing votes, Lenin's supporters eked out slim victories for control of the party. Thereafter his faction of Bolsheviks, so named after the Russian word for *majority* (which they had temporarily formed), constantly struggled to suppress the Mensheviks, the dominant voice in Russian Marxism. Neither of these groups, however, had as large a constituency within Russia as the Socialist Revolutionaries, whose objective was to politicize peasants rather than industrial workers as the prelude to a populist revolution. All these groups prepared for the revolutionary moment through study, propaganda efforts, and organizing.

During this period some trade union members, known as *syndicalists*, and anarchists kept Europe in a panic with terrorist acts; they also antagonized Marxists. Demonstrating their theory that all forms of government should be abolished, anarchists assassinated Spanish premier Antonio Canovas del Castillo in 1897, Empress Elizabeth of Austria-Hungary in 1898, King Umberto of Italy in 1900, and President William McKinley of the United States in 1901, to name a few famous victims. Syndicalists advocated the use of direct action, such as general strikes and sabotage, to bring industry and government under the control of labor unions. Their ideas were set forth most clearly in French engineer Georges Sorel's *Reflections on Violence* (1908), which explained how a general strike of workers could paralyze the industrial economy and how widespread violence could transform society. By the time of the book's publication, syndicalists had aroused some worker support for their goals. In Italy, for example, sporadic strikes among agricultural and industrial workers in the 1890s were followed by a general strike in 1904. Elsewhere anarchist plots, strikes, and protests over the high cost of living revealed rising worker activism.

Working people's voices had never been so powerful as in these two decades, and the power caused the upper and middle classes grave anxiety. Despite growing acceptance of representative institutions and despite the spread of education, most people in the "best circles" still believed that they alone should hold political power. Politicians from the old landowning and military elites of eastern and central Europe were often the most adamant in their rejection of mass politics, and many of them hoped to reverse the trend toward constitutionalism, worker activism, and reform.

Rights for Women and the Battle for Suffrage

Women did not benefit from the gains of liberalism such as parliamentary representation and equal access to the free press. They often could not vote, exercise free speech, or own property. In Austria and Germany they could not attend political meetings or belong to political groups. In France during the Third Republic, the police often prohibited women's political meetings and talks, citing laws dating from the French Revolution that forbade women to gather publicly. British women could serve on school councils but were deprived of most other representation.

Such restrictions strengthened the movement committed to gaining rights for women. Throughout the nineteenth century, women singly and in groups had struggled for rights, and by the end of the century their efforts involved millions of activists with a variety of goals. German women, influenced by the cultural ideal of *Bildung* (the belief that proper education can build strength of character and that this individual development has public importance), agitated to reform education and to acquire teaching positions more forcefully than they sought the vote. In several countries women continued to monitor the regulation of prostitution. Their goal was to prevent prostitutes from being imprisoned on suspicion of having syphilis when men with syphilis faced no such incarceration or inspection. Other women took up pacifism as their special cause. Many of them were inspired by Bertha von Süttner's popular book, *Lay Down Your Arms* (1889), which emphasized the terror inflicted on women and families by the ravages of war. (Later von Süttner would influence Alfred Nobel to institute a peace prize and then win the prize herself in 1903.)

By the 1890s, however, many activists concluded that only the right to vote would correct the problems they were combating in piecemeal fashion. Thus they launched a suffrage movement with the express purpose of reducing male privilege by giving women an equal say in society. They argued that men had promised to protect disfranchised women but that this system of supposed chivalry had led to exploitation and abuse. Power and privilege—no matter how couched in expressions of goodwill—worked to the detriment of those without them. "So long as the subjection of women endures, and is confirmed by law and custom, . . . women will be victimized," a leading suffragist claimed. Other activists believed that women had attributes needed to counterbalance masculine qualities in the running of society. The characteristics that came from mothering should shape a country's destiny as much as qualities that stemmed from work in industry and trade, they asserted.

Women's rights activists were predominantly, though not exclusively, from the middle class. Those whose husbands or fathers could afford servants and other conveniences simply had more time to be activists, and a higher level of education allowed them to read the works of feminist theorists such as Harriet Taylor and John Stuart Mill. Working-class women, especially socialists, felt conflicted over whether to engage in women's rights campaigns. Most distrusted middle-class men and women and saw suffrage for women as subordinate to economic concerns. Although some workingwomen, such as those in the textile industries of Manchester, England, put together a vigorous suffrage movement connecting the vote to improved working conditions, socialists and suffragists usually differed over issues of class and gender.

In the 1890s, major suffrage organizations with paid officials and permanent offices emerged out of the voluntary reform groups and women's clubs that had existed earlier in the century. From charity work performed as part of their mission, women had acquired skills in fundraising, public speaking, and organization building. They also devoted their lives to "the Cause" for personal reasons. British suffrage leader Millicent Garrett Fawcett (1847–1929) vowed to change things after enduring the humiliation of having her stolen purse officially labeled her husband's property. Fawcett pressured members of Parliament for the vote, recruited new members, and participated in national and international congresses on behalf of suffrage. Similarly, American Susan B. Anthony (1820–1906) traveled throughout the United States, organized suffrage societies, edited a newspaper, raised money for the movement, and founded the International Woman Suffrage Association in 1904.

In 1906 in Finland, suffragists achieved their first major victory when the Finnish parliament granted women the vote. But the failure of parliaments elsewhere in Europe to enact similar legislation provoked some suffragists to violence and bold public activism. Part of the British suffragist movement adopted a militant political style when Emmeline Pankhurst (1858–1928) and her daughters founded the Women's Social and Political Union (WSPU) in the belief that women would accomplish nothing unless they threatened men's property. Starting in 1907, members of the WSPU held parades in English cities, and in 1909 they began a campaign of violence, blowing up railroad stations, slashing works of art, and chaining themselves to the gates of Parliament. Easily disguising themselves as ordinary shoppers, they carried little hammers in their muffs to smash the plate-glass windows of department stores and shops. Parades and demonstrations made suffrage a public spectacle, resulting in violent attacks on the marchers by outraged men. Arrested for disturbing the peace, the marchers went on hunger strikes in prison. Like striking workers, these women were willing to use

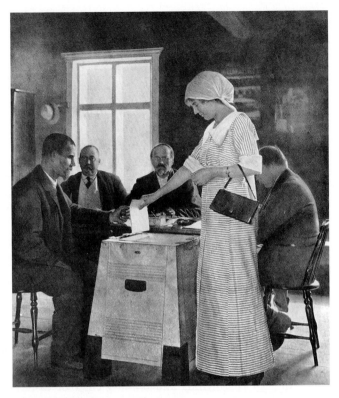

Woman Suffrage in Finland
In 1906, Finnish women became the first in Europe to receive the vote in national elections when the socialist party— usually opposed to feminism as a middle-class rather than a working-class project—supported woman suffrage. The Finnish vote elated activists in the West, now linked together by many international organizations and ties, because it showed that more than a century of lobbying for reform could lead to gains.
Mary Evans Picture Library.

confrontational tactics to obtain rights. As politicians hedged the question of the vote for women, militant suffragists added to the tensions of conflict-ridden urban life.

Liberalism Modified

Governments in western Europe, where liberal institutions were seemingly well entrenched, sought to control the conflicts of the late nineteenth century with pragmatic policies that often (and paradoxically) struck at liberalism's very foundations. After ending laissez-faire in trade by instituting protective tariffs, some politicians and reformers decided that government needed to intervene in more than economic matters to maintain productivity and peace. The scope of social welfare programs broadened, giving government officials more access to information about the family, public health, and domestic relations so they could devise protective legislation, administer disability plans, and establish food and medical programs for needy children. Officials hoped these policies would guarantee a contented workforce and better productivity, which in turn would counter economic uncertainty and political unrest. Although many programs addressed urban needs insufficiently, they added to the growing apparatus of the welfare state in which government actively promoted social well-being.

Testing Liberalism in Britain. In 1905, the British Liberal Party won a solid majority in the House of Commons and seemed determined to enact social legislation to gain working-class support. "We are keenly in sympathy with the representatives of Labour," one Liberal politician announced. "We have too few of them in the House of Commons." Liberal chancellor of the exchequer David Lloyd George (1863–1945) wanted to make a "new departure" in social policy and initiated a system of relief for the unemployed in the National Insurance Act of 1911. Conservatives in the House of Lords resisted higher taxation on the wealthy to pay for this and other social programs, leading to a Liberal threat to create more peers (lords) and thus dilute the power and prestige of the nobility. The newcomers could be counted on to vote for reform. Under this threat the lords approved the Parliament Bill of 1911, which eliminated their veto power. Many wealthy businessmen deserted the Liberal Party because of its alliance with Labour, however.

A modified liberalism advanced in Britain on social issues, but the Irish question tested British commitment to such values as self-determination and individual rights. The House of Lords had blocked previous bills granting home rule to Ireland, and after the fall of their leader Charles Parnell Irish nationalists began to rebuild their organization using methods similar to those of activists in the colonies. In the 1890s, groups formed to foster Irish culture. In 1901, the circle around the modernist poet William Butler Yeats (1865–1939) and the charismatic patriot and actress Maud Gonne (1865–1953) founded the Irish Na-

tional Theater. Gonne took Irish politics into everyday life by opposing British efforts to woo the young. Every time an English monarch visited Ireland, he or she held special receptions for children. Gonne and other Irish volunteers sponsored competing events, handing out candies and other treats for patriotic youngsters. "Dublin never witnessed anything so marvelous," enthused one home rule supporter, "as the procession . . . of thirty thousand school children who refused to be bribed into parading before the Queen of England."

Speaking Gaelic instead of English, singing Gaelic songs, using Catholicism as a rallying point, and generally reconstructing an "Irish way of life," the promoters of Irish culture threw into question the educated class's preference for everything English. This cultural agenda took political shape with the founding in 1905 of Sinn Fein ("Ourselves Alone"), a group that strove for complete Irish independence. In 1913, Parliament approved home rule for Ireland, but the outbreak of World War I prevented the legislation from taking effect and cut short dreams of independence.

Political Troubles in Italy. While British Liberals modified their policies to enhance social cohesion, their Italian counterparts drifted more rapidly from liberalism's moorings. After the struggles of the 1840s, '50s, and '60s, the newly unified Italy faced unexpected political troubles, with the north–south split and the consequences of economic modernization foremost among them. Corruption plagued Italy's constitutional monarchy, which had not yet developed either the secure parliamentary system of England or the authoritarian monarchy of Germany to guide its growing industrial economy. To forge a national consensus in the 1890s, Prime Minister Francesco Crispi (r. 1887–1891, 1893–1896) used patriotic rhetoric, bribes to gain support from the press, and imperial adventure, culminating in an attempt to conquer Ethiopia in 1896 after an earlier failure to do so. But at the battle of Adowa, the spirited Ethiopian army delivered a humiliating defeat and forced the Italians out. Crispi's attempts to unite the public behind him through imperialism failed and led instead to riots and strikes, followed by armed government repression.

A new prime minister, Giovanni Giolitti, who held office for three terms between 1903 and 1914, followed a policy known as *trasformismo* (from the word for "transform"), by which he used bribes, public works programs, and other benefits to localities to influence their deputies in parliament in the absence of well-developed political parties. Political opponents called Giolitti the "Minister of the Underworld" and accused him of preferring to buy the votes of local bosses rather than to spend money to develop the Italian economy. Giolitti's attempt to achieve consensus met instead with unrest in the rapidly industrializing cities of Turin and Milan and in the depressed agrarian south. Urban and rural workers alike demanded change, especially of the restricted suffrage that allowed only three million of more than eight million adult men to vote. Giolitti appeased the protesters by instituting social welfare programs and, in 1912, virtually complete manhood suffrage.

Anti-Semitism and Nationalism in Mass Politics

In the two decades leading up to World War I, anti-Semitism and nationalism suggested pat answers to complex questions. Leaders invoked these concepts to maintain interest-group support, to direct hostility away from themselves, and to win elections. The public responded vehemently, coming to see Jews as villains responsible for the perils of modern society and the nation-state as the hero in the struggle to survive. In both republics and monarchies, anti-Semitism and nationalism played key roles in mass politics by providing a focus for the creation of a radical right increasingly committed to combating the radical left of social democracy. Adopting the imperiled nation as its theme and using the Social Darwinist category of race to identify threats to the nation, the right fundamentally changed the older notion of nationalism based on liberal ideas of rights. Liberals had hoped that voting by the masses would make politics more harmonious as parliamentary debate and compromise smoothed out class differences. But anti-Semites and nationalists, scorning tolerant liberal values as effete, often preferred fights in the street to consensus building in parliaments.

Russification. The Russian tsar Nicholas II confronted modern life with an unswerving belief in orthodoxy in religion, autocracy in politics, and anti-Semitism and Russification in social policy. In this he followed the lead of his father, Alexander III, whose reign had opened in 1881 with an outbreak of vicious pogroms against Jews. Taught as a child to hate Jews, Nicholas stepped up the persecutions, and in his reign many high officials eagerly endorsed anti-Semitism to gain his favor. Pogroms became a regular feature of the Easter holiday in Russia, and Nicholas increasingly limited where Jews could live and how they could earn a living. He tightened restrictions on other groups and supported even more severe Russification, under which Poles, Ukranians, Tatars, and the empire's many other minorities were coerced into learning and speaking Russian, converting to the Russian Orthodox religion, and ignoring, at least publicly, their own cultural heritage.

The Dreyfus Affair in France. Violence toward Russian Jews shocked liberals in western Europe, but anti-Semitism was worming its way into mass politics across the West. The most notorious instance occurred in France and quickly was labeled the Dreyfus Affair. In 1894, a French army captain, Alfred Dreyfus, was charged with spying for Germany. Dreyfus had attended the elite École Polytechnique in Paris and become an officer in the French military, whose upper echelons were traditionally aristocratic, Catholic, and monarchist. Evidence that documents were being passed to Germany led the military command, amidst much other blundering, to fix on a Jewish officer—Dreyfus. His conviction and harsh exile to Devil's Island (off French Guiana in South America) failed to stop the espionage, but his plight aroused little immediate notice, either in the Jewish community or among the public at large.

Dreyfus's family protested his innocence, but the republican government maintained, "There is no Dreyfus Affair." Then several newspapers received proof that the army had used perjured testimony and fabricated documents to convict Dreyfus. In 1898, the celebrated French novelist Émile Zola published "J'accuse" ("I accuse") on the front page of a Paris daily. Zola cited a list of military lies and cover-ups perpetrated by highly placed government officials to create an illusion of Dreyfus's guilt. The article was explosive because it named names; but it was also a ringing defense of liberal principles in government. "I have but one passion, that of Enlightenment," wrote Zola.

**Public Opinion in the Dreyfus Affair:
"Ah! The Dirty Beast!"**

The French army used forged documents and perjured testimony to convict Captain Alfred Dreyfus of espionage. In a climate of escalating anti-Semitism, the conviction of a Jew struck many in the public as yet another narrow escape for the country. Only intense detective work by pro-Dreyfus activists and lobbying by Dreyfus's family convinced republican leaders that the system of equal rights was imperiled not by Dreyfus but by the bigotry of the army and those right-wing politicians who had trumped up the case against him. Photothèque des Musées de la Ville de Paris.

"J'accuse" caused the public to become violently divided over the question of Dreyfus's guilt or innocence.

Public riots, quarrels among families and friends, and denunciations of the army eroded public confidence in the republic and in French institutions. While republicans and the conservative opposition fought out the Dreyfus Affair, socialists made inroads into local government, winning control of mayoralties and city councils. The government finally pardoned Dreyfus in 1899 and then ousted from office the aristocratic and Catholic officers held responsible for what increasingly appeared a humiliation of the republic. Early in the twentieth century it ended religious teaching orders to ensure a public school system that was secular and that taught liberal values of tolerance. When the smoke cleared, republicans had gained control as well over the army. They had secured their triumph, however, by fanning the flames of anticlericalism and hatred. The Dreyfus Affair made anti-Semitism a standard tool of politics by producing hate-filled slogans that would be used repeatedly to blame Jews for various dissatisfactions, whether social, economic, or political. The racial side of Social Darwinism had passed from being part of social and imperial policy to the mainstream of politics.

The Right in Germany. The ruling elites in Germany also used anti-Semitism as a political weapon to garner support from those who feared the consequences of Germany's sudden and overwhelming industrialization. These elites, unlike French conservatives, still controlled the highest reaches of government and influenced the kaiser's policy. But the basis of their power was rapidly eroding, as agriculture, from which they drew their fortunes and social prestige, declined as a percentage of gross national product from 37 percent in the 1880s to only 25 percent early in the 1900s. As new opportunities lured rural people away from the land and as industrialists grew wealthier than they, the agrarian elites came to loathe industry and the working class. As a Berlin newspaper noted, "The agrarians' hate for cities . . . blinds them to the simplest needs and the most natural demands of the urban population." In contrast to Bismarck's astute wooing of the masses through social programs, William II's aristocracy often encouraged anti-Semitism, both in the corridors of power and in the streets.

Conservatives and a growing radical right claimed that Jews, who made up less than 1 percent of the German population, were responsible for the disruption of traditional society and charged them with being the main beneficiaries of economic change. In the 1890s, nationalist and anti-Semitic pressure groups flourished, spewing diatribes against Jews and "new women" but also against Social Democrats, whom they branded as internationalist, socially destructive, and unpatriotic. In the German elections of 1893, the new Agrarian League played to the fears of small farmers by accusing Jews of causing agricultural booms and busts. Candidates from other parties noted the popular response to these charges and made anti-Semitism and hate-filled speeches against an array of groups a regular feature of their campaigns, too.

These antiliberal movements profoundly affected German political life. First, instead of working for parliamentary compromise among various interests, they fueled extremist hatreds and violent feelings of nationalism. Second, instead of meeting the problems of rapid economic change with some measure of social unity and a rational program, these movements created classes of enemies whose defeat would allegedly cure all modern ills. Finally, the other great powers, facing severe economic competition from Germany for the first time and watching the increased saber rattling of its politicians, began to fear an outbreak of war at German hands and to prepare for it.

Ethnic Politics in Austria-Hungary. People in the Dual Monarchy also expressed their political and economic discontent in militantly nationalistic and anti-Semitic terms, but here nationalism had a different effect because of the presence of so many competing ethnic groups. Foremost among the nationalists were the Hungarians, who wanted autonomy for themselves while forcibly imposing Hungarian language and culture on all other ethnic groups in Hungary. The demands for greater Hungarian influence (or *Magyarization*, from Magyars, the principal ethnic group) seemed only just to them: Budapest was a thriving industrial city, and the export of Hungarian grain from the vast estates of the Hungarian nobility balanced the monarchy's foreign trade deficit. With vociferous nationalism and separatism mounting, the Independence Party provoked a series of crises in the Hungarian parliament that made a shambles of regular government processes.

Although capable of causing trouble for the empire, Hungarian nationalists, who mostly represented agrarian wealth, were vulnerable both to the resistance of other nationalities and to the demands of a growing industrial proletariat. On the land, the policy of Magyarization resulted in the formation of strong political groups among Slovaks, Romanians, and Ruthenians. Strikes erupted to protest horrendous labor conditions, and in the fall of 1905, one hundred thousand activists demonstrated in front of the Hungarian parliament for the vote. In the face of this resistance, Hungarians intensified Magyarization, even decreeing that all tombstones be engraved in Magyar. Emperor Francis Joseph temporarily brought the Hungarian nationalists to bay by threatening them with the introduction of universal manhood suffrage,

Principal Ethnic Groups in Austria-Hungary, c. 1900

which would allow the Magyars' lower-class opponents to vote. Although numerous nationality groups and the many Jews who settled in Budapest assimilated Magyar ways, the uncompromising and chauvinist nature of Hungarian policies toward both imperial government in Vienna and different ethnic groups within the empire made for instability throughout Austria-Hungary.

The insurgency of Hungary further changed the course of Habsburg politics by arousing other nationalists to intensify their demands for rights. Croats, Serbs, and other Slavic groups in the south organized and called for equality with the Hungarians. The central government gave more privileges to the Czechs and allowed them to increase the proportion of Czech officials in the government simply because growing industrial prosperity in their region gave them more influence. But every step toward recognition of Czech ethnicity provoked outrage from the traditionally dominant ethnic Germans, causing more tensions in the empire. When in 1897 Austria-Hungary decreed that government officials in the Czech region of the empire would have to know Czech as well as German, the Germans rioted.

Tensions mounted as politicians in Vienna linked the growing power of Hungarian and Czech politicians to Jews. A prime instigator of this "politics of the irrational"—as historians often label this ultranationalist and anti-Semitic phenomenon—was Karl Lueger (1844–1910), whose newly formed Christian Social Party attracted members from among the aristocracy, Catholics, artisans, shopkeepers, and white-collar workers. Thus Lueger used hatred to appeal to those groups for whom modern life meant a loss of privilege and security; in 1895, he was elected mayor of Vienna after using rough language and verbal abuse against Jews and ethnic groups in his campaign. Lueger's ethnic nationalism and anti-Semitism destabilized the multinational coexistence upon which Austria-Hungary was based.

By the turn of the century, influential parties of the right, built on aggressive nationalism and anti-Semitism, had appeared in Germany as well as Austria-Hungary. Jewishness became a symbol that Austrian and German politicians often harped on in their election campaigns, calling Jews the "sucking vampire" of modernity and blaming them for the unevenness of economic well-being, the tumult of migration and social dislocation, and just about anything else other people did not like. Rabid nationalism also inflamed the atmosphere, making politics a thing not of parliaments but of the streets, bloated with rhetoric and racism.

Jewish Responses to Modernity

Throughout the nineteenth century, the prevailing view in the West was that a Jewish identity was inferior to a Christian one, but this view provoked varying responses from Jews themselves. Jews in western Europe had responded to the spread of legal emancipation that followed in the wake of the Enlightenment by adopting liberal political and cultural values, intermarrying with Christians, and in some cases converting to Christianity. Such assimilation gave Jews the opportunity to give up the cultural ways that the dominant Christian culture saw as inferior. By contrast, Jews in Russia and Romania were increasingly singled out for persecution, legally disadvantaged, and forced to live in ghettos. If Jews wanted refuge, the cities of central and eastern Europe provided the best opportunity to succeed. They often adopted the cosmopolitan culture of Vienna or Magyar ways in Budapest. By 1900, Jews were both prominent in cultural and economic affairs in cities across the continent and discriminated against, even victimized, elsewhere.

Historians have debated why Jews disproportionately made such significant contributions to almost all fields of cultural and professional endeavor. Using the case of Jews in central Europe, some scholars maintain that in German culture such professions as medicine, the law, and the arts offered Jews a chance to demonstrate their acquisition of *Bildung*, which Germans prized above political participation. Many Jews also favored the German Empire because classical German culture seemed more appealing than the Catholic ritual they saw promoted by the Dual Monarchy of Austria-Hungary. Even escalating anti-Semitism did not stop Jews from dominating cultural achievement in Vienna, Budapest, and Prague. The celebrated composer Gustav Mahler, the budding writer Franz Kafka, and the pioneer of psychoanalysis Sigmund Freud were shaped in the crucible of Habsburg society.

Most Jews, however, were not so accomplished or prosperous as these cultural giants, and their escalating migration to the United States and other countries, in reaction to both pogroms and economic change, filled towns and cities with poor day laborers and struggling artisans (Map 25.1). Amidst this vast migration and continued persecution, a spirit of Jewish nationalism arose. "Why should we be any less worthy than any other . . . people," one leader asked. "What about our nation, our language, our land?" Jews began organizing resistance to pogroms and anti-Semitic politics, and intellectuals drew upon Jewish folklore, philology, and history to establish a national identity parallel to that of other Europeans.

In the 1880s, the Ukrainian physician Leon Pinsker, seeing the Jews' lack of national territory as fundamental to the persecution heaped on them, advocated the migration of Jews to Palestine. In 1896, Theodor Herzl (1860–1904), strongly influenced by Pinsker, published *The Jewish State*, which called not simply for migration but for the creation of a Jewish nation-state. A Hungarian-born Jew, Herzl experienced anti-Semitism firsthand as a Viennese journalist and a writer in Paris during the Dreyfus Affair. As an alternative to shedding Jewish identity, he became driven to found a Jewish state, searching Europe for financial backing, technical advice, and a political structure for the venture. His constituency should have been prosperous Jews, but many of them had assimilated and thought his ideas mad. However, with the

MAP 25.1 Jewish Migrations in the Late Nineteenth Century
Pogroms in eastern Europe, increasingly violent anti-Semitism across the continent, and the search for opportunity led Jews to many parts of the world. They migrated to European cities and, as Zionism progressed, to Palestine. The development of manufacturing in the United States offered a wealth of new opportunities, especially the chance to live where the rule of law was somewhat better established than in Russia.

support of poorer eastern European Jews, he succeeded in calling the first International Zionist Congress (1897), which endorsed settlement in Palestine and helped gain financial backing from the Rothschild banking family. By 1914, some 85,000 Jews had resettled in Palestine. Nonetheless, from many perspectives European domestic politics remained explosive.

❖ European Imperialism Challenged

Inflamed nationalism across the West made it difficult for nations to calm domestic politics and the traumas of modern industrial life. In 1897, the poet Rudyard Kipling marked the fiftieth anniversary of Queen Victoria's reign with "Recessional," a somber poem comparing the British Empire to ancient cities whose glory had long since faded:

> *Far-called our navies melt away—*
> *On dune and headland sinks the fire—*
> *Lo, all our pomp of yesterday*
> *Is one with Nineveh and Tyre.*

Kipling's turn to pessimistic sentimentalism was apt, first because holding imperial territory was aggravating relations among the European powers and second because colonized peoples were challenging European control. Japan had become an Asian power, and nationalist movements for independence were gaining strength, a development that eventually led to new rebellions against European rule.

The Trials of Empire

After centuries of global expansion, imperial adventure soured for Britain and France as the twentieth century opened, and being an imperial power proved difficult for such newcomers as Italy and Germany. "Where thirty years ago there existed one sensitive spot in our relations with France, or Germany, or Russia," the British economist J. A. Hobson wrote in 1902, "there are a dozen now; diplomatic strains are of almost monthly occurrence between the Powers." Increasing competition among a greater number of nations for colonies and escalating tensions between the French and British in Africa and elsewhere had raised serious questions about the future of imperialism. For their part, colonized people were fighting back with stubborn vigor.

Boer War. Accustomed to crushing resistance to their imperial ambitions, the British experienced a bloody defeat in 1896, when Cecil Rhodes, prime minister of the Cape Colony in southern Africa, directed his right-hand man, Dr. Leander Jameson, to lead a raid into the neighboring territory of the Transvaal. The foray was intended to stir up trouble between the Boers, descendants of early Dutch settlers, and the more recent immigrants from Britain and elsewhere who had come to southern Africa in search of gold and other riches. Rhodes hoped the raid would justify a British takeover of the Transvaal and the Orange Free State, which the Boers independently controlled. The Boers, however, easily routed the raiders, forcing Rhodes to resign in disgrace. The defeat was a blow to the British public, whose patriotism featured imperial pride as a cornerstone.

Other Europeans gloated over the British loss. Kaiser William II telegraphed his congratulations to Transvaal president Paul Kruger for "maintaining the independence of the country against attacks from without." The British were not accustomed to, nor did they accept defeat easily: for the next three years they fought the Boer War directly against the Transvaal and the Orange Free State. Britain finally annexed the area after defeating the Boers in 1902, but the cost of war—in money, destruction, and loss of life—horrified many Britons and caused them to see imperialism as a burden (Map 25.2).

Setbacks and Newcomers. Almost simultaneously, Spain lost Cuba, Puerto Rico, and the Philippines as a result of its defeat in the Spanish-American War of 1898. Urged on the United States by the expansionist-minded Theodore Roosevelt, then assistant secretary of the navy, and the inflammatory daily press, this war revealed the fragility of established European empires and the unpredictability of imperial fortunes. Even the triumphant United States, encouraged by Kipling to "take up the white man's burden" by bringing the benefits of Western civilization to those liberated from Spain, had to wage a bloody war against the Filipinos, who wanted independence, not just another imperial ruler. Reports of American brutality in the Philippines further disillusioned the European public, who liked to imagine native peoples joyously welcoming the bearers of civilization.

Despite these setbacks, emerging powers had an emotional stake in gaining colonies. In the early twentieth century, Italian public figures bragged about the Italians becoming Nietzschean supermen by conquering Africa and restoring Italy to its ancient position of world domination. After its disastrous war against Ethiopia in 1896, Italy won a costly victory over Turkey in Libya. But these wars roused Italian hopes for national grandeur only to dash them.

Germany likewise demanded a place at the imperial table and an end to the virtual British-French monopoly of colonial power. Foremost among the new competitors for empire, German bankers and businessmen were ensconced throughout Asia, the Middle East, and Latin America. Colonial skirmishes Germany had once ignored became matters of utmost concern. But Germany, too, instead of winning unalloyed glory, met humiliation and constant problems, especially in its dealings with Britain and France. As Italy and Germany aggressively pursued new

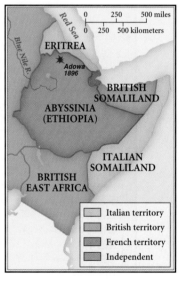

The Struggle for Ethiopia, 1896

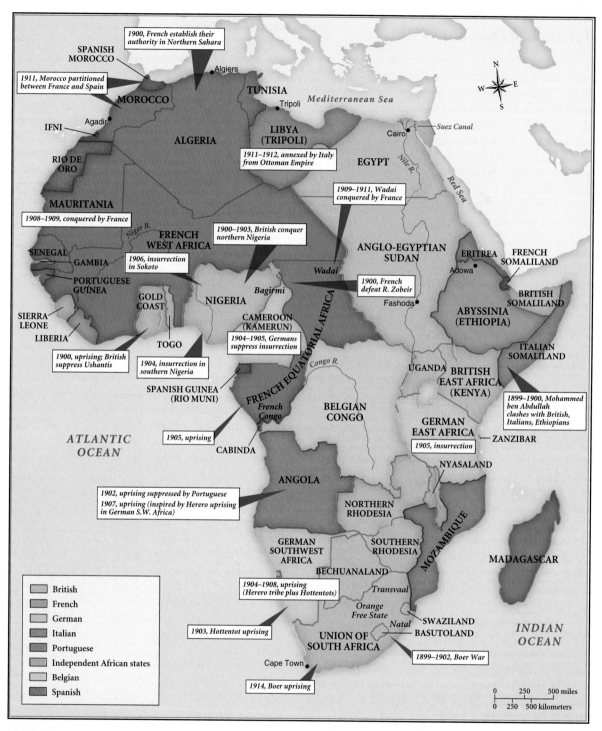

MAP 25.2 Africa in 1914

Uprisings intensified in Africa in the early twentieth century as Europeans tried both to consolidate their rule through bureaucratization and military action and to extract more wealth from the Africans. At the same time as Europeans were putting down the rebellions against their rule, a pan-African movement arose, attempting to unite Africans as one people. As in Asia and the Middle East, the more the colonial powers tried to impose their will, the greater the political forces—including the force of political ideas—that took shape against them.

territory, the rules set for imperialism at the Congress of Berlin a generation earlier gave way to increasingly heated rivalry and nationalist fury.

Japan Victorious. Europeans' confident approach to imperialism was also eroded by the rise of Japan as a power. The Japanese had started building an empire by invading the Chinese island of Formosa (present-day Taiwan) in 1874 and continued by forcing trading treaties on Korea in 1876 (Map 25.3). In 1894, Japan sparked the Sino-Japanese War, which ended China's domination of Korea. The Eu-

ropean powers, alarmed at Japan's victory, forced it to relinquish other gains, a move that outraged and affronted the Japanese. Japan's insecurity had risen with Russian expansion to the east and south in Asia. Pushing into eastern Asia, the Russians had built the Trans-Siberian Railroad through Manchuria and sponsored anti-Japanese groups in Korea, making the peninsula appear, as a Japanese military leader put it, like "a dagger thrust at the heart of Japan." Angered by the continuing presence of Russian troops in Manchuria, the Japanese attacked tsarist forces at Port Arthur in 1904.

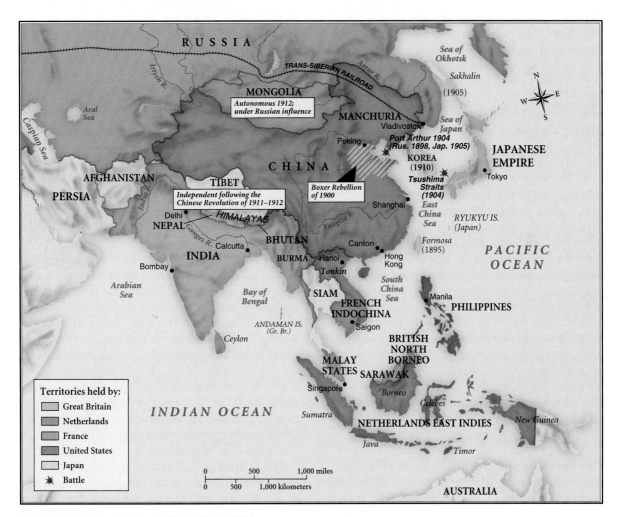

MAP 25.3 Imperialism in Asia, 1894–1914
Most of the modernizing states converged on Asia. The established imperialists came to blows in East Asia as they struggled for influence in China and as they met a formidable new rival—Japan. Simultaneously liberation movements like the Boxers were taking shape, committed to throwing off restraints imposed by foreign powers. Ultimately in 1911, Sun Yat-Sen overthrew the Qing dynasty that had left China unprepared to resist foreign takeover and started the country on a different course.

The conservative Russian military proved inept in the ensuing Russo-Japanese War, even though it often had better equipment or strategic advantage. In an astonishing display of poor leadership, Russia's Baltic Fleet sailed halfway around the globe only to be completely destroyed in the battle of Tsushima Straits (1905). Opening an era of Japanese domination in East Asian politics, the victory was the first by a non-European nation over a European great power in the modern age, and it gave the West an additional reason to fear the future. As one English general ominously observed of the Russian defeat: "I have today seen the most stupendous spectacle it is possible for the mortal brain to conceive—Asia advancing, Europe falling back." Japan went on to annex Korea in 1910 and to eye other areas in which to challenge the West.

Russian Empire Threatened

Russia, a mighty empire that had expanded southward in Asia and settled much of Siberia during the nineteenth century, concealed its weaknesses well. In reality it tottered on the brink of chaos in 1905 as revolution erupted alongside military defeat. State-sponsored industrialization in the 1890s had made the country appear modern to outside observers, and the Russification policy imitated Western-style state building by attempting to impose a unified, national culture on Russia's diverse population. Industrialization, however, also produced urban unrest as Marxist and union activists incited workers to demand better conditions. In 1903, skilled workers led strikes in Baku, where Armenians and Tatars united in a demonstration that showed how urbanization and Russification could facilitate political action among the lower classes. These and other worker protests challenged the autocratic regime.

The Revolution of 1905.   The secret police kept a lid on discontent by spying on people and by organizing its own unions staffed by police informants. In January 1905, a crowd led by one of these informants gathered one Sunday outside the tsar's Winter Palace in St. Petersburg to try to make Nicholas aware of brutal working conditions. Instead of allowing the demonstration to pass, troops guarding the palace shot into the crowd, killing hundreds and wounding thousands.

Thus began the Revolution of 1905, and news of Bloody Sunday spurred other urban workers to rebel. In almost a year of turmoil across Russia, workers struck over wages, hours, and factory conditions and demanded political representation in the government. Delegates from revolutionary parties such as the Social Democrats and the Socialist Revolutionaries encouraged more direct blows against the central government, but workers rejected their leadership and organized their own councils, called *soviets*. In February, Grand Duke Sergei, the tsar's uncle, was assassinated; in June sailors on the battleship *Potemkin* mutinied; in October a massive railroad strike ground rail transportation to a halt

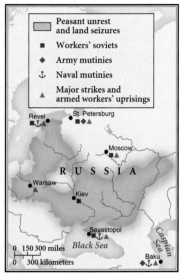

Russian Revolution of 1905

and the Baltic states and Transcaucasia rebelled; and in November uprisings broke out in Moscow. The tsar's Cossack troops kept killing strikers across the country, but their deaths only fueled the protest.

Because Nicholas II, almost alone among European monarchs, ruled his empire as an absolutist unhampered by a constitution, the revolution coalesced artisans and industrial workers, peasants, professionals, and the upper classes against the Russian nobility. Using the unrest to press their goals, liberals from *zemstvos* (local councils) and the *intelligentsia* (a Russian word for well-educated elites) demanded political reform, in particular the replacement of autocracy with a constitutional monarchy and representative legislature. They believed the reliance on censorship and the secret police that was characteristic of Romanov rule relegated Russia to the ranks of the most backward states. Preferring a military solution, Nicholas responded with half-hearted reforms—a response that triggered more street fighting. In the words of one protester, the tsar's attitude turned "yesterday's benighted slaves into decisive warriors."

Attempts at Political Reform.   Impelled by the continuing violence, the tsar created a representative body—the Duma. Although very few could vote for representatives to the Duma, its mere existence, coupled with the right of public political debate, liberalized government and allowed people to present their grievances to a responsive body. As important, during this time political parties took shape. After these constitutional parties threw their support to the reorganized government, revolutionary activity abated and the tsar's troops crushed the remaining pockets of resistance.

People soon began to wonder, however, if anything had really changed. From 1907 to 1917, the Duma convened, but twice when the tsar disliked its recommendations he sent the delegates home and forced new elections. Prime Minister Pyotr Stolypin (1863–1911), a successful administrator and landowner, was determined to eliminate the sources of discontent by ending the *mir* system of communal farming and taxation and canceling the land redemption payments that had burdened the peasants since their emancipation in 1861. He also made government loans available to peasants, who were then able to purchase land and to own farms outright. Although these reforms did not eradicate rural poverty, they did allow people to move to the cities in search of jobs and created a larger group of independent peasants. By 1917, some two-thirds of the peasantry had taken steps to gain title to their land, and 10 percent had acquired consolidated holdings.

Stolypin succeeded only partially in his other goal of restoring law and order. He clamped down on revolutionary organizations, executing their members by hanging them with "Stolypin neckties." The government urged more pogroms and stifled ethnic unrest by stepping up Russification. But rebels continued to assassinate government officials—four thousand were killed or wounded in 1906–1907—and Stolypin himself was assassinated in 1911. Stolypin's reforms had promoted peasant well-being, which encouraged what one historian has called a "new peasant assertiveness." The industrial proletariat also grew, and another round of strikes broke out, culminating in a general strike in St. Petersburg in 1914.

Despite the creation of the Duma and other reforms, the imperial government and the conservative nobility had no solution to the ongoing social turmoil and felt little inclination to share power. Their ineffectual response to the Revolution of 1905 would foster an even greater revolution in 1917.

Growing Resistance to Colonial Domination

The Japanese military victory over two important dynasties—the Qing in China and the Romanov in Russia—within a single decade had repercussions in the colonies, further eroding the security Westerners had once found in imperialism. The Japanese victories and the ability of Russian revolutionaries to force a great European power to reform inspired nationalist-minded opponents to European imperialism. The success of a non-Western, constitutional government fed protest throughout the globe.

Boxers in China. Uprisings began in China after its 1895 defeat by Japan forced the ruling Qing dynasty to grant more economic concessions to Western powers. Humiliated by these events, peasants organized into secret societies to restore Chinese integrity. One organization, based on beliefs in the spiritual values of boxing, was the Society of the Righteous and Harmonious Fists (or Boxers), whose members maintained that ritual boxing would protect them from a variety of evils, including bullets. Encouraged by the Qing ruler Dowager Empress Tz'u-hsi (Cixi) (1835–1908) and desperate because of worsening economic conditions, the Boxers rebelled in 1900, massacring the missionaries and Chinese Christians to whom they attributed China's troubles. The colonial powers put down the Boxer Rebellion and encouraged the Chinese troops in their service to ravage the areas in which the Boxers operated. Defeated once more, the Chinese were compelled to pay a huge indemnity, to destroy many of their defensive fortifications, and to allow more extensive foreign military occupation.

The Boxer Rebellion thoroughly discredited the Qing dynasty; in 1911 a successful group of revolutionaries finally overthrew the dynasty and the next year declared China a republic. Their leader, Sun Yat-Sen (1866–1925), who had been educated in Hawaii and Japan, used Western concepts to express traditional Chinese values while simultaneously promoting a cluster of Western programs: "nationalism, democracy, and socialism." Together they added up to freedom from the Qing dynasty, revival of the Chinese tradition of correctness in behavior between governors and the governed, modern economic reform, and a threat to European channels of trade and domination.

Boxer Rebellion
The Boxers sought to fortify the Chinese government against the many powers threatening its survival. They used brightly colored placards to spread information about their mission and its importance and to build support. The placards also depicted battles with imperialist forces and showed Boxer triumphs over foreign missionaries and other menacing groups. Photo courtesy Thames & Hudson, Ltd., London.

Sun's stirring leadership and the changes brought about by China's revolution seriously derailed the course of Western imperialism.

Nationalists in India.   In India, the Japanese victory over Russia and the Revolution of 1905 stimulated politicians to take a more radical course than that offered by the Indian National Congress. A Hindu leader, B. G. Tilak (1856–1920), fervently anti-British and less moderate than Congress reformers, preached blatant noncooperation: "We shall not give them assistance to collect revenue and keep peace. We shall not assist them in fighting beyond the frontiers or outside India with Indian blood and money." Tilak promoted Hindu customs, asserted their distinctiveness from British ways, and inspired violent rebellion in his followers. This brand of nationalism broke with that based on assimilating to British culture and promoting gradual change. Trying to repress Tilak, the British sponsored the Muslim League, a rival nationalist group favored for its restraint and its potential to divide Muslim nationalists from Hindus in the Congress.

Faced with political activism on many fronts, however, Britain conceded the right to vote based on property ownership and to representation in ruling councils. Because the independence movement had not fully reached the masses, these small concessions temporarily maintained British power by appeasing the best-educated and most influential dissidents among the upper and middle classes. But the British hold on India was weakening.

Young Turks in the Ottoman Empire.   Revolutionary nationalism was simultaneously sapping the Ottoman Empire, which for centuries had controlled much of the Mediterranean. In the nineteenth century, several rebellions had plagued Ottoman rule, and more erupted early in the twentieth century because of growing resistance to the empire and to European influence. Just as the Habsburgs used the transnational appeal of Catholicism to quash nationalist aspirations, similarly Sultan Abdul Hamid II (r. 1876–1909) tried to revitalize the multiethnic empire by using Islam to counteract the rising nationalism of the Serbs, Bulgarians, and Macedonians. Instead he unwittingly provoked a burgeoning Turkish nationalism in Constantinople itself. Turkish nationalists rejected the sultan's pan-Islamic solution and built their movement on the uniqueness of their culture, history, and language, as many European ethnic groups were doing. Using the findings of Western scholarship, they first traced the history of the group they called Turks to change the word *Turk* from one of derision to one of pride. Nationalists also tried to purge their language of words from Arabic and Persian, and they popularized the folklore of rural Turkish peoples scattered across territories from eastern Europe through Asia. The events of 1904–1905 electrified these nationalists with the vision of a modern Turkey becoming "the Japan of the Middle East," as they called it. In 1908, a group of nationalists called the Young Turks took control of the government in Constantinople, which had been fatally weakened by nationalist agitation and by the empire's economic dependence on Western financiers and businessmen.

The Young Turks' triumph motivated other groups in the Middle East and the Balkans to demand an end to Ottoman domination in their regions as well. These groups adopted Western values and platforms, and some, such as the Egyptians, had strong contingents of feminist-nationalists who mobilized women to work for independence. But the Young Turks, often aided by European powers with financial and political interests in the region, brutally tried to repress the uprisings in Egypt, Syria, and the Balkans that their own success had encouraged.

Their rebellions became part of the tumult shaping international relations in the decade before World War I. Empires, whether old or young, were the scene of growing resistance in the wake of Japanese, Russian, and Turkish events. In German East Africa, colonial forces countered native resistance in 1905 with a scorched-earth policy, which eventually killed more than 100,000 Africans. The French closed the University of Hanoi, executed Indochinese intellectuals, and deported thousands of suspected nationalists merely to maintain a tenuous grip on Indochina. A French general stationed there summed up the fears of many colonial rulers in the new century: "The gravest fact of our actual political situation in Indochina is not the recent trouble in Tonkin [or] the plots undertaken against us but in the muted but growing hatred that our subjects show toward us more and more."

❖ Roads to War

These international developments simultaneously aggravated competition among the great powers and caused Western nationalism in its many varieties to swell. In the spring of 1914, U.S. president Woodrow Wilson (1856–1924) sent his trusted adviser Colonel House abroad to assess the tensions among the European powers. "It is militarism run stark mad," House reported, adding that he foresaw an "awful cataclysm" ahead. Government spending on what people called the "arms race" had stimulated European economies; but arms were not stockpiled only for economic growth. As early as the mid-1890s, the socialist Eduard Bernstein had called the situation a "cold war" because the hostile atmosphere made physical combat seem imminent. By 1914, the air was even more charged, with militant nationalism in the Balkan states and conflicts in domestic politics also setting the stage for war. Although historians have long debated whether World War I could have been avoided, they have never reached a consensus. Considering the feverish background of prewar change, they have had to content themselves with tracing the steps Europeans took along the road toward mass destruction.

Competing Alliances and Clashing Ambitions

As the twentieth century opened, the Triple Alliance that Bismarck had negotiated among Germany, Austria-Hungary, and Italy confronted an opposing alliance between France and Russia, created in the 1890s. The wild card in the diplomatic scenario was Great Britain, traditional enemy of France, nowhere more than in the contest for colonial power. Constant rivals in Africa, Britain and France edged to the brink of war in 1898 at Fashoda in the Sudan. The French government, however, backed away and both nations were frightened into getting along for mutual self-interest. To prevent another Fashoda, they entered into secret agreements, the first of which (1904) guaranteed British claims in Egypt and French claims in Morocco. This agreement marked the beginning of the British-French alliance called the *Entente Cordiale*. Despite the alliance, Britain's response to a European war remained in question; even French statesmen feared that their ally might remain neutral.

Germany's Imperial Demands. From being a "satisfied" nation under Bismarck, who had worked to balance great-power interests and had spared Germany from the draining fight for colonies, Germany under William II became dissatisfied with its international status and inflamed rather than calmed the diplomatic atmosphere. Convinced of British hostility toward France and emboldened by Germany's growing industrial might, the kaiser used the opportunity presented by the defeat of France's ally Russia to contest French claims in Morocco. A man who boasted and blustered and was easily prodded to rash actions by his advisers, William landed in Morocco in 1905, thus challenging French predominance in what became known as the First Moroccan Crisis.

To resolve the situation, an international conference met in Spain in 1906, where Germany confidently expected to gain concessions and new territories. Instead the powers, now including the United States, decided to support French rule. The French and British military, faced with German aggression in Morocco, drew closer together.

Germany found itself weak diplomatically and strong economically, a situation that made its leaders more determined to compete for territory abroad. When the French finally took over Morocco in 1911, Germany triggered the Second Moroccan Crisis by sending a gunboat to the port of Agadir and demanding concessions from the French. This time no power—not even Austria-Hungary—backed the German move. No one acknowledged this dominant country's might, nor did the constant demands for recognition encourage anyone to do so. The British and French now made binding military provisions for the deployment of their forces in case of war, thus strengthening the Entente Cordiale. Smarting from its setbacks on the world stage, Germany refocused its sights on its role on the continent and on its own alliances.

Crises in the Balkans. Germany's stream of territorial claims along with public uncertainty about the binding force of alliances unsettled Europe, particularly the Balkans. German statesmen began envisioning the creation of a *Mitteleuropa* that included central Europe, the Balkans, and Turkey under their sway. The Habsburgs, now firmly backed by Germany, judged that expansion into the

MAP 25.4 The Balkans, 1908–1914

Balkan peoples—mixed in religion, ethnicity, and political views—were successful in developing and asserting their desire for independence, especially in the First Balkan War, which claimed territory from the Ottoman Empire. Their increased autonomy sparked rivalries among them and continued to attract attention from the great powers. Three empires in particular—the Russian, Ottoman, and Austro-Hungarian—simultaneously sought greater influence for themselves in the region, which became a powderkeg of competing ambitions.

Balkans and the resulting addition of even more ethnic groups would weaken the claims of any single ethnic minority in the Dual Monarchy. Russia, however, saw itself as the protector of Slavs in the region and wanted to replace the Ottomans as the dominant Balkan power, especially after Japan had crushed its hopes for expansion to the east. Austria's swift annexation of Bosnia-Herzegovina during the Young Turk revolt in 1908 enraged not only the Russians but the Serbs as well, because these southern Slavs wanted Bosnia as part of an enlarged Serbia. The Balkans thus whetted many appetites (Map 25.4).

Even without the greedy eyes cast on the Balkans by outside powers, the situation would have been extremely complex given the tensions created by political modernity. The nineteenth century had seen the rise of nationalism and ethnicity as the basis for the unity of the nation-state, and by late in the century ethnic loyalty challenged dynastic power in the Balkans. Greece, Serbia, Bulgaria, Romania, and Montenegro emerged as autonomous states, almost all of them composed of several ethnicities as well as Orthodox Christians, Roman Catholics, and Muslims. All these states sought more Ottoman and Habsburg territory that included their own ethnic group—a complicated desire given the complex ethnic structure everywhere.

In the First Balkan War, in 1912, Serbia, Bulgaria, Greece, and Montenegro joined forces to gain Macedonia and Albania from the Ottomans. The victors divided up their booty, with Bulgaria gaining the most territory, but soon they turned against one another. Serbia, Greece, and Montenegro contested Bulgarian gains in the Second Balkan War in 1913. Much to Austrian dismay, these allies won a quick victory, though Austria-Hungary managed in the peace terms to prevent Serbia from annexing parts of Albania. Grievances between the Habsburgs and the Serbs now seemed irreconcilable. Moreover, the peace conditions did not demilitarize the region, and Balkan peoples, especially angry Slavs who continued to look to Russia for help, imagined further challenges to Austria-Hungary. The Balkans had become a perilous region along whose borders both Austria-Hungary, as ruler of many Slavs, and Russia as their protector stationed increasing numbers of troops. The situation tempted strategists to think that a quick war there—something like Bismarck's wars—could resolve tension and uncertainty.

Gute Freunde, getreue Nachbarn.

Good Friends, Trusted Neighbors (1909)
This cartoon provides a vision of European countries turning from neighborliness to warfare. By trying to keep up with one another's stock of arms, they have soon utterly destroyed the neighborhood—a sober warning from a German newspaper that within five years would prove to be an accurate prediction. The war would do more than physical damage, but this was not to be foreseen.
Mary Evans Picture Library.

The Race to Arms

Between the Napoleonic Wars of the early nineteenth century and World War I a hundred years later, technology, nationalism, and imperialism transformed the practice of and rationale for war. During that period global rivalries, aspirations for national greatness, and in some cases even the struggle for independence made constant readiness for war seem necessary. On the seas and in foreign lands the colonial powers battled to establish control, and they developed railroad, telegraph, and telephone networks everywhere to link their conquests and to move troops as well as commerce. Governments began to conscript ordinary citizens for periods of two to six years into large standing armies, in contrast to smaller eighteenth-century forces that had served the more limited military goals of the time.

By 1914, escalating tensions in Europe boosted the annual intake of conscripts: Germany, France, and Russia called up 250,000 or more troops each year; Austria-Hungary and Italy, about 100,000. The per capita expenditure on the military rose in all the major powers between 1890 and 1914; the proportion of national budgets devoted to defense in 1910 was lowest in Austria-Hungary at 10 percent and highest in Germany at 45 percent.

The modernization of weaponry also transformed warfare. Swedish arms manufacturer Alfred Nobel patented dynamite and developed a kind of gunpowder that improved the accuracy of guns and produced a less clouded battlefield environment by reducing smoke from the process of firing. The industrial revolution in chemicals affected long-range artillery, which by 1914 could fire on targets as far as six miles away. Greater accuracy and heavy firepower made military offensives more difficult to win than in the past because neither side could overcome such weaponry by attacking on foot or on horseback. Military leaders devised strategies to protect their armies from overwhelming firepower; in the Russo-Japanese War, trenches and barbed wire blanketed the front around Port Arthur. New weapons were used in that conflict and in the Boer War, including howitzers, Mauser rifles, and Hotchkiss machine guns. Vickers in Britain, Creusot in France, Krupp in Germany, and Skoda in Austria-Hungary manufactured ever-growing stockpiles of these weapons.

Naval construction also played a sensational role in nationalist politics. To defend against more powerful, accurate weaponry, ships were made out of metal rather than wood after the mid-nineteenth century. In 1905, the English launched the H.M.S. *Dreadnought*, a warship with unprecedented firepower and the centerpiece of a program

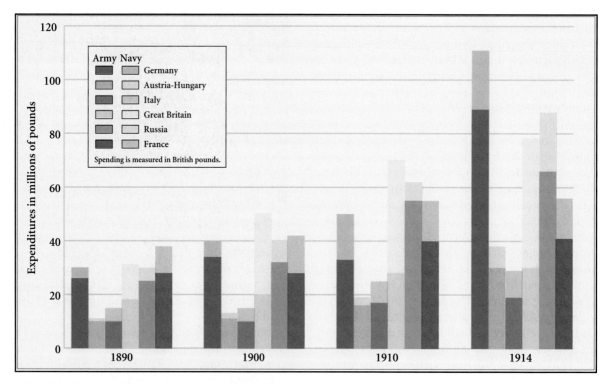

FIGURE 25.1 The Growth in Armaments, 1890–1914

The turn of the century saw the European powers engaged in a massive arms race. Several comparisons offer themselves, particularly the resources newly devoted to navies and the soaring defense spending of the Germans. Historians often ask whether better diplomacy could have prevented the outbreak of world war in 1914. The enormous military buildup, however, made some people living in the early twentieth century as well as some later historians see war as inevitable.

The Hammond Atlas of the Twentieth Century. (London: Times Books, 1996) 29.

to update the navy by constructing at least seven battleships per year. Germany had been following British navy building step by step and had made itself not just a land but a sea power. Grand Admiral Alfred von Tirpitz (1849–1930) encouraged the insecure William II to see the navy as the essential ingredient in making Germany a world power and oversaw the modernization and immense buildup of the fleet. Tirpitz admired the American naval theorist Alfred Thayer Mahan (1840–1914) and planned to build bases as far away as the Pacific, following Mahan's conclusion that command of the seas had historically been the key factor in determining international power. German ambitions, especially Tirpitz's drive to build battleships, alarmed the British and further motivated them to ally with France in the Entente Cordiale. Britain raised its naval spending from $50 million per year in the 1870s to $130 million in 1900; Germany, from $8.75 million to $37.5 million; France, from $37 million to $62.5 million (Figure 25.1). The Germans announced the fleet buildup as "a peaceful policy," but, like the British buildup, it led only to a hostile international climate and intense competition in weapons manufacture.

Because military buildup could help a country's social and economic stability by providing jobs and profit, military policy was made with an eye to internal politics. When critics of the arms race suggested a temporary "naval holiday" to stop British and German building, British officials opposed the moratorium by warning that it "would throw innumerable men on the pavement." Colonial leagues, nationalist organizations, and other patriotic groups lobbied for military spending, while enthusiasts in government publicized large navies as beneficial to international trade and domestic industry.

Public relations campaigns helped generate popular support for the arms race as they had for colonial expansion. When Tirpitz wanted to enlarge the German fleet, he made sure the press connected the buildup to the cause of national power and pride. The press accused Social Democrats, who wanted an equitable tax system more proportionate to wealth, of being unpatriotic. The Conservative Party in Great Britain, eager for more battleships, made popular the slogan "We want eight and we won't wait."

Despite the massive expenditures needed to establish military might in 1914, most of the public was convinced of the relationship between military power and national prestige and believed war was on its way to settle lingering international tensions. The remarks of Marshall Joseph Joffre (1852–1931) of France typified the sentiments of many military men of the time. When asked in 1912 if he thought about war, he said that he did constantly. "We shall have war," he maintained. "I will make it. I will win it."

1914: War Erupts

June 28, 1914, began as an ordinary day for Austrian Archduke Francis Ferdinand (1863–1914) and his wife, Sophie, as they ended a state visit to Sarajevo in Bosnia. The archduke, in full military regalia, was riding in a motorcade to bid farewell to various officials when a group of young Serb nationalists threw bombs in an unsuccessful assassination attempt. The full danger did not register,

Archduke Francis Ferdinand and His Wife in Sarajevo, June 1914
Archduke Francis Ferdinand, heir to the Austro-Hungarian monarchy, was a thorn in the side of many politicians because he did not want to favor Hungarian interests over other ethnic ones in his kingdom. His own family life was also unusual for royalty in those days in that his wife, Sophie, and he had married for love and did not like to be apart. Thus the couple were traveling together to Bosnia in 1914 and were jointly assassinated—the immediate prelude to the outbreak of World War I.
Mary Evans Picture Library.

IMPORTANT DATES

1894–1895 Japan defeats China in the Sino-Japanese War

1894–1899 Dreyfus Affair lays bare anti-Semitism in France

1899–1902 Boer War fought between Dutch descendants and the British in South African states

1900 Sigmund Freud publishes *The Interpretation of Dreams*

1901 Irish National Theater established by Maud Gonne and William Butler Yeats; death of Queen Victoria

1903 Emmeline Pankhurst founds the Women's Social and Political Union to fight for woman suffrage in Great Britain

1904–1905 Japan defeats Russia in the Russo-Japanese War

1905 Revolution erupts in Russia; violence forces Nicholas II to establish an elected body, the Duma; Albert Einstein publishes his "Special Theory of Relativity"

1906 Women receive the vote in Finland

1907 Pablo Picasso launches cubist painting with *Les Demoiselles d'Avignon*

1908 Young Turks revolt against rule by the sultan in the Ottoman Empire

1911–1912 Revolutionaries overthrow the Qing dynasty and declare China a republic

1914 Assassination of the Austrian archduke Francis Ferdinand and his wife by a Serbian nationalist precipitates World War I

and after a stop the archduke and his wife set out again. In the crowd was another nationalist, Gavrilo Princip, who for several weeks had traveled clandestinely to reach this destination, dreaming of reuniting his homeland of Bosnia-Herzegovina with Serbia and smuggling weapons with him to accomplish his end. The unprotected and unsuspecting couple became Princip's victims, as he shot both dead.

Some in the Habsburg government saw an opportunity to put down the Serbians once and for all. Evidence showed that Princip had received arms and information from Serbian officials, who directed the terrorist organization Black Hand from within the government. Endorsing a quick defeat of Serbia, German statesmen and military

leaders urged the Austrians to be unyielding and reiterated promises of support in case of war. While many heads of state and politicians were vacationing, the Austrians sent an ultimatum to the Serbian government, demanding public disavowals of terrorism, suppression of terrorist groups, and the participation of Austrian officials in an investigation of the crime. The ultimatum was severe. "You are setting Europe ablaze," the Russian foreign minister remarked of the humiliating demands made upon a sovereign state. Yet the Serbs were conciliatory, accepting all the terms except the presence of Austrian officials in the investigation. Kaiser William was pleased: "A great moral success for Vienna! All reason for war is gone." His relief proved unfounded. Austria-Hungary, confident of German backing, used the Serbs' resistance to only one of the ultimatum's terms as the pretext for declaring war against Serbia on July 28.

Complex and ineffectual maneuvering now consumed statesmen, some of whom tried very hard to avoid war. The tsar and the kaiser sent pleading letters to one another not to start a European war. Sir Edward Grey, British foreign secretary, proposed an all-European conference to no avail. The German chancellor as well as the kaiser displayed firm support for Austria in hopes of convincing the French and British to shy away from the war. The failure of either to fight, German officials believed, would subsequently keep Russia from mobilizing. At the same time, German military leaders had become fixed on fighting a short, preemptive war that would provide territorial gains leading toward the goal of a *Mitteleuropa*; simultaneously they hoped that martial law would justify arresting the leadership of the German Social Democratic Party, which threatened conservative rule.

The European press caught the war fever of the expansionist, imperialist, and other pro-war organizations, even as many governments were torn over what to do. Likewise, military leaders, especially in Germany and Austria-Hungary where there was less supervision of the military by the civilian government, promoted mobilization rather than diplomacy in the last days of July. The Austrians declared war and then ordered mobilization on July 31 without fear of a Russian attack. They did so in full confidence of German military aid, because as early as 1909 the German chief of staff Helmuth von Moltke had promised that his government would defend Austria-Hungary, believing

MAPPING THE WEST Europe at the Outbreak of World War I, August 1914

All the powers expected a great, swift victory when war broke out. Sharing borders, many saw a chance to increase their territories; and as rivals for trade and empire, they were almost all convinced that war would bring them many advantages. But if European nations appeared well prepared and invincible at the start of the war, relatively few would survive the conflict intact.

Russia would not dare intervene. But Nicholas II ordered the Russian army to mobilize in defense of Russia's Slavic allies the Serbs. Encouraging the Austrians to attack Serbia, the German general staff mobilized on August 1.

German strategy was based on the Schlieffen Plan, named after its author, Alfred von Schlieffen

(1833–1913), a former chief of the general staff. The plan essentially outlined a way to combat antagonists on two fronts by concentrating on one foe at a time. It called for a rapid and concentrated blow to the west against Russia's ally France, which would lead to that nation's defeat in six weeks, accompanied by a light holding action to the east.

The western armies would then be deployed against Russia, which, it was believed, would mobilize far more slowly. The attack on France was to proceed through Belgium, whose neutrality was guaranteed by the European powers.

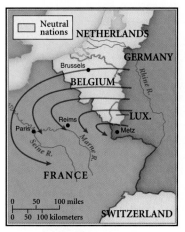

The Schlieffen Plan

But German strategy hit an unexpected snag when the Belgian government rejected an ultimatum to allow the uncontested passage of the German army through the country. Now the riddle of Britain's position was solved. The subsequent violation of Belgian neutrality brought Britain into the war on the side of Russia and France, which was simultaneously mobilizing as part of its alliance with Russia. Although the kaiser at the last minute demanded a war limited to Russia to avoid fighting the British, the military vetoed him because of its unalterable plan for a two-front war. "Who rules in Berlin?" one statesman wondered upon viewing the German government's attempts at peace and the military's push toward war.

Conclusion

Rulers soon forgot their last-minute hesitations in the general celebration that erupted with the war. "Old heroes have reemerged from the books of legends," wrote a Viennese actor after watching the troops march off. "A mighty wonder has taken place, we have become *young*." Both sides exulted, believing in certain victory. A short conflict, people maintained, would resolve tensions ranging from the rise of the working class to political problems caused by global imperial competition.

The arms race had stimulated militant nationalism and brought many Europeans to favor war over peace. The crisis of modernity had helped blaze the path to war: the *Rite of Spring* ballet that opened in Paris in 1913 had taken as its theme the ritualistic attraction of death. Facing continuing violence in politics, incomprehensibility in the arts,

and problems in the industrial order, Europeans had come to believe that war would set events back on course and save them from the perils of modernity. "Like men longing for a thunderstorm to relieve them of the summer's sultriness," wrote one Austrian official, "so the generation of 1914 believed in the relief that war might bring." Such a possibility caused Europeans to rejoice. But tragically, their elation was short-lived. Instead of bringing the refreshment of summer rain, war opened an era of political turmoil, widespread suffering, massive human slaughter, and even greater doses of modernity.

Suggested References

Private Life in an Age of Modernity

Historians are engaged in serious study of the transformations of everyday life that industrial and imperial advance had brought about by the early twentieth century. In particular, personal and domestic life, as seen in the works of Hull, Walkowitz, and Duberman et al., have taken on greater importance as components of social movements and political developments.

Accampo, Elinor A., Rachel G. Fuchs, and Mary Lynn Stewart, eds. *Gender and the Politics of Social Reform in France, 1870–1914.* 1995.

Duberman, Martin, Martha Vicinus, and George Chauncey Jr. *Hidden from History: Reclaiming the Gay and Lesbian Past.* 1989.

Engelstein, Laura. *The Keys to Happiness: Sex and the Search for Modernity in Fin-de-Siècle Russia.* 1992.

Gillis, John. *A World of Their Own Making: Myth, Ritual, and the Quest for Family Values.* 1996.

Hull, Isabell. *The Entourage of Kaiser Wilhelm II, 1888–1918.* 1982.

Walkowitz, Judith. *City of Dreadful Delight: Narratives of Sexual Danger in Late-Victorian London.* 1993.

Modernity and the Revolt in Ideas

Some of the most controversial historiography sees the road to World War I as paved with cultural conflict. Many of the studies here suggest that new forms of art, music, dance, and philosophy were as central to the challenges Europe faced as were ethnic, economic, and international turmoil.

Eksteins, Modris. *Rites of Spring: The Great War and the Birth of the Modern Age.* 1989.

Everdell, William R. *The First Moderns. Profiles in the Origins of Twentieth-Century Thought.* 1997.

Jensen, Robert. *Marketing Modernism in Fin-de-Siècle Europe.* 1994.

Kern, Steven. *The Culture of Space and Time, 1880–1918.* 1983.

*Mann, Thomas. *Buddenbrooks.* 1901.

Nehamas, Alexander. *Nietzsche: Life as Literature.* 1985.

Nineteenth- and twentieth-century philosophy: http://www .epistemelinks.com/index.asp.

Silverman, Debora L. *Art Nouveau in Fin-de-Siècle France: Politics, Psychology, and Style.* 1989.

Politics in a New Key

Historians are uncovering the dramatic changes in political life and assessing the consequences of the rise of mass politics across Europe, including the development of suffragist movements. Some studies cited here investigate a second major political phenomenon: the formation of a politics of hatred and the rise of aggressive, warlike nationalism to replace nationalism based on rights and constitutional values.

Burns, Michael. *Dreyfus: A Family Affair.* 1992.

Chickering, Roger. *We Men Who Feel Most German: A Cultural Study of the Pan-German League, 1886–1914.* 1984.

Dennis, David B. *Beethoven in German Politics, 1870–1989.* 1996.

Kent, Susan. *Gender and Power in Britain, 1640–1990.* 1999.

Kornberg, Jacques. *Theodor Herzl: From Assimilation to Zionism.* 1993.

MacKenzie, David. *Violent Solutions: Revolutions, Nationalism, and Secret Societies in Europe to 1918.* 1996.

Schorske, Carl E. *Fin-de-Siècle Vienna: Politics and Culture.* 1981.

Scott, Joan. *Only Paradoxes to Offer: French Feminism and the Rights of Man.* 1996.

European Imperialism Challenged

In the midst of raucous political and social debate, the European powers faced growing resistance to their domination and increasingly serious setbacks. Many historians now judge Europe to have played a less commanding role in the rest of the world than the leading empires claimed. Imperial instability, as some studies show, paved the road to war. The fascination with the major non-Western contender—Japan—can be traced on the Japanese history Web site.

Cohen, Paul A. *History in Three Keys: The Boxers as Event, Experience, and Myth.* 1997.

Gouda, Frances. *Dutch Culture Overseas: Colonial Practice in the Netherlands Indies, 1900–1942.* 1995.

Japanese history: http://www.csuohio.edu/history/japan/ index.html.

Kansu, Aykut. *The Revolution of 1908 in Turkey.* 1997.

McDonald, David MacLaren. *United Government and Foreign Policy in Russia, 1900–1914.* 1992.

Meyers, Ramon H., and Mark R. Peattie, eds. *The Japanese Colonial Empire, 1895–1945.* 1984.

*Pruitt, Ida. *A Daughter of Han: The Autobiography of a Chinese Working Woman.* 1945.

Sinha, Mrinalini. *Colonial Masculinity: The "Manly Englishman" and the "Effeminate Bengali" in the Late Nineteenth Century.* 1995.

Weeks, Theodore R. *Nation and State in Late Imperial Russia: Nationalism and Russification on the Western Frontier.* 1996.

Roads to War

The question of why World War I broke out remains widely debated. There are always newcomers to the discussion devoted to assessing the responsibility for the war's beginning, but while these historians fix on a single country, other historians like to look at the full range of diplomatic, military, social, and economic conditions.

Ascher, Abraham. *The Revolution of 1905: Russia in Disarray.* 1988.

Berghahn, Volker. *Germany and the Approach of War.* 1993.

Cecil, Lamar. *Wilhelm II, Prince and Emperor, 1859–1900.* 1989.

Fenyvesi, Charles. *When the World Was Whole.* 1990.

Ferguson, Niall. *The Pity of War: Explaining World War I.* 1999.

Hoensch, Jorg K. *A History of Modern Hungary, 1867–1986.* 1988.

Lambi, Ivo. *The Navy and German Power Politics.* 1984.

Manning, Roberta. *The Crisis of the Old Order in Russia.* 1982.

Tech, Mikulás, and Roy Porter, eds. *The National Question in Europe in Historical Context.* 1993.

Williamson, Samuel. *Austria-Hungary and the Origins of the First World War.* 1991.

*Primary sources

War, Revolution, and Reconstruction

1914–1929

Grieving Parents
Before World War I the German artist Kaethe Köllwitz gained her artistic reputation with wood-cuts of handloom weavers whose livelihoods were threatened by industrialization. From 1914 on, she depicted the suffering and death that swirled around her and never with more sober force than in these two monuments to her son Peter, who had died on the western front in the first months of battle. Today one can still travel to his burial place in Vladslo, Belgium, to see this father and mother mourning their loss, like millions across Europe in those heartbreaking days.
The John Parker Picture Library.

JULES AMAR FOUND HIS TRUE VOCATION in World War I. A French expert on making industrial work more efficient, Amar switched his focus after 1914 as hundreds of thousands of men returned from the battlefront missing body parts. Plastic surgery developed rapidly, as did the construction of masks and other devices to hide deformities. But Amar, who designed artificial limbs and appendages in these traumatic years, sought to devise prostheses that would allow the wounded soldier to return to normal life by "mak[ing] up for a function lost, or greatly reduced." So the arms that he designed used hooks, magnets, and other mechanisms with which the veteran could hold a cigarette, play a violin, and most important work with tools such as typewriters. Mangled by the weapons of modern technological warfare, the survivors of World War I would be made whole, it was thought, by skills and technology such as Amar's.

Amar dealt with the human tragedy of the "Great War," so named by contemporaries because of its staggering human toll—forty million wounded or killed in battle. The Great War was also what historians call a "total war," meaning one built on full mobilization of soldiers, civilians, and the technological capacities of the most highly industrialized nations. The Great War did not settle problems or restore social order as the European powers hoped it would. Instead, the war produced political cataclysm and social and cultural upheaval. In Russia, revolutionaries overturned the tsarist regime even before the war ended. In Germany, defeat and rebellion forced the kaiser to

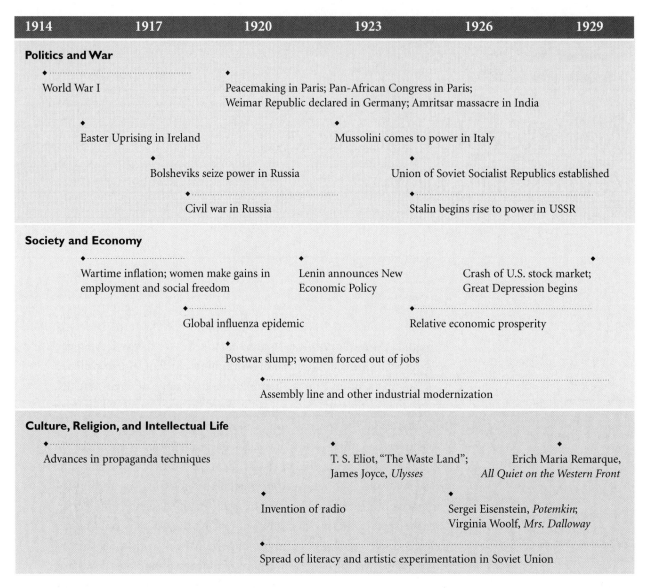

1914	1917	1920	1923	1926	1929

Politics and War

World War I

Peacemaking in Paris; Pan-African Congress in Paris;
Weimar Republic declared in Germany; Amritsar massacre in India

Easter Uprising in Ireland

Mussolini comes to power in Italy

Bolsheviks seize power in Russia

Union of Soviet Socialist Republics established

Civil war in Russia

Stalin begins rise to power in USSR

Society and Economy

Wartime inflation; women make gains in
employment and social freedom

Lenin announces New
Economic Policy

Crash of U.S. stock market;
Great Depression begins

Global influenza epidemic

Relative economic prosperity

Postwar slump; women forced out of jobs

Assembly line and other industrial modernization

Culture, Religion, and Intellectual Life

Advances in propaganda techniques

T. S. Eliot, "The Waste Land";
James Joyce, *Ulysses*

Erich Maria Remarque,
All Quiet on the Western Front

Invention of radio

Sergei Eisenstein, *Potemkin*;
Virginia Woolf, *Mrs. Dalloway*

Spread of literacy and artistic experimentation in Soviet Union

abdicate, leaving that once proud nation starving, demoralized, and buffeted by the winds of political extremism. Through ethnic uprisings and peace treaties, the long-lived Ottoman and Austro-Hungarian Empires were dismembered at the war's end. The crushing burden of war on the European powers accelerated the rise of the United States to global leadership, while service in the war intensified the demands of colonized peoples for autonomy.

For all the vast changes that the Great War ushered in, it also hastened transformations under way before it started. Nineteenth-century optimism, already tinged with a sense of decline, gave way to a more pervasive postwar cynicism. Many

Westerners turned their backs on politics and attacked life with frenzied gaiety in the Roaring Twenties, snapping up new consumer goods, drinking in entertainment provided by films and radio, and enjoying personal freedoms that Victorianism had forbidden. Others found reason for hope in the new political systems the war made possible: Soviet communism and Italian fascism. Building on prewar trends, communist and fascist leaders sought to mobilize the masses for political, even radical, ends. Modern communication technologies such as radio, film, and the press gave them the means to ally themselves with the cultural avant-garde to promote a utopian mass politics that paradoxically was antidemocratic, militaristic, and eventually totalitarian. Already weakening during the prewar period, the "gentlemanly" political tone of William Gladstone's day had been devastated by total war.

Seen as a solution to the conflicts of modernity, a war that was long anticipated and even welcomed in some quarters destabilized Europe and the world far into the next decades. From statesmen to ordinary citizens, many Europeans like Amar would spend their best peacetime efforts to make war-ravaged society function normally, while others saw that task as utterly futile, given the globally transformative force of the Great War. During the 1920s, both types were looking backward, constructing the future from the haunting fragments of an unforgettable past.

❖ The Great War, 1914–1918

When war erupted in August 1914, the ground had been prepared with long-standing alliances, the development of strategies for war, and the buildup of military technologies such as heavy artillery, machine guns, and the airplane. Seeing precedents in Prussia's rapid victories over Denmark, the Austrian Empire, and France in the 1860s and 1870 and the swift blows that Japan dealt Russia in 1904–1905, most people felt that this would be a short, decisive conflict. But the unforeseen happened: this war would last for more than four years, and it would be a total war, mobilizing soldiers, civilians, and the entire industrial capacity of the West. Although some British leaders with

A French Regiment Leaves for the Front, August 1914
Bands played, crowds cheered, and bicyclists led the way as bayonet-equipped soldiers marched eagerly to war. The mood changed quickly as machine guns and poison chemicals brought the bravest men down. People in cities, working to provide munitions and supplies, soon felt the pinch of inflation and later many lacked food. Men returned permanently disabled, even mentally deranged from their experience. And as four major empires—Ottoman, Russian, Austro-Hungarian, and German— collapsed, the war's bright beginnings disappeared from memory.
© Collection Viollet.

experience of the Boer War suggested that "the next war" would be an especially "nasty business," most of society did not anticipate the horror that lay ahead. It was precisely the unprecedented horror that made World War I "great."

Blueprints for War

World War I pitted two sets of opponents formed roughly out of the alliances developed during the previous fifty years. On one side stood the Central Powers (Austria-Hungary and Germany), which had evolved from Bismarck's Triple Alliance, and on the other the Allies (France, Great Britain, and Russia), which had emerged as a bloc from the Entente Cordiale between France and Great Britain and the 1890s treaties between France and Russia. In 1915, Italy, originally part of the Triple Alliance, joined the Allies in hopes of postwar gain. The two sides expanded globally almost from the start: in late August 1914, Japan, eager to extend its empire into China, went over to the Allies, while in the fall Turkey united with the Central Powers against its traditional enemy, Russia.

Joined by other, smaller countries, the antagonists fought with the same ferocious hunger for power, prestige, and prosperity that had inspired imperialism. Of the Central Powers, Germany aspired to a far-flung empire to be gained by annexing Russian territory and incorporating parts of Belgium, France, and Luxembourg. Some German leaders wanted to annex Austria-Hungary as well. Austria-Hungary hoped to retain its great-power status, threatened by the different nationalisms within its borders that were based on ethnicity rather than loyalty to the Habsburg crown.

Among the Allies, Russia wanted to reassert its status as a great power and as the protector of the Slavs by adding a reunified Poland to the Russian Empire, annexing the Austro-Hungarian territory peopled by Ukrainians, and reorganizing the rest of Austria-Hungary into a triple monarchy that recognized Slavic political claims. The French too craved territory, especially the return of Alsace and Lorraine, taken from them after the Franco-Prussian War, and wanted new, more secure boundaries with Germany. The British sought to keep the North Sea coast from falling to another great power and to cement their hold on Egypt and the Suez Canal, as well as to secure the rest of their

world empire. By the Treaty of London (1915), France and Britain promised Italy territory in Africa, Asia Minor, the Balkans, and elsewhere in return for joining the Allies.

All the powers with colonies enlisted or conscripted tens of thousands of colonized men into their service. Britain deployed Indian regiments in western Europe in the first days of the war and enlisted Arabs against the Turks. The French relied heavily on Senegalese and North African recruits, promising them citizenship for their service. The Germans used colonial soldiers in Europe and later in Africa and Asia.

By August 1914, machine guns and rifles, airplanes, battleships, submarines, and motorized transport—cars and railroads—were at the disposal of armies; new technologies like chlorine gas, tanks, and bombs would develop between 1914 and 1918. Countries differed, however, in their experience with and quantities of weapons of war as well as knowledgeable in their use. British generals who had fought in the Boer War knew the destructive capacity of these weapons, while the Germans were far more advanced in strategy and weaponry than either the Russians or the Austrians. The war itself became a lethal testing ground, as both new and old weaponry were used, often ineffectively.

One military concept prevailed on both sides: officers believed in a "cult of the offensive," in which spirited attacks and high troop morale would be decisive. Despite the availability of newer, more powerful war technology, an old-fashioned vision of war made officers unwilling to abandon the more familiar sabers, lances, and bayonets. Given the technological potential of European industrialization, the war thus opened on a completely unrealistic note, with Napoleonic weaponry and strategy, uniforms, polished swords, and cheerful military plans seen as central to victory. The "cult of the offensive" would cost millions of lives.

The Battle Fronts

The first months of the war crushed hope of quick victory. All the major armies mobilized rapidly. The Germans, guided by the Schlieffen Plan (see page 973), reached Luxembourg on August 2 and Belgium on August 4, 1914. The plan counted on unchallenged passage through these small countries. Meanwhile, the main body of French troops,

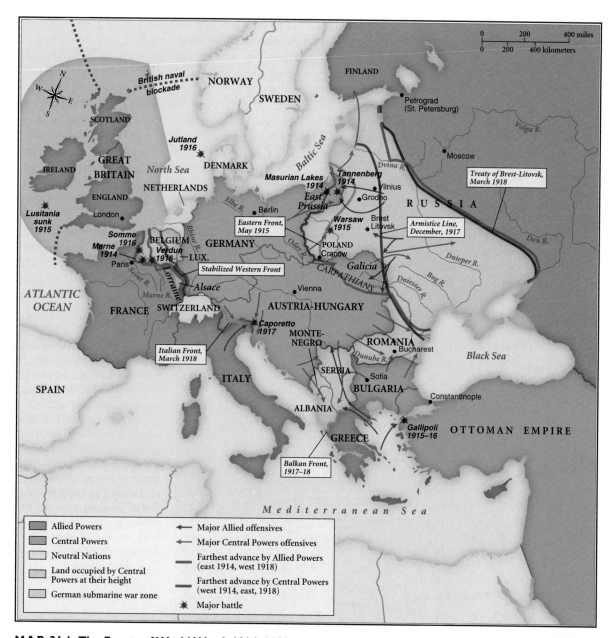

MAP 26.1 The Fronts of World War I, 1914–1918

Because the western front remained relatively stationary, devastation of land and resources was intense. All fronts, however, destroyed segments of Europe's hard-won industrial and agricultural capacity, while the immobile trenches increased military casualties. Men engaged in trench warfare for so long developed an intense camaraderie based on their incredible suffering and deprivation.

tricked by German diversionary tactics, attacked the Germans in Alsace and Lorraine instead of meeting the invasion from the north. In the late summer heat, both the Schlieffen Plan and the French offensive disintegrated because of bad planning and worse luck.

1914–1915: Indecisive Offensives. The Belgians unexpectedly resisted, slowing the German advance and allowing British and French troops to reach the northern front (Map 26.1). In September, the British and French armies engaged the Germans along the Marne River in France (Map 26.2).

Neither side could defeat the other, and the fighting continued late into the autumn along the Marne and up to Ypres in Belgium. Casualties were shocking: in the first three months of war, more than 1.5 million men fell on the western front alone. Firepower turned what was supposed to be an offensive war of movement into a stationary, defensive impasse. For the next four years the two sides faced off along a line that stretched from the North Sea through Belgium and northern France to Switzerland. Soldiers dug in, excavating parallel lines of trenches up to thirty feet deep that would serve millions of men as nightmarish homes.

On the eastern front, the "Russian steamroller"—so named because of the number of men mobilized, some twelve million in all—drove far more quickly than expected, into East Prussia on August 17 and into parts of Austria-Hungary, while Russia's Serbian allies repelled Austria-Hungary's troops in Serbia. The Russians believed that no army could stand up to their massive numbers, no matter how ill equipped and poorly trained they were. Their success was short-lived. The Germans crushed the tsar's army in East Prussia at Tannenberg and in campaigns around the Masurian Lakes. The Germans then turned south to Galicia, where Russian and Austro-Hungarian armies were fighting costly battles. Although the Russian army was capable of fighting the dual monarchy's armed forces, the technologically superior German army often stopped the Russians cold. Victory boosted German morale and made heroes of the military leaders Paul von Hindenburg (1847–1934) and Erich Ludendorff (1865–1937), who thereupon

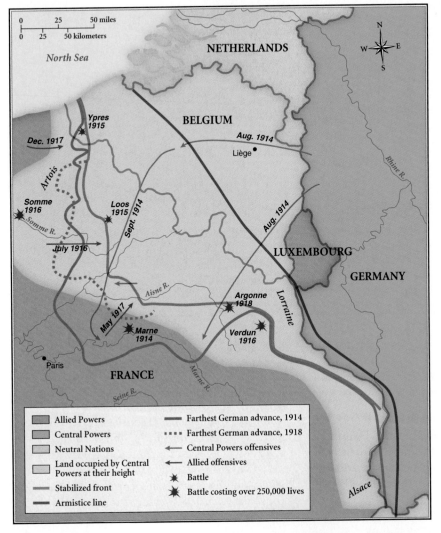

MAP 26.2 The Western Front

The western front occupied some of the richest parts of France, with long-lasting consequences. Destruction of French villages, roads, bridges, livestock, and property was the worst in Europe, while the trauma of the French people endured for generations. The effects of horrendous casualties, ever-present artillery fire, provisioning and hospital needs, and the demands of military and medical personnel changed everyone's way of life and made most people fear another war more than anything else.

The Toll of Trench Warfare

On both sides the war took an enormous toll in male lives, leaving politicians and citizens alike concerned about society's future. Depictions of shattered bodies that heavy firepower ripped to bits, however, hardly reached the home front and thus the illusion remained that the war was about individual prowess and that individual soldiers had a fighting chance of survival. Simultaneously troops from the colonies were often depicted as bringing an innate savagery to the battlefront, though these soldiers had even less chance of surviving because they were often placed in the front lines.

Left: Imperial War Museum, London; right: Robert Hunt Library.

demanded more troops for the eastern front. Despite heartening victories, by year's end German triumphs in the east had failed to knock out the Russians and had also misdirected the Schlieffen Plan, which called for only light holding action to the east until the western front had been won.

War at sea proved equally indecisive. Confident in Britain's superior naval power, the Allies blockaded the entries to the Mediterranean and North Seas to prevent supplies from reaching Germany and Austria-Hungary. William II and his advisers planned a massive submarine, or U-boat (*Unterseeboot*, "underwater boat"), campaign against Allied and neutral shipping around Britain and France. In May 1915, German submarines sank the British passenger ship *Lusitania* and killed 1,198 people, including 124 Americans. Although the atmosphere in the United States crackled with outrage, Woodrow Wilson (1856–1924; president 1913–1921) maintained a policy of neutrality. The Germans, not willing to provoke Wilson further, called off unrestricted submarine warfare. In May 1916, the navies of Germany and Britain finally

clashed in the battle of Jutland. Although inconclusive, the battle demonstrated that the German fleet could not dislodge the British as rulers of the sea.

Ideas of a negotiated peace were discarded while the cult of the offensive remained unmodified. "No peace before England is defeated and destroyed," the kaiser railed against his cousin King George V. "Only amidst the ruins of London will I forgive Georgy." Politician and powerful journalist Georges Clemenceau (1841–1929), who would become premier of France for the second time in 1917, called for a "war to the death." General staffs continued to prepare fierce attacks several times a year. Campaigns opened with heavy artillery pounding enemy trenches and gun emplacements. Troops then scrambled "over the top" of their trenches, usually to be mowed down by machine-gun fire from defenders secure in their own trenches.

Indecisive offensives continued. On the western front, the French desperately wanted to oust the Germans from their northern industrial regions. Throughout 1915, they assaulted the enemy at Ypres, Loos, and Artois; but they accomplished little, and casualties of 100,000 and more for a single campaign became commonplace. On the eastern front, troops on both sides fared no better than their counterparts in Belgium and France. In the spring of 1915, Russian armies captured parts of Galicia and lumbered toward Hungary. The Central Powers struck back in Poland later that year, bringing the front closer to Petrograd (formerly St. Petersburg), the Russian capital. The Austro-Hungarian armies routed the Serbs in 1915 and then engaged the newly mobilized Italian army.

1916: Mounting Catastrophe.

The next year was even more disastrous. When the Germans judged that a definitive blow against the French would induce the British to withdraw from the war, they turned their attention in early 1916 to the fortress at Verdun. (See Map 26.2.) The fall of the fortress, they calculated, would cripple French morale. Launching massive assaults from February through April, the Germans fired as many as a million shells in a single day. Combined French and German losses totaled close to a million men. Nonetheless the French held.

Hoping to relieve their allies, the British unleashed an artillery pounding of German trenches in the Somme region in June 1916 that was supposed to ensure a bloodless victory for Britain. But on July 1, twenty thousand British soldiers died going "over the top"—the artillery had failed to penetrate the deeply dug German fortifications. In several months of battle at the Somme, 1.25 million men were killed or wounded, but the final result was stalemate. By the end of 1916, the French had absorbed more than 3.5 million casualties. To help the Allies engaged at Verdun and the Somme, the Russians struck again, driving once more into the Carpathians, recouping territory, and menacing the Habsburg Empire. Only the German army stopped the Russian advance. Amidst the huge losses, the Habsburg army recruited men in their mid-fifties and the German general staff was impelled to take over Austrian military operations. The war was sapping Europe's strength and individual sovereignty.

The View from the Trenches.

Had the military leaders thoroughly dominated the scene, historians judge, all armies would have been utterly demol-

ished in nonstop offensives by the end of 1915. Yet historians have recently come to see that ordinary soldiers in this war were not automatons in the face of what seemed to them suicidal orders. Whereas governments and officers tended to see war as "kill or be killed," troops at the front often put into effect their own practice of "live and let live." Some battalions went for long stretches with hardly a casualty, a far cry from the common historical picture of relentless bloodshed. Diaries show that throughout the war, and despite the increasing threat of punishment, these low rates stemmed from agreements among troops to avoid battles. Enemies facing each other across the trenches frequently ate their meals in peace, for example, even though the trenches were within hand grenade reach. A German soldier described trenches "where friend and foe alike go to fetch straw from the same rick [stack] to protect them from cold and rain—and never a shot is fired." Throughout the war, soldiers fraternized on both fronts. They played an occasional game of soccer, yelled across the trenches, sang together at Christmas and Easter, exchanged mementos, and made gestures of agreement not to fight. A British veteran of the trenches explained to a new recruit that the Germans "don't want to fight any more than we do, so there's a kind of understanding between us. Don't fire at us and we'll not fire at you." Burying enemy dead in common graves with their own fallen comrades, many ordinary soldiers came to feel more warmly toward enemies who shared the trench experience than toward civilians back home. One infantryman wrote: "It is only on the home front that the atmosphere is still warlike. . . . At the [battle]front there is far too much mutual understanding of one for the other."

Newly forged bonds of male camaraderie alleviated some of the misery of trench life and aided survival. Sharing the danger of death and the deprivations of front-line experience weakened traditional class distinctions. In some cases upper-class officers and working-class draftees became friends in that "wholly masculine way of life uncomplicated by women," as one soldier put it. According to diaries and letters, soldiers picked lice from one another's bodies and clothes, revered section leaders who tended their blistered feet, and came to love one another, sometimes even passionately. Positive memories of this front-line community survived the war and influenced postwar politics.

Troops of colonized soldiers from Asia and Africa had different experiences of the trenches, especially as they were often put in the very front ranks where the risks were greatest. European observers noted that these soldiers suffered particularly from the rigors of a totally unfamiliar climate, strange food, and the ruin inflicted by Western war technology. Yet, as with class divisions, racial barriers sometimes fell, for instance, whenever a European understood enough to alleviate the distress that cold inflicted. Colonial troops' perspectives changed too, for in this war they got to see their "masters" completely undone and "uncivilized."

When the men in the trenches did fight one another, they lived in a veritable hell of shelling and sniping, flying body parts, rotting cadavers, and blinding gas. Some were reduced to hysteria or succumbed to shell shock through the sheer stress and violence of battle. Under these conditions many soldiers felt alienated from civilization and became cynical: "It might be me tomorrow," a young British soldier wrote his mother in 1916. "Who cares?" War was "so damned impersonal," depending less on swords and spirit than on wire cutters, artillery shells, gas masks, and tanks. Having gone to war often to escape ordinary life in industrial society, soldiers learned, as one German put it, "that in the modern war . . . the triumph of the machine over the individual is carried to its most extreme form." They took this hard-won knowledge into battle, pulling their comrades back when an offensive seemed lost or too costly.

The Home Front

World War I was taking place off the battlefield too. Even before the war had reached the stage of catastrophic impasse, it had become "total." Total war meant the indispensable involvement of civilians in the war industry: manufacturing the shells and bullets, machine guns and artillery, poisonous gases, cars and trains, bombs and airplanes, and eventually tanks that were the backbone of technological warfare. Increased production of artificial limbs, crutches, canes, wheelchairs, and coffins was also a wartime necessity. Because soldiers would have utterly failed without them, civilians had to work overtime for, believe in, and sacrifice for victory. To keep the war machine operating smoothly, governments directed the political, cultural, and economic lives of citizens in unprecedented ways. They oversaw factories, transportation systems, and resources ranging from food to coal to textiles. Such control would have outraged many liberals before the war but was accepted as a necessary condition for victory.

Politics Suspended.   At the outset, many socialists and working-class people who had formerly criticized the military buildup announced their support for the war. For decades socialist parties had preached that "the worker has no country" and that nationalism was an artificial ideology meant to keep workers disunited and subjected to the will of their employers. Socialists of the Second International had envisioned that their deputies would vote against military budgets and that their members would refuse to fight. But workers had joined in the euphoria of imperialism and the arms race before the war, and in August 1914 the socialist rank and file, along with most of the party leaders, were as patriotic as the rest of society. Their eager support of wartime governments ended the Second International's role as the vanguard of socialist leadership.

Initially political parties also put aside their differences; all-party solidarity was known in Germany as the *Burgfriede* ("domestic peace") and in France as the *union sacrée* ("sacred union"). Feminists divided over whether to maintain their traditional condemnation of militarism or to support the war. Although many feminists actively opposed the conflict, Emmeline Pankhurst and her daughter Christabel were among those who became militant nationalists, even changing the name of their suffrage paper to *Britannia*. Still other women flocked to philanthropic organizations assisting the war effort. Parties representing the middle classes shelved their distrust of the socialists and working classes to present a united front. In the name of victory, national leaders wanted to end political division of all kinds: "I no longer recognize [political] parties," William II declared on August 4, 1914. "I recognize only Germans."

Mobilizing for Total War.   Governments took charge of the economy, as the lack of long-range planning hampered armies across Europe. All countries were caught without ready replacements for their heavy losses of weapons and military equipment, and governments soon stepped in to ensure steady production of war supplies and their timely arrival at the front. War ministries set up boards to allocate labor on the home front and the battlefront, sponsor efficiency studies of individual industries, oversee the regulation of factory work, and give industrialists financial incentives to encourage productivity. In Austria-Hungary, the Hungarian Emergency Measures Act allowed the drafting of both men and women for military or industrial service; in Germany, all men between the ages of seventeen and sixty could be drafted. In 1916, the National Service Act made all British citizens eligible for war service. The conscription of civilians into the labor force further blurred distinctions between military and civilian life.

Governments mobilized the home front with varying degrees of success. The Russian bureaucracy reluctantly and ineffectively cooperated with industrialists and other groups that could aid the war effort. Desperate for factory workers, the Germans forced Belgian citizens to move to Germany, housing them in prison camps until they could be rotated into factory work. In Germany, Austria, France, and Britain, officials eventually controlled food allocations through rationing because the war had curtailed farming and cut off trade. Municipal governments arranged for local workshops to organize sewing and other essential tasks; they also set up canteens and day-care centers so men and women could focus fully on war production. Rural Russia, Austria-Hungary, Bulgaria, and Serbia, where youths, women, and old men struggled to sustain farms, had no such relief programs. Simultaneously, governments and industrialists retreated from the trend toward protective legislation by ignoring laws that limited the length of women's workday, the kind of work they were allowed to do, and their performance of dangerous tasks. But this was one of the few steps away from big government that politicians took in World War I.

Governments throughout Europe passed sedition laws that made it a crime to criticize official policies. To ensure civilian acceptance of longer working hours and shortages of consumer goods, governments created propaganda agencies to tout the war as a patriotic mission to resist villainous enemies. British propagandists fabricated atrocities the German "Huns" supposedly committed against Belgians, and they invented statements—for example, the kaiser's remark that British soldiers formed

War Propaganda, 1915
"Never Forget!" screams the headline of this propaganda poster depicting an assaulted woman in despair. Intended to incite sentiment against the Germans, the poster suggested what German passage through neutral Belgium came to be called—"the rape of Belgium." Propaganda offices for the Allies sent out reports of women attacked and children massacred as the German armies moved through Belgian territories.
Mary Evans Picture Library.

a "contemptible little army"—to incite the troops. British soldiers ridiculed the propaganda film *Battle of the Somme* (1916), with its staged scenes of war obviously filmed in a studio. The film drew packed civilian audiences, however, and its fake screen images bolstered the desire to smash the Germans. German propaganda warned that French African troops would rape German women if Germany was defeated. In Russia, Nicholas II changed the German-sounding name of St. Petersburg to the Russian Petrograd in 1914. But propaganda sometimes backfired. Worried about the loyalty of their many ethnic minorities, the Russians plastered Polish towns with posters promising national independence if the Poles would help fight the

Germans. But by mistakenly printing the Polish flag upside down on the posters, the Russians weakened rather than strengthened their cause.

Playing on fears and arousing hatred, propaganda rendered a compromise peace unlikely. Nonetheless, some individuals sought to shatter the nationalist consensus supporting the war. Activists in the international women's movement met in The Hague in 1915, determined to end the war. "We can no longer endure . . . brute force as the only solution of international disputes," declared Dutch physician Aletta Jacobs in her opening speech. Governments on both sides prevented many women from attending, because the slightest public moves toward a negotiated peace were seen as "defeatism." Those who reached The Hague, however, spent the remainder of the war urging statesmen to work out a peace settlement.

In Austria-Hungary, nationalist groups agitating for ethnic self-determination hampered the empire's war effort. The Czechs undertook a vigorous anti-Habsburg campaign at home, while in Paris, Thomas Masaryk (1850–1937) and Edouard Beneš (1884–1948) established the Czechoslovak National Council from which they lobbied Western governments for recognition of Czech rights. For Poles the war had finally split the powers that had partitioned their country in the eighteenth century. Jozef Pilsudski (1867–1935) set up the Polish Military Organization in Austrian Galicia, which he trained as the basis for an independent Polish army. In the Balkans, Croats, Slovenes, and Serbs formed a committee to plan a South Slav state carved from Habsburg possessions and other Balkan territory. The Allies encouraged such independence movements as part of their strategy to defeat the Habsburgs.

Society at War.   The war restructured the workforce. In the war's early days many women had lost their jobs when luxury shops, textile factories, and other nonessential establishments closed. With men at the front, many women headed households with little support and few opportunities to work. But governments and businesses soon recognized the amount of labor it would take to wage technological war. As more and more men left for the trenches, women who had lost their jobs in nonessential businesses as well as many low-paid domestic workers took over higher-paying jobs in formerly restricted munitions and metallurgical

German Welder Being Trained
As men were siphoned off to the battlefront in World War I, women took their places in factories, transportation, and services—all of them working overtime to supply the insatiable needs of modern, technological warfare. Women thus gained higher pay and learned new productive skills such as welding. A new working-class woman emerged from the experience of war.
Ullstein Bilderdienst.

industries. In Warsaw they drove trucks, and in London they conducted streetcars. Some young women drove ambulances and nursed the wounded near the front lines.

The press praised women's patriotism in adopting new roles, but women's assumption of men's jobs suggested not just social change but social disorder. From the start, a steady flood of wounded and weak men returned home to women who had adapted resourcefully and taken full charge. Some women demonstrated uncustomary strength and enthusiasm for war: "Oh, it's you that have all the luck, out there in the blood and muck," went one woman author's jingle. Workingmen commonly protested that women, in the words of one metalworker, were "sending men to the slaughter." Men feared that when the war was over women would remain in the workforce, robbing men of work and usurping their role as breadwinner. Many people, even some women, objected to women's loss of femininity. "The feminine in me decreased more and more, and I did not know whether to be sad or glad about this," wrote one Russian nurse about learning to wear rough male clothing near the battlefield. The factory woman emerged from long hours working with toxic substances looking like something that "makes you afraid with her hands and face turned yellow, her colourless hair and the corpse-like look which the handling of explosives gives her," as one male worker complained. Some criticized young female munitions workers for squandering their pay on ribbons, furs, and jewelry. These wartime tensions over traditional gender roles echoed prewar changes in relations between the sexes and presaged rifts to come.

Although many soldiers from different social backgrounds felt bonds of solidarity in the trenches, wartime conditions increasingly pitted civilians against one another along class lines. Workers toiled longer hours eating less, while many in the upper classes bought abundant food and fashionable clothing on the black market (outside the official system of rationing) and lived conspicuously well. Governments allowed many businesses high rates of profit, a step that resulted in a surge in the cost of living and thus contributed to social strife. Shortages of staples like bread, sugar, and meat grew worse, as the brutal "turnip winter" of 1916–1917—when turnips were often the only available food—progressed. A German roof workers' association pleaded for relief: "We can no longer go on. Our children are starving. . . . It is simply beyond our strength." Craftspeople producing nonessential consumer goods suffered the most. Civilians held governments responsible for these everyday difficulties; ultimately some of their bitterness festered into revolution.

Civilians in occupied areas and in the colonies suffered the most oppressive working conditions. The combatants deported or conscripted able-bodied people in territories they occupied, the Germans, for instance, sent civilians from Belgium and northern France to Germany to work. The French forcibly transported some 100,000 Vietnamese to work in France for the war effort.

Africans were made to do grueling labor for the armies in the African colonies. Of the million Kenyans and Tanzanians so conscripted, at least 100,000 died from disease and overwork. Colonized people also saw their taxes skyrocket and prices rise. All such actions, like increasing class divisions, led to further politicization.

❖ 1917–1918: Protest, Revolution, and War's End

By 1917, the situation was becoming desperate for politicians, the military, and civilians, and discontent on the home front started shaping the course of the war. Neither patriotic slogans before the war nor propaganda during it had prepared people for wartime suffering. Cities across Europe experienced civilian revolt, nationalist struggles continued to plague Britain and Austria-Hungary, and soldiers mutinied. In Petrograd, the combined protest of soldiers and civilians turned into the Russian Revolution, toppling the tsar's dynasty for good. Nor would revolt stop when the war did: instead it continued to spread in the military and among workers.

War Protest

On February 1, 1917, the German government, hard-pressed by the public clamor over mounting casualties and by the military's growing control over decision making, resumed unrestricted submarine warfare. Despite politicians' fear of bringing in the United States, Generals Ludendorff and Hindenburg, whose prestige was on the rise, bullied the kaiser into unleashing the U-boats. The military made the irresistible promise to end the war in six months by cutting off imported food and military supplies to Britain and thus forcing the island nation to surrender before the United States could come to its rescue. The British responded by mining harbors and the seas and by developing depth charges, antisubmarine bombs that exploded underwater. But the most effective measure was the convoy system of shipping, in which a hundred or more warships and freighters traveling the seas together could drive off the

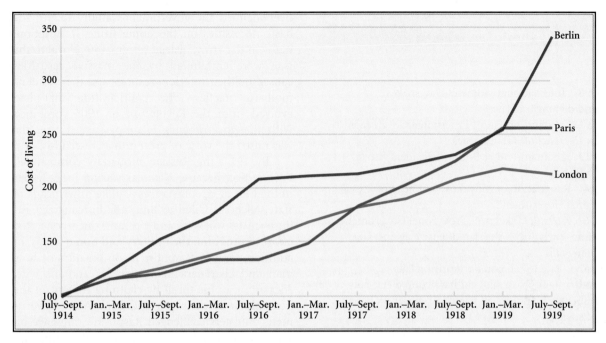

FIGURE 26.1 The Rising Cost of Living during World War I

The diversion of resources to the military resulted in a soaring cost of living for civilians. As men went to the front and as some remaining agricultural workers could find higher pay in factories, a decline in agricultural output led to scarcity and thus rising prices for food. Finally, housing came to be in short supply as resources were directed to the war effort rather than used to construct needed buildings. Even after the war prices rose in Germany because the Allies maintained their blockade to keep the pressure on the peacemaking process.

Jay Winter and Jean-Louis Robert, *Capital Cities at War: Paris, London, Berlin* 1914 –1919 (Cambridge: Cambridge University Press, 1997), 259.

submarines. The Germans' submarine gamble failed to thwart the British. Moreover, unrestricted submarine warfare brought the United States into the war in April 1917, after German U-boats had sunk several American ships.

Political opposition increased in Europe, and deteriorating living conditions sparked outright revolt by civilians. "We are living on a volcano," warned an Italian politician in the spring of 1917. High prices and food shortages plagued everyday life (Figure 26.1). "Wages are not rising [but] food prices have risen by 100 and 200 percent," a Budapest paper complained in the summer of 1915. "We cannot bear this any longer!" Food shortages in cities of Italy, Russia, and Germany as well as in Vienna provoked riots by women who were unable to feed their families. As inflation mounted, tenants conducted rent strikes, factory hands and white-collar workers alike walked off the job, and female workers protested the skyrocketing cost of living and their fatigue from overwork.

Combatant countries were rife with dissension and conflicting goals. By 1917, the war had

strengthened nationalist movements and the new emperor of Austria-Hungary secretly asked the Allies for a negotiated peace to avoid a total collapse of his empire. In the summer of 1917, the German Reichstag announced its desire for a "peace of understanding and permanent reconciliation of peoples." Woodrow Wilson further weakened civilian resolve in Germany and Austria-Hungary in January 1918 by issuing his Fourteen Points, a blueprint for a new international order that held out the promise of a nonvindictive peace settlement to war-weary citizens of the Central Powers. The Allies faced dissent too. In the spring of 1917, French soldiers mutinied, refusing to participate in any more bloody and fruitless offensives. And in Russia, wartime protest turned into outright revolution.

Revolution in Russia

Of all the warring nations, Russia sustained the greatest number of casualties—7.5 million by 1917. Slaughter on the eastern front had driven hundreds of thousands of peasants into the Russian

Revolution in Russia

1917

March 8   International Women's Day, strikes and demonstrations

March 12   Establishment of Provisional Government

March 15   Nicholas II abdicates

April 17   Lenin and other Bolshevik leaders return to Russia

May 14   Resignation of Milyukov, first head of Provisional Government

May 16   Kerensky takes over Provisional Government

Late June–early July   Russian offensive against Germany fails

Mid-July   Attempted popular uprising fails

September 9–14   Kornilov military coup d'état fails

November 6–7   Bolshevik seizure of power on behalf of soviets

November 25   Constituent assembly elections held

1918

January 18   Constituent assembly closed down by Bolsheviks

1918–1922   Civil war

1924   Union of Soviet Socialist Republics formally established

1928–1929   Stalin takes full power

interior, where officials were unprepared to deal with the refugees' hunger, homelessness, and disease. In March 1917,* crowds of workingwomen swarmed the streets of Petrograd demanding relief from harsh conditions. As these women were turned away from stores, they fell in with other protesters commemorating International Women's Day and began looting shops for food. Factory workers joined them in the streets, and the rioters enlisted support from other citizens and soldiers guarding the streets. Compared with the other great powers, Russia was industrially and commercially backward. Thus, the demands of the war

---

*Until February 1918, Russia remained on the Julian calendar, which was thirteen days behind the Gregorian calendar used by the rest of Europe. Hence the first phase of the revolution occurred in March according to the Gregorian or European calendar (but February in the Julian calendar), the later phase in November using the Gregorian calendar (October according to the Julian). All dates used in this book follow the Gregorian calendar.

overwhelmed the government's ability to provide basic necessities on the home front. In addition, many in the army, instead of remaining loyal to the tsar, were embittered by the massive casualties caused by their inferior weapons and their leaders' foolhardy tactics. The politicization that had evolved since the Revolution of 1905 combined with the government's incompetence during the war raised the voice of protest to a crescendo.

By 1917, the Russian monarchy commanded little respect because Nicholas was an inept leader in the best of circumstances. Unlike other heads of state, Nicholas failed to unify the bureaucracy, industrialists, workers, and peasants in a concerted effort to provision the military and home fronts. In addition, Grigori Rasputin, a combination of holy man and charlatan, held Nicholas and his wife, Alexandra, in his thrall by claiming to control the hemophilia of their son and heir. When government ministers challenged Rasputin's influence on state matters, Nicholas sided with Rasputin and dismissed his officials. "Is this stupidity or treason?" one member of the Duma asked of the corrupt, impotent wartime administration. Educated and influential leaders withdrew their support. When the riots erupted in February 1917, Nicholas was away, attempting to rally his forces at the front; but when railroad workers diverted his train on its way back to Petrograd, he knew the situation was hopeless. He abdicated, he and his family were taken into custody, and the three-hundred-year-old Romanov dynasty came to an end.

The Provisional Government. Politicians from the old Duma formed a new ruling entity called the Provisional Government, but continuing hardships and the competing aspirations of many groups—workers, homemakers, students, liberal politicians, and soldiers—made it difficult for the new body to govern. At first hopes were high, even utopian, that under the Provisional Government, as one revolutionary poet put it, "our false, filthy, boring, hideous life should become a just, pure, merry, and beautiful life." Composed essentially of moderates, the Provisional Government had to pursue the war successfully, manage internal affairs better, and set government on a firm constitutional footing to establish its credibility. However, it did not rule alone, as the Russian Revolution felt the tug of many different political forces.

Lenin Addressing the Second All-Russian Congress of Soviets
In the spring of 1917, the German government craftily let Lenin and other Bolsheviks travel from their exile in Switzerland back to the scene of the unfolding revolution in Russia. A committed revolutionary instead of a political reformer, Lenin used his oratory and skilled maneuvering to convince many in the soviets to follow him in overthrowing the Provisional Government, taking Russia out of the war, and implementing his brand of communism.
Novosti (London).

Spontaneously elected soviets—councils of workers and soldiers—competed with the government for political support and often challenged its policies. Soviets had sprung up during the Revolution of 1905 and quickly revived in 1917 to press for improved conditions and a speedy resolution of the war. Lively and informed, the soviets contrasted the people's needs with the privileges of the upper-class men in the Provisional Government. In the first euphoric rush of revolution, the soviets ended the deference society usually paid the wealthy and officers, urged respect for workers and the poor, and temporarily gave an air of celebration and carnival to this political cataclysm. The peasantry, another competing force for power, began to confiscate gentry estates and withheld produce from the market because of the lack of consumer goods for which to exchange food. Urban food shortages intensified.

In hopes of further destabilizing Russia, in April 1917 the Germans provided safe rail transportation for Lenin and other prominent Bolsheviks to return from their exile in Switzerland to Petrograd through German territory. Lenin, described by contemporaries as "humorless, uncompromising, and detached," had devoted his entire existence to bringing about socialism through the

force of his small band of Bolsheviks. As a political exile he had no parliamentary experience, but he had developed his position by maneuvering among socialist factions, by writing propaganda and theoretical works, and through the sheer strength of his will. Upon his return to Petrograd, Lenin issued the April Theses, a radical document that called for Russia to withdraw from the war, for the soviets to seize power on behalf of workers and poor peasants, and for all private land to be nationalized. The Bolsheviks challenged the legitimacy of the Provisional Government with the slogans "All power to the soviets" and "Peace, land, and bread." Committed to ending private property and to establishing Bolshevik leadership, Lenin wanted to block the success of the liberal policies of the Provisional Government.

By early summer the Provisional Government saw a battlefield victory as the only way to ensure its position against competitors at home and to bargain with the Central Powers for an advantageous peace. On July 1, the Russian army attacked the Austrians in Galicia but was defeated once again. The new prime minister, the Socialist Revolutionary Aleksandr Kerensky (1881–1970), used his commanding oratory to arouse patriotism, but he lacked the political skills needed to fashion an effective wartime government. In Petrograd groups of workers, soldiers, and sailors—many of them Bolsheviks—agitated for the soviets to replace the Provisional Government. So strong had the soviets grown under the coordination of the Petrograd soviet that they seemed to constitute a dual power along with the Provisional Government. To restore order, the government rounded up Bolshevik leaders and accused them of being German agents, forcing many others into hiding. Soon, however, the government needed the Bolsheviks to head off a military coup led by General Lavr Kornilov.

As Bolshevik popularity in the cities rose, the stature of other politicians fell. By fall 1917, Kerensky's Provisional Government was thoroughly discredited. Its leadership had failed both to enact a well-defined land reform and to call a constituent assembly to develop a permanent blueprint for government. Its conduct of the war had been disastrous, leaving the army, as one Russian critic put it, "a huge crowd of tired, poorly clad, poorly fed, embittered men."

The Bolshevik Takeover. In November 1917, the Bolshevik leadership, urged on by Lenin, staged an uprising against Kerensky to prevent him from holding elections that might have stabilized the Provisional Government. The Bolsheviks took over key facilities (including the Winter Palace), drove out Kerensky's government, and seized power and placed it in the hands of a congress of soviets while claiming the right to form a government.

In January 1918, elections were finally held for a constituent assembly. Russian citizens, voting freely, elected representatives from a variety of political parties. The Bolsheviks, who by then had supported the elections, did not fare well, gaining fewer seats than the Socialist Revolutionaries. Within days, the Bolsheviks used troops to disrupt the assembly and took over the government by force. They seized town and city administrations, closing down the *zemstvos* (local councils) and other institutions in the countryside where Socialist Revolutionary support was keen. Soon after, the Bolsheviks asked Germany for peace.

The Germans agreed, but their idea of peace was the Treaty of Brest-Litovsk (March 1918), which placed vast regions of the old Russian Empire under German occupation. (See Map 26.1.) The treaty partially realized the German ideal of a central European region, or *Mitteleuropa*, under German control. It also showed the remaining Allied powers how tough the Germans were as victors and how unreliable the Russians were as allies. Because the loss of millions of square miles put Petrograd at risk, the Bolsheviks relocated the capital to Moscow. Lenin agreed to the catastrophic terms of the treaty not only because he had promised to bring peace to Russia but also because he believed that the rest of Europe would soon rebel against war and overthrow the capitalist order. Signaling a new beginning, the congress that approved the Treaty of Brest-Litovsk formally adopted the name *Communist* (taken from Marx's writings) to distinguish itself from the socialists/social democrats who had voted for the disastrous war in the first place.

Civil War in Russia

Programs for rapid change and violent civil war soon followed the Bolshevik takeover. In the winter of 1918–1919, the Bolshevik government, observing Marxist doctrine, abolished private property. At the same time it allowed peasants to work the land they had seized in the first year of revolution to shift their allegiance away from the Socialist Revolutionary Party. The government also nationalized factories in order to restore production, which had fallen off precipitously even as factories came under the control of workers' councils. The Provisional Government had allowed both men and women to vote in 1917; Russia was thus the first great power to legalize universal suffrage. However, once the Bolsheviks limited slates to candidates from the Communist Party, the right to vote became a hollow privilege.

Resistance to Bolshevik policies mushroomed into full-fledged civil war (Map 26.3) with the pro-Bolsheviks (or "Reds") pitted against an array of antirevolutionary forces (the "Whites"). Among the Whites, the tsarist military leadership, composed of many landlords and supporters of aristocratic rule, took to the field whatever troops it could muster. Dispossessed businessmen and the liberal intelligentsia lent their support to the anti-Bolsheviks. The revolutionary picture was complicated by issues of nationality, class, and politics. Many non-Russian nationality groups, formerly incorporated into the empire through force, Russification, and other bureaucratic efforts, fought the Bolsheviks because they saw their chance for independence. Before World War I ended, Russia's former allies, notably the United States, Britain, France, and Japan, landed troops in the country. Motives for the invasion varied. Some wanted to keep Entente supplies out of German hands; others fought to help tsarist loyalists overturn the Bolsheviks. To compete with the Bolsheviks, the counterrevolutionary groups desperately needed a strong leader and unified goals. Instead, the groups competed with one another; the pro-tsarist forces, for example, alienated those aspiring to nation-state status, such as the Ukrainians, Estonians, and Lithuanians. Ultimately, without a common purpose, the opponents of revolution could not win.

The civil war shaped communism. Leon Trotsky (1879–1940), Bolshevik commissar of war, built a highly disciplined army by ending democratic procedures, such as the election of officers, that had originally attracted soldiers to Bolshevism.

Lenin and Trotsky introduced the policy of war communism, whereby urban workers and troops moved through the countryside, brutally confiscating grain from the peasantry to feed the army and workforce. The Cheka (secret police) set up detention camps for political opponents and black marketers and often shot them without trial. The expansion of the size and strength of the Cheka and the Red Army—the latter eventually numbered five million men—accompanied the expansion of the bureaucracy, making government more authoritarian and undermining the promise of Marxism that revolution would bring a "withering away" of the state.

As the Bolsheviks clamped down on opposition during the bloody civil war, they organized their supporters to foster revolutionary Marxism across Europe. In March 1919, they founded the Third International, also known as the Comintern (Communist International), for the explicit purpose of replacing the old International with a

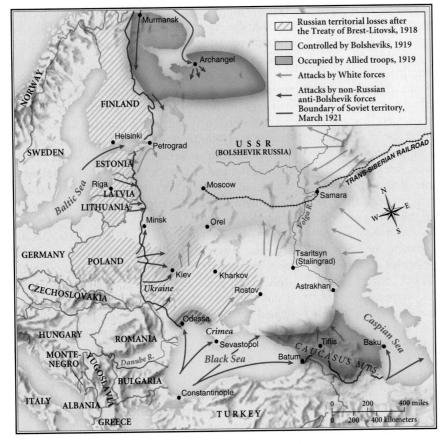

MAP 26.3 The Russian Civil War, 1917–1922
Nationalists, aristocrats, middle-class citizens, and property-owning peasants tried to combine their interests to defeat the Bolsheviks, but they failed to create an effective political consensus. The result was more suffering for ordinary people, whose produce was confiscated to fight the civil war. The Western powers and Japan also sent in troops to put down this revolution that so threatened the economic and political order.

centralized organization dedicated to promoting communism. By mid-1921, the Red Army had successfully shored up Bolshevism in Russia and secured the Crimea, the Caucasus, and the Muslim borderlands. When the Japanese withdrew from Siberia in 1922, the civil war ended in central and east Asia. The Bolsheviks were now in charge of a state as multinational as the old Russian Empire had been.

The Russian Revolution, as led by the Bolsheviks, promised bold experiments in social and political leadership. But although the revolution had turned out the inept Romanovs and the privileged aristocracy, civil war turned Russia into a battlefield where disease, hunger, and death prevailed. Moreover, the brutal way the Bolsheviks came to power by crushing opposition of all stripes ushered in a political style and direction far different from earlier socialist hopes.

Ending the War: 1918

Having pulled Russia out of World War I, the Bolsheviks left the rest of Europe's leaders confronting a new balance of forces. Facing war protest as well, these leaders were also left fearing that communism might lie in their future.

German military leaders continued to uphold the cult of the offensive despite the groundswell of discontent. Indeed, the generals developed a new offensive strategy to break the stalemate. Instead of attacking along a front extending for miles, concentrated forces would pierce single points of the enemy's relatively thin defense lines and then wreak havoc from the rear. In the fall of 1917, the Central Powers overwhelmed the Italian army at Caporetto using these tactics. In the spring of 1918, they made one final attempt to smash through the Allied lines, but the offensive ground to a bloody halt within weeks. By then the British and French had started making limited but effective use of tanks supported by airplanes. Although the first tanks were cumbersome, their ability to withstand machine-gun fire made offensive attacks possible. In the summer of 1918, the Allies, now fortified by the Americans, pushed back the Germans all along the western front and headed toward Germany. The German armies, suffering more than two million casualties between spring and summer, rapidly disintegrated.

By October 1918, the desperate German command helped create a civilian government, hoodwinking inexperienced and weak politicians to take responsibility for the defeat and to sue for peace. This change in tactics acknowledged growing pressures for constitutionalism in Germany but also served to deflect blame from the military, whose generals proclaimed themselves still fully capable of winning the war. Weak-willed civilians, they could claim, had dealt the military a "stab in the back" and were, in the words of Ludendorff, "largely responsible for things having turned out as they have. . . . They must now eat the soup they have served us." Amidst this blatant political deceit and flux, naval officers called for a final sea battle. As rumors of the plans leaked, sailors at the naval base at Kiel mutinied against what they saw as a suicide mission. Their rebellion capped years of indignities at the hands of high-ranking officers whose champagne-filled diet contrasted with the sailors' meager fare of turnips and thin soup. The sailors' revolt spread to the workers, who demonstrated in Berlin, Munich, and other major cities. The uprisings provoked Social Democratic politicians to declare a German republic in an effort to prevent revolution. On November 9, 1918, Kaiser William II fled.

The Central Powers were collapsing on all fronts. Since the previous winter, Austria-Hungary had kept many combat divisions at home simply to maintain civil order. By the fall of 1918, crowds in Prague and other disaffected parts of the empire were vandalizing imperial insignia on public buildings. At the end of October, Czechs and Slovaks declared an independent state, and the Croatian parliament simultaneously announced Croatia's independence.

Finally, on November 11, 1918, at 5:00 A.M., an armistice was signed. The guns fell silent on the western front six hours later. In the course of four years, European civilization had been sorely tested, if not shattered. Conservative figures put the battlefield toll at a minimum of ten million deaths and thirty million wounded, incapacitated, or eventually to die of their wounds. In every European combatant country, industrial and agricultural production had plummeted from prewar output. Moreover, much of the reduced output had been put to military use, and food and supplies for civilians had often fallen below subsistence levels.

Asia, Africa, and the Americas, which depended on European trade, also felt the painful impact of Europe's declining production. From 1918 to 1919, the weakened global population suffered another devastating blow when an influenza epidemic rampaged around the world, leaving at least twenty million more dead.

Besides illness, hunger, and death, the war also provoked tremendous moral questioning. Soldiers returning home in 1918 and 1919 flooded the book market with their memoirs, trying to give meaning to their experiences. People had expressed a range of feelings about the Great War in prose and verse almost from the start: some 2,500 war poets published in Britain alone. Whereas many had begun by emphasizing heroism and glory, others were cynical and bitter by war's end. They insisted the fighting had been absolutely meaningless. Total war had drained society of resources and population and had inadvertently sown the seeds of future catastrophes.

❖ The Search for Peace in an Era of Revolution

Revolutionary fervor swept the continent, especially in the former empires of Germany and Austria-Hungary. In Moscow, Lenin welcomed the emperors' downfall as a phase of world revolution that would usher in an age of working-class internationalism. Indeed, until 1921 the triumph of socialism seemed plausible. Immediately following the war, many of the newly independent peoples of eastern and central Europe fervently supported socialist principles, and workers and peasants in Germany were in a revolutionary mood. Yet as revolutionaries attempted to realize their political program, they faced liberal and right-wing opponents. Many of the latter hoped for a political order based on military authority of the kind they had relied on during the war. Faced with a volatile mix of revolution and counterrevolution, diplomats from around the world arrived in Paris in January 1919 to negotiate the terms of peace. For eighteen months they planned Europe's reconstruction according to their own competing interests, often without recognizing the magnitude of the changes brought about by the war.

Europe in Turmoil

Urban people and returning soldiers ignited the protest that swept Europe in 1918 and 1919. In January 1919, the red flag of socialist revolution flew from city hall in Glasgow, Scotland, while in cities of the collapsing Austro-Hungarian Empire workers set up councils to direct factory production and to influence political events. As in Russia, many soldiers did not disband at the armistice but formed volunteer armies or paramilitary bands, making Europe ripe not for parliamentary politics but for revolution by force.

In November 1918, Germany was politically unstable, partly because of the shock of defeat. Germans initially took to the streets in droves to rally around the civilian politicians who were ending the war. By December, however, independent socialist groups and workers' councils were vying with the dominant Social Democrats for control of the government. Demonstrators, suffering under the Allies' continuation of the wartime blockade, demanded economic policies that would assuage workers' misery and give veterans their back pay. Whereas in 1848 revolutionaries had marched to city hall or the king's residence, these protesters took over newspapers and telegraph offices, thus controlling the flow of information. Some were inspired by one of the most radical socialist factions, the Spartacists, led by cofounders Karl Liebknecht (1871–1919) and Rosa Luxemburg (1870–1919). Unlike Lenin, the two Spartacist leaders favored political uprisings that would give workers political experience and thus eliminate the need for an all-knowing party leadership. They argued for *direct* worker control of institutions, but they shared Lenin's dislike for parliamentary politics.

Social Democratic leader Friedrich Ebert (1871–1925), who headed the new government, believed that the parliamentary republic would best realize Social Democratic objectives. Splitting with his former socialist allies, he called on the German army and the Freikorps—a roving paramilitary band of students, demobilized soldiers, and others—to suppress the workers' councils and demonstrators. He thus gave official credence to the idea that political differences could be settled with violence. "The enthusiasm is marvelous," wrote one young soldier. "No mercy's shown. We shoot even the wounded. . . . We were much more humane against the French in the field." Members of the Freikorps hunted down Luxemburg and Liebknecht and murdered them. A measure of calm returned to Berlin and other cities.

In February 1919, a constituent assembly met in the city of Weimar, where it approved a constitution and founded a parliamentary republic. The reaction could not have been worse. The military leadership dreamed of a restored monarchy and a return to the military prestige of imperial days. "As I love Germany, so I hate the Republic," wrote one officer. Contempt for republican institutions motivated Freikorps officers to attempt a coup (*putsch*), known as the Kapp Putsch after one of its right-wing leaders, in the spring of 1920. The military command refused to crush the coup: "Soldiers do not fire on soldiers." So Ebert called for a general strike that stopped the coup by showing its lack of popular support. Although revolutions from both the right and the left failed, the Weimar Republic's grip on power was far from solid, and it had set the dangerous precedent of relying on street violence, paramilitary groups, and protests to solve political problems.

In the late winter of 1919, leftists proclaimed soviet republics—governments led by workers' councils—in Bavaria and Hungary. The Hungarian regime, led by Béla Kun (1885–1937), gained some middle-class nationalist support by resisting Allied plans to reduce the size of Hungary drastically. But Kun's zeal to nationalize production and the brutality of his secret police alienated many Hungarians, and the soviet republic was overthrown in August. Meanwhile in Bavaria, leaders of the German soviets fell before the assault of the volunteer armies and Weimar troops.

The Bolsheviks tried to establish a Marxist regime in Poland in the belief that its people wanted a workers' revolution. Instead the Poles resisted and drove the Red Army back in 1920, while the Allied powers rushed supplies and advisers to Warsaw. Though this and other revolts failed, they provided further proof that total war had loosened political and social order.

Peacemaking

As political turmoil engulfed peoples from Berlin to Moscow, the Paris peace conference opened in January 1919. Visions of communism spreading westward haunted the assembled statesmen, but the desperation of millions of war-ravaged citizens, the status of Germany, and the reconstruction of a secure Europe topped their agenda. Leaders such as French Premier Georges Clemenceau had to satisfy their angry citizens, who demanded revenge or, at the very least, compensation for their suffering. France had lost 1.3 million people—almost an entire generation; and more than a million buildings, six thousand bridges, and thousands of miles of railroad lines and roads had been destroyed while the war was fought on its soil. Great Britain's representative, Prime Minister David Lloyd George, caught the mood of the British public by campaigning in 1918 with such slogans as "Hang the kaiser." Italians arrived on the scene unconditionally demanding the territory promised to them in the 1915 Treaty of London.

The stance of the United States further complicated the remaking of Europe. This new world power had helped achieve the Allied victory, and its presence at the conference indicated a dramatic realignment of power away from any individual European country. President Woodrow Wilson also had a special agenda. It was conciliatory, however, seeking to incorporate his Fourteen Points, on which the truce had been based, into the final settlement. Steeped in the language of freedom, the Fourteen Points called for open diplomacy, arms reduction, an "open-minded" settlement of colonial issues, and the self-determination of peoples.

This was no small ambition, for on top of the death and destruction on both sides, Allied propaganda had made the Germans seem like inhuman monsters. Many citizens demanded a harsh peace. Moreover, some experts feared that Germany was using the armistice only to regroup for more warfare. Indeed, Germans widely refused to admit that their army had lost the war. Eager for army support, Ebert had given returning soldiers a rousing welcome: "As you return unconquered from the field of battle, I salute you." Thus, conservative leaders among Wilson's former allies campaigned to make him look naive and deluded. "Wilson bores me with his Fourteen Points," Clemenceau complained. "Why, the good Lord himself has only ten."

Nevertheless, Wilson's Fourteen Points appealed to European moderates and convinced Germans that the settlement would not be vindictive. In fact, Wilson's commitment to *settlement* as opposed to *surrender* contained tough-minded stipulations, for he recognized that Germany was still

MAP 26.4 Europe and the Middle East after the Peace Settlements of 1919–1920
The political landscape of central, east, and east central Europe changed dramatically as a result of the Russian Revolution and the Peace of Paris. The Ottoman, German, Russian, and Austro-Hungarian Empires were either broken up altogether into multiple small states or territorially reduced in size. The settlement left resentments among Germans and Hungarians and created a group of weak, struggling nations in the heartland of Europe. The victorious powers took over much of the oil-rich Middle East.

the strongest state on the continent. He merely pushed for a treaty that balanced the strengths and interests of the various European powers. Many of the historians, economists, and other experts accompanying Wilson to Paris agreed that, harshly dealt with and humiliated, Germany might soon become vengeful and chaotic—a lethal combination that could lead to the growth of unsavory political sects.

The Peace of Paris, 1919–1920. After six months, the statesmen and their teams of experts produced the Peace of Paris, composed of a cluster of individual treaties (Map 26.4). These treaties shocked the countries that had to accept them, and in retrospect historians see how they destabilized eastern and east-central Europe. (See "Contrasting Views," page 998.) The treaties separated Austria from Hungary, reduced Hungary by almost

Arguing with the Victors

The end of World War I aroused hopes around the world. The conquered expected a fair-minded treaty based on Wilson's Fourteen Points, while a variety of other peoples saw in that same document the promise of "self-determination." In particular, men living under colonial domination, such as many in Africa and the Arab states, had taken part in the conflict because the Allies had promised new rights in return for fighting this bloody and destructive war. The emir Faisal had led troops to bring about freedom and Arab unity (Document 1). Like some representatives at the Pan-African Congress, even those Africans who had not fought saw peacemaking as a process that should forge a better future. Many wanted full political rights and parliamentary representation if not outright independence (Document 2).

Thus when the thousands of politicians and expert bureaucrats from the victorious powers gathered in Paris, they were besieged by numerous outsiders to Western government, each making a claim and taking a side for freedom, peace, rights, and special attention to their needs—right or wrong. Feminist-pacifists wanted to ensure the pacifist cause (Document 3), while a Polish representative articulated a concern that Jews had taken too many good jobs in the new Poland (Document 4). Caucuses and congresses were held simultaneously with the conference to present a variety of proposals to the peacemakers, but to very little avail.

1. Claiming Independence for the Middle East

Arabs had hotly debated whether to join with the colonizers in World War I, but promises of independence won them over. Some Arabs argued for independence of individual areas in the Middle East and for resolutions to competing claims of the Arabs and of new Jewish settlers in the region. Emir Faisal, who had commanded Arab forces in the war, presented the pan-Arab ideal.

The aim of the Arab nationalist movement is to unite the Arabs eventually into one nation. . . . I came to Europe on behalf of my father and the Arabs of Asia to say that they are expecting the powers at the Conference not to attach undue importance to superficial differences of condition among us and not to consider them only from the low ground of existing European material interests and supposed spheres of influence. They expect the powers to think of them as one potential people, jealous of their language and liberty, and they ask that no step be taken inconsistent with the prospect of an eventual union of these areas under one sovereign government.

Source: Stephen Bonsal, *Suitors and Suppliants: The Little Nations at Versailles* (Port Washington: Kennikat Press, 1969), 32–33.

2. The Voice of Pan-Africanists

African and African American leaders believed it would be opportune for them to meet in a Pan-African Congress while the Paris Peace Conference was going on. For some time an idea of a single African people had been forming among leading black intellectuals, and Pan-African meetings had taken place from the late nineteenth century on. The demands were legion, but above all the congress, by mid-February 1919, had resolved to seek better treatment from the colonial powers.

Resolved

That the Allied and Associated Powers establish a code of law for the international protection of the natives of Africa. . . .

The Negroes of the world demand that hereafter the natives of Africa and the peoples of African descent be governed according to the following principles:

1. The land: the land and its natural resources shall be held in trust for the natives and at all times they shall have effective ownership of as much land as they can profitably develop. . . .

3. Labor: slavery and corporal punishment shall be abolished and forced labor except in punishment for crime. . . .

5. The state: the natives of Africa must have the right to participate in the government as fast as

their development permits, in conformity with the principle that the government exists for the natives, and not the natives for the government.

Source: Quoted in W. E. B. Du Bois, *The World and Africa* (New York: International Publishers, 1946), 11–12.

3. Pacifists' Goals for the Peace Process

Pacifist women were angered that the peace conference would be held in Paris instead of in a noncombatant or neutral country. Situating it where wartime hatred was at a fevered pitch, they argued, would not allow the conquered to receive a fair hearing. The women themselves met in Switzerland to debate the shape of the peace so that German and Austrian women would attend. The German and Austrian representatives were crucial, the pacifists believed, for a continuing blockade of the Central Powers after the armistice was increasing suffering and causing deaths. The pacifist women speeded the dispatch of their resolutions to Paris when the Versailles portion of the Peace of Paris was announced.

The International Congress of Women regards the famine, pestilence, and unemployment extending throughout great tracts of central and eastern Europe and into Asia as a disgrace to civilization.

It therefore urges the Governments of all the Powers assembled at the Peace Conference immediately to develop the inter-allied organizations formed for purposes of war into an international organization for purposes of peace, so that the resources of the world—food, raw materials, finance, transport—shall be made available for the relief of the peoples of all countries from famine and pestilence.

To this end it urges that immediate action be taken . . . to raise the blockade.

The terms of the peace tacitly sanction secret diplomacy, deny the principles of self-determination, recognize the rights of victors to the spoils of war, and create all over Europe discords and animosities, which can only lead to future war. . . . By the financial and economic proposals a hundred million people of this generation in the heart of Europe are condemned to poverty, disease, and despair, which must result in the spread of hatred and anarchy within each nation.

Source: James Weber Linn, *Jane Addams: A Biography* (New York: Greenwood, 1968), 342–43.

4. Anti-Semitism at the Peacetable

A Polish leader lobbied the Allies to exercise a police power in the newly independent Poland, where major problems would be rural crowding and inability to make ends meet on the land.

We have too many Jews, and those who will be allowed to remain with us must change their habits. I recognize that this will be difficult and will take time. The Jew must produce and not remain devoted exclusively to what we regard as parasitical pursuits. Unless restrictions are imposed upon them soon, all our lawyers, doctors, and small merchants will be Jews. They must turn to agriculture, and they must at least share small business and retail stores with their Polish neighbors. I readily admit that there is some basis in the Jewish contention that in days past it was difficult for them to own land or even to work the fields of others as tenants; that they were often compelled by circumstances beyond their control to gain their livelihood in ways which are hurtful to Polish economy. Under our new constitution all this will be changed, and for their own good I hope the Jews will avail themselves of their new opportunities. I say this in their own interest as well as in the interest of restored Poland. Now, and I fear for decades to come, Poland will be too poor to permit one-tenth of its population to engage in pursuits which to say the least are not productive.

Source: Bonsal, *Suitors and Suppliants,* 124.

QUESTIONS FOR DEBATE

1. Describe the various contending claims beyond those of the official combatant powers. Did the victorious powers heed these voices when forging the peace?
2. How were the various demands at the peace conference related to the politics and conditions of World War I?
3. Do any of the demands seem more justifiable in addressing the peacetime needs of Europe and the world?

two-thirds of its inhabitants and three-quarters of its territory, broke up the Ottoman Empire, and treated Germany severely. They replaced the Habsburg Empire with a group of small, internally divided, and relatively weak states: Czechoslovakia, Poland, and the Kingdom of the Serbs, Croats, and Slovenes, later renamed Yugoslavia. Austria and Hungary were both left reeling at their loss of territory and resources and struggling for a sense of identity. Many Austrians, their multiethnic empire gone, desperately wanted to merge with Germany, but the settlement expressly forbade such a union.

After a century and a half of partition, Poland was reconstructed from parts of Russia, Germany, and Austria-Hungary, with one-third of its population ethnically non-Polish. The statesmen in Paris also created a Polish Corridor that connected Poland to the Baltic Sea and separated East Prussia from the rest of Germany. The Allies had high hopes that central and east-central Europe would be stable; however, many of the new states became rivals and were for the most part politically and economically weak.

The treaties with Austria and Hungary were crucial for the future of Europe. At the time, however, the Treaty of Versailles with Germany was the centerpiece of the Peace of Paris. This treaty only partially quenched the French thirst for revenge. France recovered Alsace and Lorraine, and the victors would temporarily occupy the left, or western, bank of the Rhine and the coal-bearing Saar basin. Wilson accepted his allies' expectations that Germany would pay substantial reparations for the civilian damage it inflicted in the war. The specific amount was established not by the peacemakers in 1919 but by Allied commissions, which only in 1921 agreed on the crushing sum of 132 billion gold marks. Germany also had to surrender the largest ships of its merchant marine, reduce its army, almost eliminate its navy, stop manufacturing offensive weapons, and deliver a large amount of free coal each year to Belgium and France. Furthermore, it was forbidden to have an air force and had to give up its colonies.

The average German saw in these terms an unmerited humiliation that was compounded by Article 231 of the treaty, which described Germany's "responsibility" for damage done during a conflict "imposed on [the Entente] by the aggression of Germany and her allies." The outraged German people interpreted this as a "war guilt" clause, and the government set up a special propaganda office to refute it and to contest the terms of what Germans came to call a *Diktat*, or dictated peace. Article 231 allowed the victors to collect reparations from economically viable Germany rather than from decimated Austria, which had deployed the first troops. War guilt also made Germany an outcast in the community of nations.

The League of Nations. The Peace of Paris set up an organization called the League of Nations, whose responsibility for maintaining peace—a principle called *collective security*—was to replace the divisive secrecy of prewar power politics. As part of Wilson's vision, the league would guide the world toward disarmament, arbitrate its members' disputes, and monitor labor conditions around the world. Returning to prewar isolationism, the United States Senate, in a humiliating defeat for the president, failed to ratify the peace settlement and refused to join the league. Moreover, both Germany and Russia initially were excluded from the league and were thus blocked from acting in legal concert with other nations.

The covenant, or charter, of the League of Nations organized the administration of the colonies and territories of Germany and the Ottoman Empire—such as Togo, Cameroon, Tanganyika, Syria, and Lebanon—through a system of mandates. The European powers exercised political control over mandated territory, but local leaders retained limited authority. The league covenant justified the mandate system as providing governance by "advanced nations" over territories "not yet able to stand by themselves under the strenuous conditions of the modern world." The war, however, had depleted the great powers' financial resources and mental resolve to make a success of the mandate system. Their new responsibility was complicated by the fact that colonized and other people of color, who had served and fallen on the battlefield, began to challenge the claims of their European masters. They had seen how savage and degraded were these people who claimed to be racially superior, politically more advanced, and leaders of global culture. "Never again will the darker people of the world occupy just the place they had before," the African American leader W. E. B. Du Bois predicted in 1918. The mandate system continued the practice of apportioning the globe among European powers, but like the Peace of Paris it aroused anger and resistance. In the next decades, colonized peoples would rise up in greater numbers against this domination.

Economic and Diplomatic Consequences of the Peace

The financial and political settlement in the Peace of Paris had repercussions in the 1920s and beyond. Western leaders worried deeply about two intertwined issues in the aftermath of the war. The first was economic recovery and its relation to war debts, the conditions of international trade, and German reparations. The second was ensuring that peace lasted.

Economic Dilemmas.   France, the hardest hit by wartime destruction and billions of dollars in debt to the United States, estimated that Germany owed it at least $200 billion. The British, by contrast, worried about maintaining their empire and restoring trade with Germany, not about exacting huge reparations. Nevertheless, both France and Britain depended on some monetary redress to pay their war debts to the United States because Europe's share of world trade had plunged during the war. Although the United States wanted the debts paid, it used a soft tone toward the fragile Weimar Republic and a harsh one toward its Allied debtors, for whom U.S. sympathy had dwindled.

Germany claimed that the demand for reparations strained its government, already beset by political upheaval. Indeed, as early as 1919 British economist John Maynard Keynes had predicted a chain of disasters if the German standard of living were to fall because of the financial burden of reparations. But hardship was not the result of the Peace of Paris alone. The kaiser had refused to raise taxes, especially on the rich, to pay for the war, so the new republic had to deal with the resulting inflation, to pay reparations, and to finance the staggering domestic war debt. As an experiment in democracy, the Weimar Republic needed to woo the citizenry, not alienate it by hiking taxes. In 1921, when Germans refused to present a realistic payment scheme, the French occupied several cities in the Ruhr. Germany then accepted a payment plan that appeared for the sake of voters in receiver

countries to amount to $33 billion but that really came to only $12.5 billion over thirty-six years.

Embroiled with powers to the west, the German government deftly sought economic and diplomatic relations in eastern Europe. It reached an agreement to foster economic ties with Russia, desperate for western trade, in the Treaty of Rapallo (1922, renewed in the Treaty of Berlin in 1926). Its relations with powers to the west, however, continued to deteriorate. In 1923, after Germany defaulted on coal deliveries, the French and Belgians sent troops into the Ruhr basin, planning to use its abundant resources to recoup their wartime expenditures. Urged on by the government, Ruhr citizens fought back, shutting down industry and services by staying home from work. The German government printed trillions of marks to support the workers, to provide funds to the closed industries, and to pay its own war debts with practically worthless currency. Soon Germany was in the midst of a staggering inflation that demoralized its citizens and gravely threatened the international economy: at one point a single U.S. dollar cost 4.42 trillion marks, and wheelbarrows of money were required to buy a turnip. Wreaking psychological havoc, the inflation also wiped out people's savings and ruined those living on fixed incomes.

The spirit of the League of Nations demanded a resolution to this economic chaos through negotiations. The Dawes Plan (1924) and eventually the Young Plan (1929) reduced payments to the victors and restored the value of German currency. These plans also evened the balance of Germany's trade between east and west, a balance the Treaty of Rapallo had threatened. Only the French were unhappy, but their postwar weakness forced them to accept the reductions.

Ensuring Peace.   Following the Peace of Paris, statesmen recognized that ensuring peace entailed disarmament, bringing Germany back into the fold, and securing the new countries of eastern Europe. It took hard diplomatic bargaining outside the league to produce two plans in Germany's favor. At the Washington Conference in 1921, the United States, Great Britain, Japan, France, and Italy agreed to reduce their number of battleships and to stop constructing new ones for ten years. Four years later, in 1925, the league sponsored a meeting of the great powers, including Germany, at Locarno, Switzerland. The German diplomat Gustav Stresemann, who claimed that the Versailles treaty unfairly penalized Germany, negotiated a treaty at Locarno that provided Germany with a seat in the League of Nations as of 1926. In return, Germany agreed not to violate the borders of France and Belgium and to keep the nearby Rhineland demilitarized (unfortified by troops).

To the east, the door seemed open to a German attempt to regain territory lost to Poland, to form a merger with Austria, or to launch aggression against the states spun off from Austria-Hungary. To meet these unwelcome possibilities, Czechoslovakia, Yugoslavia, and Romania formed the "Little Entente" in 1920–1921. This was a collective security agreement to protect themselves from their two powerful neighbors Germany and Russia and to guard against Hungarian expansionism. Then, between 1924 and 1927, France allied itself with the Little Entente and with Poland. As diplomatic tensions relaxed, the major European powers, Japan, and the United States signed the Kellogg-Briand Pact (1928), which formally rejected international violence. The nations failed, however, to commit themselves to concrete action to prevent its outbreak.

The "Little Entente"

The publicity and planning that yielded the international agreements during the 1920s sharply contrasted with old-style diplomacy, which was conducted in secret and subject to little public scrutiny or democratic influence. The new openness suggested a diplomatic revolution and promised a peaceful age in international relations. Historians both praise and fault this era of apparent international cooperation. Some scholars praise it for promoting solid negotiations among the great powers, launching a system of collective security, reintegrating Germany into the community of nations, and showing an awareness that international politics and economics are related. Other scholars denounce the diplomats of this era who fed the press reports calculated to arouse the masses. For example,

much of the German populace was lashed into a nationalist frenzy by the press and opposing parties whenever Germany's diplomats, who were successfully working to undo the Treaty of Versailles, seemed to compromise. Although meetings such as the one at Locarno appeared to promote the goal of collective security, they also exposed the diplomatic process to nationalist demagogues who could rekindle political hatreds.

❖ A Decade of Recovery: Europe in the 1920s

Treaties ended the war but not the wartime spirit. Words and phrases from the battlefield punctuated everyday speech. Before the war the word *lousy* had meant "lice-infested"; but English-speaking soldiers returning from the trenches now applied it to anything bad. Raincoats became *trenchcoats*, and terms like *bombarded* and *rank and file* entered peacetime usage. Many feared the *Bolshies* and the *Reds* and wondered when rationing would end and they would have enough to eat. Maimed, disfigured veterans were present everywhere, and those without limbs were sometimes carried in baskets— hence the expression *basket case*. They overflowed hospitals, rest homes, and mental institutions, and family life centered on their care.

The 1920s was devoted to coming to terms with the social and political legacy of the war. A key question was how to restore civilian government when total war had generally strengthened military values, authoritarian government, and a controlled economy. Although people referred to the 1920s as the Roaring Twenties, the Jazz Age, and the Crazy Years, the sense of cultural release masked the serious problem of restoring social stability and implementing democracy. Three autocratic governments had collapsed as a result of the war, but how newly empowered citizens would react politically after the shock of war remained a burning question.

The Promise of Democratic Rebirth

The threat of revolution coexisted with a sense of democratic rebirth because of the League of Nations, the emergence of new nations from crumbled empires, and the formation of a constitutional

German republic. The extension of suffrage to women, widely granted at the war's end, also suggested the beginnings of a more democratic political order. Woman suffrage resulted in part from decades of activism; more immediately, many gov-

Women Gain Suffrage in the West	
1906	Finland
1913	Norway
1915	Denmark, Iceland
1917	Netherlands, Russia
1918	Czechoslovakia, Great Britain (limited suffrage)
1919	Germany
1920	Austria, United States
1921	Poland
1925	Hungary (limited suffrage)
1945	Italy, France
1971	Switzerland

Otto Dix, *The Sleepwalkers*
Artists in the defeated countries were especially attuned to the tragic absurdity of the war. German ex-soldier Otto Dix sketched smashed faces and corpses in varying states of decay, depicting people who had survived as grotesque or benumbed "sleepwalkers" who picked their way through the postwar wreckage. The simple horror of death and disfigurement made painted whores of those seeking a return to ordinary life.
"The Sleepwalkers" by Otto Dix from *The Nature of War* by John Keegan and Joseph Darracott. Holt, Rinehart and Winston, 1981. Private Collection, Essen.

ernments gave women the vote to reward them for their war efforts and to make revolution less tempting. In the first postwar elections, women were voted into parliaments, and the impression grew that they had also made extraordinary gains in breaking down barriers in the workplace. French men pointedly denied women the vote, insisting they would use their vote to bring back the rule of kings and priests. Governments continued building the welfare state by expanding payments to families with children and insurance programs for workers. New government benefits attested to a spreading belief that more evenly distributed wealth—sometimes referred to as *economic democracy*—was important to social stability in postwar society.

In addition to bringing about political and economic changes, the war had blurred class distinctions, giving rise to expectations that life would be fairer afterward. The massive casualties had generated social mobility by allowing commoners to move up to the ranks of officers, positions often monopolized by the prewar aristocracy. Members of all classes had rubbed shoulders in the trenches. The identical, evenly spaced crosses of military cemeteries made all the dead seem equal, as did the mass "brothers' graves" at the battlefront where rich and poor lay side by side in a single burial pit. Middle-class daughters worked outside the home; their mothers did their own housework because servants could earn more money in factories. The "servant problem," born of wartime opportunities, thus made middle-class and working-class households more similar. Finally, the Bolsheviks' refusal to honor prewar Russian bonds hurt tens of thousands of European investors, adding to the social leveling of war.

The slow trend toward economic democracy was not easy to maintain, however, because the cycles of boom and bust that had characterized the late nineteenth century reemerged. A short postwar boom prompted by rebuilding war-torn areas and filling consumer needs unsatisfied during the war was followed by an economic downturn that was most severe between 1920 and 1922. Skyrocketing unemployment led some to question the effectiveness of their governments and the fairness of society. By the mid-1920s, many of the economic opportunities for women had disappeared and they made up a smaller percentage of the workforce than in 1913.

Changes in the Political Landscape

Hard times especially corroded the new republics of eastern Europe, which were unprepared for independence in the sophisticated world market. Intensely nationalistic and competitive with one another, none but Czechoslovakia had a mature industrial sector, and agricultural techniques were often primitive. Like late-nineteenth-century politicians, leaders in these new countries reacted to adversity by enacting tariffs to protect domestic manufacturing and domestic markets.

Eastern Europe: Poland. The development of Poland exemplified the postwar political landscape in eastern Europe. Nationalism was increasingly defined in ethnic terms, and the reunified Poland consisted of one-third Ukrainians, Belorussians, Germans, and other ethnic minorities—many of whom had grievances against the dominant Poles. Moreover, varying religious, dynastic, and cultural traditions divided the Poles, who for 150 years had been ruled by three other powers. Polish reunification occurred without a common currency, political structure, or language—even the railroad tracks were not a standard size.

With virtually no economic or other support from the Allies, a constitutional government nonetheless took shape. Under a constitution that professed equal rights for all ethnicities and religions, the new democratic government, run by the Sejm

(parliament), tried to legislate the redistribution of large estates to the peasantry, but declining crop prices and overpopulation made life in the countryside difficult. Urban workers were better off than the peasantry (two-thirds of the population lived by subsistence farming) but worse off than laborers across Europe. The economic downturn brought strikes and violence in 1922–1923, and the inability of coalition parliaments to effect economic prosperity led to a coup in 1926 by strongman Jozef Pilsudski. Ultimately Pilsudski made it possible for a country choked by the endless debates of dozens of political parties and impaired by ethnic strife and anti-Semitism to function. Economic hardship and strong-arm solutions went hand in hand in east-central Europe. It was only with incredible difficulty that a reunified Poland survived the postwar years.

National Minorities in Postwar Poland

Legend:
- Polish
- Czech
- Slovak
- Belorussian
- Ukranian
- German
- Latvian
- Lithuanian
- Magyar (Hungarian)
- Romanian

Central Europe: Germany. Germany was a different case. The industrially sophisticated Weimar Republic confronted daunting challenges to making Germany democratic, even after putting down the postwar revolution. Although the German economy picked up and Germany became a center of experimentation in the arts, political life remained precarious because so many people felt nostalgia for imperial glory and loathed the Versailles treaty's restrictions. On the surface, Weimar's political system—a bicameral parliament and a chancellor responsible to the lower house— appeared similar to the parliamentary system in Britain and France, but extremist politicians heaped daily abuse on Germany's leaders, and contempt for parliamentary politics was widespread. Anyone who cooperated with the parliamentary system, wrote a wealthy newspaper and film magnate, "is a moral cripple." Right-wing parties, supporting the defunct monarchy or envisioning a new authoritarian state, constituted a threat to democracy instead of a healthy opposition. They favored violence rather than consensus building, and nationalist thugs murdered democratic leaders. One prominent victim was foreign minister Walter Rathenau, who had streamlined the German economy during the war; Rathenau, as a Jew and an industrialist, was part of two groups increasingly blamed for Germany's woes.

Support for the far right came from wealthy landowners and businessmen, white-collar workers whose standard of living had dropped during the war, and members of the lower-middle and middle classes hurt by inflation. Bands of disaffected youth and veterans proliferated, among them a group called Brown Shirts led by ex-soldier and political newcomer Adolf Hitler (1889–1945). In the wake of the Ruhr occupation of 1923, the Brown Shirts were one of the many elements that favored and even plotted the overthrow of the Weimar government. In November, Ludendorff and Hitler launched a coup d'état from a beer hall in Munich. Government troops suppressed the Beer Hall Putsch, but Hitler spent less than a year in jail and Ludendorff was acquitted. For conservative judges as for former aristocrats and most of the prewar bureaucrats who remained in government, such men were national heroes. After the mid-1920s, as the German economy surged, violent tactics and extreme political movements temporarily lost some of their appeal.

Western Europe: France and Britain. In France and Britain, parties of the right had less effect than elsewhere because parliamentary institutions were better established and the upper classes were not plotting to restore an authoritarian monarchy. In France, politicians from the conservative right and moderate left successively formed coalitions and rallied general support to rebuild war-torn regions and to force Germany to pay for the reconstruction. Hoping to stimulate population growth after the devastating loss of life, the French parliament made distributing birth-control information illegal and abortion a severely punished crime.

Britain encountered postwar boom and bust and continuing strife in Ireland. Ramsay MacDonald (1866–1937), elected the first Labour prime minister in 1924, represented the new-formed political ambitions of the working masses. Like other postwar British leaders, he had to swallow the

paradoxical fact that although Britain had the largest world empire, many of its industries were obsolete or in poor condition. A showdown came in the ailing coal industry, where prices fell and wages plummeted once the Ruhr mines reopened. On May 3, 1926, workers conducted a nine-day general strike against wage cuts and dangerous conditions in the mines. The strike provoked unprecedented middle-class resistance. University students, homemakers, and businessmen shut down the strike by driving trains, working on docks, and replacing workers in other jobs. The strike thus failed to help the miners, as citizens from many walks of life revived the wartime spirit to defend the declining economy.

In Ireland, the British government met bloody confrontation over the continuing failure to implement home rule. Irish republicans had attacked government buildings in Dublin on Easter Monday 1916 in an effort to wrest Irish independence from Britain. Leaders of the Easter Uprising were not prepared for full-scale revolt; their effort was easily defeated and many of them were hanged. The severity with which the British punished the rebels intensified demands for home rule, and in January 1919, republican leaders announced Ireland's independence from Britain and created a separate

The Irish Free State and Ulster, 1921

parliament called the Dail Eireann. The British government refused to recognize the parliament and sent in the Black and Tans, a volunteer army of demobilized soldiers so called for the color of their uniforms. Terror reigned in Ireland, as both the pro-independence forces and the Black and Tans waged guerrilla warfare, taking hostages, blowing up buildings, and even shooting into crowds at soccer matches.

By 1921, public outrage forced the British to negotiate. The treaty drawn up by the British government reversed the Irish declaration of independence and made the Irish Free State a self-governing dominion owing an oath of allegiance to the British crown. Ulster, a group of six northern counties containing a majority of Protestants, gained a separate status: it was self-governing but still had representation in the British Parliament. This division of Ireland and the terms of the division, though agreed upon at the time, subsequently led to new efforts for full independence of the Irish Free State. The rights of the Catholic minority in the north also became a major political issue there.

European powers encountered rebellion in overseas empires as well. Colonized peoples who had fought in the war expected more rights and even independence. Indeed, European politicians and military recruiters had actually promised the vote and many other reforms in exchange for support. But colonists' political activism, now enhanced by increasing education, trade, and experience with the West, mostly met a brutal response. Fearful of losing India, British forces massacred protesters at Amritsar in 1919 and put down revolts against the mandate system in Egypt and Iran in the early 1920s. The Dutch jailed political leaders in Indonesia; the French punished Indochinese nationalists. European politicians simultaneously began seeking compromises that would allow them to keep their empires intact. For many Western governments, maintaining empires abroad was crucial to ensuring democracy at home, as any hint of declining national prestige fed antidemocratic forces.

Reconstructing the Economy

For much of the West, worldwide economic competition was as big a challenge to recovery as were global political struggles. During the war the European economy had lost many of its international markets to India, Canada, Australia, Japan, and the United States. Nonetheless the war had forced European manufacturing to become more efficient and had expanded the demand for automotive and air transport, electrical products, and synthetic goods. The prewar pattern of mergers and cartels continued after 1918, giving rise to gigantic food-processing firms such as Nestlé in Switzerland and petroleum enterprises such as Royal Dutch Shell. Owners of these large manufacturing conglomerates wielded more financial and political power than entire small countries and hired rafts of public relations officials to perform a kind of indus-

trial diplomacy. By the late 1920s, Europe had overcome the wild economic swings of the immediate postwar years and was enjoying renewed prosperity.

Despite this growth, the United States was the trendsetter in economic modernization. Many European businessmen made pilgrimages to Henry Ford's Detroit assembly line, which by 1929 produced a Ford automobile every ten seconds. Ford touted this miracle of productivity as resulting in a lower cost of living and increased purchasing power for workers. Indeed, whereas French, German, and British citizens in total had under two million cars, some seventeen million cars were on U.S. streets in 1925.

Scientific management, sometimes called the science of work, also aimed to raise productivity. By timing and studying the motions workers used to accomplish tasks, the American efficiency expert Frederick Taylor demonstrated that people worked inefficiently. He developed methods to streamline workers' tasks and motions for maximum productivity. European industrialists adopted Taylor's methods during the war and after, but they were also influenced by European psychologists who emphasized the mental aspects of productivity and the need for a balance of work and leisure activities, such as cinema and sports, for both workers and managers.

The urgency behind this attention to productivity was both economic and political. Many industrial experts feared that Bolshevism would inspire class conflict, and they believed that increased productivity and prosperity would bind workers and management together. In theory, managers would reap enhanced output and profits, and workers would be rewarded with shorter hours, higher wages, and more consumer goods. In practice, streamlining did help reduce working hours in many industries, a result that encouraged union leaders to embrace modernization and the "cult of efficiency." For many workers, however, the emphasis on efficiency seemed inhuman, with restrictions on time and motion so severe that often they were allowed to use the bathroom only on a fixed schedule. "When I left the factory, it followed me," wrote one worker. "In my dreams I was a machine."

The managerial sector in industry had expanded during the war and continued to do so thereafter. Workers' initiative became devalued, with managers alone seen as creative and innovative. Managers reorganized work procedures and classified workers' skills. They categorized "female" jobs as those requiring less skill and therefore deserving of lower wages, thus adapting the old segmentation of the labor market to the new working conditions. With male workers' jobs increasingly threatened by labor-saving machinery, unions usually agreed that women should receive lower wages to keep them from competing with men for scarce high-paying jobs.

Union bureaucracy continued to balloon during World War I to help monitor labor's part in the war. Union leaders cooperated with their former antagonists in management and government to settle questions ranging from the creation of a lighter, less potent beer to plans for the reintegration of veterans into industry. Union bureaucracies became specialized, composed of negotiators, membership organizers, educators and propagandists, and political liaisons. Unions could mobilize masses of people, as they demonstrated when they blocked the 1920 Kapp Putsch against the Weimar government and organized the 1926 general strike in Great Britain. Although their lobbying efforts were often less successful than those of manufacturers' associations, unions played a key role in mass politics.

Restoring Society

With combined joy and trepidation, postwar society met the returning millions of brutalized, incapacitated, and shell-shocked veterans. Many veterans harbored hostility toward those who had remained home. Civilians had rebelled against wartime conditions, these soldiers charged, instead of patriotically enduring them. The world the veterans returned to differed from the home they left: women had cut their hair, wore tailored clothes, smoked, held jobs, and had money of their own. In contrast, veterans often had no jobs; and some soldiers found that their wives and sweethearts had abandoned them—a wrenching betrayal for those who had risked their lives to protect the homeland.

United by patriotism when the war erupted, civilians, especially women, sometimes felt estranged from these returning warriors, who had inflicted so much death and who had lived daily with filth, rats, and decaying animal and human

Otto Dix, *Cabaret: To Beauty* (1922)
Postwar fun, based on drinking, dancing, smoking, and sexual courting, took place in the newly popular cabaret or nightclub. Many cabarets in Berlin and elsewhere featured dramatic song and dance performances—sometimes of African American dancers and instrumentalists who represented the promise and exoticism of the United States. But continuing his theme of wartime trauma, Otto Dix in 1922 portrayed the cabaret as a setting for nothing more than further human alienation, no matter what the fancy garb or carefree activity.
Erich Lessing/Art Resource, NY.

flesh. Civilian anxieties were often valid. Tens of thousands of German, central European, and Italian soldiers refused to disband; a few British veterans even vandalized university classrooms and assaulted women streetcar conductors and factory workers. Women who had served on the front could empathize with the soldiers' woes. But many suffragists in England, for instance, who had fought for an end to separate spheres before the war, now embraced gender segregation, so shocked were they by the vision of brutalized veterans. Likewise, Social Democratic women in Germany began to de-emphasize political integration with men and to work instead for welfare organizations to aid women and families. Many feminist activists across the West eliminated rights for working and professional women from their agendas and

Le Corbusier's Paris of the Future
While the war profoundly disillusioned many in the West, peace aroused utopian hopes for a better future.
For modern architects like Swiss-born Le Corbusier (1887–1965), the "future city" and the "radiant city"
would organize space, and thus life, for ordinary people. Horizontal windows, roof gardens, and very plain
facades were hallmarks of this new design—a radical break with ornate prewar styles in building.
Fondation Le Corbusier/A.D.A.G.P.

instead fought for a separate, protected place in the family insured by welfare programs. Combined with the widespread victory of woman suffrage, this switch in emphasis caused commentators and even suffragists to pronounce feminism dead as a political issue.

Fearing the spread of Bolshevism, governments tried to make civilian life as comfortable as possible to reintegrate men into society and prevent revolution. Politicians believed in the stabilizing power of traditional family values and supported social programs to alleviate pent-up anger among veterans and civilians and reward their endurance. These programs included pension plans for veterans, stipends for war widows, benefits for out-of-work men, and housing for veterans—"homes for heroes," politicians called them.

The new housing was a vast improvement over nineteenth-century working-class tenements but most often benefited the more highly paid skilled workers. In Vienna, Frankfurt, Berlin, and Stockholm, modern housing projects provided collective laundries, day-care centers, and rooms for group socializing; they featured gardens, terraces, and balconies to provide a soothing, country ambiance

that offset the hectic nature of industrial life. Inside they boasted modern kitchens, indoor plumbing, central heating, and electricity. Borrowing the clean lines of East Asian and African dwellings to create a sense of modernity, domestic architects avoided ornate moldings, plasterwork, and curlicues—now seen as "old-fashioned." Architects for these projects became part of an intensive planning effort, and by the late 1920s some created housing developments on a gigantic scale to cut costs and to deal with the problem of urban crowding. German architect Ludwig Hilbersheimer and Swiss-born French architect Le Corbusier favored "high-rise" apartments that adapted the principles of New York's skyscrapers to the domestic environment and satisfied the criterion of urban planning that called for an efficient use of space.

Despite government efforts to restore traditional family values, war had dissolved many middle-class conventions, among them attempts to keep unmarried young men and women apart. Freer relationships and more open discussions of sex occurred in the 1920s. Unmarried women of wealthy families no longer needed chaperones when on the streets or in the company of young men. Middle-class youth of both sexes visited jazz clubs together, attended movies, and began keeping company in cars. Revealing bathing suits, short skirts, and body-hugging clothing emphasized women's sexuality, seeming to invite men and women to join together and replenish the postwar population. Still, the context for sexuality remained marriage. In 1918, British scientist Marie Stopes published the best-seller *Married Love*, which featured frank discussions of sexual relations. In 1927, the wildly successful *Ideal Marriage: Its Physiology and Technique* by Dutch author Theodor van de Velde appeared. Translated into dozens of languages, van de Velde's book, as Stopes's had, described sex in rhapsodic terms and offered precise information about birth control and sexual physiology.

Changing ideas about sex were not limited to the middle and upper classes; one Viennese reformer described working-class marriage as "an erotic-comradely relationship of equals" rather than the economic partnership of past centuries. The flapper, a sexually liberated workingwoman, vied with the dedicated housewife to represent the ordinary woman in the public's eyes. Meanwhile such writers as the Briton D. H. Lawrence and the American Ernest Hemingway glorified men's sexual vigor in books like *Women in Love* (1920) and *The Sun Also Rises* (1926). Images of sexually compatible men and women served to bridge the gap between home and battlefront that had caused such anxiety as the war ended. Mass culture's focus on heterosexuality encouraged the return to normality after the gender disorder that troubled the prewar and war years.

As images of men and women changed, people paid more attention to bodily improvement. The increasing use of toothbrushes and toothpaste, safety and electric razors, and deodorants reflected new standards for personal hygiene and grooming. For Western women, a multibillion-dollar cosmetics industry sprang up almost overnight. Women went to beauty parlors regularly to have their short hair cut, set, dyed, conditioned, straightened, or curled. They also tweezed their eyebrows, applied makeup, and even submitted to cosmetic surgery. Ordinary women painted their faces as formerly only prostitutes had done and competed in beauty contests that judged physical appearance. Instead of wanting to look plump and prosperous, people aimed to become thin and tan. The proliferation of boxers, hikers, gymnasts, and tap dancers spurred people to exercise and to participate in amateur sports. The consumer focus on personal health coincided with modern industry's need for a physically fit workforce.

As prosperity returned, people could afford to buy more consumer goods. Thanks to the gradual postwar increase in real wages, middle- and upper-class families snapped up sleek modern furniture, washing machines, and vacuum cleaners. Thousands of other modern conveniences such as electric irons, refrigerators, and stoves became standard in better-off working-class households. Installment buying, popularized from the 1920s on, helped ordinary people finance these purchases. Housework became more mechanized, and family intimacy increasingly depended on machines like radios, phonographs, and the less expensive automobiles. At the same time, these new domestic products that enhanced mass communication brought unforeseen changes in the public world of culture and mass politics.

❖ Mass Culture and the Rise of Modern Dictators

Wartime propaganda had aimed to unite all classes against a common enemy. In the 1920s, the process of incorporating diverse groups into a homogeneous Western culture, increasingly seen as a "mass culture," continued. The instruments of mass culture—primarily radio, film, and newspapers—expanded their influence in the 1920s. Whereas some intellectual leaders such as the Spanish poet José Ortega y Gasset urged elites to form an experimental avant-garde that refused to cater to "the drab mass of society," others wanted to use modern media and art to reach and even control the masses. Mass media had the potential for creating an informed citizenry and thus enhancing democracy. In the troubled postwar climate, however, mass media, coupled with political experimentation and outright brutality, also paved the road to dictatorship. Authoritarian rulers—Benito Mussolini, Joseph Stalin, and ultimately Adolf Hitler—aimed to control the masses in unprecedented ways.

Culture for the Masses

An array of media had received a big boost from the war. Bulletins from the battlefront had whetted the public's craving for news and real-life stories, and sales of nonfiction books soared. After years of deprivation, people were driven to achieve material success, and they devoured books that advised how to gain it. Henry Ford's biography, a story of social mobility and technological accomplishment, became a best-seller in Germany. With postwar readers avidly pursuing practical knowledge, institutes and night schools became popular, and school systems promoted reading in geography, science, and history. Photographs, the radio, and movies also contributed to the formation of national culture.

In the 1920s, filmmaking changed from an experimental medium to an international business. Since the mid-1890s, pioneering filmmakers had written, directed, produced, and starred in their own movies and hired little-known performers. The war years, when the U.S. film industry began to outstrip the European, gave rise to specialization: directors, producers, marketers, photographers, film editors, and many others subdivided the process. A star system turned film personalities into celebrities, highly admired and living like royalty. Stars and directors worked within a "studio," or large corporate structure, that set up theater chains and marketed films worldwide. To help sell films, fan magazines and paraphernalia like dolls and dishes bearing stars' faces made movies part of daily life. Films of literary classics and political events developed people's sense of a common heritage. The British government sponsored documentaries that articulated national goals. Bolshevik leaders also supported filmmaking, underwriting the innovative work of director Sergei Eisenstein (1898–1948). His films *Potemkin* (1925) and *Ten Days That Shook the World* (1927–1928) presented a Bolshevik view of history to Russian and international audiences.

Films incorporated familiar elements from other cultural forms. The piano accompaniment that went along with the action of silent films derived from music halls; comic characters, farcical plots, and slapstick humor were borrowed from street or burlesque shows and from new trends in postwar living. Thus popular comedies and romances of the 1920s satirized men and women who botched the job of achieving emotional intimacy or featured the flapper and made her more visible to the masses. Movies attracted some 100 million weekly viewers, the majority of them women. Popular films and books crossed national borders easily, in the process enhancing cosmopolitanism and global culture for an international audience.

Cinematic portrayals also played to postwar fantasies and fears. In Germany, where filmmakers used expressionist sets and costumes to make films frightening, the influential hit *The Cabinet of Doctor Caligari* (1919) depicted events in an insane asylum as horrifying symbols of state power. Austrian-born Fritz Lang (1890–1976), who worked in Berlin and later Hollywood, showed technological forces in modern life as wildly and destructively out of control in films such as the classic *Metropolis* (1926). Popular detective and cowboy films portrayed heroes who could restore wholeness to the disordered world of murder, crime, and injustice. Depiction of the plight of gangsters appealed to war veterans, who had been exposed to the cheap value of life in the modern world. The films of German director G. W. Pabst awakened anxieties about cross-class sexual attraction; they also presented complex women characters, who did not fit such simple stereotypes as the flapper. English comedian, actor, and producer Charlie Chaplin (1889–1977) created the character of the "Little Tramp," who won international popularity as the defeated hero, the anonymous modern man, trying to keep his dignity in a mechanical world.

Film remained experimental well into the 1920s, but radio was even more so. Developed from Guglielmo Marconi's wireless technology, introduced at the turn of the century, radio broadcasts in the first half of the 1920s were heard by mass audiences in public halls (much like film theaters) and featured orchestras and song followed by audience discussion. The radio quickly became a relatively inexpensive consumer item, and the public concert or lecture could now penetrate the individual's private living space age. (See "Taking Measure," page 1011.) Specialized programming for men (such as sports reporting) and for women (such as advice on home management) soon followed. By the 1930s, radio was available for politicians to reach the masses wherever they might be—even alone at home.

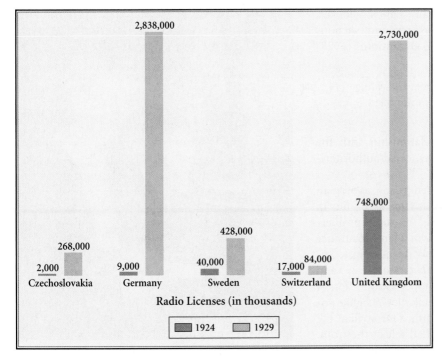

2,838,000

2,730,000

748,000

268,000

428,000

2,000   9,000   40,000   17,000 84,000

Czechoslovakia   Germany   Sweden   Switzerland   United Kingdom

Radio Licenses (in thousands)

☐ 1924   ☐ 1929

TAKING MEASURE
The Growth of Radio,
1924–1929
The spread of radio technology, like the earlier development of printing, advanced the cultural and political unity of citizens in a nation-state. The most industrially and commercially developed societies witnessed the most rapid diffusion of radios, which were both programmed and taxed by governments. Because of this centralized control, historians can compare the country-by-country use of radio in Europe and in much of the rest of the world.

Cultural Debates over the Future

Cultural leaders in the 1920s either were obsessed by the horrendous experience of war or—like the modernists before the war—held high hopes for creating a fresh, utopian future that would have little relation to the past. The vision of those haunted by the war was bleak or violent, and this was especially a theme in German art. The German artist Kaethe Köllwitz (1867–1945), whose son died in the war, portrayed in her woodcuts bereaved parents, starving children, and other heart-wrenching, antiwar images.

Other artists employed satire, irony, and flippancy to express postwar rage and revulsion at civilization's apparent failure. George Grosz (1893–1959), stunned by the carnage like so many other German veterans, joined Dada, an artistic and literary movement that had emerged during the war. Dada produced works marked by nonsense, incongruity, and shrieking expressions of alienation. Grosz's paintings and cartoons of maimed soldiers and brutally murdered women reflected his psychic wounds and his self-proclaimed desire "to bellow back." Dadaist bellowing continued the modernist tradition of shocking audiences, but now the shocks were more savage and often more hateful of

ordinary people. Avant-garde portrayals of seediness and perversion in everyday life flourished in cabarets and theaters in the 1920s and reinforced veterans' visions of civilian decadence.

A battle erupted in defeated Germany over the war's lessons for postwar life. Popular writers such as Ernst Jünger glorified life in the trenches and called for the militarization of society to restore order. Erich Maria Remarque cried out for an end to war in his controversial *All Quiet on the Western Front* (1928). This international best-seller depicted the life shared by enemies on the battlefield, thus dampening the national hatred stoked by wartime propaganda. For the British, World War I was the Great War, but the battle over the war's meaning in German novels paralleled the Weimar Republic's contentious politics.

Poets reflected on postwar conditions in more general terms, using styles that rejected the comforting rhymes or accessible metaphors of earlier verse. T. S. Eliot, an American-born poet who for a time worked as a banker in Britain, portrayed postwar life as petty and futile in "The Waste Land" (1922) and "The Hollow Men" (1925). The Irish nationalist poet William Butler Yeats joined Eliot in mourning the replacement of traditional society with its moral conviction and religious values by a new, superficial generation gaily dancing to jazz and engaging in promiscuous sex and vacuous conversation. Yeats's "Sailing to Byzantium" (1928) starts:

That is no country for old men. The young
In one another's arms, birds in the trees
—Those dying generations

Both poets had an uneasy relationship with the modern world and at times advocated authoritarianism rather than democracy.

The postwar arts produced many a utopian fantasy turned upside down; *dystopias* of life in postrevolutionary, traumatized Europe proliferated. Franz Kafka, an employee of a large insurance company in Prague, saw the world as a vast, impersonal machine. His novels *The Trial* (1925) and *The Castle* (1926) evoked the hopeless condition of the individual confronting a relentless, coglike society; his theme seemed to capture for civilian life the helplessness that soldiers had felt at the front. Kafka's expressionistic and bizarre stories, such as "Metamorphosis," in which a salesman wakes up one morning to discover he has turned into a gigantic insect, resonated as nightmarish fables of postwar modernity.

It was especially hard to maintain social optimism and a sense of coherence as an old society collapsed so rapidly and as innovation in politics, technology, and cultural life accelerated dizzyingly. Some writers, picking up on the prewar turn to psychology, confined their work to depicting the complex inner life of individuals. French author Marcel Proust, in his multivolume novel *Remembrance of Things Past* (1913–1927), explored the workings of memory, the passage of time, and sexual modernity through the life of a narrator, eventually identified as the author. At the beginning of the first volume, the narrator is obsessed with his mother's company as he tries to fall asleep at night. He witnesses progressively disturbing obsessions, such as violent sexuality and personal betrayals of love. The haunted inner life analyzed by Freud was infiltrating fiction: for Proust redemption lay in producing beauty from the raw material of life, not in promoting outmoded conventions of decency and morality.

Irish writer James Joyce and British writer Virginia Woolf shared Proust's vision of an interior self built on memories and sensations. Joyce's

Virginia Woolf
Along with Marcel Proust and James Joyce, Virginia Woolf represented the peak of literary modernism with its emphasis on interior states of mind and disjointed, dreamlike slices of reality. Woolf's novels and essays also captured the unappreciated centrality of women, who provided an array of personal services to their more highly valued husbands. Woolf boldly announced that for a woman to be as creative as a man depended on her being partially relieved of the burdens of family—most notably having "a room of one's own."
Gisele Freund/Photo Researchers, Inc.

Ulysses (1922) and Woolf's *Mrs. Dalloway* (1925) illuminated the fast-moving inner lives of their characters in the course of a single day. In one of *Ulysses'* most celebrated passages, a long interior monologue traces a woman's lifetime of erotic and emotional sensations. For Woolf the war had dissolved the solid society from which absorbing stories and fascinating characters were once fashioned. Her characters experience fragmented conversations, momentary sensations, and incomplete relationships.

There was another side to the story, one based not on the interior life of traumatized society but on the promise of technology. Avant-garde artists before the war had celebrated the new, the futuristic, the utopian. Like Jules Amar crafting prostheses for shattered limbs, they were optimistic that technology could make an entire society whole after the slaughter. The aim of art, observed one of them, "is not to decorate our life but to organize it." The group of German artists called the Bauhaus (after the idea of a craft association, or *Bauhütte*) created streamlined office buildings and designed functional furniture, utensils, and decorative objects, many of them inspired by forms from "untainted" East Asia and Africa. Many artists worked in large collectives where, under the guidance of intellectuals such as the Bauhaus's Walter Gropius (1883–1969), they staged shows of modern products that also turned a profit. Before the war Russian artists had been in the vanguard of nonrepresentational and geometric art. Temporarily entranced by the Communist experiment, they optimistically wrote novels about cement factories and ballets about steel—the latter an element common to artificial limbs and advanced, utopian design.

Artists fascinated by technology and machinery were drawn to the most modern of all countries—the United States. Hollywood films, glossy advertisements, and the bustling metropolis of New York tempted careworn Europeans. They were especially attracted to jazz, the improvisational music that emanated from Harlem. African American jazz musicians showed a resiliency of spirit, although Europeans could still feel superior to those of dark skin color in "primitive" costumes. Performers like Josephine Baker (1906–1976) and Louis Armstrong (1900–1971) became international sensations when they toured Europe's capital cities. Like jazz, the New York skyscraper pointed to the future. Skyscrapers seemed to show how engineering and architectural genius could break the bounds of city space instead of being confined by it. Europeans found in New York a potent example of avant-garde expression that rejected a terrifying past and boldly shaped the future.

The Communist Utopia

Communism also promised a shining future and a modern, technological culture. But the Bolsheviks encountered powerful obstacles to consolidating their rule. In the early 1920s, peasant bands called Green Armies revolted against the policy of war communism that confiscated their agricultural produce. Industrial production stood at only 13 percent of its prewar output; the civil war had produced massive casualties; shortages of housing affected the entire population; and millions of refugees clogged the cities and roamed the countryside. In the early spring of 1921, workers in Petrograd and sailors at the nearby naval base at Kronstadt revolted, protesting their short rations and the privileged standard of living that Bolshevik supervisors enjoyed and calling for "soviets without Communists"—that is, a return to the early promises of the Bolsheviks for a worker state.

Lenin raged that the rebels were merely reactionary "petit bourgeois" and Trotsky had many of them shot, but the Kronstadt revolt pushed Lenin to institute reform. During the revolt Lenin announced the first steps in his New Economic Policy (NEP), which imposed a fixed tax on production of grain rather than confiscating it. Subsequent laws returned parts of the economy to the free market, a temporary compromise with capitalist methods that allowed peasants to sell their grain freely and to profit from free trade in consumer goods. Although the state still controlled large industries and banking, the NEP encouraged people to produce, sell, and even, in the words of one leading Communist, "get rich." Consumer goods and more food to eat soon became available. Some peasants and merchants did indeed get rich, but many more remained impoverished. The rise of "NEPmen," who bought and furnished splendid homes and who cared only about conspicuous consumption, belied the Bolshevik credo of a classless utopia.

Protest erupted within Communist ranks. At the 1921 party congress, a group called the Worker Opposition objected to the party's usurpation of economic control from worker organizations and pointed out that the NEP was an agrarian program, not a proletarian one. Because of the NEP, critics complained, prostitutes, criminals, and bourgeois speculators thrived. In response to such charges of growing bureaucratization, Lenin suppressed the Worker Opposition faction in 1921 and set up procedures for purging dissidents.

Bolshevik leaders tightened their grip on politics by making the Communist revolution a cultural reality that would inform people's daily lives and reshape their thoughts. Party leaders invaded the countryside to set up classes in a variety of political and social subjects, and volunteers harangued the public about the importance of literacy—only 40 percent on the eve of World War I. To facilitate social equality between the sexes, as had been part of the Marxist vision of the future, the state made birth control, abortion, and divorce readily available. As commissar for public welfare, Alexsandra Kollontai (1872–1952) promoted birth-control education and programs to offer day care for children of working parents.

The bureaucracy swelled to bring modern culture to every corner of life, and *hygiene* and *efficiency* became watchwords, as they were in the rest of Europe. Such agencies as the Zhenotdel (Women's Bureau) sought to teach women about their rights under communism and about modern sanitary practices. "Americanization" was seen favorably because it had methods for sweeping away the past. Thus semiofficial institutes and associations brought the methods of Henry Ford and Frederick Taylor into factories, the army, the arts, and everyday life. *Timeists*, as efficiency experts were called, aimed to replace tsarist backwardness with technological modernity.

Journalists, writers, and artists argued heatedly about whether the old elite culture could be integrated into the Communist one, a strategy Lenin favored, or whether it had to be thrown out, as some avant-garde intellectuals believed. In the 1920s, Bolshevik culture maintained the rebelliousness of prewar experimental theater, abstract art, and free verse. The short-lived government agency Proletkult aimed to develop proletarian culture through such undertakings as workers' universities, a workers' encyclopedia, a workers' theater, and workers' publishing.

Many Russian artists experimented with blending high art, technology, and mass culture. Composers punctuated their music with the sound of train or factory whistles. The poet Vladimir Mayakovsky edited a journal advocating utilitarian art, wrote verse praising his Communist passport and essays promoting toothbrushing, and staged uproarious farces for ordinary citizens. Alexsandra Kollontai's novels about love and work in the new Communist society employed a direct, straightforward style so less-educated women might read them. The Bolsheviks confiscated mansions and imperial buildings and turned them into workers' clubs and galleries that displayed works of art to the masses.

As with war communism, many resisted the reshaping of culture to "modern" or "Western"

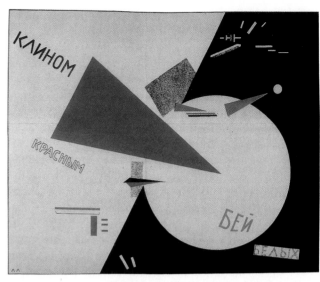

Eli Lissitsky, *Beat the Whites with the Red Wedge* (1919)
Russian artist Eli Lissitsky traveled Europe to bring news of Soviet experimentation. In particular the Soviets were taken with the new physics and their works of art surrounded the viewer with geometric forms. But abstract art was also political: in this 1919 painting, the "red" wedge uses the force of physical principles to defeat the objectively greater counter-revolutionary power of the "whites."
David King Collection.

standards. Bolsheviks threatened everyday customs and the distribution of power within the family. As Zhenotdel workers moved into the countryside, for example, they attempted to teach women to behave as men's equals. Peasant families were still strongly patriarchal, however, and Zhenotdel activists threatened gender relations. In Islamic regions incorporated from the old Russian Empire into the new Communist one, Bolsheviks urged Muslim women to remove their veils and change their way of life, but the Muslims often murdered or assaulted both Zhenotdel workers and women who followed their advice.

In the spring of 1922, Lenin suffered a debilitating stroke, and in January 1924, amidst ongoing cultural experimentation, factional fighting, and repression, the architect of the Bolshevik Revolution died. The party congress declared the day of his death a permanent holiday and changed the name of Petrograd to Leningrad. Lenin's funeral, stunning for its pomp, gave a new direction to Communist political life by elevating the deceased leader into a secular god. After Lenin's death, no one was allowed to criticize anything associated with Lenin's name, a situation that paved the way for future abuses of power by Communist leaders.

Joseph Stalin (1879–1953), who served in the powerful post of general secretary of the Communist Party, led the deification of Lenin. Both organizing the Lenin cult and dealing with thousands of local party officials gave him enormous national patronage, and his welding in 1924 of Russian and non-Russian regions into the Union of Soviet Socialist Republics gave him a claim to executive accomplishment. Lenin had become wary of Stalin's growing influence and ruthlessness and in his last will and testament asked that "the comrades find a way to remove Stalin." Stalin and the inner circle of the Communist Party, however, prevented Lenin's will from being publicized. Stalin proceeded to discredit his chief rival, Trotsky, as an unpatriotic internationalist who was unwilling to concentrate on the tough job of culturally and economically modernizing the Soviet Union. Bringing in several hundred thousand new party members who owed their positions in government and industry to him, Stalin by 1928–1929 had achieved virtually complete dictatorship in the USSR.

Fascism on the March

The political chaos and postwar discontent in Italy brought to power Benito Mussolini (1883–1945), who, like the Bolsheviks, promised an efficient utopia. Italian ire was first aroused when the Allies at Paris refused to honor the territorial promises of the Treaty of London. Domestic unrest swelled when peasants, who had made great sacrifices in the war, protested their serflike status in Italian society. Workers seized factories to draw attention to their economic plight, made worse by the slump of the early 1920s. Since the late nineteenth century, many Europeans had come to blame parliaments for their ills. So Italians were responsive when Mussolini, a socialist journalist who turned to the radical right, built a personal army (the Black Shirts) of veterans and the unemployed to overturn parliamentary government. In 1922, his supporters, known as Fascists, started a march on Rome, threatening a coup. Faced with the prospect of losing his crown, King Victor Emmanuel III (r. 1900–1946) asked the dynamic Mussolini to become prime minister and revive the country.

Mussolini and the Black Shirts

For movements like fascism the best society was one controlled by militarized politics that killed its critics and those of opposing political persuasions. Fascism saw parliamentary democracies as effeminate and doomed in the modern world, which would need dictators and obedient warriors to make it strong, efficient, and machinelike. Thus, in the name of promoting state power, Mussolini gained adherents both within and outside of Italy. Farabolafoto.

The Fascist movement flourished in the soil of poverty, social unrest, and wounded national pride. It attracted to its bands of Black Shirts many young men who felt cheated of glory by the Allies and veterans who missed the vigor of military life. The *fasces*, an ancient Roman symbol depicting a bundle of sticks wrapped around an ax with the blade exposed, served as the movement's emblem; it represented both unity and force to Mussolini's supporters. Fascism offered a less-developed ideology than Marxism but fashioned its rejection of theory into a virtue. "Fascism is not a church," Mussolini announced upon taking power in 1922. "It is more like a training ground." Fascism was thus defined by its grounding of peacetime politics in an instinctual male violence and by what it opposed: the "antinationalist" socialist movement and parliamentary rule.

Mussolini consolidated his power by putting himself at the head of government departments, by making criticism of the state a criminal offense, and by violently steamrolling parliamentary opposition. His Fascist bands demolished socialist newspaper offices, attacked striking workers, and used their favorite tactic of forcing castor oil (which caused diarrhea) down the throats of socialists. They even murdered certain powerful opponents such as the moderate socialist parliamentary deputy Giacomo Matteotti.

Despite their brutality, the sight of the Black Shirts marching through the streets like disciplined soldiers signaled to many Italians that their country was ordered and modern. Large landowners and businessmen approved Fascist attacks on strikers, and they financially supported the movement. Their generous funding allowed Mussolini to build a large staff by hiring the unemployed and thus to make it look as if Fascists could spark the economy when no one else could.

In addition to violence, Mussolini used mass propaganda and the media to foster support for a kind of military campaign to remake Italy. Peasant men huddled around radios to hear him call for a "battle of wheat" to enhance farm productivity. Peasant women, responding to his praise for maternal duty, adulated him for appearing to value womanhood. In the cities the government launched modernist architecture projects, designed new statues and public adornments, and used public relations promoters to advertise its achievements. Some intellectuals liked the Fascists' avoidance of debate in favor of action and clamored to take part in Mussolini's promotion of avant-garde culture. Mussolini claimed that he made the trains run on time, and this one triumph of modern technology made people hopeful that he could restore order out of wartime and postwar chaos.

Mussolini added a strong dose of traditional values and prejudices to his modern order. Although an atheist, he recognized the importance of Catholicism to most Italians. In 1929, the Lateran Agreement between the Italian government and the church made the Vatican a state under papal

MAPPING THE WEST Europe and the World in 1929 ▶

The map reflects the partitions and nations that came into being as a result of war and revolution, while it obscures the increasing movement toward throwing off colonial rule. This was the true high point of empire: the drive for empire would diminish after 1929 except for Italy, which still craved colonies, and Japan, which continued searching for more land and resources to fuel its rapid growth.

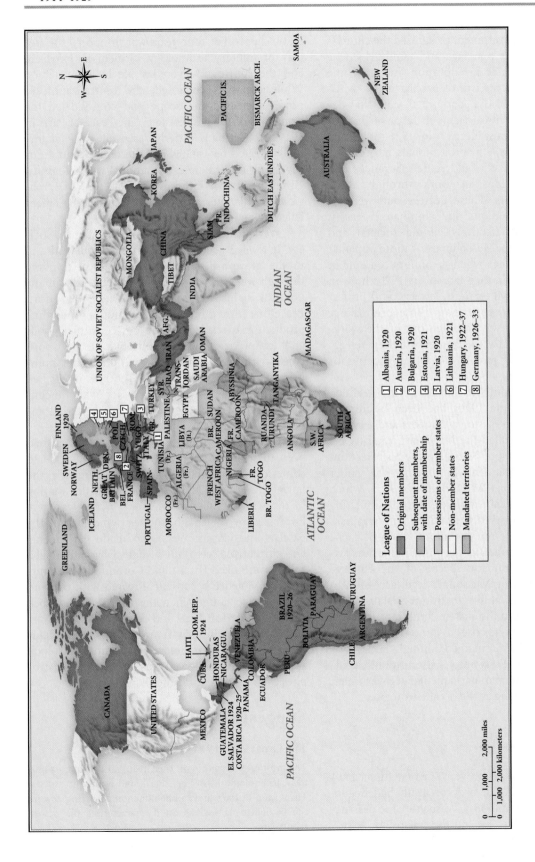

League of Nations

- Original members
- Subsequent members, with date of membership
- Possessions of member states
- Non-member states
- Mandated territories

1. Albania, 1920
2. Austria, 1920
3. Bulgaria, 1920
4. Estonia, 1921
5. Latvia, 1920
6. Lithuania, 1921
7. Hungary, 1922–37
8. Germany, 1926–33

0   1,000   2,000 miles
0   1,000   2,000 kilometers

sovereignty. The government recognized the church's right to determine marriage and family doctrine and endorsed its role in education. In return the church ended its criticism of Fascist tactics. Mussolini also introduced a "corporate" state that denied individual political rights in favor of duty to the state. Corporatist decrees in 1926 organized employers, workers, and professionals into groups or corporations that would settle grievances and determine conditions of work through state-controlled channels. These decrees outlawed independent labor unions and eliminated peasant political groups, effectively ending societal and workplace activism. Mussolini drew more applause from business leaders when he announced cuts in women's wages; and then late in the 1920s he won the approval of civil servants, lawyers, and professors by banning women from those professions. Mussolini did not want women out of the workforce altogether but wanted to ensure their relegation to low-paying jobs as part of his scheme for reinvigorating men.

Mussolini's admirers included Adolf Hitler, who throughout the 1920s had been building a paramilitary group of storm troopers and a political organization called the National Socialist German Workers' Party, or Nazis. During his brief stint in jail for the Beer Hall Putsch in 1923, Hitler wrote *Mein Kampf* ("My Struggle," 1925), which articulated a political psychology for manipulating the masses and worked the vicious anti-Semitism of prewar Viennese politics into a vision of racial annihilation. For practical purposes, Hitler was fascinated by the dramatic success of the Fascists' march on Rome, by Mussolini's legal accession to power, and by his ability to thwart socialists and trade unionists. But the austere conditions that had allowed Mussolini to rise to power in 1922 no longer existed in Germany. Although Hitler was welding the Nazi Party into a strong political instrument, the Weimar parliamentary government was actually working as the decade wore on.

Conclusion

The year 1929 was to prove just as fateful as 1914 had been. In 1914, an orgy of death had begun, leading to tens of millions of casualties, the destruction of major dynasties, and the collapse of aristo-

cratic classes. For four years war promoted the free play of military technology, virulent nationalism, and the control of everyday life by bureaucracy. While dynasties collapsed, the centralization of power increased the scope and consolidated the principles of the nation-state. The Peace of Paris in 1919 left Germans bitterly resentful, while it formally created new states in eastern and central Europe built on principles of nationalist ethnic unity. Given the intense intermingling of ethnicities, religions, and languages in the area, such a settlement failed to guarantee a peaceful future.

War furthered the development of mass society. It leveled social classes on the battlefield and in the graveyard, standardized political thinking through wartime propaganda, and extended many political rights to women for their war effort. Peacetime turned improved techniques of wartime production toward churning out consumer goods and technological innovations like air transport, cinema, and radio transmission for greater numbers of people. Modernity in the arts intensified after the war, exploring the recesses of the unconscious and probing the nightmarish battering endured by all segments of the population.

By the end of the 1920s, the legacy of war had been to so militarize politics that strongmen had come to power in Hungary, Poland, Romania, the Soviet Union, and Italy, with Adolf Hitler waiting in the wings in Germany. Many Westerners were impressed by the tough, modern efficiency of the Fascists and Communists who made parliaments and citizen rule seem out-of-date, even effeminate. Many overlooked Fascist and Communist commitment to violence because, compared with the war, it seemed so tame. When the United States stock market crashed in 1929 and economic disaster circled the globe, authoritarian solutions, technological culture, and militarism continued to look appealing. What followed was a series of catastrophes even more devastating than World War I.

Suggested References

The Great War, 1914–1918

The most recent histories of the Great War consider its military, technological, psychic, social, and economic aspects. This vision of the war as a phenomenon occurring beyond the battlefield as well as on it characterizes the newest scholarship.

Bourke, Joanna. *Dismembering the Male: Men's Bodies, Britain, and the Great War.* 1996.

*Brittain, Vera. *Testament of Youth.* 1933.

Downs, Laura Lee. *Manufacturing Inequality: Gender Division in the French and British Metalworking Industries, 1914–1939.* 1995.

Echenberg, Myron. *Colonial Conscripts: The "Tirailleurs Sénégalais" in French West Africa, 1857–1960.* 1990.

Ellis, John. *A Social History of the Machine-Gun.* 1986.

*Hasek, Jaroslav. *The Good Soldier Schweik.* 1920.

Leed, Eric J. *No Man's Land: Combat and Identity in World War I.* 1979.

Panchasi, Roxanne. "Reconstructions: Prosthetics and the Rehabilitation of the Male Body in World War I." *Differences.* 1995.

Roshwald, Aviel, and Richard Stites, eds. *European Culture in the Great War: The Arts, Entertainment, and Propaganda, 1914–1918.* 1999.

Schmitt, Bernadotte E., and Harold C. Vederler. *The World in the Crucible, 1914–1919.* 1984.

Winter, Jay, and Jean-Louis Robert, eds. *Capital Cities at War: Paris, London, Berlin, 1914–1919.* 1997.

World War I Documents Archive: http://www.lib.byu.edu/%7Erdh/wwi/.

1917–1918: Protest, Revolution, and War's End

Histories of the war's end account for the cataclysmic setting: deprivation, ongoing mass slaughter, and the eruption of revolution. Peacemaking also occurred, and that too was complex. In all, the violence of the postwar scene has made historians call into question the idea that wars end with an armistice.

Lewis, David Levering. *W. E. B. Du Bois: Biography of a Race, 1868–1919.* 1993.

Neuberger, Joan. *Hooliganism: Crime, Culture, and Power in St. Petersburg.* 1994.

Pipes, Richard. *A Concise History of the Russian Revolution.* 1995.

Schwabe, Klaus. *Woodrow Wilson, Revolutionary Germany, and Peacemaking, 1918–1919: Missionary Diplomacy and the Realities of Power.* 1985.

Smith, Leonard. *Between Mutiny and Obedience: The Case of the French Fifth Infantry Division during World War I.* 1994.

Stites, Richard. *Revolutionary Dreams: Utopian Vision and Experimental Life in the Russian Revolution.* 1989.

Wohl, Robert. *A Passion for Wings: Aviation and the Western Imagination.* 1994.

A Decade of Recovery: Europe in the 1920s

Two themes shape the history of the 1920s: recovery from the trauma of war and revolution and ongoing modernization of work and social life. The great technological innovations of the prewar period such as films and airplanes receive sophisticated treatment by historians for their impact on people's imagination. The radio is another phenomenon just beginning to find its historians.

Grossman, Atina. *Reforming Sex: The German Movement for Birth Control and Abortion Reform, 1920–1930.* 1995.

Kah, Douglas, and Gregory Whitehead. *Wireless Imagination: Sound, Radio, and the Avant-Garde.* 1992.

Kent, Susan. *Making Peace: The Reconstruction of Gender in Postwar Britain.* 1994.

Miller, Michael. *Shanghai on the Metro: Spies, Intrigue, and the French between the Wars.* 1994.

Nolan, Mary. *Visions of Modernity: American Business and the Modernization of Germany.* 1994.

Rabinbach, Anson. *The Human Motor: Energy, Fatigue, and the Origins of Modernity.* 1990.

Roberts, Mary Louise. *Civilization without Sexes: Reconstructing Gender in Postwar France, 1917–1927.* 1994.

Schwartz, Vanessa, and Leo Charney, eds. *Cinema and the Invention of Modern Life.* 1995.

Mass Culture and the Rise of Modern Dictators

Mass communications advances in cinema and radio provided new tools for the rule of modern dictators who arose from the shambles of war and revolution. Many of the most interesting recent studies look at the cultural components of the consolidation of dictatorial power, while not forgetting the violence that was a particular feature of authoritarian rule in the postwar twentieth century.

Berghaus, Gunter. *Futurism and Politics: Between Anarchist Rebellion and Fascist Reaction, 1909–1944.* 1996.

De Grazia, Victoria. *How Fascism Ruled Women.* 1994.

Harsch, Donna. *German Social Democracy and the Rise of Nazism.* 1994.

*Kollontai, Alexsandra. *Love of Worker Bees.* 1923.

Lyttleton, Adrian. *The Seizure of Power: Fascism in Italy, 1919–1929.* 1987.

Schnapp, Jeffrey. *Staging Fascism: 18BL and the Theater of Masses for Masses.* 1996.

Tumarkin, Nina. *Lenin Lives! The Lenin Cult in Soviet Russia.* 1997.

---

*Primary sources.

CHAPTER

27

An Age of Catastrophes

1929–1945

Nazis on Parade
By the time Hitler came to power in 1933, Germany was mired in the economic depression. Hated by Communists, Nazis, and conservatives alike, the republic had few supporters. To a nation still reeling from its defeat in World War I, the Nazis looked as if they would restore national power by defeating enemies—not the Allies but the Jews, Slavs, gypsies, and other groups both within and outside Germany's borders. Hitler took his cue from Mussolini by promising an end to democracy and tolerance.
Hugo Jaeger/LIFE/TimePix.

WHEN ETTY HILLESUM MOVED TO AMSTERDAM in the early 1930s to attend law school, an economic depression gripped the world. A resourceful young Dutch woman, Hillesum pieced together a living as a housekeeper and part-time language teacher. The pressures and pleasures of everyday life kept her from fully absorbing the headline accounts of Adolf Hitler's spectacular rise to power in Germany on a platform demonizing her fellow Jews for the economic slump. World War II, however, ruptured her normal existence. After the German army conquered the Netherlands in 1940, Dutch Jews suffered severe deprivation and persecution, a situation that forced Hillesum to the shattering realization she noted in her diary in July 1942: "What they are after is our total destruction." The Nazis occupied the Netherlands and started relocating Jews to camps in Germany and Poland. Hillesum went to work for Amsterdam's Jewish Council, which was compelled to organize the transportation of Jews to the east. Changing from self-absorbed student to heroine, she did what she could to help other Jews and minutely recorded the deportation. "I wish I could live for a long time so that one day I may know how to explain it." When she was taken prisoner, she smuggled out letters, witnessing the brutal treatment in the transit camps and serving as "the ears and eyes of a piece of Jewish history." Etty Hillesum never fulfilled her ambition to become a professional writer: she died in the Auschwitz death camp in November 1943.

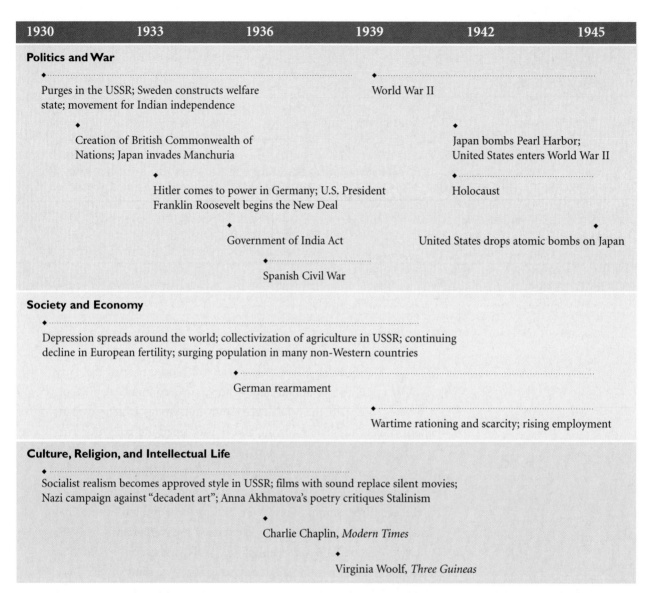

1930	1933	1936	1939	1942	1945

Politics and War

Purges in the USSR; Sweden constructs welfare state; movement for Indian independence

World War II

Creation of British Commonwealth of Nations; Japan invades Manchuria

Japan bombs Pearl Harbor; United States enters World War II

Hitler comes to power in Germany; U.S. President Franklin Roosevelt begins the New Deal

Holocaust

Government of India Act

United States drops atomic bombs on Japan

Spanish Civil War

Society and Economy

Depression spreads around the world; collectivization of agriculture in USSR; continuing decline in European fertility; surging population in many non-Western countries

German rearmament

Wartime rationing and scarcity; rising employment

Culture, Religion, and Intellectual Life

Socialist realism becomes approved style in USSR; films with sound replace silent movies; Nazi campaign against "decadent art"; Anna Akhmatova's poetry critiques Stalinism

Charlie Chaplin, *Modern Times*

Virginia Woolf, *Three Guineas*

The U.S. stock market crash of 1929 opened a horrific era in world history. During the Great Depression of the 1930s, suffering was global, intensifying social grievances throughout the world. In Europe, many people turned to military-style strongmen for answers. Adolf Hitler roused the German masses to rededicate themselves to national greatness. Authoritarian, militaristic, and fascist regimes spread to Portugal, Spain, Poland, Hungary, Japan, China, and elsewhere, trampling on representative institutions. Joseph Stalin oversaw the Soviet Union's rapid industrialization, but in the process he justified the killing of millions of citizens as the necessary price of Soviet growth.

The international scene became doubly menacing because elected leaders in the democracies reacted cautiously to the simultaneous phenomena of the depression and fascist aggression. In an age of mass media, civilian leaders appeared weak and fearful of conflict, while dictators in uniform looked bold and decisive. Only the German invasion of Poland in 1939 finally roused the democracies to strong action.

But their efforts could not divert catastrophe. World War II erupted in Europe, and by 1941 the war had spread to the rest of the world. The United States, Great Britain, and the Soviet Union allied in combat against Germany, Italy, and Japan. Tens of millions would perish in this war because both technology and ideology had become more deadly than it had been just two decades earlier. Half the dead were civilians, among them Etty Hillesum, whose only crime was being a Jew.

❖ The Great Depression

The depression triggered by the U.S. stock market crash of 1929 was not the longest in history: many Europeans still labeled the brutal downturn that began in 1873 and lasted almost a quarter of a century the "Great Depression." However, as the slump threw tens of millions out of work and brought suffering to rural and urban folk alike, opinion changed. The whole world felt the depression's impact as commerce and investment in industry fell off, social life and gender roles were upset, and the birthrate plummeted. From peasants in Asia to industrial workers in Germany and the United States, the lives of large segments of the global population were ravaged.

Economic Disaster

In the 1920s, U.S. corporations and banks as well as millions of individual Americans had recklessly invested their money, or more often borrowed money to invest in the stock market, which seemed to churn out endless profits. Using readily available credit, they bought shares in popular new companies with complete confidence in a Yale economist's predictions that the stock market was on a "permanently high plateau." The Federal Reserve Bank— the nation's central bank, which controlled financial policy—tightened the availability of credit in an attempt to stabilize the market, however, and brokers demanded that their clients immediately pay back the money they had borrowed to buy stock. As stocks were sold to pay brokerage bills, the market collapsed. Between early October and mid-November 1929, the value of businesses listed on the U.S. stock market dropped from $87 billion to $30 billion.

The crash spawned a global depression because the United States, a leading international creditor, had financed the relative economic growth of the past five years in the West. Suddenly strapped for credit, U.S. financiers cut back on

loans and called in short-term debts, undermining banks and industry at home and abroad. The fact that the United States had become the leading industrial power, producing 45 percent of the world's manufactured goods, compounded the collapse; in the interwar years, Japanese industry also took away business that had formerly been Europe's. From the aging industries of Britain to the fledgling factories of eastern Europe, a decline in consumer buying and overproduction further eroded the European economy. In particular, working-class wages, so central to a healthy economy, had not risen in proportion to the prosperity of the late 1920s. This was especially true in the United States; thus, despite its position as the world's leading

Italian Newspaper Depicts the Crash on Wall Street
The crash of the U.S. stock market was ultimately felt around the world, from Italian cities to the Asian countryside. Credit, on which modern industry and modern farming depended, dried up. Governments threw up huge tariff walls to protect national industries and thus curtailed trade, while they initially cut back on aid to unemployed people, which further reduced consumer purchasing and inflicted financial hardship and psychological pain.
Mary Evans Picture Library.

manufacturer, by 1932 U.S. steel production had slumped to only 12 percent of its level before the crash. The Great Depression left no sector of the world economy unscathed.

Government actions made the depression worse and longer than it might otherwise have been. To spur their economies, governments used standard tools such as budget cuts and high tariffs against foreign goods, but these policies further dampened trade and spending in the great industrial powers. (See "Taking Measure," below.) In 1933, an estimated 14 million U.S. workers were unemployed, and more than five thousand banks had closed, wiping out savings and reserves. In Germany, almost 6 million workers, or about one-third of the workforce, were unemployed, and many others were underemployed. France had a more self-sufficient economy. Big businesses like the innovative Citroën car manufacturer began to fail, however, and by the mid-1930s more than 800,000 French people had lost their jobs. Great Britain, with its textile, steel, and coal industries near ruin because of out-of-date techniques and foreign competition, had close to 3 million unemployed in 1932—the worst year, by many British accounts, of this "devil's decade."

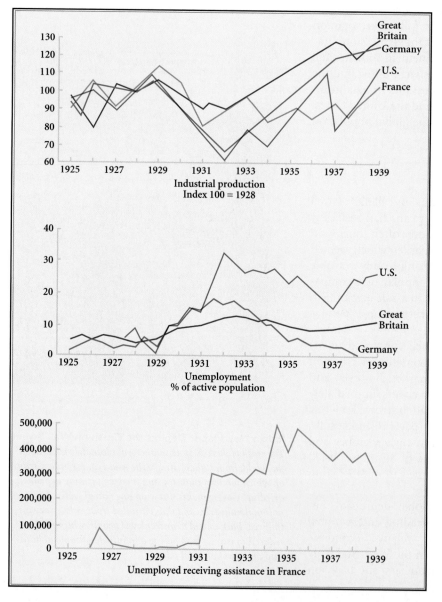

Industrial production
Index 100 = 1928

Unemployment
% of active population

Unemployed receiving assistance in France

TAKING MEASURE
Industrial Production and Unemployment, 1925–1939
The depression had many dimensions, both measurable and psychological. A calamitous fall in production in the most advanced industrial countries—Germany and the United States—was accompanied by rising unemployment. Whatever the resistance to providing government assistance, the trend toward the welfare state continued, moving from veterans' and old-age pensions to unemployment compensation, as the case of France demonstrates. Although less-industrialized countries around the world experienced smaller cuts in production, for them even the smallest decline was a setback on the road to modernizing their economy.
Based on *Atlas historique, histoire de l'humanité de la préhistoire à nos jours* (Paris: Hachette, 1987).

In the agricultural sector, where prices had been declining for several years because of abundant harvests and technological innovation, creditors confiscated farms and equipment. Millions of small farmers had no money to buy the chemical fertilizers and motorized machinery they needed to remain competitive, and they too went under. Eastern and southern European peasants, who had pressed for the redistribution of land after World War I, especially suffered because they could not afford to operate their newly acquired farms. The Polish Sejm (parliament), for example, had awarded more than six million acres from the vast estates of the Catholic church and nobility after World War I. Many of the 700,000 new landowners fell into debt trying to make their farms viable. Eastern European governments often ignored the farmers' plight and instead used scarce capital to start new industries in hopes that industrial prosperity would improve the entire economy. Most of the agricultural population were left to fend for themselves in these desperate times, a situation that increased tensions in rural society.

Social Effects of the Crash

The picture of society during the Great Depression was more complex than utter ruin, however. First, the situation was not uniformly bleak. Despite the slump, modernization proceeded. Bordering English slums, one traveler in the mid-1930s noticed, were "filling stations and factories that look like exhibition buildings, giant cinemas and dance halls and cafés, bungalows with tiny garages, cocktail bars, Woolworth's [and] swimming pools." Municipal and national governments continued road construction and sanitation projects. Running water, electricity, and sewage pipes were installed in many homes for the first time. New factories manufactured synthetic fabrics, electrical products such as stoves, and automobiles—all of them in demand. With government assistance, eastern European industry developed: Romanian industrial production, for example, increased by 55 percent between 1929 and 1939, and this increase looked like the beginning of a real success story. As war approached later in the decade, munitions production soared across Europe and helped create jobs.

Second, the majority of Europeans and Americans had jobs throughout the 1930s. Despite the depression, service workers, managers, and business magnates often enjoyed considerable prosperity. Some members of the old aristocracy were able to maintain their high standards of living by selling their country estates and moving to the cities. Lower on the social scale, people with steady employment benefited from a drastic drop in prices.

Those with jobs, however, felt the threat of becoming unemployed and having to scrape, like thousands of others, for a bare existence. In towns with heavy industry, sometimes more than half the population was out of work. In England in the mid-1930s, close to 20 percent of the population lacked adequate food, clothing, or housing. "We was like animals, we was like animals at home, all of us hungry," a day laborer recalled of life in the 1930s. "I used to sit eating cabbage stalks cos I was that hungry." In a 1932 school assignment a German youth wrote: "My father has been out of work for two and a half years. He thinks that I'll never find a job because there are 700,000 young people alone unemployed in Germany." Despite the prosperity of many people, a thundercloud of fear and resentment settled over Western society.

Changing Roles for Men and Women. Economic catastrophe upset social life and strained gender relations. Sometimes unemployed men stayed home all day, increasing the tension in small, overcrowded apartments. Women could often find low-paying jobs doing laundry and cleaning house for others. While these women were out working, men who stayed at home sometimes took over housekeeping chores but often felt that this "women's work" demeaned their masculinity. As many women became breadwinners, men could be seen standing on street corners begging. This rearrangement of gender expectations fueled the discontent of unemployed men throughout Europe.

In cities the future looked especially grim for young men, who faced severe unemployment. Restlessness and enforced idleness led many of them to form gangs that rode the subways and seemed menacing to passengers. Others loitered in parks, intruding in areas usually frequented by mothers and their children and old people. Men who lived in rural areas saw their traditional roles erode as well. The percentage of farmworkers in the western European population decreased, and patriarchal authority, once central in overseeing farm labor and allocating property among inheritors, continued its decline. Demagogues everywhere berated parliamentary politicians for their failure to stop the collapse of traditional agrarian values. The climate was thus primed for Nazi and fascist politicians who promised to restore prosperity and male dignity.

The Population "Crisis." Politicians of all stripes did agree on one issue: the consequences of the falling birthrate. They forecast national collapse, as a declining birthrate combined with a declining economy to give the impression of social deterioration and lack of confidence in the national future.

After a brief postwar upturn, the birthrate had indeed dropped; in many industrial countries by the early 1930s, it stood at half or less than half of turn-of-the-century levels. The reason was clear: in difficult economic times, people chose to have fewer children. There were other reasons too. Mandatory education and more years of required schooling, enforced more strictly after World War I, resulted in greater expenses for parents. Working-class children no longer brought in wages to supplement the family's income; instead they cost money while they went to school. As knowledge of birth control spread to the working and lower-middle classes, cutting family size became more common. By 1939, Britain's Family Planning Association, founded by Maria Stopes and others, numbered more than sixty clinics. In the United States, Margaret Sanger, working with the medical profession, led a similar organization to make birth-control information and devices accessible.

The population "crisis" invigorated racist politics and rhetoric, which held that "superior" peoples were failing to breed, while "inferior" peoples were lurking to take their place. This racism took a violent form in eastern Europe, where the rural population rose because of increased life expectancy despite an overall drop in birthrate. But increased population compounded the burdens of eastern European farm families, who faced an unprecedented struggle for survival. Rural unrest weakened the fragile states created after World War I. Early in the 1930s, Polish peasants refused to pay new taxes and blockaded debt-laden farms about to be confiscated. Throughout eastern Europe, financial woes helped infect peasant political parties with anti-Semitism. The parties blamed Jewish bankers for farm foreclosures and Jewish civil servants (of whom there were actually very few) for new taxes and inadequate relief programs. They maintained that Christians should fill the good jobs Jews held. Other minority peoples fared little better; the dominant nationality groups in Hungary, Yugoslavia, Romania, and elsewhere purged ethnic minorities from jobs. Thus population issues along with economic misery fueled ethnic hatred and anti-Semitism.

Global Dimensions of the Crash

The effects of declining purchasing power and ready credit extended beyond the West, further accelerating the pace of change and spread of discontent in European empires. World War I and postwar investment had generated economic growth in Asia, Africa, and Latin America. Economic expansion had brought profound demographic alterations not only in rising population but in high rates of rural emigration and explosive urban growth. Between 1920 and 1940, Shanghai ballooned from 1.7 million to 3.75 million residents, Calcutta from 1.8 million to 3.4 million, and Cairo from 865,000 to 1.5 million.

The depression affected both town and countryside beyond the West, cutting the demand for copper, tin, and other raw materials and for the finished products made in urban factories. It drove down the price of foodstuffs like rice and coffee, and this proved disastrous to people who had been forced to grow a single cash crop. However, the economic picture was uneven in the colonies as well as in Europe. For instance, established industrial sectors of the Indian economy like textiles gained strength, with India achieving virtual independence from British cloth, while fledgling industry like electrical energy usually suffered and per capita use remained low.

Economic distress added to other, smoldering grievances. Millions of African and Asian colonial troops had fought for Britain and France in World War I, but these countries had given little back to their colonial populations. In fact, the League of Nations charter had pointedly omitted any reference to the principle of racial equality demanded by people of color at the Versailles conference. Simultaneously, the growing economic power of Japan continued to provide colonized people a model of success by a non-Western power. Moved by the Wilsonian ideal of self-determination and inspired by Japan's example, colonial people increasingly set their sights on winning a Western-style autonomy—

at exactly the time that Western powers most needed to keep their colonies' allegiance *and* the profits of their economic development.

The British government loosened its formal political ties to its dominions (that is, those territories enjoying self-rule: Canada, New Zealand, Australia, the Irish Free State, and the Union of South Africa) with the Statute of Westminster (1931), which instituted the British Commonwealth of Nations. The commonwealth's tariffs against outsiders effectively created a beneficial group of trading partners. India was excluded from the commonwealth and became the arena for a momentous struggle against colonial domination.

Upper-class Indians, who had organized to gain rights from Britain in the late nineteenth century, were joined in the 1930s by millions of working people, including hundreds of thousands of returning soldiers. Mohandas ("Mahatma," or "great-souled") Gandhi (1869–1948) emerged as the charismatic leader for Indian independence. Of privileged birth and trained in England as a Western-style lawyer, Gandhi embraced Hindu self-denial, rejecting the elaborate trappings of British life in favor of simple clothing made of thread he had spun. He advocated *civil disobedience*—deliberately but peacefully breaking the law—which he professed to model on British suffragists' tactics and on the teachings of Jesus, Buddha, and other spiritual leaders. In 1930, he led a march to India's salt flats to protest the British monopolies in salt and other necessities that raised prices for Indians to boost colonial revenue. As Gandhi illegally picked up the forbidden salt, a nationalist-feminist poet shouted "Hail, lawbreaker." He encouraged all Indians to wear homespun clothing and thus boycott British-made textiles. Such "peaceful noncooperation" contrasted significantly with the deference Indians had traditionally shown the British.

Gandhi's tactics and leadership proved devastatingly effective in the long run, but the British did not surrender without a struggle. The colonial government jailed Gandhi repeatedly and tried to split the independence movement by encouraging the Muslim League, led by Mohammed Ali Jinnah. Hindu-Muslim antagonism, which the British had promoted since the nineteenth century, formed a counterpoint to Gandhi's campaign. By 1935, public pressure sympathetic to Gandhi led Parliament to pass the Government of India Act, which granted much of India internal self-government.

Gandhi Leading the Salt March

Mohandas Gandhi appealed to the masses, not just to the middle- and upper-class constituency of the Indian National Congress, which had emphasized reform and participation in government. Instead, Gandhi addressed the entire colonial system that prevented ordinary Indian people from using the country's national resources such as salt. Violating British laws, which prohibited Indians from gathering this natural product, Gandhi led the people in an act of civil disobedience—his march to the sea to touch the salt.
© Bettman/Corbis.

The drive for complete independence was momentarily checked.

In the Middle East, the economic and political ambitions of peoples of the old Ottoman Empire made quicker headway. Led by Westernizer Mustafa Kemal (1881–1938), or Atatürk ("first among Turks"), the Turks took advantage of European vulnerability both after World War I and during the depression to found an independent republic in 1923 and to craft a capitalist economy. In an effort to nationalize and modernize Turkish culture, Kemal moved the capital from Constantinople to Ankara in 1923, changed the ancient

Greek *Constantinople* to the Turkish *Istanbul* in 1930, mandated Western dress for men and women, introduced the Latin alphabet, and abolished polygamy. In 1936, women received the vote and were eligible to serve in the parliament. Persia similarly loosened the European grip on its economy by forcing the negotiation of oil contracts; at the same time it updated its government and in 1935 changed its name to Iran. Persistent uprisings compelled Britain to end its mandate in Iraq in 1930, although it retained crucial oil concessions. In 1936, Britain agreed to end its military occupation of Egypt (though not the Suez Canal), fulfilling the promise of self-rule granted in 1922. Conflict escalated in Palestine where British efforts to make a safe home for Zionist immigrants and to encourage the rights of native Arabs had created conditions for violence.

Obsessed by rising trade barriers in Europe and their own population decline, the French made fewer concessions to colonized people. Their trade with their colonies increased as that with Europe lagged, and the demographic surge in Asia and Africa bolstered French optimism; as one official put it, "One hundred and ten million strong, France can stand up to Germany." Western-educated native leaders such as Ho Chi Minh, founder of the Indochinese Communist Party, contested their people's subjection, but in 1930 the French government brutally crushed the peasant uprising he led. In Algeria, French settlers resisted a nationalist movement inspired by liberal values as well as Islamic and pan-Arab revivals advocated by other reform groups.

In general, British and French pursuit of economic recovery through empire split these two nations from their former allies in World War I. Preoccupied and divided, they let authoritarian and totalitarian forces spread unchecked throughout Europe during the crisis-ridden 1930s.

❖ Totalitarian Triumph

Representative government collapsed in many countries under the sheer weight of social and economic crisis. After 1929, Italy's Benito Mussolini, the Soviet Union's Joseph Stalin, and Germany's Adolf Hitler were able to mobilize vast support for their violent regimes. To some extent citizens had

been conditioned to accept the military directives of wartime. But many people admired Mussolini and Hitler for the discipline they brought to social and economic life, and they overlooked the brutal side of dictatorship. Cultural leaders and working people around the world respected Stalin's administration in the USSR because it promised full employment, free social services, and education for the masses. In an age of crisis, utopian hopes also led many to support political violence. Unity and obedience—not freedom and rights—were seen as keys to rebirth.

Scholars often apply the term *totalitarianism* to the Fascist, Nazi, and Communist regimes of the 1930s. They use it to refer to highly centralized systems of government that attempt to control society and ensure conformity through a single party and police terror. (See "Terms of History," page 1030.) Forged in the crucible of war and its aftermath, totalitarian governments broke with liberal principles to wage war on their own citizens.

The Rise of Stalinism

In the 1930s, Joseph Stalin led the astonishing transformation of the USSR from a rural society into a formidable industrial power. Having taken firm control against Lenin's express wishes, Stalin ended the New Economic Policy (NEP), Lenin's temporary compromise between Marxism and capitalism. The Soviet Union became an industrial, Communist nation directed by a new generation of technocrats with few connections to the prewar socialist movement. The costs of industrialization and the consolidation of Stalin's power were staggering. Stalin became the unquestioned leader of a single-party state, while more than ten million people, by Stalin's own count, starved, were executed, or were worked to death in labor camps during the 1930s.

Rapid Industrialization. In the spring of 1929, Stalin presented the first of several five-year plans to the Communist Party congress. Outlining a program for massive increases in the output of coal, iron ore, steel, and industrial goods, Stalin called the plan, which laid out strict, meticulously calculated production goals, an emergency measure to end Soviet backwardness. He warned that without it, "the advanced countries . . . will crush us." He thus established central economic planning—a policy used on both sides in World War I by which government directed production, allocated resources, and mobilized the workforce. This policy had also helped Japan industrialize, and increasingly Western economists and industrialists favored some degree of economic planning. Between 1928 and 1940, the number of Soviet workers in industry, construction, and transport grew from 4.6 million to 12.6 million. From 1927 to 1937, production in metallurgy and machinery rose 1,400 percent. Stalin's first five-year plan had helped make the USSR a leading industrial nation.

Central planning helped create a new elite of bureaucrats and industrial officials; the number of managers in heavy industry grew by almost 500 percent between 1928 and 1935. Mostly party officials and technical experts, these managers dominated Soviet workers by limiting their ability to change jobs or move from place to place. Nonetheless, skilled workers as well as bureaucrats benefited substantially from the redistribution of privileges that accompanied industrialism and central planning. Compared with people working the land, those in industry and especially those with mechanical skills received better housing, higher wages, and access to the limited consumer goods. Communist officials, meanwhile, enjoyed perquisites such as country homes, better health care, foods unavailable to the masses, and luxurious vacations.

Unskilled workers, however, faced a grim plight. Newcomers from the countryside were often herded into barracklike dwellings, even tents, and subjected to dangerous factory conditions. Many took pride in the skills they acquired: "We mastered this profession—completely new to us—with great pleasure," a female lathe operator recalled. More often, however, workers lacked the technical education and even the tools necessary to accomplish goals prescribed by the five-year plan. Almost everyone, from workers and managers to inspectors and government overseers, falsified production figures and other supposedly scientific data to protect their jobs—and in some cases their lives. Because fulfilling the plan had top priority as a measure of progress toward Communist utopia, official lying and corruption became ingrained in the economic system.

In a single decade the Soviet Union went from being an illiterate peasant society to an advanced industrial economy, an extraordinary achievement that had taken other Western countries a century or more to accomplish. Suffering was intense but tolerated because Soviet workers, unlike their counterparts around the world, were employed and believed in the ethos of "constant struggle, struggle, and struggle" to achieve a Communist society, in the words of a worker. Youth in particular accepted the rigors of Stalin's industrialization as a heroic challenge. After the romance of the revolution and civil war, wrote one young man, "the older generation had left to our lot only a boring, prosaic life that was devoid of struggle and excitement." For workers, NEP had endorsed old-fashioned inequality; under Stalin, one maintained, "man himself is being rebuilt."

Collectivization of Agriculture. Stalinism, as this tough, even brutal vision of modernization came to be called, politicized work life in city and countryside alike as part of forced industrialization. Stalin demanded more grain from peasants (who had prospered under NEP), both to feed the urban workforce and to export as a way to finance industrialization. Peasants resisted government demands by cutting production or withholding produce from the market. Faced with such recalcitrance, Stalin called for the "liquidation of the kulaks." The name *kulak*, which literally means "fist," was a derogatory term for prosperous peasants, but in practice it applied to anyone who opposed his plans to end independent farming.

Stalin generated enthusiasm for the attack on the peasantry by presenting it as a revolutionary challenge. In the winter of 1929–1930, party workers armed with quotas scoured villages for produce; officials soon arrived and forced villagers to identify the kulaks among them. Propaganda units instilled hatred for anyone connected with kulaks. One Russian remembered believing they were "bloodsuckers, cattle, swine, loathsome, repulsive: they had no souls; they stank." Stalin ordered these "enemies of the state" evicted, imprisoned, exiled, or murdered. Whole families and even entire villages were robbed of their possessions and left to starve. "In the station square," one writer recalled, "Ukrainian kulaks . . . lay down and died. One got used to seeing the dead there in the morning, and the hospital stable-boy . . . would come along with his cart and pile the corpses in."

Totalitarianism

*T*otalitarianism is a term loaded with controversy, but when first introduced in Italy, Mussolini's government adopted it as a mark of pride. In 1923, Mussolini proposed a law by which the political party that garnered the most votes would seat 75 percent of the delegates in Italy's parliament. Italy had many political parties whose delegates formed coalitions that acted together to govern. Mussolini hoped to end that practice so that his small but powerful party could take most of the parliamentary seats and rule alone. Its temporary popularity would be transformed into real dominance.

The Italian journalist Giovanni Amendola cried foul, claiming that this proposal would eliminate both majority rule and minority coalitions in favor of a "totalitarian" system. Amendola, later beaten to death by Mussolini's thugs, warned that such a totalitarian system "denies you the right to possess a conscience—of your own, not one imposed by others."[1] Then, in a surprising turn, the Fascists embraced the term and proclaimed the superiority of an all-encompassing state led by a virile and forward-looking party. Their model was the "total state" under conditions of "total war" when the principles of conscience, rights, and freedom gave way to efficient military rule of the masses.

---

[1]Giovanni Amendola, quoted in Abbott Gleason, *Totalitarianism: The Inner History of the Cold War* (New York: Oxford University Press, 1995), 14.

The Nazis picked up on the term, hailing the effective totalitarian party that could mobilize workers and soldiers to make them like steel in body and in spirit. The flabby democratic state that had to respond to the wishes of a mass citizenry for programs such as insurance plans and workmen's compensation would disappear as it had during wartime. Some German theorists even looked admiringly at the Soviet Union with its five-year plans and forced industrialization as another model for "total mobilization" and the "total state." They pointed approvingly at its coercion in matters of political belief as a modern way to create state power.

As refugees fled Europe in the 1930s, they contributed another ingredient to the definition of totalitarianism, a system they professed to abhor. Refugee intellectuals saw totalitarianism as stemming from the rational thought of the eighteenth century and the aim of the scientific revolution and the Enlightenment to dominate nature. Analogously, to their mind, the system of free trade and capitalist industrialization aimed at domination of the economy and resources. By these arguments, the Soviets were less implicated in totalitarianism than the Fascists and Nazis; as the cold war took shape in 1945, people who defended the USSR and hailed its contribution in the war to defeat Hitler and Mussolini turned against the term's adequacy to describe these three towering dictatorships. In the cold war the United States wanted to view the Soviet system as identical to Nazism, while the USSR's defenders now envisioned the term *totalitarianism* as cold war propaganda and rejected its use. One modification that pleased some was the term *democratic totalitarianism*, used to distinguish Stalin's from Hitler's and

---

Confiscated kulak land formed the basis of the *kolkhoz*, or collective farm, where peasants were to create a Communist agricultural system using cooperative farming and modern machinery. Agricultural collectivization provoked resistance: some country men formed guerrilla bands, and women on the *kolkhoz* hid barnyard animals and preserved rural traditions that the modernizers detested. Many peasants deserted communism for good in the 1930s. Officials nonetheless announced that, as in the city, rural work life was becoming Communist.

The Purges. Once work life was politicized, economic failure took on political meaning. Factory workers, many newly arrived from the countryside, often were unable to meet the required quotas. In the countryside, party officials' ignorance of agriculture and a lack of equipment and scientific personnel made collectivization an utter disaster. Soviet citizens starved as the grain harvest declined from 83 million tons in 1930 to 67 million in 1934. Stalin blamed failure on "wreckers," saboteurs of communism, and he instituted purges—state

Mussolini's regimes. So heated became the debate over the concept and application of *totalitarianism* as a descriptive historical term, however, that many scholars ceased to use it.

Others, however, believe the term merits rethinking now that the cold war is over. A totalitarian state, as its definition evolved late in the twentieth century, was one that intensified government's concern with private life and individual thought, leaving no realm of existence outside the state's will. Censorship of speech, suppression of parliamentary and freely chosen representative rule, and violent elimination of disagreement were crucial ingredients of a totalitarian system. Because the state was seen as a unified, massively powerful entity, laws regulating reproduction and family life were central. Not only did the labor and armed forces expand, but through the control of fertility—especially by outlawing or enforcing birth control and abortion—the state showed its power to determine life's most intimate activity. Hitler, Mussolini, Stalin, and later Mao Zedong of China all made their control of reproduction pivotal to their regimes. Totalitarian regimes also relied on violence to forge unity: control of military or paramilitary weaponry and technology of modern communications allowed for the programming of thought and the elimination of enemies, including those whose thinking did not fall in line with the regime's ideas. Many believe that totalitarianism can work only in a society where the state uses advanced technology and advanced communications to dominate intimate behavior and control individual thought.

Nonetheless it is important to note the vast differences among totalitarian states: the socialist economy of the Soviet Union differed from the economies of both Nazi Germany and Fascist Italy. Moreover, systems lumped under the term *totalitarian* had different intellectual roots. Nationalism was key in the rise of fascism and Nazism, whereas communism began as an international workers' movement and forced people of many ethnicities to live together. Anti-Semitism also infected totalitarian societies in varying degrees: in Italy, Jews were rarely persecuted (and frequently protected from Nazis); Stalin purged individual Jews without singling out the entire race for extermination; Nazism had the elimination of the Jews as central to its mission. Even the democracies, like totalitarian countries, intervened more and more in daily life. Although not uniform in policy, the various states of the United States performed forced sterilization on many African American women in the pre–World War II period even as they outlawed birth control.

For all its limitations, the term *totalitarian* can help us think about the twentieth-century state in the context of total war, increasingly destructive technology, and sophisticated means of communication in an age of mass society. The implications of totalitarianism challenge a growing global commitment to individual and human rights—thus this historic term remains central to political concerns today.

FURTHER READING

Arendt, Hannah. *The Origins of Totalitarianism.* 1951.

Gleason, Abbott. *Totalitarianism: The Inner History of the Cold War.* 1995.

Tormey, Simon. *Making Sense of Tyranny: Interpretations of Totalitarianism.* 1995.

violence in the form of widespread arrests, imprisonments in labor camps, and executions—to rid society of these villains. These purges continued as long as Stalin lived and encompassed nearly all segments of society.

Bourgeois engineers were the first group condemned for causing low productivity. Soviet citizens expressed their relief that the wreckers had been punished, and they searched their own workplaces, as one young enthusiast believed, for "concrete bearers of evil . . . workers guilty of foul-ups, breakdowns, defects." Trials of prominent figures followed. When in 1934 Sergei Kirov, the popular first secretary of the Leningrad Communist Party, was murdered, Stalin used his death (which he may have instigated) as the pretext to try former Bolshevik leaders. The secret police soon claimed they had uncovered a massive conspiracy led by Stalin's old enemy Leon Trotsky to overthrow Soviet rule. At a series of "show trials" from 1936 to 1938—trials based on trumped-up charges, fabricated evidence, and confessions extracted after threats and torture—former Bolsheviks were coerced to confess that they had corresponded with the exiled Trotsky. Most of those found guilty were shot.

The spirit of purge swept society. One woman poet described the scene: "Great concert and lecture halls were turned into public confessionals. . . . People did penance for [everything]. . . . Beating their breasts, the 'guilty' would lament that they had 'shown political short-sightedness' and 'lack of vigilance' . . . and were full of 'rotten liberalism.'" Purges occurred in local bureaucracies, universities, technical schools, and other training grounds for political and technological jobs. As international tensions intensified later in the 1930s, Stalin convinced hesitant party members to accept more purges by pleading the dangers from "German-Japanese agents of Trotskyism." In 1937 and 1938, military leaders were arrested and executed without public trials; in some ranks every officer was killed. From industry and education to the party and the army, not even the Soviet power structure escaped the great purges.

Simultaneously the government developed an extensive system of prison camps over several thousand miles stretching from Moscow to Siberia. Called the *Gulag*—an acronym for the administrative arm of the camps—the system held as many as eight million prisoners, according to some estimates, during any one year in the 1930s. Of these, one million died annually as a result of the harsh conditions, which included insufficient clothing, food, and housing along with twelve- to sixteen-hour workdays at mining, heavy construction, and other crushing labor. Beatings and murder of prisoners rounded out Gulag life, as it became another aspect of Soviet violence.

This bloody period of Soviet history has provoked intense historical debate. Were the purges carefully planned and directed solely by Stalin, who watched the trials from a secret booth in the courtroom? Or were they initiated by the Communist Party's rank and file? Some historians view the purges as the machinations of a psychopath, whereas others see them as a clear-headed attempt on Stalin's part to eliminate barriers to total control. More recently, historians have judged the purges as discrete events that emanated from power struggles among party officials and were fueled by the treachery of those looking for a quick route to the top. People in the lower ranks de-

nounced their superiors to cover the way they themselves had falsified statistics, been lenient on kulaks, or lacked the proper vigilance. Still other interpretations see many denunciations and confessions as sincere expressions of workers' commitment to rooting out enemies of their proletarian utopia. At stake in these debates is not only attributing responsibility for horrendous suffering and loss of life but for understanding the source of Communist policy in the 1930s and 1940s and thus the nature of the Soviet regime. At least we may be certain as to the outcome: ongoing arrests, incarcerations, and executions eliminated any rivals to Stalin's power.

Reshaping Soviet Society. The 1930s marked a sharp reversal of revolutionary experimentation in cultural and social life. This retreat curtailed, among other things, modernism in the arts, creativity in urban planning, and commitment to egalitarian gender ideals and sexual freedom. Much like the rest of Europe, the Soviet Union experienced a rapid decline in its birthrate in the 1930s. This drop, combined with the need to replace the millions lost since 1914, motivated Stalin to end the reproductive freedom of the early revolutionary years and turn state policy toward increasing the birthrate. Birth-control information, contraceptive devices, and abortions became difficult to obtain. Gold wedding rings and more lavish wedding ceremonies came back into fashion, and people were forced to remain married and encouraged to reproduce. The state criminalized homosexuality and touted motherhood as not only a joy but a patriotic duty. Whereas Bolsheviks had once derided the family as a "bourgeois" institution, propaganda now referred to the family unit as a "school for socialism"—that is, a miniature of the Soviet state.

Socialism under Stalin provided women a mixed experience. Those in rural areas made gains in literacy and in access to health-care facilities. They applauded new provisions for child support, as more and more men left the countryside for opportunities in factory work. Positions in the lower ranks of the party opened to women as the purges continued, and women increasingly were accepted into the professions. The stress on women, particularly those in the industrial workforce, increased however. Working long hours in factories, they also stood in long lines for scarce consumer goods and performed all household and child-care tasks under harsh conditions.

Cultural life was equally paradoxical under Stalin, as it simultaneously involved an end to avant-garde experimentation and a modern awareness of popular culture's power to shape a collective psyche. Modernist intellectuals continued to promote their ability to mobilize the masses by appealing to the unconscious and the emotions in their work. Stalin endorsed this role by calling artists and writers "engineers of the soul." In another form of central planning, he established the Union of Soviet Writers to control all matters related to the private and professional lives of writers. The union assigned housing, office space, supplies, equipment, and secretarial help and even determined the types of books authors could write.

N. J. Altman, *Anna Akhmatova* (1914)
This modernist painting portrays the poet Anna Akhmatova when she was a centerpiece of literary salon life in Russia and the subject of several avant-garde portraits. In the 1930s and 1940s, Akhmatova gave poetic voice to Soviet suffering, recording in her verse ordinary people's endurance of purges, deprivation, and warfare. As she encouraged people to resist the Nazis during World War II, Stalin allowed her to revive Russian patriotism instead of socialist internationalism.
State Russian Museum, St. Petersburg/The Bridgeman Art Library.

In return, the "comrade artist" adhered to the official style of "socialist realism," derived from the 1920s focus on the common worker as a type of social hero. This mandated style infused such monumental works as Mikhail Sholokhov's *And Quiet Flows the Don* (1928–1940), which explored the consciousness of a rural hero and his work on behalf of socialism. Painters, filmmakers, composers, and journalists aimed to "depict life in its revolutionary development," as union officials described the style. Some artists, such as the poet Anna Akhmatova (1889–1966), refused to accept this system.

> *Stars of death stood above us, and Russia,*
> *In her innocence, twisted in pain*
> *Under blood-spattered boots . . .*

wrote Akhmatova in those years. Many others, including the composer Sergei Prokofiev (1891–1953), found ways to accommodate their talents to the state's demands. Prokofiev composed the score for Sergei Eisenstein's 1938 film *Alexander Nevsky*, a work that transparently compared Stalin to the towering medieval rulers of the Russian people. When his ballet *Romeo and Juliet* was censored, Prokofiev wrote children's music, including the delightful *Peter and the Wolf*. Aided by adaptable artists, workers, and bureaucrats, Stalin stood triumphant as the 1930s drew to a close. Having brutally eliminated competitors, Stalin alone represented the revolutionary future.

Hitler's Rise to Power

Hitler ended German democracy. Since the early 1920s, he had tried to rouse the German masses to crush the fragile Weimar Republic. In his coup attempt, in his influential book *Mein Kampf* ("My Struggle," 1925), and in his leadership of the Nazi Party, he drummed at a message of anti-Semitism and the rebirth of the German "race." Hitler's message was hardly unique, but when the Great Depression struck Germany his party began to outstrip its rivals in elections. In the midst of financial collapse and unemployment, some big businessmen, notably film and press mogul Alfred Hugenberg, joined forces with Hitler to protest the restructuring of German reparations in the Young Plan. Hugenberg's press relentlessly attacked the

Weimar government, blaming it for the disastrous economy and inflaming wounded German pride over the defeat in World War I.

Simultaneously, parliamentary government virtually ground to a halt in the face of economic crisis. The conservative chancellor Heinrich Brüning (1885–1970) proposed to stabilize the economy with a balanced budget, reduced government expenditures, and increased taxes and protective tariffs, but the Reichstag failed to approve such emergency plans. Hitler's followers made parliamentary government look even more inept by rampaging through the streets, wrecking stores owned by Jews, and beating up Communists and Social Democrats. By targeting Social Democrats and Communists as a single, monolithic group of "Bolshevik" enemies, the Nazis won the approval of the middle classes, who feared Russian-style revolution and the loss of their property.

As a result of the publicity Hugenberg's media showered on it and of its own street tactics, Hitler's National Socialist German Workers' Party (NSDAP)—the Nazi Party—which had received little more than 2 percent of the vote in 1928, won almost 20 percent in the Reichstag elections of 1930 and more than doubled its representation in 1932. As newspapers vilified the Weimar Republic for its weakness, favorable press reports, brass-knuckle politics, and military parades gave the illusion of Nazi vigor. Many of Hitler's supporters, like Stalin's, were young and idealistic. In 1930, seventy percent of party members were under forty, a stark contrast to the image of Weimar politicians as aged and inef-

fectual. Although businessmen provided substantial sums of money, every class supported the Nazis. The largest number of supporters came from the industrial working class because they had the most voters, but white-collar workers and the lower-middle class joined the party in percentages out of proportion with their numbers in the population.

The elections of 1930 and 1932 stunned conservatives like Brüning because they showed the rising appeal of radicals—both Nazis and Communists made gains. Hitler's propaganda techniques had served him well with the masses against old-fashioned contenders. His propaganda chief, Joseph Goebbels, sent thousands of recordings of Hitler's speeches to the countryside and provided Nazi mementos to the citizenry. Teenagers painted their fingernails with swastikas, a symbol used by the Nazis, and in the German army, a bastion of traditional conservatism, soldiers flashed metal match covers with Nazi insignia.

Nazi rallies were masterpieces of political display in which Hitler mesmerized the crowds. He began by talking slowly until he had a sense of the audience; then, as one witness reported, "suddenly he bursts forth. His words go like an arrow to their target; he touches each private wound on the raw, liberating mass unconscious, expressing its innermost aspirations, telling it what it most wants to hear." Hitler fashioned himself the Führer, or leader, of the masses, to whom he appealed as a strong, vastly superior being. Frenzied and inspirational, he represented neither the calculating politician nor the rational bureaucrat but "the creative

Toys Depicting Nazis

As a totalitarian ideology, Nazism was part of everyday life. Nazi insignia decorated clothing, dishes, cigarette lighters, and even fingernails. People chose their loved ones according to Nazi rules, sent young people to Nazi clubs and organizations, and bought Nazi toys like these for their children's playtime. Nazi songs, Nazi parades and festivals, and Nazi art filled leisure hours.
Imperial War Museum, London.

element," one poet put it. In actuality, however, Hitler viewed the masses only as tools. In *Mein Kampf* he discussed his philosophy of how to deal with them:

> The receptivity of the great masses is very limited, their intelligence is small. In consequence of these facts, all effective propaganda must be limited to a very few points and must harp on those in slogans until the last member of the public understands what you want him to understand.

With Hitler, as with Stalin, mass politics had reached terrifying and cynical proportions.

The Communist and Nazi success in the 1932 Reichstag elections made the leader of one of those parties the logical choice as chancellor. Germany's conservative elites—from the military, industry, and the state bureaucracy—loathed the Communists and favored Hitler as a common type they could easily manipulate. Ultimately, elite leaders persuaded the aging president Paul von Hindenburg (1847–1934) to invite Hitler to become chancellor in January 1933.

The Nazification of German Politics

Vowing to uphold the Weimar constitution, Hitler took office amidst jubilation in Berlin, as tens of thousands of storm troopers holding blazing torches paraded through the streets. Millions celebrated Hitler's ascent to power. "My father went down to the cellar and brought up our best bottles of wine. . . . And my mother wept for joy," one German recalled. "'To think that I should live to see this!' she said. 'Now everything will be all right.'" Hitler moved rapidly and brutally to fulfill his program by creating a new kind of antidemocratic state, crushing racial and other enemies, whom he saw as a menace to building a new, prosperous German order.

Terror in the Nazi State. Within a month of Hitler's taking power, the elements of Nazi political domination were in place. When the Reichstag building was gutted by fire in February 1933, he blamed the Communists and used the fire as the excuse for suspending civil rights, declaring censorship of the press, prohibiting meetings of opposition writers and artists, and disrupting the work of other politi-

cal parties. Hitler had made clear throughout his career that *all* political parties except the NSDAP were his enemies. "Our opponents complain that we National Socialists, and I in particular, are intolerant and intractable," he declared. "They are right, we are intolerant! I have set myself one task, namely to sweep those parties out of Germany."

New elections were held in March. The Nazis won 288 Reichstag seats, but Social Democrats and Communists still retained more than 200 seats, and right and center parties claimed another 158. Storm troopers lashed out violently at this political failure, beating up opponents and destroying property. They prevented Communist delegates from attending Reichstag sessions and so intimidated the others that at the end of March, Hitler was able to pass the Enabling Act, which suspended the constitution for four years and allowed subsequent Nazi laws to take effect without parliamentary approval. Hitler had shown himself vigorous in meeting political crisis, and solid middle-class Germans approved the Enabling Act as a way to pull the country out of its economic and political morass.

Political violence became institutionalized to advance the creation of a *Volksgemeinschaft* ("people's community") of like-minded, racially pure Germans—"Aryans" in Nazi terminology. Heinrich Himmler, who headed the elite SS (*Schutzstaffel*) organization that protected Hitler and other Nazi leaders, commanded the Reich's political police system. The Gestapo, organized by Hermann Goering, and the Order of the Death's Head also enforced complete obedience to Nazism. These organizations had vast powers to arrest, execute, or imprison people in concentration camps, the first of which opened at Dachau near Munich in March 1933. The Nazis filled it and later camps with socialists, homosexuals, Jews, and others. They touted these camps as places where "antisocial" elements would be housed so that they could no longer interfere with the *Volksgemeinschaft*. In the muscular logic of the Nazis, individual rights interfered with the *Volksgemeinschaft*. One Nazi leader proclaimed:

> [National socialism] does not believe that one soul is equal to another, one man equal to another. It does not believe in rights as such. It aims to create the German man of strength, its task is to protect the German people, and all . . . must be subordinate to this goal.

Hitler deliberately blurred authority among the agencies of order and terror so that confusion and bitter competition reigned within the government and among the population at large. He thus prevented the emergence of coalitions against him and allowed himself to arbitrate the confusion.

At the same time, these rivalries threatened his regime, and Hitler responded with violence to discipline his closest followers as well as the masses. Ernst Roehm, leader of the SA (paramilitary troops), called for a "second revolution" to end the corrupt influence of the old business and military elites on the Nazi leadership, especially on Hitler. He hoped to make the SA the nucleus of a new German army. Despite their long-standing collaboration, Hitler ordered the assassination of Roehm, along with hundreds of SA leaders, individual enemies, and innocent civilians. The bloody Night of the Long Knives (June 30, 1934) eroded the SA's challenge to the army and the SS and led conservative business and military leaders to support Hitler yet again. Nazism's terroristic politics were in place as the foundation of his "Third Reich"—a German empire succeeding those of Charlemagne and William II. Further, massive violence was still to come.

Nazi Economic and Social Programs. Hitler continued his drastic reform of Germany with economic and social programs. Putting people back to work was crucial to the survival of his regime. Economic revival built popular support, strengthened military industries, and provided the basis for German expansion. The Nazi government pursued what economists call *pump priming*, that is, stimulating the economy through government spending. Under the guise of making farm equipment, Germany built tanks and airplanes; the Autobahn highway system was developed to serve military as well as civilian ends. From farms to factories, the government demanded high productivity and set goals for national economic independence and self-sufficiency. Skilled workers prospered in the drive to rearm; and unemployment declined from a peak of almost 6 million in 1932 to 1.6 million by 1936. As labor shortages began to appear in certain areas, the government conscripted single women into service as farmworkers and domestics.

The Nazi Party reorganized work life to increase efficiency and to curtail labor activism. Government officials and industrial managers classified jobs, determined work procedures, and set pay levels, rating women's jobs lower than men's regardless of the level of expertise required. In May 1933, the government closed down labor unions and seized their property. All workers, from the lowly unskilled to the top professionals, were compelled to join the Nazi-controlled German Labor Front, which was used to snuff out worker independence.

Imitating Stalin, Hitler announced a four-year plan in 1936 with the secret aim of preparing Germany for war by 1940. Government officials allocated raw materials, sponsored the production of synthetics, and intensified labor management; defense spending soared to 50 percent of all government expenditures by 1938. The four-year plan produced large trade deficits, which Hitler believed the spoils of future conquests would eliminate. Hitler had unprecedented power over the workings of everyday life, especially gender roles. In June 1933, a bill took effect that encouraged Aryans (those people defined as racially German) to marry and have children. The bill provided for loans to Aryan newlyweds, but only to those couples in which the wife left the workforce. The loans were forgiven on the birth of the pair's fourth child. Nazi marriage programs enforced a nineteenth-century ideal of femininity; females were supposed to be subordinate so men would feel tough and industrious despite military defeat and economic depression. Although some women complained about having to forfeit their jobs, others, remembering the miserable war and postwar years, believed that Hitler would elevate Nazi women, rewarding one, as a party leader put it, "who joyfully sacrifices and fulfills her fate."

Proposing to make life better for the German *Volk*, or people, Nazism in fact impoverished ordinary life. Although Goebbels, the minister of propaganda, ensured that 70 percent of households had "people's radios" by 1938, the programming broadcast was severely censored. Books like Remarque's *All Quiet on the Western Front* were banned, and in May 1933 a huge book-burning ceremony rid libraries of works by Jews, socialists, homosexuals, and modernist writers out of favor with the Nazis. Modern art in museums and private collections was either destroyed or confiscated. Civil servants, teachers, and other government officials were forced to adhere to Nazism. Another law took jobs from Jews and women and bestowed them on party members as rewards. In 1936, membership in the Hitler Youth, an organization that indoctrinated the young, became mandatory for all boys and girls over age ten. These children learned to report the names of adults they suspected of disloyalty to the regime, even their own parents. In public, citizens had to worry about the presence of informers—more than 100,000 were on the Nazi payroll—and so they employed what was called the "German look," a surreptitious glance around a public space for spies or party faithful.

Hitler partially fulfilled his promise to create a well-ordered national community. People boasted that they could leave their bicycles out at night without fear of robbery. And, in general, the improved economy led people to believe that Hitler was working an economic miracle while restoring pride in Germany, the prewar sense of authority, and the harmonious community of an imaginary past. For hundreds of thousands if not millions of Germans, however, Nazi rule in the 1930s brought anything but community.

Nazi Racism

The Nazis defined Jews as an inferior "race" dangerous to the superior Aryan or Germanic "race." According to Hitler, Jews were responsible for most of Germany's problems, including defeat in World War I and the intensity of the depression. Hitler attacked many ethnic and social groups, but he propelled the nineteenth-century politics of anti-Semitism to new and frightening heights. In the rhetoric of Nazism, Jews were "vermin," "abscesses," "parasites," and "Bolsheviks," whom the Germans would have to eliminate to become a true *Volksgemeinschaft*. By defining the Jews both as evil financiers and businessmen and as working-class Bolsheviks, Hitler fashioned an enemy for many segments of the population to hate passionately.

Nazi policy was called "racial," and it led to laws against "non-Aryans"—a group that, like "Aryans," was never defined. Racial classifications were made to appear scientific, however, by lists of physical and other characteristics that determined a person's "race." In 1935, the government enacted the Nuremberg Laws, legislation that specifically deprived Jews of citizenship, defined Jewishness according to a person's ancestry, ended special consideration for Jewish war veterans, and prohibited marriage between Jews and other Germans. To hold jobs, workers had to present their baptismal certificates and other evidence of their Aryan her-

itage. Whereas women defined as Aryan had increasing difficulty obtaining abortions or even birth-control information, these were readily available to the outcast groups, including Jews, gypsies, Slavs, and mentally or physically disabled people. By 1939, special courts forced Jews and other so-called inferior groups to undergo sterilization and reproductive experiments performed by Nazi doctors. In the name of improving the Aryan race, doctors helped organize the T4 project, which used carbon monoxide poisoning and other means to kill large numbers of people—200,000 handicapped and elderly—late in the 1930s, thus preparing the way for even larger mass exterminations that would occur later.

Some Jews thought the Nuremberg Laws would at least regularize their status and end street violence; instead the persecution escalated. One young Jewish woman fled her home in 1936 after being warned that the Gestapo had scheduled her arrest for daring to work in broadcasting, but her parents greeted this news with disbelief: "My mother thought I must be depressed over an unhappy love affair." Jews were forced into slave labor, evicted from their apartments, and prevented from buying most clothing and food. In 1938, a Jewish teenager, reacting to the harassment of his parents, killed a German official. In retaliation for this single murder, Nazis attacked some two hundred synagogues, smashed windows of Jewish-owned stores, broke into apartments of known or suspected Jews and stole or destroyed possessions, and threw more than twenty thousand Jews into prisons and camps. The night of November 9–10 became known as *Kristallnacht*, or the Night of Broken Glass.

Faced with this relentless persecution, which some historians have called a "social death," by the outbreak of World War II in 1939 more than half of Germany's 500,000 Jews had emigrated, often leaving behind all their possessions and paying huge fees to the government in exchange for exit visas. In the 1930s, Hitler's policies favored the migration of Jews rather than their extermination, and many emigrants—such as physicist Albert Einstein and filmmaker Fritz Lang—advanced the scientific, cultural, and scholarly accomplishments of their adopted countries, especially England and the United States. The confiscation of emigrants' property enriched their neighbors and individual Nazis; it also helped finance Germany's revival.

❖ Democracies on the Defensive

Nazism, communism, and fascism offered bold new approaches to modern politics and new kinds of economic and social policies. Their leaders' energetic, military style of mobilizing the masses challenged the other great powers to devise equally effective solutions to the problems created by the depression. However, leaders in the United States, France, and Great Britain also had to combat the political appeal of these new regimes, for Hitler, Mussolini, and Stalin had made representative government and democratic values appear effeminate, decadent signs of declining peoples. Thus the 1930s saw democracies on the defensive in a variety of arenas—economic, political, and cultural.

Confronting the Economic Crisis

As it wore on, the depression baffled as much as it alarmed politicians. Many favored tried and true remedies, but some governments undertook notable experiments to solve social and economic crises and still maintain democratic politics. The result across the West was to advance the trend toward the welfare state—that is, one that guarantees a certain level of economic well-being for individuals and businesses.

New Deal in the United States. The Great Depression had struck first in the United States, where President Herbert Hoover (1874–1964) confidently predicted that the economic downturn was only temporary because of the fundamental health of American business. When his rosy forecast proved false, the conservative Hoover opposed direct help to the unemployed, believing that "handouts," as he called assistance, would weaken the nation's moral fiber. In June 1932, some ten thousand World War I veterans marched on Washington, D.C., demanding relief; Hoover ordered the army to drive them away with tanks.

With unemployment close to fifteen million, the situation was grim when a more innovative politician, Franklin Delano Roosevelt (1882–1945), the wealthy, patrician governor of New York, defeated Hoover in the presidential election of 1932. Fulfilling his promise to voters, in his first hundred days in office Roosevelt pushed through a torrent of legislation, some of it inspired by the central control of the economy achieved during World War I: relief for businesses and instructions for firms to cooperate in stabilizing prices; price supports for hard-pressed farmers; public works programs for unemployed youth; and refinancing agencies for homeowners' mortgages. The Social Security Act of 1935 set up a fund to which employers and employees contributed. It provided retirement benefits for workers, unemployment insurance, and payments to dependent mothers, their children, and people with disabling physical conditions.

Collectively announced as his New Deal, Roosevelt's programs angered business people and the wealthy, who saw them as "socialist." But even as the depression remained severe, Roosevelt (quickly nicknamed FDR) maintained widespread support. Like Mussolini, Hitler, and other successful politicians of the 1930s and thereafter, he was an expert at using the new mass media. His radio series of "fireside chats" to the American people developed technology's possibility for injecting a sense of intimacy into mass politics. In sharp contrast to Mussolini and Hitler, however, Roosevelt aimed in his public statements to sustain—not to denounce—faith in democratic rights and popular government. At his inauguration in 1933, he declared, "The only thing we have to fear is fear itself." Americans, he exhorted on accepting renomination in 1936, should focus not on their present miseries but on the greatness that lay before them: "This generation of Americans has a rendezvous with destiny." Eager to separate themselves from Hoover's position, First Lady Eleanor Roosevelt rushed to greet the next group of veterans marching on Washington and FDR received the delegation at the White House. The Roosevelts insisted that justice, human rights, and liberal values must not be surrendered in difficult times. "We Americans of today . . . are characters in the living book of democracy," FDR told a group of teenagers in 1939. "But we are also its author." Lynchings, racial violence, and harsh discrimination continued to cause enormous suffering in the United States during the Roosevelt administration, nor did the economy fully recover. But the president's media success and bold programs kept the masses committed to a democratic future.

Eleanor Roosevelt Talks to the Nation
Eleanor Roosevelt, the wife of FDR and mother of five children, gradually became a political activist in her own right. Her work on behalf of the poor and against discrimination earned her both incredible acclaim and real hatred. Using the print and radio media, she rallied citizens during the depression and the war and eventually worked for United Nations causes. Here she is shown on January 1, 1940, at the headquarters of the American Red Cross in Washington, D.C., appealing for donations to a war relief drive.
Hulton Getty Picture Library/Liaison Agency.

A Fireside Chat with FDR
President Franklin Delano Roosevelt was a master of words, uttering many memorable phrases that inspired Americans during the depression and World War II. Aware of growing media power in the making and breaking of politicians, the press never showed Roosevelt's disabilities even when he used crutches or fell down. Instead, FDR became a symbol of U.S. resolve, ingenuity, and growing power. Here he addresses the nation on August 23, 1938, over a radio hookup while Eleanor Roosevelt and the president's mother, Sarah, observe.
© Hulton Getty/Liaison Agency.

Sweden's Welfare State. While FDR's New Deal policies met resistance and demanded compromise, Sweden developed a coherent program for solving economic and population problems that gained world attention for the way it reconceived the government's role in promoting social welfare and economic democracy. Although Sweden had industrialized later than western Europe and the United States, it had a tradition of community responsibility for working through social and economic difficulties. Sweden succeeded in turning its economy around in the 1930s. A neutral power that had profited from World War I and then suffered post-war inflation, depression, and population decline, Sweden instituted central planning of

the economy and social welfare programs. It also devalued the currency to make Swedish exports more attractive on the international market. Using pump-priming programs of public works to maintain consumer spending and to encourage modernization, the Social Democratic leaders saw Swedish productivity rise 20 percent between 1929 and 1935, a time when other democracies were still experiencing decline.

Sweden addressed the population problem with government programs, as did many other Western governments, but without the racist and antidemocratic coercion. Alva Myrdal (1902–1986), a social scientist and leading member of parliament, believed fertility rates were dependent on the economy and individual well-being. It was undemocratic, she maintained, "that the bearing of a child should mean economic distress to anybody in a country . . . who wants children." Acting on Myrdal's advice to promote "voluntary parenthood," the government started a loan program for married couples in 1937 and introduced prenatal care, free childbirth in a hospital, a food relief program, and subsidized housing for large families. By the end of the decade, almost 50 percent of all mothers received government aid. Long a concern of feminists and other social reformers, care of families became integral to the tasks of the modern state, which now saw itself as responsible for citizen welfare in hard times.

Liberalism Threatened in Britain and France. Unlike neutral Sweden, Britain and France emerged victorious but financially and morally exhausted from World War I. Because the most powerful democracy, the United States, had withdrawn from world leadership after the war by refusing to participate in the League of Nations, Britain and France had greater responsibility for international peace and well-being than their resources could sustain.

Britain was already mired in economic difficulties when the Great Depression hit. Faced with falling government revenues, Prime Minister Ramsay MacDonald, though leader of the Labour Party, reduced payments to the unemployed. At a time when married women were the first to be laid off and were often barred from holding any job, Parliament in 1931 effectively denied unemployment insurance to such women even though they had contributed to the unemployment fund. To protect jobs and domestic markets, the government imposed huge protective tariffs, setting duties on some goods at 100 percent of their value. The tariff discouraged a revival of international trade and did not relieve British misery.

Only in 1933, with the economy continuing to worsen, did the government begin to take effective steps. A massive program of slum clearance and new housing construction provided employment and infused money into the economy. By 1938, an extension of the National Insurance Act was providing minimal health benefits to twenty million workers and their families. The depression did not lift until Britain increased production to rearm in preparation for war late in the 1930s.

Depression struck later in France, but the country endured a decade of public strife in the 1930s. By 1932, severe postwar demoralization and stagnant population growth had joined with wage cuts and rising unemployment to create social and political turmoil. Deputies with opposing views on the economic crisis frequently came to blows in the Chamber of Deputies, and governments were voted in and out with dizzying rapidity. Parisians took to the streets to protest the government's belt-tightening policies, and the press trumpeted the disorderly mass rallies. Right-wing paramilitary groups mushroomed, attracting the unemployed, students, and veterans. They aimed to end representative government, which in their eyes was a "bastion of corruption."

In February 1934, the paramilitary groups joined Communists and other outraged citizens in riots around the parliament building. "Let's string up the deputies," chanted the crowd. "And if we can't string them up, let's beat in their faces, let's reduce them to a pulp." Hundreds of demonstrators were wounded and killed; inside the Chamber of Deputies, democratic representatives hurled ink bottles at one another. The antirepublican right lacked both substantial support outside Paris and a leader like Hitler or Mussolini capable of unifying its various groups. Thus France escaped the fate of Germany and Italy, but only for the present—the political chaos of the 1930s foreshadowed the fall of the Third Republic in 1940.

Mobilizing the Masses

Preserving representative government, the capitalist economy, and—for countries like Britain, France, the Netherlands, and Belgium—their empires motivated people in the democratic countries to mobilize mass support. In France, a coalition known as the "Popular Front" emerged to fight fascism and the effects of the depression. Across the democracies, writers and other intellectuals formed a kind of cultural front to brace the masses in hard, menacing times.

The Popular Front in France. Shocked into action by the force of fascism, French liberals, socialists, and Communists rallied in support of democracy. By 1936, these groups had established an antifascist coalition known as the Popular

Front. Until that time such a merging of groups had been impossible in democratic countries because of Stalin's strict opposition to Communist collaboration with liberals and socialists, who by this time disavowed Communist-style revolutions. As fascism spread throughout Europe, however, Stalin reversed course and allowed Communists to join such efforts.

For just over a year in 1936–1937 and again very briefly in 1938, the French Popular Front had enough electoral support to form a government, with the socialist leader Léon Blum (1872–1950) as premier. Like the American New Dealers and the Swedish Social Democrats, the Popular Front instituted long-overdue reforms. Blum extended family subsidies, state services, and welfare benefits, and he appointed women to his government (though women still were not allowed to vote). In June 1936, the government guaranteed workers two-week paid vacations, a forty-hour work week, and the right to collective bargaining. Working people would long remember Blum as the man who improved their living standards and provided them with benefits and vacations.

Family at Normandy Beach
In the midst of the depression of the 1930s, the working classes nonetheless gained a taste of leisure when the French government under Léon Blum mandated paid vacations for all workers. As other governments followed this lead, tourism became a booming business in the West. Citizens from all walks of life traveled to see their own country, witness its geographic differences, and visit its historic monuments.
Private Collection.

During its brief life the Popular Front made republicanism responsive to the masses by offering a youthful, but democratic, political culture. "In 1936 everyone was twenty years old," one man recalled, evoking the atmosphere of idealism. Local cultural centers sprang up for activities such as popular theater. Inspired to express their opposition to fascism, citizens celebrated democratic holidays like Bastille Day with new enthusiasm. Speakers at these events contrasted their spontaneous solidarity and good humor with fascist militarism and abuse of human rights.

Despite support from workers, the Popular Front governments were politically weak. Fearing for their investments, bankers and industrialists greeted Blum's appointment by sending their capital out of the country, leaving France financially strapped. "Better Hitler than Blum" was the slogan of the upper classes. Blum tried to win support from powerful financial interests by holding down taxes on the wealthy, in effect forcing the lower levels of society to pay for Popular Front programs. But Blum's government fell when it lost the left by refusing material support in the fight against fascism elsewhere, most notably Spain. As in Britain, memories of World War I caused leaders to block crucial support to foreign democratic forces and to keep the domestic military budgets small as a way of ensuring peace. The collapse of the antifascist Popular Front in late June 1937 showed the difficulties that pluralistic and democratic societies faced in crisis-ridden times.

Survival Strategies in Central Europe. Fledgling democracies to the east, hit hard by the depression, also fought the twin struggle for economic survival and representative government. In 1932, Engelbert Dollfuss (1892–1934) came to power in Austria; two years later he dismissed the parliament and ruled briefly as a dictator. Despite his authoritarian stance, Dollfuss would not submit to the Nazis, who assassinated him in 1934. In Hungary, where outrage over the Peace of Paris remained intense, a crippled economy resulted in right-wing general Gyula Gömbös (1886–1936) coming to power in 1932. Gömbös admired fascism and reoriented his country's foreign policy toward Mussolini and Hitler. He stirred up anti-Semitism and ethnic hatreds and left considerable pro-Nazi feeling after his death in 1936.

In democratic Czechoslovakia, the depression hit the primarily German population of the industrialized Sudeten region especially hard. As a result Nazism gained an enthusiastic following. The Slovaks, who were both poorer and less educated than the urbanized Czechs, built a strong Slovak Fascist Party. In Poland, Romania, Yugoslavia, and Bulgaria, ethnic tensions simmered and the appeal of fascism grew as the Great Depression lingered.

Cultural Vision in Hard Times

Just as culture had been mobilized in the war, postwar cultural leaders mobilized to meet the crisis of hard times and political menace. But the message was different: instead of turning away from public life as many had done in the 1920s, writers, filmmakers, and artists of the 1930s responded vigorously to the depression. Some empathized with the situations of factory workers, homemakers, and shopgirls struggling to support themselves or their families, others with the ever-growing number of unemployed and destitute. In 1931, French director René Clair's *À nous la liberté* ("Give Us Liberty") related prison life to work on a factory assembly line. Charlie Chaplin's film *Modern Times* (1936) showed the Little Tramp again, this time as a worker in a modern factory who was so molded by his monotonous job that he assumed anything he could see, even a co-worker's body, needed mechanical adjustment. These representations of the modern factory and hard times illuminated life in the 1930s with humor and sympathy that made Chaplin a hit even in the Soviet Union.

Media sympathy poured out to victims of the crisis, with women portrayed alternately as the cause and as the cure for society's problems. *The Blue Angel* (1930), a German film starring Marlene Dietrich, showed how a vital, modern woman could destroy men—and civilization. A woman's power was contrasted to the ineffectuality of an impractical professor. Although in dramas unemployment and the population crisis were often blamed on overpowering women, in comedies and musicals heroines behaved bravely, pulling their men out of the depths of despair and setting things right again. In such films as *Sally in Our Alley* (1931) and *Keep Smiling* (1938), the British comedienne Gracie Fields, for example, portrayed spunky working-class women who kept on smiling despite hard times.

Techniques of modern art like montage, which overlaid two or more photos or parts of photos, were used to grab visual and psychic attention in the cultural battles of the 1930s. Because of its urgency, however, the message came to take precedence over the form. Some intellectuals turned away from experimentation with nonrepresentational forms as they drove home their antifascist, pacifist, or pro-worker beliefs. Popular Front writers created realistic studies of human misery and the threat of war that haunted life in the 1930s. American novelist John Steinbeck (1902–1968) portrayed the desperate migration of ruined American farmers in *The Grapes of Wrath* (1939). The British writer George Orwell (1903–1950) described his experiences among the poor of Paris and London, wrote investigative pieces about the unemployed in the north of England, and published an account of atrocities committed by both sides during the Spanish Civil War (1936–1939). In some cases, the

Paul Klee, *Dancing with Fear* (1938)
Swiss-German artist Paul Klee explored modern art's ability to evoke universal truths behind surface reality. Delightful shapes and colors often marked his work, although he was always concerned with how technology would affect people's values. As the danger of Nazism's triumph mounted, Klee grew depressed and produced dark visions of fear and death.
"Tänze vor Angst," 1938, 90 (G 10) by Paul Klee. Paul-Klee-Stiftung, Kunstmuseum Bern, photo: Peter Lauri. © ARS, New York.

Soviet system inspired writers and artists, whether Communist or not, to adopt socialist realism for their depiction of working people.

Art became increasingly politicized. Some writers found it crucial to reaffirm their belief in Western values such as rationalism, rights, and concern for the poor. German writer Thomas Mann (1875–1955), a Christian, went into exile when Hitler came to power and began a series of novels based on the Old Testament hero Joseph to convey the struggle between humanist values and barbarism. The fourth volume, *Joseph the Provider* (1944), eulogized Joseph's welfare state, in which the granaries were full and the rich paid taxes so the poor might live decent lives. One of the last works of English writer Virginia Woolf, *Three Guineas* (1938), rejected experimental form for a direct attack on militarism, poverty, and the oppression of women, claiming they were interconnected parts of a single, devastating ethos undermining Europe in the 1930s.

While writers rekindled moral concerns, scientists in research institutes and universities continued to point out limits to human understanding—limits that seemed at odds with the megalomaniacal pronouncements of dictators. Astronomer Edwin Hubble (1889–1953) in California determined in the early 1930s that the universe was an expanding entity. Czech mathematician Kurt Gödel (1906–1978) maintained that any mathematical system contains some propositions that are undecidable. The German physicist Werner Heisenberg developed the "uncertainty," or "indeterminacy," principle in physics. Scientific observation of atomic behavior, according to this theory, actually disturbs the atom and thereby makes precise formulations impossible. Even scientists, Heisenberg asserted, had to settle for statistical probability. The attempt to learn the secrets of the universe led to doubts about human understanding itself. Viennese-born philosopher Ludwig Wittgenstein (1889–1951) explored the limits of language. He also questioned the traditional philosophical quest to find the essence of such terms as *thought, knowledge,* and *belief.*

Religious leaders also spurred many to recommit to religious activism. This impulse contested the violent secularization in Germany and the Soviet Union and helped foster a spirit of resistance to dictatorship among religious people. The Swiss theologian Karl Barth (1886–1968) encouraged rebellion against the Nazis, teaching that the faithful had to take seriously scriptural justifications of resistance to oppression. In his 1931 social encyclical, a letter addressed to the world on social issues, Pope Pius XI (r. 1922–1939) condemned the failure of modern societies to provide their citizens with a decent life and supported government intervention to create better moral and material conditions. The encyclical, *Quadragesimo Anno,* seemed to some an endorsement of the heavy-handed intervention of the fascists, but it also inspired some European theologians and pastors to ally themselves with the poor and politically oppressed. German Catholics frequently opposed Hitler, and religious commitment inspired many other individuals to resist fascism through the churches. During the 1930s, however, neither the traditional authority of the churches nor the cultural power of the art and mass media could block the ascendency of militarism and dictatorship.

❖ The Road to World War II

In the wake of economic catastrophe, Hitler, Mussolini, and Japan's military leaders marched the world toward another catastrophic war. Each of these leaders believed that his nation deserved to rule a far larger territory as part of its special destiny. At first many ordinary citizens and statesmen in Britain and France hoped that the League of Nations would be able to contain aggression by imposing embargoes or other sanctions. Others, believing that the powers had rushed into World War I, counseled the appeasement of Mussolini and Hitler. The widespread desire for peace in the 1930s sprang from fresh and painful memories: the destruction of World War I, the social and cultural chaos of the 1920s, and the economic turmoil of the Great Depression. But it left many people blind to Japanese actions in China and to Hitler's professed expansionist goals. By early 1938, Fascists were fighting to overthrow the Spanish republic, Japan had invaded the Asian mainland, and Hitler was menacing eastern Europe. Some historians claim that World War I, the turbulent interwar years, and World War II make up a single "Thirty Years' War" of the twentieth century. According to this view, the dramatic events of the 1930s, traditionally seen as the prelude to World War II, were actually the middle years of this conflict.

The Road to World War II

1929   Global depression begins with U.S. stock market crash
1931   Japan invades Manchuria
1933   Hitler comes to power in Germany
1935   Italy invades Ethiopia
1936   Civil war breaks out in Spain; Hitler remilitarizes the Rhineland
1937   Japan invades China
1938   Germany annexes Austria; European leaders meet in Munich to negotiate with Hitler
1939   Germany seizes Czechoslovakia; Hitler and Stalin sign nonaggression pact; Germany invades Poland; Britain and France declare war on Germany

Japan Strikes in Asia

Japan's military leaders chafed to control more of Asia and saw China, Russia, and other powers as obstacles to the empire's prosperity and the fulfillment of its destiny. Renewed military vigor was seen as key to pulling agriculture and small business from the depths of economic depression. The army took the lead: in September 1931, a railroad train in the Chinese province of Manchuria blew up, and Japanese officers used the explosion, which they had actually set, as an excuse to invade the territory. Setting up a puppet government in Manchuria, the army invaded more of China to push its goal of political and economic penetration of the Asian continent (Map 27.1).

Japanese leaders also believed that their society had put up with interference and competition from the Western powers long enough. During the difficult years of the Great Depression, the Japanese press aroused public sentiment against the kind of Western domination that had occurred at the Washington Conference in 1921, when Japan had been forced to agree to keep its fleet smaller than Western navies. Journalists called for aggressive expansion to restore the economy. Businessmen wanted new markets and resources for their burgeoning but wounded industries. In this uncertain time the military extended its influence in the government, advocating Asian conquest as part of Japan's "divine mission." By 1936–1937, Japan was spending 47 percent of its budget on arms.

The situation in East Asia had international repercussions. Great-power economic interests were threatened, as Japanese aggression compounded the effect of the growing market in Japanese goods. China asked the League of Nations to adjudicate the question of Manchuria. The league condemned the invasion, but it imposed no sanctions that would have put economic teeth into its condemnation. Meanwhile, the rebuff outraged the Japanese public and goaded the government to ally with Hitler and Mussolini. In 1933, China and Japan agreed to a truce, with Japan occupying territory on the Asian mainland. In 1937, however, Japan attacked China again, justifying its offensive as a first step toward what it called "a new order" in East Asia that would liberate the region from Western imperialism. Hundreds of thousands of Chinese were massacred in the "Rape of Nanjing"—an atrocity so named because of the brutality toward girls and women and the grim acts of torture perpetrated by the Japanese. The offensive set Japan and the United States on a collision course. President Roosevelt immediately announced an embargo on U.S. export of airplane parts to Japan and later enforced stringent economic sanctions on the crucial raw materials that drove Japanese industry. Nonetheless, the Western powers, including the Soviet Union, did not effectively resist Japan's territorial expansion in Asia and the Pacific.

Rejecting the Legacy of Versailles

Like Japanese leaders, Mussolini and Hitler called their countries "have-nots." The Allies had reneged on Britain's promise to hand over territories to Italy after World War I, and Mussolini threatened "permanent conflict" to right that wrong by expanding Italy's borders. Hitler's agenda, as stated in *Mein Kampf*, included reestablishing control over the Rhineland, breaking free from the Versailles treaty's military restrictions, and bringing Germans living in other nations into the Third Reich's orbit. Superior "Aryans," moreover, needed *Lebensraum*, or living space, to thrive. This space, according to Nazi plans, would be taken from the "inferior" Slavic peoples and Bolsheviks, who would be moved to Siberia or would serve as slaves to "Aryans." Both dictators portrayed themselves as peace-loving men who resorted to extreme measures only to benefit their country and humanity.

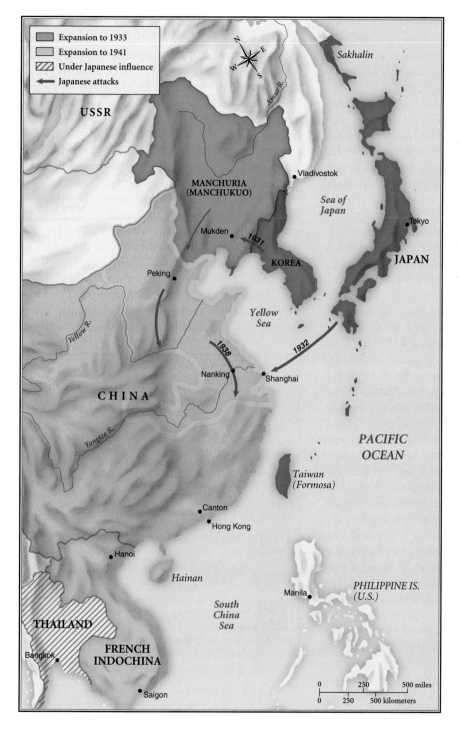

MAP 27.1 The Expansion of Japan, 1931–1941

Japanese expansion in the twentieth century approximated that of Russia and the United States in the nineteenth century: that is, it incorporated neighboring regions of Korea, Taiwan, and Manchuria with the vast area of China an inviting target. Governments of modernizing states believed that actual possession of territories was necessary for the resources, workforce, and markets they provided. But Japan's ambition fell afoul of the United States' own Pacific goals and made these two powers suddenly become deadly rivals.

Moreover, their anticommunism appealed to statesmen across Europe.

In the autumn of 1933, Hitler announced Germany's withdrawal from the League of Nations and from an international disarmament conference, which had been working fruitlessly for two years on proposals for limiting weapons. Hitler tried to unify Germany and Austria, but Austrian dictator Dollfuss resisted this first attempt at *Anschluss* (unification) and was assassinated for his obstruction.

In 1935, Hitler loudly rejected the clauses of the Treaty of Versailles that limited German military strength; he reintroduced military conscription and publicly started rearming, although Germany had been rearming in secret for years.

Mussolini also chose 1935 to assert Italian power: he invaded Ethiopia, one of the very few African states not overwhelmed by European imperialism. The attack was intended to demonstrate his regime's youth and vigor and to raise Italy's standing among the colonial powers. "A new cycle is beginning for our country," one soldier exclaimed. "The Roman legionnaires are again on the march." The poorly equipped Ethiopians resisted but could not withstand the Italian army, and their capital, Addis Ababa, fell in the spring of 1936. The League of Nations voted sanctions against Italy, but Britain and France opposed an embargo with teeth in it—one on oil—and thus kept the sanctions from being effective. The policy led to war, not peace, for the imposition of sanctions drove Mussolini into Hitler's arms, while British and French policy suggested a lack of resolve to fight aggression.

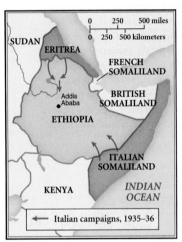

The Ethiopian War, 1935–1936

Profiting from the diversion of Italy's attack on Ethiopia, in March 1936 Hitler had defiantly sent his troops into what was supposed to be a permanently demilitarized zone in the Rhineland. The inhabitants greeted the Germans with wild enthusiasm, and the French, whose security was most endangered by this action, protested to the League of Nations instead of countering with an invasion as they had done in the Ruhr in 1923. Without the support of the British, who accepted the fait accompli, the French general staff, committed to a strategy of defense, counseled against an attack on Germany despite France's military superiority at the time. The two dictators thus appeared both as political leaders and as powerful military heroes forging, in Mussolini's muscular phrase, a "Rome-Berlin Axis." Next to them, the politicians of France and Great Britain looked not just cautious but timid.

The Spanish Civil War, 1936–1939

In what seemed like an exception to the trend toward authoritarian government, Spanish republicans overthrew their king in 1931. For centuries, Spain had declined economically and politically compared with the rest of Europe; large landowners and the Catholic clergy, who had the impoverished peasantry at their mercy, continued to dominate without modernizing the rural economy. The republicans hoped to modernize Spain by promoting industry and efficient, independent farming, but the government they established failed to enact land redistribution, which might have ensured popular loyalty and diminished the power of landowners and the church. This failure was all the more damaging because the antimonarchist forces included an array of liberals, anarchists, Communists, and other splinter groups constantly vying for power and harassing one another. In contrast,

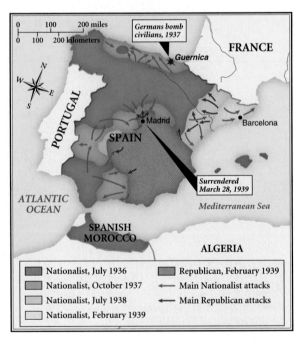

MAP 27.2 The Spanish Civil War, 1936–1939
Pro-republican and antirepublican forces bitterly fought one another to determine whether Spain would be a democracy or an authoritarian state. Germany and Italy sent military assistance, notably airplanes to experiment with bombing civilians, while volunteers from around the world arrived to fight for the losing cause of the republic. Defeating these ill-organized groups, General Francisco Franco instituted a pro-fascist government that sent many to jail and into exile.

right-wing forces from the large landowners and clergy acted in concert and drew on their substantial financial resources.

In 1936, pro-republican forces temporarily banded together in a Popular Front coalition to win elections and prevent the republic from collapsing under the weight of internal squabbling and growing monarchist opposition. With the Popular Front victory, euphoria swept the country: prisoners were set free, unemployment abated, and coveted municipal jobs were doled out. But the right recovered and revolted under the leadership of General Francisco Franco (1892–1975). Franco had the support of a host of right-wing groups, including monarchists, clergy, landowners, and ultimately the fascist Falange Party.

The military uprising led to the Spanish Civil War, which pitted the republicans, or Loyalists, against the fascist Falangists and the far more powerful forces of the authoritarian right. In a war of ever shifting battle lines, republicans held Madrid, Barcelona, and other commercial and industrial areas, whereas the rebels found most support in the agricultural west and south (Map 27.2). The struggle became a rehearsal for World War II when Hitler and Mussolini sent military personnel in support of Franco and the right to test new weapons and to practice new tactics, particularly the terror bombing of civilians. In 1937, the German Condor Legion of aviation aces, who entered the country on tourist visas, attacked the town of Guernica with low-flying planes, mowing down civilians in the streets. This gratuitous slaughter inspired Pablo Picasso's memorial mural to the dead, *Guernica* (1937), in which the intense suffering is starkly displayed in monochromatic grays and whites to capture a sense of moral decay as well as physical death.

The Spanish republican government appealed everywhere for assistance. Only the Soviet Union answered, but Stalin withdrew his troops and tanks in 1938 as government ranks floundered. Britain and France again showed their war-weariness by refusing to provide aid despite the outpouring of popular support for the cause of democracy. Instead a few thousand volunteers from a variety of countries—including many students, journalists, and artists—fought for the republic. As these volunteers put it, "Spain was the place to stop fascism," while refugee-volunteers from Mussolini's

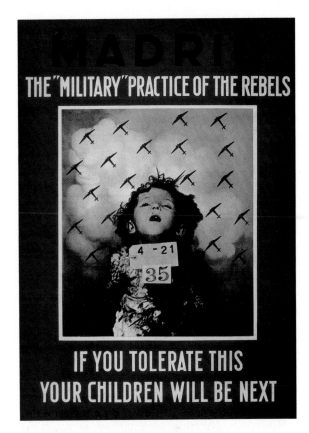

The Spanish Republic Appeals for Aid
The government of the Spanish Republic sent out modern advertising and propaganda to attract support from the remaining democracies—especially Great Britain and France. Antiwar sentiment remained high among the British and French, however. Thus, despite the horrifying and deliberate bombing of civilians by Franco's German allies, aid for the republic failed to arrive.
Imperial War Museum, London.

Italy found hope in thinking that their fighting meant, "Today in Spain, tomorrow in Italy." Besides being less well supplied than the Falangists and dependent on male and female volunteers, the republican ranks again splintered into competing groups of liberals, Trotskyites, anarchists, and Communists. In this bitter contest both sides committed widespread atrocities against civilians. The aid Franco received ultimately proved decisive, and his troops defeated the republicans in 1939. The ensuing dictatorship, which would remain in place until 1975, reinforced the European trend toward authoritarian government.

Hitler's Conquest of Central Europe, 1938–1939

The fall of central Europe that ultimately led to World War II began with Hitler's annexation of Austria in 1938. Many Austrians had actually wished for such a merger after the Paris peace settlement stripped them of their empire. In March 1938, Austrian Chancellor Kurt von Schuschnigg (1897–1977), hoping to maintain independence, called on Austrians to vote for or against Anschluss, or merging with the Third Reich. Fearing negative results, Hitler ordered an invasion.

His troops entered Austria as easily as tourists, and Austrian enthusiasm made the Anschluss appear to support the Wilsonian idea of "self-determination." The annexation fit into Hitler's plans in two ways: it began the unification of "Aryan peoples" into one greater German nation and it marked the first step in taking over the resources of central and eastern Europe. Austria was declared a German province, the Ostmark, and Hitler's thugs ruled once-cosmopolitan Vienna. An observer later commented on the scene:

> University professors were obliged to scrub the streets with their naked hands, pious white-bearded Jews were dragged into the synagogue by hooting youths and forced to do knee-exercises and to shout "Heil Hitler" in chorus. Innocent people in the streets were trapped like rabbits and herded off to clean the latrines in the S.A. barracks.

The Anschluss enhanced the image of German omnipotence, advancing Hitler's plan to "keep Europe gasping."

With Austria firmly in his grasp, Hitler turned to Czechoslovakia and its rich resources. Overpowering this democracy did not appear as simple a task as seizing Austria. Czechoslovakia had a large army and formidable border defenses and armament factories, and most Czech citizens were prepared to fight for their country. Hitler gambled correctly that the other Western powers would not interfere: many in the West thought that Czechoslovakia, a creation of the postwar peace settlement, unjustly denied Germans and other national minorities their right to self-determination.

Throughout the spring and summer of 1938, Hitler and his propaganda machine poured tremendous abuse on Czechoslovakia and its president, Edouard Beneš, for allegedly "persecuting" the German minority. Hitler wooed Czechoslovakia's neighbors into accepting his claims, partly by convincing the Poles and Hungarians that they had something to gain from the country's dismemberment. By October 1, 1938, he warned, Czechoslovakia would have to grant autonomy (amounting to Nazi rule) to the German-populated border region, the Sudetenland, or face German invasion.

As the October deadline approached, British Prime Minister Neville Chamberlain (1869–1940), eager to keep the peace, met with Hitler. Mussolini and French Premier Edouard Daladier (1884–1970) joined Hitler and Chamberlain at their last meeting in Munich and agreed not to oppose Germany's claim to the Sudetenland. Hitler topped off the Munich Conference by signing an agreement that Germany would never go to war with Great Britain. The strategy of preventing a war by making concessions for legitimate grievances (in this case, the alleged affront to Germans in the Peace of Paris) was called *appeasement*. At the time it was widely seen as a positive act, and the agreement between Germany and Great Britain prompted Chamberlain to announce that he had secured "peace in our time." Amidst great publicity, crowds lined the streets of European capitals and hailed their returning leaders for averting world war, despite the deal that in essence gave part of a sovereign country to Hitler. By contrast, the Czech ambassador to Germany wept. Stalin, excluded from the Munich deliberations, learned from the conference that the democracies were not going to fight to protect eastern Europe.

Hitler, meanwhile, was disgruntled that the agreement had thwarted his ambition to invade Czechoslovakia. Having portrayed himself as a man of peace, he waited another six months, until March 1939, and then sent German troops over the border (Map 27.3). Britain and France responded by promising military support to Poland, Romania, Greece, and Turkey in case of Nazi invasion. In May 1939, Hitler and Mussolini countered this agreement by signing a pledge of offensive and defensive support called the Pact of Steel.

Historians have sharply criticized the Munich Pact because it bought Hitler time to build his army and seemed to give him the green light for further aggression. Some historians believe that a

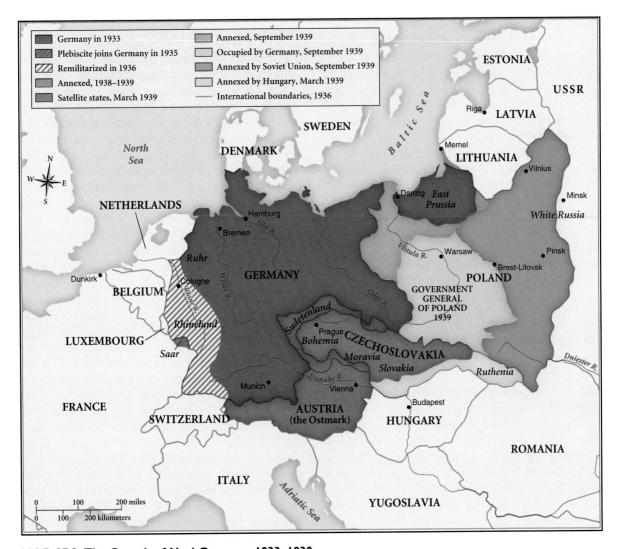

MAP 27.3 The Growth of Nazi Germany, 1933–1939

German expansion was rapid and surprising, as Hitler's forces and Nazi diplomacy brought the annexation of the new states of central and eastern Europe. Although committed to defending the sovereignty of these states through the League of Nations, French and British diplomats were more concerned with satisfying Hitler in the mistaken belief that doing so would prevent his claiming more of Europe. In the process Hitler acquired the human and material resources of adjacent countries to support his Third Reich.

confrontation might have stopped Hitler and that even if war had resulted, the democracies would have triumphed. According to this view, each military move by Germany, Italy, and Japan should have been met with stiff opposition, and the Soviet Union should have been made a partner to this resistance. Others counter that appeasement provided France and Britain precious time to beef up their own armies, which the Munich crisis caused them to do, and to prepare their citizens for an-

other war. Support for war was almost nonexistent, and even statesmen who knew of Hitler's ambitions respected, sometimes even admired, and almost always sought to pacify him in the belief that even though he was "mad" he could be dealt with rationally to meet Germany's just claims.

Such thinking received a final jolt on August 23, 1939, when Germany and the USSR signed a nonaggression agreement. The Nazi-Soviet Pact astonished public opinion in the West, given

Hitler's ambition to wipe the Bolsheviks off the face of the earth and official Soviet abhorrence of fascism. But Stalin needed extra time to reconstitute his military because he had just destroyed his officer corps in the purges. The pact provided that if one country became embroiled in war, the other country would remain neutral. Moreover, the two dictators secretly agreed to divide Poland and the Baltic States—Latvia, Estonia, and Lithuania—at some future date, with Hitler claiming western Poland and Stalin the Baltic States in addition to Finland and eastern Poland. The Nazi-Soviet Pact ensured that should war come, the democracies would be fighting a Germany with no fear of attack on its eastern borders. In the belief that Great Britain and perhaps even France would not fight because his aggression had met no resistance so far, Hitler now aimed his forces at Poland.

❖ World War II, 1939–1945

The global catastrophe that quickly came to be called the Second World War opened when Hitler launched an all-out attack on Poland on September 1, 1939. The Poles had rejected his demand that they return the free city of Danzig and yield to Germany the Polish Corridor—a strip of land to connect East Prussia with the rest of the Reich. Hitler had couched the ultimatum in nationalistic terms, claiming that Germans in Polish territory were in danger. "I needed an alibi," Hitler blatantly admitted, "especially with the German people." In contrast to 1914, no jubilation in Berlin accompanied the invasion; when Britain and France declared war two days later, the mood in other capitals was similarly grim. World War II began with dire predictions about its ultimate consequences: the British government had estimated in 1938 that the first two months of war would produce 1.8 million casualties and that London would be bombed daily by at least seven hundred tons of bombs. Although Japan, Italy, and the United States did not join the battle immediately, their participation eventually spread the fighting throughout the world. By the time World War II ended in 1945, many Europeans were starving, much of the continent lay in ruins, and unparalleled atrocities and genocide had killed 6 million Jews and countless others.

The German Onslaught

German ground forces quickly defeated the ill-equipped Polish troops by launching an overpowering *Blitzkrieg* ("lightning war"), in which the Germans concentrated airplanes, tanks, and motorized infantry to encircle Polish defenders and capture the capital, Warsaw, with overwhelming speed. Allowing the army to conserve supplies, Blitzkrieg assured Germans at home that the human costs of gaining Lebensraum, that is, sufficient "living space" for the full flowering of the Aryan race, would be low.

On September 17, 1939, the Soviets invaded Poland from the east to make their own conquest. By the end of the month, the Polish army was in shambles. Having divided the country according to the Nazi-Soviet Pact, Hitler issued a peace initiative in October so that future clashes would look like the fault of the democracies. The refusal of Britain and France to negotiate an immediate end to the conflict allowed Hitler to sell the war within the Reich as one of self-defense, especially from what propagandists called the "warlike menace" of world Jewry. Meanwhile, the USSR attacked Finland for refusing to provide a base for the Soviet military. As sympathy for the valiant Finns mounted, the League of Nations expelled the Soviet Union.

Hitler ordered an attack on France for November 1939, but his generals, who feared that Germany was ill prepared for total war, were able to postpone the offensive until the spring of 1940. During the period from November to April, known as the "phony war," the combatants engaged in little direct conflict. Then in April 1940, the Blitzkrieg crushed Denmark and Norway; the battles of Belgium, the Netherlands, and France followed in May and June.

In France, panic and defeatism infected the army. On June 5, Mussolini, eyeing future spoils for Italy, invaded France from the southeast. Much to the shock of the rest of the world, the French defense rapidly collapsed. Nor could the British army withstand the German onslaught. Trapped on the beaches of Dunkirk in northern France, 370,000 British and French soldiers were rescued in a heroic effort by an improvised fleet of naval ships, fishing boats, and pleasure craft. A dejected French government surrendered on June 22, 1940, leaving Germany to rule the northern half of the country, including Paris. In the south, named Vichy France after the spa town where the government sat, the reactionary and aged World War I hero Henri Philippe Pétain (1856–1951) was allowed to govern. Stalin used the diversion in western Europe to annex the Baltic States and to seize Bessarabia and Bukovina from Romania.

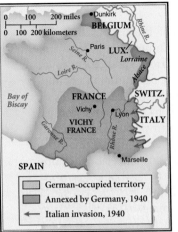

The Division of France, 1940

Britain now stood alone. Blaming Germany's rapid victories on Chamberlain's policy of appeasement, the British swept him out of office and installed as prime minister Winston Churchill (1874–1965), an early advocate of resistance to Hitler. After Hitler ordered the bombardment of Britain in the summer of 1940, Churchill rallied the nation by radio—now in more than nine million British homes—to reverse the pacifist spirit. Sacrifices to protect the ideals of liberty, he vowed, would yield Britain's "finest hour." He promised nothing, however, except "blood, toil, tears, and sweat."

In the battle of Britain, or Blitz as the British called it, the German air force (Luftwaffe) bombed public buildings and monuments, harbors and weapons depots, and military bases and industry. Refusing to negotiate, scorning surrender, and using the wealth of their colonies, the British held fast as the government poured resources into anti-aircraft weapons, its highly successful code-detecting group called Ultra, and development of its advantage in radar (a technology it had perfected in the 1930s). At year's end, the British air industry was outproducing the Germans by 50 percent.

By the fall of 1940, German air losses forced Hitler to abandon his plan for a naval invasion of Britain. He consoled himself by attacking British bases in the Mediterranean, Middle East, and North Africa and by forcing Hungary, Romania, and Bulgaria to join the Axis. This strategy gained Germany access to more food and oil for its army. Hitler then signed the Tripartite Pact with Italy and Japan (1940) and the Nonaggression Pact with Turkey (1941).

In spring 1941, Hitler, emboldened by his newly expanded power base, made his fatal decision to attack what he called the "center of judeobolshevism"—the Soviet Union. In June 1941, Operation Barbarossa began when the German army crossed the Soviet border. Hitler declared himself "happy to be delivered from [the] torment" of allying with Bolsheviks and promised to "raze Moscow and Leningrad to the ground."

Deployed along a two-thousand-mile front, 3 million German and other Axis troops quickly penetrated Soviet lines. When intelligence reports revealed troops massed on his border, Stalin simply disappeared for several days. Then he rallied to direct the defense; by July, however, the German army had rolled to within two hundred miles of Moscow and would eventually reach its suburbs. Using a strategy of rapid encirclement, German troops had killed, captured, and wounded more than half the 4.5 million Soviet soldiers defending the borders. Amidst success, Hitler blundered. Considering himself a military genius and the Slavic people inferior, he proposed attacking Leningrad, the Baltic States, and the Ukraine simultaneously, whereas his generals wanted to concentrate on Moscow. Following this cumbersome strategy lost precious time, and the German army got bogged down in the autumn rains. Driven by Stalin, local party members, and rising patriotic resolve, the Soviet people fought back in the winter, which turned Nazi soldiers to frostbitten wretches. In these early years of the war, Hitler feared that equipping his army for the Russian winter would suggest that the limits of Blitzkrieg had been reached and that a prolonged campaign lay in store—the scenario that did in fact materialize. Meanwhile his ill-supplied armies succumbed to the weather and disease. "What is all this for?" one German wrote in his diary in December 1941. "When will we ever get back home?"

War Expands: The Pacific and Beyond

As the German army entrenched in the Soviet Union, an all-out dramatic attack ignited war in the Pacific. On Sunday, December 7, 1941, Japanese navy planes bombed American naval and air bases at Pearl Harbor in Hawaii, seriously damaging or sinking all eight battleships there, and then decimated a fleet of airplanes in the Philippines. In an address to Congress Roosevelt pronounced it "a date which will live in infamy" and summoned the representatives to declare war on Japan. The outbreak of war in Europe intensified U.S.-Japanese competition, as Japan had taken control of parts of the British Empire, bullied the Dutch in Indonesia, and invaded Indochina to procure raw materials for its industrial and military expansion. Under Prime Minister Hideki Tojo (1884–1948), the militarist Japanese government decided it should settle matters with the West once and for all and forcibly unite Asians in a regional "coprosperity sphere." By spring 1942, the Japanese had conquered Guam, the Philippines, Malaya, Burma, Indonesia, Singapore, and much of the southwestern Pacific.

On December 11, 1941, Hitler, faithful to the Tripartite Pact, declared war on the United States—an appropriate enemy, he proclaimed, as it was "half Judaized and the other half Negrified." Mussolini followed suit. The United States was not prepared for a prolonged struggle: its armed forces numbered only 1.6 million, and no plan existed for producing the necessary guns, tanks, and airplanes. Earlier in 1941, Roosevelt had taken steps to assist Britain, notably with a program called Lend-Lease that provided supplies without immediate cash payment. American aid was crucial in the battle of the Atlantic—the struggle to protect vital British shipping from constant German attack. Fully 80 percent of Americans approved of the Lend-Lease plan.

But isolationist sentiment remained strong, led by the America First movement. Also working against war-preparedness was ambivalence toward the Soviet Union. Since the 1930s, many U.S. and British leaders and a good part of the general public had resisted joining forces with the USSR even against Hitler. Stalin himself reciprocated the mistrust. When Hitler declared war first on the USSR and then on the United States, his four enemies came together in the Grand Alliance of Great Britain, the Free French (an exile government led by General Charles de Gaulle and based in London), the Soviet Union, and the United States. The alliance evolved slowly over the course of the war through diplomatic negotiations and meetings of its leaders. Given the urgency of war and the partners' competing interests, the Grand Alliance and the larger coalition with twenty other countries—known collectively as the Allies—had much inter-

nal strife to overcome in their struggle against the Axis—Germany, Italy, and Japan.

The Holocaust

As the German army swept through eastern Europe, it slaughtered Jews, Communists, Slavs, and others deemed "racial inferiors" and enemies in Nazi ideology. In Poland, the SS murdered nobility, clergy, and intellectuals and relocated hundreds of thousands of Polish citizens to forced labor camps. Across the continent, the army rounded up civilians to work on German farms, in German industry, and in concentration and labor camps throughout the Reich—all to feed the voracious Nazi war machine. Herded into urban ghettos and living on minimal rations, many eastern European Jews were forced temporarily to work for the Nazis, but the Jews also became special targets of SS violence. Around Soviet towns, Jews were usually shot in pits, some of which they had been forced to dig themselves. After shedding their clothes and putting them in ordered piles for later Nazi use, ten thousand or more at a time were killed, often with the help of anti-Semitic Ukrainians or Lithuanians. More than thirty thousand were massacred at Babi Yar in the Ukraine after the fall of Kiev at the end of September 1941 (Map 27.4). However, the "Final Solution"—the Nazis' diabolical plan to exterminate all of Europe's Jews—was not yet fully under way.

In addition to the massacres, a bureaucratically organized and efficient technological system for rounding up Jews and transporting them to extermination sites had taken shape by the fall of 1941. On the eve of war in 1939, Hitler had predicted "the destruction of the Jewish race in Europe." In 1942, he exploded in rage before mass audiences: "There was a time when the Jews in Germany also laughed at my prophecies. . . . But take my word for it: they will stop laughing everywhere." Historians have demonstrated that although no clear order written by Hitler exists, he discussed the Final Solution's progress, issued oral directives for it, and from the beginning made lethal anti-Semitism a basis for Nazism.

The Holocaust was also a product of modern social and legal science and technology, managed by efficient scientists, doctors, lawyers, and government workers. Six camps in Poland were developed specifically for the purposes of mass murder—Auschwitz-Birkenau, Majdanek, Chelmno, Belzec,

Sobibor, and Treblinka. Some, like Auschwitz-Birkenau, served both as extermination and labor camps where inmates produced synthetic rubber and fuel. Others, such as Chelmno, existed solely for extermination. SS troops supervised all the camps. Improvising with sealed-up houses and trucks and using techniques developed in the T4 project in the late 1930s, Nazis and collaborators at Chelmno first gassed Christian Poles and Soviet prisoners of war. The Nazis burned the corpses in huge pits until the specially designed crematoria for mass burning started functioning in 1943. By then, Auschwitz had the capacity to burn 1.7 million bodies per year. About 60 percent of new arrivals—particularly children, women, and old people—were selected directly for murder in the gas chambers; the other 40 percent labored until, utterly used up, they too were sent to their deaths.

Extermination camps received their victims from across the continent. In the ghettos in various European cities, councils of Jewish leaders, such as the one in Amsterdam where Etty Hillesum worked, were ordered to determine those to be "resettled in the east." Many of them did so in the belief that life outside the ghetto could hardly be worse than life within. Effective resistance was nearly impossible, as Jews in the ghettos were weakened by hunger and disease and could not obtain enough necessary weapons. Moreover, the Jews who had emigrated outside Europe—mostly men and some younger women—left behind in the ghettos a surplus of women and older people. Any kind of resistance meant certain death. When Jews rose up against their Nazi captors in Warsaw in 1943, they were mercilessly butchered. The Nazis took pains to cloak their true purposes in the extermination camps. Bands played when trainloads of victims arrived; some were given postcards with reassuring messages to mail home. Then the selection process began, with men and women segregated. Many mothers, unaware that their children were automatically doomed, refused to be separated from them and thus went directly to the gas chamber. Those who avoided immediate selection had their heads shaved, were showered and disinfected, and were then given prison garments. So began life in "a living hell," as one survivor wrote.

Overworked inmates usually took in less than five hundred calories per day and experienced unimaginably bleak conditions, leaving them vulnerable to typhus and other diseases that swept through the camps. The brutality of inspections and roll calls, of mentally disturbed and criminal prison guards, and of inhumane medical experiments failed to crush the spirit of those like Etty Hillesum. Women observed religious holidays, celebrated birthdays, and re-created other sustaining aspects of domestic life. Language lessons or storytelling sessions maintained human culture in an inhuman setting. Prisoners forged new friendships that helped in the struggle for survival. An onion or part of a turnip could serve as a precious gift to someone sick with typhus. Thanks to those sharing a bread ration and doing him favors, wrote the Auschwitz survivor Primo Levi, "I managed not to forget that I myself was a man."

Historians debate what the Allies should have done about the Holocaust during the war. Some fault them for delaying the invasion of Europe or for failing to bomb the death camps about which they were informed. Others have calculated that

MAP 27.4 Concentration Camps and Extermination Sites in Europe

This map shows the major extermination sites and concentration camps in Europe, but the entire continent was dotted with thousands of lesser camps to which the victims of Nazism were transported. Some of these lesser camps were merely way stations on the path to ultimate extermination. In focusing on the major camps historians often lose sight of the ways in which evidence of deportation and extermination blanketed Europe.

many ordinary Germans knew of the genocide and ask why so few protested and why the Jews' own leaders cooperated in the deportations. Anti-Semitism had intensified since the end of the nineteenth century, and the Holocaust came about because of the high level of industrial, scientific, and legal organization that accompanied human hatred. Six million Jews, the vast majority from eastern Europe, along with an estimated five to six million gypsies, homosexuals, Slavs, and countless others were murdered. (See "New Sources, New Perspectives," page 1056.)

Societies at War

Even more than World War I, World War II depended on industrial productivity geared totally toward war and mass murder. The Axis countries remained at a disadvantage throughout the war despite their vast conquests. Although the war accelerated economic production some 300 percent between 1940 and 1944 in all belligerent countries, the Allies produced twice the armaments of the Axis powers in 1941 and more than three times Axis output in 1943. Even while its lands were occupied and many of its cities besieged, the Soviet Union increased its production of aircraft 40 percent between 1942 and 1943; by the spring of 1943 it was turning out 2,000 tanks per month (Figure 27.1).

Both Japan and Germany made the most of their lower capacity, most notably in the strategy of Blitzkrieg. Hitler had to avoid imposing wartime austerity because he had come to power promising

Persecution of Warsaw Jews
Hitler was determined to exterminate by violent means Jews, Slavs, gypsies, homosexuals, and others he deemed "undesirable"; he often enlisted community leaders to cooperate in deportation and even executions. In the 1930s, people fled Germany and then countries the Nazis conquered. In the city of Warsaw, where Jews were crowded into ghettos and deprived of food and fuel, the Jewish uprising brought massive retaliation.
© Bettman/Corbis.

	1939	1940	1941	1942	1943	1944	1945
Aircraft							
Great Britain	7,940	15,049	20,094	23,672	26,263	26,461	12,070
United States	5,856	12,804	26,277	47,826	85,998	96,318	49,761
USSR	10,382	10,565	15,735	25,436	34,900	40,300	20,900
Germany	8,295	10,247	11,776	15,409	24,807	39,807	7,540
Japan	4,467	4,768	5,088	8,861	16,693	28,180	11,066
Major Vessels							
Great Britain	57	148	236	239	224	188	64
United States	——	——	544	1,854	2,654	2,247	1,513
USSR	——	33	62	19	13	23	11
Germany (U-boats only)	15	40	196	244	270	189	0
Japan	21	30	49	68	122	248	51
Tanks							
Great Britain	969	1,399	4,841	8,611	7,476	5,000	2,100
United States	——	c. 400	4,052	24,997	29,497	17,565	11,968
USSR	2,950	2,794	6,590	24,446	24,089	28,963	15,400
Germany	c. 1,300	2,200	5,200	9,200	17,300	22,100	4,400
Japan	c. 200	1,023	1,024	1,191	790	401	142

FIGURE 27.1 Weapons Production of the Major Powers, 1939–1945
World War II devoured people and weapons, necessitating dramatic changes in the workforce and everyday life. As agricultural production was often hit hard by invading forces, people lived on reduced rations. Raw materials were channeled into the manufacture of weapons, and it was the real difference in productivity that spelled victory for the Allies: Germany and Japan were outproduced in almost every category. While the Allies filled their factories with women workers, German policies keeping women from well-paid industrial work could not be turned around in time to boost production.
From *The Hammond Atlas of the Twentieth Century* (London: Times Books, 1996), 103.

to end economic suffering, not increase it. The use of millions of slave laborers and resources from occupied areas improved the German standard of living, but those benefits disappeared after Blitzkrieg failed in the Soviet Union. Although Japan's government had built public support for the war, it maintained the erroneous belief that a few costly attacks would discourage Americans from pursuing war so far from home. Neither Japan nor Germany took the resources and morale of its enemies into full account.

Allied governments were overwhelmingly successful in generating civilian participation, especially among women. In the Axis countries, where government policy encouraged large families and motherhood was particularly exalted, women followed the fascist doctrine of separate spheres, avoiding paid work in wartime even though they were desperately needed in offices and factories. "The weakening of the family system would be the weakening of the nation," Japanese leaders argued. In contrast, Soviet women constituted more than half the workforce by war's end. They dug massive antitank trenches around Moscow and other threatened cities, and 800,000 volunteered for the

military, even serving as pilots. As the Germans invaded, Soviet citizens moved entire factories eastward; some five hundred were moved from Moscow in October 1941 alone. Stalin encouraged a revival of Russian nationalism, allowing religious services because the Orthodox church provided people with hope and inspired patriotism and sacrifice.

The democracies used propaganda to mobilize loyalty; even more than in World War I, propaganda saturated society in movie theaters and on the radio. Accustomed to listening to politicians on the air, people were glued to their radios for war news. Films depicted aviation heroes and infantrymen as well as the workingwomen and wives left behind. Government agencies monitored filmmaking and allocated supplies to approved films. In the United States, military leaders loaned authentic props only if they could censor the scripts. Advertisers of consumer goods connected their products to the war effort: "If your dealer doesn't have your favorite LIFE SAVERS," read one advertisement, "please be patient. . . . It is because the shipment he would have received has gone to the Army and Navy."

Museums and Memory

Holocaust Memorial Museum
Designed to evoke a sense of awe at the unprecedented suffering caused by the mass murder of the Jews, the Holocaust Memorial Museum in Washington, D.C., displays pictures of thousands of Germany's victims. Other museums around the world focus on different aspects of Hitler's policy of extermination, emphasizing the many nationalities of his victims or the variety of reasons for their slaughter. Johnson/Liaison.

What is the difference between history and memory? What is the difference between a historical monument and a history textbook? Or the difference between the history of the Holocaust and a Holocaust museum?

Recently historians have come to focus on the role of historical monuments and museums that house historical artifacts. Both of these institutions are testimonials to historical events because they provide records of those events and show that people were deeply moved by them. Monuments to World War I keep the memory of the Great War alive in villages and cities from which its fallen soldiers came, while Holocaust museums are found in dozens of countries, many far from the region where the Holocaust took place. Photographs and objects from the times make us feel as if we have had real and vivid contact with the past.

But is the impression conveyed by a tragic photo or the memory of an event the same as its history? Historians wrestle with this question and for the most part regard photographs and oral testimony as useful historical evidence. However, many judge such institutions as the Holocaust museum as only partially about the history of the Holocaust. Instead, the Holocaust museum tells a great deal about the nation or group that builds it. It tells about the "memory" that the nation or group wants average people to have of the Holocaust. Or it may convey a consensus view reached when officials from the government and survivors or their representatives come to an agreement about what the museum or monument should look like.

Holocaust memorials have had a complicated development that is instructive to historians. Some Holocaust memory sites sprang up spontaneously in concentration camps as memorials consecrated by survivors themselves. Stones, writings, plaques, flowers and plants, and other objects were used to testify to what had happened in the camp. In many cases, these initial memorials

Between 1939 and 1945, people lost much of their privacy as governments organized many aspects of everyday life. Bureaucrats regulated the production and distribution of food, clothing, and household products, all of which were rationed and generally of lower quality. In England by 1943, the wartime Ministry of Food employed 39,000 people just to manage what people ate. These bureaucrats gave hints for meals without meat, sugar, fat, dairy products, and other staples and taught were replaced when local and national governments stepped in to take over the site, sometimes waiting years between destroying the spontaneous memorials and replacing them with an official museum. The concentration camp at Dachau, near Munich, is one that fell into disrepair until a group of survivors, including many Catholic clergy, demanded the camp be made into a permanent museum and memorial, with the crematorium and other grisly features preserved.

Although townspeople and local government resisted, Dachau and its crematorium became one of the most visited camps and indeed came to symbolize the Holocaust in all its horror. Yet Dachau was not primarily an extermination site for Jews, Slavs, and gypsies but a grim concentration camp where Hitler put political prisoners, many of them Catholic clergy. It is so often visited because it is on the tourist route, close to a beautiful city. Indeed, among the plaques in this "on-site" museum, one invites visitors to tour the other cultural institutions and scenery of the area while another asks them to remember that vast numbers of those interned were Polish and Catholic. All of these factors in the politics of memories—official and unofficial, competing and contested—need to be taken into account by historians.

Museums also serve to create an "official" memory for the people of a single nation-state who themselves have competing memories. The process of creating this memory provokes incredible public and private debate over what the museum should look like, what it should include, and even how it will fit with goals of tourism. The on-site museum at Auschwitz creates a Polish memory of the Holocaust by emphasizing the millions of Poles who died, while the museum at Buchenwald under the Communist East German regime emphasized the number of working-class people who died there and the uprising of its many socialist prisoners who ultimately liberated the camp.

In the case of Holocaust museums, official memories can clash with memories of actual survivors who, for instance, do not like what is often the most aesthetic or avant-garde in terms of art and architecture. They generally reject abstract art because a "realistic" depiction of their suffering seems most important. As for architectural design, the American Holocaust Museum was redone so that it would not look grimly "out-of-place" but rather fit in with the tranquil style of the central museum mall in Washington, D.C. Historians take into account these "official" memories, but they also look at the way certain objects like shoes or eyeglasses are displayed to create a certain memory effect. They note that costume designers puff up prison uniforms to make them look more lifelike and to make people feel emotionally that they are involved with the Holocaust.

Holocaust museums have offered a powerful, vivid, and emotionally charged experience of history. In contrast, history prides itself on eliminating emotions and biases in reaching historical judgments, ascertaining facts, and calculating cause and effect. Though each provides an important representation of the past, the relationship between memory and history remains fraught with questions—and never more so than in the case of the Holocaust.

QUESTIONS FOR DEBATE

1. Why do museums and public exhibitions of art and artifacts arouse more debate than do history books?

2. Do you trust a history book more than you trust a museum? How do we compare and evaluate the presentation of the past in either one?

FURTHER READING

Gillis, John R. *Commemorations: The Politics of National Identity.* 1994.

Sherman, Daniel J., and Irit Rogoff, eds. *Museum Culture: Histories, Discourses, Spectacles.* 1994.

Young, James Edward. *The Texture of Memory: Holocaust Memorials and Meaning.* 1993.

that women and children should embrace deprivation so their fighting men would survive. Governments hired more businessmen, economists, statisticians, and other specialists to influence civilian thought and behavior. Government-sponsored media directed people in techniques of home canning or growing "victory gardens" to add to the food supply. With governments standardizing such items as food, clothing, and entertainment, World War II furthered the development of mass society.

Propaganda and government policies promoted racial thinking and hatred on both sides. On the home front, homogenized news reports instilled hatred for the enemy. Since the early 1930s, the German government had drawn ugly caricatures of Jews, and anti-Semitic, anti-Slav, and anti-gypsy sentiment was a hallmark of Nazism. Similarly, Allied propaganda during the war depicted Germans as sadists and perverts and the "Japs" as uncivilized, insectlike fanatics. The U.S. government forced citizens of Japanese origin into concentration or internment camps in the western states. In the Soviet Union, Muslims and minority ethnic groups were uprooted and relocated as potential Nazi collaborators. In the Soviet-occupied parts of Poland, industrialists, union members, professionals, and thousands of others were sent to the Gulag, if not murdered outright. Soldiers and civilians on both sides were preoccupied with enemies, sharply depicted in stereotypical racial and ethnic terms.

Colonized peoples were drawn into the war, many of them against their will, through conscription into the armies and forced labor. Some two million Indian men served the Allied cause, as did several hundred thousand Africans. As the Japanese swept through the Pacific and parts of East Asia, they too conscripted men into their army. Both sides bombarded colonized societies with propaganda, as radio stations and newspapers proliferated during the war. Ironically this propaganda politicized colonized peoples in unprecedented numbers. Because of forced labor and artificially low wages and profits to native workers and entrepreneurs, politicization aroused interest not only in the war but also in postwar liberation.

From Resistance to Allied Victory

Professional armies ultimately defeated the Axis powers, but civilian resistance in Nazi-occupied areas also contributed to the Allied triumph. General Charles de Gaulle (1890–1970) directed the Free French government and its forces from his haven in England; some 20 percent of these were initially troops made up of colonized Asians and Africans. Other French resisters fought in Communist-dominated groups, some of whom gathered information to aid the Allied invasion of the continent. The Polish resistance was unified

against the Nazis, whereas in Yugoslavia, Serbs and Croats often attacked each other as much as they did the fascists until the Communist forces of Josip Broz (known as Marshall Tito) came to dominate the resistance. Rural groups called partisans, or the *maquis*, planned assassinations, disrupted communications, and bombed bridges, rail lines, and military facilities and supplies.

People also fought back through everyday activities. Homemakers circulated newsletters telling how to foil the plans of the occupying powers through demonstrations at prisons where civilians were detained and marketplaces where food was rationed. In central Europe, hikers smuggled Jews and others over dangerous mountain passes. Danish villagers created vast escape networks. Resisters played on stereotypes of femininity: women often carried weapons to assassination sites in the correct belief that Nazis would rarely suspect or search them; they also seduced and murdered enemy officers. In Paris a woman chemist made explosives for the French resistance in her university laboratory. Other actions subtly undermined the demands of fascist leaders. Couples in Germany and Italy limited family size in defiance of pro-birth policies. German teenagers danced the forbidden American jitterbug, thus defying the Nazis and forcing the police to monitor their groups. Resistance underscored the importance of the liberal ideal of

Hidden Revolver
Resistance to Nazism took many forms, from the concerted uprising in Warsaw to small acts of protest to assassinations of Nazi officers and collaborators. In a militarized state with informers everywhere, retaliation against Nazis sparked human ingenuity, whether in obtaining enough food or killing the enemy. Weapons were hidden in baby carriages, under clothing, or in books—as in this example from the Dutch resistance.
Erich Lessing/Art Resource, NY.

Battle of Leningrad

In the face of Nazi invasion, Soviet citizens reacted heroically, moving entire factories to the interior of the country and building fortifications. Nowhere was their resolve so tested as in Leningrad (St. Petersburg), when hundreds of thousands died during a Nazi siege lasting more than two years. Before the invasion of Normandy in 1944, the people of the USSR bore the brunt of Nazi military might in Hitler's attempt to defeat what he called "judeobolshevism."
Sovfoto.

individual political action and helped rebuild the community solidarity that authoritarian rule had fractured.

The spirit of resistance produced renowned heroes such as Swedish diplomat Raoul Wallenberg (1912–1947?), whose dealings with Nazi officials saved thousands of Hungarian Jews. But traitors abounded—collaborators who contributed to the initial Nazi victories and who cooperated with the Nazis during the occupation for personal advantage. From Vidkun Quisling, a Norwegian promoter of Nazism and prime minister during the occupation of his country, to countless other individuals in all walks of life who betrayed Jews in hiding or informed on resistance networks, Nazi Germany profited from the services of collaborators.

The Axis Crushed. The Allies started tightening a noose around the Axis in mid-1942 (Map 27.5). A major turning point came in August when the German army began a siege on Stalingrad, a city whose capture would give access to Soviet oil and cut access to the country's interior. Months of ferocious fighting led to house-to-house combat, as neither side would surrender despite massive casualties. Finally, the Soviet army captured the ninety

thousand German survivors in February 1943. Meanwhile, the British army in North Africa held against the Germans in Egypt and Libya and together with U.S. forces invaded Morocco and Algeria in the autumn of 1942. In July 1943, Allied forces landed in Sicily, hoping for a quick victory over Italy as the king ousted Mussolini. However, the Germans came to their ally's aid, occupied northern Italy, and fought bitterly for the peninsula until April 1945, when Allied forces finally triumphed. After Italy's liberation, partisans shot Mussolini and his mistress and hanged their dead bodies for public display.

The victory at Stalingrad marked the beginning of the costly Soviet drive westward—during which the Soviets bore the brunt of the Nazi war machine. As the Americans and British invaded North Africa and Europe and pounded German cities with strategic bombing to demoralize civilians and destroy the war industry, coordination among the Allies became imperative. In November and December 1943, Roosevelt, Churchill, and Stalin met at Teheran, Iran, to agree on the opening of a western European front, for which Stalin had been pressing and which Churchill had resisted. On June 6, 1944, the combined Allied forces

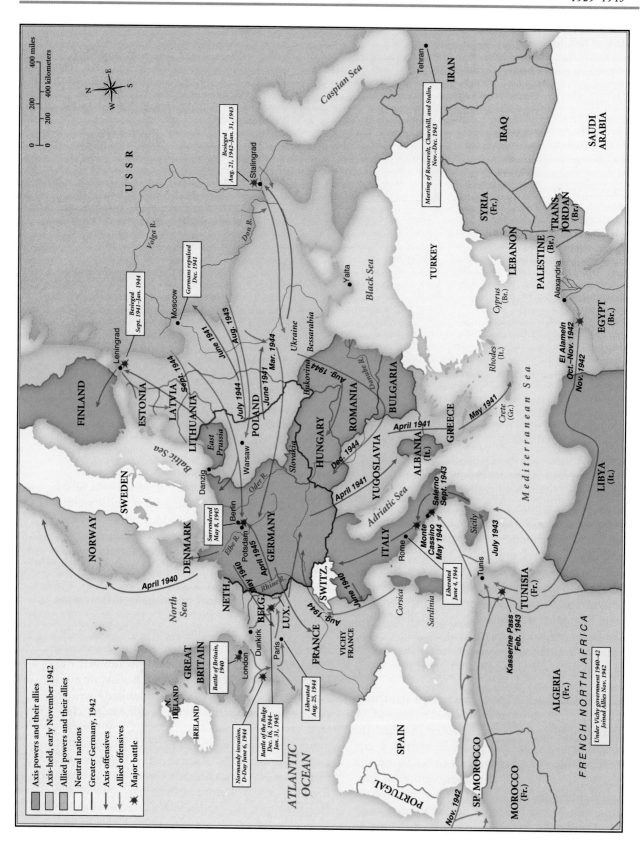

Legend
- Axis powers and their allies
- Axis-held, early November 1942
- Allied powers and their allies
- Neutral nations
- Greater Germany, 1942
- Axis offensives
- Allied offensives
- Major battle

400 miles
200
0

400 kilometers
200
0

USSR

Besieged Aug. 21, 1942–Jan. 31, 1943 — Stalingrad

Caspian Sea

Tehran

IRAN

IRAQ

SAUDI ARABIA

Meeting of Roosevelt, Churchill, and Stalin, Nov.–Dec. 1943

SYRIA (Fr.)

TRANS JORDAN (Br.)

LEBANON (Br.)

PALESTINE (Br.)

Alexandria

EGYPT (Br.)

Volga R.

Don R.

Germans repulsed Dec. 1941 — Moscow

Besieged Sept. 1941–Jan. 1944 — Leningrad

TURKEY

Yalta

Black Sea

Cyprus (Br.)

El Alamein Oct.–Nov. 1942

Nov. 1942

Mediterranean Sea

June 1941
Aug. 1943
June 1941
Mar. 1944
Ukraine
Bessarabia

July 1944
Sept. 1944
POLAND
June 1941

ESTONIA
LATVIA
LITHUANIA

FINLAND

Baltic Sea

SWEDEN

NORWAY

East Prussia

Warsaw

Danzig

Oder R.

DENMARK

April 1940

Surrendered May 8, 1945 — Berlin

Potsdam
Elbe R.
April 1945

GERMANY

HUNGARY

Slovakia

ROMANIA

BULGARIA

Bukovina
Aug. 1944
Danube R.
Dec. 1944

YUGOSLAVIA

April 1941

ALBANIA (It.)

GREECE

April 1941
May 1941

Crete (Gr.)

Rhodes (It.)

Adriatic Sea

ITALY

Salerno Sept. 1943
Monte Cassino May 1944
Rome
Liberated June 4, 1944

Sicily
July 1943

Tunis

Kasserine Pass Feb. 1943

TUNISIA (Fr.)

Corsica

Sardinia

SWITZ.

FRANCE

VICHY FRANCE

June 1940

Aug. 1944

Liberated Aug. 25, 1944

Paris

Dunkirk

BELG.
LUX.
NETH.
May 1940
Rhine R.

GREAT BRITAIN

Battle of Britain, 1940

London

Battle of the Bulge Dec. 16, 1944–Jan. 31, 1945

Normandy invasion, D-Day June 6, 1944

N. IRELAND
IRELAND

North Sea

ATLANTIC OCEAN

SPAIN

PORTUGAL

SP. MOROCCO

MOROCCO (Fr.)

Nov. 1942

ALGERIA (Fr.)

LIBYA (It.)

FRENCH NORTH AFRICA

Under Vichy government 1940–42 Joined Allies Nov. 1942

◀ **MAP 27.5 World War II in Europe and Africa**
World War II inflicted massive loss of life and destruction of property on civilians, armies, and all the infrastructure—including factories, equipment, and agriculture—needed to wage total war. Thus, the war swept the European continent as well as areas in Africa colonized by or allied with the major powers. Ultimately the Allies crushed the Axis by moving from east, west, and south to inflict a total defeat.

under the command of U.S. General Dwight Eisenhower reached the heavily fortified French coastline of Normandy. The Nazis had been deceived into concentrating their forces to the north. After taking the beaches, Allied troops fought their way through the Norman hedgerows as the air force pummeled the German-held cities of western France. In late July, Allied forces broke through German defenses and a month later helped liberate Paris, where rebellion had erupted against the Nazis. As the liberating armies marched through French cities, officials gave them the illusion of being ethnically French by moving to the rear the tens of thousands of troops from the colonies who had contributed to victory. British, Canadian, U.S., and other Allied forces then fought their way eastward to join the Soviets in squeezing the Third Reich to its final defeat.

In July 1944, a group of German military officers, fearing their country's military humiliation, attempted to assassinate Hitler by exploding a bomb at a meeting. The Führer was only wounded, and the conspirators and many hundred others were cruelly tortured and then killed. Despite crushing military defeat, Hitler continued to preach German victory, maintaining that the Allies were merely "stumbling into their ruin." Driven mad by his hate-filled ideology, he believed that Germans were proving themselves unworthy of his greatness and deserved to perish in a cataclysmic conflagration. He thus refused all negotiations that might have spared Germans further death and destruction. The Soviet armies entered Poland, pausing only to allow the Germans to put down a spontaneous uprising of the Polish resistance in August 1944. (The elimination of the Polish resistance would give the Soviets a freer hand after the war.) Facing more than twice as many troops as on the western front, Stalin's forces met fierce German fighting in Hungary during the winter of 1944–1945. Hitler's refusal to surrender resulted in mas-

sive bombing of Germany. As the Soviet army took Berlin, Hitler committed suicide with his wife, Eva Braun. Their bodies were burned in the courtyard of the German chancellery. Although many soldiers remained committed to the Third Reich, Germany finally surrendered on May 8, 1945.

Japan Defeated. In keeping with their "Europe first" strategy, the Allies had sent most men and material to the European theater. Following the German surrender, they were able to focus solely on the Pacific war (Map 27.6). In 1940 and 1941, Japan had ousted the Europeans from many colonial holdings in Asia, but in May 1942, the U.S. forces stopped the Japanese in the battle of the Coral Sea. In battles at Midway Island and Guadalcanal later that year the Allies turned the tide, despite their diminished forces, by destroying some of Japan's formidable naval power. Unlike the United States, Japan lacked the capacity to recoup losses of ships or of manpower. The Allies stormed one Pacific island after another, gaining more bases from which to cut off the import of supplies and to launch bombers toward Japan itself. The Japanese ruled out surrender even after the fall of Saipan in 1944 delivered a blow to the military government. The Japanese instead resorted to *kamikaze* tactics, in which pilots deliberately crashed their planes into American ships, killing themselves in the process.

The United States stepped up its bombing raids on the Japanese mainland. In the spring of 1945, its firebombing of Tokyo killed more than 100,000 civilians. Meanwhile a U.S.-based international team of more than 100,000 scientists, technicians, and other workers engaged in the Manhattan Project, which succeeded in developing the atomic bomb. The still controversial decision to use atomic weapons was based on cruel experience: in battles at Iwo Jima and Okinawa, Japanese troops had fought fiercely, inflicting horrendous losses and dying almost to the man rather than surrender. This suicidal and destructive strategy caused Allied military leaders to calculate that defeating Japan might cost hundreds of thousands of Allied lives and take months, if not years. To avoid this unacceptable toll and, some argue, to stop the war in the East before the Soviet Union could take territory, the U.S. government unleashed atomic weapons on Japan's civilian population. On August 6 and 9, 1945, U.S. pilots dropped atomic bombs

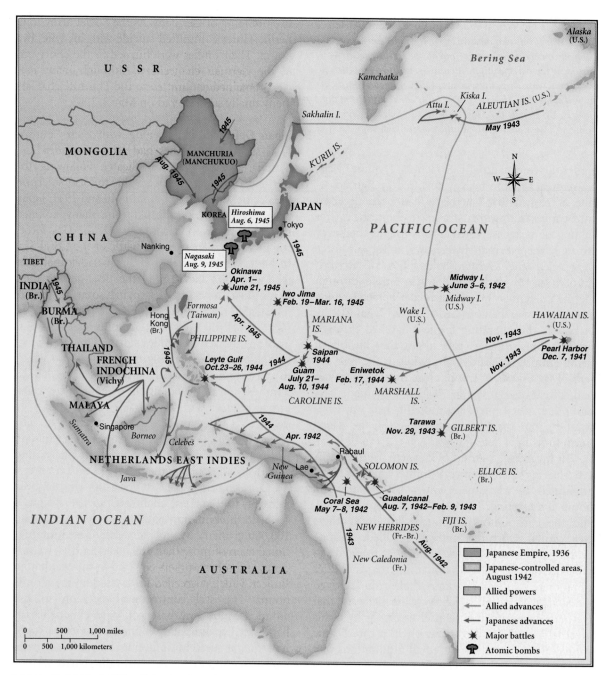

MAP 27.6 World War II in the Pacific

As in Europe, the early days of World War II gave the advantage to the Axis power, Japan, as it took the offensive in conquering islands in the Pacific and territories in Asia—many of them colonies of European states. Britain countered by mobilizing a vast Indian army, while the United States, after the disastrous losses at Pearl Harbor and in the Philippines, gradually gained the upper hand by costly assaults, island by island. The Japanese strategy of fighting to the last person instead of surrendering when a loss was in sight was one factor in President Truman's decision to drop the atomic bomb in August 1945.

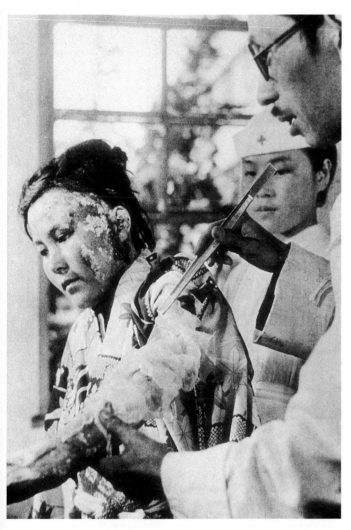

Hiroshima Victim
On August 6 and 9, 1945, the United States dropped the first atomic weapons on Hiroshima and Nagasaki, Japan, killing tens of thousands instantly and leaving tens of thousands more to die of their injuries and the aftereffects. A few days later Japan surrendered, but controversy has swirled around the decision to drop the bomb ever since. Some see it as a racist act, no atomic weapons having been dropped on Germany, while others see it as a justified act of warfare in a conflict that threatened to cost countless more casualties because of Japan's policy of no surrender.
Gamma Liaison.

on Hiroshima and Nagasaki, respectively, killing 140,000 people instantly, with tens of thousands more deaths from burns, wounds, and other afflictions in the days and weeks to come. Although hardliners in the Japanese military wanted to continue the war, on August 14, 1945, Japan surrendered.

❖ Toward a Postwar Settlement

The Great Depression had inflicted global suffering, while the Second World War left fifty to sixty million dead, an equal number of refugees without homes, and probably the most tragic moral legacy in human history. Envisioning a postwar political, social, and cultural settlement was thus top priority. Unlike World War I, however, there would be neither a celebrated peace conference nor a definitive, formal agreement among all the Allies about the final resolution of the war. In fact, the victorious Allies distrusted one another in varying degrees, with the United States and the Soviet Union on the brink of another debilitating and dangerous war.

Wartime Agreements about the Peace

The Grand Alliance was composed of nations with vastly different political and economic systems, and wartime agreements reflected continuing differences about the shape of postwar Europe. Entered into during a catastrophic war, many agreements would later be contested or arouse intense political debate. In 1941, on a warship off Newfoundland, Roosevelt and Churchill had forged the Atlantic Charter, which condemned aggression, reaffirmed the ideal of collective security, and endorsed the right of all people to choose their governments. Not only did the Allies come to focus on these points, but so did colonized peoples to whom, Churchill said, the charter was not meant to apply.

In the heat of war, the Allied leaders kept meeting, hammering out wartime as well as postwar agreements. In October 1944, Churchill went to the USSR to plan with Stalin the postwar distribution of territories. The Soviet Union would control Romania and Bulgaria, Britain would control Greece, and they would jointly oversee Hungary and Yugoslavia. These agreements went against Roosevelt's faith in collective security and seemed to threaten American commitments to self-determination and open doors in trade. In February 1945, the "Big Three"—as Roosevelt, Churchill, and Stalin were quickly labeled—met in the Crimean town of Yalta. Roosevelt advocated the institution of the United Nations to replace the League of Nations as a global peace mechanism. He also supported future Soviet influence in Korea,

IMPORTANT DATES

1929 The U.S. stock market crashes; global depression begins; Soviet leadership initiates war against prosperous farmers, the kulaks; Germany's Thomas Mann wins the Nobel Prize for literature

1933 Hitler comes to power in Germany

1936 Show trials begin in the USSR; Stalin purges top Communist Party officials and military leaders; the Spanish Civil War begins

1938 Virginia Woolf publishes *Three Guineas*

1939 Germany invades Poland; World War II begins; the Spanish Civil War ends

1940 France falls to the German army

1940–1941 The British air force fends off German attacks in the battle of Britain

1941 Germany invades the Soviet Union; Japan attacks Pearl Harbor; the United States enters the war

1941–1945 The Holocaust

1944 Allied forces land at Normandy, France

1945 The fall of Berlin; United States drops atomic bombs on Hiroshima and Nagasaki; World War II ends

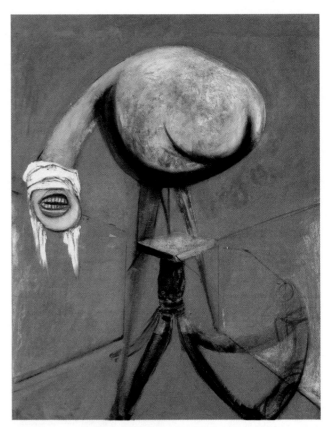

Francis Bacon, *Three Studies for Figures at Base of Crucifixion* (c. 1944), center panel
At the end of the war, English artist Francis Bacon depicted the traditional Western subject of the crucifixion, but in a way that converted the individual person into a grotesque monster. His figures often reflect horror, disgust, and debasement and thus seem to describe the human condition at the end of World War II and the Holocaust.
Tate Gallery, London/Art Resource, NY.

Manchuria, and the Sakhalin and Kurile Islands in return for Stalin's pledge of help against future Japanese aggression. The last meeting of the Allied leaders took place at Potsdam, Germany, in the summer of 1945. By this time, President Harry S. Truman (1884–1972) had succeeded Roosevelt, who had died in April; Prime Minister Clement Attlee (1883–1967), whose Labour Party had just won the British elections, replaced Churchill. At Potsdam the leaders agreed to give the Soviets control of eastern Poland, to cede a large stretch of eastern Germany to Poland, and to adopt a temporary four-way occupation of Germany that included France as one of the supervising powers. Yet as victory unfolded, the Allies scrambled to outmaneuver one another. Making peace proved a prolonged and bitter process—and one that was hardly over in 1945.

Europe's Uncertain Future

Allied leaders had more than the boundaries of Europe to account for. European dominion was at an end. Forced into armies or into labor camps for war production, colonial peoples were in full rebellion or close to it. For a second time in three decades, colonial peoples had seen their masters killing one another, slaughtered by the very technology that was supposed to make European civilization superior. The Japanese also inspired rebellion by organizing governments in Asia run by anti-Western, indigenous leaders. Deference to Europe was virtually finished, with independence a matter of time.

Western values were imperiled as well. Not only were normal liberal politics at a standstill, if not in chaos, in 1944–1945, but the high European standard of living had been replaced by wartime deprivation, even starvation. Rational, Enlightenment, democratic Europe had succumbed to

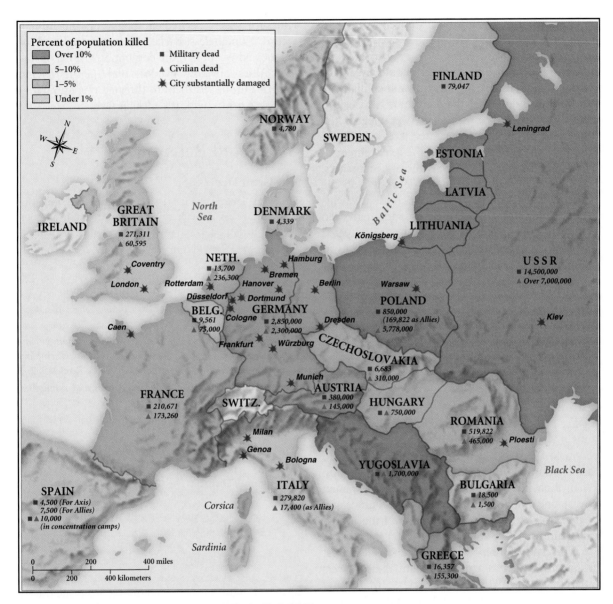

MAPPING THE WEST Europe at War's End, 1945

While all of Europe was severely shocked during the age of catastrophe, wartime damage left scars that would last for decades. Major German cities were bombed to bits, while the Soviet Union suffered an unimaginable toll of perhaps twenty-five million deaths due to the war alone. Everything from politics to family life needed rebuilding. The chaos fueled postwar tensions stemming both from the quest to punish those held responsible for such suffering and from the superpowers' determination to gain the political allegiance of recovering countries in the cold war.

From *The Hammond Atlas of the Twentieth Century* (London: Times Books, 1996), 102.

permanent wartime values, and it was this Europe that George Orwell captured in his novel *1984* (1949). Poor food and worn clothing, grimy streets and dwellings, people prematurely aged and care-worn—all characterized both London of the 1940s and Orwell's fictional state, Oceania. Like his hero

Winston Smith, Orwell worked for the wartime Ministry of Information (called the Ministry of Truth in the novel) and churned out doctored news for wartime audiences. Information and truth hardly mattered, in the language Orwell called "Newspeak," where old words were replaced by sanitized ones. As in Orwell's novel, words had taken on new meaning during the war: *disengagement* replaced *retreat*, *battle fatigue* substituted for *insanity*, and *liberating* a country could mean invading it and slaughtering its army and civilians.

Millions rejoiced at the demise of Nazi evil in 1945, but Orwell saw as part of war's legacy the deadening of creativity, the intrusion of big government into everyday life, and the replacement of democracy by the rule of bureaucratic managers. For Orwell, bureaucratic power depended on the perpetuation of conflict, and fresh conflict was indeed brewing in the race for Berlin and Japan even before the war ended. As Allied powers competed for territory, a new struggle called the *cold war* was taking root.

Conclusion

The Great Depression brought massive social dislocation and fear. It provided a setting in which dictators thrived because they promised to restore national greatness, bring economic prosperity, and destroy the people's enemies. Enticed by the mass media, people turned from representative institutions toward dynamic, if brutal, leaders. Memories of World War I permitted Hitler and Mussolini to menace Europe unimpeded throughout the 1930s. When a coalition formed to stop them, it was an uneasy one among the imperial powers France and Britain, the Stalinist Soviet Union, and the industrial giant the United States.

The costs of a bloody war—one waged against civilians as much as armies—taught these powers different lessons. The United States, Britain, and France were convinced that a minimum of citizen well-being was necessary to prevent a recurrence of fascism. Soviet citizens hoped that life would become easier and more open for them. The devastation of the USSR's population and resources, however, made Stalin increasingly obsessed with national security and reparations. Britain and France confronted the final eclipse of their imperial might, underscoring Orwell's insight that the war had transformed society irrevocably. Neither the murder of millions of Jews, Slavs, and others in death camps nor the militarization of society would ever disappear from the European legacy. The deliberate, technological murder of innocents like Etty

Hillesum was a permanent blight on the human record. Nonetheless, backed by vast arsenals of sophisticated weaponry, the competing visions of former Allies on how to deal with Germany and eastern Europe led them to threaten one another—and the world—with yet another war.

Suggested References

The Great Depression

Historians look to the depression as a complex event with economic, social, and cultural consequences, but in addition they see its impact as yet another indication of the tightening of global economic connections. To follow some of the political implications for European empires, see in particular Columbia University's South Asia Web site, which explores Gandhi's economic resistance to British colonialism.

Brown, Ian. *The Economies of Africa and Asia in the Interwar Depression*. 1989.

Evans, Richard J., and Dick Geary. *The German Unemployed: Experiences and Consequences of Mass Unemployment from the Weimar Republic to the Third Reich*. 1987.

James, Harold. *The German Slump: Politics and Economics, 1924–1936*. 1986.

Johnson, H. Clark. *Gold, France, and the Great Depression, 1919–1932*. 1997.

Roszkowski, Wojciech. *Landowners in Poland, 1918–1939*. 1991.

Rothermund, Dietmar. *The Global Impact of the Great Depression, 1929–1939*. 1996.

South Asia and Gandhi: http://www.columbia.edu/cu/libraries/indiv/area/sarai.

Totalitarian Triumph

The vicious dictators Stalin, Hitler, and Mussolini are among the most popular subjects for historians and readers alike. Recent historical works have moved beyond this fascination to study their mobilization of art and the media and to consider people's reactions to totalitarian regimes. Historians are especially intrigued with the mixture of modernism and traditionalism or even antimodernism in the dictators' programs and policies.

Ades, Dawn, et al. *Art and Power: Europe under the Dictators, 1930–1945*. 1995.

Berezin, Mabel. *Making the Fascist Self: The Political Culture of Interwar Italy*. 1997.

Engel, Barbara Alpern, and Anastasia Posadskaya-Vanderbeck, eds. *A Revolution of Their Own: Voices of Women in Soviet History*. 1998.

Fest, Joachim. *Hitler*. 1974.

Fitzpatrick, Sheila. *Stalin's Peasants.* 1994.

Fritzsche, Peter. *Germans into Nazis.* 1998.

Groys, Boris. *The Total Art of Stalinism: Avant-Garde, Aesthetic Dictatorship, and Beyond.* 1992.

Hildebrand, K. *The Third Reich.* 1984.

Kaplan, Marion. *Between Dignity and Despair: Jewish Life in Nazi Germany.* 1998.

Koonz, Claudia. *Mothers in the Fatherland: Women, the Family, and Nazi Politics.* 1987.

Kotkin, Stephen. *Magnetic Mountain: Stalinism as Civilization.* 1995.

Kuromiya, Hiroaki. *Stalin's Industrial Revolution: Politics and Workers, 1928–1932.* 1988.

Democracies on the Defensive

The democracies attacked the depression from a variety of perspectives ranging from state policy to film and the arts, yet another indication of how complex politics can be. Further departure from liberal policies, whether in trade or in the development of the activist welfare state, also have attracted historical study.

Kalvemark, Ann-Sofie. *More Children or Better Quality? Aspects of Swedish Population Policy.* 1980.

Kennedy, David M. *Freedom from Fear: The American People in Depression and War, 1929–1945.* 1999.

Lavin, Maud, et al. *Montage and Modern Life, 1919–1942.* 1992.

Rearick, Charles. *The French in Love and War: Popular Culture in the Era of the World Wars.* 1997.

Richards, Jeffrey, ed. *The Unknown 1930s: An Alternative History of the British Cinema, 1929–39.* 1998.

The Road to World War II

The road to war encircled the globe, involving countries seemingly peripheral to the struggles among the antagonists. The perennial question for many historians is whether Hitler could have been stopped, but with globalization there is new attention to the beginnings of war beyond the West as a prelude to decolonization.

Crozier, Andrew. *The Causes of the Second World War.* 1997.

Iriye, Akira. *The Origins of the Second World War in Asia and the Pacific.* 1987.

Knight, Patricia. *The Spanish Civil War.* 1991.

*Mangini González, Shirley. *Memories of Resistance: Women's Voices from the Spanish Civil War.* 1995.

Watt, D. Cameron. *How War Came: The Immediate Causes of the Second World War.* 1989.

World War II, 1939–1945

In a vast literature historians have charted the war's innumerable and global horrors, with issues of the Holocaust, industrial killing, and the nature of racial thinking drawing particular attention. The United States Memorial Holocaust Museum provides online exhibits giving the history of the Holocaust in different locations. While looking at the social aspects of war, historians have intently debated the development of the cold war within the "hot" war.

Browning, Christopher. *The Path to Genocide: Essays on Launching the Final Solution.* 1992.

*Dawidowicz, Lucy S. *A Holocaust Reader.* 1976.

Dower, John W. *War without Mercy: Race and Power in the Pacific War.* 1986.

Fussell, Paul. *Wartime: Understanding and Behavior in the Second World War.* 1989.

Goodwin, Doris Kearns. *No Ordinary Time: Franklin and Eleanor Roosevelt, the Home Front in World War II.* 1994.

Holocaust Museum: http://usholocaustmuseum.org.

Lewis, Peter. *A People's War.* 1986.

Ofer, Dalia, and Lenore J. Weitzman, eds. *Women in the Holocaust.* 1998.

Rhodes, Richard. *The Making of the Atomic Bomb.* 1986.

*Vassiltchikov, Marie. *Berlin Diaries, 1940–1945.* 1988.

Weinberg, Gerhard. *A World at Arms: A Global History of World War II.* 1994

*Primary sources.

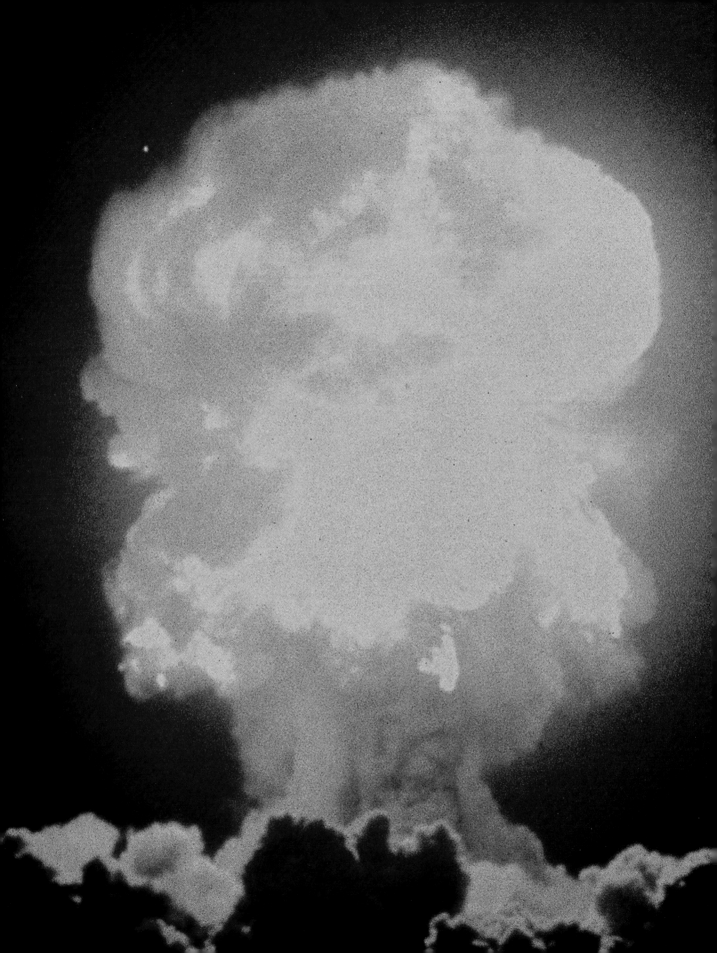

The Atomic Age

c. 1945–1960

The Atomic Age

The atomic bombs dropped on Hiroshima and Nagasaki in 1945 were followed by several decades of increasingly powerful detonations for testing purposes. The Soviet Union practiced underground testing, while the United States carried out atmospheric tests in the Pacific region. Protests against testing developed in the 1950s, many of them citing the hazards of radioactivity and the growing threat of nuclear annihilation. Simultaneously, nuclear power was converted to peacetime use, notably serving both as a source of energy and as a therapy for cancer.
Mark Meyer/Liaison Agency.

IN LATE AUGUST 1949, THE SOVIET UNION DETONATED its first atomic bomb. Two days after President Harry S. Truman announced the news of this test, Billy Graham, a young Baptist minister, based his sermon at a revival meeting on the fearsome event. Graham warned that U.S. officials believed "we have only five to ten years and our civilization will be ended." He announced that Russia had aimed bombs to strike New York, Chicago, and Los Angeles, where the revival was taking place. "Time is desperately short . . . . Prepare to meet thy God," he warned. People flocked to hear Graham, launching the evangelist's astonishing career of spiritual and political influence in the United States and around the globe.

Graham's message—"We don't know how soon, but we do know this, that right now the grace of God can still save a poor lost sinner"— captured the extremes of postwar sentiment in an atomic age. On the one hand, the postwar situation was tragic. Fifty million people had died globally; Europe and Japan were prostrate and their peoples starving; evidence of genocide and other inhumanity was everywhere; the menace of nuclear annihilation loomed. It was to this menace that Graham referred. The old international order was gone, replaced by the rivalry of the United States and the Soviet Union for control of a devastated Europe, whose political and economic systems had collapsed. The nuclear arsenals of these two "superpowers"—a term coined in 1947—grew massively in the 1950s, but they were enemies who did not fight outright. Thus their terrifying rivalry was called the *cold war.*

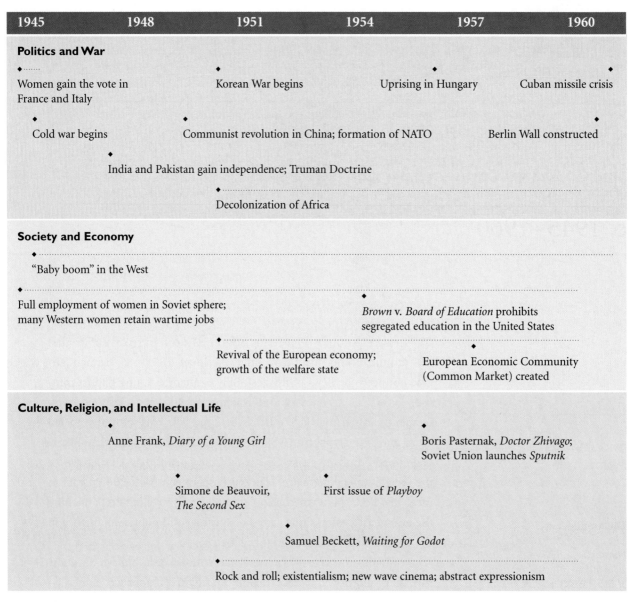

1945	1948	1951	1954	1957	1960

Politics and War

Women gain the vote in France and Italy

Cold war begins

India and Pakistan gain independence; Truman Doctrine

Korean War begins

Communist revolution in China; formation of NATO

Decolonization of Africa

Uprising in Hungary

Cuban missile crisis

Berlin Wall constructed

Society and Economy

"Baby boom" in the West

Full employment of women in Soviet sphere; many Western women retain wartime jobs

Revival of the European economy; growth of the welfare state

Brown v. *Board of Education* prohibits segregated education in the United States

European Economic Community (Common Market) created

Culture, Religion, and Intellectual Life

Anne Frank, *Diary of a Young Girl*

Simone de Beauvoir, *The Second Sex*

First issue of *Playboy*

Boris Pasternak, *Doctor Zhivago*; Soviet Union launches *Sputnik*

Samuel Beckett, *Waiting for Godot*

Rock and roll; existentialism; new wave cinema; abstract expressionism

The cold war divided the West politically, economically, and culturally, causing acute anxiety even for someone like Graham from the victorious and wealthy United States.

On the other hand, the defeat of Nazism inspired an upsurge of hope, a revival of religious feeling like Graham's, and a new commitment to humanitarian goals. Heroic effort had defeated fascism, and that defeat raised hopes that a new age would begin. Atomic science promised advances in medicine, and nuclear energy was trumpeted as a replacement for coal and oil. The creation of the United Nations heralded an era of international cooperation. Around the globe, colonial peoples won independence from European masters, while in the United States the civil rights movement gained new momentum. The welfare state expanded, and by the end of the 1950s economic rebirth, stimulated in part by the cold war, had made much of Europe more prosperous than ever before. An "economic miracle" had occurred.

Extremes of hope and fear infused the atomic age, as society, culture, and the international order were transformed. Gone was the definition of a West comprising Europe and its cultural offshoots such as the United States and an East comprising

Asian countries like India, China, and Japan. During the cold war, *West* came to stand for the United States and its client countries in western Europe, while *East* meant the Soviet Union and its tightly controlled bloc in eastern Europe. Still another terminology arose in the 1950s. The *first world* was the capitalist bloc of countries; the *second world*, the socialist bloc; and the *third world*, the countries emerging from imperial domination. As the world's people redefined themselves politically and culturally, they did so in an atmosphere of immense progress and equally immense peril. By the early 1960s, an array of new nations had arisen in Africa and Asia, and population growth soared. However, simultaneously millions were dying in wars of liberation, while the superpowers took the world to the brink of nuclear disaster when the United States discovered Soviet missile sites on its doorstep—ninety miles from Florida, on the island of Cuba. From the dropping of the atomic bomb on Japan in 1945 to the Cuban missile crisis of 1962, Graham's dread that "we are moving madly toward destruction" gripped much of the world.

❖ World Politics Transformed

The turmoil of wartime and the postwar years ended the global leadership of Europe. Many countries lay in ruins by the summer of 1945, and conditions would deteriorate before they got better. Bombed and bankrupt, victorious Britain could not feed its people. In contrast, the United States, whose territory was virtually untouched in the war, emerged as the world's sole economic giant, and the Soviet Union, despite suffering immense destruction, retained formidable military might. These two nations drew the entire world into a diplomatic battle of nerves that became known as the cold war. Having occupied Europe as part of the victorious alliance against Nazism and fascism, the two superpowers next used Germany—at the heart of the continent and its politics—to divide Europe in two. By the late 1940s, the USSR imposed Communist rule throughout most of eastern Europe and in the 1950s quashed rebellions against its dominance. Western Europeans found themselves at least partially constricted by the very U.S. economic power that helped them rebuild, as the United States maintained air bases and nuclear weapon sites across western Europe. The age of bipolar world politics had begun, with Europe as its testing ground.

Europe Prostrate

In contrast to World War I when devastation was limited to the front lines around the trenches, armies in World War II had fought a war of movement that leveled thousands of square miles of territory. Across the continent, whole cities were clogged with rubble; homeless survivors wandered the streets. In Sicily and on the Rhine River, almost no bridge remained standing; in France, motorized vehicles lacked the necessary parts to operate. In the Soviet Union, seventy thousand villages and more than a thousand cities lay in shambles.

Everywhere people were suffering. In the Netherlands, where both the Nazi occupation and the struggle for liberation had been unusually severe, the Dutch faced imminent death until a U.S. airlift of food provided some relief. In Britain, soap and other basic commodities were difficult to obtain, and many died in the bitterly cold winter of 1946–1947 because of a shortage of fuel. Italian bakers sold bread by the slice. When Allied troops passed through German towns, the famished inhabitants lined the roads in hopes that someone would toss them something to eat. "To see the children fighting for food," one British soldier noted, "was like watching animals being fed in a zoo." As Allied troops settled in to occupy the devastated continent, there were no uprisings as after World War I. Until the late 1940s, people were exhausted by the struggle for bare survival.

The tens of millions of refugees suffered the most. Many had been inmates of prisons and death camps; others, especially ethnic Germans, had fled westward to escape the victorious but destructive Red Army as it pushed toward Berlin. Native Germans in the Western-occupied zones viewed refugees as competitors for food and work. "Unwanted, even hated," they were treated "like dirt," one journalist on the scene reported. Many refugees ultimately found homes in countries that experienced little or no war damage, such as Denmark, Sweden, Canada, and Australia. Following the exodus of refugees from the east, western Europe became one of the world's most densely populated regions (Map 28.1).

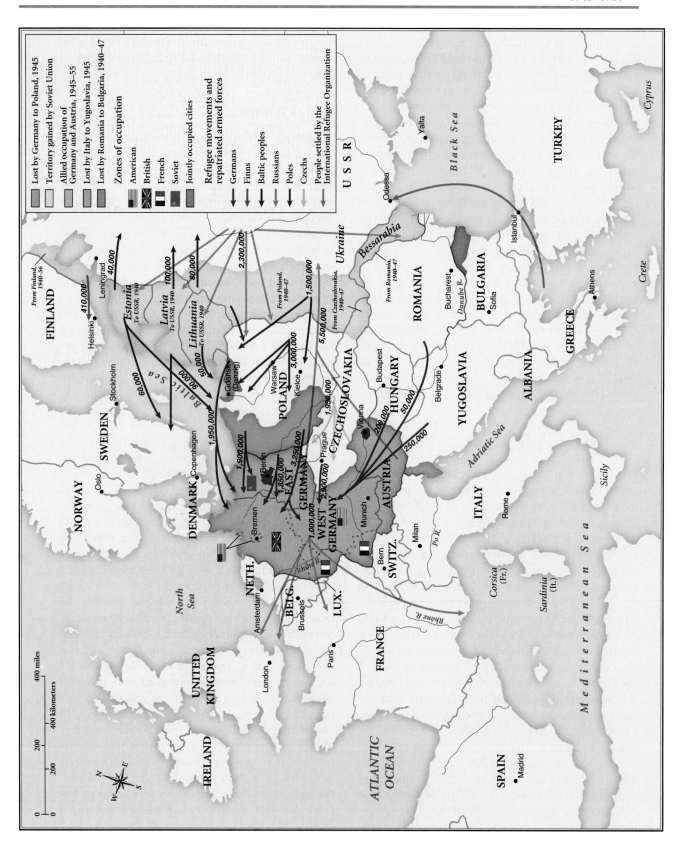

◀ **MAP 28.1 The Impact of World War II on Europe**
European governments, many of them struggling to provide food and other necessities for their populations, found themselves responsible for hundreds of thousands, if not millions, of new refugees. Simultaneously, millions of prisoners of war, servicemen, and slave laborers were returned to the Soviet Union, many of them by force. This situation unfolded amidst political instability and even violence.

The USSR drove many people from eastern Europe, yet it lobbied hard for the repatriation of several million Soviet prisoners of war and forced laborers. This was the first signal of Stalin's determination to revive Communist orthodoxy, which had weakened during the war. The Allies transported the majority of the Russian refugees back to the Soviet Union, where exile or execution for being "contaminated" by Western ideas awaited. As stories of executions filtered out, the Allies slowed the process, leaving hundreds of thousands of Soviet prisoners of war and former slave laborers to join the ocean of refugees in western Europe.

Survivors of the concentration camps also discovered that their suffering had not ended with Germany's defeat. In *The War* (1986), French author Marguerite Duras, drawing on her diary, described the returnees' arrival at Paris train stations: skeletal, diseased, and disoriented. Many surviving Jews often had no home to return to, as property had been confiscated and entire communities destroyed. Moreover, anti-Semitism had become official policy under the Nazis. In the summer of 1946, a vicious crowd in Kielce, Poland, rioted against returning Jewish survivors, killing at least 40 of the 250. Elsewhere in eastern Europe, such violence was common. Some Jewish survivors were not released from death camps for more than a year after the liberation because no one knew what to do with them. Meanwhile some officials across Europe even denied that unprecedented atrocities had been committed and wanted to refuse Jews any help.

Jews sought safety in various places. Some hoped to settle in the United States, but the federal government, fearing anti-Semitic backlash, let only about 12,000 Jews into the country. Many survivors crammed into the port cities of Italy and other Mediterranean countries, eventually to escape Europe for Palestine, where Zionists had been settling for half a century. As they had in the 1930s, the British balked at this vast migration to the Middle East, for they saw their interests threatened by likely Arab-Jewish conflict over control of the region. Unwilling or unable to help Hitler's most abused victims, many European countries had simply lost the capacity for moral and economic leadership.

New Superpowers: The United States and the Soviet Union

Only two powerful countries were left in 1945: the United States and the Soviet Union. The United States was now the richest country in the world. Its industrial output had increased a remarkable 15 percent annually between 1940 and 1944, a rate of growth that was reflected in workers' wages. By 1947, the United States controlled almost two-thirds of the world's gold bullion and more than half of its commercial shipping, up from almost one-fifth of the total in the 1930s. (Other countries had also profited from the war: Norwegian electrical output and Swedish exports to Nazi Germany were vast. India, Egypt, and Australia had made so much money supplying British war needs that they were able to buy out many British firms.) Continuing to spend heavily on industrial and military research, the United States enhanced its postwar economic position still more.

A confident mood swept the United States at the end of the war. Although some feared a postwar depression and many shared Billy Graham's worries about nuclear annihilation, a wave of suburban housing development and consumer spending kept the economy buoyant. Temporarily reversing the trend toward a lower birthrate, a "baby boom" exploded from the late 1940s through the early 1960s as couples responded to the economic abundance by having more children.

Casting aside the post–World War I policy of nonintervention, Americans embraced their position as global leaders. Many had learned about the world while tracking the war's progress; hundreds of thousands of soldiers, government officials, and relief workers had direct experience of Europe, Africa, and Asia. Leaders in the United States expressed trust in their ability to guide the rest of the world. "America must be the elder brother of nations in the brotherhood of man," *Life* magazine advised.

The Soviets also emerged from the war with a well-justified sense of accomplishment. Withstanding horrendous losses, they had resisted the most massive onslaught ever launched against a modern nation and thus earned an important position in world affairs. Instead of the international isolation dealt Russia after World War I, Soviet leadership expected equality in decision making with the United States, and indeed many Europeans and Americans had great respect for the Soviet contribution to Hitler's defeat. Ordinary Soviet citizens believed that a victory that had cost the USSR as many as 25 million lives would bring some improvement in the everyday conditions and a continuation of the war's relatively relaxed politics. "Life will become pleasant," one writer prophesied. "There will be much coming and going, and a lot of contacts with the West." Others foresaw the opening of private shops and restaurants as well as the distribution of plots of land to individual farmers. The Stalinist goals of industrialization and defense against Nazism had been won, and thus many Soviets expected an end to decades of hardship.

Stalin took a different view and chose to increase repression to bring about recovery. Mobilization for total war had encouraged individual responsibility while relaxing "Communist" oversight, and Stalin moved ruthlessly to reassert control. In 1946, his new five-year plan set increased production goals and mandated more stringent collectivization of agriculture. Although industrial production had doubled by 1950, per capita gross national product was still less than one-third that of the United States. Stalin cut back the army by two-thirds to beef up the labor force and also turned his attention to the low birthrate, a result of wartime male casualties and women's long, arduous working days, which discouraged them from adding child care to their already heavy responsibilities. He introduced an intense propaganda campaign emphasizing that workingwomen should hold down jobs and also fulfill their "true nature" by producing many children.

Origins of the Cold War

In the immediate postwar years, the United States and the Soviet Union engaged in a cold war that would afflict the world for more than four decades. How did these two titans, allies in the most colossal military victory of all times, turn against each other so quickly? Because no peace treaty officially

ended the conflict with Germany as a written record of contest and compromise or of things gone wrong (as in the Peace of Paris), the origins of the cold war remain a matter of debate. Historians point to consistent U.S., British, and French hostility that began with the Bolshevik Revolution and continued through the war. Others point to Stalin's aggressive policies, notably the Nazi-Soviet alliance in 1939 and his quick claims on the Baltic states and Polish territory when World War II broke out. Although controversy continues, scholars today fault both sides. (See "New Sources, New Perspectives," page 1076.)

United States–Soviet Union Mistrust. Agreements during the war that held the Grand Alliance together were never reached easily, and Stalin felt that Churchill and Roosevelt were deliberately letting the USSR bear the brunt of Hitler's onslaught on the continent as part of their anti-Communist policy. Some Americans believed that dropping the atomic bomb on Japan would serve as a warning to Stalin not to try more land grabs. At war's end Stalin continued to see a world hostile to Soviet security, and indeed the new U.S. president, Harry Truman, was far more prepared than Roosevelt to refuse anything the Soviets wanted or needed. Given what Stalin interpreted as a menace from the West and his own country's exhausted condition, he saw the USSR as needing not just a temporary military occupation but a permanent "buffer zone" of European states loyal to the USSR as a safeguard. Across the Atlantic, Truman saw the initial Soviet occupation of eastern Europe as heralding an era of Communist expansion. By 1946, members of the U.S. State Department were describing Stalin as the final "neurotic" Asian ruler prepared to continue the centuries-old Russian thirst for "world domination."

The cold war thus became a series of moves and countermoves in an atmosphere of mutual suspicion that had deep roots. In retrospect it is hardly surprising that animosity developed, because the shared occupation of so rich an area as Europe by two such different countries as the United States and the Soviet Union was unprecedented. There were simply no rules, although some historians see the contest as in fact a case of traditional European or "Western" national rivalries. In line with its geopolitical needs, the USSR proceeded to repress democratic government in central and eastern Europe between 1945 and 1948. Coalition or popular-front type government, which included liberals, socialists, Communists, and peasant party leaders, at first predominated in Hungary, Poland, and Czechoslovakia. However, Stalin imposed Communist rule almost immediately in Bulgaria and Romania. In Romania, he cited citizen violence in 1945 as the excuse to demand an ouster of all non-Communists from the civil service and cabinet. When the Allies protested, a single member of the Peasant Party and another from the Liberal Party were allowed to join eighteen Communists in the government. In response to these events, party membership in Romania soared from 2,000 in 1945 to more than 800,000 a year later. In Poland the Communists fixed the election results of 1945 and 1946 to create the illusion of approval for communism. Nevertheless, the Communists had to share power between 1945 and 1947 with the popular Peasant Party of Stanisław Mikołajczyk, which had a large constituency of rural workers and peasant landowners.

Truman Doctrine and Marshall Plan. The United States acknowledged Soviet influence in areas it occupied, but western European leaders worried that Communist power would spread even farther. The difficult conditions of postwar life made Communist programs promising better conditions and the confiscation of fascist property increasingly attractive to western European workers, while Communist leadership in the resistance gave the party a powerful allure. U.S. and British concern mounted when Communist insurgents threatened to overrun the right-wing monarchy the British had installed in Greece in 1944. The British propped up this repressive government until the terrible winter of 1946–1947 made it financially impossible for them to keep sending aid. Britain could no longer sustain its own people, let alone an unpopular foreign regime. U.S. leaders feared that Europe was on the brink of "going Communist."

The United States now put its new interventionist spirit to work. In March 1947, Truman reacted to the Communist threat by announcing what quickly became known as the *Truman Doctrine*, the countering of political crises with economic and military aid. The president requested $400 million in military aid for Greece and Turkey, where the Communists were also pressuring. Fearing that

---

The Cold War

1945–1949 USSR establishes satellite states in eastern Europe

1947 Truman Doctrine announces American commitment to contain communism; U.S. Marshall Plan provides massive aid to rebuild Europe

1948–1949 Soviet troops blockade Berlin; United States airlifts provisions to Berliners

1949 Western democracies form North Atlantic Treaty Organization (NATO); Soviet bloc establishes Council for Mutual Economic Assistance (COMECON); USSR tests its first nuclear weapon

1950–1953 Korean War

1950–1954 U.S. senator Joseph McCarthy leads hunt for American Communists

1953 Stalin dies

1955 USSR and Eastern bloc countries form military alliance, the Warsaw Pact

1956 Khrushchev denounces Stalin in "secret speech" to Communist Party Congress; Hungarians revolt unsuccessfully against Soviet domination

1959 Fidel Castro comes to power in Cuba

1961 Berlin Wall erected

1962 Cuban missile crisis

Americans would balk at backing Greece, U.S. congressmen would agree to the program only if Truman would "scare hell out of the country," as one put it. Truman thus publicized the aid program as necessary to fortify the world against a tide of global Soviet conquest. In the fall of 1948, the United States supplied the Greek government with 10,000 transport vehicles, close to 100,000 rifles, and 140 planes. The show of American support convinced the Communists to back off, and in 1949 the Greek rebels declared a cease-fire.

"The seeds of totalitarian regimes are nurtured by misery and want," the president warned in the same speech that introduced the Truman Doctrine. His linkage of poverty to the rise of dictatorship led to the *Marshall Plan*, a program of massive U.S. economic aid to Europe. Secretary of State George C. Marshall announced the plan in a Harvard commencement address in June 1947. He cited the deterioration of economic exchange during the war as a threat to political stability. By the early 1950s,

Government Archives and the Truth about the Cold War

The cold war involved a veritable battle of words over history. The United States alleged that Stalin was a monster perpetrating massacres even greater than those of Hitler and that the Soviet Union aimed for world domination. The Soviet Union claimed that the United States dropped the atomic bomb on Japan out of racist contempt for people of color and in preparation for a nuclear destruction of the Soviet Union and its allies. In those days, truth in history seemed to depend on whose side one favored or whose propaganda was most effective.

Government archives have enlightened some of these cold war accusations. As the modern nation-state grew in the nineteenth century, historians came increasingly to rely on official government archives to answer questions arising from such contests of words. Participants and eyewitnesses, it was believed, were not reliable because of their bias. Instead, trained scholars, ridding themselves of bias, would carefully examine government records, preserved in official repositories where tampering could not take place.

The opening of USSR archives in the late 1980s and 1990s after the fall of Soviet communism gave answers to many cold war questions. In 1956, in the midst of superpower rivalry, Nikita Khrushchev first threw official light on the slaughter connected with Stalin's regime. In his partial revelation of truths, Lenin and Stalin were seen as distinctly different political beings, with Lenin an ideologue and benefactor and Stalin a creature of excess. The Soviet archives, however, revealed a more vicious Lenin, one who demanded from the start of the Bolshevik regime the kind of brutality that Khrushchev had pinned on Stalin alone. Lenin and his contemporaries started the reliance on wholesale massacre of the upper classes, peasants, dissenters, and even ordinary citizens. At the same time, the archives discredited the U.S. claim that the Soviet Union in the 1950s was out to conquer the world. Instead, scholars found both Stalin and Khrushchev fearful of a U.S. nuclear attack and eager to come to terms. Their bluster and brinkmanship, the archives showed, often arose from a need to appear dominant to Soviet satellite states and to the new challenger for Communist leadership—the People's Republic of China.

Much official U.S. archival material still remains closed to scholars, but the Freedom of Information Act (1966, amended 1974) allows historians to press for access and at times to obtain it. Official U.S. documents have opened up debate about the dropping of the atomic bomb, with some scholars concluding that it was not merely a matter of ending the war with Japan in the most expeditious way. Instead, brandishing atomic weapons served U.S. cold war ends. Tapes released from the Kennedy administration have shown the president differing from his generals, most of whom wanted a nuclear war during the Cuban missile crisis. Kennedy, far from being the consistent cold warrior he sought to portray, pulled back from the brink.

For all that new archival evidence can reveal, reliance on this material has many pitfalls. One train of thought leads to the belief that if an archive contains no written evidence of an event, the event is open to question. For instance, if there is no written order from Hitler to start the Holocaust, some have argued, it means that he did not know about the event or even that it did not occur. Second, faith in archives also makes them susceptible to forgeries and the planting of

the United States had sent Europe more than $12 billion in food, equipment, and services.

The Marshall Plan claimed that it was not directed "against any country or doctrine but against hunger, poverty, desperation, and chaos." Stalin, however, saw it as a U.S. political ploy that caught him without similar economic aid to offer to his client countries in eastern Europe. The Soviet Union reacted by suppressing the remaining coalition governments and assuming political control in central and eastern Europe. In Poland, where the government found the possibility of Marshall Plan

Russian Secret Archives
The opening of archives across the former Soviet bloc had many consequences. In the former East Germany, for instance, names of secret police informers were made public and many people had their reputations utterly tarnished for their collaboration with the Communist government. The opening of the archives also exposed the cases of those convicted with trumped up evidence (some pictured here), most of them sent to camps and to their deaths long since. The probable existence of such secret archives and concealed official information around the world has made historians and the families of victims fight for access.
ITAR-TASS/Sovfoto.

evidence. In a case of a former Soviet operative, Vasili Mitrokhin, who smuggled tens of thousands of hand-copied documents from Russia in the 1990s, questions arise as to how someone with a fairly low security clearance could have the prolonged access to top Soviet secrets that would enable him to do such extensive copying. Are these documents a plant of the Soviet secret police to show its virtuosity in global espionage?

Finally, excessive faith in archival documents, some critics say, skews history by suggesting that the most important kind of history comes from official government sources. These critics point out that important historical evidence lies as well in sources ranging from newspapers, family account books, diaries, and personal letters to novels, paintings, and architecture. The choice depends on the kind of history one believes most representative and influential.

QUESTIONS FOR DEBATE

1. Are archives overseen by government officials more or less likely to be biased than other sources? How can we know the extent to which they are telling the truth?

2. Make a list of the most reliable sources for discovering historical truth and provide reasons for your ranking these sources as reliable.

FURTHER READING

Christopher Andrew and Vasili Mitrokhin, *The Mitrokhin Archive: The KGB in Europe and the West.* 1999.

Stephane Courtois et al., *The Black Book of Communism: Crimes, Terror, Repression,* trans. Johnathan Murphy and Mark Kramer. 1999.

Vladislav Zubok and Constantine Pleshakov, *Inside the Kremlin's Cold War: From Stalin to Khrushchev.* 1996.

aid attractive, Stalin purged Mikołajczyk in 1947 in the name of creating a "people's government"—the code name for a Communist-controlled state. In Hungary, the prime minister and head of the popular Small-Holders Party was forced out while on a trip to Switzerland in 1947. Czechoslovakia, which by eastern European standards had prospered under a Communist-led coalition, welcomed the Marshall Plan as the beginning of East-West rapprochement. This illusion ended, however, during a purge of non-Communist officials that began in the autumn of 1947. By June 1948, the socialist president, Edouard

Beneš, had resigned and been replaced by a Communist figurehead. Nonetheless, the populace remained so passive that Communist leaders called the takeover "like cutting butter with a knife." The Soviet Union had successfully created a buffer of satellite states in eastern Europe directed by "people's governments." Stalin capped his victory by organizing the Cominform, a centralized association of Communist parties around the world under Moscow's direction.

The only exception to the Soviet sweep in eastern Europe came in Yugoslavia, under the Communist ruler Tito (Josip Broz, 1892–1980). During the war, Tito led the powerful anti-Nazi Yugoslav "partisans." After the war, he drew on support from Serbs, Croats, and Muslims to mount a Communist, but not a Soviet, revolution. Eager for Yugoslavia to develop industrially rather than simply serve Soviet needs, he remarked: "No matter how much each of us loves the land of Socialism, the USSR, he can, in no case love his country less.... We study and take as an example the Soviet system, but we are developing socialism in our country in somewhat different forms." Furious, Stalin ejected Yugoslavia from the Cominform. To Stalin, commitment to communism meant obedience to him.

Yugoslavia after the Revolution

Yugoslavia emerged from its Communist revolution as a federation of six republics and two independent provinces within Serbia. This settlement recognized the country's cultural diversity but was also based on the belief that only tough measures would quell ethnic and religious animosities. Tito's forceful personality held these groups together until his death in 1980; his strong organization also enabled Yugoslavia to hold the Soviets at bay.

The Division of Germany

The cold war became most menacing in the superpowers' struggle for control of Germany. The terms of the agreements reached at Yalta provided for Germany's occupation by troops divided among four zones, each of which was controlled by one of the four principal victors in World War II—the United States, the Soviet Union, Britain, and France. As the Soviet Union and the United States took firm stands over the future of this once rich and still potentially powerful country, at issue was the heart of the European continent.

The sides disagreed on fundamental matters in German history. Many in the United States had come to believe that there was something inherently wrong with the character of Germans, who had provoked two world wars and the Holocaust. At the height of the war, Roosevelt had often spoken of using desperate means to end their apparent militaristic tendencies. After the war, the U.S. occupation forces undertook a reprogramming of German cultural attitudes by controlling the press and censoring the content of all media in the U.S. zone to ensure that they did not express fascist or authoritarian values. Stalin took a different tack in the Soviet-occupied zone to suppress what he perceived as the "evils" of German society. He believed that Nazism was merely another form of advanced capitalism and he therefore confiscated and redistributed the estates of wealthy Germans.

A second disagreement arose over the use of Germany's economic potential. American leaders hoped for an economic coordination among the zones to benefit the occupying countries and to support Germany itself. According to their plan, surplus produce from the Soviet-occupied areas would feed urban populations in the western zones; in turn, industrial goods would be sent to the USSR. The Soviets upset this plan. The Grand Alliance had agreed that the USSR deserved reparations from German resources, so the Soviets immediately dismantled industries and sent machinery, vehicles, and other equipment to the Soviet Union. They transported skilled workers, engineers, and scientists to the USSR to work as virtual slave laborers. The Soviets also manipulated the currency in their zone, enabling the USSR to buy German goods at unrealistic prices.

Amidst these growing cold war tensions, the three Western Allies agreed to merge their zones into a West German state. Instead of continuing to curtail German power as wartime agreements called for, the United States embarked on an economic buildup under the Marshall Plan to make the western zone a buffer against the Soviets. By 1948, notions of a permanently weakened

Germany came to an end. To achieve the new government the United States enlisted many former Nazi officials as spies and rechanneled the hatred of Bolshevism that had been a keystone of Nazism into serving the cold war.

Stalin struck back at the Marshall Plan on July 24, 1948, when Soviet troops blockaded Germany's capital, Berlin. Like Germany as a whole, the city had been divided into four occupation zones, even though it was located more than one hundred miles deep into the Soviet zone and was thus cut off from Western territory. The Soviets declared that Berlin was now part of their zone of occupation and refused to allow vehicles to travel through the entire Soviet zone, including Berlin. They expected the West to capitulate to the new situation, as it had done elsewhere in eastern Europe.

Instead, the United States responded decisively, flying in millions of tons of provisions to the stricken city. During the winter of 1948–1949, the Berlin airlift—Operation Vittles, as U.S. pilots called it—even funneled coal to the city to warm some two million isolated Berliners (Map 28.2). Reports of people's sufferings, of pilots' valiant deeds, and of Soviet belligerence transformed the cold war in the popular imagination, as many Westerners increasingly came to see the conflict as a moral crusade. By the time the Soviets ended the blockade on May 12, 1949, a divided Berlin had become the symbol of the cold war. By then, the reorganization of international politics after the collapse of Europe had become clear: over the security of an eastern European bloc of satellite states the Soviet Union would risk war, and the United States would do no less on behalf of a western Europe that ended at Berlin.

The logical consequence of the division of Germany and this new bipolarity was the formation of competing military alliances (Map 28.3). The United States, Canada, and their European allies formed the North Atlantic Treaty Organization, or NATO, in 1949. NATO provided a unified

MAP 28.2 Divided Germany and the Berlin Airlift, 1946–1949

Berlin, controlled by the United States, Great Britain, France, and the Soviet Union, was deep in the Soviet zone of occupation and became a major point of contention among the former allies. When the USSR blockaded the western half of the city, the U.S. responded with a massive airlift. To stop movement between the two zones, the USSR built a wall in 1961 and used troops to patrol it.

MAP 28.3 European NATO Members and the Warsaw Pact in the 1950s

The two superpowers intensified their rivalry by creating large military alliances: NATO, formed in 1949, and the Warsaw Pact, formed in 1955 after NATO invited West German membership. International politics revolved around these two alliances, which faced off in the heart of Europe. War games for the two sides often assumed a massive war concentrated in central Europe over control of Germany.

military force for the member countries, which also included Britain, France, Belgium, the Netherlands, Luxembourg, Italy, Denmark, Portugal, Iceland, and Norway. In 1955, after the United States forced France and Britain to invite West Germany to join NATO, the Soviet Union retaliated by establishing the military organization commonly called the Warsaw Pact, which included Albania, Bulgaria, Czechoslovakia, East Germany, Hungary, Poland, and Romania. These two massive regional alliances formed the military muscle for the new cold war politics. Replacing the individual might of the great European powers, the strength of each was seen to determine the fate of the world in the atomic age.

❖ The Political and Economic Recovery of Europe

The ideological clash between East and West served as a background to a remarkable economic and political recovery that took place between 1945 and 1960. The first order of business on the political front was a highly charged eradication of the Nazi past and an attempt to deal with its memories. western Europe revived its democratic political structures, its individualistic culture, and its productive capabilities. Eastern Europe restlessly endured a far less prosperous and far more repressive existence under Stalinism, although even these conditions of everyday life had improved as peasant societies were forced to modernize. By 1960, people across the continent had escaped the poverty of the depression, and Europeans had left behind wartime deprivation to enjoy a higher standard of living—an "economic miracle" it was even called—than ever before in human history. In both western and eastern Europe, the state took increasing responsibility for the health and well-being of citizens. The atomic age also became the age of the welfare state.

Dealing with the Nazi Past

In May 1945, Europeans lived under a complex system of political jurisdiction: local resistance leaders, Allied armies of occupation, international relief workers, and the remnants of bureaucracies often worked at odds to restore society. Amidst confusion, starvation, and a thriving black market was an array of goals. While bureaucrats made feeding civilians a priority, international agencies dealt with the tens of millions of refugees. Resistance fighters' immediate purpose was to set up new governments, take over the collaborationist media, and purge Nazis, often by violent means. Occupying armies that covered much of the continent were often a law unto themselves: the Soviets were especially feared for inflicting rape and robbery. Distributing food and clothing, other armed forces tried to instill order.

The desire for revenge against Nazis hardened with the discovery of the death camps' skeletal survivors and the remains of the millions murdered in the camps as the Soviet army approached. Swift vigilante justice by civilians released pent-up rage and aimed to punish collaborators and fascist sympathizers for their complicity in the Holocaust and other occupation crimes. Villagers often shaved the heads of women suspected of associating with Germans and made them parade naked through the local streets. Members of the resistance did not wait for courtroom justice but executed tens of thousands of Nazi officers and collaborators on the spot. In this atmosphere of revenge and purge, crowds of men descended on village and town halls to get certification that they had been in the resistance. The celebration of resistance heroes—some of them self-proclaimed—and the purge of evildoers became the founding acts of a reborn European political community.

Government officials with clean records and Allied representatives undertook a more systematic "denazification." Investigators in Belgium identified 700,000 people suspected of collaboration out of a total population of 8 million. These investigations often showed how hard it was to draw a line between acts of collaboration with totalitarianism and cooptation in the name of survival. At a different level, the trials conducted at Nuremberg, Germany, by the victorious Allies in the fall of 1945 used the Nazis' own documents to provide a horrifying panorama of crimes by Nazi leaders. Each country contributed its most esteemed legal experts for these unusual trials, which underscored principles of justice and public accountability for crimes even in wartime. Although international law lacked a precedent for defining genocide as a crime, the judges at Nuremberg found sufficient

The Punishment of Collaborators
Women who had romantic involvements with Germans were called "horizontal" collaborators to
suggest that they were traitorous prostitutes. With heads shaved and often stripped of their clothing,
they were forced to parade through cities and towns enduring verbal and other abuse. The public
shaming of these women, a vivid part of the memory of the war, served as the background for the
film Hiroshima Mon Amour, *which gripped audiences late in the 1950s.*
Robert Capra/Magnum Photos Inc.

cause to sentence half of the twenty-four defendants to death, among them Hitler's closest associates such as Hermann Goering, and the remainder to prison terms. The Nuremberg trials introduced the notions, which have persisted to the present, of prosecution for crimes against humanity and an international politics based on demands for human rights.

After Nuremberg, Allied prosecution of Nazi and fascist leadership continued, but that huge task never succeeded completely. Some of the leaders most responsible for war crimes disappeared. Patriotic Germans, many of whom were brutalized by invading armies, were skeptical about denazification even as they were forced to march through concentration camps to acknowledge the inhumanity of Nazism. As women in Germany endured starvation and savage rape and additionally performed the arduous labor of clearing rubble, the belief took hold that Germans were the main victims of the war. German civilians also interpreted

the trials of Nazis as the characteristic retribution of victors rather than the well-deserved punishment of the guilty. Allied officials themselves, eager to restore government services, often relied on the expertise of high-ranking fascists and Nazis. Scientists of any political hue were welcomed in the United States to advance military capability, while many Nazi bureaucrats kept their jobs in the new West Germany to help the West wage the cold war more effectively. The Nazi past haunts European debates, cultural life, and politics to this day, yet political expediency led Westerners at the time to forgive some Nazis quite easily.

Rebirth of the West

Against all political and economic odds, western Europe revived. Reform-minded civilian governments reflected the coalitions that had opposed the Axis. They conspicuously emphasized democracy to show their rejection of the totalitarian

Women Clearing Berlin

The amount of destruction caused by World War II was staggering, requiring the mobilization of the civilian population in Berlin, where women were conscripted to sort the rubble and clear it away. Scenes like this were ultimately used as propaganda in the cold war to make it seem as if the Germans were the victims rather than the perpetrators of the war. Such depictions also made the Germans appear weak and helpless before a threatened menace, as in the photos of weak and ravaged Belgian women in World War I propaganda.
AKG Photo, London.

regimes that had earlier attracted so many Europeans—with such dire consequences. Rebuilding devastated towns and cities spurred industrial recovery, while bold projects for economic cooperation like the European Common Market and the conversion of wartime technological know-how to peacetime use produced a brisk trade in consumer goods and services in western Europe by the late 1950s.

The Challenge of Postwar Politics. Resistance leaders had the first claim on office in postfascist western Europe. In France the leader of the Free French, General Charles de Gaulle, governed briefly as chief of state; he quit over limitations on the president's power that were reminiscent of the Third Republic. The French approved a constitu-tion in 1946 that established the Fourth Republic and finally granted the vote to French women. Meanwhile, Italy replaced its constitutional monarchy with a full parliamentary system that also allowed women the vote for the first time. As in France, a resistance-based socialist government initially governed. Then late in 1945 this was replaced by the conservative leadership of the Christian Democrats, who headed a coalition including Communists and socialists. Christian Democrats, who had a strong presence in postwar politics across western Europe, descended from the traditional Catholic centrist parties of the prewar period. They adopted this name to gain wider support that would include Protestants and workers and allow them to pursue liberal economic programs and democratic reform.

Tentative Steps toward Democracy. It was the Communist Party, however, that seemed to attract the most vocal loyalty of a consistently large segment of the western European population. Symbol of the common man, the ordinary Soviet soldier was a hero to many western Europeans outside occupied Germany, as were the resistance leaders — most of them Communist until late in the war when the impending Nazi collapse lured mainline politicians to join the anti-Nazi bandwagon. People still remembered the common man's plight in the depression of the 1930s. Thus, in Britain, despite the successes of Winston Churchill's Conservative Party leadership, the Labour government of Clement Attlee appeared more socialist by fulfilling promises that it would share prosperity equitably among the classes through expanded social welfare programs and the nationalization of key industries.

The political air became more charged as the cold war took hold. Increasingly urged on by Moscow, the French Communist chief called the French Fourth Republic a "reactionary dictatorship" and summoned the French people to overthrow it. Amidst ongoing hardship in everyday life, strikes broke out across the West, and de Gaulle responded by creating a new anti-Communist party, Rally of the French People (RPF). By the late 1940s, cooperation between ruling Christian Democrats and Communists in other countries fell apart. Rejecting the language of consensual politics, one intellectual called anyone who opposed communism "a dog." In the words of one French journalist, western Europe looked as if "blood was going to flow."

In West Germany, however, communism had no appeal. In 1949, centrist politicians helped create a new state, the German Federal Republic. Its first chancellor was the seventy-three-year-old Catholic anti-Communist Konrad Adenauer. Working with other democrats, Adenauer drafted a constitution that would prevent the emergence of a dictator and guarantee individual rights. Adenauer also allied himself with Ludwig Erhard, an economist who had stabilized the postwar German currency so that commerce could resume. Erhard used his academic expertise and commitment to the free market to "turn a lunar landscape into a flourishing beehive," in the words of one German commentator. The economist and the politician successsfully guided Germany away from both fas-

cism and communism and restored the representative government that Hitler had overthrown.

Paradoxically, it was in the United States, as it promoted democratic values against totalitarianism, that postwar politics most imperiled individual freedom and actually threatened peacetime democracy. The 1949, explosion of the Soviet atomic bomb and the successful Communist revolution in China brought to the fore Joseph McCarthy, a U.S. senator from Wisconsin, who announced that Communists were infiltrating American institutions. Facing a reelection struggle, McCarthy warned of a great conspiracy to overthrow the United States. His false claim to have

Hollywood Stars Protest in Washington
The appearance of top stars like Lauren Bacall and Humphrey Bogart to protest the persecution of writers, filmmakers, and actors late in the 1940s did not dampen the government's hunt for Communists. In the search for anyone critical of U.S. policy, people from many walks of life lost their jobs, were imprisoned, or endured public humiliation. Homosexuals of any political belief were special targets for what seemed to resemble the Soviet attempt to force everyone to hold the same political thoughts.
UPI/Corbis-Bettmann.

names of hundreds, even thousands, of conspirators led to a hysteria that curtailed free speech in the United States. As during the Soviet purges, people were called before panels to confess, testify against friends, think about whether they had ever had Communist thoughts or sympathies. The atmosphere was electric with fear because only five years before, such mass media as *Time* and *Life* magazines had run glowing stories about Stalin and the Soviet system. By 1952, more than six million people had been subpoenaed, investigated, or imprisoned or had lost their jobs. McCarthy had books like Thomas Paine's *Common Sense*, written in the eighteenth century to support the American Revolution, removed from government shelves, and he personally oversaw book burnings. Although the Senate finally voted to censure McCarthy in the winter of 1954, the assault on freedom had been devastating and anticommunism dominated political life.

Economic Miracles.   Given the incredible devastation, the economic rebirth of western Europe was even more surprising than the revival of democracy. In the first weeks and months after the war, the job of rebuilding often involved menial physical labor that mobilized entire populations. With so many men dead, wounded, or detained as prisoners of war, German housewives, called "women of the ruins," earned their living clearing rubble by hand. The task was vast: up to 95 percent of major cities had been bombed to bits. Neighborhoods set up survival networks to provide daily necessities, and the resulting grassroots organizing, so at odds with Nazi practice, influenced German politics in the decades to come.

Initially governments diverted labor and capital into rebuilding infrastructure—transportation, communications, industrial capacity. However, the scarcity of goods sparked unrest and made communism attractive politically because it proclaimed less interest in the revival of big business than in the ordinary person's standard of living. But as the Marshall Plan sustained the initial recovery with American dollars, food and consumer goods became more plentiful, and demand for automobiles, washing machines, and vacuum cleaners boosted economies. The growth in production of all kinds wiped out most unemployment. Labor-short northern Europe even arranged for "guest" workers to migrate from impoverished regions like Sicily to help rebuild cities. The outbreak of war in Korea in 1950 further stimulated the European economy.

The 1950s witnessed astonishing rates of economic growth. (See "Taking Measure," below.) Between 1950 and 1954, the West German economy grew at an unmatched 8.2 percent annual rate. In the second half of the 1950s, France's economy

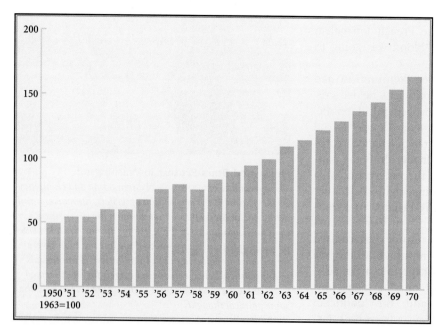

TAKING MEASURE
World Manufacturing Output, 1950–1970
During the "long boom" from the 1950s to the early 1970s, the world experienced increased industrial output, better agricultural production, and rising consumerism. This era of prosperity resulted not only from the demand generated by the need to rebuild Europe but also from the adaptation of war technology to peacetime uses. The General Agreement on Trade and Tariffs (GATT) was also implemented after the war, lowering tariffs and thus advancing trade.
Hammond Atlas of the Twentieth Century (London: Times Books, 1987), 127.

took off at an annual rate of 8 percent. Late in the 1950s, Italy likewise rebounded with new ventures in the production of oil and synthetic products. Britain's annual growth was a mere 3 percent because the country did not face massive reconstruction and merely repaired without modernizing its basic industries. More important, although Britain's immediate postwar capital investment was very high, its trade was oriented toward the less vigorous Commonwealth economies. Thus it missed out trading with the booming western European countries.

The postwar recovery also featured the adaptation of wartime technology to consumer industry and the continuation of military spending. Civilian travel expanded as nations organized their own air systems based on improved airplane technology. Developed to relieve wartime shortages, synthetic goods such as nylon now became part of peacetime civilian life. Factories churned out a vast assortment of plastic products, ranging from pipes to household goods and rainwear. In the climate of cold war, governments ordered bombs, fighter planes, tanks, and missiles; and they also continued to sponsor military research (Figure 28.1). Spending for armaments helped stabilize the economy by creating jobs, as it had in Germany and the United States in the late 1930s. The cold war ultimately prevented a repeat of the 1920s when reduced military spending threw people out of jobs and thus fed the growth of fascism.

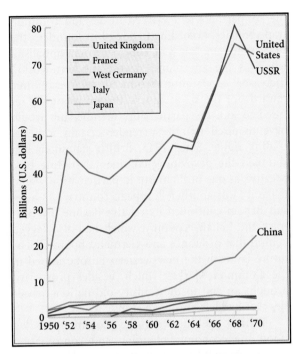

FIGURE 28.1 The Arms Race, 1950–1970
As soon as the war ended, the United States and the Soviet Union started a massive arms buildup that would continue into the 1980s. Because it had not suffered destruction during the war, the United States could afford spending hundreds of billions of dollars. The Soviet Union could not, and its citizens were comparatively deprived by these expenditures. By the end of the twentieth century, the United States and Russia held vast arsenals of nuclear and other weapons and along with France led the way in selling arms to the rest of the world.

The Common Market.   International cooperation and planning that led to the creation of the Common Market and ultimately the European Union of the 1990s provided a final ingredient in recovery. The Bretton Woods Agreement of 1944, eventually signed by forty-four nations, with the Soviet Union a notable exception, envisioned a world bank and planned the International Monetary Fund (IMF). The IMF's goal was to ensure the stability of currencies by using pooled monies to prop up any weak currency and thus to further trade. One aim was to preempt the kind of economic instabilities that had led to social and political turmoil in the 1930s.

Drastic economic change was the order of the day. The Marshall Plan demanded as the condition for assistance that recipients cooperate in more far-reaching economic policy. In 1951, Italy, France, Germany, Belgium, Luxembourg, and the Nether-

lands formed the European Coal and Steel Community (ECSC). This organization managed coal and steel production and prices and, most important, arranged for West German output to benefit western Europe. According to the ECSC's principal architect, Robert Schuman, the economic unity created by the organization would make another war "materially impossible." Simply put, the bonds of common productivity and trade would keep France and Germany from another cataclysmic war.

In 1957, the "six," as the ECSC members were called, took another major step toward regional prosperity when they signed the Treaty of Rome. The treaty provided for the sharing of atomic resources through a commission called EUROCOM and a trading partnership called the European Economic Community (EEC), known popularly as the Common Market. The EEC reduced tariffs among the six partners and worked to develop common trade policies. According to one of its founders, the EEC aimed to "prevent the race of nationalism, which is the true curse of the modern world." Increased cooperation produced great economic rewards for the six members. Britain pointedly refused to join the partnership; membership would have required that it surrender certain imperial trading rights. Since 1945, British statesmen had shunned the developing continental trading bloc because, as one of them put it, participation would make it "just another European country." As a result Britain continued its relative decline. By contrast, the Italian economy, which had also lagged behind that of France and Germany, boomed. The future lay with the new western Europe joined in the Common Market, which, besides prosperity, brought an end to the century-old national rivalries that had left Europe in ruins.

Behind the move to the Common Market stood the economic planning and coordination that had brought liberal economics under the government umbrella during wartime. Government experts (whether under Hitler or Roosevelt) had planned everything from transportation to the coordination of production in different regions. Called *technocrats* after 1945, these specialists were to base decisions on expertise rather than on personal interest; those working for the Common Market were to disregard the self-interest of any one nation. French economist Jean Monnet, who inspired and helped create the Common Market, believed that rational administration by supranational agencies composed of disinterested experts reduced the potential for irrationality and violence in politics, both domestic and international.

Cooperation and expert planning had an American aura that had also drawn Europeans to jazz and skyscrapers. Monnet attacked socially conservative government practices in favor of American ones. In summertime meetings he encouraged European government leaders to take the daring step of removing their jackets and rolling up their sleeves. "I'll do the same—it's a habit I picked up in America," he said. Some critics insisted, some even today, that expert planning diminished democracy by putting massive control in the hands of bureaucracy, not legislatures. Still others deplored the end of liberal economics and the free market, a development that to them smacked of socialism.

The Welfare State: Common Ground East and West

On both sides of the cold war, governments intervened forcefully to ameliorate social conditions. This policy of intervention became known as the *welfare state*, indicating that states were no longer interested solely in maintaining order and augmenting their power. The welfare state had been gradually building for almost a century, as in the creation of government pensions in Bismarck's newly created Germany or in the British national health-care system that began to give twenty million workers medical benefits during the depression. After World War II, governments further opened their purse strings to fund more and more social programs.

The welfare state encouraged population growth with direct financial aid. The European population had declined during the war, and almost all countries now desperately urged couples to reproduce. In France, where fertility had been dropping for more than a century, de Gaulle called on women to produce "twelve million healthy babies." Imitating the sweeping Swedish programs of the 1930s, nations expanded or created family allowances, health-care and medical benefits, and programs for pregnant women and new mothers. The French gave larger allowances for each birth after the first; for many French families this allowance provided as much as a third of the household income.

Britain's maternity benefits and child allowances, announced in a wartime report, favored women who did not work outside the home and provided little coverage of any kind to working-women. The West German government passed strict legislation that discouraged employers from hiring women. In fact, West Germans bragged about removing women from the workforce, claiming it distinguished democratic practices from Communist ones that were said to demand women's work outside the home. One result of the cutback in pensions and benefits to married women was their high rate of poverty in old age.

In eastern Europe and the Soviet Union, where wartime loss of life had been enormous, women worked nearly full time and usually outnumbered men in the workforce. Child-care programs, family allowances, and maternity benefits were designed to encourage pregnancies by such women. The scarcity of consumer goods, the housing shortages, and the lack of household conveniences in the Eastern bloc, however, discouraged workingwomen from having large families. Because women had sole responsibility for onerous domestic duties on top of their paying jobs, their already heavy workload increased with the birth of each additional child.

Other welfare-state programs aimed to improve people's health. State-funded medical insurance and subsidized medical care covered health-care needs everywhere except in the United States. Countries as diverse as Great Britain and the Soviet Union had nationalized health-care systems in which doctors and hospital employees worked for the state and the country's entire population was covered. In other nations, citizens' medical expenses were reimbursed through social security plans. The combination of better material conditions and state provision of health care dramatically extended life expectancy and lowered rates of infant mortality. Contributing to the overall progress, the number of medical doctors and dentists more than doubled between the end of World War I and 1950, and vaccines greatly reduced the death toll from such diseases as tuberculosis, diphtheria, measles, and polio. In England, schoolchildren stood on the average an inch taller than children the same age had a decade earlier. And as

people lived longer, governments began to establish programs for the elderly. All in all, per capita expenditures on civilian well-being shot up after the war. Belgium, for example, which had spent $12 per capita in 1930, led western European countries with $148 per capita in 1956; Britain, which had led in 1930 with welfare expenditures of $59, now lagged behind with $93 because of its near-bankrupt condition.

Welfare-state initiatives in other areas played a role in the higher standard of living. A growing network of government-built atomic power plants brought more thorough electrification of eastern Europe and the Soviet Union. Governments legislated better conditions and more leisure time for workers. Beginning in 1955, Italian workers received twenty-eight paid holidays annually; in Sweden they received twenty-nine vacation days, and the number grew in the 1960s. Planning also helped provide a more varied diet and more abundant food, with meat, fish, eggs, cheese, milk, and fresh fruit supplementing the older grain-based foods. In Czechoslovakia, annual per capita consumption of meat was 125 pounds in 1960 and in Hungary, 105.

Housing shortages posed a daunting challenge for both the welfare state and the individual. After three decades of economic depression and war, people had trouble finding a decent place to live. Because the war had been so destructive and had

Postwar Housing in Poland
Wartime devastation only added to the growing shortage of housing that had begun with the diversion of resources to fight World War I and that had increased during the depression of the 1930s, when housing construction almost entirely halted. In the post–World War II years, shortages were so grave that slapdash, cheap buildings with far less than one room per person went up from England to Eastern Europe. It was not until the 1960s that the Soviets began building anywhere near the housing units needed, some million or more per year.
Sovfoto.

diverted resources into military needs, postwar Europeans often lived with three generations sharing one or two rooms. Eastern Europeans faced the worst conditions, whereas Germans and Greeks fared better because only 20 to 25 percent of prewar housing had been lost. To rebuild, governments sponsored a postwar housing boom. In western Europe, they provided incentives to private builders but also, as in the Eastern bloc, the state itself undertook building projects. New cities formed around the edges of major urban areas in both East and West. Many buildings went up slapdash, and restored towns took on an undistinguished look and a constantly deteriorating condition. Westerners labeled the new apartments in Poland "environmentally horrible." Despite the building boom, housing shortages had not disappeared by the 1960s. Nevertheless the modernized appearance of many European cities suggested that the century's two cataclysmic wars had definitively swept away a good deal of the old Europe.

Recovery in the East

Creating a Soviet bloc according to Stalin's prewar vision of industrialization was an immense undertaking. Before the war, the economies of the successor states to Austria-Hungary such as Poland and Hungary had remained largely rural and dominated by small peasant farmers. Stalin called on the crushing methods that had served him before to transform these economies.

Stalin Unleashed. In eastern Europe, Stalin enforced collectivized agriculture and badly needed industrialization through the nationalization of private property. In Hungary, for example, where one thousand families owned more than one-quarter of the arable land, Communists seized and reapportioned all estates over twelve hundred acres. Having gained support of the poorer peasants through this redistribution, Communists later pushed them into cooperative farming. In the Transylvania area of Romania, Communists first seized the land of the German minority there and redistributed it to poorer Romanian farmers. Then they converted the property of wealthier peasants into collective farms. The process was brutal and slow, and rural Romanians would look back on the 1950s as "dreadful." Some of those same people

also felt that ultimately their lives and their children's lives had improved. "Before we peasants were dirty and poor, we worked like dogs. . . . Was that a good life? No sir, it wasn't. . . . I was a miserable sharecropper and my son is an engineer," said one Romanian peasant.

Stalin prodded all the socialist economies in his bloc to match U.S. productivity. An admirer of American industrial know-how, he once claimed that "the union of Russian revolutionary drive with American business ability" was "the essence of Leninism." The Soviet Union also formed regional organizations, instituting the Council for Mutual Economic Assistance (COMECON) to coordinate economic relations among the satellite countries and Moscow. Modernization of production in the Eastern bloc opened new technical and bureaucratic careers, and modernizers in the satellite states touted the virtues of steel plants and modern transport. The terms of the COMECON relationship thwarted development of the satellite states, for the USSR was allowed to buy goods from its clients at bargain prices and sell to them at exorbitant ones. Nonetheless these formerly peasant states became oriented toward technology and bureaucratically directed industrial economies. People moved to cities where they received better education, health care, and, ultimately, jobs.

Like Soviet industrialization in the 1930s, repression accompanied the drive for modernization. The Catholic clergy, which often protested the imposition of communism, was crushed. Old agrarian elites, professionals, intellectuals, and other members of the middle class were discriminated against, imprisoned, or executed. Prisoners in East German camps did hard labor in uranium and other dangerous mines; one imprisoned Romanian intellectual spent years in water up to his chin cutting bamboo for an aborted canal linking the Black Sea and the Danube. Although its Western allies often objected to the arrogance of the rich and powerful United States, the Soviet Union dominated its alliances through physical coercion along with state-instituted programs to build loyalty to the regime. Thus citizens in satellite countries found themselves obliged to attend adult education classes, women's groups, and public ceremonies.

Science and culture were the building blocks of Stalinism in the satellite countries as well as in the USSR. An intense program of Russification and

Re-Creating Hungarian Youth
People across Europe focused on the well-being of young people after World War II, and in the Soviet sphere this took the form of education in Communist ways. Youth groups, such as those in the early Stalinist USSR, served this end, and vivid posters in the Soviet realist style carried inspirational messages: "Forward for the Congress of the Young Fighters of Peace and Socialism," reads this typical message to Hungarian youth in 1950.
Magyar Nemzeti Múzeum, Budapest (Hungarian National Museum).

de-Christianization began. The Soviets forced students in eastern Europe to read histories of the war that ignored native resistance and gave the Red Army sole credit for fighting the Nazis. They replaced national symbols with Soviet ones. For example, the Hungarians had to accept a new flag with a Soviet red star beaming rays onto a hammer and sickle; the Hungarian colors were reduced to a small band on the flag. Utter historical distortion, revivified anti-Semitism, and rigid censorship re-

sulted in what one staunchly socialist writer characterized as "a dreary torrent of colorless, mediocre literature." For information people had to rely on the *Great Soviet Encyclopedia*, started in 1949, which claimed the Russians to be forerunners in every field of endeavor from automobile technology to physics. Although modernization was a priority, Soviet ideology continued to take its toll by undercutting the potential for steady scientific advances.

In the USSR itself, Stalin instituted new purges to ensure obedience and conformity. Marshall Zhukov, a popular leader of the armed forces, was shipped to a distant command, while Anna Akhmatova, the great poet whose popular writing had emphasized perseverance and individual heroism during the war, died confined to a crowded hospital room because she refused to glorify Stalin in her postwar poetry. The tsarist tradition of Russification and anti-Semitism revived. Soviet agents rooted out "Jewish influences" and "bourgeois decadence" in the arts: they put writers and artists out of work, evicted them from their apartments, and denied them the privileges that came with artistic achievement.

After Stalin. In March 1953, while leading the rebuilding of the Soviet Union and planning more purges, Stalin died. As people openly mourned this man they considered their savior from backwardness and Nazism, troubles were already apparent in the empire he ruled so tyrannically. Political prisoners in the labor camps who had started rioting late in the 1940s now pressed their demands for reform. Consumer goods were much scarcer than in the West because of the government's high military spending and the enormous cost of recovery. Amid deprivation and discontent, Soviet leaders and bureaucrats enjoyed country homes, luxury goods, and plentiful food, but many of them had come to distrust Stalinism and were ready for some changes. The Stalinist system faced daunting challenges, but without Stalin.

It was a fateful time. A power struggle ensued within the Soviet government, and protests took place across the empire. Labor camp inmates stopped working to emphasize their need for better food and the right to receive letters. Amid turmoil some prisoners of the Gulag labor camps were freed and the production of consumer goods beefed up—a policy called "goulash communism" because in part it resulted in more food for ordinary people. The old ways could not hold. In 1955, Nikita Khrushchev (1894–1971), an illiterate coal miner before the revolution, outmaneuvered other rivals to emerge the undisputed leader of the Soviet Union, but he did so without the usual executions. The next year he attacked Stalinism. Addressing the Twentieth Party Congress, he listed what he called Stalin's "perversions" of the Communist revolution. Khrushchev denounced the "cult of personality" Stalin had built about himself and announced that Stalinism did not equal socialism. The "secret speech"—it was not published in the USSR but became widely known—sent tremors through Communist parties around the world and signaled that Stalin's death might bring a real change of direction.

In this climate of uncertainty, protest erupted once more in early summer 1956, when discontented Polish railroad workers struck for better wages. Popular support for their cause forced the return of Wladislaw Gomulka, a Communist victim of an earlier Stalinist purge. Gomulka initiated a more liberal Communist program. Inspired by the Polish example, Hungarians rebelled against forced collectivization in October 1956—"the golden October," they would call their uprising. As in Poland, economic issues, especially announcements of reduced wages, sparked some of the first outbreaks of violence, but the protest soon targeted the entire Communist system. Intellectuals and students turned universities into major political centers. Residents of Budapest filled the streets and smashed the huge statue of Stalin. Tens of thousands of protesters convinced the Hungarian army, sent to disperse them, to join the rebellion and succeeded in returning a popular hero, Imre Nagy, to power. When Nagy announced that Hungary might leave the Warsaw Pact, Soviet troops moved in, killing tens of thousands and causing hundreds of thousands more to flee to the West. Nagy was hanged. The U.S. refusal to intervene showed that, despite a rhetoric of "liberation," it would not risk World War III by militarily challenging the Soviet sphere of influence.

A Partial Thaw. The failure of eastern European uprisings overshadowed significant changes in Soviet policy. In the process of defeating his rivals, Khrushchev ended the Stalinist purges, reformed

the courts (which came to function according to procedures, not like the stage for show trials of the past), and set a policy of more limited sentences for political offenders and criminals. The gates of the Gulag opened still farther, and the secret police lost many of its arbitrary powers. These reforms contributed to what came to be called the climate of "thaw" in the Soviet Union.

The thaw, however, was fragile. It depended not only on the death of Stalin but also on the Soviet sense of security acquired from increased productivity, military buildup, and stunning successes in aerospace development. In 1957, the Soviets successfully launched the first artificial earth satellite, *Sputnik*, and in 1961 they put the first cosmonaut, Yuri Gagarin, in orbit around the earth. The Soviets' edge in space technology shocked the Western bloc and motivated the creation of the U.S. National Aeronautics and Space Administration (NASA). Soviet successes indicated that the USSR was on the way to achieving Stalin's goals of Westernization and modernization. Nevertheless, Khrushchev continued to fear and bully dissidents. For example, he forced Boris Pasternak to refuse the 1958 Nobel Prize in literature because his novel *Doctor Zhivago* (1957) cast doubt on the glory of the revolution and affirmed the value of the individual.

Yet Khrushchev himself made several trips to the West and was more widely seen by the public than Stalin. More confident and more affluent, the Soviets took steps to reduce their diplomacy's paranoid style and concentrated their efforts on spreading the message of Leninism and socialist progress to the emerging nations of Asia, Africa, and Latin America.

❖ Decolonization in a Cold War Climate

World War II dealt the final blow to the ability of European powers to maintain their vast empires and their global influence. During the war the Allies had again relied heavily on Asian and African troops and had encouraged anti-Axis independence movements. In the postwar world, however, the Western powers attempted to stamp out nationalist groups and reimpose their control—with fatal results. As before, colonized peoples had been on the front lines defending the West; and as before, they had witnessed the full barbarism of Western warfare. Excluded from victory parades and other ceremonies so the powers could maintain the illusion of Western supremacy, adult men in the colonies still did not receive the political rights promised them. Instead, people in Asia, Africa, and the Middle East, often led by individuals steeped in Western values and experienced in war, embraced the cause of independence and often clashed with the West in bloody warfare.

The path to achieving a modern nation-state, however, was often fraught with conflict off the battlefield as well. In Africa, a continent whose peoples spoke more than five thousand languages, the European conquerors' need for convenient administrative units had led to regional designations such as Rhodesia and Nigeria, obliterating living arrangements that had relied on ethnic ties and local cultures. In addition, religion played a divisive role in independence movements. In India, Hindus and Muslims, both desiring independence, battled one another even though they shared the goal of eliminating the British. In the Middle East and North Africa, pan-Arab and pan-Islamic movements might seem to have been unifying forces. Yet many Muslims were not Arab, not all Arabs were Muslim, and Islam itself encompassed many competing beliefs and sects. Differences among religious beliefs, ethnic groups, and cultural practices— many of them invented or promoted by the colonizers to divide and rule—overlapped and undermined political unity. Despite these complications, peoples in what was coming to be called the third world succeeded in throwing off the imperial yoke imposed by Britain, France, Belgium, and the Netherlands.

Loss of empire threatened Europe's economy and upset a European sense of identity based on a belief in Western superiority. At the same time, the decolonizing world offered a new field for competition between the United States and the Soviet Union, thus increasing the possibility of nuclear war and magnifying the drama of decolonization. Many leaders of newly independent nations turned a cold shoulder to each of the global giants and envisioned instead a consortium of nonaligned countries exerting its own leverage in world affairs.

The End of Empire in Asia

By the end of World War II, leaders in Asia began to mobilize the mass discontent that had intensified during the war and were able to drive out foreign rulers. The biggest loser would be Britain, which by the 1960s would decline from a global imperial power to a small island nation. In need of postwar resources, Winston Churchill was determined not to let the colonies go their own way, but the victorious Labourites under Clement Attlee promoted decolonization as important to social justice. Such debate became moot as national liberation movements increasingly took matters into their own hands and as white settlers often resisted the independence of people they still wanted to rule.

Independence in South Asia. The British had promised to grant India its independence in the 1930s, but they postponed it when war broke out. They even declared war against the Nazis on the Indians' behalf. Some two million Indian men were mobilized, anchoring the war in the Middle East and Asia. Local industry became an important wartime supplier and Indian business leaders bought out British entrepreneurs short of cash. But during this period of economic prosperity for some, food shortages drove people to overcrowded cities, and political fissures between Hindus and Muslims, long encouraged by the British, widened.

When, after the war, the Labour government sent its statesmen to preside over the end of the British Empire in India, they decreed that two countries should emerge from the old colony, so great was the mistrust between the Congress and League Parties. Thus, in 1947 India was created for Hindus and Pakistan for Muslims. Yet during the independence year, political tensions exploded among opposing members of the two religions. Hundreds of thousands were massacred in the great shift of populations between the two nations. In 1948, a radical Hindu assassinated Gandhi, who though a Hindu himself had continued to champion religious reconciliation. Confronting nationalist movements elsewhere, Britain retained control of Hong Kong; but before two decades of the postwar era had passed, almost half a billion Asians had gained their freedom from the rule of fifty million British.

"People's Very Own Army"

Dramatic posters had spread the word during World War II of a range of Communist activities to help the Chinese people fight the Japanese invaders. In this depiction, Communists are neighbors, protectors, and providers of medical cures and supplies. They deal with all kinds of people, the poster claims, and are cheerfully helpful. As a result of their efforts, China would prosper.

Peasant Revolts in China (LWC Series), 1973. p. 106, ill. 41. Photo courtesy Thames & Hudson, Ltd., London.

Communist Revolution in East and Southeast Asia.

In 1949, a Communist takeover in China brought in a government that was no longer the plaything of the traditional colonial powers. Mao Zedong (1893–1976) led his army of Communists to victory over Jiang Jieshi's unpopular, corrupt Nationalist government, which the United States had bankrolled. Chinese communism in the new People's Republic of China emphasized above all the welfare of the peasantry rather than the indus-

trial proletariat and was thus distinct from Stalinism, Leninism, and Marxism. Mao instituted social reforms such as civil equality for women but at the same time copied Soviet collectivization, rapid industrialization, and brutal repression of the privileged classes. Although China began to distance itself from the USSR in the mid-1950s, the Western bloc saw only monolithic red from Leningrad to Beijing.

The United States and the Soviet Union were deeply interested in East Asia, the United States because of the region's economic importance and the USSR because of its shared borders. Thus the Chinese victory spurred both superpowers to increase their involvement in Asian politics. They faced off indirectly in Korea, which had been split at the thirty-eighth parallel after World War II. In 1950, the North Koreans, supported by the Soviet Union, invaded the U.S.-backed South. The United States maneuvered the UN Security Council into approving a "police action" against the North. The UN eventually deployed 400,000 troops from member nations to help the South Korean army repel the invaders. The combined military forces quickly drove well into North Korean territory,

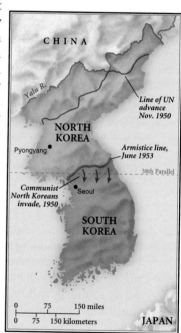

The Korean War, 1950–1953

where they were met by the Chinese rather than the Soviet army. After two and a half years of stalemate, the opposing sides finally agreed to a settlement in 1953: Korea would remain split at its prewar border, the thirty-eighth parallel.

The United States lost more than 50,000 men—almost as many as would die in the Vietnam War—and increased its military spending from $10.9 billion in 1948 to almost $60 billion in 1953 to hold the line on Communist expansion. It outpaced Soviet expenditures by $10–$20 billion annually from 1951 to 1960. Communist potential in decolonizing areas led the American secretary of state, John Foster Dulles, to characterize Asian countries as a row of dominoes: "You knock over the first one and what will happen to the last one is that it will go over [to communism] very quickly." The expansion of the cold war to Asia prompted the creation of an Asian counterpart to NATO. Established in 1954, the Southeast Asia Treaty Organization (SEATO) included Pakistan, Thailand, the Philippines, Britain, Australia, New Zealand, France, and the United States. One side effect was the rapid reindustrialization of Japan to provide the United States with supplies.

The cold war spread to Indochina, where nationalists had been struggling against the postwar revival of French imperialism. Their leader, the European-educated Ho Chi Minh (1890–1969), preached both nationalism and socialism and built a powerful organization, the Viet Minh, to fight colonial rule. He advocated the redistribution of land held by big landowners, especially in the rich agricultural area in southern Indochina where some six thousand owners possessed more than 60 percent of the land. The French army fought all efforts at independence, but the Viet Minh surprised the French with its tenacious resistance. Finally, these peasant guerrillas forced the technologically advanced French army to withdraw after the bloody battle of Dien Bien Phu in 1954.

Indochina, 1954

The Geneva Convention of 1954 carved out an independent Laos and divided Vietnam into North and South, each free from French control. The Viet Minh was ordered to retreat to an area north of the seventeenth parallel. But superpower intervention undermined the peace treaty. President Truman had seen the Indochinese conflict as part of the anti-Communist crusade rather than as a nationalist issue; he began providing aid to the French well before their defeat at Dien Bien Phu. President

Eisenhower's advisers wanted him to drop an atomic bomb on the Viet Minh, and, although threatening to do so, the president refused direct military intervention. The decolonizing world was becoming a battleground not only for independence but also for the cold war. Avoiding major conflict in Europe, the superpowers and their allies volleyed back and forth, risking the nuclear brink while subjecting native peoples to the force of their military might. In fighting to prevent national liberation in the name of fighting communism, the United States in particular was acquiring a reputation as an "imperialist" power of the old school, nowhere more so than in Vietnam.

The Struggle for Identity in the Middle East

The power of oil and the ability of small countries to see the opportunity for maneuvering between antagonists in the cold war gave new impetus to independence struggles in the Middle East. The legacy of the Holocaust, however, complicated the political scene. As in the rest of the world after the war, Middle Eastern peoples renewed their commitment to independence and resisted attempts by the major powers to regain imperial control. Weakened by the war, British oil companies wanted to tighten their grip on profits, as the value of this energy source soared. The cold war gave Middle Eastern leaders an opening to bargain with the superpowers, playing them off one against another, especially over resources to re-establish war torn economies. The Western powers' commitment to secure a Jewish homeland in the Middle East further stirred up Arab determination to regain economic and political control of the region.

When World War II broke out, 600,000 Jewish settlers and twice as many Arabs lived, in intermittent conflict, in British-controlled Palestine. In 1947, an exhausted Britain ceded the area to the United Nations to work out a settlement between the Jews and the Arabs. In the aftermath of the Holocaust, the UN voted to partition Palestine into an Arab region and a Jewish one (Map 28.4). Conflicting claims, however, led to war, and Jewish military forces prevailed. On May 14, 1948, the state of Israel came into being. "The dream had come true," Golda Meir, the future president of Israel,

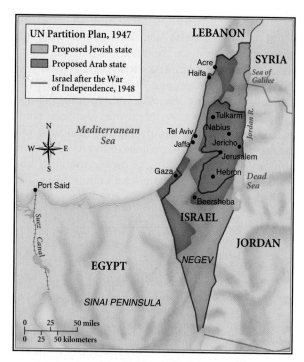

MAP 28.4 The Partition of Palestine and the Creation of Israel, 1947–1948

The creation of the Jewish state of Israel in 1948 against a backdrop of ongoing wars among Jews and indigenous Arab peoples made the Middle East a powder keg until the present day. The struggle for resources and for securing the borders of viable nation-states was at the heart of these bitter contests, threatening to pull the superpowers into a third world war.

remembered, but "too late to save those who had perished in the Holocaust." Israel opened its gates to immigrants, driving its ambitions against those of its Arab neighbors.

One of those neighbors, Egypt, had gained its independence from Britain at the end of the war. Britain, however, retained its control of Middle Eastern oil and its dominance of Asian shipping through the Suez Canal, which was owned by a British-run company. In 1952, Colonel Gamal Abdel Nasser became Egypt's president after the ouster of its king. Nasser's dreams for Egypt included economic modernization and true national independence. A prime goal was reclaiming the Suez Canal, "where 120,000 of our sons had lost their lives in digging it [by force]," he stated. In July 1956, Nasser nationalized the canal.

Britain immediately demanded the canal's return and won support from Israel and France. In

October, the three countries attacked Egypt, bringing the Suez crisis to a head while the Hungarian revolt was in full swing. The British branded Nasser another Hitler and called on the United States for help. Anxious to avoid military conflict with the Soviet Union, which had threatened the British, French, and Israelis if they did not withdraw, the Americans declined. In refusing support, the United States struck an anti-imperialist posture for developing nations whose economic and political partnership it sought—unlike its response in Asia. American opposition made the British back down from what one British diplomat called "a squalid and most humiliating episode." Nasser's triumph inspired confidence that the Middle East could confront the West and win.

New Nations in Africa

In sub-Saharan Africa, nationalist leaders roused their people to challenge Europeans' increasing demand for resources and labor, which resulted in poverty for African peoples. "The European Merchant is my shepherd, and I am in want," went one African version of the Twenty-third Psalm. Disrupted in their traditional agricultural patterns, many Africans flocked to shantytowns in cities during the war, where they kept themselves alive through scavenging, craft work, and menial labor for whites. Protests multiplied, and underemployed city dwellers formed one power base for politicians committed to decolonization. Ironically, the ethnic groups fostered by the imperialist powers constituted another.

Already in 1945, delegates to the sixth Pan-African Congress had declared that "if the Western world is still determined to rule mankind by force, then Africans, as a last resort, may have to use force to achieve freedom." Kwame Nkrumah led the diverse inhabitants of the relatively prosperous, British-controlled West African Gold Coast in passive resistance, in imitation of Gandhian methods. After years of arresting and jailing the protesters, the British withdrew, allowing the state of Ghana to come into being in 1957. Nigeria, the most populous African region, became independent in 1960 after the leaders of its many regional groups and political organizations reached agreement on a federal-style government. In these and other African states where the population was mostly black, independence came less violently than in mixed-race territory (Map 28.5).

The eastern coast and southern and central areas of Africa had numerous European settlers, who violently resisted independence movements. In British East Africa, where white settlers ruled in splendor and where blacks lacked both land and economic opportunity, violence erupted in the 1950s. African men, almost all of whom had assisted the British as soldiers in World War II, formed rebel groups named the Land Freedom Army but known as Mau Mau. They maintained their solidarity through ceremonies, oaths, and rigid discipline. With women serving as provisioners, messengers, and weapon stealers, Mau Mau bands formed from the Kikuyu ethnic group tried to re-

cover land from whites. In 1964, after the British had slaughtered some ten to fifteen thousand Kikuyus, Kenya gained formal independence. In 1948, the Afrikaners took control of the South African government and formalized white supremacism in the brutal system of *apartheid* ("apartness"), which would last until the 1990s. Among the most urbanized and wealthiest of African nations, South Africa also had the most numerous Western-educated elites, many of whom formed the leadership of an ongoing and increasingly powerful resistance movement.

France—although eager to regain its great-power status after its humiliating defeat and occupation in World War II—easily granted certain demands for independence, such as those of Tunisia, Morocco, and West Africa, where there

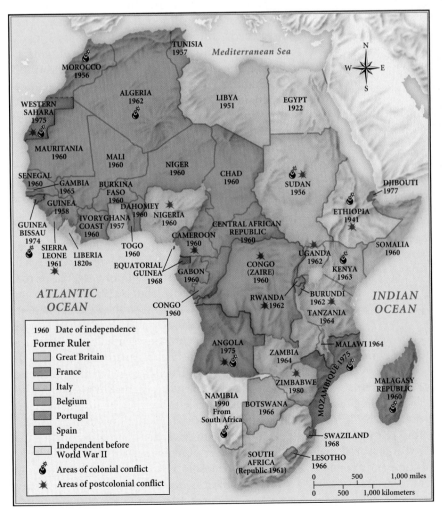

MAP 28.5 The Decolonization of Africa, 1951–1990
The liberation of Africa from European rule was an uneven process, sometimes occurring peacefully and at other times demanding armed struggle to drive out European settlers, governments, and armies. The difficult process of nation building following liberation involved setting up state institutions, including educational and other services. Creating national unity also took work, except where the struggle against colonialism had already brought people together.

Jomo Kenyatta, First President of the New Kenyan Nation

Jomo Kenyatta (1964–1978) had been educated in England and wrote Facing Mount Kenya, *a work that explained Kikuyu life as a distinct culture to Westerners. After a costly struggle that had resulted in his imprisonment by the British, Kenyatta became president of the new republic but closed down much political debate by outlawing opposition parties. His one-party government brought social calm, which made Kenya a good place for Western investments.*
© Bettman/CORBIS.

were fewer settlers, more limited economic stakes, and less military involvement. Elsewhere, French struggles against independence movements were costly, prolonged, and bloody. The ultimate test of the French empire came in Algeria. When Algerian nationalists rebelled against the restoration of French rule in the final days of World War II, the French army massacred tens of thousands of protesters. The liberation movement resurfaced as the Front for National Liberation in 1954. Those forces attacked European settlers and their Arab supporters

with ferocious intensity. Meanwhile the French dug in, sending more than 400,000 troops and fighting back savagely. Asked what would happen were France to grant Algeria independence without a fight, one general replied, "The army would rebel." Neither side fought according to the rules of warfare: the French tortured natives, while Algerian women, shielded by gender stereotypes, planted bombs in European clubs and cafés and carried weapons to assassination sites.

Shedding its colonies at a rapid rate, France drew the line at Algeria. "The loss of Algeria," warned one statesman, "would be an unprecedented national disaster." Although many agreed, the Algerian War also threatened French social stability, as protests in Paris greeted reports of the army's barbarous practices. French settlers in Algeria and the military met the antiwar movement with terrorism against citizens in France. They threatened coups, set off bombs, assassinated politicians, and promoted other kinds of violence in the name of *Algérie Française* (French Algeria).

France's Fourth Republic collapsed over Algeria. In 1958, Charles de Gaulle, supported by the army and approved by the Chamber of Deputies, came back to power. In return for leading France out of its Algerian quagmire, de Gaulle demanded the creation of a new republican government, one with a strong president who chose the prime minister and could exercise emergency power. From the strengthened presidential office of the Fifth Republic, de Gaulle led the French toward a new, postcolonial identity by paradoxically invoking images of French grandeur and the legacy of French culture as he planned to decolonize Algeria. Terrorism against him escalated, but by 1962 de Gaulle had negotiated independence with the Algerian nationalists. Hundreds of thousands of *pieds noirs* ("black feet"), as the French condescendingly called Europeans in Algeria, as well as their Arab supporters fled to France. The Dutch and Belgian empires also disintegrated. Violent resistance to the reimposition of colonial rule led to the establishment of the large independent states of Indonesia and Zaire.

As Europe received immigrants from former colonies, heated discussions over race and the rights of citizenship in the postcolonial era began reshaping political ideas. In the context of these tumultuous changes, structures emerged in which the new states could operate on the world stage.

The United Nations convened for the first time in 1945, and one notable change ensured it a greater chance of success than the League of Nations: both the United States and the Soviet Union were active members from the outset. The charter of the UN outlined a collective global authority that would adjudicate conflicts, provide military protection if any members were threatened by aggression, and oversee the fate of nonindependent states. Although the UN was a forum for cold war jockeying, notably in the transformation of the Belgian Congo into Zaire, many newly independent nations joined the General Assembly and eventually gained increasing global influence. In 1955, Achmed Sukarno, who succeeded in wrenching Indonesian independence from the Dutch, sponsored the Bandung Convention of nonaligned nations to set a common policy for achieving modernization and facing the major powers. Both the UN and the meetings of emerging nations began shifting global issues away from those of the Western powers. North-south inequities, ethnicity and human rights, and "postcolonialism" nudged their way into public consciousness alongside the "proletariat" and the fate of the West in the atomic age.

❖ Cultural Life on the Brink of Nuclear War

Both the Holocaust and the cold war shaped postwar leisure and political culture, as the responsibility for Nazism, the cause of ethnic and racial justice, and the merits of the two superpowers set people against one another. There was a veneer of normalcy in the baby boom and the apparent restoration of gender roles, and growing affluence sometimes papered over both the horrors of the Holocaust and the omnipresent threat of nuclear annihilation. Yet this was a time of intense self-scrutiny as Europeans debated decolonization and the Americanization that seemed to accompany the influx of U.S. dollars, consumer goods, and cultural media. Behind the prosperity, the cold war menaced. In October 1962, the world held its breath while the leaders of the Soviet Union and the United States provoked the real possibility of nuclear conflagration over the issue of missiles on the island of Cuba.

Restoring "Western" Values

After the depravity and inhumanity of Nazism, cultural currents in Europe and the United States reemphasized universal values, spiritual renewal, and political choice. Some, like Billy Graham, saw the churches as central to the restoration of values through an active commitment to "re-Christianizing" Europe and the United States. Their success was only partial, however, as the trend toward a more secular culture continued. Thus, in the early postwar years people emphasized the triumph of a Western heritage, a Western civilization, and Western values over fascism, and they characterized the war as one "to defend civilization [from] a conspiracy against man." This definition of *West* often emphasized the heritage of Greece and Rome and the rise of national governments in England, France, and western Europe as they encountered "barbaric" forces, be these nomadic tribes or Nazi armies. The West was a flexible entity, including those who could be shown to have aimed for common standards of constitutional or representative government and "civilized" behavior. The first Western civilization textbooks had appeared in the United States late in the 1930s to document the superiority of Western culture, threatened by fascists and by nationalist movements in Asia and Africa. University courses in Western civilization flourished after the war to reaffirm those values. At the same time, the postwar renewal of humanitarianism pushed issues of cultural pluralism and human rights to the forefront of culture.

Holocaust and Resistance Literature. Memoirs of the death camps became compelling reading material. Rescued from the Third Reich in 1940, Nelly Sachs won the Nobel Prize in literature in 1966 for her poetry about the Holocaust. Anne Frank's *Diary of a Young Girl* (1947), the poignant record of a teenager hidden with her family in the back of an Amsterdam warehouse, was emblematic of the survival of Western values in the face of Nazi persecution. Confronted with the small miseries of daily life and the grand evils of Nazism, Anne never stopped believing that "people are really good at heart." Some continued to admire the Nazis, so the flood of memoirs was doubly important in revealing the grim truth. This literature called for a new commitment to tolerance and pluralism.

Histories of the resistance also tapped into the public's need for inspiration after an orgy of savagery. Governments erected permanent plaques at spots where resisters had been killed; their biographies filled magazines and bookstalls; organizations of resisters commemorated their role in winning the war. Although resistance efforts were publicized, discussion of collaboration with Nazis was tacitly forbidden. French filmmakers, for instance, avoided the subject for decades after the war for fear of reopening wounds. Many a politician with a Nazi past moved into the new cultural mainstream even as the stories of resistance took on mythical qualities.

Existential Philosophy. By the end of the 1940s, existential philosophy became the rage among the cultural elites and students and in universities. It explored the meaning (or lack of meaning) of human existence in a world where evil flourished. Two of its leaders, Albert Camus (1913–1960) and Jean-Paul Sartre (1905–1980), had written for the resistance during the war, although Nazi censors had also allowed the production of Sartre's plays. Taking their starting point from the German philosophers Friedrich Nietzsche (1844–1900) and Martin Heidegger (1889–1976), existentialists confronted the question of what "being" was about, given what they perceived as the absence of God and the breakdown of morality. Their answer was that "being," or existing, was not the automatic process either of God's creation or of birth into the natural world. One was not born with spiritual goodness in the image of a creator, but instead, through action and choice, one created an "authentic" existence. Camus's novels, such as *The Stranger* (1942) and *The Plague* (1947), dissected the evils of a corrupt political order and pondered human responsibility in such situations. Whereas Camus focused on mental attitudes and choices in the face of evil, Sartre's writings emphasized political activism. Sartre's idea of an activist existence validated resistance under totalitarianism. Despite the fact that they had never confronted the enormous problems of making choices while living under fascism, young people in the 1950s found existentialism compelling and made it the most fashionable philosophy of the day. A decade later the spirit of existentialism became part of the inspiration for

students who sought to reform society through political confrontation.

In 1949, Simone de Beauvoir (1908–1986), Sartre's lifetime companion, published the twentieth century's most important work on the condition of women, *The Second Sex*. Beauvoir believed that most women had failed to take the kind of action necessary to lead authentic lives. Instead they lived in the world of "necessity," devoting themselves exclusively to reproduction and motherhood. Failing to create an authentic self through considered action and accomplishment, they had become its opposite—an object or "Other." Moreover, instead of struggling to define themselves and assert their freedom, women passively accepted their own "Otherness" and lived as defined by men. In the 1960s, Beauvoir's theory would guide the women's movement beyond struggles for legal and political reform and underscore the powerful cultural and psychological components of women's experience.

Beauvoir's classic book was a smash hit, in large part because people thought Sartre had written it. Both were celebrities, for the intellectual world increasingly attracted media attention. The media spread the new commitment to humane values just as it had spread support for Nazism or for its wartime enemies. Photos in glossy magazines, a constant stream of articles in newspapers, and interviews on radio built a cohesive, enlightened sector of the public concerned with the death camp literature, stories of the resistance, or the latest trend in philosophy.

Race and Human Rights. While Europeans debated decolonization among peoples of color in Africa and Asia, intellectuals spawned new theories of what liberation would mean for decolonized peoples. Already the first half of the century had witnessed the rise of pan-Africanism and theories exploring the distinctness of black culture forced to breed in the context of colonial rule. But it was in the 1950s and 1960s that the immensely influential writing of Frantz Fanon (1925–1961), a black psychiatrist from the French colony of Martinique, began analyzing liberation movements. He called the mental functioning of the colonized person "traumatized" by the violence and the brutal imposition of a culture other than one's own as the only standard

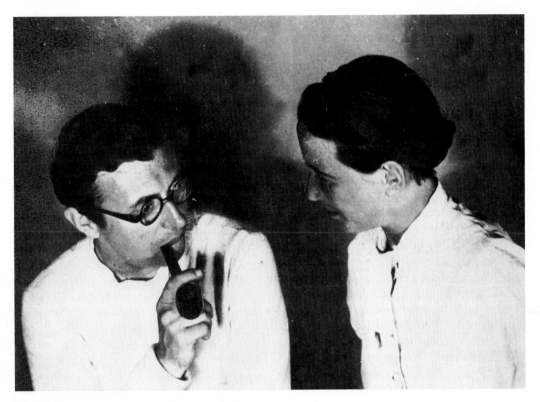

Jean-Paul Sartre and Simone de Beauvoir
The postwar period saw the rise of glossy, richly illustrated weekly magazines featuring news and
pop culture. The faces of even the most complex philosophers became well known to the public, while
their private lives intrigued readers. The public personae of these two existentialists, who were seen
to promote the revival of human values after the nightmare of fascism, hid the tortured relationship
Sartre and de Beauvoir actually had.
Editions Gallimard.

of value. Ruled by guns, the colonized person knew only violence and would thus naturally decolonize by means of violence. Translated into many languages, Fanon's *Black Skin, White Masks* (1952) and *The Wretched of the Earth* (1961) posed the question of how to "decolonize" one's mind.

Simone de Beauvoir had seen blacks in the United States as another example of an oppressed "Other," while African Americans had become only too aware of the cultural values common to both sides in the war: Nazis murdered those they considered of inferior "races" like Jews and blacks, while the United States dropped an atomic bomb on the Japanese people of color but not on the white race in Germany. In principle blacks had fought in the war to defeat the Nazi idea of white racial superiority. Thus, in the 1950s the commit-

ment to the civil rights cause embodied in such long-standing organizations as the National Association for the Advancement of Colored People (NAACP, founded 1909) intensified.

In 1954, the U.S. Supreme Court declared segregated education unconstitutional in *Brown* v. *Board of Education*, a case initiated by the NAACP. On December 1, 1955, in Montgomery, Alabama, Rosa Parks, an African American seamstress and part-time secretary for the local branch of the NAACP, boarded a bus and took the first available seat in the so-called white section at the front of the bus. When a white man found himself without a seat, the driver screamed at Parks, "Nigger, move back." Sitting in the front violated southern laws, which encompassed a host of inequitable, even brutal policies toward African Americans. Parks confronted that system through the studied practice of civil disobedience, and her action led to a boycott of public transportation that pushed the civil rights movement into the African American community as a whole.

The culture of rights and human values generated further organizing. Led by groups such as the Student Non-Violent Coordinating Committee (SNCC), the Southern Christian Leadership Conference (SCLC), and the NAACP, blacks and some white allies boycotted discriminatory businesses, "sat in" at segregated facilities, and registered black voters disfranchised by local regulations. Many talented leaders emerged, foremost among them Martin Luther King Jr. (1929–1968), a minister from Georgia whose oratorical power galvanized activists to Gandhian nonviolent resistance against brutal white retaliation, including bombings, arson, and murder. For a few years the postwar culture of nonviolence would shape the civil rights movement. Soon, however, the voices of postcolonial activists and thinkers like Fanon would merge with those of the African American civil rights movement to revolutionize thinking about race and rights.

Rising Consumerism and Shifting Gender Norms

Government spending on reconstruction, productivity, and welfare helped prevent the kind of social, political, and economic upheaval that had followed World War I. Nor did the same tensions prevail among men and women. A rising birthrate, bustling youth culture, and upsurge in consumerism edged out wartime behavior. Men returned from World War II much less frustrated than they had been in the 1920s, because of the decisive result of World War II. In England, for instance, where World War I veterans had wrecked some university classrooms and attacked working-women, faculty were surprised at how docilely young men returned to their studies after World War II.

Nonetheless the war affected men's roles and sense of themselves. Young men who had missed World War II adopted the rough, violent style of soldiers. The 1920s had seen the streets filled with illegal armies such as the German freikorps; in the

Zbigniew Cybulski, the Polish James Dean
Zbigniew Cybulski depicted a tortured young resistance fighter in Andrzej Wajda's film Ashes and Diamonds *(1958). On the last day of World War II Cybulski's character is to assassinate a Communist resistance leader, and his human dilemma around the act is set amidst the chaos in Poland at war's end. Like existentialist philosophers and other cinema directors at the time, Wajda captured the debate over human values and the interest in young heroes of the postwar era.*
Photofest.

1950s, roaming gangs merely posed as tough military types. Their delinquency did not necessarily involve actual crime but rather the swaggering control of urban space that occupying armies displayed. While Soviet youth admired aviator aces, elsewhere groups such as the "teddy boys" in England (named after their Edwardian style of dressing) and the gamberros in Spain took their cues from new forms of pop culture in music and film.

The leader of rock and roll style and substance was the American singer Elvis Presley. Sporting slicked-back hair and an aviator-style jacket, Presley bucked his hips and sang sexual lyrics to screaming and devoted fans. In a German nightclub late in the 1950s, members of a group of Elvis fans called the Quarrymen performed, fighting and yelling at one another as part of their show. They would soon become known as the Beatles. Rebellious young American film stars like James Dean in *Rebel without a Cause* and Marlon Brando in *The Wild One* created the beginnings of a conspicuous postwar youth culture.

The rebellious and rough masculine style appeared also in literature. In his autobiography explaining how he and Francis Crick had discovered the structure of the gene in 1953, James Watson portrayed himself as a fanatic bad boy. His book, *The Double Helix*, described how he had rifled people's desk drawers (among other dishonest acts) to become a scientific hero. Irish novelist and playwright Samuel Beckett's play *Waiting for Godot* (1952) has two tramps, perhaps like POWs, standing around talking nonstop while trusting that something—or someone—good will eventually come along. Beckett proposed that such hope was absurd. In the revival of West German literature, Heinrich Böll published *The Clown* (1963), a novel whose young hero takes to performing as a clown and begging in a railroad station. Böll protested that West Germany's postwar goal of respectability had allowed the resurgence of precisely those groups of people who had produced Nazism. Across the Atlantic, the American "Beat" poets, who looked dirty, bearded, and sometimes crazy, like prisoners or camp survivors, critiqued traditional ideals of the upright and rational male achiever.

Both high and low culture revealed that two horrendous world wars had weakened the Enlightenment view of men as rational, responsible breadwinners. The 1953 inaugural issue of the American magazine *Playboy* ushered in a widely imitated depiction of a changed male identity. *Playboy* differed from typical pornographic magazines: along with pictures of nude women, it featured serious articles, especially on the topic of masculinity. This segment of the media presented modern man as sexually aggressive and independent of dull domestic life—

just as he had been in the war. Breadwinning for a family only destroyed a man's freedom and sense of self. The notion of men's liberty had come to include not just political and economic rights but freedom of sexual expression; this definition would become increasingly integrated into political culture.

In contrast, Western society promoted a postwar model for women that differed from their experience of war as essential workers and heads of families in the absence of their men. Instead postwar women were made to symbolize the return to normalcy—a domestic, nonworking norm. Late in the 1940s, the fashion house of Christian Dior launched a clothing style called the "new look." It featured a pinched waist, tightly fitting bodices, and voluminous skirts. This restoration of the nineteenth-century female silhouette invited a renewal of clear gender roles. Women's magazines publicized the "new look" and urged a return to domesticity. Clad in crinolines, hats, gloves, and dainty shoes and reshaped by an array of constricting undergarments, "feminine" women portrayed the return to normalcy. Even in the hard-pressed Soviet Union, recipes for homemade face creams passed from woman to woman, and beauty parlors did a brisk business. New household products such as refrigerators and washing machines raised standards for women's accomplishment in the home by giving them the means to be "perfect" housewives.

However, "new look" propaganda did not mesh with reality. Dressmaking fabric was still being rationed in the late 1940s; even in the next decade women could not get enough of it to make voluminous skirts. In Europe, where people had barely enough to eat, the underwear needed for "new look" contours simply did not exist. Consumers had access only to standardized undergarments available with ration tickets. European women continued to work outside the home after the war; indeed, mature women and mothers were working more than ever before (Figure 28.2). The female workforce was going through a profound revolution as it gradually became less youthful and more populated by wives and mothers who would work outside the home all their lives. In the face of real women's long hours at work, heroines in Soviet fiction were still portrayed as ready to embrace a leisured version of femininity and maternal

The "New Look"
Immediately after the war, the French fashion industry swung into action to devise styles for the return to normal life. Cinched, even corseted waists and voluminous skirts suggested the nineteenth century rather than the depression and war years, when some women had started regularly wearing trousers. The highly restrictive femininity was also part of the cold war, as the leisured ideal demanded by the "new look" for middle-class Western women contrasted with the more practical styles in the Soviet Union, where women had to work to rebuild their devastated country.
Liaison Agency.

subservience: "I can't be the boss forever," one woman said as she encouraged her husband to resume his prewar authority. "I'll be having children." Despite being bombarded with images of nineteenth-century middle-class femininity, women in Europe and the United States continued working to support their families.

The advertising business presided over the creation of cultural messages as well as over the rise of a new consumerism that accompanied recovery. Guided by marketing experts, western Europeans were imitating Americans, by driving some forty million motorized vehicles, including motorbikes, cars, buses, and trucks. The demand for cars made the automobile industry a leading economic sector. The number of radios in homes grew steadily—for example, by 10 percent a year in Italy between 1945 and 1950—and the 1950s marked a high tide of radio influence. The development of television in the 1920s and 1930s was interrupted by the war, but peacetime saw its rapid spread in the United States, which had twenty million sets by 1953. In Britain only 20 percent of the population owned TVs in the early 1950s, but 75 percent of all households owned one by 1961. Britain and the United States, however, were the great exceptions: the French had only sixty thousand sets in the mid-1950s; the Italians, only five thousand. Only in the 1960s did television become an important consumer item for most Europeans. In the 1950s, radio was still king.

The Culture of Cold War

Radio was at the center of the cold war. As superpower rivalry heated up, radio's propaganda function came to the fore. During the late 1940s and early 1950s, the Voice of America, with its main studio in Washington, D.C., broadcast in thirty-eight languages from one hundred transmitters and provided an alternative source of news for people in eastern Europe. The Soviet counterpart broadcast in Russian around the clock but initially spent much of its wattage jamming U.S. programming. Russian programs stressed a uniform Communist culture and values; the United States by contrast, emphasized diverse programming and promoted debate about current affairs.

Its issues and events conveyed by radio and other media, the cold war acquired a far-reaching

	Member Countries of Council of Mutual Economic Assistance[1]		Member Countries of European Economic Community[2]	
	1950	1960	1950	1960
Female as % of total population	54.9	53.9	51.8	51.6
Female labor force as % of total labor force	48.5	48.7	31.1	31.4
Distribution of female labor force (%):				
Agriculture	63.3	50.0	26.1	16.8
Industry	16.9	22.6	29.3	31.3
Services	19.8	27.4	44.6	51.9

[1] Albania, Bulgaria, Czechoslovakia, East Germany, Hungary, Poland, Romania, and USSR

[2] Belgium, Denmark, France, West Germany, Ireland, Italy, Luxembourg, Netherlands, and United Kingdom

FIGURE 28.2 Women in the Workforce, 1950–1960

In contrast to the situation after World War I, women did not leave the workforce in great numbers after World War II. In fact, Europe faced labor shortages. In countries of the Soviet bloc, women vastly outnumbered men because so many men had died in the war, and the task of rebuilding demanded every available worker. In Western Europe, women's workforce participation was lower, and countries like West Germany tried to keep women out of the labor pool to distinguish themselves from the Communist bloc. Note the increase in women's service-sector employment in just one decade.

World Employment 1996–1997: National Policies in a Global Context (Geneva: International Labour Office, 1996), 7.

emotional impact. The news featured reports about nuclear testing, military buildups, and hostile diplomatic incidents. The public heard tests of emergency power facilities that sent them scurrying for cover; in school, children rehearsed for nuclear war, and families built bomb shelters in their backyards. Reports of Soviet and American leaders facing one another down became part of everyday life. Amidst constant stories of the possibility of nuclear annihilation, mathematician and philosopher Bertrand Russell reported living daily in "confused agitation."

Popular culture centered on the cold war. Books like George Orwell's *1984* (1949) were claimed by ideologues on both sides as vindicating their beliefs. Ray Bradbury's popular *Fahrenheit 451* (1953), whose title indicated the temperature at which books would burn, condemned cold war

curtailment of intellectual freedom. In the USSR, official writers churned out spy stories, and espionage novels topped best-seller lists in the West. *Casino Royale* (1953) by the British author Ian Fleming introduced James Bond, who survived tests of wit and physical prowess at the hands of Communist and other political villains. Traveling to exotic places, Agent 007 brilliantly improvised with sophisticated, futuristic weaponry provided by government scientists—themselves employed in the cold war. Soviet pilots would not take off for flights when the work of Yulian Simyonov, the Russian counterpart of Ian Fleming, was playing on radio or television.

Consumer culture as a whole came under the cold war banner, as people debated the "Americanization" they saw taking place in Europe. While many Europeans were proponents of American

Bomb Shelter

Americans expressed their fear of nuclear annihilation by building tens of thousands of individual bomb shelters. Stocked with several months' supply of canned food and other goods, the shelters were to protect a family from the nuclear blast itself and from the disorder that might follow nuclear war. The government also prepared shelters to shield top officials and to ensure the continuation of civil society despite vast casualties and massive destruction.
Bettman/Corbis.

business practices, the Communist Party in France led a successful campaign to ban Coca-Cola for a time in the 1950s. A more widespread strategy involved producing elite consumer items. The French *new wave* cinema developed in reaction to mass-market Hollywood films. Directors like François Truffaut and Jean-Luc Godard focused on the maker, or *auteur*, of a film to contrast their work with movies concocted by anonymous studio executives. The *auteur* produced new wave films much as an author created a literary work. In addition, new wave directors introduced the history of film into their work in the form of film themes and symbols from the earliest days of film. In literature, French writers pioneered the *new novel* as an antidote to best-sellers that pumped up the U.S.-style mass market. Although the first in this genre, Nathalie Sarraute's *Tropismes,* was written in 1939,

most new novels appeared in the 1950s and thereafter. Sarraute wrote in terms of human "gestures," "subconversations," and fleeting glimpses of the interior of the human psyche.

Both sides tried to win the war by pouring vast sums of money into culture, though the United States did it by secretly channeling government money into foundations to promote U.S. symphonies, award fellowships to artists and writers, and start popular magazines around the world. As leadership of the art world passed to the United States, art became part of the cold war. *Abstract expressionism,* practiced by American artists such as Jackson Pollock, produced abstract works by dripping, spattering, and pouring paint in contrast to abstract works that still had elements of realism, such as those of Picasso. Abstract expressionists spoke of the importance of the artist's self-discovery, spiritual growth, and sensations in the process of painting. "If I stretch my arms next to the rest of myself and wonder where my fingers are, that is all the space I need as a painter," commented Dutch-born Willem de Kooning on his relationship with his canvas. Said to exemplify Western "freedom," such painters were given shows in Europe and awarded commissions at the direction of U.S. government agencies. Shrouded in a culture of secrecy and deception, information about both sides in the cold war is only now emerging from archives and memoirs.

The USSR openly promoted Communist culture around the world. When a show of abstract art opened in the Soviet Union, Khrushchev yelled

Mark Rothko, *Light Red over Black* (1957)
Lithuanian-born Mark Rothko spread large, luminous fields of color across his canvases in an attempt to capture universal spiritual values. Usually his paintings contained only two or three of these fields, prompting the viewer to experience long periods of contemplation. Rothko was part of a school of artists that aimed in the 1950s to reach enduring truths with such primal or "primitive" forms.
Tate Gallery, London/Art Resource, NY.

IMPORTANT DATES

1945	Cold war begins
1947	India and Pakistan win independence from Britain
1948	State of Israel established
1949	Mao Zedong leads Communist revolution in China; Simone de Beauvoir publishes *The Second Sex*
1950	Korean War begins
1953	Stalin dies; Korean War ends
1954	*Brown* v. *Board of Education* prohibits segregated schools in the United States; Vietnamese forces defeat the French at Dien Bien Phu
1956	Egyptian leader General Abdel Nasser nationalizes the Suez Canal; uprising in Hungary against USSR
1957	Boris Pasternak publishes *Doctor Zhivago*; USSR launches *Sputnik*
1958	Fifth Republic begins in France
1962	The United States and USSR face off in the Cuban missile crisis

that it was "dog shit." Pro-Soviet critics in western Europe saw U.S.-style abstract art as "an infantile sickness" and supported official socialist realist art with "human content," showing the condition of the workers and the oppressed races in the United States. In Italy, the *neorealist* technique was developed by filmmakers such as Roberto Rossellini in *Open City* (1945) and Vittorio De Sica in *The Bicycle Thief* (1948). Such works challenged Hollywood-style sets and costumes by using ordinary characters living in devastated, impoverished cities. By depicting stark conditions, neorealist directors conveyed their distance both from middle-class prosperity and from fascist bombast. "We are in rags? Let's show everyone our rags," said one Italian director. Values of the Communist resistance resonated not only in the post-fascist world but in the escalating climate of bipolarity. Reacting to the Soviet publicity of racial oppression in the United States, U.S. agents made certain that most films had African Americans as extras. Seen or unseen, the cold war entered the most unsuspected aspects of cultural life.

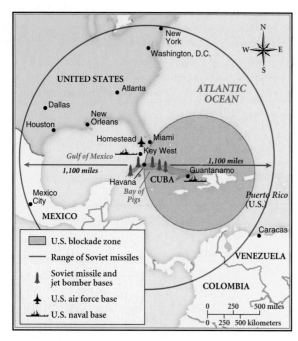

MAP 28.6 The Cuban Missile Crisis, 1962

Just off the coast of the southeastern United States, Cuba posed a threat to North American security once the Soviet Union began stocking the island with missiles. The United States reacted vigorously, insisting on the dismantling of missile sites and an end to the Soviets' supplying Cuba with further weaponry. Although his generals were prepared for nuclear war with the Soviet Union, President Kennedy refused to take this step despite his cold war stance on many other issues. Soviet Premier Khrushchev similarly backed down from a military confrontation.

Kennedy, Khrushchev, and the Atomic Brink

It was in this pervasive climate of cold war that John Fitzgerald Kennedy (1917–1963) became U.S. president in 1960. Kennedy represented American affluence and youth but also the nation's commitment to cold war. Kennedy's media advisers and ghostwriters recognized how perfect a match their articulate, good-looking president was to the power of television. A war hero and early fan of the fictional cold war spy James Bond, Kennedy intensified the arms race and escalated the cold war. In 1959, a revolution in Cuba had brought to power Fidel Castro, who allied his government with the Soviet Union. In the spring of 1961, Kennedy, assured by the Central Intelligence Agency (CIA) of success, launched an invasion of Cuba at the Bay of

Pigs to overthrow Castro. The invasion failed miserably and humiliated the United States. A few months later Kennedy had a chilling meeting with Khrushchev in Vienna, at which the Soviet leader brandished the specter of nuclear holocaust over the continuing U.S. presence in Berlin.

In the summer of 1961, East German workers, supervised by police and the army, stacked bales of barbed wire across miles of the city's east–west border to begin construction of the Berlin Wall. The divided city had served as an escape route by which some three million people had fled to the West. As a concrete wall replaced the barbed wire, people resorted to jumping through apartment windows to freedom and, when the windows were blocked, jumping from roofs. Kennedy responded at home with a call for more weapons and an enhanced civil defense program. In October 1962, matters came to a head when the CIA reported the installation of Soviet medium-range missiles in Cuba (Map 28.6). Kennedy now responded forcefully, calling for a blockade of ships headed for Cuba and threatening nuclear war if the missiles were not removed. For several days the world stood on the brink of nuclear disaster. Then, between October 25 and 27, Khrushchev and Kennedy negotiated an end to the crisis. The Soviets promised to remove the missile installations. Kennedy spent the remainder of his short life working to improve nuclear diplomacy; Khrushchev did the same. The two leaders, who had looked deeply into the nuclear future, clearly feared what they saw.

Conclusion

World War II began the atomic age and transformed international power politics. Two superpowers, the Soviet Union and the United States, each controlling atomic arsenals, replaced the former

MAPPING THE WEST The Cold War World, c. 1960 ▶

Superpower rivalry between the United States and the Soviet Union resulted in the division of much of the industrial world into cold war alliances. Simultaneously the superpowers vied for the allegiance of the newly decolonized countries of Asia and Africa by providing military, economic, and technological assistance. Wars such as those in Vietnam and Korea were also products of the cold war.

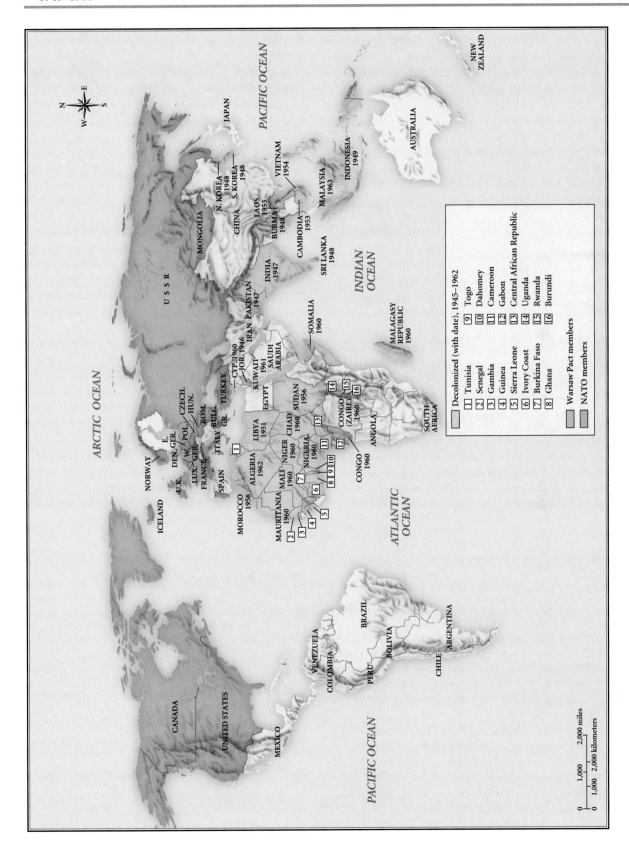

European leadership and engaged in a menacing cold war. The cold war saturated everyday life, giving birth to cold war religion in the preachings of the Reverend Billy Graham and to a secular culture of bomb shelters, spies, and witch-hunts. The postwar reconstruction of Europe created a cold war division into an Eastern bloc dominated by the Soviets and a freer West mostly allied with the United States.

Yet both halves of Europe recovered almost miraculously. The east, where wartime devastation was greatest, experienced less prosperity and achieved recovery at greater human cost than did western Europe. Wartime technology served as the basis for new consumer goods and improved health. Western Europe formed a successful Common Market that would become the foundation for the trend toward European unity. Yet as a result of the war Germany recovered as two countries, not one, and the former European powers shed their colonies. Newly independent nations emerged in Asia and Africa, opening the possibility for a more equitable distribution of global power.

As the West as a whole grew in prosperity, its cultural life focused on eradicating the evils of Nazism and on surviving the atomic rivalry of the superpowers. In the midst of consumerism and a heated cold war culture, many came to wonder whether cold war was really worth the threat of nuclear annihilation.

Suggested References

World Politics Transformed

In the past decade, the opening of Soviet archives and closer research in American records have allowed for more informed views of the diplomacy and politics of the cold war in Europe and around the world. Although few defend Stalin, we now benefit from balanced assessments of superpower rivalry. Two Web sites contain biographies of the main players, time lines, and miscellaneous details of cold war events.

Cold war: http://library.thinkquest.org/10826.mainpage .htm; http://history.acusd.edu/gen/20th/coldwar0.html.

Cronin, James. *The World the Cold War Made: Order, Chaos, and the Return of History.* 1996.

Eisenberg, Carolyn Woods. *Drawing the Line: The American Decision to Divide Germany, 1944–1949.* 1996.

Gaddis, John. *We Now Know: Rethinking Cold War History.* 1997.

Hogan, Michael J. *A Cross of Iron: Harry S Truman and the Origins of the National Security State, 1945–1954.* 1998.

*Pasternak, Boris. *Doctor Zhivago.* 1958.

Vadney, T. E. *The World Since 1945.* 1992.

Zubkova, Elena. *Russia after the War: Hopes, Illusions, and Disappointments, 1945–1957.* 1998.

Zubok, Vladislav, and Constantine Pleshakov. *Inside the Kremlin's Cold War: From Stalin to Khrushchev.* 1996.

The Political and Economic Recovery of Europe

Though painstaking and complex, recovery in its material and political forms yielded a distinctly new Europe whose characteristics historians are still uncovering. Because of the opening of the archives, historical attention has focused on charting Soviet occupation, recovery, and Communist takeover.

Herf, Jeffrey. *Divided Memory: The Nazi Past in the Two Germanies.* 1997.

Kenney, Padraic. *Rebuilding Poland: Workers and Communists, 1945–1950.* 1997.

Marrus, Michael. *The Unwanted: European Refugees in the Twentieth Century.* 1985.

Medvedev, Roy. *Khrushchev.* 1983.

Moeller, Robert, ed. *West Germany under Construction: Politics, Society, and Culture in the Adenauer Era.* 1997.

Naimark, Norman M. *The Russians in Germany: A History of the Russian Zone of Occupation, 1945–1949.* 1995.

Pinder, John. *European Community: The Building of a Union.* 1991.

Decolonization in a Cold War Climate

Novelists, philosophers, and historians debate the impact and issues of decolonization. Powerful evocations of the brutality of the process appear most often in novels such as *Cracking India*, recently made into the film *Earth*.

Brown, L. Carl. *International Politics and the Middle East.* 1984.

Dunbabin, J. P. D. *The Post-Imperial Age: The Great Powers and the Wider World.* 1994.

*Fanon, Frantz. *The Wretched of the Earth.* 1961.

Flaghan, Simha. *The Birth of Israel: Myths and Realities.* 1987.

Hargreaves, J. D. *Decolonization in Africa.* 1996.

*Primary source.

McIntyre, W. David. *British Decolonization, 1946–1997: When, Why, and How Did the British Empire Fall?* 1999.

*Sidhwa, Bapsi. *Cracking India: A Novel.* 1992.

Cultural Life on the Brink of Nuclear War

Cold war culture, including the growth of consumerism, make the 1950s a fertile field for research, especially as new sources become available. Historians like Saunders have focused on governments' direction of high culture to the point that some artists and writers were made "stars" because of government intervention.

*Beauvoir, Simone de. *The Mandarins.* 1956.

Boyer, Paul. *By the Bomb's Early Light: American Thought and Culture at the Dawn of the Atomic Age.* 1985.

Cohen-Solal, Annie. *Sartre.* 1987.

Heineman, Elizabeth D. *What Difference Does a Husband Make? Women and Marital Status in Nazi and Postwar Germany.* 1999.

Kuisel, Richard. *Seducing the French: The Dilemma of Americanization.* 1993.

Lapidus, Gail. *Women in Soviet Society: Equality, Development, and Social Change.* 1978.

McDowell, Colin. *Forties Fashion and the New Look.* 1997.

Marcus, Milicent. *Italian Film in the Light of Neorealism.* 1986.

Marling, Karal Ann. *As Seen on TV: The Visual Culture of Everyday Life in the 1950s.* 1994.

Saunders, Frances Stonor. *Who Paid the Piper?* 1999.

Swann, Abram de. *In Care of the State: Health Care, Education, and Welfare in Europe and the United States in the Modern Era.* 1988.

Challenges to the Postindustrial West

1960–1980

IN JANUARY 1969, JAN PALACH, a twenty-one-year-old philosophy student, drove to a main square in Prague, doused his body with gasoline, and set himself ablaze. In his coat—deliberately put to one side—was a paper demanding an end to Soviet-style repression in Czechoslovakia. It promised more such suicides unless the government lifted state censorship. The manifesto was signed: "Torch No. 1." Across a stunned nation black flags were flown, close to a million people flocked to Palach's funeral, and shrines to his memory seemed to spring up overnight. For the next months, as repression continued, more Czech youth followed Palach's grim example and became torches for freedom.

In an age of conspicuous technological growth, Jan Palach's self-immolation was a primal and horrifying scene. It was part of a massive uprising of youth, women, minorities, and many others in the 1960s and 1970s against repression, war, poverty, inequality, and technology itself. From Czechoslovakia to the United States and around the world, protests arose against the way in which industrial nations in general and the superpowers in particular were directing society.

Political repression outraged these activists, and they objected to the human consequences of technology's dizzying pace. Technological advances, reformers believed, had given enormous power to a handful of engineers, financiers, managers, and bureaucrats—the new (but unelected) leaders of a "postindustrial society." The term *postindustrial* indicated the emergence of the service sector—including finance, engineering, and

Shrine to Jan Palach
Jan Palach was a martyr to the cause of an independent Czechoslovakia, free to pursue a non-Soviet destiny. His self-immolation on behalf of that cause roused the nation. As make-shift shrines sprang up and multiplied throughout the 1970s and 1980s, they served as common rallying points that ultimately contributed to the overthrow of Communist rule.
© Mark Garanger/Corbis.

1960	1964	1968	1972	1976	1980

Politics and War

◆ Test-ban treaty; assassination of U.S. president Kennedy

◆ Spread of political terrorism; growth of black power, environmental, gay rights, pacifist, and feminist movements

◆ Nikita Khrushchev ousted in the USSR; U.S. Civil Rights Act

◆ SALT I signed   ◆ Helsinki accords

◆ Willy Brandt becomes West German foreign minister and develops Ostpolitik

◆ Americans taken hostage in Iran

◆ Revolution in Czechoslovakia; uprisings throughout Europe and the United States; Martin Luther King Jr. assassinated

◆ Treaty ending war in Vietnam; Yom Kippur War

Society and Economy

◆ Emergence of multinational corporations; postindustrial society and economy in West

◆ OPEC raises price of oil and imposes oil embargo in the West

◆ Migration from formerly colonized areas into the West; further decline in birthrate, rising rates of divorce, new family patterns; growth of Japanese economy

◆ Launch of *Intelsat*

◆ First test-tube baby born

◆ First successful human heart transplant   ◆ Miniaturization of computer

Culture, Religion, and Intellectual Life

◆ English rock group the Beatles lead the way toward a new mass youth culture

◆ Spread of TV culture in Europe; construction of new universities

◆ Forum on "pop art" in New York City   ◆ U.S. astronauts walk on the moon; Sony produces first affordable color VCR

◆ Vatican II   ◆ Christa Wolf, *Divided Heaven*   ◆ Aleksandr Solzhenitsyn, *Gulag Archipelago*

health care—as the dominant force in the economy in the West, replacing heavy industry. Many of the protesters were being educated to enter this service elite. As critics, however, they saw conformity, mindlessness, and bondage resulting from work in which the majority of people used neither mental nor physical skill but in many cases merely watched over an ever-growing number of machines. Protest in these postindustrial decades aimed at recovering human power and control.

While reformers questioned the values of technological society, whole nations challenged the superpowers' monopoly of international power. An agonizing war in Vietnam sapped the will and resources of the United States, and China confronted the Soviet Union with increasing belligerence and confidence. The oil-producing states of the Middle East formed a cartel and reduced the flow of oil to the leading industrial nations in the 1970s. The resulting price increases turned a slowdown in the postwar economy into a recession. Other third-world countries resorted not to economic leverage but to terrorism to achieve their ends; some countries deployed both. Even the wealth, military might, and technological leadership of the superpowers could not guarantee that they would always emerge victorious in this age of increasingly global competition. Nor during these decades could the superpowers prevent the erosion of their legitimacy—an erosion often brought on by the individual acts of citizens, like the human torches. In their economies, societies, and international and domestic politics, the superpowers faced challenges at virtually every turn.

❖ The Technology Revolution

Three decades after World War II, continuing technological advances steadily boosted prosperity and changed daily life in industrial countries. In Europe and the United States, people awoke to instantaneous radio and television news, worked with computers, and used revolutionary contraceptives to control reproduction. Satellites orbiting the earth reported weather conditions, relayed telephone signals, and collected military intelligence. Smaller gadgets—electric popcorn poppers, portable radios and tape players, automatic garage door openers—made life more pleasant. The reliance of humans on machines led one scientist and philosopher, Donna Haraway, to insist that people were no longer self-sufficient individuals, but rather *cyborgs*—that is, humans who needed machines to sustain ordinary life processes. However, as with the invention of textile machinery and the railroads in the eighteenth and nineteenth centuries, the full range of social implications would not take shape all at once.

The Information Age

Information technology catalyzed social change in these postindustrial decades just as innovations in textile making and the spread of railroads had in the nineteenth century. Some commentators have suggested that the development of information technology was even more revolutionary because of its

potential for conveying knowledge, culture, and politics globally. Mass journalism, film, and radio had begun to forge a more homogeneous society based on shared information and images in the first half of the twentieth century; in the last third of the century, television, computers, and telecommunications made information more accessible and, some critics said, culture more standardized. Politics and the economy felt the impact of information technology as well.

The Spread of Television Culture. Americans embraced television in the 1950s; following the postwar recovery, it was Europe's turn. Between the mid-1950s and the mid-1970s, Europeans rapidly adopted television as a major entertainment and communications medium. In 1954, one percent of French households had television; in 1964, nearly 40 percent did; and by 1974, almost 80 percent. With the average viewer tuning in about four and a half hours a day, the audience for newspapers and theater declined. "We devote more . . . hours per year to television than [to] any other single artifact," one sociologist commented in 1969. Virtually every Western home boasted a TV set. As with radio, European governments funded television broadcasting with tax dollars and controlled TV programming to avoid what they perceived as the substandard fare offered by American commercial TV; instead they featured drama, ballet, concerts, variety shows, and news. Governments believed this new medium should be used to preserve the humanist tradition by presenting viewers with "choice," as one British official put it, "the widest possible range of subjects treating the entire field and all the variety of the human conscience and experience." Thus the welfare state, in Europe at least, assumed a new obligation to fill its citizens' leisure time—and also gained more power to shape daily life.

With the emergence of communications satellites and video recorders in the 1960s, statesponsored television encountered competition. Satellite technology allowed for the transmission of sports broadcasts and other programming to a worldwide audience. Feature films on videotape became readily available to television stations (although not yet to individuals) and competed with made-for-television movies and other programs. European governments continued to produce high-quality television, but they often found themselves outpaced by private pay stations that either churned out American-style sitcoms or bought American comedies and dubbed in the native language. The competition increased in 1969 when the Sony Corporation introduced the first affordable color videocassette recorder to the consumer market. What statesmen and intellectuals considered the junk programming of the United States—soap operas, game shows, sitcoms—amused a vast Western audience because it dealt with the joys, sorrows, tensions, and aspirations of daily life. Critics charged that both state-sponsored and commercial television avoided extremes to keep sponsors happy, instead spoon-feeding audiences only "official" or "moderate" opinions. They complained that although TV provided more information than had ever been available before, the resulting shared culture represented the lowest common denominator.

Soviet-bloc television also exercised a powerful, widespread cultural influence. Even in one rural area of the Soviet Union, 44 percent of the inhabitants watched television every day in the late 1970s; another 27 percent tuned in every three or four days; others continued to prefer radio. By the end of the 1970s, Soviet announcers were broadcasting government-approved news to some thirty million TV sets in both rural and urban areas, uniting a far-flung population. Educational programming also united the population of the USSR by broadcasting shows designed to advance Soviet culture. At the same time, with travel impossible or forbidden to many, shows about foreign lands were among the most popular—as were postcards from these lands, which became household decorations.

Governments used the media not only to disperse culture but also to achieve political ends. Heads of state could usually preempt regular programming. In the 1960s, French president Charles de Gaulle addressed his fellow citizens frequently, employing the grandiose gestures of an imperial ruler to stir patriotism. As electoral success increasingly depended on cultivating a successful media image, political staffs came to rely on media experts as much as they did policy experts. To ensure political neutrality in West Germany, an official committee regularly monitored state television announcers, watching for subtle signs of bias. Nonetheless, mere coverage on television news made national politics an ever-larger presence in daily life.

The Computer Age Opens. Just as revolutionary as television was the computer, which reshaped work in science, defense, and ultimately industry. Computers had evolved dramatically since the first electronic computer, Colossus, which the British used in 1943 to decode Nazi military and diplomatic messages. Awesome in its day, Colossus was primitive by later standards—gigantic, slow, able only to decode, and so noisy that it sounded like "a roomful of [people] knitting away with steel needles," in the words of one Western observer. With growing use in civilian industry and business after the war, computing machines shrank from the size of a

Venice Skyline

Television swept Europe in the 1960s and 1970s, increasingly uniting people by the daily news, theater, films, and game shows. Satellite transmission allowed programming to cross national boundaries, further welding peoples and cultures of the Common Market. In a divided Germany, the exchange of programming bridged even the Berlin Wall and was an early contributor to the erosion of cold war divisions. Tom Bross/Stock Boston.

gymnasium in the 1940s to that of a small desk in the late 1970s. By the mid-1980s they would be no larger than an attaché case and fantastically more powerful than Colossus.

The expanding capabilities and tumbling prices of computers depended on the development of increasingly sophisticated digital electronic circuitry implanted on tiny silicon chips, which replaced the clumsy radio tubes used in 1940s and 1950s computers. Within a few decades the computer could perform hundreds of millions of operations per second and even respond to sound. The price of the integrated circuit at the heart of computer technology would eventually fall to less than a dollar; as a result, businesses and households would gain access to enormous amounts of information and computing ability at a reasonable cost. Commentators throughout the West spoke of an information revolution.

Computers changed the pace and patterns of work not only by speeding up and easing tasks but also by performing many operations that workers had once done themselves. In garment making, for example, experienced workers no longer painstakingly figured out how to arrange patterns on cloth for maximum efficiency and economy. Instead a computer specified instructions for the optimal positioning of pattern pieces, and trained workers, usually women, followed the machine's directions. By the end of the 1970s, the miniaturization of the computer had made possible a renewal of the eighteenth-century "cottage industry." As in earlier times, people could work in the physical isolation of their homes but be connected to a central mainframe. Some companies were even using electronic mail among employees in the late 1970s.

Did computers transform society for the better? Whereas the Industrial Revolution had seen physical power replaced by machine capabilities, the information revolution witnessed brainpower augmented by computer technology. Many believed computers would profoundly expand mental life, providing, in the words of one scientist, "boundless opportunities . . . to resolve the puzzles of cosmology, of life, and of the society of man." Others maintained that computers programmed people, reducing human capacity for inventiveness, problem solving, and initiative. As the 1970s closed, such predictions were still untested as this information revolution moved toward a more dramatic unfolding in the 1980s and 1990s.

The Space Age

The Space Age
1957 Soviet Union launches the first artificial satellite, *Sputnik*
1961 Soviet cosmonaut Yuri Gagarin orbits the earth; capsule carrying Alan Shepard Jr. makes first U.S. suborbital flight
1965 United States launches first commercial communications satellite, *Intelsat I*
1969 United States astronauts Neil Armstrong and Edwin Aldrin walk on moon's surface
1970s–present Soviet Union and United States individually and in collaboration with various countries perform space station experiments, lunar probes, and other scientific experiments
1971 Soviet Union attempts unsuccessfully to put *Salyut 1*, a space station, into orbit
1973 United States puts *Skylab*, an experimental space station, into orbit
1976 *Viking* spacecraft explores Mars
1979–1986 Spacecraft *Voyager* makes successful flybys of Jupiter, Saturn, and Uranus

The Space Age

When the Soviets launched the satellite *Sputnik* in 1957, they ignited competition with the United States that was quickly labeled the "space race." Although President Eisenhower had little interest in what he considered merely an expensive attempt to gain global status, his successor, John F. Kennedy, became obsessed by the idea of "beating" the Soviets in space. He proclaimed it an American goal to put a man on the moon by the end of the 1960s. Throughout the decade, increasingly complex space flights tested humans' ability to survive the process of space exploration, including weightlessness. Astronauts walked in space, endured weeks (and, later, months) in orbit, repaired malfunctioning equipment, docked with other craft, fixed satellites, and carried out experiments for the military and private industry. Meanwhile a series of unmanned rockets filled the earth's gravitational sphere with weather, television, intelligence, and other communications satellites.

In July 1969, a worldwide television audience watched as U.S. astronauts Neil Armstrong and

Children's toys and games revolved increasingly around space. Science fiction writing, already a popular genre for several decades, reached ever-larger audiences. Films portrayed space explorers answering questions about life that were formerly the domain of church leaders. American filmmaker Stanley Kubrick's breathtaking 1968 hit movie based on Arthur C. Clarke's *2001: A Space Odyssey* explored human morality and intelligence through a prism of extraterrestrial life and space travel. Likewise, in the internationally popular television series *Star Trek*, members of the starship *Enterprise*'s diverse crew wrestled with the problems of maintaining humane values against less-developed, often menacing civilizations. In the Eastern bloc, Polish author Stanislaw Lem's novel *Solaris* (1971) similarly portrayed space age individuals engaged in personal quests and likewise drew readers and ultimately viewers into a futuristic fantasy.

This space age grew out of cold war concerns, but it also offered the possibility of more global political cooperation, for—like the U.S. atomic bomb project during World War II—the diffusion of rocket technology resulted from international efforts. From the 1960s on, U.S. spaceflights often involved the participation of other countries such as Great Britain and the Netherlands. In 1965, Western European nations established the European Space Research Organization to develop rocket technology in competition with the superpowers. Using rocket and other space technology, an international consortium headed by the United States launched the first commercial communications satellite, *Intelsat I*, in 1965, and by the 1970s more than four hundred stations worldwide and some 150 countries worked together to maintain global satellite communications. Interlocking space, computer, and other information technology systems still served cold war ends, but the international collaboration needed to sustain these systems also countered virulent nationalism.

Lunar landings and experiments in space advanced pure science despite space race hype. Astronomers, for example, previously dependent on remote sensing for their work, used mineral samples from the moon to calculate the age of the solar system more precisely. Unmanned spacecraft provided data on cosmic radiation, magnetic fields, and infrared sources. *Viking* transmitted stunning pictures of Mars in 1976, and *Voyager*, in its flyby of

Valentina Tereshkova, Russian Cosmonaut
People sent into space were heroes, representing modern values of courage, strength, and well-honed skills. Insofar as the space age was part of the cold war race for superpower superiority, the USSR held the lead during the first decade. The Soviets trained both women and men, and the 1963 flight of Valentina Tereshkova—the first woman in space—supported Soviet claims of gender equality in contrast to the U.S. program.
Archive Photos.

Edwin "Buzz" Aldrin walked on the moon's surface—the climactic moment in the space race. As Armstrong stepped out of *Apollo 11*'s lunar module, he remarked, "That's one small step for man, one giant leap for mankind." Astronauts and cosmonauts were perhaps the era's most admired heroes. Beginning with Soviet cosmonaut Yuri Gagarin, these space explorers had to live up to high public expectations. American astronaut John Glenn later became a senator and presidential contender. The Soviets promoted the first woman in space, Valentina Tereshkova, as a role model for women—and never more so than when she married another cosmonaut and became a mother.

The space race also drove Western cultural developments. A whole new fantasy world developed.

Saturn, Jupiter, and Uranus beginning in 1979, supplied masses of new data about the earth's solar system. Such findings from outer space reinforced the "big bang" theory of the origins of the universe, first posited in the 1930s by American astronomer Edwin Hubble and given crucial support in the 1950s by the discovery of a low level of radiation permeating the universe in all directions. Based on the work of Einstein and Planck, the "big bang" theory explains the development of the universe from a condition of extremely high density and temperature some ten billion years ago. Nuclei emerged when these conditions dissipated in a rapid expansion of space—the so-called big bang.

Although the media touted the human conquerors of space, breakthroughs in space exploration and astronomy were utterly dependent on technology. As the first American astronauts themselves acknowledged, their chief role had been to rouse public interest. Scientists could gain accurate knowledge of the heavens only with the aid of mathematics and remarkable new instruments such as the radiotelescope, which depicted space by receiving, measuring, and calculating nonvisible rays. The scientific use of sophisticated technologies was not limited to astronomy and physics, moreover, but extended to the life sciences, which investigated the origins and evolution of life itself.

The Revolution in Biology

Advances in the biological sciences brought dramatic new health benefits, but they raised serious questions about scientific intervention in life processes. In 1952, scientists Francis Crick, an Englishman, and James Watson, an American, discovered the configuration of DNA, the material in a cell's chromosomes that carries hereditary information. Apparently solving the mystery of the gene and thus of biological inheritance, they showed how the "double helix" of the DNA molecule splits in cellular reproduction to form the basis of each new cell. This genetic material, biologists concluded, provides a chemical pattern for an individual organism's life. Beginning in the 1960s, genetics and the new field of molecular biology progressed rapidly. Growing understanding of nucleic acids and proteins permitted important progress in knowledge of viruses and bacteria and made possible a host of new antibiotics and antiviral serums to combat polio and

such dangerous childhood diseases as mumps and measles. Tetanus, syphilis, and tuberculosis no longer ravaged the West.

In the wake of this biological revolution came questions about the ethics of humans' tampering with the natural processes of life. For example, understanding how DNA works allowed scientists to bypass natural animal reproduction by a process called *cloning*—obtaining the cells of an organism and dividing or reproducing them (in an exact copy) in a laboratory. But *should* scientists interfere with so basic and essential a process as reproduction? ethicists and politicians asked. Similarly, the possibility of genetically altering species and even creating new ones (for instance, to control agricultural pests) led to concern about how such actions would affect the balance of nature. Thus, although science functioned on a theoretical plane, its consequences rippled through the social, cultural, and moral realms as well. Invoking Mary Shelley's *Frankenstein*, one critic noted that people still fear "that our scientists, well-intentioned and decent men and women all, will go on being titans who create monsters."

In a related medical field, Dr. Christiaan Barnard of South Africa performed the first successful heart transplant in 1967, and U.S. doctors later developed an artificial heart that allowed critically ill recipients to live for several years after a transplant, although often severely disabled. These medical miracles, however, prompted questions and even protests. For example, given the shortage of reusable organs, what criteria should doctors use in selecting recipients? Commentators also debated whether the enormous cost of new medical technology to save a few people would be better spent on helping the many who lacked even basic medical and health care. Such quandaries moved medicine further into the arena of social policy.

Reproductive Technologies and the Sexual Revolution

Technology also influenced the most intimate areas of human relations—sexuality and procreation. In traditional societies, community and family norms dictated marital arrangements and sexual practices, in large part because too many or too few children threatened the crucial balance between population size and agricultural productivity. As Western societies industrialized and urbanized, however, not only did these considerations become less urgent but the growing availability of reliable birth-control devices permitted young people to begin sexual relations earlier, with less risk of pregnancy. In the 1960s these trends accelerated. The birth-control pill, first produced in the United States and tested on women in developing areas, came on the Western market after U.S. and British health authorities approved it in the early 1960s. By 1970, "the pill" provided a more reliable means than condoms and diaphragms for controlling reproduction, and its use spread to all industrialized countries. Worldwide, millions sought out voluntary surgical sterilization through tubal ligations and vasectomies. New techniques brought abortion, traditionally performed by amateurs, into the hands of medical professionals, making it a safe procedure for the first time.

Childbirth and conception itself were similarly transformed. Whereas only a small minority of Western births took place in hospitals in 1920, more than 90 percent did by 1970. Obstetricians now performed much of the work midwives had once done. As pregnancy and birth became a medical process, innovative new procedures and equipment made it possible to monitor women and fetuses throughout pregnancy, labor, and delivery. The number of medical interventions rose: cesarean births increased 400

percent in the United States in the 1960s and 1970s, and the number of prenatal visits per patient in Czechoslovakia, for example, rose 300 percent between 1957 and 1976. In 1978, the first "test-tube baby," Louise Brown, was born to an English couple. She had been conceived when her mother's eggs were fertilized with her father's sperm in a laboratory dish and then implanted in her mother's uterus. This complex process, called *in vitro fertilization*, ultimately spared many couples the agony of unwanted childlessness. Donor-supplied "banks" provided sperm or eggs for the in vitro method if the couple who wanted to conceive could not produce their own. If a woman could not carry a child to term, the laboratory-fertilized embryo could be implanted in the uterus of a surrogate, or substitute, mother. Researchers even began working on an artificial womb to allow for reproduction entirely outside the body—from storage bank to artificial embryonic environment.

A host of disturbing ethical and political controversies—and some tragedies—accompanied these breakthroughs. In the early 1960s, a West German drug firm, without prior testing, distributed the tranquilizer thalidomide, claiming that it safely prevented miscarriages. Pregnant women used the drug widely, with disastrous results: thousands of disabled and mentally handicapped children were

Thalidomide Children
In the last third of the century, increasingly destructive side effects of powerful medicines became apparent. Women who had taken the drug thalidomide gave birth to children with severe disabilities, and the public condemned companies selling untested products. The race to profit from scientific and technological developments sometimes ignored human well-being. Deutsche Press Agentur/Archive Photos.

born. The Catholic church firmly opposed all mechanical and chemical means of birth control as a sinful intervention in a sacred process. Many Catholics and other opponents of abortion maintained that life begins at conception, and they branded abortion as murder. In vitro fertilization also stirred disapproval, appearing to some as "playing God" with life.

The expanding media and medical professions meanwhile helped democratize knowledge of birth-control procedures after World War II and made public discussions of sexual matters explicit, technical, and widespread. Popular use of birth control allowed Western society to be saturated with highly sexualized music, literature, and journalism without a corresponding rise in the birthrate—impressive evidence of the increasing separation of sexuality from reproduction. Abundant statistical surveys showed that regular sexual activity began at an ever-younger age, and people talked more openly about sex—another component of cultural change. Finally, in a climate of increased publicity to sexuality, more open homosexual behavior became apparent, along with continued efforts to decriminalize it across the West. The Western media trumpeted the "commercialization of sex" and announced the arrival of a "sexual revolution." From the late nineteenth century to the 1960s, however, sexual revolution had been trumpeted with each advance in birth-control technology, showing once again the social and political impact of technological transformation.

❖ Postindustrial Society and Culture

Reshaped by soaring investments in science, the spread of technology, and growing prosperity, Western countries in the 1960s started on what social scientists labeled a *postindustrial* course. Instead of being centered on manufacturing and heavy industry, postindustrial society emphasized the distribution of such services as health care and education. The service sector was the leading force in the economy, and this meant that intellectual work, not industrial or manufacturing work, had become primary. Moreover, all parts of society and industry interlocked, forming a system constantly in need of complex analysis. Thus, unlike the preindustrial age

dominated by landlords or the industrial age dominated by manufacturers, postindustrial society brought to the fore highly educated professional and technical experts who could calculate needs, gather information, and make predictions. One Soviet scientist characterized his work as "not simply an act of creativity but a complex system of coordinati[on]" that demanded management. (See "Terms of History," page 1120.)

Postindustrial society changed the day-to-day lives and material conditions of millions of workers. Many working-class people, formerly cramped in tenements, could now afford to buy their own homes; by the 1970s, more than one-third of Western European workers owned homes. Corporations boosted workers' participation in management decisions and employed industrial psychologists to alleviate tensions. The rise of "industrial parks" at the edges of cities made room in city centers for corporate headquarters, banks, and university and government buildings. The postindustrial characteristics of individuals and society would carry over from the 1960s and 1970s into the next century.

Multinational Corporations

One of the major innovations of the postindustrial era was the rise of multinational corporations. These companies produced for a global market and conducted business worldwide, but unlike older kinds of international firms, they established major factories in countries other than their home base. For example, by 1970, Standard Oil of New Jersey employed about 150,000 people, some 90,000 (60 percent) of them outside the United States. Of the five hundred largest businesses in the United States in 1970, more than one hundred did over a quarter of their business abroad; IBM, for instance, operated in more than one hundred countries. Although U.S.-based corporations led the way, European and Japanese multinationals like Volkswagen, Shell, Nestlé, and Sony also had a broad global scope.

Some multinational corporations had bigger revenues than entire nations. They appeared to burst the bounds of the nation-state, as they set up shop in whatever part of the world offered cheap labor. Their interests differed starkly from those of ordinary people with a local or national outlook. In the first years after the war, multinationals preferred European employees, who constituted a highly

Postindustrial

In 1973, U.S. sociologist Daniel Bell's book *The Coming of Postindustrial Society* announced a momentous change in Western society. The economies of the major powers had stopped being predominantly manufacturing and had become instead "postindustrial." By this Bell meant not that there was no more industrial production of cars, household goods, and materials such as steel but rather that service industries like health care, education, banking, and other financial services had outstripped manufacturing. In terms of both number of employees and income generated, service industries were forming an ever larger sector of the economy, and Bell saw this postindustrial trend continuing. And, in fact, statistics from the 1990s testified to the accuracy of Bell's prediction: in the United States, for example, workers in manufacturing made up only 15 percent of the workforce.

Postindustrial society, in Bell's analysis, had a second component that has also been borne out over time. Like observers in Western Europe, Bell pointed to the critical importance of information and knowledge in the operation of society. Decisions in individual enterprises as well as in technological society as a whole could no longer spring from hunches and small bits of information. Instead the management of any entity depended on *systems analysis*, which took into account every factor pertinent to the system, be it a factory, a financial institution, or a government. Under these circumstances those who knew how to obtain, manipulate, and produce vast quantities of knowledge—even a single worker—could be far more important than the owner of a firm. Bell had captured the knowledge or information-based characteristics of the age.

The term *postindustrial* was part of a trend prevalent in these years to use the prefix *post* with an array of words, employed first in the term *postwar*. *Postwar* came to mean the period between the end of the war and economic recovery from it, 1945 to about 1960. On the one hand the term seemed simple enough to understand, but on the other hand some people found that the entire second half of the twentieth century was infused with the spirit of World War II, extending the meaning of postwar to encompass far more than a fifteen-year period and economic definition. Most notably, Europe and the world still reverberated with the legacy of the Holocaust and wartime devastation many decades later. *Post*s proliferated in these decades: *postmodern, post-historical, post-Marxist, post-Western*, and even *post-human*, to name a few of the most important uses.

The term *postmodern* arose after the various rebellions of the 1960s had challenged the rational, educated labor pool, had a strong consumer tradition, and eagerly sought secure work. Then in the 1960s, multinationals moved more of their operations to the emerging economies of formerly colonized states. This development afforded new options for hiring should labor costs rise or taxes and regulations increase. Although multinational corporations provided jobs in developing areas, profits usually enriched foreign stockholders.

Initially critics denounced what they perceived as a new imperialism in the guise of corporate invasion. However, many European firms believed that they could stay competitive only by expanding, and they adeptly and aggressively reacted to the changing international business climate by stepping up mergers. In chemicals, glass, electrical products, transport, metallurgy, and many other industries, huge conglomerates came to dominate European production. In France, for example, a massive glass conglomerate merged with a metallurgical company to form a new group specializing in all phases of construction—a wise move given the postwar building boom. Whereas U.S. production had surpassed the combined output of West Germany, Great Britain, France, Italy, and Japan in the immediate postwar years, by the mid-1970s these countries had rebounded. By 1972, both the nationalized British Steel company and the privately owned and German-based Thyssen firm were approaching the revenues of U.S. Steel and Bethlehem Steel—giants of their time.

European firms were often backed and sometimes even owned by their governments. These companies increased their investment in research progressive, and technology-proud attitudes connected with the Enlightenment, the first wave of modernity. Enlightenment thinkers associated modernity with the triumph of science and Enlightenment faith that precise knowledge would yield an ever better future. In the 1960s, students and environmentalists maintained that bombs, pollution, and the rising tide of cancer—not progress—had been the most spectacular results of modernity. Over the next decades *postmodernity* would criticize even more aspects of the Enlightenment.

Post-human also began to emerge as an idea during these decades, associated at first with the development of artificial organs and body parts and the imminent development of robots to do factory work. Not only had machines replaced people in factories, critics observed, but ordinary people could not live without machines in their lives. The so-called "virtual reality" of the internet age contributed yet another sense of *post-human*, as people developed relationships that were purely electronic.

Post-Marxism can be dated to these years when socialist countries introduced elements of the market economy. Hungary was notable in opening the road to post-Marxism economically, while Czechoslovakia and Poland mounted continuing protests to Soviet rule. All of these set the stage for the collapse of communism in the 1980s and 1990s, ushering in a more thoroughly post-Marxist period. Some maintain that the challenges to Marxism from the 1950s on stemmed from the inability of the Communist system to meet the technological demands of the postindustrial age. As technology and information determined the well-being of industries, consumers, and social programs, ideology got in the way of efficiency, causing the government, the economy, and the social order to collapse.

The emergence of a postindustrial social and economic order may well leave us wondering what will succeed it as an organizing principle for human productivity. The emergence of such concepts as postmodern, post-human, and post-Marxist suggests that theorists are seeing further change already at hand. Historians, however, counterbalance these analyses by suggesting that most proclamations of change and most visions of the future have deep roots in the past.

FURTHER READING

Bell, Daniel. *The Coming of Post-Industrial Society: A Venture in Social Forecasting.* 1973.

Hayles, N. Katherine. *How We Became Posthuman: Virtual Bodies in Cybernetics, Literature, and Informatics.* 1999.

Seidman, Steven, ed. *The Postmodern Turn: New Perspectives on Social Theory.* 1994.

and used international cooperation to produce major new products. This new emphasis on research was a crucial ingredient in postindustrial society. Ventures like the British-French Concorde supersonic aircraft, which, beginning with its first flight in 1976, flew from London to New York in under four hours, and the Airbus, a more practical series of passenger jets inaugurated in 1972 by a consortium of European firms, attested to the strong relationship among government, business, and science (Map. 29.1). Jointly pursuing technological and production innovations, European firms commanded large enough research budgets to compete successfully with U.S.-based multinational giants. "The prime function . . . of an industrial company," said one British executive, "[is] to spend every possible penny it can afford on technical development."

The New Worker

In its formative stage, industrial production had depended on workers who often labored to exhaustion, endured malnourishment, and lived in a state of poverty that sometimes led to violence. This scenario changed fundamentally in postwar Europe. To begin with, the proportion of people toiling in factories and mines and on farms dropped. Whereas the farm population had been declining as a percentage of the workforce for almost two centuries, the substantial reduction of the blue-collar workforce was new. It resulted from resource depletion in coal mines, the substitution of oil for coal and of plastics for steel, the growth of international competition, and automation in manufacturing processes.

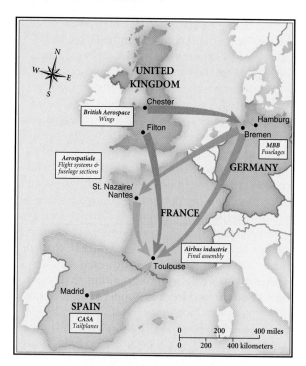

MAP 29.1 The Airbus Production System
The international consortium Airbus marked an important step in the economic and industrial integration of Europe. It also advanced the revitalization of the individual national economies by establishing new manufacturing centers away from capital cities and by modernizing older ones. Its formation presaged the international mergers and cooperative production that would characterize the late twentieth and early twenty-first centuries; today Airbus is a global enterprise with parts and service centers around the world, including the United States, China, and India.

Redefining Labor. Within firms the relationship of workers to bosses shifted. Managers increasingly blamed old-fashioned hierarchical decision making for diminished productivity. Following the lead of Swedish manufacturers, employers started grouping workers into teams that set their own production quotas, organized and assigned tasks, enforced their own quality standards, and competed with other teams to see who could produce more. As workers adopted attitudes and gained responsibilities that had once been managerial prerogatives, traditional definitions of labor became obsolete. Union membership declined along with blue-collar work, although strikes remained important for raising labor issues and unions continued to play a key role in factory organization (outside West Germany and most of the Soviet bloc, where unions were illegal).

When strikes occurred, however, they were often short-lived and symbolic.

In both U.S.-led- and Soviet-bloc countries, a new working class emerged, consisting of white-collar service personnel. Its rise undermined old social distinctions based on the way one worked: those who performed service work or had managerial functions were not necessarily better paid than blue-collar workers. The ranks of service workers swelled with researchers, health-care and medical workers, technicians, planners, and government functionaries. Scientists and technicians constituted 3.6 percent of the U.S. workforce in 1965, up 50 percent from a decade earlier. Employment in traditional parts of the service sector—banks, insurance companies, and other financial institutions—also surged because of the vast sums of money needed to finance technology and research. Entire categories of employees such as flight attendants devoted much of their skill to the psychological well-being of customers. The consumer economy provided more and more jobs in sales and repair, in restaurants and personal health, fitness, and grooming, and in hotels and tourism. By 1969, the percentage of service-sector employees had passed that of manufacturing workers in several industrial countries: 61.1 percent versus 33.7 percent in the United States; 49.8 percent versus 41.9 percent in the Netherlands; and 48.8 percent versus 41.1 percent in Sweden.

Postindustrial work life had some different ingredients in the Soviet bloc. Late in the 1960s, Communist leaders announced a program of "advanced socialism"—more social leveling, greater equality of salaries, and nearly complete absence of private production. The percentage of farmers remained higher in the Soviet bloc than in western Europe. A huge difference between professional occupations and those involving physical work remained as well in socialist countries. Less mobility existed between the two classifications, but much as in the U.S.-led bloc, gender also shaped the workforce into two groups, with men generally earning higher pay for better jobs and women relegated to lower pay and lesser jobs. Somewhere between 80 and 95 percent of women worked in socialist countries, but they generally held the most menial and worst-paying jobs.

As the postwar boom accelerated, West Germany and other Western nations absorbed immigrant,

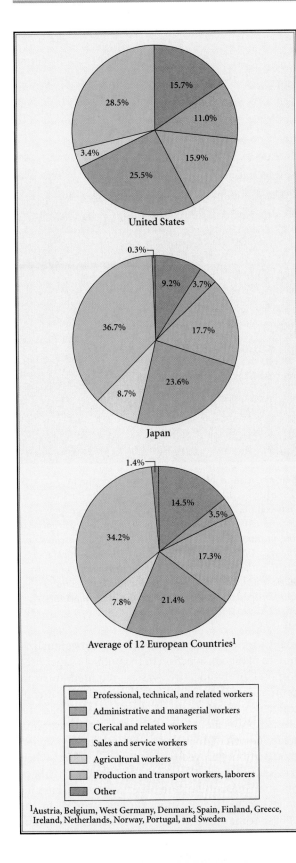

United States

15.7%
28.5%
11.0%
3.4%
15.9%
25.5%

Japan

0.3%
9.2% / 3.7%
36.7%
17.7%
8.7%
23.6%

Average of 12 European Countries[1]

1.4%
14.5%
3.5%
34.2%
17.3%
7.8%
21.4%

■ Professional, technical, and related workers
■ Administrative and managerial workers
■ Clerical and related workers
■ Sales and service workers
■ Agricultural workers
■ Production and transport workers, laborers
■ Other

[1]Austria, Belgium, West Germany, Denmark, Spain, Finland, Greece, Ireland, Netherlands, Norway, Portugal, and Sweden

◀ **TAKING MEASURE** Postindustrial Occupational Structure, 1984

Striking changes occurred in the composition of the workforce in the postwar period. Agriculture continued its declining importance as a source of jobs, but by the 1980s the percentage of these workers in the most advanced industrial countries had dropped well below 10 percent. The most striking development was the expansion of the service sector, which came to employ more than half of all workers. In the United States, the agricultural and industrial sectors, which had dominated a century earlier, now offered less than a third of all jobs.
Yearbook of Labour Statistics (Geneva: International Labour Office, 1992), Table 2.7.

or "guest," laborers. Coming from Turkey, Greece, southern Italy, Portugal, and North Africa, these workers collected garbage, built roads, held factory jobs, and cleaned homes. In an environment where desirable work usually involved mental operations and clean conditions, these jobs appeared more lowly than before. Although males predominated among migrant workers, female migrants who worked performed similar chores for less pay. Often their menial work was "off the books," thus cutting them off from social security and other employee benefits. Migrants *looked* different from the native population and were thus pegged as lower class, although by the 1980s many had obtained better-paying, higher-status jobs and integrated themselves into the host culture. (See "Taking Measure," left.)

From Farming to Agribusiness. Farm life was updated, even bureaucratized. By the 1970s, one could travel for miles in Europe without seeing a farmhouse. Small landowners sold family plots to farmers engaged in *agribusiness*. Governments, farmers' cooperatives, and planning agencies took over decision making from the individual farmer; they set production quotas and handled an array of marketing transactions. Western European agriculture rebounded rapidly from its low productivity of the late 1940s, when refugees did much farm work without machinery or fertilizer. In the 1960s, agricultural output rose an average of 3 percent per year in Greece and Spain and 2.5 percent in the Netherlands, France, and Great Britain. Genetic research and the skyrocketing use of machinery contributed to growth. Between 1965 and 1979, the number of tractors in Germany more than tripled from 384,000 to 1,340,000 and in Spain rose from 22,000 to almost 250,000. The six Common Market countries used more than 8.3 million tons of chemical fertilizer in 1969. Although politicians continued to invoke the well-being of the family farmer to win elections, such appeals increasingly became successful exercises in nostalgia.

As farming modernized, it required constant adaptation to market trends and the newest technology. For example, in the 1970s a French farmer, Fernande Pelletier, with the help of her husband, son, and daughter-in-law, made a living on her hundred-acre farm in southwestern France in the new setting of international agribusiness. Advised by a government expert, Pelletier produced whatever foods might sell competitively in the Common Market—from lamb and veal to foie gras and walnuts. She also compared interest rates, whether on the purchase of machinery or of baby animals; learned how to diversify her labor-intensive farming; and joined with other farmers in her region to buy heavy machinery and to sell her products. Agricultural solvency required as much managerial and intellectual effort as did success in the industrial sector.

The Boom in Education and Research

Education and research were key to running postindustrial society and the means by which nations maintained their economic and military might. In the West, common sense, hard work, and creative intuition had launched the earliest successes of the Industrial Revolution. By the late twentieth century these qualities alone no longer sufficed. Rather, success in business or government demanded the humanistic or technological expertise of a highly educated manager and ever-growing staff of researchers. "Today one is educated and therefore powerful," one French official put it. "It's the accumulation of knowledge, not of wealth, that makes the difference."

Those corporations and governments that invested the most in research became military and industrial leaders. The United States funneled more than 20 percent of its gross national product into research in the 1960s, in the process siphoning off many of Europe's leading intellectuals and technicians in a so-called brain drain. Complex systems—for example, nuclear power generation with its

Shepherd and Nuclear Plant in Yugoslavia
Twentieth-century society continued to offer stark contrasts between the increasingly high-tech capabilities of government and business and the daily life of ordinary people. On the one hand, machines like TV sets filled the household, and the vast majority of people worked with mechanical tools. On the other hand, even working in the shadow of a vast nuclear installation, this shepherd symbolizes a simultaneous immunity to or escape from the spirit of the machine.
Steve McCurry/Magnum Photos, Inc.

many components, from scientific conceptualization to plant construction to the publicly supervised disposal of radioactive waste—required intricate professional oversight. Scientists and bureaucrats frequently made more crucial decisions than did elected politicians in the realm of space programs, weapons development, and economic policy. Soviet-bloc nations proved less adept at linking their considerable achievements in science to actual applications because of the bureaucratic red tape involved in getting an innovation approved. In the 1960s, some 40 percent of Soviet-bloc scientific findings became obsolete before the government approved them for application to technology.

The new criteria for success fostered unprecedented growth in education, especially in universities and scientific institutes (where most research was conducted) and other postsecondary institutions. The number of university students in the United States spurted from 1.2 million in 1950 to 7 million in 1969—an increase of nearly 600 percent. In Sweden it rose by about 580 percent and in West Germany 250 percent during that period. Great Britain established a new network of polytechnic universities to encourage the technical research that elite universities often scorned and to accommodate the baby boomers now coming of age. France set up administrative schools for future high-level bureaucrats. Khrushchev's successors tried to rid Soviet science of the priority Stalinism often gave to ideology over evidence from research. By the late 1970s, the Soviet Union had built its scientific establishment so rapidly that the number of its advanced researchers in the natural sciences and engineering surpassed that of the United States. Meanwhile, institutions of higher learning in the United States and Western Europe added courses in business and management, information technology, and systems analysis.

In principle, education made the avenues to success more democratic by basing them on talent instead of wealth. In fact, societal leveling did not occur in most western European universities. During these decades only about 10 percent of university students were the children of workers or peasants; thus to some extent a university degree certified that one was from the "right" social circles. Moreover, instruction often remained rigid and old-fashioned. Although eighteenth-century Europeans had pioneered educational reform, by the 1960s and 1970s U.S. innovations to foster creative teaching and learning had made little impact elsewhere. Students reported that teachers lectured even young children, who were required to take notes, and pupils spoke in class only to echo the teacher or to recite homework memorized the night before. At the university level, as one angry student put it, the professor was "a petty, threatened god" who puffed himself up "on the passivity and dependence of students." Such judgments would provoke young people to rebel late in the 1960s against the traditional authority of teachers, officials, and parents.

Redefining the Family

Just as education changed dramatically to meet the needs of postindustrial society, the contours of the family shifted from what they had been a century earlier: family roles were transformed, and the relationship between parents and children—long thought to be natural and unchangeable—looked alarmingly different. Even though television and media commentators often delivered messages about what the family should be, technology, consumer goods, and a constant flow of guest laborers and migrants from the former colonies made for enormous variety in what households actually were.

Changes in the Household. In the 1960s, the family appeared in many new forms: households were now headed by a single parent, by remarried parents merging two sets of unrelated children, by unmarried couples cohabitating, or by traditionally married parents who had fewer children. Households of same-sex partners also became more common. At the end of the 1970s, the marriage rate had fallen 30 percent in the West from its 1960s level. The average marriage lasted one-third longer than it had a century earlier because of increased longevity. The rate of divorce, especially in areas of northern Europe, nonetheless rose, suggesting yet another change in attitudes toward marriage.

After almost two decades of baby boom, the birthrate dropped significantly. On average, a Belgian woman, for example, bore 2.6 children in 1960 but only 1.8 by the end of the 1970s. Although the birthrate fell, the percentage of children born outside of marriage soared; in Switzerland, for example, it doubled during these years. Combined with high rates of abortion—435 per 1,000 live births in Czechoslovakia and 146 per 1,000 in Sweden—the new patterns of reproduction aroused social concern.

Daily life within the family changed. For one thing, technology became more readily available as consumer items saturated domestic space. Radio and television filled a family's leisure time and often formed the basis of its common social life. Machines such as dishwashers, washing machines, and clothes dryers became more affordable and more widespread, reducing (in theory) the time women had to devote to household work and raising standards of cleanliness. More women worked outside the home during these years to pay for the prolonged economic dependence of children. To advance in a knowledge-based society, these children did not enter the labor force until their twenties but instead attended school and required their parents' support. Some social scientists interpreted the phenomenon of mothers working outside the home to meet these rising costs as women's abandonment of the family. They charged that selfish and greedy women who worked caused many social problems and personal disorders.

Whereas the early modern family organized labor, taught craft skills, and monitored reproductive behavior, the modern family seemed to have a primarily psychological mission—bringing it more in line with the postindustrial nature of work. Parents were to provide emotional nurture while their children learned intellectual skills in school; spouses offered each other comfort after the grueling discipline of office or factory work. If families could not handle this responsibility alone, psychologists, social workers, and social service agencies were available to provide counseling and assistance. Television programs portrayed a variety of family experiences on soap operas, sitcoms, and family-oriented game shows and gave viewers an opportunity to see how other families dealt with the tensions of modern life. Postindustrial experts in media and health care reshaped the family as much as they changed the nature of work outside the home.

Youth and the Generation Gap. Postindustrial society transformed teenagers' lives. A century earlier, teens had been full-time wage earners; now most were students, financially dependent on their parents. The young sometimes remained financial "minors" into their twenties, a situation that produced new tensions for both young and old. Simultaneously youth gained new roles as consumers. Advertisers and industrialists saw the baby boomers as a huge market and wooed them with consumer items associated with rock music—records, portable radios, stereos. The rock music industry became a multibillion-dollar business. Pop music of the previous generation had described the route from youthful attraction to love and finally to adult marriage. In contrast, rock music celebrated youthful rebellion against adult culture in biting, critical, and often explicitly sexual lyrics. The mixture of high-tech music and pop-star marketing contributed to the growing "generation gap."

The new models for youth were themselves the products of advanced technology and savvy marketing. The Beatles were a little known English bar band in 1962 when they hired a new manager, Brian Epstein. Epstein remade their image and their music, booked them in major theaters across Europe and the United States, and encouraged them to produce tamer songs. Beatle John Lennon claimed to write two different kinds of music, one a formulaic kind for mass consumption and another, more innovative kind to please himself. "What's your message for American teenagers?" the Beatles were asked. "Buy some more Beatle records," they responded. Television and more sophisticated international marketing campaigns boosted the Beatles far beyond the popularity of earlier rock-and-roll stars, even Elvis. By the mid-1960s, public appearances of the Beatles summoned thousands of fans whose hysteria intensified during the group's performances.

Sex roles for the young did not change, however. Despite the popularity of a few individual women rockers, promoters focused on men, whom they depicted as surrounded by worshiping female "groupies." Targeting teenagers as avid consumers of sexuality and gender stereotypes, several recording empires sold billions of records and dominated rock music. Encouraged to see themselves as resisting adult values and their parents' demands, young people were financially part of families but bound emotionally to a commercial youth culture.

Art, Ideas, and Religion in a Technocratic Society

Cultural trends evolved with technology itself. Like modernists in the past, a new generation of artists addressed growing consumerism and technology with their art. Even as colonies continued officially to rip away from the old colonial powers, their influence on the Western mind remained powerful, leading musicians, scholars, and religious leaders to turn in their direction. Conversely, many of these intellectuals enjoyed growing international recognition and global markets—like the multinationals themselves—and they buttressed their prestige by employing statistical and other scientific methods.

Expanding Artistic Boundaries. "Pop art," whose leading practitioners were Richard Hamilton of Britain and Robert Rauschenberg of the United

Rolling Stones Tour Europe
The Rolling Stones took the youth revolution in music to a new level of raw energy and social critique. Much like the modernist avant-garde early in the twentieth century, they were dissonant and shocking. Unlike modernists, however, the Stones were commercially successful, all of them becoming multimillionaires, international celebrities, and models to youth around the world.
Dominique Berretty.

States, featured images from everyday life and employed the glossy techniques and products of what these artists called "admass," or mass advertising, society. "There's no reason," they maintained of modern society's commercialism, "not to consider the world as one gigantic painting." Rauschenberg sold little in the 1950s because his totally white paintings, executed with house paint, had no appeal; but he saw the reflections appearing in the monochromatic white as a new kind of art that broke down artistic boundaries. He eventually turned to collages made from comic strips, magazine clippings, and fabric to fulfill his vision that "a picture is more like the real world when it's made out of the real world."

In 1962, New York's Museum of Modern Art held a forum to consider the phenomenon of pop art. This event marked the beginning of the movement's acceptance and commercial success. By then

such maverick American artists as Jasper Johns (b. 1930) and Andy Warhol (1927?–1987) had joined Rauschenberg. Pop art in the 1960s parodied modern commercialism. It showed, for example, how the female body, the classic form that attracted nineteenth-century male art buyers, was used to sell everything mass culture had to offer in the 1960s and 1970s. Swedish-born artist Claes Oldenburg (b. 1929) depicted the grotesque aspects of ordinary consumer products in *Giant Hamburger with Pickle Attached* (1962) and *Lipstick Ascending on Caterpillar Tractor* (1967).

"High" art picked up "low" objects to depict, but the effect was even more striking when the depictions were made of scraps of metal, cigarette butts, dirt, and, later, excrement. Artists again argued that these details were still another side of reality that they needed to capture. Such an attitude could have surprising results: the Swiss sculptor Jean

Niki de Saint-Phalle, *Fontaine Stravinsky* (1983)
Niki de Saint-Phalle's exuberant and playful art, seen in the fountains of Paris and cities around the world, captured the accessibility of pop art. Her other work drew inspiration from Caribbean and African styles and celebrated women of decolonizing countries. Living during the rebirth of activism, de Saint-Phalle lined up suspended bags of paint and machine-gunned them to create a spattered canvas—her answer to the alleged "macho" style of abstract expressionists like Jackson Pollock.
Barbara Alper/Stock Boston.

Tinguely (1925–1991) used rusted parts of old machines to make moving fountains. His partner Niki de Saint-Phalle then constructed huge, gaudy figures—many of them inspired by the folk traditions of the Caribbean and Africa—to decorate them. Their colorful fountains adorned main squares in Stockholm, Montreal, Paris, and other cities.

The American composer John Cage (1912–1992) had been working to the same ends when he added sounds produced by such everyday items as combs, pieces of wood, and radio noise into his musical scores. Buddhist influence led Cage also to incorporate silence in music and to compose by randomly tossing coins and then choosing notes by the corresponding numbers in the ancient Chinese *I Ching* ("Book of Changes"). Using silence was one way to capture the full range of sound and to continue the trend away from classical melody that had begun with modernism. Cage's orchestral scores allowed the players themselves to decide when and how they would participate in the musical production.

Other composers, called *minimalists*, simplified music by featuring repetition and sustained notes as well as by rejecting the "masterpiece" tradition of lush classical compositions. Some stressed modern technology; they introduced tape recordings into vocal pieces and used computers and synthesizers both to compose and to perform their works. German composer Karlheinz Stockhausen (b. 1928) introduced electronic music into classical composition in 1953, as did Cage soon after. Influenced by his own travels, Stockhausen continued the modern style of fully exploring non-Western tonalities in such 1970s pieces as *Ceylon*. But even though this music echoed the electronic and increasingly interconnected state of human society, its audiences diminished. By the 1970s, the amateur tradition of performing the latest style of music in the home had virtually disappeared, in part because of the technological demands. Some listeners found it difficult to appreciate the new patterns of sound, whether presented by amateurs or professionals. At the same time, improved recording technology and mass marketing brought music of all varieties to a wider home audience than ever before.

Heyday of Social Science. The social sciences reached the peak of their prestige during these decades, often because of their increasing use of statistical models and predictions. Sociologists and psychologists produced empirical studies that purported to demonstrate rules for understanding individual, group, and societal behavior. American psychologist B. F. Skinner (1904–1990) proposed to modify behavior through a system of accurately monitoring what people actually did, then rewarding positive behaviors and punishing negative ones. Critics worried that behaviorists trampled on concepts of human freedom in their advocacy of "social engineering" of ordinary people by so-called experts. Yet any promise of certainty in an age of rapid change was popular.

Sociologists, anthropologists, and psychologists also undermined some of the foundations for the belief that individuals had true freedom and for the assertion that Western civilization was any more sophisticated or just than non-Western societies. French anthropologist Claude Lévi-Strauss (b. 1908) developed a theory called *structuralism*. The theory insisted that all societies function within controlling structures—kinship and exchange, for example—that operate according to coercive rules similar to those of language. Structuralism challenged existentialism's tenet that humans could create a free existence and shook the social sciences' former faith in the triumph of rationality. In the 1960s and 1970s, the findings of the social sciences generally paralleled concerns that technology was creating a society of automatons and that complex managerial systems would eradicate individualism and human freedom.

Changes in Religion. Debates about free will coincided with new Christian preachings about the changing times. Responding to what he saw as a crisis in faith caused by affluence and secularism, Pope John XXIII (r. 1958–1963) in 1962 convened the Second Vatican Council, known as Vatican II. The bishops participating in Vatican II modernized the liturgy, democratized many church procedures, and at the last session in 1965 renounced church doctrine that Catholics should regard the Jewish people as guilty of killing Jesus. These new policies countered elitist, authoritarian, and anti-Semitic aspects of traditional religion that many people interpreted as having buttressed fascism. The Catholic church thus opened itself to some new influences. Although Pope John's successor, Paul VI (r. 1963–1978), kept Catholic opposition to artificial birth control alive in the encyclical *Humanae Vitae* (1968), he became the first pontiff to visit Africa, Asia, and South America. He also encouraged Catholicism in the Soviet bloc, paving the way for religion to become a primary focal point for anti-communism there.

Simultaneously a Protestant revival occurred in the United States, and growing numbers of people joined sects that stressed the literal truth of the Scriptures. In western Europe, Christian churchgoing remained at a low ebb. In the 1970s, for example, only 10 percent of the British population went to religious services—about the same number that attended live soccer matches. The composition of the Western religious public was also metamorphosing because of immigration of people from the colonies, which increased the strength of the non-Christian religions. Muslims, Jews, and Hindus were among the major religious groups making their way to Europe and the United States to find economic opportunity and to escape the hardships of decolonization in an age of cold war.

❖ Contesting the Cold War Order in the 1960s

Affluence, scientific sophistication, and military might elevated the United States and the Soviet Union to the peak of their power early in the 1960s. By 1965, however, the six nations of the Common Market had replaced the United States as the leader in worldwide trade and often acted in their own self-interest by making overtures across the U.S.-Soviet divide. Communist China, along with countries in Eastern Europe, contested Soviet leadership, blurring the political boundary between the capitalist and Communist worlds. In the decolonizing regions, the superpowers had difficulty finding suitable and pliable allies. The struggle for Indochinese independence had never ended, and by the mid-1960s Marxist-Leninist ideology, peasant aspirations, and Western technological capitalism converged to produce a devastating war in Vietnam. But in some respects the most serious challenge to the cold war order came from rising citizen discontent within the West. Persistent injustice and repression so outraged people like Jan Palach that in the 1960s they rose up in protest against the consequences of technological development, the lack of fundamental rights, and the nuclear holocaust latent in the cold war.

Cracks in the Cold War Consensus

In the summer of 1963, less than a year after the shock of the Cuban missile crisis, the United States and the Soviet Union signed a test-ban treaty outlawing the explosion of nuclear weapons in the atmosphere and in the seas. The acceptance of the treaty suggested that the superpowers would reduce international tensions to focus on domestic politics. The new Soviet middle class of bureaucrats and managers demanded a better standard of living and a reduction in cold war animosity, and U.S.-led-bloc reformers called for more effective democracy and the more equal distribution of wealth. Amidst growing postindustrial prosperity clear signs emerged, particularly across Europe, that individuals and entire nations alike were not as interested as U.S. and Soviet leaders were in pursuing the cold war.

Western Europe. In western European countries, voters elected politicians who promoted an increasing array of social programs designed to ensure economic democracy. A significant minority shifted their votes away from the Christian Democratic coalitions to Socialist, Labor, and Social Democratic Parties in hopes of placing more attention on ordinary people's needs during rapid change than on the cold war. In Britain, Harold Wilson, the Labour prime minister, came to power in 1964, calling for technical education and a focus on the needs of the expanding middle class of service workers. Wilson could not reverse the economy's half-century-long decline, however. British productivity remained the lowest among industrialized powers, and Commonwealth trading partners increasingly turned to Japanese and American goods.

Germany's leadership passed to Ludwig Erhard, who had guided the country's "economic miracle."

Here too Social Democratic politicians had enough influence to shift money from defense spending to domestic programs. Willy Brandt (1913–1992), the Socialist mayor of West Berlin, became foreign minister in a coalition government in 1966. Brandt pursued reconciliation with fellow Germans in Communist East Germany. This policy, known as *Ostpolitik*, ended frigid relations with the Soviet bloc and thus unsettled cold war thinking. With German and other markets saturated by goods from the economic resurgence, West German business leaders wanted, as one industrialist put it, "the depoliticization of Germany's foreign trade"—mainly the opening of the Soviet bloc to consumerism and new business opportunities.

French president Charles de Gaulle also moved to break the cold war stranglehold on Europe. Although France had but a 4 percent share of the world economy, de Gaulle forcefully advocated the interests of France and of a cooperative Europe in opposition to the superpowers. He poured more money into French nuclear development, and he steered a middle course between the United States and the Soviet Union. He withdrew French forces from NATO (after the United States tried to dissuade him from developing nuclear weapons independent of NATO) and signed trade treaties with the Soviet bloc. However, he also protected France's good relations with Germany to prevent further encroachments from the Soviet bloc. At home, de Gaulle's government mandated the cleaning of all Parisian buildings and sponsored the construction of modern housing. He described France as "the princess in the fairy story or the Madonna in the frescoes . . . dedicated to an exalted and exceptional destiny." With his haughty demeanor and stubborn pursuit of French grandeur, de Gaulle offered the European public an alternative to superpower toadying. Following his lead, western Europe began reasserting itself.

Eastern Europe. Brandt's Ostpolitik and de Gaulle's assertiveness had their echoes in the Soviet bloc, where since 1953 the uneven progress of cold war thaw and hardening had stirred the winds of change. Pushing de-Stalinization, Khrushchev took the dangerous course of trying to reduce Communist officialdom's privileges, and he sanctioned the publication of dissident Aleksandr Solzhenitsyn's *One Day in the Life of Ivan Denisovitch* (1962), which revealed firsthand the terrible conditions in the labor camps. Khrushchev's blunders—notably his humiliation in the Cuban missile crisis, his ineffectual schemes to improve Soviet agriculture, and his inability to patch the rift with China—became intolerable to his Kremlin colleagues. In 1964 they ousted him in favor of two party bureaucrats, Leonid Brezhnev (1906–1982) and Alexei Kosygin (1904–1980). Nevertheless, attempts at reform continued. As premier, Kosygin encouraged plant managers to turn a profit. Soviet policy called for ratcheting up the defense budget while producing televisions, household appliances, and cheap housing to alleviate the discontent of a better-educated citizenry. The government also loosened restrictions to allow cultural and scientific meetings with Westerners, another move that relaxed the cold war atmosphere in the mid-1960s.

The Soviet satellites in eastern Europe grasped the opportunity presented by Moscow's relaxed posture. Members of COMECON (the Soviet bloc's economic organization) refused to become agricultural backwaters supporting Soviet growth. Romania promoted industrialization, Poland allowed private farmers greater freedom to make money, and Hungarian leader János Kádár (1912–1989) introduced elements of a market system into the national economy. East Germany, benefiting from economic ties to West Germany, strove to advance technological education. Each of these countries in its own way was differentiating itself from the Soviet model.

In the arts, Soviet-bloc writers continued for a time to thaw the frozen monolith of socialist realism. Ukrainian poet Yevgeny Yevtushenko (b. 1933) exposed Soviet complicity in the Holocaust in *Babi Yar* (1961), a passionate protest against the slaughter of tens of thousands of Jews near Kiev during World War II and the refusal of Soviet authorities to commemorate the tragedy. In East Berlin, Christa Wolf (b. 1929) challenged the

Hagop Hagopian, *No to the Neutron Bomb!* (1977)
In an era of ongoing cold war, culture continued to be on the front line, with the Soviets persecuting those who produced abstract or critical art. Artists were adept, however, at incorporating Soviet icons in work critical of the regime. They might, for instance, depict Lenin's portrait but with citizens turning their back on it instead of being inspired by it. Or, as in this painting, they bravely critiqued the course of the arms race.
The Jane Voorhees Zimmerli Art Museum. Rutgers, The State University of New Jersey. The Norton and Nancy Dodge Collection of Nonconformist Art from the Soviet Union. Photo: Jack Abraham.

celebratory nature of socialist art. Her novel *Divided Heaven* (1965) shows a couple divided by the Berlin Wall; the man chooses to escape to the West but the woman stays behind to support socialism and ultimately commits suicide.

Repression returned later in the 1960s, however, as the Soviet government took to bulldozing outdoor art shows and otherwise harassing artists. Visual artists held secret exhibitions in their apartments, even turning their living spaces into a new kind of art known as "installations." In installations, art includes the arrangement of many everyday objects in large spaces—a form very distinct from the space of a canvas or a sculpture. These artists' paintings depicted Soviet citizens as worn and tired in grays and other monochromatic color schemes instead of the brightly attired and heroic figures of socialist realism. Still victims of the cold war, writers relied on *samizdat* culture, in which uncensored publications were reproduced by hand or by mimeograph and passed from reader to reader. These cultural forms of resistance laid part of the foundation for the more successful movement against Soviet rule in the 1980s.

The United States. Even in the United States, other issues challenged the cold war for front-page attention. The assassination of President John F. Kennedy in November 1963 shocked the nation and the world. But only momentarily did it still escalating demands for civil rights for African Americans and other minorities. White segregationists reacted with extraordinary violence to sit-ins at lunch counters, efforts to register black voters, and freedom marches. They firebombed black churches, schools, homes, and buses and murdered individual activists. This violent racism was a weak link in the American claim to moral superiority in the cold war, and in response to the murders and destruction, Kennedy had introduced civil rights legislation. Pressured by the growing momentum of African American activism, he forced the desegregation of schools and universities, calling civil rights for blacks "a moral issue . . . as old as the Scriptures" and appealing to Americans to end racism "in the Congress, in your state and local legislative body, and, above all, in our daily lives." In a massive rally in Washington, D.C., in August 1963, hundreds of thousands of marchers assembled around the Lincoln Memorial, where they heard the electrifying words of the African American minister Martin Luther King Jr.:

> *I have a dream that . . . all of God's children, black men and white men, Jews and Gentiles, Protestants and Catholics, will be able to join hands and sing in the words of the old Negro spiritual, "Free at last! Free at last! Thank God Almighty, we are free at last!"*

Lyndon B. Johnson (1908–1973), Kennedy's successor, turned rhetoric into reality when he steered the Civil Rights Act through Congress in

Peace Corps Volunteers in the Ivory Coast
The Peace Corps, founded by President Kennedy, tapped the idealism of young Americans in the 1960s; under the auspices of this program they went to all parts of the newly independent world and to regions where new economic development was taking place. Whether fostering literacy or working on agricultural projects, Peace Corps volunteers participated in the reformist spirit of the times, though their efforts were sometimes seen as a continuation of Western paternalism.
Jim Pickerell/Black Star.

1964. This legislation forbade segregation in public facilities and created the Equal Employment Opportunity Commission (EEOC) to fight job discrimination based on "race, color, national origin, religion, and sex." Southern conservatives had tacked on the provision against sex discrimination in the vain hope that it would doom the bill. Modeling himself on his hero Franklin Roosevelt, Johnson envisioned what he called a Great Society in which new government programs would give the forty million Americans living in poverty some share of American abundance. He sponsored myriad reform programs: Project Head Start for disadvantaged preschool children, the Job Corps for training youth, Volunteers in Service to America (VISTA) to support volunteers in poverty-stricken areas, and projects for urban development. These programs brought hope to many Americans, who agreed with black novelist Ralph Ellison that Johnson was "the greatest American president for the poor and the Negroes."

Vietnam and Turmoil in Asia

Outside the U.S.-led and Soviet blocs, some countries looked to the superpowers for military and economic support, playing the cold war card. Israel and Taiwan unequivocally depended on the United States to protect them; Cuba and certain African states turned to the Soviet Union. Yet elsewhere during the 1960s, third world nations increasingly distanced themselves from the superpowers. Many were still tied by technical systems such as radio and telephone networks and by trade to their former rulers; where the cold war was concerned, however, they sought to be nonaligned.

Communist China's independent way was the biggest surprise to both the Soviet Union and the United States. Mao Zedong, ever hostile to Western capitalism, also detested Soviet bureaucratization and claims to leadership. Moreover, he rebuked Khrushchev for backing down in Cuba. In 1966, Mao unleashed the Cultural Revolution, a movement to remake individual personality according to Mao's vision of socialism. Mao wanted the Chinese to experience revolution on a permanent basis instead of stagnating in Soviet-style bureaucratic corruption. China's youth were empowered to haul away people of every class for "reeducation"—which translated to personal humiliation, incarcer-

ation, and millions of deaths. Economic goals lost their importance as the Chinese became obsessed with reinventing revolutionary political culture.

Both superpowers had interests in East and Southeast Asia, but they often failed to see the complex changes under way in the region. American policymakers, for example, did not detect the growing dispute between the two Communist giants because they had an inflexible vision of monolithic communism. While China plunged into Mao's bloody cultural and economic experiments, the peoples of Southeast Asia were coming to grips with decades of demographic upheaval. Despite war and nationalist revolution, the region's population more than tripled between 1920 and 1970, reaching 370 million by the end of the 1970s. This explosive growth confounded nationalist leaders, typically military men with little experience in governing a booming population. Like the 85 percent of third world leaders who rose from the military, most East and Southeast Asian rulers were dictators without the technological expertise to make their countries economically viable.

Superpower intervention in this unstable part of the world was loaded with risk, and nowhere was this truer than in the tragic U.S. intervention in Vietnam (Map 29.2). Since the Geneva settlement in 1954, the United States had propped up corrupt and incompetent leaders, in the 1960s escalating its commitment to a non-Communist South Vietnam. North Vietnam, China, and the Soviet Union backed the rebel Vietcong, as the South Vietnamese Communists came to be called. Although Kennedy beefed up the U.S. military presence, the strength of the Vietcong seemed to grow daily.

In August 1964, Lyndon Johnson induced the U.S. Congress to pass a resolution endorsing the bombing of North Vietnam—the Vietcong's lifeline. By 1966, the United States had more than a half-million soldiers in South Vietnam. Before the war ended in 1975, the United States would drop more bombs on North Vietnam than the Allies had launched on Germany and Japan combined during World War II. Television reports carried the optimistic predictions of Johnson's advisers that each fresh attack and every new draft call-up revealed a "light at the end of the tunnel." Massive air attacks, some boasted, would "bomb North Vietnam back to the Stone Age." Yet the strategy failed. Despite regular announcements of enormous North

Vietnamese "body counts," American casualties also mounted relentlessly. The Vietcong escalated its guerrilla warfare and then melted away into jungles and cavernous hillsides.

Johnson offered massive aid to Indochina if the Vietcong and North Vietnamese would stop fighting. After decades of anticolonial struggle, the insurgents rejected a negotiated peace. North Vietnam's leaders calculated that the United States would give in first as the American public recoiled

from the horrors of televised slaughter: South Vietnamese officials casually executed people in the streets, and children screamed in mortal pain as they were engulfed by flaming napalm, a jellied gasoline that asphyxiated its victims while they burned. Branded as murderers by international opinion, American forces simultaneously looked inept before images of pajama-clad Asians on bicycles who held at bay the technologically advanced Yankees.

By 1968, a swelling American antiwar movement challenged the killing on humanitarian grounds. In an age of ideological war, lack of support at home spelled the beginning of the end for the U.S. war effort. Johnson abandoned his soaring political ambition and announced in March 1968 that he would not run for president again. As he left office in January 1969, peace remained elusive and the war's social and economic costs to the United States continued to mount. The U.S. superpower was tarnished, irreparably it seemed at the time; so too was the Soviet Union.

The Explosion of Civic Activism

In the midst of cold war, technological advance, and bloody conflict, a new social activism emerged in the West. Students, blacks and other racial minorities, women, antiwar protesters, environmentalists, and homosexuals raised their voices to demand that Western reality match its ideals. The civil rights movement in the United States ignited fiery protests in the streets, in universities, and in the halls of government. In the Soviet bloc dissident movements demanded political democratization and social change. These movements nearly swept up France and Czechoslovakia in revolution in 1968; they cast doubts on the superpower status of the United States and the Soviet Union; and they contested the cold war order.

Civil Rights. A broad cross section of Americans embraced the bold activism of the civil rights movement and transformed it. In 1965, César Chávez (1927–1993) led Mexican American migrant workers in the California grape agribusiness to strike for better wages and working conditions. Controversy swirled around the protest: "A hoax, a fantasy, a charade," one white columnist called the work action and the hunger strikes. Deeply religious and ascetic, Chávez helped Hispanic Americans define their

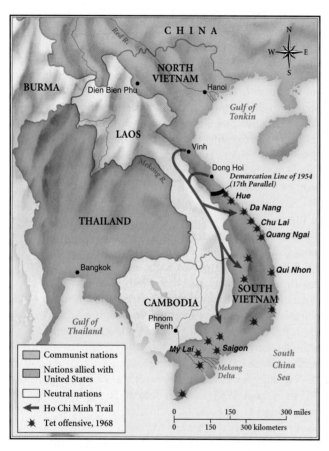

MAP 29.2 The Vietnam War, 1954–1975
The local peoples of Southeast Asia had long resisted incursions by their neighbors. They also resisted French rule from the end of the nineteenth century, never more fiercely than in the war that liberated them after World War II. Ill prepared by comparison with the French, the Vietnamese nonetheless triumphed in the battle of Dien Bien Phu in 1954. But the Americans soon became involved, trying to stem what they saw as the tide of Communist influence behind the Vietnamese liberation movement. The ensuing war in Vietnam in the 1960s and 1970s spread into neighboring countries, making the region the scene of vast destruction.

identity and struggle against deportation, inferior schooling, and discrimination.

Meanwhile the African American civil rights movement took a dramatic turn as riots protesting police brutality erupted in Watts, a black district of Los Angeles, in the summer of 1965. City after city experienced similar outbursts of anger and frustration. Some activists transformed their struggle into a militant affirmation of racial differences. They urged blacks not to push for mere equality but for a celebration of their race under the banner "Black is beautiful." The issue they faced was one they felt they had in common with decolonizing people: how to shape an identity different from that of white oppressors. Imitating whites amounted to self-hatred, and thus blacks should celebrate their African heritage and work for "black power" by reclaiming rights instead of begging for them nonviolently. Some formerly pacifist black leaders turned their rhetoric to violence: "Burn, baby, burn," chanted rioters who destroyed the grim inner cities around them in the belief that civil rights legislation alone offered only slight relief to their plight.

Student Protest. As a result of the new turn in black activism, white American university students who had participated in the early stages of the civil rights movement found themselves excluded from leadership positions. Many soon joined the swelling protest against technological change, consumerism, sexual repression, the educational establishment, and the Vietnam War, including conscription into the U.S. forces fighting in Southeast Asia. European youth caught the fever. In the mid-1960s, university students in Rome occupied an administration building after right-wing opponents assassinated one of their number during a protest against the 200-to-1 student-teacher ratio. Polish high school and university students created Michnik Clubs, named for the outspoken dissident Adam Michnik, to study Western political theory, science, and economics but faced constant harassment by the secret police. In Prague in 1965, students held a carnival-like procession celebrating the American Beat poet Allen Ginsberg as their May King, and on May Day in 1966 they chanted, "The only good Communist is a dead one." In commemorating the tenth anniversary of the 1956 uprisings, some students were arrested and expelled from the university. The Federation of [West] German Socialist Students (SDS), led by Rudi Dutschke and the "situationists" in Strasbourg, France, called on students to wake up from the slumbering pace of student life and reform the world. Situationists believed that bureaucratic, mass society numbed people, and they watched for opportunities or created "situations"—emblazoning university walls with challenging slogans, for example—to jolt individuals to action.

Students attacked the traditional university curriculum. They questioned how studying Plato or Dante would help them after graduation. They also took part in forcing from the curriculum required humanities courses in the arts, philosophy, and literature. Students turned the defiant rebelliousness of 1950s youth culture into a political style by mocking education: "How to Train Stuffed Geese," French students called the way universities taught them. "No professors over forty" and "Don't trust anyone over thirty" were powerful slogans of the day. Long hair, blue jeans, communal living, and a repudiation of personal hygiene announced students' rejection of middle-class values, as did their denunciation of sexual chastity. With the widespread use of the pill, abstinence became unnecessary as a method of birth control, and students made the sexual revolution explicit and public with open promiscuity and experimentation.

The young created a counterculture nourished with heavy doses of sex, rock and folk music, and drugs. Early in the 1960s, then Harvard professor Timothy Leary provided his students with the hallucinogen LSD. Marijuana use became common among student protesters, and amphetamines and barbiturates added to the drug culture, which had its own rituals, songs, and gathering places. Electronic rock music and mind-altering chemicals—produced by the very technology that youth culture scorned—induced new sensations, created a sense of personal creativity, and restored a belief in the individual experience. Businesses made billions of dollars selling blue jeans, dolls dressed as "hippies," natural foods, and drugs, as well as packaging and managing the stars of the counterculture.

Women's Protest. Women active in the civil rights and student movements soon realized that protest organizations devalued women just as society at large did. Male protesters adopted the leather-jacketed machismo style of their film and rock heroes, but women in the movements were often judged by the status of their male-protester lovers. "A woman was to 'inspire' her man," African American activist Angela Davis complained, adding that women aiming for equality supposedly "wanted to rob [male protesters] of their manhood." Such biting criticisms of masculine supremacy among African American activists elicited a response among white women, who admired the strength of African American women and also had their own grievances against the youth culture's exploitation of them. "We demand that our problems be discussed substantively," announced a speaker in Frankfurt, West Germany, interrupting a student meeting. "It is no longer enough that women are occasionally allowed to say a few words to which, as good antiauthoritarians, you listen—and then go on with the order of the day."

More politically conventional middle-class women eagerly responded to the international bestseller *The Feminine Mystique* (1963) by American journalist Betty Friedan. Friedan popularized Simone de Beauvoir's philosophy by focusing on the changes in middle-class women's lives wrought by technology and affluence. Friedan maintained that middle-class women led useless existences, allowing their talents to stagnate while laborsaving devices and their children's daily absence in school made them useless.

Throughout the West, middle-class activists were working on the legal aspects of reproductive and civil rights. In France they helped end the ban on birth control in 1965. In Sweden, where for decades generous welfare benefits and access to birth control had improved women's lives, the Frederika Bremer Association lobbied to make tasks both at home and in the workplace less gender-segregated. The National Organization for Women (NOW) was formed in the United States in 1966 "to bring women into full participation in the mainstream of American society now."

Whereas these organizations followed official procedures for contesting unequal rights, some middle-class women joined street activists on behalf of such issues as abortion rights or the decriminalization of gay and lesbian sexuality. Many flouted social conventions in their attire, language, and attitudes. Renouncing brassieres, hair curlers, high-heeled shoes, cosmetics, and other adornments, they spoke openly about taboo subjects such as their sexual feelings, explained the "politics of housework," and even announced that they had resorted to

Gay Activists in London
The reformist spirit of the 1960s and 1970s changed the focus of homosexuals' activism. Instead of concentrating mostly on legal protection from criminal prosecution, gays and lesbians began affirming a special and positive identity. As other groups who had endured discrimination began making similar affirmations, "identity politics" was born. Critics charged that traditional universal values were sufficient and that homosexuals and others constituted "special-interest" groups. Gays, women, and ethnic or racial minorities countercharged that the universal values first put forth in the Enlightenment seemed to apply only to a privileged few.
© Hulton Getty/Liaison Agency.

illegal abortions. In France, for example, several hundred prominent women, including Simone de Beauvoir, went public with such information. This brand of feminist activity was meant to shock polite society—and it did. At a Miss America contest in 1968, women protesters crowned a sheep the new beauty queen. West German women students tossed tomatoes at male protest leaders in defiance of standards for ladylike behavior. Many women of color, however, broke with feminist solidarity and spoke out against the "double jeopardy" of being "black and female."

1968: Year of Crisis

The West seethed with protest and calls for reform; it erupted in 1968, propelled by forces on the other side of the world. In January, on the first day of Tet, the Vietnamese New Year, the Vietcong and the North Vietnamese attacked more than one hundred South Vietnamese towns and American bases, inflicting heavy casualties. The Tet offensive, as it came to be called, caused many Americans to conclude that the war might be unwinnable. The antiwar movement of students, clergy, and pacifists suddenly gained crucial momentum from a disillusioned public. Meanwhile in Czechoslovakia, a quieter movement against Soviet cold war domination had taken shape, but the atmosphere in that country, as elsewhere around the world, soon became explosive.

Violence Erupts.   On April 4, 1968, Martin Luther King Jr. was assassinated by a white racist, and more than a hundred cities in the United States erupted in violence as African Americans vented their anguish and rage. On campuses, strident confrontation over the intertwined issues of war, technology, racism, and sexism closed down classes. At Columbia University in New York City, where the administration had proposed destroying a Harlem neighborhood to build a gym, students took over buildings and suffered violent police attacks in order, as one student put it, "to recapture a school from business and war and rededicate it to learning and life."

At the same time, student protest was escalating in France. In January, students at Nanterre had gone on strike, invading administrative offices and demanding a say in university governance. They called themselves a "proletariat"—an exploited working class—and considered themselves part of a New Left. When students at the more prestigious Sorbonne in Paris showed solidarity with students of Nanterre in street demonstrations, the police arrested and assaulted hundreds of them. The Parisian middle classes reacted with unexpected sympathy to the student uprising because of their own resentment of bureaucracy. They were also horrified at

seeing the elite and brutal police force, the CRS, beating middle-class students and passersby who expressed their support.

By May the violence had accelerated into outright revolt, and French students handed out advice for evading tear gas and fragmentation grenades used by the CRS:

> *VARIOUS PROTECTIVE MEASURES*
> *Garbage can cover as a shield. . . . Lemon—wet a handkerchief with it, suck on it. Bicarbonate of soda around the eyes, in diluted form on a handkerchief. Goggles, motorcycle or ski, or a swimming mask.*

French workers joined in: some nine million went on strike, occupying factories and calling not only for higher wages but also for "participation" in everyday decision making. To some, the revolt of youth and workers looked as if it might spiral into another French revolution.

The normally decisive president Charles de Gaulle seemed paralyzed at first, but he soon took steps to undermine support for the student revolt. In June he announced a raise for workers, and businesses offered them a strengthened voice in decision making. Many citizens, having grown tired of the street violence, the destruction of private property, and the breakdown of social services (for example, garbage was not collected for weeks), were ready to dissociate themselves from the student protesters. After skillfully using the media to solidify the separation of students from the wider population, de Gaulle sent tanks into Paris. Although demonstrations continued throughout June, the student movement had been closed down.

Prague Spring.   The Soviets had weathered protests and even uprisings before, but the 1968 revolt began within the Czechoslovak Communist Party. In the autumn of 1967 at a Party congress, Alexander Dubček (1921–1992), head of the Slovak branch of the party, had called for more social and political openness. First Party Secretary Antonín Novotný (1904–1975) responded with ridicule: "We've had more than enough of democracy." In a culture where anti-Semitism and ethnic prejudice remained formidable political weapons, Novotný taunted Dubček as an inferior Slovak. Yet the call for reform struck a chord among frustrated party officials, technocrats, and intellectuals; Czechoslovaks

Prague Spring

When the Soviets and other Warsaw Pact members cracked down on the Prague Spring, they met determined citizen resistance. People refused assistance of any kind to the invaders. Indeed, despite dejection at the repression of Dubček's government, protest on a small and large scale was ongoing from then until the final fall of Communist rule two decades later.
Prache-Levin/Sygma.

began to dream of creating a new society—one based on "socialism with a human face." Party officials drove Novotný from power and replaced him with Dubček.

Dubček changed the Communist style of government, ending censorship, instituting the secret ballot for party elections, and allowing competing political groups to form. The "Prague Spring" had begun—"an orgy of free expression," one Czech journalist called it. People bought uncensored publications, packed uncensored theater productions, and engaged in almost nonstop political debate. "Nobody talks about football [soccer] . . . anymore," one taxi driver complained. Meanwhile, Dubček's new government faced the enormous problem of negotiating policies acceptable to the USSR and the entrenched party functionaries. Radicals pressed for fundamental change, but those with a vested

interest in the Communist system wanted more limited reform.

On top of the internal uncertainty, the Polish, East German, and Soviet regimes threatened the reform government daily. Announcing new recognition of civil rights and the separation of the Communist Party from the government, Dubček warned that democracy demanded "a conscious civic discipline" and "statesmanlike wisdom of all citizens." When Dubček failed to attend a meeting of Warsaw Pact leaders, Soviet threats became intense. Finally on the night of August 20–21, 1968, Soviet tanks rolled into Prague in a massive show of antirevolutionary force.

Citizens tried to halt the return to Communist orthodoxy by using free expression as sabotage. They painted graffiti on tanks and confused invading troops by removing street signs. Illegal radio stations broadcast testimonials of resistance, accounts of Soviet brutality, and warnings to people about to be arrested. They refused to sell food or other commodities to Soviet troops. As the Soviets gradually removed reformers from power, Jan Palach and other university students immolated themselves. Protest of one type or another never stopped, forcing the new Czechoslovak government to maintain repression. Meanwhile, Soviet determination to retain control over the Soviet bloc was expressed in the Brezhnev Doctrine, announced in November 1968. Reform movements, Brezhnev declared, were not merely domestic matters but rather "a common problem and concern of all socialist countries." Further moves toward change would meet similar repression.

Prague Spring, 1968

Protest in 1968 changed the style and direction of high politics in Western societies. It challenged superpower dominance on which the cold war was based. Whether burning draft cards in the United States or scribbling graffiti on public buildings in Europe, students made all government open to question. Yet change did not necessarily occur in the way reformers had hoped. Governments turned to conservative solutions, while disappointed reformers considered more radical avenues to social transformation.

❖ The Erosion of Superpower Mastery in the 1970s

The 1970s brought an era of *détente*—a lessening of cold war tensions—as the United States pulled out of the Vietnam War and as the superpowers negotiated to limit the nuclear arms race. Despite this relaxation in the cold war, the superpowers appeared to lose their dominance. By the early 1970s, student protest evolved into ongoing reform movements, while other groups, such as those for Basque independence in Spain and for Catholic rights in Northern Ireland, took violent action. This violence affected the superpowers as it threw their allies off

balance. Although the United States and the Soviet Union still controlled the balance of power, their grip was also loosening because of their own internal corruption, the challenge of terrorism, and competition from the oil-producing states, Japan, and the Common Market.

The Superpowers Tested

As the 1970s opened, both superpowers faced daunting internal and external challenges to their dominance, and both underwent crises of leadership as economic and political uncertainty mounted. Domestic politics remained heated during this decade; the uncertainties of economic modernization grew; and coalitions formed by other countries began to undermine superpower mastery. Neither superpower had leaders wholly competent to face these challenges.

The United States in Crisis. In November 1968, the conservative Richard Nixon (1913–1994) was elected president of the United States. Nixon claimed to have a "secret plan" to bring peace to Southeast Asia, but even as peace talks dragged on, warfare continued to ravage Vietnam and to mount up debt in the United States. In 1970, Nixon ordered U.S. troops to invade Cambodia, the site of North Vietnamese bases. Campuses erupted again in protest, and on May 4 the National Guard killed four students and wounded eleven others at a demonstration at Kent State University in Ohio. Nixon called the victims "bums," and a growing reaction against the counterculture made many Americans agree with him that the guardsmen "should have fired sooner and longer."

The United States and North Vietnam finally signed a peace treaty on January 27, 1973. By terms of the agreement, Nixon withdrew American troops, but he still continued to supply South Vietnam's forces. The Communists did not relent either, and in 1975 South Vietnam collapsed under a determined North Vietnamese offensive. Vietnam was forcibly reunified.

Small and great powers reeled from decades of conflicts in Southeast Asia. Tens of thousands of U.S. and South Vietnamese loyalists fled the region. In adjacent Cambodia the Communist Khmer Rouge government inflicted a horrendous reign of terror in which it slaughtered a million people in an attempt to turn the country back to an agrarian society. The Vietnam War had cost the United States billions of dollars, more than fifty thousand lives, and its moral authority. Many countries now viewed the United States not as a defender of liberty but as an oppressor of third world people. Moreover, the "domino theory," which had justified intervention since the 1950s, was proven false: although Cambodia and Laos went Communist, Thailand did not, and Communist Vietnam became Communist China's enemy.

Simultaneously the United States pulled off a foreign policy triumph when Henry Kissinger, Nixon's secretary of state and a believer—like Bismarck—in Realpolitik, decided to take advantage of the ongoing conflict between China and the USSR. In 1972, Kissinger's efforts to bring the United States and China closer resulted in Nixon's visiting the *other* Communist power. Pictures of Mao Zedong and Nixon shaking hands rocked the world, for they seemed to promise the possibility that diplomatic miracles would end the cold war. Within China the meeting helped stop the brutality and excesses of the Cultural Revolution, which had left the country prostrate. Gradually, Chinese pragmatists interested in technology, trade, and relations with the West replaced hard-line ideologues.

The world benefited from this diplomatic breakthrough. Fearful of the Chinese and of the cold war's economic toll, Soviet leader Brezhnev made overtures to the U.S.-led bloc. In 1972, the superpowers signed the Strategic Arms Limitation Treaty (SALT I), which set a cap on the number of antimissile defenses each country could have. In 1975, in the Helsinki accords on human rights, the Western bloc officially acknowledged Soviet territorial gains in World War II in exchange for the Soviet bloc's guarantee of basic human rights.

While pursuing a degree of mutual reconciliation with these foreign enemies, the enigmatic Nixon focused on reelection at any price. After his landslide victory in the 1972 presidential race, evidence came to light that Nixon's reelection committee had paid several men—caught in the act and arrested—to wiretap the telephones at Democratic Party headquarters in Washington's Watergate building. Televised congressional hearings revealed not only that the president's office had jeopardized the Constitution's guarantee of free elections but also that Nixon himself had attempted to cover up the truth about the Watergate break-in. Between 1968 and 1972, Nixon had forged a powerful conservative consensus based on the idea that activist groups calling for expanded rights were but a minority. The so-called silent majority had supported Nixon in all but one state in 1972, but in the summer of 1974 the Watergate scandal forced Nixon to resign in disgrace—the first U.S. president ever to do so.

Dissent and Repression in the Soviet Bloc. The Soviet leadership also tried conservative solutions to meet mounting criticism. By the early 1970s, the hard-liner Brezhnev had eclipsed Kosygin's influence in the Soviet Union and freely clamped down on critics. Following the events in Czechoslovakia in 1968, the Soviet dissident movement was at a low ebb. "The shock of our tanks crushing the Prague Spring . . . convinced us that the Soviet colossus was invincible," explained one pessimistic liberal. Other voices persisted, however. In 1974, Brezhnev expelled Solzhenitsyn from the USSR after the publication of the first volume of *Gulag Archipelago* (1973–1976) in the U.S.-led bloc. Composed from myriad biographies, firsthand reports, and other sources of information about prison camp life, Solzhenitsyn's story of the Gulag (the Soviet system of internment and forced-labor camps) documented the brutal conditions Soviet prisoners endured under Stalin and his successors. The book appeared at a time when western European Ostpolitik was spreading dissatisfaction with the economy and the repression of free speech in the Eastern bloc. The expulsion of Solzhenitsyn showed that the Soviet hierarchy would severely punish revelations regarding the Gulag.

The Kremlin persecuted many ordinary people who did not have Solzhenitsyn's international reputation. Soviet psychologists, complying with the government, certified the "mental illness" of people who did not play by the rules; thus dissidents wound up as virtual prisoners in mental institutions. The crudest Soviet persecutions, however, involved anti-Semitism: Jews were subject to educational restrictions (especially in university admissions), severe job discrimination, and constant assault on their religious practice. It was "not dramatic" persecution, as one Jewish writer put it, "but daily . . . always present." A commonplace accusation by Soviet officials was that Jews were "unreliable, they think only of emigrating. . . . [T]heir allegiance is elsewhere. It's madness to give them an education, because it's state money wasted." Ironically, even dissidents blamed Jews for the Bolshevik Revolution, for the terror of Stalinist collectivization, and for the supposed destruction of Russian literature. As attacks intensified in the 1970s, Soviet Jews protested and sought to emigrate to Israel or the United States, but the government severely restricted emigration, often claiming that Jews who had finished their compulsory military service could not leave because they knew "state secrets."

Dissent persisted in satellite states. Throughout the 1970s, workers and intellectuals in Poland generated protest writing and formed activist groups. In an open letter to the Czechoslovak Communist Party leadership in 1975, playwright Václav Havel accused Marxist-Leninist rule of making people materialistic, not socialist, and indifferent to civic life. The only viable conduct under Communist repression, Havel wrote, was either to disengage from public life or to work for the special privileges awarded to successful technocrats. In 1977, Havel, along with a group of fellow intellectuals and workers, signed Charter 77, a public protest against the Communist regime. The police imprisoned and tormented many of the charter's signatories, including Havel; philosopher Jan Patocka died after his "interrogation."

By this time the brain drain of eastern European intellectuals had become significant. The modernist composer Gyorgy Ligeti had left Hungary in 1956, after which his work was celebrated in concert halls and in such classic films as *2001: A Space Odyssey*. From exile in Paris, Czech writer Milan Kundera enthralled audiences with *The Book of Laughter and Forgetting* and other novels that chronicled the lives of tortured characters caught in the grim realities of Communist institutions. The presence of these exiles and escapees to the United States and western European capitals helped erode any lingering support for communism. In France, for example, a group of "new philosophers" loudly demanded that leftists justify their commitment to Soviet communism in light of the brutal practices revealed by Solzhenitsyn and others. Communist parties in the West broke their last remaining ties to the Soviet Union, but even after declaring an independent path, their success at the polls dwindled.

The West, the World, and the Politics of Energy

While the superpowers wrestled with internal political embarrassments and the intricacies of nuclear diplomacy, other nations were developing new economic muscle. Since 1960, the six Common Market countries, led by West Germany, had surpassed the United States in percentage of gross world product. This achievement made the Common Market a countervailing economic power to the Soviet Union and the United States. Although the Common Market maintained the lead, its economic ascent slowed in the 1960s; by 1965, the rate of West German economic growth had fallen from a high of 9.4 percent between 1951 and 1955 to less than 5 percent—still a substantial rate. In the face of this downturn, which brought rising unemployment, politicians used pump-priming techniques to stimulate industrial investment and also put foreign "guest" laborers and married women out of work in favor of native-born men.

The opening of eastern European markets helped bolster western European prosperity; by the end of the decade, western European exports to the Soviet bloc totaled some $45 billion annually, producing a burden of debt that Communist countries could ill afford. In 1973, Britain joined the Common Market, followed by Ireland and Denmark. The market's exports now amounted to almost three times those of the United States.

Meanwhile, the United States, still the leading single producer in most fields, had become a major debtor. Rising purchases of military and imported goods brought inflation and a trade deficit. Dollars flooded the international currency markets, and in 1971, the Bretton Woods currency system, created during World War II to maintain stable international markets, collapsed. The international monetary crisis actually strengthened European integration still further as Common Market countries agreed to cooperate to prevent financial chaos. The Common Market's economic clout allowed it to force the United States to relinquish its single-handed direction of Western economic strategy.

Economic and geopolitical power spread not only beyond the United States but beyond the West. Japan emerged from its postwar reconstruction to challenge the United States and western Europe as

"AND ANYWHERE KHALID WENT, THE LAMB WAS SURE TO GO!"

The Middle East and the Politics of Oil

When Middle Eastern countries took control of the price and volume of oil they sold, Western leaders were taken aback, so thoroughly accustomed were the United States and its allies to setting the conditions of trade. OPEC leaders were lampooned in cartoons as the global economic crisis unfolded. Stagflation hit Western economies hard, while everyone came to terms with the new force of oil in international politics. Rosen-Albany Times-Union, NY/Rothco.

a manufacturing and exporting giant. In the 1960s, its rate of growth accelerated from an annual average of 9 percent in the 1950s to more than 11 percent, thanks in part to heavy buying by the United States for the wars in Korea and Vietnam. Even without oil and other key natural resources, Japan had become the world's largest shipbuilder by the 1970s, and only the United States and the Soviet Union surpassed it in iron and steel production.

In the 1970s, the Middle East's oil-producing nations also dealt Western dominance a critical blow. Tensions between Israel and the Arab world provided the catalyst. On June 5, 1967, Israeli forces, responding to Palestinian guerrilla attacks, seized Gaza and the Sinai peninsula from Egypt, the Golan Heights from Syria, and the West Bank from Jordan. Although Israel won a stunning victory in this Six-Day War, the Arab humiliation led the Arab states to try to forge a common political

Israel after the Six-Day War, 1967

and economic strategy. This strategy ranged from the populist militancy of the defeated Egyptian leader Gamal Abdel Nasser to the more conservative and somewhat more pro-Western leadership in Saudi Arabia to the radical factions of the Palestine Liberation Organization (PLO), which used terrorism against Israel. In 1973, Egypt and Syria attacked Israel on Yom Kippur, the most holy day in the Jewish calendar. Egypt initially made headway, but Israel, with material assistance from the United States, stopped the assault and counterattacked.

Having failed militarily against Israel and the United States, the Arab nations turned decisively to economic clout. The Organization of Petroleum Exporting Countries (OPEC), a relatively loose consortium before the Yom Kippur War, quadrupled the price of its oil and imposed an embargo, cutting off all exports of oil to the United States in retaliation for its support of Israel. For the first time since imperialism's heyday, the *producers* of raw materials—not the industrial powers—controlled the flow of commodities and set prices to their own advantage. The West was now mired in an oil crisis.

Throughout the 1970s, oil-dependent Westerners watched in astonishment as OPEC upset the balance of economic power. Instead of being controlled by the Western powers, the oil-producing nations helped provoke an economic recession by restricting the flow of oil and charging more for it (Figure 29.1). These actions caused unemployment to rise by more than 50 percent in Europe and the United States. Economic policymakers found old theories ineffective. Whereas previous recessions had brought falling prices as goods went unsold, this recession resulted in soaring inflation. By the end of 1973, the inflation rate jumped to over 8 percent in West Germany, 12 percent in France, and 20 percent in Portugal; in 1974, it reached 13 percent in Britain and Italy and 8 percent in the United States. Eastern-bloc countries, dependent on Soviet oil, fared little better. Though formally outside the bloc, Yugoslavia felt the effects, with 40 percent inflation by the end of the decade. Skyrocketing interest rates in the U.S.-led bloc discouraged both industrial investment and consumer buying. With prices, unemployment, and interest rates soaring—the unusual combination of economic conditions was dubbed *stagflation*—a sense of discouragement settled over Westerners. They realized not only that energy resources were finite but also that their economic prosperity had limits.

Political Alternatives in Hard Times

The unprecedented economic situation and the changing global balance of power inspired new waves of citizen activism. Some of these movements took the cause of reform to shocking extremes. Frustrated by long-standing grievances or the slow pace of change, some turned to violence, including bombings, kidnapping, and murder—a politics of terror reminiscent of the late nineteenth century but devastating to the superpowers' goal of maintaining the status quo.

Environmental Politics. A sense of limits to global resources encouraged the formation of environmental political parties. An escapee from Nazi Germany, E. F. "Fritz" Schumacher, produced one of the bibles of the environmental movement, *Small Is Beautiful* (1973), which spelled out how technology and industrialization threatened the earth and its inhabitants. Environmentalists like Schumacher and the American Rachel Carson, author of *Silent Spring* (1962), advocated the immediate rescue of rivers, forests, and the soil from the ravages of factories and chemical farming. Instead of massive agribusiness, which required huge doses of chemical fertilizers and produced single crops for the market, they pleaded for small-scale, diverse, organic (pesticide-

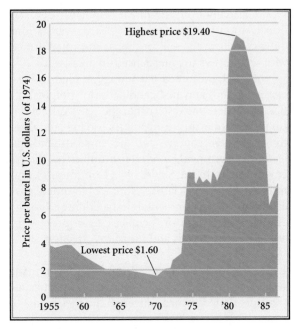

FIGURE 29.1 Fluctuating Oil Prices, 1955–1985
Colonization allowed the Western imperial powers to obtain raw materials at advantageous prices. Even with decolonization, European and American firms often had such entrenched roots in newly independent economies that they were able to set the terms for trade. OPEC's oil embargo and price hikes of the 1970s were signs of change, which included the exercise of decolonized countries' control over their own resources. Not only did OPEC's action lead to a decade of painful economic downturn, it also encouraged some European governments to improve public transportation and to impose policies that would make individual consumers cut back their dependence on oil.

free) farming. For industry, environmentalists demanded that factories be scaled back and made more environmentally responsible. These attitudes challenged almost two centuries of faith in industrial growth and in the infinite ability of humanity to extract progress from the natural world.

Initially the environmental movement had its greatest political effect in West Germany. As student protest subsided in the 1970s, environmentalism united members of older and younger generations around the 1960s political tactic called *citizen initiatives*, in which groups of people blocked everything from public transportation fare increases to plans for urban growth. In the 1970s, citizen initiative groups targeted nuclear power and nuclear installations; they took their cue from Chancellor Willy Brandt, whose Ostpolitik sought to extricate

West Germany from the threat of nuclear devastation. Demonstrations against nuclear power stations drew crowds in the tens of thousands, often armed with wirecutters to enter fenced-in areas.

In 1979, the Green Party was founded in West Germany and launched candidates for political office. Elsewhere in western Europe, environmentalists influenced mainstream politics, forcing candidates to voice their concern for the environment and leading governments to establish ministries for the environment. In the Soviet bloc, Communist commitment to industrial development blinded governments to environmental destruction and to the effects of pollution on people; citizen protest focused on basic needs and individual freedom.

Expansion of Feminism.   Feminist activism made real gains in the 1970s. Environmental parties attracted many women angered at the birth of thalidomide babies and concerned about the chemical contamination of their family's food. Men could escape to the moon or into their careers, a West German ecologist maintained, but not women, "who must give birth to children, willingly or unwillingly, in this polluted world of ours." Other women's activism had notable successes in the 1970s. In Catholic Italy, feminists won the right to divorce, to gain access to birth-control information, and to obtain legal abortions. The demand for these rights as well as for equal pay, job opportunities, and protection from rape, incest, and battering framed the major legal struggles of thousands of women's groups in the 1970s.

In the U.S.-led bloc, personal change also became a goal for women. Consciousness-raising sessions in which groups of women shared individual experiences with marriage, with children, and in the workforce became popular. Such sessions alleviated

Soldiers and Civilians in Northern Ireland
Separatist, civil rights, and terrorist movements made everyday life unpredictably dangerous in the last third of the century, as activists increasingly directed their violence against ordinary people. The world wars had often targeted civilians, and those leading internal struggles did so even when the declared wars were over. In Belfast, Northern Ireland, British troops fought to put down the Irish Republican Army and restore unity. Civilians were often drawn into the conflict. It was only late in the 1990s that both sides called a halt to the killing and agreed to negotiate.
Brian Aris/Camera Press London.

some of the isolation women felt at home; participants realized that women shared many similar experiences. Soviet-bloc women, who often formed the majority of the workforce and shouldered responsibility for all domestic work, received inspiration from feminist stories spread through the *samizdat* network. The new camaraderie among many women in both the Soviet and U.S.-led blocs prepared them for political participation.

In 1977, fifteen thousand activist women from around the globe poured into Houston to mark the International Year of Women. The meeting brought together Westerners interested in political and economic rights and cultural equality and third world women who called for an end to violence, starvation, and disease. The utter poverty afflicting women in less-developed countries called into question the commonality on which Western feminist politics was based. The issue of sexual orientation also challenged many mainstream activists in Houston, as lesbians exposed the greater privileges heterosexual women enjoyed. After Houston the media publicized the "death of feminism," both because of the convention's relative calm and because of the invisible roots feminism had sunk into mainstream local, national, and global politics. In 1978, East German author Christa Wolf spoke of a confident new attitude pervading the movement: "[Women] feel that their new role has already begun to solidify; their lust for life is great, their hunger for reality insatiable." Organization, raised consciousness, and some economic gains backed women's entry into local and national government from the 1970s on. (See "Contrasting Views," page 1146.)

Politics by Violence. Terrorist bands took a radically different path, responding to the conservative political climate and worsening economic conditions with kidnappings, bank robberies, bombings, and assassinations. Disaffected and well-to-do youth, steeped in the most extreme theories of society's decay, often joined these groups. Eager to bring down the Social Democratic coalition that led West Germany throughout the 1970s, the Baader-Meinhof gang assassinated prominent businessmen as well as judges and other public officials. Practiced in assassinations of public figures and random shootings of pedestrians, Italy's Red Brigades kidnapped and then murdered the head of the dominant Christian Democrats in 1978. Advocates of

independence for the Basque nation in northern Spain assassinated Spanish politicians and police.

In Britain, nationalist and religious violence in the 1970s pitted the Catholics in Northern Ireland against the dominant Protestants. Catholics experienced job discrimination and a lack of civil rights. In 1969, Catholic student protest turned into demonstrations on behalf of union with the Irish Republic. As violence in Northern Ireland escalated, the British government sent in troops. On January 30, 1972, which became known as "Bloody Sunday," British troops fired at demonstrators and killed thirteen, setting off a cycle of violence that left five hundred dead in that single year. Protestants fearful of losing their dominant position combated a reinvigorated Irish Republican Army (IRA),

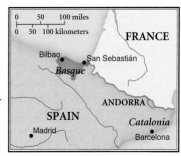

Nationalist Movements of the 1970s

which carried out bombings and assassinations to achieve the union of the two Irelands in order to end the oppression of Catholics.

Terrorists failed in their goal of overturning the existing democracies. In Italy, Christian Democrats and Communists managed to govern together throughout the terrorist crisis. In West Germany, Willy Brandt resigned in 1974 amidst a spy scandal within his government, the economic downturn, and ongoing terrorism. Another Social Democrat, the more pragmatic Helmut Schmidt, replaced him but continued Brandt's policies of rapprochement with East Germany and the Soviet Union.

Sorely tried as it was, parliamentary government scored some important successes in the 1970s. The Iberian Peninsula, suffering under dictatorship since the 1930s, regained its freedom and set out on a course of greater prosperity. The death of Spain's Francisco Franco (1892–1975) ended more than three decades of dictatorial rule. Franco's hand-picked successor, King Juan Carlos (b. 1938), surprisingly steered his nation to Western-style

Feminist Debates

The new feminist movement of the late twentieth century provoked the most pronounced and widespread debate over gender in recorded history. Discussion often reached a heated pitch, much like other reform movements of the day. Hardly the single movement described by journalists, feminism had a variety of concerns often depending on nationality, ethnicity, sexual orientation, and class. These could produce conflict among activists and serious divisions on goals and policies, as the authors of the Combahee River Statement demonstrated (Document 1). At times, concerns over issues like equal opportunity in the workplace were directed at government policies, though secretly, as in the case of the Soviet worker (Document 2). Italian feminists saw all the disabilities imposed by government as characteristic of larger problems (Document 3), while Germans explicitly connected the cause of feminism to that of environmentalism (Document 4).

1. Criticizing Feminism

In the United States, black women, like several other minority groups, found themselves marginalized in both the feminist and civil rights movements. In 1977 some of them issued the Combahee River Statement.

A Black feminist presence has evolved most obviously in connection with the second wave of the American women's movement beginning in the late 1960s. Black, other third world, and working women have been involved in the feminist movement from its start, but both outside reactionary forces and racism and elitism within the movement itself have served to obscure our participation. . . .

Black feminist politics also have an obvious connection to movements for Black liberation, particularly those of the 1960s and 1970s. . . . It was our experience and disillusionment within these liberation movements, as well as experience on the periphery of the white male left, that led to the need to develop a politics that was antiracist, unlike those of white women, and antisexist, unlike those of Black and white men. . . .

Above all else, our politics initially sprang from the shared belief that Black women are inherently valuable, that our liberation is a necessity not as an adjunct to somebody else's but because of our need as human persons for autonomy.

Source: "The Combahee River Collective Statement" in *Feminism in Our Time: The Essential Writings, World War II to the Present*, Miriam Schneir, ed. (New York: Vintage, 1994), 177–179.

2. Criticizing Socialism

Official policy in the Soviet Union stated that socialism had brought women full equality, eliminating the need for feminism. Thus in 1930, the government abolished the women's bureau, or Zhenotdel, and had branded feminism "bourgeois." In the 1970s, however, Russian women in clusters announced their dissatisfaction with so-called equality under socialism. Tatyana Mamonova, the editor of a collection of Russian women's writings—which originally circulated in samizdat form—was ultimately expelled from the country for publicizing views such as those of this railroad worker.

Today a woman has no outlet for complaints because women's sections have been abolished as "unnecessary." It is becoming increasingly clear that the current equality means only giving women the right to perform heavy labor. . . . [I]n our day the woman, still not freed from the incredible burden of the family, strains herself even harder in the service of society. The situation . . . is true not only in large cities but also in villages. On collective and state farms, women do the hardest and most exhausting work while the men are employed as administrators, agronomists, accountants, warehouse managers, or high-paid tractor and combine drivers. In other words, men do the work that is more interesting and more profitable and does not damage their health.

Source: Tatyana Mamonova, ed., *Women and Russia: Feminist Writings from the Soviet Union* (Boston: Beacon Press, 1984), 8.

3. Policy and Patriarchy

In Italy, as in the Soviet Union, feminism had an underground quality to it involving mimeographed tracts and graffiti on buildings; women formed their own bookshops and published small newspapers. But women also lobbied hard to get legislation on divorce and abortion changed. With socialism powerful among some intellectuals and in unions, the Feminist Movement of Rome saw issues in theoretical terms and connected the disabilities imposed on women with both class and sexual customs in a 1976 article in its paper.

Patriarchal society is based on authoritarian-exploitative relationships, and its sexuality is sadomasochistic. The values of power, of the domination of man over the other [woman], are reflected in sexuality, where historically woman is given to man for his use. . . .

The idea of woman as man's property is fundamental to her oppression and she is often the only possession that dominant men allow exploited men to keep. . . .

In other words woman is given to the (exploited) man as compensation for his lack of possessions. . . .

We denounce as the latest form of woman's oppression the idea of a "sexual revolution" where woman is forced to go from being one man's object to being everybody's object, and where sadomasochistic pornography in films, in magazines, in all the forms of mass media that brutalize and violate woman, is bandied about as a triumph of sexual liberty.

Source: "Male Sexuality—Perversion," *Movimento Femminista Romano* (1976), quoted in *Italian Feminist Thought: A Reader*, ed. Paola Bono and Sandra Kemp (Oxford: Blackwell, 1991), 68–69.

4. Feminism and Environmentalism

"Green" feminists took a different approach, such as this announced by Delphine Brox-Brochot in "Manifesto of the 'Green' Women." Brox-Brochot was speaking in 1975 to people in Bremen, West Germany, in the context of men's landing on the moon and other accomplishments in space.

Man has actually landed on the moon—an admirable feat. . . . We "Green" women . . . believe that men belong to our environment. In order to rescue that environment for our children, we want to confront this man, this adventurer and moon explorer. A female cosmonaut from a so-called socialist republic doesn't justify this energy-wasting enterprise for us at a time when three-fourths of the earth's population is suffering from malnutrition.

Our inability to solve immediate problems may tempt us into escape—to the moon, into careerism, escape into ideologies, into alcohol or other drugs. But one group cannot escape completely: women, society's potential mothers, who must give birth to children, willingly or unwillingly, in this polluted world of ours.

Source: Delphine Brox-Brochot, "Manifesto of the 'Green' Women," in *German Feminism: Readings in Politics and Literature*, ed. Edith Hoshino Altbach et al. (Albany: State University of New York Press, 1984), 314.

QUESTIONS FOR DEBATE

1. To what extent should we see the feminist movements of the 1960s and 1970s as primarily an offshoot of other reform movements of the day and thus a product of their time?

2. Is it more appropriate to speak of feminism in these decades as a unified movement or as a set of multiple movements with multiple goals?

3. Were there distinctly national issues within feminism that made the movement more a product of national politics than of gender politics?

IMPORTANT DATES

1962   Forum on "pop art" at the Museum of Modern Art in New York City

1962–1965   Vatican II reforms Catholic ritual and dogma

1963   U.S. president John F. Kennedy assassinated

1964   Nikita Khrushchev ousted in the USSR, replaced by Leonid Brezhnev and Alexei Kosygin

1966   Willy Brandt becomes West German foreign minister and develops Ostpolitik, a policy designed to bridge tensions between the two Germanies

1967   South Africa's Dr. Christiaan Barnard performs first successful human heart transplant

1968   Revolution in Czechoslovakia against communism; student uprisings throughout Europe and the United States

1969   U.S. astronauts walk on the moon's surface

1972   SALT I treaty between the United States and Soviet Union

1973   North Vietnam and the United States sign treaty ending war in Vietnam; OPEC raises price of oil and imposes oil embargo on the West

1973–1976   Aleksandr Solzhenitsyn publishes *Gulag Archipelago*

1977   Feminists gather in Houston to mark the first International Year of Women

1978   The first test-tube baby is born in England

1979   Iranians take U.S. hostages in Teheran

constitutional monarchy, facing down threatened military coups. Portugal and Greece also ousted right-wing dictators, thus paving the way for their integration into western Europe and for substantial economic growth.

Yet the dominance of the West was deteriorating. In 1976, Jimmy Carter (b. 1924), a wealthy farmer and governor of Georgia, narrowly won the U.S. presidential election (the first after Watergate) by selling himself as an outsider to Washington corruption. Carter's domestic and foreign policies met with some success; but they did little to return the economy to its pre-Vietnam and pre–oil embargo prosperity or stem global terrorism.

The last two years of Carter's administration witnessed still another challenge to Western dominance in the form of Islamic militancy. Late in the 1970s, students, clerics, shopkeepers, and unemployed men in Iran began a religious agitation that forced Shah Reza Pahlavi (1919–1980) into exile in January 1979. Repressively and brutally ruled by the U.S.-backed shah, Iran had enormous but unevenly distributed wealth and a large population of discontented, poor Shi'ite Muslims. The militants installed a fundamentalist Muslim leader, Ayatollah Ruhollah Khomeini (1900?–1989), whose political messages had arrived from his Parisian exile via cassette technology to consolidate opposition to the shah. Khomeini called for a transformation of the region into a truly Islamic society awaiting the coming of the Mahdi, or Messiah. Iran, he believed, could lead this transformation if it renounced the Western ways advocated by the shah and followed the strict rule of Islam. In the autumn of 1979, revolutionary supporters of Khomeini took hostages at the American embassy in Teheran and would not release them. The paralysis of the United States in the face of Islamic militancy along with the soaring inflation following another round of OPEC price hikes suggested that the 1980s and 1990s might cripple the West even more.

Conclusion

The 1960s and 1970s left the West with a sense of emergency. In these decades, an unprecedented level of technological development transformed businesses, the nature of warfare, the exploration of space, and the functioning of government. It also had an enormous impact on everyday life. Work changed, as society reached a stage called *postindustrial*, in which the service sector predominated. New patterns of family life, new relationships among the generations, and revised standards for sexual behavior also characterized these years. Optimism abounded in the potential of humans to perpetuate progress and affluence. Yet technological change produced stubborn problems: concentrations of bureaucratic and industrial power, social inequality, environmental degradation, even uncertainty about humankind's future.

A surge of rebellion among youth, ethnic and racial minorities, and women condemned these conditions along with the threats posed by the continued cold war. By the end of the 1970s, war in Vietnam, protests throughout the Soviet bloc, the power of oil-producing states, and the growing

Revolutionary Fervor in Iran

The installation of an Islamic government in Iran gained the real enthusiasm of citizens, for whom the rule of the shah had brought modernization and Westernization, but a clamp-down on freedom and striking inequalities of wealth. Islamic rule meant distinctly different roles for men and women; women, for instance were required to wear more restrictive clothing and to adopt a more subservient demeanor after years of Westernization and liberalization. At the same time, the strict separation of the sexes brought new opportunity for jobs in medicine, teaching, and other professions as women were trained to treat an all-female clientele who could no longer use men's services.
Alfred/Liaison Agency.

political force of Islam had weakened superpower preeminence. The U.S.-led bloc also confronted terrorism, and the Soviet Union, long able to repress dissent in a growing economy, was putting more resources into military buildup than it could ultimately support. While the superpowers faltered, society approached the global age—one prepared by the array of technology of the 1960s and 1970s. The phenomena of rising citizen activism, globalism, and rapid technological advance posed real challenges to a world on the verge of a new millennium.

Suggested References

The Technology Revolution

Wartime technological development came to have profound consequences for the peacetime lives of individuals and for society. The works below describe the new technologies and analyze their importance, with authors divided on whether the new developments should be feared or embraced.

Hecht, Gabrielle. *The Radiance of France: Nuclear Power and National Identity after World War II.* 1998.

Kimbrell, Andrew. *The Human Body Shop: The Cloning, Engineering, and Marketing of Life.* 1997.

Mazlich, Bruce. *The Fourth Discontinuity: The Co-Evolution of Humans and Machines.* 1994.

*Rhodes, Richard, ed. *Visions of Technology: A Century of Vital Debate about Machines, Systems, and the Human World.* 1999.

Singer, Edward Nathan. *The Twentieth Century Revolution in Technology.* 1998.

*Stanworth, Michelle, ed. *Reproductive Technologies: Gender, Motherhood, and Medicine.* 1987.

Postindustrial Society and Culture

Changes in the way people worked became striking in the 1960s, causing social observers to analyze the meaning of the transformation. Many critics agree that technology's creation of a postindustrial workplace changed not only the way people worked but also how they lived in families and interacted with peers.

Bennett, Tony, ed. *Rock and Popular Music: Politics, Policies, Institutions.* 1993.

Evans, Christopher. *The Micro Millennium.* 1979.

Hochschild, Arlie. *The Time Bind: When Work Becomes Home and Home Becomes Work.* 1997.

Proctor, Robert. *Cancer Wars: The Politics behind What We Know and Don't Know about Causes and Trends.* 1994.

*Primary sources.

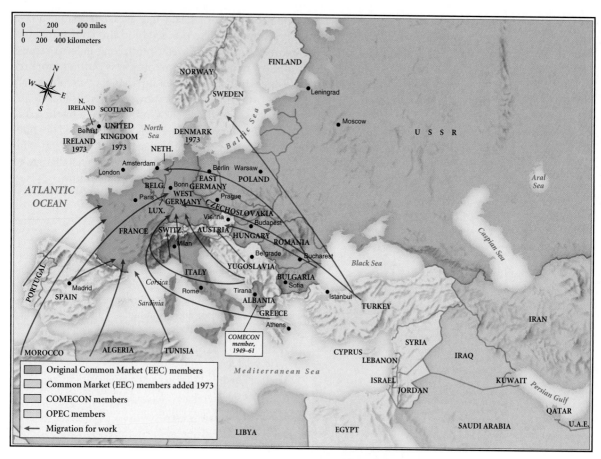

MAPPING THE WEST Europe and the Mediterranean, 1980

Despite the continuation of the cold war and the division of Europe into two antagonistic regions, the superpower grip diminished during the 1960s and 1970s. Within the Soviet bloc, several governments introduced features of a market economy and communications technology brought news of life in the U.S.-led bloc. U.S. allies protested American policies in Vietnam, with anti-American elements very much in evidence in the uprisings of 1968. Mediterranean countries played their role in the West's transformation during these decades, not only in the oil embargo but in sending tens of thousands of migrants to work in labor-short Europe and often to settle there permanently.

Sampson, Anthony. *The New Europeans.* 1968.

Sinfield, Alan. *Literature, Politics, and Culture in Post-war Britain.* 1989.

Contesting the Cold War Order in the 1960s

Historians look to domestic politics, international events, social change, and cultural life to capture the texture of this tumultuous decade. But the momentous changes on so many fronts still need synthetic treatment. A Martin Luther King Web site introduces visitors to the biography, speeches, sermons, and major life events of the slain civil rights leader.

Caute, David. *Sixty-Eight.* 1988.

*Dubček, Alexander. *Hope Dies Last: The Autobiography of Alexander Dubček.* 1993.

Fineberg, Jonathan. *Art since 1940: Strategies of Being.* 1995.

*Guy-Sheftall, Beverly, ed. *Words of Fire: An Anthology of African-American Feminist Thought.* 1995.

Katsiaficas, George. *The Subversion of Politics: European Autonomous Social Movements and the Decolonization of Everyday Life.* 1997.

*Lévi-Strauss, Claude. *Tristes Tropiques.* 1961.

The Martin Luther King, Jr. Papers Project at Stanford University: http://www.stanford.edu/group/King.

Tarrow, Sidney. *Democracy and Disorder: Protest Politics in Italy, 1965–1975.* 1989.

The Erosion of Superpower Mastery in the 1970s

As the superpowers continued their standoff, historians found that myriad global changes affected their status. Some of the most compelling reading is found in personal testimonies such as Chang's account of Maoism and the Cultural Revolution, while the dissident art of the Soviet Union is striking for its deft and moving critique of life under Communism. Many interesting Web sites explore the development of green parties over the past three decades, the most inclusive being that of the global organization with links to green parties of all continents and countries.

Battah, Abdalla M., and Yehuda Lukachs, eds. *The Arab-Israeli Conflict: Two Decades of Change.* 1988.

*Chang, Jung. *Wild Swans: Three Daughters of China.* 1991.

Green parties worldwide: http://www.greens.org.

Huelsberg, Werner. *The German Greens: A Social and Political Profile.* 1988.

Koshar, Rudy. *Germany's Transient Pasts: Preservation and National Memory in the Twentieth Century.* 1998.

Laqueur, Walter. *The Age of Terrorism.* 1987.

Olson, James S., and Randy Roberts. *Where the Domino Fell: America and Vietnam, 1945–1990.* 1996.

Rosenfeld, Alla, and Norton T. Dodge. *From Gulag to Glasnost: Nonconformist Art from the Soviet Union.* 1995.

Smith, Dennis B. *Japan since 1945: The Rise of an Economic Superpower.* 1995.

*Solzhenitsyn, Aleksandr Isaevich. *The Gulag Archipelago.* 1973–1976.

Swain, Geoffrey, and Nigel Swain. *Eastern Europe since 1945.* 1993.

The New Globalism: Opportunities and Dilemmas

1980 to the Present

Paraguay-France Championship Soccer Match

Professional sports had become a force for global unity and national rivalry alike by the twenty-first century. The pool of highly paid and internationally celebrated athletes was a global melting pot of race, ethnicity, gender, and religion, while the diffusion of sports news and programming, such as the Paraguay-France soccer championship match, encouraged a common, global culture.

Owen Franken/Stock Boston.

I N THE MID-1980S, THE SOVIET MAGAZINE *OGONYOK* ("Small Fires"), instead of making up patriotic "letters to the editor" as was the custom under communism, began printing actual reports from readers. Identifying herself as a "mother of two," one woman protested that the cost-cutting policy of reusing syringes in hospitals was spreading AIDS. "Why should little kids have to pay for the criminal actions of our Ministry of Health?" she asked. Other readers complained of corrupt factory managers, of "the radioactive sausages" foisted on the public after the disastrous explosion at the Chernobyl nuclear plant, and of endless lines at grocery stores and the lack of food. Sales of *Ogonyok* soared from a few hundred thousand to four million, and the experiment in printing real letters flooded the offices with hundreds of thousands of pieces of mail. The *Ogonyok* example was not unique: all across the Soviet bloc people were exploring political participation and resistance. They wrote, picketed, and protested; in so doing they created an unprecedented public activism that, with incredibly little bloodshed, toppled the Soviet empire in 1989 and ended the cold war.

The collapse of communism in Europe had unexpected repercussions, including the eruption of ethnic violence in the region, the deterioration of everyday life, and the decline of public services. The latter result was part of a general trend in the West, as Great Britain, the United States, and the other advanced industrial economies reversed the century-long trend toward the welfare state. Government support for citizens' health, housing, and social security diminished, as politicians

1980	1984	1988	1992	1996	2000

Politics and War

Islamic revolution in Iran

Student uprising in Beijing's Tiananmen Square; collapse of Soviet empire

Retrenchment of the welfare state in Great Britain, the United States, other western nations

Germany reunified

International congress of women at Beijing

Rise of Solidarity in Poland

War in the Persian Gulf

First postapartheid elections in South Africa

Civil war in the former Yugoslavia

USSR formally dissolved

Society and Economy

Gorbachev's policy of perestroika; nuclear accident at Chernobyl

Genocide in Rwanda

AIDS epidemic reaches global proportions

Privatization and economic dislocation in post-Soviet economies; Internet revolution

Collapse of Thai currency and upset of Asian "tigers"

Euro becomes currency of the European Union; world population reaches six billion

Culture, Religion, and Intellectual Life

Growing influence of Islam in culture and politics; postmodernism in architecture, literature, and cultural theory; international diffusion of culture

looked back to the liberal values of the nineteenth century, not the liberalism of the twentieth. However, government increased subsidies and incentives for business, as the West found itself in a new struggle of global competition. This war targeted the rising economic power of Japan, China, and other Asian countries, and for a time it came to replace the cold war, at least in public rhetoric. As international business mergers accelerated in the 1990s and as the Internet connected enterprises around the world in a matter of seconds, however, international unity rather than competition became the order of the day among former rivals in business and politics alike.

The end of the cold war thus hastened the arrival of the "global age"—marked by the vast international and national migration of tens of millions of people, the expanding global marketplace, and an accelerated cultural exchange of popular music, books, films, and television entertainment. The global age also encompassed the international impact of disasters such as AIDS and environmental degradation. To some it signaled an end of superpower rivalry and the dominance of the United States. Others pointed to the rise of new forces that rivaled those of the West, such as the economic power of the Asian countries and the cultural might of Islam. Only as the century drew to a close did observers equate globalism with the revolutionary power of the Internet. Whatever the meaning of the many new phenomena, there is no question that the twenty-first century will bring extraordinary challenges that have worldwide resonance.

For historians, understanding the recent past is a challenge in itself. Every day of the past two decades has been filled with news—news that now receives virtually instantaneous reporting because of modern communications technology. Unlike journalists, historians do not attempt to choose from this mass the most talked-about story of the moment or the one that will attract the greatest readership. Rather, they are interested in judging what will be important in the long run and which items from the unfiltered mass of technologically transmitted news are actually true. Historians want to identify social, cultural, and political events that are uniquely important or generally significant for people's everyday lives. Historians make the most reliable evaluations when these phenomena are no longer "news"—that is, after a good period of time has shown their staying power and influence.

In the first edition of this book we held our breath in the face of rapidly changing events and judged that the fall of communism in Europe and the increasing interconnectedness of the world's peoples and cultures were the challenges not only of the moment but of history. In this second edition we persist in that judgment although the end of the Soviet Union and the coming of globalism have brought greater perils than we anticipated only five or six years ago. Other forces like the Internet missed our notice altogether, despite the fact that the system had been around for several decades. As an experiment in history, you might note the important events of the months in which you take this course, put your list away for several years or more, and then see if those events—along with the events discussed in this chapter—stand the test of time.

❖ Global Challenges

It is now a commonplace belief that we live in a global age, but once our historical vision widens to encompass the globe we see a picture of uneven development and much room for debate about the state of our planet and its peoples. Despite a rapidly changing economy, access to jobs, and prosperity for many, the end of the cold war ushered in many challenges. First, the health of the world's peoples and their environment encountered a multipronged attack as nuclear disaster, acid rain, and surging population threatened the planet's ecosystem. Second, economic prosperity and physical safety continued to elude great masses of people, especially in the southern half of the globe. Third, a greater number of states than ever before exercised economic and political power, especially through multinational agencies like the World Bank and the World Trade Organization—a shift from the bipolarism of the cold war when there were two reigning superpowers. Simultaneously, nonstate or transnational allegiances such as Islamic or ethnic movements also vied for power and influence, often calling into question not only the concept of national borders but the very nation-state on which modern history has focused.

Pollution and Population

Whereas industrialization and a growing population had once appeared wholly positive, people became aware of their dangers and limits. For each warning of imminent catastrophe—either from overcrowding or ecological disaster—some scientists and social theorists pointed to the solutions that humans had usually been able to devise for even the direst calamities.

Threats to the Environment. Despite the best efforts of the spreading ecology movement, technological development continued to threaten the environment. The dangers were laid bare starkly in 1986, when the nuclear plant at Chernobyl in the Soviet Union exploded and spewed radioactive dust into the atmosphere. The reactor, like most in the USSR, had been constructed with minimal safety features. Many plant workers died within the year; others perished more slowly from the effects of radiation. Levels of radioactivity rose for hundreds of miles in all directions, and by the 1990s cancer rates in the region were soaring, particularly among children.

Other environmental problems were more insidious but also had devastating global effects. Fossil-fuel pollutants such as those from natural gas, coal, and oil mixed with atmospheric moisture to

Chernobyl Memorial Demonstration

The explosion at the nuclear plant at Chernobyl in Ukraine caused death and illness and led to a regional surge in cancer cases that has lasted to the present day. Coming in the midst of reform in the Soviet Union, the explosion pointed to the dangers in the entire nuclear system, which had been built with minimal safety precautions to save money. Citizens protested more widely, revealing their anger at the condition of their daily lives.
Sovfoto/Eastfoto.

produce acid rain, a poisonous brew that destroyed forests in industrial areas. Acid rain damaged more than 70 percent of Europe's Norway spruce trees. In eastern Europe, where fossil fuels were burned with virtually no safeguards, forests looked as if they had been ravaged by fire, and children suffered a range of ailments such as chronic bronchial disease. In less industrial areas, the world's rain forests were hacked down at an alarming rate, as people sought land to develop for cattle grazing or for growing cash crops. Clearing the forests depleted the global oxygen supply and threatened the biological diversity of the entire planet.

By the late 1980s, scientists from around the world had identified other challenges to the environment. The public's use of chlorofluorocarbons (CFCs), chemicals found in aerosol and refrigeration products, had blown a hole in the ozone layer. Part of the blanket of gases surrounding the earth, ozone prevents harmful ultraviolet rays from reaching the planet. Simultaneously, automobile and industrial emissions of chemicals were adding to the thermal blanket of which ozone was a part. The result was *global warming*, an increase in the temperature of the earth's lower atmosphere. Changes in temperature and dramatic weather cycles of drought or drenching rain indicated that a *greenhouse effect* might be permanently warming the earth. Some researchers forecast dire effects for the earth's future.

The global public stepped up pressure on governments to check pollution, and the affluent West possessed the resources to begin to undo some of the damage that had accompanied industrialization and technological change. Automobile manufacturers in western Europe and the United States began building cars with lower carbon monoxide emissions, and industrialists scaled back on factory pollution of air and waterways. Consumers began recycling such products as newspapers, glass and plastic containers, and cardboard. In Europe, municipal governments turned streets into automobile-free pedestrian zones, established more "green" areas in cities, and even banned cars altogether when ozone levels reached a danger point. European countries and Japan led the world in providing efficient public transportation, thus reducing the number of polluting automobiles on the streets. In the United States, the automobile industry's political influence blocked the expansion of mass transit, however, and prevented restrictions on automobile use.

Population Growth. Nations with less-developed economies struggled with the pressing issue of surging population. Whereas by 1995 Europe was actually experiencing negative growth (that is, more deaths than births), the less industrially developed countries accounted for 98 percent of all population growth globally. The annual growth rate of world population had been about 2 percent since 1950. By late 1999, the globe's population had reached 6 billion and the growth rate was estimated at 1.5 percent, with a doubling at this rate forecast for 2045.

(See "Taking Measure," below.) Migration, urbanization, and social dislocation plagued nations without the industrial and commercial resources to feed these swelling numbers.

The population increased partly because the spread of Western medicine enabled people to live much longer. In nonindustrial countries, life expectancy rose by an average of sixteen years between 1950 and 1980. The superpowers did not fare particularly well by this measure of social health: life expectancy in the Soviet Union fell steadily in the 1970s to 1990s, from a peak of seventy years in the mid-1970s to fifty-three for Russian men in 1995; by 1995, the United States had fallen from the top twenty in longevity for both women and men. Meanwhile, fertility rates, which had been dropping in the West for decades, were also declining in the less-developed world by 1995, as some 58 percent of couples were estimated to use birth control. Women in North Africa, who had produced an average of 6.8 children in the 1950s and 1960s, were giving birth to an average of 5.6 by the mid-1980s. In China the number fell precipitously, from 6.2 to 2.0 in 1995, largely because of government restrictions on pregnancy. Nonetheless, the Chinese population skyrocketed. Where women entered the economic arena, as in South Korea, family limitation advanced. Many took heart at the slowdown in population increase as a sign of the potential for diverting calamitous growth.

Western medicine and better health found their way into the less-developed world in the form of vaccines and drugs for diseases such as malaria and smallpox. However, half of all Africans did not benefit from basic public health facilities such as safe drinking water. Drought and poverty, along with the maneuvers of politicians in some cases, spread famine in regions like the Sudan. Critics analyzed these conditions as the result of a growing divide not between East and West but among countries of the wealthy North and the far poorer South. Medical practice in the industrialized nations focused on high-tech solutions to health problems. Specialists performed heart bypass surgery, transplanted organs, and treated cancer with radiation and chemotherapy. Preventive care received less attention; for example, in the late 1970s the Netherlands spent less than 3 percent of its total medical expenditures on preventive medicine. Expensive, technological, in-hospital treatment of the sick became the rule in wealthy nations, and studies showed that a disproportionate amount of these services went to the upper classes, especially men. At the other end of the scale, the unemployed suffered more chronic illnesses than those who were better off, but they received less care. Within industrial countries as well

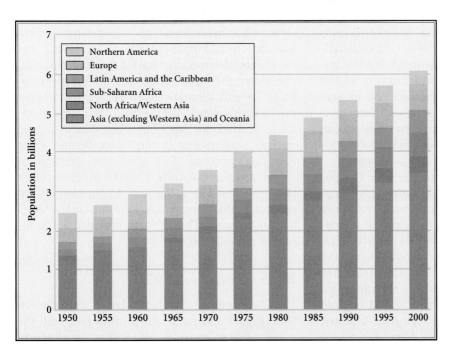

TAKING MEASURE
World Population Growth, 1950–2000

In the twenty-first century, a major question is whether the global environment can sustain billions of people indefinitely. In the early modern period, local communities had lived according to unwritten rules that balanced population size with the productive capacities of individual farming regions. Centuries later the same need for balance had reached global proportions. As fertility dropped around the planet because of contraception, population continued to grow because of improved health. The political, social, and environmental results remain unclear.

as outside them, the distribution of health services became a hotly debated issue in the general argument of whether technological solutions could remedy global problems.

North versus South?

During the 1980s and 1990s, world leaders tried to address the growing economic schism between the earth's northern and southern regions. Although Australians and New Zealanders were exceptions, southern peoples generally suffered lower living standards and measures of health than northerners. Recently emerging from colonial rule and economic exploitation by the North, citizens could not yet count on their new governments to provide welfare services or education. Latin American nations grappled with government corruption, multibillion-dollar debt, widespread crime, and grinding poverty. In Brazil, bands of homeless children roamed city streets. The drug trade plagued Colombia; illegal commerce diverted resources that might have been channeled toward investment, social reforms, and the development of democracy. Other countries, prominent among them Mexico, began to strengthen their economies by marketing their oil and other natural resources more effectively.

In sub-Saharan Africa, environmental destruction resulted from the conversion of land to the production of cash crops. The region suffered from drought, continuing famine, and civil war. In lands such as Rwanda, military rule, ideological factionalism, and ethnic antagonism encouraged under imperialism produced a lethal mixture of conflict and genocide in the 1990s. Millions perished; others were left starving and homeless. Although African countries began turning away from military dictatorship and toward parliamentary government, global economic advance was uneven on that continent.

In South Africa, native peoples struggled for political rights and economic opportunity against entrenched white racism. In 1990, the moderate South African leader F. W. de Klerk released the imprisoned political leader Nelson Mandela (b. 1918), who had been held for almost three decades because of his antiapartheid politics. By then the media had made Mandela's plight a focus of worldwide concern, and multinational corporations had reduced their economic activity in the segregated country. De Klerk's government followed Mandela's release

with a gradual dismantling of such aspects of apartheid as segregated parks and beaches. In 1993, the government and the African National Congress (ANC) agreed to a democratic constitution that granted the vote to the nonwhite majority while guaranteeing whites and other minorities civil liberties. The path to reform was complicated by divisions among African ethnic groups, most notably between the Xhosa, who held most of the positions of power in the ANC, and the Zulu, who opposed the ANC. Strong evidence suggested that conflict among Africans was fanned by white supremacists in the police and army and in paramilitary groups. In 1994, the ANC won a landslide victory and Mandela, the country's president, endorsed the tolerant new constitution, promoted a multiracial democracy in which international business flourished, and oversaw the election of a second postapartheid president in 1999.

Southern countries' drive to modernize could serve as a force for political stability, but sometimes internal struggles over national policy ignited turmoil. In India, Rajiv Gandhi (1944–1991), the grandson of India's first prime minister, Jawaharlal Nehru, worked for education, women's rights, and an end to bitter local rivalries; his assassination in 1991 by Tamil nationalists raised questions about whether India would continue to have the strong leadership necessary to attract investment and thus to continue modernization. That question was soon answered, as India developed its leadership in communications and other technology. In Pakistan and the Philippines, too, the impulse for modernization grew, but unstable social conditions and inept political systems discouraged investment. Moreover, the United Nations slapped both Pakistan and India with economic sanctions when they detonated nuclear weapons late in the 1990s. Because these emerging economies as a whole continued to increase their share of gross domestic product during the 1980s and 1990s, Western domination eroded proportionally. However, the hardships in the South by comparison with the North provided a new focus for global politics.

Islam Confronts the West

The Iran hostage crisis that began in 1979 showed that religion and nationalism could join with the power of oil to make the Middle East an arbiter of

Muslims at Prayer in Marseille, France
As migration increased during the 1980s and 1990s, Europe became more ethnically and racially diverse than it had been for centuries. In most European countries, immigrants could eventually become citizens, while others such as Switzerland and Germany used the criterion of common ancestry to determine who would have political and civil rights. Cultural exchange and interaction accelerated during these decades, and debates over what constituted cultural values and cultural identity multiplied.
Steve McCurry/Magnum Photos, Inc.

international order. The charismatic leaders of the 1980s—Iran's Ayatollah Khomeini, Libya's Muammar Qaddafi, and Iraq's Saddam Hussein—despite important differences, all promoted a pan-Arabic or pan-Islamic world order that gathered increasing support. According to a Muslim intellectual, the capitalist West had used up "that stock of values which gave it its predominance. . . . The turn of Islam has come." Nor did the Soviet Union, before its demise, offer a useful alternative. Muslims should confront the superpowers, Khomeini urged, by taking the position "Neither East, nor West, only the Islamic Republic."

Khomeini's program had wide appeal. Turning from the Westernization that had flourished under the shah, his regime required women to cover their bodies almost totally in special clothing again, restricted their right to divorce, and eliminated a range of other rights. Such changes became a stand-

ard component of Islamic revolution because these restrictions were believed to restore the pride and Islamic identity that imperialism had stripped from Middle Eastern men. Khomeini built widespread support among the Shi'ite Muslims. Even though they constituted the majority in many Middle Eastern countries—72 percent of the population in Bahrain, 60 percent in Iraq, and 95 percent in Iran—they had long been ruled by the Sunnis. The tables turned when Khomeini proclaimed the ascendancy of the Shi'ite clergy in Islamic revolutionary society.

Power in the Middle East remained fragmented, however, and Islam did not achieve its unifying goals (Map 30.1). The Iranian Shi'ites expressed their newfound power and anti-Western feeling by refusing to release the hostages taken in 1979 from the U.S. embassy; their prolonging of the hostage crisis through 1980 contributed to the collapse of the Carter presidency and the election of Ronald

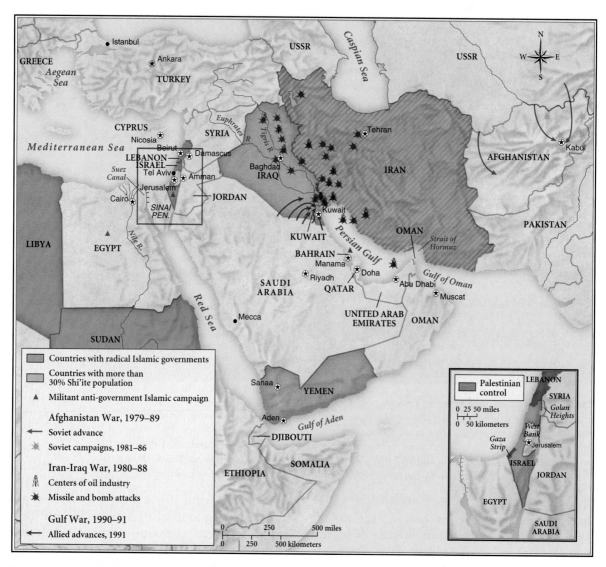

MAP 30.1 The Middle East, 1980–1991

Tensions among states in the Middle East, especially the ongoing conflict between Palestinians and Israelis, became more complicated in the 1980s. As Islam took center stage in politics, Middle Eastern populations additionally divided over such issues as the extent of religious determination of state policies, the rule of religion in everyday life, and access to human rights including freedom of speech and of movement. Conflicts erupted around some of these questions because, as elsewhere, they were also the vehicle for political ambition. The increasing demands of globalization in the 1990s pulled other citizens in the direction of secularization, high-tech international partnerships, and a reduction in the costly politics of violence.

Reagan. Meanwhile, in September 1980, Iraq's president, Saddam Hussein, launched an attack on Iran. Hussein feared that Iraq's Shi'ite minority might rebel against his regime, and he sought to channel their aggression through a patriotic crusade against the non-Arab Iranians. The Iraqi leader also coveted oil-rich territory in Iran. After eight years of com-

bat, the war's primary outcome was massive loss of life on both sides.

The Soviet Union became embroiled against the force of Islam when it supported a coup by a Communist faction against the Communist government in Afghanistan in 1979. The factionalism provided an opening for stiff resistance by Afghanis whose traditional way of life had been threatened by communism's modernizing thrust. By 1980, tens of thousands of Soviets were fighting in Afghanistan, using the USSR's most advanced missiles and artillery to overcome Muslim leaders. After the withdrawal of Soviet forces and the collapse of the USSR, power in Afghanistan remained contested, though by the late 1990s the fundamentalist Taliban party had succeeded in imposing a strict regime, creating millions of political and religious refugees.

As the USSR's empire fell apart, Saddam Hussein was the first to test the post–cold war waters. At the end of the Iran-Iraq war in 1988, Iraq staggered under a heavy debt, unresolved territorial disputes with Iran, the bitter loss of hundreds of thousands of soldiers and civilians, and a lowered standard of living. Hussein viewed the annexation of neighboring Kuwait, whose 600,000 citizens enjoyed the world's highest per capita income, as a solution to Iraq's troubles and a means of smothering internal discontent. In August 1990, he invaded the oil-rich country. While stirring fears among world leaders that he would take other nations, he appealed to the masses in the region as a pan-Arab hero.

Contrary to Hussein's expectations, the deployment of Iraqi troops on the Saudi Arabian border galvanized international resistance. The USSR joined the United Nations' effort to stop the Iraqi invasion, signaling a post–cold war shift in the winds of diplomacy whereby small warring nations would no longer be able to exploit superpower animosities. A multinational force led by the United States pummeled the Iraqi army. Iraq's defeat in the Persian Gulf War heightened pressure on all Middle Eastern leaders to negotiate a peaceful solution to their decades-long disputes.

Yet many of those same leaders used international terrorism to advance their causes. Assassinations and bombings of public buildings and transportation took their toll in lives, especially among the Western powers. Reaching Africa, Asia, and Latin America, terrorism reshaped international politics and perhaps even the definitions of the terms *war* and *peace.*

The Rise of the Pacific Economy

The last third of the twentieth century saw an incredible global diffusion of industry and technology, especially in Asia and some countries in Latin America such as Chile. Just as economic changes in the early modern period had redirected European affairs from the Mediterranean to the Atlantic, explosive productivity from Japan to Singapore in the 1980s began to spread economic power from the Atlantic region to the Pacific. In 1982, the Asian Pacific nations accounted for 16.4 percent of global gross domestic product, a figure that had doubled since the 1960s. More surprising, by the mid-1990s China was achieving economic growth rates of 8 percent and more, while Japan had developed the second largest national economy after the United States.

South Korea, Taiwan, Singapore, Hong Kong, and China were popularly called "tigers" for the ferocity of their growth. Japan, however, led the charge. Investment in high-tech consumer industries drove the Japanese economy. Thus in 1982, Japan had 32,000 industrial robots in operation; Western Europe employed only 9,000, the United States, 7,000. In 1989, the Japanese government and private businesses invested $549 billion to modernize industrial capacity, a full $36 billion more than American public and private investment combined. Such spending paid off substantially, as Japanese companies turned out high-quality consumer products that found an eager international market. Just as the U.S. military had done during its wars in Asia between 1950 and the 1970s, now U.S. buyers snapped up automobiles, televisions, videocassette recorders, cameras, and computers from Japanese or other Asian Pacific companies.

"Tigers" of the Pacific Rim, c. 1985

As the profits rolled in, Japanese enterprises bought large sections of American cities and swallowed up Western businesses, furthering globalization. Huge financial institutions flourished: by the end of the 1980s, Japan was home to the world's eight largest banks as well as a brokerage house that was twenty times larger than its nearest American competitor. Furthermore, whereas Japanese military expenses remained low by constitutional mandate, the United States throughout much of the 1980s poured mounting sums into its cold war military budget—but failed to raise taxes to pay for this expenditure. Thus the Japanese and other Asians who purchased U.S. government bonds actually financed America's ballooning national debt. Forty years after its total defeat in World War II, Japan was bankrolling its former conqueror.

Despite rising national prosperity, individual Asian workers, particularly outside of Japan, paid dearly for this newly created wealth. For example, women in South Korea and Taiwan labored in sweatshops to produce clothing for such U.S.-based companies as J. C. Penney and Calvin Klein. Using the lure of a low-paid and docile female workforce, governments were able to attract electronics and other industries. However, educational standards rose, along with access to birth control and other medical care for these women. Despite the persistent grip of authoritarian government, some of the tigers ranked high by UN standards for human development.

A single party that centralized decision making for the economy and much else in the society had dominated Japan's business-oriented government for most of the postwar period. The results were mixed. Japanese workers were expected to subordinate their interests to those of the business firm, just as business followed coordinated government instructions. The rewards for this discipline were great, and Japanese success was held up as a model to the West. Yet resistance to the patriarchal political elite developed: in 1989, Japanese women led the way in voting out of office a prime minister who kept a mistress. Women also entered the parliament and cabinet, long a bastion of elderly men. Government attempts to maintain cultural homogeneity brought charges of racism from abroad. The country also had to deal with the reality that hundreds of thousands of non-Japanese had illegally entered the country to perform the menial labor shunned by native workers. Critics began to express concern about environmental deterioration, the quality of life in overcrowded cities, and the growing menace of domestic terrorism.

Mounting economic difficulties plagued Japan and the other Asian tigers in the 1990s. Financial scandals and widespread corruption, long a problem in postwar Japanese politics, repeatedly brought down the political leadership. The stock market plunged, as did the value of the yen. Domestic consumers cut back, and those interested in saving sent their money abroad for higher returns. Japan's relations with its major trading partner, the United States, were often strained. From 1997 on, Japan's depressed economy threatened to pull the rest of the region, if not the world, into a deep recession. A severe business crisis struck the Pacific rim as currency speculation and irresponsible and corrupt financial practices first brought down the Thai currency in 1997 and then toppled politicians and industrial leaders in Indonesia, South Korea, and elsewhere in the region. Many Asian leaders vacillated amidst a growing recognition that for the first time in modern history global civilization's industrial and financial health depended on countries outside the West.

✦ The Welfare State in Question

Stagflation remained a powerful economic threat as the 1980s opened, and along with the realignment of global economic power it forced non-Communist governments in the West to put their economic houses in order. In the postwar world, the Keynesian practice of pump priming through government spending had been the spark that recharged a flagging economy. The unprecedented mix of the energy crisis, soaring unemployment, and double-digit inflation made new remedies imperative. Voters frustrated by threats of a declining standard of living elected conservative politicians, who maintained that decades of supporting a welfare state were at the heart of economic problems. Across the West, tough times intensified feelings that the unemployed and new migrants were responsible for the downturn. Nineteenth-century emphases on competitiveness, individualism, and revival of privilege for the "best circles'" replaced the twentieth-century trend toward advancing economic democracy to combat totalitarianism. The return of prosperity in the 1990s was accompanied by a measurable decline in the well-being of sectors of the working class and the poor. Whereas a few decades earlier, poverty was feared as a source of totalitarianism, the new politics dismissed it as a problem created by and restricted to the lower classes.

Thatcher Reshapes Political Culture

More than anyone else, Margaret Thatcher (b. 1925), the outspoken leader of Britain's Conservative Party from 1979 to 1990, reshaped the West's political and economic ideas. Coming to power amidst continuing economic decline, revolt in Northern Ireland, and labor unrest, the combative prime minister eschewed the politics of consensus building, vowing instead to transform Britain through the force of her own ideas. "I don't spend a lifetime watching which way the cat jumps," she announced. "I know really which way I want the cats to go." In parliamentary speeches, Thatcher lashed out at union leaders, Labour politicians, and people who received welfare-state benefits as enemies of British prosperity.

Thatcher believed that only a resurgence of private enterprise could revive the sluggish British economy. Her anti-welfare-state policies struck a revolutionary chord, and she called herself "a nineteenth-century liberal" in reference to the economic individualism of that age. In her view, business leaders and entrepreneurs were the key members of society. Although immigrants often worked for the lowest wages and contributed to profits, she characterized as inferior the unemployed and immigrants from Britain's former colonies, saying that neither group contributed to national wealth. More than two-thirds of the public read newspapers that expressed part or all of this general attitude; thus even members of the working class blamed labor leaders or newcomers for Britain's trauma.

The policies of "Thatcherism" were based on *monetarist* or *supply-side* theories associated most prominently with U.S. economist Milton Friedman. Monetarists contend that inflation results when government pumps money into the economy at a rate higher than a nation's economic growth rate. Thus they advocate a tight rein on the money supply to keep prices from rising rapidly. Supply-side economists maintain that the economy as a whole flourishes when business prosperity "trickles down" throughout the society. To implement such theories,

Margaret Thatcher
As British prime minister for more than a decade, Margaret Thatcher profoundly influenced European history by cutting back the welfare state. Thatcher was convinced and convinced others that the welfare state did not advance society and its citizens but made them lazy by rewarding those who had not contributed to the nation. Her tenure in office encouraged other politicians from Ronald Reagan to Helmut Kohl to execute similar cuts in programs; in this way, more than any other head of state she set the general course in domestic policy for the late twentieth century.
Stuart Franklin/Sygma.

the British government cut income taxes on the wealthy to spur new investment and pushed up sales taxes to compensate for the lost revenue; the result was an increased burden on working people, who bore the brunt of the sales tax. Thatcher vigorously pruned government intervention in the economy: she sold publicly owned businesses and utilities such as Britoil, British Airways, and Rolls-Royce; refused to prop up "outmoded" industries such as coal mining; and slashed education and health programs.

In the first three years of Thatcher's government, the British economy did not respond well to her shock treatment. The quality of universities, public transportation, highways, and hospitals deteriorated, and leading scholars and scientists left the country in a renewal of the brain drain. In addition, social unity fragmented—in 1981, blacks and Asians rioted in major cities—and Thatcher's popularity sagged. A turning point came in March 1982, when Argentina invaded the British Falkland Islands in the South Atlantic. Thatcher invoked patriotism to unify the nation and refused to surrender the islands without a fight, even though they were thousands of miles away. The gamble paid off, as the prime minister's public support soared. The appeal to national sentiment had replaced the progress of economic democratization as a unifying social force.

By the mid-1980s, inflation had dissipated in Britain. Historians and economists debate whether the change resulted from Thatcher's policies or from the lack of spending power that burdened the poor and unemployed. In any case, Thatcher's program became the standard. Even when the Labour Party gained power again late in the 1990s, it did so under the banner of competitiveness and "workfare" (a term suggesting that those receiving government benefits should work for them) instead of welfare. As enacted by Labour (and Democrats in the United States), the cutbacks traditionally associated with the right came to be called the "Third Way," which merged conservative and liberal programs into an alternative policy. Britain had been one of the pioneers of the welfare state, and now it pioneered in changing course.

The Reagan Revolution and Its Aftermath

Moved by the same social and political vision as Thatcher, Ronald Reagan (b. 1911; president 1981–1989) worked a similar revolution. The former actor was at his best in carefully planned television appearances. In front of the camera the "Great Communicator" furthered the idea that a so-called moral majority existed in the land that had somehow lost its grip on affairs to amoral, spendthrift forces. Reagan vowed to promote the values of the "moral majority," which included commitment to Bible-based religion, dedication to work, sexual restraint, and unquestioned patriotism.

In domestic affairs, Reagan pursued a radical course on a par with Thatcher's. His program of "Reaganomics" produced a whopping income tax cut of 25 percent between 1981 and 1983, combined with massive reductions in federal spending for student loans, school lunch programs, and mass transit. Like Thatcher, Reagan believed that tax cuts would lead to investment and a reinvigorated economy; federal outlays for welfare programs, which he felt only encouraged sloth, would generally be unnecessary thereafter.

In foreign policy, Reagan spent most of his time in office preoccupied with the Communist threat. The longtime cold warrior labeled the Soviet Union an "evil empire" and demanded huge military budgets to counter the Soviet arms buildup of the 1970s. Reagan announced the Strategic Defense Initiative (SDI, but known popularly as "Star Wars"), a costly plan to put lasers in space to defend the United States against a nuclear attack. The combination of tax cuts and military expansion had pushed the federal budget deficit to $200 billion by 1986.

The impact of Reagan's military buildup on U.S. global power and domestic health is a heatedly debated topic. Critics held Reaganomics accountable for the escalating violence and drug use in schools across the country and the growing numbers of homeless Americans sleeping on the streets. In his best-selling book *The Rise and Fall of the Great Powers* (1988), historian Paul Kennedy points out that nations at the top have always had trouble balancing military commitments with economic resources. Thus, although Reagan's administration spent less of the gross national product on the military than Eisenhower's had (7.5 percent as opposed to 10 percent), it did so at a time when the United States faced stiff competition from such global powers as Japan and West Germany. The system of military procurement itself took place outside the bounds of the competitive market system Reagan glorified. Citizens of both the United States and the USSR would feel the economic effects of policies based on "imperial overstretch," Kennedy predicted.

The election of Democrat Bill Clinton (b. 1946) as U.S. president in 1992 did not fundamentally change the move away from the welfare state. As in Britain, an ethic of workfare continued in the United States, and the goal of competitiveness in an increasingly global economy justified crumbling urban schools and the relative decline in the lower segments of society. In fact, the economy soared in the 1990s, lifting people in the professions and top management to ever greater wealth. From this vantage point, cuts in social programs were a real success, though others attributed rising wealth to technology's boosting worker productivity.

Alternatives to Thatcherism

Other Western European leaders found retrenchment of the welfare state necessary as well but did so with less politically divisive rhetoric. Facing welfare costs and the legacy of stagflation from the 1970s, the center-right West German leader Helmut Kohl (b. 1930), who took power in 1982, reduced welfare spending, froze government wages, and cut corporate taxes. By 1984, the inflation rate was only 2 percent, and West Germany had acquired a 10 percent share of world trade. Unlike Thatcher, Kohl did not fan class and racial hatreds. The politics of divisiveness was particularly unwise in Germany where terrorism on the left and on the right continued to flourish. Moreover, the legacy of Nazism loomed menacingly. "Let's gas 'em," said unemployed German youth of immigrant Turkish workers. The revival of Nazi language appalled many in Germany's middle class rather than gaining their support.

France took a different political path through the 1980s than either Germany or Britain but ended up in a similar position. By 1981, stagflation had put more than 1.5 million people out of work and reduced the economic growth rate to an anemic 1.2 percent. The French elected a socialist president, François Mitterrand (1916–1996), who nationalized banks and certain industries and stimulated the economy by wage increases and social spending— the opposite of Thatcherism. New public buildings like museums and libraries arose along with new subway lines and improved public transport. Financial leaders reacted by sending capital abroad rather than investing it at home, while many ordinary citizens continued to support the protections offered by state programs. In Mitterrand's second term, conservatives captured the majority of seats in the assembly, which entitled them to choose the prime minister. Until the end of the century, conservatives and socialists continued to share power. Thus French policy alternated between the need to encourage investment by cutting the costs of social

programs and the citizenry's commitment to social security programs and a vibrant public life. By 2000, the French economy was the most prosperous in Europe.

At the same time, France suffered continuing high unemployment as businesspeople refused to invest in new jobs laden with high costs such as social security. As elsewhere, political repercussions accompanied changing social and economic conditions, and political racism emerged as an expression

SOS-Racism
"Don't touch my pal" reads this slogan that was emblazoned on banners, posters, and buttons in France. As threats mounted to the safety of migrants across Europe, countermovements demanding tolerance and promoting their well-being grew. SOS-Racism was one of the most powerful, holding marches with hundreds of thousands of participants. Nonetheless, strongly racist political parties preaching hatred of all foreigners thrived and in Austria actually controlled the government by late 1999.
G. Merillon/Gamma Liaison.

of discontent. Beginning with the 1985 national elections, Jean-Marie Le Pen's National Front party, which promised to deport African and Muslim immigrants and cut French ties with nonwhite nations, won 10 percent or more of the vote. The class antagonisms that had once shaped politics changed to expressions of racial and ethnic hatred.

Meanwhile, a cluster of smaller states without heavy defense commitments enjoyed increasing prosperity after the recession of the early 1980s ended. In Spain, tourist dollars helped rebuild the southern cities of Granada and Córdoba. Under a moderate socialist prime minister, Felipe Gonzalez—who, like Mitterrand and other socialist leaders, supported the aspirations of the middle class—the country joined the Common Market in 1986. The Italian economy grew despite pervasive political corruption, and in Ireland a surge of investment in education for high-tech jobs combined with low wages to bring new business to the country. Prosperity and the increasingly unacceptable death toll led to a political rapprochement between Ireland and Northern Ireland in 1999. Austria prospered, too, in part by reducing government pensions and aid to industry and agriculture. Austrian chancellor Franz Vranitsky summed up the changed focus of government in the 1980s and 1990s: "In Austria, the shelter that the state has given to almost everyone—employee as well as entrepreneur—has led . . . a lot of people [to] think not only what they can do to solve a problem but what the state can do. . . . This needs to change." The century-long growth of the welfare state seemed to be over by the 1990s, but the future mission of government was unclear.

Maintaining a broad array of social programs despite the reigning mood, Sweden stood out as an exception. The government offered each immigrant a choice of subsidized housing in neighborhoods inhabited primarily by Swedes or primarily by people from the immigrant's native land. Such programs were expensive: the tax rate on income over $46,000 was 80 percent. When productivity flagged, the government denied benefits to unemployed workers who refused retraining or a job offer. The Swedes also reduced their costly dependence on foreign oil by cutting consumption in half between 1976 and 1986. Despite anti-inflationary success and a highly productive workforce, Sweden dropped from fourth to fourteenth place among nations in per capita income by 1998. Businesspeople were beginning to look to countries where taxation was far lower. Once Soviet communism was dead, Sweden's "middle way" came to seem extreme.

❖ The Collapse of Soviet Communism

The most consequential event of these decades was the breakup of the Soviet empire in 1989 followed by the collapse of the USSR itself in the 1990s. Emblematic of other trends, the end of bipolarity hastened globalization, while socialist collapse undermined the largest single system providing government benefits to citizens. But what most struck people at the time was the suddenness of it all. In 1979—a mere decade earlier—Communist leaders in eastern Europe and the Soviet Union held firmly to power and were wedded to the past. The fate of peoples in the USSR rested in the hands of Leonid Brezhnev and a group of elderly bureaucrats who had matured during Stalin's "construction of socialism" in the 1930s. Although Poland and Hungary experimented with limited economic reform, U.S.-led-bloc analysts found no reason to think that radical change would happen in the near future. In the United States the CIA erroneously reported that the bloc was in robust economic health.

Yet protest by workers, artists, and others had never really stopped across the Soviet realm despite repression of the Prague Spring. CIA reports to the contrary, the Soviet economy was not robust but deteriorating. Communications, international trade, and democratic movements were pulling apart a vast region that communism had structured for almost half a century. Ironically, the triumph of democracy in the former Soviet empire opened an era of painful adjustment, uncertainty, and violence for hundreds of millions of people.

Rebellion in Poland

Dissent against Soviet rule reached crisis stage in the summer of 1980, when Poles reacted furiously to government-increased food prices by going on strike. As the protest spread, workers at the Gdańsk shipyards, led by electrician Lech Walesa and crane operator Anna Walentynowicz, created an independent labor movement called Solidarity. The organization soon embraced much of the adult population, including a million members of the Communist Party.

The Poles had engaged in various forms of resistance to Communist rule for decades. The Catholic church, which numbered 28 million members out of a total population of 35 million, had long unified people around opposition to socialist secularization. Moreover, worker protest in the 1970s had been common, as steep energy prices, scarce consumer goods, inflation, and government ineptitude worsened the conditions of everyday life. In the summer of 1980, opposition to Poland's rulers, who directed both politics and the economy, coalesced. Intellectuals banded together in the Workers' Defense Committee (KOR) and joined the attack. Karol Wojtyła (b. 1920), the former archbishop of Cracow, had become Pope John Paul II in 1978, and he lent his authority to the anti-Communist cause. Solidarity workers occupied factories and waved Polish flags as well as giant portraits of the pope and the Virgin Mary.

Having achieved mass support at home and worldwide sympathy through media coverage, Solidarity pledged to support moderate economic reform. Its leaders insisted, however, that the government recognize it as an independent union—a radical demand under communism. As food became scarce and prices rose, tens of thousands of women marched in the streets crying, "We're hungry!" As the Communist Party teetered on collapse, the police and the army, with Soviet support, imposed a military government and in the winter of 1981 outlawed Solidarity. Continued efforts by reporters and dissidents, using global communications, kept Solidarity alive as a force both inside and outside of Poland.

Stern and puritanical, General Wojciech Jaruzelski took over as the head of Poland's new regime in 1981. Dissent persisted in various forms: in *Danton*, a 1982 film ostensibly about the French Revolution, Polish filmmaker Andrzej Wajda cast as Robespierre, the fanatic instigator of the Reign of Terror, an actor who looked just like the Polish leader. Jaruzelski insisted that "the place of People's Poland is and will remain among the socialist powers," but his hope was not so much to revive socialist enthusiasm at home as to ward off Soviet intervention. The general could not push repression too far: he needed new loans from the U.S.-led bloc to keep the sinking Polish economy afloat. Instability infected Polish politics once Solidarity was born, and the stage was set for communism's downfall.

Reform in the Soviet Bloc

The rise of Solidarity exposed the economic woes of people living in the Soviet bloc. Far from insulating their citizens from the ups and downs of capitalism, Soviet-style economies suffered from rampant decay by the early 1980s and their people felt the full consequences. Years of stagnant and then negative growth led to a deteriorating standard of living. After working a full day, Soviet homemakers stood in long lines to obtain basic commodities; housing and food shortages necessitated the three-generation household, in which grandparents took over tedious homemaking tasks from their working children and grandchildren. "There is no special skill to this," a seventy-three-year-old grandmother and former garbage collector remarked. "You just stand in line and wait." Even so, they often went away empty-handed, and more than one foreign visitor complained that she had never eaten so many varieties of cabbage salad. Basic household supplies like soap disappeared instantly from stores, and the quality of medical care varied according to status. One cheap and readily available product—vodka—often formed the center of people's social lives. Alcoholism reached crisis levels, diminishing productivity and tremendously straining the nation's morale.

Economic stagnation had many other ramifications. Ordinary people decided not to have children, and fertility fell below replacement levels throughout the Soviet bloc, except for the Muslim areas of Soviet Central Asia. The country was forced to import massive amounts of grain because 20 to 30 percent of the grain that was produced in the USSR rotted before it could be harvested or shipped to market, so great was the inefficiency of the state-directed economy. Industrial pollution, spewed out by enterprises responsible only for meeting production quotas, reached scandalous dimensions. A massive and privileged party bureaucracy hobbled industrial innovation and failed to achieve socialism's professed goal of a decent standard of living for working people. To match American military growth, the Soviet Union diverted 15 to 20 percent of its gross national product (more than double the U.S. proportion) to armaments. As this combustible mixture of problems heated up, a new generation was coming of age that had no memory of World War II or Stalin's purges. One Russian observer found members of the younger generation "cynical, but less afraid." "They believe in nothing," a mother said of Soviet youth in 1984. "They won't be pushed around," added another.

In 1985 a new leader, Mikhail Gorbachev (b. 1931), opened an era of unexpected change. In 1956, Gorbachev, then only twenty-five, had attended the party congress at which Khrushchev had first condemned Stalin's excesses. Later, as a trusted official, he traveled widely in the Soviet bloc and got a first-hand glimpse of life in the West during trips to France, Italy, and West Germany. The son of peasants, Gorbachev had risen through the party ranks as an agricultural specialist, and he quickly proposed broad plans to reinvigorate the Soviet economy. His program of *perestroika* ("restructuring") aimed to streamline production and management. The economy had depended not on innovation but on labor-intensive production, and outmoded machinery hampered Soviet industrial output. Against the will of managers, who benefited from the status quo, Gorbachev hoped to reverse economic decay by improving productivity, increasing the rate of capital investment, encouraging the use of up-to-date technology, and gradually introducing such market features as prices and profits.

Along with perestroika, Gorbachev proclaimed a policy of *glasnost* (usually translated as "openness" or "publicity"). For the Soviet leader, *glasnost* meant speaking "the language of truth," disseminating "wide, prompt, and frank information," and allowing Soviet citizens new measures of free speech. When officials complained that glasnost threatened their status, Gorbachev replaced more than a third of the party's leadership in the first months of his administration. The pressing need for glasnost became most evident after the Chernobyl catastrophe in 1986, when bureaucratic cover-ups delayed the spread of information about the accident, with lethal consequences for people living near the plant.

After Chernobyl even the Communist Party and Marxism-Leninism were opened to public criticism. Party meetings suddenly witnessed complaints about the highest leaders and their policies. Television shows such as *The Fifth Wheel* adopted the outspoken methods of American investigative reporting; one program showed an interview with an executioner of political prisoners and exposed the plight

Gorbachevs and Reagans at the Ranch
Ronald Reagan raised the temperature of the cold war with a massive arms buildup in the 1980s that caused the U.S. budget deficit to soar. When Mikhail Gorbachev came to power in the USSR, he changed course, encouraging freer speech, seeking innovation in the economy, and reducing cold war tensions. The two leaders' regular meetings helped slow down the arms race.
Ruelas, L.A. Daily News/Sygma.

of Leningrad's homeless children. "Work is getting pretty easy around here," remarked TV censor Natalya Strepetova, who had less and less to do at her job.

Political factions arose, not only for and against Gorbachev, but across the political spectrum. In the fall of 1987, one of Gorbachev's erstwhile allies, Boris Yeltsin, quit the governing Politburo after denouncing perestroika as inadequate for real reform. Yeltsin's political daring, which in the past would have consigned him to oblivion (or Siberia), inspired others to organize in opposition to the crumbling ruling orthodoxy. By the spring of 1989, in a remarkably free balloting, not a single Communist was chosen for office in Moscow's local elections.

Glasnost and perestroika dramatically affected superpower relations as well. Recognizing how severely the cold war arms race was draining Soviet resources, Gorbachev almost immediately began scaling back missile production. His unilateral actions gradually won over Ronald Reagan. The two leaders met at Geneva, Switzerland, in the autumn of 1985 to initiate a personal relationship and begin defusing the cold war. "I bet the hard-liners in both our countries are bleeding when we shake hands," said the jovial Reagan at the summit's conclusion. Although future meetings did not go as smoothly, a major breakthrough from the U.S. point of view occurred in early 1989, when Gorbachev at last withdrew his country's forces from the debilitating war in Afghanistan. By the end of the year, the United States was beginning to cut back its own vast military buildup.

The End of Soviet Rule

Tremors shook the Communist world in the spring of 1989. Inspired by Gorbachev's visit to China's capital, Beijing, thousands of students massed in Tiananmen Square to demand democracy. They used telex machines and electronic mail to rush their messages to the international community, and they effectively conveyed their goals through the cameras that Western television trained on them. China's aged Communist leaders, while pushing economic modernization and even allowing market operations, refused to consider the introduction of democracy. As workers began joining the Democracy forces, the government crushed the movement and executed as many as a thousand rebels.

The End of Communism in Europe

June 1989 Solidarity defeats Communists in Polish elections

August 1989 Czechoslovakia opens borders to western Europe

October 1989 Hungary dismisses Communist Party as official party

November 1989 East German Politburo resigns; Berlin Wall opened; Alexander Dubček calls for the ouster of Stalinists and a reform government comes to power in Czechoslovakia

December 1989 Nicolae Ceauşescu driven from power and executed in Romania

Spring 1990 Lithuania announces its secession from the USSR and other Baltic States follow

October 1990 Germany reunited; Gorbachev announces transition to a market economy; Boris Yeltsin defeats Communist candidate to become president of the Russian Republic

August 1991 After coup attempt in Moscow, operations of Communist Party suspended

---

The "Velvet Revolution." Despite the setback to the forces of democracy in China, the spirit of revolt advanced in eastern Europe in 1989 and brought decades of Communist rule to an end. Indeed, the year 1989 has been designated the twentieth century's *annus mirabilis* ("year of miracles") because of the sudden and unexpected disintegration of Communist power throughout the region (Map 30.2). Events in Poland took a dramatic turn first. In the spring the Polish government, weakened by its own bungling of the economy and lacking Soviet support for further repression, again legalized Solidarity and promised free elections. In parliamentary elections in June, Solidarity candidates drove out the Communists. "Our defeat," Jaruzelski admitted, "is total." By early 1990, Jaruzelski had been replaced as president by Walesa, who began Poland's rocky transition to a market economy.

As it became evident that the Soviet Union would not intervene in Poland, the fall of communism repeated itself in country after country. In Hungary, which had experimented with "market socialism" since the 1960s, popular demands for liberalization spread from economics to politics at the

MAP 30.2 The Collapse of Communism in Europe, 1989–1991

In one form or another, resistance to communism had been continuous since the 1940s; thus the 1989 overthrow of Communist government in the USSR satellite countries of Eastern Europe occurred with surprising rapidity. In 1991, Communist Yugoslavia began to break up into individual states composed of competing ethnicities and religions. Then the USSR itself fell apart, as the Baltic states seceded, followed by the official dissolution of the rest of the USSR on January 1, 1992.

beginning of 1989. Critical journals appeared, and the populace boycotted the traditional May Day parade. In the fall, the Parliament dismissed the Communist Party as the official ruling institution and people tore down Communist symbols throughout the country.

In Czechoslovakia, which after 1968 had been firmly restored to Soviet-style rule, people watched the progress of glasnost expectantly. Although they could see Gorbachev on television calling for free speech, he never mentioned reform in Czechoslovakia. In the spring of 1989, however, a petition campaign secured the release of dissident leader and playwright Václav Havel. Demonstrators protested in the streets for democracy, but the government cracked down by turning the police on them. The turning point came on November 24 when Alexander Dubček, leader of the Prague Spring of 1968, addressed the crowds in Prague's Wenceslas Square with a call for the ouster of Stalinists from the

government. Almost immediately, Communist leadership resigned. Capping the country's "velvet revolution," as it became known for its lack of bloodshed, the formerly Communist-dominated parliament elevated Havel to the presidency.

The most potent symbol of a divided Europe—the Berlin Wall—stood in the midst of a divided Germany. East Germans had attempted to escape over the wall for decades, despite their country's reputation as having the most dynamic economy in the socialist world. When Austria and Hungary opened their common border in August 1989, thousands of East Germans turned what looked like vacation travel to Hungary into escape. From Hungary they passed to Austria and on to West Germany, where the government had long promised citizenship to *all* Germans. But it was protest at home that ultimately toppled the regime, unsupported now by Soviet tanks. Throughout the fall, increasing crowds that ultimately reached half a million had rallied in East

Destroying the Berlin Wall
The most disturbing symbol of cold war, the Berlin Wall came down in 1989 as dramatically as it had gone up in 1961. The next decade saw not only the reunification of Germany but the massive rebuilding of Berlin as the nation's capital.
© Reuters Newmedia Inc./Corbis.

German cities, confusing politicians who on November 9 issued an ambiguous statement more or less permitting passage through the crossings in the Berlin Wall. The shock of suddenly free access was overwhelming, as guards allowed tens of thousands of Berliners to flood through, all of them celebrating the opening of the wall. Protest turned to festive holiday: West Berliners handed out bananas, a consumer good that had been in short supply in the Eastern zone, and that fruit became the unofficial symbol of reunion. Almost immediately Berliners released years of frustration at their division by assaulting the wall with sledgehammers and bringing home chunks as souvenirs. The government finished its complete destruction in the fall of 1990.

Almost as soon as the Berlin Wall tumbled, the world's attention fastened on the political drama in

Romania. Since the mid-1960s, Nicolae Ceaușescu had ruled as the harshest dictator in Communist Europe since Stalin. In the name of modernization he destroyed whole villages; to build up the population he outlawed contraceptives and abortions, a restriction that led to the abandonment of tens of thousands of children. Most Romanians lived in utter poverty as Ceaușescu channeled almost all the country's resources into building himself an enormous palace in Bucharest. Yet in early December 1989, an opposition movement rose up, and when authorities moved to suppress it, the spirit of resistance spread. Most of the army turned against the government and crushed the forces loyal to Ceaușescu. On Christmas Day viewers watched on television as the dictator and his wife were tried by a military court and then executed. Soon after, Western photographers displayed what Ceaușescu had wrought, from orphanages packed with thousands of unwanted, uncared-for children to the mass graves of those who had earlier dared to dissent.

Reunification of Germany. The collapse of communism in Europe paved the way for the reunification of Germany. Chancellor Helmut Kohl of West Germany based the campaign for reunification on the promise of a more comfortable way of life. In July 1990, he arranged for East German currency to be exchanged on a one-to-one basis with West German marks. A shrewd politician, Kohl acted on what he called his "grass-roots instinct that the East Germans wanted their microwaves now, and not in three years." After the economic foundations were in place, full political union took place on October 3, 1990, far earlier than anyone had expected at the end of 1989.

German Reunification, October 1990

The realities of unification did not live up to the dream. East German industry passed into the hands of West German managers, whose efficiencies in downsizing the workforce caused unemployment to soar, especially among women and youth. As early as September 1990, many social services, such as day-care centers that allowed women to work to support their families, closed down. Imitating the capitalist U.S. and western European leaders meant eliminating institutions these countries did not favor. Although restoration of buildings and industrial modernization proceeded in the nation's former Communist half, social tensions flared. West Germans blamed their new co-citizens for the diversion of resources to the east, and East Germans took out their frustrations through murder, violent attacks, or hateful rhetoric against immigrants. As Germany tried to keep its high standard of living amidst these stresses, the economy declined late in the 1990s relative to others in Europe. Throughout the former Soviet bloc, the transition to democracy and free markets gave rise simultaneously to social instability, economic upheaval, and nationalist expressions of discontent.

The Breakup of Yugoslavia and the Soviet Union

After a few delirious months, the problems of post-Communist life intensified, turning events in ever more violent directions as first Yugoslavia and then the Soviet Union itself fell apart. Like Hungarians and Czechs in the nineteenth-century Habsburg Empire, nationality groups in the USSR began to demand political and cultural autonomy in the 1980s. The Soviet empire had held together more than one hundred ethnic groups, and the five republics of Soviet Central Asia were home to fifty million Muslims. Similarly in Yugoslavia, Communist rulers had enforced unity among religious and ethnic groups, and intermarriage among them occurred regularly. But ethnicity became an effective political slogan for ambitious politicians with the coming of democracy, and violent instability continued into the new millennium.

MAP 30.3 The Former Yugoslavia, c. 2000

After a decade of destructive civil war, UN forces and UN-brokered agreements attempted to protect the civilians of the former Yugoslavia from the brutal consequences of post-Communist rule. Ambitious politicians, most notably Slobodan Milosevic, used the twentieth-century Western strategy of fostering ethnic and religious hatred as a powerful tool to build support for themselves while making those favoring peace look softhearted and unfit to rule.

Yugoslavia in 1990, before Destruction of the Mostar Bridge (top) and after (bottom)
In modern history the construction of a nation-state has depended on the growth of institutions such as armies and bureaucracies and the promotion of a common national culture. In an effort to dominate Bosnia and Croatia, Serbs destroyed non-Serb architecture, books, and such ancient symbols as the Mostar Bridge.
Top: Sygma; bottom: Stephane Cardinale/Sygma.

Yugoslavia. Ethnic tensions erupted in Yugoslavia in 1990 when a Serb Communist, Slobodan Milosevic, won the presidency of his republic and began to assert Serb ascendancy. Other nationalities resisted. "Slovenians . . . have one more reason to say they are in favor of independence," warned one of them. In the spring of 1991, first Slovenia and then Croatia seceded, but the Croats soon lost almost a quarter of their territory to the Serb-dominated Yugoslav army (Map 30.3). An even more devastating civil war engulfed Bosnia-Herzegovina, where the republic's Muslim majority tried to create a multicultural and multiethnic state. Many Bosnian Serb men formed a guerrilla army, backed by the covert support of Milosevic's government, and gained the upper hand; the Muslim Bosnians were prevented by a UN arms embargo from equipping their forces adequately to resist. Late in the 1990s, the Serb forces started attacking people of Albanian ethnicity living in the Yugoslav province of Kosovo. From 1997 to 1999, hundreds of thousands of Albanian Kosovars fled their homes as Serb militias and the Yugoslav army began attacking the civilian population. NATO pilots bombed the region in an attempt to drive back the army and Serb militias. Amidst incredible violence and suffering, UN peacekeeping forces stepped in to enforce an interethnic truce, but people throughout the world felt that this intervention came far too late, reflecting great-power self-interest rather than a true commitment to maintaining peace and protecting human rights.

During the 1990s, civilians died by the tens of thousands, as Yugoslav republics broke away and as Serbs pursued a policy they called "ethnic cleansing"—that is, genocide—against the other nationalities. They raped women as another form of "conquest" to leave them pregnant with Serb babies. Men and boys were often taken away and massacred. Each competing force also aimed at the cultural heritage of its opponent. Military units destroyed libraries and museums, architectural treasures like the Mostar Bridge, and cities rich with medieval history such as Dubrovnik. Ethnic cleansing thus entailed destroying actual people as well as all traces of their complex past. Many in the West explained violence in the Balkans as part of "age-old" blood feuds manifesting the backwardness of an almost "Asian" society. Others saw ethnic rivalry using genocide to achieve national power as a modern phenomenon, while still others blamed the former great powers for stirring up many of these tensions in the first place. Across both western and eastern Europe, the language of racial, ethnic, and religious hatred was shaping political agendas, nowhere more violently than in the former Communist states.

The Soviet Union. Horrendous as ongoing genocide was, the utter collapse of the Soviet Union in 1992 launched a string of secessions with the potential for widespread destabilization of regional and perhaps global politics. Perestroika had failed to revitalize the Soviet economy; people confronted soaring prices, the specter of unemployment, and even greater scarcity of goods than they had endured in the past. Although Gorbachev announced late in 1990 that there was "no alternative to the transition to the market," his plan was too little, too late and satisfied no one. The Russian parliament's election of Boris Yeltsin as president of the Russian Republic over a Communist candidate provoked a coup in 1991 by a group of eight antireform hard-liners, from the Soviet vice president to the powerful head of the Soviet secret police, or KGB. Holding Gorbachev under house arrest, coup leaders claimed to be rescuing the Soviet Union from the "mortal danger" posed by "extremist forces." Yeltsin, however, standing atop a tank outside the Russian Republic's

parliament building, called for mass resistance. Hundreds of thousands of residents of Moscow and Leningrad filled the streets, the heads of the other republics declared their support for Yeltsin and Gorbachev, and units of the army defected to protect Yeltsin's headquarters. People used fax machines and computers to coordinate internal resistance and send messages to the rest of the world. The coup was in complete disarray in the face of citizen determination not to allow a return of Stalinism, or indeed of any form of Soviet orthodoxy.

The Soviet Union disintegrated. People tore down statues of Soviet heroes; Yeltsin outlawed the party newspaper, *Pravda*, and sealed the KGB files. At the end of August the Soviet parliament suspended operations of the Communist Party itself. One republic after another followed the lead of the Baltic States, which declared their independence in September 1991. Blood was spilled throughout the disintegrating Communist world in a variety of ethnic conflicts. In the Soviet republic of Tajikistan, native Tajiks rioted against Armenians living there; in Azerbaijan, Azeris and Armenians clashed over contested territory; and in the Baltic States, anti-Semitism revived as a political tool. The USSR finally dissolved on January 1, 1992. Twelve of the fifteen former Soviet republics banded together in a Commonwealth of Independent States (CIS; Map 30.4).

The coup and drive for dissolution of the USSR so tainted Gorbachev's regime that he ceded power to Yeltsin. But increasingly plagued by corruption, the Russian economy went into an ever-deepening crisis. Yeltsin's political allies bought up national resources, stripped them of their value, and sent billions of dollars out of the country. By 1999, Yeltsin's own family appeared deeply implicated in stealing the wealth once seen as belonging to all the people. Ethnic and religious battles continued for the entire decade of the 1990s, as the government undertook disastrous policies. Military action against Muslim dissenters in the province of Chechnya inflicted destruction and massive casualties on both sides. In Russia, the political right appealed to nationalist sentiments and won increasing support. Political disorder was matched by social disarray, as organized crime interfered in the distribution of goods and services and assassinated legitimate entrepreneurs, legislators, and anyone who criticized them. As a result, western powers drastically reduced their aid to rebuild Russian infrastructure.

MAP 30.4 Countries of the Former Soviet Union, c. 2000

Following an agreement of December 1991, twelve of the countries of the former Soviet Union formed the Commonwealth of Independent States (CIS). Dominated by Russia and with Ukraine often disputing this domination, the CIS worked to bring about common economic and military policies. As nation-states dissolved rapidly in the late twentieth century, regional alliances and coordination were necessary to meet the political and economic challenges of the global age.

Developing a free market and a republican government brought suffering to Russia as it had more than a century earlier to other Western peoples. The conditions of everyday life grew increasingly dire as salaries went unpaid, food remained in short supply, and essential services disintegrated. People took drastic steps to stay alive. Hotel lobbies became clogged with women turning to prostitution

People Selling Belongings in the Former Soviet Union
The collapse of a state that not only employed and paid its citizens but also took responsibility for feeding, housing, and clothing them brought unbelievable hardship. Because the breakup of the USSR was total, no institutions existed to step in and hire or provision huge cities like Moscow and St. Petersburg. People desperately took to the streets selling dishes, clothes, and other possessions.
Swersey/Gamma Liaison.

because they were the first people fired as industry privatized and service jobs were cut back. Unpaid soldiers sold their services to the Mafia. Ordinary citizens stood on the sidewalks of major cities selling their household possessions. There were, of course, many plusses: people were able to travel freely for the first time and the media were more open than ever before in Russian history. Some, many of them young and highly educated, profited from contacts with technology and business. However, their frequent emigration to more prosperous parts of the world further depleted Russia's human resources.

The dismantling of communism was thus more complicated and painful than anyone had imagined. "I knew in my heart that it would collapse," said one ex-dissident, commenting sadly on the exodus of youth from his country, "but it never crossed my mind that the future would look like this." Alongside such human costs lay the question of who would control the massive Soviet arsenal of nuclear weapons and how global politics would shape up without cold war guidelines.

❖ Global Culture and Western Civilization at the Dawn of a New Millennium

As the final years of the millennium unfolded into a global age, thinkers began to posit a variety of scenarios for the future. On the one side was a view that the end of the cold war meant "an end of history" because the great ideological struggles were over and Western values and liberal democracy had triumphed. Attached to this view was a related one: the rest of the world was absorbing Western cultural values rapidly as it developed technologically and adopted more and more features of representative government and human rights. An opposing view predicted a "clash of civilizations" in which increasingly incompatible religions and cultures would lead to future global strife. For example, the power of Islam, as it gathered more than one billion followers, would confront Western values rather than absorb them. The latter view also seemed plausible given the growing number of small states populated by different ethnic and racial groups who refused to live under the same national and cultural umbrella.

The actual movement of peoples and cultures in the late twentieth century suggests that neither view holds. International migration, the movement of disease and climate, the information revolution, and the global sharing of culture have produced neither a successful Western homogenization nor a convincing argument for the cultural purity of any group. In the 1980s and 1990s, Western society changed as rapidly as it did when it came into intense contact with the rest of the globe hundreds of years earlier. Moreover, national boundaries in the traditional European center of the West were weakening politically and economically with the growing strength of the European Union and the simultaneous splintering of large nations into small states based on claims to ethnic uniqueness. Basque separatists of western France and separatist parties in different areas of Italy gained strength; Quebec threatened to secede from Canada. Culture respected national boundaries less as East, West, North, and South became saturated with one another's cultural products. Observers even labeled the new millennium an era of "denationalization." But there is no denying that even while the West absorbed peoples and cultures, it continued to exercise not only economic but also cultural power over the rest of the globe. (See "Contrasting Views," page 1178.)

Redefining the West: The Impact of Global Migration

The movement of people globally was massive in the last third of the twentieth century. Uneven economic development, political persecution, and warfare (which has claimed as many as 100 million victims worldwide since 1945) sent tens of millions in search of safety and opportunity. The most desperate of these migrants were displaced persons and refugees. (See "Taking Measure," right.) Many fled to the West. In the 1970s alone, more than 4.7 million people moved to the United States. By 1982, France had about 4.5 million foreign residents. But other parts of the world were as full as the West of people on the move. The oil-producing nations of the Middle East employed millions of foreign workers, who generally constituted one-third of the labor force. Singapore and Nigeria were also home to millions of foreign-born inhabitants. The ongoing violence in Africa sent Rwandans, Zairians, and others to South Africa, as its government became dominated by blacks. War in Afghanistan made Iran one of the most popular asylums, with close to 2 million refugees in 1995.

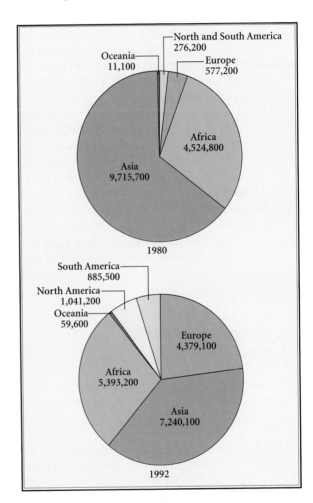

TAKING MEASURE World Refugee Population, 1980–1992

The global age has been characterized by widespread migration for both economic opportunity and physical safety from the wars, civil conflicts, and famine that menaced millions of people. As globalization advanced, migrants and refugees traveled greater distances, with North America and Europe receiving a larger percentage than they had in the 1980s and earlier. By the 1990s, some politicians began to realize that in losing large numbers of people their countries were sending vast human resources to other parts of the world. The Hammond Atlas of the Twentieth Century (London: Times Books, 1996) 183; David Levinson, ed., *Ethnic Relations: A Cross-Cultural Encyclopedia* (Santa Barbara: ABC-CLIO, 1994) 201.

The Debate over Globalization

Globalization has transformed the workings of government and industry, provoked the rise of thousands of organizations devoted to supporting and combating it, and expanded educational offerings to meet its needs. As part of the controversy over its value were hardheaded economic arguments on both sides: whereas a Harvard professor advocated the global scale of business (Document 1), two environmental scientists saw globalization as a disaster for the future of agriculture in India (Document 2). Another component of globalization—migration—aroused real opposition. According to a British newspaper editor, it led to political instability (Document 3). Rightist French politician Jean-Marie Le Pen preached "cultural diversity" for the world, by which he meant that the many peoples and cultures should be kept separate, with strict control of migration and of immigrants (Document 4).

1. Globalization Builds the Economic Future

Rosabeth Moss Kanter, a renowned management consultant and professor, cited the advantages of globalization in 1994.

[G]lobalization encourages the formation of alliances and partnerships—cooperative relationships that extend each partner's global reach while each contributes its local competence. . . . Some countries require local partners in order for companies to do business there. But even where this is not required, many companies recognize the benefits of establishing alliances to combine technologies or develop market access quickly. Connection to a global network allows smaller companies to gain the purchasing power or market clout of larger ones.

Source: Rosabeth Moss Kanter, afterword to *Global Strategies: Insights from the World's Leading Thinkers,* ed. Percy Barnevik and Rosabeth Moss Kanter (Cambridge: Harvard Business Review Books, 1994), 230.

2. Destruction of an Agricultural Way of Life

Scientists Vandana Shiva and Radha Holla-Bhar protested the ways in which economic globalization affected the environment and local farmers in their native India.

Until very recently in India, biodiversity was something held entirely in common by local communities of people. Resources and knowledge about forest or agricultural properties were freely shared. Whether it was seeds of the farm or plants of the forest, all were clearly understood to be part of the cultural, spiritual, and biological commons.

The idea that the commons could be divided up, purchased, and owned by individuals or companies for their own commercial purposes was unknown to Indian farmers until the early 1960s, when certain international conventions established "plant breeder's rights." These new "rights" allowed commercial plant breeders to take traditional indigenous varieties of seed, for example, "improve" them (often by very minor alterations of genetic structure), and then patent and commercialize them, eventually selling back the patented seeds to the communities that first provided them freely.

This globalization of the South's biodiversity commons was a windfall for northern corporations, which began a race to patent and privatize as much of this natural commons as possible, without ever paying royalties to the original breeders and farmers . . . who gathered all the knowledge about them.

The issue came to a crisis during the GATT [General Agreement on Tariffs and Trade] negotiations [1986], when the United States and other northern countries imposed their new rules of Trade-Related Intellectual Property Rights.... The northern countries argued that when southern farmers attempted to retain free use of their own seeds, developed by them over thousands of years, it was a form of piracy....

Before GATT, Indian law excluded the private ownership of patent rights and biological materials. This helped ensure that entitlements to food and nutrition remained as broad-based as possible.

Source: Vandana Shiva and Radha Holla-Bhar, "Piracy by Patent: The Case of the Neem Tree," in *The Case against the Global Economy and for a Turn toward the Local*, ed. Jerry Mander and Edward Goldsmith (San Francisco: Sierra Club Books, 1996), 146–48.

3. The Perils of Global Migration

In 1995, Martin Woollacott, deputy editor of the influential British newspaper the Guardian, *found the global migration of peoples and their settlement in diasporas or communities of migrants from a different native land far from positive.*

Diasporas have many beneficial effects on both host and migrant communities, but they may also breed pathological attitudes among a small minority. Some may fight their own wars on foreign soil. Or diaspora communities can provide inadvertent cover, in their separateness from the main society, for terrorists and extremists from inside or outside who want to attack their hosts.... The global village can be a violent place. Its curse is that new combination of intimacy and aggression, with societies so penetrated by each other physically and culturally that awful damage can be wreaked at close quarters in a way that was not possible in the past.

Source: M. Woollacott, "Living in the Age of Terror," *Guardian*, August 22, 1995.

4. Guarding the Nation from Global Mixture

In France, Jean-Marie Le Pen led a popular political party, the National Front party, committed to renewed nationalism in the face of globalization. Here is an excerpt from his platform.

The French will have priority when it comes to being hired. In the event of group redundancies, they will be the first to keep their jobs. The immigrants who will be induced to going back to their country of origin will liberate numerous jobs for the French. Through the application of new protectionism, jobs will be protected against unauthorized competition from countries where wages and social protection are low....

Foreigners whose resident's permit has expired and immigrant unemployed people with no more unemployment allowance rights will be repatriated to their country of origin in human and dignified conditions. Expulsions of illegal immigrants and delinquents will be effectively upheld. French people will be given priority for social allowances, housing and jobs. Family allowances and the Minimum Revenue for Insertion (RMI) will be reserved for our compatriots, and will therefore be revalued. In order to avoid all disguised immigration the right of asylum will be strictly limited, family regrouping will be abolished and French naturalization will become more difficult.

Source: mosaique@mosaique.worldnet.net. Copyright Mosaïque, March 1995.

QUESTIONS FOR DEBATE

1. Describe and analyze the areas in which globalization seems to raise the most questions.

2. In what ways are issues around globalization centuries-old points of contention?

3. Is it possible or desirable to change the course of globalization?

4. List the benefits of globalization and assess whether the benefits outweigh the costs, some of which are presented in these documents.

Post-decolonization turmoil produced millions of refugees who left their homelands in search of better work. Migrants often earned desperately needed income for family members who remained in the native country, and in some cases they propped up the economies of entire nations. In the southern African country of Lesotho, where the soil had been ruined by overuse during colonial rule, between 40 and 50 percent of national income came from migrant workers, particularly from those who toiled in the mines of South Africa. In countries as different as Yugoslavia, Egypt, Spain, and Pakistan, money sent home from abroad constituted up to 60 percent of national income. Many governments allowed foreigners to work in the host country for periods ranging from one or two to ten or more years. In places where immigration was restricted, millions of people nevertheless successfully crossed borders: from Mexico and China to the United States, over unguarded African frontiers, between European states. Such migrants, unprotected by law, risked exploitation and abuse of their human rights. Those at greatest risk were the eastern European and Asian prostitutes, many of whom were coerced into international sex rings that controlled their passports, wages, and lives.

Foreign workers were a convenient scapegoat for native peoples suffering from economic woes such as unemployment caused by downsizing. Political parties with racist programs came to life in Europe, where unemployment was in double digits at various times in the 1980s and 1990s. The National Front party in France, the Progress Party in Norway, and the Zentrum Party in the Netherlands thrived in the 1990s, while in Austria the party of the racist right became the dominant political force after its victory in the 1999 elections. These groups called for the elimination of blacks and Arabs from Europe in the name of creating racially and ethnically "pure" nations. Tensions between foreigners and natives often exploded in violence. In eastern Europe, which had accepted large numbers of Indochinese refugees, economic crisis brought outbursts against Vietnamese and other Asians. European countries rounded up illegal immigrants and deported them. Obtaining political asylum became more difficult despite worldwide violence.

Among migrants to the West, women had little to say in decisions about leaving home; a patriarchal head of the household generally made such choices.

Once abroad, migrant women suffered the most from unstable working conditions. West Germany, for example, prohibited them from working during economic crises. Even in prosperous times, foreign-born women usually obtained more menial, lower-paying jobs than migrant men or native Europeans. They formed the backbone of labor in oppressive sweatshops, whether in New York or Paris. Moreover, the host society often denigrated as "backward" or "primitive" the familial customs the migrants sought to uphold. Women were more likely than men to be refused political asylum. Rape and other violence against them, even during civil war, were classified as part of everyday life, not politics.

The offspring of immigrants also had a difficult time adjusting to their new surroundings. Young people generally struggled for jobs, and unemployment hit them especially hard because "whites" and "real" citizens received preference. They also struggled with questions of identity. To advance in school or at work, immigrant youth had to embrace their new society in varying degrees, and they often felt torn between two cultures. Young black immigrants in particular began to forge an international or transnational identity, one that combined elements of African, Caribbean, American, and European cultures. As tens of millions of people migrated in the 1980s and 1990s, the former belief in a national identity based on a single, unique culture was losing ground.

Uncertain Borders of the Nation-State

The Western nation-state had been an increasingly powerful source of identity for five hundred years, never more so than in the twentieth century. By the twenty-first century, however, the nature of European national borders was changing not only through the force of mass migration and decolonization but because of international cooperation, technology, transnational allegiances, and other factors that made the nation-state and excessive patriotism seem outmoded. The forces eroding the Western tradition of a single national identity affected not only immigrants but vast numbers of the world's peoples.

European Union.   Regional alliances like NATO and the Warsaw Pact had appeared to override national interests, but nothing compared with the

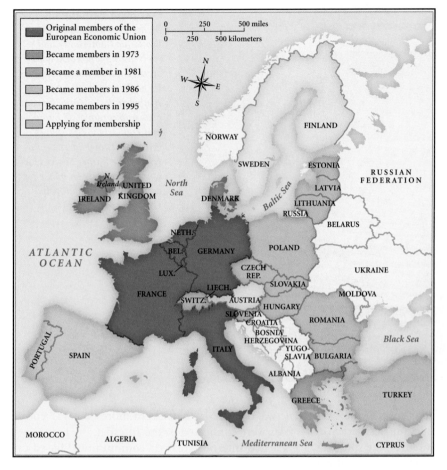

MAP 30.5 The European Union in 2000

The European Union appeared to increase the economic health of its members despite the rocky start to the common currency—the euro. The EU decidedly helped end the traditional warfare its members had undertaken against one another for centuries, and common passports, common business laws, and borders open to member countries facilitated trade and migration of workers. But many critics feared the further loss of cultural distinctiveness among peoples in an age of mass communications if the economic union turned into a political one, while others predicted "Americanization" if political cooperation among European countries was lacking.

turn-of-the-millennium merging of individual nation-states into the European Union (Map 30.5). "[A united] Europe will not be created at a stroke [of a pen] or according to a single plan," Robert Schuman, an outspoken French promoter of European unity, had prophesied in the 1950s. Indeed, the experience of the European Community (EC) proved that a unified Europe remained an evolving entity with an unpredictable future. In 1992, the twelve countries of the EC ended national distinctions in the spheres of business activity, border controls, and transportation. Citizens of EC member countries carried a common burgundy-colored passport, and governments, whether municipal or national, had to treat all member nations' firms the same. In 1994 by the terms of the Maastricht Treaty, the EC became the European Union, and in 1999 a common currency, the European Currency Unit (ECU or euro) came into being. Common policies governed everything from the number of American soap

operas aired on television to pollution controls on automobiles to standardized health warnings on cigarette packages.

Some national leaders opposed tighter integration as an infringement on national sovereignty. Margaret Thatcher, Britain's prime minister, warned that terrorists would pass freely across borders, opposed the use of a common currency, and criticized moves toward closer pan-European unity, but her forceful opposition seemed so out of step with the times that her own party forced her resignation in 1991. Meanwhile, intellectuals across the continent worried that an emerging "Eurospeak" jargon threatened the distinctiveness of national languages and portended a dull standardization of culture. But countries continued to join the original twelve. Sweden, Finland, and Austria joined the EU in 1995; Turkey and Cyprus were officially scheduled for entry. Most former Communist-run nations also sought inclusion. Though members initially balked

European Parliament
By the 1990s, the European Economic Community had evolved into a political body of more than a dozen members. Its parliament—the greatest symbol of the potential for complete unification of all Europe—met regularly in Strasbourg, France. Meanwhile, the countries of the former Soviet bloc applied virtually en masse for admission to the European Union.
AKG Photo, London.

at competing with the lower labor costs in the east, some of the former Communist countries were also promised future admission. Moreover, the splintering of Czechoslovakia into two states in 1993 along with the fragmentation of Yugoslavia and the former Soviet Union disturbed those who saw the European future in terms of one large region, not increasing numbers of small states. As union tightened, a highly advanced industrial megastate complete with its own bureaucracy overlaid the traditionally distinct individual nations of the western heartland. More diverse and multiethnic, European countries simultaneously grew more uniform.

The Challenge of the Internet. Rapid technological change in electronic communications also made traditional national borders appear easily permeable, if not obsolete. In 1969, the U.S. Department of Defense developed a computer network to carry communications in case of nuclear war. This system and others like it in universities, government, and business grew into an unregulated system of more than ten thousand networks globally. These came to be known as the *Internet*—shorthand for *inter-*

networking. By 1995, users in more than 137 countries were connected to the Internet.

The Internet created "communities" based on business needs, shared cultural interests, or other factors that transcended common citizenship in a particular nation-state. Communicating via the Internet allowed users often to escape state regulation such as censorship. A global marketplace in goods and services ranging from advanced weaponry to organ transplants opened up to the computer literate. With this technology, political and other causes could become transnational too. While enthusiasts claimed that this could promote world democracy, critics charged that communications technology favored elites and disadvantaged those without computer skills. They also argued that the ordinary person's most intimate records were now the easy prey not only of the state but of international forces.

Internet and other communications technology promoted business mergers on a vast international scale in the 1990s. Almost instantaneous information on inventory, wages, costs, and transportation could be accessed worldwide. This ease of access allowed businesses to move in and out of countries

Hong Kong Skyline
No longer could the East be used as an exotic foil to help those in the West lay claim to a superior civilization. The 1980s saw Hong Kong, Singapore, China, and other Pacific economies soar and develop the most modern technological capabilities. Skylines changed, reshaped by mountainous glass and steel skyscrapers, and cities like Hong Kong came to symbolize everything postmodern.
Jane Tyska/Stock Boston.

rapidly depending on wages and political conditions. As a result, the labor force gained an international quality, with workers of one country pitted against others in a similar job category on the other side of the globe. Moreover, high technology reduced those without computer skills to minimum-wage jobs as clerks and fast-food attendants. Such trends of the 1990s were creating a two-tiered labor market so reminiscent of the way women had traditionally been exploited that critics spoke of a new "feminization" of work around the world.

Operating on the Internet, global corporations, often seen as out of reach and out of touch, neither inspired nor displayed national loyalty, and mounting business scandals—ranging from Wall Street junk-bond scams to the corrupt dealings of much of the Italian elite—eroded confidence in the ethics of capitalism. "I don't care about ethics," said one German "cyberpunker" at his arraignment for infiltrating a variety of national computer banks. "If it's Russian interests or Western interests, I don't care about that stuff." As people questioned which values of Western civilization still held, some Westerners acknowledged their lack of compassion for the stateless migrant or a destitute fellow citizen. Without an

appreciation of face-to-face society, it was charged, technoculture dragged the Darwinian view of the struggle for survival to new depths of inhumanity.

Nonetheless, huge population centers arose precisely *because* of technoculture, and observers pointed to the growing importance of "global cities" like New York, Hong Kong, Tokyo, and London. These cities swelled in the 1990s; and their postmodernist architecture soared to new heights, drastically changing the modernist skylines of but a century earlier. In these cities, high-level information specialists such as lawyers, accountants, financiers, and a variety of analysts formed a decision-making loop in the technological network. Their financial power changed the complexion of most cities, making them unaffordable to lower levels of information management and service workers. Immigrants continued to flock to the global cities and generally filled the lowest levels of jobs.

The Spread of AIDS.   Disease, like technology, operated on a global terrain. In the early 1980s both Western values and Western technological expertise were challenged by the spread of a global epidemic disease: acquired immune deficiency syndrome, or

An AIDS Educator in Thailand
AIDS spread rapidly around the world, demonstrating the mobility of both people and disease. Activism centered on forcing governments to support AIDS research and to fund AIDS treatment. Other activists, like this man instructing sex workers in Thailand, focused on prevention through education.
Peter Booker/Panos Pictures.

AIDS. An incurable, highly virulent killer, AIDS initially afflicted heterosexuals in central Africa; its first European victim, Danish physician Grethe Rask, died in 1977 after working among the sick in that region. The disease later turned up in Haitian immigrants to the United States and in homosexual men worldwide. As researchers focused attention on the mysterious ailment in the early 1980s, they discovered that it effectively shut down the body's entire immune system. By the late 1990s, no cure had yet been discovered, though protease-inhibiting drugs helped alleviate the disease.

The mounting death toll made some equate AIDS to a Black Death of the twentieth century, reinforcing prejudices and stereotypes about some of its most vulnerable victims. As millions contracted the disease in Africa, treatment was not forthcoming because the ill were too poor. In fact, the deadly Ebola virus and dozens of others smoldered like a global conflagration in the making. The failure of corporate and government "megasystems" to deal effectively with the important challenges of ad-

vanced technological society such as the spread of AIDS showed that while global forces could promote technological advance, they could not necessarily replace the nation-state's concern for its citizens' well-being.

The Global Diffusion of Culture

Culture has long transcended political boundaries, and in fact archaeologists point to its diffusion as a constant of tens of thousands of years of human history. In the ancient world, the Romans studied the work of Greek philosophers; in the nineteenth century, Western scholars immersed themselves in Eastern languages. Asian civilizations borrowed too as religions, agricultural products, and manufactured goods circulated strikingly in the last millennium. But in the postwar period cultural exchange accelerated vastly through new forms of transportation and communication: tourism, for instance, became the largest single industry in Britain and in many other Western countries by the early 1990s. Throngs of visitors from Japan and elsewhere testified to the powerful place the West still held in the world's imagination. Chinese students in Tiananmen Square had rallied around their own representation of the Statue of Liberty (which itself was a gift from France to the United States). In Japan, businesspeople wore Western-style clothing and watched soccer, baseball, and other Western sports using English terms. In Asia, ruling families became Western-style celebrities instead of sacred, godlike figures, while the Pacific Rim tigers became heavy borrowers of Western culture.

The Globalization of Pop Culture. Remarkable innovations in communications have also integrated cultures and made the earth seem a much smaller place, though one with a distinctly Western flavor. Videotapes and satellite-beamed telecasts transport American television shows to Hong Kong and Japanese movies to Europe and North America. American rock music sells briskly in Russia and elsewhere in the former Soviet bloc. When more than 100,000 Czechoslovakian rock fans, including President Václav Havel, attended a Rolling Stones concert in Prague in 1990, it was clear that despite a half-century of supposedly insular Communist culture, Czechs and Slovaks had tuned in to the larger world. Sports stars like the Brazilian soccer player Pelé and the American basketball hero Michael Jordan became better known to countless people than their own national leaders. In today's world, millions of people might even, at the same moment, be spectators at a "live" event anywhere on the planet, whether World Cup competition or an Academy Awards broadcast from Hollywood.

The political power of the United States and the Western presence in the global economy have given Western culture an edge. U.S. success in "marketing" culture, along with the legacy of British imperialism, helped make English the dominant international language. Such English words as *stop, shopping, parking, okay, weekend,* and *rock* infiltrated dozens of non-English vocabularies. With British and American pop music filling the airwaves worldwide, people anywhere could tune their radios to hear songs in English. English is the official language of the European Union and of the new Central European University in Budapest; unofficially, it is the language of travel. In the 1960s, French president de Gaulle, fearing the corruption of the French lan-

guage, had banned such new words as *computer* in government documents; in the mid-1990s, the French government updated the ban. Neither directive, however, could stop the influx of English into scientific, technical, diplomatic, and daily life. Other European countries, among them Germany and the Netherlands, built on their polyglot traditions by rapidly assimilating new words.

Western Europe, the United States, and Australia boasted the largest publishing firms. The giant media empire of Australian-born Rupert Murdoch not only published books, magazines, and newspapers, but produced movies and television shows through its filmmaking and TV network subsidiaries. The news media concocted an extremely successful formula for "selling" news broadcasts that combined reports of late-breaking local, national, and international events with slice-of-life stories about ordinary people. Often focusing on third world suffering, whether because of war, famine, disease, or general underdevelopment, contemporary newscasts reinforced the apparent benefits of life in the West.

Globalism and the Arts. The West continued to devour material from others, as it had done since the age of expansion beginning in the late fifteenth century. Publishers successfully marketed the outpouring of written work by major non-Western artists and intellectuals, and Hollywood made many of their novels into internationally marketed films. Such literature won both popular and critical acclaim and exerted a strong influence on European and North American writers. The lush, exotic fantasies of Colombian-born Nobel Prize winner Gabriel García Márquez (b. 1928), for example, attracted a vast Western readership. His novels, including *One Hundred Years of Solitude* (1967) and *Love in the Time of Cholera* (1988), portray people of titanic ambitions and passions who endure war and all manner of personal trials. Whereas well-regarded European writers of the day, such as the philosopher and novelist Iris Murdoch (1919–1999) or the "new" novelist Nathalie Sarraute (1900–1999) often wrote fiction in a style that was inaccessible to a mass readership, García Márquez's *magical realism* continued an older tradition of comprehensible narrative with larger-than-life characters.

Another Nobel Prize recipient who won high regard in the West was Egyptian writer Naguib

Mahfouz (b. 1911). Having immersed himself in his youth in great Western literature, Mahfouz authored more than forty books. His celebrated *Cairo Trilogy*, written in the 1950s, describes a middle-class family—from its practice of Islam and seclusion of women to the business and cultural life of men in the family. British colonialism forms the trilogy's backdrop; it impassions the protagonists and shapes their lives and destinies. In the eyes of many Arab observers, Mahfouz was a "safe" choice for the Nobel Prize, not only because he produced a literature about the history of colonialism but also because he had adopted a European style. "He borrowed the novel from Europe; he imitated it," charged one fellow Egyptian writer. "It's not an Egyptian art form. Europeans . . . like it very much because it is their own form." The globally read Egyptian Nawal el-Saadawi was also accused of producing exotic accounts of women's oppression to appeal to Western feminists. Thus, although non-Western literature reshaped Western taste, it sometimes provoked charges of inauthenticity in its authors' homelands.

Immigrants to Europe described how the experience of Western culture felt to the transnational person. The popular writer Buchi Emecheta (b. 1944), in her novel *In the Ditch* (1972) and her autobiography *Head above Water* (1986), explored her experiences as a newcomer to Britain. Her *Joys of Motherhood* (1979) was an imaginary foray back in time to probe the nature of mothering under colonial rule in her native Lagos in West Africa. While critiquing colonialism and the welfare state from a non-Western perspective, Emecheta, like many writers and politicians from less-developed countries, felt the lure of Western education and Western values. International conflict around artistic expression became dangerous. Salman Rushdie (b. 1947), also an immigrant to Great Britain (from India), produced the novel *The Satanic Verses* (1988), which ignited outrage among Muslims around the world because it appeared to blaspheme the prophet Muhammad. From Iran the Ayatollah Khomeini promised both a monetary reward and salvation in the afterlife to anyone who would assassinate the writer. In a display of Western cultural unity, international leaders took bold steps to protect Rushdie until the threat was lifted a decade later.

The mainstream was widened and sometimes fraught with conflict as groups outside the accepted circles engaged in artistic production. From within the West, novelist Toni Morrison (b. 1931), who in 1993 became the first African American woman to win the Nobel Prize in literature, described the nightmares, daily experiences, and dreams of the descendants of men and women who had been brought as slaves to the United States. But many parents objected to the inclusion of Morrison's work in curricula. Critics charged that, unlike Shakespeare's universal Western truth, the writing of African Americans, Native Americans, and postcolonial authors represented only a partial vision, not great literature.

Cultural arbiters were often relieved when the novels of Eastern-bloc dissidents powerfully endorsed Western values. Many of these writers first published their works in the West, and their writings were eventually smuggled back to their homelands. Milan Kundera (b. 1929) left Czechoslovakia in 1975 after Communist police had harassed him for his rebellious writing. Settling in Paris, Kundera produced *The Book of Laughter and Forgetting* (1979) and *The Unbearable Lightness of Being* (1984). In these works he dwelt on the importance of remembering the oppressive climate of the Eastern bloc in the face of a natural tendency to repress and to forget. In Kundera's fictional world, life often drifts toward immateriality and a quest for ease. The culture of forgetting and an easy attitude toward life, however, were just what repressive governments wanted. Writers who remained in the Soviet bloc were often suspicious of those who found success in the West. In the land of prosperous book contracts, said one Polish writer, there was no such thing as literature; rather, writing was merely a "line of business." And indeed, the dissidents were often wildly successful.

Some dissident writers chose not to leave the Communist world, and they survived by turning out a literature that was acceptable, even if the government did not embrace it wholeheartedly. East German writer Christa Wolf (b. 1929) explored subjects, such as individuality, personal guilt, and the search for self-identity, that went against the grain of East Germany's Communist ideology. In such works as *The Quest for Christa T.* (1970), she touched on themes that appealed deeply to Westerners in the 1970s and 1980s. While probing Western values in the context of communism, however, Wolf never crossed the fine line that would have brought her atonal, like the chant of monks and like Wagner—a collage of sound and music from everywhere. Her music, however, lacked the harshness of modernists from the middle of the century and represented a turn toward accessibility in classical music.

Postmodernism. Some called this hyper-mixing of influences *postmodernism*, and one definition of postmodernism included multiplicity without a central unifying theme or privileged canon. Striking examples of postmodern art abounded in Western society, including the AT&T building in New York City, the work of architect Philip Johnson (b. 1906). Although the structure itself, designed in the late 1970s, looked sleek and modern, its entryway was a Roman arch, and its cloud-piercing top suggested the eighteenth-century Chippendale style. The blueprints of Johnson and other postmodernists appealed to the human past and drew from cultural styles that spanned millennia and continents without valuing one style above others. The Guggenheim Museum in Bilbao, Spain, designed by American Frank Gehry (b. 1929), was similarly bizarre by classical or even "modern" standards as it represented forms, materials, and perspectives that by rules of earlier decades did not belong together. These were aesthetic examples of the postmodern, which also gave rise to films and novels without the unity of a single narrative or plot.

Other intellectuals defined the postmodern in political terms as an outgrowth of the demise of the eighteenth-century ideals of human rights, individualism, personal freedom, and their guarantor—the Western nation-state. A structure like the Bilbao Guggenheim was just an international tourist attraction that had no Spanish roots or purpose; consumption, global technology, mass communications, and international migration made citizenship, nationalism, and rights irrelevant to its meaning. It was a rootless structure, unlike the Louvre in Paris. Moreover, the end of formal imperialism meant an end to the white privilege behind modern civil rights as defined in the eighteenth century. The 1982 American film *Blade Runner*, for example, depicted a dangerous, densely packed, multiethnic Los Angeles patrolled by police with high-tech gear—a metropolis with no place for national or personal identity or human rights. For postmodernists of a political bent, computers had replaced the autonomous, free self and bureaucracy had rendered

Toni Morrison Receiving Nobel Prize
The first African American woman to receive the Nobel Prize, Toni Morrison had used her literary talent to depict the condition of blacks under slavery and after emancipation. Morrison also published cogent essays on social, racial, and gender issues in the United States.
Pressens Bild/Gamma Liaison.

into open opposition to the government. Consequently, the East German regime allowed her to continue publishing. With the collapse of communism, Wolf was condemned for the privileges she had enjoyed under Communist rule and for her lack of forceful dissent.

Others in the Communist world mixed global cultures no matter how dangerous or unpopular. The acclaimed composer Sofia Gubaidulina (b. 1931)—a Tatar, granddaughter of a teacher of Islam, and herself a Christian strongly influenced by Asian mysticism—created music with electronic guitars, tam-tams, and accordion along with screams and whispers. Her music was tonal and

Christo and Jeanne-Claude, Umbrellas

Attuned to global differences and similarities in landscape, environment, and ways of life, the artists Christo and Jeanne-Claude created an art that enhanced people's sensual experience of the everyday world. Their installation of umbrellas in California (top) and Japan (bottom) featured colors that complemented distinctive rural terrain, just as their wrapping of the Reichstag in Berlin (1971–1995) had enhanced urban architecture. As global citizens, they recycled the vast quantities of materials once their works were dismantled.

Top: *Christo and Jeanne-Claude: The Umbrellas, Japan-USA, 1984–91. California site.* Photo: Wolfgang Volz. © Christo 1991; bottom: *Christo and Jeanne-Claude: The Umbrellas, Japan-USA, 1984–91. Ibaraki, Japan site.* Photo: Wolfgang Volz. © Christo 1991.

representative government obsolete—an international elite of the strong, technologically trained would replace the parliament.

A third definition of the postmodern involved investigating the "unfreedom" or irrationality that shaped human life. Thus French psychoanalyst Jacques Lacan, who deeply influenced Western literary criticism in the 1980s, maintained that people operate in an unfree, predetermined world of language. Patriarchal rules of language exist before we are born and are rooted in our psychic structure. In becoming social, communicating beings we must bow to these laws. Another prominent French thinker, Michel Foucault, professed to deplore the easy acceptance of such liberal ideas as the autonomous self, the progressive march of history, and the advance of freedom. For him the sexual revolution had not been liberating at all; rather, sexuality was merely a way in which humans expressed power over one another and through which society, by allowing greater sexual expression, actually controlled individuals. Freedom, in short, had lost credibility: even in the most intimate part of human experience, people were locked in a grid of social and individual constraint. For some people struggling with the legacy of colonialism, racism, and sexism, the message from these thinkers that the rational, independent, and superior Westerner was illusory was actually a hopeful one.

Conclusion: The Making of the West Continues

Although some postmodernists proclaimed an end to centuries of faith in progress, they themselves worked within the modern Western tradition of constant criticism and reevaluation. Moreover, said their critics, the daunting problems of contemporary life—population explosion, resource depletion, North-South inequities, nuclear power, global pollution, and ethnic hatred—demanded the exercise of humanistic values and the renewal of a rational commitment to progress now more than ever. Postmodernists and other philosophers countered with the question of "unintended consequences," that is, the question whether one could begin to know the consequences of an act. Who would have predicted, for example, the human misery resulting from the fall of the Soviet empire?

IMPORTANT DATES

1979 Islamic revolution in Iran

1980 An independent trade union, Solidarity, organizes resistance to Polish communism; Prime Minister Margaret Thatcher begins dismantling the welfare state in Britain

Early 1980s AIDS epidemic strikes the West; rise of the Pacific economy

1981 Ronald Reagan becomes U.S. president

1985 Mikhail Gorbachev comes to power in the USSR

1986 Explosion at Soviet nuclear plant at Chernobyl; Spain joins the Common Market

1989 Chinese students revolt in Tiananmen Square and government suppresses them; fall of the Berlin Wall

1990s Internet revolution

1990–1991 War in the Persian Gulf

1991 Civil war erupts in the former Yugoslavia

1992 Soviet Union is dissolved

1993 Toni Morrison becomes the first African American woman to win the Nobel Prize

1994 Postapartheid elections held in South Africa

1995 International congress of women at Beijing

1997 Collapse of Thai currency and upset of the Asian "tigers"

1999 Boris Yeltsin resigns as president of Russia; euro monetary system introduced in the European Union; world population reaches six billion

---

The years since 1980 proved both sides correct. The collapse of communism signaled at least the eclipse of an ideology that was perhaps noble in intent but deadly in practice. Events from South Africa to the Middle East to Northern Ireland indicated that certain long-feuding groups were wearying of conflict and groping for peace, even as other peoples took up arms against their neighbors. Yet the unintended consequences of communism's fall were bloodshed, sickness, and hardship, while the global age ushered in by the Soviet collapse has brought "denationalization" to many regions of the world. Africa and Asia also faced disease and the erosion of their economic and social fabric as they faced Westernization and the global age.

Peoples and cultures of the rest of the world have indeed played their roles in the making of the

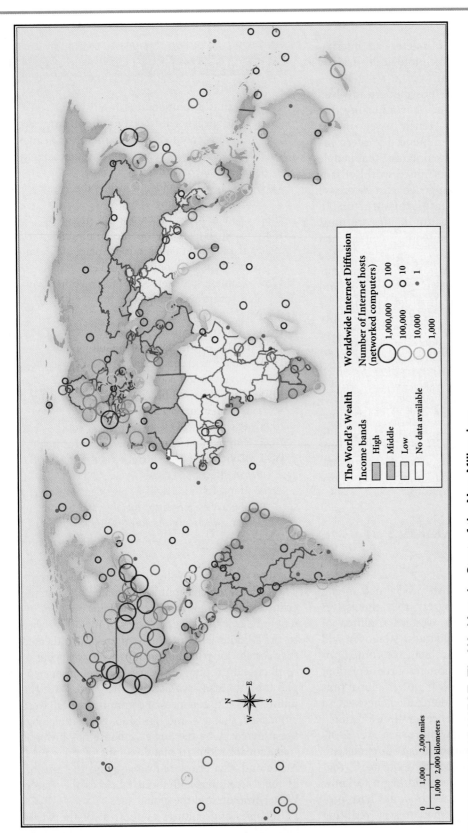

MAPPING THE WEST The World at the Start of the New Millennium

By the twenty-first century, the Internet had transformed communications and economic organization into an interconnected global network. People in the so-called North had greater access to this network in 1999 and for the most part enjoyed greater wealth. Despite globalization, historians still find local and national conditions of political, social, and economic life important in telling the full story of peoples and cultures.

From www.mids.org (Austin: Matrix Information and Directory Services, Inc.)

West—at some times more than others. At the dawn of the millennium, the West must look in many directions to find its way. Western traditions of democracy, human rights, and economic equality have much to offer. Given that these were usually intended only for certain people, global debates about their value abound. The nation-state, which protected those values for privileged Westerners, is another legacy that must be rethought in an age of transnationalism, when more people than ever are demanding the dignity of citizenship without its being attached to a specific ethnicity. At the same time, the West faces questions of its own cultural identity—an identity made from the far-flung cultural, natural, and human resources of Asia, Africa, and the Western Hemisphere. Non-Westerners have challenged, criticized, refashioned, and made enormous contributions to Western culture; they have also served the West's citizens as slaves, servants, and menial workers. One of the greatest challenges to the West and the world in this global millennium is to determine how peoples and cultures can live together on terms that are enriching for everyone.

A final challenge to the West is living with the inventive human spirit. In the past five hundred years the West has benefited from its scientific and technological advances. Longevity and improved material well-being have spread around the world. In the past century, communication and information technology brought people closer to one another than ever before. Simultaneously, through the use of technology the last century was the bloodiest in human history. War and genocide were among its hallmarks, and even now the world's leaders urge their scientific communities to search for ever more destructive weapons, posing perhaps the greatest challenge to the West and to the world. The making of the West has been a constantly inventive undertaking but also a deadly one. What mixture of peoples and cultures will face the paradoxical challenge of technology to protect the creativity of the human race in the twenty-first century?

Suggested References

Global Challenges

Historians see the challenges of the past two decades as enormously diverse, ranging from conditions in the environment to issues of leadership in international affairs. However, as Rives and Yousefi show, challenges such as the globalization of work have benefits as well as costs.

Appleyard, Reginald. *International Migration: Challenges for the Nineties.* 1991.

Feshbach, Murray. *Ecological Disaster: Cleaning Up the Hidden Legacy of the Soviet Regime.* 1995.

Keylor, William R. *The Twentieth-Century World: An International History.* 1992.

*Khadduri, Majid, and Edmund Ghareeb. *War in the Gulf, 1990–1991.* 1997.

Moin, Baqr. *Khomeini: Life of the Ayatollah.* 1999.

Rives, Janet, and Mahmood Yousefi. *Economic Dimensions of Gender Inequality: A Global Perspective.* 1997.

UN Population Data: http://www.unfpa.org/swp/swpmain.htm.

The Welfare State in Question

The transformation of the welfare state involved powerful political personalities and raised fundamental issues about the nature of citizenship. Much cutting-edge history concerns an analysis of citizens' relationship to their state and their relationship to one another in an age of global migration and dramatic economic change. The work of Paul Gilroy in particular has brought these questions to the fore.

Ash, Timothy Garton. *In Europe's Name: Germany and the Divided Continent.* 1993.

Caciagli, Mario, and David I. Kertzer, eds. *Italian Politics: The Stalled Transition.* 1996.

Gilroy, Paul. *"There Ain't No Black in the Union Jack": The Cultural Politics of Race and Nation.* 1987.

Sassen, Saskia. *Globalization and Its Discontents: Essays on the New Mobility of People and Money.* 1998.

Schaller, Michael. *Reckoning with Reagan: America and Its President in the 1980s.* 1992.

Thompson, Juliet S., and Wayne C. Thompson. *Margaret Thatcher: Prime Minister Indomitable.* 1994.

The Collapse of Soviet Communism

Historians will be telling and retelling this story, for the full consequences of communism's collapse are still unfolding. As new archives open, scholars, such as Kligman, focus on recounting some of the most horrendous aspects of Communist rule. Others, like Wachtel, explain the post-Communist situation in terms of very long-standing trends such as the obstacles to creating cultural unity among peoples of the former Yugoslavia.

Funk, Nanette, and Magda Mueller. *Gender Politics and Post-Communism: Reflections from Eastern Europe and the Former Soviet Union.* 1993.

*Primary sources.

Glenny, Misha. *The Fall of Yugoslavia: The Third Balkan War.* 1996.

*Gorbachev, Mikhail. *Memoirs.* 1996.

Jarausch, Konrad. *The Rush to German Unity.* 1994.

Kazanov, Anatoly M. *After the USSR: Ethnicity, Nationalism, and Politics in the Commonwealth of Independent States.* 1995.

Kligman, Gail. *The Politics of Duplicity: Controlling Reproduction in Ceaușescu's Romania.* 1998.

Sternhal, Suzanne. *Gorbachev's Reforms: De-Stalinization through Demilitarization.* 1997.

Strayer, Robert. *Why Did the Soviet Union Collapse?* 1998.

Wachtel, Andrew B. *Making a Nation, Breaking a Nation: Literature and Cultural Politics in Yugoslavia.* 1998.

Weigel, George. *Witness to Hope: The Biography of Pope John Paul II.* 1999.

Global Culture and Western Civilization at the Dawn of a New Millennium

The fate of cultural identity in an age of globalization engages a wide range of investigation and theorizing. From the nation-state to our individual relationships, as Applegate and Turkle, among others, suggest, long-standing identities are open to rethinking.

Agre, Philip. *Computation and Human Experience.* 1997.

Applegate, Celia. "A Europe of Regions: Reflections on the Historiography of Sub-National Places in Modern Times." *The American Historical Review.* 1999.

Bales, Kevin. *Disposable People: New Slavery in the Global Economy.* 1999.

Dery, Mark. *Escape Velocity: Cyberculture at the End of the Century.* 1996.

*Emecheta, Buchi. *The Joys of Motherhood.* 1979.

Huntington, Samuel P. *The Clash of Civilizations and the Remaking of the World Order.* 1996.

Iriye, Akira. *Cultural Internationalism and World Order.* 1997.

*Morrison, Toni. *Paradise.* 1998.

Piening, Christopher. *Global Europe: The European Union in World Affairs.* 1997.

Public Broadcasting: http://www.pbs.org.

Redmond, John, and Glenda S. Rosenthal. *The Expanding European Union: Past, Present, Future.* 1998.

Turkle, Sherry. *Life on the Screen: Identity in the Age of the Internet.* 1995.

Useful Facts and Figures

PROMINENT ROMAN EMPERORS

Julio-Claudians

27 B.C.–14 A.D.	Augustus
14–37	Tiberius
37–41	Gaius (Caligula)
41–54	Claudius
54–68	Nero

Flavian Dynasty

69–79	Vespasian
79–81	Titus
81–96	Domitian

Golden Age Emperors

96–98	Nerva
98–117	Trajan
117–138	Hadrian
138–161	Antonius Pius
161–180	Marcus Aurelius

Severan Emperors

193–211	Septimius Severus
211–217	Antoninus (Caracalla)
217–218	Macrinus
222–235	Severus Alexander

Period of Instability

235–238	Maximinus Thrax
238–244	Gordian III
244–249	Philip the Arab
249–251	Decius
251–253	Trebonianus Gallus
253–260	Valerian
270–275	Aurelian
275–276	Tacitus
276–282	Probus
283–285	Carinus

Dominate

284–305	Diocletian
306	Constantius
306–337	Constantine I
337–340	Constantine II
337–350	Constans I
337–361	Constantius II

(Continued)

361–363	Julian
363–364	Jovian
364–375	Valentinian I
364–378	Valens
367–383	Gratian
375–392	Valentinian II
378–395	Theodosius I
	(the Great)

The Western Empire

395–423	Honorius
406–407	Marcus

407–411	Constantine III
409–411	Maximus
411–413	Jovinus
412–413	Sebastianus
423–425	Johannes
425–455	Valentinian III
455–456	Avitus
457–461	Majorian
461–465	Libius Severus
467–472	Anthemius
473–474	Glycerius
474–475	Julius Nepos
475–476	Romulus Augustulus

PROMINENT BYZANTINE EMPERORS

Dynasty of Theodosius

395–408	Arcadius
408–450	Theodosius II
450–457	Marcian

Dynasty of Leo

457–474	Leo I
474	Leo II
474–491	Zeno
475–476	Basiliscus
484–488	Leontius
491–518	Anastasius

Dynasty of Justinian

518–527	Justin
527–565	Justinian I
565–578	Justin II
578–582	Tiberius II
578–582	Tiberius II (I) Constantine
582–602	Maurice
602–610	Phocas

Dynasty of Heraclius

610–641	Heraclius
641	Heraclonas
641	Constantine III
641–668	Constans II
646–647	Gregory
649–653	Olympius
669	Mezezius

668–685	Constantine IV
685–695	Justinian II (banished)
695–698	Leontius
698–705	Tiberius III (II)
705–711	Justinian II (restored)
711–713	Bardanes
713–716	Anastasius II
716–717	Theodosius III

Isaurian Dynasty

717–741	Leo III
741–775	Constantine V Copronymus
775–780	Leo IV
780–797	Constantine VI
797–802	Irene
802–811	Nicephorus I
811	Strauracius
811–813	Michael I
813–820	Leo V

Phrygian Dynasty

820–829	Michael II
821–823	Thomas
829–842	Theophilus
842–867	Michael III

Macedonian Dynasty

867–886	Basil I
869–879	Constantine

887–912	Leo VI
912–913	Alexander
913–959	Constantine VII Porphygenitus
920–944	Romanus I Lecapenus
921–931	Christopher
924–945	Stephen
959–963	Romanus II
963–969	Nicephorus II Phocas
976–1025	Basil II
1025–1028	Constantine VIII (IX) alone
1028–1034	Romanus III Argyrus
1034–1041	Michael IV the Paphlagonian
1041–1042	Michael V Calaphates
1042	Zoe and Theodora
1042–1055	Constantine IX Monomchus
1055–1066	Theodora alone
1056–1057	Michael VI Stratioticus

Prelude to the Comnenian Dynasty

1057–1059	Isaac I Comnenos
1059–1067	Constantine X (IX) Ducas
1068–1071	Romanus IV Diogenes
1071–1078	Michael VII Ducas
1078–1081	Nicephorus III Botaniates
1080–1081	Nicephorus Melissenus

Comnenian Dynasty

1081–1118	Alexius I
1118–1143	John II
1143–1180	Manuel I
1180–1183	Alexius II

1183–1185	Andronieus I
1183–1191	Isaac, Emperor of Cyprus

Dynasty of the Angeli

1185–1195	Isaac II
1195–1203	Alexius III
1203–1204	Isaac II (restored) with Alexius IV
1204	Alexius V Ducas Murtzuphlus

Lascarid Dynasty in Nicaea

1204–1222	Theodore I Lascaris
1222–1254	John III Ducas Vatatzes
1254–1258	Theodore II Lascaris
1258–1261	John IV Lascaris

Dynasty of the Paleologi

1259–1289	Michael VIII Paleologus
1282–1328	Andronicus II
1328–1341	Andronicus III
1341–1391	John V
1347–1354	John VI Cantancuzenus
1376–1379	Andronicus IV
1379–1391	John V (restored)
1390	John VII
1391–1425	Manuel II
1425–1448	John VIII
1449–1453	Constantine XI (XIII) Dragases

PROMINENT POPES

314–335	Sylvester
440–461	Leo I
590–604	Gregory I (the Great)
687–701	Sergius I
741–752	Zachary
858–867	Nicholas I
1049–1054	Leo IX
1059–1061	Nicholas II
1073–1085	Gregory VII
1088–1099	Urban II
1099–1118	Paschal II
1159–1181	Alexander III
1198–1216	Innocent III
1227–1241	Gregory IX

1243–1254	Innocent IV
1294–1303	Boniface VIII
1316–1334	John XXII
1447–1455	Nicholas V
1458–1464	Pius II
1492–1503	Alexander VI
1503–1513	Julius II
1513–1521	Leo X
1534–1549	Paul III
1555–1559	Paul IV
1585–1590	Sixtus V
1623–1644	Urban VIII
1831–1846	Gregory XVI

(Continued)

1846–1878	Pius IX
1878–1903	Leo XIII
1903–1914	Pius X
1914–1922	Benedict XV
1922–1939	Pius XI

1939–1958	Pius XII
1958–1963	John XXIII
1963–1978	Paul VI
1978	John Paul I
1978–	John Paul II

THE CAROLINGIAN DYNASTY

687–714	Pepin of Heristal, Mayor of the Palace
715–741	Charles Martel, Mayor of the Palace
741–751	Pepin III, Mayor of the Palace
751–768	Pepin III, King
768–814	Charlemagne, King
800–814	Charlemagne, Emperor
814–840	Louis the Pious

West Francia

840–877	Charles the Bald, King
875–877	Charles the Bald, Emperor
877–879	Louis II, King

879–882	Louis III, King
879–884	Carloman, King

Middle Kingdoms

840–855	Lothair, Emperor
855–875	Louis (Italy), Emperor
855–863	Charles (Provence), King
855–869	Lothair II (Lorraine), King

East Francia

840–876	Ludwig, King
876–880	Carloman, King
876–882	Ludwig, King
876–887	Charles the Fat, Emperor

GERMAN KINGS CROWNED EMPEROR

Saxon Dynasty

962–973	Otto I
973–983	Otto II
983–1002	Otto III
1002–1024	Henry II

Franconian Dynasty

1024–1039	Conrad II
1039–1056	Henry III
1056–1106	Henry IV
1106–1125	Henry V
1125–1137	Lothair II (Saxony)

Hohenstaufen Dynasty

1138–1152	Conrad III
1152–1190	Frederick I (Barbarossa)

1190–1197	Henry VI
1198–1208	Philip of Swabia
1198–1215	Otto IV (Welf)
1220–1250	Frederick II
1250–1254	Conrad IV

Interregnum, 1254–1273: Emperors from Various Dynasties

1273–1291	Rudolf I (Habsburg)
1292–1298	Adolf (Nassau)
1298–1308	Albert I (Habsburg)
1308–1313	Henry VII (Luxemburg)
1314–1347	Ludwig IV (Wittelsbach)
1347–1378	Charles IV (Luxemburg)
1378–1400	Wenceslas (Luxemburg)
1400–1410	Rupert (Wittelsbach)
1410–1437	Sigismund (Luxemburg)

Habsburg Dynasty

1438–1439	Albert II		1637–1657	Ferdinand III
1440–1493	Frederick III		1658–1705	Leopold I
1493–1519	Maximilian I		1705–1711	Joseph I
1519–1556	Charles V		1711–1740	Charles VI
1556–1564	Ferdinand I		1742–1745	Charles VII (not a Habsburg)
1564–1576	Maximilian II		1745–1765	Francis I
1576–1612	Rudolf II		1765–1790	Joseph II
1612–1619	Matthias		1790–1792	Leopold II
1619–1637	Ferdinand II		1792–1806	Francis II

RULERS OF FRANCE

Capetian Dynasty

987–996	Hugh Capet
996–1031	Robert II
1031–1060	Henry I
1060–1108	Philip I
1108–1137	Louis VI
1137–1180	Louis VII
1180–1223	Philip II (Augustus)
1223–1226	Louis VIII
1226–1270	Louis IX (St. Louis)
1270–1285	Philip III
1285–1314	Philip IV
1314–1316	Louis X
1316–1322	Philip V
1322–1328	Charles IV

Valois Dynasty

1328–1350	Philip VI
1350–1364	John
1364–1380	Charles V
1380–1422	Charles VI
1422–1461	Charles VII
1461–1483	Louis XI
1483–1498	Charles VIII
1498–1515	Louis XII
1515–1547	Francis I

1547–1559	Henry II
1559–1560	Francis II
1560–1574	Charles IX
1574–1589	Henry III

Bourbon Dynasty

1589–1610	Henry IV
1610–1643	Louis XIII
1643–1715	Louis XIV
1715–1774	Louis XV
1774–1792	Louis XVI

After 1792

1792–1799	First Republic, 1792–1799
1799–1804	Napoleon Bonaparte, First Consul
1804–1814	Napoleon I, Emperor
1814–1824	Louis XVIII (Bourbon Dynasty)
1824–1830	Charles X (Bourbon Dynasty)
1830–1848	Louis Philippe
1848–1852	Second Republic
1852–1870	Napoleon III, Emperor
1870–1940	Third Republic
1940–1944	Vichy government, Pétain regime
1944–1946	Provisional government
1946–1958	Fourth Republic
1958–	Fifth Republic

MONARCHS OF ENGLAND AND GREAT BRITAIN

Anglo-Saxon Monarchs

829–839	Egbert
839–858	Ethelwulf
858–860	Ethelbald
860–866	Ethelbert
866–871	Ethelred I
871–899	Alfred the Great
899–924	Edward the Elder
924–939	Ethelstan
939–946	Edmund I
946–955	Edred
955–959	Edwy
959–975	Edgar
975–978	Edward the Martyr
978–1016	Ethelred the Unready
1016–1035	Canute (Danish nationality)
1035–1040	Harold I
1040–1042	Hardicanute
1042–1066	Edward the Confessor
1066	Harold II

Norman Monarchs

1066–1087	William I (the Conqueror)
1087–1100	William II
1100–1135	Henry I

House of Blois

1135–1154	Stephen

House of Plantagenet

1154–1189	Henry II
1189–1199	Richard I
1199–1216	John
1216–1272	Henry III
1272–1307	Edward I
1307–1327	Edward II
1327–1377	Edward III
1377–1399	Richard II

House of Lancaster

1399–1413	Henry IV
1413–1422	Henry V
1422–1461	Henry VI

House of York

1461–1483	Edward IV
1483	Edward V
1483–1485	Richard III

House of Tudor

1485–1509	Henry VII
1509–1547	Henry VIII
1547–1553	Edward VI
1553–1558	Mary
1558–1603	Elizabeth I

House of Stuart

1603–1625	James I
1625–1649	Charles I

Commonwealth and Protectorate (1649–1660)

1653–1658	Oliver Cromwell
1658–1659	Richard Cromwell

House of Stuart (Restored)

1660–1685	Charles II
1685–1688	James II
1689–1694	William III and Mary II
1694–1702	William III (alone)
1702–1714	Anne

House of Hanover

1714–1727	George I
1727–1760	George II
1760–1820	George III
1820–1830	George IV
1830–1837	William IV
1837–1901	Victoria

House of Saxe-Coburg-Gotha

1901–1910	Edward VII

House of Windsor

1910–1936	George V
1936	Edward VIII
1936–1952	George VI
1952–	Elizabeth II

PRIME MINISTERS OF GREAT BRITAIN

Term	Prime Minister	Government
1721–1742	Sir Robert Walpole	Whig
1742–1743	Spencer Compton, Earl of Wilmington	Whig
1743–1754	Henry Pelham	Whig
1754–1756	Thomas Pelham-Holles, Duke of Newcastle	Whig
1756–1757	William Cavendish, Duke of Devonshire	Whig
1757–1761	William Pitt (the Elder), Earl of Chatham	Whig
1761–1762	Thomas Pelham-Holles, Duke of Newcastle	Whig
1762–1763	John Stuart, Earl of Bute	Tory
1763–1765	George Grenville	Whig
1765–1766	Charles Watson-Wentworth, Marquess of Rockingham	Whig
1766–1768	William Pitt, Earl of Chatham (the Elder)	Whig
1768–1770	Augustus Henry Fitzroy, Duke of Grafton	Whig
1770–1782	Frederick North (Lord North)	Tory
1782	Charles Watson-Wentworth, Marquess of Rockingham	Whig
1782–1783	William Petty FitzMaurice, Earl of Shelburn	Whig
1783	William Henry Cavendish Bentinck, Duke of Portland	Whig
1783–1801	William Pitt, the Younger	Tory
1801–1804	Henry Addington	Tory
1804–1806	William Pitt (the Younger)	Tory
1806–1807	William Wyndham Grenville (Baron Grenville)	Whig
1807–1809	William Henry Cavendish Bentinck, Duke of Portland	Tory
1809–1812	Spencer Perceval	Tory
1812–1827	Robert Banks Jenkinson, Earl of Liverpool	Tory
1827	George Canning	Tory
1827–1828	Frederick John Robinson (Viscount Goderich)	Tory
1828–1830	Arthur Wellesley, Duke of Wellington	Tory
1830–1834	Charles Grey (Earl Grey)	Whig
1834	William Lamb, Viscount Melbourne	Whig
1834–1835	Sir Robert Peel	Tory
1835–1841	William Lamb, Viscount Melbourne	Whig
1841–1846	Sir Robert Peel	Tory
1846–1852	John Russell (Lord)	Whig
1852	Edward Geoffrey–Smith Stanley Derby, Earl of Derby	Whig
1852–1855	George Hamilton Gordon Aberdeen, Earl of Aberdeen	Peelite
1855–1858	Henry John Temple Palmerston, Viscount Palmerston	Tory
1858–1859	Edward Geoffrey–Smith Stanley Derby, Earl of Derby	Whig
1859–1865	Henry John Temple Palmerston, Viscount Palmerston	Tory
1865–1866	John Russell (Earl)	Liberal
1866–1868	Edward Geoffrey–Smith Stanley Derby, Earl of Derby	Tory
1868	Benjamin Disraeli, Earl of Beaconfield	Conservative
1868–1874	William Ewart Gladstone	Liberal
1874–1880	Benjamin Disraeli, Earl of Beaconfield	Conservative
1880–1885	William Ewart Gladstone	Liberal
1885–1886	Robert Arthur Talbot, Marquess of Salisbury	Conservative
1886	William Ewart Gladstone	Liberal
1886–1892	Robert Arthur Talbot, Marquess of Salisbury	Conservative
1892–1894	William Ewart Gladstone	Liberal
1894–1895	Archibald Philip–Primrose Rosebery, Earl of Rosebery	Liberal

(Continued)

Term	Prime Minister	Government
1895–1902	Robert Arthur Talbot, Marquess of Salisbury	Conservative
1902–1905	Arthur James Balfour, Earl of Balfour	Conservative
1905–1908	Sir Henry Campbell-Bannerman	Liberal
1908–1915	Herbert Henry Asquith	Liberal
1915–1916	Herbert Henry Asquith	Coalition
1916–1922	David Lloyd George, Earl Lloyd-George of Dwyfor	Coalition
1922–1923	Andrew Bonar Law	Conservative
1923–1924	Stanley Baldwin, Earl Baldwin of Bewdley	Conservative
1924	James Ramsay MacDonald	Labour
1924–1929	Stanley Baldwin, Earl Baldwin of Bewdley	Conservative
1929–1931	James Ramsay MacDonald	Labour
1931–1935	James Ramsay MacDonald	Coalition
1935–1937	Stanley Baldwin, Earl Baldwin of Bewdley	Coalition
1937–1940	Neville Chamberlain	Coalition
1940–1945	Winston Churchill	Coalition
1945	Winston Churchill	Conservative
1945–1951	Clement Attlee, Earl Attlee	Labour
1951–1955	Sir Winston Churchill	Conservative
1955–1957	Sir Anthony Eden, Earl of Avon	Conservative
1957–1963	Harold Macmillan, Earl of Stockton	Conservative
1963–1964	Sir Alec Frederick Douglas-Home, Lord Home of the Hirsel	Conservative
1964–1970	Harold Wilson, Lord Wilson of Rievaulx	Labour
1970–1974	Edward Heath	Conservative
1974–1976	Harold Wilson, Lord Wilson of Rievaulx	Labour
1976–1979	James Callaghan, Lord Callaghan of Cardiff	Labour
1979–1990	Margaret Thatcher (Baroness)	Conservative
1990–1997	John Major	Conservative
1997–	Tony Blair	Labour

RULERS OF PRUSSIA AND GERMANY

1701–1713	*Frederick I
1713–1740	*Frederick William I
1740–1786	*Frederick II (the Great)
1786–1797	*Frederick William II
1797–1840	*Frederick William III
1840–1861	*Frederick William IV
1861–1888	*William I (German emperor after 1871)
1888	Frederick III
1888–1918	*William II
1918–1933	Weimar Republic
1933–1945	Third Reich (Nazi dictatorship under Adolf Hitler)
1945–1952	Allied occupation
1949–1990	Division of Federal Republic of Germany in west and German Democratic Republic in east
1990–	Federal Republic of Germany (united)

*King of Prussia

RULERS OF AUSTRIA AND AUSTRIA-HUNGARY

1493–1519	*Maximillian I (Archduke)
1519–1556	*Charles V
1556–1564	*Ferdinand I
1564–1576	*Maximillian II
1576–1612	*Rudolf II
1612–1619	*Matthias
1619–1637	*Ferdinand II
1637–1657	*Ferdinand III
1658–1705	*Leopold I
1705–1711	*Joseph I
1711–1740	*Charles VI
1740–1780	Maria Theresa
1780–1790	*Joseph II
1790–1792	*Leopold II
1792–1835	*Francis II (emperor of Austria as Francis I after 1804)
1835–1848	Ferdinand I
1848–1916	Francis Joseph (after 1867 emperor of Austria and king of Hungary)
1916–1918	Charles I (emperor of Austria and king of Hungary)
1918–1938	Republic of Austria (dictatorship after 1934)
1945–1956	Republic restored, under Allied occupation
1956–	Free Republic

*Also bore title of Holy Roman Emperor

LEADERS OF POST–WORLD WAR II GERMANY

West Germany (Federal Republic of Germany), 1949–1990

Years	Chancellor	Party
1949–1963	Konrad Adenauer	Christian Democratic Union (CDU)
1963–1966	Ludwig Erhard	Christian Democratic Union (CDU)
1966–1969	Kurt Georg Kiesinger	Christian Democratic Union (CDU)
1969–1974	Willy Brandt	Social Democratic Party (SPD)
1974–1982	Helmut Schmidt	Social Democratic Party (SPD)
1982–1990	Helmut Kohl	Christian Democratic Union (CDU)

East Germany (German Democratic Republic), 1949–1990

Years	Communist Party Leader
1946–1971	Walter Ulbricht
1971–1989	Erich Honecker
1989–1990	Egon Krenz

Federal Republic of Germany (reunited), 1990–

1990–1998	Helmut Kohl	Christian Democratic Union (CDU)
1998–	Gerhard Schroeder	Social Democratic Party (SPD)

RULERS OF RUSSIA, THE USSR, AND THE RUSSIAN FEDERATION

c. 980–1015	Vladimir
1019–1054	Yaroslav the Wise
1176–1212	Vsevolod III
1462–1505	Ivan III
1505–1553	Vasily III
1553–1584	Ivan IV
1584–1598	Theodore I
1598–1605	Boris Godunov
1605	Theodore II
1606–1610	Vasily IV
1613–1645	Michael
1645–1676	Alexius
1676–1682	Theodore III
1682–1689	Ivan V and Peter I
1689–1725	Peter I (the Great)
1725–1727	Catherine I
1727–1730	Peter II
1730–1740	Anna
1740–1741	Ivan VI
1741–1762	Elizabeth
1762	Peter III
1762–1796	Catherine II (the Great)
1796–1801	Paul
1801–1825	Alexander I
1825–1855	Nicholas I
1855–1881	Alexander II
1881–1894	Alexander III
1894–1917	Nicholas II

Union of Soviet Socialist Republics (USSR)*

1917–1924	Vladimir Ilyich Lenin
1924–1953	Joseph Stalin
1953–1964	Nikita Khrushchev
1964–1982	Leonid Brezhnev
1982–1984	Yuri Andropov
1984–1985	Konstantin Chernenko
1985–1991	Mikhail Gorbachev

Russian Federation

1991–1999	Boris Yeltsin
1999–	Vladimir Putin

*USSR established in 1922

RULERS OF SPAIN

1479–1504	Ferdinand and Isabella
1504–1506	Ferdinand and Philip I
1506–1516	Ferdinand and Charles I
1516–1556	Charles I (Holy Roman Emperor Charles V)
1556–1598	Philip II
1598–1621	Philip III
1621–1665	Philip IV
1665–1700	Charles II
1700–1746	Philip V
1746–1759	Ferdinand VI
1759–1788	Charles III
1788–1808	Charles IV
1808	Ferdinand VII
1808–1813	Joseph Bonaparte
1814–1833	Ferdinand VII (restored)
1833–1868	Isabella II
1868–1870	Republic
1870–1873	Amadeo
1873–1874	Republic
1874–1885	Alfonso XII
1886–1931	Alfonso XIII
1931–1939	Republic
1939–1975	Fascist dictatorship under Francisco Franco
1975–	Juan Carlos I

RULERS OF ITALY

1861–1878	Victor Emmanuel II
1878–1900	Humbert I
1900–1946	Victor Emmanuel III
1922–1943	Fascist dictatorship under Benito Mussolini (maintained in northern Italy until 1945)
1946 (May 9–June 13)	Humbert II
1946–	Republic

SECRETARIES-GENERAL OF THE UNITED NATIONS

		Nationality
1946–1952	Trygve Lie	Norway
1953–1961	Dag Hammarskjold	Sweden
1961–1971	U Thant	Myanmar
1972–1981	Kurt Waldheim	Austria
1982–1991	Javier Pérez de Cuéllar	Peru
1992–1996	Boutros Boutros-Ghali	Egypt
1997–	Kofi A. Annan	Ghana

UNITED STATES PRESIDENTIAL ADMINISTRATIONS

Term(s)	President	Political Party
1789–1797	George Washington	No party designation
1797–1801	John Adams	Federalist
1801–1809	Thomas Jefferson	Democratic-Republican
1809–1817	James Madison	Democratic-Republican
1817–1825	James Monroe	Democratic-Republican
1825–1829	John Quincy Adams	Democratic-Republican
1829–1837	Andrew Jackson	Democratic
1837–1841	Martin Van Buren	Democratic
1841	William H. Harrison	Whig
1841–1845	John Tyler	Whig
1845–1849	James K. Polk	Democratic
1849–1850	Zachary Taylor	Whig
1850–1853	Millard Filmore	Whig
1853–1857	Franklin Pierce	Democratic
1857–1861	James Buchanan	Democratic
1861–1865	Abraham Lincoln	Republican
1865–1869	Andrew Johnson	Republican
1869–1877	Ulysses S. Grant	Republican
1877–1881	Rutherford B. Hayes	Republican
1881	James A. Garfield	Republican
1881–1885	Chester A. Arthur	Republican
1885–1889	Grover Cleveland	Democratic
1889–1893	Benjamin Harrison	Republican
1893–1897	Grover Cleveland	Democratic
1897–1901	William McKinley	Republican
1901–1909	Theodore Roosevelt	Republican
1909–1913	William H. Taft	Republican
1913–1921	Woodrow Wilson	Democratic
1921–1923	Warren G. Harding	Republican
1923–1929	Calvin Coolidge	Republican
1929–1933	Herbert C. Hoover	Republican
1933–1945	Franklin D. Roosevelt	Democratic
1945–1953	Harry S. Truman	Democratic
1953–1961	Dwight D. Eisenhower	Republican
1961–1963	John F. Kennedy	Democratic
1963–1969	Lyndon B. Johnson	Democratic
1969–1974	Richard M. Nixon	Republican
1974–1977	Gerald R. Ford	Republican
1977–1981	Jimmy Carter	Democratic
1981–1989	Ronald W. Reagan	Republican
1989–1993	George H. W. Bush	Republican
1993–	William J. Clinton	Democratic

MAJOR WARS OF THE MODERN ERA

1546–1555	German Wars of Religion
1526–1571	Ottoman wars
1562–1598	French Wars of Religion
1566–1609, 1621–1648	Revolt of the Netherlands
1618–1648	Thirty Years' War
1642–1648	English Civil War
1652–1678	Anglo-Dutch Wars
1667–1697	Wars of Louis XIV
1683–1697	Ottoman wars
1689–1697	War of the League of Augsburg
1702–1714	War of Spanish Succession
1702–1721	Great Northern War
1714–1718	Ottoman wars
1740–1748	War of Austrian Succession
1756–1763	Seven Years' War
1775–1781	American Revolution
1796–1815	Napoleonic wars
1846–1848	Mexican-American War
1853–1856	Crimean War
1861–1865	United States Civil War
1870–1871	Franco-Prussian War
1894–1895	Sino-Japanese War
1898	Spanish-American War
1904–1905	Russo-Japanese War
1914–1918	World War I
1939–1945	World War II
1946–1975	Vietnam wars
1950–1953	Korean War
1990–1991	Persian Gulf War
1991–1997	Civil War in the former Yugoslavia

POPULATION OF MAJOR CITIES, 1750–1990

City	1750	1800	1850	1900	1950	1990
Amsterdam	210,000	217,000	224,000	511,000	804,000	713,000
Athens	10,000	12,000	31,000	111,000	565,000	772,000
Berlin	90,000	172,000	419,000	1,889,000	3,337,000	3,438,000
Brussels	60,000	66,000	251,000	599,000	956,000	954,000
Budapest	xxxxxxxx[1]	54,000	178,000	732,000	1,571,000	2,017,000
Dublin	90,000	165,000	272,000	373,000	522,000	920,000
Geneva	22,000	22,000	31,000	59,000	145,000	167,000
St. Petersburg	150,000	336,000	485,000	1,267,000	xxxxxxxx	4,437,000
Lisbon	148,000	180,000	240,000	356,000	790,000	678,000
London	675,000	1,117,000	2,685,000	6,586,000	8,348,000	6,803,000
Madrid	109,000	160,000	281,000	540,000	1,618,000	2,991,000
Moscow	130,000	250,000	365,000	989,000	xxxxxxxx	8,747,000
Paris	576,000	581,000	1,053,000	2,714,000	2,850,000	2,152,000
Prague	59,000	75,000	118,000	202,000	922,000	1,212,000
Rome	156,000	163,000	175,000	463,000	1,652,000	2,828,000
Stockholm	60,000	76,000	93,000	301,000	744,000	679,000
Warsaw	23,000	100,000	160,000	638,000	601,000	1,654,000
Zurich	11,000	12,000	17,000	151,000	390,000	342,000
New York	22,000	60,000	696,000	3,437,000	7,892,000	7,322,000
Montreal	6,000	xxxxxxxx	58,000	268,000	1,022,000	1,017,000
Mexico City	xxxxxxxx	137,000	170,000	345,000	2,234,000	8,235,000
Buenos Aires	11,000	40,000	99,000	664,000	2,981,000	2,960,000
Cairo	xxxxxxxx	211,000	267,000	570,000	2,091,000	6,452,000
Alexandria	xxxxxxxx	15,000	60,000	320,000	919,000	3,413,000
Istanbul	xxxxxxxx	600,000	xxxxxxxx	1,125,000	983,000	6,220,000
Damascus	xxxxxxxx	130,000	150,000	140,000	335,000	1,451,000
Jerusalem	xxxxxxxx	xxxxxxxx	xxxxxxxx	42,000	83,000	524,000
Tokyo	xxxxxxxx	xxxxxxxx	xxxxxxxx	1,819,000	6,778,000	8,163,000
Delhi	xxxxxxxx	xxxxxxxx	xxxxxxxx	209,000	914,000	8,419,000

[1] xxxxxxxx = population statistics unavailable

Source: B. R. Mitchell, ed. *International Historical Statistics* (1998).

Index

All Quiet on the Western Front
(Remarque), 1011
Alsace (AHL says), 611, 862, 1000
World War I and, 980
Amar, Jules, 977
Amendola, Giovanni, 1030
America First movement, 1052
American Indians. *See* Native Americans
Americanization, 1097, 1103, 1181 *(m)*
American War of Independence
(Revolutionary War; 1775–1783), 633,
714, 717–719, 717 *(i)*
Americas, the (New World; Western
Hemisphere), 586. *See also* Atlantic
system; Caribbean region; Latin
America; North America
European colonization of (seventeenth
century), 587–589, 588 *(m)*
settlement of, 651–654
Amiens, Treaty of (1802), 774
Amsterdam, 572, 587, 629, 630
Anabaptists, 621 *(i)*
Anarchism, 884
Anarchists, 921, 952, 953
And Quiet Flows the Don (Sholokhov),
1033
Andreas-Salomé, Lou, 944
Anglican Church. *See* Church of England
Anna Karenina (Tolstoy), 928
Anne (Great Britain; r. 1702–1714), 666
Anne of Austria, 605, 605 *(i)*, 606
A nous la liberté (film), 1042
Anschluss (AN shlus), 1045, 1048
Anthony, Susan B. (1820–1906), 954
Anticlericalism, in France, 737 *(i)*
Anti-Corn Law League, 828
Anti-Semitism, 912, 946. *See also* Holocaust
in the 1930s, 1026
in Austria-Hungary, 958–959
in early twentieth century, 956–959
in France, 924
in Germany, 957–958, 1033, 1037
in Russia and the Soviet Union, 956,
1089
in totalitarian societies, 1031
after World War II, 1073
Antiwar movement (1960s), 1134, 1137
Antwerp, 1576 sack of, 570
Apartheid, 1095, 1158
Aphorisms, Nietzsche's, 946
Appeasement, policy of, 1048
April Theses (Lenin), 991
Arab nations, in the 1970s, 1142
Architecture. *See also* Housing
in the 1920s, 1008, 1013
baroque, 591
in the nineteenth century, 816
Areopagitica (Milton), 635
Argentina, 1164
Arianism (Arian Christians), 621 *(i)*

Aristocracy (nobility)
after 1848 revolutions, 842
Bohemian, 614
in Brandenburg-Prussia, 612
British, 699
the Enlightenment and, 698–699
in France
French Revolution, 732, 747
Napoleon, 769
religious division, 565–566
Hungarian, 615
late-nineteenth-century, 908–909
manners in the seventeenth century
and, 637–639
in Poland, 698–699
in Russia, 616, 699
in Spain, 698–699
Armed forces. *See also* Military, the; Navy;
War; *and specific wars*
English, Cromwell and, 620, 624, 625
French, 773
in 1790s, 749
under Louis XIV, 610
Peace of Westphalia (1648) and,
579–580
Prussian, 670–671, 707, 710
Russian, 855
seventeenth-century, 613 *(f)*
Thirty Years' War and, 578
in World War I, 984–985
in World War II, 1050–1052,
1059–1063
Arms race
1950–1970, 1085 *(f)*
before World War I, 969–971, 970 *(f)*
Armstrong, Louis, 1013
Armstrong, Neil, 1115
Art and artists, 876. *See also* Painting(s);
Sculpture, nineteenth-century
in the 1920s, 1011
Asian, 919
Dutch, 629, 629 *(i)*
eighteenth-century, 701, 701 *(i)*
globalism and, 1185
industrial and imperial change and
(1870s–1880s), 917–919
in late sixteenth and early seventeenth
centuries, 589–592
in the late twentieth century,
1126–1128, 1131–1132
under Louis XIV (France),
606–607
Mannerism, 590–591, 590 *(i)*
modern, 948–950
rococo, 661, 661 *(i)*
Rousseau on, 693–694
seventeenth-century, 634–637
Articles of Confederation (1777), 719
Art nouveau, 950
Aryans, 1035, 1036, 1044

Asia
in the 1960s, 1133–1134
decolonization in, 1091–1093
imperialism in, 963–964, 963 *(m)*
new imperialism and, 904–905
white settlements in, 654–655
Asian art and architecture, 919
Assemblies. *See* Legislative Assembly
Assembly of Notables (France), 731–732
Assembly of the Land (Russia), 616, 617
Assignats, 738
Astell, Mary (1666–1731), 679
Astrology, 598
Astronauts, 1115–1116, 1116 *(i)*
Astronomy, 947
revolution in (sixteenth–seventeenth
centuries), 593, 594–597
space exploration and, 1116–1117
Atatürk, (AHT uh turk) (Mustafa Kemal)
(1881–1938), 1027–1028
Atheism (atheists), 677, 689, 743
Atlantic Charter, 1063
Atlantic revolutions, 726
Atlantic system, 646, 647–656, 648 *(m)*
slavery and, 647, 649–651
world trade and, 651–655
Atomic bombs, 1069 *(i)*
in World War II, 1061, 1063
Attlee, Clement (1883–1967), 1064, 1083,
1091
Augustinus (Jansen), 609
Augustus I, elector of Saxony, 563
Auschwitz-Birkenau extermination and
labor camp, 1052, 1053
Austerlitz, battle of (1805), 774
Australia, 1093
Austria (Austrian Empire, to 1867), 1166.
See also Austria-Hungary; *and
individual emperors and political
leaders*
1830 revolts in Italian states and, 798
in the 1930s, 1041
as absolutist state, 614–615
Belgian independence movement and,
728–729
Congress of Vienna (1814–1815) and,
782, 784
Crimean War (1853–1856) and, 851,
853
dual monarchy and, 863
ethnic divisions in (1848), 838–840
French Revolution and, 738, 742, 747,
748, 750, 751, 755, 755 *(m)*, 757
German annexation of (1938), 1048
German unification and, 859–860
Hungary and, 615, 671, 671 *(m)*, 828
industrialization in, 807, 808
Italian unification and, 856–857
liberalism in, 828
Napoleon and, 774

continued

continued

continued

Tripartite Pact (1940), 1051, 1052
Triple Alliance, 927, 967, 980
Tristan, Flora (1801–1844), 829
Trotsky, Leon (TROT skee) (1879–1940), 993, 1013, 1031, 1032
Truffaut, François (troo FO) (1932–1984), 1104
Truman, Harry S. (1884–1972), 1064, 1069, 1093
cold war and, 1074, 1075
Truman Doctrine (1947), 1075
Trusts, 897
Tsushima Straits, battle of (1905), 964
Tuberculosis, 813
Tunisia, 901
Turgenev, Ivan (toor GAY nyif) (1818–1883), 854, 855, 877
Turgot, Jacques (1727–1781), 714
Turkestan, 905
Turkey, 966–967
in 1920s–1930s, 1027–1028
German Nonaggression Pact with (1941), 1051
World War I and, 980
Turks, 966
Turner, Joseph M. W. (1775–1851), 793–794, 817, 817 (i)
Two Sicilies, kingdom of the, 837
2001: A Space Odyssey (film), 1116
Two Treatises of Government (Locke), 633
Typhus (typhoid), 868
Tz'u-hsi (Cixi; dowager empress of China; 1835–1908), 965

U-boats. *See* Submarine warfare
Ukraine, 617
in World War II, 1051
Ulster, 625
Ulster (Northern Ireland), 1005, 1005 (m)
Ultra, 1051
Ultras (France), 785
Ulysses (Joyce), 1012
Umbrellas (Christo and Jeanne-Claude), 1188 (i)
Undset, Sigrid (1882–1940), 940
Unemployment
in the 1970s, 1142–1143
Great Depression (1930s) and, 1024, 1024 (f), 1025, 1040
Union of Indochina, 905, 905 (m)
Union of Soviet Socialist Republics. *See* Soviet Union
Unions. *See* Labor unions
United Nations, 1063, 1097, 1173–1174
Korean War and, 1092
United States, 865–867, 968. *See also* Superpowers; *individual presidents*
in the 1960s, 1132–1133
1970s crises and, 1139–1140

in the 1980s, 1164–1165
China and, 1140
civil rights movement in, 1099–1100, 1132, 1134–1135
Civil War (1861–1865), 865
cold war and. *See* Cold war
economy of
1920s, 1006
in the 1920s, 1023
Great Depression (1930s), 1023–1024, 1038
after World War II, 1073
expansion of, 865, 866 (m)
French Revolution and, 751
industry in, 895
Korean War and, 1092
Paris Peace Conference (1919) and, 996
politics after World War II, 1083–1084
religion in, 785
Revolutionary War (1775–1783), 633, 714, 717–719, 717 (i), 719
space exploration, 1115–1116
student movement in (1968), 1137
Suez Canal crisis (1956) and, 1094
Vietnam War and, 1092–1093, 1133–1134, 1135
war with Mexico, 865
after World War I, 1001
World War I and, 988, 994
after World War II, 1073
World War II and, 1051–1052, 1055
Universal Exhibition (Manet), 878
Universal Exposition of 1889, 894 (i)
Universities, 686, 702
in the 1960s, 1125, 1135
women in, 872
Upper class. *See also* Aristocracy
late-nineteenth-century, 908–910
Urbanization, 805, 809–814, 913
USSR. *See* Soviet Union
Utilitarianism, 789
Utopia (More), 790
Utopian socialists, 790

Vaccination, 673
Vallain, Jeanne Louise, 742 (i)
Valois (vahl WAH) dynasty, 566
Van de Velde, Theodor, 1009
Van Gogh, Vincent (van GO) (1853–1890), 918, 919
Vasari, Giorgio (vuh ZAHR ee) (1511–1574), 567 (i)
Vatican, the, 1016, 1018
Vatican II (Second Vatican Council; 1962), 1129
Vega, Lope de (VAY guh, LO pe de) (1562–1635), 590
Velázquez, Diego (ve LAS kez, dee AY go) (1599–1660), 580 (i)

"Velvet revolution" (Czechoslovakia), 1170
Vendée rebellion (vahn DAY) (1793), 745–746, 746 (m)
Venetia, 784, 836, 857
Venice (Venetians), 570, 750
Verdi, Giuseppe (VAYR dee, joo SEP ee) (1813–1901), 837, 847, 847 (i), 849, 873
Verdun, battle of (1916), 984
Vermeer, Jan (vuhr mihr) (1632–1675), 636
Versailles
palace at, 607–608, 607 (i)
Treaty of (1919), 1000
German rejection of, 1044–1046
women's march to (1789), 723–725, 725 (i)
Vertical integration of industries, 897
Vesalius, Andreas (ve SAY lyoos) (1514–1564), 597
Vichy France, 1051
Victor Emmanuel II (Italy; r. 1861–1878), 847, 856, 858
Victor Emmanuel III (Italy; r. 1900–1946), 1015
Victoria (Great Britain; r. 1837–1901), 842, 864, 864 (i), 904, 922, 952
death of, 951
Vienna, 869 (i)
Ottoman siege of (1683), 615, 615 (i), 618
Vietcong, 1133, 1134
Viet Minh, 1093
Vietnam, 1140
Vietnamese, 988
Vietnam War (1954–1975), 1092–1093, 1130, 1133–1134, 1134 (m), 1135, 1137, 1139–1140
Vigée-Lebrun, Marie-Louise-Elizabeth (vee ZHAY luh broen) (1755–1842), 701
Violence, political (1970s), 1145, 1148
Virginia, 588–589, 630, 650
Virgin Mary (mother of Jesus)
cult of, 640
doctrine of the Immaculate Conception, 880
VISTA (Volunteers in Service to America), 1133
Volksgemeinschaft (FOLKS ge min shahft), 1035, 1037
Voltaire (François Marie Arouet) (vol TAYR) (1694–1778), 677, 683–686, 688, 688 (i), 689, 689 (i), 692, 696, 707, 711
Voting rights (suffrage), 924
in France, 737
in Germany, 862
in Great Britain, 799, 922

Elevation

Feet	Meters
Over 13,120	Over 4,001
6,561–13,120	2,001–4,000
1,641–6,560	501–2,000
661–1640	201–500
0–660	0–200
Below sea level	Below sea level

⍟ National capital
• Major city

0   150   300 miles
0   150   300 kilometers

NORWAY

Bergen

Oslo

SWEDEN

Stockholm

Göteborg

North Sea

Aarhus

DENMARK

Copenhagen

Baltic Sea

Gdańsk

SCOTLAND

Glasgow   Edinburgh

NORTHERN
IRELAND

Belfast

IRELAND

Dublin

Cork

UNITED

Liverpool

KINGDOM

Birmingham

WALES   ENGLAND

Thames R.

London

English Channel

NETHERLANDS

Amsterdam

Rotterdam

Antwerp

Brussels

BELGIUM

Elbe R.

Berlin

POLAND

Oder R.

GERMANY

Frankfurt

Prague

CZECH REP.

Brno

Rhine R.

Paris

Seine R.

Luxembourg

LUXEMBOURG

LIECHTENSTEIN

Munich

Vienna

Bratislava

Danube R.

ATLANTIC
OCEAN

FRANCE

Loire R.

Zürich   Vaduz

Bern

SWITZERLAND

Innsbruck

AUSTRIA

Graz

Budapest

Lyon

Rhône R.

A L P S

Milan

SLOVENIA

Ljubljana

Zagreb

Po R.

CROATIA

Bay of
Biscay

Oporto

PYRENEES

Ebro R.

ANDORRA

Andorra
la Vella

Marseille

MONACO

San
Marino

SAN
MARINO

BOSNIA AND
HERZEGOVINA

Adriatic Sea

APENNINES

Split

Sarajevo

PORTUGAL

Lisbon

Madrid

SPAIN

Barcelona

Corsica

ITALY

Rome

Naples

*Tyrrhenian
Sea*

Seville

Sardinia

BALEARIC IS.

*Ionian
Sea*

Gibraltar
(Br.)

Algiers

Palermo

Sicily

Tunis

Rabat

MOROCCO

ALGERIA

TUNISIA

Valletta

MALTA

Tripoli

LIBYA